economics

Michael A. Leeds
Temple University

Peter von Allmen
Moravian College

Richard C. Schiming
Minnesota State University, Mankato

PEARSON

Addison
Wesley

Boston San Francisco New York
London Toronto Sydney Tokyo Singapore Madrid
Mexico City Munich Paris Cape Town Hong Kong Montreal

For Holland and Helen Hunter, who taught me that economics is about people as well as equations. — **Michael A. Leeds**

For Barb and Jim Burnell, and Gene Pollock, whose love of economics and teaching fostered the same in me. — **Peter von Allmen**

To Patty. — **Richard C. Schiming**

Editor-in-Chief	Denise Clinton
Senior Acquisitions Editor	Adrienne D'Ambrosio
Editorial Assistant	Jennifer Moquin
Director of Development	Kay Ueno
Senior Development Editor	Rebecca Ferris-Caruso
Senior Administrative Assistant	Dottie Dennis
Supplements Editor	Jason Miranda
Director of Media	Michelle Neil
Senior Media Producer	Melissa Honig
MyEconLab Content Lead	Douglas A. Ruby
Executive Marketing Manager	Stephen Frail
Director of Market Development	Dona Kenly
Managing Editors	Nancy Fenton/James Rigney
Senior Production Supervisor	Katherine Watson
Senior Design Managers	Charles Spaulding/Gina Hagen Kolenda
Senior Manufacturing Buyer	Carol Melville
Illustration and Composition	Argosy Publishing

Library of Congress Cataloging-in-Publication Data
Leeds, Michael (Michael A.)
    Economics / Michael A. Leeds, Peter von Allmen, Richard Schiming.
    p. cm.
    Includes index.
    ISBN 0-201-88262-0
    1. Economics. I. Von Allmen, Peter. II. Schiming, Richard. III.
    Title.
    HB171.5.L3724 2006
    330--dc22   2005030358

Printed in the United States of America

3 4 5 6 7 8 9 10—QWT–09 08 07

Text and photo credits appear on page C-1, which constitutes a continuation of the copyright page.

About the Authors

Michael A. Leeds is Associate Professor in the Fox School of Business and Management of Temple University. He received his B.A. in Economics from Haverford College and his Ph.D. from Princeton University. He has received numerous teaching awards from the Fox School and is currently the director of its honors program. His areas of interest include labor economics, applied microeconomics, and the economics of sports.

Peter von Allmen is Professor of Business and Economics at Moravian College. He received his B.A. from the College of Wooster and his Ph.D. from Temple University. His research includes the use of quantitative methods in the teaching of economics, the economics of sports, and family labor supply models. He teaches microeconomics and industrial organization at the undergraduate and MBA levels, economics of health and health care, freshman writing, and labor economics.

Richard C. Schiming is Professor of Economics at Minnesota State University, Mankato. He received his B.A. in Economics from Valparaiso University and his Ph.D. from Ohio State University. His areas of teaching interest are macroeconomics and money and banking. His research is focused primarily on issues in economic education.

Brief Contents

Table of Contents

"What? Another 'Principles of Economics' Text?"

There have been so many introductory economics texts written over the years that you could not be blamed for wondering what one more could add to the mix. We have read and enjoyed any number of introductory textbooks. The same, however, cannot be said of students. The vast majority are turned off by the very qualities that first attracted us to economics. Like most people who go on to pursue an advanced degree in economics, we were drawn in by the analytical rigor and the mathematical purity. Our experience has shown that few students share this enthusiasm for the technical aspects of economics. Students still regard economics with a mixture of awe and boredom. They are cowed by its complexity and abstraction. Befuddled students tell their professors that while they understand the theory, they just don't understand all the graphs and equations that we so enthusiastically throw on the board.

Behind Every Economics Principle Lies a Fascinating Story.

In this textbook, we introduce economics to students using an approach that has been very successful in our own teaching. Long after our students have forgotten the definitions and diagrams they memorized, they remember the stories that we tell. In addition to being serious theoreticians or policy analysts, economists are still essentially storytellers. In "field classes" that we have taught, we have found that economics can excite even reluctant students if we place the material into an appealing context. We apply this approach to introductory economics by taking great pains to present material in the context of a story taken from the news, business, history, or contemporary life at the very outset of each chapter and by continually reinforcing the application of theory to these real-world examples. How can students be motivated to master material if they cannot relate it to their lives? Students relate to the material more completely by seeing *how* economic reasoning applies even before they see the techniques themselves. This approach shows readers that economics is not just a dry set of theories but a way to view the world around them. The rhythm that stories create helps students remember the basic points both during the academic term and long after the course has ended.

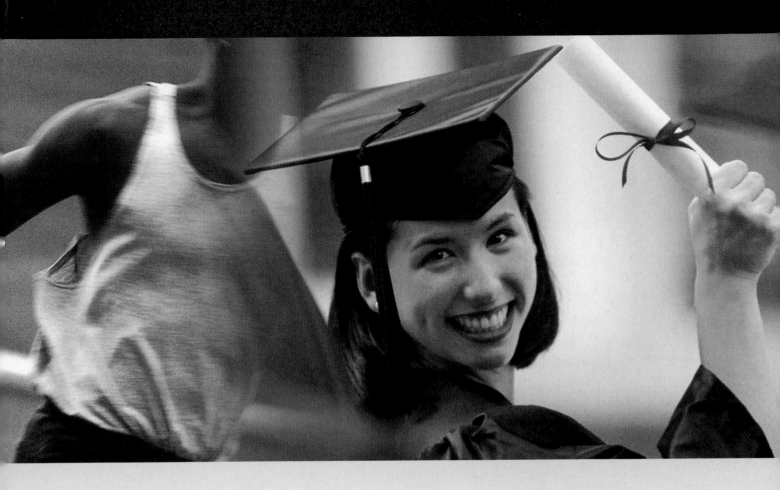

Economics' innovative approach to the core principles of economics is driven by an integrated learning and assessment system. The textbook builds on three pedagogical pillars for successful learning:

■ **ASSESS FOR SUCCESS.**
Economics treats assessment as an ongoing and essential part of the learning process. Tightly integrated tools help instructors hold students accountable for their learning.

■ **DRAW STUDENTS IN.**
Economics introduces concepts in the context of stories that capture students' interest and help them better understand and remember what they've read.

■ **MAKE THE CONNECTION.**
Economics challenges students to put economics to work as they analyze government policies, think critically about the news, and make personal decisions.

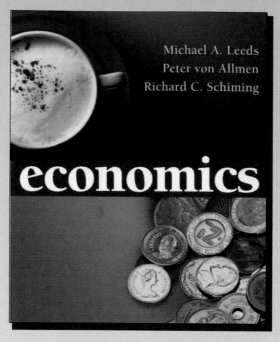

Michael A. Leeds
Peter von Allmen
Richard C. Schiming

economics

Overview

The text begins with a set of six core chapters designed to introduce all the critical tools and concepts required to study either microeconomics or macroeconomics. Chapter 1 describes economics as an area of study and introduces key conceptual building blocks. Chapters 2 and 3 overview the U.S. economy and introduce the student to economic methodology. We introduce the basics of the critical demand and supply framework in Chapter 4 and then follow it with a treatment of elasticity in Chapter 5 that emphasizes the intuition and usefulness of elasticities. We close the introductory section with applications of the demand and supply model by considering the motivation for and effects of government intervention in markets. This discussion includes the concepts of consumer and producer surplus, which we revisit at several later points in the textbook.

Role of Consumers and Firms

Across the microeconomics chapters, we carefully expand and reinforce the economics toolkit as well as apply it to an increasingly broad set of economic problems and issues. We build on students' understanding of demand concepts in an in-depth examination of consumer choices in Chapter 7. We then turn our attention "inside the firm" and cover production and cost concepts in Chapter 8, in the context of a small guitar manufacturer.

Market Structure, Pricing, and Public Policy

Chapter 9 begins our study of markets. We analyze perfect competition here using the famous Pike Place Fish Market in Seattle. Students learn why firms are price takers, and the general rule for maximizing profits. In Chapter 10, we turn to monopoly and show how the monopoly power of the Atlanta Braves and their vendors allows the team to set prices rather than take them as given from the market. Three chapters cover monopolistic competition (Chapter 11), oligopoly (Chapter 12), and antitrust and regulation (Chapter 13). These chapters offer a concise yet well-rounded treatment of how firms compete when they have some level of market power as well as competitors, and how the government might respond if a market becomes highly concentrated.

Resource Markets, Market Failure, and Public Goods

Chapters 14 and 15 analyze resource markets. Students learn—through the example of Google's financial capital history and a realistic example of a small manufacturer—about the importance of decision-making within a firm. Chapter 14 describes the essential elements of finance, including how firms attract financial capital and choose among funding options. Chapter 15 covers labor markets. Here, we show how firms and individuals make decisions regarding labor demand and supply. Chapter 16 covers the U.S. distribution of income by considering the case of one its most visible and wealthy citizens, Oprah Winfrey, and her philanthropic efforts. Chapter 17's introduction to market failure includes a discussion of public goods, common property resources, and externalities. It also describes how government intervention might be used to increase overall economic efficiency when markets fail.

Measuring Macroeconomic Health

We begin our coverage of macroeconomics by introducing students to the key features of macroeconomics: unemployment, inflation, and GDP. We open with unemployment because it is the most tangible and immediately relevant of the three concepts to students' lives. Our coverage of inflation notably includes recent changes in the way the Bureau of Labor Statistics calculates inflation without straying too far from the simple, appealing story of the fixed market basket. Finally, the Gross Domestic Product chapter introduces students to the business cycle and fluctuations around potential GDP.

Aggregate Demand, Aggregate Supply, and Fiscal Policy

Our careful and balanced look at the implications of changes in aggregate demand and aggregate supply emphasizes the basic building blocks of the standard model so that the student grasps how the pieces interrelate. The chapters take an even-handed approach to the short-run and the long-run versions of the model: We do not side with either school of thought. We then use the model to explain the theory and practice of both fiscal and monetary policy.

In Chapter 21, we build the basic model by explaining the characteristics of both aggregate demand and aggregate supply and how they combine to determine both short-run and long-run macroeconomic equilibrium. We then use the model in Chapter 22 to explore how changes in aggregate demand and aggregate supply explain both the short-run health of the macroeconomy and how an economy can adjust to the full employment level of output in the long run. We focus on the development of the short-run model in the context of the economic challenges of the Great Depression in Chapter 23. An appendix to Chapter 23 uses the Keynesian cross model to explain macroeconomic equilibrium. In Chapter 24, we show how changing taxes and government spending can move an economy closer to the full employment level of output. We rely on aggregate demand and aggregate supply to illustrate fiscal policy. We take a close look at the causes and consequences of the federal budget deficit and national debt in Chapter 25.

Money and Monetary Policy

The first chapter in the money and banking sequence (Chapter 26) defines money by focusing on the basic principles, characteristics, and functions of money assets, using a local currency called Ithaca Hours as an illustration. We also describe bank operations in a fractional reserve world. Chapter 27 explores how banks create money by accepting deposits and making loans. We also investigate the tools of monetary policy used by the Fed in the particular context of the response to the 9/11 crisis. In Chapter 28, we look at the short-run and long-run roles that money plays in the macroeconomy by focusing on the impact of changes in the money supply on interest rates.

Long-Run Economic Health

Chapter 29 explores the conflict between active and passive stabilization policies in macroeconomic theory and policy in the context of the response to the recession of 2001. We take students through recent and current controversies in macroeconomic thought. Chapter 30 covers growth theory and policies designed to promote growth. Although some texts—particularly those that emphasize long-run theories—present growth early in their books, we use this chapter as a link between the macroeconomic and international sections of the text. We do so by emphasizing differences in growth among countries and asking why some countries have grown faster than others. We also pay close attention to development and how it relates to (and differs from) growth.

International Trade and Finance

Chapters 31 and 32 present economic theories of international trade and international finance. The chapters are written so that instructors of both macroeconomics and microeconomics may cover the material without assigning supplemental readings. Chapter 31 carefully establishes the costs and benefits of trade as well as the impact of barriers to trade. We make extensive use of consumer and producer surplus to show who wins and loses from trade. Chapter 32 covers the impact of trade blocs on trade patterns.

ASSESS FOR SUCCESS

Economics treats assessment as an ongoing piece of the learning process. Throughout the chapter, and in the **MyEconLab** Study Guide at the end of each chapter, students are directed to **MyEconLab**, the full-featured online homework and tutorial system that accompanies *Economics.*

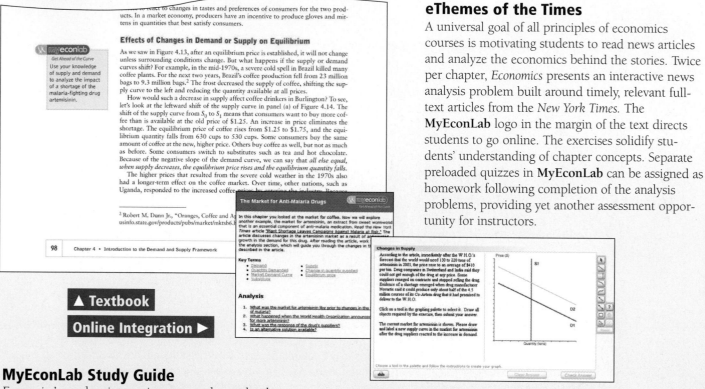

▲ **Textbook**

Online Integration ▶

eThemes of the Times

A universal goal of all principles of economics courses is motivating students to read news articles and analyze the economics behind the stories. Twice per chapter, *Economics* presents an interactive news analysis problem built around timely, relevant full-text articles from the *New York Times.* The **MyEconLab** logo in the margin of the text directs students to go online. The exercises solidify students' understanding of chapter concepts. Separate preloaded quizzes in **MyEconLab** can be assigned as homework following completion of the analysis problems, providing yet another assessment opportunity for instructors.

MyEconLab Study Guide

Economics' seamless integration among the textbook, assessment materials, and online resources sets new standards in the principles of economics market. Each chapter concludes with a set of problems correlated to those that students encounter online in **MyEconLab**. Even the numbering is the same, so instructors can easily assign exercises for homework or quizzes. Instructors can use **MyEconLab** to assign the end-of-chapter **MyEconLab** Study Guide exercises online—and **MyEconLab** will grade and track student work in an online gradebook.

▲ **Textbook**

◀ **Online Integration**

DRAW STUDENTS IN

Each chapter of *Economics* introduces theory and models in the context of a story—taken from the news, business, history, or contemporary life—that is followed through the chapter. The stories engross students and improve their retention by providing context.

Stories That Engage

In Chapter 4, for example, a trip to a coffee shop in Burlington, Vermont, adds flavor to the concepts of supply and demand while making these key tools tangible to students.

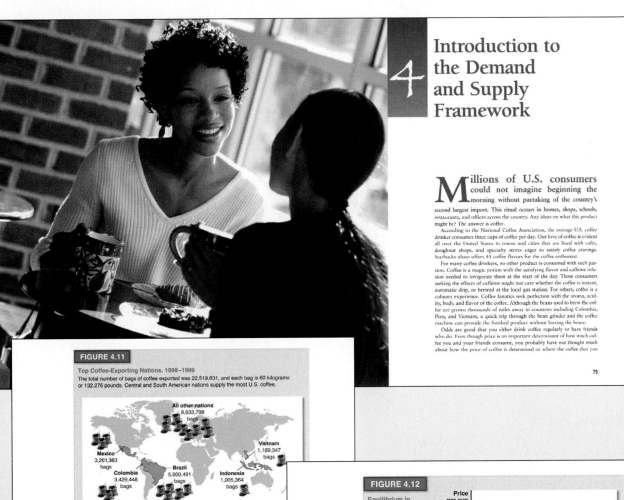

Introduction to the Demand and Supply Framework

Millions of U.S. consumers could not imagine beginning the morning without partaking of the country's second largest import. This ritual occurs in homes, shops, schools, restaurants, and offices across the country. Any ideas on what this product might be? The answer is coffee.

According to the National Coffee Association, the average U.S. coffee drinker consumes three cups of coffee per day. Our love of coffee is evident all over the United States in towns and cities that are lined with cafés, doughnut shops, and specialty stores eager to satisfy coffee cravings. Starbucks alone offers 45 coffee flavors for the coffee enthusiast.

For many coffee drinkers, no other product is consumed with such passion. Coffee is a magic potion with the satisfying flavor and caffeine infusion needed to invigorate them at the start of the day. Those consumers seeking the effects of caffeine might not care whether the coffee is instant, automatic drip, or brewed at the local gas station. For others, coffee is a culinary experience. Coffee fanatics seek perfection with the aroma, acidity, body, and flavor of the coffee. Although the beans used to brew the coffee are grown thousands of miles away in countries including Colombia, Peru, and Vietnam, a quick trip through the bean grinder and the coffee machine can provide the finished product without leaving the house.

Odds are good that you either drink coffee regularly or have friends who do. Even though price is an important determinant of how much coffee you and your friends consume, you probably have not thought much about how the price of coffee is determined or where the coffee that you

79

FIGURE 4.11

Top Coffee-Exporting Nations, 1998–1999
The total number of bags of coffee exported was 22,519,831, and each bag is 60 kilograms or 132.276 pounds. Central and South American nations supply the most U.S. coffee.

All other nations
8,633,798 bags

Vietnam
1,189,347 bags

Mexico
3,261,383 bags

Colombia
3,429,448 bags

Brazil
5,000,491 bags

Indonesia
1,005,364 bags

Source: U.S. Department of Commerce, December 1999

of workers in the coffee industry rise, *ceteris paribus*, the cost of producing rises as well. As a result, coffee shops are less willing to go to the expense ducing and selling output at any price than they were before the wage incre the supply curve shifts leftward. If wages fall, the supply curve shifts right

For coffee sellers, one of the primary inputs is the beans used to brew th Figure 4.11 shows the major sources of U.S. coffee imports. Most of the U. supply comes from Central and South American countries, including

Chapter 4 • Introduction to the Demand and Supply Frame

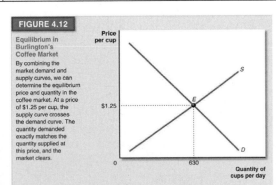

FIGURE 4.12

Equilibrium in Burlington's Coffee Market
By combining the market demand and supply curves, we can determine the equilibrium price and quantity in the coffee market. At a price of $1.25 per cup, the supply curve crosses the demand curve. The quantity demanded exactly matches the quantity supplied at this price, and the market clears.

Price per cup

$1.25

630

Quantity of cups per day

today's price in the paper. Where, then, does the price come from? It turns out that
as market forces determine the price of coffee.
the willingness and ability of

Within the textbook and online, *Economics* encourages students to apply economic concepts to the analysis of news, national policy debates, and personal decisions. Three techniques reinforce the material in each chapter.

Test + Extend Your Knowledge

Students check whether they have assimilated what they have read in two *Test + Extend* segments in each chapter. Students who cannot answer the "test" portion are informed that they must go back over the material. Students who have mastered the material have the chance to apply their knowledge in a new context in the "extend" portion. Many segments link students to interesting Web sites that illustrate chapter topics and give students the opportunity to build their economic research skills

TEST + *EXTEND* Your Knowledge

1. TEST Explain whether and how each of the following enters the circular flow of economic activity:
a. A teller's salary at Citizens Bank
b. The corporate headquarters built for the H. J. Heinz Company
c. The $10 that a kindergartner in Pittsburgh received for her birthday from her grandfather

2. EXTEND The "Country at a Glance" tables in the Data and Research section of the World Bank Web site (using the link at www.aw-bc.com/leeds/ch03) provide information on production for many countries. Use these tables to find the distribution of output among the agriculture, manufacturing, and services categories in: (a) an industrialized country other than the United States (such as Japan or the Netherlands); and b) a developing country (such as Bolivia or Uganda). How does the distribution of output in these countries differ from one another? Why do you think they differ?

and household income. In 2003, government purchases of goods and services accounted for more than 18 percent of all U.S. economic activity. To accurately depict the U.S. economy, our circular flow model must account for the actions of government. Before discussing the role of government as a whole in the circular flow, we briefly describe the different levels of government.

Levels of Government

When most people speak of government, they typically mean the nation's central or federal government. In fact, the

LifeLessons

Sometimes, More Driving Can Help You Save On Gasoline

Have you ever noticed that the price of gas can vary quite a bit from one state to another? In addition to federal (nationwide) gas taxes of 18.4 cents per gallon, there are state taxes ranging from a low of 8 cents per gallon in Alaska to 35.1 cents per gallon in Hawaii. These taxes are often used to pay for road maintenance. Florida and Georgia are neighboring states, yet state taxes are 12.2 cents per gallon in Georgia and 29.6 cents per gallon in Florida. The difference may be enough to entice Floridians living near the Georgia state line to bear the opportunity cost of their time (and the gasoline needed to make the trip) to drive to Georgia to make their gasoline purchases. The resources used when consumers in Florida drive to Georgia and back to make gasoline purchases is yet another source of waste created by the tax. That is, consumers use resources (time and gasoline)—that could be otherwise employed—to make the trip across the border to pay the lower tax in Georgia. Thus, consumers should carefully consider these costs to ensure that the costs of the trip exceed the benefits. Despite the costs they impose, differences in tax rates across local governments are quite common.

Life Lessons

Economic principles govern the decisions by major corporations and governments that involve billions of dollars and affect millions of lives. They also apply to hundreds of decisions that individuals make in their everyday lives. *Life Lessons* examine the economics behind these everyday decisions, such as the opportunity cost of traveling to purchase low-priced gas or the benefits of being flexible when shopping for airline tickets.

Strategy and Policy

These features delve into firm and government policies and issues—such as the effectiveness of anti-smoking efforts in Ukraine and the shopping habits of U.S. teens—and challenge students to analyze them using economic tools. Instructors can use the accompanying *Critical Thinking* questions as the basis of written assignments.

18 to 28 years old	0.37	0.42	0.24
29 or more years old	0.28	0.33	0.15

 Strategy and Policy
Getting Smokers to Quit When They're Young[2]

Governments around the world are concerned with cigarette smoking among teens. One reason is that smoking has well-known adverse health effects. Another is that the addictive properties of tobacco turn many teens who start smoking into long-term smokers. Historically, governments have tried to discourage smoking through taxes on cigarettes. A study by the Alcohol and Drug Information Centre in Ukraine shows how difficult this problem can be from a policy perspective. It also highlights how important it is to get young smokers to quit before they reach adulthood. Table 5.5 shows results from the study. It indicates that the price elasticity of demand for cigarettes is inelastic at all ages, but becomes more inelastic as smokers age and as their income increases. While teen smokers have an elasticity of between 0.52 and 0.70, adults over age 28 have an elasticity of only 0.15 to 0.28. They are less than one-half as sensitive to price increases as teens.

According to the report, at current prices for cigarettes in Ukraine, a 100-percent increase in the cigarette tax would result in an 8.8-percent increase in the total cost per pack. Based on the elasticities shown, the short-run impact would be about a 6-percent decrease in teen smokers, but only a 1.32-percent decrease in high-income smokers over 28 years old. However, in the long run, the benefits of such a tax would be con-

Get Ahead of the Curve

MyEconLab—the online homework and tutorial system that is packaged with every new copy of *Economics*—puts students in control of their own learning with study and practice tools correlated with the online, interactive version of the textbook and other media resources. Within **MyEconLab's** structured environment, students practice what they learn, test their understanding, and then pursue a Personalized Study Plan that **MyEconLab** generates for them based on their performance on practice tests.

At the core of MyEconLab are the following features:

- **Practice Tests**—Practice tests enable students to test their understanding and identify the areas in which they need to do further work. Many questions ask students to work with graphs: interpreting them, manipulating them, and even drawing them. Instructors can use the supplied pre-built tests or create their own tests.

- **Personalized Study Plan**—Based on a student's performance on a practice test, **MyEconLab** generates a Personalized Study Plan that shows where further study is needed.

- **Additional Practice Exercises**—The Personalized Study Plans direct students to additional exercises for each topic. Additional practice exercises are keyed to each section of the textbook and link students to the eText with animated graphs.

- **Tutorial Instruction**—Launched from the additional practice exercises, tutorial instruction is provided in the form of solutions to problems, step-by-step explanations, and other media-based explanations.

- **Powerful Graphing Tool**—Integrated into the practice tests and additional practice exercises, the graphing tool lets students manipulate and even draw graphs so that they grasp how the concepts, numbers, and graphs are connected. (**MyEconLab's** powerful graphing application evaluates and grades these graphs.)

- **MyEconLab features three types of graphing problems**

Draw Graphs—**MyEconLab's** Draw Graph problems automatically grade the graphs students draw.

Model-based Graphs—Students can change data inputs and watch graphs shift. Multiple-choice, true/false, and short–answer questions quiz students on their interpretations of the graph.

Data Graphs—Students can plot up to five variables against each other, giving them a clear picture of how economic indicators relate to each other.

Get Ahead of the Curve

MyEconLab provides flexible tools that allow instructors to easily and effectively tailor online course materials to suit their needs. Instructors can create and assign tests, quizzes, or graded homework assignments. **MyEconLab** saves time by automatically grading all questions and tracking results in an online gradebook. **MyEconLab** can even grade assignments that require students to draw a graph.

After registering for **MyEconLab**, instructors have access to downloadable supplements such as instructor's manuals, Microsoft PowerPoint lecture notes, and test banks. Test banks can also be used within **MyEconLab**, giving instructors ample material from which they can create assignments.

For more information about **MyEconLab**, or to request an Instructor Access Code, visit **www.myeconlab.com**.

Additional MyEconLab Resources

■ **Textbook content**—Quick reference to specific pages of the text that correspond to each Study Plan exercise. **MyEconLab** is also available in a version that contains a full, searchable online text. Ask your Addison-Wesley representative for details.

■ **eStudy guide**—The entire Study Guide in electronic format and printable.

■ **Econ Tutor Center**—Staffed by qualified, experienced college economics instructors, the Econ Tutor Center is open five days a week, seven hours a day. Tutors can be reached by phone, fax, e-mail, or White Board technology. The Econ Tutor Center hours are designed to meet your students' study schedules, with evening hours Sunday through Thursday. Students receive one-on-one tutoring on examples, related exercises, and problems.

■ **Research Navigator**—(CourseCompass version only) Extensive help on the research process and four exclusive databases of accredited and reliable source material including the *New York Times*, the *Financial Times*, and peer-reviewed journals.

■ **Animated figures**—Over 125 figures from the textbook presented in step-by-step animations with audio explanations of the action.

■ **Glossary Flashcards**—Every key term is available as a flashcard, allowing students to quiz themselves on vocabulary from one or more chapters at a time.

■ **Weekly News**—Featuring a new microeconomic or macroeconomic current events article, with discussion questions posted online weekly. Instructor answer keys are available.

A Complete Instructor and Student Support Package

Instructor's Manual

In addition to numerous ideas for enlivening your lectures, the *Instructor's Manual* provides in-depth solutions to questions and exercises from the book. Material for the microeconomics chapters was authored by Myra Moore of the University of Georgia; the macroeconomics chapter materials were written by Robert Eyler of Sonoma State University.

The *Instructor's Manual* contains:

- chapter overviews
- chapter outlines
- learning objectives to provide instructors with a bird's-eye view
- in-depth lecture launchers with innovative ideas for engaging and motivating students
- tips on circumventing common student errors
- ready-to-assign questions for class discussion and activities
- answer keys for the *Test + Extend* exercises, *Strategy and Policy* critical thinking questions, and end-of-chapter problems

Study Guide

With exercises to reinforce key concepts and helpful learning tools, the *Study Guide* is an essential companion to the text. Material for the microeconomics chapters was authored by Morris Knapp of Miami Dade College; the macroeconomics chapter materials were written by John Krieg of Western Washington University. Students will find helpful overviews of the chapter contents, learning objectives, and listings of key terms corresponding to each chapter. Checkpoint tips advise students on common conceptual pitfalls related to chapter contents and build their graph-building and interpretation skills. The Self-Test, which includes fill-in-the-blank, true/false, multiple-choice, and problem-based questions, provides the additional exercises students need to cement their understanding of key concepts. Sample midterm and final exams provide a final check before critical points in the semester.

Test Banks

Four printed test banks—two each for the microeconomic and macroeconomic volumes—provide a wealth of testing material. The top-notch question-writing team includes Emil Berendt of Friends University, S. Hussain Ali Jafri of Tarleton State University, Leonie Stone of SUNY Geneseo, Laura A. Wolff of Southern Illinois University Edwardsville, and Anthony Zambelli, Cuyamaca College. Each chapter offers a wide selection of multiple-choice, short-answer, and essay questions. Questions have been accuracy-checked and vetted with real students.

Instructor's Resource Disk with Microsoft PowerPoint Lecture Presentation, Computerized Test Banks, and Instructor's Manual

Compatible with Windows and Macintosh computers, this CD-ROM provides numerous resources. The Microsoft PowerPoint Lecture Presentation was developed by Michael Youngblood of Rock Valley College. Work key figures and graphs from the text into your lectures with these customizable slides. The CD features graphs from the text and outlines key terms, concepts, and figures. For added convenience, the CD also includes the Microsoft Word files of the entire *Instructor's Manual* and computerized *Test Bank* files. The easy-to-use testing software (TestGen with QuizMaster for Windows and Macintosh) is a valuable text preparation tool that allows professors to view, edit, and add questions.

Overhead Transparencies

Incorporate important figures and graphs into your course with this selection of full-color overhead transparencies.

Study Card

This handy laminated reference card contains key definitions, concepts, equations, and graphs.

In addition to access to **MyEconLab**, the student's ultimate online tool that is automatically packaged with each text, the following supplementary materials are available to aid and enhance students' mastery of concepts:

Economist.com Edition

The premier online source of economic news analysis, Economist.com provides your students with insight and opinion on current economic events. Through an agreement between Addison-Wesley and *The Economist*, students can receive a low-cost subscription to this premium Web site for 12 weeks, including the complete text of the current issue of *The Economist* and access to *The Economist's* searchable archives. Other features include Web-only weekly articles, news feeds with current world and business news, and stock market and currency data. Professors who adopt this special edition will receive a complimentary one-year subscription to Economist.com.

Wall Street Journal Edition

When packaged with this text, Addison-Wesley offers students a reduced-cost, 10- or 15-week subscription to the *Wall Street Journal* print edition and the *Wall Street Journal Interactive Edition*. Adopting professors will receive a complimentary one-year subscription to both the print and interactive versions.

Financial Times Edition

Featuring international news and analysis from journalists in more than 50 countries, *The Financial Times* will provide your students with insights and perspectives on economic developments around the world. For a small charge, a 15-week subscription to *The Financial Times* can be included with each new textbook. Adopting professors will receive a complimentary one-year subscription, as well as access to the online edition at FT.com.

The Dismal Scientist Edition

The Dismal Scientist provides real-time monitoring of the global economy, allowing your students to go beyond theory and into application. For a nominal fee, a 3-month subscription to *The Dismal Scientist* can be included with each new textbook. Each subscription includes complete access to all *The Dismal Scientist's* award-winning features. Adopting professors receive a complimentary one-year subscription.

PearsonChoices Alternative Editions . . . your text, your way!

With ever-increasing demands on time and resources, today's college faculty and students want greater value, innovation, and flexibility in products designed to meet teaching and learning goals. We've responded to that need by creating *PearsonChoices*, a unique program that allows faculty and students to choose from a range of text and media formats that match their teaching and learning styles—and students' budgets.

Books à la Carte Edition

For today's student on the go, we've created a highly portable version of *Economics* that is three-hole punched. Students can take only what they need to class, incorporate their own notes, and save money! Each Books à la Carte text arrives with a laminated study card, perfect for students to use when preparing for exams, plus access to **MyEconLab**.

SafariX Textbooks Online

SafariX Textbooks Online is an exciting new service for college students looking to save money on required or recommended textbooks for academic courses. By subscribing to "Web Books" through SafariX Textbooks Online, students can save up to 50 percent off the suggested list price of print textbooks. Log on to www.safarix.com for details about purchasing *Economics*.

Acknowledgments

When we first agreed to write this text, it quickly became clear that none of us fully understood the magnitude of a two-semester principles book, even though two of us had already been through the process of writing a text before. We are indebted to countless others for pitching in with their hard work and innovative ideas. First and foremost, we are thankful for our excellent team at Addison-Wesley. Denise Clinton and Sylvia Mallory provided strategic input at critical junctures throughout the project. Peg Monahan helped shape early drafts and kept us mindful of our audience every step of the way. Adrienne D'Ambrosio championed the project within the editorial group and personally directed many of the market development activities. Stephen Frail's economics forums and grasp of market nuances were incredible assets. Dottie Dennis provided expert market research and administrative support. We benefited from Dona Kenly's market development efforts. Above all, special thanks goes to Senior Development Editor Rebecca Ferris-Caruso, whose diligence, expertise, and guidance in developing the manuscript were incredible; she is the best development editor in the business.

Nancy Fenton, Scott Harris, and Katy Watson managed the critical details throughout the production process. Regina Kolenda and Charles Spaulding created the striking interior and cover designs. Michelle Neil and Melissa Honig did an awe-inspiring job on the MyEconLab material and provided us with a seamless print and online program. Jason Miranda and Kirstey Dickerson steered the complex print supplements and managed this challenging process.

We are also most grateful for the work of our research assistants, Marianne Ball, Erin McCormick, Irina Pistolet, Elizabeth Wheaton, and especially Catherine Leblond, who read drafts, critiqued problems, and searched for data. Catherine's dedication kept her with us from her undergraduate and master's training in economics at Northwestern through her law school work at Stanford. Of course, each of us is indebted to our families—Eva, Daniel, and Melanie Leeds; Heather, Dan, Tom, and Eric von Allmen; and Patricia Hargrove, and Rachel and Lawrence Schiming, all of whom offered much-needed support through long hours and short deadlines.

A principles of economics textbook is the product of the talents and hard work of many talented colleagues. We are especially grateful to the accuracy-checking efforts during the demanding production process of Eric Chiang, Florida Atlantic University; Michael Nieswiadomy, University of North Texas; Erick Elder, University of Arkansas, Little Rock; and William Mosher, Clark University. We are further gratified that some of our toughest critics as manuscript reviewers signed on to develop an impressive array of supplementary materials to accompany the textbook. We are especially indebted to Emil Berendt, Robert Eyler, S. Hussain Ali Jafri, Morris Knapp, John Krieg, Myra Moore, Laura A. Wolff, Michael Youngblood, and Anthony Zambelli, as well as the MyEconLab content developers—Kenneth Baker, University of Tennessee, Knoxville; David Schodt, St. Olaf College; Leonie Stone, SUNY Geneseo; Cathleen Leue, University of Oregon; and Catherine Leblond.

Finally, and most importantly, we are truly thankful to have had so many manuscript reviewers and class testers, whose names are listed here, who took the time and care to read earlier drafts of the manuscript and offer comments, criticism, and suggestions. We strived to incorporate this invaluable input, and believe that it improved the final product enormously.

Reviewers

Alper Altinanahtar, *Texas Tech University*

Ryan Amacher, *University of Texas at Arlington*

Alan Ammann

Donna Anderson, *University of Wisconsin, La Crosse*

Kevin Baird, *Montgomery County Community College*

Rita Balaban, *College of Charleston*

King Banaian, *St. Cloud State University*

Cynthia Bansak, *San Diego State University*

Bharati Basu, *Central Michigan University*

Jeff Bauer, *University of Cincinnati Clermont College*

Klaus Becker, *Texas Tech University*

Joe Bell, *Southwest Missouri State University*

Bruce Bellner, *Ohio State University*

Emil Berendt, *Friends University*

Tibor Besedes, *Louisiana State University*

Jay Bhattacharya, *Okaloosa-Walton College*

Doug Bice, *University of Michigan*

Dixie Blackley, *Le Moyne College*

John Blair, *Wright State University*

Craig Blek, *Imperial Valley College*

Genevieve Briand, *Eastern Washington University*

Charles Britton, *University of Arkansas*

Gregory Brock, *Georgia Southern University*

Stacey Brook, *University of Sioux Falls*

Bruce Brown, *California Polytechnic University, Pomona*

Darrell Brown, *Ivy Tech State College*

Robert Carlsson, *University of South Carolina*

Scott Carson, *University of Texas of the Permian Basin*

Shawn Carter, *Jacksonville State University*

Joel Carton, *Texas Tech University*

Jill Caviglia-Harris, *Salisbury University*

Eric P. Chiang, *Florida Atlantic University*

Nan-Ting Chou, *University of Louisville*

Gary Clayton, *Northern Kentucky University*

Pam Coates, *San Diego Mesa College*

Michael Cohick, *Collin County Community College*

Elchanan Cohn, *University of South Carolina*

Bob Consalvo, *Southern Vermont College*

Sean Corcoran, *California State University, Sacramento*

Richard Croxdale, *Austin Community College*

Dean Draney, *St. Philip's College*

Dennis Edwards, *Coastal Carolina University*

Jeffrey Edwardson, *Texas A & M University*

Erick Elder, *University of Arkansas, Little Rock*

Larry Ellis, *Appalachian State University*

Sharon Erenburg, *Eastern Michigan University*

Elizabeth Erickson, *University of Akron*

Erick Eschker, *Humboldt State University*

Ayse Y. Evrensel, *Southern Illinois University Edwardsville*

Robert Eyler, *Sonoma State University*

Farzad Farsio, *Montana State University, Billings*

Bichaka Fayissa, *Middle Tennessee State University*

Maya Federman, *Pitzer College*

Nicholas Feltovich, *University of Houston*

Bob Figgins, *University of Tennessee at Martin*

Philip Forbus, *University of South Alabama*

Timothy Fuerst, *Bowling Green State University*

Marc Fusaro, *East Carolina University*

Shirley Gedeon, *University of Vermont*

Otis Gilley, *Louisiana Tech University*

Susan Glanz, *St. John's University*

Patrick Gormely, *Kansas State University*

Richard Gosselin, *Houston Community College*

John Graham, *Rutgers University*

Darren Grant, *University of Texas at Arlington*

Anthony Gyapong, *Penn State Abington*

Bob Harmel, *Midwestern State University*

Gail Hawks, *Miami Dade College, Wolfson*

Barry Haworth, *University of Louisville*

Denise Hazlett, *Whitman College*

George Heitmann, *Muhlenberg College*

Rick Hirschi, *Brigham Young University of Idaho*

Kevin M. Hollenbeck, *Western Michigan University*

Alexander Holmes, *University of Oklahoma*

John Horowitz, *Ball State University*

Jack Hou, *California State University, Long Beach*

Murat Iyigun, *University of Colorado*

S. Hussain Ali Jafri, *Tarleton State University*

Marianne Johnson, *University of Wisconsin, Oshkosh*

Wayne Joerding, *Washington State University*

Paul Jorgensen, *Linn-Benton Community College*

Chris Kauffman, *University of Tennessee, Knoxville*

Thomas Kelly, *Baylor University*

Jim Kelsey, *Whatcom Community College*

Ara Khanjian, *Ventura College*

Mark Killingsworth, *Rutgers University*

John Krieg, *Western Washington University*

Stephan Kroll, *California State University, Sacramento*

Patricia Kuzyk, *Washington State University*

Tom Larson, *California State University, Los Angeles*

Susan Laury, *Georgia State University*

Stephen Layson, *University of North Carolina at Greensboro*

Frances Lea, *Virginia Community College*

Sang Lee, *Southeastern Louisiana State*

Cathleen Leue, *University of Oregon*

Ronnie Liggett, *University of Texas—Arlington*

Stephen Lile, *Western Kentucky University*

Solina Lindahl, *California State Polytechnic University, San Luis Obispo*

Christine B. Lloyd, *Western Illinois University*

Melody Lo, *University of Southern Mississippi*

Michael Loewy, *University of South Florida*

K.T. Magnusson, *Salt Lake Community College*

John Marangos, *Colorado State University*

Daniel Marburger, *Arkansas State University*

Marenglen Marku, *Virginia Polytechnic Institute*

Danny Martinez, *Salt Lake Community College*

Leah Greden Mathews, *University of North Carolina at Asheville*

Steve McCafferty, *Ohio State University*

Tammy McDonald, *University of Massachusetts, Boston*

Alla Melkumian, *Western Illinois University*

Edward Merkel, *Troy State University*

William Mertens, *University of Colorado at Boulder*

John Min, *Northern Virginia Community College*

Shahruz Mohtadi, *Suffolk University*

Kristen Monaco, *California State University, Long Beach*

Myra Moore, *University of Georgia*

William Mosher, *Clark University*

Robert Mulligan, *Providence College*

Antu Panini Murshid, *University of Wisconsin at Milwaukee*

George Nagy, *Hudson Valley Community College*

Doug Nelson, *Spokane Community College*

John Neri, *University of Maryland*

Charles Newton, *Houston Community College/Southwest College*

Pamela Nickless, *University of North Carolina at Asheville*

Jerome P. Niemiec, *Texas State University*

Farrokh Nourzad, *Marquette University*

Joan Osborne, *Palo Alto College*

John Pharr, *Cedar Valley College*

Susan Pozo, *Western Michigan University*

Greg Pratt, *Mesa Community College*

Marilyn Pugh, *Prince George's Community College*

James Ragan, *Kansas State University*

Peter Rangazas, *Indiana University-Purdue University Indianapolis*

Kathryn Roberts, *Chipola College*

Paul Roscelli, *Canada College*

Alannah Rosenberg, *Saddleback College*

Barbara Ross, *Kapi'olani Community College*

Stephen Rubb, *Sacred Heart University*

Rose Rubin, *University of Memphis*

Martin Sabo, *Community College of Denver*

Ted Scheinman, *Mount Hood Community College*

David Schodt, *St. Olaf College*

Gerald Scott, *Florida Atlantic University*

James Self, *Indiana University, Bloomington*

Reza Sepassi, *Florida Community College*

Thomas Shea, *Springfield College*

Calvin Shipley, *Henderson State University*

Mark Showalter, *Brigham Young University*

Geok Simpson, *University of Texas—Pan American*

Sara Solnick, *University of Vermont*

Martin Spechler, *Indiana University-Purdue University Indianapolis*

Tesa Stegner, *Idaho State University*

Claire Starry, *Southern New Hampshire University*

Nick Stratis, *Florida State University*

Richard Stratton, *University of Akron*

Charles Stull, *Kalamazoo College*

Bryce Sutton, *University of Alabama at Birmingham*

Manjuri Talukdar, *Northern Illinois University*

Mark Thoma, *University of Oregon*

Lloyd Thomas, *Kansas State University*

Andrew Tucker, *Tallahassee Community College*

John Vahaly, *University of Louisville*

Kristin Van Gaasbeck, *California State University, Sacramento*

Jennifer VanGilder, *California State University, Bakersfield*

Glenn Waddell, *University of Oregon*

John Wade, *Eastern Kentucky University*

Angela Waits, *Gadsden State Community College*

Samson Wakjira, *Truman State University*

Claudia Wehbe, *Florida International University*

Mark Wheeler, *Western Michigan University*

Mark Witkowski, *University of Arkansas—Little Rock*

Laura Wolff, *Southern Illinois University Edwardsville*

Wei Xiao, *University of New Orleans*

Virginia York, *Gulf Coast Community College*

Douglas Young, *Montana State University*

Anthony Zambelli, *Cuyamaca College*

Class Testers

Faiz Al-Rubaee, *University of North Florida*

Marwan Abu-Sawwa, *Florida Community College at Jacksonville*

Alper Altinanahtar, *Texas Tech University and South Plains College*

Birjees Ashraf, *Houston Community College*

Ken Baker, *University Tennessee, Knoxville*

Rita Balaban, *College of Charleston*

Emil Berendt, *Friends University*

Trisha Bezmen, *Old Dominion University*

Charles Biles, *Humboldt State University*

Jim Bishop, *Daytona Beach Community College*

David Black, *University of Toledo*

Robert Black, *Houghton College*

Marc Borchers, *Hillsborough Community College*

Abdelkrim Boukahil, *University of Wisconsin, Whitewater*

Gail Burkett, *Palm Beach Community College*

Marilyn Butler, *Sam Houston University*

Anoshua Chaudhuri, *San Francisco State University*

Daniel Cobb, *St. Louis Community College, Meramec*

Olga Cordero-Brana, *University of Hawaii, Hilo*

Ron Coleman, *San Antonio College*

Rosalee Danielson, *College of DuPage*

Sammi Dakhlia, *University of Alabama*

Jackie Donofrio, *Monroe Community College*

Ron Dunbar, *Madison Area Technical College*

Scott England, *Metropolitan State College of Denver*

Nancy Eschen, *Florida Community College at Jacksonville*

Brian Evans, *Foothill College and Holy Family University*

Ali Faegh, *Houston Community College*

Mitch Fisher, *College of DuPage*

Arthur Fleisher, *Metropolitan State College of Denver*

Jack Gazzo, *Mississippi Gulf Coast Community College*

Susan Glanz, *St. John's University*

Tom Gresik, *Notre Dame*

Bill Goffe, *State University of New York—Oswego*

Richard Gosselin, *Houston Community College*

Troy Guider, *Mississippi Gulf Coast Community College*

Ghunaym Ghunaym, *Albany State University*

Anthony Gyapong, *Penn State University, Abington*

Christopher Hallstrom, *University of Portland*

Gail Hawks, *Miami Dade College, Wolfson*

Mike Hilmer, *Virginia Polytechnic Institute*

Leslie Horton, *Quinsigamond Community College*

Michael Iannone, *The College of New Jersey*

Noel Jacoby, *Lake City Community College*

S. Hussain Ali Jafri, *Tarleton University*

Paul Jorgensen, *Linn Benton Community College*

Jonathan Kaplan, *California State University, Sacramento*

Emelie Kenney, *Siena College*

Maurice Knapp, *Miami Dade College, Wolfson*

Bruce Koller, *Diablo Valley Community College*

Jeffrey Krans, *Keuka College*

Douglas Krupka, *Georgia State University*

Andrew Lambert, *Palm Beach Community College*

Tom Larson, *California State University, Los Angeles*

Suk Hun Lee, *Loyola University Chicago and University of Wisconsin, Milwaukee*

Ronnie Liggett, *University of Texas, Arlington*

James Luke, *Lansing Community College*

Sirous Malek, *Collin County Community College*

Andrew Mauer-Oats, *Northwestern University*

Marenglen Marku, *Virginia Polytechnic Institute*

Wayne Martin, *Kansas Community College*

Danny Martinez, *Salt Lake City Community College*

John R. McArthur, *Wofford College*

Alla Melkumian, *Western Illinois University*

John Min, *Northern Virginia Community College*

Trudy Morlino, *Georgia Perimeter College*

Nivedita Mukherji, *Oakland University*

Solomon Namala, *Cerritos College*

Charles Newton, *Houston Community College Southwest*

Louise Nordstrom, *Nichols College*

Joan Osborne, *Palo Alto College*

Alexandre Padilla, *Metropolitan State College of Denver*

Robert Potter, *University of Central Florida*

Tammy Potter, *Gadsden State Community College*

Renee Quick, *Wallace State Community College*

Rudy Radulovich, *Florida Community College at Jacksonville*

James Ragan, *Kansas State University*

Charles Reichheld, *Cuyahoga Community College*

Jeff Reynolds, *Northern Illinois University*

Sammie Root, *Texas State University—San Marcos*

Ann Ritchey, *Mount Union College*

Kathryn Roberts, *Chipola Junior College*

Barbara Ross, *Kapi'olani Community College*

Nicholas Rupp, *East Carolina University*

Abed Saleh, *Miami Dade College, Kendall*

1 Economics: The Science of Everyday Life

Hit the alarm: time to get up and embark on the new semester. Classes start tomorrow, and you have a long list of things to do before then. You need to confirm your class schedule, catch up with friends, buy books, and get a new parking sticker. Your first stop is the registrar.

As you pass the student center bookstore, you see that a long line already snakes out the door. The line at the administration building is just as bad—there are so many people milling around in the main room that it takes you a while to make sure you are in the line for schedules and not for student aid. When you finally get to the front, the news is not good.

"What?!" you say. "Are you sure? I'm not registered for anything?" Because of a mix-up in the registrar's office, you are not currently enrolled in any classes for the semester. You have no choice but to re-register for courses today. The psychology course you wanted is now closed. The only available history course meets at the same time as the biology class that you need to fulfill your science requirement. And the only daytime open section of the calculus course that you must take to satisfy the math requirement meets at 8:00 A.M. You have some hard choices to make.

You begin by tackling the history versus biology dilemma. It's one or the other, the registrar tells you. You can't have both. "The history class is a special topics course that probably won't be offered again, but the biology course is offered every semester," she tells you. You reluctantly give up the biology course and register for history. Next, the math course: Calculus at 8:00 A.M.—ouch! You need to work late at your part-time job three nights a week, and if there's one thing you don't want to sacrifice, it's sleep. "One evening section has an open seat," the registrar says. Sounds good. Fortunately, you have some flexibility with regard to which nights you work. 7:00 to 10:00 P.M. is a lot better than 8:00 A.M. Better to rearrange your work schedule to keep that night open each week than to risk sleeping through class. The art class you want is still open—it seems that there are plenty of seats in Abstract Pottery Design. Three down, one to go.

Now for the psychology class. "You have to let me in," you say. "I *need* this class." The registrar replies that because you are a sophomore with no declared major, "need" is probably overstating the case. "But I need a social science class for my distribution requirement. Why can't I have everything I want? Isn't that what I pay tuition for?"

"Let's see," she ponders, "a social science class for the person who needs an answer to the question, 'Why can't I have everything I want?' Ah, here we are: Principles of Economics."

In this chapter, we will introduce several key economic concepts that illustrate the need to make choices and the trade-offs that individuals face every day. We will emphasize these concepts throughout the book.

ALONG THE WAY, YOU WILL ALSO LEARN:

- Economics is about scarcity and the ways in which scarce resources are allocated among competing uses.

- Economics as a field is split into two main branches: one that focuses on the health of the overall economy and one that focuses on individuals and firms.

- To make good decisions, you must compare the costs and the benefits of all possible actions against one another.

- Economists use models that are simplifications of reality to describe behavior and make predictions.

- Economics is valuable as a discipline, in part because economic forces affect our lives every day.

AT THE END OF THE CHAPTER, THE MYECONLAB LOGO WILL DIRECT YOU ONLINE

- MyEconLab is a resource-packed online homework and tutorial system that can help you perform better in your economics course. To log in for the first time, see page 30 for instructions.

- MyEconLab can help you apply important concepts from the chapter to real-world issues. Watch for the logo to indicate online features about economic reasoning and graphing.

- At the end of each chapter, you'll find a special study section that will help you get the most out of your textbook and your instructor's MyEconLab course.

▶What Is Economics?

Welcome to economics. In this class, you will learn that making choices is fundamental to our lives. You will also learn about the process everyone goes through to make those choices. For individuals, families, firms, and nations, economics is about making the best possible decisions: We cannot have everything. In this section, we describe scarcity, and the two main branches of the economics discipline and the types of problems they seek to solve.

Scarcity

Economics
The study of how scarce resources are allocated among competing uses.

We begin our study of economics with some basic vocabulary. **Economics** is the study of how scarce resources are allocated among competing uses. **Scarcity** means that there are not enough resources available to produce and consume all the goods and services we desire.

Scarcity
There are not enough resources available to produce and consume all the goods and services we desire. We therefore must make choices about *what* to produce, *how* we produce it, and *for whom* we produce.

This definition differs from the common definition of the word "scarcity" to indicate that there is very little of something. For example, land suitable for agriculture is a scarce economic resource in the United States, even though the United States is one the world's largest producers of many agricultural goods. Though abundant, land is not available in limitless quantities. As such, we must make choices about how to use (or to not use) this land. Scarcity is central to the definition of economics, because it implies that we must make choices about *what* to produce, *how* we produce it, and *for whom* we produce it. At a societal level, nations must decide how to allocate health care, education, and natural resources. At the firm level, business owners must decide how to allocate machinery and labor resources among all of the products they might produce. At a personal level, you must decide how to allocate your time and income among all of the goods and services you consume—including even the process of choosing a class schedule for the coming semester.

Microeconomics and Macroeconomics

The study of economics is divided into two general areas: microeconomics and macroeconomics.

Microeconomics
The study of how individual consumers or households interact with firms in markets.

Microeconomics. Microeconomics is the study of how individual consumers or households interact with firms in markets. Microeconomics also investigates how firms use resources, such as labor, and how individual workers decide how much time to allocate to labor. Your choices between buying a new or used book, driving a small or large car, or going to graduate school instead of seeking employment are all examples of microeconomic decisions by an individual consumer. At the firm level, microeconomic analysis typically focuses on how a firm makes choices to maximize its profits—for example, by setting the price and quantity of its output. Microeconomics also determines the number of firms that we can expect to be able to earn profits selling goods in a specific market, and predicts whether that market produces the goods and services that society wants. For example, an ongoing question in the computer industry is whether Microsoft's domination of the market for operating systems is in the best interest of consumers. Consumers might have better products and lower prices if many more firms sold operating systems for personal computers. Yet compatibility problems among those systems might mean that the additional choices make society worse off rather than better off. These are among the concepts studied in microeconomics.

Macroeconomics
The study of the major spending and producing units in the economy.

Macroeconomics. Macroeconomics is the study of the major spending and producing units in the economy. Macroeconomics aggregates all consumers together to form the demand side of the economy, all producers together to form the supply side, and all markets together to form the overall economy. Macroeconomics focuses on scarcity issues at the societal level. No economy has the resources to produce all the output necessary to satisfy the unlimited wants of everyone in the national economy. Because every national economy is part of the larger global economy, macroeconomists also focus on the economic relationships among nations. We read about macroeconomic issues such as changes in overall employment, inflation, and economic growth in the newspapers every day. It is vital to understand these issues as we make our own personal economic decisions. For example, if the economy is not growing and overall employment is falling, it might be better to stay at a job that you don't like until you have already found a new position. Otherwise, you risk being without work for an extended period of time. Macroeconomic analysis is important because it can help the government enact policies that minimize economic slowdowns and keep the economy running smoothly.

Whether you study microeconomics, macroeconomics, or both, a few basic, universal concepts govern the economic behavior of individuals and institutions. In the remainder of this chapter and the five following chapters, we introduce this core set of economic ideas, concepts, and definitions. Your careful study of these building blocks will be useful throughout the course, as you will see them again in almost every chapter.

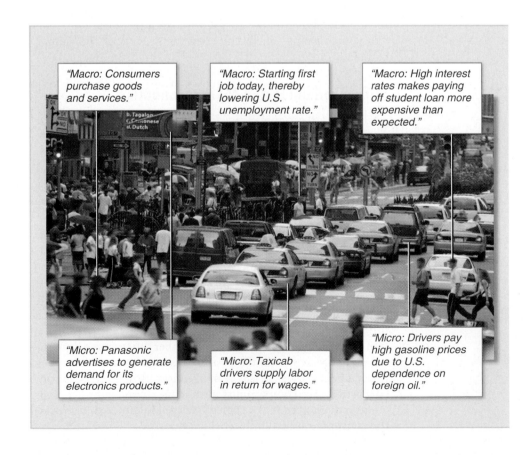

Positive versus Normative Economics

In addition to distinguishing between microeconomics and macroeconomics, economists divide their analysis into two general categories: positive and normative.

Positive
Type of economic analysis that involves "what is," or purely objective relationships that can be tested with data.

Positive Economic Analysis. Positive economic issues are those that are testable or verifiable. Thus, positive analysis is limited to descriptive statements or explicit predictions that do not require value judgments. Some examples of positive economic questions are:

- What is the cheapest airfare from Chicago to Dallas?
- What will happen to the cost of a $100,000 loan if interest rates increase by one percent?
- What will happen to prices in the U.S. economy if some countries decide not to purchase American-made products?
- What will happen to total consumer spending if the government cuts taxes by 10 percent?

For each question, there is a single answer that we can obtain without any need for individual interpretation.

Normative
Type of economic analysis, often can be described as "what ought to be." Normative economic analysis is subjective.

Normative Economic Analysis. Normative economic analysis is subjective, in that it requires the observer to make value judgments. With normative economic issues, even the choice of which questions to ask involves personal values. Sometimes positive analysis is described as "what is" and normative analysis as "what ought to be." In the context of your course selection dilemma, a positive question is, "Can I take both the history and biology classes I want?" The answer to this question is purely objective: no, because they are scheduled at the same time. However, if you were to ask a classmate which class is better, the answer is subjective, in that it depends on the classmate's opinion regarding the relative appeal of the two areas of study or the professors assigned to teach them. Questions involving normative issues, such as the following, are subject to debate:

- Should we subsidize the medical bills of low-income patients so that they can buy AIDS medication when needed?
- Should firms be allowed to market products that are very helpful to some consumers but harmful to others?
- Should the government adopt policies that cause hardship in the near term but increase long-term growth?
- Should the government make reducing unemployment its primary policy goal?

For each of these questions, a portion of the answer or portion of the information relevant to the answer can be obtained using objective analysis, yet each question requires us to make a value judgment.

A Positive Focus. The distinction between normative and positive analysis allows decision makers to focus their attention on positive issues first, in order to identify and clarify the implications of possible solutions. The decision makers can then apply their own norms to make the best possible decision. Throughout this text, we generally focus on positive economic analysis. We do so not because we dislike normative questions, but because solid positive analysis is a prerequisite for successful normative analysis.

1. TEST For each of the following statements, identify whether it is related primarily to microeconomics or macroeconomics:
   a) The price of bananas went up, so I bought apples instead.
   b) Total employment today is lower than it was last year.
   c) Designer shoes are not worth the money.
   d) Prices in England are lower than in the United States.
   e) Americans do not save enough.
   f) Dogs are a better value than cats as pets.

2. *E X T E N D* Identify whether each of these statements is positive or normative.
   a) The price of bananas went up, so I bought apples instead.
   b) Total employment today is lower than it was last year.
   c) Designer shoes are not worth the money.
   d) Prices in England are lower than in the United States.
   e) Americans do not save enough.
   f) Dogs are a better value than cats as pets.

▶ The Allocation of Goods and Services

Economic system
Set by national governments to establish the basic ground rules according to which consumers and producers interact to allocate goods and services among competing uses.

Let's return to the definition of economics from page 5: Economics is the study of how scarce resources are allocated among competing uses. Because resources are scarce, we need some mechanism—or an economic system—to allocate them. An **economic system** sets the basic ground rules for consumer and producer interactions. National governments establish economic systems to allocate goods and services among competing uses. **Goods and services** are all those resources and activities that consumers, firms, and the government consider valuable. In this section, we examine the two main types of economic systems: market-based and transition economies.

Goods and services
Resources and activities that consumers, firms, and the government consider to have value.

Market-Based Exchange Systems

In economics, the word "market" has a different meaning than you might have encountered in the past. Buyers and sellers use markets to exchange goods and services. A market can be a physical place, such as a jewelry shop, but this is not always the case. For example, every year, millions of buyers and sellers use eBay to exchange goods and services online. Most eBay transactions occur without the buyer and seller ever meeting. Other examples include the market for gasoline in a small town, the market for commercial airliners, and a stock market. In the small town, buyers consist of consumers in that town and the surrounding areas, and sellers might consist of two or three gas stations. In contrast, the market for commercial airliners is worldwide. Because planes cost millions of dollars and are easy to transport, airlines are willing to search for them across a much wider area than you might for gasoline. In other types of markets, no tangible good changes hands at all. In the stock market, for example, buyers and sellers exchange shares of stock that represent partial ownership of corporations. Buyers of stock do not actually receive a part of the company to hold. Instead, they receive a paper certificate that represents ownership.

Market-based system
Allocates resources based on prices determined by the forces of supply and demand.

A **market-based system** allocates goods and services based on prices. The prices are determined by the forces of supply and demand. *Supply* is the quantity of a good or service that sellers are willing and able to produce at various prices over a given period of time. *Demand* is the quantity of a good or service that buyers are willing and able to purchase at various prices over a given period of time. For instance, your

What Is a Market?
The market for oranges consists of oranges supplied by sellers who grow the oranges and demand for oranges from consumers.

choice of how many pairs of shoes to buy depends on how many pairs of shoes are available at various prices (supply) and your willingness and ability to pay for shoes (demand). If we combine the supply of shoes available from all sellers, and the demand for shoes of all buyers, we can analyze the entire shoe market. Most goods and services are exchanged in markets similar to the shoe market, where buyers and sellers must agree on a price in order to make an exchange. As you will learn in Chapter 4, prices are determined by the natural interaction of supply and demand.

Without markets, producers and consumers would be like trains on different tracks. Producers want to produce one set of goods, consumers want to buy another, and never the twain shall meet. Fortunately, the incentives inherent in a market system easily resolve this problem. Producers do not produce goods and services simply because they are able to do so. They respond to consumer demand, in the hope of earning profits. Thus, we say that market-based economies are *demand-driven*. In a **demand-driven economy**, producers respond to the desires of consumers, rather than forcing consumers to mold their choices to what firms want to produce. No firms produce books made of lead; they can do so, but no one wants to buy such a book. Consumers send signals to firms by using their limited incomes to purchase those goods they find most appealing, and by not choosing less desirable options.

Economists assume that consumers are rationally self-interested. Having **rational self-interest** means that consumers endeavor to make choices that give them the greatest satisfaction. In turn, the potential to earn profits motivates firms to do the best job they can of meeting consumer needs. As you will learn throughout the course, the incentives present in a market-based economy are one of the primary reasons that market-based economies prosper.

Demand-driven economy
An economy in which producers are forced to respond to the desires of consumers, rather than one in which consumers are forced to mold their choices to what producers want to produce. Market-based economies are demand-driven.

Rational self-interest
Quality that causes consumers to endeavor to make choices that give them the greatest satisfaction.

Most, but not all, goods and services are exchanged using markets in a market-based economy. There are times when even market-based economies use alternative means to allocate goods and services. As we will discuss in Chapter 6, under some conditions, markets fail to allocate resources in the way that society deems most desirable. In fact, your course selection is one such exception to a market-based transaction. At most colleges, seats in classes are allocated on a first-come, first-served basis. Can you imagine what registration would be like if seats were instead sold on a market to the highest bidder? More importantly, governments typically step in to make allocation decisions if society believes that a market-based outcome will be undesirable. Governments thus help low-income families pay for food, shelter, and medicine. Market-based economies are therefore more precisely described as *mixed economies*. In a **mixed economy**, most goods and services are allocated using markets, but some goods and services are allocated by the government.

Mixed economy
Allocates most goods and services using markets, but some goods and services are allocated by the government.

Transition Economies

Centrally planned economy
An economy in which the government, rather than the market, allocates resources.

In a **centrally planned economy**, the government, rather than the market, allocates resources. Central planning was a hallmark of communist and socialist states. While it was once prevalent in much of the world, today only a few countries—such as Cuba and North Korea—openly advocate central planning. A major reason for the decline of centrally planned economies is that they do not provide sufficient incentives. Producers have no incentive to satisfy the desires of consumers, because they do not receive benefits in the form of profits. Workers have little incentive to work hard, as their compensation is not adequately tied to their performance. Governments decide what goods will be produced and how they will be produced. Historically, the result of central planning was stagnation, and eventually, declining standards of living.

Transition economies
Economies in the process of switching from an allocation scheme that relies on central planning to one that uses markets.

Since 1989, the term *transition economy* has been applied to most of the formerly communist countries. **Transition economies** are economies in the process of switching from an allocation scheme that relies on central planning to one that uses markets. Some examples of transition economies are the Czech Republic, Poland, and Russia. Transition economies are important because the welfare of hundreds of millions of individuals depends on the successes of these nations in creating and maintaining market-based systems. Understanding the global economy is an essential aspect of economics; for this reason, you will find examples of international economic issues and problems throughout this text, as well as two chapters at the end of this book that are devoted to international trade and finance.

▶ Opportunity Cost

Opportunity cost
The most desired alternative you have forgone to obtain or do something else.

We now build on our understanding of how economic systems allocate scarce goods and resources by examining the decision-making process. Because resources are scarce and people must choose between competing uses, economists have developed a way to think about the cost of those choices. When choosing among alternatives, you must consider each option's opportunity cost. **Opportunity cost** is the value of the most desired alternative you forgo in order to obtain a good or service or undertake another activity. Whenever you choose to do one thing, you give up many different alternatives. For example, by choosing to enroll in the history class, you gave up chances to enroll in any other open classes, enroll in fewer classes, receive a partial tuition refund, and take another part-time job. However, the most important

ARLO & JANIS: © Newspaper Enterprise Association, Inc.

sacrifice to consider is the activity that you would have chosen to pursue if you had not enrolled in the history class. Thus, the opportunity cost of taking the history class is the biology class that you also wanted to take.

Have you ever heard the expression, "There is no such thing as a free lunch"? It is a widely used saying in economics that refers to opportunity costs. Even if someone gives you a good at no cost, you still give up the time required to consume it. The opportunity cost may be the time that you could have spent talking with a friend, going on a bike ride, or studying for your calculus exam. The next-best alternative represents the opportunity cost of the good, because you cannot pursue that alternative if you accept the good.

Opportunity costs also apply to firms and nations. The money that a firm spends to buy a machine to fill soda cans cannot be used for another purpose, such as hiring more workers. If the firm then uses that machine to produce cans of ginger ale, it cannot use the same machine to produce cans of tonic water at the same time. The firm thus faces an opportunity cost when it buys the machine and when the firm uses the machine to produce ginger ale.

Similarly, if a nation decides to provide health care to all of its citizens, the resources used to provide that service cannot be used to build schools, improve roads, or fight crime. The interrelationships among problems can complicate policy decisions. Consider low-income families who need more health care services than they can afford. The government can either help them to pay for the services, or use those same resources to fund job-training programs that will, over time, reduce poverty. Opportunity costs exist for every activity undertaken and every purchase made, no matter how small.

From an individual's standpoint, the opportunity cost of a good or activity determines its value. The decision of whether to buy your calculus book new or used is based on whether the new book is worth more to you than the other things you could afford to do if you bought a used book.

▶Cost-Benefit Analysis

Opportunity costs are only one factor in decision making. Economic analysis requires more than measuring costs: Good economic decision makers must compare the costs *and* benefits of proposed actions, and allocate resources based on that analysis. Even though costs are frequently measured in dollars, we know now that the best way to think about cost is as opportunity cost. Firms generally measure benefits in terms of dollars as well—a firm's benefit is typically an increase in revenue. For consumers, benefits are increases in personal satisfaction or happiness, and are harder to measure than firm benefits.

Cost-benefit analysis

Systematically compares costs to benefits to determine whether an activity should be pursued and, if so, the extent to which it should be pursued.

Cost-benefit analysis systematically compares the costs and benefits of an activity to determine whether it should be pursued and, if so, the extent to which it should be pursued. Selling an additional unit of output brings benefits to a firm, in the form of revenue. However, the firm must compare the benefits to the cost of producing it. Thus, most decisions by individuals, firms, and the government concern how much of an activity they should undertake. When trying to decide whether one of these entities should do a little more or a little less of an activity, economists typically use *marginal analysis*. **Marginal analysis** compares the costs and benefits of the last unit of an activity, rather than all the units combined. It is one of the most important concepts in economics, because—whether we recognize it or not—we use marginal analysis all the time in our own decision making.

Marginal analysis

Compares the costs and benefits of the last unit of an activity, rather than of all units combined.

To illustrate the value of marginal analysis, let's suppose you're a bowling enthusiast. Suppose that each game you bowl costs $3.00 and takes about 30 minutes of your time—the monetary and opportunity costs. You decide how many games to bowl by comparing these costs to the extra happiness you get from an additional game. Because your arm starts to tire and there are other activities you like to pursue, you get less additional satisfaction from bowling each additional game. With a constant cost per game and a declining benefit for each additional game, you eventually reach the point where the cost of another game exceeds the benefits. You then stop bowling for the day. The key to your decision is the value and cost of one more game, not the overall value you place on bowling.

Marginal cost

The cost of consuming or producing an additional unit.

Marginal benefit

The benefit of consuming or producing an additional unit.

In general, for each additional unit that we consume or produce, we compare the **marginal cost**, or the cost of consuming or producing that additional unit, to the **marginal benefit**, or the benefit associated with consuming or producing one more unit. In our bowling example, the marginal cost of the additional unit is equal to the opportunity cost. If it costs $3.00 to bowl another game and takes 30 minutes, the true marginal cost is what you give up by using these resources (money and time) to bowl rather than doing something else. The marginal benefit is the change in your satisfaction. To compare the marginal cost and marginal benefit for a firm, we compare the additional cost of producing and selling one more unit of output to the additional revenue that the firm will earn by selling that unit. Whether you study microeconomics, macroeconomics, or both, you will find that this concept of marginal analysis will help you to understand the behavior of individuals, firms, and even governments.

▶ Economic Models

Economic model

A tool that economists use to understand and explain economic events, and to predict the outcome of economic actions.

Economic models are another important tool for economists. To illustrate: Suppose that as you leave the registrar's office a new student stops you and asks you how to get to the library. Odds are that your directions will not include the precise length of the hallway one must walk down, the number of stairs to exit the building, or the number of trees that will be passed. Instead, you give the student only the information essential to find the library, and no more. So it is with economic models. **Economic models** are tools that economists use to understand and explain economic events and to predict the outcome of economic actions. Models are necessary because we cannot fully describe all the complexities that make up a single transaction. Imagine trying to sum all transactions that make up a firm's sales or overall consumption in the economy. Doing so would be too time-consuming, too expensive, and would require mountains of overly detailed information. Thus, we need a way to simplify economic analysis so that we can quickly answer important questions. Models allow us to make solid predictions about how participants in the economy will act under different circumstances.

Simplifying Assumptions

Economic models serve as a framework of analysis. They are like a simplified story designed to allow economists to analyze complex behavioral, technical, and institutional relationships. Consider the microeconomic questions of determining how many workers should be employed to operate a given number of machines. In such cases, economists often assume that laborers are all equally productive. When we make this assumption, we do not literally mean that all people are alike. Assuming that all workers are equally productive allows us to focus on the important questions of how machines and people work together to create products. While accounting for each worker's unique qualities would be more realistic, we would become bogged down in figuring out which workers were used first, and who worked with whom. Models are also essential at the macroeconomic level. The U.S. economy is made up of almost 300 million consumers, and a seemingly endless variety of products and services. To analyze the impact of a policy change on each consumer and firm would be impossible. Instead, we aggregate consumers' actions based on models that organize and simplify basic principles of behavior.

Assumptions
Simplifications used to construct an economic model.

We refer to the simplifications built into models as **assumptions**. To focus on a specific aspect of an economic relationship, we make simplifying assumptions about what is happening in other markets, the size of firms, and the information possessed by consumers. Let's examine a microeconomic example. In the retail market for coffee, a useful simplifying assumption might be that coffee shop owners attempt to maximize the profits from the sale of their products. This assumption is almost always true and saves the time and expense of surveying every shop owner individually. Yet it would be risky to assume that all consumers buy at least one cup of coffee, regardless of price. This assumption would also simplify our model, but it is certainly incorrect and would likely lead to inaccurate predictions about coffee purchases. At the macroeconomic level, we assume that as household income increases, consumers spend more. While this is not true for every single household, it is true for most.

Obviously, we must be careful when making assumptions. Too many simplifying assumptions can rob a model of its power to predict, or can limit its usefulness to a small set of circumstances. The best models use a limited number of assumptions and, as a result, provide a great deal of explanatory power. Because assumptions are so important to economic models, we will be very explicit about the assumptions we make throughout the text.

Ceteris Paribus

Sound economic analysis depends on the ability of researchers to attribute changes that they model to specific causes. We cannot control all aspects of an economy or of the people and firms that inhabit it. As a result, economic models almost always

Ceteris paribus
A Latin phrase that means "all else equal."

make use of the Latin term **ceteris paribus**, which means "all else equal," when evaluating changes in causal factors. The *ceteris paribus* assumption indicates that if we are considering the relationship between one variable and another, we must hold all other variables fixed. That is, we change or evaluate change in only one factor at a time to determine its effect.

To see why economists value the *ceteris paribus* assumption, let's consider a situation with three variables, all of which change at the same time. Suppose the following three events occur in the same year: Your school increases the number of credits required to graduate by 20, your tuition rises by $1,000 per year, and a competing school lowers its tuition by $500. The next year, enrollment is down by 10 percent at your school. Because all the changes in credit hours and prices occurred at the same time, there is no easy way to separate out the effects of the change in each variable on enrollment. Thus, school administrators would have difficulty trying to predict the effect of another $1,000 tuition increase the following year on enrollment. The only way to know the true effect of a $1,000 increase in tuition is to keep all other factors that could affect enrollment constant—that is, to hold "all else equal." In the theories we describe and use in this text, we will always identify what changes occur and what remains constant in the models.

Testing Hypotheses

Models are particularly important for economics and other social sciences such as psychology or sociology. As in the "hard sciences" of chemistry or physics, social scientists follow the scientific method. The scientific method involves making assumptions, formulating a hypothesis about the subject under study, and testing the hypothesis under laboratory conditions. A chemist can control the interaction of compounds and a physicist can control the interaction of forces at work on an object. However, economists have far less ability to control the interactions of people and organizations and must test their hypotheses using historical data from real-world events. In this text, we rely on carefully formulated theoretical models that have gained acceptance over time, in part by withstanding the rigors of repeated empirical testing.

▶ The Importance of Studying Economics

Now that we have described the analysis that economists undertake and the tools they employ, we can turn to practical applications. You and your classmates have varying motivations for taking this economics course. You might be taking the course because you think it is an important tool for understanding the world around you. In fact, there are *many* reasons why you should study economics. Whether you focus narrowly on the events of your own life at school or broadly on the events of the world, you will encounter economic forces at work. Understanding these forces will enrich your life as a citizen, employee, or employer, and perhaps also guide your career choice.

The Consumer and Citizen Perspective

If you pick up any major city newspaper, watch the news on television, or check the news on your Web browser, you will encounter stories involving economics. For example, during the Severe Acute Respiratory Syndrome (SARS) outbreak in Asia in 2003, widespread panic nearly shut down the Chinese economy. Relatively few people contracted the disease and the number of fatalities was smaller still. However, the economic impact was dramatic. Consumers stayed home, and business and pleasure travel was severely curtailed. China lost as much as 40 percent of its annual $67 billion tourism income due to fear of the disease. If you were planning to go to Asia as an exchange student, or if you simply wanted to buy an MP3 player manufactured in China, you felt the economic impact of an illness that was mostly confined to an economy half a world away.

The economic aspects of some situations are less obvious. You might be surprised to find a group of economists fretting over reports from the Weather Channel regarding the temperature in Florida on a February day. Such behavior makes more sense if you know that if the temperature falls below freezing for any length of time, the citrus crop will spoil, setting off a chain of unwelcome events. Grapefruit and orange prices will rise. Consumers will face higher prices for orange juice at the grocery store. Florida farmers will lose much of their revenue and risk bankruptcy. Finally, the state government might have to raise taxes to provide assistance to farmers and their families.

It is also common to find news stories about broad social problems such as unemployment. It might seem that we should try to eliminate all unemployment. However, there are costs to all our actions. If the government devoted the necessary resources to ensure that all citizens that wanted to work could find jobs, fewer resources would be available for other important programs. Such a program might also require a level of government interference in markets that most Americans would not want.

Whatever issue you encounter, it almost always has an economic aspect worth examining. Thus, understanding current events requires that we understand the economic forces that affect those events. As the famous economist John Maynard Keynes once said, "Practical men, who believe themselves to be quite exempt from any intellectual influences, are usually the slaves of some defunct economist."

The Employee Perspective

Most individuals have a direct connection with the economy through their roles as employees. Wage levels, the taxes that are deducted from your paycheck, and the rules that govern overtime pay are economic outcomes influenced by the labor market. In fact, the wheels are already in motion to determine your own participation in the labor market, based on your investment in a college education. Economic forces even affect the major that students choose as they weigh the costs and benefits of different majors, and whether to pursue graduate study. You might not choose to pursue marketing, even though it is your favorite subject, if you learn that it is very hard to find jobs in marketing. Instead, you might decide to pursue a degree in nursing upon learning that the demand for nursing services is predicted to increase dramatically as the population ages. In every occupation, the overall health of the economy will affect your chances of obtaining your dream job.

The Manager and Employer Perspective

No matter what kind of organization they run, managers need to decide how to allocate scarce resources. As the manager of a pet food manufacturing facility that is having trouble keeping up with demand for its products, should you increase output by hiring more employees for an extra production run or by opening a new plant?

As head of a nonprofit hospital, should you use your scarce resources to launch a fundraising drive for a new hospital wing or devise a reorganization plan that will make better use of existing facilities? In a government position, you might need to make decisions about how to allocate the scarce resources within your jurisdiction as an attempt to please the competing desires of your constituents. In every aspect of your life, you will need to appraise the economic implications of your choices.

Career Opportunities in Economics

If you are considering pursuing economics as a major, you should know that it has many applications. Economics majors work in many different occupations in government, businesses, consulting firms, charitable foundations, and academia. You can apply an economics degree to any occupation involving resource allocation decisions. Careers in economics can be roughly divided into two areas: theoretical and applied work.

Theoretical Work. Economists who do theoretical work are most often found in academia. Theoretical economists develop new models that describe relationships or outcomes that have not yet been explained or explained adequately. For example, Stanford University economist Sherwin Rosen developed a model to explain why the earnings of elite athletes or singers are so much greater than those of other professional athletes and entertainers who are almost as good. His theory on the "economics of superstars" is based on the idea that fans want to see the people who are the best at their jobs, not those who are second-best. However, performances by golfer Tiger Woods or comic Chris Rock are scarce. As a result, the people at the top of their professions earn disproportionately high salaries. In macroeconomics, economic theory has developed and changed enormously over time. At one time, economists believed that the government could easily adopt temporary policies such as tax cuts to increase consumer spending. More recent developments indicate that if consumers know that tax cuts are temporary, they might not change their behavior. As a result, policy makers have had to rethink how to best change consumer spending.

Applied Work. Economics can be applied in almost any area. An applied economist who works in a large corporation might analyze the effectiveness of a marketing campaign or might be part of the general management team. Economists who work for state and local governments measure the costs and benefits of policy changes within their jurisdictions. In many cases, applied economists employ statistics to analyze data from past and current events, enabling economists to advise the best course of action for the future. This science of making predictions about future conditions based on past and present information is called **economic forecasting**.

Economic forecasting
The science of making predictions about future conditions based on past and present information.

Weather forecasters use models of evaporation, wind direction and intensity, and lunar cycles to predict weather. Economists use information such as current employment, inventory levels, and consumers' optimism about the future of the economy to make predictions about the state of the economy, a specific industry, or an individual firm in the coming year.

Many economists act as advisors or consultants. Firms or institutions that do not have sufficient work for a full-time staff economist often hire contracted expertise from a consulting firm. Consulting firms maintain staffs of highly trained economists who provide valuable input for firms and institutions on an as-needed basis. For example, Macy's might use economic consultants to estimate the costs and benefits of building a new store in an area with growing population.

Off We Go

At this point, you have a sense of economics as a discipline, a grasp of some of its most fundamental concepts, and an appreciation of why it is such a vital area of inquiry. As you read through this textbook and attend class each week, keep the ideas from this chapter in mind. Before we close, consider these tips that will guide your way through the course:

- Go to class. Studies have shown that class attendance significantly increases students' grades. It will increase your understanding of the material and help you to stay focused on what your instructor wants you to get from the course. While there, take the very best notes that you can and review them regularly. Your notes will prove to be a valuable study resource. More importantly, note-taking encourages you to be an active learner.
- When studying, aim for understanding, not just memorization. Memorization is a very poor tool for learning anything, but is especially poor for economics. The type of knowledge you gain in this discipline does not lend itself to memorization.
- Use the Study Guide, MyEconLab resources, and end-of-chapter problems to test your understanding before exams. You will be surprised at how much you can increase your understanding by committing yourself to doing extra problems. Active learning is always better than passive listening or reading.
- Have fun with it! If you keep your eyes and mind open, you will indeed discover that economics truly is all around you, and you will encounter new ways to use what you learn. Applying what you learn in class today to your next shopping trip to the mall or at work tomorrow will make you a better consumer and employee, which brings its own form of satisfaction.
- Don't procrastinate. Each concept in economics builds on the previous one. You will do far better by maintaining a steady pace than by cramming the night before the midterm or the final. One good strategy is to form a study group with your classmates. You will be surprised by how much you can teach each other as you progress through the course.

Strategy and Policy
Water, Water Everywhere

The concept of opportunity costs might seem irrelevant when it comes to water. Water is one of the world's most plentiful resources. Have you ever heard the famous line "Water, water everywhere Nor any drop to drink"?[1] Most of the water that covers the earth is salty and thus not readily usable for human consumption or agriculture. As populations grow in countries around the world, rivers, lakes, and underground aquifers have come under enormous demand. In the western United States, cities such as Phoenix and Las Vegas have grown at spectacular rates, increasing demand for already scarce water in a desert climate. One of the waterways under the most stress is the Colorado River. Seven western states obtain part of their water resources from the Colorado River. An agreement known as the Colorado River Compact, which dates back to 1922, first established usage rights

---

[1] Samuel Taylor Coleridge, "The Rime of the Ancient Mariner."

among these competing states. To date, California (which is the farthest downstream) has benefited because other states have not fully used their allocations. In the future, however, California's water shortages are likely to become more intense as upstream states take their full share of the river's annual flow.

The same scenario is being played out all over the world. The BBC estimates that one in five people worldwide now lack access to safe drinking water.[2] Mighty rivers such as the Jordan in the Middle East, the Volta in West Africa, and the Yellow River in China are all under intense pressure from pollution, population increases, and agriculture. Conflicts over water rights are especially difficult when rivers cross national boundaries. Increased damming of the Euphrates and Tigris rivers by Turkey has created tensions with downstream neighbors Syria and Iraq. At the same time, competition for the waters of the Nile increases steadily with the development and population increases of Egypt, Ethiopia, and Sudan. On every continent, the competition for clean fresh water grows every day.

Critical-Thinking Questions

1. Why might prices be an ineffective way to allocate water?
2. What technological changes might help to alleviate the shortages?

SUMMARY

- **Defining economics.** Economics is the study of the allocation of scarce resources among competing uses. Microeconomics focuses on the behavior of consumers and producers, and their transactions as they interact in markets. Macroeconomics focuses on the collective behavior of consumers, firms, government, and workers in the national and international economy.

- **The allocation of goods and services.** Goods and services can be allocated using markets. Prices in markets are determined by the forces of supply and demand, or by a central plan in which governments make production and allocation decisions. Market-based economies are fundamentally distinct from centrally planned economies in that market-based economies are demand-driven.

- **Opportunity cost.** The relevant cost of pursuing any activity is the opportunity cost, which is the value of the next-most preferred alternative forgone. Opportunity costs allow individuals, firms, and governments to consider what must be sacrificed to consume or produce a given good or service.

- **Cost-benefit analysis.** Cost-benefit analysis is the process of systematically comparing costs and benefits to determine whether to pursue an activity. With allocation decisions, we must consider both the costs and the benefits associated with additional consumption. Decisions of this type require that we focus on the marginal cost and benefit of consuming one additional unit, rather than all of the units as a whole.

- **Economic models.** An economic model is a framework of analysis designed to allow economists to analyze complex behavioral, technical, and institutional relationships. Economic models are based on a set of simplifying assumptions designed to make analysis easier without decreasing a model's ability to analyze or predict.

- **The importance of studying economics.** Economics is an important academic discipline. Economic research allows analysts to make appropriate government policy,

---

[2] Source: "World Water Crisis," news.bbc.co.uk/hi/english/static/in_depth/world/2000/world_water_crisis/default.stm. Accessed December 13, 2004.

enables firms to formulate their best possible strategy, and provides individuals with insight into how to make personal and financial decisions. As a practical tool, economic analysis allows for better-informed employers, employees, and consumers. Economic analysis falls into two broad categories: theoretical and applied.

■ **Off we go.** Economics is truly all around us every day. As you work through the textbook and course, be sure to keep your eyes open for ways in which you can apply what you learn. Try to avoid falling behind and relying on memorization. The best way to ensure success is to keep up with assignments, attend class regularly, and be an active learner.

▶ KEY TERMS

Assumptions 13	Economic system 8	Microeconomics 5
Centrally planned economy 10	Economics 5	Mixed economy 10
	Goods and services 8	Normative 7
Ceteris paribus 14	Macroeconomics 6	Opportunity cost 10
Cost-benefit analysis 12	Marginal analysis 12	Positive 7
Demand-driven economy 9	Marginal benefit 12	Rational self-interest 9
Economic forecasting 16	Marginal cost 12	Scarcity 5
Economic model 12	Market-based system 8	Transition economy 10

▶ PROBLEMS

1. Describe the economic factors associated with choosing a college or university.
2. Write three examples of microeconomic questions, and three examples of macroeconomic questions.
3. Suppose that you are assigned to a team that will study the wisdom of compressing garbage into large sealed drums and dumping them into the deepest parts of the ocean. Describe and differentiate among some of the positive and normative economic issues that must be addressed.
4. What does it mean to say that an economy is demand-driven?
5. In the last 25 years, most of the world's centrally planned economies have failed. Why do you suppose central planning does not seem to work as an economic system?
6. Make a list of the potential opportunity costs of attending college. Add to this the direct monetary cost (tuition, room and board, and books) to estimate the full cost of attending college for one year.
7. If you were awarded one free year of college and could enroll in as many classes as you wanted, how many would you take? Why?
8. Evaluate this statement: "In England, all health care is paid for by the government, so health care is free for consumers." What specific types of costs do consumers pay even if they do not actually write a check each time they visit the doctor?
9. If the marginal benefit of pizza declines with each slice that you consume, why do you ever eat more than one slice?
10. What are the costs and benefits of making assumptions when formulating a model?

Appendix for Chapter 1

Graphing and Algebra Review

You will encounter many graphs throughout this book. With the exception of some simple bar charts, the graphs will mostly be plots or sketches of straight lines. Depending on the preferences of your instructor, you might use basic algebra. You will, however, find no advanced mathematics in this textbook; you will not do much more than work with simple linear equations. If it has been some time since you worked with graphs or studied algebra, or if math is not a strong point for you, take some time to review this appendix. We will describe the use of tables and graphs, linear equations, determining the slope of a curve, and calculating percentage change.

Variables are letters or symbols that represent economic concepts, such as P for price, or Q for quantity. In economic models, we divide variables into two classes: dependent variables and independent variables. It is easy to distinguish between them: The value of the **dependent variable** *depends* on the value of the **independent variable**. For example, suppose we are examining the relationship between wages and the number of hours that an individual chooses to work. The wage offered is the independent variable and hours worked is the dependent variable. Now suppose we are examining the relationship between the number of hours that an individual studies for an exam and the exam grade that he receives. In this case, hours spent studying is the independent variable, and the exam grade is the dependent variable.

Variable
A letter, symbol, or name that represents a value or an economic concept.

Dependent variable
A variable that is influenced by external forces (independent variables).

Independent variable
A variable thought to influence the value of another variable (the dependent variable).

Using Tables and Graphs to Show Relationships

We will make frequent use of graphs and tables to show the relationship between two variables. For example, suppose we want to show the relationship between the hours spent studying (work) and the exam grade received (reward). We can construct a table that shows the various hours studied in one column and the exam grade in another column, as in Table 1A.1.

Data
Facts or information organized in a manner suitable for display, processing, or analysis.

The observations recorded for the independent variable (hours of study) and the dependent variable (exam grade) represent data. **Data** are pieces of information, often in the form of numerical statistics that are suitable for analysis. In this case, the data are a record of exam grades and time spent studying. Any outside observer can use the table to see how studying affects grades. Tables make information easy to review and compare. For example, we could construct the same table for a student at another school, or the same student in a different course, to compare information.

Line graph
An algebraic representation of the relationship between two variables using a single line.

A graph is another useful way to show relationships between economic variables. A **line graph** uses a single line to show the relationship between a dependent and an independent variable. To construct a line graph, we track the independent variable on the horizontal axis, and the dependent variable on the vertical axis. We then plot each point from our table on the graph, and use a line to connect the points. We plot the data from Table 1A.1 to make a line graph that shows the relationship between hours of study and exam grades in Figure 1A.1.

TABLE 1A.1

Relationship Between Hours Studied and Exam Score

Hours Spent Studying	Exam Grade
0	60
1	70
2	80
3	90
4	100

Equations of Straight Lines

Although it is not necessary to employ algebra to use this text, your instructor might use equations to show the relationships between variables. To keep models simple, we often use straight lines to depict relationships in introductory economics, even if the true relationship is not exactly linear. In an equation, the dependent variable is shown on the left-hand side of the equal sign, and the independent variable is on the right-hand side of the equal sign.

In a single linear equation, the slope and the intercept completely describe the relationship between the independent and the dependent variables. The basic form of a linear equation is:

$$Y = b + mX \tag{1A.1}$$

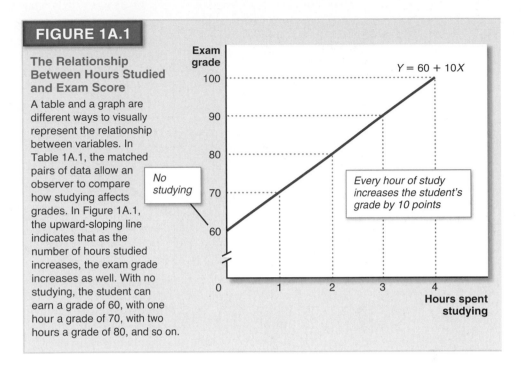

FIGURE 1A.1

The Relationship Between Hours Studied and Exam Score

A table and a graph are different ways to visually represent the relationship between variables. In Table 1A.1, the matched pairs of data allow an observer to compare how studying affects grades. In Figure 1A.1, the upward-sloping line indicates that as the number of hours studied increases, the exam grade increases as well. With no studying, the student can earn a grade of 60, with one hour a grade of 70, with two hours a grade of 80, and so on.

In graph: Exam grade; $Y = 60 + 10X$; No studying; Every hour of study increases the student's grade by 10 points; Hours spent studying

Slope

A measurement of the rate of change along a line. The slope of a line is equal to the change in Y divided by the change in X.

Parameters

Numerical constants that have a set value not determined by the researcher.

In Equation 1A.1, Y is the dependent variable, X is the independent variable, b is the Y-intercept, and m is the slope. The Y-intercept of a line tells you the value of Y when X equals zero. The **slope** tells you by how much Y changes when X changes by one unit. You may recall the phrase "rise over run" as a description of slope. The slope of a line is equal to the change in Y divided by the change in X. We call the slope and intercept **parameters**, not variables, because they do not vary each time the equation is used and because the investigator cannot choose them. In this text, they will typically be given to you.

For example, suppose you are given the information that Janine buys four gallons of gas each week regardless of whether she is volunteering that week for the Share-A-Ride Program, plus three additional gallons for each person that she drives. We can represent her consumption of gasoline with an equation, by allowing Y to represent the number of gallons of gas consumed and X to represent the number of people she offers to drive. Thus, we set $b = 4$ as the Y-intercept, and $m = 3$ as the slope, and write the following equation:

$$Y = 4 + 3X \qquad (1A.2)$$

The parameters b and m tells us that if X is equal to zero, Y is equal to 4, and that for every one-unit increase in X, Y increases by 3:

$$Y = 4 + 3(0) = 4$$
$$Y = 4 + 3(1) = 7$$
$$Y = 4 + 3(2) = 10$$
$$Y = 4 + 3(3) = 13$$

We can produce a line graph based on the relationship described by the equation. As with any line graph, for each value of X, we plot the appropriate value of Y based on the equation. Figure 1A.2 shows the graph of the equation $Y = 4 + 3X$. Notice that the line intersects the Y-axis at $Y = 4$ gallons of gas, which is the

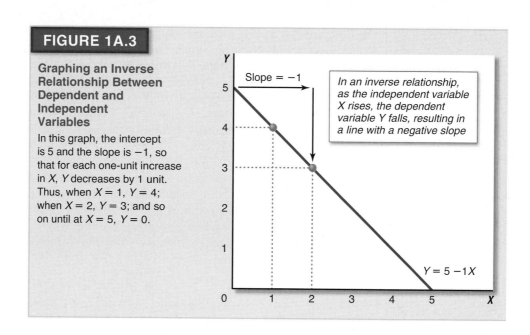

FIGURE 1A.2

The Relationship Between Passengers and Gasoline Consumption

The equation representing Janine's gasoline consumption has an intercept of 4 and a slope of 3. When $X = 0$, $Y = 4$, because Janine uses 4 gallons of gas regardless of whether she volunteers for Share-A-Ride. We see that she uses an additional 3 gallons for each person that she transports: 7 when she transports one person, 10 for two people, 13 for three people, and so on.

Gallons of gasoline

$Y = 4 + 3X$

For every one-unit increase in the independent variable, X, the dependent variable, Y, increases by 3 units

Number of passengers

FIGURE 1A.3

Graphing an Inverse Relationship Between Dependent and Independent Variables

In this graph, the intercept is 5 and the slope is −1, so that for each one-unit increase in X, Y decreases by 1 unit. Thus, when $X = 1$, $Y = 4$; when $X = 2$, $Y = 3$; and so on until at $X = 5$, $Y = 0$.

Slope = −1

In an inverse relationship, as the independent variable X rises, the dependent variable Y falls, resulting in a line with a negative slope

$Y = 5 - 1X$

Y-intercept, and that for each one-unit increase in X (that is, for each person she drives), Y increases by 3 units.

In general, the slope and intercept can take on any value. For instance, we frequently encounter inverse relationships in economics; where the dependent variable falls as the independent variable rises. In such cases, the slope of the line is negative, as in Equation 1A.3, which is illustrated in Figure 1A.3.

$$Y = 5 - 1X \qquad (1A.3)$$

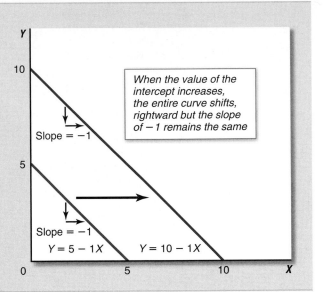

FIGURE 1A.4

The Effect of a Change in Intercept on the Curve

When the intercept increases from 5 to 10, the entire curve shifts rightward, because for every value of X, the corresponding Y-value is 5 units more than before. When run is positive but rise is negative, we see a downward-sloping curve, indicating that an increase in one variable is associated with a decrease in the other variable.

In Equation 1A.3, the Y-intercept is 5, and the slope is –1, which means that Y decreases by 1 for every one-unit increase in X:

$$Y = 5 - 1(0) = 5$$
$$Y = 5 - 1(1) = 4$$
$$Y = 5 - 1(2) = 3$$

and so on, until:

$$Y = 5 - 1(5) = 0$$

Changes in the Intercept Term

A change in the Y-intercept shifts the entire line to a new location. If the Y-intercept in Equation 1A.3 increases from 5 to 10, the new equation is:

$$Y = 10 - 1X \qquad (1A.4)$$

The entire line shifts up, because for every value of X, Y is 5 units more than before. Figure 1A.4 shows the original line in blue, and the new line for Equation 1A.4 with the new intercept in red. Notice that the slope of the line does not change.

Changes in the Slope

When the value of m changes, the slope of the line changes. In Equation 1A.2, if the slope increases from $m = 3$ to $m = 4$, the new equation is:

$$Y = 4 + 4X \qquad (1A.5)$$

The value of Y increases by 4 units for each one-unit increase in X, and the line becomes steeper. Figure 1A.5 shows the original line from Figure 1A.2 in dark blue, with the new, steeper line from Equation 1A.5 in light blue.

The Effect of a Change in Slope on the Curve

If the intercept of 4 remains the same, but the value of the slope increases from 3 to 4, then when $X = 6$, the corresponding value of Y will increase from 22 to 28. Thus, we see that for every one-unit increase in X, the value of Y increases by increments of 4 rather than 3 units, resulting in a line with a steeper incline.

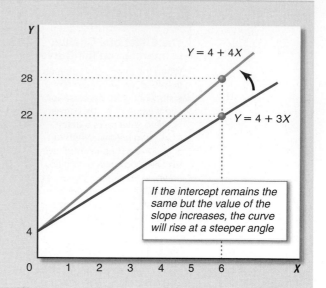

If the intercept remains the same but the value of the slope increases, the curve will rise at a steeper angle

FIGURE 1A.6

Lines with Zero and Infinite Slopes

Horizontal lines have a zero slope, and vertical lines have an infinite slope. In both cases, no relationship exists between the dependent variable (Y) and the independent variable (X).

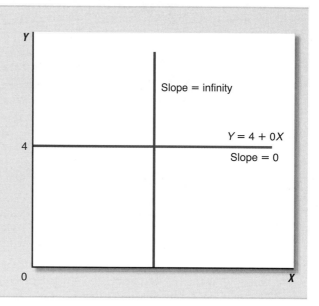

There are two special slopes worth noting. The first occurs when the line is horizontal. In this case the slope of the line is zero, because changes in X do not affect Y. To illustrate, return to Equation 1A.5 and change the slope to 0. The new equation is:

$$Y = 4 + 0X = 4 \qquad (1A.6)$$

The dependent variable Y always equals 4, and the line is horizontal.

At the opposite extreme, if the line is vertical, we say that the slope is infinite or undefined (economists almost always say infinite). Figure 1A.6 shows lines with

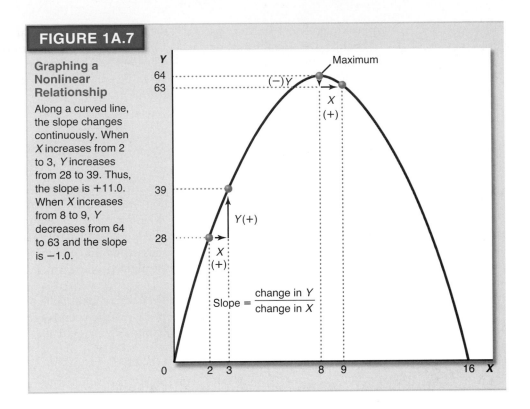

FIGURE 1A.7

Graphing a Nonlinear Relationship

Along a curved line, the slope changes continuously. When X increases from 2 to 3, Y increases from 28 to 39. Thus, the slope is +11.0. When X increases from 8 to 9, Y decreases from 64 to 63 and the slope is −1.0.

slopes of zero in blue and infinity in red. In both cases, the lack of a positive or negative value for the slope indicates that there is no relationship between the dependent and independent variables.

Estimating the Slope of a Curve

Get Ahead of the Curve

Use your knowledge of tables and graphs to display and interpret oil consumption data.

When lines are not straight, the rate of change (or slope) of the line is not constant. Such cases are common in economics. Profits, labor productivity, and opportunity cost are just a few examples of models in which change is not clear. In these cases, we will often want to make statements about the rate of change in one variable as the other increases or decreases. Without the use of calculus, it is very difficult to find the precise rate of change or slope at any given point on the line. Fortunately, we can easily calculate an estimate that serves our purposes. For example, in Figure 1A.7, we see that at first, as X increases, Y also increases, and so the line is positively sloped. The relationship is not constant, however, because the increases in Y get smaller and smaller as X rises, and the slope of the line decreases (becomes less positive) until Y reaches a maximum where X = 8 and Y = 64. Beyond the maximum point, Y decreases as X increases. Because Y decreases by more each time X increases, the slope of the line gets steeper (becomes more negative) the farther we move beyond the maximum, until at X = 16, Y has fallen all the way to zero.

To approximate the slope of a curve, choose two points of interest, and draw (or imagine) a straight line segment between them. Now determine the change in Y given the change in X to determine the approximate slope. Figure 1A.7 shows two such calculations. From them, we can see that the slope of the line between X = 2 and X = 3 is approximately 11.0, and the slope between X = 8 and X = 9 is approximately -1.0. More precisely, the slope that you calculate is the average rate of change over the interval on the X-axis. This slope's calculation will be sufficient for our purposes. Two notes of caution: You must have two points to make this estimate. The farther apart the two points are, the greater the chance that your estimate of the slope will differ from the actual slope at the points you have chosen.

►Using Percentages

When variables change, economists are often more interested in the size of the change relative to the variable's starting level than in the absolute magnitude of the change. One way to resolve this dilemma is to represent changes as percentages, because percentages are not specified in units. Changes in economic variables are thus frequently presented and discussed as percentages. Calculating percentages and percentage changes is very straightforward, and requires only a bit of arithmetic.

Suppose that Eric earns $500 per week and spends $80 per week on groceries. We determine the percentage of his income that he spends on groceries by dividing the expenditure by his income and then multiplying by 100:

$$\text{Percent of income spent on groceries} = (\$80/\$500) \times 100 = 16\%$$

Notice that there are no units associated with the percentage. Because dollars appear in both the numerator and the denominator, the two cancel each other out.

Suppose that Eric receives a raise to $600 per week. His co-worker, Michelle, receives a raise at the same time, from $700 to $820 per week. You might say that because Eric's raise is $100, and Michelle's is $120, Michelle received a better raise. However, we cannot immediately tell whether Michelle's pay increased more relative to what she originally earned versus the same information for Eric's increase and original wage, because the two starting points are different. We can avoid this confusion by describing the changes as percentages. To calculate a percentage change, subtract the original value from the new value, then divide the difference by the original value and multiply by 100:

Eric's percentage increase $= [(\$600-500)/500] \times 100 = (100/500) \times 100 = 20\%$
Michelle's percentage increase $= [(\$820-700)/700] \times 100 = (120/700) \times 100 = 17.1\%$

Even though Michelle received a larger increase in absolute terms, Eric received a better raise on a percentage basis, that is, based on his previous salary.

►Key Terms

Data 22	Line graph 22	Slope 23
Dependent variable 21	Parameters 23	Variable 21
Independent variable 21		

PROBLEMS

1. Plot the data in the following table on a line graph. What is the slope of the resulting line?

X	Y
1	2
2	4
3	6
4	8
5	10

2. Suppose that consumption (Y) and income (X) are related such that $Y = 0.9X$.
   a. What is the slope of this line?
   b. What is the Y-intercept?
   c. If consumption were 1,000, what would be the value of income?

3. Plot the equation $Y = 20 - 2X$ on a graph. At what point does the line reach the X-axis? Suppose the Y-intercept increases to 30. Draw the new line.

4. Plot the equation $Y = 15$ on a graph. What is the slope of this line? On the same graph, plot the line $X = 15$. What is the slope of this line?

5. Plot the equation $Y = 10 + X$. Then, assume that the slope of the line doubles. Plot the new line. Using the new line, determine the increase in Y if X increases from 4 to 5.

6. The following data show Damon's test grades and the time he spent studying.

Test	Hours Studied	Score
1	2	75
2	3	85
3	4	90
4	1	50
5	7	90
6	0	0

   a. Which is the dependent and which is the independent variable?
   b. Plot the points on a graph. Be sure to put the dependent variable on the vertical axis.
   c. Does the relationship appear linear? Explain.
   d. Determine the slope between 2 and 3 hours of studying.

7. Suppose Jane's income increases from $400 to $800 per week in 2006. What is the percentage increase in her income?

8. Suppose Tanya's income decreases from $800 to $400 per week in 2006. What is the percentage decrease in her income?

9. Answer true or false, and explain your reasoning: "The unemployment rate is 4.5 percent in the United States and in Germany. Thus we know that the same number of people are unemployed in each country."

10. Suppose the U.S. labor force is 150 million people. If three percent are unemployed, how many workers are unemployed?

TO LOG INTO MyEconLab FOR THE FIRST TIME:

1. Log into MyEconLab and take Practice Test chapter-A. Follow these instructions to log in for the first time.
2. Click on "Take a Test" and select Test A for this chapter.
3. Take the diagnostic test and MyEconLab will grade it automatically and create a personalized Study Plan, so you can see which sections of the chapter you should study further.
4. The Study Plan will serve up additional practice problems and tutorials to help you master the specific areas where you need to focus. By practicing online, you can track your progress in the Study Plan.
5. After you have mastered the sections, "Take a Test" and select TestB for this chapter. Take the test, and see how you do!

Section 1.1, Exercise 1 How can you best explain the concept of scarcity?

Section 1.1, Exercise 2 Identify whether each of the following statements is positive or normative:

a. The United States should give food to countries where there is famine.
b. Higher interest rates mean that borrowers must pay more for loans.
c. The primary goal of the government should be economic growth.
d. If wages rise, consumers will have more income to spend.

Section 1.2, Exercise 1 How are prices determined in a market economy?

Section 1.3, Exercise 1 It's Saturday morning, and you have to make a choice: sleep for another two hours, help clean the house, or play basketball with your friends. You don't like to clean the house, so you would never voluntarily choose that. If you decide to sleep, what is the opportunity cost of your choice?

Section 1.3, Exercise 2 Your friend offers you a choice of a cola, an iced tea, or a glass of milk. You don't really like milk, so after some thought, you decide to take the iced tea. What is the opportunity cost of your choice?

Section 1.3, Exercise 3 What do economists mean when they say that there is no such thing as a free lunch?

Section 1.4, Exercise 1 You have five hours to spend studying, and you must choose between studying economics and studying math. Every hour that you spend on each subject increases your exam score for that test, but there is a cost, because you can't study the other subject at the same time. The following table shows your marginal benefits and costs.

Hours Studying Economics	Marginal Benefit (increase in points on economics exam)	Marginal Cost (loss of points on math exam)
0	0	0
1	20	5
2	15	10
3	12	12
4	5	15
5	2	18

If you value points on both exams equally, for how many hours should you study economics, and why?

Section 1.4, Exercise 2 Cars emit carbon monoxide and other greenhouse gases, which are bad for the environment, but reducing emissions is costly. Many environmental groups argue that legal emission standards should be lowered. How would an economist decide the optimal level of emissions?

Appendix, Exercise 1 For each of the following functions, graph the function and label the intercept(s) and slope.

a. $Y = 500 - 2X$
b. $Y = 10X$
c. $Y = 100 + 4X$
d. $Y = 900 - 3X$
e. $Y = -50 + 5X$

Appendix, Exercise 2 For each of the following equation pairs, graph the original equation; indicate whether the intercept, slope, or both have changed; and graph the new equation.

   a. $Y = 500 - 2X$; $Y = 1{,}000 - 2X$
   b. $Y = 10X$; $Y = 20X$
   c. $Y = -50 + 5X$; $Y = -100 + 10X$

Appendix, Exercise 3 If you earn $500 per week and pay $150 a week to rent your apartment, what percentage of your income is spent on rent?

Appendix, Exercise 4 If your income rises to $600, by what percentage has it increased?

Appendix, Exercise 5 Nancy earns $500 per week, and Andrew earns $450 per week. Each receives a raise of $100 per week. Calculate each worker's raise in percentage terms. Who got the better raise?

2 Efficiency and Allocation in the Global Economy

You learned in Chapter 1 that society's limited resources cannot fulfill unlimited desires and that economics is the study of how we make choices under conditions of scarcity. Because we can't do everything, choosing to pursue one activity—such as building a car or providing an X-ray—is also choosing not to pursue another activity, such as engineering a fighter plane or researching a new vaccine.

Governments make such choices all the time, and the consequences ripple around the world, affecting everything from your grandmother's medicine cabinet in Duluth to the price of steel in Beijing. When U.S. President George W. Bush said, in response to the September 11, 2001, attacks, "America will do what is necessary to ensure our nation's security," he was announcing a commitment of resources. Such commitments do not come without substantial cost. Undertaking a massive, long-term military operation requires extensive resources. Once these resources are committed to military uses, they cannot be employed to produce goods and services in other industries.

The conflict over the allocation of public resources is a constant in human history. If a country spends too much of its resources on wars, it might not be able to adequately meet the needs of its citizens at home. If it concentrates all of its resources on domestic needs, the country might not be able to defend itself. In a current example, even as the United States has devoted hundreds of billions of dollars to military operations in the Middle

East, more than 40 million Americans lack adequate health care. In this chapter, we focus on the allocation decision made by the United States to distribute scarce resources between the production of vaccinations and guns, and the related trade-offs. Although guns and vaccinations are very dissimilar goods, production of both requires allocation of scarce economic resources.

Most Americans support the idea of guaranteed basic medical care, such as check-ups, vaccinations, and essential medications. Offering such care to everyone would cost billions of dollars. For instance, the Canadian government spends heavily to allocate the necessary resources to keep medications more affordable than they are in the United States. As a result, some elderly people in the northern United States have recently turned to the international market, crossing the border into Canada to fill needed prescriptions. At the same time, some Canadians cross the border into the United States to obtain access to high technology procedures which are less available in Canada. These incidents brought to light many complexities regarding the health care systems in the United States and Canada. When a society chooses to devote resources to one activity, another must be forgone.

At both a microeconomic and a macroeconomic level, the choices we make as a nation concerning *what, how,* and *for whom* to produce have an enormous impact on our daily lives. We address the question of *for whom* goods and services are produced in Chapter 4. In this chapter, we begin our exploration of choices and their consequences, which will help determine *what* will be produced and *how* it will be produced.

ALONG THE WAY, YOU WILL ALSO LEARN:

- The basic resources used in production.
- Why economies with productive efficiency must produce less of one good to produce more of another.
- How current choices affect economic growth.
- How economists define efficiency and equity, the tension that sometimes exists between the two, and the natural incentives for efficiency in market economies.
- The benefits of specialization and trade.

AT THE END OF THE CHAPTER, THE MYECONLAB LOGO WILL DIRECT YOU ONLINE

- MyEconLab is a resource-packed online homework and tutorial system that can help you perform better in your economics course. To log in for the first time, see page 30 for instructions.
- MyEconLab can help you apply important concepts from the chapter to real-world issues. Watch for the logo to indicate online features about comparative advantage and the production possibilities frontier.
- At the end of each chapter, you'll find a special study section that will help you get the most out of your textbook and your instructor's MyEconLab course.

▶ Factors of Production

We begin our look at *what* and *how* goods and services are produced by examining the resources used in production. Economies use four basic categories of resources, or **inputs**, to produce all goods and services: land, labor, physical capital, and entrepreneurship. We define each input category in detail in the following sections. Collectively, these four inputs are also known as the **factors of production**. The answers to the questions of *what* and *how* a nation can produce are determined in part by how much of these factors it possesses, or its **factor endowment**. Our discussion of each input relates it to our example of the U.S. trade-off between military expenditures and vaccine production.

Land

Land is, in part, what the term implies: a natural resource that can be used for agriculture, mining, housing, industrial production, and recreation. Economists also include in this category other natural resources, such as water, gas and oil deposits, minerals, and forests. In the context of the nation's decision to produce more guns or more vaccinations, any given parcel of land or natural resource can be used either in the production of guns or vaccinations, but not both.

Labor

Labor is the entire pool of physical and mental talents available to produce goods and services. The **labor force** is the number of individuals 16 and over that are willing and able to work. Our definition focuses on the productive ability of the people in the labor force. A fundamental characteristic of labor is that it is embodied in the seller. That is, it is not possible for individuals to loan their productivity to someone else, or for workers to provide their labor without opportunity cost. You cannot, for example, show up for work *and* be out playing golf at the same time.

The U.S. population is about 290 million, but only about 60 percent of the population is in the labor force—not everyone is willing and able to work. The government definition of the labor force excludes the youngest members of society, as well as retired or institutionalized individuals. An alternative definition might be that labor is the sum of all the physical and mental abilities in an economy. However, economists typically do not use this definition, instead relying on the government definition.

The knowledge, experience, and innate ability that allows individuals to produce output is called **human capital**. People typically increase human capital through education and training that improves their ability to produce output. Nearly all jobs require some amount of human capital. Chefs need knowledge about cooking techniques and kitchen equipment. Veterinarians must master animal anatomy. Electricians must know safe wiring techniques. Increasing the level of human capital increases the productivity of workers in society. In the context of our guns-or-vaccinations example, highly trained medical researchers could apply their knowledge toward military endeavors, such as defending against germ or biological warfare, or they could develop a vaccine against the common cold—but not both.

Physical Capital

Physical capital
See capital goods.

Capital goods
The buildings and equipment used to produce other goods and services.

Consumption goods
Goods that can only be consumed and cannot be used to produce other goods.

Financial capital
The money that a firm raises.

Physical capital refers to buildings and equipment that can be used to produce other goods and services. For example, computers, software, drill presses, dump trucks, office buildings, and factories are all types of physical capital. We also refer to such resources as **capital goods**. Ice cream, in contrast, is not a capital good. Although we might like ice cream and want to produce it, we cannot use ice cream to produce other goods. Ice cream is a consumer good, because we buy it for our own use to satisfy our demand for dessert. Consumer goods, such as ice cream are also called *consumption goods*. By definition, **consumption goods** cannot be used to produce other goods. Returning to our example: Military hardware, such as guns and jeeps, is physical capital used to produce national defense. Vaccine doses are consumption goods.

Sometimes, the term "capital" is used to mean money. You might hear, for instance, that a firm is trying to raise capital to expand its operations. The money that the firm raises is **financial capital**. The buildings and equipment that the firm purchases as part of the expansion are physical capital. In this chapter and throughout the text, unless we specifically state otherwise, we use the term "capital" to mean "physical capital."

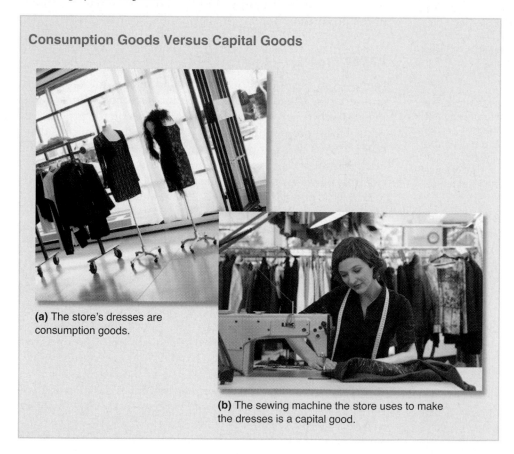

Consumption Goods Versus Capital Goods

(a) The store's dresses are consumption goods.

(b) The sewing machine the store uses to make the dresses is a capital good.

Entrepreneurship

Entrepreneurs
Individuals who apply their creative talent and resources to start and operate businesses.

Entrepreneurs organize, operate, and assume the risk of business ventures using land, labor, and physical capital to produce innovative goods and services. Visionary entrepreneurs often anticipate the future needs of the market and are the first to supply the goods and services that fulfill those needs. Entrepreneurial skill has played a vital role in the development of the U.S. economy. Consider the contributions of Henry Ford, who revolutionized the automobile industry, and Steve Jobs and Bill Gates, computer industry pioneers.

Management
A form of labor and a science where certain highly trained workers organize, supervise, and lead others.

The skills of a manager are closely aligned with those of the entrepreneur. **Management** is a form of labor, and in many complex organizations it is also a science, in which highly trained managers organize, supervise, and lead others. Skillful leadership increases the productivity of the rest of the labor force. For this reason, economists sometimes consider management to be a separate category from the rest of the labor force.

DILBERT: © Scott Adams/Dist. by United Feature Syndicate, Inc.

Production Technology

The total volume of output an economy is able to produce depends on its factor endowments—how much land, labor, capital, and entrepreneurship it has—and how it employs those inputs. With greater endowments of the factors of production or better technology, the economy can produce more output.

Typically, a nation must acquire both education and technology to increase productive capacity. Suppose, for example, that a new technology takes the form of a statistical software package designed to analyze product defect rates. This technological advance will have no impact on output unless the individuals operating the new software learn how to use it and how to interpret the software's output. In the late twentieth century, technology boomed in the United States. For productive capacity to increase, however, education levels had to increase as well. In 1976, 64 percent of American adults had completed high school, and 14 percent had completed college. By 2003, the percentage of Americans who had completed high school had risen to 85, and 27 percent had completed college. Thus, we attribute the growth in the economy over that period not only to an increase in technology, but also to our ability to utilize that technology.

Production possibilities frontier (PPF)
The curve that shows the combinations of goods and services that an economy can produce in a given time period.

▶ The Production Possibilities Frontier

In this section, we will build our first economic model. It is designed to analyze scarcity, economic trade-offs, opportunity cost, and growth. The **production possibilities frontier (PPF)** is a curve that shows the combinations of goods and services an economy can produce in a given time period. Our focus here is to analyze the trade-off between military and health expenditures. We begin by stepping back and examining how these two expenditures fit into the economy as a whole, and the balance of goods and services that a nation produces.

Gross Domestic Product

Gross Domestic Product (GDP)
The value of all the new final goods and services produced annually in an economy.

GDP per capita
GDP divided by the number of people in the population; in other words, output per person.

Military and health expenditures are only two of the many goods and services produced by an economy. To determine their relative weight in the economy, we need a measure of the economy's overall output. **Gross Domestic Product (GDP)** is the market value of all the new final goods and services produced in a given period in an economy. In 2004, U.S. GDP was $11.7 trillion. You will often see GDP figures reported as output per person rather than as total output. We calculate output per person, **GDP per capita**, by dividing total GDP by the total population. The GDP per capita in the United States was about $40,000 in 2004. The distinction between GDP and GDP per capita is helpful when comparing economies of differing sizes. We also use GDP per capita to compare a given economy in one time period with that same economy in another period after an increase (or decrease) in population.

Trade-offs Between Goods

We can depict the choices regarding military and health-care spending using a simple model. Recall from Chapter 1 that economic models usually require simplifying assumptions. In this case, we want to focus on a society's trade-offs regarding a very limited number of goods and services without becoming distracted by the thousands of goods and services that are actually produced. As we examine these choices, we assume that the total quantity of resources available is fixed, that all resources are fully employed, and that the level of technology and human capital does not change. Our model assumes that only two goods are produced in the economy: doses of influenza vaccine and guns.

Panel (a) of Figure 2.1 shows some of the possible combinations of doses of vaccines and guns that could be produced in the United States. (In reality, the United States is capable of producing much greater quantities than we show here. Smaller numbers simplify the model.) Combination A shows that all the resources in the economy are devoted to gun production. The economy produces 120 guns and 0 doses of vaccines. In each row, you can see how the number of doses produced increases as fewer guns are produced. When the economy devotes fewer resources to gun production in combination B, vaccine production jumps from 0 to 100,000 doses. Thus, the cost of the first 100,000 vaccines (in terms of guns) is 20 guns. Gun production must fall from 100 to 60 in order to produce 200,000 doses of vaccine (combination C). Thus, we can say that the cost of the second 100,000 doses is 40 guns. The second 100,000 doses cost more in terms of guns (40) than do the first 100,000, which cost 20 guns. To increase vaccine production to 300,000 vaccines, gun production must fall by another 60 guns, all the way to 0 (combination E); here, all of the economy's resources are devoted to producing vaccines. The more vaccines produced, the more expensive they are in terms of lost gun production. In other words, the opportunity cost of vaccines, as measured by the number of guns forgone, increases as vaccine output increases.

Building the Production Possibilities Frontier. Society must choose one of these combinations of gun and vaccine quantities. Before discussing *what* to produce, we

FIGURE 2.1

The Production Possibilities Frontier (PPF)

The table in panel (a) shows some of the different production possibilities in the economy. Panel (b) shows the same information in graph form. The economy is capable of producing any combination of guns and vaccines that lies on or inside the frontier (gold area). Movement along the curve indicates constantly changing trade-offs, from devoting all resources to producing a maximum of 120 guns (with no vaccine) to devoting all resources to producing a maximum of 300,000 vaccines (with no guns). Points outside the frontier such as *F* are not feasible.

(a)

Combination	Quantity of guns	Quantity of vaccines
A	120	0
B	100	100,000
C	60	200,000
D	20	280,000
E	0	300,000

(b)

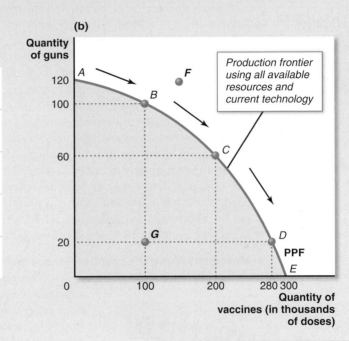

must be very clear about how much of one good we give up to have more of another. Showing the data in panel (a) in graph form clearly illustrates how the cost of producing more of one good changes depending on the current mix of outputs.

Economists use data like those in panel (a) of Figure 2.1 to draw the production possibilities frontier in panel (b) of the same figure. The graph illustrates the number of doses of vaccines and guns that our example economy can produce in one year. The number of doses of vaccine produced is shown on the horizontal axis, and the number of guns is shown on the vertical axis. We refer to the curve as a "frontier," because it represents the boundary outside of which an economy cannot produce. Along a single PPF, we continue to assume that the total quantity of resources available is fixed, that all resources are fully employed, and that the level of technology and human capital does not change during the year. The downward slope of the curve indicates that there is an opportunity cost to increasing the production of either good. At any point on the curve, we must produce less of one good in order to produce more of the other. More importantly, the slope of the curve indicates the minimum amount of one good that must be sacrificed to increase production of the other.

Points Along the PPF

In Figure 2.1 panel (b), we see that the economy can produce as many as 120 guns if all resources are devoted to producing guns. It can produce up to 300,000 doses of vaccine if all resources are devoted to producing vaccines. The economy can produce any combination of guns and vaccines that lies on or inside the PPF. It cannot produce combinations of vaccines and guns that lie outside the PPF. Producing at point *F* in panel (b) of Figure 2.1 requires more resources than the economy has at its disposal.

Combinations that lie directly on the frontier, such as *A* through *E*, illustrate productive efficiency. **Productive efficiency** means that all the economy's resources are fully employed using the current technology. No resources go unused, and we cannot increase the production of either good without sacrificing production of some of the other. Operating at any point inside the frontier, such as point *G* in panel (b) of Figure 2.1 is inefficient. When the economy simultaneously produces 100,000 doses of vaccine and 20 guns, it underutilizes its scarce resources. At point *G*, there is unemployment (some of the resources are not being used) or underemployment (some of the resources are being used inefficiently). In contrast, if the economy operates at point *B* on the PPF, it produces 100 guns, 80 more guns than at point *G*, without giving up any doses of vaccine. Some resources are not used or not used in the most productive way at point *G*. Therefore, no doses of vaccine must be sacrificed to move from *G* to *B*. Once at point *B*, producing more guns will require giving up some vaccine production. Thus, when the economy is producing efficiently, there is an opportunity cost associated with a move to any new point on the frontier.

Movement Along the Frontier. Notice that the PPF is bowed outward, as shown by the curve in panel (b) of Figure 2.1. This means that the trade-off between guns and vaccines is constantly changing, because as we produce more and more guns (and move upward along the PPF), we exhaust those resources that are best suited to producing guns. To compensate, we must utilize other resources that are less and less suited for gun production but more and more suited for vaccine production, such as biochemists. Similarly, as we move down the PPF, we must employ both labor and physical capital increasingly well suited to gun production, and increasingly poorly suited to the production of vaccines.

Because not all resources are equally useful in the production of guns and vaccines, the cost of shifting resources from producing one good to the other is not always the same. The **law of increasing opportunity cost** states that *as more and more resources are devoted to the production of one good (good A) at the expense of another good (good B), the opportunity cost of producing more of good A increases.* When countries are forced to specialize in producing commodities such as guns and other defense goods, the opportunity cost to society can be great. During World War II, Americans were forced to drive with tires with replacement treads, because so much of the nation's rubber was devoted to military uses. Even more striking is that U.S. auto production fell from over 3 million

Productive efficiency
When all of the economy's resources are fully employed, no resources go unused, and the production of any good cannot be increased without sacrificing production of another good.

Law of increasing opportunity cost
States that as we devote more and more resources to the production of one good at the expense of another, the opportunity cost of producing more of that good increases.

FIGURE 2.2

Shifting Resources and Increasing Opportunity Costs

As gun production increases, the initial cost as measured in doses of vaccine is relatively small. The first 20 guns cause vaccine production to fall by only 20,000 vaccines. However, the final 20 guns come at great cost. Indeed, vaccine production must fall from 100,000 doses to 0 in order to increase gun production from 100 to120.

When the final 20 guns are produced, vaccine production falls from 100,000 to 0

When the first 20 guns are produced, vaccine production falls by 20,000

units in 1941 to just 600 in 1944, as nearly all auto industry resources were converted to military production.

We can see the principle of increasing opportunity cost in Figure 2.2 by evaluating the cost of an increase in gun production at various points along the frontier. The first 20 guns that we give up (as gun production falls from 120 to 100) causes vaccine production to increase from 0 to 100,000 doses. Yet, forgoing the last 20 guns increases vaccine production by only 20,000 doses (from 280,000 to 300,000). In general, the more we produce of any good, the greater the sacrifice we must make to produce still greater quantities of it.

Modeling Economic Growth

Now that you've mastered the PPF model, we can use it to analyze an economy's output over time. An economy can grow over time by employing the factors of production introduced earlier in the chapter. Here we will discuss possible sources of growth and illustrate economic growth in terms of a shift of the production possibilities frontier.

myeconlab

Get Ahead of the Curve

Use the production possibilites frontier to analyze economic growth in Japan.

Shifts of the Frontier

Over time, an economy's PPF can shift to a new position if more resources become available or as technology and human resources improve. For example, if workers' human capital increases, the economy can produce both more vaccines and more guns. The increase in capital shifts the PPF outward, as shown by PPF_2 in Figure 2.3.

Additional capital can also change the shape of the PPF, as shown by PPF_3 in Figure 2.3. If the new capital is especially well suited to producing vaccines, the PPF will shift farther on the doses of vaccine axis than on the guns axis. However, if the

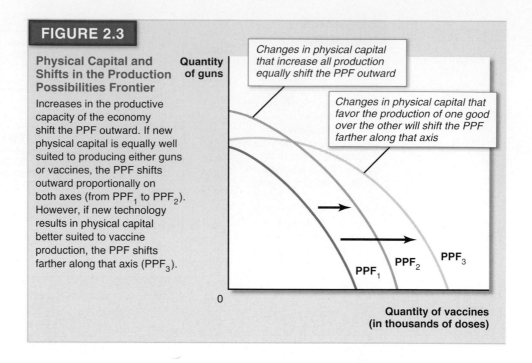

FIGURE 2.3

Physical Capital and Shifts in the Production Possibilities Frontier

Increases in the productive capacity of the economy shift the PPF outward. If new physical capital is equally well suited to producing either guns or vaccines, the PPF shifts outward proportionally on both axes (from PPF$_1$ to PPF$_2$). However, if new technology results in physical capital better suited to vaccine production, the PPF shifts farther along that axis (PPF$_3$).

Quantity of guns

Changes in physical capital that increase all production equally shift the PPF outward

Changes in physical capital that favor the production of one good over the other will shift the PPF farther along that axis

PPF$_1$ PPF$_2$ PPF$_3$

0

Quantity of vaccines (in thousands of doses)

new physical capital resembles the existing capital, the curve will retain the same general shape (PPF$_2$). The same is true for technological developments. The development and implementation of new technology are among the most important sources of increased overall production. That is, more advanced machinery capable of producing higher-quality goods at faster speeds shifts the PPF outward. Sometimes this new technology replaces existing, less productive capital, as in the case of computers with word processing software effectively replacing typewriters. In other instances, new technology works with existing capital or labor to increase its productivity. Consider a new software program that increases the processing speed of an existing personal computer. In either case, improvements in technology increase the productivity of the inputs, and the PPF shifts outward.

Changes in Population

Recall that the PPF assumes that the economy's resources are fixed. One implication of this assumption is that population is constant. If we ignore trade among nations, it follows that the output that is produced in a nation is equal to that which is consumed. Thus, if the PPF shifts outward, we have more output divided among the same number of people, and GDP per-capita increases. An increase in GDP per capita means an increase in the standard of living.

If the population grows over time, the changes in our model are not as clear-cut. When the population grows, the productive capacity of the economy increases. However, the output that is produced must be divided among more people. If an increase of 10 percent in the population causes output to increase by 10 percent, people are no better off. Consider what would happen, though, if the new workers were more skilled and more able to take advantage of cutting-edge technology and existing capital. In this case, the 10-percent increase in population might cause output to grow at an even faster rate, such as 20 percent. For example, a 10-percent increase in computing speeds might allow skilled mail-order workers to process 20 percent more orders. The increased output benefits both the firm and the consumers.

Choices and Long-Run Growth

As we noted, there are several possible sources of long-run growth in an economy. Growth can result from an increase in the level of human capital in the labor force, an increase in technology, an increase in the quantity of capital, or even from the discovery of some new natural resource, such as an oil deposit. In this section, we focus on the effect of a deliberate choice on the part of an economy to produce more capital and the effect of that choice over time on the nation's growth prospects.

The specific position that an economy occupies on the production possibilities frontier can alter the location of the frontier over time. Suppose a nation has the option of choosing to produce either consumption goods (such as TV sets and furniture) or capital goods (such as machinery or buildings). If it produces mostly consumption goods, it will not add much to its capital stock over time. A country's **capital stock** is its usable productive capital. By concentrating on consumption goods at the expense of accumulating capital stock, its ability to produce does not increase appreciably. In this case, most resources are used for goods and services that are consumed, rather than for goods that can in turn produce more goods. If instead the nation devotes much of its current production to capital goods, then its production possibilities frontier shifts outward at a more rapid pace. By investing heavily in the production of capital goods, a nation can eventually produce more consumption goods *and* more capital goods than if it had not.

For example, following World War II, Japan invested very heavily in replacing destroyed manufacturing plants and equipment with newer capital and technology. The immediate opportunity cost of this investment was fewer consumption goods. In the long run, however, Japan's productive capacity increased dramatically. The Japanese economy flourished from the 1950s through the mid-1980s. By operating at a point such as A on PPF_{50} in Figure 2.4, Japan was able to shift from PPF_{50} outward to PPF_{85}, to a point such as B.

Capital stock
The set of usable productive capital.

FIGURE 2.4

Outward Shift of Japan's Production Possibilities Frontier

From 1950 through the 1980s, Japan invested heavily in capital goods by producing at point A; as production increased, the economy grew very rapidly. As a result, Japan could move to a point such as B in 1985, producing both more capital and more consumption goods within any given time period.

TEST + *E X T E N D* Your Knowledge

1. TEST If the United States experiences an increase in technology but no change in population, do you expect GDP per capita to rise or fall? If U.S. employment increases from 135 million to 140 million workers between 2008 and 2009, while output stays constant at $12 trillion, how will output per worker change?

2. EXTEND Find data for per-capita GDP (look on the Bureau of Economic Analysis Web site under "Supplementary Tables" using the link at www.aw-bc.com/leeds/ch02) and output per worker (look on the U.S. Department of Labor Bureau of Labor Statistics Web site under "Productivity and Costs" using the link at www.aw-bc.com/leeds/ch02) for the past 20 years. Which has been rising more quickly? If this trend continues, how do you predict that the U.S. standard of living will change?

▶ Efficiency and Equity

We've established that productive efficiency means that the economy operates on the PPF and that resources are not fully utilized if the economy operates inside the PPF. But where on the PPF should an economy operate? In other words, *what* should the economy's resources be used to produce? And what are the implications of choosing one point over another?

Allocative Efficiency

Allocative efficiency
When an economy produces the combination of goods and services that it values most highly.

The answer to these questions lies in the very definition of economics. They require that we consider the allocation of scarce resources among competing uses. An economy achieves **allocative efficiency** when it produces the combination of goods and services that it values most highly.

To identify an economy's optimal combination of goods and services, we must look closely at the shape of the PPF and at the trade-offs that it implies. We can see this by considering the United States' choices in the production of vaccines and guns.

Thinking on the Margin. Figure 2.6 shows a hypothetical PPF for the United States, similar to that in Figure 2.2. The United States can choose to produce any number of combinations of capital goods and consumption goods. The typical shape of the PPF tells us that as we increase capital good production from A to B, from B to C, and finally from C to D, we must forgo increasing quantities of consumption goods. The movement from A to B requires much less sacrifice than the movement from C to D. If the United States chooses to produce the combination of goods indicated by point D (where the PPF meets the horizontal axis), it will have enormous quantities of capital goods (such as heavy machinery). However, it will then have sacrificed all consumption goods such as shampoo and DVD players.[1] The lack of food, clothing, and other personal items will impose great hardship on society, dramatically compromising the quality of life. Choosing point A provides a high level of consumption, but fails to increase the country's productive capacity and does not

---

[1] For now, we ignore the possibility of obtaining other goods by trade. Later, we revisit this model and discuss trade.

LifeLessons

It Pays to Work Hard in Your Principles Class

Whatever their majors, most students begin their college experience with introductory classes. Although you may be anxious to get on with studies in your favorite subject area (or spend time with friends), hard work early in your college career can later pay big dividends. Nations benefit in the long run from short-term sacrifices of consumption goods in order to increase their capital stock. You will also benefit from investing in your own human capital by sacrificing some leisure time now to get the most out of your introductory classes. The better your command of fundamental skills such as writing and mathematics and of the material learned in introductory courses like this one, the easier it will be to succeed in political science, history, sociology, and business courses, as well as in upper-level economics classes.

In economics, intermediate-theory classes provide in-depth coverage of many of the same concepts discussed in this basic principles text. Upper-level classes such as labor economics, public finance, and urban economics apply the tools that you learn here to specific areas of the discipline.

In the context of the production possibilities frontier, assume that there are two goods you can produce in your first year of college: classroom success and fun. Figure 2.5 shows your production possibilities frontier. The increased resources that you allocate toward success in the classroom now will allow for greater success *and* more fun in the future. Notice that the production possibility curve shifts outward to PPF_2, but with a bias toward the success in classes axis. Allocating your time at point A in your first year will allow you to choose point B as a senior.

FIGURE 2.5

Shifts in the Production Possibilities Frontier in College

PPF_1 represents your production possibilities frontier during your first year in college. If you choose an allocation that devotes a lot of resources to classroom success in your first year, such as point A, your production possibilities frontier shifts outward with a bias towards classroom success to PPF_2 in your senior year. You then have the possibility of choosing point B, where you have both more fun *and* enjoy more classroom success than if you had focused more on fun in your first year.

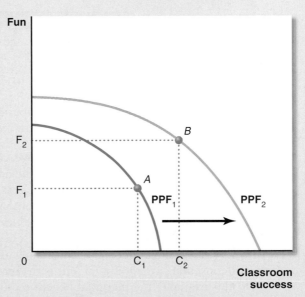

FIGURE 2.6

Choosing a Point on the Production Possibilities Frontier

When choosing what to produce, a society weighs the value of increasing production of one good against the cost of how much of the other good it must forgo. As capital goods production increases from *A* to *B* (200 to 300 units), from *B* to *C* (300 to 400 units), and finally from *C* to *D* (400 to 450 units), increasing quantities of consumer goods must be forgone. If the United States chooses to produce at point *A*, its future consumption and output growth will be reduced. With such a low investment in physical capital, its capacity to produce will not grow as fast as at points *B* and *C*. To increase production of capital goods from 300 units (point *B*) to 400 units (point *C*), consumer goods production must fall from 600 to 300 units.

allow the economy to increase future output and consumption. Such decisions are, by definition, extreme. How can we determine the optimal point on the PPF?

Marginal Benefit and Marginal Cost. We can identify the most desirable point along an economy's PPF by comparing the added benefit of consuming a little bit more of one good with the opportunity cost of providing a little bit more of the other good. Most of our economic decisions involve relatively small changes in how we allocate our time, effort, money, or resources as compared to the total amount of the resource we have at our disposal. Recall from Chapter 1 that marginal benefit is the benefit of producing or consuming an additional unit. The cost of producing or consuming an additional unit is the marginal cost.

In this example, the marginal benefit to society of increasing the production of capital goods (such as the benefit of a move from point *B* to point *C*) is the value society places on the additional 100 units of capital goods. Extra capital goods mean that firms in the economy benefit from their increased ability to produce other goods as a result of the change. The marginal cost to society of producing more capital goods is the value of the consumer goods that it must give up to obtain them. In this case, it is the value of the 300 units of consumer goods lost from point *B* to point *C*. Notice that we compare the *value* of the lost consumer goods to the *value* of the new capital, not the *number* of goods gained or lost. If the marginal cost of moving down the PPF is less than the marginal benefit, then the *net benefit* (the total benefit minus the total cost) is positive, and society is better off. If the marginal cost is greater than the marginal benefit, the net benefit is negative, and society is worse off. *Society is best off when the marginal benefit of a choice equals its marginal cost.* Note that this does not mean that a society is best off when the *total* benefit equals the *total* cost.

The Trade-off Between Efficiency and Equity

Economists use the concept of efficiency to evaluate the well-being of society, because inefficiency implies that resources are wasted. When an economy operates efficiently, it can produce more total goods and services than when it does not. One nice feature of productive efficiency is that it is a positive economic question. That is, we can objectively measure efficiency gains and losses.

The problem with using efficiency as our only measuring stick is that we do not take into consideration whether an outcome is fair or equitable. Though it looks like the word "equality," *equity* has a slightly different meaning. Equality means that all people receive an equal share. **Equity** indicates that an allocation is fair or just. Equity is a normative concept based on subjective opinion. Fairness might mean perfect equality, but perfect equality may or may not be fair. Before we can judge whether the outcome of a policy is equitable, we must first decide on the criteria for fairness.

We can return to our example of flu vaccines to illustrate how a society must resolve fairness issues. In the fall of 2004, the United States experienced a severe shortage of flu vaccine. As a result, the government needed to establish criteria by which the available doses were allocated. You could argue that it would be fair to have the doses distributed on a first-come, first-served basis. To do so, however, ignores the fact that some individuals benefit much more than others. For an otherwise healthy individual, a bout with the flu is probably nothing more than an annoyance and a few days of work or school missed. For a high-risk or elderly patient, the flu can be life-threatening. Thus, another fairness criterion that might be more acceptable to most members of society is to have those in the highest-risk groups served first, and lower-risk groups vaccinated afterwards. The government decided that vaccinating high-risk groups first would be more fair than a first-come, first-served policy, and the Centers for Disease Control published guidelines specifying who should receive preference.

Equity
When an allocation is fair or just. Different people may have very different conceptions of what truly is fair or just.

► Individual Choices and Gains from Trade

Up to this point, we have focused on output decisions in a single economy. We will now use the production possibilities frontier to explore the impact of trade on nations. People have long recognized that trade can make two nations better off when each produces something that the other nation cannot produce or cannot produce well. Consider the Finns, makers of Nokia cellular phones, and the Ugandans, who grow coffee. It does not take an economist to recognize that in this simplified example, for Finns to be able to drink coffee and Ugandans to be able obtain cellular phones, the two nations must trade with each other.

Comparative and Absolute Advantage

Before we model trade, we'll define the subject more broadly. David Ricardo, a nineteenth-century English philosopher and economist, provided the brilliant insight that trade is based on the principle of comparative advantage. Comparative advantage is based on opportunity cost—the cost of producing another good in terms of what could be produced instead. A **comparative advantage** exists if one individual or group has a lower opportunity cost of pursuing an activity than another individual or group. When two parties have different opportunity costs of producing goods, each party should specialize in production of the good in which it has a comparative advantage.

We first illustrate how two parties gain from trade through a simple example of trade between individuals where each individual has an absolute advantage in the production of one good. An **absolute advantage** means that the individual or group is able to produce more of a good than another individual or group. We will then show how the same principle applies to nations—for instance, when one nation has an absolute advantage in the production of both goods, but each has a comparative advantage in a different good.

Imagine that—as in the television show *Survivor*—teams of individuals are isolated on an island. Each team consists of two players, and to survive, both must procure food and water. The simplest way to obtain food is by fishing. To obtain water, the players must hike up to a spring in the mountains. On Team Alpha, Bindee is skillful at fishing, and can catch 10 fish per day. Her teammate, Josh, can catch only 3 fish per day. Josh, though, excels at fetching water. He can carry 15 gallons per day, while Bindee can manage only 5.

Bindee's production possibilities are shown in panel (a) of Figure 2.7, and Josh's are shown in panel (b). For simplicity, we assume that the trade-off rates are constant, so the PPFs are straight lines instead of bowed out. At first, Bindee and Josh don't specialize in the tasks they are best at, and each fishes and fetches water. For Bindee, the opportunity cost of obtaining 1 more fish is always one-half gallon of water. For Bindee to catch an additional fish, the time and effort required equals the time and effort she would expend collecting one-half gallon of water. Because her time and energy are fixed resources, Bindee can't have both the extra fish and the

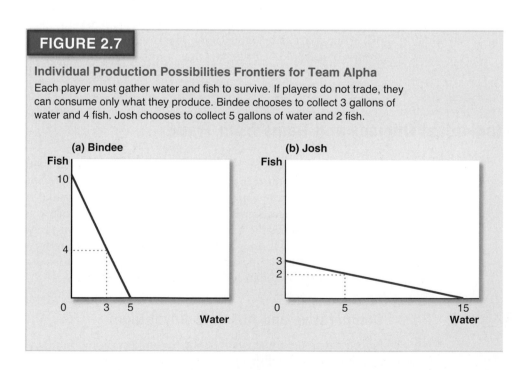

FIGURE 2.7

Individual Production Possibilities Frontiers for Team Alpha
Each player must gather water and fish to survive. If players do not trade, they can consume only what they produce. Bindee chooses to collect 3 gallons of water and 4 fish. Josh chooses to collect 5 gallons of water and 2 fish.

extra half-gallon of water. She must sacrifice one to get the other. For Josh, the opportunity cost of obtaining 1 more fish is constant at 5 gallons of water. If he wants to catch an additional fish, he must make do with 5 fewer gallons of water. After weighing the options, Bindee elects to collect 3 gallons of water and 4 fish. Josh elects to collect 5 gallons of water and 2 fish. Together, their total output is 8 gallons of water and 6 fish.

Now suppose that Bindee and Josh form an alliance. Each of them specializes in the task he or she does best. Because Bindee gives up less water than Josh to obtain an extra fish, they conclude that Bindee should fish and Josh should collect water. With specialization, the total output of fish and water increases. Bindee spends all her time fishing, and, at the end of the day, she brings back 10 fish. Josh spends all his time collecting water and returns with 15 gallons.

Josh and Bindee can now trade with each other so that both end up with water and fish. Both are willing to trade the good they produced for the other good, as long as the quantity they must give up is less than the opportunity cost of acquiring the good themselves. Bindee is willing to trade no more than 2 fish for a gallon of water. Josh is willing to accept no less than one-fifth of a fish per gallon of water. The exact exchange rate will depend on their skill as negotiators. In the end, Josh trades 7.5 gallons of his water for 5 of Bindee's fish. Each ends up with 5 fish and 7.5 gallons of water. This new allocation represents an improvement for both compared to when they were each performing both tasks: Bindee gets 1 additional fish and 4.5 additional gallons of water, while Josh gets 3 additional fish and 2.5 additional gallons of water. Specialization allows each to consume more than they can produce by themselves. Figure 2.8 summarizes Bindee and Josh's gains from trade.

The example illustrates one of the most powerful lessons in economics. Individuals can reap enormous benefits from specialization and exchange. International trade among nations is based on the same principle. Nations can increase their overall welfare by specializing in the activities at which they are most productive. In addition, nations trade with other nations for goods that they can produce on their own only at a relatively high opportunity cost.

The Great Leap Forward

The consequences of ignoring comparative advantage and the gains from specialization and trade may be far more serious than in our island game. Within a single economy, voluntary exchanges between individuals and firms significantly improve well-being. Perhaps the most dramatic example of ignoring this principle comes from China's Great Leap Forward from 1958 to 1960. The leaders of the Chinese Communist Party were impatient with the progress that had been made since they came to power. They sought to "leap over" traditional methods of economic growth by reforming human nature.

One of the centerpieces of this initiative was the Party's rejection of the notion that people should have specialized skills. Instead, it sought to create a "new person" who could perform a variety of tasks. Each person, family, and village would then be self-sufficient. This practice involved the creation of countless backyard furnaces. Each household was supposed to make its own steel. The result was abysmal failure. Lacking the skills or the size advantages of large steel manufacturers, individuals made little steel of any value. In striving to perform tasks for which they were ill suited, the Chinese people were kept from tasks for which they were well suited. One consequence of this ill-fated policy was a famine in which up to 50 million people perished in only a few years.

FIGURE 2.8

Gains from Trade Based on Specialization

If players specialize and trade, each can focus on the commodity for which he or she has a comparative advantage. Bindee spends her day fishing, catching 10 fish, while Josh collects water and brings back 15 gallons of water. They trade some of their output, and each ends up with 5 fish and 7.5 gallons of water.

	Without Trade		With Specialization and Trade	
	Produce	**Consume**	**Produce**	**Consume**
Bindee	4 fish	4 fish	10 fish	5 fish
	3 water	3 water	0 water	7.5 water
Josh	2 fish	2 fish	0 fish	5 fish
	5 water	5 water	15 water	7.5 water

Comparative Advantage and Trade Between Nations

We can extend the lessons learned in the island trade game to an example of comparative advantage involving nations. Consider a simple world in which two nations, the Republic of Korea (also known as South Korea) and Argentina, can each produce either DVDs or beef. Suppose that South Korea can produce either 90 million DVDs or 15 million pounds of beef each month. Argentina can produce either 120 million DVDs or 30 million pounds of beef. Both nations resolve to be self-sufficient and spend one-third of their resources producing DVDs and two-thirds of their resources producing beef. South Korea would produce 30 million DVDs and 10 million pounds of beef while Argentina would produce 40 million DVDs and 20 million pounds of beef.

Unlike in our island trade example, where each person had an absolute advantage in one good, we can see that Argentina has an absolute advantage in producing *both* goods: Argentina can produce more DVDs *and* more beef than South Korea. Argentina and South Korea can still successfully specialize by recognizing that each has a different comparative advantage. South Korea must sacrifice six

Get Ahead of the Curve

Apply your knowledge of the production possibilities frontier and comparative advantage to the nations ravaged by the 2004 Asian tsunami.

TABLE 2.1

Gains from International Trade Based on Comparative Advantage

DVDs are measured in millions. Beef is measured in millions of pounds.

	Without Specialization and Trade		With Specialization and Trade	
	Produce	**Consume**	**Produce**	**Consume**
South Korea	30 DVDs	30 DVDs	90 DVDs	40 DVDs
	10 beef	10 beef	0 beef	10 beef
Argentina	40 DVDs	40 DVDs	0 DVDs	50 DVDs
	20 beef	20 beef	30 beef	20 beef

DVDs to obtain one pound of beef, while Argentina must sacrifice four DVDs to obtain one pound of beef. Argentina has the lower opportunity cost and should specialize in beef production. Beef production is Argentina's comparative advantage. Because South Korea must sacrifice one-sixth of a pound of beef to produce a DVD, while Argentina must sacrifice one-fourth of a pound of beef for each DVD, DVD production is South Korea's comparative advantage.

As in the case of the island trade game, when South Korea and Argentina trade, both are better off. Table 2.1 shows the benefits of trade. Because South Korea is relatively better at producing DVDs than beef, it focuses all of its production on DVDs and produces no beef. Argentina, which has a comparative advantage in beef production, produces only beef. As a result of this specialization, the total production of DVDs and beef is greater. If South Korea wants to trade for beef, it will be willing to trade no more than six DVDs for one pound of beef. If Argentina wants to trade for DVDs, it will accept no less than four DVDs for one pound of beef. If South Korea and Argentina are equally skilled bargainers, the terms of trade will be halfway between the 4:1 minimum of Argentina and the 6:1 maximum of South Korea. Suppose that this is true; and they agree to trade 50 million DVDs for 10 million pounds of beef, a 5:1 ratio.

As a result, South Korea can consume 40 million DVDs and 10 million pounds of beef. Argentina can consume 50 million DVDs and 20 million pounds of beef. Each country benefits from trade. Each country can consume as much beef as it could without trade, but each now has 10 million more DVDs. Note that Table 2.1 shows only one possible outcome of trade between the two countries. Depending on the bargaining power of each, the terms of trade might not be five DVDs for one pound of beef. Yet, as long as each is better off after the exchange than it would be without trading, each has an incentive to trade.

Trade in modern societies is more complicated than the direct trade of one commodity for another. As described in Chapter 1, most economies use market-based exchange to trade goods and services. Throughout the text, we will see that the use of markets to facilitate the exchange of goods and services between individuals, firms, and nations does not alter the fundamental concept that trade improves well-being. The principles are as relevant in modern complex economies as in a simple island survivor game, with one important exception. In the examples here, we used PPFs that were straight lines, indicating constant opportunity cost. In reality, PPFs are bowed outward, as we described earlier. The nation as a whole is better off with trade than without. However, there are costs to individuals in that nation when resources are shifted from one form of production to another, such as from DVD production to beef production.

1. TEST Suppose Argentina can now produce 200 million DVDs or 100 million pounds of beef, while Korea's production possibilities remain unchanged. Does Korea still have a comparative advantage in the production of any good?

2. EXTEND Babe Ruth was arguably the best hitter in the history of baseball. It is less well known that he was one of the best pitchers in the game from 1915 through 1918. Look up his statistics using the link at www.aw-bc.com/leeds/ch02 and explain why the Red Sox and Yankees ended Babe Ruth's pitching career by converting him to a full-time outfielder.

Strategy and Policy
Efficiency and Equity in Health Care

Matters of equity and fairness come into sharp focus when one examines the topic of health care. The United States spends more than twice as much per capita on health care as nearly every other country. Although the United States devotes about 14 percent of its GDP to health care, more than 44 million Americans, many of them children, are without any form of health insurance. In contrast, Canada and the United Kingdom spend far less on health care. Yet, both offer universal coverage, leaving no citizens without care.

Individuals in the United States who are without employer-based health insurance may still purchase health care. However, the cost is often prohibitive. Does this mean that America is inefficient and allocates its resources poorly? Few people would argue that it is a good thing for so many Americans to be without health insurance. Does the large number of U.S. citizens lacking health care indicate that the United States is less efficient than Canada or the United Kingdom? The United States might simply choose to allocate its health-care resources differently than other countries do.

Figure 2.9 shows a production possibilities frontier indicating the possible choices between intensive care and extensive care. A health-care system that provides *intensive* care devotes its resources toward helping those who need a great deal of care—that is, those who are very ill. In contrast, *extensive* care means providing basic care to a large proportion of the population. In panel (a) of Figure 2.9, the United States is producing at point *A*. It devotes much of its health-care expenditures to sophisticated, intensive care. The U.S. health-care system is well equipped to treat patients who are very ill and need complex diagnoses and treatments. In contrast, a nationalized health-care system, like that of the United Kingdom, operates at point *B* in panel (b). It devotes much of its resources to extending basic health benefits to all of its citizens. The implications of the different choices are that U.S. consumers who have health insurance are very well cared for and have access to enormous resources to diagnose and treat severe illnesses. Those without insurance receive little or no care. In contrast, citizens of the United Kingdom have better access to basic care, such as the treatment of minor illnesses, than an uninsured American. But widely accessible basic care comes at the cost of lower access to technologically advanced treatment.

In a market economy with no government provision of goods or services, health care is allocated only to those who are willing and able to pay for it. Therefore, equity concerns cannot be addressed directly. As a society, though, voting preferences

FIGURE 2.9

Extensive Versus Intensive Health-Care Choices

In choosing to produce at point *A* in panel (a), the United States elects to devote a large quantity of its productive capacity to intensive health care. Insured individuals have access to many resources to diagnose and treat severe illnesses, while uninsured people may lack even basic health care. The United Kingdom, in contrast, produces at point *B* in panel (b), choosing more extensive health care. Basic health care is available to all citizens, but people who need intensive care for grave medical problems have access to fewer resources than insured persons in the United States.

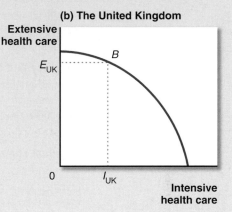

might reveal that we do not want any citizens to go without certain forms of care. There is no guarantee that market solutions will provide everyone with an acceptable level of health care as well as other goods and services. As a result, most market-based economies are, in some sense, mixed economies, as described in Chapter 1. We will return to the role of the government in a market economy in Chapter 3.

Critical-Thinking Questions

1. You saw earlier in the chapter that economies with different specialties benefit from trade with one another. Why don't we observe this phenomenon in the provision of health care?
2. Discuss the fairness issues related to the health-care choices of the United States and the United Kingdom.

 SUMMARY

- **Factors of production.** The four factors of production are land, labor, physical capital, and entrepreneurship. Land is a natural resource used for agriculture, mining, housing, production, and recreation. Labor is the number of people willing and able to work. Physical capital includes those goods that can be used in the production of other goods and services. Entrepreneurship, which is considered separately from labor, is an indication of how some individuals focus on the creation of new products and how best to organize the other productive inputs, rather than on actual production. Better education and technology increase the productivity of labor and capital.

- **The production possibilities frontier.** A PPF shows the possible output choices for a society, and the trade-offs that must be made in terms of production of one good if we decide to produce more of another. The value of the total output of the economy is called the Gross Domestic Product (GDP). An economy is producing efficiently when it produces on the frontier. Once on the frontier, to obtain more of one good or service, the economy must forgo some of another good or service. The law of increasing opportunity costs dictates that along the frontier, increases in the quantity of one good or service come at an increasing opportunity cost in terms of the other good.

- **Modeling economic growth.** When the productivity or resources of a society increase, the PPF shifts outward. How rapidly the PPF shifts over time depends on the choices society makes. All else held equal (*ceteris paribus*), an economy that emphasizes capital goods production will grow faster than one focused more on consumption goods production.

- **Efficiency and equity.** Allocative efficiency requires that an economy produce the combination of goods and services that society values most highly. Equity or fairness is a normative concept, and so can be defined in many ways. Because equity and efficiency are different concepts and yet both are desirable, there might be tension between what society deems the most efficient solution and the most equitable solution.

- **Individual choices and gains from trade.** Individuals must decide how to allocate their resources. Such choices require a comparison of the marginal benefit (the value of what is gained) to the marginal cost (the value of what is lost). Individuals can increase their well-being by trading with others who have different resources or skills. Entire economies benefit when members of society specialize according to their comparative advantage and trade with each other rather than trying to produce everything they want to consume. Nations also improve their well-being when they trade with other nations by specializing according to comparative advantage.

KEY TERMS

Absolute advantage 48	Factors of production 35	Land 35
Allocative efficiency 44	Financial capital 36	Law of increasing
Capital goods 36	Gross Domestic Product	opportunity cost 40
Capital stock 43	(GDP) 38	Management 37
Comparative advantage 48	GDP per capita 38	Physical capital 36
Consumption goods 36	Human capital 35	Production possibilities
Entrepreneurs 36	Input 35	frontier (PPF) 37
Equity 47	Labor 35	Productive efficiency 40
Factor endowment 35	Labor force 35	

PROBLEMS

1. How can a nation increase its stock of human capital if the population remains constant?
2. Why is education such an important tool for long-run economic growth?
3. For each term below, specify whether it is part of capital, labor, land, or entrepreneurial skill.
   a. Coal
   b. Reading ability
   c. A cement mixer
   d. An auto mechanic
   e. A president of a small business

4. In the following table, create an additional column that shows the opportunity cost (measured in skateboards) of increases in rollerblade production. Graph the PPF.

Rollerblades	Skateboards
0	100
1	90
2	75
3	50
4	0

5. On the PPF to the left, what is the opportunity cost of the first hot dog? What is the opportunity cost of increasing hot dog production from 2 to 3?

6. On the PPF shown in Problem 5, which points are productively efficient? If this were the PPF for your grill at a barbeque, how might you go about finding a point of allocative efficiency?

7. What does it mean to say that an allocation demonstrates productive efficiency? If we know that a resource allocation is productively efficient, does this mean it is also equitable?

8. Suppose that the trade-off between guns and doses of vaccine for the United States is constant. An additional gun can always be produced at an opportunity cost of 20,000 doses of vaccine, right up to the maximum of 100 guns. Draw the PPF. What principle does this result violate?

9. What are the costs and benefits of a nation specializing in the production of consumption goods (as opposed to capital goods) in the near term?

10. Why do we often observe that there are shortages of many consumption goods in nations involved in prolonged wars?

11. Suppose that initially, every member of society has the same wealth. Ten years later, some are much wealthier than others. Does this mean that economic activity during the 10-year period was inefficient? Does it mean that it was inequitable? Explain.

12. Marla can produce 10 chairs per day if she makes only chairs, or 5 tables per day if she makes only tables. Justine can produce 5 chairs per day or 5 tables per day. Assume that the tradeoff rate in production is constant.
   a. For each, calculate the opportunity cost of producing a chair and the opportunity cost of producing a table.
   b. Does Justine have an absolute advantage in the production of either good?
   c. Does Justine have a comparative advantage in the production of either good?

13. Rodney and Laura each work eight hours per day. Rodney can produce three hats per hour spent in hat production, and one shirt per hour spent in shirt production. Laura can produce three hats per hour spent in hat production and three shirts per hour spent in shirt production.
   a. With no trade, what is the opportunity cost of producing an additional shirt for Rodney? What is the opportunity cost of an additional shirt for Laura?
   b. Which (if any) individual has a comparative advantage in hat production? Will Laura benefit from trading with Rodney? Explain.

14. Suppose that an economy can produce any of the following combinations of corn (measured in bushels) and tractors.

	Corn	Tractors
A	100	0
B	80	12
C	60	20
D	40	26
E	20	30
F	0	32

a. Plot the PPF.

b. Does the opportunity cost of producing another tractor increase as more tractors are produced?

c. What is the opportunity cost (in tractors) of increasing corn production from 40 bushels to 60 bushels?

d. Suppose that there are two identical economies with this PPF. One concentrates on corn production in the short run, producing at point B. The other concentrates on tractor production, producing at point E. What long-run changes do you predict in the PPFs for these two countries?

Section 2.2, Exercise 1 The following table shows the production possibilities for a country that can produce either computers or wheat.

Computers (millions of machines)	Wheat (millions of bushels)
5	0
4	100
3	175
2	225
1	250
0	260

a. Graph the production possibilities frontier, putting computers on the vertical axis.

b. If the economy is currently on the PPF and is producing 175 million bushels of wheat, what is the opportunity cost of 1 million more computers?

Section 2.2, Exercise 2 Refer to the graph that you drew in Problem 1.

a. Find a point that is outside the PPF and label it P_1. Find a point that is inside the PPF and label it P_2.

b. How can you best describe the points that you just found?

Section 2.2, Exercise 3 The following table shows the production possibilities for a country that can produce either automobiles or wool.

Automobiles (millions of cars)	Wool (millions of yards)
30	0
25	200
15	350
10	450
5	525
0	575

a. Graph the production possibilities frontier, putting automobiles on the vertical axis.
b. Explain what happens to the opportunity cost of producing wool as society devotes more and more resources to wool production.

Section 2.3, Exercise 1 Consider an economy that produces two goods: steel and corn. In each of the following cases, draw a representative PPF and show the effect of the stated change:

a. The population of the country increases.
b. There is a discovery of new iron ore, which is an input to steel production but not to corn production.
c. There is an improvement in technology that makes all inputs more productive.
d. A drought permanently reduces the amount of arable land (which is an input to corn production but not to steel production).

Section 2.3, Exercise 2 Consider an economy that can produce consumption goods, which can be used now, or capital goods, which can be used to produce more goods of all kinds in the future. Show graphically what will happen to the PPF next year under each of the following circumstances.

a. The economy chooses to produce mostly consumer goods this year.
b. The economy chooses to produce mostly capital goods this year.

Section 2.3, Exercise 3 If an economy chooses to produce mostly capital goods in the present, how does this decision affect consumption choices in the present, and in the future?

Section 2.5, Exercise 1 Michael can produce 20 pizzas or 40 loaves of bread in 10 hours. Nina can produce 30 pizzas or 50 loaves of bread in 10 hours. Assume that the tradeoff rate in production is consistent.

a. Graph the PPF for each person, putting pizza on the horizontal axis.
b. What is Michael's opportunity cost of producing a pizza? What is Nina's opportunity cost of producing a pizza?
c. Does anyone have an absolute advantage? Explain.
d. Does anyone have a comparative advantage in any good? Explain.
e. Describe what Nina and Michael should do to maximize their benefits.

Section 2.5, Exercise 2 The countries of Economica and Societa each produce cloth and telephones. The following table shows their production possibilities if they devote all of their resources to one good, and if they can switch resources from the production of one good to the other at a constant opportunity cost. (That is, Economica can produce 1,000 yards of cloth or 2,000 telephones, or any combination thereof.)

	Cloth	Telephones
Economica	1,000	2,000
Societa	4,000	1,000

a. Graph the PPF for each country, putting cloth on the horizontal axis.
b. What is Economica's opportunity cost of producing cloth? What is Societa's opportunity cost of producing cloth?

Section 2.5, Exercise 3 Refer to the table in the previous exercise.

a. Does either country have an absolute advantage? Explain.
b. Does either country have a comparative advantage in either good? Explain.
c. Describe what the two countries should do to maximize their benefits.
d. Find a price of cloth (in terms of telephones) at which both countries can gain from trade.

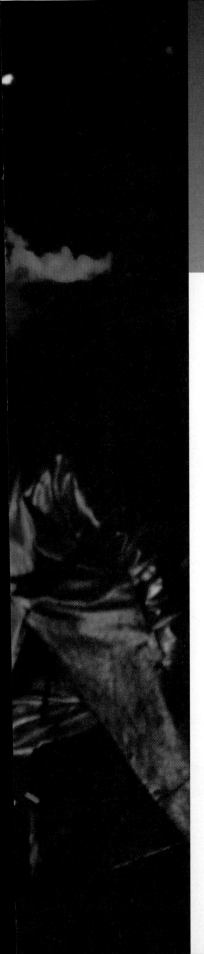

3 The American Economy in a Global Setting

In 1962, the Pittsburgh Steelers put the U.S. Steel emblem and the word "Steel" (later changed to "Steelers") on their helmets. This action solidified their place in the hearts of Pittsburgh sports fans, many of whom worked in steel mills. Like Detroit, Pittsburgh took its identity from one specific industry and the product it turned out. Detroit was Motown, and Pittsburgh was Steel City. The mills ran day and night, turning out massive amounts of steel and so much pollution that the city's street lamps often had to be turned on in the middle of the day. All that came to a halt in the 1970s and 1980s, when competition from more efficient steel makers in other states and other countries began to overwhelm Pittsburgh's aging factories. One after another, steel mills closed, and tens of thousands of steelworkers lost their jobs.

Hundreds of thousands of other people, many far from Pittsburgh, were also affected when the steelworkers lost their jobs. The numerous companies that provided goods and services to the Pittsburgh steel industry, from raw materials to transportation, saw their markets dry up. At home, the shops that sold groceries and clothing to steelworkers found themselves without customers. Between 1970 and 1990, the population of Pittsburgh fell by almost 30 percent. The metropolitan area as a whole lost almost 300,000 people. The local government was helpless to stem the tide. With tax revenues tumbling, it struggled to provide even the most basic services.

Pittsburgh today is a city of about 325,000 people, less than half its size in 1950. Still, the city has managed to survive and, in some sectors, to thrive. While Pittsburgh's economy has stabilized, the steel industry there has not. Auto manufacturers survived the challenge posed by foreign producers, but Pittsburgh's steel mills are gone forever. In their place are banks, pharmaceutical companies, and a number of high-tech service sector firms. Moreover, those people who blame foreign steel for the loss of Pittsburgh's steel mills might be surprised to learn that many of the largest employers in Pittsburgh today are foreign-owned. The 10 largest firms in the Pittsburgh area include companies from the United Kingdom (GlaxoSmithKline and the Royal Bank of Scotland, which owns Citizens Bank), Germany (Bayer), Japan (Sony), and even Luxembourg (Arcelor).

In this chapter, we look at the forces that tie together economies at the city, regional, and national levels. In the process, we develop a model that further illustrates the choices society makes regarding *what, how,* and *for whom* to produce. The essence of this model is "what goes around comes around." When firms thrive, households prosper. When households struggle, so do firms. We also look at why the financial health of local governments is linked to the financial health of local firms and households. In addition, we examine why the federal government weathers such storms better than local governments. Finally, we examine the international forces that connect the economies of different nations.

ALONG THE WAY, YOU WILL ALSO LEARN:

- How households and firms are connected by a circular flow of economic activity.
- How the product and resource markets connect households and firms.
- What role government plays in the economy.
- What role financial markets play in the economy.
- How imports and exports affect the circular flow of economic activity.

AT THE END OF THE CHAPTER, THE MYECONLAB LOGO WILL DIRECT YOU ONLINE

- MyEconLab is a resource-packed online homework and tutorial system that can help you perform better in your economics course. To log in for the first time, see page 30 for instructions.
- MyEconLab can help you apply important concepts from the chapter to real-world issues. Watch for the logo to indicate online features about the government and international sectors of the circular flow.
- At the end of each chapter, you'll find a special study section that will help you get the most out of your textbook and your instructor's MyEconLab course.

▶ The Circular Flow of Economic Activity

Pittsburgh's bitter experience in the 1970s and 1980s illustrated a vital economic concept that underlies much microeconomic and all macroeconomic analysis: Firms and households interact so closely with one another that the health of each group depends upon the health of the other. Steel manufacturers paid their employees with the revenues from their sales. When those sales dried up, the firms paid lower salaries and wages. Similarly, firms in the Pittsburgh area were able to sell their wares only while the local workforce had enough purchasing power to buy them. Decreases in purchasing power cycled from firms to workers and vice versa.

Economists illustrate goods, services, and incomes as flowing in a circle, from households to firms and back again. One way to visualize this circular flow of economic activity is to think of the transactions between firms and households as water flowing through a circular set of pipes. The amount of water flowing through the pipes at any point in time corresponds to the level of economic activity. The pipes connect households with firms through the product market and the resource market. The **product market** refers to the entire system of markets in which households purchase goods and services from firms. The **resource market** consists of markets for factors of production that firms use to make the goods and services they sell on the product market.

Figure 3.1 demonstrates the **circular flow model** of economic activity. According to the circular flow model, (1) households send revenue to the product market, where (2) it is transferred to firms in exchange for goods and services. The story does not end there. Much of the revenue that firms receive from customers goes (3) directly back to households through the resource market as (4) income to their employees. Firms also provide income to households in a less direct fashion by using revenue to pay other businesses for rent on their buildings and for the equipment required to produce their goods and services. The other firms in turn use much of their revenue to pay their own employees. Firms also use revenue to repay any loans they have taken out from the local bank or other lenders. Finally, any remaining revenue goes as profit to the owners, who have their own households. Ultimately, almost all of the money finds its way to households. Households use the income to make the purchases that provide firms with their revenue. These actions initiate yet another cycle of the circular flow of income.

Product market
The system of markets in which households purchase goods and services from firms.

Resource market
The system of markets for factors of production.

Circular flow model
Represents goods, services, and incomes in the economy as flowing in a circle, from households to firms and back again.

FIGURE 3.1

The Circular Flow of Economic Activity

In the basic circular flow model, income from households flows to firms as household members buy goods or services from businesses via the product market. The income that businesses receive flows back to the households through the resource market, where they are exchanged for production-related resources, thus completing the circular flow. The yellow arrows show the flow of money in the economy. The blue arrows show the flow of goods and services.

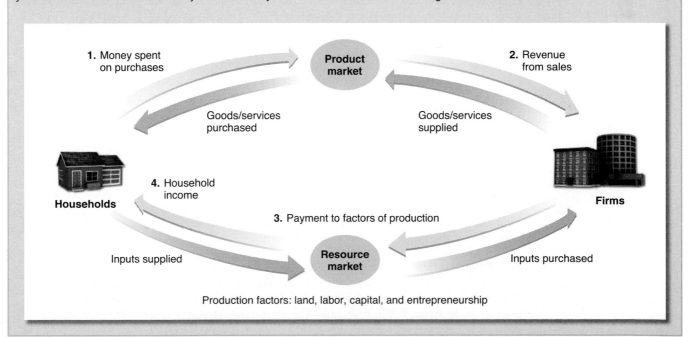

1. Money spent on purchases
2. Revenue from sales
Product market
Goods/services purchased
Goods/services supplied
Households
4. Household income
3. Payment to factors of production
Firms
Inputs supplied
Inputs purchased
Resource market
Production factors: land, labor, capital, and entrepreneurship

The interconnection of households and firms lies behind many microeconomic and macroeconomic models. In the following sections, we closely examine the components of the circular flow, including the two main sectors: firms and households. We first examine how these sectors interact in the product market and then in the resource market.

►Households and Firms: The Product Market

Before looking more closely at the circular flow model, let's take a closer look at the two main sectors of the economy: households and firms. Once you have a better understanding of what households and firms are, we can then explain how they interact in the product market.

Households

Households participate in the product market as purchasers of goods and services. Their members buy everything from concert T-shirts and peanut butter to refrigerators and automobile repairs. Most people are part of a household of some kind. A typical image of a household is two parents, two children, and perhaps a dog. According to government statistics, however, reality is quite different. About one-third of all U.S. households are not families, which the Census defines as people related by birth, marriage, or adoption. Most of the households that do not include a family consist of individuals living alone.

Many households that are families do not have the traditional structure. About one-fourth of all households are headed by a single man or woman with no spouse present. That means that only about half (52 percent) of all families meet the stereotypical two-parent image. Moreover, this figure is declining. Thanks to falling birth rates and longer lifespans, the average U.S. household is also growing steadily older. Since 1980, the median age of Americans has risen by almost six years, from about 30 to almost 36. The aging of the baby boom generation will lead to still greater changes. Projections for the year 2020 suggest that more than 50 million Americans—16 percent of the U.S. population—will be at least 65 years old. This graying of America will inevitably lead to changes in government policy and in the sorts of products that U.S. households consume.

U.S. households are also on the move. Fueled in part by the decline in traditional industries such as steel, the population of Pittsburgh has declined since 1980, and the population of Pennsylvania has grown only 4 percent. Over this same period, the U.S. population as a whole grew by over 28 percent. Where did people go? Many of them went to the south and southwest, where populations increased dramatically. For example, Florida's population has grown by more than 70 percent, and Arizona's population has more than doubled.

Firms

Like households, firms take many different forms. In this section, we provide an overview of the most common types of firms.

Sole proprietorships
Firms with only one owner, who bears full responsibility for the firm's success or failure.

Sole Proprietorships. Some firms—in particular, small firms—have only one owner who bears full responsibility for the firm's success or failure. Such **sole proprietorships** give the entrepreneurs that run them large rewards if they prosper. But they also present large risks. If the firm fails, the proprietor is solely responsible for all the firm's debts and expenses. The proprietor bears the consequences for all decisions made by the firm, from what to produce to what color wallpaper to use in the office.

Partnerships. Some firms are owned collectively by a small number of people who share the firm's profits. Such firms, known as **partnerships**, allow individuals to pool their resources. They are then able to reach a scale of operation that the limited finances of a sole ownership could not achieve. Each of the partners bears responsibility for the firm's performance. Partnerships can be small "mom and pop" operations, or they can be very large businesses that have many partners. Most major accounting firms and large law firms are partnerships.

Corporations. Some firms have a large number of owners, each of whom has only a small share of the overall responsibility for the firm. These firms, known as **corporations**, sell shares of the company in the form of **stock**, or certificates representing partial ownership of a firm. Some corporations are *privately held*. Their stock is not openly bought and sold, but remains in the hands of relatively few individuals. Others are *publicly held*. These firms' stock can be bought and sold by the public at large. An **initial public offering (IPO)** occurs when a corporation first sells its stock to the public.

Stockholders have a say in the operation of the firm that is proportional to the amount of stock they own. Stockholders receive their portion of the firm's profits in the form of **dividends**, periodic payments that are determined by the number of shares they own. An important and unique feature of corporations is that stockholders do not have any financial liability beyond the value of the stock they own. If the firm goes bankrupt, stockholders do not have to repay any of the firm's debts. Their only loss is that the stock they own becomes worthless.

We tend to think of corporations as much larger organizations than either proprietorships or partnerships. Indeed, one basic reason for a firm to *incorporate* (become a corporation) is to raise funds that will enable it to grow. However, some very small firms become corporations to reduce the risks that accompany the other forms of organization.

The recent IPO by Google, Inc., is one example of a firm that was originally owned by a small number of people. Initially, Google, Inc., was a partnership of two Stanford University graduate students, Larry Page and Sergey Brin. They literally ran the company from a dormitory room. They formed a corporation only after an investor gave them a $100,000 check made out to Google, Inc. Because the original owners held an IPO, thousands of stockholders now own a small part of Google. Page and Brin retained a significant portion of the ownership for themselves, making them fantastically wealthy (at least in terms of their stock ownership).

The Product Market

"Product market" is a misleading name for the setting in which households make purchases from firms. First, the product market is not really a single market. It is a name we give to all the different ways in which firms and households get together to buy and sell goods and services. Wal-Mart, the local bakery, and kctchupworld.com all are part of the product market. Second, products constitute a decreasing portion of what people buy in the U.S. economy. Increasingly, firms and households exchange services more than physical products.

The evolution of the product market in Pittsburgh, discussed earlier, eliminated many steelworkers' jobs in Pittsburgh. However, it also created new jobs in finance, pharmaceuticals, and other areas.

Partnerships
Firms led by a small number of people who share the firm's profits and responsibility for its failures.

Corporations
Firms that have a large number of owners, each of whom has only a small share of the overall responsibility for the firm.

Stock
A certificate representing partial ownership of a firm.

Initial public offering (IPO)
The first sale of stock by a firm to the general public.

Dividends
Periodic payments to shareholders that are determined by the number of shares of stock one holds.

Changes in the U.S. Economy. While not as wrenching as Pittsburgh's experience, the U.S. economy as a whole has gone through changes. Figure 3.2 shows that the United States produces a far different array of goods and services than it did in the years following World War II. The chart shows the proportion of overall economic activity that falls into each of five basic categories: agriculture/mining, construction/manufacturing, transportation/public utilities, government, and services/trade/FIRE (finance, insurance, and real estate). Services cover a variety of activities in which no tangible product is produced or exchanged.

Figure 3.2 shows the dramatic changes that took place between 1947 and 2004. Today, only about 25 percent of overall production takes the form of construction and manufacturing, down from more than 30 percent. Agriculture and mining have fallen even more significantly, from 11.2 percent to less than 2.5 percent of GDP. While the traditional sectors declined in importance, other sectors have risen dramatically. The total of services, FIRE, and wholesale and retail trade has risen to more than 56 percent of GDP. The service sector alone represents almost as much of GDP as manufacturing, accounting for slightly over 23 percent of GDP.

The Emergence of the Service Sector. Does the large rise in services mean that the U.S. is becoming an economy of low-paid janitors and waitresses? In fact, the growth of the service sector does not mean that the U.S. economy is generating only low-paying jobs. The service sector consists of a variety of occupations—some of

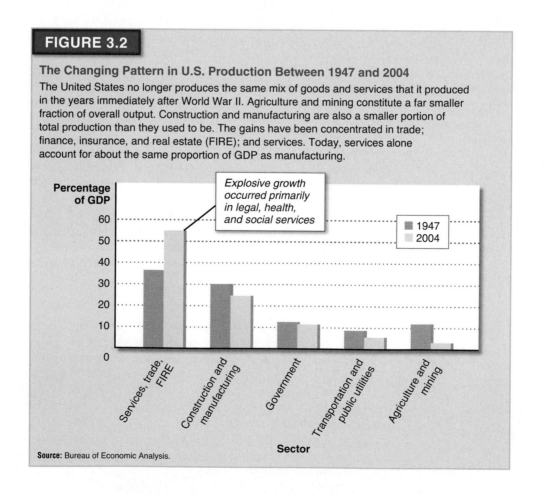

FIGURE 3.2

The Changing Pattern in U.S. Production Between 1947 and 2004

The United States no longer produces the same mix of goods and services that it produced in the years immediately after World War II. Agriculture and mining constitute a far smaller fraction of overall output. Construction and manufacturing are also a smaller portion of total production than they used to be. The gains have been concentrated in trade; finance, insurance, and real estate (FIRE); and services. Today, services alone account for about the same proportion of GDP as manufacturing.

Source: Bureau of Economic Analysis.

them highly lucrative. The most dramatic growth in services between 1947 and 2004 came in three relatively highly paid areas. In 2004, the proportion of GDP attributable to legal services was three times its 1947 level. Over the same time period, health services rose by a factor of about four, while social services rose to almost 18 times their 1947 level. While not all service jobs pay well, the growth in these areas shows that the United States is not becoming a nation of burger flippers, as some critics claim.

Firm-to-Firm Transactions. To this point, we have considered households to be the only consumers in the product market. In fact, household consumption accounts for only 62 percent of the purchases on the product market. Who makes the rest of the purchases? Purchases by governmental bodies account for another 16 percent, while 8 percent of the purchases are by foreign consumers, firms, and governments. The remaining 14 percent or so consists of purchases by firms from other firms. In Chapter 2, you saw that one of the basic inputs to the production process is physical capital: the buildings, machinery, and equipment that firms use to produce output for households. Most firms fit into the standard picture of the circular flow, selling their output to households. However, some firms, such as the steel plants that used to be in Pittsburgh, sell virtually all of their output to other firms. Other firms, such as Citizens Bank or Sony, deal with a mixture of firms and households. Thus, household and firm purchases make up more than 75 percent of purchases on the product market.

Households and Firms: The Resource Market

We now turn to the interactions of firms and households in the resource market. Each firm, whether it is a bank or a steel plant, uses a variety of inputs to produce its output. In paying for these inputs, such as the wages and salaries it pays its workers, the firm returns to households much of the revenue it received from them on the product market. By returning incomes from firms to households, the resource market completes the circular flow of income from households to firms and back again.

Exchange on the Resource Market

Figure 3.3 shows the relative size of payments to the different inputs in the resource market. This figure shows the percentage of each category as a percentage of total payments to productive resources in 2004. We next discuss each input in turn.

Payments to Labor. By far the greatest percentage of payment in the resource market goes to labor. Wages, salaries, and other forms of worker compensation have long been the largest single category of income. In 2004, payments to labor accounted for more than 70 percent of all income earned on the resource market in the U.S. economy.

Rent
Payment to owners of land.

Payments to Landowners. Payment to landowners, called **rent**, is among the smallest of the sources of income. Rent has steadily fallen as a percentage of total income in the U.S. economy. In 2004, it accounted for less than 2 percent of total income.

Payments to Capital. Many purchases by households and firms are too expensive to be bought with cash on hand. In order to purchase big-ticket items, many households

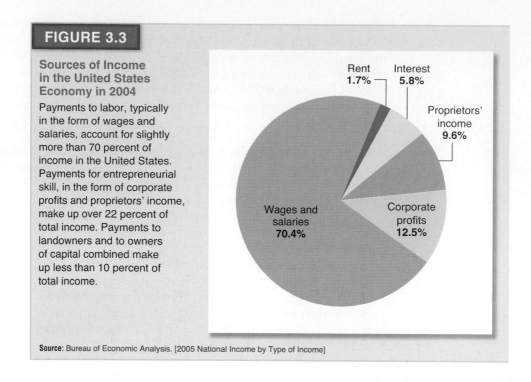

FIGURE 3.3

Sources of Income in the United States Economy in 2004

Payments to labor, typically in the form of wages and salaries, account for slightly more than 70 percent of income in the United States. Payments for entrepreneurial skill, in the form of corporate profits and proprietors' income, make up over 22 percent of total income. Payments to landowners and to owners of capital combined make up less than 10 percent of total income.

Rent
1.7%

Interest
5.8%

Proprietors' income
9.6%

Wages and salaries
70.4%

Corporate profits
12.5%

Source: Bureau of Economic Analysis. [2005 National Income by Type of Income]

and firms must first borrow. One of a bank's main functions is to bring together borrowers and lenders. Thus, Bayer or GlaxoSmithKline might come to Citizens Bank for a loan to build an addition to facilities in Pittsburgh, or one of their employees might borrow money to buy a new car.

Citizens Bank gets its funds in turn by attracting deposits from people who save part of their incomes. Banks attract deposits by offering to share some of the interest payments on their loans with depositors. The interest paid on loans is the source of the interest payments to depositors on their checking and savings accounts. Figure 3.3 shows that interest payments to households accounted for about 6 percent of total household income in 2004. Interest is one of the most volatile sources of income. It has ranged from about 1 percent to almost 10 percent of income over the last 75 years.

Proprietor's income
The profit earned by a sole proprietorship or partnership.

Corporate profits
The net income of corporations.

Payments for Entrepreneurial Skill. Most of the remainder of household income comes from firms' profits, the reward to the owners for their entrepreneurial skill. The profits of a sole proprietorship or a partnership are called **proprietor's income**. This category accounted for about 9.5 percent of total income in 2004. The profits of corporations, known as **corporate profits**, accounted for about 12.5 percent of total income.

Using the Circular Flow Model

The circular flow model provides many important insights into the economy and public policy. It tells us, for example, that the economic health of households and firms are strongly linked with one another. When the steel industry in Pittsburgh went into decline, the entire economy of Pittsburgh and the surrounding area struggled. Households suffered, mostly because fewer workers were employed and wages fell. Some households also were hurt by declines in other forms of income, such as the decline in corporate profits. Steel's decline hurt other firms as well. With steel plants and other firms closing down, firms that did business with the steel companies also lost sales and profits.

Declining household incomes also harmed firms. With household income declining and people leaving Pittsburgh, the demand for goods and services from local firms fell as well.

The circular flow model discussed up to this point is a self-contained unit. In the rest of this chapter, we consider extensions of the basic model that allow funds and goods and services provided by the government or foreign countries to move through the circular flow. In particular, we extend the basic model by incorporating the government, financial, and international sectors.

TEST + *E X T E N D* Your Knowledge

1. TEST Explain whether and how each of the following enters the circular flow of economic activity:
  a) A teller's salary at Citizens Bank
  b) The corporate headquarters built for the H. J. Heinz Company
  c) The $10 that a kindergartner in Pittsburgh received for her birthday from her grandfather

2. EXTEND The "Country at a Glance" tables in the Data and Research section of the World Bank Web site (using the link at www.aw-bc.com/leeds/ch03) provide information on production for many countries. Use these tables to find the distribution of output among the agriculture, manufacturing, and services categories in: (a) an industrialized country other than the United States (such as Japan or the Netherlands); and (b) a developing country (such as Bolivia or Uganda). How does the distribution of output in these countries differ from one another? Why do you think they differ?

▶ The Government Sector of the Economy

We begin our extension of the circular flow model with the government sector. Federal, state, and local governments have become a major source of firm revenue and household income. In 2004, government purchases of goods and services accounted for about 18 percent of all U.S. economic activity. To accurately depict the U.S. economy, our circular flow model must account for the actions of government. Before discussing the role of government as a whole in the circular flow, we briefly describe the different levels of government.

Levels of Government

When most people speak of government, they typically mean the nation's central or federal government. In fact, the term "government" refers to a set of institutions whose authorities range from small towns to an entire nation. In the United States, most governments fall into one of three categories: local, state, or federal. While there is some overlap, each level of government has responsibility for a particular set of duties and funds these activities with a particular set of taxes.

Local Government. Local governments typically provide amenities and services such as parks, museums, schools, and police protection. Large cities such as Pittsburgh often provide an even broader array of services. Most local governments rely on **property taxes,** or taxes on land and structures, to provide these services. They use property taxes because, unlike households or firms, property is immobile. While

Property tax
A tax on land and structures.

Sales tax
A tax on transactions between merchants and customers.

Income tax
A tax levied on personal income or corporate earnings.

Get Ahead of the Curve
Use your knowledge of the government sector of the circular flow to analyze the debate over school finance in Texas.

Balanced budget
When a government's expenditures equal its revenues.

firms and workers can travel or move to a nearby town to escape income and sales taxes, property owners cannot move the land on which they are located. Local governments typically do not impose **sales taxes**, which are taxes on transactions between merchants and customers. People could avoid local sales tax by going to a different town to shop. Local governments seldom impose **income taxes**, which are levies on personal or corporate earnings. Households and firms can move to nearby towns to avoid income taxes. Typically, only the largest cities, which dominate their regional economy, use either sales or income taxes.

State Government. State governments provide services for which no single municipality can take responsibility. For example, neither the government of Pittsburgh nor that of the nearby town of Sewickley takes into account the benefits that the roads connecting the two places bring to the residents. As a result, cities tend to spend less on such projects than many residents desire. At times, states also assume responsibility for local services when impoverished communities cannot afford to provide adequate services. For example, many state governments assist the school systems in struggling communities. Unlike local governments, many state governments rely on sales taxes to finance their activities. People often find it harder to leave the state to avoid sales taxes than to go to a neighboring town. While people might move out of state to avoid state income taxes, most residents cannot easily go to another state to shop.

Federal Government. The federal government provides goods and services that states and municipalities either cannot or will not provide. Examples include national defense and the interstate highway system. Most city and state governments are limited in what they can spend, because they are legally required to have balanced budgets in which they can spend no more than they raise in tax revenue. A **balanced budget** occurs when a government's expenditures equal its revenues. In order to balance budgets, states and cities must frequently cut back on their spending or raise taxes when their revenues decline. Sales and property tax revenues frequently fall during economic downturns. As a result, states and cities find it difficult to help their populations when they need it during bad economic times. The federal government faces no such constraint, in part because lenders have confidence that it can repay its debts. The federal government can levy a broader variety of taxes than either state or local governments. Although people may move between towns or states, very few would consider leaving a country to avoid taxes.

The federal government is also a more stable source of funds than local and state governments, because it is less vulnerable to local downturns. For example, when steel plants in Pittsburgh closed, Pittsburgh and Pennsylvania were less able to raise revenue. Their loss, however, was North Carolina's gain. When modern plants built in North Carolina displaced plants in Pennsylvania, the federal government's ability to raise revenue remained roughly the same, while the two states' abilities changed.

Government Spending, Government Revenue, and the Circular Flow

The government interacts with firms and households both directly and indirectly. Direct interaction includes giving money to or taking money from the other sectors of the economy (households and firms). Indirect interaction with households and firms takes place through the product and resource markets. We explore each of these interactions in turn.

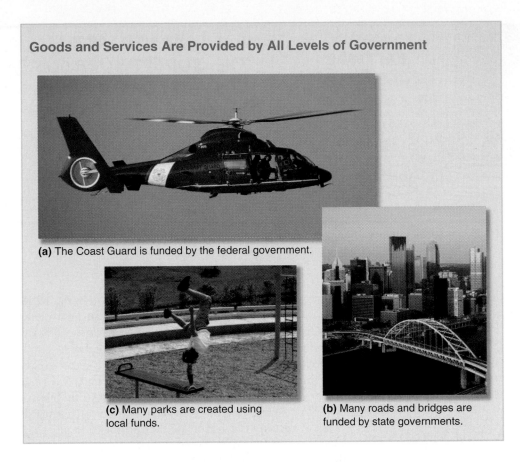

Goods and Services Are Provided by All Levels of Government

(a) The Coast Guard is funded by the federal government.

(c) Many parks are created using local funds.

(b) Many roads and bridges are funded by state governments.

Government Spending, Transfer Payments, and Taxes. Government affects the household and firm sectors directly by adding or taking away income. It adds to incomes by providing transfers. **Transfer payments** are a shift of funds from one group or sector to another. They do not involve any exchange or transaction. A worker's salary and a firm's sales revenue are not transfer payments, as each results from a market transaction. Medicare payments to elderly patients and support payments to firms threatened by foreign producers are transfer payments. The government expects nothing in exchange for a transfer.

The government also collects taxes from the private sector. Taxes are a leakage from the circular flow, reducing the levels of income and revenue for firms and households. Transfer payments are injections into the circular flow, increasing income and revenue for firms and households.

The government also affects the circular flow via the product and resource markets. Like households, governments buy goods and services in the product market. Like firms, governments hire workers and purchase other inputs in the resource market. Unlike the other two sectors, governments also raise funds on the product and resource markets through taxes on transactions. **Government expenditure** involves these market transactions, in which the government spends money to acquire goods and services on the product and resource markets. Examples include school buses and the services provided by schoolteachers.

Spending, Taxes, and the Budget Deficit. One of the great macroeconomic controversies of the last half-century is about how the federal government has consistently spent more money than it has taken in. We call this excess of spending over

Transfer payments
Funds shifted from one group or sector to another without involving an exchange or transaction.

Government expenditure
A market transaction in which the government spends money to acquire goods and services on the product or reserve market.

EASTSIDE ELEMENTARY

WE LEARNED ABOUT THE BUDGET SURPLUS IN HISTORY TODAY.

E-mail:BobThaves@aol.com
©2002 Thaves / Dist. by NEA, Inc.
www.frankandernest.com

4-16 THAVES

FRANK & ERNEST: © Thaves/Dist. by Newspaper Enterprise Association, Inc.

Budget deficit
The excess of spending by the government over tax revenue.

Budget surplus
The excess of tax revenue over government spending.

Security
A certificate that promises to pay the bearer a specific sum of money on a particular date.

incoming taxes the **budget deficit**. For a brief period in the 1990s, revenues exceeded spending, and a **budget surplus** occurred. While state and local governments can run deficits or surpluses, the federal budget deficit has generally dwarfed those at other levels and will be the focus of our attention in this book.

When the federal government runs a deficit, it typically makes up the shortfall of revenue by borrowing. This does not mean that the U.S. Congress goes to the local bank for a home improvement loan when it wants to refurbish the Capitol building. Instead, the Treasury Department issues a variety of interest-bearing IOUs known as *securities*. A **security** is a certificate that promises to pay the bearer a specific sum of money on a particular date. Some securities, such as U.S. savings bonds, are readily available to the general public. Others are denominated in such large amounts that the government sells them to only a few members of the corporate and banking world.

▶ The Financial Sector of the Economy

We now look at the role of the financial sector in the circular flow model. In the simple model of the circular flow depicted in Figure 3.1, income and expenditure move steadily between households and firms. All household income in the resource market returns to firms as expenditures on goods and services in the product market. If we measured the level of activity at any two points in the circular flow, we would get the same reading. The reading actually stays constant only if households spend all their incomes on goods and services. If households save some of their incomes, the savings leak out of the circular flow, like water leaking out of a pipe, and do not return to firms as revenue. How realistic is it to assume that no leakage occurs? What role do financial markets play?

Generally, American households spend almost 97 percent of their incomes and save the other 3 percent. Three percent seems like a very small portion of total income. However, losing 3 percent of GDP every time that income cycles through the circular flow would quickly cause the flow to dry up.

While they do leak income from the circular flow, savings never completely leave it. After all, most of us do not keep our savings under our mattresses. Instead, we keep it in checking or savings accounts, in mutual funds, or in a variety of similar forms. For simplicity, we refer to all these savings institutions as *banks*. The banks do not hold onto these funds, either. They lend some of the funds that households have deposited to other households for car loans, home improvement loans, and the like. They also lend funds to firms, which use these funds to invest in plants and equipment. Some of the savings support spending by the government to cover its budget deficit. All this lending leads to additional expenditure, thereby replacing the leakage.

Consider what bank owner George Bailey said to worried depositors in the classic movie *It's a Wonderful Life*, explaining to a customer why he cannot repay all the depositors all their money right away:

"No, but you . . . you . . . you're thinking of this place all wrong. As if I had the money back in a safe. The money's not here. Your money's in Joe's house . . . right next to yours. And in the Kennedy house, and Mrs. Macklin's house, and a hundred others. Why, you're lending them the money to build, and then, they're going to pay it back to you as best they can."

The Bailey Savings and Loan is one small example of what goes on in the financial sector, which brings savers and borrowers together to recycle funds into the economy. The leakage of savings from the circular flow is offset by the injection of investment. In addition, the leakage makes the investment possible.

► The International Sector of the Economy

The international sector is the final piece of our circular flow model. For good and for ill, the role of the international sector has increased in the U.S. economy. As noted earlier in this chapter, foreign steel makers may have played some role in the decline of Pittsburgh's steel industry. We have seen that foreign firms have also played a major part in Pittsburgh's recovery. In a final irony, while U.S. Steel no longer produces steel in Pittsburgh, it remains headquartered there and has purchased steel mills in Europe.

Closed economy
An economy in which households and firms do not engage in international trade.

Until now, we have been looking at a closed economy. A **closed economy** is one in which households and firms do not engage in international trade. That is, all purchases are from domestic producers and all sales are to domestic consumers. A closed economy model cannot account for how some firms sell laptops to Algeria, and some households buy their shoes from Italy. As a result, in this section we modify our model so as to analyze an **open economy**, or one that engages in international trade.

Open economy
An economy in which households and firms engage in international trade.

Trade and the Circular Flow

Imports
Goods and services that domestic households, firms, and governments buy from foreign producers.

Goods and services that households, firms, and governments buy from foreign producers are called **imports**. American households and firms buy both American-made goods and imports with their incomes. Consequently, some of the income that flows from firms to households actually goes to firms and households outside the United States. As a result, imports cause some income to leak from the national circular flow.

Firms often sell their output to foreign firms and households. Domestically made goods and services that are sold to foreign households, firms, and governments are called **exports**. Exports inject income from foreign firms and households into the circular flow of the U.S. economy. The pipes that connect the households and firms that constitute the U.S. economy are in turn connected to a broader array of pipes representing the circular flow of economies of countries throughout the world.

Imports bring foreign-made goods and services into the U.S. economy and take expenditure, revenue, and income out of the economy. The reduced income, in turn, further reduces the flow through the pipes, as the level of internal domestic economic activity declines. Exports increase the flow through the pipes as the level of domestic economic activity increases. The difference between the injection of exports and the leakage of imports, called **net exports** (sometimes also known as the *trade balance*) by economists, represents the net addition of the international sector to production by the U.S. economy.

When a country's net exports are positive, it exports more than it imports. We call this situation a **trade surplus**. When it imports more than it exports, net exports are negative, and we say that the nation is running a **trade deficit**.

U.S. Imports and Exports

Except for a brief period immediately after World War II, the United States has consistently run a trade deficit over the last century. Americans have regularly bought more goods and services from foreign countries than foreigners have bought from Americans. According to figures from the International Trade Commission, the United States ran a trade deficit of over $650 billion in 2004. Even with a large trade deficit, the United States still exports billions of dollars of goods and services. Table 3.1 shows the trade surplus or deficit that the U.S. ran for specific products in 2004, breaking the trade balance into three broad categories: agricultural goods, manufactured goods,

Exports
Goods that domestic producers sell to foreign households, firms, and governments.

Net exports
The difference between the injection of exports and the leakage of imports.

Trade surplus
The excess of exports over imports.

Trade deficit
The excess of imports over exports.

myeconlab

Get Ahead of the Curve

Use your understanding of U.S. imports to consider how cattle imports from Canada affect the international sector of the circular flow.

TABLE 3.1

U.S. Exports and Imports in 2004 by Product Group (in Billions of Dollars)

Product Group	Exports	Imports	Balance
Agricultural goods	61.4	54.2	+7.2
Manufactured goods	624.0	1,174.8	−550.8
Airplanes and airplane parts	39.8	16.2	+23.6
Scientific instruments	33.0	28.4	+4.6
Clothing	4.4	72.3	−67.9
Vehicles	65.2	187.7	−122.5
Mineral fuels	18.6	206.7	−188.1
Coal	2.8	2.4	+0.4
Crude oil	0.3	136.0	−135.7

Source: Bureau of Economic Analysis, "Exports and Imports of Goods By Principle SITC Commodity Groupings: 2004."

LifeLessons

No Economy Is an Island

As the United States pulled out of its economic downturn of 2001, the rest of the world celebrated. While they may have been happy in part to see better times for Americans, the governments of Thailand and Poland did not celebrate because they had been worried about the well-being of residents of Fresno or Dubuque. They celebrated because they were worried about the residents of Bangkok and Warsaw. Our model of the circular flow has shown that nations can no longer ignore economic developments in other countries. The well-being of nations is closely linked through the international sectors of their economies. In particular, countries that export many of their goods to the United States rely on the health of the U.S. economy in order to keep their own economies strong.

During the U.S. downturn of 2001, household incomes and purchases fell. Lower purchases harmed U.S. firms as well as firms in other countries that exported their product to the United States. With sales to the United States in decline, the circular flow of economic activity in other countries declined as well. The United States thus serves as a global engine for growth on which other countries rely.

The United States is not the only country that has a global impact. In 2004, the economy of the People's Republic of China grew by approximately 9.5 percent. Consider that the U.S. economy grew by about 4.5 percent between 1998 and 1999, at the peak of its expansion. This rapid growth in China may have helped finally pull Japan out of the economic doldrums that have lasted over a decade. Japan's exports to China grew by about 29 percent in 2004. These exports contributed significantly to Japan's overall economic growth.

and mineral fuels. Even at this broad level, we see that the trade balance is highly uneven. An overall trade deficit does not mean that a country imports more than it exports of every good. For example, Table 3.1 shows that the United States had huge deficits in manufactured goods and mineral fuels, but a surplus in agricultural goods.

A sampling of more specific goods within the broad categories of manufactured goods and mineral fuels shows that the overall deficits mask surpluses in some specific products. The United States imports far more clothing and vehicles than it exports. It has a substantial surplus in such areas as airplanes and airplane parts and scientific instruments. Even in the fuels category, the United States managed to eke out a small surplus in the coal trade. This surplus was overshadowed, though, by a deficit of close to $136 billion in crude oil. This figure accounts for more than one-fifth of the overall deficit.

Strategy and Policy
Unexpected Victims of Taxation

In the 1990s, the federal government thought it had come up with an ideal way to raise revenue. It imposed a 10-percent tax on luxury items costing more than $100,000. One of the centerpieces was a tax on yachts. Who could possibly complain about taxing an industry that caters to the rich and powerful? Unfortunately, the people who designed the tax ignored the principles of the circular flow and encountered unintended consequences.

By increasing the cost of yachts, the tax discouraged the purchase of new U.S. yachts by households on the product market. Many potential yacht buyers responded to the tax by buying boats in other countries, buying used boats, or buying boats just under the $100,000 limit. The decline in sales on the product market in turn caused firms to employ fewer resources to produce yachts. Firms purchased less physical capital, fewer materials, and less labor on the resource market. In particular, while yachts are made for the well-to-do, many workers are employed in making them. Thus, the tax on yacht sales did not disappoint just wealthy would-be yacht owners. It led to many workers' losing their jobs, causing them and their families to fall into poverty. Faced with the evidence that the tax was affecting the working class as well as the very rich, the government eventually revoked the tax.

Critical-Thinking Questions

1. Use the circular flow model diagram to show why the tax reduced incomes in the economy.
2. Suppose that the government provided transfer payments to the yacht workers while they searched for new jobs. Show how these payments would have affected the circular flow.

▶SUMMARY

■ **The circular flow of economic activity.** Economists represent the economy as a circular flow in which households exchange money for goods and services from firms in the product market while firms exchange money for inputs from households in the resource market. Income cycles from households to firms and back again. The economic well-being of households and firms thus depend on each other.

■ **Households and firms: The product market.** Households are the primary consumers of goods and services. Many households no longer resemble the stereotypical family of four. Firms also come in a variety of forms: sole proprietorship, partnership, and corporation. Each type of firm has specific advantages and disadvantages. Households purchase goods and services from firms on the product market. In the United States, the services sector has become an increasingly important part of the product market.

■ **Households and firms: The resource market.** Firms hire the inputs they need on the resource market. This process returns income that firms receive on the product market to households. By far the largest payment by firms goes to workers in the form of wages, salaries, and other forms of compensation for the labor input. Payments are also made to landowners in the form of rent, to capital in the form of interest and to entrepreneurial skill as profits.

■ **The government sector of the economy.** The U.S. government sector consists of the federal government, state governments, and local governments. The federal government spends more than all state and local governments combined. In part, this spending is due to the federal government's greater ability to raise revenue. Governments enter the circular flow directly through direct taxes such as income tax and transfer payments, and indirectly by taxing transactions, as with a sales tax, or by purchasing goods and services. When the government spends more than it takes in, a budget deficit results. When it spends less than it takes in, a budget surplus results.

■ **The financial sector of the economy.** Because households do not spend all their income, some funds leak out of the circular flow. Financial markets restore these funds to the circular flow by making savings available to households, firms, or the government, which use the funds to undertake projects that they otherwise could not afford.

■ **The international sector of the economy.** Households and firms often buy foreign-made products or sell the products they make to households and firms in other nations. Imports are a leakage from the circular flow, while exports are an injection. When a nation exports more than it imports, it has a trade surplus. When it imports more than it exports, a trade deficit occurs. The United States has a large overall trade deficit, but it still exports many goods and services.

▶ KEY TERMS

Balanced budget 68	Imports 71	Rent 65
Budget deficit 70	Income tax 68	Resource market 61
Budget surplus 70	Initial public offering	Sales tax 68
Circular flow model 61	(IPO) 63	Security 70
Closed economy 71	Net exports 72	Sole proprietorships 62
Corporate profits 66	Open economy 71	Stock 63
Corporations 63	Partnerships 63	Trade deficit 72
Dividend 63	Product market 61	Trade surplus 72
Exports 72	Property tax 67	Transfer payments 69
Government expenditure 69	Proprietors' income 66	

▶ PROBLEMS

1. How do the following fit into the circular flow of economic activity?
   a. The pay that you receive for your part-time job with a local advertising firm.
   b. Medicare payments that your grandfather receives for his diabetes treatment.
2. In what ways do the product and resource markets resemble one another? In what ways do they differ?
3. What insights does economic theory provide for analyzing the statement, "Tax big business, not the people."
4. Why is the level of economic activity the same no matter where we measure it in the circular flow?
5. Trace the flow of money that Becky pays for a doll through the circular flow to the wages her neighbor earns working for a doll manufacturer.
6. What are the advantages and disadvantages of being a corporation as compared to a sole proprietorship?
7. What must be true about net exports if the United States is currently running a trade deficit?
8. In which market (product or resource), if any, are the following found?
   a. College tuition
   b. Textbooks
   c. Salary paid to a teaching assistant
   d. A scholarship received by a needy student
9. The circular flow model shows households buying goods and services from firms, but household purchases account for only about 60 to 70 percent of all purchases on the product market. Where do the rest of the purchases come from?
10. Why is the federal government able to run deficits and most state and local governments are not?

11. If the government runs a deficit, that means it does not have enough money to pay for the goods and services it provides. Where does the money come from?

12. Why does New York City have a sales tax, but Chicopee, Massachusetts, does not?

13. Why don't we include Social Security payments to retirees as government expenditure?

14. What was the likely impact of the war with Iraq on the U.S. federal budget deficit?

15. If you decided to save five percent of each paycheck you receive in a savings account, how would you be, in effect, providing loans to other people? Why don't such deposits dry up the money in the circular flow?

16. In the simplest circular flow model with only firms and households, how do financial markets keep the circular flow of economic activity from running dry?

17. The Bureau of Economic Analysis reported that during the first six months of 2002, the United States exported $10 billion of goods and services to Australia and imported $6 billion of goods and services from Australia.
    a. Is this a trade surplus or a trade deficit for the United States?
    b. How would this imbalance affect the circular flow of income and expenditure in the United States?

18. Why are imports a leakage from the circular flow, even though they allow domestic consumers to buy items they might not otherwise buy?

HERE'S HOW MyEconLab CAN HELP YOU GET A BETTER GRADE

1. Log into MyEconLab and take Practice Test 3-A (to log in for the first time, see page 30 for instructions).

2. Based on your test results, MyEconLab will identify the areas where you need further work and create a personal Study Plan for you.

3. Your Study Plan contains the exercises listed below and others like them that will target the specific chapter topics you need to focus on. You'll receive instant feedback and find links to tutorials, animations, and the online textbook to help you study.

4. When you're ready, go take Practice Test 3-B and demonstrate how your results have improved.

Section 3.1, Exercise 1 The following table gives a list of items. Identify whether each item is sold primarily in the product market or the resource market.

Item	Market
Pizza	
Agricultural land	
Production machinery	
Winter coats	
Workers with computer skills	
Automobiles	
Textbooks	

Section 3.1, Exercise 2 Explain the circular flow of money in the economy.

Section 3.1, Exercise 3 Explain the circular flow of resources and products in the economy.

Section 3.3, Exercise 1 The following table gives a list of payments to various resources. In each case, identify the type of resource (land, labor, capital, and entrepreneurship) that is being paid.

Transaction	Resource Paid
A fast-food server receives weekly wages	
You pay rent to the owner of your apartment	
A corporate executive earns a salary	
General Electric earns an annual profit	
A bank receives interest on a loan	
A small business owner earns a profit	

Section 3.3, Exercise 2 Using the circular flow model, explain why a fall in consumer income is likely to affect firms.

Section 3.3, Exercise 3 Using the circular flow model, explain why a decrease in the number of firms is likely to affect consumers.

Section 3.4, Exercise 1 What is the primary source of funds for local governments? For state governments? For the federal government?

Section 3.4, Exercise 2 Why do the revenues of the federal government vary less than those of state and local governments?

Section 3.4, Exercise 3 Why do we consider savings to be a leakage from the circular flow of income, and how do financial markets reinject funds?

Section 3.6, Exercise 1 What is the role of the international economy in the circular flow of economic activity?

Introduction to the Demand and Supply Framework

4

$\mathbf{M}$**illions of U.S. consumers could not imagine beginning the morning without partaking of one of the country's largest imports.** This ritual occurs in homes, shops, schools, restaurants, and offices across the country. Any ideas on what this product might be? The answer is coffee.

According to the National Coffee Association, the average U.S. coffee drinker consumes three cups of coffee per day. Our love of coffee is evident all over the United States in towns and cities that are lined with cafés, doughnut shops, and specialty stores eager to satisfy coffee cravings. Starbucks alone offers 45 coffee flavors for the coffee enthusiast.

For many coffee drinkers, no other product is consumed with such passion. Coffee is a magic potion with the satisfying flavor and caffeine infusion needed to invigorate them at the start of the day. Those consumers seeking the effects of caffeine might not care whether the coffee is instant, automatic drip, or brewed at the local gas station. For others, coffee is a culinary experience. Coffee fanatics seek perfection with the aroma, acidity, body, and flavor of the coffee. Although the beans used to brew the coffee are grown thousands of miles away in countries including Colombia, Peru, and Vietnam, a quick trip through the bean grinder and the coffee machine can provide the finished product without leaving the house.

Odds are good that you either drink coffee regularly or have friends who do. Even though price is an important determinant of how much coffee you and your friends consume, you probably have not thought much about how the price of coffee is determined or where the coffee that you drink is grown. As you savor your next cup of coffee, consider that in the eyes of coffee producers, the industry is in turmoil. The emergence of many new growers in nations such as Vietnam and Côte d'Ivoire has forced coffee prices to new lows. As a result, changes are brewing.

In Chapter 2, we explored resource allocation and the choices that are inherent in any economic decision. In this chapter, we narrow our focus to the market system of resource allocation. Our primary task here is to introduce the demand and supply framework that we will use throughout the remainder of the text.

We've established that, for an economy to operate efficiently, it must produce a combination of goods that lies on the production possibilities frontier. Yet in Chapter 2, we did not look at an individual market to see how much would be produced or the price at which the goods would be sold. These considerations are the basics of demand and supply. Our particular focus in this chapter is on the workings of the market for coffee in the small city of Burlington, Vermont. Whether you are brewing your own cup each morning or purchasing a cup at the university cafeteria, the Starbucks on the corner, or a cozy café on Church Street in Burlington, Vermont, you are a participant in the coffee market and are contributing to the demand for this good.

ALONG THE WAY, YOU WILL ALSO LEARN:

- What consumer demand is, and how price affects the demand for a good or service.
- How producers' response to price determines the supply in a market.
- What it means for a market to be in equilibrium.
- The limitations of demand and supply analysis.
- How the fundamental questions of what, how, and for whom to produce are answered in market economies.

AT THE END OF THE CHAPTER, THE MYECONLAB LOGO WILL DIRECT YOU ONLINE

- MyEconLab is a resource-packed online homework and tutorial system that can help you perform better in your economics course. To log in for the first time, see page 30 for instructions.
- MyEconLab can help you apply important concepts from the chapter to real-world issues. Watch for the logo to indicate online features involving supply and demand analysis.
- At the end of each chapter, you'll find a special study section that will help you get the most out of your textbook and your instructor's MyEconLab course.

 Demand

Demand
The willingness and ability to pay for a certain quantity of a good or service at a given set of prices over a given period of time.

By deciding how many cups of coffee to purchase today or how many pounds of coffee beans to purchase during your next trip to the grocery store, you gauge both your ability to pay for coffee at various prices and how much you like coffee. In the language of economics, you determine your *demand* for coffee. The term **demand** means the willingness and ability to pay for a certain quantity of a good or service

Individual demand
The willingness and ability of a specific person to pay for a particular good or service at various prices over a given period of time.

Market demand
The quantity that all consumers are willing and able to buy of a particular good or service at various prices over a given period of time.

Quantity demanded
The quantity that consumers are willing and able to purchase at a given price.

Individual demand curve
A graph that shows the quantity of a good or service that an individual will demand at various prices.

at a given set of prices over a given period of time. In practice, demand is the quantity of a good or service that consumers would like to purchase at a given set of prices over a given period of time, *ceteris paribus*. Recall that the term *ceteris paribus* means "all else equal." In this context, it means that the prices of other goods, income, expectations of future prices, and tastes and preferences are held constant. **Individual demand** is the quantity of a particular good or service that a specific person will purchase at various prices, while **market demand** refers to the quantity that *all* consumers in the market purchase at various prices. Note that we do not say that demand tells us how much consumers *do* purchase—we don't know yet how much is available for purchase. Demand tells us only how much consumers *would* purchase at each price if that quantity were available. Later in the chapter, we'll turn to a discussion of how much of a good is available for purchase at each price.

Suppose you are a student in Burlington, Vermont, a small city with a large number of coffee shops. If all of the shops charge $1.50 for a large cup of coffee, you might be willing and able to buy three cups per day—two in the morning, and one after lunch. At a higher price of $2.00, you might prefer to skip one of those morning cups and purchase only two cups per day. If the price were only $1.00, you might buy four cups per day. Economists call the quantity that you are willing and able to purchase the **quantity demanded**. By plotting these quantities on the horizontal axis of a graph and the price on the vertical axis, we can determine an individual demand curve for coffee, as shown in Figure 4.1. The **individual demand curve** shows the quantity of a good or service that an individual would like to buy at various prices. This curve shows that as price decreases, you (the consumer) are willing and able to purchase more coffee. If the price is $3.00 or more, you decide not to purchase any coffee. As the price falls, the quantity that you are willing and able to purchase increases until the price falls to $0, at which point you decide to consume six cups per day. Thus, *as the price falls, the quantity demanded increases*.

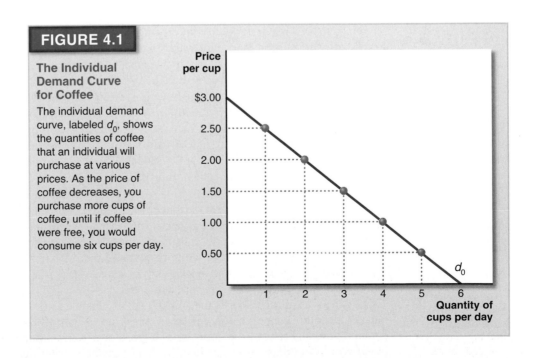

FIGURE 4.1

The Individual Demand Curve for Coffee

The individual demand curve, labeled d_0, shows the quantities of coffee that an individual will purchase at various prices. As the price of coffee decreases, you purchase more cups of coffee, until if coffee were free, you would consume six cups per day.

FIGURE 4.2

Individual and Market Demand Schedules and Curves

The succession of demand schedules in panel (a) and graphs in panel (b) shows how the market demand curve results from adding the quantities that each individual purchases at various prices. We typically sum hundreds or thousands of individual demand curves to obtain the total market demand.

(a) Individual and market demand schedules

Price of coffee	José	+	Tran	+	You	=	Market
$1.00	2		2		4		8
$2.00	1		1		2		4

(b) Individual and market demand curves

The Market Demand Schedule and the Market Demand Curve

Now let's see how economists use information on individual demand to predict behavior at the market level. Panel (a) of Figure 4.2 shows how many cups of coffee you and your friends José and Tran are willing and able to purchase at the prices of $1.00 and $2.00. In reality, there are many more than three consumers in the coffee market. Nevertheless, we assume for now that there are only three, because the process of determining market demand from individual demand is the same no matter how many consumers there are in a market.

The quantity of coffee demanded in this market of three consumers is the sum of the quantities demanded by the three buyers—José, Tran, and you. There are two ways to determine the quantities demanded for the entire market. First, we can add the individual quantities in the individual demand schedule shown in panel (a) of Figure 4.2. An **individual demand schedule** tells us the quantity a consumer would purchase at each price. If we read across the row where the price is $2.00, for example, we see that José and Tran would each like to buy one cup and you would buy two cups, so total market quantity demand is equal to four cups. Alternatively, we can plot the information found in the individual demand schedules, and then add the horizontal distances of the individual demand curves at each price, as shown in panel (b) of Figure 4.2. Adding these curves horizontally means that we add the total quantity demanded at each price. The graph shows the same result as in the table. At a price of $2.00, the total quantity demanded in the market is four cups. With either method, we can say that at $1.00, eight cups of coffee are demanded.

Let's now examine a larger market for coffee. Panel (a) of Figure 4.3 shows the market demand schedule for coffee in the whole city of Burlington. A **market demand schedule** tells us the quantity of a good or a service that all consumers combined would purchase at each price. In this case, the market demand schedule tells

Individual demand schedule
Tells what quantity of a good or service a consumer would purchase at each price.

Market demand schedule
A table that tells the quantity of a good or a service that all consumers purchase at each price.

The Demand for Coffee in the City of Burlington, Vermont

Both the market demand schedule in panel (a) and the market demand curve in panel (b) show the quantity of coffee that consumers are willing and able to purchase at various prices. In this market, no coffee would be purchased at prices of $4.40 or higher. If coffee were free, consumers would drink 880 cups per day.

(a) Market demand schedule

Combination	Price	Quantity
A	$4.40	0
B	2.25	380
C	1.75	530
D	1.50	580
E	1.25	630
F	1.00	680
G	0.75	730
H	0.00	880

(b) Market demand curve

us how many cups of coffee the residents of Burlington would purchase at different prices. Notice that at lower prices, the quantity demanded is higher, because consumers who get less satisfaction from a cup of coffee begin to find it worthwhile to purchase one, and consumers who are already buying some coffee are willing to purchase more.

Panel (b) of Figure 4.3 illustrates the information in panel (a) by plotting the information from the market demand schedule on the price–quantity axes. The result is the market demand curve for coffee. The **market demand curve** shows the quantity demanded at each price for all consumers in the market combined. The number of cups of coffee sold per day appears along the horizontal (quantity) axis. The vertical axis shows the price (measured in dollars per cup). The market demand schedule in panel (a) shows that at a price of $0.75, the quantity demanded is 730 cups. The same information appears in the graph. Reading across from the $0.75 price level on the vertical axis, we encounter a point on the demand curve that is directly above 730 cups of coffee. *Both the market demand curve and the market demand schedule show the quantity that consumers are willing and able to purchase at various prices.* The advantage of the market demand curve in panel (b) is that we can quickly gauge the relationship between price and quantity without having to analyze and interpret tabular data.

Market demand curve
A graph that shows the quantity demanded at each price for all consumers in the market combined.

The Law of Demand

From panel (b) of Figure 4.3, we see that the quantity demanded at a price of $4.40 is zero. At such a high price, no consumers in Burlington are willing and able to purchase a cup of coffee. They would drink something else—tea, perhaps—instead. At the other extreme, Figure 4.3 shows that at a price of $0, the quantity demanded rises to 880 cups. At a price of $1.25, all consumers combined want to buy 630 cups. Both the individual and market demand curves thus slope downward, indicating that, *all else equal, as the price decreases, the quantity demanded increases.* Economists refer to this negative or *inverse* relationship between price and quantity as the **Law of Demand**.

Law of Demand
The negative or inverse relationship between price and quantity demanded. When the price increases, quantity demanded decreases; when the price decreases, quantity demanded increases, *ceteris paribus*.

One feature of Figure 4.3 may trouble you. Shouldn't consumers demand an infinite quantity of coffee if it is free? Consumers would not want an unlimited number of free cups for two reasons. First, even though the cup is free, we must assess the opportunity cost of consuming it. The time spent consuming a cup of coffee cannot be used to do other things or to consume other products. Second, as we saw in Chapter 2, the marginal benefit that a consumer receives from any good or service decreases with each additional unit consumed. That first cup of coffee in the morning wakes you up and brings the pleasure of good taste. Even though the second cup is identical to the first, it will bring less additional benefit, because you already received some satisfaction from the first cup. Indeed, after several cups, the effects of the caffeine might become undesirable. Even switching to decaffeinated coffee will result in declining marginal benefit, as you become full and tire of consuming more and more of the same drink. The marginal benefit of additional cups declines as the number of cups consumed increases for each individual consumer. This relationship holds true for every consumer and the entire market. In fact, it is the reason behind the Law of Demand.

Movement Along the Demand Curve

Change in quantity demanded
A change in the amount of a good or service that consumers are willing and able to buy as a result of a price change.

When the price of coffee changes, we can locate the new quantity demanded by moving to a different position on the demand curve. In Figure 4.4, if the price of a cup of coffee increases from $1.25 to $1.75, the quantity demanded decreases from 630 to 530 cups. We call the change in the amount of a good or service that consumers are willing and able to buy as a result of a change in its price a **change in quantity demanded**. It is illustrated by a movement along the demand curve.

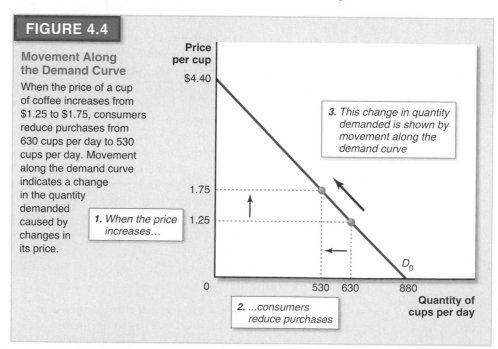

FIGURE 4.4

Movement Along the Demand Curve

When the price of a cup of coffee increases from $1.25 to $1.75, consumers reduce purchases from 630 cups per day to 530 cups per day. Movement along the demand curve indicates a change in the quantity demanded caused by changes in its price.

1. When the price increases...

2. ...consumers reduce purchases

3. This change in quantity demanded is shown by movement along the demand curve

FIGURE 4.5

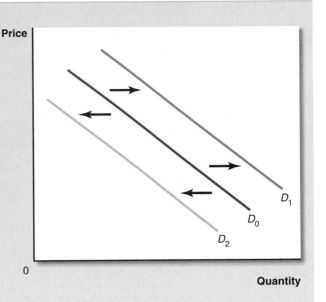

Changes in Demand

If demand increases, the entire demand curve shifts to the right from D_0 to D_1, indicating that consumers will now purchase greater quantities at every price. If demand decreases, the entire demand curve shifts to the left from D_0 to D_2, indicating that consumers will now purchase lower quantities at every price.

Changes in Demand

We've established that changes in the price of coffee move us to a new position on a given demand curve. Changes in a variety of other factors may change the entire price–quantity relationship. We refer to a change in the quantity that consumers will purchase at each price as a **change in demand**. A change in demand shifts the entire demand curve to a new location, as shown in Figure 4.5. Changes in quantity demanded result from changes in price—a movement along the curve. An increase in the demand for coffee—a rightward shift of the demand curve—implies that consumers want to buy more coffee *at every price. Do not confuse a change in demand, indicated by a shift of the demand curve, with a change in quantity demanded, indicated by a movement along the demand curve.*

Let's examine the following factors that can shift the demand curve to a new position:

- Changes in consumers' incomes
- The prices of substitutes (such as tea) and of complements (such as cream)
- Tastes and preferences (what consumers like and dislike)
- Expectations about future prices
- The number of consumers in the market

Changes in Consumers' Incomes. Suppose that all consumers' incomes increase by $500 per year. More consumers can afford coffee, and those who already buy coffee can afford to buy even greater quantities. People normally buy more of a good or service at every price when their incomes rise. **Normal goods** are thus goods for which increases in income result in increased demand. Figure 4.6 shows that if coffee is a normal good, the entire demand curve shifts rightward. Consumers respond to higher incomes by purchasing 750 rather than 630 cups at a price of $1.25. Farther up the new demand curve, consumers are now willing and able to buy 630 cups of coffee at a price of $1.40.

For **inferior goods**, increases in income result in fewer purchases at every price. A store brand of cola is an example of an inferior good, because consumers buy less of it when their incomes rise. In fact, what is an inferior good to one person could

Change in demand

A change in the quantity that consumers will purchase at each price. A change in demand shifts the entire demand curve.

Normal good

A good for which increases in income result in increased demand.

Inferior good

A good for which increases in income result in lower demand.

FIGURE 4.6

An Increase in Income Shifts the Demand Curve to a New Position

When consumer income increases for a normal good, such as coffee, consumers purchase more coffee at every price. In the graph, this relationship appears as a rightward shift of the entire demand curve from D_0 to D_1. The new demand curve shows that at a price of $1.25 per cup of coffee, consumers increase their purchases from 630 cups to 750 cups.

be a normal good to another. For example, if you consider coffee to be a normal good, you will buy more coffee when your income increases. Yet if your friend Tran considers coffee to be an inferior good, she will buy less coffee when her income increases. The converse is also true. *The demand decreases as income decreases for normal goods, and consumption increases as income decreases for inferior goods.* Note that the definitions of the words "normal" and "inferior" here are specifically in the context of economics, and describe only the changes in consumption resulting from a change in income.

Prices of Substitutes and Complements. If the prices of a good's substitutes or complements change, consumers reallocate their budgets to satisfy their desires in the least costly way. **Substitutes** are goods or services that consumers view as similar, or that serve a similar purpose, such as butter and margarine. What about goods or services that are used together? Economists call goods or services that consumers use together in some way **complements**. For example, most consumers view peanut butter and jelly as complements. When the price of a substitute or complement good changes, the demand for the good also changes. Say, for instance, that the price of tea increases. Some tea drinkers who view coffee and tea as good substitutes for one another will switch to coffee. The demand for coffee will increase, shifting the demand curve for coffee rightward. Conversely, if the price of tea falls, some coffee drinkers switch to tea, shifting the demand curve for coffee to the left.

To see how changes in the price of complements affects consumption, consider the behavior of Kim. Each week, Kim purchases one quarter-pound bag of coffee beans to grind and brew at home, and one quart of cream to add to the coffee she makes. Thus, coffee and cream are complements for Kim. When the price of a complement to coffee increases, the demand for coffee falls. To see why, think of complementary goods as a single commodity: If the price of cream increases, the price of coffee with cream also increases. We know from the Law of Demand that if the price of a cup of coffee with cream increases, fewer cups will be bought. Thus, the demand for coffee falls when the price of a complement rises.

Substitutes
Goods or services that are similar to one another from the consumer's perspective.

Complements
Goods or services that consumers use together in some way.

Fox Trot

FOXTROT © 2002 Bill Amend. Reprinted with permission of UNIVERSAL PRESS SYNDICATE. All rights reserved.

Tastes and Preferences. As the tastes and preferences of coffee drinkers change, the demand for coffee changes as well. There are many reasons why tastes may change. Information about the health effects of drinking coffee may alter consumers' preferences for it. Changes in preferences may also be a function of fads and lifestyle changes.

Perhaps the only trends that come and go faster than the latest food and drink fads are diets. The low-carbohydrate Atkins Diet craze that became all the rage in 2003 was not a new idea, but it certainly became a popular one. So many Americans started counting "carbs" that firms began to offer low-carbohydrate versions of popular staples such as breads, pastas, and even soft drinks. Coca-Cola C2™ and Pepsi Edge® are low-carbohydrate versions of the two popular colas aimed at satisfying the increased demand for low-carb products by carb-counting dieters. Even Krispy Kreme, maker of delicious but definitely non-diet doughnuts, planned to introduce a low-carb version of its signature product after experiencing its first bout of declining profits. In the face of ever changing consumer tastes, these manufacturers can take comfort in the fact that soon, another new diet craze will sweep the nation, and carb counting (as well as the low-carb versions of their products) will go the way of the grapefruit diet.

Expectations About Future Prices. Changes in expectations about future prices may also affect current demand. Suppose that an earthquake in Colombia causes consumers to expect coffee prices to increase in the future. They will attempt to purchase more coffee right away to avoid the higher prices they expect in the future, shifting the current demand curve to the right. The opposite occurs if consumers expect prices to fall. Consumers hold off on purchases, awaiting the anticipated lower prices, shifting the current demand curve to the left.

Number of Consumers in the Market. The number of consumers in a market is an important determinant, on page 89, for the level of demand in that particular market. Let's say the population of Burlington increases by 10 percent, and the newcomers have the same taste for coffee as existing residents. The quantity demanded will be 10 percent higher at every price due to the change in market size, as indicated by the rightward shift of the demand curve.

Table 4.1 summarizes the effects of changes in factors that can shift the demand curve.

LifeLessons

Sometimes It Pays to Swim Against the Tide

Another factor that shifts the demand curve for many products over the course of a year is seasonality. The market demand for bathing suits, for instance, is greatest in the early summer. Most people prepare for the beach or the pool by replacing suits that are worn out, no longer fit, or are out of fashion.

We can use the model of demand and supply to confirm that the best time to get a good price on a bathing suit is in the fall, when demand is low and stores are left with many unsold suits. In Figure 4.7, we see the bathing suit market in the first half of the year, with high demand, and a price of $70. When the warm weather fades, consumer preferences for warm-weather clothing fall. The demand curve for bathing suits shifts leftward from D_0 to D_1 as consumers turn their attention to fall and winter fashions. When the demand curve shifts leftward, stores cannot sell enough suits at the original price of $70, and they must reduce prices to clear their inventory.

In this case, shopping off-season can mean much lower prices. The same is true for other seasonal wear, such as skis or winter coats, or even for cars at the end of the model year. The next time you hear of a sale for which merchandisers have "discounted by as much as 50 percent to make way for new stock!" you will know that they are simply responding to the economics of demand and supply, and to the inevitable leftward shift of the demand curve as the season draws to a close.

FIGURE 4.7

A Decrease in Demand in the Bathing Suit Market

When the season changes from warm to cold weather, the demand for bathing suits falls. The decrease in demand from D_0 to D_1 causes prices to fall to $40, as consumers allocate more of their budgets to cold-weather clothes.

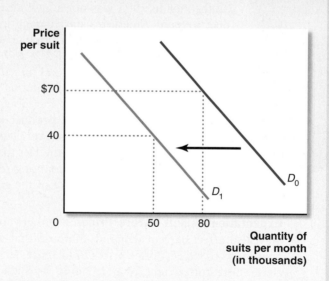

TABLE 4.1

Factors That Shift the Demand Curve

Factors	Direction of the Shift
Increase in income	
Normal goods	Rightward
Inferior goods	Leftward
Decrease in income	
Normal goods	Leftward
Inferior goods	Rightward
Prices of substitutes	
Substitute price increases	Rightward
Substitute price decreases	Leftward
Prices of complements	
Complement price increases	Leftward
Complement price decreases	Rightward
Tastes and preferences	
Good becomes more popular	Rightward
Good becomes less popular	Leftward
Expectations	
Higher prices expected in the future	Rightward
Lower prices expected in the future	Leftward
Population	
Increase in the number of consumers in the market	Rightward
Decrease in the number of consumers in the market	Leftward

TEST + *E X T E N D* Your Knowledge

1. TEST Suppose that the following events occur over the course of one month. For each event, use a graph to show how the demand for coffee would change (if at all).

a. A widely published news story cites a scientific study that found that coffee prevents aging.

b. Consumers receive a tax rebate check of $500 in the mail.

c. The price of doughnuts triples, due to a mold problem with the current stock of flour.

d. The price of coffee rises.

2. EXTEND Draw a coffee demand curve that is a straight, vertical line. What does the steepness of the curve imply about consumers' demand for coffee? Under what circumstances might this be true (at least over a relatively small price range)?

▶ Supply

Supply
The quantity of a good or service that producers are willing and able to produce or offer at a given set of prices over a given period of time.

Individual firm supply schedule
A table shows the quantity that a firm is willing and able to supply at various prices over a specific period of time.

Individual firm supply curve
A graph that shows the quantity that a given firm is willing and able to supply at each price over a specific time period.

Market supply schedule
A table that shows the quantity of a good or service that all firms in a market are willing and able to produce and sell at various prices over a given period of time.

Market supply curve
A graph that shows the quantities that sellers are willing and able to sell at various prices over a specific time period.

We now turn our attention to the supply side of the market. More than 2.9 billion pounds of coffee are consumed in the United States every year. We have seen that individual consumers decide how much coffee to buy by comparing the benefit they receive from one more cup to the price of that additional cup. But where does all that coffee come from? How do coffee producers decide how much coffee to produce at various prices? **Supply** is the quantity of a good or service that producers are willing and able to produce or offer at a given set of prices over a given period of time. The basis of a firm's decision regarding how much coffee to produce is similar to that of consumers and demand. Consumers and producers both must focus on the additional, or *marginal,* unit to maximize their well-being.

We know that consumers compare the marginal benefit to the marginal cost, which in this case is the price. Producers view exchange from the opposite perspective. They compare the marginal cost—the extra cost of producing an additional unit—to the marginal benefit, which is the price they receive.[1] Figure 4.8 shows the *individual firm supply schedule* and the *individual firm supply curve.* In markets where there is vigorous competition among a large number of firms, the price at which an individual firm is willing to supply output is equal to the marginal cost of production. The **individual firm supply schedule** and the **individual firm supply curve** show the quantity that a single firm is willing and able to offer for sale at various prices. Thus, at a price of $1.25 per cup, the firm will offer 60 cups per day for sale (point *E*). If the price were to increase to $1.50, the marginal benefit (the price) would exceed the marginal cost if it were to still offer only 60 cups. Instead, at the increased price of $1.50, the firm would offer 80 cups. If the price were to fall to $1.00 and the firm still offered 60 cups for sale, the marginal cost would exceed the marginal benefit. The firm would reduce its quantity supplied to 40 cups. In general, if the price exceeds the marginal cost, the firm will produce an additional unit.

The Market Supply Schedule and the Market Supply Curve

The **market supply schedule** shows the quantity of a good or service that all firms in a market are willing and able to produce and sell at various prices over a given period of time. Panel (a) of Figure 4.9 shows the market supply schedule for coffee in Burlington. For example, when the price is $1.00, producers make 504 cups of coffee available. As the price rises, the coffee shops that are less efficient at producing coffee—those that are able to produce at the higher cost—begin to offer a small number of cups for sale.

As we did with the demand schedule, we can plot the data in the supply schedule to determine the market supply curve for coffee, measured in cups per day, as shown in panel (b) of Figure 4.9. The **market supply curve** shows the quantities that sellers are willing and able to offer for sale at various prices over a specific time period. We create the market supply curve in much the same way as the market demand curve: It is the horizontal sum of all of the individual firm supply curves. The information shown in panels (a) and (b) of Figure 4.9 is identical. At a price of $0.75, coffee producers are willing and able to supply 378 cups. At a price of $1.25, they are willing and able to supply 630 cups. If the price rises to $1.50, they supply 756 cups to the market.

---

[1] Here we assume that the additional benefit derived from producing and selling an additional unit is equal to the price. While this is not always the case, it is a good assumption in markets where there is vigorous competition.

FIGURE 4.8

The Individual Firm Supply Schedule and Curve

The individual firm supply schedule in panel (a) and the individual firm supply curve in panel (b) show the quantity that a firm is willing and able to offer for sale at each price. At each price, the firm compares the marginal benefit of selling another cup of coffee (the price) to the marginal cost of producing it. In competitive markets, individual firm supply is equal to the marginal cost of production.

(a) Individual firm supply schedule

Point	Price	Quantity
A	$4.50	320
B	2.50	160
C	1.75	100
D	1.50	80
E	1.25	60
F	1.00	40
G	0.75	20

(b) Individual firm supply curve

The Law of Supply

Law of Supply
States that, all else equal, an increase in price will result in an increase in the quantity supplied.

Over relatively short time horizons, we can say that *ceteris paribus, the relationship between price and quantity supplied is almost always positive.* According to the **Law of Supply**, all else equal, an increase in price will typically result in an increase in the quantity supplied. As the price rises, coffee shops are more willing and able to produce and sell coffee, because higher prices offset higher production costs.

Over long periods of time, the relationship between price and quantity supplied may not be positive due to shifts in the supply curve. Production methods and input prices might change, resulting in greater quantities sold at lower prices rather than higher prices. To illustrate this idea, you need look no further than the calculator that you have in your backpack. Handheld calculator prices have fallen over time, even as the quantity sold has increased substantially. The decrease in the price of the electronics (the memory chips and circuit boards) that are used to produce them has caused the price of calculators to drop.

Movement Along the Supply Curve

Change in quantity supplied
A change in the amount that producers are willing and able to sell when price changes.

Firms generally respond to higher prices by producing more output. In the context of the supply curve, this means an upward movement along the supply curve. We refer to a change in the amount that producers are willing and able to sell when price changes as a **change in quantity supplied.** Firms respond to lower prices by selling less output, and the quantity supplied decreases. In Figure 4.9, if the price of coffee increases from $1.50 to $1.75, firms increase the quantity supplied from 756

FIGURE 4.9

The Supply of Coffee in the City of Burlington, Vermont

The market supply schedule in panel (a) shows the quantity that suppliers are willing to produce at various prices. At any given price, we can simply move across the graph until we intersect the supply curve shown in panel (b), and then drop straight down to read the quantity. The positive slope of the supply curve indicates that as the price increases, suppliers are willing and able to sell greater amounts of coffee.

(a) Market supply schedule

Combination	Price	Quantity
A	$4.50	2268
B	2.50	1260
C	1.75	882
D	1.50	756
E	1.25	630
F	1.00	504
G	0.75	378

(b) Market supply curve

cups per day to 882 cups per day. If the price falls to $0.75, the quantity supplied also falls—to 378 cups per day.

Changes in Supply

Along a single supply curve, all factors related to the production of the good other than the price and quantity are held constant. These include:

- Price of inputs (such as wages)
- Technology
- Natural disruptions such as unusually bad weather
- The number of firms in the market
- Expectations about future prices

A change in any of these factors can change the location of the supply curve: that is, the quantity of output that firms are willing and able to sell at a given price. Figure 4.10 shows that an increase in supply shifts the supply curve from S_0 to S_1, and a decrease in supply shifts the supply curve leftward from S_0 to S_2. We will examine changes in supply that result from government policies in Chapter 6. Let's take a closer look at each of the remaining factors.

Price of Inputs. One of the most important inputs in production is labor. For most products, labor costs make up a significant portion of production costs. If the wages

FIGURE 4.10

Changes in Supply

An increase in supply shifts the market supply curve rightward from S_0 to S_1. A decrease in supply shifts the market supply curve leftward from S_0 to S_2. When supply increases, sellers will offer more units for sale at every price. When supply decreases, sellers will offer fewer units for sale at every price.

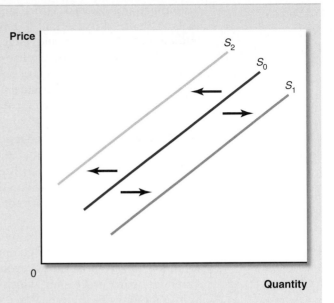

FIGURE 4.11

Top Coffee-Exporting Nations, 1998–1999

The total number of bags of coffee exported was 22,519,831, and each bag is 60 kilograms or about 132 pounds. Central and South American nations supply the most U.S. coffee.

Source: U.S. Department of Commerce, December 1999

of workers in the coffee industry rise, *ceteris paribus*, the cost of producing output rises as well. As a result, coffee shops are less willing to go to the expense of producing and selling output at any price than they were before the wage increase, and the supply curve shifts leftward. If wages fall, the supply curve shifts rightward.

For coffee sellers, one of the primary inputs is the beans used to brew the coffee. Figure 4.11 shows the major sources of U.S. coffee imports. Most of the U.S. coffee supply comes from Central and South American countries, including Brazil,

Colombia, and Mexico. Other large coffee-producing nations are African nations, such as Cotê d'Ivoire and Uganda, and Asian nations such as Vietnam and Indonesia. Wholesalers and large coffee companies like Maxwell House™ and Folgers™ import the beans. They either sell the coffee directly to consumers in ground or whole-bean form, or sell to smaller producers, such as individual coffee shops, who then sell to consumers. Later in the chapter, we discuss how changes in the number of bean-producing countries have affected the market for coffee beans.

Technology. Changes in production technology and the technology imbedded in inputs are important sources of changes in supply. Consider improved technology, such as an improvement in fertilizer that reduces producers' costs. This technology could permit coffee to be produced more cheaply than before. Coffee shops would then be induced to make more coffee available at every price, and the supply curve shifts rightward.

The most familiar examples of changes in technology and the resulting changes in supply are related to the computer industry. The introduction of the personal computer in the early 1980s revolutionized the way that people worked. Tasks as simple as word processing, which we now take for granted, were forever altered by the move from the typewriter to the computer. But, by today's standards, the first personal computers were slow and expensive. Advances in microchip and other personal computer technologies have resulted in a price decline of 30 percent per year. Thus, even with the rapid demand growth, supply has increased such that computer sellers can offer more powerful machines at lower prices year after year.

Natural Disruptions. Particularly in agricultural markets, natural forces such as hurricanes and other major storms, droughts, and unusually warm or cold weather for long periods can affect supply. In the coffee bean market, if a drought causes a poor coffee bean harvest, the supply curve will shift to the left. With beans more scarce, their price will rise. The increased cost of beans means that for coffee shops, a vital input is now more expensive. The supply curve for coffee will shift leftward as well. The same leftward shift of the supply curve might occur in the New England market if a major snowstorm prevents harvested beans from reaching retailers in that portion of the country.

The Number of Firms in the Market. Changes in the number of firms in the market can shift the supply curve. If more firms enter the market, the market supply curve shifts rightward, and greater quantities are available at each price. If firms decide to leave the market, the market supply curve will shift leftward. There is, however, an important difference between changes in the number of consumers in a market and changes in the number of firms. When firms enter or leave a market, they usually do so for reasons directly related to the expected profits available in that industry. That is, firms enter the local coffee market *because* of changes in the coffee market (such as increased demand that leads to higher prices). In contrast, the number of consumers in a given market often changes for reasons unrelated to that market. For example, if the population of Burlington increases because the University of Vermont decides to expand, the additional coffee drinkers that move to town will cause demand to increase. People don't move to Burlington because of the coffee, but their presence will affect the market.

Expectations about Future Prices. Finally, as with demand, expectations about future prices can affect current supply. If firms expect coffee prices to fall in the future, they will try to sell more at higher prices today, shifting the supply curve

TABLE 4.2

Factors That Shift the Supply Curve

Factors	Direction of the Shift
Change in input prices	
Lower input prices	Rightward
Higher input prices	Leftward
Change in technology	
Increase in production technology	Rightward
Decrease in production technology	Leftward
Natural disruptions	
Bad events (e.g., hurricane)	Leftward
Good events (e.g., excellent growing season)	Rightward
Number of firms in the market	
More firms	Rightward
Fewer firms	Leftward
Expectations	
Lower prices expected in the future	Rightward
Higher prices expected in the future	Leftward

rightward. If firms expect higher prices in the future, they will withhold supply as they wait for higher prices, shifting the supply curve leftward.

Table 4.2 summarizes the factors that can shift the supply curve. In the next section, we describe how the forces of demand and supply interact to generate a single price at which money is exchanged for goods or services, and how that single price changes when one of the curves shifts.

▶ Equilibrium

The combined forces of demand and supply in a market determine the quantity of a product or service sold in a given time period, as well as the price per unit. If we compare the data for coffee shown in panel (a) of Figure 4.3 and panel (a) of Figure 4.9, we see that at a price of $1.25, the quantity demanded (Q_D) and the quantity supplied (Q_S) are identical at 630 cups per day.

We can also find this point using a graph that shows the demand and supply curves. To illustrate the demand and supply sides of the coffee market in Burlington, Figure 4.12 combines the market demand curve from panel (b) of Figure 4.3 with the market supply curve from panel (b) of Figure 4.9. At a price of $1.25, consumers are willing and able to purchase 630 cups, and suppliers are willing and able to sell 630 cups. A price of $1.25 balances the market, in the sense that all those willing and able to buy or sell coffee at that price can do so. We say that $1.25 is the equilibrium price for coffee. The **equilibrium price** is the price at which the quantity demanded is equal to the quantity supplied. At this price, we say that the market *clears*, meaning that the quantity demanded equals the quantity supplied.

Equilibrium price
The price at which the quantity demanded is equal to the quantity supplied.

The Self-Correcting Market

We've seen that a price of $1.25 balances the desires and abilities of consumers and producers. Yet why does this price actually prevail on the market? No government office proclaims the official price of coffee, nor do we read an announcement about

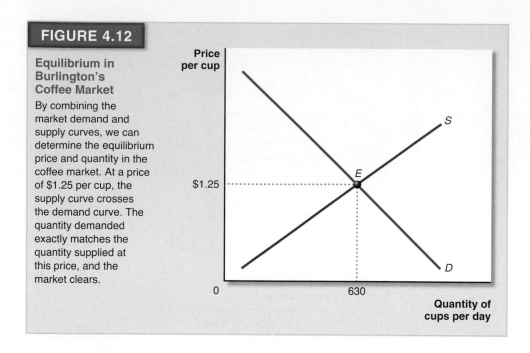

FIGURE 4.12

Equilibrium in Burlington's Coffee Market

By combining the market demand and supply curves, we can determine the equilibrium price and quantity in the coffee market. At a price of $1.25 per cup, the supply curve crosses the demand curve. The quantity demanded exactly matches the quantity supplied at this price, and the market clears.

today's price in the paper. Where, then, does the price come from? It turns out that no official declaration is necessary, as market forces determine the price of coffee. The forces of demand and supply—in other words, the willingness and ability of consumers and producers to consume and produce at various price levels—work together to determine the price of coffee and other goods and services with no direct intervention or assistance from the government or any other oversight body.

Surpluses. To see how this process works, let's suppose that coffee shops in Burlington mistakenly believe the price of coffee to be $1.50 instead of the actual equilibrium price of $1.25. Panel (a) of Figure 4.13 shows that the quantity demanded by consumers falls from the equilibrium quantity of 630 cups to 580 cups per day, while the quantity supplied by the coffee shops is 756 cups per day. If the quantity demanded is less than the quantity supplied at the current price, there is a **surplus**, or **excess supply**. In this case, we have a surplus of 756 − 580 = 176 cups.

Surplus
Exists if the quantity demanded is less than the quantity supplied at the current price.

Excess supply
See *Surplus.*

The surplus frustrates coffee producers. They are unable to sell all that they desire at a price of $1.50. Some coffee shops undercut their competition by offering their coffee at the lower price of $1.40 per cup. When this happens, quantity demanded increases to 600, since consumers are more willing and able to purchase coffee. Quantity supplied decreases to 706, as producers are less willing and able to provide coffee. Again, panel (a) of Figure 4.13 shows that some producers remain frustrated even at a price of $1.40 because there still is excess supply of 106 cups per day. They respond by lowering their prices further. The process continues until the equilibrium price of $1.25 is reached. At that point, no producer is frustrated, and there is no more pressure to reduce prices. Thus, the market is *self-correcting*, as market forces cause the surplus to disappear.

Shortages. The same process takes place in reverse when prices are too low. Panel (b) of Figure 4.13 shows that at a price of $1.00 per cup, consumers in Burlington are willing and able to purchase 680 cups of coffee. The coffee shops, however, are

FIGURE 4.13

Surpluses and Shortages in Burlington's Coffee Market

In panels (a) and (b), you can see that when the price is either above or below $1.25 per cup, the market is in disequilibrium. In panel (a), if the price of coffee is too high—for example, at $1.50 or even $1.40—then quantity supplied exceeds quantity demanded and a surplus results. The only way to eliminate the surplus is for the price to fall to $1.25, the value at which the number of willing sellers equals the number of willing buyers. In panel (b), the price is set too low and demand exceeds supply, resulting in a shortage. In both panels, market forces work on their own to restore the equilibrium.

Shortage
Exists if the quantity demanded is greater than the quantity supplied at the current price.

Excess demand
See *Shortage.*

willing and able to sell only 504 cups. When the quantity demanded is greater than the quantity supplied at the current price, the difference between the quantity demanded and the quantity supplied is called a **shortage** or **excess demand.** At a price of $1.00, there is a shortage of 176 cups. Customers are frustrated because they cannot purchase all the coffee they desire. Sellers realize that more people than they can profitably satisfy want to buy their coffee. Some customers try to ensure that they get the coffee they want by offering to pay more. Coffee shops are happy to oblige, as the shops can continue to sell all the coffee they produce at the higher price. The higher price reduces the shortage. While producers are more willing and able to sell coffee at the higher price, consumers are less willing and able to buy. As before, the process continues until the equilibrium price of $1.25 is restored.

The Advantages of Self-Correcting Markets. One of the primary advantages of using the market system to allocate resources is that markets are largely self-correcting and do not require constant monitoring in order to function efficiently. If goods and services were allocated using central planning (as described in Chapter 1) rather than market forces, many resources would be required to update and modify the plan as external forces changed. Even with substantial resources devoted to planning, goods and services were commonly misallocated in the old Soviet Union. The plans became outdated almost as soon as they were put into action. For example, to have a central plan dictate that three years from now the United States should produce 5 million pairs of gloves and 3 million pairs of mittens, does not allow

FIGURE 4.14

Demand and Supply Changes in the Coffee Market

In panel (a), a decrease in supply is shown as a leftward shift of the supply curve. The quantity that sellers are willing and able to sell drops at every price. The shift causes the equilibrium price to increase to $1.75 and the equilibrium quantity to fall to 530 cups per day. In panel (b), the supply curve shifts to the right. With the new supply curve, S_2, the equilibrium price falls to $1.00 and the quantity increases to 680. In panel (c), the demand curve shifts to the right. With the new demand curve, D_1, the equilibrium price rises to $1.75 and the quantity increases to 882.

(a) A decrease in supply

(b) An increase in supply

(c) An increase in demand

producers to react to changes in tastes and preferences of consumers for the two products. In a market economy, producers have an incentive to produce gloves and mittens in quantities that best satisfy consumers.

Effects of Changes in Demand or Supply on Equilibrium

As we saw in Figure 4.13, after an equilibrium price is established, it will not change unless surrounding conditions change. But what happens if the supply or demand curves shift? For example, in the mid-1970s, a severe cold spell in Brazil killed many coffee plants. For the next two years, Brazil's coffee production fell from 23 million bags to 9.3 million bags.[2] The frost decreased the supply of coffee, shifting the supply curve to the left and reducing the quantity available at all prices.

How would such a decrease in supply affect coffee drinkers in Burlington? To see, let's look at the leftward shift of the supply curve in panel (a) of Figure 4.14. The shift of the supply curve from S_0 to S_1 means that consumers want to buy more coffee than is available at the old price of $1.25. An increase in price eliminates the shortage. The equilibrium price of coffee rises from $1.25 to $1.75, and the equilibrium quantity falls from 630 cups to 530 cups. Some consumers buy the same amount of coffee at the new, higher price. Others buy coffee as well, but not as much as before. Some consumers switch to substitutes such as tea and hot chocolate. Because of the negative slope of the demand curve, we can say that *all else equal, when supply decreases, the equilibrium price rises and the equilibrium quantity falls.*

The higher prices that resulted from the severe cold weather in the 1970s also had a longer-term effect on the coffee market. Over time, other nations, such as Uganda, responded to the increased coffee prices by entering the industry. Because

---

[2] Robert M. Dunn Jr., "Oranges, Coffee and Apartments," at usinfo.state.gov/products/pubs/market/mktsb6.htm.

existing growers could not keep new growers out of the market, the supply curve shifted to the right. In recent years, wholesale coffee prices have dropped sharply as new suppliers continue to emerge. The large increase in supply has shifted the supply curve rightward from S_0 to S_2 as shown in panel (b) of Figure 4.14. The rightward shift of the supply curve causes the equilibrium quantity to rise to 680 and the equilibrium price to fall to $1.00. If these low prices cause some producers to exit the industry, the quantity of coffee supplied will dwindle, and prices will rise again.

We can also show the impact of an increase in demand on the equilibrium price and quantity. Beginning with the original equilibrium price and quantity shown in Figure 4.12, suppose that the demand for coffee increases due to a rise in consumer income. With consumers more able to afford coffee, the quantity demanded becomes greater at every price. The demand curve shifts rightward, as in panel (c) of Figure 4.14. The new demand curve, D_1, indicates a higher equilibrium price of $1.75 and quantity of 882 cups. More generally, *all else equal, when demand increases, both price and quantity increase.* Conversely, *when demand falls, both price and quantity fall.*

Changes in Both Demand and Supply

In the previous examples, *either* the supply curve *or* the demand curve shifted. When *both* curves shift, the outcome is harder to predict with certainty. Suppose, for example, that the popularity of coffee continues to rise. As a result, the market demand curve shifts rightward. In the same period, a bumper crop of coffee beans causes the market supply curve to also shift rightward. In Figure 4.15, demand increases from D_0 to D_1 and supply increases also, from S_0 to either S_1 or S_2. Given these shifts, the equilibrium quantity will certainly increase. Whether the price increases or decreases after the curves shift depends largely on the relative sizes of the curve shifts. We see that the demand curve shifts moderately to the right to D_1. If the supply curve shifts rightward by a relatively small amount to S_1, price will

FIGURE 4.15

An Increase in Both Demand and Supply

When both the demand and supply curves shift rightward, the equilibrium will increase, in this case to either 1,000 or 1,300 depending on how large the supply curve shift is. Whether price rises or falls is also dependent on the relative sizes of the curve shifts. If the supply curve shifts by a relatively small amount compared to demand, price will rise to $1.50. If the supply curve shift is large relative to the change in demand, price will fall to $1.00.

FIGURE 4.16

An Increase in Demand and Decrease in Supply

When the supply and demand curves shift in opposite directions, we can predict the direction of the price change, but the direction of the quantity change depends on the relative size of the shifts. In the graph, demand increases and supply decreases. Price will rise, but the effect on quantity is uncertain. When the decrease in supply is relatively small, as in the shift from S_0 to S_1, price will rise to $2.00 and quantity will also rise to 800. When the decrease in supply is relatively large, as in the shift from S_0 to S_2, price will increase to $2.90, but quantity will fall to 500.

increase to $1.50 and the new equilibrium quantity is 1000. If the increase in supply is relatively large, and the new supply curve is S_2, price will fall to $1.00 and the new equilibrium quantity is 1300. Because buyers will pay more for each cup, and sellers offer more units at any given price, the quantity will certainly rise. If instead both curves had shifted leftward, we know that quantity would have decreased. The direction of the price change would depend on the relative sizes of the shifts. *In general, when both curves shift in the same direction, we can say whether quantity will increase or decrease, but the change in price is uncertain.*

Suppose that instead of shifting in the same direction, the demand and supply curves shift in opposite directions. In Figure 4.16, we see that the demand curve has shifted to the right from D_0 to D_1. Instead of a bumper crop, a drought causes the supply curve to shift leftward. Whether supply shifts to S_1 or S_2, the price will increase. If the leftward shift is relatively small, as in the case of S_1, quantity will increase. If the leftward shift is large, as in the case of S_2, quantity will decrease. Because buyers will pay more for each unit, and sellers will provide fewer units at any given price, the price will certainly rise. Whether the quantity increases or decreases depends on the relative size of the shifts. What if the direction of the shifts had been reversed, and demand had decreased and supply increased? The effect on price would be the opposite—it would certainly fall—and the direction of the quantity change would again be ambiguous. *In general, when the curves shift in opposite directions, we can say whether price will increase or decrease, but the change in quantity is uncertain.* Table 4.3 summarizes the effect on price and quantity when both the supply and demand curves shift.

The Limits of Demand and Supply Analysis

As versatile as the demand and supply model is, it can sometimes be difficult to use. At times, the forces of demand and supply can be difficult to observe or measure.

TABLE 4.3

Changes in Equilibrium Price and Quantity When Both Supply and Demand Shift

Market Change	Increase in Supply Supply shifts rightward	Decrease in Supply Supply shifts leftward
Increase in demand Demand shifts rightward	• Quantity will increase • Price may increase, decrease, or remain unchanged	• Quantity may increase, decrease, or remain unchanged • Price will increase
Decrease in demand Demand shifts leftward	• Quantity may increase, decrease, or remain unchanged • Price will fall	• Quantity will decrease • Price may increase, decrease, or remain unchanged

TEST + *E X T E N D* Your Knowledge

1. TEST Suppose that scientists develop a new strain of coffee plant that can grow and thrive in cooler climates than current plants. How will this innovation affect the market? Draw a graph that shows the change in the world coffee market and discuss how this change might affect consumers and producers.

2. EXTEND Suppose that researchers also discover that the beans from these new plants have the added benefit of reducing the risk of heart attacks. Show this change on the graph as well. With the two effects combined, can we say for sure whether price will rise or fall? What can we say about quantity?

Incorrectly applying demand and supply analysis can lead to erroneous conclusions and inappropriate policy prescriptions. We discuss a few of these problems next.

Thin Markets

When buyers and sellers are not in close contact with one another, or when there are so few buyers or sellers that demand or supply is sporadic, we say that markets are "thin." In such cases, the demand and supply model is likely to be cumbersome and not very useful. For example, before the advent of Internet shopping and the emergence of online booksellers such as Barnes & Noble and Amazon.com in the out-of-print book market, the market for older books was not well organized. The supply, scattered across the country in used bookshops, was not always catalogued and rarely publicized. Buyers, who were also scattered across the country, had only sporadic demand for an occasional book. When a consumer did look for an out-of-print book, chances were good that the local used-book seller would not have the title the buyer sought. If a copy was available, neither the buyer nor the seller had much of an idea of what the book was worth. There was no mechanism by which to gauge the market demand or supply. Similar to an auction for a unique item, when no market price is readily observable, the buyer and seller must mutually agree on a price each time a transaction occurs.

A Thin Market Illustrates the Limits of Demand and Supply Analysis

(a) Before Internet shopping, the out-of-print book market was an example of a thin market. The total supply and buyers of a particular used book were scattered throughout the country. Price comparisons were not feasible, and thus, no market price existed.

(b) Online bookstores allow buyers to compare prices from independent used-book sellers throughout the country. A market price can be established, and the supply and demand model is useful for analyzing the market.

With the organization of the out-of-print market by the major online sellers, individual buyers and sellers can now locate or offer books in the virtual marketplace of the Internet and in much larger numbers. Small bookshops that carry out-of-print books can list their inventories with major sellers such as barnesandnoble.com. Small shops can see the prevailing prices of books while helping consumers locate the books they want and compare prices.

Output that Cannot Be Measured

The demand and supply model is also difficult to apply in cases where output is not measured in easily quantified units. An example of this is education, one of the most important goods or services produced in our economy. Measuring the output of the many resources that are employed in the education industry is a challenge. This analysis is further complicated because the benefits of education (such as higher salary) accrue over a lifetime, but the costs (such as books and tuition) are largely paid up front. The demand and supply framework is difficult to apply here because it is a *static* model, whereas the output is based on *dynamic* events. A **static model** looks at a market at a given moment in time, while a **dynamic model** looks at changes that occur in markets over time. Two people may agree that a high school education is highly valuable. However, they might measure the success of their school districts very differently. One might place a high value on a vocational

Static model
Designed to look at a market at a given moment in time.

Dynamic model
Looks at changes that occur in markets over time.

education designed to ensure that students land high-wage jobs immediately after high school. Another might value a college preparatory program focused on building skills students need to succeed in college. This approach will generate greater benefits, but at a more distant future time. Thus, the value of a specific outcome such as mathematics proficiency is very difficult to determine at either a group or individual level. Because education is intangible and the benefits and timing of benefits received are uncertain, the relationship between prices and outputs makes analysis difficult.

Fluctuating Market Conditions

Part of the dilemma of static versus dynamic analysis is the challenge that arises when external factors change. For example, when evaluating a single demand curve, we assume that income, tastes and preferences, prices of other goods, market size, and expectations are constant. We cannot, however, ask the world to stand still while we analyze the implications of the current level of demand and supply. Although we assume "all else equal," the truth is that markets fluctuate all the time. The value of any given analysis is fleeting at best. We must be diligent when working with the demand and supply model to recognize and take into account important changes that do occur.

Consider what happens when people observe rising prices and increased sales over time. They might mistakenly conclude that the demand curve slopes upward. In fact, the positive relationship between sales and price is a series of equilibrium points, as the demand and supply curves shift over time. Suppose that you stop in Burlington once each year, and record the price of coffee and the quantity of cups sold. The data you record are plotted in panel (a) of Figure 4.17. Could the data that

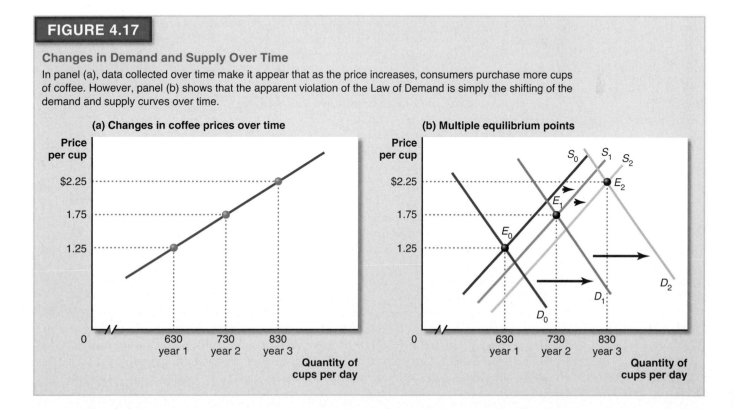

FIGURE 4.17

Changes in Demand and Supply Over Time

In panel (a), data collected over time make it appear that as the price increases, consumers purchase more cups of coffee. However, panel (b) shows that the apparent violation of the Law of Demand is simply the shifting of the demand and supply curves over time.

show consumers purchasing more coffee as price increases be a violation of the Law of Demand? In fact, they are not. As more consumers move to Burlington, the demand for coffee increases, shifting the demand curve in panel (b) to the right from D_0 to D_1 to D_2. With the growth of the town, more coffee shops open, which shifts the supply curve rightward from S_0 to S_1 to S_2. However, because the increases in demand are larger than the increases in supply, the price rises over time. Thus, although the annual observations make it appear that consumers purchase more coffee as the price increases, panel (b) of Figure 4.17 shows that the Law of Demand still holds. The apparent positive relationship occurs because demand and supply both shifted steadily rightward.

Strategy and Policy

Investing Based on Expectations Can Be Risky

During the technology boom of the early and mid-1990s, high-technology stock prices soared. Some of these price increases were based on sound economic data related to past and current performance of these companies. However, much of the increase—in fact, *all* the increase at some firms—was based not on actual company performance, but expectations of future performance. At the time, there was widespread belief that the capacity of the Internet and computer-based businesses would lead to explosive growth in the economy for years to come. We know that expectations are an important determinant of demand and supply for goods and services. The same is true for stocks. When shareholders (people who own stock in a company) believe that the stock price will rise in the future, they have an incentive to keep the stock rather than sell it. The more shareholders believe this to be true, the less stock will be available at any given price.

In the context of a demand and supply graph, the supply curve shifts leftward. At the same time, those same expectations of higher prices in the future increase demand. More investors want to buy the stock because they believe prices will be even higher in the future. The increase in the value of technology stocks was in some ways doomed to reverse itself. Some of the companies whose stocks increased by several hundred percent had no sales revenue at all. Buyers were making choices based *only* on expectations, and with very few hard facts to support their decisions.

As the 1990s drew to a close, many experts were warning that a dramatic decrease in prices was inevitable. Over the next two years, as investors returned to more traditional means of evaluating stocks, prices fell dramatically. Figure 4.18 shows just how dramatically the change in expectations can affect a single stock. Early in 1999, the company Verticalnet, Inc., began offering shares of its stock to the public. Verticalnet, Inc., offers products and services designed to help firms manage their purchases of materials needed for production. As with many technology stocks, investors believed that the stock price would rise over time. The belief that the price would rise increased demand. The increase in demand caused the price to increase. As Figure 4.18 shows, the price of shares of Verticalnet stock soared from about $100 per share to almost $1,200 per share in January 9, 2000. After consumers came to realize that the company would never have enough earnings to support such a price, demand decreased rapidly. By the summer of 2001, the stock was trading at less than $5 per share. Investors who were slow to sell their other technology stocks found that, as with Verticalnet, Inc., their values had dropped dramatically. In some cases, the value of the retirement funds held as stocks fell by so much that investors

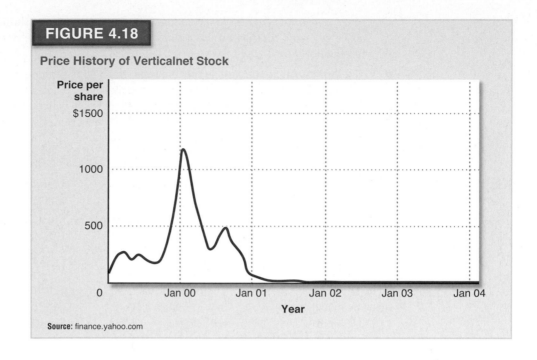

FIGURE 4.18

Price History of Verticalnet Stock

Price per share

$1500

1000

500

0   Jan 00   Jan 01   Jan 02   Jan 03   Jan 04

Year

Source: finance.yahoo.com

were forced to delay retirement. Thus, in this example, we can learn another life lesson: If it seems too good to be true, it probably is.

Critical-Thinking Questions

1. Use a demand and supply diagram to show how changes in expectations about prices on the part of sellers (supply) and buyers (demand) increased the price of Verticalnet to almost $1,200 per share in January 2000.
2. On the same graph, show how a dramatic decrease in the expectations of buyers caused prices to fall to $5.00 per share in the summer of 2001.

►SUMMARY

- **Demand.** Consumer demand represents the willingness and ability to purchase an item at various prices. The Law of Demand states that, *ceteris paribus*, price and quantity demanded are inversely related. Changes in the price of a good or service cause changes in quantity demanded: As price decreases, quantity demanded increases; and as price increases, quantity demanded decreases. Market demand is the sum of all individual demands. The position of the demand curve is determined by income, prices of substitutes and complements, tastes and preferences, expectations about future prices, and the number of consumers in the market. Seasonality can also affect the position of the demand curve.

- **Supply.** Supply schedules and curves describe firms' willingness and ability to supply goods and services to a market at various prices. Because increases in price increase the quantity of a good supplied, supply curves are positively sloped. Thus, the Law of Supply dictates that, all else equal, when price rises, the quantity supplied rises. Changes in input prices, technology, expectations, the number of firms in the market, and natural events such as weather affect the location of the supply curve.

- **Equilibrium.** When the quantity supplied and the quantity demanded are equal, we say that a market is in equilibrium. The equilibrium price is determined by market forces and will change if either the supply or the demand curve shifts. When price is above the equilibrium, a surplus results. A shortage occurs if the price is set below the equilibrium.

- **The limits of demand and supply analysis.** Demand and supply analysis is not appropriate in all cases. The demand and supply model is not well suited to thin markets, in which there are very few buyers or sellers (or in which they have difficulty finding one another); to markets in which output cannot be easily measured; or to markets in which external factors are constantly changing.

▶KEY TERMS

Change in demand 85	Individual demand schedule 82	Market demand schedule 82
Change in quantity demanded 84	Individual firm supply curve 90	Market supply curve 90
Change in quantity supplied 91	Individual firm supply schedule 90	Market supply schedule 90
Complements 86	Inferior good 85	Normal good 85
Demand 80		Quantity demanded 81
Dynamic model 102	Law of Demand 84	Shortage or excess demand 97
Equilibrium price 95	Law of Supply 91	Static model 102
Individual demand 81	Market demand 81	Substitutes 86
Individual demand curve 81	Market demand curve 83	Supply 90
		Surplus or excess supply 96

▶PROBLEMS

1. Begin by drawing a graph similar to Figure 4.1, and then show the effect of each of the following on the demand for coffee:
   a. A decrease in the price of cream for use with coffee.
   b. A decrease in income.
   c. The development of a new drink that is caffeinated and tastes similar to coffee.
   d. An expectation on the part of coffee buyers that future prices will be higher.
2. In your own words, explain the Law of Demand as it applies to diamond jewelry.
3. Explain the difference between a change in the quantity of running shoes demanded and a change in demand for running shoes.
4. Suppose we are studying the market for soccer balls in the United States. In each of the following cases, indicate whether the demand or supply curve will shift, and the direction of the shift (rightward, leftward).
   a. The United States women's team wins the World Cup.
   b. Income falls.
   c. The price of soccer nets increases.
   d. A change in technology decreases the cost of producing the soccer balls.
   e. The United States population increases.
5. Draw a demand and supply curve similar to Figure 4.12, and show the effect of an increase in the number of consumers in the coffee market on the market. What will happen to price and quantity?
6. List three goods that you believe are normal goods for most consumers and three goods that you believe are inferior goods for most consumers. Finally, can you think of a good for which demand would typically not change at all with a change in income?

7. The demand for shorts in summer is shown in the following figure.

a. At what price will the quantity demanded fall to zero?
b. How many pairs of shorts are consumed if they are free?
c. When the price increases from $20 to $25, what happens to the quantity demanded?
d. What do you predict will happen to this demand curve if consumer income increases?

8. Suppose coffee buyers are completely insensitive to price changes for all prices below $4.00 per cup. At any price from free to $3.99 per cup, all consumers combined will drink 300 cups per day. Once coffee reaches $4.00, though, all consumers will switch to espresso. Draw the demand curve based on this information. Is this curve consistent with the Law of Demand? Why or why not?

9. The following market demand and market supply schedules describe the market for lawn tractors in Des Moines, Iowa.

Price	Quantity Demanded	Quantity Supplied
$4000	0	4000
3000	1000	3000
2000	2000	2000
1000	3000	1000
0	4000	0

a. What are the equilibrium quantity and price?
b. Draw the market demand and supply curves, and label the equilibrium price and quantity.

10. Suppose the supply of peanut butter falls substantially after a drought in peanut-producing areas. What is the effect on the price of peanut butter? What products may experience a change in demand as a result of the change in the peanut butter market? Why?

11. Suppose that a hurricane sweeps through Colombia just before a major coffee harvest, destroying much of the crop. Draw a demand and supply graph showing the effect of the crop damage on prices and output. Are producers in other countries made better off or worse off by this change? What about consumers?

12. Continuing the scenario in problem 9, answer the following questions.
    a. Suppose that the incomes of all homeowners in Des Moines increase. What do you predict will happen in this market? Redraw your graph from problem 9, and include the effect of the increase in income.
    b. Suppose that the wages of lawn tractor producers increase (that is, input prices increase). Redraw your graph from problem 9, and include the effect of the input price increase.
13. Continuing the scenario in problem 11, suppose that at the same time that the coffee crop is destroyed, coffee decreases in popularity in America, due to the introduction of a new caffeinated drink that many consumers prefer to coffee. Also suppose that the United States coffee supply increases, due to the introduction of a new country exporting coffee to the U.S. Show these effects on a single demand and supply graph. Can you say with certainty in which direction quantity will change? What about price? Explain.
14. Use a demand and supply graph to show the changes in the demand for skis over the course of the year. Use two demand curves (summer and winter) to show the effect of the seasons on the prices of skis. Explain your result.
15. In Figure 4.12, suppose that the price is somehow set above the equilibrium price. What would happen to the quantity supplied and the quantity demanded? What do you predict will happen to price?
16. In Figure 4.7, how would seasonal demand changes in the winter affect the price if the government fixed the price of suits at $70 year-round? Show your answer using a graph.
17. In problem 7, if the supply curve for shorts in summer were fixed at 300 (the supply curve is vertical at $Q = 300$), what would the equilibrium price be? Redraw the figure with the new supply curve.
18. Suppose that the supply schedule of shorts is as follows:

Price	Quantity
$ 5	0
10	200
15	300
20	400
25	500
30	600
35	700

    a. Carefully plot the points to create the supply curve, and then recreate the demand curve from problem 7 on the same graph.
    b. What is the equilibrium price and quantity?
19. The book *Murder at Ebbets Field* by Troy Soos is currently out of print. Describe the difficulty in determining a fair price for this book, assuming that you could not use Internet. Then log on to Barnes & Noble (www.barnes andnoble.com) and look under the "Out of Print" books section to check the supply of this book and its price.

HERE'S HOW MyEconLab CAN HELP YOU GET A BETTER GRADE

1. Log into MyEconLab and take Practice Test chapter-A (to log in for the first time, see page 30 for instructions.)
2. Based on your test results, MyEconLab will identify the areas where you need further work and create a personal Study Plan for you.
3. Your Study Plan contains the exercises listed below and others like them that will target the specific chapter topics you need to focus on. You'll receive instant feedback and find links to tutorials, animations, and the online textbook to help you study.
4. When you're ready, go take Practice Test chapter-B and demonstrate how your results have improved.

Section 4.1, Exercise 1 The following table shows the demand schedule for two-liter bottles of cola per day.

Price per Bottle	Quantity Demanded
$3.00	0
2.50	10
2.00	20
2.50	30
2.00	40
1.50	50
1.00	60
0.50	70
0.00	80

a. Use the table to graph the demand for cola.
b. If the price of cola decreases from $2.50 to $2.00, how would you best describe the change?

Section 4.1, Exercise 2 Boxed macaroni and cheese is considered by many to be an inferior good. It has many substitutes, such as various frozen dinners.

a. What would happen to the demand for macaroni and cheese if consumer incomes rise?
b. What would happen to the demand for macaroni and cheese if the price of frozen dinners falls?

Section 4.3, Exercise 1 The following table lists the supply and demand for pizzas per week in a college town.

Number of Pizzas Demanded	Price per Pizza	Number of Pizzas Supplied
1000	$10	400
900	12	450
800	14	500
700	16	550
600	18	500
500	20	650

a. Use the table to graph the supply and demand curves and find the equilibrium price and quantity of pizza.
b. Assume that during the summer, most of the students leave town. Show the probable effect on the market and on the equilibrium price and quantity of pizza.

Section 4.3, Exercise 2 The following table lists one month's supply and demand for bushels of corn in Chicago.

Number of Bushels Demanded	Price per Bushel of Corn	Number of Bushels Supplied	Shortage or Surplus
200,000	$0.50	87,500	
175,000	0.75	100,000	
150,000	1.00	112,500	
125,000	1.25	125,000	
100,000	1.50	137,500	
75,000	1.75	150,000	

a. Find the shortage or surplus at each price.
b. If the price of corn is $1.50, is there a shortage or a surplus? What do you expect to happen to the price of corn next?

Section 4.3, Exercise 3 Consider the market for cars. For each of the following cases, draw a graph and show whether supply or demand will shift. Show also the effect on the equilibrium price and quantity of cars.

a. There is an increase in income, and cars are a normal good.
b. The wages of autoworkers rise.
c. It is September, and consumers know that cars usually go on sale in November.
d. There is an increase in the price of gasoline.

e. There is a reduction in the price of airplane tickets.

f. Some automakers leave the industry.

Section 4.3, Exercise 4 The following graph shows the market for tea.

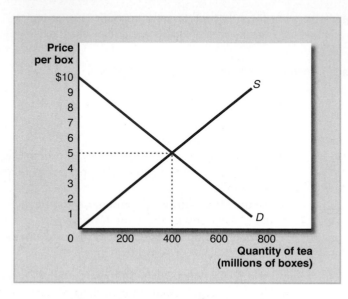

a. Find the equilibrium price of tea, and label it P_1. Then determine a price of tea at which there would be a *shortage* of tea, and label it P_2.

b. Carefully explain what will happen in the market if the current price is P_2.

Section 4.3, Exercise 5 Consider the market for sport utility vehicles (SUVs), which is currently in equilibrium, as shown on the following graph.

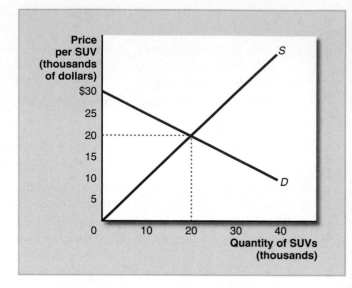

a. Suppose that there is an increase in the price of gasoline. At the same time, the price of steel—an input to SUV production—falls. Show the effect on the market by shifting the appropriate curve(s).

b. What can you determine about the change in equilibrium price and quantity, based on the information given?

Section 4.4, Exercise 1 In some markets, it is difficult to use demand and supply analysis accurately.

a. Give an example of a market for which this is the case.

b. Explain why is it difficult to use demand and supply analysis in some markets.

5 Elasticity

Karen has just spent a hectic morning working at her job in downtown Kansas City without taking a break. She is now famished, but she is also pressed for time. She has a little more than an hour to get to her car, drive more than 40 miles to the University of Kansas in Lawrence, find a parking space, and make her afternoon class on time. Karen decides that she has to get something to eat on the way from the office to the parking garage. There are lots of places to eat in the local area, including three reasonably priced burger restaurants, Connie's Salad Bar, and one local health food restaurant.

Karen is only one of thousands of consumers in the immediate area who also want to grab a quick lunch. At the beginning of the school year, an off-campus morning job with high pay seemed like a fabulous idea. However, the commute in all types of weather is tiring, and being perpetually in the lunchtime market for fast food in a city center is beginning to wear on her budget and her waistline. She'd like to duck into Connie's Salad Bar and grab one of the packaged gourmet salads to go, but those salads cost more than a burger and are hard to eat in the car. Connie's is trying to compete with the burger restaurants and offers a reasonably easy-to-eat falafel veggie pita sandwich for a little less than a burger. The problem with this choice is that she has to stand in the sandwich line to get it. Karen decides to see how long the line is before she gives up and goes to Wendy's, Burger King, or McDonald's.

For Karen and all of her fellow downtown lunch customers, the market for a lunch choice is defined by two important characteristics: It has to be close by, and it has to provide fast service. We will soon see that those two limitations severely affect how choosy Karen can be, how much she is willing to pay, and how firms determine their pricing policies.

In this chapter, we expand our discussion of supply and demand by investigating consumers' and producers' sensitivity to price changes. We use Karen's lunchtime dilemma to conduct much of our investigation.

ALONG THE WAY, YOU WILL ALSO LEARN:

- The keys to defining a market and finding its edges.
- How economists measure sensitivity of quantity demanded to price changes.
- Why the demand for some products is more price-sensitive than the demand for others.
- How economists measure the sensitivity of demand to changes in income and the prices of other goods, particularly substitutes and complements.
- How price elasticity of supply measures the sensitivity of producers to changes in the prices of goods.

AT THE END OF THE CHAPTER, THE MYECONLAB LOGO WILL DIRECT YOU ONLINE

- MyEconLab is a resource-packed online homework and tutorial system that can help you perform better in your economics course. To log in for the first time, see page 30 for instructions.
- MyEconLab can help you apply important concepts from the chapter to real-world issues. Watch for the logo to indicate online features about elasticity and calculating the price of elasticity of demand.
- At the end of each chapter, you'll find a special study section that will help you get the most out of your textbook and your instructor's MyEconLab course.

Defining the Market

Market edges
Identify the firms and the commodities that form the supply side of the market.

Before we can analyze the demand or supply for any good or service, we must define what we mean by "the market." As defined in Chapter 1, buyers and sellers use markets to exchange goods and services. A market is an entity that enables buyers and sellers to communicate with one another, either directly or electronically. We can represent a market by drawing a circle around a set of goods or services to indicate that they are "in" the market from the perspective of the consumer. Goods and services in the market include items that are, from the consumer's perspective, potential substitutes. Thus, a firm's research to define its market involves measuring consumer responses, tastes, and preferences. The perimeter of the circle is the edge of the market. **Market edges** identify the firms and the commodities that form the supply side of the market. The demand side of the market consists of consumers. In searching for market edges, consumers consider two important factors: geography, and product characteristics such as size, flavor, color, and price. Now let's apply the concept of market edges to the question of where Karen might go for lunch.

Geography

Americans purchase more than 50 million fast-food meals each day. In 2003, Americans spent more than $148 billion on fast food. While there are over 200,000

U.S. fast-food restaurants, they are not all part of the same market. Geography is an important determinant of market edges, because we prefer to eat hot food either where it is produced (in a sit-down restaurant) or close by (as with takeout). In addition, as the distance a consumer travels for a meal increases, so too does the opportunity cost of their time, which eventually exceeds the value of the meal. In contrast, goods such as computers are ordered online or by phone and transported over long distances all the time. In other words, the geographic limits consumers place on the market for such nonperishable goods as computers are much larger than those on the fast-food market. As a result, restaurants need look no farther than a few miles to find the edges of the markets they serve. However, the ease of online ordering means that consumers in California and in New Jersey belong to the same retail computer market. From a supplier's perspective, if a firm knows the geographic limits of its market, it can gauge the number of competitors it faces.

Product Characteristics

Karen's quest for a *quick* and *affordable* lunch also limits the characteristics of the food she might consider purchasing. She does not have the time or the money to eat a five-course meal at a four-star restaurant. In this case, the price itself helps to define the market. A four-star restaurant charges prices so different from other options that it clearly will not attract consumers who might choose fast food. On the other hand, preparing her own lunch is too time-consuming, so the grocery store is an unattractive option. Stopping at a convenience store is a possibility, but it has no seating, and she does not want to eat standing up. As expected, the health food restaurant and Connie's are both mobbed. The remaining three options—Wendy's, Burger King, and McDonald's—all serve lunch, offer fast service, and are within her budget. Because they match the product characteristics she is searching for and are within the relevant geographic area, they represent the supply side of the market. These restaurants are well aware of their competition, and so must set prices accordingly. Karen and all consumers with similar tastes and preferences represent the fast-food restaurants' potential consumers. Together, all consumers constitute the demand side of the market. In the next section, you will see why it is so important for firms to understand consumer demand and price sensitivity.

▶ Demand Elasticities

We begin our study of price sensitivity by taking a closer look at demand. (Later, we turn our attention to supply.) One of the most important ways that economists analyze demand is by examining consumers' responsiveness to changes in price. Consumers' sensitivity or insensitivity to changes in price is vitally important to firms and policy makers. As you will see, consumer reactions determine whether a firm's sales revenue increases or decreases when the price of a good changes. The Law of Demand states that if price increases, quantity demanded decreases. For firms, the key is the relative size of these changes. Thus, knowing in advance how sensitive consumers are to price changes is an important part of a firm's strategy.

Elasticity
A measure of consumer sensitivity to changes in prices and income. Elasticities are calculated as the percentage change in quantity that results from a percentage change in another variable, such as price or income.

Economists use *elasticities* to measure the sensitivity of consumer preferences to changes in prices and income. Specifically, an **elasticity** shows the percentage change in quantity that results from a percentage change in any one of three important underlying factors: the price of a good itself, consumer income, and the prices of other goods. In this section, we focus on the price elasticity of demand, interpret the meaning of elasticity values, develop a shortcut calculation, and illustrate price elasticity ranges.

Calculating Price Elasticity of Demand

Price elasticity of demand
Expresses the sensitivity of the quantity demanded for a good or service to changes in its price.

Total revenue
Price times the quantity sold; it represents the total amount of money that sellers receive for their output.

The **price elasticity of demand** expresses the sensitivity of the quantity demanded for a good or service to changes in its price. Suppose the price of a kid's meal served at your favorite family restaurant increases from $3.00 to $4.00. The restaurant can use a price elasticity to estimate how many fewer meals it will sell (the change in quantity demanded). The price elasticity will also allow the restaurant to determine how the total revenue earned from sales of kids' meals will change. **Total revenue** is equal to the price of the good times the quantity sold.

Price Elasticity of Demand Formula. The price elasticity expresses price sensitivity as the ratio of the percentage change in quantity demanded to the percentage change in price. The most straightforward way to express this ratio is:

$$E_d = \frac{\text{Percentage change in quantity demanded}}{\text{Percentage change in price}} \qquad (5.1)$$

where E_d is the symbol for price elasticity.

Reading Equation 5.1 as a sentence, we say: "The price elasticity of demand equals the percentage change in quantity demanded divided by the percentage change in price."

Price Elasticity of Demand Analysis. Price elasticities of demand are actually less than or equal to zero, because price and quantity are inversely related. When the price *increases*, quantity demanded *decreases*. However, it is common practice to drop the negative sign (to take the absolute value). Doing so allows us to say that demand is more elastic when the numerical value of the elasticity is larger, not "more negative." For example, if a 10-percent increase in the price of fast-food meals causes the quantity demanded to fall by 5 percent, we express the elasticity as 0.5, not –0.5. If demand is more price-sensitive (more elastic), a price increase of 10 percent might result in a decrease in quantity demanded of 10 percent; this elasticity is 1.0 instead of –1.0. Throughout our discussion of price elasticities, we will thus consistently ignore the minus sign when computing percentage changes.

Notice that the elasticities above have no units. To see why, we expand Equation 5.1 to calculate the percentage changes. One way to calculate a percentage change is to divide the change in a variable by its starting point and then multiply by 100. For example, suppose that the price of a meal increases from $5.00 to $6.00, and as a result, the quantity demanded decreases from 1,000 meals to 900 meals. The percentage change in meals is calculated as follows:

$$(\text{Change in number of meals/starting point}) \times 100 =$$

$$\frac{(900 \text{ meals} - 1,000 \text{ meals})}{1,000 \text{ meals}} \times 100 = \frac{-100 \text{ meals}}{1,000 \text{ meals}} \times 100 = -10\%$$

Because we divide quantity of meals by quantity of meals, the units (the number of meals) cancel out, and the resulting percentage change carries no units. Similarly, you can see that the currency units similarly cancel out in the denominator, because we use the change in price divided by the original price to compute the percentage change in price. Finally, when we divide the two percentage changes, the percentage signs also cancel out, leaving a unit-free number. The elasticity of demand is calculated as follows:

$$\text{Percentage change in price} = \frac{[(\$6.00 - \$5.00)]}{\$5.00} \times 100 = 20\%$$

$$\text{Percentage change in quantity} = \frac{[(900 - 1,000)]}{1,000} \times 100 = -10\%$$

$$E_d = 10/20 = 0.5$$

Proportions and Percentages

You have seen that an elasticity is the ratio of two percentage changes. An elasticity is also the ratio of two proportional changes. This is true because a percentage is simply a proportion multiplied by 100. In the previous calculations, the percentage change in price was 20 percent. The proportional change is 0.20. The proportional change in quantity is –0.10. If we divide −0.10 by 0.20, we get −0.50. Again we drop the negative signs, and get the same answer as when we used percentages:

$$E_d = 0.10/0.20 = 0.50$$

To keep the formulas simple, we will show changes in proportions, although we will still refer to elasticities as ratios of percentage changes.

Using the Midpoint Formula

There is a shortcoming in our price elasticity of demand equation that we must address before we discuss additional applications of the elasticity of demand. Specifically, our calculations are sensitive to the direction in which we travel along the demand curve. In Figure 5.1, we would expect the elasticity to be the same regardless of whether we move from point A to point B or from point B to point A. However, this is not the case. If we use Equation 5.1 to calculate elasticities for points along the demand curve in Figure 5.1, we see that a $1.00 price increase from $6.00 to $7.00 results in an elasticity of 1.50:

$$E_d = [(3 - 4)/4]/[(7 - 6)/6] = (1/4)/(1/6) = 6/4 = 1.50$$

If the price falls from $7.00 to $6.00, instead of increasing from $6.00 to $7.00, the elasticity changes:

$$E_d = [(4 - 3)/3]/[(6 - 7)/7] = (1/3)/(1/7) = 7/3 = 2.33$$

The elasticity changes depending on which way we travel along the demand curve, because the base value (or starting point) is different. When the price rises, the denominator in the elasticity formula is $(7 - 6)/6 = 1/6$. When the price falls, the denominator becomes $(6 - 7)/7 = -1/7$ (or just 1/7 if we drop the negative sign), a smaller proportional change. It would be burdensome if we had to state

FIGURE 5.1

Direction of Movement and Corresponding Elasticity

The price elasticity of demand equals the percentage change in quantity demanded divided by the percentage change in price. The direction of a price change affects the value of the corresponding elasticity because the starting point—and thus the denominators in the equation (highlighted in red)—are different.

(a) An increase in price

$E_d = [(3-4 / 4] / [(7-6) / 6] = 1.50$

(b) A decrease in price

$E_d = [(4-3 / 3] / [(6-7) / 7] = 2.33$

Arc elasticity
See *Midpoint elasticity*.

Midpoint elasticity
The change in quantity divided by the average of the old and new quantities, divided by the change in price divided by the average of the old and new prices.

which direction the price was changing every time we asked about the elasticity of demand in a certain price range. We avoid this step with a relatively simple change in the formula, which yields an average, or *midpoint elasticity* (sometimes called the **arc elasticity**). The **midpoint elasticity** shown in Equation 5.2 is the change in quantity demanded divided by the average of the old and new quantities over the change in price divided by the average of the old and new prices. The advantage of the midpoint elasticity is that its value is the same for a given price change regardless of the direction of change. We will use the midpoint elasticity formula throughout this chapter. A weakness of this formula is that it is the average elasticity between the two prices rather than at any single point. If the two prices are close to one another, this approach does a good job of estimating the elasticity at the average price. Here we show the midpoint elasticity for a price increase in fast-food meals from $5.00 to $6.00:

$$E_d = \frac{\text{Change in quantity demanded/Average quantity demanded}}{\text{Change in price/Average price}} \qquad (5.2)$$

$$E_d = [(\$900 - 1{,}000)/950]/[(\$6.00 - \$5.00)/\$5.50] = 0.577$$

Determining Price Elasticity Ranges and Revenue Effects

Elasticities of demand are divided into five categories that correspond to differing price sensitivities. In this section, we will learn how elasticities change with consumer behavior. By identifying ranges of elasticities that have similar implications

FIGURE 5.2

Perfectly Inelastic and Elastic Demand

In panel (a), a rise in price for fast food results in a 0 percent decrease in quantity demanded, indicating that consumers will purchase the same number of meals no matter what the price is. When elasticity is 0, the demand curve is perfectly inelastic. In panel (b), when consumers are infinitely sensitive to price changes, the demand curve is horizontal. Demand is perfectly elastic, and consumers will purchase an unlimited quantity of meals at the given price of $5.00, but no meals at a higher price.

for firms, we can simplify the firms' decision-making processes. Specifically, you will learn about the important relationship between the elasticity of demand and changes in total revenue for the firm after a price change.

Perfectly Inelastic Demand. At one extreme, suppose that consumers do not respond at all to an increase in price. We show this case in the vertical demand curve in panel (a) of Figure 5.2. Consumers purchase 1,000 meals per day at any price between $0 and $10.00. Because consumers are completely insensitive to price changes, the percentage change in quantity demanded is zero for any percentage change in price. That is, the numerator in Equation 5.1 equals zero, so the elasticity is zero. When the elasticity is zero, consumers are completely insensitive to price changes, and economists say that the demand curve is **perfectly inelastic**.

Perfectly inelastic
Describes demand that occurs when the elasticity is zero, so consumers are completely insensitive to price changes.

To see how a supplier (a restaurant, in this case) uses this information, assume that panel (a) of Figure 5.2 depicts the fast-food market in a small town with only one restaurant, which currently charges $5.00 per meal. Total revenue for the restaurant is equal to price times the quantity sold and is the total amount of money that the seller receives for its output. Thus, total revenue is $5,000 ($5.00 per meal × 1,000 meals). What if the restaurant owner realizes that consumers do not buy less when the price increases? The owner can double the price to $10.00, sell the same 1,000 meals, and increase revenue to $10,000. A restaurant that faces a perfectly inelastic demand curve can dramatically increase revenues without increasing output simply by acting on the knowledge that consumers' actions are not price-sensitive.

Although it is hard to imagine that the demand for fast food is perfectly inelastic, consider the demand for kidney dialysis. For patients, failure to receive the procedure can be fatal. As a result, the demand for such a procedure may be close to perfectly inelastic.

Perfectly elastic
Demand is perfectly elastic (or *infinitely elastic*) when its elasticity approaches infinity.

Perfectly Elastic Demand. At the other extreme, assume that consumers stop buying the product entirely when the price rises. In this case, they behave according to the horizontal demand curve shown in panel (b) of Figure 5.2. The horizontal demand curve indicates that even the slightest price change causes a very large change in quantity demanded, as quantity falls to zero. With a large numerator and an infinitesimally small denominator, the elasticity approaches infinity. We say that demand is **perfectly elastic** or **infinitely elastic** when elasticity approaches infinity. In this case, if the restaurants increase price by even the smallest amount, they will not sell any output. If they sell 1,000 meals for $5.00, overall revenue is $5,000. If they charge $5.01, total revenue falls to $0. Although the restaurants can charge $4.99, they have no incentive to do so, because they can already sell all the meals they want for $5.00 each. In panel (b), the firm has no incentive to choose a price other than $5.00.

Inelastic
When demand is inelastic, consumers are relatively insensitive to price changes. Elasticities between 0 and 1 are considered inelastic.

Inelastic Demand. Inelastic demand implies that consumers are relatively insensitive to price changes. If the percentage change in quantity demanded is smaller than the percentage change in price and the elasticity lies between 0 and 1, we say that demand is **inelastic**. For example, when demand is inelastic, a two-percent price increase would result in a decrease of less than two percent in quantity demanded. This was the case in our original calculation, where the midpoint elasticity was 0.577. Because the percentage change in quantity demanded is less than the percentage change in price, total revenue moves in the same direction as the price change. Thus, if the firm increases the price, total revenue will increase as well. A firm will always want to take advantage of this circumstance if it occurs. If the firm increases price, we know from the Law of Demand that it will sell less output. If the firm can increase revenue by selling less output, it will surely do so.

Unit-elastic
Describes demand when the percentage change in price and quantity demanded are the same, so that elasticity equals 1.

Unit-Elastic Demand. When the percentage change in price and quantity demanded are the same and the elasticity is equal to 1, demand is **unit-elastic**. Suppose that when the price changes from $4.50 to $5.50, quantity demanded falls from 165 to 135. Using the midpoint formula to calculate the percentage changes:

Percentage change in quantity demanded $= (135 - 165)/150 = -0.20$

Percentage change in price $= (5.50 - 4.50)/5.00 = 0.20$

Thus, the elasticity of demand is:

$$E_d = 0.20/0.20 = 1.0$$

An interesting outcome of this relationship is that the total revenue for a firm remains unchanged after the price change. Originally, total revenue was $4.50 \times 165 = \$742.50$. After the price decrease, total revenue is $5.50 \times 135 = \$742.50$.

Elastic
When demand is elastic, consumers are relatively sensitive to price changes. Elasticities greater than 1 fall in the elastic range.

Elastic Demand. When demand is elastic, consumers are relatively sensitive to changes in price. If the percentage change in quantity demanded is larger than the percentage change in price and the elasticity is greater than one (that is, between one and infinity), we say that demand is **elastic**. Total revenue rises if price decreases and

FIGURE 5.3

The Relationship Between Elasticity and Total Revenue

Depending on the elasticity of demand, total revenue may increase, decrease, or stay the same after a price change. The direction and size of the arrows represent the effects of a price increase.

Demand Elasticity	Price Change	Quantity Change	Total Revenue Change	
Perfectly inelastic	↑	None	↑	The greatest increase in total revenue, because consumers still purchase the same quantity.
Inelastic	↑	↓	↑	The percentage decrease in quantity demanded is smaller than the percentage increase in price; total revenue increases.
Unit-elastic	↑	↓	None	Percentage increase in price and quantity demanded are equal, and so offset one another, leaving total revenue unchanged.
Elastic	↑	↓	↓	The percentage decrease in quantity demanded is larger than the percentage increase in price; total revenue decreases.
Perfectly elastic	↑	Infinite	Falls to zero	Any increase in price causes quantity, and therefore total revenue as well, to fall to zero.

falls if price increases. The changes in price and total revenue are always opposite with elastic demand, because consumers react so strongly to price changes. A firm will produce less output and have less revenue after a price increase when demand is elastic.

Figure 5.3 summarizes the impact of a price increase on various elasticity ranges and the resulting total revenue.

Making Decisions with Demand Elasticities

Suppose that one of the fast-food chains is considering price changes at some locations. Managers are aware that consumers in Kansas City might have different price sensitivities than those in St. Louis. Their goal is to make the best decision about pricing changes based on location-specific sales data.

We know from earlier in the chapter that when consumers in Kansas City faced a price increase from $5.00 to $6.00, they reduced their purchases from 1,000 to 900 meals, a decrease of 100 meals. In St. Louis, when the price rises from $5.00 to $6.00, the quantity demanded falls by 750 meals from 11,250 to 10,500. Because the same price change results in a decrease of only 100 meals in Kansas City, simply comparing the market demand in St. Louis to that of Kansas City leads us to believe that demand in St. Louis is much more sensitive to a change in price. But to answer the question correctly, we must consider the change in quantity demanded relative to the size of the market in which it occurred.

Because they are free from units of measurement, elasticities are a good tool to use when comparing price sensitivity in markets of different sizes, or when different currencies or quantities are involved. For example, we can use elasticities to resolve the question of whether Kansas City consumers are more sensitive to price changes

Get Ahead of the Curve

Apply the concept of elasticity to choices teens make.

than St. Louis consumers are. We saw that the Kansas City demand elasticity was 0.577 for a price change of $5.00 to $6.00. Using Equation 5.2, the elasticity in St. Louis is:

$$\text{Percentage change in quantity demanded} = (10{,}500 - 11{,}250)/10{,}875$$
$$= -0.069 \text{ or } -6.9\%$$

$$\text{Percentage change in price} = (6.00 - 5.00)/5.50 = 0.182 \text{ or } 18.2\%$$

$$E_d = 0.069/0.182 = 0.38$$

Because the St. Louis elasticity of 0.38 is smaller than the elasticity of 0.577 in Kansas City, demand in St. Louis is *less* elastic (or *more* inelastic) than demand in Kansas City. This result may seem surprising, given that the change in quantity demanded that results from the $1.00 price increase is so much larger in St. Louis. Elasticities allow us to see that the larger quantity response is due to the difference in the market size, not to greater price sensitivity. In this case, many more people live and work in St. Louis than in Kansas City. The management now knows that consumers in St. Louis are less price-sensitive, and can plan strategy accordingly.

Varying Elasticities on Linear Demand Curves

As we interpret elasticities from the firm's perspective, we must consider whether elasticities are fixed or fluctuating. Does a demand function with a linear demand curve (that is, a line along which the slope is constant) have a constant elasticity? In fact, elasticity continually changes as we move along a straight-line demand curve. Consider the demand curve shown in Figure 5.4. When the price of a fast-food meal increases from $2.00 to $3.00, quantity demanded falls from 8 meals to 7, and the elasticity is calculated as follows, using the midpoint formula:

$$E_d = [(7 - 8)/7.5]/[(3 - 2)/2.5] = (0.133)/(0.4) = 0.33$$

Because the elasticity lies between 0 and 1, demand at this point is price-inelastic. When the price increases from $6.00 to $7.00, and quantity demanded falls from 4 units to 3, the demand elasticity is calculated as follows, using the midpoint formula:

$$E_d = [(3 - 4)/3.5]/[(7 - 6)/6.50] = (0.286)/(0.154) = 1.86$$

Here, the elasticity is greater than 1, which means that demand is price-elastic. The reason for the change in elasticity lies in the changing ratio of price to quantity.

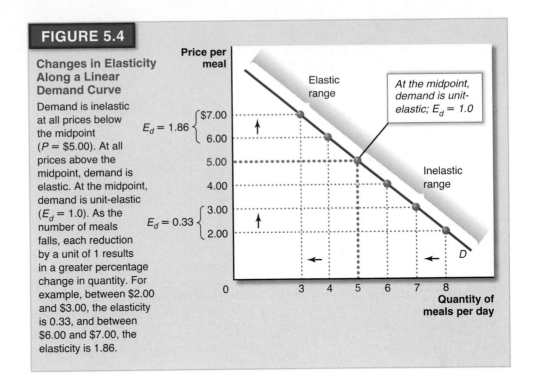

FIGURE 5.4

Changes in Elasticity Along a Linear Demand Curve

Demand is inelastic at all prices below the midpoint ($P = \$5.00$). At all prices above the midpoint, demand is elastic. At the midpoint, demand is unit-elastic ($E_d = 1.0$). As the number of meals falls, each reduction by a unit of 1 results in a greater percentage change in quantity. For example, between $2.00 and $3.00, the elasticity is 0.33, and between $6.00 and $7.00, the elasticity is 1.86.

Decreasing the number of meals by one from 8 to 7 means that on a percentage basis, quantity falls by less than when the number of meals falls from 4 to 3. The farther up the demand curve we travel, the smaller the number of meals becomes. As the number of meals falls, a reduction by one causes a greater percentage change in quantity. The opposite occurs with regard to price as we move up the demand curve. The farther up the demand curve we travel, the smaller the percentage change in price of each successive move. At the midpoint of this linear demand curve, where price equals $5.00, the elasticity is equal to 1.0; the demand for meals is unit-elastic.

Although linear demand curves do not have constant elasticities, we can still say something about the nature of the demand elasticity by looking at the slope of the demand curve. As the demand curve becomes steeper, the quantity response for any given price change falls. Thus, as a general rule: *at any given price, all else equal, the steeper the demand curve, the more inelastic is demand.* For example, Figure 5.5 shows two demand curves for markets A and B that intersect at a price of $10.00. A $2.00 price decrease to $8.00 results in an increase in quantity demanded from 10 units to 13 units on D_A, and in an increase in quantity demanded from 10 to 20 units on D_B. The elasticities are:

$$E_{dA} = [(13 - 10)/11.5]/[(8 - 10)/9] = 1.17$$
$$E_{dB} = [(20 - 10)/15]/[(8 - 10)/9] = 3.00$$

The flatter demand curve, D_B, is therefore much more elastic than D_A, given the same price change. That is, consumers in market B are more price-sensitive than consumers in market A.

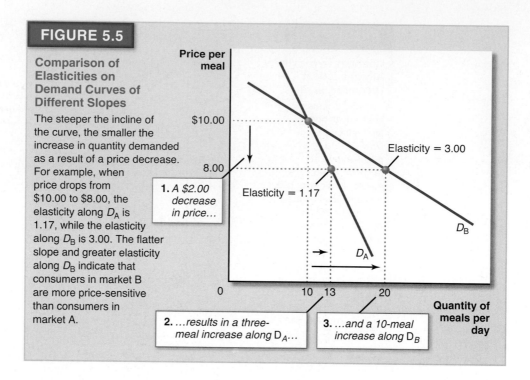

FIGURE 5.5

Comparison of Elasticities on Demand Curves of Different Slopes

The steeper the incline of the curve, the smaller the increase in quantity demanded as a result of a price decrease. For example, when price drops from $10.00 to $8.00, the elasticity along D_A is 1.17, while the elasticity along D_B is 3.00. The flatter slope and greater elasticity along D_B indicate that consumers in market B are more price-sensitive than consumers in market A.

Price per meal

$10.00

8.00

Elasticity = 3.00

1. *A $2.00 decrease in price...*

Elasticity = 1.17

D_B

D_A

0   10 13   20

Quantity of meals per day

2. *...results in a three-meal increase along* D_A*...*

3. *...and a 10-meal increase along* D_B

TEST + *EXTEND* Your Knowledge

1. TEST Based on the elasticities in the text, if restaurants in both St. Louis and Kansas City were to raise their prices by eight percent, what would be the percentage change in quantity for each?

2. EXTEND Suppose that consumers in Sydney, Australia, reduce their purchases of hamburgers from 600 to 525 units when the price increases from A$5.00 to A$6.00. Are consumers more price-sensitive or less price-sensitive than consumers in Kansas City?

►Determinants of Demand Elasticity

You've learned how to calculate price elasticities of demand and understand the important revenue implications of the various elasticity ranges for firm strategy. Why is the demand for some products more elastic than the demand for others? The three main factors that determine price elasticities are:

- The availability of substitutes
- The share of consumer income devoted to a good
- The consumer's time horizon

We discuss each of these factors in turn.

Availability of Substitutes

For most commodities, the single most important determinant of the price elasticity of demand is the availability of substitutes. Recall from our discussion of market definition and edges that consumers determine which products are potential

TABLE 5.1

Selected Price Elasticities

	Product or Service	Price Elasticity	Elasticity Range
1	Wine	0.05	Inelastic
2	Beer	0.11	Inelastic
3	Spirits	0.11	Inelastic
4	Industrial fuel consumption—electric	0.14	Inelastic
5	Restaurants	0.19	Inelastic
6	Industrial fuel consumption—gas	0.27	Inelastic
7	Potatoes	0.27	Inelastic
8	Industrial fuel consumption—liquid	0.30	Inelastic
9	Wool	0.33	Inelastic
10	Beef	0.65	Inelastic
11	Chicken	0.65	Inelastic
12	Fast-food restaurants	1.00	Unit-elastic
13	Cereal and bakery products	1.00	Unit-elastic
14	Airline travel	1.25	Elastic
15	Apples	1.27	Elastic
16	Fresh tomatoes	2.22	Elastic
17	Fresh peas	2.83	Elastic

Sources: Rows 1–3, 13: "Cross-County Alcohol Consumption Comparison: An Application of the Rotterdam Demand System," E. A. Selvanathan, *Applied Economics*, October 1991, vol. 23, issue 10, page 1,613.
Row 14: "Price and Income Elasticities For Airline Travel," J. M. Cigliano, *Business Economics*, September 1980, vol. 15, no. 4, page 17.
Rows 7, 11, 15–17: *The Structure of American Industry*, Walter Adams, Macmillan, 1990.
Rows 4, 6, 8: *The Structure of World Energy Demand*, Robert Pindyck, Massachusetts Institute of Technology Press, 1979.
Rows 5, 12: "The Restaurant and the Fast Food Race: Who's Winning?" Douglas M. Brown, *Southern Economic Journal*, April 1990, vol. 56, no. 4, pages 984–995.

substitutes for others. As the number of products in a market increases, so does the potential for consumers to substitute one good for another. *Ceteris paribus, demand is more elastic for goods or services that have more substitutes.* For example, if consumers can easily switch from Wendy's to Burger King, they are more likely to change their purchasing decisions when one restaurant raises its price by switching to the other. If no other brands are available, consumers must then consider the alternative of doing without the good. In this case, quantity demanded will not fall as much when the price increases. Thus, if a firm has many competing products that consumers regard as close substitutes for its output, their consumers are very sensitive to price changes. All else equal, if a firm has no competitors in the market, consumers' demand is more inelastic.

Real Product Elasticity Estimates. Table 5.1 shows estimated price elasticities for several well-known product categories as well as for several specific commodities. Note that in some cases, the table shows demand elasticities for broadly defined categories of products, such as restaurants. The elasticity for restaurants as a group is in the inelastic range because it includes many goods that are by definition substitutes. As such, there are few potential substitutes left that might increase the price elasticity. When we narrow the product group from all restaurants to fast-food restaurants, the elasticity increases from 0.19 to 1.00. With the product defined more narrowly, there are now many more potential substitutes (such as other types of restaurants). Also note that goods that have few ready substitutes for most consumers—such as electricity and gasoline—are very price-inelastic. At the other end of the spectrum, for many foods—such as fresh vegetables like tomatoes and peas—there are numerous substitutes. As a result, the demand for these is highly price-elastic.

Fast-Food Substitutes and Elasticity. With so many substitutes readily available, why is the demand for fast food not highly price-elastic? The answer lies in how we define the market. While the demand for *fast food as a whole* is unit-elastic, the demand for fast food *at a particular restaurant* is much more elastic. Whether out on a short lunch break, stopping to grab a bite to eat while traveling, or in need of a quick snack before catching a bus, consumer demand for fast food is roughly unit elastic. The reason is that fast food does not have many close substitutes as a product group. Fast-food restaurants sell a fairly standard array of meals that are fully prepared, hot, and designed specifically to meet the tastes of busy Americans. Fewer and fewer of us have the time and energy to cook all of our own meals, despite health warnings concerning the fat content of french fries, oversized burgers, and thick shakes.

Because most fast-food markets include several restaurants offering similar products, sellers must compete for business. Figure 5.6 depicts the market for fast food at a large mall's food court and at a single restaurant in the food court. Assume that all other prices, like those at more upscale restaurants nearby, are held constant. The market demand curve in panel (a) shows that a 9.5-percent increase (using the midpoint formula) in price at all the restaurants in the food court (as we have defined the market) will reduce the quantity of fast food demanded by about 10.5 percent (using the midpoint formula). The changes in price and quantity offset each other; in other words, while some consumers do switch to other food types, overall restaurant revenue stays about the same. The elasticity of demand for the market is 10.5/9.5 = 1.105.

It is unlikely in most industries that all the firms will reach and honor an agreement to raise all prices together—besides, it's illegal! Thus, we consider the more likely possibility that only one restaurant raises its price. Panel (b) of Figure 5.6 shows the demand curve for a hypothetical Burger King in the food court. Its demand curve is much more elastic than the combined demand for all the restaurants at the food court. Suppose the price of a Burger King combination meal increases by 9.5 percent, (using the midpoint formula), from $5.00 to $5.50. The quantity of combination meals consumers now demanded in a typical hour falls from 100 to 70, a 35.3-percent decrease (using the midpoint formula). Because a 9.5-percent price increase results in a 35.3-percent decrease in quantity, the elasticity for this particular restaurant is 35.3/9.5 = 3.72. In this case, the price elasticity of demand for a typical restaurant is more than three times as large as the price elasticity of demand for the market. The high elasticity of demand reflects the wide variety of substitutes. Any time the number of competing firms in the market rises, the price elasticity of demand for each individual firm increases as well, because consumers have access to more close substitutes.

Share of Consumer Income

Price elasticities also depend on the product's cost relative to the buyer's income. For example, the demand for individually wrapped pieces of bubble gum, which cost about $0.02 each, is highly inelastic. The demand for cashmere sweaters, which cost $100 each, is much more elastic. Suppose that every day after lunch, you purchase a piece of bubble gum for two cents. A price hike of one cent, to $0.03, translates to a 50 percent increase. Spending the extra penny has a minimal impact on your

FIGURE 5.6

The Availability of Substitutes and the Elasticity of Demand

In panel (a), consumers of fast food at the mall are reluctant to switch to other types of restaurants. Thus, a 50-cent increase in the price of fast food results in a modest decrease of only 10.5 percent in the quantity of meals demanded. In panel (b), however, when other fast-food substitutes for Burger King are readily available, a 50-cent rise in price soon causes consumers to switch to competing fast-food restaurants. Quality demanded falls by 35.3 percent. The elasticity at the individual restaurant level is 3.72—much higher than elasticity at the market level, which is only 1.10.

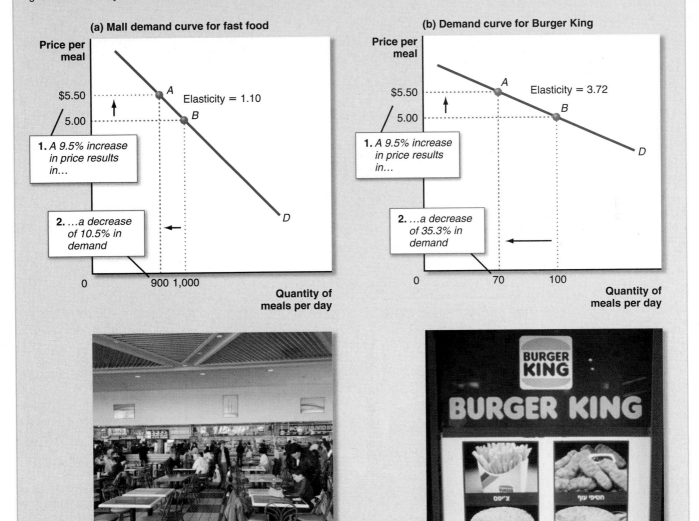

(a) Mall demand curve for fast food

Price per meal

$5.50 .... A
                Elasticity = 1.10
5.00 .... B

1. A 9.5% increase in price results in...

2. ...a decrease of 10.5% in demand

0   900 1,000

Quantity of meals per day

(b) Demand curve for Burger King

Price per meal

$5.50 .... A
                Elasticity = 3.72
5.00 .... B
                         D

1. A 9.5% increase in price results in...

2. ...a decrease of 35.3% in demand

0   70   100

Quantity of meals per day

total budget, so you will still probably buy the same amount of gum. If cashmere sweaters experience the same 50-percent increase, going from $100 to $150 apiece, you will almost certainly purchase fewer of them. Your response may be driven in part by the availability of substitutes (sweaters in other fabrics, such as wool or cotton). However, your sensitivity to price in this case is more likely due to the impact of this 50-percent increase on your overall budget.

LifeLessons

To Choose, You Need Choices

For a typical sports fan, a trip to the baseball stadium involves the purchase of more than a ticket. Most fans want a cold drink and some classic ballpark food to go with it. The cost of a hot dog and a soda generally runs about $6.00: $3.75 for the hot dog, and $2.25 for the soda. The cost of a comparable hot dog and soda at a local convenience market is about $2.50: $1.50 for the hot dog and $1.00 for the soda. Why does the same food cost more than twice as much at the stadium?

The answer lies in the definition of the market and the resulting list of possible substitutes. The convenience market charges low prices because it competes with many nearby food sellers. It might be only a mile or two from the stadium, but it might as well be in another world. The hot dog stand at the park competes only with the other vendors at the park, most of which are operated by the same company. The hot dog vendor knows that if you walk away from his stand, you will soon discover that pizza is $4.00 per slice at the stadium. The edges of the market extend no farther than the gates of the stadium.

Even if you could leave the park and return with a meal purchased elsewhere (which most stadiums prohibit), you would risk missing an exciting play. Or you could stop at the convenience store on the way to the game. That way, you can arrive at the park full and satisfied—and maybe even with enough cash left over for that $20 hat.

Whenever consumers face constraints on choices that limit substitutes, demand is less elastic and prices are higher than if the constraints did not exist. Whether you are making a trip to the only all-night convenience store for aspirin or buying an umbrella on a rainy day from a street vendor, when you cannot be choosy, you usually end up paying more.

RUDY PARK: © Darrin Bell and Theron Heir/Dist. by United Feature Syndicate, Inc.

Consumer's Time Horizon

The time horizon of purchases and consumption also affects elasticities. For example, consumers often use goods with complements that do not have to be replaced at the same time. Consider a car that lasts for years and a tank of gasoline that may be consumed in a few days. Consumers purchase some goods specifically to go with others, which sometimes prevents them from responding immediately to a price change in one or both goods. For example, Jared works full time. He is a single father of three busy children, and has a relatively long commute to work in an area that offers no public transportation. If the price of gasoline rises substantially, he wants

TABLE 5.2

Selected Short-Run and Long-Run Price Elasticities

	Product or Service		Short-Run Price Elasticity	Long-Run Price Elasticity
1	Residential fuel consumption	Gas	0.15	1.01
		Oil	0.18	1.10
		Electric	0.19	1.00
2	Medical care and hospitalization insurance		0.28	3.86
3	Cigarettes		0.40	0.48
4	Jewelry and watches		0.44	0.72
5	Non-durable toys		0.58	1.72
6	Car tires, tubes, accessories, and parts		0.63	0.37
7	Railway—commuter line		0.67	0.81
8	New cars and net purchases of used cars		0.96	0.15
9	China, glassware, tableware, and utensils		1.16	1.31

Sources: Rows 2, 4–8: *Consumer Demand in the United States*, Hendrik Houthakker, Lester Taylor, Harvard University Press, 1966. Rows 1, 9: *The Structure of World Energy Demand*, Robert Pindyck, Massachusetts Institute of Technology Press, 1979. Row 3: "Cigarette Taxation and Demand: An Empirical Model," Hai-Yen Sung, The-Wei Hu, Theodore Keeler, *Contemporary Economic Policy*, July 1994, vol. 12, no. 3, page 91.

to cut back on his driving, but he cannot do so easily. He still needs to use his car to commute to work, to drop off and pick up the children, and to drive to the grocery store. A more fuel-efficient car or perhaps a home closer to work might be options in the future. However, it would be difficult and expensive to buy a new car or to move immediately after the price of gas rises. As a result, Jared's demand for gasoline is very inelastic in the near term, but more elastic over a longer time period.

Table 5.2 shows the short-run and long-run demand elasticities for a number of commodities. In most cases, short-run elasticities are smaller than long-run elasticities. If, for example, the price of home heating oil increases sharply in mid-January, consumers are unlikely to install new windows, to change to natural gas or electric heat, or to move to Florida in the near term.

Though less common, there are some interesting cases where the short-run elasticity is greater than the long-run elasticity. Notice in Table 5.2 that the short-run demand elasticity for new cars is 0.96, but the long-run elasticity is 0.1525. In this case, the larger short-run elasticity is a reflection of the nature of the durability of the good. **Durable goods** typically last for a long time. Most new-car buyers are replacing an existing car with a new one. Thus, in the short run, demand is more elastic, because a consumer can repair an existing car. In the long run, though, the car must be replaced, which makes long-run demand much more inelastic than the short-run demand.

Durable goods
Goods that typically last for a long time. Short-run demand for durable goods is usually more elastic than long-run demand.

▶Income and Cross-Price Elasticities of Demand

We can use elasticities to evaluate the impact of changes in a variety of variables on the demand for a product. For instance, firms are often interested in the sensitivity of quantity demanded to changes in income. Recall that changes in income shift the entire demand curve, which changes the quantity demanded at every price. The government may want to know how the number of computers purchased changes as consumer income increases, because changes in income might affect revenue from sales taxes. We may also be interested in how sensitive the quantity demanded is to changes in the prices of related goods. Firms need information on how consumers react to changes in substitute and complementary goods in order to set their own prices appropriately. In this section, we examine two additional elasticities of demand: *income* and *cross-price elasticities*.

Income Elasticity

Suppose that the president of Ford Motor Company knows that the demand for the company's cars rises and falls regularly with the overall ups and downs of the economy. He plans his production schedule accordingly. The president of Johanna Farms Milk, however, has no such worries. People buy roughly the same amount of milk regardless of whether the economy is booming or in a recession. If consumers purchase fast food instead of fancier restaurant meals, fast-food sellers could actually increase their sales when incomes fall. The differences in consumers' purchasing patterns for these products stems from their **income elasticity of demand**, which shows the percentage change in quantity demanded that results from a percentage change in income.

Income elasticity of demand
Shows the percentage change in quantity demanded that results from a percentage change in income.

Income Elasticity Equation. The income elasticity equation is similar to a price elasticity equation, but substitutes percentage changes in income for percentage changes in price. As with the midpoint formula for price elasticities, we use the average income and average quantity for consistency. The result is again a unit-free number.

$$E_I = \frac{\text{Percentage change in quantity demanded}}{\text{Percentage change in income}} \qquad (5.3)$$

When we evaluated price elasticities, we dropped the negative sign to make the resulting elasticities easier to interpret. We do not do so here, because the income elasticity of demand for a good can be positive, negative, or zero. Its sign tells us something important about the consumer's attitude toward the good. Recall from Chapter 4 that a consumer buys more of a normal good in response to an increase in income. Because both income and quantity rise for a normal good, its income elasticity of demand is positive. If Karen's income elasticity for fast food is +1.20, fast food is a normal good for her. If her income increases by one percent, her purchases of fast food will increase by 1.2 percent. If Jacob's income elasticity is –1.20, he responds to an increase in income by purchasing *less* fast food. He considers fast food to be an inferior good; the income elasticity of demand is negative. With inferior goods, if the denominator of Equation 5.3 is positive (income increases), the numerator must be negative, as quantity decreases. If Tamara's income elasticity of demand for fast food equals zero, her demand for fast food is completely insensitive to changes in income. Thus, zero represents the dividing line between normal and inferior goods.

Luxuries and Necessities. Whether a good is normal or inferior is not an inherent, unchanging characteristic. The same product can be inferior under some circumstances and normal under others. While Karen buys more fast food when her income rises from $500 to $600 per week, Jacob responds to a similar increase by buying less fast food. Moreover, as Karen's income continues to increase, she might begin to treat fast food as inferior. For example, she might choose to eat at fine restaurants and to reduce her consumption of fast food when she receives her next raise to $700 per week.

Economists use a value of +1.0 as a dividing line between luxuries and necessities. A commodity whose income elasticity is greater than 1 is a **luxury**. If a commodity's income elasticity is less than 1, it is a **necessity**. We use "luxury" and "necessity" as technical terms—indicating an elasticity range, rather than making a value judgment about the quality of the goods in question. If the income elasticity of demand for a commodity is positive but less than 1.0 (say, 0.25), a consumer will buy a little more of it when his or her income increases.

Table 5.3 shows the estimated income elasticities of demand for a number of commodities; these elasticities represent the average response of consumers to a change in income. Notice that when consumers obtain additional income, they do not buy much more chicken or butter. However, increases in income cause a disproportionately large increase in consumption of goods like airline tickets. The income elasticity of 1.91 in Table 5.3 indicates that consumers' air travel increases significantly when compared to their income increases. Conversely, we can observe goods with high- and low-income elasticity when income falls. When consumers experience a decrease in income, they might cut back on air travel. However, they may not be able to reduce their milk consumption by much, as indicated by the income elasticity of only 0.50 for milk.

TABLE 5.3

Selected Income Elasticities

	Product or Service	Income Elasticity
1	Pork	0.14
2	Potatoes	0.15
3	Raw wool	0.27
4	Chicken	0.28
5	Butter	0.37
6	Milk	0.50
7	Wine	0.63
8	Beer	0.71
9	Oranges	0.83
10	Lettuce	0.88
11	Beef	1.05
12	Fresh peas	1.05
13	Apples	1.32
14	Peaches	1.43
15	Cream	1.72
16	Airline travel	1.91

Sources: Rows 7, 8: "Cross-County Alcohol Consumption Comparison: An Application of the Rotterdam Demand System," E. A. Selvanathan, *Applied Economics*, October 1991, vol. 23, issue 10, page 1,613.
Rows 1–6, 9–15: "Price and Income Elasticities For Airline Travel," J. M. Cigliano, *Business Economics*, September 1980, vol. 15, no. 4, page 17.
Row 16: *The Structure of American Industry*, Walter Adams, Macmillan, 1990.

Fast-Food Income Elasticity. What about the income elasticity for fast food? According to one research study, the income elasticity of demand for fast food is 0.68, making it a necessity.[1] (Be mindful that "necessity" is a technical term rather than a normative descriptor.) Although some consumers might claim to *need* a Big Mac, the income elasticity simply tells us that they will not respond to increased income by making many additional trips to fast-food restaurants. Even if their income falls, their preferences for fast food are such that they won't cut back consumption by much. Also note that a necessity for one person may be a luxury for another. Remember that Karen's income elasticity is 1.20, indicating that for her, fast food is a luxury good, while Jacob regards fast food as an inferior good.

Cross-Price Elasticity

Cross-price elasticities
Show the percentage change in quantity demanded of one good given a percentage change in the price of a different good.

Cross-price elasticities show the percentage change in quantity demanded of one good given a percentage change in the price of a different good. Just as changes in income shift the demand curve, recall that when the price of a substitute or complement for a good changes, it shifts the demand curve for that good. Thus, we can use a cross-price elasticity to determine whether two goods are substitutes or complements. Because they indicate how easily consumers can substitute between goods, cross-price elasticities are also very useful when we define markets or search for market edges.

Calculating Cross-Price Elasticities. We calculate cross-price elasticities with the same basic equation as for price elasticities, but with one important difference. With price elasticities, we compare the percentage changes in the quantity demanded and price of a single good. For cross-price elasticities, we compare the percentage change in the quantity demanded of one good to the percentage change in the price of another. For example, the owner of a Burger King restaurant in town would want to know the cross-price elasticity of the demand for his burgers with respect to the price of the burgers at Wendy's. The cross-price elasticity indicates whether changes in Wendy's prices would affect sales. The formula for cross-price elasticity is:

$$E_{XY} = \frac{\text{Percentage change in the quantity demanded of good X}}{\text{Percentage change in the price of good Y}} \qquad (5.4)$$

Suppose the owner of the Burger King notices that when the price of a Wendy's hamburger (which corresponds to Y in Equation 5.4) increases by 25 percent, the sales of Burger King burgers (X in Equation 5.4) increase by 10 percent. The cross-price elasticity is:

$$E_{XY} = 10/25 = 0.40$$

Interpreting Cross-Price Elasticities. The owner can learn about the relationship between two products by looking at the sign of the cross-price elasticity. In our cross-price elasticity calculation, an increase in the price of one good causes the demand for the other to increase. This positive relationship indicates that the two goods are substitutes: Consumers respond to the higher price of a Wendy's hamburger by switching to Burger King. If the cross-price elasticity is negative, an increase in the price of one good causes a decrease in demand for the other, and

---

[1] Douglas M. Brown, "The Restaurant Fast Food Race: Who's Winning?" *Southern Economic Journal,* April 1990, vol. 56, no. 4, pages 984–95.

the goods are complements. Suppose that the owner of the Wendy's notices that after increasing burger prices from $1.00 to $1.20, the quantity of fries demanded falls from 1,000 to 800. In this case, she knows that the goods are complements, because the cross-price elasticity between burgers (Y) and fries (X) is:

$$E_{XY} = [(800 - 1,000)/900]/[(1.20 - 1.00)/1.10] = (-0.22)/(0.182) = -1.21$$

By comparing the signs and magnitudes of cross-elasticities in any given market, she can tell whether products are strong or weak substitutes, or complements. The larger the magnitude of the cross-price elasticity, the more the price of one good affects purchases of the other. For example, if the cross-price elasticity between Wendy's burgers and Burger King's burgers is 0.75, but the cross-price elasticity between Burger King's and McDonald's burgers is 2.50, we can conclude that consumers view McDonald's and Burger King's burgers as closer substitutes than Wendy's and Burger King's burgers. If the cross-price elasticity between burgers and fries is −1.21 and the cross-price elasticity between burgers and onion rings is −0.50, consumers believe that fries are stronger complements to burgers than onion rings.

Independent goods
Two goods between which the cross-price elasticity is equal to zero, indicating that there is no relationship between them.

How would a change in the price of pencils affect the demand for cheeseburgers? Most likely, it would not change the demand for cheeseburgers at all. The two goods are neither substitutes nor complements, but independent. If two goods are **independent**, the cross-price elasticity between them is equal to zero, indicating that there is no relationship. Table 5.4 summarizes the important characteristics of the three demand elasticities we have introduced.

TEST + *E X T E N D* Your Knowledge

1. TEST Table 5.3 reports that the income elasticity of airline travel is 1.91. If consumers receive a 15-percent increase in income, by how much will airline travel increase? What type of good is airline travel?

2. EXTEND What do you predict about the income elasticity of long-distance bus travel? When income increases, will consumers ride the bus more or less often? Show the effect of an increase in consumer income on long-distance transportation using supply and demand graphs for both the airline market and the bus transportation market.

 ## Elasticity of Supply

Elasticity of supply
Shows the percentage change in quantity supplied that results from a percentage change in price.

We also use elasticities to investigate how sensitive producers are to changes in the price of their output. The **elasticity of supply** shows the percentage change in quantity supplied that results from a percentage change in price.

Elasticity of Supply Equation

The elasticity of supply formula is essentially the same as for price elasticity of demand. However, we now consider price sensitivity along the supply curve rather than the demand curve. The formula is shown in Equation 5.5. Because price and quantity supplied vary directly, supply elasticities are positive.

$$E_S = \frac{\text{Percentage change in quantity supplied}}{\text{Percentage change in price}} \tag{5.5}$$

TABLE 5.4

Summary of Demand Elasticities

Elasticity	Sign or Range	Indication
Price elasticity of demand		
Perfectly inelastic	$E = 0$	Consumers are completely insensitive to price changes.
Inelastic	$0 < E < 1$	Consumers are relatively insensitive to price changes.
Unit-elastic	$E = 1$	Price and quantity changes are proportional.
Elastic	$E > 1$	Consumers are relatively sensitive to price changes.
Perfectly elastic	$E = \infty$	Consumers respond to even the smallest price increase by stopping consumption altogether.
Income elasticity		
Normal goods	$E_I > 0$	Consumers buy more as income increases.
Inferior goods	$E_I < 0$	Consumers buy less as income increases.
Cross-price elasticity		
Substitutes	$E_{XY} > 0$	If the price of Y increases, consumers buy more of X.
Complements	$E_{XY} < 0$	If the price of Y increases, consumers buy less of X.
Independent goods	$E_{XY} = 0$	If the price of Y increases, consumers do not change their consumption of X.

Elasticity of Supply Calculation

Suppose that because of an increase in market demand, fast-food prices increase by 5 percent. If a fast-food restaurant responds by increasing its quantity supplied by 10 percent, the price elasticity of supply is equal to 2.0:

$$E_S = \frac{\text{Percentage change in quantity supplied}}{\text{Percentage change in price}} = 10/5 = 2.0$$

Varying Elasticities on Linear Supply Curves

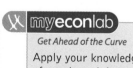

Get Ahead of the Curve

Apply your knowledge of supply and demand elasticities to rising prices for gasoline in California.

As with demand elasticities, linear supply curves do not have constant elasticities. The proportions of price and quantity change as we move along the curve. However, we can say that at any *given price, all else equal, the steeper the supply curve, the more inelastic is supply.* When supply is perfectly inelastic, the supply curve is vertical. If supply is perfectly elastic, the supply curve is horizontal. Figure 5.7 shows the elasticity of supply changes along a linear supply curve. In this case, the elasticity falls from a high of 1.91 between a price of $1.00 and $2.00 to a low of 1.19 between $4.00 and $5.00.

FIGURE 5.7

Changes in Elasticity Along a Linear Supply Curve

In panel (a), the elasticities in the table are calculated using the midpoint formula. In each case, the elasticity represents the percentage change in quantity given a percentage change in price. Panel (b) shows that the elasticity of supply changes as we move along a linear supply curve, because proportions of price and quantity are also changing. All else equal, the steeper the curve, the more inelastic the supply.

(a) The elasticity of supply for various price changes

Price (in $)	Quantity	Supply Elasticity
1	2	
		1.91
2	9	
		1.40
3	16	
		1.25
4	23	
		1.19
5	30	

(b) Changing elasticity along a linear supply curve

Determinants of Supply Elasticities

A firm's ability to respond to changes in the price of the goods it sells depends on how easily it can adjust its purchases of inputs and the prices of those inputs. For instance, the elasticity of supply for fast food depends in part on the markets for the labor, beef, chicken, bread, potatoes, and even packaging materials used to produce the final product. If the prices that restaurants pay for inputs increase rapidly as the restaurants expand their output, the cost of increasing output also rises rapidly. Restaurant owners remain profitable only if they can cover the higher costs by charging higher prices. As a result, supply would be relatively inelastic.

Production technology, including the firm's ability to substitute one input for another as input prices change, is also an important determinant of supply elasticities. Suppose a fast-food restaurant learns that its current packaging supplier will raise paper bag prices by 10 percent in response to an increase in orders. If the restaurant can easily switch to a lower-cost supplier, it will do so, and supply will be elastic. If, however, the restaurant is contractually bound to purchase from the approved franchise supplier, the owner has little choice but to pay the extra cost. Supply is then less elastic. Only when the contract expires will the firm be able to negotiate a new agreement with the current or a replacement supplier. Thus, supply tends to be more elastic over longer periods of time.

TABLE 5.5

Price Elasticities for Cigarettes by Age and Income Group for Ukraine

Age Group	Low-Income Individuals	Middle-Income Individuals	High-Income Individuals
14 to 17 years old	0.65	0.70	0.52
18 to 28 years old	0.37	0.42	0.24
29 or more years old	0.28	0.33	0.15

Strategy and Policy
Getting Smokers to Quit When They're Young[2]

Governments around the world are concerned with cigarette smoking among teens. One reason is that smoking has well-known adverse health effects. Another is that the addictive properties of tobacco turn many teens who start smoking into long-term smokers. Historically, governments have tried to discourage smoking through taxes on cigarettes. A study by the Alcohol and Drug Information Centre in Ukraine shows how difficult this problem can be from a policy perspective. It also highlights how important it is to get young smokers to quit before they reach adulthood. Table 5.5 shows results from the study. It indicates that the price elasticity of demand for cigarettes is inelastic at all ages, but becomes more inelastic as smokers age and as

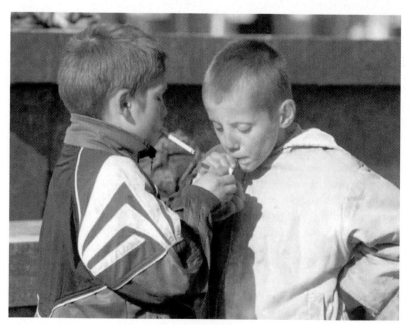

their income increases. While teen smokers have an elasticity of between 0.52 and 0.70, adults over age 28 have an elasticity of only 0.15 to 0.28. They are less than one-half as sensitive to price increases as teens.

According to the report, at current prices for cigarettes in Ukraine, a 100-percent increase in the cigarette tax would result in an 8.8-percent increase in the total cost per pack. Based on the elasticities shown, the short-run impact would be about a 6-percent decrease in teen smokers, but only a 1.32-percent decrease in high-income smokers over 28 years old. However, in the long run, the benefits of such a tax would be considerably greater if the teens who quit did not start smoking again as they aged.

---

[2] Data for this section are taken from the Economic Analysis of Tobacco Demand and Price and Income Elasticity of Cigarettes, International Centre For Policy Studies, Alcohol and Drug Information Centre (ADIC—Ukraine), at *www.adic.org.ua/adic/reports/econ/ch-3/3–4.htm* (accessed 12/25/04).

Critical-Thinking Questions

1. In the United States, many government anti-smoking messages are designed to reduce smoking among young people. Based on the results of the Ukraine study on demand elasticities, comment on the likely effectiveness of such a campaign aimed at older adults.
2. Why are price elasticities for cigarettes lower among higher-income individuals?

▶ **SUMMARY**

- **Defining the market.** Before analyzing any given market, we must determine which goods and services make up that market. We define market edges both geographically and in terms of product characteristics. Goods that a consumer could reasonably substitute for other goods are in the same market.

- **Demand elasticities.** Elasticities are unit-free measures of price sensitivity. The price elasticity of demand shows the percentage change in quantity given a percentage change in price, and range between 0 and infinity. Values between 0 and 1 make up the inelastic range. Goods or services with demand elasticities greater than 1 are elastic. A demand elasticity of 1 is unit-elastic. To avoid confusion stemming from the direction of a price change, we use the midpoint formula for calculations.

- **Determinants of demand elasticity.** Three factors determine elasticity: the availability of substitutes, the share of consumer income, and the time horizon. All else equal, the more substitutes that are available, the more elastic is demand. Goods that occupy a large share of a consumer's income have a more elastic demand. Elasticities are greater over longer periods of time for most goods, because time allows consumers to change the mix of goods that they consume.

- **Income and cross-price elasticities.** Income and cross-price elasticities are useful for evaluating consumer sensitivity to changes in income and in prices of other related goods. Income elasticities are positive for normal goods and negative for inferior goods. Cross-price elasticities are positive for goods that are substitutes, and negative for goods that are complements.

- **Elasticity of supply.** Elasticity of supply shows the percentage change in quantity supplied given a percentage change in price. Like demand elasticities, supply elasticities are unit-free numbers. The greater the elasticity of supply, the more sensitive producers are to price changes. Supply elasticities are influenced by changes in input prices as production increases and by the ability of the supplier to switch to other inputs if prices do increase.

▶ **KEY TERMS**

Arc elasticity 118
Cross-price elasticity 132
Durable goods 129
Elastic 120
Elasticity 115
Elasticity of supply 133
Income elasticity of demand 130

Inelastic 120
Independent goods 133
Luxury 131
Market edges 114
Midpoint elasticity (arc elasticity) 118
Necessity 131

Perfectly elastic (infinitely elastic) 120
Perfectly inelastic 119
Price elasticity of demand 116
Total revenue 116
Unit-elastic 120

1. For each product, describe the most important factors that influence the definition of the market (such as cost and perishability):
   a. Gasoline
   b. Ice cream cones
   c. Commercial airliners
   d. Live music
   e. Books

2. There are nearly 100 different breakfast cereals on the market. Use the concept of market definition to describe why manufacturers would choose to make so many varieties of cereal.

3. For each case, compute the price elasticity of demand:
   a. Price increases by 5 percent, and quantity demanded remains unchanged.
   b. Price increases by 5 percent, and quantity demanded decreases by 3 percent.
   c. Price decreases by 10 percent, and quantity demanded increases by 5 percent.
   d. Price increases by 2 percent, and quantity demanded falls to zero.
   e. Price decreases by 10 percent, and quantity demanded increases by 10 percent.

4. For each case, compute the elasticity using the midpoint formula:
   a. Price increases from $1.00 to $2.00, and quantity demanded decreases from 40 to 30.
   b. Price increases from $1.00 to $4.00, and quantity demanded decreases from 100 to 40.
   c. Price decreases from $3.50 to $2.50, and quantity demanded increases from 3,000 to 3,500.
   d. Price decreases from $4.00 to $2.75, and quantity demanded increases from 1 to 2.

5. Suppose that when price increases from $4.00 to $6.00, quantity demanded decreases from 12 to 8. What is the price elasticity of demand in this range? Use the midpoint formula to make your calculation.

6. For each commodity, state whether you believe demand is relatively elastic or inelastic and explain why:
   a. Heinz ketchup
   b. Blue jeans
   c. Business demand for airline tickets
   d. Cell phones
   e. Thumbtacks
   f. Houses

7. Suppose that a five-percent increase in the price of chicken sandwiches results in the following changes in sales at a local Wendy's:
   a. Chicken sandwich sales fall by 7.5 percent.
   b. Salad sales increase by 0.5 percent.
   c. Burger sales increase by 3 percent.
   d. Drink sales fall by 3 percent.
   e. French fry sales fall by 2 percent.
   f. Baked potato sales are unchanged.
   Compute the price elasticity of chicken sandwiches and all the relevant cross-price elasticities. What can you say about the market edges for chicken sandwiches based on your results?

8. At some stadiums, consumers are allowed to bring food in from outside the facility. What can you predict about the elasticity of demand for concession food at these stadiums compared to ones where no outside food is allowed? Why?

9. Why are economists uncomfortable with designating some goods as luxuries and others as necessities?

10. Suppose that consumers experience a 10 percent increase in income, and purchases of sunglasses increase by 5 percent. What is the income elasticity for sunglasses? Based on your answer, are sunglasses normal or inferior goods?

11. Suppose that the price of margarine increases by 10 percent and the quantity of butter demanded increases by 8 percent. What is the cross-price elasticity? What does this cross-price elasticity indicate about butter and margarine as commodities?

12. Tina's Earring Hut increases the price of birthstone earrings from $100 to $110, and the quantity of birthstone necklaces sold falls from 75 to 60 per week as a result. What is the cross-price elasticity? What does this result indicate about earrings and necklaces?

13. What do you predict about the sign and magnitude of the income elasticity for facial tissues? Why?

14. If Mario's income elasticity for jellybeans is +0.50, and his income increases by 30 percent, by what percentage will he increase his purchases of jellybeans?

15. Suppose that a newspaper reports that the quantity of iPods sold increased by 10 percent last year. In each of the following cases, assume that the listed change is the cause of the change in iPod sales, and compute the relevant elasticity:

   a. A 5-percent increase in the price of CD players
   b. A 10-percent increase in the price of CDs
   c. A 5-percent decrease in the price of online music subscriptions
   d. An 8-percent increase in income
   e. A 4-percent decrease in the price of an iPod

   Based on the information, which goods are complements and which goods are substitutes for iPods? Are iPods a normal or inferior good?

16. What factors are important in determining the elasticity of supply? Explain, using examples.

17. Suppose that the price of hammers increases by 8 percent, causing sellers to increase the quantity supplied by 14 percent. What is the elasticity of supply? Is this value in the elastic or inelastic range?

18. Draw a supply curve that is perfectly inelastic. Choose two points on the curve and calculate the elasticity to confirm that your graph is correct.

19. Using the data in Figure 5.7, what is the supply elasticity if the price increases from $5.00 to $6.00, and the quantity supplied increases from 30 to 37 units?

20. Would you prefer to sell a good for which demand is relatively price-elastic or relatively price-inelastic? Why?

HERE'S HOW MyEconLab CAN HELP YOU GET A BETTER GRADE

1. Log into MyEconLab and take Practice Test chapter-A (to log in for the first time, see page 30 for instructions.)

2. Based on your test results, MyEconLab will identify the areas where you need further work and create a personal Study Plan for you.

3. Your Study Plan contains the exercises listed below and others like them that will target the specific chapter topics you need to focus on. You'll receive instant feedback and find links to tutorials, animations, and the online textbook to help you study.

4. When you're ready, go take Practice Test chapter-B and demonstrate how your results have improved.

Section 5.1, Exercise 1 Why would goods like McDonald's and Wendy's hamburgers be considered part of the same market, but Ferrari and Ford automobiles would usually not be considered to be part of the same market?

Section 5.2, Exercise 1 Currently, the price of bread is $2.00 per loaf, and the grocery store is selling 1,000 loaves per week. The manager estimates that selling bread at $1.80 per loaf would increase sales to 1,100 loaves per week.

a. Calculate the price elasticity of demand. Is demand elastic or inelastic at this point?
b. Calculate the midpoint elasticity of demand. Is demand elastic or inelastic at this point?

Section 5.2, Exercise 2 At a price of $0.25 per pound, 500 pounds of salt are sold monthly. At a price of $0.50 per pound, 400 pounds of salt are sold per month.

a. Calculate the price elasticity of demand. Is demand elastic or inelastic at this point?
b. Calculate the midpoint elasticity of demand. Is demand elastic or inelastic at this point?

Section 5.2, Exercise 3 Matt and Will are buying books. Matt says, "I always spend $100 on books, whether the price rises or falls." Will says, "I always buy 10 books, whether the price rises or falls."

a. What is Matt's price elasticity of demand for books?
b. What is Will's price elasticity of demand for books?

Section 5.2, Exercise 4 A movie theater estimates that the price elasticity of demand for evening movie tickets is –0.90.

a. If the theater wishes to maximize revenue from evening tickets, should it raise the price, lower it, or keep it the same?
b. The same theater estimates that the price elasticity of demand for matinée tickets is −20. If the theater wishes to maximize revenue from matinée tickets, should it raise the price, lower it, or keep it the same?

Section 5.2, Exercise 5 The following table shows the demand schedule for two-liter bottles of cola per day.

Price (per bottle)	Quantity Demanded
$3.00	0
2.50	10
2.00	20
2.50	30
2.00	40
1.50	50
1.00	60
0.50	70
0.00	80

a. Calculate the midpoint elasticity of demand between $2.50 and $2.00.
b. Calculate the midpoint elasticity of demand between $1.00 and $0.50.
c. Find the point at which the price elasticity of demand is unitary.
d. How does elasticity change along the demand curve?

Section 5.2, Exercise 6 Basic commodities, like wheat, are known to have low price elasticities, such as 0.75. Suppose that a good harvest increases the supply of wheat.

 a. What will happen to the price of wheat?
 b. What will happen to farm revenue from wheat sales?

Section 5.4, Exercise 1 Basic commodities, like wheat, are known to have small income elasticities, such as 0.90. Over time, consumer incomes tend to rise.

 a. As income rises, what will happen to the demand for wheat and the quantity of wheat purchased?
 b. What will happen to the proportion of their incomes that consumers spend on wheat?

Section 5.5, Exercise 1 The following table gives the demand and supply schedules for pizza.

Number of Pizzas Demanded	Price (per pizza)	Number of Pizzas Supplied
1,000	$10	400
900	12	450
800	14	500
700	16	550
600	18	600
500	20	650

 a. Calculate the price elasticity of demand at the equilibrium point. Use the midpoint formula.
 b. Calculate the price elasticity of supply at the equilibrium point. Use the midpoint formula.

6 Market Efficiency and Government Intervention

You just can't decide. Should you buy a laptop for school? On the plus side, a laptop of your own would make it a lot easier to take notes in class, work on research papers, organize your schedule, enjoy music, and send instant messages to friends. However, a laptop costs $1,200. You could continue to use the computer labs at school to do your work. The social aspect of running into friends at the lab is appealing. Yet using the school's computers can be pretty inconvenient during the end-of-semester crunch. When the school's network goes down, you can't print your work, and sometimes you lose your work entirely. It seems like buying a laptop is just barely worth it, but you plan to make the purchase.

Your friend Charlie faces the same decision. He doesn't have a laptop and is currently using the school's computers for all of his work. As an English major, he has many more papers to write than you do. He is tired of the crowded labs and the inconvenience of having to work on literature papers during lab hours, instead of whenever he feels inspired to write. In addition, Charlie commutes on the train, where he could make much better use of his time with a laptop. Though he seems more committed to the laptop idea than you, both of you decide to take the plunge.

The true cost of the laptop becomes apparent at the computer store. In addition to the $1,200 you pay for the computer itself, you must pay tax on the computer. The tax adds another $50 to the cost. Suddenly, your $1,200 laptop is a $1,250 laptop. The thought of working in the computer lab is starting to seem more appealing. The extra $50 is more than you can spend right now, and you decide instead to do without your own computer. But Charlie hates the thought of losing all that potential work time on the train. For him, the increase in cost is frustrating, but not enough to turn him away. He would have paid as much as $1,400 for the machine.

"I guess the law of demand does work," you grumble, leaving the store empty-handed. "Except in this case, my purchases went from one to zero when the price tag on the machine stayed the same. The tax did me in." Without the extra charge, you would have bought a laptop. Charlie didn't like paying an extra $50, but he still seems happy to have the machine in his backpack.

In this chapter, we continue to develop the supply and demand model as a tool for market analysis. You learned in Chapter 4 that the model has wide applicability and can often explain complex interactions in a very straightforward way. We will pair the model with our knowledge of elasticities to show how consumers and producers both benefit when a consumer buys a product. We will also learn how governmental intervention in markets with charges such as taxes and license fees creates inefficiencies.

ALONG THE WAY, YOU WILL ALSO LEARN:

- Why exchange at a single market price creates value for consumers and producers.

- How a free market outcome without any form of government intervention can maximize the value that is created.

- How outside forces, such as the government, can intervene to alter market outcomes.

- How differences in the elasticity of supply and demand affect consumer and producer well-being, as well as efficiency losses from government intervention.

- That in some cases, market outcomes result in less than the maximum consumer and producer surplus.

AT THE END OF THE CHAPTER, THE MYECONLAB LOGO WILL DIRECT YOU ONLINE

- MyEconLab is a resource-packed online homework and tutorial system that can help you perform better in your economics course. To log in for the first time, see page 30 for instructions.

- MyEconLab can help you apply important concepts from the chapter to real-world issues. Watch for the logo to indicate online features about the economic effects of price floors and taxes.

- At the end of each chapter, you'll find a special study section that will help you get the most out of your textbook and your instructor's MyEconLab course.

► The Benefits of Market-Based Exchanges

One of the most fundamental benefits of market-based exchanges is that they typically make both consumers and producers better off. To illustrate, let's return to our example of the laptop purchase decision. For the moment, ignore the additional $50 that tax adds to the price of the laptop and assume that the machine costs exactly $1,200. If you choose to purchase a laptop, you show by your actions that you prefer the computer to the $1,200 that you must forgo to purchase it. At the same time, the computer store indicates that it prefers the $1,200 to the laptop. Thus, both parties benefit from the exchange. In this section, we focus on this simple insight, which

FIGURE 6.1

The Relationship Between Market Price and Marginal Benefit

Panel (a) shows how willingness to pay affects values of consumer surplus for a few representative consumers. When we plot these data in panel (b), consumer surplus is represented by the shaded blue area between the equilibrium price of $1,200 and the demand curve. Consumer surplus represents the combined difference for all consumers between the marginal benefit that they receive and the price that they pay. The total consumer surplus is equal to $\frac{1}{2}$ (500 × $400), or $100,000.

(a) The value of a laptop for various consumers

Consumer	Marginal Benefit or Willingness to Pay	Price	Consumer Surplus
Gerald	$1,500	$1,200	$300
Charlie	1,400	1,200	200
Nancy	1,300	1,200	100
You	1,225	1,200	25
Margie	1,200	1,200	0

(b) Consumer surplus in a competitive market

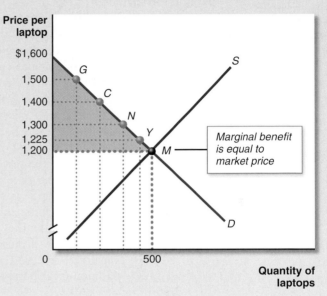

is central to market economies. Let's begin by examining the perspectives of both the consumer and producer. We'll also evaluate the overall gains from exchange in the market.

Consumer Surplus

The marginal benefit of an additional unit of a good or service is equal to a consumer's willingness to pay for it. The demand curve represents the marginal benefit. In fact, we could re-label the demand curve as the marginal benefit curve. Panel (a) of Figure 6.1 shows various consumers' marginal benefit from the laptop purchase. These values help to form the demand curve for laptops shown in panel (b) of Figure 6.1. As a specific example, Gerald is a computer science major. He relies heavily on his machine and cannot afford to be tied up in the lab when it is crowded. He would be willing and able to pay $1,500 for a machine (point G in panel (b) of Figure 6.1). However, Gerald must pay only the equilibrium price of $1,200. Gerald's marginal benefit exceeds the price he must pay by $300. Charlie is willing to pay $1,400. His marginal benefit, shown by point C in panel (b) of Figure 6.1, is $200 greater than the actual price. Nancy is willing and able to pay $1,300 for a laptop computer. Her marginal benefit (point N in panel (b) of Figure 6.1) exceeds the price by $100. Her marginal benefit is much less than Charlie's or Gerald's, but purchasing the computer still leaves her better off. For you, a computer is worth $1,225, so the $25 difference between marginal benefit and price is even smaller (point Y). Your friend

Margie values the computer at exactly $1,200 (point *M*). She purchases the computer, because her marginal benefit equals the price. At a price of more than $1,200, she will not buy the computer. We call Margie the *marginal consumer*. The **marginal consumer** is indifferent between buying and not buying and receives no consumer surplus from purchasing the good or service.

Marginal consumer
A consumer who is indifferent between buying and not buying, and who receives no consumer surplus from purchasing the good or service.

Consumer surplus
The combined difference for all units purchased between the marginal benefit for consumers and the price.

If we add the difference between the marginal benefit and price for every consumer in the market, we obtain the total consumer surplus. **Consumer surplus** is value that flows to consumers because they are not all charged the maximum that they are willing to pay. If there were only five consumers in the market, we could add the surpluses of all consumers to obtain the total surplus. In panel (a) of Figure 6.1, the total would be $625. In reality, there are many consumers with widely varying tastes. We can approximate the total consumer surplus for the entire market by computing the area of the triangle shaded in blue in panel (b) of Figure 6.1. This is the area between the demand curve and the market price, up to the equilibrium quantity. The formula for the area of a triangle is one-half of the base times the height. The base is the distance between $Q = 0$ and $Q = 500$, or 500. The height is the distance between $p = \$1,200$ and $p = \$1,600$, or $400. Thus, the total consumer surplus in panel (b) is $\frac{1}{2}(500 \times \$400)$, or $100,000.

How would an improvement in computer production technology affect consumer surplus? It would cause the price of a computer to fall and consumer surplus to increase. In Figure 6.2, the price of laptops falls from $1,200 to $1,000. Consumer surplus increases from the area shaded in blue to include the area shaded in light blue. At the lower price, more consumers are able to buy a computer at a price that is lower than the maximum they are willing to pay. Conversely, if the price of the computer rises, consumer surplus falls. Thus, if the price rises by $100, from $1,200 to $1,300, consumers like you and Margie—for whom surplus was initially less than $100—will no longer purchase a laptop. Total consumer surplus is now $\frac{1}{2}(375 \times \$300)$, or $56,250.

FIGURE 6.2

The Inverse Relationship Between Price and Consumer Surplus

When the supply curve shifts from *S* to S_1, the price falls and the quantity of laptop computers demanded increases from 500 to 620. At the new lower price of $1,000, consumers who value a laptop at less than $1,200 but more than $1,000 now purchase a computer. The consumers who were willing to purchase a machine at $1,200 now buy one for $1,000. As a result, consumer surplus increases by the area shaded in light blue. The value of the surplus is now $\frac{1}{2}(620 \times \$600)$, or $186,000.

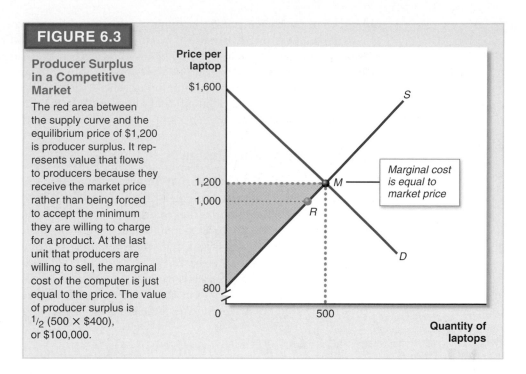

FIGURE 6.3

Producer Surplus in a Competitive Market

The red area between the supply curve and the equilibrium price of $1,200 is producer surplus. It represents value that flows to producers because they receive the market price rather than being forced to accept the minimum they are willing to charge for a product. At the last unit that producers are willing to sell, the marginal cost of the computer is just equal to the price. The value of producer surplus is $\frac{1}{2}$ (500 × $400), or $100,000.

Producer Surplus

We now turn to the supply side of the market. Producers focus on the difference between the marginal cost of producing an additional unit of a good and the price that they receive in return. We have established that the supply curve shows the quantity that sellers are willing and able to produce and offer for sale at various prices. As noted in Chapter 4, we can also think of the supply curve as the marginal cost curve. Thus, the benefit to producers from selling an additional unit is the difference between the price that the firm receives and its marginal cost. Consider Redline Computers, a very efficient computer manufacturer that can produce a computer at a marginal cost of $1,000. Point R on the supply curve in Figure 6.3 represents Redline's marginal cost. When they sell a computer at the market price of $1,200 instead of $1,000, it receives a consumer surplus of $200.

The surplus that producers earn on the goods that they sell is the key to success: The more producers earn on their sales, the more profitable they are. Similar to the marginal consumer, the marginal cost of the last unit that producers are willing to sell is just equal to the price. The sum of all such producer surpluses is the area shaded in red in Figure 6.3. This area represents the producer surplus for the market. **Producer surplus** is the extra benefit that flows to producers because they receive the market price, rather than having to sell each unit for the marginal cost of producing it. We can calculate the size of this area using the same method as for consumer surplus. The total producer surplus is $\frac{1}{2}$(500 × $400), or $100,000.

Producer surplus
The combined difference for all units sold between the market price and the marginal cost of production.

Gains from Exchange

The sum of consumer and producer surplus represents the total gains from exchange in a market. At a price of $1,200, the total surplus is $200,000. Total surplus in Figure 6.3 is maximized when the price is set at the $1,200 equilibrium point, where the supply and demand curves meet. The marginal benefit of the last unit sold is just equal to the marginal cost of producing it. If a smaller quantity were produced and sold, the marginal benefit of the last unit would exceed the marginal cost, and society would benefit from an increase in production. If a larger quantity were produced and sold, the marginal cost of production would exceed the marginal benefit, and society would be better off if output were lower. Thus, the sum of consumer and producer surplus is maximized at the point where the supply and demand curves cross. This solution results in an efficient allocation of resources. That is, the gains from exchange are as large as they can possibly be in this product market.

The Competitive Equilibrium

We've determined that the equilibrium shown in Figure 6.3 is highly desirable. But how do we achieve such an outcome? Recall from Chapter 4 that when there are many buyers and sellers in a market (markets are not thin), no single consumer or firm can influence the price. The equilibrium price will come about naturally as buyers search for the lowest prices and sellers attempt to attract customers. In fact, one of the hallmarks of market-based exchange is that vigorous competition among buyers and sellers in a market leads to prices at efficient levels, as shown in Figure 6.3. In the next section, we will see that various forms of government intervention have the undesired effect of reducing these gains from exchange.

TEST + *E X T E N D* Your Knowledge

1. TEST Redraw Figure 6.3, but now assume that the demand curve is perfectly elastic (a horizontal line) at $1,200. How does this change affect the size of the consumer surplus and producer surplus? Is society better off if transactions take place?

2 . E X T E N D Recreate Figure 6.3 again with the same equilibrium price and quantity, but with a demand curve that is perfectly inelastic (a vertical line). How does this change affect consumer surplus? Explain your result.

▶ Consumer and Producer Surplus Application: Taxes and the Competitive Equilibrium

We know that in a competitive equilibrium, the sum of consumer and producer surplus is maximized. In this section, we consider the consequences of taxes in a competitive market. You will learn how taxes alter the naturally occurring equilibrium, reducing overall efficiency.

Per-Unit Taxes

In Chapter 3, you learned that governments impose taxes for a variety of reasons. Governments use tax revenue to raise revenue to fund social programs, schools, roads, and other government services. Some taxes (sometimes called "sin taxes") attempt to reduce consumption of a good that the government wants to discourage consumers from using, such as cigarettes.

Per-unit tax
Adds a fixed dollar amount to the price of each unit of a good sold.

The simplest tax is a *per-unit tax*. A **per-unit tax** adds a fixed-dollar amount to the price of each unit of a good sold. To illustrate, suppose that in order to fund a new education initiative in low-income areas, the government imposes a $100 per-unit tax on each laptop sold. The tax, which we denote by the letter t, shifts the

FIGURE 6.4

The Effect of a Per-Unit Tax on Laptop Sales

A $100 tax on laptops shifts the supply curve to the left, from S to S^t, such that the vertical distance between the curves is equal to the tax. On the new supply curve, we see that the supply and demand intersect price at the new $P^t = \$1,250$, because consumers pay the old price plus only half the tax, or $50. Sellers receive the new price less the entire $100 tax, or $1,150. The tax revenue generated is equal to the tax amount of $100 per laptop times the number of laptops sold, and is shaded in yellow. The deadweight loss is the loss of consumer and producer surplus, shown in gray.

supply curve leftward. In Figure 6.4, the curve shifts from S to S^t. The vertical distance between the old and new supply curve is $100, the amount of the tax. Yet when the supply curve shifts up by $100, the price of a machine does not increase by $100. In this example, it increases by only $50 from P^* to P^t or from $1,200 to $1,250. Consumers now have to pay $50 more for each computer. Why don't consumers pay the entire $100? We explain this point by examining the effect of the tax on consumers and producers.

Tax Incidence

The reason why the $100 per-unit tax causes only a $50 price increase lies in the downward slope of the demand curve. When consumers pay a higher price, the quantity demanded decreases. The new quantity is determined by the intersection of the demand curve, D, and the new supply curve, S^t. Producers receive the new equilibrium price $(P^t - t)$ for each machine they sell. In this case, they receive $P^t - t = \$1,250 - \$100 = \$1,150$. Consumers pay the price including the tax, P^t, or $1,250. Consumers pay $50 more than before the tax was imposed, and producers receive $50 less. Sellers are willing to pay part of the tax. If they tried to pass the entire tax on to consumers, quantity (and their revenue) would fall even more. Because consumers pay $50 more than before, we say that the *incidence of the tax on consumers* is one-half of the tax, or $50. The **incidence of a tax on consumers** is the increase in the price that consumers pay due to the tax. Producers receive $50 less than before the tax. As a result, we say that the *incidence of the tax on producers* is also one-half the tax, or $50. The **incidence of a tax on producers** is the decrease in the price received by producers as a result of the tax. Although the incidence of the tax on producers and consumers is split equally in this case, it need not be. We will return to the determinants of tax incidence later in this section.

Incidence of a tax on consumers
The increase in the price that consumers pay due to a tax.

Incidence of a tax on producers
The decrease in the price received by producers as a result of a tax.

The difference between what consumers pay and what producers receive amounts to $100 per laptop, which is exactly equal to the tax. The total revenue generated by the tax is equal to the shaded area in yellow in Figure 6.4, which is $100 times 400 (the number of machines sold) or $40,000. Notice that part of the rectangle was once consumer surplus (the area above the original price), and part of the rectangle was once producer surplus (the area below the original price). Because the incidence of the tax falls on both producers and consumers, the revenue generated comes from both the producer and consumer surpluses.

Deadweight Loss

If you examine the effect of the tax on consumer and producer surplus in Figure 6.4 closely, you will see that consumers and producers lose more from their combined surplus than the value of the tax revenue. We know that the area shaded in yellow represents tax revenue that the government can transfer to others—for instance, to aid needy families. If the increase in well-being from those who benefit from the tax offsets the loss of surplus by those who pay the tax, value is not lost when consumers purchase their computers. In this case, the tax is simply a transfer of value from one group to another. However, the tax creates a loss to society that is not transferred to others in the economy. Before the tax, the consumer surplus was the area above the price and below the demand curve, and the producer surplus was the area below the price and above the supply curve. After the tax is in place, the quantity of computers sold falls, and the area shaded in gray in Figure 6.4 is no longer a part of consumer or producer surplus. This area is a loss to society, because it is not transferred to any other party.

Deadweight loss
A loss in consumer and/or producer surplus that results when the price and quantity are not set at the competitive equilibrium.

This type of loss in consumer and producer surplus that results when the price and quantity are not set at the competitive equilibrium is a **deadweight loss**. The revenue generated when the government imposes the tax helps those with low incomes. However, society as a whole loses some of the value created by the computer market, in the form of deadweight loss. For example, when you decided not to purchase the laptop after the tax was imposed, your purchase and the consumer surplus you would have received are part of that deadweight loss. That machine is worth $1,225 to you. With no tax, the price is $1,200, resulting in a $25 surplus when you purchase a computer. With the tax, the price increases to $1,250, and the value to you is less than the new price. As a result, you do not purchase a laptop. The loss that all consumers and producers combined experience when the tax is imposed creates the deadweight loss.

To find the size of the deadweight loss, we can calculate the area of the gray triangle. The change in quantity (the height) is 100, and the change in price (the base) is $100. Thus the area is $\frac{1}{2}(\$100 \times 100)$, or $5,000.

Elasticity and Tax Incidence

We know that the elasticities of demand and supply reveal consumers' and producers' price sensitivity. A per-unit tax changes the price that buyers pay and sellers receive. As a result, the elasticities of demand and supply are important determinants of the incidence of a tax and the size of the deadweight loss.

We can show the importance of elasticity on a graph if we recall that at a given price and quantity, a curve with a relatively flat slope indicates a response that is more elastic (more price-sensitive). Steeply sloped curves indicate a response that is relatively inelastic (less price-sensitive). To demonstrate how varying demand elasticities alter the incidence of a tax, let's consider per-unit taxes on gasoline.

To begin, let's focus on demand elasticity. Panels (a) and (b) of Figure 6.5 show the effects of a 50-cent-per-gallon tax on gasoline. As before, the tax shifts the supply curve leftward such that the vertical distance between the two supply curves, S and S^t, equals the tax. To keep the focus on demand, the supply curves S and S^t have the same position and slope, and the initial equilibrium price and quantity are the same in both panels. In panel (a), the demand for gasoline is highly inelastic (as it is in reality). Notice that most of the incidence of the tax falls on consumers. Because consumers do not reduce their purchases much when the price increases, they end up paying most of the tax. The small decrease in quantity also creates a relatively small deadweight loss, which is shaded in gray. In panel (b), demand is highly elastic. With price-sensitive consumers, quantity falls by a larger amount than in panel (a), and the incidence falls mostly on sellers. Notice also that the gray area indicating deadweight loss is larger in panel (b). The larger decrease in quantity means that more of the combined consumer and producer surplus is lost.

In panels (c) and (d) of Figure 6.5, we focus on the relationship between the elasticity of supply and tax incidence. To isolate the effects of changes in the price sensitivity of sellers, the demand curves in both panels are the same. In panel (c), we see that the supply curves S and S^t are relatively inelastic, and in panel (d), the supply curves show supply as relatively more elastic. When supply is relatively inelastic, more of the incidence of the tax falls on sellers. When supply is more elastic, it falls more on buyers. As with demand, as the elasticity increases, so too does the size of the deadweight loss.

We summarize the effects of elasticity on tax incidence as follows:

1. All else equal, the incidence of a tax on consumers rises as the elasticity of demand falls.
2. All else equal, the incidence of a tax on producers rises as the elasticity of supply falls.
3. For any given supply curve, as the demand elasticity increases, the deadweight loss increases.
4. For any given demand curve, as the supply elasticity increases, the deadweight loss increases.

Government Intervention via Price Floors, Price Ceilings, and Quotas

In the previous section, you saw that a tax reduces the overall efficiency of the economy. The goal of the tax was to raise revenue for the government. Thus, the deadweight loss created by a per-unit tax was a result of unintended changes in the competitive equilibrium price and quantity. In this section, we will discuss three tools that governments use to alter market outcomes: price floors, price ceilings, and quotas. We will show that these tools also reduce efficiency.

Price Floors

Price floor
A minimum price imposed by the government to redistribute income from buyers to sellers.

We begin with the case of a government deciding that the market price of a good or service is too low. The government might then try to redistribute income from buyers to sellers by imposing a minimum price, or **price floor**. Price floors are most commonly used in two areas: agriculture and labor. Price floors in agriculture are intended to protect farmers' incomes if the market price of their output is too low for them to operate profitably. In effect, the government says that it will punish—

FIGURE 6.5

Elasticity and Tax Incidence

A $0.50 per-gallon tax on gasoline shifts the supply curve to the left. The vertical distance between the original supply curve, S, and the supply curve with the tax, S^t, is equal to the tax. In panel (a), the demand for gasoline is inelastic, and most of the tax falls on consumers (light yellow area). The decrease in quantity demanded and the deadweight loss (shaded in gray) generated by the tax are small. By contrast, we can see in panel (b) that when demand is relatively elastic, most of the incidence falls on sellers (dark yellow area). The decrease in quantity demanded and the deadweight loss generated are relatively large.

(a) Demand is inelastic

(b) Demand is elastic

In panels (c) and (d), we see the effect of changes in elasticity of supply on the tax incidence. In panel (c), where sellers are insensitive to price change, supply is relatively inelastic, and sellers bear the burden of most of the price increase generated by the tax (dark yellow area). However, when sellers are sensitive to an increase in price, as in panel (d), supply is elastic, and the resulting decrease in quantity produced is relatively large as is the corresponding deadweight loss. In this situation, much of the incidence of the tax falls on consumers.

(c) Supply is inelastic

(d) Supply is elastic

LifeLessons

Have you ever noticed that the price of gas can vary quite a bit from one state to another? In addition to federal (nationwide) gas taxes of 18.4 cents per gallon, there are state taxes ranging from a low of 8 cents per gallon in Alaska to 35.1 cents per gallon in Hawaii. These taxes are often used to pay for road maintenance. Florida and Georgia are neighboring states, yet state taxes are 12.2 cents per gallon in Georgia and 29.6 cents per gallon in Florida. The difference may be enough to entice Floridians living near the Georgia state line to bear the opportunity cost of their time (and the gasoline needed to make the trip) to drive to Georgia to make their gasoline purchases. The resources used when consumers in Florida drive to Georgia and back to make gasoline purchases is yet another source of waste created by the tax. That is, consumers use resources (time and gasoline)—that could be otherwise employed—to make the trip across the border to pay the lower tax in Georgia. Thus, consumers should carefully consider these costs to ensure that the costs of the trip exceed the benefits. Despite the costs they impose, differences in tax rates across state governments are quite common.

TEST + *EXTEND* Your Knowledge

1. TEST If the demand curve for laptops is perfectly inelastic (a vertical line), what portion of the $100 tax will be paid by consumers? What portion will be paid by sellers? Illustrate using a graph.

2. EXTEND Suppose that the demand for plots of land is perfectly elastic, and the supply is perfectly inelastic. Use a graph to show the effects of a tax on land. What is the incidence of the tax on consumers?

typically, with a fine—everyone who charges less than the minimum price it has set. Just as the floor in your home keeps this textbook from falling any farther when you drop it, a price floor keeps the price of an item from falling any further in the market than the allowable minimum.

Prune Burger, Anyone? Suppose that the U.S. government believes that prune prices are too low. It tries to help prune growers by imposing a price floor.[1] Figure 6.6 shows the impact of the price floor on the market for prunes. The price floor forces consumers to pay the higher price, P_f, instead of the equilibrium price, P_e. If the market operated freely, the excess supply at P_f would cause the price to fall back to the equilibrium price, P_e. However, the price floor prevents consumers from bidding down the price, and thus makes them worse off. With the higher price, the consumer surplus is reduced to the area above P_f and below the demand curve. In Figure 6.6, consumer surplus declines by the area between P_f and P_e that lies below the demand curve.

---

[1] Okay, they really grow plums and let them dry into prunes, but you know what we mean!

FIGURE 6.6

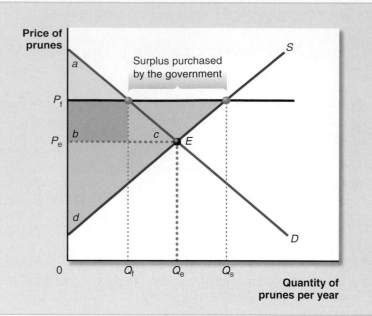

Price Floor in the Prune Market

Without the price floor, the market equilibrium occurs at E with a price of P_e and a quantity of Q_e. When the government installs a price floor in the prune market, the price increases from P_e to P_f. At the new price, producers are willing to supply Q_s, but consumers wish to purchase only Q_f, resulting in a surplus. Because there are no willing buyers for the $(Q_s - Q_f)$ units, the government purchases the surplus. As a result, original consumer surplus, *abc*, is reduced to the blue-shaded area, and original producer surplus, *bcd*, expands, so that the total increase in producer surplus includes both the light- and dark-shaded red areas above the supply curve and below P_f.

The price floor is both a blessing and a curse for prune growers. For those prune growers who are able to sell all their produce, the higher price brings greater revenue than before. Producer surplus increases by the area shown in dark red. The excess supply that accompanies the price floor, however, means that some unlucky prune growers cannot sell all of their produce, and some may sell none at all. Remember that the demand curve tells us the quantity that buyers are willing and able to purchase at various prices. Although sellers are happy to produce more at the established price floor, buyers are not willing and able to buy the additional quantity. Because they cannot sell their output, a higher price does not help these prune growers.

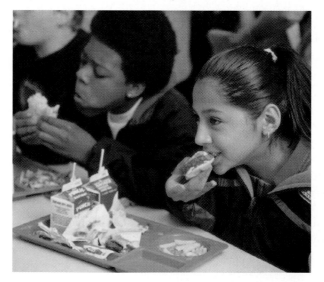

For the price floor to help prune farmers as a whole, the government must help the unlucky producers who cannot sell their output. For example, it might purchase the $Q_s - Q_f$ units that consumers do not purchase at the established price floor. If so, the producer surplus expands to the entire area between the supply curve and the price floor up to Q_s (the light and dark red shaded areas).

While this story might seem highly unlikely, it is in fact true. The government recently sought to eliminate the surplus created by the price floor for prunes by buying the surplus prunes $(Q_s - Q_f)$ and test-marketing them as ingredients for hamburgers in school lunches.[2] When the government buys the surplus, farmers get to sell all their output at the established floor price. The area in Figure 6.6 between Q_s and Q_f above marginal cost (shaded in light red), is added to the existing producer surplus.

[2] Philip Brasher, "Prune Burgers on School Lunch Menus?" *Philadelphia Inquirer* online, January 30, 2002.

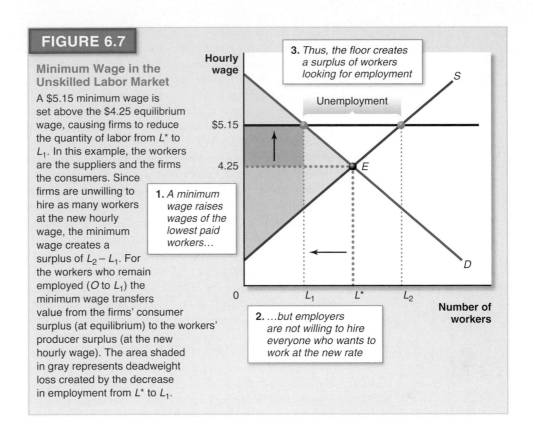

FIGURE 6.7

Minimum Wage in the Unskilled Labor Market

A $5.15 minimum wage is set above the $4.25 equilibrium wage, causing firms to reduce the quantity of labor from L^* to L_1. In this example, the workers are the suppliers and the firms the consumers. Since firms are unwilling to hire as many workers at the new hourly wage, the minimum wage creates a surplus of $L_2 - L_1$. For the workers who remain employed (O to L_1) the minimum wage transfers value from the firms' consumer surplus (at equilibrium) to the workers' producer surplus (at the new hourly wage). The area shaded in gray represents deadweight loss created by the decrease in employment from L^* to L_1.

3. *Thus, the floor creates a surplus of workers looking for employment*

Unemployment

Hourly wage

$5.15

4.25

E

S

D

1. *A minimum wage raises wages of the lowest paid workers...*

0   L_1 L^* L_2

Number of workers

2. *...but employers are not willing to hire everyone who wants to work at the new rate*

Minimum Wages. The most widely known price floor is the minimum wage. As of 2005, with few exceptions, U.S. workers must be paid at least $5.15 per hour. Employers cannot pay less, no matter what the equilibrium wage would be in the absence of the price floor.

In Figure 6.7, the minimum wage is a horizontal line at $5.15 per hour. If the equilibrium wage is below the price floor, establishing a minimum wage has three direct effects. First, as the government hoped, it increases the wages for L_1 of the lowest-paid workers from $4.25, the equilibrium wage they earn without the price floor, to $5.15. Second, it reduces employment from L^* to L_1. The distance between L_1 and L^* represents workers who used to be employed, but now cannot find jobs. Third, $L_2 - L^*$ workers who were previously not employed by choice would now like to work at the increased wage but cannot find jobs. Why don't we read the new quantity from the supply curve? After all, more workers are willing to work at the new, higher wage. Although there is plenty of supply (available workers) at the new price, buyers (potential employers) are *willing and able* to hire only L_1 workers. Thus, the quantity supplied is greater than the quantity demanded. $L_2 - L_1$ workers who would like to be employed at the minimum wage cannot find jobs.

In fact, whenever the price (or wage, in this case) is not at the equilibrium level, we can always find the correct quantity by remembering a simple maxim: *The short side of the market rules.* Whichever curve indicates the lower quantity is the curve we should use to determine the quantity. Thus, the final effect is that the floor creates a surplus. There are more workers who would like to work at the minimum wage than will find jobs.

The introduction of a price floor in the labor market creates a loss to society that we can measure as a decrease in consumer and producer surplus. Notice that in

Figure 6.7 before the minimum wage is imposed, the consumer surplus that employers receive is the area above the price and below the demand curve. The producer surplus that flows to workers is the area below the price and above the supply curve. After the floor is in place, the quantity of workers hired falls. The area shaded in dark red is transferred from employers to workers. Those workers who keep their jobs receive an increase in pay and are better off. The area shaded in gray in Figure 6.7 is the deadweight loss, because it represents the decrease in consumer and producer surplus in the labor market.

Economists disagree over the impact of minimum wage laws. The official 2004 U.S. poverty threshold for a family of three is $15,219. Yet, this income level is nearly 50 percent more than the minimum wage workers annual pay. About 10 percent of U.S. families have incomes below the poverty level. Thus, some argue that increasing the minimum wage is greatly needed to help raise low-income families out of poverty. Those who argue against increasing the minimum wage believe the increased income for some would come at too high a cost. We know from our analysis in Figure 6.7 that employment falls when the minimum wage increases. In addition, employers might reduce the hours each employee works. And others might cut costs by decreasing the quality of working conditions or eliminating training programs that might provide better long-term benefits to low-wage workers. Finally, because many minimum wage workers are teenagers who are members of families not living in poverty, the minimum wage may not help those who truly are needy.

Why does the government enact policies that create deadweight losses? The decisions to establish agricultural price floors or minimum wages are normative. As a society, we show that assisting farmers and low-wage earners is important to us by continuing to set and enforce price and wage minimums, even with the knowledge that they create deadweight loss.

The Effectiveness of Price Floors. Price floors do not always affect markets. If the equilibrium wage is above the minimum wage, then the floor has no effect on the market. In 1999 and 2000, when the U.S. national unemployment rate was below 4.5 percent, most entry-level positions were paying well above the minimum wage. Most firms were already paying more than the minimum wage, because the demand for labor was so high.

Recall that the tax on laptops meant that you and other consumers with the same willingness and ability to pay decided not to purchase a computer. The minimum

DILBERT: © Scott Adams/Dist. by United Feature Syndicate, Inc.

wage and the price floor for prunes give us additional examples of the potential hazards of government intervention. A price floor may achieve its stated goal of increasing wages or prices. However, it might also create other problems (such as reduced employment and the reduction in consumer and producer surpluses). In addition, government intervention in one market may have repercussions in another market. If, for example, the government guarantees high prices in the prune market, it might cause some farmers to abandon other markets, such as the apple market to enter the prune market. Such effects clearly conflict with the goals of the government policy. They create an even greater supply of prunes, but at the cost of reducing the supply of apples.

Price Ceilings

Price ceiling

A maximum price that a producer may charge for a good or service, imposed by the government.

If the government believes that prices are too high, it can intervene by setting maximum prices, or price ceilings. A **price ceiling** is the opposite of a price floor: It represents the maximum price a producer may charge for a good or service. Suppose, for example, that a city government determines that there is not enough low-cost housing available. It may seek to create more low-cost housing by setting maximum rents for apartments, a policy known as rent control.

Figure 6.8 shows a hypothetical market for two-bedroom apartments. In the absence of rent control, the equilibrium rental price is $1,500 per month. We show the impact of a rent ceiling of $900 per month by drawing a horizontal line at the $900 ceiling price. As with the price floor, the ceiling has two immediate effects—one desirable, the other not. The desirable effect is that a maximum rent reduces the cost of housing. But how many apartments will be available for rent at this lower

FIGURE 6.8

A Price Ceiling in the Market for Apartments

Price ceilings in the form of artificially low apartment rents can create shortages. In this graph, the ceiling price of $900 per month reduces the quantity of available apartments from 900 to 600, even though consumers would like to rent 1,200 apartments at the lower price. The difference, 1,200–600, is the shortage generated by the price ceiling. The area shaded in light blue is the value in the form of lower rents that is transferred from the initial producer surplus of apartment owners to the new consumer surplus of renters. The size of the deadweight loss is $1/2$ ($900 × 300), or $135,000.

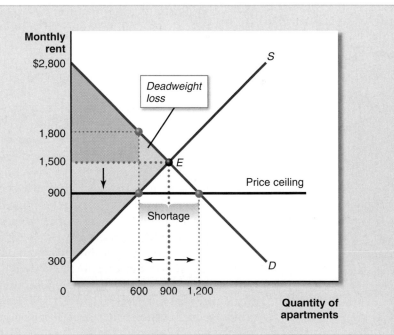

price? To find the answer, we must investigate what suppliers and consumers are willing to do. At the price ceiling, many more apartments (Q_d) are demanded, but fewer (Q_s) are supplied. Because we cannot force landlords to rent their apartments at the lower price (they could convert them to office space, for instance), the quantity supplied dictates the number of transactions. Again, *the short side of the market rules*. The undesirable effect is a shortage of affordable housing.

As with the other forms of government intervention, the price ceiling transfers some of the existing surplus between parties and creates a deadweight loss. In Figure 6.8, the area shaded in light blue was once part of producer surplus. The price ceiling transfers this surplus to the lucky apartment renters who find a low-cost apartment. But the shortage of available apartments means that the area shaded in gray is lost from consumer and producer surplus and so is a deadweight loss.

Rent control was very popular in the United States in the 1970s and early 1980s. At its peak of popularity, 200 different municipalities had rent controls. Since then, the shortages that economists predicted have become a reality. The number of moderately priced units available in controlled areas is lower than in uncontrolled areas. In addition, owners of apartment buildings that were rent-controlled did not have the proper incentive to keep them well-maintained. They were already experiencing excess demand at the rent-control price. As a result, many local governments abandoned rent control as a policy measure.[3]

Quotas

We begin illustrating the final form of government intervention with an example. Suppose that your college's office of computing and information technology issues a memo stating that the wireless network is completely overloaded by the number of students accessing it with laptops. Until the capacity of the routers can be increased, the number of new laptops permitted on campus will be limited to 300. No additional network access will be allowed.

Quota
A maximum quantity of a good or service that can be bought and sold over a specific period of time.

Such a limit on quantity is a **quota**, or a maximum quantity that can be bought and sold over a specific period of time. You may have heard the term "quota" used to indicate a *minimum* quantity that must be obtained. In economics, we typically use the term to indicate a *maximum* allowable quantity. Quotas are sometimes used to limit international trade. For example, in the early 1980s, the U.S. and Japanese governments agreed on limits for the number of Japanese cars that could be imported into the United States. Quotas can be applied whenever a governing body determines that the market equilibrium is not in the best interest of the overall society.

Let's see how the limit on network access cards for laptops affects the market for laptops at the college. To simplify the model, we assume that the laptop is useful only if it can be connected to the network. Unable to accommodate all users, the college institutes a policy that only machines bought at the college bookstore can be equipped with the necessary network card. A maximum of 300 machines are available. Figure 6.9 shows the effect of the quota. In the absence of any restrictions, the

---

[3] William Tucker, "*Policy Analysis: How Rent Control Drives Out Affordable Housing*," Cato Policy Analysis No. 274, May 31, 1997, at *www.cato.org/pubs/pas/pa-274.html*. Accessed January 6, 2005.

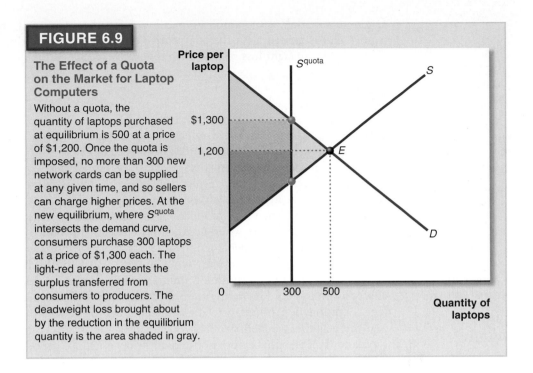

FIGURE 6.9

The Effect of a Quota on the Market for Laptop Computers

Without a quota, the quantity of laptops purchased at equilibrium is 500 at a price of $1,200. Once the quota is imposed, no more than 300 new network cards can be supplied at any given time, and so sellers can charge higher prices. At the new equilibrium, where S^{quota} intersects the demand curve, consumers purchase 300 laptops at a price of $1,300 each. The light-red area represents the surplus transferred from consumers to producers. The deadweight loss brought about by the reduction in the equilibrium quantity is the area shaded in gray.

equilibrium quantity of laptops purchased is 500, and the equilibrium price is $1,200. After the quota is imposed, no more than 300 are available at any one time. Thus, the supply curve becomes a vertical line (perfectly inelastic) at Q = 300. Even though other sellers could make more laptops available and consumers would be willing to pay to purchase them, the school policy effectively means that no transactions beyond 300 units are permitted. The new supply curve, S^{quota}, crosses the demand curve at $1,300. Thus, only consumers willing to pay at least $1,300 will purchase a laptop. If you refer to panel (a) of Figure 6.1, you can confirm that neither you nor Margie will purchase a computer at this price. Nancy, who previously enjoyed a consumer surplus of $100 when the price was $1,200, now becomes the marginal consumer. The area in light green is transferred from consumers to producers. Once again, the reduction in quantity from an equilibrium of 500 to 300 units reduces the overall consumer and producer surplus, and creates a deadweight loss equal to the area shaded in gray.

Get Ahead of the Curve

Use your knowledge of competitive markets and welfare to analyze the economic effects of the European Commission's proposed eliminations of a price floor for sugar.

▶ Concluding Thoughts on Market Efficiency

You saw in the previous sections that per-unit taxes and other government policies that alter the competitive equilibrium can reduce efficiency in the economy. In this section, we preview three other potential sources of inefficiency that are often analyzed in microeconomics.

Monopoly
When a single firm is the sole supplier of a good or service to a market. A monopolist typically restricts the quantity of output and charges a price that is greater than marginal cost, generating deadweight loss.

Monopoly Power

Throughout this chapter, we have assumed that markets are competitive, which implies many sellers competing with one another. An important result of this competition is that the market supply curve represents the marginal cost of production. However, the solution might be quite different if the supply side of the market were controlled by a monopoly. A **monopoly** occurs when a single firm is the sole supplier of a good or service to a market. A monopolist typically restricts the quantity of output and charges a price that is greater than the competitive price. As with the other instances in this chapter, a deadweight loss results when the price exceeds marginal cost.

Externalities

Externalities
Events that occur when the production or consumption of a good or service generates unintended and uncompensated costs or benefits.

For better or worse, the activities of others sometimes affect us in unintended ways. **Externalities** occur when the production or consumption of a good or service generates unintended or uncompensated costs or benefits.

Negative externality
When the production or consumption of a good or service generates unintended costs.

A common **negative externality**, or cause of unintended costs, is pollution. Air, water, or noise pollution that results from either producing a good (such as the noise produced by a construction firm) or consuming a good (such as riding a loud motorcycle) reduces efficiency. The producer of the noise does not factor in the cost that his actions impose on others when deciding how much to produce or consume. Because the marginal costs are understated, these goods are *overproduced* (or *overconsumed*). Overall well-being in the economy would increase if less of this activity took place.

Positive externality
When the production or consumption of a good or service generates unintended benefits.

A **positive externality** results in unintended benefits. Consider a buyer who purchases a rundown home in an otherwise nice neighborhood and restores it to excellent condition. The homeowner benefits from her labor when the house is finished, and the neighbors benefit from the removal of the local eyesore. The person who buys and fixes the house does not take these benefits into account. Because the marginal benefits are understated, goods that produce positive externalities are *underproduced (or underconsumed)*. Overall efficiency in the economy would be greater if more of this activity took place.

Public Goods and Common Property Resources

Public goods
Can be freely consumed by anyone whether they pay for it or not and one person's consumption of the good does not detract from another's doing so.

Another potential efficiency loss is created when consumers do not pay prices consistent with the benefits received. A **public good** can be freely consumed by anyone, whether they pay for it or not. Moreover, one person's consumption of the good does not detract from another's doing so. Consider national defense. There is no way to protect one home against a missile attack but not that of a neighbor who pays nothing toward national defense. Each individual hopes that others will pay for the public good, enabling him or her to benefit from the public good for free. Unless the government intervenes, public goods will be underproduced. Overall economic efficiency would be increased if more of these goods were produced.

Common property resources are similar to public goods, except that consumers are rivals. That is, one person's consumption can affect the ability of another to consume the good as well. The computer network at your school is a form of a common property resource for those who can access the system. All students typically have free access to the network at no additional cost per minute of use. Because students are not charged for usage, they have no incentive to restrict their use. However, if all students use the network very intensively, it will run slower. It will also be more prone to crashes and viruses that make the network less useful for all. Common property resources tend to be *overconsumed*.

Strategy and Policy _____
Powerless in California

Before California lifted regulations on energy producers, the industry performed two distinct duties: generating energy and delivering it to consumers. In an effort to create more competition in the power industry, California separated the two

FIGURE 6.10

The Effect of a Price Ceiling on Power Shortages in California

To protect consumers from high energy prices, the California legislature installed price ceilings in the delivered residential electricity market. When demand was low (D_L), the ceiling did not affect the equilibrium. In 2000, increased demand, D_H, caused the equilibrium price to rise from P_C to P_1, higher than the delivery firms were allowed to charge. Quantity demanded continued rising to Q_D, while the quantity supplied was only Q_S, resulting in a shortage (Q_D-Q_S).

The price ceiling set an artificially low price given the new demand, D_H

functions. Under the new scheme, consumers were supposed to benefit from the ability to shop around for the best prices in the market for electricity. To protect consumers, legislators placed a ceiling on the price that the delivery firms could charge to transport electricity from the generating company to households. At first, this policy had little impact on California's economy, because a prolonged recession limited the demand for energy. With the economic recovery of the late 1990s, Californians' demand for energy began to grow. Extreme weather conditions in 2000 caused the demand for energy to rise even further.

In Figure 6.10, which depicts the California market for electricity, the price ceiling is set at the initial equilibrium price of P_C. At the initial low level of demand, D_L, the price ceiling had no effect on the equilibrium price and quantity. But in 2000, demand increased so much (to D_H) that the equilibrium price of delivered energy rose from P_C to P_1 and exceeded the price that energy delivery firms were allowed to charge. The price ceiling caused the quantity demanded to rise to Q_D, resulting in a shortage, Q_D-Q_S. Faced with excess demand for power, the utility companies had to find a way to ration supply. This solution frequently came in the form of "rolling blackouts" that disrupted power and economic activity throughout California that summer.

As with the rental market for apartments, the price ceilings in the electricity delivery market set an artificially low price, decreased quantity supplied, and created a shortage. Once again, you can see that government intervention must be exercised with great care and wisdom, or we run the risk of creating problems that are as vexing as those that we initially set out to solve.

Critical-Thinking Questions

1. Would a deadweight loss have resulted if demand had decreased in 2000 instead of increased? Explain.
2. Why do you suppose the government enacted the policy if, in the end, it hurt consumers rather than helped them?

- **The benefits of market-based exchange.** Consumers and producers are both made better off when they exchange goods and services voluntarily using competitive markets. Consumer surplus is the combined benefit that consumers receive because for all but the marginal unit, the marginal benefit of consumption exceeds the price. Producer surplus is the benefit that producers receive; for all but the marginal unit, the price that sellers receive is greater than the marginal cost of production. The competitive equilibrium is the intersection of the supply and demand curves. When price is set at this point, the sum of consumer surplus and producer surplus is maximized.

- **Consumer and producer surplus application: taxes and the competitive equilibrium.** If the output and price in a market are forced away from the competitive equilibrium, the gains from exchange are reduced. The reduction in gains, a deadweight loss, represents value that is lost from consumer and producer surplus. Per-unit taxes are levied on each unit sold, with the result that some of the consumer and producer surplus is transferred to the government as tax revenue. The taxes also create a deadweight loss because the equilibrium quantity is reduced. The incidence of the tax depends on the elasticity of demand and supply.

- **Price floors, price ceilings, and quotas.** Governments sometimes intervene in markets and intentionally alter the price or quantity in an attempt to help consumers or producers. Price floors (minimum prices), price ceilings (maximum prices), and quotas (maximum quantities) alter prices or output, and as a result create deadweight loss. Although these policies may achieve their intended result, they often also have the unintended effect of changing incentives and rewards in other related markets, which reduces their overall benefit.

- **Concluding thoughts on market efficiency.** Monopoly power reduces efficiency compared to the competitive equilibrium because monopolists charge prices in excess of marginal cost. The existence of externalities and common property resources reduces overall efficiency because goods are underproduced, underconsumed, overproduced, or overconsumed.

▶ KEY TERMS

Consumer surplus 146	Marginal consumer 146	Producer surplus 147
Deadweight loss 150	Monopoly 159	Public goods 160
Externalities 160	Negative externality 160	Quota 158
Incidence of a tax on consumers 149	Per-unit tax 148	
	Price ceiling 157	
Incidence of a tax on producers 149	Price floor 151	
	Positive externality 160	

▶ PROBLEMS

1. Draw a market supply and demand curve for televisions, with the equilibrium price at $300. Label the consumer and producer surplus on your graph. If the government places a $10 per-set tax on televisions, how are consumer and producer surplus affected? Show this on your graph.
2. In the graph that you drew for Problem 1, identify the area that represents deadweight loss and the source of this deadweight loss.
3. The following table shows the marginal benefit each consumer receives from the purchase of a dictionary. For each consumer, calculate the consumer surplus. If these consumers represent all demand, what is the total consumer surplus in this market?

Consumer	Marginal Benefit	Price
Juanita	$50	$20
James	$45	$20
Sunni	$30	$20
Marco	$20	$20

4. Suppose that consumer demand for the medication Crixivan (used to combat the affects of HIV) is vertical. Thus, consumers will pay any price to get a specific quantity, and only that quantity. What can we say about consumer surplus in this case? (Assume that the supply curve is a typical upward-sloping line.) Use a graph to illustrate your response.

5. What does it mean to say that someone is a "marginal consumer"?

6. Suppose that the equilibrium price of socks is initially $3.00 per pair. After the government imposes a per-unit tax of $0.50 per pair, the price rises to $3.20. What is the incidence of the tax on consumers?

7. Why do many states not tax "necessities," such as medicine, food, and clothing?

8. Suppose that the demand for laptops is a horizontal line at $1,200, indicating that consumers will purchase zero units at any price above $1,200. Use a graph to show the effect of the $100 per-laptop tax on producers.

9. If a $1.00 per-unit tax on cigars increases the price paid by consumers from $4.00 to $4.50 each, and decreases the equilibrium quantity of cigars from 300 per day to 200 per day, what is the size of the deadweight loss created? Compute a numerical answer and show using a supply and demand diagram.

10. Draw a supply and demand curve for potatoes, with the equilibrium price at $6.00 per bag.
    a. If the government installs a price floor of $7.00 per bag, how will it affect consumer and producer surplus? Show the deadweight loss.
    b. How would your answer change if the price floor were set at $5.00 per bag?

11. What does it mean to say that "the short side of the market rules"?

12. Draw a supply and demand curve for vitamins, with the equilibrium price at $10.00 per bottle.
    a. Suppose that the government believes that this price is too high to promote good health among its citizens, and installs a price ceiling of $8.00 per bottle. Show the effect of this policy on consumer and producer surplus, and label any deadweight loss created by the policy.
    b. Which consumers are better off with the price ceiling in place? Are some consumers worse off? If so, describe why.

13. Suppose that citizens decide to take up very healthy eating habits and exercise, while consuming fewer vitamins. As a result, demand for vitamins falls, and the new equilibrium price of vitamins is $7.50 per bottle. What is the effect of a price ceiling set at $8.00?

14. What is the effect of a price ceiling on milk if the demand for milk is perfectly inelastic?
    a. Show the changes in consumer and producer surplus plus any deadweight loss that may occur on a graph. Give an explanation for the deadweight loss.
    b. How do your results change if the supply of milk is perfectly inelastic? Assume that the demand curve is downward-sloping.

15. Use a supply and demand graph to show how it could be that a government-imposed restriction would not alter the market equilibrium, in each of these cases:
    a. A price floor
    b. A price ceiling
    c. A quota
16. If the production of a good generates negative externalities, is efficiency improved if more or less of the good is produced? What if the good generates positive externalities?

myeconlab STUDY GUIDE

HERE'S HOW MyEconLab CAN HELP YOU GET A BETTER GRADE

1. Log into MyEconLab and take Practice Test chapter-A (to log in for the first time, see page 30 for instructions.)

2. Based on your test results, MyEconLab will identify the areas where you need further work and create a personal Study Plan for you.

3. Your Study Plan contains the exercises listed below and others like them that will target the specific chapter topics you need to focus on. You'll receive instant feedback and find links to tutorials, animations, and the online textbook to help you study.

4. When you're ready, go take Practice Test chapter-B and demonstrate how your results have improved.

Section 6.1, Exercise 1 Elise is very thirsty, and is willing to pay $5.00 for a cola. She discovers that the store's price of a cola is only $1.25. What is Elise's consumer surplus?

Section 6.1, Exercise 2 The following table shows consumers' willingness to pay for a particular book.

Consumer	Willingness to Pay
Tom	$100
Sally	$80
Sue	$60
Matt	$40
Rob	$20

a. Suppose that the market price of the book is $60. How many copies will be sold, and what is the value of total consumer surplus?

b. If the price of the book rises to $100, how many copies will be sold, and what is the value of consumer surplus?

Section 6.1, Exercise 3 The following graph shows the supply and demand for flat-screen TVs.

a. Calculate consumer surplus, and show the area on the graph.

b. Calculate producer surplus, and show the area on the graph.

c. What are the gains from exchange in this market?

Section 6.2, Exercise 1 Suppose that the market for flat-screen TVs is currently in equilibrium, as shown in the graph in the previous problem, and that the government imposes a $150 tax per unit.

a. Show the effect of the tax on a graph.

b. If the new price is $1,110, what is the incidence of the tax on consumers? On producers?

c. Assume that the new quantity is 90,000. Calculate consumer surplus, producer surplus, and government revenue from the tax.
d. What is the combined consumer and producer surplus in this market now?
e. What is the size of the deadweight loss?
f. Based on the price change from the tax, what can you say about the relative size of the elasticity of supply and the elasticity of demand in this market?

Section 6.3, Exercise 1 The following graph shows the market for wheat, which is currently in equilibrium at a price of $4.00 per bushel.

a. Select an effective price floor, and show its effect on the quantity of wheat demanded and quantity of wheat supplied.
b. Identify the size of the surplus on the graph.
c. What happens to consumer surplus when the price floor is imposed? Identify the area on your graph.
d. Assuming that the government does *not* buy the surplus, what happens to producer surplus when the price floor is imposed? Identify the area on your graph.
e. Who gains and who loses from the price floor?

Section 6.3, Exercise 2 Consider the wheat market described in the previous problem. Suppose that the government wishes to make sure that all farmers gain and thus purchases any surplus wheat at the floor price.

a. What happens to producer surplus when the price floor is imposed? Identify the area on your graph.
b. Who gains and who loses from the price floor?

Section 6.3, Exercise 3 The following graph shows the market for gasoline, which is currently in equilibrium at a price of $2.00 per gallon.

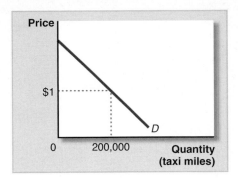

a. Select an effective price ceiling, and show its effect on the quantity of gasoline demanded and quantity of gasoline supplied.
b. Identify the size of the shortage on the graph.
c. What happens to consumer surplus when the price ceiling is imposed? Identify the area on your graph.
d. What happens to producer surplus when the price ceiling is imposed? Identify the area on your graph.
e. Who gains and who loses from the price ceiling?

Section 6.3, Exercise 4 Large cities, such as New York City, usually require that taxicabs be licensed, and restrict the number of taxis by issuing a limited number of licenses, which are usually called medallions. This quantity restriction is essentially a quota on taxi service.

Suppose that the market is currently in equilibrium at a price of $1.00 per mile, and that a cab can drive only 100 miles per day. At a price of 1.00 per mile, the total quantity demanded is 200,000 miles.

a. If medallions are not restricted, how many taxis will there be in equilibrium?
b. Now suppose that the city restricts the number of medallions to 1,000. Show the effect on the market.
c. What will happen to the price per mile of taxi service?
d. Who gains and who loses from the quota?

7 Consumer Behavior

It's nice to dream about being able to buy whatever you want without worrying about whether you can afford it. The advertising that surrounds us certainly encourages this dream. Most of us, however, would quickly find ourselves in deep trouble if we tried to live it. In reality, we need to think about how much money we have to spend and then plan how we are going to allocate it. In short, we have to make budgets.

Let's say that you are a lover of both gourmet pizza and the latest indie bands. Every month you have exactly $100 in spending money. You could easily eat $100 worth of pizza in one month, and you could just as easily spend the whole $100 on CDs. Unfortunately, at this point in your life you have no way to increase your monthly income beyond $100. And that sum has to cover both pizza *and* CDs, not one or the other. How much pizza should you purchase with your scarce resources? How will that decision affect your consumption of other goods, such as CDs? What are the implications of this simple consumer dilemma?

In this chapter, we show how economists model these kinds of trade-offs in the consumer decision-making process. As with most microeconomic problems, we will focus closely on decisions made at the margin. To see how consumers use marginal analysis, we develop a model of your decision process—which mirrors all consumer decision making in two distinct stages. The first stage shows what you *are able to do* as a consumer on a budget. The second stage shows what you *would like to do*. Your consumption decision—how many pizzas and CDs to buy with $100—lies in finding the best match between what you are able to do and what you want to do.

ALONG THE WAY, YOU WILL ALSO LEARN:

- How to represent the individual consumer's choices using budget analysis.

- How consumers reveal their preferences through the choices they make.

- How consumers respond to changes in prices, income, and other external forces.

 AT THE END OF THE CHAPTER, THE MYECONLAB LOGO WILL DIRECT YOU ONLINE

- MyEconLab is a resource-packed online homework and tutorial system that can help you perform better in your economics course. To log in for the first time, see page 30 for instructions.

- MyEconLab can help you apply important concepts from the chapter to real-world issues. Watch for the logo to indicate online features about the budget line and consumer choice.

- At the end of each chapter, you'll find a special study section that will help you get the most out of your textbook and your instructor's MyEconLab course.

 Budget Analysis

Consumer behavior
The decision-making process that consumers use to allocate their scarce resources.

We now begin our investigation of consumer behavior. **Consumer behavior**, in economics, refers to the decision process that consumers use to allocate their scarce resources.

Most individuals and households allocate their incomes very carefully. Consumers must consider how to allocate their limited income among many possible choices. Even the wealthiest individuals cannot buy everything they wish. Your decision regarding how many pizzas and CDs to buy will be made in this context of limited resources: You have only so much time, money, and energy to spend shopping. In our simple example, we consider only the monetary constraint. You have a monthly budget that limits your spending to the $100 that you earn from a part-time job, and you cannot exceed the $100 budget (no borrowing is allowed, and you have no other sources of income). To keep the model simple, we'll also assume income cannot be saved, so that each month you spend the entire $100.

The process of allocating scarce resources is the very foundation of economics. Your effort to buy the right number of pizzas and CDs might seem trivial, but it illustrates a universal problem: Budget limitations always mean making choices. Those choices might concern how many cars a family purchases, how many roads a state builds, or—as you saw in Chapter 2—how much health care a nation provides for its citizens. At every level of analysis and in every nation, budget limitations constrain people's choices.

Budget Line Determination

We will use budget analysis to address the question of how best to allocate your scarce resources between two goods: pizza and music CDs. In the real world, there are many other goods that you might want to consume; by limiting your choices to two, we can more easily show how the choice process works.

We've established that you have $100 of spending money per month to allocate to pizza and CDs. The price of a personal-size gourmet pizza is $10. The price of a

FIGURE 7.1

The Budget Line

Panel (a) shows the various combinations of pizzas and CDs that you could consume in one month. Panel (b) shows the same information in graph form. Given an income of $100 and a price of $10 per pizza and per CD, the green budget line shows all the combinations of pizzas and CDs that you can afford. You cannot choose combination *D*, because it exceeds your monthly income. With a combination such as *F*, some income would go unused. The budget line's slope is equal to −1 times the price of the good on the *x*-axis (CD's) divided by the price of the good on the *y*-axis (pizzas). In this case, the price ratio is −1.0, indicating that for each extra pizza, you must give up one CD, and vice versa.

(a) Possible consumption bundles

Number of Pizzas	Number of CDs
10	0
9	1
8	2
7	3
6	4
5	5
4	6
3	7
2	8
1	9
0	10

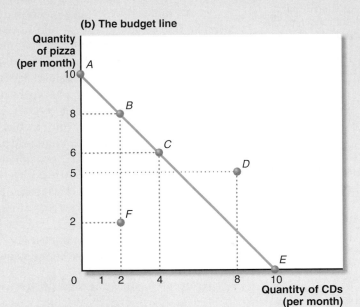

(b) The budget line

Budget line
Shows all the consumption opportunities available to a consumer, given income and fixed prices. Its slope represents the trade-offs that the consumer faces when deciding how much to spend on each good or service.

CD through a music discounter is also $10. Panel (a) of Figure 7.1 shows the combinations of the two goods that you can afford to purchase. Panel (b) shows the same information in graph form. In panel (b), the negatively sloped diagonal line is the budget line. A **budget line** shows the boundary of all the consumption opportunities available to you, given income and fixed prices. (Note that the axes of our budget line measure the *quantities* of each good, not the price or the money spent on that good.)

Budget Line Characteristics

The budget line in Figure 7.1 illustrates several characteristics common to all budget lines:

1. Every point on the line represents a specific basket of goods that you can purchase at the current prices with your budgeted income of $100. For example, the coordinates of point *B* are (2, 8). If you choose this point, you purchase two CDs and eight pizzas. If instead you choose to buy four CDs and six pizzas, point *C* represents your decision.

2. The budget line is straight and has a negative slope. The value of the slope is equal to minus one times the ratio of the prices of the goods: the price of *X*

divided by the price of Y. In this case, the slope is -1.0.[1] This constant, negative slope reflects the trade-off that you face: Moving down the budget line, you must give up one pizza for each additional CD you buy. (You can also think of this trade-off in terms of opportunity cost. Remember that opportunity cost measures the cost of what you must forgo.) Therefore, moving from point B to point C means giving up two pizzas if you want to purchase two more CDs.

3. Because budget lines are straight lines, they are simple to plot on a graph. After we have determined the intercepts, we can connect them with a straight line to obtain the complete set of possible **consumption baskets**, or combinations of goods and services you can choose, given current prices and your income.

Consumption basket
The combination of goods or services a consumer can choose, given prices and income.

4. The budget line's vertical and horizontal intercepts (points A and E, respectively) set the outer limits of the purchases you can make of each good. The vertical intercept indicates how much pizza you can buy if you allocate all your income to pizza and purchase no CDs (point A). In this case, you can buy 10 pizzas = $100/$10. The horizontal intercept shows the other extreme—allocating all your income to CDs. If you spend all your income on CDs and buy no pizza (point E), you can buy 10 CDs = $100/$10.

5. You cannot purchase any combination of goods outside the budget line, such as D, because you do not have enough income. Purchasing five pizzas and eight CDs costs $5 \times \$10 + 8 \times \$10 = \$130$, which exceeds your income by $30. Points inside the budget line, such as F, are obtainable but are not desirable in our model because we assume that income cannot be saved for future consumption.

6. When plotting budget lines, find the intercepts by dividing income by the price of each good. Plot the intercepts, and connect them with a straight line. Because budget lines are straight and negatively sloped, you can also use the intercepts to find the slope if you compute $-1 \times \dfrac{\text{Vertical Intercept}}{\text{Horizontal Intercept}}$. For example, the vertical axis intercept in Figure 7.1 is 10. The horizontal axis intercept is 10. Thus, the slope is $-10/10 = -1.0$.

Changes in Income and Price

Get Ahead of the Curve

Apply the budget line model to consumer choices in response to higher gasoline prices.

We can use the budget line to illustrate income changes. When income changes, the entire budget line shifts to a new position with no change in slope. The new line shows the updated consumption possibilities. Suppose, for example, that you get a raise at work, and your $100 monthly income increases to $200. Figure 7.2(a) shows your original budget line in dark green as well as your new one in light green. As your income increases, your budget line shifts to the right. If you spend all your income on pizza, you can now buy 20 pizzas at $10 each. If, instead, you spend it all on CDs, you can buy 20 CDs at $10 each. Although you still face the same trade-off between pizzas and CDs (the price ratio is the same), you can now consume more of both goods.

If the price of one good changes, the budget line pivots to reflect the new trade-off rate. For example, suppose that the CD discounter lowers the price of CDs to $5 to clear out inventory. Because there was no change in the price of pizza, the vertical intercept remains unchanged at 10 pizzas. However, if you purchase only CDs, you can now buy 20 instead of 10. These two points create a new budget line, shown in light green in panel (b) of Figure 7.2. The budget line rotates outward

---

[1] We calculate the slope of a straight line as the change in Y divided by the change in X; in this case, $(6 - 8)/(4 - 2) = -1$.

FIGURE 7.2

The Effect of Changes in Income and Price on the Budget Line

In panel (a), when income increases from $100 to $200, the dark-green budget line shifts to the right. In its new location (light-green curve), the maximum number of pizzas and CDs that you can purchase increases. However, the slope of the budget line does not change, because prices remain the same. Similarly, if income decreases, the budget constraint shifts to the left and maintains the same slope. In panel (b), your income is $100. When the price of CDs decreases from $10 to $5, the budget line rotates outward. The new slope is equal to the new price ratio, or −$5/$10 = −0.5. You must give up one-half pizza to obtain one additional CD, and the maximum number of CDs you can purchase if you don't buy any pizza has increased from 10 to 20. If the price per CD increases to $20, the budget line rotates inward with an increased slope of −$20/$10 = −2.0. You must now give up two pizzas to obtain one more CD. The maximum number of CDs you can purchase if you don't buy any pizza has decreased from 10 to 5.

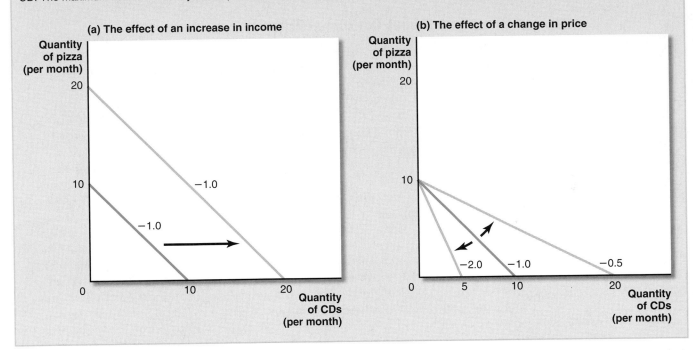

along the horizontal axis to 20 CDs while remaining anchored at the 10-pizza point on the vertical axis. The slope of the line changes from −1.0 to −$5/$10 = −0.5. In order to buy one more CD, you must now give up only one-half pizza instead of one. If the price of CDs increases to $20 instead of falling to $5, the budget line rotates inward along the horizontal axis. The slope of this budget line is −$20/$10 = −2.0, as shown in light green in panel (b) of Figure 7.2.

TEST + *E X T E N D* Your Knowledge

1. TEST Joe buys concert tickets for $25 each and science fiction novels for $10 each. If Joe's budget for concert tickets and novels is $200 per month, what is the maximum number of concerts he can attend if he buys no novels? Draw the budget line, placing concerts on the horizontal axis. What is the slope of the budget line?

2. EXTEND To promote its grand opening, a new bookstore in Joe's neighborhood advertises a 50 percent off sale on science fiction novels for the first month that the store is in business. If Joe buys all of his books at the new store that month, how does this sale alter his budget constraint? Draw the new constraint and label the slope.

► Utility Theory

Budget lines show what we are able to consume. They do not provide any information about what we *want* to consume, which is the focus of this section. We use our information concerning what we want to do as well as what we can do to construct a model of consumer behavior. Such information is valuable both for economists who seek to understand consumer behavior and for firms. The better that firms understand how consumers make decisions, the better they can tailor their products and marketing efforts to maximize profits.

Assumptions About Consumer Behavior

Like all economic models, the model of consumer behavior rests on simplifying assumptions. As noted in Chapter 1, the world is far too complex for us to model it completely. To make the model as widely applicable as possible, we make only a few fundamental assumptions.

Maximizing Well-Being. The first assumption that we make in consumer theory is that *consumers maximize their well-being.* Maximizing well-being is central to the model of consumer behavior. It would be extremely difficult to predict behavior consistently if individuals did not focus on their well-being. Does this assumption mean that people are motivated only by greed? It is true that desire for higher levels of income and consumption generally plays an important role in the maximization process. However, it is not the only source of well-being. Our tastes and preferences are complex; what contributes to our well-being (and thus drives our behavior) is not always directly related to accumulating more money to spend on goods and services. For example, altruistic behavior, such as charitable giving, is consistent with maximizing one's own well-being. If you made a donation to relief efforts in Indonesia after the 2004 tsunami, it contributed to the well-being of others as well as to your own well-being, because you received the satisfaction of having helped others in a time of great need. Remember, consumers maximize their well-being, not their income. While our example focuses on maximizing well-being through consumption of goods, well-being involves much more than just consumption.

Utility
Well-being, including the benefits that consumers derive from consuming goods and services.

Rather than the imprecise term "well-being," economists typically refer to the benefits that consumers enjoy as **utility**. As we work with our model of utility, keep in mind that utility is in the eye of the beholder. That is, each consumer has his or her own preferences. You might have a strong preference for music over pizza. A friend might feel just the opposite, and purchase lots of pizza but few CDs.

Rational Consumers. We also assume that *consumers are rational.* "Rationality" has a special meaning in economics: behaving in a consistent manner. It might seem irrational for someone to paint her house with zebra stripes. However, this decision does not violate the economic definition of rationality, as long as the person consistently prefers the zebra-stripe pattern to all others. To an economist, rational behavior can thus include actions that we consider bizarre. One famous study actually showed that inmates in an asylum—people who are completely irrational by our everyday standards—behave in an economically rational way.[2]

---

[2] Gary Becker, "De Gustibus Non Est Disputandum [There's No Accounting for Taste]," *American Economic Review,* vol. 67, no. 2 (March 1977), pages 76–90.

Perfect Foresight. When consumers make purchases, they do so based on the satisfaction that they believe they will obtain from consuming the good or service. However, consumers do not know this information with certainty. When they make a purchase, the actual satisfaction they derive may be quite different from what they expected. Lots of purchases do not provide the satisfaction that the buyer had expected. The purchase was not irrational, because the purchaser acted according to the best information available at the time. The economics of uncertainty is widely studied. To keep the focus on consumer choices when faced with limited resources, we will assume that consumers do know with certainty the satisfaction that they would obtain from consuming a good or service.

Total Utility

Our notion of utility is based on the writings of British philosophers in the seventeenth and eighteenth centuries. At the time, philosophers like Jeremy Bentham believed that someday we would be able to measure an individual's well-being in the same way we use a thermometer to measure our body temperature. Economists no longer believe such an instrument can be devised. To simplify this discussion, however, we will assume temporarily that we have a utility meter to measure people's well-being. You will soon see, though, that we can predict consumer behavior without actually measuring utility.

Total utility is the total satisfaction that a consumer derives from the consumption of goods or services. Of course, a person's well-being cannot actually be divided up into units, but if we could measure utility, we might find that you derive utility from consuming pizza over one month according to the data in panel (a) of Figure 7.3. These data show that as you begin to consume pizzas, your utility level increases with each pizza you eat. The first pizza provides lots of satisfaction, so total utility increases from 0 to 25 units. The second pizza increases total utility to 45 units, and so on. We depict this information in graph form in panel (b) of Figure 7.3, which

Total utility
The total satisfaction that a consumer derives from the consumption of goods or services.

Consumers Maximize Their Utility Choosing to Consume the Goods That Provide the Most Utility

FIGURE 7.3

The Total Utility of Pizza Consumption

The data in the table in panel (a) show the total utility of consuming various quantities of pizzas. Panel (b) shows the same data in graph form, with each bar representing the total utility you received for each pizza consumed. As you eat more pizzas, your total utility (shown just below the line) increases up to the 11th unit. Note that the marginal utility (shown just above the line) or satisfaction derived from eating one additional pizza, gradually decreases as the quantity consumed increases.

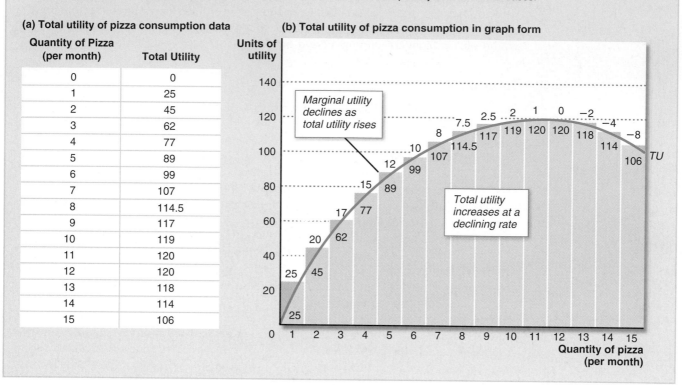

(a) Total utility of pizza consumption data

Quantity of Pizza (per month)	Total Utility
0	0
1	25
2	45
3	62
4	77
5	89
6	99
7	107
8	114.5
9	117
10	119
11	120
12	120
13	118
14	114
15	106

(b) Total utility of pizza consumption in graph form

shows the total utility of consuming up to 15 pizzas. Each bar in the graph represents the total utility from consuming a given amount of pizza. We connect the bars with a smooth curve. In practice, economists use the curve rather than the bar graph, as it is much less cumbersome.

Marginal Utility

The level of total utility you obtain from eating pizza or listening to CDs is certainly interesting, but is it relevant to your decision of how much of each good to buy? Remember that consumers make most decisions on the margin. That is, individuals focus on the added benefit of an additional unit rather than the total benefit of all units put together. In our example, after you have decided to eat pizza, the question is how much pizza to eat. Therefore, what interests us most is the *additional* utility that you derive from consuming one more pizza. The satisfaction received from consuming one additional unit of a good or service—or the satisfaction we lose from consuming one unit less—is the *marginal utility* of the good or service. More formally, **marginal utility** is the change in total utility associated with a one-unit change in consumption.

Marginal utility
The change in total utility associated with a one-unit change in consumption.

FIGURE 7.4

The Marginal Utility of Pizza Consumption

The data in panel (a) are shown in graph form in panel (b). Each bar represents the marginal utility you receive from each unit of pizza consumed. As you eat more and more pizzas, your marginal utility decreases, and eventually it becomes negative; in this example, at the thirteenth pizza. Thus, in accordance with the principle of diminishing marginal utility, the additional utility you receive becomes smaller the more you eat, until finally you are made worse off by eating another pizza.

(a) Marginal utility of pizza consumption data

Pizzas	Marginal Utility
0	
1	25
2	20
3	17
4	15
5	12
6	10
7	8
8	7.5
9	2.5
10	2
11	1
12	0
13	−2
14	−4
15	−8

(b) Marginal utility of pizza consumption in graph form

Diminishing marginal utility

The decrease in marginal utility associated with consuming successive units of a good. As consumers consume more of a good or service, holding consumption of all other goods and services constant, the marginal utility they derive from each additional unit must eventually decline.

Diminishing Marginal Utility. In Figure 7.3, you can see that total utility increases at a decreasing rate. The additional utility derived from the consumption of each pizza is less than the added utility derived from the previous one. This inverse relationship between the extra utility you get from consuming an additional pizza and the total amount of pizza you consume illustrates the principle of *diminishing marginal utility,* the most important aspect of consumer theory. The **diminishing marginal utility** principle states that *as consumers consume more of one good or service and hold consumption of all other goods and services constant, the marginal utility they derive from each additional unit must eventually decline.* In fact, marginal utility can decrease to the point where total utility remains constant or even decreases with the consumption of an additional unit. For example, whether you consume 12 pizzas or 11, total utility remains the same, at 120. Consuming more than 12 pizzas causes total utility to fall.

To analyze diminishing marginal utility more closely, consider Figure 7.4, which shows the marginal utility of each additional pizza you consume, in table and graph formats. Marginal utility measures the change in utility over an interval. That is, it measures the additional utility of going from zero pizzas to one pizza or from one pizza to two pizzas, not the utility *at* one pizza or *at* two pizzas. As a result, we indicate the change in utility between the units, rather than at each pizza, in panel (a) of Figure 7.4. Panel (b) of Figure 7.4 shows the marginal utility of consuming more pizzas in a graph. This graph confirms our observation in Figure 7.3 that total utility increases up through the eleventh pizza and your marginal utility declines after the first pizza. Because total utility does not increase when you consume the twelfth pizza, the marginal utility of the twelfth pizza is zero.

The Diamond–Water Paradox. We can use the concept of marginal utility to resolve what at first glance might seem to be a paradox regarding the pricing of two goods: water and diamonds. Water is essential for life; humans can live for only a few days without it. In contrast, diamonds are typically only for show. Apart from a few industrial uses, they have no essential function. The total utility of water is far higher than the total utility of diamonds. Then why are water prices so low and diamonds prices so high?

The most important reason for the price difference lies in differences between the marginal utilities. The total utility that we derive from consuming water is very high. However, the marginal utility of the last gallon of water we consume is typically very low, in part because we usually consume so much water. Figure 7.5(a) shows that the total utility we receive from diamonds is far lower than the total utility we receive from water, which is shown in panel (b). The abundance of water means that one more

---

FIGURE 7.5

The Diamond–Water Paradox

The total utility for water is much greater than the total utility for diamonds, because water is vital to life and diamonds are not. Yet diamonds have much higher prices than water. The key to the diamond–water paradox lies in the abundance of water compared to diamonds. Although total utility for water is higher than for diamonds, the marginal utility of the last unit of diamonds consumed is much greater than that of water, as seen in the difference in the slopes of the total utility curves. The marginal utility we derive from the last gallon of water consumed is low because we consume so much already. The marginal utility we receive from the last diamond is very high, because we consume so few.

(a) Total and marginal utilities for diamonds

Units of utility

Total utility

Relatively steep slope indicates a high marginal utility for the last unit of diamonds

0   D_1 Quantity of diamonds (in carats)

(b) Total and marginal utilities for water

Units of utility

Total utility

Relatively small slope indicates a low marginal utility for the last unit of water

0   W_1 Quantity of water (in gallons)

BORN LOSER: © Newspaper Enterprise Association, Inc.

gallon of water adds very little utility, and one less unit takes away very little. The marginal utility of the last diamond is very high, because most people do not have very many diamonds to begin with. The difference in marginal utility translates into a difference in price. Water is inexpensive in most areas because it is so plentiful. The low price of water indicates that the marginal value of the last unit is low, yet the total benefit from consuming water is very large. In economic terms, the total utility gained from consuming water is very high. Diamonds are expensive because they are so scarce. That is, the marginal utility of the last diamond is typically very high, because they are scarce and most people have so few. Note that the total utility from consuming diamonds is relatively small compared to water. Thus, the diamond–water paradox of high-priced diamonds and low-priced water depends on the scarcity of diamonds relative to water. If water became more scarce, no paradox would exist.

Maximizing Utility

We assume that consumers want to maximize their utility and that none of us can afford everything we want. To maximize our total utility when consuming goods and services, we must compare the additional utility that a good brings us with the cost it imposes. In this section, we show how consumers choose a utility-maximizing basket of goods and services.

To show how consumers make choices, we need a decision rule that incorporates both the prices of the goods and your income. Remember the importance of making decisions based on opportunity costs. In our pizzas-and-CDs example, the cost is the opportunity cost in the form of CDs you must sacrifice to get more pizza (and vice versa). Thus, we must compare the price of pizzas and the marginal utility that they provide to the price of CDs and the marginal utility they provide.

Determining Marginal Utility per Dollar

Marginal utility per dollar
The marginal utility of a given unit of consumption of a good or service divided by the price of the good or service.

We begin by computing the marginal utility per dollar of each unit of consumption of a good or service. The **marginal utility per dollar** is the marginal utility a consumer receives for a given unit of consumption divided by the price of the good or service. This calculation adjusts the marginal utility derived from an additional unit by the cost of that gain in utility. For example, we know from Figure 7.4 that the marginal utility of the second pizza is 20. Thus, with a price of $10 per pizza, the marginal utility per dollar of the second pizza is 20/10 = 2.0. Similarly, the marginal utility of the sixth pizza is 10. The marginal utility per dollar of the sixth pizza is 10/10 = 1.0. The marginal utility per dollar declines when you consume more of a good or service, just as marginal utility does, because the price stays constant at $10.

Identifying the Utility-Maximizing Consumption Basket

We can apply the concept of marginal utility per dollar to find the utility-maximizing basket by using the data in Table 7.1. When you are ready to spend the first $10 and have no pizza or CDs to start with, you have a choice of obtaining 50 units of utility from a CD (shown in column 3), or 25 units of utility from a pizza (in column 6). The clear choice is to purchase a CD, because the CD gives you more satisfaction per dollar of expenditure. With the second $10, you could purchase a second CD and get an additional 37 units of utility or purchase a pizza (your first pizza) and receive 25 units of utility. Again, a CD is the better choice. The same is true for your third choice. However, the marginal utility of a fourth CD is 20, which is less than the marginal utility of your first pizza, 25. Because this first pizza would provide more additional utility than a fourth CD, you should buy the pizza. This process continues until you purchase six CDs and four pizzas. At this point, you exhaust your income and the marginal utility per dollar of each good is equal. Total utility is maximized at 248 units (171 units from the 6 CDs and 77 units from the 4 pizzas).

Normally, you have to satisfy both conditions—spending all your money and setting the marginal utility per dollar equal—to maximize your utility. You could set the marginal utility per dollar equal with other combinations. For example, you could spend only $60 to buy two pizzas and four CDs. However, that would

TABLE 7.1

Marginal Utility and Total Utility per Dollar Spent on Pizza and CDs When Both Goods Are Priced at $10 Each

Quantity of CDs (1)	Marginal Utility per Dollar of the Last CD (2)	Total Utility from CDs (3)	Quantity of Pizza (4)	Marginal Utility per Dollar of the Last Pizza (5)	Total Utility from Pizza (6)
0	0.0	0	0	0.0	0
1	5.0	50	1	2.5	25
2	3.7	87	2	2.0	45
3	3.1	118	3	1.7	62
4	2.0	138	4	1.5	77
5	1.8	156	5	1.2	89
6	1.5	171	6	1.0	99
7	1.0	181	7	0.8	107
8	0.5	186	8	0.75	114.5
9	0.2	188	9	0.25	117
10	0.1	189	10	0.2	119

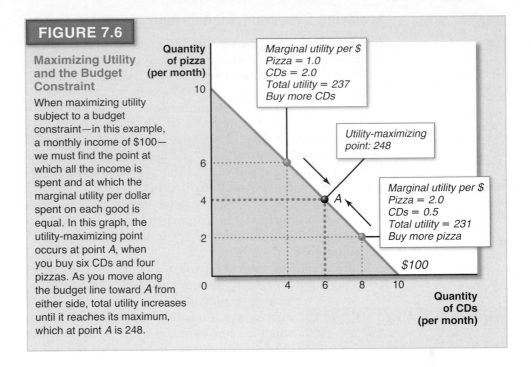

FIGURE 7.6

Maximizing Utility and the Budget Constraint

When maximizing utility subject to a budget constraint—in this example, a monthly income of $100—we must find the point at which all the income is spent and at which the marginal utility per dollar spent on each good is equal. In this graph, the utility-maximizing point occurs at point *A*, when you buy six CDs and four pizzas. As you move along the budget line toward *A* from either side, total utility increases until it reaches its maximum, which at point *A* is 248.

Figure labels:
- Quantity of pizza (per month)
- Marginal utility per $ Pizza = 1.0 CDs = 2.0 Total utility = 237 Buy more CDs
- Utility-maximizing point: 248
- *A*
- Marginal utility per $ Pizza = 2.0 CDs = 0.5 Total utility = 231 Buy more pizza
- $100
- Quantity of CDs (per month)

increase your total utility level to 183. Because we do not consider the possibility of saving to increase future utility in our analysis, maximizing utility here requires that you spend all your income.[3]

You can also spend the entire $100 and still fail to maximize your utility. With Table 7.1, we can compare the marginal utility per dollar of the many combinations of CDs and pizza that cost exactly $100. For example, you could spend $100 by purchasing four CDs and six pizzas. If you do so, the marginal utility per dollar of the fourth CD is 2.0, the marginal utility per dollar of the sixth pizza is 1.0, and your total utility is 237, as shown in Figure 7.6. Compare that with the combination of CDs and pizza with equal marginal utilities per dollar—six CDs and four pizzas. Purchasing six CDs and four pizzas maximizes your utility: 248 is the highest possible utility on the table, given your income. As a rule, when the marginal utility per dollar is not equal across all goods, you should allocate income away from the good with the lowest marginal utility per dollar toward the good with the highest marginal utility per dollar. In this case, when all income has been spent, the following guidelines apply:

- If the marginal utility per dollar spent on the last pizza is greater than the marginal utility per dollar spent on the last CD: Buy more pizza.
- If the marginal utility per dollar spent on the last CD is greater than the marginal utility per dollar spent on the last pizza: Buy more CDs.
- If all income is spent and the marginal utility per dollar is equal for the last pizza and the last CD, utility is maximized.

---

[3] Equalizing marginal utility per dollar might not always be possible, because some items are not divisible into very small units. For example, the marginal utility per dollar derived from owning one car may be slightly greater than the marginal utility per dollar of all the other goods you consume, but the marginal utility per dollar of a second car would be much less. Because you can't buy (and would not want!) 1.5 cars, the best decision is to buy one.

Achieving Consumer Equilibrium

Consumer equilibrium
The point where the marginal utility per dollar spent is equal across all goods or services consumed.

The rule of allocating income toward goods with the highest marginal utility per dollar applies no matter how many goods are in the consumer's consumption basket. In general, the **consumer equilibrium** occurs at the point where the marginal utility per dollar spent is equal across all goods.

This process is based on the principle of diminishing marginal utility: The more we consume of any good, the lower the marginal utility of the last unit. With a constant price for each good, as we consume additional units, the marginal utility per dollar of each good decreases. In addition, the closer the ratios are to equality, the higher the utility level will be. As Figure 7.6 shows, if consumption is not optimal, moving toward the optimal basket increases utility.

Equimarginal principle
Consumers maximize their utility when purchasing goods or services such that the marginal utility per dollar of the last unit of all goods or services are equal and all income is spent.

We conclude this discussion with the **equimarginal principle**: When a consumer purchases goods such that the marginal utility per dollar spent on the last unit of all goods are equal and all income is spent, the consumer is maximizing utility and is in equilibrium.

At this point, you might be saying to yourself, "Why does this information matter to me? I don't carry a utility meter around and check it every time I feel like

buying a pizza!" The good news is that economics does not require you to do so, any more than LeBron James must solve complex equations governing the laws of physics before shooting a basketball. Yet when LeBron makes a game-winning basket, he behaves *as if* he had solved those equations. Just as physics can be used to explain the way the natural world operates—even actions taken without conscious consideration of the laws of physics—economics can explain how consumers behave. According to our model of consumer behavior, you can list the affordable combinations of pizza and CDs in order from most preferred to least preferred. You now know that when you are confronted with two different combinations of CDs and pizzas, you can always follow the previous guidelines to determine whether one combination provides greater utility than the other, or if you like both combinations the same amount. We do not need to know *how much* more you prefer one basket to another. For our model to explain the real world, all we need to know is that when you are standing in the mall with a pizza shop to your right and a music store to your left, you can decide in which direction to walk. Don't feel perplexed by the abstract nature of the model. Just remember that despite its simplicity, the model does a good job of predicting human behavior. For example, it is very useful when trying to predict consumer behavior when the relative prices of two goods change.

▶ From Utility Maximization to Individual Demand

In Chapter 4, you saw that demand curves are downward-sloping. All else held equal, if the price of coffee rises, you purchase fewer cups. We can now show that downward-sloping demand curves result from consumers maximizing their utility subject to budget constraints. We then apply this knowledge to two final factors influencing consumer decision making.

LifeLessons

It's Not Just What It Costs, It's What It's Worth

Author Oscar Wilde once described a cynic as "a man who knows the price of everything, and the value of nothing." In the context of our discussion of consumer choice, such a person might be described as knowing everything about the budget constraint, and nothing about tastes and preferences.

Think about a time when you needed to shop for a nice outfit for a special occasion. Did you search and search for the cheapest thing you could find, without regard to whether you liked it? Not likely. We make consumption decisions using information on prices, but not *solely* based on prices. Similarly, have you ever had someone tell you that you should not buy something "because it's too expensive"? They are really saying that the price is too high compared to the marginal utility that they would receive. As a result, it would not be worth it to *them* to make the purchase. Because preferences are individual-specific, a good that one person feels is not worth buying might be a bargain for another. Consider making a decision whether to purchase a pair of jeans. Thirty dollars for a pair of tried-and-true Levi's might suit your needs. Designer jeans by Diesel might seem like a deal to another consumer at $150. In fact, for most of the goods that you purchase, the good is worth more to you than you pay for it. Recall that marginal utility declines as you purchase additional units. Only at the margin—the last unit purchased—is your marginal utility equal to the price. For all units up to this point, it is "worth it" to make the purchase.

TEST + *EXTEND* Your Knowledge

1. TEST In Frank Herbert's novel *Dune*, people go to the planet Arrakis to mine an addictive product known as "spice." The more spice a person consumes, the more he or she craves it. Make a marginal utility table (using numbers that you create) for "spice" and draw the corresponding utility curve.

2. EXTEND Use the concepts in this section either to support or to refute the following statement: "If the marginal utility per dollar of consuming additional units of water were constant, we would demand unlimited quantities of water."

Demand Curves and Utility

We begin our examination of the relationship between utility and the demand curve by looking at the effect of a decrease in the price of pizza. With an income of $100 and the original prices of $10 for CDs and pizza, you maximized utility by consuming six CDs and four pizzas. If the price of pizza falls to $5, the marginal utility per dollar changes for pizza, and the equality is thrown out of balance. How does this price change affect your purchases of CDs and pizza?

We must recalculate the marginal utility per dollar at the new $5 pizza price. Assuming that your preferences have not changed, the marginal utility per dollar for CDs calculated in Table 7.1 remains unchanged. However, with the price of pizza cut in half, the marginal utility per dollar of pizza doubles. We show the new values in column 5 of Table 7.2.

Using the data in Table 7.2, we see that the original consumption basket of six CDs and four pizzas now violates the equimarginal principle. In addition, if you chose that same combination of goods, you would now have $20 left over. We return to equilibrium by following the same equimarginal principle—finding the point where marginal utilities per dollar are once again equal. You begin by purchasing the good with

TABLE 7.2

Marginal Utility and Total Utility per Dollar Spent on Pizzas and CDs After the Price of Pizza Falls to $5

Quantity of CDs (1)	Marginal Utility per Dollar of the Last CD (2)	Total Utility from CDs (3)	Quantity of Pizza (4)	Marginal Utility per Dollar of the Last Pizza (5)	Total Utility from Pizza (6)
0	0.0	0	0	0.0	0
1	5.0	50	1	5.0	25
2	3.7	87	2	4.0	45
3	3.1	118	3	3.4	62
4	2.0	138	4	3.0	77
5	1.8	156	5	2.4	89
6	**1.5**	171	6	2.0	99
7	1.0	181	7	1.6	107
8	0.5	186	**8**	**1.5**	114.5
9	0.2	188	9	0.5	117
10	0.1	189	10	0.4	119

the highest marginal utility per dollar and continue until all income is exhausted. If you increase your consumption of pizzas to eight and keep CD consumption at six, the marginal utilities per dollar are again equal at 1.5. Also, your utility level is higher than before the price change, because you have more pizza but do not have to give up any CDs. Total utility increases from 248 to 285.5 after the price change.

You did not change your consumption of CDs, but there is no requirement that this be so. If faced with the same price change, another person who values the two goods differently might buy a few more pizzas, but also buy more CDs. Again, the change in an individual's consumption is dependent on his or her relative preferences for the two goods.

The price change gives us two points on the consumer's individual demand curve for pizza, shown in Figure 7.7. Our model of consumer behavior results in a downward-sloping demand curve, consistent with the Law of Demand. When the price of a good falls, marginal utility per dollar rises. As a result, we increase our consumption of that good. When the price of a good increases, marginal utility per dollar falls and we consume less of that good.

Income and Substitution Effects

We can enhance our model of consumer behavior and our understanding of the demand curve by recognizing that the decisions consumers make are the combined influence of changes in the relative prices of goods and changes in purchasing power that occur when prices change.

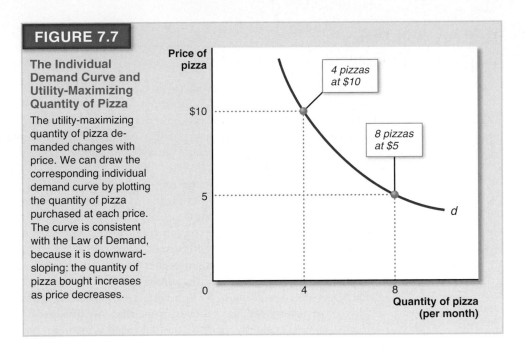

FIGURE 7.7

The Individual Demand Curve and Utility-Maximizing Quantity of Pizza

The utility-maximizing quantity of pizza demanded changes with price. We can draw the corresponding individual demand curve by plotting the quantity of pizza purchased at each price. The curve is consistent with the Law of Demand, because it is downward-sloping: the quantity of pizza bought increases as price decreases.

Substitution effect
Indicates that consumers almost always substitute away from the good or service that has become relatively more expensive and toward the good or service that has become relatively cheaper.

Income effect
The increase in a consumer's purchasing power that results from a decrease in the price of a good or service that the consumer purchases.

Substitution Effect. Recall that when the price of a good changes, we change our consumption of the good for two reasons. As we saw with your decisions regarding pizza and CDs, when the price of pizza falls, both conditions for utility maximization are violated. Pizza is now relatively less expensive than before. You bring the marginal utility per dollar for pizza and CDs back into equality by consuming more pizza. Purchasing more of the good or service that has become relatively cheaper is called the **substitution effect**. Consumers almost always substitute away from the good that has become relatively more expensive and toward the good that has become relatively cheaper.

Income Effect. The other force at work is the income effect. The **income effect** means that a decrease in the price of a good or service results in an increase in purchasing power, which is comparable to receiving extra income. The consumer can spend that income on any good or service of his or her choosing—either pizza or CDs, in our example.

For normal goods, the income effect is positive, which means that you purchase even more of the good after its price decreases. In this case, the income effect reinforces the substitution effect. As a result, the quantity response is larger than it would be with the substitution effect alone.

For inferior goods, the income effect is negative, which means that consumers shift away from the now-cheaper good toward other goods. As a result, the income effect partially offsets the substitution effect. The quantity response to the price change is smaller than it would be with the substitution effect alone. The income effect implies, for example, that a decrease in the price of chicken increases the purchasing power of shoppers, leading them to buy more beef.

Strategy and Policy

Shopping with Friends[4]

Some stores are more welcoming to groups of teen shoppers than others. A few stores go so far as specifically limiting the number of teens allowed in the store at one time. Those that are less welcoming may be afraid that the "pack mentality" of several teens together creates peer pressure to engage in unacceptable behavior such as shoplifting. However, such retailers may be missing out on other beneficial effects of the pack mentality.

Whether they embrace them or rebuff them, retailers know that teens are an important and powerful consumer group. Teen shoppers spend nearly $150 billion of their own and their parents' money each year. An important characteristic of *how* teens shop is that they often do so with friends. Recent research indicates that when teens shop in groups, retailers can benefit. Teens exert powerful positive peer influence on one another when shopping. They provide both information and reinforcement about the wisdom of specific purchases.

Peer pressure is nothing new. You have probably been in many situations where friends have influenced your behavior—either positively or negatively. Yet peer influence is not explicitly part of the standard consumer model. That teen consumers' tastes and preferences are influenced in a positive way by having "purchase pals" may be welcome news to retailers. Research using data from more than 300 teen shoppers showed that teens who reported enjoying shopping with friends tended to spend more than those who did not. Also, a tendency to shop often with friends led teens to spend more than those who did not. Certainly part of the increase might be due to information that teen shoppers get from friends about product characteristics. But it might also be that young shoppers do not want to appear cheap in front of their friends, or don't want to be left out when a group of friends makes purchases. In the language of consumer theory, their tastes and preferences are altered (toward increased consumption) when shopping with friends.

Critical-Thinking Questions

1. How might retailers take advantage of the findings of this study?
2. For which types of stores do you think these findings are most important? Least important?

SUMMARY

- **Budget analysis.** All consumers must make choices based on limited incomes by allocating their incomes across all the goods and services that they consume or would like to consume. This budget limitation acts as a constraint on their efforts to maximize their well-being, or utility.

- **Consumer behavior and utility theory.** The model of consumer preferences rests on the assumptions that consumers are utility-maximizers, are rational, and have perfect foresight. The total satisfaction they derive from consumption is total utility. Marginal utility is the additional satisfaction derived from consuming one additional unit of a good or service. As more and more units are consumed, the marginal utility derived from the last unit declines.

---

[4] Based on Tamara F. Mangleburg, Patricia M. Doney, and Terry Bristol, "Shopping with Friends and Teens' Susceptibility to Peer Influence," *Journal of Retailing*, March 2004, vol. 80, no. 2, pages 101–117.

- **Achieving consumer equilibrium.** Consumers maximize utility subject to their budget constraints. In doing so, they allocate income to the good or service that provides them with the highest marginal utility. The equimarginal principle states that consumers will allocate their income such that the marginal utility per dollar spent on the last unit of each good or service is the same and all income is spent.

- **From utility maximization to individual demand.** By changing the price of one good or service and holding income and other prices constant, we show how consumers respond to price changes. These responses form the individual's demand for the commodity.

▶KEY TERMS

Budget line 169	Equimarginal principle 180	Substitution effect 183
Consumer behavior 168	Income effect 183	Total utility 173
Consumer equilibrium 180	Marginal utility 174	Utility 172
Consumption basket 170	Marginal utility per	
Diminishing marginal	dollar 177	
utility 175		

▶PROBLEMS

1. Antonio likes to chew gum while he plays baseball. The following table shows the utility he derives from chewing various amounts of gum in the course of one game:

Pieces of Gum	Total Utility
0	0
1	20
2	45
3	60
4	70
5	75
6	75
7	60

   a. Draw a graph of the total utility that Antonio derives from gum chewing.
   b. Create a table showing the marginal utility that he receives from each piece of gum.
   c. Draw the marginal utility graph similar to 7.4(b).
   d. At what point does diminishing marginal utility set in?
   e. At what point does marginal utility reach zero?
   f. Assume that gum costs five cents per piece ($0.05). Make a new column in your table showing the marginal utility per dollar.

2. Sunita buys mystery novels and comic books. Mystery novels cost $4 each, and comic books cost $2 each. Her budget for all reading materials is $20 per month. The marginal utility (MU) she receives from units of each is shown in the following table:

Q	$MU_{\text{Mysteries}}$	MU_{Comics}
0	—	—
1	80	20
2	40	16
3	20	13
4	8	10
5	4	4

a. Add a column showing marginal utility per dollar for each commodity.
b. Find the consumption combination that satisfies the requirements for consumer equilibrium.
c. Notice that the marginal utility of an additional unit falls so much faster for novels than for comic books? Why might this be so?

3. Ignacio likes to collect skateboards and read books. He has $500 per year to allocate toward consumption of skateboards and books. Skateboards cost $100 each, and books cost $50 each.
a. What is the maximum number of skateboards Ignacio can buy?
b. What is the maximum number of books he can buy?
c. Draw the budget constraint, placing books on the vertical axis and skateboards on the horizontal axis.
d. What is the slope of the budget constraint? What does the slope tell you about the trade-off rate between the two goods?

4. Koki buys running shoes and concert tickets. Running shoes cost $75 per pair, and concert tickets cost $50 each. Draw the budget constraint, assuming that Koki's income is $1,500 per month. On the same graph, show how the constraint changes if her income falls to $1,200 per month.

5. Jacob uses his allowance of $5.00 per week to buy baseball cards and candy bars. Candy bars are $0.50 each and baseball cards are $0.50 per pack. Draw the budget constraint with candy bars on the horizontal axis. Show how the budget line changes if the price of baseball cards increases to $1.00 per pack.

Use the data in the following table to answer Problems 6 and 7.

Quantity of Ice Cream Cones	Total Utility
0	0
1	25
2	55
3	70
4	77
5	77
6	70

6. The above table shows the quantity of ice cream cones Marci consumes, and the total utility she derives from consumption.
a. Create an additional column indicating the marginal utility.
b. At what point does diminishing marginal utility set in?
c. At what point does diminishing total utility set in?
d. Graph total and marginal utility on separate graphs.
e. Describe the relationship between marginal utility and total utility in this case.

7. Use the data in the table above in Problem 6 to create a new table showing marginal utility per dollar, assuming that ice cream cones cost $2 each.
8. What assumptions do we make about consumer behavior with respect to consumers' actions? For each assumption you list, give an example that violates the assumption.
9. Use the concept of marginal utility to explain why restaurants that offer free refills on drinks do not end up having to provide an unlimited quantity.
10. Every day, Sylvia buys a can of soda to go with her lunch. She puts $0.50 into the vending machine, and tries to press two different buttons at exactly the same time so that the soda that appears is essentially a random choice between the two. Is she irrational?
11. Why are newspaper vending machines designed so that after paying you can take as many papers as you want but candy vending machines are not?
12. The following table shows the utility that Darius gets from consuming hot dogs and soda. If hot dogs cost $1.00 each, sodas cost $0.50 each, and Darius has $6.00 to spend, how should he allocate his income so as to maximize his utility?

Quantity	Total Utility from Soda	Total Utility from Hot Dogs
0	0	0
1	20	30
2	29	48
3	35	60
4	40	70
5	43	75

13. Use the table from Problem 12 to answer the following questions:
    a. If Darius has $3.00, how many of each good will Darius buy? (*Hint:* Begin at zero units of each good and spend each dollar such that it generates the largest increase in utility.)
    b. What is true about the marginal utility per dollar spent on the last soda and last hot dog at his chosen allocation?
14. Suppose coffee costs $1.00 per cup and donuts cost $0.50 each. If the marginal utility Jamal receives from the last cup of coffee he buys is 20 and the marginal utility of the last donut is 30, is he maximizing his utility? If not, which good should he buy more of?
15. How would you rewrite the consumer equilibrium condition (the equimarginal principle) if there were four commodities—X, Y, Z, and M—instead of only two?

16. David buys five goods. The total utility (*TU*) he derives from consuming the various units of each good are shown in the following table. His income is $41. The price of good A is $3.00, the price of good B is $2.50; the price of good C is $5.00; the price of good D is $6.00; and the price of good E is $1.50. Use the income, prices, and information in the following table to find David's consumer equilibrium. At the equilibrium, how many units of each good does he buy?

	TU from Good A	*TU* from Good B	*TU* from Good C	*TU* from Good D	*TU* from Good E
1	16	30	24	25	5
2	30	50	44	49	8
3	42	65	59	69	10
4	50	75	66	69	10
5	48	80	70	64	7

17. How do shoe stores manage to keep selling store-brand sneakers even if consumers know that they are not as durable or comfortable as name-brand sneakers?

18. Use marginal utility to explain why ski resorts do not allow individuals to transfer their lift tickets to others during the course of a day.

19. Suppose that you can allocate your budget across three goods. Your marginal utility for two of the goods declines, as in any typical case. For the third good, however, your marginal utility remains constant. Does this mean that you should buy only this third good? Why or why not?

Appendix for Chapter 7

Indifference Curves and Deriving the Demand Curve

As an alternative to finding utility-maximizing baskets by equating the marginal utility per dollar of each good consumed, we can use graphical analysis to show the choices that individuals make. In this appendix, we develop the indifference curve, and show how it can be used with budget constraints to identify utility-maximizing consumption combinations.

▶ Indifference Curves

Indifference curve
Compares consumption alternatives for two goods or services, showing combination baskets that each give the consumer the same level of total utility.

An **indifference curve** compares consumption alternatives for two goods or services, showing baskets that give the consumer the same level of total utility. The consumer is "indifferent" to all points on the curve, because he or she is just as well off at one point as at another. Thus, each indifference curve represents a specific level of utility.

Figure 7A.1 shows two indifference curves representing combinations of pizza and CDs for a particular consumer, Jennifer. Along each curve, her utility is constant—she has the same utility level when consuming at point A on U_1 as at point B or point C. She would be better off if she could move up to the next indifference curve, U_2. She could then have more of one good without sacrificing any of the other, or even more of both goods. For example, compare point B' on U_2 to point B on U_1. Jennifer could have two more pizzas and another CD if she moved to B'. When two or more indifference curves are shown on the same graph, the indifference curve farthest from the origin represents the highest level of utility (in this case, U_2). We typically show only a few curves in any one graph to give an idea

Indifference map
The set of all a consumer's indifference curves, which covers all possible consumption combinations.

of the consumer's preferences. However, there are actually an infinite number of these curves. Together, all a consumer's indifference curves, which cover all possible consumption combinations, form an indifference map. An **indifference map** is similar to a topographic map, in that it shows which direction a consumer should travel (specifically, which good or service to consume more of) to maximize utility.

▶ Properties of Indifference Curves

The indifference curves shown in Figure 7A.1 exhibit the standard properties of indifference curves. In the following sections, we review these properties, and note which might not always hold.

Indifference Curves Are Negatively Sloped

Most indifference curves are negatively sloped. The negative slope implies a trade-off between the two goods or services. Remember that utility is held constant along the curve. So, if Jennifer gives up some of one good, she must be compensated with more of the other good. For example, if she moves from point A to point B, and then from point B to point C in Figure 7A.1, she is sacrificing pizza to obtain CDs. The trade-off is driven by the notion that if consumers are maximizers, they will prefer more to less of the goods they consume. If indifference curves are positively sloped, having more of both goods gives Jennifer the same utility level as having less of both. This is the case if one of the products is a "bad," like garbage, instead of a desirable good.

Indifference Curves Are Usually Convex to the Origin

Most indifference curves are convex. That is, they are bowed inward toward the origin. Convexity is directly related to the notion of diminishing marginal utility. To

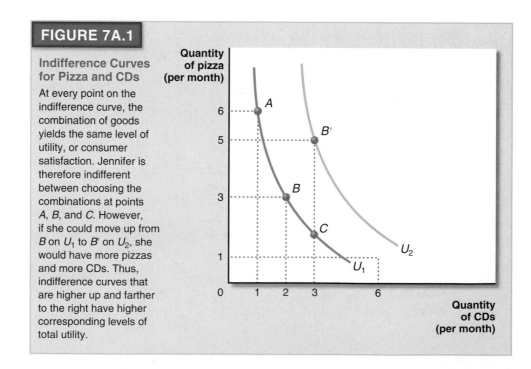

FIGURE 7A.1

Indifference Curves for Pizza and CDs

At every point on the indifference curve, the combination of goods yields the same level of utility, or consumer satisfaction. Jennifer is therefore indifferent between choosing the combinations at points A, B, and C. However, if she could move up from B on U_1 to B' on U_2, she would have more pizzas and more CDs. Thus, indifference curves that are higher up and farther to the right have higher corresponding levels of total utility.

FIGURE 7A.2

An Indifference Curve with a Convex Shape and Negative Slope

As we move down the indifference curve, total utility remains constant, but the marginal utility of the last good consumed on both the vertical and horizontal axes changes. For total utility to remain constant, at each point on the curve, a loss of utility for the last pizza consumed must be compensated for by an equal gain in utility for the last CD. The marginal rate of substitution declines as you move from *A* to *B* and *B* to *C*.

$MRS = \frac{-3}{1} = -3$

$MRS = \frac{-2}{1} = -2$

see why, let's return to Jennifer's tastes and preferences for pizza and CDs. At point A in Figure 7A.2, Jennifer has 10 pizzas but only 2 CDs. Thus, the marginal utility of the tenth pizza is fairly low given that she already has 9 pizzas. In contrast, the marginal utility of the second CD is much higher. Remember that, along an indifference curve, total utility is constant. Thus, when moving along the curve, whatever the marginal utility derived from an increase in one good (for example, more CDs) must be exactly offset by the loss in utility caused by the decrease in consumption of the other. As Jennifer moves from point A to point B, she is willing to exchange three pizzas for one CD. We know that the marginal utility of the last pizza is now higher, while the marginal utility of the last CD is lower. As a result, the trade-off will not be the same when she makes her next move. When moving from B to C, she is willing to exchange two pizzas for one CD. This exchange rate is the **marginal rate of substitution (MRS)**, the rate at which an individual will exchange the good on the vertical axis for the good on the horizontal axis, holding utility constant. This exchange rate also describes the slope of the indifference curve. For example, the move from A to B is:

$$MRS = (7 - 10)/(3 - 2) = -3$$

The MRS from *B* to *C* is:

$$MRS = (5 - 7)/(4 - 3) = -2$$

Notice that the *MRS* declines as we move down the curve. This declining marginal rate of substitution is always present when the curves are convex.

Marginal rate of substitution (*MRS*)
The rate at which an individual will exchange the good or service on the vertical axis for the good or service on the horizontal axis, holding utility constant. This exchange rate also describes the slope of the indifference curve.

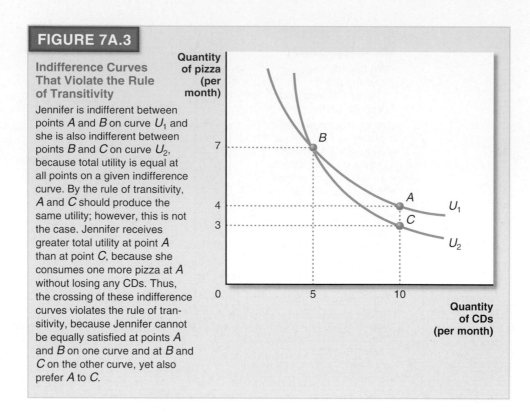

Indifference Curves That Violate the Rule of Transitivity

Jennifer is indifferent between points *A* and *B* on curve U_1 and she is also indifferent between points *B* and *C* on curve U_2, because total utility is equal at all points on a given indifference curve. By the rule of transitivity, *A* and *C* should produce the same utility; however, this is not the case. Jennifer receives greater total utility at point *A* than at point *C*, because she consumes one more pizza at *A* without losing any CDs. Thus, the crossing of these indifference curves violates the rule of transitivity, because Jennifer cannot be equally satisfied at points *A* and *B* on one curve and at *B* and *C* on the other curve, yet also prefer *A* to *C*.

Indifference Curves Do Not Intersect

Indifference curves can never intersect one another. If they did, they would violate an important assumption regarding consumer preferences known as *transitivity*. **Transitivity** is a logical property stating that if the consumer prefers *A* to *B*, and prefers *B* to *C*, he or she must also prefer *A* to *C*. When indifference curves intersect, consumer preferences are not transitive. To see why, suppose that Jennifer's preferences are described by the two indifference curves in Figure 7A.3. Based on U_1, she is indifferent between points *A* and *B*. Based on U_2, she is indifferent between points *B* and *C*. Transitivity requires that she also be indifferent between *A* and *C*. This is logically impossible, however, given that the points lie on two separate indifference curves that indicate two different levels of utility.

When the assumptions about consumer behavior hold, the resulting set of indifference curves is a set of thin, nonintersecting, convex lines, indicating higher utility as the consumer moves further from the origin. Because it would take many indifference curves to describe every possible utility level, we usually show only two or three to represent the rest.

Transitivity
A logical property requiring that if a consumer prefers A to B, and B to C, he or she must also prefer A to C.

Indifference Curves Can Be Used to Show the Utility-Maximizing Solution

Indifference curves show the exchanges that Jennifer is *willing* to make at each utility level. Recall that budget lines show the exchanges that she is *able* to make. We can combine the two to show the choice that she *will* make to maximize her utility subject to her budget constraint. Keep in mind that Jennifer's objective is to maximize utility; the budget line is the constraint. Economists call the process of maximizing utility subject to the individual's budget constraint **constrained maximization**.

Constrained maximization
The process of maximizing utility subject to the constraint of the consumer's budget.

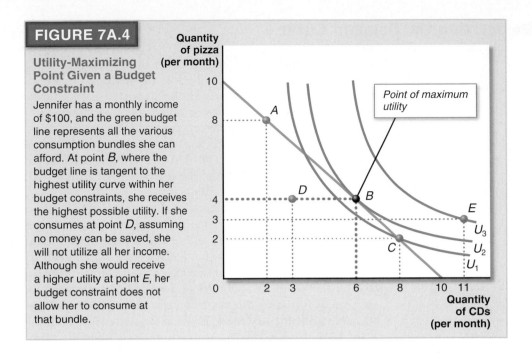

FIGURE 7A.4

Utility-Maximizing Point Given a Budget Constraint

Jennifer has a monthly income of $100, and the green budget line represents all the various consumption bundles she can afford. At point *B*, where the budget line is tangent to the highest utility curve within her budget constraints, she receives the highest possible utility. If she consumes at point *D*, assuming no money can be saved, she will not utilize all her income. Although she would receive a higher utility at point *E*, her budget constraint does not allow her to consume at that bundle.

Tangent
Describes a curved line that just touches a straight line at one single point. The slopes of tangent lines are equal at the point of tangency.

Jennifer maximizes her utility by choosing the basket that places her on an indifference curve that is as far from the origin as possible, yet still within the limit set by her budget constraint. Jennifer has a budget and therefore cannot consume more than her income allows.

Figure 7A.4 shows three indifference curves that illustrate Jennifer's preferences for pizza and CDs. It also shows her budget constraint, assuming that the price of pizzas and of CDs is $10 each, and that she has $100 of income to spend: This is the same budget constraint as that shown in Figure 7.1. Recall that the slope of the budget line is equal to the ratio of the prices of the two goods (with a negative sign added, because the line is negatively sloped to indicate that consumers must trade one good for another). In this case, the slope is –1.0. Thus, Jennifer is able to trade the goods one-for-one at any point on the line. The slope of the indifference curve (*MRS*) is not constant—the slope declines throughout as the quantity of CDs increases. So while the rate at which she is able to make exchanges remains constant, the rate at which she is willing to make exchanges does not.

The green budget line in Figure 7A.4 shows all the possible combinations of pizza and CDs that Jennifer can consume, given the prices and her $100 income. For example, she can consume at points *A*, *B*, or *C*. Given that her goal is to maximize utility, the best choice is clear. She should consume at point *B*. At this point, her budget line touches the highest possible indifference curve, U_2. When a curved line just touches a straight line at one single point, we say that the lines are **tangent**. The slopes of tangent lines are equal at the point of tangency. Thus, the rate at which Jennifer is willing to trade CDs for pizza is the same as the rate at which she is able to trade CDs for pizza at point *B*. She can make no additional change that increases her utility.

The two remaining points in the graph (*D* and *E*) are not on the budget line. Although Jennifer can afford to consume the basket of goods indicated by point *D* (four pizzas and three CDs), it does not exhaust her income. Because no savings are allowed in our model, we know that she never chooses this point. Moving to point *E* would increase her utility level to U_3, but she cannot afford to do so.

Deriving the Demand Curve

Recall that an individual demand curve shows the quantity demanded of a good (such as CDs) at various prices, while the prices of other goods (such as pizza), income, tastes, and preferences are held constant. We can use indifference curves and budget lines to show how Jennifer's choices change when the price of CDs changes, holding other parameters constant. The demand curve shows the quantity demanded at various prices. As a result, we need change only the price of one good while holding everything else constant to derive the demand curve for that good. To draw the demand curve, we plot the corresponding utility-maximizing baskets on a new graph that shows prices and quantities.

The graph in panel (a) of Figure 7A.5 reproduces the indifference curves of Figure 7A.4 with the initial budget line and two additional budget lines. The original budget line has a slope of –1.0, and reflects a price of $10 for each good and a $100 income. When Jennifer faces this budget line, she chooses to consume five CDs. What does she do if CDs are more expensive? The steeper budget line, with a horizontal axis intercept of about 7.7 ($7.7 \approx 100/13$), reflects an increase in the price of CDs from $10 to $13. At this price, she purchases only three CDs. If the price of CDs falls to $8, the new budget line is the flatter line with a horizontal axis intercept of 12.5 ($12.5 = 100/8$). At this lower price, Jennifer maximizes her utility by purchasing seven CDs. To draw her demand curve, transfer the quantity of CDs to the graph in panel (b) of Figure 7A.5, record the price on the vertical axis for each

FIGURE 7A.5

Using Changing Budget Lines to Draw a Demand Curve

Holding the price of pizza constant at $10, the budget line's slope changes as the price of CDs changes. The varying budget lines are tangent to indifference curves at different points, generating different utility-maximizing consumption combinations. To draw the demand curve for CDs, we record the prices on the vertical axis. We then plot the points relating the prices and the corresponding quantities of CDs bought. The line that connects all these points is Jennifer's demand curve for CDs, given the price of pizza and her level of income.

quantity, and connect the points. The resulting line is Jennifer's individual demand curve for CDs, given the price of pizza and an income of $100.

►SUMMARY

- **Indifference curves.** These lines show a consumer's preferences for two goods by mapping out all the combinations of the goods that a consumer regards as providing the same utility level. Each indifference curve depicts the combinations of goods for one utility level. An indifference map shows the set of indifference curves for a consumer for a given set of products.

- **Properties of indifference curves.** Indifference curves are usually negatively sloped and are typically convex to the origin (bowed inwards). Indifference curves never cross or touch one another for a given set of preferences. Indifference curves can be used (along with budget constraints) to show the utility-maximizing basket.

- **Deriving the demand curve.** Altering the price of one of the two goods also changes the budget constraint, because it alters the price ratio. If we alter the price of a good repeatedly and evaluate the changes in consumer behavior using the utility-maximizing points on the indifference map, we can sketch out the demand curve.

►KEY TERMS

Constrained maximization 192	Indifference map 190	Tangent 193
Indifference curve 189	Marginal rate of substitution (MRS) 191	Transitivity 192

►PROBLEMS

1. Why are indifference curves typically negatively sloped and convex?
2. Using the concept of marginal utility, explain why a consumer would be willing to move from point *A* to point *B* in Figure 7A.1.
3. Suppose that Janine buys only pencils and pens. She is indifferent between any of the following combinations of pencils and pens:

	A	*B*	*C*	*D*	*E*
Pencils	20	15	12	10	8
Pens	2	3	4	7	12

   a. Sketch the indifference curve. Put pens on the horizontal axis.
   b. What is the marginal rate of substitution between *A* and *B*; *B* and *C*; *C* and *D*; and *D* and *E*?
   c. Suppose that Janine has exactly $16 to allocate between these two goods, and that pens and pencils both cost $1 apiece. Plot the budget constraint and label the utility-maximizing point.

4. Suppose that an order of tacos costs $2, an order of fries costs $1, and your lunch budget is $20 per week. Draw a figure similar to Figure 7A.4 such that you maximize your utility by purchasing seven tacos and six orders of fries. (Draw your own indifference curve).

5. Not all indifference curves have the shapes described in the chapter.
   a. Suppose that you have to choose between two goods: ice cream (which you like), and eel soup (which you do not like). Draw a set of indifference curves that reflects your preferences. (*Hint:* Think about the trade-offs that you are willing to make.)
   b. What would the indifference curves for left and right shoes look like?
   c. What would indifference curves look like for butter and margarine for a consumer who cannot taste the difference?

HERE'S HOW MyEconLab CAN HELP YOU GET A BETTER GRADE

1. Log into MyEconLab and take Practice Test chapter-A (to log in for the first time, see page 30 for instructions.)
2. Based on your test results, MyEconLab will identify the areas where you need further work and create a personal Study Plan for you.
3. Your Study Plan contains the exercises listed below and others like them that will target the specific chapter topics you need to focus on. You'll receive instant feedback and find links to tutorials, animations, and the online textbook to help you study.
4. When you're ready, go take Practice Test chapter-B and demonstrate how your results have improved.

Section 7.1, Exercise 1 Tim has $150 per week to spend on CDs and pizza. Pizza costs $2 per slice, and CDs cost $15 per disc.

a. What is the equation of Tim's budget constraint?
b. Graph Tim's budget constraint, labeling the intercepts and slope.

Section 7.1, Exercise 2 Carolyn has $400 per month to spend on movies and concerts. Movies cost $10 per ticket, and concerts cost $50 per ticket.

a. Graph Carolyn's budget constraint, labeling the intercepts and slope.
b. Suppose that the price of concert tickets falls to $40. Graph the new budget constraint.
c. Return to the original prices, and suppose that Carolyn's income increases to $500 per month. Graph the new budget constraint.

Section 7.2, Exercise 1 The following table shows a consumer's utility from hamburgers.

Quantity of Hamburgers	Total Utility
0	0
1	15
2	25
3	29
4	31
5	31
6	30

a. Calculate marginal utility.
b. What is the maximum number of hamburgers that this consumer would eat if they were free?

Section 7.2, Exercise 2 The following table shows the marginal utility of movies viewed per month for Carolyn.

Quantity of Movies	Marginal Utility
0	–
1	50
2	30
3	20
4	10
5	5
6	0

a. Calculate Carolyn's total utility from movies.
b. Graph Carolyn's marginal and total utility from movies.

Section 7.3, Exercise 1 Rob is eating chocolate-chip cookies and milk. He gets 100 units of utility from his tenth cookie, and 400 units of utility from his fifth glass of milk. The price of milk is $1.00 per glass, and the price of a cookie is $0.50. Rob is currently spending all of his income.

a. Is Rob maximizing his utility? Demonstrate how you know.
b. Should Rob adjust his consumption choices, and if so, how?

Section 7.3, Exercise 2 Kristin likes to spend her summer at the pool, reading mysteries and eating ice cream. The following table shows the total utility that Kristin receives from consuming paperback books and ice-cream cones. The price of a paperback book is $10, and the price of an ice-cream cone is $1.

Quantity of Books	Marginal Utility per Dollar of the Last Book	Total Utility from Books	Quantity of Ice-Cream Cones	Marginal Utility per Dollar of the Last Ice-Cream Cone	Total Utility from Ice-Cream Cones
0		0	0		0
1		50	1		100
2		95	2		150
3		135	3		175
4		170	4		187
5		200	5		193
6		225	6		196
7		245	7		198
8		260	8		199
9		270	9		199
10		275	10		196

a. Calculate marginal utility per dollar for each good.
b. If Kristin's income is $56, what is her utility-maximizing choice of ice cream and books?
c. If Kristin's income rises to $99, what is her new utility-maximizing choice of ice cream and books?

Section 7.4, Exercise 1 Refer to the table in the previous exercise.

a. Suppose that Kristin's income is $56, and that the price of ice cream increases to $4. What is Kristin's utility-maximizing choice now?
b. Graph Kristin's demand for ice cream.

Section 7.4, Exercise 2 Alyssa buys four sweaters when the price is $25. When the price falls to $15, she buys seven sweaters.

a. Graph the approximate shape of Alyssa's demand curve.
b. Carefully describe the income and substitution effects of the drop in the price of sweaters.

Appendix, Exercise 1 Pam is choosing between magazines and books. Her indifference curves and budget constraint are shown on the following graph.

a. Identify Pam's utility-maximizing point.
b. Suppose that the price of books falls. Draw a new budget constraint and show the approximate effect on her utility-maximizing choice.

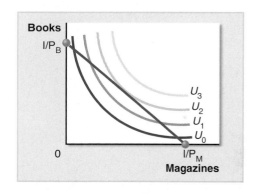

Appendix, Exercise 2 Stephanie buys DVDs and movie tickets. Movie tickets cost $10, and DVDs cost $15. Stephanie is currently spending all of her income buying 10 DVDs and 10 movie tickets. Asked about her choice, she says, "I really love movies. I received twice as much utility from the tenth movie as I did from the tenth DVD."

a. Graph Stephanie's budget constraint, putting movie tickets on the horizontal axis. What is the price ratio?
b. What is Stephanie's *MRS* (of DVDs for movie tickets)?
c. Is it possible that Stephanie is maximizing utility with her current choices? If not, how should her choice be changed?

8 Firm Production and Cost

Seth has played the guitar ever since he was in middle school. He also has a natural aptitude as a woodworker. Although his primary occupation is as a cabinetmaker, he has been making his own guitars for many years. He has started making special orders for other musicians. In fact, there seem to be a lot of musicians that want to buy one of his guitars. Finally, Seth decides, it's time to figure out what it would take to make a living with his guitar-making business. He isn't sure how many people he should hire and how many guitars his new company, Seth's Guitarworks, should try to produce each year. There are a lot of decisions to make.

As consumers, we don't often think about the many decisions that must be made when producing the goods that we consume. A guitar player, for instance, is most concerned with the sound and feel of a finished instrument. But for the firm that manufactures the guitar, choosing the best combination of physical capital and labor is as important as the guitar itself. In the beginning, at least, Seth's Guitarworks will produce a small quantity of instruments almost completely by hand, with simple tools and many hours of labor devoted to each guitar. A large corporation using a factory equipped with sophisticated machinery that automates much of the production process might, in contrast, be able to produce a similar guitar at lower cost with relatively few hours of labor. In general, the level of technology employed, the skills required of the workers, and even the physical size and cost of the machinery needed all help determine whether an industry will comprise many small firms, or only a few very large ones.

In this chapter, we shift our focus from the demand side of the market to the supply side, and from the consumer's perspective to the firm's perspective. We will establish many of the building blocks and tools that will be important as we consider the firm's role in markets in later chapters.

ALONG THE WAY, YOU WILL ALSO LEARN:

- What firms are and why they exist.
- The choices that managers make to turn labor and capital into products.
- How economists measure the productivity of labor in the short run.
- How economists measure costs in the short run.
- Why firms might want to change size, and how long-run costs are determined.

AT THE END OF THE CHAPTER,
THE MYECONLAB LOGO WILL DIRECT YOU ONLINE

- MyEconLab is a resource-packed online homework and tutorial system that can help you perform better in your economics course. To log in for the first time, see page 30 for instructions.
- MyEconLab can help you apply important concepts from the chapter to real-world issues. Watch for the logo to indicate online features about short- and long-run production decisions.
- At the end of each chapter, you'll find a special study section that will help you get the most out of your textbook and your instructor's MyEconLab course.

 ## The Motivation of Firms

Firm
An organization that employs resources (capital, labor, and materials) to produce goods and services.

Profits
The difference between the total revenue that a firm receives from selling its output and the total cost it incurs to produce that output.

Accounting profits
A measure of profit that takes into account explicit costs and the cost of interest payments on loans and depreciation.

Explicit costs
The costs of inputs that are incurred through payment to the owner of the resource.

Implicit cost
A cost of production that requires no direct money payment by the firm.

What exactly is a firm? Why do firms exist? A **firm** is an organization that employs resources (capital, labor, and materials) to produce goods and services. Firms range from huge corporations with thousands of employees to the sole proprietorships or limited partnerships (discussed in Chapter 3) with only a handful of employees.

When you read the question "Why do firms exist?," you may have immediately thought to answer, "Firms exist to make money." If so, your answer is correct. On the supply side, firms produce guitars and thousands of other goods and services with the goal of maximizing their profits. **Profits** are the difference between the total revenue that a firm receives from selling its output and the total cost it incurs to produce that output. The central question we begin addressing in this section is *how* the firm should combine resources to earn the greatest profit.

The Firm's Profits

To illustrate how a firm determines profits, let's again consider Seth, our successful cabinetmaker contemplating leaving his current job to enter the guitar-manufacturing business. His opportunity costs are significant, in that he must forgo his current salary to start the business. His possible accounting and economic profits vary. **Accounting profits** include explicit costs and the cost of interest payments on loans and depreciation. **Explicit costs** are the cost of inputs that are obtained through payment to the owner of the resource, such as the cost of labor and materials. (An **implicit cost** requires no direct money payment by the firm.) **Depreciation** is the allowance that a firm makes for the decrease in the value of its capital stock over

TABLE 8.1

Accounting Profits Versus Economic Profits

Total revenue for Seth's Guitarworks Less explicit costs and depreciation	$130,000
Materials	−35,000
Labor	−20,000
Capital and depreciation	−5,000
Accounting profits:	70,000
Less implicit opportunity costs	−50,000
Economic profits:	20,000

Depreciation
The allowance that a firm makes for the decrease in the value of its capital stock over the course of a year.

Economic profits
Are calculated as revenue minus explicit costs, depreciation, and opportunity costs.

the course of the year. Firms must account for depreciation because, over time, capital equipment wears out and needs to be replaced. **Economic profits** subtract the same explicit costs and depreciation costs from revenues that accounting profits do, but they also include an important implicit cost: opportunity cost.

Let's now measure these profit concepts for Seth's business venture. Suppose that Seth can earn $130,000 in one year of producing and selling guitars. The cost of materials is $35,000; he pays $20,000 to an assistant; and the cost of his capital equipment, including an allowance for depreciation, is $5,000. As a result, it seems that Seth is earning $70,000 ($130,000 −$35,000 −$20,000 −$5,000). Yet, if we include the opportunity cost of Seth's labor in producing the guitars (the $50,000 that he could otherwise earn as a cabinetmaker), his economic profits are only $20,000 ($130,000 −$35,000 −$20,000 −$5,000 −$50,000). Table 8.1 summarizes the calculation of Seth's accounting and economic profits.[1] Managers and owners of firms report accounting profits in their statements to the government (for tax purposes) and, in the case of corporations, to shareholders. However, managers and owners make decisions based on economic profits. As a result, we must factor opportunity costs into the decision process.

The Firm's Production of Goods

Production
The transformation of inputs—capital, labor, and materials—into output.

Production is the transformation of inputs—capital, labor, and materials—into output. To look beyond the simple statement that "firms exist to make money," we must examine the choices that firm managers make regarding how to combine inputs to maximize profits.

Let's once again consider Seth. Our career woodworker has now turned into an entrepreneur, the owner of Seth's Guitarworks. His goal is to maximize profits by producing guitars using optimal combinations of capital and labor. Seth now rents a barn workshop, and has taken out a loan to purchase the necessary capital. He has hired permanent employees with specific skills, including a sales force. He combines

---

[1] Another form of opportunity cost is forgone interest on financial capital. For example, if Seth purchases machinery to produce guitars at a cost of $100,000, the opportunity cost of purchasing the machinery is the interest that he would have earned if he had left the $100,000 in the bank.

the capital and labor to produce the guitars, makes the monthly rent and loan payments, and pays the employees using revenue generated by the sales force. The residual revenue is profit that he can keep for himself.

The Firm's Transactions Costs

Transactions costs
The costs of making all the exchanges necessary to produce an item.

Seth *could* produce guitars without a firm. However, by forming a firm, Seth can make *more* profit than otherwise, because he can reduce the cost of organizing, supervising, planning, and coordinating production. Together, these costs are called **transactions costs**, or the costs of making all the exchanges necessary to produce an item. These might be administrative costs, such as the cost of negotiating labor contracts and rental agreements. They might also include the opportunity cost of the time required to travel between subcontractors, and the time needed to hire and train a labor force.

An internalized transaction is a process or exchange that occurs within a firm rather than in the market (for instance, when a firm hires a clerk to process the payroll instead of having another firm perform the payroll function). When a transaction is internalized, the firm gives up a powerful incentive mechanism—the market. (A firm with its own payroll clerk cannot also try to minimize costs by having the payroll processing firm bid for the right to provide those same services.) In Seth's case, he needs to put tuners on the guitars before they are shipped. While the guitar itself is made mostly of wood, the tuners are made of metal and contain small gears that tighten or loosen the guitar strings. Producing a metal guitar tuner requires very different technology, equipment, and know-how than producing a wooden guitar body does. If Seth decides to make his own tuners and does a poor job, it is his problem to solve. What if he purchases tuners from an outside vendor that turn out to be poorly made? He can use the power of the market to solve his problem by either switching or threatening to switch to another supplier. As a rule, *firms should internalize transactions if doing so reduces costs, and use the market if internalizing transactions raises costs.* The key advantage of producing in the context of a firm is that firms can reduce transactions costs. Reducing transactions costs is essential to minimizing total cost, and in turn, to maximizing profits.

▶ Production: Turning Inputs into Outputs

Firms can typically choose from among many possible ways to combine inputs. Though production of guitars (or cars, pizzas, and most other goods) involves the use of many different inputs, our primary focus will be on capital and labor. We've established that firms seek to maximize profits. In this section, we outline the remaining key assumptions of a production model.

Capital and Labor

Recall that we introduced capital and labor in Chapter 2. We use the term "capital" to indicate physical capital (not financial capital, or money the firm raises). Capital (K) includes the plant and equipment used to produce goods and services.[2] In a guitar factory, capital includes everything from the hand and power tools to the ventilation fans used to reduce dust.

---

[2] Economists use K as the symbol for capital even though it is spelled with a C: the letter C is used to represent cost.

Labor (L) is the entire pool of physical and mental talents available to produce goods and services. As with capital, this single variable summarizes many different inputs, from skilled artisans to accountants to the person who sweeps the sawdust from the factory floor. In a more detailed study, we would include each type of labor as a unique input. To keep the model simple, however, we assume that all workers are equally productive.

Time Period

Depending on the length of time under consideration, a firm might face many choices of how to combine capital and labor, only a few choices, or no choice at all. We simplify the role that time plays in the model of production by specifying two time periods: the short run and the long run.

Short run
A span of time so brief that there is at least one fixed input.

Fixed input
An input that a firm is incapable of increasing or decreasing in the time period under consideration (usually capital).

Variable input
An input that can be changed in the short run (usually labor).

Long run
The time period in which a firm can change all inputs.

Distinguishing the Short Run from the Long Run. The **short run** is a span of time so brief that there is at least one fixed input. A **fixed input** is one that a firm is incapable of increasing or decreasing in the time period under consideration. In contrast, inputs that can be changed in the short run are **variable inputs**.

In the case of two inputs, we typically assume that capital (such as buildings and equipment) is fixed, and that labor is variable. Capital includes the inputs that are relatively difficult for a firm to change. Labor represents all inputs that the firm can change fairly easily. Because we assume that capital is fixed, we also assume that in the short run, the number of firms in the industry is fixed. Indeed, in order for a new firm to enter, it must increase its capital stock, which we specifically assume to be fixed in the short run. The **long run** is the time period in which a firm can change all inputs. In the long run, a firm can choose how much labor and how much capital to use. Technology, which is typically associated with capital, is also variable in the long run. Firms may alter the level and mix of inputs in the long run, as they seek to produce their chosen output levels most efficiently. In addition, the number of firms in the industry in the long run is variable.

Determining the Time Period. The definitions of short run and long run create a useful framework for decision making. Think of the long run as the firm's planning horizon. Firms always operate in the short run. The long run is a set of options that the firm may pursue if it needs to grow or to scale back to meet demand most effectively.

Notice that our definitions of the short run and long run never mention whether the short run is measured in weeks, months, or years. This lack of specificity is quite intentional.[3] Depending on the industry, the state of technology, and the initial size of the firm, the long-run planning horizon may be as short as a day or two, or as long as several years. Suppose that the owner of a hot dog stand finds that she cannot produce all the hot dogs that she could sell in the short run. Increasing capacity—a long-run decision—might be as simple as stopping at a kitchen supply store on the way home to buy a four-burner stove to replace her two-burner stove.

In contrast, consider the case of CF Martin & Co., a guitar manufacturer with a longstanding reputation for quality. In the 1990s, it could no longer meet the demand for its products with its existing 95,000-square-foot plant in Nazareth,

---

[3] If you have taken an accounting course, you might have learned that the long run is defined as a period of more than one year. In economics we make no such distinction.

Pennsylvania. In response, the company nearly doubled the size of the plant. The expansion took more than a year to complete.[4] The implementation of long-run decisions requires an even lengthier time horizon in industries such as power generation, automobile manufacturing, and shipbuilding, where meaningful increases in plant size or construction of new plants are measured in years.

Production Model Assumptions

In summary, the assumptions behind the economic model of production are as follows:

- Firms want to maximize profits.
- In order to maximize profits, firms must try to produce each output level at minimum cost.
- All workers are equally productive.
- In the short run, capital is fixed; in the long run, all inputs are variable.

▶ Short-Run Production

Production function
A description of the relationship between the quantity of inputs used and the output produced, using either a table or a graph.

Total product (*TP*)
A synonym for the quantity of output, *Q*, in discussions of production and cost.

Total product curve
Shows the relationship between the quantity of labor used (on the horizontal axis) and the quantity of output produced (on the vertical axis) for a fixed amount of capital.

With the assumptions underlying our model of production in place, we can now focus on the short-run production decisions of Seth's Guitarworks. In the short run, Seth has a fixed amount of capital available to produce guitars, but he can add or subtract labor whenever he wishes.

The Total Product of Labor and the Production Function

We've established that production is the conversion of inputs into output. A **production function** is a mathematical relationship between the quantity of inputs used and the output produced. We can show the production function using either a table or a graph. When discussing production and cost, **total product (*TP*)** is a synonym for the quantity of output (*Q*). Both *TP* and *Q* represent the amount of guitars that Seth and his labor force produce per time period. Panel (a) of Figure 8.1 shows the production function in table form as a list of the quantity of guitars that Seth can produce in one month using anywhere from 0 to 10 workers. The righthand column, labeled "Quantity of Guitars," gives the *total product* of the workforce. Panel (b) of Figure 8.1 illustrates the total product curve. Like the data in Table 8.1, the **total product curve** shows the relationship between the quantity of labor, or workers

[4] Source: CF Martin & Co. Web site, www.martinguitar.com/news/index.html; accessed January 30, 2005.

FIGURE 8.1

The Production Function and the Total Product Curve

The table in panel (a) shows changes in the number of guitars that Seth can produce with a fixed quantity of capital and different amounts of labor. In panel (b), the total product curve (*TP*) shows the same production function. With each additional worker that Seth hires, the quantity of guitars produced changes. Quantity of output rises quickly at first, but with the addition of the fourth worker, it begins to increase more slowly. Output reaches its peak when Seth adds the eighth worker, but the addition of a ninth worker does not increase the number of guitars produced each month.

(a) Total product of labor per month for 0 to 10 workers

Quantity of Labor	Quantity of Guitars
0	0
1	6
2	16
3	28
4	38
5	46
6	52
7	56
8	58
9	58
10	54

(b) The total product curve

Average product of labor (*AP*)
The total product divided by the number of workers who produced it.

used (on the horizontal axis), and the quantity of output produced (on the vertical axis) for a fixed amount of capital.

The Average Product of Labor

To determine how productive labor is, we can compute the **average product of labor (*AP*)**, or the total product of labor divided by the number of workers who produced it, as shown in Equation 8.1.

$$AP = \text{Total product/Number of workers who produced the output} \quad (8.1)$$

Using the information from panel (a) of Figure 8.1, we see that if Seth employs 7 workers, he produces 56 guitars. Thus, the average product of labor is 56/7 = 8 guitars per worker. With 10 workers, the average product of labor is 54/10 = 5.4 guitars per worker. It is extremely important to note that the average product of labor does not tell us how many guitars *each* worker produces; it provides only the average productivity of all workers. Economic decisions are made at the margin, so we must move beyond a simple average to find the effect of the marginal worker.

The Marginal Product of Labor

Notice that in Figure 8.1, no guitars are produced when there is no labor input. When the quantity of labor increases and is combined with the fixed quantity of capital, output rises quickly at first but then grows more and more slowly. Eventually, when the ninth worker is added to the production process, no additional output is produced. Worse yet, adding a tenth worker actually causes output to go down. Are these last few workers lazy or unskilled? That cannot be, as we assume that all labor is equally productive.

Marginal product of labor (*MPL*)
The change in output that results from a one-unit increase in the quantity of labor. Because it measures changes in actual output (as opposed to changes in sales revenue from output), it is also sometimes called the *marginal physical product of labor.*

To understand this unexpected result, we must examine *changes in output* rather than *total output* produced as labor increases. As with most decisions in economics, we want to focus on marginal changes, not the total amount. The **marginal product of labor (*MPL*)** is the change in output that results from adding one more worker (Equation 8.2). Because it measures changes in actual output (as opposed to changes in sales revenue from output), it is also sometimes called the *marginal physical product of labor.* To compute the marginal product of labor, we take the ratio of the change in output to the change in labor.

$$MPL = \text{Change in total product/Change in labor} \qquad (8.2)$$

Applying this equation shows, for example, that the marginal product of the first worker is 6 and the marginal product of the fourth worker is 10. In this case, the incremental change in labor is always one unit, or one worker.

For the first unit of labor: $MPL = (6 - 0)/(1 - 0) = 6$
For the fourth unit of labor: $MPL = (38 - 28)/(4 - 3) = 10$

Panel (a) of Figure 8.2 adds marginal and average product to the output data from panel (a) of Figure 8.1. Panel (b) of Figure 8.2 shows average and marginal product in graph form. As with marginal utility in Chapter 7, we show the marginal product values over the interval from one unit of labor to the next.

Analyzing the data in panel (a) of Figure 8.2, we can now identify how output changes as more and more workers are combined with a fixed amount of capital. The table shows important changes in the marginal product of labor, which are also reflected in the marginal product of labor curve in panel (b) of Figure 8.2. Looking at the third column of the table, we see that for the first three units of labor, each additional worker adds more to output than the previous worker. The marginal product of the third worker is 12, more than any other worker.

Specialization of labor
Instead of each worker performing multiple tasks, each worker devotes his time to a single task or a few related tasks.

Why would marginal product increase for the first few workers? The answer lies in the specialization of labor. When Seth works by himself—the second row in panel (a) of Figure 8.2—he can produce only six guitars per month, partly because he has to perform all the tasks himself. Economists say that he *underutilizes* the capital; that is, he does not use it to its full capacity. If Seth had a co-worker, together they could produce *more* than twice as much output as a single worker, because less time would be lost switching tasks, and each could specialize in certain activities. **Specialization of labor** means that instead of each worker performing multiple tasks, each worker devotes his time to a single task or a few

FIGURE 8.2

Average and Marginal Product and the Law of Diminishing Marginal Returns

The table in panel (a) shows the average and marginal product of labor for the first 10 workers at Seth's Guitarworks over the course of a month. Capital remains fixed. Panel (b) plots the same data in graph form. When Seth adds 2 new workers to his fixed physical capital, marginal product (*MPL*) increases quickly, up to point *A*. Between points *A* and *B*, when there are 3 to 8 workers, output is still increasing; however, *MPL* has begun decreasing in accordance with the Law of Diminishing Marginal Returns. After point *B*, *MPL* becomes negative, because the addition of new workers actually reduces the number of guitars produced. The average product of labor curve (*AP*) is upward-sloping to the point where *MPL* crosses it, and downward-sloping thereafter.

(a) Total, marginal, and average product of labor per month for 0 to 10 workers

Quantity of Labor	Quantity of Guitars	Marginal Product of Labor	Average Product of Labor
0	0		—
		6	
1	6		6
		10	
2	16		8
		12	
3	28		9.33
		10	
4	38		9.5
		8	
5	46		9.2
		6	
6	52		8.67
		4	
7	56		8
		2	
8	58		7.25
		0	
9	58		6.44
		−4	
10	54		5.4

(b) Marginal and average product curves

related tasks. Specialization can increase output dramatically, and it is a hallmark of all assembly line–type production.

The Law of Diminishing Marginal Returns. In panel (b) of Figure 8.2, when the third worker is hired, the marginal product curve reaches its highest point, *A*, and remains greater than zero up to point *B*. Between *A* and *B*, guitar production continues to increase when another worker is added, but output increases more and more slowly with each additional worker. In this section of the table and graph, we say that production is characterized by diminishing returns.

The **Law of Diminishing Marginal Returns** states that *as more and more units of the variable input (labor) are combined with the fixed input (capital), the marginal product of the variable input must eventually decline.* Diminishing marginal returns set in because the workers have only so much capital to utilize. Seth has a fixed quantity of capital that all workers must share. As he hires additional workers, each worker has less access to the saws, mallets, clamps, sanding equipment, and space required to work. At this stage, output increases by smaller increments with each additional worker. As Seth adds more and more labor, total output still rises, but *marginal* product—the additional output from an additional worker—declines.

Law of Diminishing Marginal Returns
As more and more units of the variable input (labor) are combined with the fixed input (capital), the marginal product of the variable input must eventually decline.

DILBERT: © Scott Adams/Dist. by United Feature Syndicate, Inc.

Notice that in the downward-sloping section of the marginal product curve in the graph in panel (b) of Figure 8.2, the marginal product curve passes through the average product curve when average product is at its highest point. Whenever the productivity of the marginal worker exceeds the average productivity, average productivity rises. Whenever the marginal value is less than the average value, the average falls. To see why, consider the heights of students arriving to a class. Suppose that the first two people in the room are both 65 inches tall. The average height of students in the room is 65 inches. If the next student (i.e., the marginal person) who walks in is 74 inches tall, the average increases to 68 inches ((65 + 65 + 74)/3 = 68). Because the marginal is greater than the average, the average rises. If the next (marginal) student who enters is shorter than the current average—say, 64 inches tall—the average height falls to 67 inches ((65 + 65 + 74 + 64)/4 = 67).

Finally, notice that when Seth hires the ninth worker, in panel (b) of Figure 8.2, output remains constant at 54 guitars, so the marginal product of the ninth worker is 0. The marginal product of the tenth worker is –4. As a result, Seth's firm produces fewer guitars with 10 workers than with 9. In panel (b) of Figure 8.2, the marginal product of labor is negative beyond point B. Seth has so many workers attempting to build guitars, in such tight quarters, with so few machines, that adding the tenth worker causes production to decline. Such a dilemma is certainly possible. Rational firm owners don't allow this scenario to occur, because to have more workers *and* less output unequivocally reduces profits.

The Law of Diminishing Marginal Returns and the Marginal Product Curve. The Law of Diminishing Marginal Returns is the single most important concept in our study of the short run, because it governs the productivity of a firm whenever one input is fixed. We summarize the relationship between the Law of Diminishing Marginal Returns and the marginal product curve as follows:

- Increasing marginal returns: Marginal product of labor curve is rising.
- Decreasing marginal returns: Marginal product of labor curve is falling.
- Negative marginal returns: Marginal product of labor curve is less than zero.

TEST + *EXTEND* Your Knowledge

► Short-Run Cost

So far, we have established that workers become less productive as the firm adds more of them to a fixed amount of physical capital. Firms are not primarily interested in how productive their workers are. But they are interested in how much it costs for workers to produce their output. In this section, we see how the productivity of workers affects the cost of production. In fact, cost theory and production theory are simply two different ways of evaluating the transformation of inputs into outputs. The difference is that production theory focuses on physical units of inputs and outputs, while cost theory focuses on what firms pay to produce their output.

Fixed and Variable Cost

In the short run, Seth's Guitarworks must work with the capital stock that it has at hand. Seth must pay a fixed amount each month to cover the rent on the barn factory and make loan payments for all the equipment used to produce the guitars regardless of whether he produces 0 guitars or 50 guitars per month.

Fixed costs (*FC*)
Costs that cannot be changed in the short run and that do not change as the quantity of output produced rises or falls.

Fixed Costs. For Seth's Guitarworks, fixed costs are $4,000 per month. **Fixed costs (*FC*)** are costs that cannot be changed in the short run and that do not change as the quantity of output produced rises or falls (monthly rent and loan payments).

Variable costs (*VC*)
Costs that vary with output—if output increases, variable costs rise, and if output decreases, variable costs fall.

Variable Costs. Seth does have a choice as to how much labor to employ in the short run. As indicated in panel (a) of Figure 8.1, Seth can use as few as 0 workers and as many as he chooses. Thus, the cost of labor is a variable cost. **Variable costs (*VC*)** change with output—if output increases, variable costs rise, and if output decreases, variable costs fall. Let's suppose that Seth must pay each worker $2,000 per month. For each additional worker Seth hires, his variable costs increase by $2,000 per month.

Total cost (*TC*)
The sum of all fixed costs plus the sum of all variable costs.

Total Cost. As with the theory of production, the theory of cost looks at the relationship between inputs and output. The difference is that we use cost theory to quantify changes in firm activity using money as a measure, rather than counting physical units of inputs or output. Together, the sum of all fixed costs plus the sum of all variable costs equals **total cost (*TC*)**. See Equation 8.3. We usually assume that capital is the fixed input in the short run, and thus the cost of capital is fixed in the

LifeLessons

Sunk cost
A special kind of fixed cost that is not recoverable.

short run. Because labor is the variable input in the short run, labor costs are variable costs.

$$\text{Total fixed cost} + \text{Total variable cost} = \text{Total cost} \qquad (8.3)$$

Total Costs at Seth's Guitarworks

To study short-run cost at Seth's Guitarworks, we create a table similar to panel (a) of Figure 8.1 that focuses on the costs of producing various quantities of output (guitars) per month, shown in panel (a) of Figure 8.3.

Column 1 shows the quantity of labor required at Seth's Guitarworks to produce the output, and column 2 shows the possible monthly output levels. Column 3 shows the fixed cost of $4,000 per month. As implied by its name, this cost is always $4,000. Column 4 shows the quantity of labor multiplied by its monthly cost of $2,000 per person, which is the variable cost of producing the output level. Finally, column 5 shows the total cost of production.

Panel (b) of Figure 8.3 shows total fixed cost (*TFC*), total variable cost (*TVC*), and total cost (*TC*) in graph form. We derive the curves by plotting the output levels from column 2 on the horizontal axis, and the cost data (measured in dollars) from columns 3, 4, and 5 on the vertical axis. The constant distance between the total cost and total variable cost curves represents total fixed cost.

Average Cost Concepts

The information in panel (a) of Figure 8.3 describes the total cost of producing output, broken down into fixed and variable costs. However, it does not give much insight into the per-unit or average cost of producing additional output. You'll now learn how to calculate average costs. This information is valuable to firms because

FIGURE 8.3

Short-Run Costs per Month at Seth's Guitarworks

The table in panel (a) shows Seth's fixed, variable, and total costs for different output levels within a one-month period. Panel (b) shows the same information in graph form. In the short run, Seth faces a total fixed cost (*TFC*) of $4,000 each month, regardless of the quantity of guitars produced. Total variable cost (*TVC*) shows the labor cost associated with various levels of output. The total cost (*TC*) is the sum of the total fixed costs and the total variable costs. As a result, the distance between the *TC* and *TVC* curves remains constant.

(a) Fixed, variable, and total costs of possible monthly output levels

(b) Total fixed, total variable, and total cost curves

Quantity of Labor (1)	Quantity of Guitars (2)	Fixed Cost (3)	Variable Cost (4)	Total Cost (5)
0	0	$4,000	$0	$4,000
1	6	4,000	2,000	6,000
2	16	4,000	4,000	8,000
3	28	4,000	6,000	10,000
4	38	4,000	8,000	12,000
5	46	4,000	10,000	14,000
6	52	4,000	12,000	16,000
7	56	4,000	14,000	18,000
8	58	4,000	16,000	20,000

it allows them to calculate profits and profits per unit easily over many different output choices.

Average total cost (*ATC*)
The firm's total cost divided by the quantity of output it produces.

Average variable cost (*AVC*)
The total variable cost divided by output.

Average fixed cost (*AFC*)
The total fixed cost divided by output.

Calculating Average Total Cost. Average total cost (*ATC*) equals the firm's total cost divided by the quantity of output it produces (Equation 8.4). We compute **average variable cost (*AVC*)** and **average fixed cost (*AFC*)** in the same way (Equations 8.4 through 8.7): Average variable cost is the total variable cost divided by output, and average fixed cost is the total fixed cost divided by output. Note that we can also compute average total cost as the sum of average fixed cost and average variable cost (Equation 8.7). Panel (a) of Figure 8.4 shows the average cost data for Seth's Guitarworks.

$$ATC = \text{Total cost/Output} \tag{8.4}$$
$$AVC = \text{Total variable cost/Output} \tag{8.5}$$
$$AFC = \text{Total fixed cost/Output} \tag{8.6}$$
$$ATC = AFC + AVC \tag{8.7}$$

Graphing Average Costs. The cost data in panel (a) appear in graph form in panel (b) of Figure 8.4. The quantity of guitars is on the horizontal axis, and average cost in dollars is on the vertical axis. There are a few important things to note about the shape of the average cost curves. First, the average fixed cost curve slopes down

FIGURE 8.4

Average Fixed, Variable, and Total Cost Curves for Seth's Guitarworks

The average cost data in panel (a) is plotted in graph form in panel (b). As the quantity of guitars produced increases and fixed costs are spread over a larger number of units, average fixed cost (AFC) decreases, and the curve slopes down toward the horizontal axis. Average total cost (ATC) equals the sum of average fixed cost and average variable cost (AVC), and is therefore initially higher than AVC. However, due to the Law of Diminishing Marginal Returns, the average variable cost eventually increases more quickly than the average fixed cost decreases, and so ATC slopes upward again.

(a) Average fixed, average variable, and average total cost of possible monthly output levels

Quantity of Labor	Quantity of Guitars	Average Fixed Cost	Average Variable Cost	Average Total Cost
0	0	—	—	—
1	6	$666.67	$333.33	$1,000.00
2	16	250.00	250.00	500.00
3	28	142.86	214.29	357.15
4	38	105.26	210.53	315.79
5	46	86.96	217.39	304.35
6	52	76.93	230.76	307.69
7	56	71.43	250.00	321.43
8	58	68.96	275.86	344.82

(b) Average fixed, average variable, and average total cost curves for Seth's Guitarworks

continuously. As more and more guitars are produced, the fixed costs are spread over more and more units of output. Each guitar is forced to "carry" less and less of the monthly rent and loan payments that make up fixed costs. Thus, average fixed cost approaches zero—but never reaches it—as output expands. Second, the average total cost and average variable cost curves are roughly U-shaped. The average total cost curve initially lies far above the average variable cost curve for a given level of output, because it is the sum of average variable cost and average fixed cost, which are higher at low output levels.

The average variable and average total cost curves eventually slope upward because of the Law of Diminishing Marginal Returns. To see why, we must introduce one more cost concept for the short run—marginal cost.

myeconlab

Get Ahead of the Curve

Use your knowledge of short-run production costs to analyze concerns about price increases in the Chinese economy.

Marginal Cost

We know that economic decisions are typically made at the margin. When making production decisions, manufacturers compare the marginal cost (MC) of producing another unit of output to the marginal benefit. As such, marginal cost is one of the most important concepts in our study of the firm. Seth's marginal cost is the extra cost that he incurs every time he produces one more guitar. Because Seth's fixed costs do not change when his output increases, marginal cost is also the change in his total variable cost when he produces each additional guitar.

Calculating Marginal Cost. To compute Seth's marginal cost, we must find out how much his costs increase when output increases and then divide by the change in quantity (Equation 8.8).

$$MC = \text{Change in Total Cost/Change in Output} \qquad (8.8)$$

The middle column of Table 8.2 shows the total cost of producing guitars at Seth's Guitarworks using the cost data from Figure 8.3, panel (a). The increase in total cost for the first 6 guitars is $2,000. To find an estimate of marginal cost per guitar for the first 6 guitars, we compute the change in total cost ($6,000 – $4,000) and divide by the change in output $(6 - 0)$.[5] The result is $333.33, shown in the right hand column. The remaining marginal cost values are calculated in the same way. As with all of our marginal concepts, the values are shown between the output levels because marginal cost changes as output changes.

Graphing Marginal Cost. Panel (a) of Figure 8.5 shows the marginal cost data from Table 8.2 in graph form. As with marginal product, the line is plotted using the midpoint of the change in the variable on the horizontal axis. For example, we see that point A represents the marginal cost of producing an additional guitar when output increases from 16 guitars to 28 guitars, and so is plotted at $(28 + 16)/2 = 22$ guitars.

The marginal cost curve typically has the shape shown in Figure 8.5: decreasing at first, and then increasing more and more steeply. This shape is like an upside-down version of the marginal product curve. Panel (b) of Figure 8.5 reproduces the marginal product of labor curve from Figure 8.2. Up to point A on the marginal cost curve in panel (a), marginal cost decreases as Seth adds labor to his fixed capital. This portion of the marginal cost curve corresponds to the rising portion of the marginal product of labor curve in panel (b). In this range, the increases in output are larger than the increases in cost, causing the marginal cost to fall.

TABLE 8.2

Total and Marginal Costs of Possible Monthly Output Levels

Quantity of Guitars	Total Cost	Marginal Cost
0	$4,000	
		$333.33
6	6,000	
		200.00
16	8,000	
		166.67
28	10,000	
		200.00
38	12,000	
		250.00
46	14,000	
		333.33
52	16,000	
		500.00
56	18,000	
		1,000.00
58	20,000	

---

[5] Ideally, we would prefer to measure marginal cost using one-unit changes in output. However, for consistency, we continue with the production data used throughout the chapter.

FIGURE 8.5

Marginal, Average Variable, and Average Total Cost Curves

Using the data in Table 8.2, we can plot the marginal, average variable, and average total costs in graph form. The marginal cost decreases at first. As marginal physical product increases with each guitar produced, the marginal cost of the last unit of output falls. Then, when the Law of Diminishing Marginal Returns causes physical output to increase more slowly, marginal cost rises. Point *A* at the minimal point of the marginal cost curve in panel (a) corresponds to the maximum point on the marginal product curve in Figure 8.2 in panel (b). Beyond point *A*, the increase in output is now less than the increase in cost, and as the marginal product curve slopes downward, the marginal cost curve slopes upward.

Diminishing marginal returns set in at point *A* on both graphs. Beyond this point, adding another worker causes output to rise, but the increase is less than that generated by the previous worker. Marginal cost begins to rise because the marginal product of labor has begun to fall. As more and more individuals work with a fixed amount of capital, their ability to produce additional output decreases. For example, if Seth employs 4 workers, they can produce 38 guitars monthly. The fourth worker must be paid $2,000, just as the third worker was, yet the marginal product of the fourth worker is 10 guitars as opposed to 12 guitars for the third worker. If we divide the change in cost by the change in output, we see that the marginal cost of the output produced by the fourth worker ($2,000/10 = $200) is greater than the marginal cost of the output produced by the third worker ($2,000/12 = $166.67). After marginal cost begins to rise, it rises continuously.

Let's return to panel (a) of Figure 8.5 for a moment to consider the relationship between the marginal cost curve and the two average cost curves. As soon as the marginal cost curve passes through the average variable and average total cost curves, the two curves begin to rise. *The marginal cost curve intersects both the average variable cost curve and the average total cost curve at their minimum points* (just as the marginal product curve always passes through the average product curve at its maximum). There is a very simple explanation for this fact. When the Law of Diminishing Returns sets in, marginal cost begins to rise (at point *A*). Up to the point where the marginal cost curve intersects the average variable cost curve, the marginal cost of output is less than the average variable cost of output, which causes average variable cost to fall. After the marginal cost curve passes through the average variable cost curve, the last unit of output is more expensive than the average unit, causing average variable cost to rise. The same is true for the average total cost curve. As soon as the cost of the marginal unit of output is greater than the average total cost of output, average total cost begins to rise.

TEST + *E X T E N D* Your Knowledge

1. TEST Assume that all labor is measured in hours and paid $10 per hour. The firm must pay for a $100 business license no matter how much output is produced. Use the information given to complete the following table. At what point do diminishing marginal returns set in?

L	Q	AP	MPL	TVC	TFC	AVC	AFC	TC	MC
0	0								
1	5								
2	12								
3	20								
4	25								
5	26								

2. EXTEND Create a table similar to the one in the "Test" section with new output figures such that the marginal product of labor is constant at five (so that every additional worker adds five units to output). How does the constant marginal product of labor affect marginal cost?

▶ Long-Run Production and Cost

Get Ahead of the Curve

Apply concepts of short- and long-run production to explain the difficulty of increasing the production of armored Humvees.

In describing the assumptions of our model of production, we established that in the long run, all in parts such as labor and capital are variable. Let's now turn our attention to Seth's long-run decisions with his booming guitar business. He has sold 45 to 50 guitars per month every month for the past year. A look back at panel (a) of Figure 8.1 shows that if demand increases much further, he will not be able to fill his orders. Seth believes that he can reduce his costs at his current level of production by adding more capital. He must think of how to build more guitars in the most economically efficient—or least costly—way. It is time to do some long-run planning.

Production in the Long Run

In the long run, Seth is not restricted to his barn workshop. He plans to build a larger facility with more automated equipment. Table 8.3 shows Seth's current production possibilities, plus the output ranges of three hypothetical plants, all larger than his barn workshop. The small plant (Plant A) is twice the size and cost of his current facility (in this instance, cost refers only to what Seth pays each month to use the building, not to what he pays for the labor that is employed within the building). The medium plant (Plant B) is three times the size and cost of his current facility. The large plant (Plant C) is four times the size and cost of his current facility.

Table 8.3 shows that the larger plants have a larger capacity. Consider the output possibilities for each plant. Plant *A* can produce a maximum of 120 guitars per month, Plant *B* a maximum of 200 guitars, and Plant *C* a maximum of 275 guitars. The larger plants can make effective use of greater quantities of labor. For example, Seth maximizes his output in Plant *A* with 20 workers. Adding workers beyond this point does not add to output: The marginal product of labor at this point is zero.

Total Product of Labor per Month for Existing Facility and for Plants A, B, and C

Quantity of Labor	Quantity of Guitars for Existing Facility	Quantity of Guitars for Plant A	Quantity of Guitars for Plant B	Quantity of Guitars for Plant C
0	0	0	0	0
5	46	45	49	56
10	54	82	89	109
15	41	108	120	146
20		**120**	151	175
25		110	177	198
30		95	193	217
35		75	**200**	231
40		50	198	244
45			182	256
50			162	263
55			138	272
60			98	**275**
65			70	270
70			50	264

The marginal product of labor in Plant B reaches zero after 35 workers, and in Plant C after 60 workers. Seth must choose his plant size based on how confident he is that his business will grow. If he is too conservative and builds a plant that is too small, he will soon need to expand again. However, he does not want to be too optimistic and end up paying to maintain a plant that is too big for his firm.

Cost in the Long Run

Long-run average cost (*LAC*)
Long-run total cost divided by output.

Because Seth can vary all his inputs in the long run, all his costs are variable costs in the long run. However, the fact that Seth has no fixed costs does *not* mean that he does not have to pay for his plant and equipment. Seth's long-run total cost includes the cost of both his labor and his capital. In the long run, we consider how changes in plant size and in the size of the labor force together affect average cost. We compute **long-run average cost (*LAC*)** by dividing long-run total cost by output (Equation 8.9).

$$LAC = \text{Long-run total cost/output} \qquad (8.9)$$

As Seth considers the potential three new plant sizes, he must determine whether any of the new options will allow him to increase revenue more than costs and thus increase profits for his firm. Here we discuss the key features of long-run cost, and how the freedom to vary capital affects the decision-making process.

Larger Plants Can Produce More Output—Bigger Means More. In the short run, the Law of Diminishing Marginal Returns determines Seth's costs. In the long run, the Law of Diminishing Marginal Returns does not apply. To understand why, remember that in the short run Seth experienced diminishing returns because each additional worker he hired had less and less capital to work with. Panel (a) of Figure 8.1 shows that adding the ninth worker adds nothing to total output. In the long run, there are no such limits. The ninth worker (and many more) can be highly productive, because Seth can also supply them with sufficient capital.

Increasing Returns to Scale. For some products, there are distinct advantages to having a large facility that produces large quantities of output. These advantages are related to the technology that becomes available at larger plant sizes. For example, when producing a guitar, automated sanding equipment and computerized cutting tools and measuring devices can work faster, for longer hours without interruption, and under conditions (such as high temperature) that humans would find unbearable. In addition, the work that is performed by people can be divided into narrowly defined, specialized tasks, allowing the firms to take full advantage of both learning-by-doing and comparative advantage. Advantages that large firms have over small firms are **economies of scale** (or **increasing returns to scale**). Economies of scale exist when the average cost of output falls as the size of the firm expands. We can also think of economies of scale in terms of changes in inputs and the resulting change in output. If all inputs are increased by a given percentage, output will increase by more than that percentage when economies of scale are present. For example, if all inputs are increased by 100 percent, output will increase by *more than* 100 percent.

Firms can often produce more efficiently by manufacturing products on an assembly line. There are three primary reasons for this improvement. First, assembly lines provide many opportunities for workers to specialize, which increases the speed at which they can perform their assigned tasks. Second, bigger machines can save labor. Assembly lines save time by presenting the product to the workers right at their workstations where appropriate tools and materials are at hand. Finally, firms can save on setup costs. When a plant specializes in producing one particular good, it spends less time switching machinery and parts to accommodate changes in output than if it produced several different kinds of goods. The more units it produces between changes in the type of output it produces, the less time it spends rearranging and the greater the efficiency.

Decreasing Returns to Scale. Not all production is characterized by economies of scale. Think of the most exclusive restaurant in town. It probably has no more than 20 tables. Why? Because cooking gourmet meals is not suited to mass production. McDonald's can produce millions of hamburger patties in central locations before shipping them to individual restaurants. The meals at gourmet restaurants are produced after they have been ordered. In industries that require a great deal of communication and interaction between workers, as well as between workers and customers, large, automated production facilities can easily be a drawback, particularly if output is customized to buyer specifications. When long-run average cost rises as output increases, we say that there are **diseconomies of scale** or **decreasing returns to scale**. Diseconomies of scale exist when the average cost of output increases as the size of the firm increases. In the case of decreasing returns to scale, if all inputs are increased by a given percentage, output increases by *less than* that percentage. For example, a 100 percent increase in all inputs might increase output by only 75 percent.

Economies of scale
Exist when the average cost of output falls as the size of the firm expands.

Increasing returns to scale
See *economies of scale*.

Diseconomies of scale
Occur when long-run average costs rise as output increases.

Decreasing returns to scale
Occur when long-run average costs rise as output increases, or when the average cost of output increases as the size of the firm increases.

Constant Returns to Scale

If the average cost of output remains the same as output increases, there are **constant returns to scale**. With constant returns to scale, expansion brings neither an advantage nor a disadvantage. In this case, an increase in inputs of a given percentage will result in an increase in output of the *same* percentage.

The long-run average cost curve shows the lowest possible average cost of producing each level of output, assuming that all inputs are variable. Think of the curve as the best possible production scenario for every possible output level. The long-run average cost curve represents the lowest possible cost at each output level, based on all possible short-run average cost curves. Remember that the long run is a planning tool that allows a firm's management team to find the least costly way of producing without the constraint of fixed capital. For Seth, it means asking himself a series of questions, such as, "If I wanted to produce 100 guitars per month, how could I accomplish that most efficiently? What about 150 guitars per month?" And so on. The answer to each of these questions becomes a point on the long-run average cost curve.

Figure 8.6 (a) shows how we derive the long-run average cost curve. In the long run, the firm can choose the least costly method of producing any level of output, so the long-run average cost curve is created by choosing the most efficient points on the various short-run average cost curves (*SAC*). This does *not* mean choosing the point

---

FIGURE 8.6

Long-Run Average Cost and Preferred Plant Size
Panel (a) shows that for any given quantity of output, we can calculate all the various short-run cost curves (*SAC*ₐ, *SAC*_b, *SRAC*_c, etc.) that correspond to different plant sizes. By connecting the cost curves, we obtain the long-run average cost curve (*LRAC*). For example, while a large plant represented by *SAC*_h is capable of producing 275 guitars, a smaller plant, *SAC*_g, can do so at a lower average cost. Panel (b) shows *LAC* initially sloping downward because as output increases, the average cost decreases. From 0 to 120 guitars, Seth's production is characterized by economies of scale. Between 120 and 200 guitars per month, *LAC* remains horizontal, indicating constant returns to scale. Beyond 200 guitars, *LAC* slopes upward, as increased production increases unit costs, indicating diseconomies of scale.

(a) Constructing the long-run average cost curve

(b) Long-run average cost and scale economies

---

at the bottom of each short run U-shaped curve. For example, Seth can choose to produce 275 guitars per month with the mix of capital and labor that puts him at the bottom of SAC_h. In the long run, he can produce 275 guitars more cheaply if he instead chooses a smaller plant size, indicated by SAC_g. Panel (b) shows the long-run average cost (LAC) curve for Seth's Guitarworks. For Seth's Guitarworks, the production technology results in scale economies for all output levels up to 120 guitars per month, as shown by the downward-sloping long-run average curve. The smallest output at which the firm can achieve the lowest possible average cost is known as the **minimum efficient scale**. In Figure 8.6, the minimum efficient scale is SAC_d, which minimizes average cost at an output level of 120 guitars. At all output levels lower than 120, the firm can reduce average cost by expanding. From 120 to 200 guitars per month, the long-run average cost curve is horizontal, indicating constant returns to scale. In this range, the average cost per guitar is constant. Finally, production of more than 200 guitars per month is characterized by decreasing returns to scale. Long-run average cost increases in this range.

> **Minimum efficient scale**
> The smallest output at which the firm can achieve the lowest possible average cost.

The shape of the long-run average cost curve is a key determinant of how many firms we can expect to find in an industry. Thus, we will rely on these concepts in following chapters when we discuss differences across industries, such as why there are so many firms in some industries, yet so few in others.

Strategy and Policy
For Increasing Productivity, It's Tough to Beat Education[6]

Managers who want to increase output have a variety of options. They can ask their workers to work more hours, they can add more workers, or they can increase capital. There is also yet another way to increase worker productivity. Highly educated employees are often more productive than less-educated employees. In fact, a study by the National Center on Education Quality of the Workforce recently found that increasing the educational attainment of workers might be the *most* effective way for firms to increase productivity. From data collected as part of the National Employer Survey, researchers found that increasing workers' average educational attainment by 10 percent (a little more than one year of schooling) increases worker productivity by 8.6 percent. In the service sector, the productivity increase was even larger (11 percent). These productivity increases compare very favorably with other options that a firm might pursue. Indeed, a 10-percent increase in capital stock raises productivity 3.4 percent, and a 10-percent increase in hours worked boosts productivity by 5.6 percent.

From a policy perspective, these results seem to represent a call for action. For a nation to prosper, its economy must grow. If the most effective way for firms to increase productivity is to hire educated workers, then the government should work to increase the educational attainment of its labor force. Exactly how to increase the educational level of the labor force is less clear. Remember that changes in worker

---

[6] "The Other Shoe: Education's Contribution to the Productivity of Establishments," administered by the Bureau of the Census, www.thelearningalliance.info/Docs/Jun2003/DOC-2003Jun24.1056450799.pdf, accessed February 1, 2005.

education and the costs and benefits of making such changes occur at the margin. The government must thus decide which individuals would benefit most from increased education—that is, should we increase the education level of the least educated, or the education level of those who are already highly educated? The government also must determine the cost of providing that education. A complicating factor in policy making is that much of the funding for education is provided at the state and local levels through real estate taxes. As a result, creating a national strategic initiative is quite difficult.

Critical-Thinking Questions

1. Why is education most effective in the service sector of the economy?
2. If firms benefit greatly from more educated workers, why might they be reluctant to provide education?

SUMMARY

- **The motivation of firms.** Firms want to maximize profits. To do so they must minimize the cost of producing each output level. Specifically, firms try to minimize the transactions cost of organizing and carrying out production. Although firms report accounting profits, they make decisions based on economic profits, which include opportunity costs.

- **Production: turning inputs into output.** Production is the transformation of inputs into output. Capital and labor are the two inputs most typically considered. Although materials are required in the production of physical outputs, they are not a choice variable in the simple model of production. In the short run, one input (usually capital) is fixed, and firms adjust output by using more or less of the variable input (usually labor). In the long run, all inputs are variable.

- **Short-run production.** When analyzing production in the short run, we typically assume that capital is a fixed input and labor is variable. Because capital is fixed, labor is subject to the Law of Diminishing Marginal Returns. This law stipulates that as more and more labor is combined with fixed capital, the marginal product of labor must eventually fall.

- **Short-run cost.** Short-run costs are another way to express the short-run production concepts. The cost of the fixed input, capital, is called fixed costs. Some of these fixed costs are also sunk costs. Labor is a variable cost, because it changes according to the desired quantity of output. Marginal cost is the cost of producing an additional unit of output, and rises as the Law of Diminishing Marginal Returns sets in.

- **Long-run production and cost.** In the long run, all inputs are variable. Because firms always exist and operate in the short run, managers use the long-run production model to plan for various output possibilities over time. Although the Law of Diminishing Marginal Returns does not apply to the long run, the productivity of labor still changes as the size of a firm increases, due to changes in economies of scale. Long-run costs are not divided into fixed costs and variable costs, because all costs are variable in the long run. The long-run average cost curve shows how costs change as the scale of an operation changes. When the long-run average cost curve is downward-sloping, a firm experiences economies of scale. When the long-run average cost curve is flat, returns to scale are constant. When the long-run average cost curve slopes upward, there are diseconomies of scale.

PROBLEMS

1. How do economists distinguish the short run from the long run?
2. Bevin folds paper airplanes. She works 8 hours each day. She can fold 16 planes per hour for the first 3 hours that she works, and 12 planes per hour for the next 2 hours. She can fold only 8 planes per hour for the final 3 hours.
   a. Make a table showing Bevin's total product for each day, using hours as the measure of labor input.
   b. On the same table, show her marginal product.
   c. At what point does her marginal productivity begin to decline?
   d. Show the marginal product curve on a graph.
3. What does the term "specialization of labor" mean? How might it help firms to be more productive?
4. Complete the following table. Then answer the questions after it.

L	Q	MPL
0	0	
1	10	
2	15	
3	25	
4	30	
5	32	
6	29	

   a. At what point do diminishing marginal returns set in?
   b. At what point do total returns begin to fall?
   c. Graph the total product and marginal product curves.
5. In the short run, which input is typically fixed? Which input is typically variable? Why do we assume that these inputs are fixed and variable? Can you think of examples where the typical cases might not hold and the opposite would be true?
6. Juan gives up his job painting houses for $1,000 per week to paint landscapes. Should he consider his previous salary in his calculation of economic profits, accounting profits, or both? What about the cost of his easel and supplies?
7. Why don't economists specify a particular time period to represent the short run?

8. Over the last 50 years, the average size (in acreage) of farms in the United States increased by more than 100 percent. Assuming that farmers are profit maximizers and so choose the most profitable farm size in the long run, what changes might be behind this increase in average size?

9. Hakim's Surfboard Company has only two costs: a monthly mortgage of $2,000 and a variable cost of $200 per board produced.
   a. Make a table showing the fixed, variable, and total costs of Hakim's output for 0 to 10 surfboards per month.
   b. On a graph, show the fixed, variable, and total costs of output.

10. In the following table, fill in the missing values of total fixed cost (*TFC*), total variable cost (*TVC*), total cost (*TC*), and marginal cost (*MC*). Then make one graph showing total cost, total fixed cost, and total variable cost, and a second graph showing marginal cost.

Q	TFC	TVC	TC	MC
0	100			
1		20		
2		25		
3		30		
4		37		
5			147	
6		60		
7			180	
8		120		

11. Answer true, false, or uncertain: If fixed costs are zero, and the marginal cost of an additional unit is always $10, then *AVC*, *ATC*, and *MC* are all constant and equal to one another. Explain your answer.

12. Describe the fixed, variable, and marginal costs associated with the production of a music CD.

13. Econometrics, Inc., recently completed a cost study for a firm in the sneaker manufacturing industry. The analysis determined that, in the long run, the least-cost method for producing sneakers is as follows:

Thousands of Pairs per Month	Average Cost per Pair
0	—
1	$25
2	20
3	15
4	15
5	15
6	20
7	25

   a. Based on the results of the study, create a graph showing the long-run average cost curve for the sneaker industry.
   b. Label the curve indicating where the industry experiences economies of scale, constant returns to scale, and diseconomies of scale.

14. Suppose you buy a pair of shoes on sale. After wearing them a few times, you lose them at the beach, so you purchase a new pair. How should you classify the cost of the first pair of shoes? How should the cost factor into your decision of how much to spend on the new pair?

15. Explain the relationship between marginal cost and marginal product. Use graphs of each curve in your explanation.

16. If marginal cost is falling, what must be true about average variable cost and average total cost?

17. In an industry where production is strongly affected by diseconomies of scale, what size of firm would have an advantage: large or small? Why?

18. Suppose that 10 students take an introductory economics exam, and the average score is 70 out of 100. Then one more student (who thus represents the marginal unit) takes the exam and earns a score of 90. How does this score affect the average? How would your answer change if the student scored a 70? What if the student scored 50?

19. Suppose that at Pat's Swimming Pools, cost must increase to three times its current level to double output in the long run. Does this represent increasing, decreasing, or constant returns to scale?

20. Juanita is the owner of a shop that makes decorative pottery. If she works alone, she can produce 5 pots per day. With one assistant, she can produce 12 pots per day. A second assistant increases output to 17 pots per day. Hiring a third increases output to 20 pots per day. A fourth leaves output unchanged at 20 pots per day, and a fifth assistant (that is, six workers total including Juanita) reduces output to 15 pots per day.
    a. Create a table that shows the total product of labor, average product of labor, and marginal product of labor for Juanita and her assistants.
    b. Draw a graph that shows the average and marginal product of labor curves.
    c. At what point do diminishing marginal returns set in?
    d. At what point do total returns begin to fall?
    e. Why (in general) does the marginal productivity of labor eventually fall?

21. Kamran's Cues, Inc., produces pool cues. The following table shows data on the fixed and variable costs of production. Complete the table and draw one graph that shows TC, TFC, and TVC, and another graph that shows ATC, AVC, AFC, and MC.

Q	TFC	TVC	TC	AFC	AVC	ATC	MC
0	$50	$0					
1	50	20					
2	50	30					
3	50	37					
4	50	47					
5	50	60					
6	50	76					
7	50	96					
8	50	122					
9	50	158					
10	50	208					

HERE'S HOW MyEconLab CAN HELP YOU GET A BETTER GRADE

1. Log into MyEconLab and take Practice Test chapter-A (to log in for the first time, see page 30 for instructions.)

2. Based on your test results, MyEconLab will identify the areas where you need further work and create a personal Study Plan for you.

3. Your Study Plan contains the exercises listed below and others like them that will target the specific chapter topics you need to focus on. You'll receive instant feedback and find links to tutorials, animations, and the online textbook to help you study.

4. When you're ready, go take Practice Test chapter-B and demonstrate how your results have improved.

Section 8.1, Exercise 1 You are currently earning a salary of $35,000, and you have savings of $50,000 on which you are earning 10 percent interest. You are considering starting a small business. You will have to use your $50,000 savings to purchase inventory, but you expect that if you were to go out of business, you would be able to recover $25,000. Your expectation is that in the first year, the business is expected to have sales of $200,000 and costs of $125,000.

   a. What is your expected economic profit or loss for the first year?

   b. Based only on the first year, would it be advisable to do this?

Section 8.1, Exercise 2 The Superbok Corporation is considering a new line of products. Engineering estimates suggest that the cost of the products will be $100,000, and that revenues will be equal to $110,000.

   a. What is the accounting profit from this line of products?

   b. If the corporation must borrow the money to finance the product at a rate of 10 percent interest, what is the economic profit?

Section 8.2, Exercise 1 In economics, what distinguishes defines the short run versus the long run?

Section 8.3 Exercise 1 The following table shows the marginal product of labor for the first seven workers at a sandwich shop.

Quantity of Labor	Marginal Product of Labor (number of sandwiches)
0	0
1	20
2	10
3	5
4	2
5	1
6	0
7	−5

a. Find total output.

b. At what point do diminishing marginal returns begin?

c. What would you expect to happen to the marginal product of each worker if the size of the store (capital) were to be increased?

Section 8.3, Exercise 2 The following table shows the short-run production function for chairs.

Quantity of Labor	Quantity of Chairs
0	0
1	10
2	40
3	70
4	90
5	100
6	105
7	105
8	100

a. Find the average product of labor.

b. Find the marginal product of labor for each quantity of labor.

Section 8.3, Exercise 3 Indicate whether each of the following statements is true or false in the short run, justify your answer.

a. If marginal cost is increasing, marginal product must be increasing.
b. If marginal cost is less than average total cost, average total cost must be falling.
c. If average total cost is falling, marginal cost must be falling.
d. If average product is falling, there must be diminishing marginal returns.
e. If average total cost is at its minimum, marginal cost must be equal to average total cost.

Section 8.4, Exercise 1

a. Using the table in Section 8.3, Exercise 1, assume that the wage rate is $5 per hour, and find the marginal cost curve.
b. When there are diminishing returns, what is happening to marginal cost?

Section 8.4, Exercise 2 Consider a firm that has just built a plant that has daily fixed operating expenses of $500. Each worker costs $10.00 per hour, and labor is measured in worker hours.

a. Based on this information, fill in the following table.
b. Show your results on two separate graphs. Put marginal, average variable, and average total cost on one graph, and put fixed, variable, and total cost on the other.

L	Q	MPL	FC	VC	TC	MC	AVC	ATC
0	0					—	—	—
10	100							
20	150							
30	175							
40	195							
50	205							
60	210							
70	212							

Section 8.5, Exercise 1 On the following graph, identify:

a. A quantity at which there are economies of scale
b. A quantity at which there are diseconomies of scale
c. The minimum efficient scale

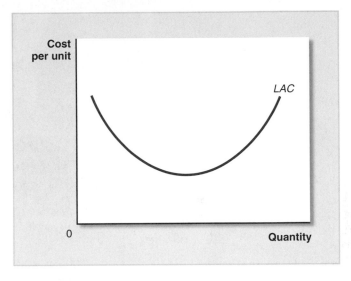

Section 8.5, Exercise 2 A firm discovers that when it doubles all of its inputs, output triples.

a. What is the shape of this firm's long-run average cost curve?
b. Does this firm have increasing, decreasing, or constant returns to scale?

Section 8.5, Exercise 3 Indicate whether each of the following statements are true or false in the long run; justify your answer.

a. If marginal cost is increasing, marginal product must be increasing.
b. If marginal cost is less than average total cost, average total cost must be falling.
c. If average total cost is falling, marginal cost must be falling.
d. If average product is falling, there must be diminishing marginal returns.
e. If average total cost is at its minimum, marginal cost must be equal to average total cost.

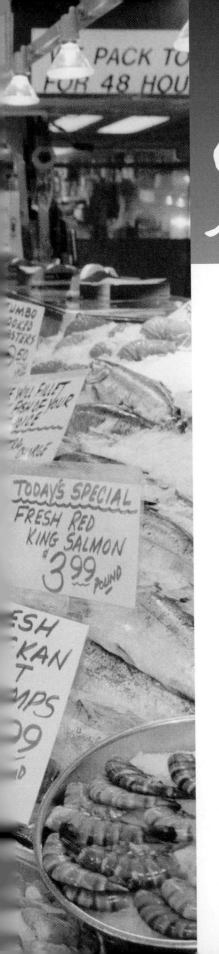

9 Perfect Competition

When Danny Washington and his brother Jarrod walk into the famous Pike Place Market in Seattle for the first time, they are overwhelmed. "Man! Look at all the people!" Danny exclaims. "Look at all the fish!" Jarrod answers. There must be hundreds of stores and stands, and thousands of people are surging through the aisles. There are many stands filled with fabulous flowers or fresh fruits and vegetables. As the boys look around, they see that the biggest attraction of Pike Place is definitely the fish.

Danny and Jarrod have come up from Los Angeles for a family reunion that will be celebrated with one of their Aunt Doris's famous seafood dinners. To help her out, they have offered to go shopping for the crabs and prawns that will be used for the appetizers and for the salmon for the main course. Danny takes out his aunt's list, and the two begin shopping.

They see fresh fish stands everywhere on the main floor of the market. Fortunately, their aunt has written down the names and locations of four vendors she likes. The two are determined to do the best job they can to stretch her budget. "Let's check out the prices at each stand first," Jarrod says. "Then we'll decide where to buy things." After finding the vendors they want and wading through the crowds to the front of displays, the boys discover something that surprises them—the vendors all sell the same types of fish for the same prices. The boys can't believe it. They even check out a couple of vendors who are not on their list. It's the same everywhere. Salmon fillets are $10.00 per pound, and prawns $7.99 per pound, at every stand. Even the Dungeness crabs are priced alike at every stand. Is this a coincidence? Or could this be some kind of conspiracy?

As you learned in Chapter 8, profit maximization—creating the largest possible difference between revenue and cost—is the primary goal of every firm. In this chapter, we begin our study of markets with a model that serves as one of the most important models in economics. With *perfect competition*, many relatively small firms compete against one another. One of the hallmarks of the perfectly competitive market structure is its efficiency, which is related to the application of resources towards their most highly valued purpose. As a result, we can use predicted outcomes of the model as a benchmark against which we can measure the performance of any industry.

ALONG THE WAY, YOU WILL ALSO LEARN:

- How we can classify markets based on their organization.
- What assumptions govern the model of perfect competition.
- How perfect competitors determine prices.
- How perfectly competitive firms maximize economic profits in the short run.
- How the perfectly competitive firm determines the supply curve.
- How perfectly competitive firms compete in the long run.
- How changes in production costs affect the perfect competitor's supply in the long run.

 AT THE END OF THE CHAPTER, THE MYECONLAB LOGO WILL DIRECT YOU ONLINE

- MyEconLab is a resource-packed online homework and tutorial system that can help you perform better in your economics course. To log in for the first time, see page 30 for instructions.
- MyEconLab can help you apply important concepts from the chapter to real-world issues. Watch for the logo to indicate online features about applying the model of perfect competition.
- At the end of each chapter, you'll find a special study section that will help you get the most out of your textbook and your instructor's MyEconLab course.

▶ Market Structure

Market structure
The number and size of buyers and sellers in the market.

Oligopoly
A market structure in which there are relatively few sellers, each with a large share of the total market.

Monopolistic competition
A market structure in which there are many sellers of products that are similar, but not identical.

In the next several chapters, you will learn how firms maximize economic profits in various market structures. **Market structure** refers to the number and size of buyers and sellers in the market. Our focus in these chapters will be primarily on sellers (supply). There are four market structures: monopoly, oligopoly, monopolistic competition, and perfect competition.

Monopoly is the least competitive market structure. Recall from Chapter 6 that monopolies are markets with a single seller of a good for which there are no close substitutes. In most communities, for example, the local electric company has a monopoly in the delivery of electricity. An **oligopoly** is a market in which there are relatively few sellers, each with a large share of the total market. Examples of oligopolies include the markets for laundry detergent, breakfast cereals, and automobiles. **Monopolistic competition** describes a market in which there are many sellers of products that are similar but not identical. The retail market for many types of clothing (such as jeans and dresses) can often be described using this model. Finally, **perfect competition** is a market structure in which there are many sellers (and buyers) of an identical product. Most examples of perfect competition come from unprocessed foods such as wheat, corn, grain, or fish. In the next section, we fully describe the assumptions that form the basis of the perfect competition model. In the three chapters that follow, we carefully describe the assumptions that lie behind the other market structures.

Perfect competition
A market structure in which there are many sellers and buyers of an identical product.

Assumptions of the Perfect Competition Model

As noted, perfect competition is a model used to describe industries in which consumers can purchase essentially the same good from a large number of firms, each of which is small relative to the size of the market. The model of perfect competition is based on a set of assumptions about firms, consumers, and information. These assumptions simplify the complex interactions that characterize real-world markets. The assumptions do not apply all of the time to any single market. However, when the assumptions do hold, the model makes accurate predictions about prices, output, economic profits, and efficiency. Before applying the model, we lay out its structure by exploring the four assumptions that characterize perfect competition.

All Sellers Offer the Same Commodity

We now return to our observations during a shopping trip through Pike Place market. As Danny and Jarrod walk from fish stand to fish stand, they need to be sure that they are making a fair comparison between goods as they shop. You probably have heard that you must compare apples to apples and not to oranges. In this case, it is salmon to salmon. The decision to purchase one pound of salmon fillets for $10.00 or five large crabs for $20.00 almost certainly varies from one individual to another, because the decision involves a comparison of two different products. Yet it is a simple matter to decide which is a better buy, a pound of salmon fillets priced at $10.00 or $11.00. All rational consumers prefer cheaper salmon to more expensive salmon of the same quality. The model of perfect competition assumes that the market is made up of firms that sell homogeneous—or undifferentiated—commodities like flounder. In other words, firms in the market sell goods that are perfect substitutes for one another.

Many Buyers and Sellers

In describing the scene at Pike Place, we noted that there are both many buyers and many sellers. Each firm supplies only a small fraction of the total output because there are no extensive economies of scale for any firm relative to the size of the market. This is the second assumption of the competitive model. With numerous participants on both the supply and demand sides of the market, we are assured that the basic conditions for competition exist. That is, there are many competitors and many consumers to compete for. If only one firm was selling fish, it would be able to set its own price. With many buyers and sellers, no single firm or consumer can influence the market-determined price.

Perfect Information

Perfect information
All the buyers and sellers are aware of market conditions; namely, the prices charged by other sellers and the quality of the various goods for sale.

The third assumption of the model of perfect competition is **perfect information**, which means that all the buyers and all the sellers are aware of market conditions. Market conditions include the prices charged by other sellers and the quality of the various goods for sale. In the fish market, each shopper and storeowner can easily check the prices posted throughout Pike Place by taking a brief stroll. For many products, you can obtain good information by taking a "virtual stroll" on the Internet. Before the advent of the Internet, information was often much more costly to obtain, which made the assumption of perfect information a relatively risky one.

Free Entry and Exit

Free entry and exit
Ensures that firms can easily enter or leave an industry if they wish. This assumption is sometimes referred to as *perfectly mobile resources,* meaning that firms can easily add and remove labor and capital.

Free entry and exit, the fourth assumption of the model, ensures that firms can easily enter or leave an industry if they wish. This assumption is sometimes stated as *perfectly mobile resources,* meaning that firms can easily add and remove labor and capital. In the section that follows, we discuss in detail why firms would want to enter a market. For now, suppose that the existing firms at Pike Place are making large economic profits. Entrepreneurs who see that they can earn more by selling fish at Pike Place than by doing something else might want to enter the industry. If some or all of the fish vendors are losing money, the assumption of free exit means that fish vendors can simply close up shop and leave the industry at no additional cost. This assumption does not hold if firms are tied into long-term contracts or are forced to purchase large quantities of capital that cannot be used elsewhere. It is difficult to exit the airline industry, for instance. An airline must maintain and rent space for a fleet of planes until it can sell them. In short, most firms prefer not to be trapped in an industry, unsurprisingly, because it constrains their choices.

Table 9.1 summarizes the assumptions of competitive markets that we've outlined. This set of assumptions defines a perfectly competitive market.

Defining a Market

Market definition
The process of identifying a product and the buyers and sellers of that product.

Market definition is the process of identifying a product and the buyers and sellers of that product. In the case of the fish market and, more generally, of perfect

TABLE 9.1

Assumptions of the Perfect Competition Model

Homogeneous Commodity	All firms sell exactly the same product. Consumers view output of all firms as perfect substitutes.
Many Buyers and Sellers	There are many buyers and sellers; no single buyer or seller can influence prices.
Perfect Information	Both the buyers and the sellers are familiar with all market conditions, in particular prices.
Free Entry and Exit	There are no costs related to entering or exiting the market, so firms can enter or exit the market freely.

competition, the process is straightforward because the product is homogeneous. Our job will be more complex in future chapters where we discuss market structures in which the product varies from one seller to another.

▶ Firms Are Price Takers

Market power
The ability of a firm to set price.

Price taker
A firm that accepts the price as set by the market.

We can now apply your understanding of the perfect competition model to the Pike Place Market. We return to our initial question: Why do all Pike Place vendors sell the same fish for the same price? From the firms' perspective, one of the most important outcomes in the perfect competition model is that they have no **market power**, meaning that the actions of any one firm cannot affect the market price. Perfectly competitive firms are **price takers** because they take the price as determined at the market level, rather than deciding on a price independently from other sellers.

That day at Pike Place, all individual firms were selling salmon fillets for $10 per pound. In panel (a) of Figure 9.1, we see that the market equilibrium price of $10 per pound is set by the intersection of the market supply and market demand curves. Because individual firms have no control over the equilibrium price of $10 per pound, each firm faces a demand curve that is horizontal, or perfectly elastic, at the market price as shown in panel (b).

The demand curve observed by an individual firm is a horizontal line in panel (b) of Figure 9.1. This demand curve indicates that each firm can sell any quantity it wants at the market price, but nothing at a higher price. The firm can also sell any quantity it wants at any price lower than the market price. However, doing so would

FIGURE 9.1

Market Demand and Supply and a Single Firm's Demand Curve for Salmon

In panel (a), the intersection of the market demand and supply curves *D* and *S* indicates that the market equilibrium price is $10 for salmon fillets at 700 pounds per day. The demand curve for an individual firm, *d*, in panel (b) is a horizontal line (perfectly elastic) with a vertical intercept at the market-determined price of $10. The horizontal line indicates that no single firm can affect market price and thus cannot either sell above the market price or maximize profits by selling below it.

(a) The market equilibrium price for salmon

(b) The firm's demand curve for salmon

conflict with the firm's goal of maximizing economic profit. Recall that the individual demand curve answers the question, "If the price were $X, or $Y, or $Z, how many would I buy?" To determine its profit-maximizing price, the firm effectively turns this question around and asks itself, "If our price were $X, or $Y, or $Z, how many would consumers buy from us?" In Figure 9.1, a firm can sell all that it wants at the market price without causing the price to fall, but can charge no more. Because the product is homogenous, and the firm is so small relative to the size of the total market, its actions do not affect the market price. Including grocery stores with fish counters, there are more than 500 fish and seafood retailers listed in the Seattle-area phone book. Each firm is very small relative to this market. Even if one of those stores were to increase its sales by 100 percent, or at the other extreme, shut down entirely, the change in supply would not be enough to change the market price.

Because firms have no control over price, they instead focus on producing the optimum output level. In the next section, we analyze how a firm determines that output level in the short run.

Perfect Competition's Short-Run Profit Maximization

Because perfectly competitive firms lack market power, they cannot choose the price at which they sell their output. To maximize economic profits, firms therefore focus on choosing the optimum output levels. In this section, we evaluate the firm's output decision in two different ways. We first show how a firm selects the profit-maximizing output level by comparing its total revenue to its total cost. We then show how the firm can also use marginal analysis to arrive at the same profit-maximizing output level. Although both methods result in the same output choice, each is valuable for our understanding of firm behavior.

The Total Cost and Total Revenue Approach to Profit Maximization

As shown in Equation 9.1, maximizing economic profits means creating the largest difference between total revenue (TR) and total cost (TC).

$$\text{Profits} = TR - TC \qquad (9.1)$$

Normal profit
When a firm's earnings just cover all of its costs, including opportunity cost (also called *zero economic profit*).

Recall from Chapter 8 that economic profits include opportunity costs, such as the best alternative use of the entrepreneur's time. Economic profits can be positive, zero, or negative. Zero economic profit is also sometimes called **normal profit**, because a firm earning zero economic profits covers all of its costs, including opportunity cost. To analyze firm behavior using this method of profit maximization, consider the decision process of Seattle Salmon, a firm that sells only salmon fillets. As a producer and seller, it operates its own fishing boat and has a stand in Pike Place.

Seattle Salmon's Total Revenue. Total revenue for Seattle Salmon is the market price, p, times the firm's output level, q. The market price for salmon fillets is $10 per pound. Because the price is constant (it does not change as the firm's output changes), a graph of total revenue is a straight, upward-sloping line, with a slope equal to the price. Selling one pound of fish brings in $10, selling two pounds of fish

FIGURE 9.2

Total Cost, Total Revenue, and the Profit-Maximizing Level

Panel (a) shows data for Seattle Salmon's total cost, total revenue, and profit at various output levels. Panel (b) plots the total revenue and total cost curves, TR and TC, using data from the table. Between four and seven pounds, the slope of TR is greater than the slope of TC, and thus profits rise until they reach their maximum. The profit-maximizing output level occurs where the distance between total revenue and total cost curves is greatest: seven pounds of salmon. Below the output level of four pounds, total cost exceeds total revenue, and Seattle Salmon operates at a loss, shown by the shaded red area.

(a) Total revenue, total cost, and profit for Seattle Salmon

Price (per pound) (1)	Quantity (in pounds) (2)	Total Revenue (3)	Total Cost (4)	Economic Profit (5)
$10	0	$0	$15.00	−$15.00
10	1	10	25.00	−15.00
10	2	20	31.00	−11.00
10	3	30	35.00	−5.00
10	4	40	40.00	0.00
10	5	50	46.00	4.00
10	6	60	54.00	6.00
10	**7**	**70**	**63.50**	**6.50**
10	8	80	76.00	4.00
10	9	90	90.00	0.00
10	10	100	106.00	−6.00

(b) Total cost, total revenue, and profit

brings in $20, and so on, so the slope is 10 in this example. We show the total revenue calculations from Equations 9.2 and 9.3 in columns 1, 2, and 3 in panel (a) of Figure 9.2 and graph these total revenue points in panel (b).[1]

$$TR = p \times q \tag{9.2}$$
$$TR = \$10 \times q \tag{9.3}$$

Seattle Salmon's Total Cost. Recall from Chapter 8 that the distinguishing feature of the short run is that at least one input is fixed. As Seattle Salmon strives to maximize its economic profits in the short run, it knows that it cannot change its stock of capital, which includes the cost of the boat, the lease for the stand, and the necessary equipment. Together, these fixed costs amount to $15 per day. The firm must bear this cost no matter how much or how little it produces and sells. The variable cost is the cost of labor. As more workers are employed, the variable cost rises, as

---

[1] In order to keep the arithmetic simple, we have made the sales and cost figures artificially low throughout the chapter. In reality, such a firm would sell hundreds of pounds of fish per day, and would have costs that are proportionally higher as well.

does the quantity of fish caught and brought to market. Column 4 in Figure 9.2 (a) shows the total costs for Seattle Salmon. Panel (b) of Figure 9.2 shows that the short-run total cost curve for Seattle Salmon has the familiar shape described in Chapter 8. At an output level of zero, the firm pays only its fixed costs. As output increases, costs first increase slowly and then more rapidly, as the Law of Diminishing Marginal Returns sets in.

Seattle Salmon's Profit-Maximizing Level. By subtracting total cost from total revenue in columns 3 and 4 of panel (a) of Figure 9.2, we can determine the firm's profit-maximizing output level. At all output levels below four pounds of fish per day, economic profits are negative for Seattle Salmon. In panel (a), we see that at four pounds per day, $TC = TR$ and the firm earns zero economic profit. Panel (b) tells the same story for the firm in graph form. At four pounds per day, the total revenue curve passes through the total cost curve, indicating that total cost and total revenue are equal, and economic profits are zero. The firm also has zero economic profit if it sells nine pounds per day, because once again total cost and total revenue are equal. At any level of output between four pounds and nine pounds per day, Seattle Salmon makes positive economic profits. To find the maximum level of economic profit, we look for the largest difference between total revenue and total cost. This occurs at an output level of seven pounds per day.

Beyond an output level of about five pounds per day, the total cost curve shows that diminishing marginal returns cause costs to rise at a very rapid rate. With only a fixed amount of capital to work with (one boat), the only way to catch more fish is by adding more fishermen. However, each additional fisherman adds fewer fish than the previous fisherman. As a consequence, increasing output by a given amount requires a greater and greater addition of fishermen, and higher and higher variable cost. Thus, additional increases in output cause the firm to experience steadily falling economic profits as output grows from seven to nine pounds. In addition, there are rapidly increasing losses when the firm produces more than nine pounds per day. Between four and seven pounds, the total cost curve is flatter than the total revenue curve, so revenue grows faster than costs, and economic profits rise. Between seven and nine pounds, the total cost curve is steeper, so costs grow faster than revenue, and economic profits fall. As a result, the distance between the curves is greatest at seven pounds, a point to which we soon return.

The Marginal Cost and Marginal Revenue Approach to Profit Maximization

We can also find the level of output that maximizes economic profit by examining how producing one more unit of output affects costs and revenues. Rather than focusing on total cost and total revenue, this approach examines marginal cost and marginal revenue. You know from Chapter 8 that marginal cost (MC) is the additional cost of producing one more unit of output. **Marginal revenue (MR)**, as shown in Equation 9.4, is the additional revenue that a firm gains from selling one more unit of output.

$$\text{Marginal revenue} = \text{Change in total revenue/Change in output} \qquad (9.4)$$

In the case of perfect competition, marginal revenue requires no calculation at all. Every time a competitive firm sells an additional unit, it receives the market price, p, in exchange. One pound of salmon generates $10 in revenue, two pounds generates $20, and so on. *For perfectly competitive firms, marginal revenue equals price.*

Marginal revenue (MR)
The additional revenue that a firm gains from selling one more unit of output. For perfectly competitive firms, marginal revenue equals price and thus also equals average revenue.

FIGURE 9.3

Using Average Cost to Compute Profit for Seattle Salmon

The data in panel (a) shows revenue and cost data for Seattle Salmon. Each unit represents one pound of fish. The graph in panel (b) confirms that profit is maximized when marginal revenue, *MR*, is equal to marginal cost, *MC*, at an output level of seven pounds of salmon. Where the average total cost curve, *ATC*, equals $9.07, *ATC* times units of output yields the total cost, represented by the yellow rectangle. Total revenue, which equals the area of rectangle *ABCD*, minus total cost equals the profit, shown by the light green rectangle. Note that in Chapter 8, we showed marginal cost values between output levels to emphasize that it represents a change from one output level to the next. In panel (a), we show the marginal cost of a specific unit of output at that output level to emphasize the profit-maximizing solution.

(a) Revenue and cost data for Seattle Salmon

Quantity of Salmon 1	Price = Marginal Revenue 2	Variable Cost 3	Total Cost 4	Marginal Cost 5	Average Variable Cost 6	Average Total Cost 7	Economic Profit 8
0	$10.00	$0.00	$15.00	—	—	—	−$15.00
1	10.00	10.00	25.00	$10.00	$10.00	$25.00	−15.00
2	10.00	16.00	31.00	6.00	8.00	15.50	−11.00
3	10.00	20.00	35.00	4.00	6.67	11.67	−5.00
4	10.00	25.00	40.00	5.00	6.25	10.00	0.00
5	10.00	31.00	46.00	6.00	6.20	9.20	4.00
6	10.00	39.00	54.00	8.00	6.50	9.00	6.00
7	**10.00**	**48.50**	**63.50**	**9.50**	**6.93**	**9.07**	**6.50**
8	10.00	61.00	76.00	12.50	7.63	9.50	4.00
9	10.00	75.00	90.00	14.00	8.33	10.00	0.00
10	10.00	91.00	106.00	16.00	9.10	10.60	−6.00

(b) Marginal revenue, marginal cost, and average total cost curves

It is also important to note that, for perfectly competitive firms, marginal revenue is equal to **average revenue**, which is equal to total revenue divided by output. Because each unit is sold for the same price, average revenue remains equal to the price or marginal revenue no matter how many units are sold.

To find the profit-maximizing output level using marginal cost and marginal revenue, we compare the benefit that a firm receives from selling one more unit (*MR*) to the cost of producing it (*MC*). As long as marginal revenue is greater than marginal cost, it is worth it for the firm to produce and sell that unit. Doing so causes revenues to rise by more than costs. The firm does not want to produce that unit if marginal cost is greater than marginal revenue, because then costs rise more than revenues, and economic profits decrease.

Determining Seattle Salmon's Marginal Revenue and Marginal Cost. Panel (a) of Figure 9.3 shows revenue and cost data for Seattle Salmon. Notice that price and marginal revenue are both shown in column 2. They are constant at $10.00 per pound of fish. The marginal cost values in column 5 show the additional cost of producing one pound of salmon. In the row shown in boldface, we see that the marginal revenue (column 2) gained from selling the seventh unit is $10.00, and the

Average revenue
Total revenue divided by output. For perfectly competitive firms, average revenue equals marginal revenue.

Get Ahead of the Curve

Analyze current problems in the U.S. airline industry with the model of the profit-maximizing firm.

marginal cost (column 5) of that unit is $9.50. The firm should produce and sell this level output (seven pounds), because the extra revenue from producing and selling it is greater than the marginal cost of producing it. If the firm produces an eighth unit, its marginal cost is $12.50, which exceeds the $10.00 marginal revenue gained from selling it. Thus, the firm's profit-maximizing output level is seven pounds of fish, and its total economic profits are $6.50, as shown in column 8.

Panel (a) of Figure 9.3 confirms that, as in Figure 9.2, Seattle Salmon maximizes economic profits when it sells seven pounds of fish per day. At that output level, the extra benefit of selling the last pound is about equal to the added cost of producing it. Recall that the distance between the total cost and total revenue curves was greatest at the profit-maximizing output in Figure 9.2.

The rule for finding the profit-maximizing output level is to continue to sell output as long as MR is greater than MC. The firm should stop at the point where producing one more unit of output leads to a zero increase in economic profits, that is, where $MC = MR$. This rule is the firm's version of setting marginal benefit equal to marginal cost. In future chapters, we will use the $MC = MR$ rule extensively as we discuss profit maximization in other market structures. Note that in Figure 9.3, the firm has no output choice at which marginal revenue is exactly equal to marginal cost. Thus, it chooses the highest output level at which MR is still greater than MC.

Notice that we can use the data for average total cost in column 7 of Figure 9.3, panel (a) to compute the firm's profits. The figure shows that average total costs of selling seven units of output are $9.07 per pound. If we multiply average total cost times output (9.07×7), we recreate the total cost figure of $63.50 shown in panel (a) of Figure 9.2.[2] This method of calculating total cost will come in handy when we show economic profits on a graph.

Graphing Seattle Salmon's Marginal Revenue and Marginal Cost. We can use a graph to apply marginal cost and marginal revenue to profit maximization. Panel (b) of Figure 9.3 shows the marginal cost, marginal revenue, and average total cost for Seattle Salmon. The profit-maximizing output level is where the marginal cost curve intersects the marginal revenue curve. Again, we see that the profit-maximizing output level is seven pounds per day. The average total cost curve shows the average total cost of each unit.[3]

Figure 9.3, panel (b) also shows the area of total cost, total revenue, and total economic profit. Total cost equals the area of the rectangle shaded yellow. As in the data from the table, total cost is the product of average total cost and the profit-maximizing quantity of seven units. Total revenue equals the area $ABCD$. These observations are easy to confirm, as the area of a rectangle is its length times its width; in this case, $p \times q$, which we already know represents total revenue. To obtain total cost, we can multiply average total cost times the number of units sold. The difference between the two rectangles is total revenue minus total cost or economic profit, the area shaded in green.

Identifying the Shutdown Point. We have established that if the firm produces and sells output, it should produce where $MC = MR$. Under some circumstances, however, the price of a good or service is so low that the firm is better off not producing at all, even though it still must pay its fixed costs. If Seattle Salmon reduces

---

[2] In this case, $9.07 \times 7 \approx 63.50$ due to rounding.
[3] The graph shown in panel (b) is an approximation of the data in the table, as we show MC precisely equal to MR at seven units of output to illustrate the profit maximizing condition. More precise computation of marginal cost and marginal revenue such that they are exactly equal requires the use of calculus.

output to zero, it still must pay $15 in fixed costs each day. Thus, if its economic losses from producing are less than $15 per day, it is better off producing at a loss in the short run. This situation will occur if Seattle Salmon's revenues exceed its variable costs, but not its total costs. The **shutdown point** occurs where Seattle Salmon can cover its variable costs, and the firm's losses are equal its fixed costs. If revenues fall below this point, the firm would minimize economic losses by shutting down—producing no output in the short run and hoping for prices to rebound.

Figure 9.4 shows the shutdown point—when price is just equal to the minimum point of *AVC*. At that point, *MC* is equal to *MR*, indicating that this point is the optimal output choice. Because marginal revenue is equal to average revenue, $6.10 represents both average revenue and average variable cost per pound at an output of 5.1 pounds per day. At that output level and price, total revenue and total variable cost are just equal at $31.11, and the firm covers only its variable cost. If prices were to fall any lower, the firm would not be able to cover all of its variable costs, and it would be better to shut the firm down. If it continued to operate, losses would equal fixed costs, plus the uncovered portion of variable costs. Think of shutting down as a temporary condition, as opposed to exiting the industry; we discuss exit from the industry later in the chapter.

The Impact of Profit Maximization on the Industry. We know from Chapter 4 that the market supply is the sum of the output supplied by individual firms. Thus, if the other firms in the market use the same production methods and materials and therefore have the same costs as Seattle Salmon, they too produce and sell seven pounds of salmon fillets per day. The equilibrium price is $10 per pound, and the equilibrium quantity for the entire market is seven times the number of firms in the market. For example, if there are 100 identical fish sellers in the salmon fillet market, the short-run market equilibrium quantity is 700 pounds per day at $10 per pound.

Shutdown point
The point at which total revenue is just equal to total variable costs.

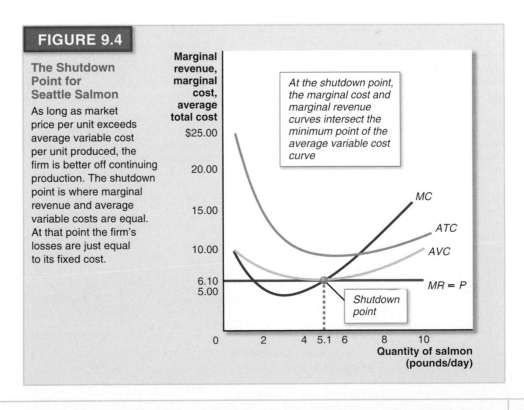

FIGURE 9.4

The Shutdown Point for Seattle Salmon

As long as market price per unit exceeds average variable cost per unit produced, the firm is better off continuing production. The shutdown point is where marginal revenue and average variable costs are equal. At that point the firm's losses are just equal to its fixed cost.

At the shutdown point, the marginal cost and marginal revenue curves intersect the minimum point of the average variable cost curve

We've established that firms choose to maximize profits by operating at an output level where marginal cost equals marginal revenue. In this section, we extend this line of reasoning to see how a firm determines its entire supply curve.

The Firm's Short-Run Supply Curve

Figure 9.1 showed that the market supply curve is the sum of all the individual firm supply curves, and is upward-sloping. Let's verify this assertion and learn more about firm behavior by deriving the firm's supply curve. The individual firm supply curve shows the quantity that a firm is willing and able to supply at various prices. As you will see, this includes prices so low that the firm does not supply any output.

Determining Seattle Salmon's Supply Curve. We know that at a price of $10 per pound, Seattle Salmon (and every firm like it) is willing to supply seven pounds of salmon per day. What happens if the price changes? Suppose that the National Institutes of Health reports that eating salmon has important health benefits. This new information is likely to shift consumers' tastes and preferences away from other, less healthy foods toward salmon. Panel (a) of Figure 9.5 shows this change as a rightward shift of the market demand curve for salmon from D_0 to D_1. The higher demand increases the equilibrium price of salmon from $10 per pound to $12 per pound. Seattle Salmon's output appears in panel (b) of Figure 9.5. The firm's output level is now too low. At seven pounds per day, price is greater than marginal cost. To restore output to a level that is consistent with the profit-maximizing rule, Seattle Salmon must increase output to eight pounds per day,

FIGURE 9.5

The Effect of an Increase in Demand on Market Equilibrium and Profit-Maximizing Choice

In panel (a), an increase in demand causes the demand curve to shift rightward. As a result, the equilibrium quantity increases from seven pounds of fish per day to eight pounds and then to nine pounds. Each increase results in a higher equilibrium price. We see in panel (b) that at the new price of $12, the individual firm's marginal cost of production, *MC*, is now lower than the new price if it produces seven pounds per day. The firm responds by increasing production to eight pounds per day. When market demand shifts to D_2, price increases to $14, and the firm maximizes profits by selling nine pounds of fish per day.

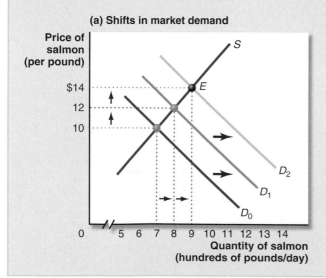

(a) Shifts in market demand

(b) The individual firm maximizes profits

where price is again equal to marginal cost. If the market demand curve in panel (a) shifts again from D_1 to D_2 and the price of salmon increases to $14 per pound, Seattle Salmon can maximize profits by selling nine pounds per day.

Keeping in mind that competitive firms always set $P = MC$ to maximize economic profits, we can identify the firm's supply curve. In Figure 9.5(b), we saw that the firm's marginal cost curve determines the output level. Thus, if the firm chooses to produce and sell output, the competitive firm's supply curve is the marginal cost curve depicted in Figure 9.6. We can see on the graph that when the price is $10.00 per pound, the firm sells seven pounds of fillets. When the price increases to $14.00 per pound, the firm increases its output to nine pounds. When the price falls to $6.10, the firm reaches the shutdown point and quantity supplied drops to zero.

Calculating Seattle Salmon's Profits. At each profit-maximizing output level, we can compute Seattle Salmon's economic profits. Table 9.2 shows the price, profit-maximizing output level, total revenue, total cost, and economic profit earned at various prices with the cost data shown in panel (a) of Figure 9.3. Again, we see that as prices rise, the firm is willing and able to sell more fish, and the profits increase. As prices fall, Seattle Salmon produces less, and economic profits decline. Eventually, when the price decreases to $9.25 per pound, the firm reaches the point where its economic profits fall to zero at 6.5 pounds of fish per day.

Table 9.2 also shows us that if the price of salmon falls to $6.00 per pound, the loss-minimizing output is five pounds per day, and Seattle Salmon loses $16.00, which is worse than the $15.00 loss if it shuts down. The table confirms that the firm should shut down at any price below $6.10 per pound.

We know that in the short run, the firm stops producing and shuts down when price falls below average variable cost. Thus, *the firm's supply curve is equal to the marginal cost curve, as long as the price is greater than or equal to average variable cost. Below the point where price equals average variable cost, quantity supplied is zero.*

FIGURE 9.6

Using Marginal Cost to Set Profit-Maximizing Output Level

Because an individual firm uses its marginal cost to set its profit-maximizing output level, the marginal cost curve is also the firm's supply curve. As market price changes, Seattle Salmon can adjust its supply of fish to maximize profit, selling more fish as prices rise and less fish as prices decline. At any price below $6.10 per pound, the firm will shut down production because price is below average variable cost.

TABLE 9.2

Various Prices and Their Corresponding Economic Profits

Price per pound (1)	Profit-Maximizing Output (or Loss-Minimizing) Level (2)	Total Revenue (3)	Total Cost (4)	Economic Profit (5)
$14.00	9.0	$126.00	$90.00	$36.00
12.00	8.0	96.00	76.00	20.00
10.00	7.0	70.00	63.50	6.50
9.25	6.5	60.13	60.13	0
8.00	6.0	48.00	54.00	−6.00
6.10	5.1	31.11	46.11	−15.00
6.00	5.0	30.00	46.00	−16.00
5.00	4.0	20.00	40.00	−20.00

TEST + *E X T E N D* Your Knowledge

1. TEST Suppose the market price of lemonade is $0.20 per glass. A lemonade stand has fixed costs of $2.00 and marginal costs increase at the rate of $0.01 per glass. As a result, the marginal cost of the second glass is $0.02, and the marginal cost of the fourth glass is $0.04. How many glasses should the stand sell to maximize economic profits? What is the firm's total revenue at the profit-maximizing quantity? Calculate the firm's total cost, average total cost, and economic profits. Draw a graph similar to Figure 9.3, and label the area that represents economic profits.

2. EXTEND How would the firm's profit-maximizing output, total revenue, total cost, and profits change if fixed costs increased to $4.00?

► Long-Run Equilibrium in Perfect Competition

In the previous section, you saw that at a price of $10.00 per pound, Seattle Salmon and all other existing firms with similar costs earn an economic profit of $6.50 per day. If there are no changes at the market level in the short run, Seattle Salmon cannot improve on this level of profit by changing either its price or output. Over time, however, other entrepreneurs will see that firms in this industry are earning substantial profits. In this section, we will show how the ability of new firms to enter the industry affects output and price in the long run, and explain the market conditions that are present in long-run equilibrium.

The Effect of Entry and Exit

As we shift from the short run to the long run, we turn our focus to changes that occur over longer periods of time, rather than at a moment in time. On the cost side, this means that firms are free to change fixed inputs such as plant size and equipment, and that technology can change. Panel (a) of Figure 9.7 shows a long-run average cost

FIGURE 9.7

Long-Run Equilibrium at the Market Level

In panel (a), at a price of $5 per pound, Seattle Salmon's economic profits are equal to zero, but the firm continues production at an output level of 8 pounds of fish per day. Panel (b) shows that as new firms enter the market, market output increases from 700 to 1,000 pounds of fish per day, and the market supply curve shifts rightward from S_0 to S_1. Firms make zero economic profits at the long-run equilibrium, so there is no incentive for entry once the price falls to $5 and the quantity supplied equals the quantity demanded.

(a) The long-run average cost curve

(b) A shift in market supply

(LAC) curve for Seattle Salmon. Recall from Chapter 8 that we construct the LAC curve by choosing the lowest cost plant option for each level of output. For this example, we assume that all existing and potential entrants face the same costs.

If existing firms are earning positive economic profits, entrepreneurs who are not currently in the industry begin to enter the industry. Panel (b) of Figure 9.7 shows that as more firms enter the industry, the market supply curve shifts rightward from S_0 to S_1. The rightward shift of the market supply curve increases the quantity supplied, and the resulting drop in market price pushes down each firm's marginal revenue curve. As the price falls from $10 to $5, the firms' economic profits as well. Firms continue to enter the industry until economic profits are driven to zero, as shown in panel (a), where price is just equal to average cost at the optimal output level. At a price of $5, the firm can do no better than to produce and sell eight pounds per day. When existing firms no longer earn positive economic profits, no other firms have any incentive to enter. *The firm and industry are in* **long-run equilibrium** *when quantity supplied is equal to quantity demanded at the market level, and firms are earning zero economic profits.*

Long-run equilibrium
Describes a firm and industry when quantity supplied is equal to quantity demanded at the market level, and firms are earning zero economic profits.

Firm Efficiency and Production Costs

In the drive to be profitable, a firm in long-run equilibrium can increase economic profits only if demand (and thus also price) increases, or if it is able to cut costs. As a result, perfectly competitive firms have a powerful incentive to be efficient producers. Only productively efficient firms thrive in competitive markets. In the long run, an inefficient firm that produces goods at a higher cost than its competitors pays the ultimate price—going out of business. Inefficient producers' departure from the industry is painful for the owners of those firms, but it is good for the overall economy, as higher-cost, inefficient producers are replaced with more efficient firms that can profitably sell output at lower prices. In the following chapters, you will see that this constant pressure to be productively efficient makes competitive markets the most efficient of all market structures. Intense competition is an engine of efficiency that ensures that firms do not stagnate and rest on their past accomplishments.

The Long-Run Supply Curve

Long-run supply curve
Shows the quantity that sellers will offer to the market at various prices over time, such that each firm earns zero economic profit.

To see how prices change in the long run, we begin by again assuming that all firms have equal costs. We can then determine the long-run supply curve for the industry. The **long-run supply curve** shows the quantity that sellers will offer to the market at various prices over time, such that each firm earns zero economic profit. The shape of the long-run supply curve depends on how costs change for firms in the industry over time. In addition, technological change plays an important role in the survival of individual firms and long-run pricing trends.

Constant-Cost Industry

To begin, suppose that the fish industry is in long-run equilibrium (as in Figure 9.7) at a price of $5 per pound, so all firms in the industry earn zero economic profits. Suppose that demand increases in the market due to an increase in consumer income. As a result, the market demand curve shifts to the right from D_0 to D_1 in panel (a) of Figure 9.8, and the price rises to $9. The increase in price creates positive economic profits for producers and entices new firms to enter the industry. In panel (b), we see that firm entry shifts the market supply curve rightward from S_0 to S_1. We know that with free entry, firms continue to enter until economic profits are driven back to zero. If new and existing firms continue to face the same input costs, the price at which economic profits are driven to zero is again $5. Firms' costs

FIGURE 9.8

The Long-Run Supply Curve in a Constant-Cost Industry
In panel (a), the initial market equilibrium is E_0. Firms' profits increase when the price rises to $9 because of an increase in market demand (see E_0'). The increase in profits causes new firms to enter the industry, shifting the supply curve rightward from S_0 to S_1, as shown in panel (b). In a constant-cost industry, firms continue to enter the industry until the price returns to $5 and the new equilibrium of E_1. Panel (c) shows the resulting horizontal long-run supply curve.

remain constant in the fish market if the cost of labor, boats, nets, and other inputs do not change. By connecting equilibrium points like E_0 and E_1, we can sketch out the long-run supply curve. In Figure 9.8, the long-run supply curve is LS in panel (c). The horizontal long-run supply curve implies that the fish industry is a **constant-cost industry**, because firms' input costs do not change as the industry expands. As a result, the price returns to its original level of $5 in the long run.

Constant-cost industry
Industry in which costs do not change as it expands. The long-run supply curve is horizontal.

Increasing-Cost Industry

The long-run supply curve need not be horizontal. If production costs increase as the industry expands, it is an **increasing-cost industry**. For example, if increased demand for fishermen causes their wages to increase as the fishing industry grows, firms' economic profits are driven back to zero at prices higher than $5, because firms now have to cover higher input costs than before. We show this kind of increasing-cost industry in panel (a) of Figure 9.9. When the price reaches $6, firms earn zero economic profits. As a result, the long-run supply curve is upward-sloping.

Increasing-cost industry
Industry characterized by increasing production costs as it expands. The long-run supply curve is upward-sloping.

Decreasing-Cost Industry

Decreasing-cost industry
Industry in which production costs fall as it expands. The long-run supply curve is downward-sloping.

If production costs fall as the industry expands, it is a **decreasing-cost industry**. This situation can occur if an industry grows large enough that it becomes economically profitable for a supplier to introduce a new technology in the industry, such as a more advanced fishing net system. If all firms employ the new net system, economic profits are driven to zero at a price lower than $5, because the firms now have to

FIGURE 9.9

The Long-Run Supply Curve in Increasing- and Decreasing-Cost Industries

Panel (a) shows an increasing-cost industry in which the cost of production increases as the industry expands. The initial equilibrium is E_0. An increase in demand from D_0 to D_1 causes the market price to increase to \$9 (at E_0'). The increase in price creates positive economic profits for existing firms and so causes new firms to enter. In panel (a), the supply curve shifts from S_0 to S_1 as firms enter the market. Firms' profits are driven to zero at higher prices than before the increase in demand. At \$6, economic profits at the firm level are zero and entry stops. The resulting long-run supply curve, LS, is upward-sloping. In panel (b), the opposite occurs. As the industry expands following the increase in demand from D_0 to D_1, production costs fall, and the supply curve shifts rightward until economic profits are driven to zero at a price of \$4. The long-run supply curve in a decreasing-cost industry is downward-sloping.

(a) Increasing-cost industry

(b) Decreasing-cost industry

cover lower costs than they did originally. In panel (b) of Figure 9.9, economic profits are driven to zero when the price reaches \$4, and the long-run supply curve is downward-sloping.

Technological Change

No firm wants to see its profits continually driven downward by falling prices. We know from our discussion of short-run profits and losses that firms cannot restore profitability by raising prices above the market level. Firms are price takers and cannot charge more than the market price. With no way to increase profitability by raising prices, the only option available is to try to cut costs, so that the firm can earn positive profits at the existing price. Thus, when a technological change allows firms to reduce production costs, firms will be quick to adopt the new technology. Their gains, however, will be short-lived, as other firms in the industry pursue the same strategy.

TEST + *EXTEND* Your Knowledge

1. TEST When personal computers were first introduced in the 1980s, they cost about $3,000 and performed very limited functions. Today, despite much greater demand, personal computers with much greater capabilities are available for less than $1,000. If we adjust prices for inflation, computer prices have fallen even more substantially than is implied by the change from $3,000 to $1,000. What might have caused such a decrease? Use a supply and demand diagram to show the long-run supply curve.

2. *EXTEND* Based on your answer to the source of falling prices for personal computers, what other products can you think of that have had similar movements in price?

Strategy and Policy
Firms Would Prefer to Avoid Perfect Competition

The push to reduce costs through improved efficiency is evident in the U.S. agricultural industry. The size of the average farm is now about 50-percent larger than it was in 1960. The National Agricultural Statistics Service reports that since then almost two million farms, mostly smaller family farms without the financial resources to adopt the newest production methods, have ceased operation. Despite government programs designed to help them, farmers are in a sense victims of their own efficiency. Since World War II, the average output per acre of land in the corn industry has more than tripled, while the labor used to farm that same land has fallen by more than 90 percent! American farmers must choose between staying efficient and leaving the industry. Firms in search of greater profits must cut costs. But as all other firms in the industry also cut costs by adopting new production methods, prices fall to the point where all firms earn zero economic profits, and the cycle begins again.

Producers in agriculture are particularly vexed because they generally cannot produce or develop the capital they use, as it is so large and expensive. Instead, major industrial suppliers such as John Deere and chemical companies that manufacture fertilizers develop cost-saving technologies. These suppliers are known as "upstream" industries because they develop, produce, and sell inputs to the agriculture industry, which is located "downstream." The upstream firms want to sell as many of these new inputs as possible, and therefore they make the inputs available to all farms. This widespread availability makes it extremely difficult for any single farm to create and maintain a cost advantage. Although agriculture producers might want to stop the cycle of decreasing costs and falling prices, no single farm can do so alone. Farms that fail to adopt the new technology run the risk of going out of business due to their high costs.

Critical-Thinking Questions

1. Should the government intervene and discourage the development of new technology for agriculture? Who benefits from new technologies?
2. Why don't farmers simply refuse to purchase the new technology?

SUMMARY

- **Market structure.** Economic models of firms vary by the structure of the market in which the firm participates. As markets become more concentrated, market power tends to increase. Perfect competition represents the least concentrated, most competitive market structure. Monopolistic competition and oligopoly markets have more than one firm, but market power exists because products are differentiated. Monopoly is the least competitive market structure.

- **The assumptions of the competitive model.** The model of perfect competition assumes a homogeneous commodity produced by many firms and sold to many buyers; perfect information; and free entry and exit by firms in the long run.

- **Firms are price takers.** Because firms are so small relative to the market and do not produce a differentiated product, individual firms have no market power, and prices are determined at the market level.

- **Perfect competition's short-run profit maximization.** Firms maximize economic profits in the short run by setting output at a level that maximizes the difference between total revenue and total cost. This output level is also where marginal revenue is equal to marginal cost.

- **Supply in competitive markets.** The individual firm supply curve is equal to the portion of the short-run marginal cost curve that lies above the average variable cost curve. At the market level, the supply curve is the horizontal sum of the individual firm supply curves.

- **The competitive firm and the market in the long run.** In the long run, firms may enter and exit an industry, and alter their capital stock. This freedom creates constant downward pressure on profits, forcing prices to the point where long-run marginal cost is equal to price and long-run average cost; that is, to the point of zero economic profits. Perfect competition promotes efficiency by forcing firms to price at marginal cost and to maintain the lowest possible production costs in the long run.

- **Perfect competition's long-run supply.** The long-run supply curve shows the quantity that all firms, combined, are willing to supply to the market at various prices. In a constant-cost industry, firm costs do not change as the industry expands and prices return to their original level. In an increasing-cost industry, production costs increase as the industry expands and prices rise. In a decreasing-cost industry, production costs fall as the industry expands and prices fall.

▶ **KEY TERMS**

Average revenue 235	Long-run equilibrium 241	Normal profit 232
Constant-cost industry 243	Long-run supply curve 242	Oligopoly 228
Decreasing-cost industry 243	Marginal revenue (MR) 234	Perfect competition 229
Free entry and exit 230	Market definition 230	Perfect information 230
Increasing-cost industry 243	Market power 231	Price taker 231
	Market structure 228	Shutdown point 237
	Monopolistic competition 228	

▶ **PROBLEMS**

1. Brian and Ahmad are teens who live in Lockport, New York, near Lake Erie. They are assured regular snowfall from November through March. To earn money, they offer to shovel driveways in their housing development after every storm. All driveways in the development are the same size, so they

charge a standard price of $20 per driveway. There are other snow-shoveling teams in the neighborhood who also charge $20 per driveway, but at that price, no additional teams want to join in.

a. Use a supply and demand diagram to show the market for shoveled driveways.

b. Illustrate on your graph what will happen if a new group of homes is built in the development.

c. Suppose that Brian and Ahmad buy a snowblower that can clear driveways at twice the speed of shovels. How will this development affect the market and other firms (teams of shovelers)?

2. How well does the market for pizza in your town match up with the assumptions of perfect competition? Be as specific as possible with respect to each assumption.

3. For each of the following products or services, make a table similar to Table 9.1 that identifies whether each assumption of the competitive model generally holds, and if not, why not.

a. Running shoes
b. Laptop computers
c. Shoeshine stands
d. Ground beef
e. No. 2 pencils
f. Gold

4. Describe what happens to a competitive firm if it charges a price in excess of the current market price.

5. Explain why the assumption of perfect information is important to the model of perfect competition.

6. Answer true or false: Firms can benefit from charging a price below the market level in a competitive market. Explain your answer.

7. Complete the following table, and indicate the best level of output for the firm if the market price is $4.00.

Firm output = q	TR	TFC	TVC	TC	Profit
0		$10	$ 0		
1			2		
2			4		
3			5		
4			6		
5			8		
6			11		
7			16		
8			23		

a. What will the firm do if the price increases to $6.00? What if the price falls to $2.00?

b. Draw a graph similar to Figure 9.2 showing the total revenue and total cost curves for output levels from zero to eight units, assuming that the price is $4.00. Label the profit-maximizing output level.

c. Use the $MR = MC$ method to show the best output level of the firm at a price of $4.00.

8. The marginal cost and average total cost schedules for Homer's Donuts are shown in the following table.

Dozens of donuts = Q	MC	TC	ATC
0	—	$4.00	—
1	$0.30	4.30	$4.30
2	0.25	4.55	2.275
3	0.40	4.95	1.65
4	0.65	5.60	1.40
5	1.00	6.60	1.32
6	1.50	8.10	1.35
7	2.25	10.35	1.48
8	4.00	14.35	1.79
9	7.00	21.35	2.37

   a. How many donuts will Homer sell if the price is $1.50 per dozen?

   b. If an increase in the number of consumers in the market shifts the market demand curve rightward, resulting in a new price of $2.25, how will Homer's Donuts respond?

   c. Create a graph showing marginal cost, average total cost, and marginal revenue, assuming a price of $1.50 per dozen donuts. Label the optimal output level for the firm and the area that represents economic profits.

9. Suppose that the market demand for bottled water is $Q = 1000 2 100p$, and the market supply is $Q = 100p$, where Q is measured in hundreds of gallons. What is the market equilibrium price and output level? If a firm has a marginal cost $MC = q$ (where q is also measured in hundreds of gallons), how many gallons will it supply?

10. What does the term "shutdown point" mean? Draw a graph for a firm that shows the marginal cost, average total cost, and average variable cost curves, and label the shutdown point. At this point, what do we know about the firm's economic profits?

11. Suppose that a firm faces a market price of $40, and has a short-run marginal cost curve of $MC = 10 + q$. How much should the firm produce? If the total cost of this output level is $1,500, what are the economic profits? If fixed costs are $450, what can we say about the firm's best strategy in the short run?

12. Assume that all firms in an industry are earning positive economic profits. Describe the process by which these economic profits are driven to zero. Be sure to address both the market level and the firm level in your answer.

13. Describe why the long-run supply curve in an industry may be upward-sloping. Give an example of an industry where you believe this to be the case.

14. In the following graphs, draw the marginal revenue curve for the firm, and the areas that represent profit, total cost, and total revenue.

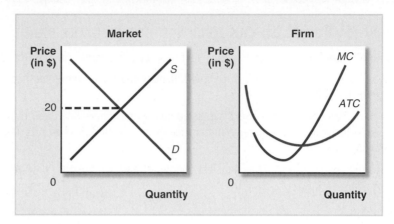

15. One of the primary outcomes of the perfectly competitive model is that firms have no market power. How will this outcome be affected if consumers can gain information about prices only by engaging in a very costly search process?
16. What do you predict will happen in a competitive market if demand falls to the point where all firms take losses, even in the long run?
17. Is the wedding gown industry a good example of a perfectly competitive market? Why or why not?
18. Initially, the market demand curve, D, in a competitive constant-cost industry is $Q_d = 100 - 20p$. With the industry in long-run equilibrium, the market supply curve, S, is $Q_s = 30p$. What are the market price and quantity? After an increase in income, market demand increases to $Q_d = 150 - 20p$. What are the new equilibrium price and quantity? What will happen as the industry returns to long-run equilibrium?
19. Describe the benefits of the perfectly competitive industry structure from a consumer's point of view. What drawbacks are there?

Section 9.1, Exercise 1 For each of the following descriptions of an industry, identify the appropriate market structure:

a. There are many chicken farmers. Each farmer sells identical eggs.

b. Many small companies sell T-shirts, all of which are slightly different from each other.

c. In a small town, there is only one company that provides garbage collection services.

d. There are a small number of automobile producers, each with a relatively large market share.

Section 9.2, Exercise 1 It is difficult to find markets that are truly perfectly competitive, because in many markets, not all assumptions of the model are met. For each of the following examples, state which assumption of the competitive model is clearly violated.

a. Bottled water is sold with brand-name labels, and consumers believe that one kind of water is different from another.

b. There are a small number of manufacturers of steel in the United States, and most firms are large in relation to the size of the market.

c. Although all standard Monopoly® games are identical and are sold at many stores, different stores sell them at different prices. It would take you a long time to drive to all the stores and find the lowest price.

d. Taxi cabs are essentially identical products, and there are many cabs, but to operate a taxi (in most large cities), you must have a taxi license. The number of taxi licenses is restricted.

Section 9.3, Exercise 1 What does it mean to say that a firm is a price taker?

Section 9.4, Exercise 1 The following table gives total short run cost of production for Bob's Picnic Tables.

Quantity	Total Cost
0	$ 575
1	625
2	650
3	700
4	775
5	875
6	1000
7	1150
8	1325
9	1525
10	1750

a. What is Bob's Picnic Tables' fixed cost?

b. If the price of a picnic table is $150, calculate total revenue for each output level.

c. Calculate profit for each output level.

d. What is Bob's short-run profit-maximizing output?

Section 9.4, Exercise 2 Susan's pool-cleaning service is a profit-maximizing, competitive firm. Susan cleans pools for $40 each. Her total cost per day is $425, of which $100 is a fixed cost. She cleans 10 pools per day.

a. What is Susan's daily profit?

b. Should Susan shut down in the short run?

Section 9.4, Exercise 3 The following table shows quantity and marginal cost data for Michael's Yard Care, a perfectly competitive firm providing landscape services. The firm can care for up to 10 lawns per day, and has daily fixed costs of $100.

Quantity	Marginal Cost
0	—
1	20
2	10
3	15
4	25
5	40
6	60
7	85
8	115
9	150
10	190

a. Use the table and the information given to find average total and average variable cost.
b. If the price of daily lawn care is $60, what is marginal revenue for Michael's Yard Care?
c. What is the firm's short-run profit maximizing output?
d. What is the firm's profit?

Section 9.4, Exercise 4 Refer to the table in the previous exercise. How would each of the following changes affect the firm's profit-maximizing output?

a. The price increases to $115.
b. Fixed costs increase to $500.
c. Marginal costs double at every level of output.
d. The price falls to $10.

Section 9.4, Exercise 5 Under what circumstances should Michael's Yard Care (see previous exercise) shut down in the short run?

Section 9.5, Exercise 1 The following graph shows cost curves for a perfectly competitive firm in the short run.

a. Identify the shutdown point.
b. Identify the breakeven point.
c. What is the short-run supply curve of the firm?

Section 9.5, Exercise 2 How will a competitive firm's short-run supply curve change under each of the following circumstances?

a. The wages of the firm's employees rise.
b. The firm's fixed costs increase.
c. The price of the inputs that the firm buys falls.

Section 9.6, Exercise 1 Suppose that in a perfectly competitive industry in which all firms have identical costs, firms are making a positive economic profit.

a. Can this be a long-run equilibrium for this industry? Explain.
b. What do you expect to see happen in the future?

Section 9.7, Exercise 1 Assume that a perfectly competitive, constant cost industry is currently in long-run equilibrium.

a. Draw a graph of the industry and a representative firm.
b. Suppose that demand increases. Identify the short-run equilibrium price and quantity of the industry and the quantity of the firm.
c. What will happen to this industry in the long run? Identify the long-run equilibrium price and quantities for the industry and the firm.

Section 9.7, Exercise 2 Assume that a perfectly competitive, increasing-cost industry is currently in long-run equilibrium.

a. Draw a graph of the industry.
b. Suppose that demand decreases. Identify the short-run equilibrium price and quantity of the industry.
c. What will happen to this industry in the long run? Identify the long-run equilibrium price and quantities for the industry.

10

Monopoly

It's late morning on a bright Saturday in May in Atlanta and baseball fans are streaming toward Turner Field, home of the Braves. Eight-year-old Max and big sister Ashley, 10, are wearing their Braves hats and carrying their mitts. Their older cousin John is taking them to their first game, and they are thrilled. For a fan, there's nothing like the energy of the crowd, the excitement of an important game, and the chance to root for the home team in person at a major league ballpark. In a baseball market like Atlanta's, this loyalty is a good thing, because the Braves are truly the only game in town. We've moved along the spectrum of market structures from the perfect competition at the Seattle fish market in the previous chapter to the other extreme: the monopoly of Major League Baseball.

When the Braves moved to Atlanta in 1966, the city's population was just under 200,000. By 1997, when young fan Max was born and the first pitch was thrown out at the newly built Turner Field, the population in the Atlanta region had grown to 3.1 million, and there was still no other major league team playing within several hundred miles. Without local competition, will the Braves organization still do its best to give the fans a good experience? When they get to the field, Ashley, Max, and John stock up on snacks and soft drinks. For each seat, sausage, ice cream bar, and bag of peanuts, John will have paid a price that has been carefully calculated to maximize profits in a monopoly market.

In this chapter we explore monopoly. A monopoly is a market in which there is only one producer that provides a good or service with no close substitutes. Because monopoly is at the opposite end of the spectrum from perfect competition, in that monopolists have no competitors, we will take care to compare the assumptions, mechanics, and outcomes of the monopoly model with those of the perfectly competitive model.

ALONG THE WAY, YOU WILL ALSO LEARN:

- The importance of market definition in characterizing monopoly markets.
- The difference between exogenous and strategic entry barriers.
- How monopolists decide on price.
- How monopolies maximize profits in the short run and the long run.
- How monopolies affect consumers and the broader economy.
- Why monopolies might charge different prices to different consumers.

 AT THE END OF THE CHAPTER, THE MYECONLAB LOGO WILL DIRECT YOU ONLINE

- MyEconLab is a resource-packed online homework and tutorial system that can help you perform better in your economics course. To log in for the first time, see page 30 for instructions.
- MyEconLab can help you apply important concepts from the chapter to real-world issues. Watch for the logo to indicate online features about monopoly pricing and price discrimination.
- At the end of each chapter, you'll find a special study section that will help you get the most out of your textbook and your instructor's MyEconLab course.

Defining the Market

To analyze a market, we must first define it. *When we define a market, we set the geographic area, time, and product characteristics that limit potential substitutes.* Think of a market as a set of concentric circles. In the innermost circle are all the goods that we consider to be in the market. In the next circle, we find the closest substitutes. As we move farther and farther from the center, we find goods that are weaker and weaker substitutes for the product as we have defined it.

How would we define the market for a Major League Baseball game in Atlanta? The two constraints in the previous sentence—location and a Major League Baseball game—go a long way toward defining the market. Let's first consider the geographical constraint of location. Restricting the market to a specific area such as Atlanta is a reflection of the fact that to "consume" a live baseball game, you must go to the site *where* it is played *at the time* that it is played. If the market were simply a Major League Baseball game, you could, in theory, travel from Atlanta to New York to see the Yankees and then fly right back after the game.

Focusing specifically on the Atlanta area, the map in Figure 10.1 shows that there are no Major League Baseball teams within 462 miles of Atlanta. The transportation costs, including the opportunity cost of your time to make the trip to the ballpark and back, make it unrealistic to include teams other than the Atlanta Braves in the market. The second constraint defines the market from the standpoint of product characteristics. You might be able to see high school games instead, but if you

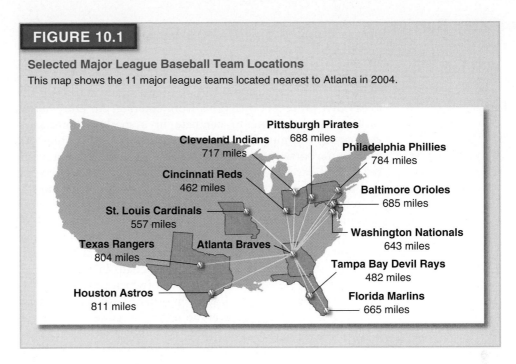

FIGURE 10.1

Selected Major League Baseball Team Locations

This map shows the 11 major league teams located nearest to Atlanta in 2004.

Pittsburgh Pirates
688 miles

Cleveland Indians
717 miles

Philadelphia Phillies
784 miles

Cincinnati Reds
462 miles

Baltimore Orioles
685 miles

St. Louis Cardinals
557 miles

Washington Nationals
643 miles

Texas Rangers
804 miles

Atlanta Braves

Tampa Bay Devil Rays
482 miles

Houston Astros
811 miles

Florida Marlins
665 miles

FIGURE 10.2

Substitutes for a Major League Baseball Game

We think of the market as a set of concentric circles. In the center circle, we have the desired good, a professional baseball game. As we move out from the center, we encounter increasingly weaker substitutes to the initial good, going from college baseball to watching a baseball game on television.

Televised baseball game

High-school and Little League baseball

College baseball

Major League Baseball game

want to see the best baseball in a major league park, then Little League, high school, and even college baseball are not in the same market. You could watch a game on television, but you do not consider a televised game a good substitute. You want to *go* to a game. Figure 10.2 shows the market for attendance at a game as we have defined the market. While substitutes exist, they all lie outside the center circle. Thus, being the only Major League Baseball team in Atlanta means that the Braves have a monopoly on Major League Baseball in that area.

Entry Barriers

Entry barrier
Obstacles that firms must overcome to compete in a market. Entry barriers can be exogenous, meaning that they are not created by incumbent firms, or strategic.

Recall that one of the key assumptions of the perfect competition model is that firms can enter and exit an industry freely. We make no such assumption when discussing monopoly; in fact, a central feature of monopoly markets is that some entry barrier exists that prevents other firms from entering. An **entry barrier** is an obstacle that firms must overcome to compete in a market. Sometimes these barriers are *exogenous*, meaning that they are not created by existing firms. Common exogenous entry barriers are economies of scale and certain government regulations. In the case of baseball, some exogenous entry barriers are the cost of forming a team, and the need to find a venue large enough to host the games.

In other cases, barriers are *strategic* in nature. That is, incumbent firms purposely make it as difficult as possible for other firms to enter the industry. Strategic entry barriers include certain legal restrictions, exclusive control over a vital production input, and certain types of government regulation. These types of entry barriers are extremely important in professional baseball. In fact, before a new major league team can play, the league's management (which consists of other team owners) must first admit the team to the league. In order to protect the interests of existing teams, new teams are almost never admitted in close physical proximity to existing teams. By establishing geographic boundaries on markets for each team, existing teams limit the number of potential competitors and ensure each existing team an exclusive market for its product. Other such barriers include the extensive contracts that the league has with both local and national television outlets. These contracts make it very difficult for a new team or league to garner a fan base.

Natural Monopoly

Natural monopoly
Exists if, due to scale economies, a monopoly will emerge if the market is left undisturbed.

In some industries, the economies of scale that arise when firms face high fixed and relatively low marginal costs create a natural barrier to entry. Under these circumstances, the long-run average cost (*LAC*) curve is downward-sloping. A **natural monopoly** occurs when the long-run average cost curve is downward-sloping until it crosses the demand curve. The term "natural monopoly" stems from the fact that, due to extensive scale economies, if the market is left undisturbed, a monopolistic market structure will evolve of its own accord. For example, strategic entry barriers are the most compelling reason for the Braves' position as a monopolist. However, the team might argue that they are also a natural monopoly due to the extremely high fixed costs of starting a professional baseball franchise and the low marginal cost of admitting an additional fan to see a game. To play a season, the Braves must set a roster of players (many of them with guaranteed contracts), enter into a lease agreement for a stadium, and pay various other fixed costs that do not depend on the level of attendance. Together, the costs exceed $100 million, and the Braves must pay all of these costs even if there is another team in the market.

Figure 10.3 shows the conditions under which the Braves could be a natural monopoly. In the figure, the high cost of starting up and maintaining a professional baseball franchise generates a long-run average cost curve that is downward-sloping beyond the point where it crosses the demand curve. In this case, adding a team and dividing the output such that each team plays for half as many fans causes the average cost of producing output to rise. Overall costs would be lower with just one team, because the marginal cost of accommodating one additional fan at a game is very low. Thus, the Braves could argue that they are a natural monopoly. In Chapter 13, we discuss natural monopolies in greater detail, including the government's role regarding their actions.

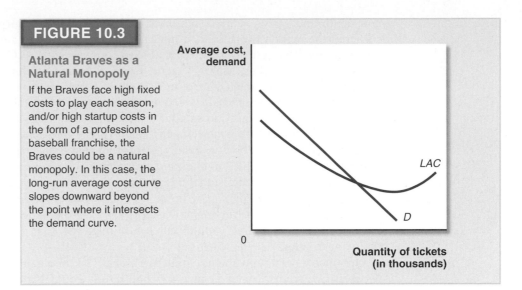

FIGURE 10.3

Atlanta Braves as a Natural Monopoly

If the Braves face high fixed costs to play each season, and/or high startup costs in the form of a professional baseball franchise, the Braves could be a natural monopoly. In this case, the long-run average cost curve slopes downward beyond the point where it intersects the demand curve.

You can think of the evolution of a natural monopoly as a race down the long-run average cost curve. Once one firm is established in the market, a new entrant will find it harder and harder to compete successfully as the output of the initial entrant grows, because it will have a higher average cost due to its lower output level. We will return to the concept of natural monopoly in this chapter when we discuss profit-maximizing output levels and efficiency.

Scale economies frequently occur because of mass production on assembly lines. Scale economies are also common in industries where the product itself is very large, as in the case of ship and airplane manufacturers. The huge physical plant that is required to assemble a Boeing 767 makes it impossible for a small firm to enter this industry. The same is true with container ships and tankers that carry oil and other liquids. They are simply too big to be built by a small firm.

Legal Restrictions

Governments have created laws can that limit entry in industries that require heavy investment in research and development. These laws encourage new products and processes by protecting the firms' rights to their new innovations. Firms can use these laws and regulations strategically to monopolize industries or product markets. Without the ability to protect their new product from those who might copy it, firms would have much less incentive to innovate. Patents and copyrights guarantee exclusive market power for a fixed period of time. **Patents** give inventors exclusive rights to produce and sell a new product for 20 years. **Copyrights** protect authors and publishers of literary, musical, dramatic, and artistic work against others copying their work. Copyrights last 95 years for businesses and 70 years beyond the death of the creator for individuals. The benefit to society of such protection is that it gives the firms property rights to their inventions and creations, which amplifies the incentive to invest in research and development. **Property rights** are the rights to gains from inventions and innovations.

Control of a Resource

One sure way to monopolize an industry is to own or to control all of a crucial input to production. Probably the most famous example of this occurred in the late

Patent
Gives inventors exclusive rights to produce and sell a new product for 20 years.

Copyright
Protects authors and publishers of literary, musical, dramatic, and artistic work against others copying their work.

Property rights
The rights to gains from firms' and individuals' inventions and innovations.

nineteenth and early twentieth centuries, when the ALCOA Corporation virtually cornered the market on bauxite, a mineral needed to produce aluminum. With no access to this key input, firms were unable to compete with ALCOA.

As we noted earlier, Major League Baseball maintains its monopoly power mostly through geographic control over markets governing how close teams' home cities can be to one another. It is very unlikely that Major League Baseball would allow another team to move to Atlanta. Furthermore, teams that own their own stadiums would not permit a new startup team to use the same facility to compete against them for market share. Finally, teams that rent their facilities from the cities in which they play, as the Braves do in Atlanta, insist that no other team be allowed to use the facility for professional baseball. Thus, even if a rival league that did not respect the existing league's geographic boundaries were started, it would have to bear the expense of constructing new facilities. In a fledgling league, a $500 million expense for a new stadium would represent a huge risk that most investors would not want to take.

Opponents are a fundamental input in baseball, because games are always played between two teams. Major League Baseball tightly controls this essential input by restricting entry into the league. Many cities would love to have Major League Baseball teams. They would even be willing to pay to gain access to the league, but the existing teams deny it to them.

Maintaining Monopoly in Baseball

Sherman Anti-Trust Act
Outlaws monopolizing an industry and firms' working together to restrain trade in an effort to control an industry.

Ironically, the Braves have been able to maintain their monopoly power through their *exemption* from a government law. Since 1890, the **Sherman Anti-Trust Act** has outlawed monopolizing an industry, or firms' working together to control an industry. For over 100 years, this sweeping piece of legislation has been the cornerstone of U.S. anti-trust policy. The United States Department of Justice has used the act to bring lawsuits against industry giants such as Standard Oil, ALCOA, IBM, and, most recently, Microsoft. We will discuss this act and other important pieces of anti-trust and regulatory legislation in detail in Chapter 13. For now, we note that through an unusual set of circumstances, Major League Baseball has been exempt from the Sherman Act since 1922.[1]

Baseball's anti-trust exemption ensures that the Braves will maintain their monopoly power and continue to use their membership in the league to their advantage. In addition to limiting the geographic market and restricting entry to the league, team owners fix the number of games that each team will play. The ability to set season length and schedules gives Major League Baseball in general and the Braves in particular market power; that is, the ability to set prices. Thus, although the owners of major league teams routinely engage in monopolistic behavior such as controlling the number of teams in the league, setting output, and even setting prices, the government is powerless to act against it.

To summarize, industries that a single firm has monopolized for a long time generally have strong entry barriers. In contrast, in the model of perfect competition, we assume that there are no entry barriers, so that firms enter an industry whenever they find it profitable to do so. We will return to the implications of these different assumptions when we discuss long-run profits later in the chapter.

---

[1] Technically, the Curt Flood Act of 1998 lifted the exemption, but the conditions of the Curt Flood Act are so restrictive that it has no real effect on league behavior, as it applies only to labor issues, and players must disband their union in order to have the act apply.

Monopoly's Demand and Marginal Revenue

The demand relationship facing a monopolist differs dramatically from that facing a competitive firm. Because the monopolist is the only supplier in the market, the demand curve for its output is the market demand curve. Unlike perfect competition, we do not need to analyze the firm and the market separately. In this case, the firm *is* the market.

Figure 10.4 shows a hypothetical market demand curve for a professional baseball game in Atlanta. For now, we make the simplifying assumption that all seats at the park are equally desirable in the eyes of consumers. Like all market demand curves, this curve shows the quantity of the good that consumers as a group are willing and able to buy at various prices. Consistent with the Law of Demand, the curve slopes downward. The location and the slope of the curve reflect consumers' willingness and ability to pay. The demand curve's vertical intercept indicates that at prices higher than $50, no fans will purchase tickets to the game. The horizontal intercept of 50 (measured in thousands) indicates that if tickets were free, 50,000 fans would want to come to the game. While there may be more than 50,000 fans, the opportunity cost of accepting a free ticket (for example, travel costs) exceeds the benefit they would receive.

The Braves have market power because they can choose to sell tickets at any price along the demand curve. While market power allows the Braves to make choices they would not be able to make under perfect competition, it does not mean that they can force consumers to buy tickets at any price. Because they face a downward-sloping demand curve, monopolists can charge a high price if they are willing to sell relatively little output. Alternatively, they can sell a great deal of output at a low price.

Price and Marginal Revenue for the Monopolist

To see this trade-off more clearly and to determine how monopolists decide upon the optimal price-quantity combination, let's consider the relationship between price and marginal revenue. Before we work through our example of the demand

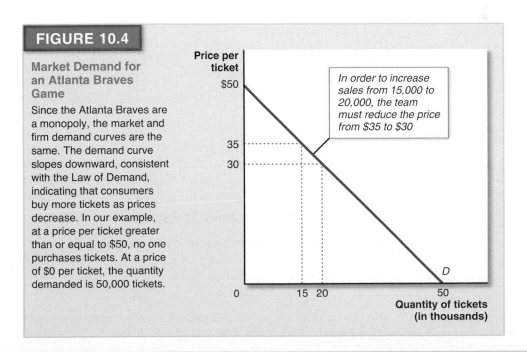

FIGURE 10.4

Market Demand for an Atlanta Braves Game

Since the Atlanta Braves are a monopoly, the market and firm demand curves are the same. The demand curve slopes downward, consistent with the Law of Demand, indicating that consumers buy more tickets as prices decrease. In our example, at a price per ticket greater than or equal to $50, no one purchases tickets. At a price of $0 per ticket, the quantity demanded is 50,000 tickets.

In order to increase sales from 15,000 to 20,000, the team must reduce the price from $35 to $30 for Braves games, recall that we assumed that all seats were equally desirable. Thus, we also assume that the team sells all of its tickets for the same price, though in reality it sells tickets to any given game at many different prices. Later in the chapter we will drop the assumption of a single price for tickets, and see how the Braves can increase their profits by charging multiple prices for tickets to the same game.

Recall that price and marginal revenue are always equal in perfect competition, because firms can sell all the output they want at the market price. As a result, the additional revenue is always equal to the market price. This is not true for the Braves. They must lower the price they charge if they want to increase their ticket sales. For example, suppose that the Braves can sell 15,000 tickets at a price of $35 per ticket. To increase the quantity demanded to 20,000, they must lower the price to $30 per ticket. If all consumers have the right to buy a ticket at the same price, the Braves cannot simply sell the additional 5,000 tickets at the $30 price and still charge $35 for the first 15,000. Because we assume all tickets sell for the same price, the Braves must sell all 20,000 at the lower price. That the Braves must reduce the price of all tickets to increase the quantity of tickets sold means that *a monopolist's marginal revenue—that is, the extra revenue it receives from selling one additional unit of output—is less than the price.*

To check this statement's accuracy, let's assume that the Braves currently charge $35 per ticket, which results in attendance of 15,000 and total revenue of $525,000. If the Braves lower the price to $34 per seat, attendance rises to 16,000 and the new total revenue is $544,000. To find the marginal revenue, we first subtract the total revenue at the old price from total revenue at the new price.[2] Then we divide the difference in revenue by the change in quantity. The calculation below shows that marginal revenue is $19,000, or just $19 per seat for the extra 1,000 seats, which is much less than the $34 price.

$$MR = \text{Change in total revenue / Change in quantity} =$$
$$[(\$544,000 - \$525,000)/(16,000 - 15,000)] = \$19 \text{ per seat}$$

It is possible for the price to be so low that the marginal revenue is negative. Suppose, for example, that the Braves reduce ticket prices from $15 to $14 per seat, and attendance increases from 35,000 to 36,000. The marginal revenue is:

$$\$14 \times 36,000 = \$504,000$$
$$\underline{-\$15 \times 35,000 = \$525,000}$$
$$\$-21,000$$

$$MR = -\$21,000/1,000 = -\$21 \text{ per seat}$$

Cutting the price brings in more fans, but because all fans now pay a lower price than before, the team's total revenue falls, something that the Braves certainly do not want to see happen. As we shall soon see, the impact of a price change on total revenue depends on the elasticity of demand in that area of the demand curve.

Changes in the Monopolist's Revenue

In each of the previous examples, there are two forces at work. Selling an additional 1,000 seats *increases* revenue because of the increase in quantity demanded, but it also *decreases* revenue because all seats are now sold at a lower price. Figure 10.5

---

[2] In this example we use a change in quantity of 1,000 seats to represent a one-unit change in output.

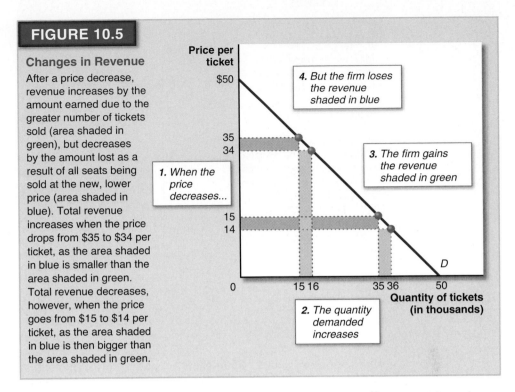

FIGURE 10.5

Changes in Revenue

After a price decrease, revenue increases by the amount earned due to the greater number of tickets sold (area shaded in green), but decreases by the amount lost as a result of all seats being sold at the new, lower price (area shaded in blue). Total revenue increases when the price drops from $35 to $34 per ticket, as the area shaded in blue is smaller than the area shaded in green. Total revenue decreases, however, when the price goes from $15 to $14 per ticket, as the area shaded in blue is then bigger than the area shaded in green.

illustrates these changes in revenue. In the first case, when the price fell from $35 to $34 per seat, total revenue went up because the gain from selling more (the area shaded in green) exceeded the loss (the area shaded in blue) from charging less. When the price fell from $15 to $14, total revenue fell because the loss (again, in blue) exceeded the gain (in green). In the end, whichever force (as measured by the two shaded areas in Figure 10.5) is greater determines whether total revenue rises or falls.

As the previous examples show, we can identify two distinct sections of the demand curve, one in which price cuts increase total revenue, and one in which price cuts reduce total revenue. These different sections are particularly easy to identify when the demand curve is a straight line. In this case, marginal revenue falls at twice the rate of the decline in price. Figure 10.6 shows the Braves' demand and marginal revenue curves. In this example, the slope of the demand curve is −1.0. Since the marginal revenue curve is twice as steep, its slope is −2.0. It cuts the horizontal axis and becomes negative at the quantity that corresponds to the midpoint of the demand curve: 25,000 tickets in this case. At all prices above the midpoint of the demand curve, marginal revenue is positive, and price decreases cause total revenue to rise. At all prices below the midpoint, marginal revenue is negative, and price decreases cause total revenue to fall.

We can use the curves in Figure 10.6 to find the implications of changes in output for marginal revenue. For instance, the Braves can sell 20,000 tickets at a price of $30 and marginal revenue of $10. At the midpoint of the demand curve, attendance is 25,000, ticket price is $25, and marginal revenue is $0. To verify that marginal revenue is $0, we check the change in revenue as we pass through the midpoint of the demand curve. When the price is $24, the quantity demanded is 26,000, and total revenue is $624,000. If price increases to $26, quantity demanded falls to 24,000, but total revenue remains unchanged at $624,000. Thus, the marginal revenue of this price change around the midpoint at $25 is zero.

Finally, because the marginal revenue—the added revenue from selling one more ticket—is negative beyond the midpoint of the demand curve, we know that the Braves will never operate below the midpoint of the demand curve. They will never

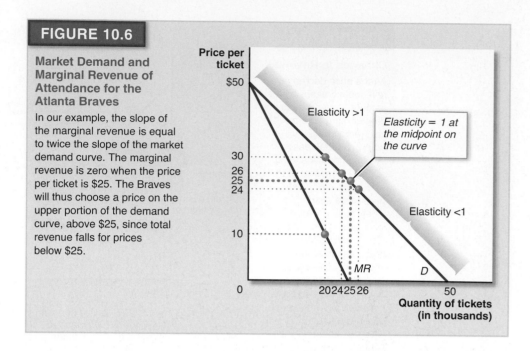

FIGURE 10.6

Market Demand and Marginal Revenue of Attendance for the Atlanta Braves

In our example, the slope of the marginal revenue is equal to twice the slope of the market demand curve. The marginal revenue is zero when the price per ticket is $25. The Braves will thus choose a price on the upper portion of the demand curve, above $25, since total revenue falls for prices below $25.

try to sell more than 25,000 tickets or charge a price of less than $25. What remains is to find out *which* price on the top half of the curve the Braves will choose. Next, we show how the monopolist chooses the best level of output to maximize profits.

Demand, Marginal Revenue, Total Revenue, and Elasticity

You know from Chapter 5 that the elasticity of demand varies along a linear demand curve. When demand is elastic, total revenue increases following a price decrease, and decreases when price increases. When demand is unit-elastic, total revenue remains constant following a price change. When demand is inelastic, total revenue will increase when price increases, and decrease when price decreases. We can use our understanding of the relationship between marginal revenue and total revenue to locate these points on the demand curve in Figure 10.6.

When the price changed from $24 to $26, total revenue remained unchanged and so marginal revenue was zero at the midpoint of $25. When total revenue remains unchanged, demand is unit-elastic. Thus, at the point where marginal revenue is equal to zero, demand is unit-elastic (equal to 1). In the upper half of the demand curve, marginal revenue is positive. When price falls, output increases more than proportionally, and total revenue increases. Thus, in the upper half of the demand curve, demand is elastic (greater than 1). In the lower half of the demand curve, marginal revenue is negative. In this range, when price falls, demand increases less than proportionally, and total revenue decreases. Thus, in the lower half of the curve, demand is inelastic (less than 1). A monopolist always operates in the elastic range of demand where marginal revenue is positive.

▶ Monopoly's Short-Run Profit Maximization

Like the perfectly competitive firm, the monopolist maximizes profit in the short run by producing the quantity that maximizes the difference between total revenue and

FIGURE 10.7

Short-Run Profit-Maximization Point for the Atlanta Braves, Using Total Revenue and Total Cost

In our hypothetical example, the Braves earn a negative profit between 0 and 10,000 tickets, as well as when 22,000 or more tickets sold, because total cost is greater than total revenue. They earn a positive profit in the shaded area, between 10,000 and 22,000 tickets are sold, because total revenue exceeds total cost. At the short-run profit-maximization point, where 18,000 tickets are sold, the total cost and total revenue curves are the farthest apart and so yield the greatest profit.

total cost for a given amount of capital. If we plot total revenue and short-run total cost on a graph, we can find the profit-maximizing output level by finding the point where the curves are farthest apart, as shown in Figure 10.7. Although we still find the profit-maximizing output by locating the largest difference between total cost and total revenue as we did in Chapter 9, Figure 10.7 and Figure 9.2 differ, because the monopolist's total revenue curve is not the same as the perfectly competitive firm's. Because perfectly competitive firms are price takers and monopolies are not, the monopolist must charge a lower price to sell additional output. Thus, the Braves' total revenue does not grow at a constant rate. In fact, it reaches a maximum at 25,000 tickets and falls thereafter. The total cost curve has the familiar S-shape, with a vertical axis intercept equal to fixed cost. If fewer than 10,000 fans attend, the Braves lose money. If 10,000 to 22,000 fans attend, the Braves earn positive profits. Beyond 22,000 fans, the Law of Diminishing Marginal Returns causes total cost to rise so sharply that the Braves again lose money. As the figure shows, the largest difference between revenue and cost occurs when attendance is 18,000. Therefore, the Braves maximize their profits at an attendance level of 18,000, as illustrated in Figure 10.8.

Monopoly's Profit-Maximizing Output: Marginal Cost and Marginal Revenue

Just as with perfect competition, the monopolist maximizes profits by producing output up to the point where the marginal revenue from the last unit produced equals the marginal cost of the last unit produced. Figure 10.8 shows the Braves' market demand and marginal revenue curves from Figure 10.6, and adds the team's marginal cost curve.[3] Note that the marginal revenue and marginal cost curves cross

myeconlab

Get Ahead of the Curve

Apply your understanding of monopoly pricing to explain the common practice of discounting Broadway tickets.

---

[3] In reality, the marginal cost of one additional fan at a baseball game is likely to be close to zero until the stadium is close to full capacity, but we show it as positive here to present a more typical example of marginal cost.

Two Views of the Home of the Braves

(a) If the Braves set these ticket prices too high, attendance will be too low to maximize profits.

(b) Since the marginal cost of having an additional fan in the stands is very low, the best strategy for the Braves is to set prices such that they generate lots of revenue from attendance.

FIGURE 10.8

Profit-Maximization Point for the Atlanta Braves, Using Marginal Revenue and Marginal Cost

In our example, marginal revenue and marginal cost are equal at the profit-maximization point, where 18,000 tickets are sold. The profit-maximizing price is determined by the demand curve, not by the marginal revenue curve, so the profit-maximization price for the monopolist is $32 rather than $14.

when attendance is 18,000, so the Braves maximize their profits when they draw 18,000 fans. At this point, marginal revenue and marginal cost are both $14. What price should the monopolist charge? While it might seem sensible to charge a price of $14 in this example, the Braves can charge much more than that. Remember that the demand curve, not the marginal revenue curve, tells us consumers' willingness and ability to pay for various levels of output. To find the profit-maximizing price, we must look directly upward from the profit-maximizing output level to the demand curve. From there we read across to the vertical axis to find the profit-maximizing price of $32.

No Monopoly Supply Curve. The determination of the profit-maximizing quantity and price in this market raises an interesting question. Where is the supply curve? The answer is that for a monopolist, there is no supply curve. Recall that a supply curve tells us the quantity that firms sell at various prices. For perfectly competitive markets, the supply curve is formed from the actions of many suppliers, so no one firm can influence the price. Competitive firms are price takers that make decisions about how much to sell by comparing their marginal cost to the price set at the market level. Monopolies *choose* the price that maximizes profits based on the demand and marginal revenue curves. As such, the relationship between price and quantity are not based solely on cost information. It is the interaction of firm cost and consumer demand that determines the price-quantity relationship for a monopoly.

The Monopolist's Profit. Although we can use Figure 10.8 to find the profit-maximizing attendance level, it does not give us enough information to calculate *how much* profit the Braves earn when attendance is 18,000. To see how much the Braves' profit is, we must add an average total cost curve to Figure 10.8, as seen in Figure 10.9. We can then use the same geometric principles as in Figure 9.3 to find the areas that represent total revenue, total cost, and total profit. Total revenue equals price times quantity. We know that the area of a rectangle is *base times height*. In the graph, we find total revenue by multiplying the base (the profit-maximizing quantity of 18,000) by the height (the profit-maximizing price of $32). Thus, the area of the rectangle is 18,000 × $32 = $576,000, which is equal to total revenue.

Total cost equals average total cost times quantity. In Figure 10.9, this is the area shaded in yellow. When 18,000 people attend the game, the average cost per person is $25. Once again using the *base times height* formula, total cost is $450,000

FIGURE 10.9

Total Revenue, Cost, and Profit for the Atlanta Braves

Total revenue is equal to price times quantity, which, at a price per ticket of $32 and attendance of 18,000 people, is the area shaded in green plus the area shaded in yellow. Total cost equals average cost of $25 times quantity, which is the area of the rectangle shaded in yellow. Total profit is equal to the difference between the two areas; that is, to the area shaded in green.

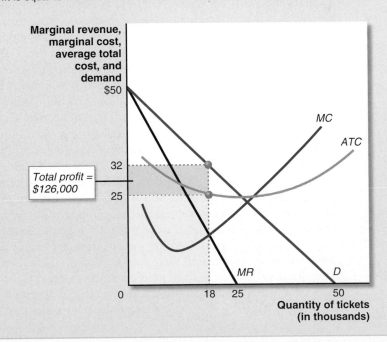

(18,000 × $25). The difference between total revenue and total cost is the area shaded in green, which represents the total profit of $126,000.

TEST + *E X T E N D* Your Knowledge

1. TEST Draw a figure similar to Figure 10.9 that shows a monopolist earning zero economic profits. (*Hint:* The *TR* and *TC* areas must be equal.)

2 . E X T E N D Go to the Web site www.baseballprospectus.com/ article.php?articleid=1333 and find the table that shows total revenue and revenue per capita for all major league teams. Which teams have the highest revenue? How do the revenue differences compare to population differences? Can you make any inferences about monopoly power and city size?

► Monopoly's Long-Run Profit Maximization

In the long run, all inputs are variable. For the Braves, this may mean a new stadium, new executive offices, or a new training facility for the players. Despite the greater flexibility of inputs in the long run, a firm still maximizes profits when the marginal cost of the last unit of output just equals the marginal revenue that it brings to the firm. The difference between maximizing profit in the short run and doing so in the long run is that in the long run, the firm can increase its output in the most efficient way; that is, it can choose the lowest-cost combination of labor and capital. In baseball, the trend is toward building smaller stadiums, because teams no longer need or want to share venues with their NFL football counterparts. By downsizing their capacity but offering more amenities and types of seating, teams hope to increase the demand for their product and realize greater profits.

At this point, we note another major difference between perfect competition and the monopoly outcome. In the previous chapter, we saw that in perfectly competitive markets, firms earn zero economic profits in the long run. When competitive firms earn positive economic profits, it entices other firms to enter the industry, which shifts the market supply curve to the right. This rightward shift causes prices to fall, a process that continues until economic profits are driven to zero. If the Braves are earning large economic profits, it certainly would look attractive to a potential owner of a major league team. Does this mean that the long-run profits will be eaten away by a flood of new teams? To find the answer, we must recall our assumptions of the monopoly model. We assume that entry barriers prevent new firms from joining the industry. Potential owners would like to enter, but they cannot. Entry barriers are the reason the long-run profitability of a monopoly can differ from that of a perfectly competitive industry. Unlike in perfect competition, long-run positive profits can persist indefinitely in a monopoly.

In Major League Baseball, the Braves have nothing to fear. As noted earlier, unique entry barriers ensure that the only competition they face will be on the field. No matter how profitable they are, the only way the Braves will ever have to compete economically against another major league team is if they grant permission for another team to compete in their market. Potential competitors cannot even appeal to the legal system for help in gaining access to markets in baseball. As noted earlier, Major League Baseball's exemption from the Sherman Anti-Trust Act prevents potential competitors from suing to gain access to the markets.

The Efficiency Effects of Monopoly

So far, our focus in this chapter has been on the firm and on the effect of monopoly power on profits. To fully analyze monopoly as a market structure, we must go beyond this focus to evaluate the effects of monopoly on consumers and on the economy as a whole.

Efficiency and Deadweight Loss

In Chapter 9, you saw that a firm produces the efficient level of output when it sets price equal to marginal cost. At the market level, this output level is efficient because it maximizes the sum of consumer and producer surplus, and there is no deadweight loss. To see how monopoly fares in terms of efficiency, let's analyze a hypothetical vendor at Turner Field in Atlanta, Betsy's Baked Braves. Betsy sells a clever dessert consisting of a pie decorated with an image of some of the more popular players, which she bakes and sells at the stadium on game days. Because she has the only permit to sell baked goods in the stadium, she has a monopoly in the market. Figure 10.10 shows the standard monopoly solution, where Betsy sets marginal revenue equal to marginal cost, and uses the demand curve to determine price. To simplify the analysis, we assume that marginal cost is constant at $6.

In the graph, marginal cost and marginal revenue are $6 and price is $9 at the profit-maximizing output level of 40 pies per hour. If the firm were perfectly competitive, it would operate where the marginal cost curve intersects the demand curve, at a price of $6 and output of 80 pies per hour. Recall that if any perfectly competitive firm charges a price above marginal cost, consumers will go elsewhere.

myeconlab

Get Ahead of the Curve

Evaluate the effects of monopoly in the media business on the variety of music played on local radio stations.

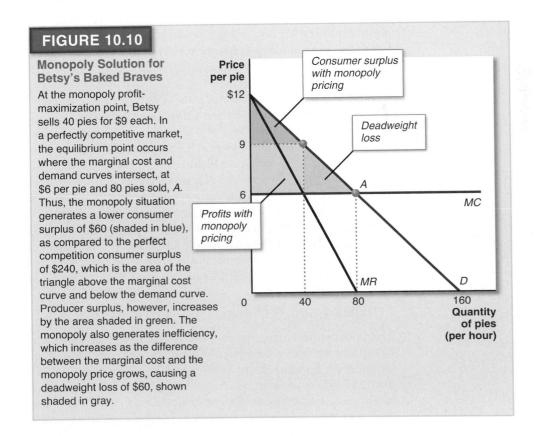

FIGURE 10.10

Monopoly Solution for Betsy's Baked Braves

At the monopoly profit-maximization point, Betsy sells 40 pies for $9 each. In a perfectly competitive market, the equilibrium point occurs where the marginal cost and demand curves intersect, at $6 per pie and 80 pies sold, *A*. Thus, the monopoly situation generates a lower consumer surplus of $60 (shaded in blue), as compared to the perfect competition consumer surplus of $240, which is the area of the triangle above the marginal cost curve and below the demand curve. Producer surplus, however, increases by the area shaded in green. The monopoly also generates inefficiency, which increases as the difference between the marginal cost and the monopoly price grows, causing a deadweight loss of $60, shown shaded in gray.

Thus, perfectly competitive sellers must set price equal to marginal cost. Because she is a monopolist facing a downward-sloping demand curve, Betsy can charge more for each pie while selling fewer of them. If she had competitors, consumers would be able to buy more pies at lower prices.

Changes in Consumer Surplus. Just because consumers pay a higher price for Betsy's pies, society is not necessarily worse off. Before making any claims about social well-being, we must first separate out the effect of the monopoly price into the loss for consumers, and the loss for society as a whole. To do so, we begin by noting that in a perfectly competitive market, if producers have a constant marginal cost of $6, pies would sell for $6. Recall from Chapters 4 and 6 that the demand curve shows what consumers are willing and able to pay for various quantities of pie, and that consumer surplus measures the benefits that flow to consumers from paying less than the maximum that they are willing to pay. In Figure 10.10, the demand curve shows that some consumers are willing and able to pay much more than the market price of $6 to buy a pie, but they do not have to pay more, since all consumers are charged $6. All consumers whose individual demand is represented by a point above $6 on the market demand curve get a bargain of sorts because they pay less than what the pie is worth to them. In Figure 10.10, the triangle which is formed by the demand curve, the marginal cost curve, and the vertical axis (the three shaded areas combined) is the consumer surplus when consumers pay the competitive price.

When Betsy charges the monopoly price, she captures some of the consumer surplus as revenue, represented by the rectangle shaded in green. Consumer surplus shrinks to the triangle shaded in blue, which is the area above the monopoly price and below the demand curve. The transfer of value from consumers to the monopolist certainly makes consumers worse off. From the perspective of the entire economy, however, it is rather like taking money out of one pocket and putting it into the other. In other words, nothing is lost to society as a whole. Benefits simply change hands. However, we have not yet accounted for the entire original consumer surplus.

Deadweight Loss. We know that a monopoly reduces consumer surplus and that the monopolist captures the area shaded in green, but what happens to the area shaded in gray? It is simply lost. The forty-first to eightieth pies are not sold, so neither consumers nor Betsy receive this value. The area shaded in gray represents the *deadweight loss*; that is, the loss in consumer and producer surplus resulting from the loss in efficiency caused by the monopoly. From a societal standpoint, this is a loss rather than a transfer, because the monopolist could produce more units at a cost below what society is willing to pay but chooses not to. Thus, deadweight loss is also sometimes called *social cost*. Monopolies cause a reduction in efficiency in the short run, because the price, or value of the product to society, exceeds marginal cost, the cost to society of producing the good. In general, the greater the monopoly price is in excess of the marginal cost, the greater the loss of efficiency.

Efficiency and Technology

You know from Chapter 9 that the adoption and use of the most current technology is an imperative for perfectly competitive firms. This is not always the case for monopolies. Suppose that a new oven is developed that could increase Betsy's productivity by 25 percent. The purchase of the new oven is a choice rather than an imperative, as she has no competitors. If Betsy decides that she is satisfied with her profits as they are, she can opt not to purchase the oven, and she will still have the entire market to herself.

Critics of this argument believe that monopolists like Betsy have every incentive to innovate and adopt new technology to protect their market power. Microsoft chairman Bill Gates argues that Microsoft's continued success in the marketplace is due to its commitment to innovation. The desire to protect its market position gives firms like Microsoft an incentive to continue to innovate and patent new production processes before a potential entrant can do so.

Proponents of the idea that monopolies are slow to adopt new technology point to historical examples such as the decline of the U.S. motorcycle industry in the 1970s. Harley-Davidson dominated the large bike segment of the market until the 1970s. At that point, Harley-Davidsons were technologically outdated and had suffered from the same nagging engine problems for years. In the late 1970s, sensing an opportunity, Japanese motorcycle manufacturers introduced large bikes to the U.S. market with great success. In 1983, Harley-Davidson sought temporary trade protection through the U.S. government. While the tariffs were in place, Harley-Davidson essentially remade itself as a company, increasing productivity by 50 percent, and cutting defects by 68 percent.[4] Critics of monopoly power argue that Harley-Davidson's ability to increase its efficiency and quality so substantially in such a short period of time provides strong evidence that the rigors of competition forced the company to be efficient.

Government Regulation

Sometimes the government decides that the private market outcome is not in the best interest of society. In such cases, it may intervene by producing the good or service instead of relying on private market suppliers, as in the case of national defense, police, and fire services. Can you imagine the confusion and inefficiency that would result if a service such as fire protection were conducted by private firms only for their own customers? Believe it or not, this was once the case. In the eighteenth century, fire companies would respond to fires only at houses that displayed a plaque indicating that the family was a customer.

Governments may also regulate an industry by enacting laws designed to limit access to markets. Licensing is one way to limit market access. For example, to legally serve alcoholic beverages, a bar or restaurant must first secure a liquor license. The government limits the number of licenses available at any one time, which restricts access to the market. Zoning laws can also limit market access. Some local governments have passed ordinances that ban restaurants with drive-through windows in an effort to keep fast-food restaurants out of specific areas. Although there might be good reasons for such laws, they reduce competition in the local restaurant market.

Regulated industry
An industry in which the government oversees a specific aspect of the firms' behavior, such as occupational safety, product safety, entry conditions, or pricing.

Governments Allow Natural Monopolies. Governments sometimes also allow monopolies when they decide that, due to scale economies, it might be most efficient to have only one firm in an industry. If it allows the monopoly to exist, however, the government then supervises the monopoly's behavior. A **regulated industry** is one in which the government oversees specific behaviors such as occupational safety, product safety, entry conditions, or pricing. Natural monopolies are allowed to remain intact, but only under supervision by the government. Electric utilities, water and sewer companies, and cable television companies are regulated industries. In exchange for the right to be a monopolist in a certain market, the right of firms to set their own prices is heavily restricted.

---

[4] Peter C. Reid, *Well Made in America: Lessons from Harley-Davidson on Being the Best*, McGraw Hill, 1991, page 148.

Because the relationship between a monopoly and the government can be complex and can affect many large industries that serve so many consumers, we present a full discussion of these market arrangements in Chapter 13.

Rent Seeking

Rent seeking
The expenditure of resources to transfer wealth or income from one group to another that does not result in increased production.

In order to gain access to and maintain monopoly profits, firms may engage in **rent seeking**, which is the expenditure of resources to transfer wealth or income from one group to another, which does not result in increased production. In the case of monopolies, firms use resources to lobby governments to grant them monopoly power. In baseball, for instance, major league team owners lobby the government to maintain the anti-trust exemption that allows the teams to ignore the rules set out in the Sherman Act. In Figure 10.10, the firm would be willing to spend its entire profits (the area shaded in green) on lobbying efforts in order to protect its position as a monopoly. Because it uses resources that are not devoted to increases in output, rent seeking is inefficient. Thus, the total loss to society in Figure 10.10 is equal to the deadweight loss plus any resources used for rent seeking.

TEST + *E X T E N D* Your Knowledge

1. TEST In Figure 10.10 what would happen to Betsy's sales if the industry were perfectly competitive and she tried to charge consumers the monopoly price of $9? Explain.

2. EXTEND Use the geometry formula for the area of a triangle $A = 1/2b \times h$ to solve for the value of consumer surplus with the competitive price of $6, and with the monopoly price of $9 in Figure 10.10. What is the value of the deadweight loss?

▶ Price Discrimination

In Figure 10.10, we noted that as a monopolist, Betsy is able to capture some of the consumer surplus. She does not claim all the consumer surplus, however, as the area

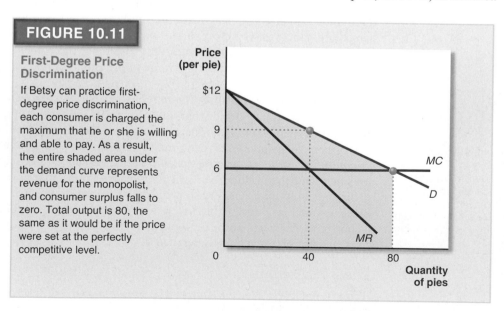

FIGURE 10.11

First-Degree Price Discrimination

If Betsy can practice first-degree price discrimination, each consumer is charged the maximum that he or she is willing and able to pay. As a result, the entire shaded area under the demand curve represents revenue for the monopolist, and consumer surplus falls to zero. Total output is 80, the same as it would be if the price were set at the perfectly competitive level.

Price discrimination
Separating customers
into groups based on their
willingness to pay, and then
charging them different
prices.

between the monopoly price and demand curve still represents value in excess of the monopoly price of $9. If Betsy could figure out who receives this extra value and force them to pay a higher price, she would be able to claim more of the consumer surplus. That is, she could transfer part of the consumer surplus to the producer. This is the essence of **price discrimination**, which means separating customers into groups based on their willingness to pay and then charging them different prices. Although the more common use of the word discrimination has to do with distasteful actions based on personal prejudices, we mean something quite different here. In this context, discrimination means, "able to tell the difference between." More specifically, it means that the producer can distinguish between those who are willing and able to pay more and those who are not.

There are three forms of price discrimination. In the following paragraphs, we define, briefly discuss, and include some common examples of each. It is important to remember that price discrimination exists only if the producer sells the same product to different consumers at different prices. Charging consumers different prices if the cost of serving them differs is *not* price discrimination. For example, if it costs a gas station owner more to have an employee pump the gas than to allow customers to pump their own, then it is not price discrimination to charge more for full-service than for self-service. However, it *is* price discrimination to charge people who drive sports cars more than those who drive sedans for the same grade of gas.

First-Degree Price Discrimination

First-degree price discrimination
Also known as personalized pricing, occurs when firms take advantage of differences in consumers' willingness to pay for the same item, and each consumer is charged the maximum that they are willing and able to pay.

In the most rarely observed form of price discrimination, **first-degree price discrimination** or *personalized pricing*, firms take advantage of the fact that consumers differ in their willingness and ability to pay for the same item by charging consumers the maximum that they are willing and able to pay. Because consumers have no incentive to reveal their maximum price, the firm cannot simply offer a single price, and must employ a different way of selling its products to get buyers to reveal what they are willing and able to pay. One possibility is to sell goods using an auction wherein consumers must reveal their willingness to pay or have no chance to purchase the item. This works only if consumers believe that no other firm sells the same item. Thus, if Betsy can convince every customer that he must pay what the pie was worth to him in order to get one, and that she will know if a customer is lying, her customers will reveal their willingness to pay. As Figure 10.11 shows, if Betsy can consistently practice first-degree price discrimination, she captures the entire consumer surplus, because every customer pays the maximum that he is willing and able to offer. In addition, Betsy's Baked Braves sells the same amount as it would if it were a perfectly competitive firm, because she continues to sell until the marginal price (the price of the last unit) is just equal to marginal cost. This point corresponds to the same output level as with perfect competition, and there is no deadweight loss. The difference is that *unlike* perfect competition, each consumer is charged a different price, and only the last unit is sold at marginal cost. Fortunately for consumers, such a pricing strategy is extremely difficult to implement, and firms can rarely extract the entire consumer surplus during a transaction.

Second-Degree Price Discrimination

Second-degree price discrimination
Also known as quantity discounting, when firms sell output at more than one price by taking advantage of each consumer's different willingness to pay for different quantities.

With **second-degree price discrimination**, also known as *quantity discounting*, firms sell output at more than one price by taking advantage of the fact that each consumer's willingness to pay for a good declines as the amount he buys rises. Firms thus sell goods and services at a discount when consumers buy larger quantities. For

LifeLessons

It Pays to Be Flexible

The next time you decide to travel, think flexible. Most airlines offer multiple prices for travel between cities. Like all price-discrimination schemes, these fares are intended to capture consumer surplus from travelers. Airlines design fares by setting a price known as a full coach fare and then offering discounts from that fare for consumers who are willing and able to accept certain restrictions on when they fly, how long they stay at their destination, how far in advance they book their tickets, and now even how much luggage they carry. In general, business travelers have more inelastic (less price-sensitive) demand than leisure travelers, who tend to be more price-conscious. The airlines design the restrictions to be very inconvenient for most business travelers, who then pay the higher fares. Suppose it is Monday, and you have just learned that you must travel from Charlotte, North Carolina, to Phoenix, Arizona, for a one-day meeting on Wednesday, two days from now. You don't have time to change planes more than once each way. Your Aunt Edna also wants to head to Phoenix, but only because she has never seen a cactus before. You are locked into a specific day; she can travel whenever she pleases. You will spend only one night there, but Aunt Edna is flexible, so she decides to order tickets now for a flight in November and to stay over a Saturday night. Let's check the fares for you and Aunt Edna. Prices quoted are the best available fares from American Trans Air on Travelocity.com on June 2, 2004:

You: $380
Aunt Edna: $315

It turns out that Aunt Edna's willingness to be flexible saves her more than 20 percent on her ticket. Such savings are quite typical. In fact, the savings are so dramatic when the round trip includes a Saturday night stay that many companies offer their employees incentives to leave on Saturday for Monday meetings. Even though it requires an extra day and a half of meals and another night in a hotel, the firms usually come out ahead.

---

example, Betsy can have a "buy one pie, get the second pie for 50 percent off" sale. The communications firms, too, sometimes charge more for the first units of calling than for subsequent units. The Braves may practice this form of price discrimination by offering discounts for season tickets or group sales.

Third-Degree Price Discrimination

Third-degree price discrimination

When a firm charges different prices in different markets for the same product or service. To put this strategy into practice, a firm needs three things: market power in both markets, different demand in the two markets, and the ability to prevent reselling.

Third-degree price discrimination, the most common form of price discrimination, occurs when a firm charges different prices in different markets for the same product or service. To put this strategy into practice, a firm needs three things: market power in both markets, different demand in the two markets, and the ability to prevent resale. If Betsy knows that senior citizens and children are generally less willing or able to pay for her pies, and charges them a lower price as a result, she practices third-degree price discrimination. To accomplish this, Betsy needs monopoly power in the pie market for both adults and children. Children and adults must differ in their willingness and ability to pay for the pies. Finally, Betsy must find a way to prevent children from buying the cheaper pies and reselling them to adults at prices lower than her adult price. Some common examples of third-degree price discrimination are children's prices at movies, senior citizen discount days at retail shops, and advance purchase discounts on airfares.

Although there are laws designed to limit firms' ability to price-discriminate, there have been relatively few legal challenges to third-degree price discrimination, as it is not seen as an impediment to competition. The exceptions typically involve firms

TABLE 10.1

Comparing Perfect Competition and Monopoly

Characteristic	Perfect Competition	Monopoly
Number of firms	Many	One
Barriers to entry	No	Yes
Firm(s) have market power (ability to set price)	No	Yes
Price at profit-maximizing output	Equal to marginal cost	Exceeds marginal cost
Firm(s) can earn positive short-run economic profits	Yes	Yes
Firm(s) can earn positive long-run economic profits	No	Yes
Firm(s) produce efficient level of output	Yes	No
Firm(s) can price discriminate	No	Yes

Get Ahead of the Curve

Use your knowledge of the monopoly model to show how patients and international markets allow drug companies to price discriminate.

claiming that cost differences require that they charge different prices. For example, dry cleaners have been criticized for charging higher prices to clean women's blouses than men's shirts, even when they are made from the same fabric; and the courts have rejected the notion that haircut prices can be based on gender alone.

Perfect Competition Versus Monopoly

Throughout the chapter, we have identified several key differences between the model of perfect competition and the monopoly model. As we apply these models and study other models in future chapters, it will be useful to keep these differences in mind. Table 10.1 summarizes the key characteristics of these two important models of firm behavior.

Strategy and Policy
Creating a Monopoly to Track Internet Addresses

Can you imagine the confusion if all firms and individuals were able to make up a universal resource locator (URL) for their Web sites without checking first to see whether that address was already occupied? URLs are the Internet addresses for Web pages that end in extensions like *.com* or *.net*. In order to prevent such chaos, a single company named Verisign has been entrusted with the task of assigning all Internet Web addresses that end in *.com* or *.net*. The benefit of such a system for all users of the Internet is that it creates a level of order that would otherwise be absent. However, as with most forms of regulation and government intervention, allowing Verisign to control Internet addresses runs the risk of creating new problems.

In September 2003, just such a problem arose when Verisign introduced a new service known as Site Finder. According to Verisign, Site Finder is designed to assist customers when they mistype a URL and accidentally enter a non-existent address. Before Site Finder went live, any person making such a mistake would receive an error message and no additional information, or perhaps another firm's redirection application, such as one developed by Microsoft. Instead of finding a competing product or offering an error message with no further information, the new product by Verisign automatically directs consumers to a Verisign site that prompts the user with a number of questions such as "Did you mean to type ...?" and then follows with nearly identical spellings that lead to active sites. Although this innovation may seem innocent enough, to Internet insiders, the change is revolutionary. "This issue has become a sort of flashpoint for the industry. This is about who controls the Internet," according to Mark Lewyn, the chairman of a firm whose products perform the same function as Site Finder.[5]

Because the same company that controls Internet addresses also operates Site Finder, its critics argue that it has an unfair advantage in the market for redirection software. The argument is similar to the one made by critics of Microsoft, who claim that its dominance of the operating system market gives it an unfair advantage in the applications market (e.g., word processing and spreadsheet software).

Critical-Thinking Questions

1. If the government were to become even more involved in regulating the Internet, how might it restore competition to the redirection software market?
2. What are the potential drawbacks of allowing Site Finder to leave the automatic connection to its redirection software in place?

▶ SUMMARY

- **Defining the market.** A firm is a monopoly if it provides a good or service in a market with no close substitutes. Thus, to determine whether a firm is a monopoly, it is important to first define the market from the consumer's perspective.

- **Entry barriers.** Most monopolists have some way to keep other firms from entering the market. These entry barriers can be exogenous, such as economies of scale and government intervention, or they can take the form of strategic actions by the firm, such as patents and copyrights.

- **Monopoly's demand and marginal revenue.** Because the monopolist does not compete against other suppliers, the market demand curve is the monopoly's demand curve. The market demand curve is downward-sloping. Thus, in contrast with perfect competition, the monopolist must reduce price to increase output. Marginal revenue is less than price, and so the marginal revenue curve lies below the demand curve.

- **Monopoly's short-run profit maximization.** In the short run, the monopolist maximizes profits by setting marginal revenue equal to marginal cost to determine the best output level and then determines price from the demand curve. No unique relationship between price and quantity supplied exists for monopolists.

- **Monopoly's long-run profit maximization.** In the long run, the monopolist's profits are not necessarily eroded by the addition of more firms to the industry. In fact, successful monopolies typically generate substantial positive long-run profits. If the

---

[5] David Macguire, "With Site Finder, Verisign Sparks Internet-Wide Criticism," *The Washington Post*, September 25, 2003.

firm's entry barriers can be sustained over long periods of time, the monopolist may show positive long-run profits.

- **The efficiency effects of monopoly.** When monopolies charge in excess of marginal cost, inefficiency results. This inefficiency, also known as deadweight loss, increases as the difference between price and marginal cost increases. Over long periods of time, monopolies may not be as diligent as competitive firms at developing and adopting new technologies, because they may be able to remain profitable without doing so. Perfectly competitive firms must always innovate and adopt new technologies as they become available so as to remain in business.

- **Price discrimination.** Monopolies may be able to use their market power to charge different prices to different consumers based on their willingness to pay. When monopolies price discriminate, they transfer a portion of the consumer surplus from consumers to themselves in the form of additional revenues.

▶KEY TERMS

Copyright 257
Entry barrier 256
First-degree price
   discrimination 271
Monopoly 253
Natural monopoly 256
Patent 257

Price discrimination 271
Property rights 257
Regulated industry 269
Rent seeking 270
Second-degree price
   discrimination 271

Sherman Anti-Trust Act
   258
Third-degree price
   discrimination 272

▶PROBLEMS

1. Draw a set of concentric circles similar to those in Figure 10.2 that defines the market for your college. To what degree do you believe that it is a monopolist?
2. Is the following statement a good example of a monopoly? "American Luggage Company has a great new briefcase that also holds computers. It is really unique in the way that it opens." Why or why not?
3. What kinds of entry barriers might exist in the popular music recording industry?
4. List possible entry barriers (if any) in the following markets:
   a. Lemonade sold at roadside stands
   b. Writing mystery novels
   c. Subway car manufacturing
   d. Newspaper publication
   e. Running shoe manufacturing
   f. Pizza sold in shops
5. Many people say that Microsoft has a near monopoly in the operating system market, but argue that consumers are better off than if there were many competing operating systems. Why might they make such a claim?
6. In Figure 10.4, why is the demand for Braves games not infinite when the price is equal to zero?
7. How do you suppose the addition of a second major league team in Atlanta will affect the demand curve for the Braves? Draw a curve similar to that in Figure 10.4 for the Braves after the new team enters the market.
8. Suppose that in Figure 10.9, the marginal cost of attendance is equal to zero. What is the new profit-maximizing output level? Suppose the Braves' only cost is a $500,000 fixed cost. Calculate the new team profits assuming a price of $25 per ticket.

9. Is it possible for a monopolist to lose money in the long run? Draw a graph to support your answer.
10. Explain why monopolists are likely to be more successful if they face a highly inelastic demand curve.
11. Using graphs, show that if a monopolist's demand curve is highly inelastic (steeply sloped), the difference between price and marginal cost is greater than if demand is elastic (relatively flat).
12. Why don't monopolists produce the socially desired level of output? Use a graph to explain your answer.
13. True or false: If the average total cost curve is horizontal, a monopoly will produce the efficient level of output. Explain your answer using a graph.
14. To decide if a firm is a natural monopolist, must we evaluate the short run or the long run? Explain.
15. What conditions are necessary for a firm to practice third-degree price-discrimination?
16. Many restaurants have specific days or times of day during which they offer senior citizen discounts. Is this a good example of third-degree price discrimination? Why or why not?
17. Suppose that the Texas Ski Company has a monopoly on skiing in Texas due to a special technology that allows it to make snow at all temperatures. Draw a graph similar to Figure 10.9 with the following characteristics: Demand is linear (a straight line). At a price of zero, 1,000 lift tickets are demanded. When the price reaches $200, the quantity of lift tickets demanded drops to zero. The marginal revenue curve intersects the vertical axis at $200, and intersects the horizontal axis at 500 tickets. Marginal cost is constant at $40 per ticket.
    a. Draw a graph showing demand, marginal revenue, and marginal cost, and show the monopoly profit-maximizing output and price on your graph.
    b. What is the price if Texas Ski prices like a competitive firm?
    c. Label the deadweight loss on your graph assuming the firm prices at the monopoly level.
    d. Show the quantity of tickets that Texas Ski sells if it can practice first-degree price discrimination.
18. Use a graph to show that a natural monopoly, if left unchecked, sets a price that generates a deadweight loss, but that if the firm is forced to price at marginal cost, its profits are negative.

Section 10.1, Exercise 1 How is a market best defined?

Section 10.2, Exercise 1 What factors are barriers to entry into a market?

Section 10.3, Exercise 1 The following table shows the demand schedule for a monopolist.

Price	Quantity Demanded
$10	0
9	1
8	2
7	3
6	4
5	5
4	6
3	7
2	8
1	9
0	10

a. Find marginal revenue.
b. Graph the demand curve and the marginal revenue curve.

Section 10.3, Exercise 2 What is the relationship between price elasticity of demand and marginal revenue for a monopolist?

Section 10.4, Exercise 1 The following table shows demand and total cost for a monopolist.

Price	Quantity Demanded	Total Cost
$500	0	$ 20,000
450	50	30,000
400	100	35,000
350	150	45,000
300	200	60,000
250	250	80,000
200	300	105,000
150	350	135,000
100	400	170,000
50	450	210,000
0	500	255,000

a. Find total revenue.
b. At what price is total revenue maximized?
c. Find profit.
d. What is the monopolist's short-run profit-maximizing output?

Section 10.4, Exercise 2 A monopolist is selling in a market with the following demand curve:

$$P = 500 - \tfrac{1}{2}Q$$

Thus marginal revenue is: $MR = 500 - Q$. The firm has constant marginal costs of $50 per unit. Find the monopolist's profit-maximizing price and quantity.

Section 10.4, Exercise 3 The following graph shows demand, marginal cost, and average total cost curves for Tinyville Trains, a local monopolist.

a. Draw the marginal revenue curve.
b. Find the short-run profit-maximizing price and quantity.
c. Identify the short-run profit for Tinyville Trains.

Section 10.4, Exercise 4 The following graph shows demand, marginal cost, and average variable cost curves for Large Locomotives, a local monopolist.

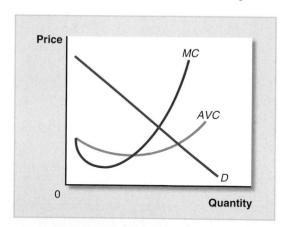

a. Draw the marginal revenue curve.
b. Find the short-run profit-maximizing price and quantity.
c. Show an average total cost curve such that Large Locomotives is making a short-run profit.

d. Show an average total cost curve such that Large Locomotives is making a short-run loss.
e. If Large Locomotives is making a short-run loss, should it shut down?

Section 10.5, Exercise 1 In perfectly competitive markets, we always expect to see economic profits of zero in the long run. Is this true for a monopolist?

Section 10.6, Exercise 1 The following graph shows a representative monopolist.

a. Show the profit-maximizing price and quantity.
b. Show the efficient price and quantity.
c. At the monopolist's profit-maximizing price and quantity, identify consumer surplus, producer surplus, and deadweight loss.

Section 10.6, Exercise 2 Monopolists gain profit at the expense of consumers. Why don't we count this transfer of surplus from consumers to producers as part of the deadweight loss?

Section 10.7, Exercise 1 Identify whether each of the following situations is an example of price discrimination, and, if so, the degree of price discrimination.

a. Laundry detergent is cheaper per ounce if you buy it in a big box rather than in a small box.

b. Students receive discounts on magazines and newspapers.

c. Movie tickets are cheaper if you see the movie during the day.

d. The price of a hamburger is higher in New York City than it is in a small town in upstate New York.

e. In some countries, it's common to haggle over prices at the market, and thus every consumer pays a different price.

Section 10.7, Exercise 2 It is common to see student discounts on things like meals, newspapers, and other small items, but it is much rarer to see significant student discounts on things like computers and cars. How can you best explain why?

11 Monopolistic Competition and Product Differentiation

Ask any 10 Philadelphians to identify the city's best-known food, and you will get an almost unanimous response: the cheesesteak. Cheesesteaks have been a Philadelphia staple since the 1930s. A Philly cheesesteak consists of very thin strips of fried, shredded steak served on a long roll with melted cheese, but that's only the beginning. Depending on the shop, a cheesesteak may be topped with ketchup, pizza sauce, peppers, onions, pepperoni slices, mushrooms, a variety of spice mixes, or all of the above. The length of the roll, the quality of the meat, the sauce and spices, and even the type of cheese varies widely from shop to shop. There are hundreds of cheesesteak shops in the Philadelphia area. Many of them advertise the virtues of their special version of the cheesesteak, and everyone seems to swear by a favorite.

The debate over who makes the best Philly cheesesteak motivated Philadelphia-area high-school senior Josh Brawer to design a tasty senior project. Accompanied by the food editor of the *Philadelphia Inquirer*, Josh and three of his friends visited 23 cheesesteak shops and ate 56 sandwiches[1]—in only four days. Among the many varieties they discovered, each of the taste testers had a favorite version of the Philly cheesesteak. However, their preferences were often quite different.

This variety from shop to shop indicates something very specific about the cheesesteak industry in Philadelphia. There are too many different shop proprietors for the industry to be considered a monopoly, yet there is too much variation in the product for the cheesesteak industry to fit

---

[1] Craig LaBan, "The Cheesesteak Project," The *Philadelphia Inquirer Magazine*, August 11, 2002, page M08.

our model of perfect competition. Visualize the range of possible market structures as a continuum with perfect competition at one end and monopoly at the other. Most industries, including the Philadelphia cheesesteak industry, fall somewhere in between. Economists refer to any industry in which the product or service varies somewhat from firm to firm but otherwise resembles perfect competition as *monopolistic competition*.

In this chapter, we will explore the market outcomes in monopolistically competitive industries. Specific topics include how producers differentiate their products, how they choose the profit-maximizing output level and price, and the effects of advertising.

ALONG THE WAY, YOU WILL ALSO LEARN:

- The assumptions that underlie the model of monopolistic competition.
- How monopolistically competitive firms maximize short-run profits.
- The long-run implications of monopolistic competition.
- How monopolistic competition outcomes compare to perfect competition outcomes.
- How advertising can affect consumer behavior and economic efficiency.

AT THE END OF THE CHAPTER, THE MYECONLAB LOGO WILL DIRECT YOU ONLINE

- MyEconLab is a resource-packed online homework and tutorial system that can help you perform better in your economics course. To log in for the first time, see page 30 for instructions.
- MyEconLab can help you apply important concepts from the chapter to real-world issues. Watch for the logo to indicate online features about advertising and product differentiation.
- At the end of each chapter, you'll find a special study section that will help you get the most out of your textbook and your instructor's MyEconLab course.

Assumptions of the Monopolistic Competition Model

As we continue with our cheesesteak example, we will fully develop the monopolistic competition model. The model of monopolistic competition is distinguished by the following assumptions:

- Free entry and exit over the long run.
- Many firms, each one small relative to the size of the overall market.
- All firms in a given market produce differentiated products that are similar but not identical.

In this section, we take a detailed look at each of these characteristics. Notice that there is much overlap between the assumptions of the monopolistic competition and perfect competition models. Although cheesesteaks differ from firm to firm, in every other sense the industry appears to have all the characteristics of perfect competition. Many markets resemble the cheesesteak market in this way. Most restaurants, clothing retailers, and movie theaters fall somewhere between perfect competition and monopoly.

Free Entry and Exit in the Long Run

Firms in monopolistically competitive markets are free to enter and exit the industry over the long run. There are no substantial entry barriers, such as patents or copyrights, that limit firms' ability to enter, as there are in the monopoly model. You will see later in the chapter that the ability of new firms to enter the industry plays an important role in determining price and product characteristics in the long run.

Many Firms

Monopolistically competitive industries comprise many firms. Unlike many monopolies, there are no extensive scale economies in production. Because each firm is small relative to the size of the total market, consumers have a choice of products from many different suppliers. The existence of a large number of firms also means that each firm will have limited market power. As a result, firms must be very aware of the prices that competing firms charge.

Product Differentiation

Product differentiation
Variation in the characteristics of products that are substitutes.

The key difference between the models of perfect competition and monopolistic competition is product differentiation. **Product differentiation** means that, although firms strive to make their products stand out from those of their competitors, the products in a given market are similar enough that consumers view them as close substitutes. These products differ in brand name but have the same generic name, such as different brands of cheesesteaks or movie theaters. The distinctive features of a product can be real—for example, differences in the spices or the quantity of meat in a cheesesteak. Distinctive features can also be perceived. Josh and his taste-testing friends all had their own opinions on which cheesesteak was the best in town. For some, the difference was based on the sauce, for others it was due to how the cook grilled the onions. The difference may even be simply the location. Some shops are more convenient than others, and therefore more desirable, even if the actual product is the same. A different example of this phenomenon is the frequency of high-priced gas stations near highway exits.

The Monopolistic Competition Model in Practice

The model of monopolistic competition can be applied widely, to markets ranging from retail consumer goods to political parties. We will carefully examine its mechanics and its implications throughout this chapter. As with any model, we must be sure to apply it only when the underlying assumptions are appropriate. For example, we should not use the monopolistic competition model to analyze the daily newspaper industry, as there are typically only one or two newspapers in a given city. It would also be inappropriate for the automobile industry. Even though there are many auto buyers and at least 10 major domestic or foreign producers, substantial entry barriers make it very difficult for new firms to gain a foothold.

Throughout the chapter, we will compare the outcomes of the monopolistic competition model to those of perfect competition and monopoly. Based on the name of this model, it is tempting to think of it as very similar to a monopoly. Yet the assumptions of the model indicate that the price charged, quantity produced, and profit earned by monopolistically competitive firms is much more similar to perfect competition than to monopoly.

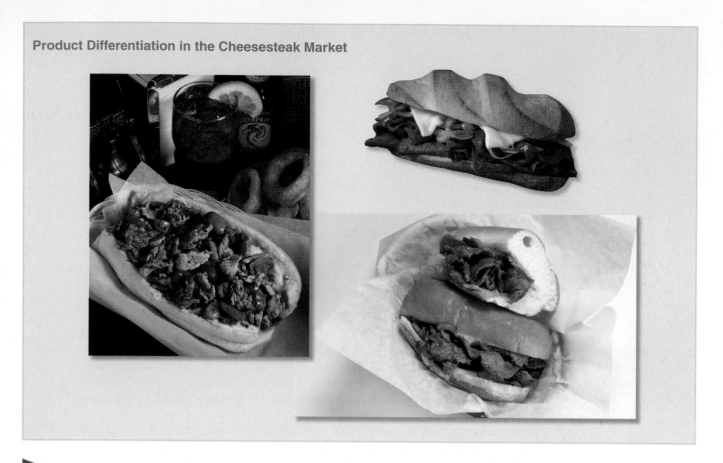

▶ Short-Run Profit Maximization for the Monopolistic Competitor

We've stressed that the key difference between perfect competition and monopolistic competition is product differentiation. We now turn to the implications of product differentiation for a firm's demand curve, marginal revenue curve, price, output, and profit in the short run. Recall that in perfectly competitive industries, consumers consider each seller's goods to be identical to all others. As a result, firms have no market power and must charge the market price to maximize profits. For firms, perfect competition means having little control over profits. However, if a firm can differentiate its product, it may be more able to attract and keep customers. Even if its prices are higher than those of a competitor down the street, it may still retain some of its consumers if its product is in some way unique. Thus, rather than being completely at the mercy of market-determined demand (and price), firms can gain a measure of control over their market. Those that fail to differentiate their products in a way that consumers desire will face decreased demand, and may eventually be driven from the market. We now illustrate this line of reasoning graphically in the context of the cheesesteak example.

Demand and Marginal Revenue

For the firm, product differentiation creates market power in the form of customer loyalty. After all the taste testing, Josh settled on a favorite: the cheesesteaks at John's Roast Pork (John's, for short). Josh prefers John's sandwiches because of the grilled-to-order onions and the seeded rolls. There are other shops close to John's that Josh must pass by to get there. However, he does not view their steaks as perfect

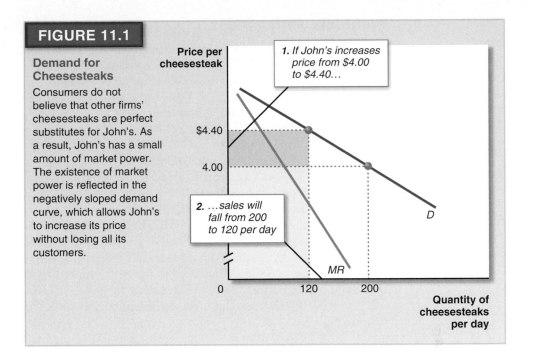

FIGURE 11.1

Demand for Cheesesteaks

Consumers do not believe that other firms' cheesesteaks are perfect substitutes for John's. As a result, John's has a small amount of market power. The existence of market power is reflected in the negatively sloped demand curve, which allows John's to increase its price without losing all its customers.

Price per cheesesteak

1. If John's increases price from $4.00 to $4.40...

$4.40

4.00

2. ...sales will fall from 200 to 120 per day

D

MR

0   120   200

Quantity of cheesesteaks per day

substitutes. He is willing to spend a little extra for the sandwich at John's in terms of the money he puts on the counter and also the opportunity cost of traveling farther to get there. There are many customers like Josh. If we add up their individual demand curves, we determine the demand curve for John's cheesesteak sandwiches, as shown in Figure 11.1. At a price of $4.00, consumers demand 200 cheesesteaks per day.

The downward slope of the demand curve in Figure 11.1 means that if John's raises prices, it will lose many of its customers. At a price of $4.40, consumers demand 120 cheesesteaks, a drop of 80 cheesesteaks. Unlike with perfect competition, however, John's will retain those customers who have a strong preference for its cheesesteaks over those of its competitors. The downward-sloping demand curve also indicates that, like a monopolist, John's must reduce its prices to increase sales. It cannot simply sell more cheesesteaks at the market price as in perfect competition. As a result, marginal revenue is less than price. Similar to the graph of a monopoly shown in Figure 10.6, the marginal revenue curve in Figure 11.1 lies below the demand curve and has a steeper slope. But compared to the demand curve facing a typical monopoly, the demand curve for cheesesteaks at John's is much more elastic, or price-sensitive. It is also important to remember that the monopolist's demand curve represents the demand for the entire market, while the demand curve of a monopolistically competitive firm is only a small portion of the overall market. The market demand for cheesesteaks would be the sum of the demand curves for John's plus all the other cheesesteak sellers in the area.

Highly elastic demand indicates that customers are quite willing to switch to substitute goods when faced with a price increase. In this case, if John's raises prices by too much, even customers like Josh are likely to head across the street to a competing shop. In general, as the number of available substitutes rises, more customers will respond to a higher price by switching to a firm's competitors. In contrast, if John's were the only cheesesteak shop in town, it could raise prices without losing as many customers due to the lack of available substitutes.

Profit-Maximizing Output

As with perfect competition and monopoly, a monopolistically competitive firm maximizes profits by selling up to the point where marginal cost is just equal to marginal revenue. After the firm determines the profit-maximizing output level, it uses the demand curve to set the price. Figure 11.2 shows the demand, marginal revenue, and marginal cost curves for John's. Using the $MC = MR$ rule, we see that John's maximizes short-run profits by selling 200 cheesesteaks per day at a price of $4.00 each.

Figure 11.2 shows the output level that maximizes economic profits. To determine the firm's short-run profits, we need information about revenue *and* costs. Figure 11.3 shows the demand curve from Figure 11.2 and incorporates the average total cost curve for John's. We can use the information in Figure 11.3 to determine the profits of a monopolistically competitive firm. Total revenue is the area that corresponds to the price of one of John's cheesesteaks (on the vertical axis) times the quantity of cheesesteaks sold (on the horizontal axis). In this example, $p \times q = \$800$. Total cost is the area shaded in yellow, which corresponds to average total cost times quantity. In this case, $ATC \times q = \$2.75 \times 200 = \$550$. The difference—the area shaded in green, or $250—represents John's profits.

Loss Minimization and the Shutdown Point

In Chapter 10, you learned that even monopolies have no guarantee of economic profits. The same is true for monopolistically competitive firms. If the demand for a business's cheesesteaks declines or if costs increase, profits will fall. Panel (a) of Figure 11.4 shows one way in which a decline in demand might affect John's economic profits. In this case, demand has fallen to a level such that the demand curve just touches the average total cost curve at the output level where $MC = MR$. At this

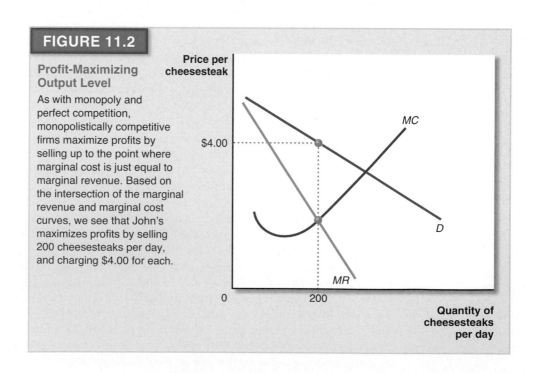

FIGURE 11.2

Profit-Maximizing Output Level

As with monopoly and perfect competition, monopolistically competitive firms maximize profits by selling up to the point where marginal cost is just equal to marginal revenue. Based on the intersection of the marginal revenue and marginal cost curves, we see that John's maximizes profits by selling 200 cheesesteaks per day, and charging $4.00 for each.

FIGURE 11.3

Short-Run Profits

In the short run, profits are determined by subtracting total cost, the yellow-shaded area, or $550, from total revenue, or $800. The difference is the firm's profit, which is the green-shaded area, or $250.

FIGURE 11.4

Minimizing Losses and Reaching the Shutdown Point

In panel (a), total revenue and total cost both equal the yellow-shaded area. Economic profits are thus zero and the firm breaks even. In panel (b), demand has fallen such that total revenue and total variable cost equal the green-shaded area. Losses are equal to the blue-shaded area, which represents total fixed costs, and the firm is at the shutdown point.

output level, both price and average total cost are $2.50, and output is 175 cheesesteaks per day. The total revenue of $437.50 is just equal to total cost—the area shaded in yellow—and the firm breaks even (earns zero economic profit).

In panel (b), demand has fallen to the point where at the optimal output of 135 cheesesteaks per day, total revenue just equals total variable cost ($2.00 × 135 = $270 or the area shaded in green), and the firm is at the shutdown point. Economic losses are $135, and are equal to fixed costs (shaded in blue); thus, the firm is indifferent between staying open and shutting down in the short run.

Monopolistic Competition in the Long Run

In our discussion so far, the way a monopolistically competitive firm maximizes profit might seem quite similar to a monopoly. The only difference is that monopolistically competitive firms have a more elastic demand curve than monopolies, due to the larger number of close substitutes. This observation is valid in the short run. In the long run, though, free entry makes the outcomes for monopolistically competitive firms quite different from the typical monopoly outcome. In this section, we focus on the motivation for firm entry and exit in a market.

Firm Entry

In Chapter 9, you saw that if a perfectly competitive firm is earning positive economic profits, other firms will enter the market in the long run. New firms continue to enter until economic profits are driven to zero. The same is true with monopolistic competition. If John's Roast Pork and other shops like it are earning positive long-run economic profits, more cheesesteak shops will open in the same area. We show the effect of new entrants on John's demand curve in panel (a) of Figure 11.5. As new competitors with similar products enter the market, the demand curve for John's cheesesteaks shifts leftward and flattens out (becomes more elastic). John's customers now eat elsewhere more frequently, and stop at John's only when it is most convenient for them. As such, the leftward shift of the demand curve represents a loss of market share. John's most loyal customers, including people like Josh who prefer its cheesesteaks to those of other producers, will still usually eat at John's. They might occasionally try a new spot with cheesesteaks that are similar to John's, however. One of the new shops might also be more conveniently located—remember that part of product differentiation is location.

New cheesesteak shops will continue to open until long-run economic profits are driven to zero, and firms no longer have a reason to enter. There is an important difference between the point at which economic profits are zero in monopolistic competition and the point at which they equal zero in perfect competition. Unlike with perfect competition, price does not fall to the minimum point of the long-run average cost curve in a monopolistically competitive industry. As panel (b) of Figure 11.5 shows, each shop will break even at an output level lower than the output level where the *LAC* curve reaches its minimum, because there is a downward-sloping demand curve. When John's follows the *MC* = *MR* rule to find the best level of output, it produces 180 sandwiches per day, which it sells for $2.60 each. At this point, the demand curve just touches the *LAC* curve. Both total revenue and total cost are equal to the area shaded in yellow and economic profits equal zero.

FIGURE 11.5

Effects of New Entrants on the Demand for Cheesesteaks at John's Roast Pork

If John's is earning positive economic profits, new firms have an incentive to enter the market. In panel (a), John's demand curve shifts to the left as the number of John's customers falls. The curve also flattens out because demand becomes more elastic. The existence of additional cheesesteak shops makes customers more price-sensitive. Firms will continue to enter the market until economic profits fall to zero. In panel (b), in the long-run, Little John's produces 180 cheesesteaks and sells them for $2.60 each. At that point, the long-run average cost (*LAC*) curve just touches the demand curve at the optimal output level. New firms thus have no incentive to enter the market.

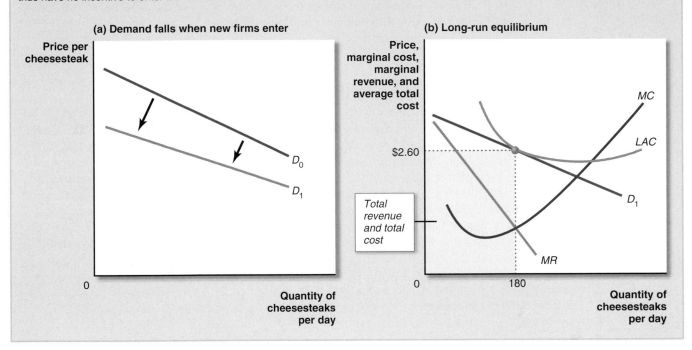

Firm Exit

If all firms incur the same costs and experience identical demand, then in the long run all firms operate at the break-even point, and no additional firms enter. In perfect competition, we often assume that this scenario is the case. For example, it is reasonable to assume that all salmon fillet sellers at Pike Place Market (discussed in Chapter 9) have the same costs. In monopolistic competition, costs are rarely identical. Costs may be similar from one cheesesteak restaurant to another. However, firms might have different expenditures for décor, for materials related to quality, and for rent payments to secure better locations. Demand is also likely to vary somewhat from one shop to another. The variations in cost and demand from firm to firm mean that we frequently see long-run turnover of firms in monopolistically competitive industries. Some firms exit the market by going out of business, and new ones enter the market.

A short walk around your local mall or downtown area should provide evidence of turnover in many retail industries. Every year, thousands of small businesses open their doors for the first time, and thousands of others close their doors for the last time. Of all new business ventures, 34 percent close within two years, and more than half close within four years. Although many new ventures succeed, market conditions factor heavily in the reasons for failure. The most common reason for small business failure cited in one government-sponsored study is "outside business conditions" (including new competition and declining prices).[2]

In summary, when firms in the industry are all in long-run equilibrium:

- Each firm maximizes profits by setting output at the point where $MC = MR$ and choosing price based on the demand curve.
- If firms all have equal costs, each firm earns zero economic profits, because price will equal average cost.
- Each firm's price is greater than the minimum point of the LAC curve.
- Firms may have different costs and unique demand curves. They might therefore have different prices and profits, and the weakest firms are forced from the market.

TEST + *E X T E N D* Your Knowledge

1. TEST Suppose that the market demand for khaki pants is $Q_d = 3,500 - 50p$. Initially, a single firm, The Pants Company, sells pants as a monopolist at a price of $25 per pair. Attracted by the large profits of The Pants Company, a new firm enters the market. The new firm sells similar khakis, but the pants have different styling and do not have the same brand recognition. Because of the new competitor, The Pants Company now faces the demand curve $Q_d = 3,000 - 75p$. At the same price of $25 per pair, how many pairs of pants will it sell?

2. EXTEND Many large retailers now offer the same products on the Internet that they do in their stores. How do the existence of large online retailers such as L.L.Bean and Lands' End affect the demand curves for small shop owners in rural areas? How might the small retailers be able to respond to online low-price sellers to maintain their profitability?

▶ Monopolistic Competition Versus Perfect Competition

Now that we've established the workings of the monopolistic competition model in both the short run and the long run, we can compare the outcomes of the model to those of perfect competition. One of the most important conclusions from our study of the model of perfect competition is that perfect competition causes the market to operate efficiently. In the short run, competitive firms allocate resources efficiently because they maximize profit by producing output up to the point where price equals marginal cost. In the long run, the lack of product differentiation combined with the entry of new firms pushes each perfectly competitive firm to produce up to the point where long-run average costs are minimized. Finally, in both the short run and the long run, perfect competition forces firms to minimize their costs of production. If they do not, lower-cost firms will take away all their customers. Compared to perfect competition, there are both costs and benefits to monopolistically competitive industries.

---

[2] Theresa Sullivan, Elizabeth Warren, and Jay Westbrook, "Financial Difficulties of Small Businesses and Reasons for Their Failure," September 1988, www.sba.gov/advo/research/rs188tot.pdf (accessed March 10, 2005); business closure statistics are from Brian Headd "Redefining Business Success: Distinguishing Between Closure and Failure," March 20, 2002, www.sba.gov/advo/stats/bh_sbe03.pdf (accessed March 10, 2005).

Allocative Efficiency

We've established that in monopolistically competitive industries, the large number of readily available substitutes (and potential substitutes through entry) pressures firms to be efficient producers. Nevertheless, a monopolistically competitive industry does not allocate resources as efficiently as a perfectly competitive industry. In the long run, perfectly competitive firms produce at the point where long-run average costs are minimized. For monopolistically competitive firms, the optimal output level is less than if they produced at the point where *LAC* is minimized. Price exceeds marginal cost and the monopolistically competitive price is greater than the competitive price—even if by only a small amount. In Figure 11.6, we see that when John's is in long-run equilibrium, it produces 180 steaks per day at a cost of $2.60 each. If it were a perfectly competitive firm producing at the point where the *LAC* reaches its minimum, it would produce 190 cheesesteaks per day, at a cost of $2.50 per cheesesteak. The difference between the actual cost and the cost with perfectly competitive pricing ($2.60–$2.50) means that cheesesteaks are not produced as cheaply as they could be. There is no intent on the part of the firm to be inefficient. The reduction in output is the result of marginal revenue being less than price for a monopolistically competitive firm. The difference between marginal cost and price results in a deadweight loss (shaded in gray), similar to the deadweight loss we saw with monopolies.

FIGURE 11.6

**The Long-Run Monopolistic Competition Equilibrium
Versus the Perfect Competition Equilibrium**

Perfectly competitive firms produce where the long-run average cost (*LAC*) curve reaches its minimum. Thus, if the cheesesteak market were perfectly competitive, John's would produce 190 cheesesteaks and sell them for $2.50 each. Under monopolistic competition, however, John's produces 180 cheesesteaks at a price of $2.60 each. As a result, it does not minimize long-run average cost and has excess capacity. The resulting deadweight loss is shaded in gray.

Policy makers tend to dismiss such a loss for two reasons. First, given that the loss is probably small compared to the cost of the government intervention that would be required to eliminate it, product differentiation occurs in almost every market. These costs include investigating the firm, calculating the magnitude of the loss, and instituting some form of corrective action (including the potential loss of efficiency associated with the action). Second, the loss comes from product differentiation, a process that allows consumers to choose from a variety of products. We discuss the benefits that consumers derive from this variety later in this chapter.

Excess Capacity

A downward-sloping demand curve causes another problem, which is related to the loss of allocative efficiency: **excess capacity**, which exists if an industry can increase output without firms making losses. Suppose that each firm incurs the same costs as John's. In Figure 11.6, we saw that John's could produce another 10 sandwiches per day if it produced where $LAC = MC = P$, as a perfectly competitive firm would. In other words, there is underproduction at both the firm and industry level, as each firm could produce more output at a lower per-unit cost if it produced at the point where LAC is minimized.

The Benefits of Variety

The consumer sees an important advantage to product differentiation that at least partially offsets the costs of excess capacity. That advantage lies in the variety itself. If the cheesesteak market were perfectly competitive, all cheesesteaks would be the same. Product homogeneity would be an unwelcome turn of events in most markets. For example, if the shirt market were perfectly competitive, you would wear the same type of shirt every day. Worse yet, it would be the same shirt that everyone else would be wearing. Consumers value variety, whether in food, blue jeans, shirts, magazines, or mystery novels. There is a trade-off that pits deadweight losses and excess capacity against the benefits of variety. The greater the variety, the greater the set of choices for consumers in any particular market.

Variety occurs in many forms. It gives us Granny Smith apples and Golden Delicious apples. It also gives us high-quality and low-quality products. Because some people prefer Granny Smith apples to other varieties, the existence of different types of apples benefits consumers. We may find it hard to believe that the existence of low-quality products also benefits consumers, but it does. Presumably, it costs more to make a high-quality item than it costs to make a poor one. If so, then the price of a product also rises with quality. If only the highest-quality items were available, consumers would be able to purchase only the expensive variety of each item. Imagine, for example, that the gourmet manufacturer Godiva were the only producer of chocolates. Many people would not be able to afford so delectable a treat and would have to forgo chocolates. Others would decide that chocolates were no longer worth the expense, and cut back or eliminate their consumption of chocolates entirely. The existence of cheaper items allows more people to consume more chocolates, making them happier than they would be with nothing but gourmet chocolates.

In Table 11.1, we summarize the model of monopolistic competition by comparing it to the models of perfect competition and monopoly. Similar to perfect competition, monopolistically competitive industries are characterized by easy entry that, in turn, drives long-run economic profits to zero. However, because the product is differentiated, firms are able to exercise a small degree of market power and set price slightly above marginal cost.

TABLE 11.1

Summary of Market Structure Characteristics for Perfect Competition, Monopolistic Competition, and Monopoly

Market Structure	Product	Entry	Price Versus *MC*	Long-Run Economic Profits
Perfect competition	Homogeneous	Easy	$P = MC$	0
Monopolistic competition	Differentiated	Easy	$P > MC$	0
Monopoly	Unique	Very difficult	$P > MC$	≥ 0

TEST + *E X T E N D* Your Knowledge

1. TEST Draw a figure similar to panel (b) of Figure 11.5, but showing that demand has fallen to the point where the firm would make losses. Label the area that represents the loss.

2. EXTEND What might cause a cheesesteak restaurant to suffer long-run losses? List at least two cost-side reasons and two demand-side reasons. Given that long-run losses are not sustainable over time, what will happen to this firm?

▶ Advertising: Information or Persuasion?

We now turn to the role of advertising in monopolistically competitive markets. How do consumers learn about the variety of choices in a market? Firms in perfectly competitive markets usually do not advertise at all, because there is nothing unique about their product or price that makes advertising profitable. Monopolists typically do not advertise extensively either. While advertising may attract some people to the product, monopolists have no competitors and no need to differentiate their products. Firms in monopolistically competitive markets need to advertise to inform consumers about how their product differs from all the others. Firms like John's use advertising to shift their demand curves rightward and make them steeper (less elastic), so that they have more customers at every price.

Brand Identity and Brand Loyalty

Brand identity
A consumer's ability to recognize a product and associate it with a specific name.

The goal of advertising is to create brand identity or brand loyalty with a customer base. **Brand identity** is a consumer's ability to recognize a product and associate it with a specific name. Examples include Kleenex™ facial tissues, Band-Aid™ adhesive strips, Scotch™ tape, and Campbell's™ soup. Brand identity translates into increased demand: Consumers know the name of the product, and perhaps some of its advantages, before deciding which brand to purchase. Even though other products may be virtually identical, consumers are less inclined to purchase them,

Brand loyalty
A consumer's willingness
to remain with a specific
product despite the existence
and advertisements of
competitors.

because they are less familiar. **Brand loyalty** is a consumer's willingness to remain with a specific product despite the existence and advertisements of competitors. Brand loyalty thus makes consumer demand for a certain good less elastic, because consumers are less likely to switch to another brand after a price increase. Next, we look at the advertising opportunities available to John's to build brand identity and brand loyalty in the cheesesteak market.

Types of Advertising

Whether the advertising that firms use to create brand loyalty is beneficial to consumers depends on the type of advertising used. In this section, we discuss different types of ads and their effect on consumers and on overall market demand.

Informational Advertising. Advertising can benefit consumers if it increases consumers' knowledge about important product characteristics and prices. Suppose that John's bakes its own rolls fresh every morning. Every other cheesesteak shop buys rolls that are usually a day or two old, from a central bakery. As a result, John's sandwiches taste fresher than those of its competitors. If John's does not advertise, information can travel only slowly (and not uniformly) from one customer to another through word of mouth. In Figure 11.7, we see that the advertisement increases demand by increasing brand identity. The demand curve at John's shifts from D_1 to D_2. The increase in demand allows John's to charge $4.50 instead of $4.00 *and* to sell 40 more cheesesteaks. Without an ad, the only way to sell more cheesesteaks would be to reduce the price. If the advertisement also increases brand loyalty, the consumer demand will also be more inelastic, because consumers will view other products as weaker substitutes than before the ad.

Consumers' demand for John's cheesesteaks increased because they received information about the product that was important to them. Advertising that contains information about a product that is important to consumers is known as **informational advertising**. Remember that one of the assumptions in competitive markets is perfect information. When ads contain meaningful information, efficiency

Informational advertising
Contains objective
information about the
characteristics of a good or
service that is useful to the
consumer making product
choices.

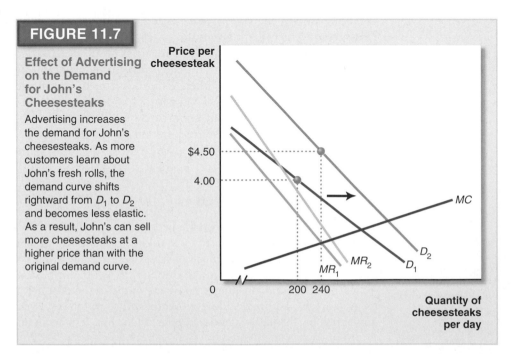

FIGURE 11.7

Effect of Advertising on the Demand for John's Cheesesteaks

Advertising increases the demand for John's cheesesteaks. As more customers learn about John's fresh rolls, the demand curve shifts rightward from D_1 to D_2 and becomes less elastic. As a result, John's can sell more cheesesteaks at a higher price than with the original demand curve.

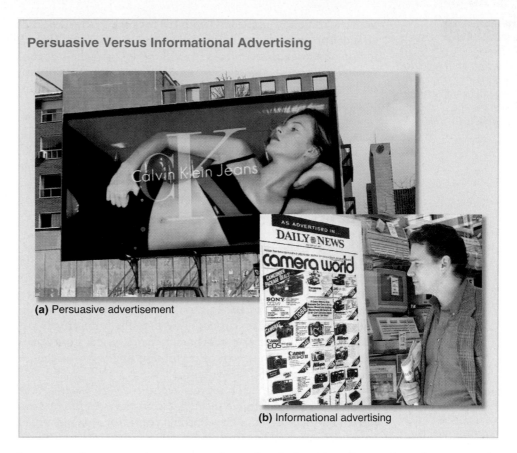

Persuasive Versus Informational Advertising

(a) Persuasive advertisement

(b) Informational advertising

increases. Consumers know more about the choices they face and can better match their tastes and preferences to the products they consume. Informational advertising in the cheesesteak market makes it easier for really hungry people to find the biggest cheesesteaks, for those who like hot and spicy food to find the steaks with the hottest peppers, and for those who like chicken instead of beef to find chicken cheesesteaks. Conversely, it allows people who *don't* like oversized sandwiches to *avoid* the restaurant with the biggest cheesesteaks in town.

Ads can also convey information about prices. If John's has a two-for-one sale, consumers can respond only if they are aware that it is taking place. If information about prices is difficult to obtain, uninformed consumers pay more for cheesesteaks than is necessary. In addition, one shop's advertisements of its low prices may cause other shops to reduce their prices as well, benefiting all consumers.

Persuasive advertising
Focuses on affecting consumer tastes through the use of subjective information.

Persuasive Advertising. Persuasive advertising attempts to alter consumer tastes and preferences by using subjective information ("We're the best!"), or by associating a product name with a celebrity, such as the brand identity that Nike has with golfer Tiger Woods. For example, suppose that John's hires a rock star who lives in the Philadelphia area to appear in its ads. Rather than conveying any meaningful information about the product, the person simply says: "To be cool like me, buy your cheesesteak at John's." The ad contains no information about the product or its price. In fact, John's is selling the same sandwich as many other shops, and at the same price. If consumers who are big fans of the rock star go to John's merely in order to identify with the star, John's demand curve shifts rightward. However, in this case, the increase in demand is not based on any meaningful information about the commodity. It may increase the well-being of consumers if they believe that they

Get Ahead of the Curve

Apply your knowledge of advertising in monopolistically competitive markets to the phone and cable industries.

are now somehow associated with the rock star. However, it does not result in more efficient production or distribution of cheesesteaks. In 2004 alone, total U.S. spending on advertising exceeded $141 billion dollars. The portion of this total that represents persuasive ads reduces overall efficiency in the economy. The resources spent on such ads simply redistribute demand from one supplier to another, independent of price and product quality.

In fact, most product advertisements have elements of both information and persuasion. The balance between the two varies greatly depending on the product. For example, car dealerships often hire superstar athletes to appear in commercials for a specific sale in which the athlete gives objective details about prices, product characteristics, and store hours.

Advertising Product Characteristics

Search goods
Goods that have characteristics that can easily be described to and verified by consumers.

Product characteristics have a lot to do with how a product is advertised. Goods whose characteristics can be described to and verified easily by consumers are **search goods**. Search goods include products like MP3 players: Information such as how many songs it holds, battery life, and other features are easily described and understood. Thus, consumers can easily compare the characteristics of one MP3 player to another. Products that can easily be described objectively often use informational ads that describe the product characteristics, price, store location, and hours. While there may be some element of persuasion in ads for search goods, the most important feature is typically information.

Experience goods
Must be consumed in order for the consumer to determine their quality.

Not all goods can be objectively described. With **experience goods**, the only way for the consumer to determine their characteristics is to use or consume them. For example, an ad for Mountain Dew™ could consist of a scientist reading the list of ingredients and describing how they are combined to create the product. But such information is meaningless to consumers. What matters to consumers is how the product tastes, which cannot be accurately described—even using an ingredient list. With experience goods, information that consumers could use to make a purchase decision (such as how the product tastes) cannot readily be conveyed in a television or print ad. As a result, experience goods are typically advertised using persuasive ads. Advertisements for soft drinks, perfumes, and hair care products tend to focus on images of happy consumers using the product instead of information about how the product is manufactured. In some cases, firms offer samples or demonstrations. For example, a ski or snowboard manufacturer could describe the difference between two models. However, the only way for a consumer to make a meaningful comparison is to try both products. Ski and snowboard manufacturers frequently host demonstration days at which potential buyers can try a ski or snowboard for a few runs. Similarly, stores frequently offer samples of fragrances for consumers to test.

Spurious Product Differences

Spurious product differences
Perceived and often intentionally created product differences that have no impact on the quality of the good or service.

Have you ever seen a product for which the package has been redesigned, but the product itself remains unchanged? It is common practice with consumer products. Sometimes, a firm will even enthusiastically announce, "same great product, exciting new packaging!" From an objective standpoint, the new, brightly colored packaging of this product is completely meaningless. The soap that is inside the package is what matters, not the design on the label. Firms' willingness to trumpet the announcement of a new label is a good indication that not all product variety is meaningful. Sometimes firms attempt to create **spurious product differences**, which are perceived differences that are unimportant to the quality of the end product. This often happens where there is no real variety, because firms want consumers to *believe* that they are consuming something better. Advertising plays a key role in these cases. In large markets where a shift in product loyalty of even a small percentage of consumers can mean millions of dollars in additional revenue for firms, the most similar products are most intensively advertised. For example, bottled water is one of the fastest-growing beverage markets. Images of clear mountain springs create perceived differences between the taste and health qualities of bottled water and tap water. In reality, many studies have found that the tap water used in comparison tests is as "healthy" as the much more expensive bottled water. In addition, consumers often cannot taste the difference. One study in Yorkshire, England, found that 60 percent of consumers could not even distinguish bottled water from the local tap water![3]

LUANN: © GEC Inc./Dist. by United Features Syndicate, Inc.

LifeLessons

Firm Spending and Product Differentiation

When firms go to great lengths to convince consumers that their products are different from others on the market, it may actually be an indicator of just how similar they really are. The soft drink industry is a good example of how product similarity relates to advertising intensity. Soft drink manufacturers often advertise very intensively. In 2004, Coca Cola™ alone spent more than $1 billion on advertising. However, taste-test results from independent labs such as Consumer Reports show that most consumers cannot distinguish one cola from another, or decaffeinated soda from caffeinated. You can try this experiment in class or with friends who are cola drinkers. Go to the store and get cans of four or five different brands of cola. Have each participant write down their favorite cola brand before tasting any of the samples. Then, with the labels disguised, give each a small cup of each brand, and ask them to choose their favorite brand. In most cases, even loyal drinkers of one specific brand have great difficulty identifying their brand over others. Think twice before paying full price for a brand-name soda!

---

[3] "Putting the Oh! In H$_2$O," *E-Mainstream*, vol. 46, no. 6 (November/December 2002), www.awwa.org/Communications/mainstream/2002/nov_dec/page_12.cfm (accessed June 6, 2005).

Thrill seekers have been visiting amusement parks for over 100 years. In 1884, a coasterlike ride with a leisurely top speed of 6 miles per hour opened at Coney Island, New York. Today, the amusement-park industry is a thriving and highly competitive industry in which parks continually attempt to outdo one another with extreme coasters in hopes of attracting guests. Designers attempt to increase demand for their own coaster types through product differentiation, and modern coasters test the limits of both physics and riders' desire for increased speed, height, twists, and turns. The Six Flags Great Adventure Park in New Jersey currently boasts a coaster named Kingda Ka, billed as the tallest and fastest coaster on earth, reaching an astonishing height of 456 feet and a top speed of 128 mph.

It's not all just about how high and how fast. Coasters can be differentiated in many ways. The indoor Rockin' Roller Coaster at Disneyworld features cars shaped like old automobiles racing through a darkened building to the tune of Aerosmith music. Some coasters offer inverted loops or twists, or suspend the rider from tracks which are above rather than below them. Others are deliberately "old school" in that they are constructed of wood rather than steel. Most large parks even have small versions of coasters designed to appeal to young riders who are not ready for the full-sized versions.

For some enthusiasts, interest in new coasters borders on obsession. The Internet contains numerous roller coaster–related Web sites that contain extensive histories, rumors, and blogs regarding new construction, information on trips, and more. For these roller coaster riders, "if you build it, they will come."

Critical-Thinking Questions:

1. If parks with existing roller coasters are highly profitable, and the industry can be described accurately using the model of monopolistic competition, what should we expect to observe in the long run?
2. How can amusement-park owners use ticket pricing strategies and other features in their parks to create brand loyalty?

SUMMARY

- **Assumptions of the monopolistic competition model.** The model of monopolistic competition maintains almost all of the assumptions of the perfectly competitive model, including the existence of many buyers and sellers and of free entry and exit in the long run. Unlike that of perfect competition, this model assumes that the product is differentiated. These variations are not so great that consumers consider competing brands to be poor substitutes, but are enough to create some level of market power for the firms.

- **Short-run profit maximization for the monopolistic competitor.** In the short run, monopolistically competitive firms maximize profits by selling output up to the point where marginal revenue is equal to marginal cost. For a monopolistically competitive firm, price exceeds marginal cost at this level of output, creating a deadweight loss (though this loss is generally small due to the availability of substitutes).

- **Monopolistic competition in the long run.** In the long run, new firms enter the industry if existing firms are earning positive economic profits. If firms are suffering economic losses, some firms will exit. Thus, monopolistically competitive firms earn zero economic profits in the long run. There is some loss of efficiency relative to perfect competition, however, because output levels are slightly lower and prices are slightly higher than if the market were perfectly competitive.

- **Monopolistic competition versus perfect competition.** Product variety creates some loss of efficiency. The benefit of product variety is the increase in satisfaction that consumers derive from not consuming the same product as all other consumers. In addition, consumers purchase a product more closely tailored to their preferences—choosing, for example, the level of quality that they most prefer.

- **Advertising: Information or persuasion?** Firms use advertising to help differentiate their products from those of their competitors. Informational advertising increases efficiency, because it allows consumers to make more informed choices. Persuasive advertising is inefficient, because it uses resources to create market power that is not based on actual product characteristics. Firms may be able to capture market share by creating spurious variations in their products. Differences such as trivial changes in packaging do not increase efficiency. Instead, they use resources simply to shift market share from one firm to another.

▶ KEY TERMS

Brand identity 293	Informational advertising 294	Search goods 296
Brand loyalty 294		Spurious product
Excess capacity 292	Persuasive advertising 295	differences 297
Experience goods 296	Product differentiation 283	

▶ PROBLEMS

1. In one or two sentences each, answer the following:
   a. In what way does the model of monopolistic competition differ from the model of perfect competition?
   b. What happens to the market power of existing firms when additional firms enter a monopolistically competitive market?
   c. If firms have market power, why are long-run economic profits driven to zero in monopolistic competition?
   d. Why might a manufacturer purposely produce goods that are of lower quality than those of its competitors?

2. Draw a figure similar to Figure 11.3 for a firm in the dress-shoe market. The firm is making positive profits by selling 100 pairs per week at a price of $50 per pair, and manufacturing shoes at an average total cost of $45 per pair.
   a. Label the area that represents profits.
   b. Calculate the profits numerically.
   c. Explain why the firm could not also be in long-run equilibrium. What is likely to happen next in this industry if most firms have profits similar to this firm?
   d. Draw a new demand and marginal revenue curve that shows the firm in long-run equilibrium.

3. Houses located along a beach or lake often sell for several times more than otherwise identical houses located a mile or two inland. Apply your understanding of monopolistic competition to explain why.

4. Note whether each market fits the model of monopolistic competition. If the model is inappropriate, explain why.
   a. Sneakers
   b. Mail-order laptop computers
   c. Blank CD-RW discs
   d. Peas
   e. Sections of *Principles of Economics* at your school

5. If the market for college education were perfectly competitive, how would it be different from what it is now? In what ways would current and future students be better off? How might they be worse off?

6. Would you (as a consumer) prefer that the market for T-shirts be perfectly competitive or monopolistically competitive? Why? (*Hint:* Remember the assumptions of each model, and note that there is no single correct answer here.)

7. Use the model of monopolistic competition to explain why new music groups want to sound different but not too different from existing popular bands.

8. Draw a graph showing the short-run profit-maximizing output for a monopolistically competitive firm that is making losses large enough to cause it to shut down. Be sure to include the *D*, *MR*, *MC*, *ATC*, and *AVC* curves.

9. If a monopolistically competitive firm is able to patent its production process (but not its product), can it become a monopolist in the industry? Why or why not?

10. Draw a graph of a monopolistically competitive firm in long-run equilibrium. Label the profit-maximizing output for this firm. How would its output level change if it had no market power and simply accepted the market price, as in perfect competition?

11. Comment on the following statement from the standpoint of allocative efficiency: "It doesn't matter whether a new sauce actually makes the cheesesteak unique. As long as consumers believe the ads and *think* that the sauce is different, then it is."

12. Answer true or false: If marginal cost is constant (the *MC* curve is a horizontal line), a monopolistically competitive firm ends up producing the same level of output and charging the same price as if it were perfectly competitive. Draw a graph to defend your answer.

13. Use a graph to show the changes in demand that a firm might experience after introducing a new type of sweater that is highly resistant to snags and unraveling. What do you predict will happen to price and output?

14. Describe a typical political campaign ad run by a candidate in a heated race for governor. What type of content is likely to be in the ad—persuasive or informational? What type of content would benefit voters most in such an ad?

15. What types of advertising techniques (informational or persuasive) are typically used to promote ice cream? Why would another type of advertising likely be ineffective?

16. Wal-Mart often faces significant opposition from local retailers when it attempts to open new stores in small-town areas. In some cases, owners of small shops have gone out of business as a result of a Wal-Mart opening nearby. Use the concepts from this chapter to discuss the benefits and costs for *consumers* of a new Wal-Mart in a small town that currently has only small retail shops. Do you believe consumers are better off or worse off with Wal-Mart in such cases?

17. Are consumers as a group better off or worse off if the government prohibits the sale of low-quality goods? In what ways might your answer depend on the nature of the product?

HERE'S HOW MyEconLab CAN HELP YOU GET A BETTER GRADE

1. Log into MyEconLab and take Practice Test chapter-A (to log in for the first time, see page 30 for instructions.)

2. Based on your test results, MyEconLab will identify the areas where you need further work and create a personal Study Plan for you.

3. Your Study Plan contains the exercises listed below and others like them that will target the specific chapter topics you need to focus on. You'll receive instant feedback and find links to tutorials, animations, and the online textbook to help you study.

4. When you're ready, go take Practice Test chapter-B and demonstrate how your results have improved.

Section 11.1, Exercise 1 How is monopolistic competition like monopoly?

Section 11.1, Exercise 2 How is monopolistic competition like perfect competition?

Section 11.2, Exercise 1 There are five gas stations in a small town, and all are identical except for location.

   a. Why would this industry be considered monopolistically competitive, given that the gas stations are identical?
   b. Would you expect that the prices charged by the stations would be the same?

Section 11.2, Exercise 2 The following graph shows demand and marginal cost for a monopolistically competitive firm in the short run.

   a. Draw the marginal revenue curve.
   b. Find the profit-maximizing price and quantity.
   c. Show the firm's profit on the graph.

Section 11.3, Exercise 1 In Dansville, there is only one movie theater. Because it is the only firm in the market, it is able to charge $12 for a movie. Average costs are $5.

   a. What is the theater's profit per ticket?
   b. Because profits exceed zero, more firms are considering entering the market. Analysts estimate that every new theater will raise average costs by $1, due to advertising costs, and lower ticket prices by $2. How many firms will there be in long-run equilibrium, and what will be the profit per ticket?

Section 11.3, Exercise 2 Suppose that the market for household cleaning services in Boise, Idaho is monopolistically competitive. One firm in the industry, Supertidy Cleaners, is in short run equilibrium, maximizing profits by charging a price of $50 per house and cleaning 20 houses per week.

   a. Sketch a graph of the equilibrium for Supertidy Cleaners including demand, marginal revenue, average total cost and marginal cost curves. Assume that ATC has its usual U-shape and is equal to $35 at the equalibrium output level.
   b. Label the area that represents the firm's profits.
   c. Label the deadweight loss.
   d. If all firms are earning profits, what do you predict will occur in the long run?

Section 11.4, Exercise 1 The following graph shows a monopolistically competitive firm in long-run equilibrium.

a. Identify the profit-maximizing price and quantity.
b. Identify the allocatively efficient price and quantity.
c. Identify the deadweight loss.

Section 11.4, Exercise 2 Refer to the graph in the previous exercise.

a. Identify the minimum efficient scale for the firm.
b. In monopolistically competitive industries, every firm is producing with excess capacity. What does this imply about average cost at the profit-maximizing point relative to minimum average cost?

Section 11.5, Exercise 1 Are the following advertisements primarily persuasive or informative?

a. Jennie's Salmon Shop is now open until midnight.
b. Delicious Chicken Snax are the tastiest in the world!
c. Try our new, heart-healthy menu!
d. You'll look more beautiful wearing Elegance Perfume.

Section 11.5, Exercise 2 One objective of advertising is to build brand loyalty.

a. What effect does increasing brand loyalty have on the firm's elasticity of demand?
b. What effect does increasing brand loyalty have on the firm's market power?

Section 11.5, Exercise 3 Why does spurious advertising reduce allocative efficiency?

12 Oligopoly

When Sega's Dreamcast, a new, high-powered video game console, hit the market in September 1999, it broke all existing records for advance sales. More than 200,000 consoles had been pre-ordered, and Dreamcast outsold rival Nintendo 64 by a three-to-one ratio. By October, the company had reported sales of more than 500,000 units. By the year's end, sales had topped one million. Dreamcast offered better graphics than existing machines and allowed players to play opponents online. It seemed destined for world domination, just like the warring characters in many of its games. Only two years later, however, it was "game over." Dreamcast went out of production, and Sega soon dropped out of the video game console market to concentrate exclusively on game development.

What happened? Why didn't the Sega machine become the dominant game system for years to come? What insights can we gain about the market structure of the video game console industry from Sega's downfall?

It's important to know that Sega was driven from the market by a very small number of powerful rivals. One of them, Sony, released its PlayStation 2 in October 2000, only 13 months after Dreamcast was introduced. Sony sold the first 500,000 available machines in only 24 hours. By the end of the year, PlayStation 2 had captured 60 percent of the market. Sony's success resulted not from a lower price, but from two highly attractive features: PlayStation 2 contained an integrated DVD player, and was compatible with the games from its predecessor, the original PlayStation. This compatibility gave PlayStation 2 many times more usable games than were available for Dreamcast.

The pending introduction of two more major rivals helped seal Dreamcast's fate, as potential game system buyers held off, waiting to see what fabulous features they could get in the new machines. In November 2001, Nintendo introduced GameCube, which had many of the same features as Dreamcast and a lower price. Then, software giant Microsoft introduced Xbox, a faster system with a hard drive and improved online-play technology.

Microsoft changed the competitive landscape dramatically, as it had more resources and more experience in computer-related technology than any other company in the market. Yet other characteristics of the market had hardly changed. The market still consisted of only three producers—Microsoft, Nintendo, and Sony—leaving consumers with the same number of choices as before. Each of the three firms continued to compete intensely by altering its product's prices and characteristics, always aware of the other firms' price and product characteristics.

In this chapter, we complete our examination of market structures with a look at oligopolies. An oligopoly is an industry in which a small number of sellers offer products that are close (sometimes even perfect) substitutes. Oligopoly markets are more concentrated than monopolistically competitive markets, but not as concentrated as monopolies. Thus, oligopoly lies between monopolistic competition and monopoly on the continuum of market structures. We will consider how the actions of one firm in an oligopolistic industry can affect the profits of the other firms in the market. We will see how oligopolies compete with each other, and we will use a tool called *game theory* to predict how oligopolies act strategically.

ALONG THE WAY, YOU WILL ALSO LEARN:

- The characteristics of oligopoly.
- How firms in oligopolies interact with each other.
- How sellers may behave when they do not cooperate with their rivals.
- How sellers may behave when they do cooperate with each other.
- How to think of the rivalry between firms as a game.
- How to measure market concentration.
- Whether oligopolies are beneficial to society.

AT THE END OF THE CHAPTER,
THE MYECONLAB LOGO WILL DIRECT YOU ONLINE

- MyEconLab is a resource-packed online homework and tutorial system that can help you perform better in your economics course. To log in for the first time, see page 30 for instructions.
- MyEconLab can help you apply important concepts from the chapter to real-world issues. Watch for the logo to indicate online features about oligopoly pricing and centralized cartels.
- At the end of each chapter, you'll find a special study section that will help you get the most out of your textbook and your instructor's MyEconLab course.

►Characteristics of Oligopoly

Before examining firm behavior and market outcomes in oligopolies in the context of our video game console example, we first describe the characteristics of this important model.

Entry Barriers

Oligopoly markets typically have substantial entry barriers. These barriers can be scale economies that arise naturally and prevent smaller firms from competing, or strategic barriers that firms create to make entry more difficult. Strategic entry barriers can include intensive advertising or legal barriers, such as patents. Whatever the source of the entry barrier, the inability of new rivals to enter an industry creates market power (the ability to set prices) for existing firms.

Products Can Be Differentiated

Oligopolistic firms can sell products that consumers view as perfect substitutes, such as cell phone minutes, or differentiated, as in the case of video game consoles. Firms often differentiate their products in an attempt to increase their market power.

Small Number of Interdependent Firms

The small number of firms in an oligopoly means that, unlike perfectly competitive firms, an oligopolist's actions can have a substantial impact on its competitors' profits. When Sony introduced PlayStation 2, Sega sales fell sharply. You will see throughout this chapter that the interdependence of oligopolies plays an important role in determining market outcomes.

Cooperation

Collusion
Occurs when supposedly competing firms form joint strategies to maximize profits.

There are so few firms in an oligopoly that they may be tempted to cooperate or collude with one another. **Collusion** occurs when supposedly competing firms form joint strategies to maximize profits. This cooperation can take many forms, including agreements on prices, geographic limits on sales, and even research and development. Later in the chapter we consider how collusion affects market outcomes.

Non-Cooperative Oligopoly

Rivals
Firms in the same industry that do not cooperate with one another.

When firms in the same industry do not cooperate with one another, we say that they are **rivals**. Rival firms use a variety of strategies to compete with one another. Some of those strategies result in efficient outcomes that benefit consumers. Others simply consume resources and reduce overall efficiency. In this section, we focus on the effects of price competition, advertising, and product offerings.

Price Competition

In oligopoly markets with differentiated products, products are substitutable yet have different characteristics and prices. For example, all video game consoles are roughly equivalent: They all allow consumers to play multiple-player video games with high-quality graphics. The similarity makes consumers sensitive to differences in prices of competing products when choosing among them.

Firms Undercut Prices. Suppose that there are only two firms (products) in the market, Sony's PlayStation 2 and Microsoft's Xbox. If consumers view these products as perfect substitutes, the firm that offers the lower price will receive all the orders. The other firm will receive no orders. Each firm will try to undercut the competition until its price equals marginal cost and no further price cuts are possible. We know that as price gets closer to marginal cost, allocative efficiency increases. Thus, price-cutting behavior benefits consumers and the economy as a whole. In this case, oligopolists end up selling at the same price as if the industry were perfectly competitive. Although our example is extreme, in that prices fall to marginal cost, price wars are common in some concentrated industries. As a result, firms often earn much less than monopoly-level profits. In the past 20 years, for example, firms in the airline industry have frequently engaged in price wars, keeping profits low.

Sticky Prices and the Kinked Demand Curve. Even if consumers view competing products in an oligopoly market as imperfect substitutes, rival firms need to be aware of each other's prices. Instead of undercutting its competitors' prices, a firm may have "sticky" prices. **Sticky prices** occur when firms are reluctant to change their prices for fear of losing market share and profit. If one firm raises its price but its rivals do not raise theirs, it will lose substantial market share. If, however, the firm reduces its price and all other firms reduce theirs as well, it will not gain market share.

We can show this reasoning graphically using a **kinked demand curve**, a tool that shows the impact of price increases and decreases for a firm in a concentrated industry. It illustrates why oligopolists may be reluctant to change their pricing strategy, and how an oligopolist's sales and market share may change, depending on the pricing behavior of its rival. It is not a model designed to show how a certain price arises in an oligopoly market.

In Figure 12.1, we start by assuming that Microsoft and Sony are the only two firms in the video game console market. Consumers regard the two products as substitutes. For simplicity, we also assume that each firm begins with 50 percent of the market and that Microsoft and Sony both charge $299 per console. Let's first focus on Microsoft and its decision-making process. Figure 12.1 shows that there are actually two demand curves that cross at the current price of $299. We say that the demand curve is "kinked" because the demand curve that is relevant for Microsoft depends on which direction it changes its price and whether Sony changes its price as well.

If Sony matches Microsoft's price decreases but not its price increases, the relevant demand curve is steeper (less elastic) at prices below $299, and flatter (more elastic) at prices above $299. Thus, the kink actually combines two demand curves. For example, suppose Microsoft raises its price to $350. If Sony responds to Microsoft's price hike by also raising its price to $350, Microsoft's sales of Xbox units fall back along the demand curve D_R. The quantity of Xboxes sold falls from 4,000 per day to 3,700 per day. Because the two firms still charge the same price, market shares remain unchanged. Total revenue for each firm increases from 4,000 × $299 = $1.196 million to 3,700 × $350 = $1.295 million, and both firms are better off.

Sticky prices
Prices that firms are reluctant to change for fear of losing market share and profit.

Kinked demand curve
Combines two demand curves: one in which the rival firm responds to price changes, and one in which it does not.

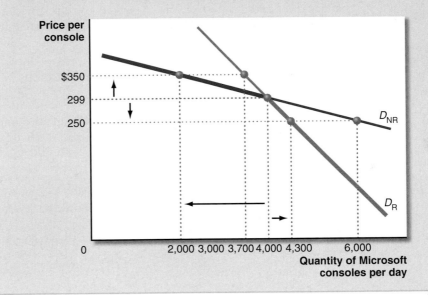

FIGURE 12.1

The Kinked Demand Curve for Microsoft's Xbox

Initially, Microsoft and Sony both control 50 percent of the market for consoles, and each sells its console for $299. The kink in the demand curve results from Sony's reaction to Microsoft's price changes. When Microsoft increases its price from $299 to $350, and Sony does not change its price, then Microsoft's sales fall along the demand curve D_{NR} from 4,000 to 2,000. If Sony had also raised its price, Microsoft's sales would have fallen along the demand curve D_R to 3,700. When Microsoft lowers its price to $250, sales increase to 4,300 if Sony decreases its price as well. If Sony does not match the price decrease, sales increase by much more, to 6,000. If Sony does not match price increases but does match decreases, Microsoft's demand curve is flatter (more elastic) above $299, and steeper (less elastic) below $299.

If Sony leaves its price unchanged at $299, when Microsoft increases its price to $350, sales of Xbox units will fall, according to D_{NR}, to 2,000, as consumers switch to the relatively less-expensive Sony systems. The dramatic decrease in sales causes Microsoft's revenue to fall to 2,000 × $350 = $700,000. Because Microsoft does not want to risk the consequences of Sony leaving its price at $299, it is reluctant to increase its price from $299 to $350.

Now let's consider the possible outcomes if Microsoft lowers the Xbox price from $299 to $250. When the price falls, the quantity demanded increases. Yet the magnitude of the increase in sales depends on how Sony responds to the price decrease. If Sony does not decrease its price to $250, Microsoft's sales move outward along the demand curve D_{NR} to 6,000 per day. However, because Sony does not want to lose so many sales to Microsoft, it is likely to match this price decrease. If this happens, Microsoft's sales move along the demand curve D_R, and it sells only 4,300 rather than 6,000 units per day. These sales figures take away much, if not all, of Microsoft's incentive to decrease price.

Nash Equilibrium. The kinked demand curve helps us to reach an important conclusion about the firms' strategies for pricing. If rivals always match price decreases but never match price increases, firms have little incentive to change prices to seek a competitive advantage. In our video game console example, as long as the costs of

Get Ahead of the Curve
Apply the model of sticky prices in an oligopoly to pricing behavior in the airline industry.

Nash equilibrium
Exists when the optimal strategy of a firm is to keep its strategy constant, given the strategy of the other firms.

production do not change, prices are likely to remain at $299. Neither firm is willing to risk the negative consequences of raising or lowering its price. Economists refer to this situation as a **Nash equilibrium**—each firm has an incentive to keep its strategy constant, given the strategy of the other firms. A Nash equilibrium is a stable solution, because no firm would choose to deviate from its current strategy unless the other firm changes strategies. It is named after John Nash, who won the 1994 Nobel Prize in Economics in part for his work on non-cooperative oligopoly. We will return to this important type of equilibrium solution later in the chapter.

In summary, consumers see price as one relevant factor in concentrated industries. As with monopolistic competition, the closer substitutes the products are, the more price-sensitive consumers are. As a result, after firms set their prices, oligopolists may be reluctant to change them in the short run, because they consider such changes to be too risky. Over longer periods of time, prices change as input prices and market demand change. We next examine strategies oligopolies use to gain market share.

Using Advertising and Product Proliferation to Reduce Competition

Firms in non-cooperative oligopolies typically formulate competitive strategies that are much more complex than simply setting prices. As discussed earlier, firms in the

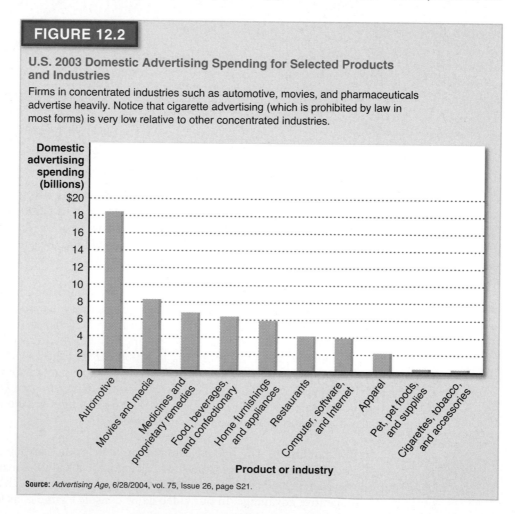

FIGURE 12.2

U.S. 2003 Domestic Advertising Spending for Selected Products and Industries

Firms in concentrated industries such as automotive, movies, and pharmaceuticals advertise heavily. Notice that cigarette advertising (which is prohibited by law in most forms) is very low relative to other concentrated industries.

Source: *Advertising Age*, 6/28/2004, vol. 75, Issue 26, page S21.

video game console market consider the prices of competing goods, equipment features, and changes in the number of competitors in the market when setting prices.

Advertising. Recall from Chapter 11 that informational advertising contains product information, including where the product can be bought, its price, and product characteristics. Such information improves economic efficiency because it allows consumers to make better-informed choices and pay lower prices. Persuasive advertising is designed to sway consumer tastes. If advertising makes consumer demand for a firm's products more inelastic, it can profitably increase prices.

Figures 12.2 and 12.3 show U.S. expenditures on advertising and the portion of product prices that is attributable to advertising for a variety of goods. When only a few firms are in contention for all the consumers in a market, the firms often draw on intensive advertising. For example, in 2003, the automotive industry spent more than $18 billion in the United States alone on advertising.

Intensive advertising is really two forms of non-price competition. First, to the extent that advertising creates brand loyalty among existing consumers, it makes them more reluctant to switch to another brand. Second, the brand loyalty that results from intensive advertising creates an entry barrier for potential new entrants. The data in Figure 12.2 indicate that any new competitor in these industries must be prepared to spend hundreds of millions if not billions of dollars on advertising. Any new entrant in the video console market would have to do so as well in order to inform consumers about its product and convince them that they should switch brands.

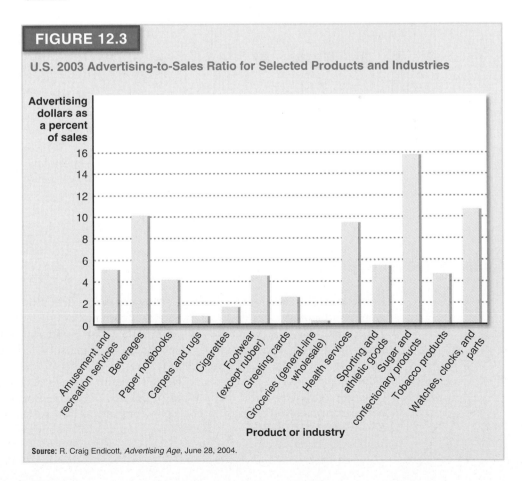

FIGURE 12.3

U.S. 2003 Advertising-to-Sales Ratio for Selected Products and Industries

Source: R. Craig Endicott, *Advertising Age*, June 28, 2004.

Product proliferation
Occurs when a firm introduces many related products so that it has a variant for every consumer, regardless of his or her tastes.

Product Proliferation. In some concentrated industries, incumbent firms erect entry barriers to potential competitors through **product proliferation**, or the firm's introduction of so many related products that it has a variant for every consumer, regardless of the consumer's tastes. One of the most striking examples is the running shoe industry. Each of the leading manufacturers (including Nike, Asics, Adidas, and New Balance) produces dozens of varieties of shoes. Nike alone produces more than 25 different styles of women's running shoes, each in several different color combinations. In addition, it produces more than 10 additional styles designed for specific events such as sprinting or javelin throwing. Many of the running shoes are slight variations on the basic design, aimed at comfort and performance while running. If we include men's and unisex styles, Nike offers well over 100 different styles of running shoes!

Think of all the possible shoe types as a spectrum similar to the color spectrum of the rainbow (red, orange, yellow, green, blue, indigo, violet). At one end are the lightest, least supportive shoes designed for short-distance competitive sprinting. At the other end are shoes with lots of support and shock resistance designed for long-distance training. Each manufacturer positions products all along this continuum because the cost of producing another, slightly different shoe is generally less than the revenue it generates. Moreover, filling a void in the spectrum may prevent a potential rival from gaining a "foothold" in the industry.

TEST + *E X T E N D* Your Knowledge

1. TEST What types of calling plan variations are available through wireless carriers? Why would they offer different types of plans rather than a single plan?

2. E X T E N D Consider the different types of wireless phone users— college students, managers and professionals, high school students, and others. Go to www.verizon.net and match available calling plans with your perception of demand from various groups.

▶ Cooperative Oligopoly

In the previous section, we discussed strategies that a firm might pursue in order to gain an advantage over its rivals. If a market contains only a few firms, they may be able to increase their profits by colluding rather than competing. Collusion can take many forms. Firms can agree to fix prices by charging some consumers more than others or by dividing the market in some way (for example, geographically). Consumers typically face higher prices as a result of such actions. While antitrust laws regulate or prohibit many types of collusive activities, some communications between firms are legal and do not harm consumers. In this section, we look at the positive and negative sides of cooperative behavior by evaluating industry standards and price-fixing schemes.

Industry Standards

Industry standard
An agreement on a common size, shape, or configuration across all manufacturers.

One way that firms often cooperate is by agreeing upon an **industry standard**—a common size, shape, or configuration. Consumers benefit when firms in an industry share information and agree to produce all products to a certain standard. Standards allow consumers to switch easily from one producer to another and to mix and match goods and services from competing firms. Imagine how hard it would be to learn to type if every keyboard manufacturer used a different layout for the keys! In the video game console industry, each manufacturer must produce products that can be connected to a standard television through plugs of a specific configuration. In doing so, they ensure that the maximum number of possible consumers can use their systems.

Network externality
Exists when consumers' utility from consuming a good increases with the number of other individuals consuming the same good.

When consumers' utility from consuming a good increases with the number of other individuals consuming the same good, economists say that there is a **network externality**. Consider the word-processing industry. In the 1990s, WordPerfect and Microsoft Word dominated the market. People who preferred WordPerfect had to use an unreliable file conversion process to access files created in Word, and vice versa. By the end of the decade, Word's market share exceeded 90 percent. Consumers who stuck with WordPerfect or other software found themselves increasingly at a disadvantage when it came to sharing files. Although the domination of a market by a single firm creates market power, consumers often benefit from the standardization.

Unfortunately, some cooperative behavior reduces competition in markets and hurts consumers. We focus next on price fixing, an illegal form of cooperation, and show why it harms consumers.

Industry Standards on Benefit Producers and Consumers

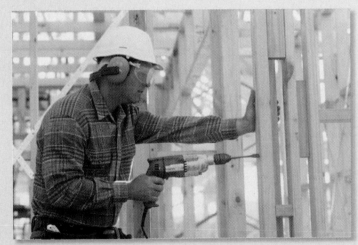

(a) In the construction industry, industry standards reduce costs and increase product quality

(b) Standards such as chair and table dimensions mean more productive conference rooms

Cartels

Cartel
A group of firms that agree to work together to increase their profits.

A **cartel** is a group of firms that agree to work together to increase their profits. The Organization of Petroleum Exporting Countries, or OPEC, is the most famous cartel in the world. Cartel behavior is prevalent in a variety of industries, ranging from diamonds to illegal drugs to the National Collegiate Athletic Association (NCAA).

Centralized cartel
A group of firms that collude in order to charge the monopoly price by agreeing to individual production quotas.

Centralized Cartel. In a **centralized cartel**, firms behave as if they are separate manufacturing plants all operating as a single monopoly. They agree to restrict overall output to what a monopoly would produce and to charge the monopoly price. Centralized cartels are illegal in the United States (a topic we return to in Chapter 13). However, international cartels such as OPEC operate openly because they fall outside the jurisdiction of U.S. courts. As such, OPEC production quotas for member nations are publicly available. Table 12.1 shows the agreed-upon production quotas for OPEC member countries effective as of March 2005.[1] By explicitly controlling the quantity of oil produced and closely monitoring any changes in price, the member nations of OPEC can strongly affect prices in the international crude oil market.

Duopoly
An industry comprising two firms that supply an entire market.

Duopoly Cartels. Figure 12.4 shows how a centralized cartel works in the case of a **duopoly**, an industry comprising two firms that supply an entire market. Consider first what would happen if the firms behaved like perfectly competitive firms and set

TABLE 12.1

OPEC Quotas as of March 2005*

Member Country	Quota Effective March 2005 (in barrels of oil per day)
Algeria	878,000
Indonesia	1,425,000
Iran	4,037,000
Kuwait	2,207,000
Libya	1,473,000
Nigeria	2,265,000
Qatar	713,000
Saudi Arabia	8,937,000
UAE	2,400,000
Venezuela	3,165,000
Total	27,500,000

Source: "OPEC Quotas," "News and Info," at www.opec.org/home/quotas/quotas.htm
*Note: Iraq does not have a quota.

[1] For a list of the current production quotas, see "OPEC Quotas" under "News & Info" at www.opec.org/home/quotas/quotas.htm.

FIGURE 12.4

Duopoly Equilibrium in a Centralized Cartel

In a duopoly, if the firms act like a perfectly competitive firm, price is determined by the intersection of the demand and supply curves, where the supply curve is the sum of MC_1 and MC_2. In the graph, the market supply and demand curves intersect at a price of $40 and equilibrium quantity of 33 million barrels. If the firms behave like a cartel, they set the sum of the marginal cost curves equal to marginal revenue. The resulting equilibrium price of $48 and total equilibrium quantity of 20 million barrels are the monopoly equilibrium price and quantity. The deadweight loss is shaded in gray.

price equal to marginal cost. To determine the market supply curve, we horizontally add the individual supply curves of the firms, which are given by the marginal cost curves MC_1 and MC_2. This curve ($MC_1 + MC_2$) intersects the market demand curve, D, at the perfectly competitive equilibrium price of $40 per barrel. The equilibrium quantity is 33 million barrels.

What price–output combination does the cartel choose? Rather than view the sum of the marginal cost curves as a supply curve as in a competitive industry, a cartel views the sum of the individual marginal cost curves as an overall "monopoly" marginal cost curve. To choose the best output level, it sets the sum of the marginal cost curves equal to marginal revenue. Thus, the two firms combined produce 20 million barrels and charge $48 per barrel. Because consumers pay the monopoly price and consume the monopoly output, a deadweight loss occurs (the area shaded gray).

To determine the output level of each individual firm in the cartel, we can use the point where the sum of the marginal cost curves meets the MR curve to determine each firm's output. On the graph, this point is labeled r. If we draw a horizontal dashed line from the axis across to point r, the points where this line cuts the individual marginal cost curves (point s for Firm 2 and point t for Firm 1) indicate the output levels for the two firms. Thus, Firm 1 produces 7 million and Firm 2 produces 13 million barrels.

Although a successful cartel charges the same price as a monopoly, the very essence of a cartel makes it unstable. Each member of the cartel has agreed to sell its output at the established price. Yet, at the cartel price, marginal revenue exceeds each firm's marginal cost of production. As a result, each firm believes it could increase profits by producing and selling a little more than the agreed-upon output. This overproduction undermines the established price. Because the cartel's demand curve is downward-sloping, when its members increase output, the price they charge must fall. As a result, cartel profits fall as well. Unless members of the cartel can punish a firm that exceeds the established output level, preventing overproduction can be difficult. The instability of cartels is good news for consumers: Unstable cartels have a hard time maintaining monopoly prices.

Market-sharing cartel
Formed from agreements
to split markets along a
definable boundary.

Market-Sharing Cartel. Cartels can use tools other than price to increase market power. Agreements to split markets along a definable boundary lead to **market-sharing cartels**. For example, in July 2001, Scandinavian Airlines (SAS) and Maersk Air were fined more than 50 million euros when it was discovered that they had secretly agreed to share the market for flights in and out of Denmark.[2] Although the actual market-sharing arrangement was complex, we can use hypothetical numbers to illustrate the effect of the cartel. Consider the market demand for flights out of Denmark, as shown in Figure 12.5. If SAS and Maersk Air act like perfectly competitive firms, the industry supply curve represents the sum of their marginal cost curves. The equilibrium price is 300 euros, and 700 passengers per day choose to fly.

If the two firms form a market-sharing cartel and divide the market equally, each operates as a monopolist for half the market. Suppose that half the customers want to fly east to Moscow, and half want to fly west to New York. SAS and Maersk agree that SAS will carry all the eastbound traffic, Maersk will carry all westbound traffic, and neither will encroach on the other's territory. Instead of a choice between two airlines, all consumers now face a monopolist. Assuming they have the same costs panel (a) of Figure 12.6 shows the marginal cost curve of SAS in such a case, and panel (b) shows Maersk's marginal cost curve. We see that when the market is divided, consumers pay 500 euros, and only 250 passengers fly in each market, for a total of 500 passengers. As expected, when firms can act as a monopoly, prices are 200 euros higher and output is 200 passengers lower than in the perfect competition outcome.

This example shows that consumers may be strongly affected by cooperative behavior. Thus, economists are very interested in how such behavior arises, and what its implications may be. In the next section, we introduce a methodology that we can use to analyze both cooperative and non-cooperative firm behavior.

FIGURE 12.5

Market Equilibrium for Flights out of Denmark with No Collusion

In a duopoly with no collusion, SAS and Maersk Air act like perfectly competitive firms. Summing their individual marginal cost curves, MC_1 and MC_2, yields the market supply curve, $MC_1 + MC_2$. In equilibrium, the market supply and demand curves intersect, generating an equilibrium price of 300 euros per ticket and equilibrium quantity of 700 passengers.

[2] Paul Belleflamme and Francis Bloch, "Market Sharing Agreements and Stable Collective Networks," October 11, 2001, www.qmw.ac.uk/~ugte186/msascn.pdf, accessed August 31, 2005.

FIGURE 12.6

Market Equilibrum for Flights out of Denmark with Collusion

SAS and Maersk act like a cartel to divide the market, with SAS carrying all the eastbound passengers and Maersk carrying all the westbound passengers. The markets are of equal size, so demand in each market is exactly half the total passenger demand at each price after the market is split. Each airline sets marginal cost equal to marginal revenue, as each has monopoly power in its half of the market. Collusion generates an equilibrium price of 500 euros per ticket in each market and total equilibrium quantity of 500 passengers; that is, the monopoly equilibrium price and quantity. The deadweight loss is shaded in gray.

Game Theory

Game theory
Analyzes firms' strategies by recognizing the interdependence of their actions; used to show the outcomes of various strategies chosen by the firms.

Payoff matrix
Shows the outcomes for each strategy that a player might follow.

We can evaluate many of the strategies used by oligopolistic firms with a technique called game theory. **Game theory** analyzes firms' strategies by recognizing the interdependence of their actions. As the name implies, game theory views corporate strategy as if it were a strategic game such as chess. Based on the strategies chosen by each player (in this case, each firm), we can evaluate the outcome, or payoff, for each player. A table called the **payoff matrix** shows the outcomes for each strategy that a player might follow. We assume that firms are aware of this payoff matrix and use it to choose the best alternative. For example, we might assume that firms form strategies to maximize profits in the current period. We can use game theory to study the outcomes of various strategies. In addition, we show how the game's outcome changes if we alter our assumptions about how firms interact with one another (for example, whether they act cooperatively). Game theory allows us to decide which strategy, if any, is best for the firm under a variety of circumstances. In the context of oligopoly, we can see how outcomes change when players collude instead of treating each other as rivals.

Determining the Dominant Strategy

To show how economists use game theory to analyze firm behavior, we return to the video game console market. Suppose that Sony and Microsoft are contemplating new advertising campaigns that describe the features of their consoles and the available games. Each is aware that the other might advertise and does not want to lose market share (and the profits they might earn by producing that output). Based on past experience, each company knows the consequences of its actions. We show these outcomes in the payoff matrix in Figure 12.7.

As the executives at each firm consider their choices, they also need to anticipate the strategy of the other firm. Consider Sony's possible strategies. If Microsoft advertises, Sony's profits increase two percent if it also advertises, or decrease by one percent if it does not advertise. As a result, when Microsoft advertises, Sony's best strategy is to advertise. If Microsoft does not advertise, Sony's profits increase by five percent if it advertises; Sony's profits remain unchanged if it does not advertise. Here again, Sony's wisest move is to advertise. Thus, in either case, Sony is better off advertising. Because Sony's best strategy is to advertise regardless of what Microsoft does, we say that advertising is a dominant strategy for Sony. A **dominant strategy** occurs when one strategy is best for a player regardless of the rival's actions.

Because we assume that Microsoft faces exactly the same set of choices and payoffs as Sony, we know that both firms will follow the same dominant strategy. Thus, the Nash equilibrium means that both firms advertise and each firm's profits rise by two percent. In this case, the Nash equilibrium is also a **dominant strategy equilibrium,** in which neither player has any reason to change strategy, because each player has a single strategy that is optimal under all circumstances.

Dominant strategy
A strategy that is best for a player regardless of his rival's actions.

Dominant strategy equilibrium
Each player has a single strategy that is optimal under all circumstances; a form of Nash equilibrium.

Multiple Nash Equilibrium Solutions in a Game

Suppose that instead of facing the options in Figure 12.7, Sony and Microsoft can each choose to develop its product by adding one of two possible new features: one that appeals to young players, or one that appeals to teens. Each firm can offer only one type of improvement, and the market demand in the youth and teen markets is too small for both firms to be profitable if they enter the same market. Figure 12.8 shows the payoff matrix. Unlike the dominant strategy equilibrium in Figure 12.7, Sony's and Microsoft's best strategies depend on the decision made by the other firm. If both enter the youth or teen market, profits fall by three percent for each.

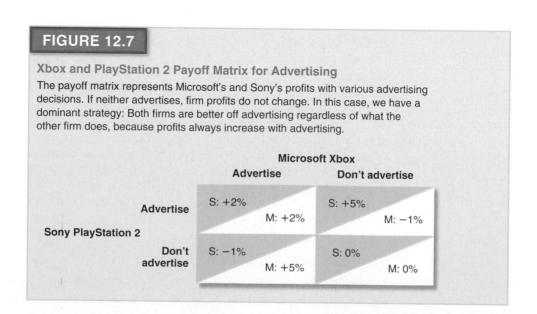

FIGURE 12.7

Xbox and PlayStation 2 Payoff Matrix for Advertising

The payoff matrix represents Microsoft's and Sony's profits with various advertising decisions. If neither advertises, firm profits do not change. In this case, we have a dominant strategy: Both firms are better off advertising regardless of what the other firm does, because profits always increase with advertising.

	Microsoft Xbox	
	Advertise	Don't advertise
Sony PlayStation 2 Advertise	S: +2% / M: +2%	S: +5% / M: −1%
Don't advertise	S: −1% / M: +5%	S: 0% / M: 0%

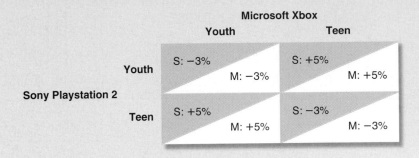

FIGURE 12.8

Nash Equilibria

If Sony and Microsoft both choose to offer a product to the same market (youth or teen), both experience a three-percent decline in profits. If they offer products to different markets, both increase profits by five percent. Thus, there are two Nash equilibria. If the firms end up in either the upper right or lower left, neither firm has an incentive to change its strategy.

However, if Sony chooses the youth market and Microsoft chooses the teen market, profits rise by five percent for each. Suppose the choices are reversed: Sony pursues the teen market while Microsoft pursues the youth market. We see again that both firms increase profits. In this case, there are two Nash equilibria—the upper right and the lower left of the payoff matrix. In both places, each firm follows a fixed strategy, as long as the other firm does so as well. The upper-left and lower-right cells, which correspond to the results of both firms entering the same market, are not equilibria. Either firm would be better off if it changed its strategy and the other firm did not. In cases where there are multiple Nash equilibria, the outcome is uncertain. Once the firms achieve one of the equilibrium points, neither firm will want to change its strategy, but if firms must make their strategies at the same time, there is no obvious way for the firms to choose a specific strategy. In such cases, the firms have an incentive to work cooperatively, or collude.

Colluding and the Prisoners' Dilemma

Prisoners' dilemma
A payoff matrix in which the dominant strategy leads all players to an outcome in which all players could be made better off through collusion.

As we saw in the previous example, firms sometimes can achieve better outcomes if they collaborate upon joint strategies. We can use game theory to explore this question. You will discover that even a dominant strategy equilibrium does not always yield an outcome that is in the players' best interest. We begin by considering a famous two-player strategy problem known as the *prisoners' dilemma*. A **prisoners' dilemma** occurs when the dominant strategy leads all players to an undesired outcome. The players must cooperate if they want to reach the best outcome, but they have no clear way to do so.

Consider two criminals, Billie and Teri, who are caught in the act of robbing a home. The police would prefer to convict at least one (and preferably both) of them of robbery. However, Billie and Teri have no stolen items in their possession when they are captured. Unfortunately, the police have no physical evidence. If neither one of them confesses and implicates her partner, they can convict Billie and Teri of criminal trespass only.

Criminal trespass is punishable by 1 month in jail, while the more serious crime of robbery is punishable by 24 to 36 months in jail. If only one of the criminals goes to jail, that individual receives the maximum sentence—36 months. If they both

DILBERT: © Scott Adams/Dist. by United Feature Syndicate, Inc.

confess, both go to jail for 24 months. If you've ever watched a detective show, you can guess how the police work. They quickly separate the two suspects, and offer each the opportunity of confessing in exchange for receiving no sentence (0 months of jail time). In doing so, the police create the payoff matrix for Billie and Teri shown in Figure 12.9.

The payoff matrix indicates that the dominant strategy for each player is to confess, as confessing always appears to lead to a lighter sentence. Thus the dominant strategy equilibrium is for each to confess. Unfortunately for our two criminals, this means that each will spend 2 years in jail. Is there a better outcome for both players? Suppose that they had a chance to agree beforehand that neither will confess (and that they trust one another enough to stick to the agreement). Each will then be sentenced to only 1 month in jail instead of 2 years. Without collusion, each is doomed by her dominant strategy to 2 years in jail.

FIGURE 12.9

Prisoners' Dilemma

The payoff matrix represents possible outcomes for our home robbers, Billie and Teri. With no collusion, the dominant solution for both Billie and Teri is to confess. However, the dominant strategy where both confess and spend 2 years in jail leads to an outcome that neither is happy with. They can reach the more desirable outcome of each spending only 1 month in jail only if they can act cooperatively by agreeing not to confess beforehand, and trust one another enough to hold to the agreement.

		Teri	
		Confess	Don't confess
Billie	Confess	B: −24 mo. / T: −24 mo.	B: 0 mo. / T: −36 mo.
	Don't confess	B: −36 mo. / T: 0 mo.	B: −1 mo. / T: −1 mo.

Firm Collusion

The problem for our two criminals is the same as for two colluding firms. They must trust one another enough to overcome the temptation to follow their own individual dominant strategies. Suppose that Sony and Microsoft are contemplating use of a new chip. The chip would improve graphics performance slightly, but would also significantly increase the cost of manufacturing the game systems and therefore the products' prices. Consumers would not notice the benefits of the new chip unless the firms advertise them, so the firms must also bear the cost of advertising. We show the payoff matrix for this situation in Figure 12.10. The percentages in the matrix indicate changes in profits from the current year to the following year.

In this case, using the new chip is again a dominant strategy for each firm. It increases each firm's profits regardless of what the other firm does. For example, if Sony believes that Microsoft will use the new chip, it can also use the chip and increase profits by one percent. Alternatively, if Sony does not use the chip, it will lose one percent of profits. If Sony believes that Microsoft will not use the chip, it can use the chip and gain profits of four percent or not use the chip and gain profits of three percent. Again, both firms face the same set of choices and payoffs. Thus, each chooses to install the new chip, and each increases profits by one percent.

While using the new chip increases profits, the dominant strategies of the two firms do not lead to the best overall solution. If neither firm installs the chip, it saves on the cost of the chip and the advertising campaign. Both firms then increase profits by three percent instead of one percent. Without some means to decide jointly that it will not install the new chip, each firm will go ahead with the installation.

Can the firms improve the outcome if they choose to cooperate rather than to compete? We illustrate this behavior in the context of game theory in Figure 12.10. Suppose that both firms are aware of the entire payoff matrix before they must commit to a strategy. The problem they face is that the dominant strategy equilibrium is in the upper-left quadrant, while both firms prefer the outcome in the lower-right quadrant to the dominant strategy equilibrium. Both firms' profits grow faster if they do not introduce the chip, only if they can be certain that the other firm will not introduce it either.

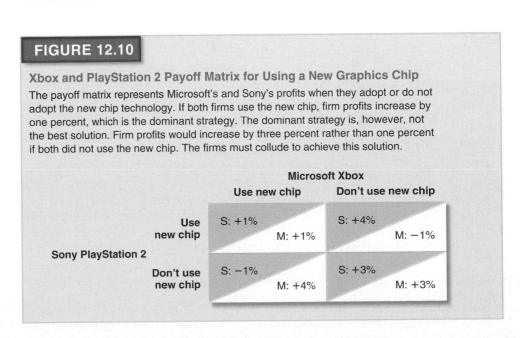

FIGURE 12.10

Xbox and PlayStation 2 Payoff Matrix for Using a New Graphics Chip

The payoff matrix represents Microsoft's and Sony's profits when they adopt or do not adopt the new chip technology. If both firms use the new chip, firm profits increase by one percent, which is the dominant strategy. The dominant strategy is, however, not the best solution. Firm profits would increase by three percent rather than one percent if both did not use the new chip. The firms must collude to achieve this solution.

		Microsoft Xbox	
		Use new chip	**Don't use new chip**
Sony PlayStation 2	**Use new chip**	S: +1% M: +1%	S: +4% M: −1%
	Don't use new chip	S: −1% M: +4%	S: +3% M: +3%

Measuring Market Concentration

Market concentration
Refers to size and distribution of firm market shares and the number of firms relative to the market.

We have seen that when a market becomes concentrated, firms may have greater market power, which allows them to set their price above marginal cost. Furthermore, if there are very few firms in a market, they may be able to collude and charge the same price as a monopolist would. Thus, for policy makers to monitor markets for collusion, they must be able to measure **market concentration**, the size and distribution of firm market shares and the number of firms relative to the market. However, we do not yet have such a measuring stick. To quantify market concentration, economists use two measures of industry concentration that can help determine which market structure model is most appropriate for a given market.

Four-Firm Concentration Ratio

Four-firm concentration ratio (CR4)
Measures market concentration by adding the market shares of the four largest firms in an industry.

The **four-firm concentration ratio (CR4)** measures market concentration by adding the market shares of the four largest firms in an industry. It has several advantages as a measurement tool: It requires very little information to calculate, it is simple to understand, and we can use it to compare different markets or to track a given market over time.

For example, we can use the CR4 to show the market concentration in the sneaker industry. The four largest firms in the sneaker industry as of 2004 were Nike, with 62 percent of the market; New Balance, with 15.5 percent; Asics, with 10 percent; and Adidas, with 4.3 percent. We can use the CR4 to show the overall market concentration:

Nike:	62 percent
New Balance:	15.5 percent
Asics:	10 percent
Adidas:	4.3 percent
CR4 =	91.8

An industry with a low CR4 is typically more competitive than an industry with a high CR4. Consider a perfectly competitive industry with 100 equal-sized firms. Each firm has 1 percent of the market, so the CR4 equals 4 (1 + 1 + 1 + 1). At the other extreme, the CR4 is 100 (100 + 0 + 0 + 0) for a monopoly.

The CR4 allows us to compare different industries. Figure 12.11 shows several industries and their CR4s. From this table, we can see that four firms make up more than 80 percent of the breakfast cereal industry. The largest four firms in the women's and girls' apparel industry make up only about 13 percent of the market. Although there is no hard-and-fast rule that associates a given market structure model with a given CR4 value, most economists agree that for markets with CR4 values exceeding 60, the oligopoly model is more applicable than monopolistic competition.

The CR4 is not a perfect measure. It does not indicate how the market shares are distributed among the four largest firms or how market shares are distributed among all smaller firms. For example, because there are only three firms in the video console market, the CR4 is 100—the same as a monopoly. Yet the conditions in the video console market are very different from a monopoly.

The Herfindahl-Hirschman Index

Herfindahl-Hirschman Index (HHI)
Measures market concentration as the sum of squared market shares.

The **Herfindahl-Hirschman Index (HHI)** is a more sophisticated measure of market share than CR4 and addresses some of CR4's weaknesses. Computing the HHI is a two-step process. First, we square the market share of each firm in the industry, not

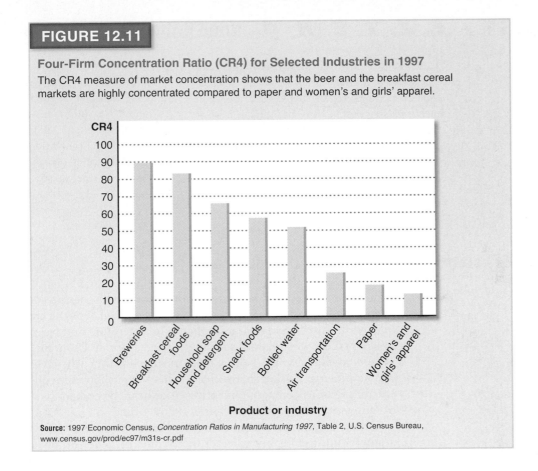

FIGURE 12.11

Four-Firm Concentration Ratio (CR4) for Selected Industries in 1997
The CR4 measure of market concentration shows that the beer and the breakfast cereal markets are highly concentrated compared to paper and women's and girls' apparel.

Source: 1997 Economic Census, *Concentration Ratios in Manufacturing 1997*, Table 2, U.S. Census Bureau, www.census.gov/prod/ec97/m31s-cr.pdf

just the four largest firms. Then we compute the sum of the squares. If, for example, there were two additional sneaker manufacturers, each with 4.1 percent of the market, we could calculate the HHI for the sneaker industry as:

$$HHI = (62^2 + 15.5^2 + 10^2 + 4.3^2 + 4.1^2 + 4.1^2) = 4{,}236.36$$

To understand the usefulness of the HHI index, let's suppose that the four largest firms each control 22.95 percent of the market. The combined share of the four largest firms remains the same, so the CR4 is still 91.8 percent. In contrast, the HHI falls by almost half to 2,140.43:

$$HHI = (22.95^2 + 22.95^2 + 22.95^2 + 22.95^2 + 4.1^2 + 4.1^2) = 2{,}140.43$$

The HHI changes dramatically, because it squares each market share, giving greater weight to firms with large market shares. After the HHI exceeds 1,800, government regulators become concerned that the market may be an oligopoly.

The HHI thus has two advantages over the CR4:

1. It can uncover changes in structure that are not revealed by the CR4.
2. It uses data on all firms, not just the largest four.

The disadvantage of the HHI is that calculating it requires market share data for all firms, which can be very difficult to obtain. In Chapter 13, we will discuss how the government uses these measures of industry concentration when it sets and enforces antitrust and regulatory policy.

1. TEST In Wooster, Ohio, there are four shops that offer formal wear and tuxedos, and six appliance repair shops. Assume that in each industry, each firm has equal market share. What are the CR4 and HHI measures of industry concentration in these markets?

2. EXTEND Look up "formal wear and tuxedos" and "appliance repair" in your local yellow pages and count the number of suppliers in your town. Assuming that firms are of equal size, what are the CR4 and HHI values in each industry? Based on your answer for Wooster, Ohio, how do the industry concentrations in the two towns compare? In which town would you expect prices to be lower for tuxedo rentals? For appliance repair?

▶ Efficiency in Concentrated Industries

In addition to the breakfast cereal and brewery industries, as shown in Figure 12.11, a few firms dominate many other U.S. industries, such as the chewing gum, automobile manufacturing, and large appliance (refrigerators and freezers) markets. Should policy makers worry about such high concentration? Economists are divided on the issue. Some economists believe that consumers suffer whenever relatively few firms command large market shares. They believe that oligopolies do not provide the benefits of vigorous competition—prices at or near the competitive level and a high rate of innovation and technology adoption over time.

Others believe that the issue is not whether there *are* many firms in the industry at any point in time, but whether there *could be*. They do not worry about concentration if the market is contestable. A market is **contestable** if entry barriers are low. If a market is contestable, consumers are likely to face low prices regardless of the firms' market shares, because existing firms must be aware that new competitors can enter at any time. Consider a monopolist that has no entry barriers to protect its position. If the firm charged high prices, it would generate profits above the competitive level, which would attract entrants. (Recall that when perfectly competitive firms are earning positive economic profits, new firms will enter.) Thus, the only way for it to remain a monopolist is to keep prices low enough that no new firms want to enter. If the firm followed the standard rule of setting marginal cost equal to marginal revenue, new firms would enter the industry and undercut the price charged by the monopoly.

Like monopolies, most oligopolies are not contestable, so they typically charge prices higher than their marginal cost, creating a deadweight loss. Output and allocative efficiency are lower than if the industry were perfectly competitive, and prices are higher. In Figure 12.12, we see that if the oligopolist uses its market power to charge the price of $30 instead of the perfect competition price of $20, it creates a deadweight loss equal to the shaded area. The deadweight loss occurs because, as with monopoly, society would be better off if more output were produced.

The government may step in to reduce the deadweight loss by forcing oligopolists to sell more output at lower prices or by breaking a large firm up into smaller competing firms. The government's success depends on factors such as the cost of the legal process, the nature of the entry barriers, and the size of the deadweight loss. The benefits of lower prices or more competing firms may not be worth a long and expensive legal battle. (We will focus on U.S. government policy regarding concentrated industries in Chapter 13.)

Contestable
Describes a market in which entry barriers are low enough that firms can gain entry to the industry.

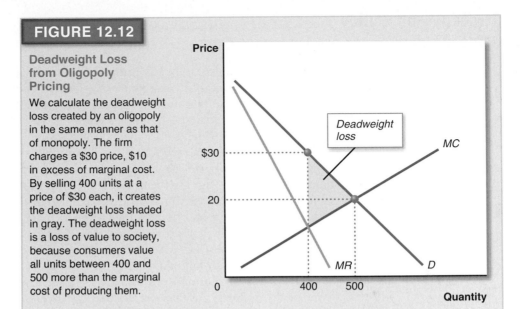

FIGURE 12.12

Deadweight Loss from Oligopoly Pricing

We calculate the deadweight loss created by an oligopoly in the same manner as that of monopoly. The firm charges a $30 price, $10 in excess of marginal cost. By selling 400 units at a price of $30 each, it creates the deadweight loss shaded in gray. The deadweight loss is a loss of value to society, because consumers value all units between 400 and 500 more than the marginal cost of producing them.

Oligopolies may also innovate and adopt new technology more slowly than competitive firms. If they do, consumers suffer. This problem may occur because established firms use industry standards to block new technologies or because there are fewer competitors to challenge them. Consumers benefit when firms compete with each other by improving their products and lowering prices to gain advantage. If firms do not compete vigorously or compete in ways that reduce efficiency (such as the creation of strategic entry barriers), they reduce overall economic well-being.

In this chapter and the previous three, we examined the four basic market structures: perfect competition, monopoly, monopolistic competition, and oligopoly. Table 12.2 summarizes the characteristics of these models. It provides a useful guideline for deciding how to analyze an industry. As we know, the predictions of each model are quite different. Thus, choosing the correct model is vital to describe firm behavior and industry outcomes such as price and quantity.

TABLE 12.2

Summary of Market Structure Characteristics

Market Structure	Product	Entry	Price Versus MC	Long Run Economic Profits	CR4; HHI
Perfect competition	Homogeneous	Easy	$P = MC$	0	Very low; very low
Monopolistic competition	Differentiated	Easy	$P > MC$	0	Less than 60; less than 1,800
Oligopoly	Homogeneous or differentiated	Difficult	$P > MC$	≥ 0	60–90; over 1,800
Monopoly	Unique	Very difficult	$P > MC$	≥ 0	100; 10,000

Until November 2003, wireless phone consumers faced a frustrating exit barrier: Phone numbers were not portable. Have you ever tried to switch from one wireless service to another and found that you had to change to a new phone number? A new law, known as the Wireless Local Number Portability (WLNP), made it much easier to change to a new provider. Under the old rules, switching to a new provider meant having to inform everyone who had the old number that it was no longer valid, and perhaps having to print new business cards and stationery to update to the new number. For people who use their phones intensively, the hassle and cost of making such a change often constituted an exit barrier that prevented them from switching to a new provider who offered a lower price. Under the WLNP, this barrier disappeared entirely. Wireless providers are now forced to compete to attract and keep their customers' business. Most customers are still bound by one- to two-year contracts that include substantial penalties for early cancellation. However, the ability of customers to switch providers without a fee at the end of the contract will lead to lower prices. Industry insiders predict that the freedom to change carriers without changing phone numbers will cause wireless prices to fall by as much as 15 to 20 percent.[3] Even customers who do not switch service providers benefit, because firms must offer lower prices to induce all customers to stay.

Critical-Thinking Questions

1. Under what circumstances might wireless providers be able to prevent prices from falling—i.e., what strategic action might they take?
2. What other entry and exit barriers might providers use to prevent switching?

SUMMARY

- **Characteristics of oligopoly.** Oligopolies are concentrated markets with few firms. Oligopoly markets usually have barriers to entry. The product may be differentiated or homogeneous. Unlike market structures with large numbers of firms, firms in an oligopoly are aware that they have few rivals and that they must formulate strategies to compete with those rivals. Firms in oligopolies interact either non-cooperatively or cooperatively.

- **Non-cooperative oligopoly.** If firms treat one another as rivals, they may use either prices or a variety of non-price strategies, such as exploiting scale economies and high fixed costs of entry, advertising, and product proliferation, to gain and protect market share.

- **Cooperative oligopoly.** Some forms of interfirm cooperation benefit consumers. Industry standards, for example, often make it easier for comsumers to switch from one brand to another. Other forms of cooperation are bad for consumers. Firms in an oligopoly market may be able to form a cartel in which firms join together to set prices and output, resulting in price and output similar to those of a monopoly.

- **Game theory.** Because the number of firms (players) is so limited, the most effective way to evaluate firms' strategies is to view them as a game. One benefit of this technique is that the same payoff matrix can be used to show both non-cooperative and cooperative outcomes.

---

[3] Grant Gross and Stephen Lawson, "WLNP is a boon to customers," *The Industry Standard*, December 1, 2003, www.thestandard.com/article.php?story=2003120102 5958933, accessed March 24, 2004.

- **Measuring market concentration.** Market concentration is measured using the four-firm concentration ratio (CR4) and the Herfindahl-Hirschman Index (HHI). In general, the higher the CR4 or HHI for an industry, the more concentrated the market shares.

- **Efficiency in concentrated industries.** Concern over oligopolies varies. Some economists focus on market share of existing firms and believe that the causal linkage between market share and market power is strong. Others focus on the contestability of the market.

▶ KEY TERMS

Cartel 314
Centralized cartel 314
Collusion 307
Contestable 324
Dominant strategy 318
Dominant strategy
  equilibrium 318
Duopoly 314

Four-firm concentration
  ratio (CR4) 322
Game theory 317
Herfindahl-Hirschman Index
  (HHI) 322
Industry standard 313
Kinked demand curve 308
Market concentration 322

Market-sharing cartel 316
Nash equilibrium 310
Network externality 313
Payoff matrix 317
Prisoners' dilemma 319
Product proliferation 312
Rivals 307
Sticky prices 308

▶ PROBLEMS

1. Suppose that there are only two accountants in the auditing services industry: Jones and Smith. Each person currently charges $100 per hour for its services. Use a kinked demand curve to show why Jones may be reluctant to change this price in either direction.

2. Suppose the firms in a concentrated industry decide to compete against one another as rivals. What type of rivalry is best for consumers? What form of rivalry might be harmful to consumers?

3. It is useful for policy makers to distinguish between persuasive and informational advertising. Do you agree or disagree with this statement? Why?

4. Mattresses come in only a small number of different sizes. Discuss how this industry standard affects consumers. Are they better off or worse off because of the standard?

5. Suppose that you are the president of a computer firm in a concentrated industry. Your production manager advocates switching to a new type of disk drive that holds five percent more data than other drives through the use of a unique technology. If you employ this new technology, your machines will have the largest disk capacity, but they will be incompatible with any disks created by your competitors' machines. What factors should you consider in deciding whether to manufacture the new drive?

6. When a firm patents a process or product that it does not intend to use or produce, it is sometimes called a *sleeping patent*. Explain why a firm in a concentrated industry might pursue such a strategy.

7. In the following graph, two firms make up the supply side of the industry. On the graph, show the price and output levels that result if the firms compete against one another as rivals so that they charge the perfectly competitive price. Also show the price, joint output, and output of each firm if the two firms operate as a centralized cartel.

8. Consider the following payoff matrix. Each firm is contemplating investing heavily in research and development (R&D). The payoffs represent changes in profits. Assume that each firm is concerned only about its own welfare (not the damage to the other player). The payoff shown in the upper left is for Firm A; the payoff shown in the lower right is for Firm B. Initially assume that players do not cooperate with one another.

   a. Does either player have a dominant strategy? If so, what is it? If not, why not?

   b. Is there a Nash equilibrium for this game?

   c. Would collusion alter the outcome?

9. Why are centralized cartels unstable? Justify your answer using a graph.

10. Suppose that all colleges and universities make a joint announcement that in order to standardize the Bachelor of Arts and Sciences degrees, all schools will move to a system of equal admissions requirements and equal rigor in their programs. What is your prediction about the change in overall consumer (i.e., student) welfare from such a strategy? That is, would social welfare improve or not? Why?

11. In the following payoff matrix, each player is deciding whether to have a sale on Memorial Day. Determine whether each player has a dominant strategy. If so, state that strategy and resulting equilibrium. If not, explain why not. Would collusion alter the outcome? The payoff shown in the upper left is for Firm A; the payoff shown in the lower right is for Firm B.

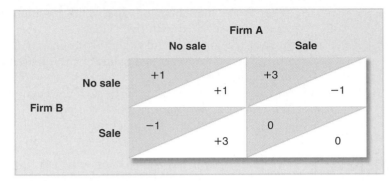

12. Suppose that two firms compete for all consumers in the local lawn service market. Both Firm A and Firm B have the option of offering a free sample cutting. If one firm offers a sample and the other does not, the first firm increases profits by three percent and the other's profits are unchanged. If both firms offer the sample, profits increase by one percent for each. If neither firm offers the sample, profits for both increase by two percent.
    a. Construct the payoff matrix for the two firms.
    b. If cooperation is not allowed, what will each firm decide to do?
    c. Will the outcome change if cooperation is allowed?

13. Suppose the market for gasoline in a small town contains six stations. Their market shares are 35, 30, 20, 5, 5, and 5 percent.
    a. Compute the CR4 and the HHI for this market. How would your answers change if one year later the market shares had shifted respectively to 22.5, 22.5, 22.5, 22.5, and 10 percent, with the last station going out of business?
    b. Suppose that given the new distribution of market share, a community activist group plans to protest to the local government that closing one station will make the market less competitive than before. Based on the changes in the CR4 and HHI, what is your opinion of this argument?

14. Suppose that the market shares of the light bulb industry are as follows:

    | Firm A | 22 percent |
    | Firm B | 20 percent |
    | Firm C | 20 percent |
    | Firm D | 18 percent |
    | Firm E | 10 percent |
    | Firm F | 10 percent |

    a. Calculate the CR4.
    b. How does the CR4 change if Firm A's market share increases by eight percent and Firm D's market share decreases by eight percent?
    c. How does the CR4 change if Firm E's market share increases by five percent and Firm F's market share falls by five percent?
    d. Use the data and your answers to parts a, b, and c to discuss the strengths and weaknesses of this measure of industry concentration.
    e. Compute the HHI for the original market shares, and for the change in market shares described in part c. How do the changes in the HHI compare to the changes in the CR4 when the market shares changed?

15. What is the maximum possible value for the HHI? What is the industry structure associated with this value?
16. Answer true or false, and explain your answer: "If an industry has only four firms, the CR4 reveals just as much information about industry concentration as the HHI."
17. Suppose there are 10 firms in the surfboard manufacturing market in Florida. Why might a Web site that posts the prices of each surfboard manufacturer lead to lower prices? Why might it lead to higher prices?

⅋ myeconlab STUDY GUIDE

HERE'S HOW MyEconLab CAN HELP YOU GET A BETTER GRADE

1. Log into MyEconLab and take Practice Test chapter-A (to log in for the first time, see page 30 for instructions.)
2. Based on your test results, MyEconLab will identify the areas where you need further work and create a personal Study Plan for you.
3. Your Study Plan contains the exercises listed below and others like them that will target the specific chapter topics you need to focus on. You'll receive instant feedback and find links to tutorials, animations, and the online textbook to help you study.
4. When you're ready, go take Practice Test chapter-B and demonstrate how your results have improved.

Section 12.1, Exercise 1 How is oligopoly different from perfect competition?

Section 12.1, Exercise 2 Oligopoly firms are said to be *interdependent*. What does this mean?

Section 12.2, Exercise 1 There are two large firms in a oligopoly market. Each has constant marginal and average costs of $50 per unit. Demand in this market is given by $Q = 500 - 2P$.

a. If these firms compete vigorously by always undercutting each other's prices, what will the market price and quantity be?
b. What profit will each firm earn?
c. What would the price and market quantity be if this were a perfectly competitive market?

Section 12.2, Exercise 2 Michael and Nina have sandwich shops on Main Street, and these are the only restaurants in town. Nina charges $3.00 for a cheeseburger, as does Michael. At that price, she sells 100 burgers per day. She believes that if she raises her price, Michael will pay no attention, but that if she lowers her price, he will follow the price cut.

a. Draw the approximate shape of Nina's demand curve, showing her current price and quantity.
b. Is it likely that Nina will change her price?

Section 12.3, Exercise 1 Which of the following products are likely to involve network externalities?

a. Cable TV stations
b. Computer operating systems, such as Microsoft Windows
c. Cellular phone providers that offer free minutes when calling other customers on the same plan
d. Movie theaters

Section 12.3, Exercise 2 There are two firms in an oligopoly market. The following graph shows the marginal cost curves for each firm and the total marginal cost, as well as the demand curve.

a. If the firms compete against each other, what will the market price and quantity be?
b. How much will each firm sell?
c. If the firms form a centralized cartel, show how the cartel will choose the profit-maximizing price and quantity.
d. How much will each firm sell now?

Section 12.4, Exercise 1 In the game shown here, two countries must decide how much oil to produce. Since demand is inelastic, low *world* production drives up prices and thus profits. However, for each firm, selling more oil at a high price earns the most money. The matrix shows profits in billions. The first number in each cell is Saudi Arabia's payoff; the second number is Kuwait's payoff.

	Kuwait	
Saudi Arabia	Low production	High production
Low production	(8, 8)	(1, 10)
High production	(10, 1)	(4, 4)

a. If the countries decide to collude to maximize profits, what will each country do? What profit will each country earn?
b. What is the dominant strategy for each country, and what profit will each country earn if they follow those strategies?
c. Is the solution you found in part a of this question a Nash equilibrium?
d. Is the solution you found in part b of this question a Nash equilibrium?

Section 12.4, Exercise 2 Two players are playing a coin matching game. Each player simultaneously reveals either heads or tails. If the coins match Call wins $10. If they don't match Flip wins $10.

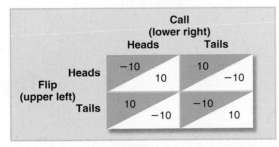

a. Is there a dominant strategy in this game?
b. Is there a Nash equilibrium in this game?

Section 12.4, Exercise 3 In the game shown here, Pepsi and Coke are trying to decide whether to advertise during the Super Bowl. If both advertise, the effect cancels out, and there is no impact on market share, but it's expensive. If neither advertises, there is no effect on market share, but it doesn't cost them anything. If one advertises but the other doesn't, market share—and thus profits—increase for the firm that advertises. (Payoffs are profits, in millions.)

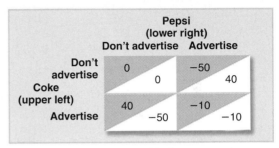

a. If the firms decide to collude to maximize profits, what will each firm do? What profit will each firm earn?
b. What is the dominant strategy for each firm, and what profit will each firm earn if they follow those strategies?
c. Is the solution you found in part a of this question a Nash equilibrium?
d. Is the solution you found in part b of this question a Nash equilibrium?

Section 12.5, Exercise 1 The following table gives the market shares for the top four firms in two industries. There are only four firms in each of these markets.

	Industry A	Industry B
Market share of Firm 1	35	85
Market share of Firm 2	25	5
Market share of Firm 3	25	5
Market share of Firm 4	15	5

a. Calculate the four-firm concentration ratio for each industry.
b. Calculate the Herfindahl-Hirschman Index for each industry.
c. Which industry is more concentrated?

Section 12.6, Exercise 1 What is a contestable market, and what effect does contestability have on oligopoly prices?

Section 12.6, Exercise 2 Why are antitrust authorities concerned about oligopoly markets?

13 Antitrust, Regulation, and Deregulation

If you attend concerts, sporting events, or theatrical presentations, you've almost certainly bought tickets from Ticketmaster. In many cases, the only way to get a ticket in advance is through Ticketmaster. The ticket giant sold 95 million tickets in 2002 and has exclusive distribution rights in the United States for 89 percent of the top 50 arenas, 88 percent of the top amphitheaters, and 70 percent of the top theaters.1 With this market dominance comes substantial market power.

String Cheese Incident, a popular jam band from Boulder, Colorado, filed suit against the massive ticket-selling company in August 2003. The band claimed, among other things, that Ticketmaster was using this market power to charge excessive service fees. The suit alleged that the $11.65 service fee charged for tickets to the band's shows at Ticketmaster venues was harmful to fans and that Ticketmaster's arrangements with concert venues were anticompetitive. The band wanted to sell tickets for its shows through its own agency, SCI Ticketing, and charge a service fee of only $4.00 per ticket. Ticketmaster filed a countersuit, claiming that the band interfered with its contracts with venues. Ticketmaster asserted that the service fee was simply the cost of doing business and maintaining the large infrastructure required to print and sell so many tickets.

Bands like String Cheese Incident had historically been permitted to sell as much as 50 percent of their concert tickets in direct-to-fan sales, even when Ticketmaster was handling the rest. The band claims that in May 2002, Ticketmaster decided to cut their allocation to just 8 percent and to

---

1 Steve Knopper, "Incident Fight Ticketmaster," *Rolling Stone*, August 28, 2003, www.rollingstone.com/news/story/_/id/5936870, accessed August 10, 2005.

allow SCI Ticketing to sell only to members of the band's fan club. With the battle lines clearly drawn, both sides turned to the courts for resolution of the dispute. In May 2004, the band settled its lawsuit against Ticketmaster, securing the right to sell between 10 and 100 percent of the tickets for its shows.[2]

Why did the band think the courts would be a logical place to resolve its dispute with Ticketmaster? What are antitrust and regulation laws, and how do they apply? How did these laws evolve? How might the government intervene in the market if it determined that Ticketmaster is a monopoly?

In Chapters 9 through 12, we discussed the benefits of competitive markets and the inefficiencies that can result in monopoly, monopolistically competitive, and oligopolistic markets. An entire branch of the U.S. legal system is designed to promote and enforce the benefits of competition. In this chapter, we explore U.S. antitrust and regulatory policy: the laws designed to promote competition and the legal remedies available when violations are discovered.

ALONG THE WAY, YOU WILL ALSO LEARN:

- The goals of U.S. regulatory and antitrust policies.
- The legal framework for U.S. antitrust policy.
- How governments enforce antitrust policy.
- How the government gauges the effect of mergers on competition.
- How antitrust laws are interpreted and enforced.
- The theory behind regulation and how it is carried out.
- What deregulation is, and why the government might deregulate an industry.

AT THE END OF THE CHAPTER, THE MYECONLAB LOGO WILL DIRECT YOU ONLINE

- MyEconLab is a resource-packed online homework and tutorial system that can help you perform better in your economics course. To log in for the first time, see page 30 for instructions.
- MyEconLab can help you apply important concepts from the chapter to real-world issues. Watch for the logo to indicate online features about government regulation and antitrust law.
- At the end of each chapter, you'll find a special study section that will help you get the most out of your textbook and your instructor's MyEconLab course.

▶ The Government's Role in Promoting Efficiency

Throughout our discussion of the various market structures, we have highlighted the impact of those structures on economic efficiency. In this section, we look at how various government policies address efficiency concerns in different types of markets.

---

[2] David Kushner, "String Theory," *Fortune Small Business*, December 1, 2004, www.fortune.com/fortune/smallbusiness/articles/0,15114,1008826,00.html, accessed April 27, 2005.

Why the Government Might Intervene

What would prompt the U.S. government to investigate and possibly take action against a company like Ticketmaster? There are three primary reasons for such governmental intervention:

- To promote productive efficiency
- To promote innovation
- To improve allocative efficiency

Promote Productive Efficiency. Recall from Chapter 2 that productive efficiency means that the economy's resources are employed in a way that results in the lowest total cost. Given that Ticketmaster has such a high market share, the ticket distribution industry is an oligopoly, and in some cases a near monopoly. If another, less-concentrated market structure can distribute tickets at a lower cost than companies like Ticketmaster, then the government should promote that alternative structure.

Innovation
The creation of new technology and the application of that technology to the production process.

Promote Innovation. Innovation is the creation of new technology and the application of that technology to the production process, or the creation of new products that better serve a market. For example, the government might consider the question, "Is Ticketmaster making the best use of new and emerging Internet technology to provide the fastest, most secure, and most accurate ticketing possible?"

Improve Allocative Efficiency. Allocative efficiency is the distribution of a nation's resources in the way most valued by society. In this case the government might be concerned with the quantity of resources used to create and maintain the ticket distribution industry. Allocative efficiency typically stems from using markets to allocate resources and allowing prices to measure the value of those resources.

Most economists agree that the best way to advance these three broad goals is through competition. However, competitive markets do not always occur naturally and sometimes are not even desirable: For instance, it may actually be more efficient for Ticketmaster to remain a monopolist with the government regulating the prices it charges than for many competing firms such as SCI Ticketing to operate independently. We will return to this topic later in the chapter.

Natural and Optimal Market Structure

Natural structure
The degree of competition in a market that would occur if the market operated on its own, with no intervention.

Optimal structure
The degree of competition in a market that maximizes allocative efficiency.

Economists distinguish between a market's natural structure and its optimal structure. The **natural structure** of a market refers to the degree of competition that would occur if the market operated on its own, with no intervention. The **optimal structure** is the degree of competition that maximizes allocative efficiency. One of government's roles is to monitor markets and intervene if it feels that the natural structure differs too much from the optimal structure. Suppose Ticketmaster's dominance of the ticket distribution market creates costs that are one percent above the optimal level. In that case, the market is likely close enough to its optimal structure that the administrative and legal costs involved in creating a more competitive environment outweigh the gains. What if Ticketmaster's dominance results in costs that are 35 percent above the best alternative market structure? Government action is then probably warranted. We consider the implications of three possible market setups for the ticket distribution market: perfect competition, monopoly, and cartel.

Ticketmaster Sales: The Perfect Competition Benchmark

We can gauge the efficiency of a market by comparing the existing price and output with the price and output that would result from marginal cost pricing under the ideal of perfect competition. Panel (a) of Figure 13.1 shows hypothetical industry conditions for the concert ticket distribution market. If the ticket distribution market is competitive, the market supply curve is the sum of the individual firms' marginal cost curves. To keep the arithmetic simple, we assume the competitive price is $5. The outcome is efficient, because the $5 marginal benefit from the last ticket sold is equal to the $5 marginal cost of producing it, which in turn maximizes the sum of consumer and producer surplus. At the $5 price, 120 million tickets are distributed. Recall from Chapter 6 that consumer surplus is the benefit that flows to consumers because they are not all charged the maximum that they are willing and able to pay. Consumer surplus is $600 million ($\frac{1}{2}$ (120 million × $10)), which is the area shaded blue in Figure 13.1. Producer surplus is the extra benefit that flows to producers because they receive the market price rather than being forced to sell each unit for the minimum cost of producing it. Producer surplus is $300 million ($\frac{1}{2}$ (120 million × $5)), which is the area shaded light red. The competitive fee of $5 and output of 120 million tickets maximize the value of the consumer and producer surpluses.

Ticketmaster Sales: The Monopoly Scenario

If the distribution of tickets is controlled by a monopoly, the monopolist chooses the price so that marginal revenue is equal to marginal cost, as you saw in Chapter 10.

FIGURE 13.1

Consumer and Producer Surplus With Competitive and Monopoly Pricing

In panel (a), when price is set at the competitive level of $5, consumer surplus (shaded blue) and producer surplus (shaded light red) are maximized. In panel (b), when consumers are charged the monopoly price of $10, output falls to 70 million tickets, and consumer surplus falls to the area shaded blue. The light red area is the producer's surplus, and the gray area represents the deadweight loss resulting from monopoly pricing.

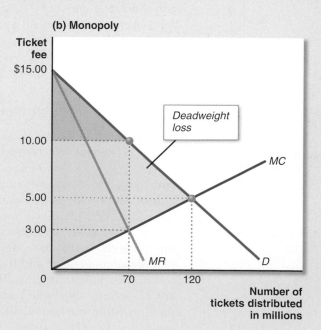

Panel (b) of Figure 13.1 shows the same market demand curve as in panel (a). We've added the monopolist's marginal revenue curve and the monopolist's marginal cost curve in place of the industry supply curve. In this example, the monopolist sets a service fee of $10 per ticket. At this price, it distributes 70 million tickets. We show the competitive price of $5 and quantity of 120 million on the same figure. The monopoly price ($10) greatly exceeds the marginal cost of the last unit sold ($3). The consumer surplus is the blue area, and the producer surplus is the light-red area. Notice that the consumer surplus area has fallen to $175 million ($\frac{1}{2}$ (70 million × $5)), much less than in Figure 13.1(a).

Part of what is lost from consumer surplus is transferred to the monopolist's revenue. This is the difference between the $10 monopoly price and the $5 perfectly competitive price times the 70 million tickets sold, or $350 million. The area shaded in gray in the figure represents the deadweight loss, the value that is lost to society because of the lower output of the monopoly. To compute the area of this triangle, we take half of the $7 difference between price and marginal cost times the reduction in ticket sales (120 − 70 million); or $\frac{1}{2}$ ($7 × 50 million), which is $175 million. The top portion of this triangle ($125 million) is lost from consumer surplus. The lower portion ($50 million) is lost from producer surplus. If the ticket market resembles panel (b) of Figure 13.1, both concertgoers and other sellers such as SCI Ticketing are worse off when Ticketmaster dominates the ticket market. With prices set at twice the competitive price, the government might investigate the ticket market to determine whether it should intervene.

Ticketmaster Sales: The Cartel Scenario

Governments sometimes also have an incentive to intervene when there is more than one firm in an industry, and those firms cooperate rather than compete. Suppose that Ticketmaster and SCI Ticketing are competing against one another. If each firm wants to offer customers the lowest price possible, we might observe the $5 competitive price, even though there are only two firms. However, if they are the only two ticket sellers, they can cooperate. The two firms can easily communicate with one another about pricing decisions and check online price listings to ensure that the agreements are followed. In this case, the two firms might decide to fix prices and sell at the monopoly price of $10 shown in Figure 13.1(b), as in the cartel model from Chapter 12. Because the deadweight loss equals the loss under pure monopoly, such cooperation is clearly not in the interest of consumers or society in general.

Because these highly concentrated industries might not yield efficient levels of output, the government has an incentive to intervene. We next examine the legal framework that defines the government's possible actions.

►The Legal Framework of U.S. Antitrust Policy

The roots of U.S. antitrust policy lie in the economic boom that followed the Civil War in the mid-1860s. The United States was still a largely agricultural nation. However, heavy industry was emerging. A few very large firms came to dominate the young steel, railroad, and oil industries. They were owned and run by such men as John D. Rockefeller and James B. Duke, who amassed great fortunes in the oil and tobacco industries, respectively. Today these families are well known for their philanthropy. In their own day, the term "robber baron" was coined in recognition of their dogged pursuit of wealth, often at the expense of consumer welfare and their competitors. Large combinations of businesses, known as *trusts*, came under fire for unethical practices. Examples include unscrupulous pricing strategies devised to put competitors out of business.

The Sherman Antitrust Act of 1890

Increased concern over the behavior of trusts and of their effect on consumer welfare led Congress to pass the Sherman Antitrust Act of 1890. As we discussed in Chapter 10, the act outlawed monopolizing an industry and collusion among firms to restrain trade. Although it was passed more than 100 years ago, the Sherman Act still forms the basis for much of U.S. antitrust policy. The essential elements of the Sherman Act are contained in two short sections shown in Table 13.1.

Two or more firms conspiring to fix prices or to restrict output can be prosecuted under Section 1 of the Sherman Act. In order for consumers and the economy in general to receive the benefits of free markets, firms must compete. They must not cooperate to set a price above the perfectly competitive level. The government can prosecute a firm that takes actions specifically designed to drive out competitors and create a monopoly under the second section of the Sherman Act. The courts may break up the monopoly into smaller firms, prohibit certain practices, or impose fines. Using the Sherman Act, individuals, firms, and the government itself can file suits against alleged violators. In the next sections, we take a brief look at two such cases.

The Addystone Pipe Case. The 1899 price-fixing case of Addystone Pipe and Steel Company illustrates how Section 1 of the Sherman Act can be applied. A group of cast-iron pipe manufacturers conspired to set prices within certain geographic areas. Their defense was that the fixed prices prevented harmful competition that would have damaged all the firms involved. The courts disagreed. Their position on price fixing has not wavered since then. One hundred years later, pharmaceutical giant F. Hoffman LaRoche was found guilty of an international price-fixing scheme in the vitamin market. The $500 million penalty was the largest fine ever imposed in an antitrust case.

The Tobacco Trust Case. The case of the Tobacco Trust, which was led by the Duke family and American Tobacco, illustrates how Section 2 of the act can be applied. From 1881 to 1906, the Tobacco Trust controlled the consumer tobacco products industry by engaging in predatory pricing. **Predatory pricing** occurs when a firm sets the price of its product below its own costs, so as to drive a rival out of the industry. In one instance, the Tobacco Trust effectively set a price of zero. Consumers paid

Predatory pricing
Occurs when a firm sets the price of its product below its own costs to drive a rival out of the industry.

TABLE 13.1

Excerpts From Section 1 and 2 of the Sherman Antitrust Act

1	Every contract, combination in the form of a trust or otherwise, or conspiracy, in restraint of trade or commerce among these several States, or with foreign nations, is declared to be illegal. Every person who shall make any contract or engage in any combination or conspiracy hereby declared to be illegal shall be deemed guilty of a felony. . . .
2	Every person, who shall monopolize, or attempt to monopolize, or combine or conspire with any other person or persons, to monopolize any part of the trade or commerce among the several States, or with foreign nations, shall be deemed guilty of a felony. . . .

only the tax on the product, leaving no chance for a rival to survive. After the rival firms were forced out of business, the trust was free to increase prices without fear of losing market share to competing firms.

This strategy violates Section 2 of the Sherman Act, as it represents anticompetitive behavior intended to monopolize a market. As a result of the suit, in 1911 the Tobacco Trust was broken into four principal firms: American Tobacco, Liggett and Meyers (L&M), R.J. Reynolds (which had been part of American Tobacco), and Lorillard. However, the initial judgment and breakup did not deter the largest cigarette firms from practicing predatory behavior. In 1946, American Tobacco, L&M, and R.J. Reynolds were convicted of essentially the same strategy, as well as collusion to drive out low-priced brands during the Great Depression. The tobacco products market is still dominated by a few large firms.

The Clayton Act

Clayton Act (1914)
Legislation prohibiting price discrimination and establishing more detailed guidelines for monopoly and collusion-related conduct and penalties.

The Sherman Act laid the foundation for oversight and litigation. However, it was not specific enough as to what it prohibited. The **Clayton Act** of 1914 attempted to remedy this shortcoming, and contained much more detailed language, prohibiting:

- Price discrimination by charging different prices to different consumers, if that discrimination lessens competition.
- **Product tie-ins**, which are contracts that require consumers who purchase one product from a firm to purchase another one as well.
- Stock of competing companies, if such an acquisition lessens competition.
- Service on the boards of directors of competing firms.

Product tie-ins
Require a customer purchasing one product to also buy another product.

Treble damages
Damages equal to three times the actual damage inflicted. Plaintiffs have a right to recover treble damages in antitrust cases under the Clayton Act.

The Clayton Act also gave the government the power to issue injunctions to stop anticompetitive practices. In addition, it established the right of plaintiffs to recover **treble damages**, or three times the actual damage inflicted. For example, behavior that causes $1 million in damages will result in a $3 million judgment under treble damages. Finally, the Clayton Act exempted labor unions from antitrust laws.

The Federal Trade Commission Act

Federal Trade Commission (FTC)
Agency created in 1914 by the Federal Trade Commission Act; works with the Department of Justice to enforce antitrust law.

In 1914, the government also passed the Federal Trade Commission Act. This act created an agency to pursue antitrust cases, the **Federal Trade Commission (FTC)**. Congress empowered the FTC to pursue abuses of trade that could lessen competition. The original charge of the FTC still holds today, as reflected in its mission statement: "The Commission seeks to ensure that the nation's markets function competitively, and are vigorous, efficient, and free of undue restrictions."[3]

Additional legislation passed during the twentieth century refined and extended the acts discussed so far. Most notable was the Robinson-Patman Act of 1936, which attempted to define price discrimination more precisely than prior acts. Table 13.2 summarizes the most important pieces of U.S. antitrust legislation and their key components.

---

[3] Federal Trade Commission, "Vision, Mission and Goals," www.ftc.gov/ftc/mission.htm.

TABLE 13.2

Summary of Key U.S. Antitrust Legislation

Year	Act	Primary Purpose
1890	Sherman Antitrust Act	Made trusts and restraint of trade illegal; made it illegal to monopolize or attempt to monopolize an industry.
1914	Clayton Act	Made price discrimination illegal; prohibited product tie-ins; prohibited stock purchases that lessen competition; prohibited individuals from serving on multiple boards.
1914	Federal Trade Commission Act	Established the Federal Trade Commission as an enforcement mechanism for antitrust issues.
1936	Robinson-Patman Act	Clarified the definition of price discrimination.

Enforcement of Antitrust Policy

The Department of Justice (DOJ) and the FTC are jointly charged with overseeing and enforcing antitrust policy. They have the power to sue firms in order to:

- Force violators to stop anticompetitive practices
- Break up existing firms into smaller ones
- Prevent the formation of very large firms
- Impose fines on companies found guilty of violating antitrust law

Enforcing antitrust policy is complex and requires much interpretation by the courts. Consider our example of the ticket-distribution market. What actions can the court take if it determines that it must intervene to improve the efficiency of the ticket distribution market? Options include fining Ticketmaster, breaking it into a few medium-sized firms that compete against one another, or leaving it as a monopoly and regulating it. The courts could also do nothing and hope that market incentives will encourage a new firm to enter the market.

Enforcing antitrust law involves a significant amount of judgment. First, the government must decide how much industry concentration is possible if consumers are still to reap the important benefits of competition. It must then formulate a policy that will improve overall welfare if the current level of concentration is beyond the acceptable limit. Finally, it must determine whether the policy is worth the cost of bringing a lawsuit plus the cost of administering whatever remedies the courts may choose. Filing and pursuing a complex antitrust case requires an enormous amount of investigative and legal resources. Some cases have literally taken decades to work their way through the courts. The U.S. government's case against Microsoft is a good illustration of how complicated a case can be. To understand why the case proved so difficult, we must first understand how the courts decide whether a firm has violated antitrust laws.

Per se illegality
Legal standard establishing some actions as illegal in and of themselves. Actions that always reduce competition are generally illegal *per se*.

Standards: *per se* Illegality and the Rule of Reason

The government's difficulty in applying the law leads it to invoke two separate standards, depending on the nature of the offense. The first standard is ***per se* illegality**:

actions that always reduce competition are generally illegal *per se*, meaning illegal in and of themselves. If such activity is discovered, no further evidence (such as proof of damages) is needed for the firm to be found in violation of the Sherman Act. Price fixing falls under this standard. If a group of firms is found to have colluded when setting prices, the courts require no further information regarding damage to consumers or other firms. The court is then free to impose penalties and force the firms to stop colluding. The burden of proof lies with the accused firms to show that they were not colluding.

The second standard is known as the rule of reason. The **rule of reason** insists that each case be judged on its own merits. Rival firms or consumers that claim to be damaged by a firm's anticompetitive practices must demonstrate that such actions were taken, *and* that they caused economic damages. In contrast to the *per se* standard, the rule of reason standard places the burden of proof on the accusers. Accusers must show that they have suffered damages as a result of a firm's behavior.

The Microsoft Antitrust Case

The 1998 case against Microsoft illustrates the complexities of antitrust actions. In May of 1998, the U.S. Department of Justice filed suit against Microsoft alleging violation of both sections of the Sherman Act. In the suit, the DOJ claimed that the company had illegally restricted competition by tying its Internet Explorer Web browser to its Windows operating system. The DOJ claimed that Microsoft had tied the two products together to gain control of the Web browser market.

Historically, product tie-ins have been illegal *per se*. Initially, the court applied this standard to Microsoft's actions and found the company guilty of using tie-ins to monopolize the market. When Microsoft appealed this ruling, the appeals court decided that the rule of reason standard was more appropriate. The initial decision was overruled. This change in standards was essentially a win for Microsoft. It overturned the previous ruling, which specified that Microsoft be broken into several smaller firms. Under the terms of the final judgment of November 2002, Microsoft remained a single firm, admitted no guilt, and agreed only to some general guidelines prohibiting retaliation against competitors.[4]

Changes in Enforcement

The Microsoft case is just one example of how the interpretation of antitrust laws has changed over the years. In the years since the Sherman Antitrust Act of 1890, antitrust laws have been enforced unevenly, with enforcement generally becoming less stringent. Two reasons for this change of attitude are technological change and globalization. Globalization and the emergence of the electronic marketplace (over the Internet) have effectively reduced entry barriers such that firms are now able to enter and compete in markets that they previously could not.

 Mergers

In addition to serving as an antitrust watchdog and policy enforcer, the FTC may seek to block or alter a merger. A **merger** occurs when two companies formally combine into a single firm.

Rule of reason
Legal standard advocating that each case be judged on its own merits. Rival firms or consumers who claim to be damaged by a firm's anti-competitive practices must demonstrate both that such actions were taken and that they caused economic damages.

 myeconlab

Get Ahead of the Curve
Examine the government's use of the Sherman Antitrust Act in 2004 against companies producing memory chips.

Merger
When two companies formally combine into a single firm. There are three basic types of mergers: conglomerate, vertical, and horizontal.

---

[4] For complete details on the Microsoft suit and the terms of the settlement, see "*United States v. Microsoft:* Current Case" at www.usdoj.gov/atr/cases/ms_index.htm.

Types of Mergers

There are three basic types of mergers: conglomerate, vertical, and horizontal.

Conglomerate merger
Occurs when firms in unrelated industries merge; rarely challenged by government.

Conglomerate Merger. A **conglomerate merger** occurs when firms in unrelated industries merge. For example, Beatrice Foods, a massive conglomerate of the 1980s, once owned Stiffel Lamps. The government rarely challenges conglomerate mergers, as they are unlikely to alter the competitive landscape in any one industry.

Vertical merger
When one firm purchases another firm that lies either above or below it in the production stream.

Vertical Merger. A **vertical merger** occurs when one firm purchases another firm that lies either above it or below it in the production stream. Think of the production stream as the trail that a product follows from raw materials to finished goods. A vertically integrated firm controls some or all the steps in the production process. Consider a family farm that uses its harvested fruit to produce pies with homemade crusts. If it then sells pies from its own farm stand, it is a vertically integrated firm. A non-integrated firm performs only one step in the production process. For example, a non-integrated producer of pies might buy partially finished goods, such as canned pie filling and premade piecrusts from other firms. It performs only the final assembly, producing the finished good that is sold to consumers. The FTC and the DOJ monitor vertical mergers, because such a merger can enable a producer to control a resource needed to manufacture a final good, creating an entry barrier to would-be competitors. After the firm controls the resource, it can draw on that advantage to become more powerful in the final good's market.

Horizontal merger
When firms that are in the same industry or market merge.

Horizontal Merger. Horizontal mergers are combinations of two firms that are in the same industry or market. For example, Chrysler Motors merged with Daimler-Benz Motors in 2000 to become Daimler-Chrysler. When firms that produce the same good switch from being competitors to being partners in a new, larger corporation, competition weakens. The government must decide whether consumers will be better off or worse off as a result.

The Government on Mergers

The government's position on mergers has changed significantly over the years. To see how stark the evolution has been, consider the following two cases. In 1966, in *The United States v. Vons Grocery Co.*, the courts blocked a horizontal merger between two grocery stores in the Los Angeles area. The new firm would have had only 7.5 percent of the local grocery market. In 1999, the FTC and the courts both changed course and approved the merger of Exxon and Mobil Oil corporations, the largest industrial merger in history. The new combined Exxon/Mobil Corporation

FRANK & ERNEST: © Thaves/Dist. by Newspaper Enterprise Association, Inc.

made the gasoline industry more concentrated, especially in light of several other large mergers that had recently taken place in the industry.

Current DOJ guidelines for horizontal mergers are such that a merger resulting in a post-merger HHI value of less than 1,800 will rarely be challenged, and even those that do increase the HHI to above 1,800 will be challenged only if remaining rivals cannot maintain a competitive environment in the face of the newly merged firm.

TEST + *E X T E N D* Your Knowledge

1. TEST Typically, airports lease arrival and departure gates to airlines. How might an airline use a strategy of long-term gate leases to dominate air traffic in a certain region of the country? How might such a strategy affect the demand for other modes of travel in the same area?

2 . E X T E N D In May 1999, the Department of Justice filed suit against American Airlines, alleging an attempt to monopolize the air traffic at the Dallas–Fort Worth airport. All documentation, including the original complaint against American, can be found at www.usdoj.gov/atr/cases/f2400/2438.htm. Go to the Web page and read the complaint. Explain why the DOJ refers to Section 2 of the Sherman Act instead of Section 1. In your opinion, do American's alleged actions represent violations or simply aggressive competition?

▶ Regulation

Until now, we have focused on antitrust policy. However, the government might decide that a firm with monopoly power should *not* be broken up or fined for its market domination. Let's revisit our example of the possible Ticketmaster monopoly. Suppose the government determined that Ticketmaster has a monopoly in the ticket distribution market. However, increasing competition in the industry would reduce efficiency, because it is a natural monopoly. What other steps could the government take?

In such circumstances, the government could decide to leave the dominating firm or firms intact and to *regulate* the industry. Recall our discussion of regulation from Chapter 10. In a regulated industry, the government oversees a specific aspect of firm behavior. Regulations may apply to occupational safety, product safety, entry conditions, and pricing. In this section, we focus on regulation of prices aimed at increasing allocative efficiency.

The government may prefer to regulate a monopoly if extensive scale economies make the industry a natural monopoly. In this case, breaking up the existing firm into smaller ones could increase the cost of production and therefore increase the price to consumers. There may also be no potential competitors willing to enter the industry, because the sunk costs of attempting to enter are too high and the risk of failure is too great. We begin our study of regulation with the two broad theories that underpin it. We then examine a specific case: the telecommunications industry.

Public interest theory
Regulation theory based on the idea that governments must address the interests, needs, or demands of the public; maintains that government should regulate firm behavior to increase overall welfare and make consumers better off.

Theories of Regulation

Economists rely on two main theories of regulation that represent the consumer and firm perspectives. We examine *public interest theory* and *capture theory* in turn.

Public Interest Theory. When an industry is regulated, the government restricts the prices firms may charge or the profits they are allowed to earn. **Public interest theory** holds that government must address the interests (needs or demands) of the public.

As a result, governments should regulate firm behavior to increase overall welfare. Consumer groups subscribe to this view. In the case of price regulation of a firm, they would work to ensure that firms do not charge monopoly prices. In regulated industries, oversight boards such as a public utility commission typically defend the interests of consumers and economic efficiency. As mentioned in Chapter 10, utilities are firms that provide natural gas, water, and electricity. **Public utility commissions (PUCs)** set the guidelines for firm behavior. For example, they set the prices firms may charge over a given period of time. During public hearings, they consider the opinions of both consumers and the firm on what action would be most appropriate. In general, a single utility company operates more efficiently than a large number of competing firms. The reasons for this efficiency include restrictions on consumers that make it difficult to change suppliers (most utilities require that customers be physically connected to their services; for instance, through underground natural gas pipes). In addition, massive infrastructure is required to operate utilities.

Public utility commissions (PUCs)
Set the guidelines for firm behavior through public hearings at which they consider the opinions of both consumers and the firm on appropriate action.

Capture theory
Regulation theory based on the idea that firms benefit from regulation because they eventually capture the regulators, so that consumers are made worse off by regulation.

Capture Theory. Sometimes firms prefer to be regulated. **Capture theory** is based on the idea that firms benefit from regulation because they eventually capture (control) the regulators (the members of the PUCs). Capture may be especially problematic if the boards are themselves made up of industry experts who come from and may return to the firms that are regulated. Restrictions such as licenses and permits create entry barriers for would-be competitors. These entry barriers actually increase the market power of the existing firms. If regulators act according to public interest theory, their behavior will be consistent with the stated purpose of regulation (increasing overall welfare). If regulation creates an environment predicted by capture theory, then consumers are made worse off by regulation. Whether public interest theory or capture theory dominates the regulatory process is uncertain.

Specific types of regulation can take many forms, yet all of them have a common goal: to promote economic efficiency and redistribute gains from firms to consumers. We can illustrate how regulation can increase efficiency by examining the regulation of the telecommunications industry.

Regulation of the Telecommunications Industry

The structure of the telecommunications industry today is entirely different from only a few decades ago. Can you imagine life without cell phones? In the early 1970s, the cell phone industry was virtually non-existent. Most phone service was through wired telephones. There was almost no competition in the industry. One very large firm, AT&T, and its local subsidiaries provided the vast majority of local and long-distance telephone service. In fact, competition was legally forbidden in most areas, because the firm was considered a natural monopoly.

AT&T's Natural Monopoly. A massive amount of capital is required to set up and operate a telephone network. As a result, the government determined that the industry operated most efficiently as a monopoly. Recall from Chapter 10 that if there are economies of scale throughout the entire range of demand, average cost rises if more than one firm provides the good. We call such industries natural monopolies because one firm naturally emerges as the sole provider. Figure 13.2 illustrates this point by presenting a simplified picture of the telecommunications industry. Output is measured as the number of minutes of calling per day. The long-run average cost (*LAC*) curve falls continuously, because the marginal cost curve (*MC*) lies below the *LAC* curve at all output levels. The firm maximizes profit where *MC* equals *MR*, here at a level of 100 million minutes of calling. The firm sets a price of 15 cents per minute. With an average cost of 10 cents per minute, profits are $5 million, the area shaded in green.

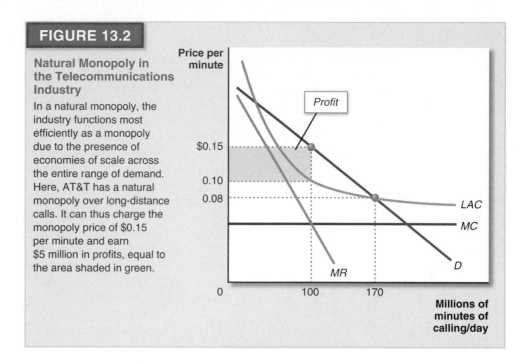

FIGURE 13.2

Natural Monopoly in the Telecommunications Industry

In a natural monopoly, the industry functions most efficiently as a monopoly due to the presence of economies of scale across the entire range of demand. Here, AT&T has a natural monopoly over long-distance calls. It can thus charge the monopoly price of $0.15 per minute and earn $5 million in profits, equal to the area shaded in green.

Suppose another firm had tried to enter the industry using the same technology. It would have faced a number of significant obstacles. First, it would have needed the funds to set up its own telecommunications network. It would then have had to lure customers away from the existing firm. To fend off the rival, AT&T could have chosen to cut its price to 8 cents per minute, increasing output to 170 million minutes. The new entrant would not be able to match this price, because its lower output would not allow it to make positive economic profits at that price. Besides, at 8 cents per minute, AT&T would satisfy all the demand in the industry. The new entrant would have no customers.

Using antitrust law to break a natural monopoly into smaller, competing firms in this case would waste society's resources and could result in higher cost per minute for telephone services. Thus, consumers might have been charged higher prices because more revenue would be needed for two firms to at least break even.

The presence of scale economies was not the only striking feature of the telecommunications industry. Demand for telephone service during the time that AT&T operated as a monopolist was highly price-inelastic. Recall that inelastic demand means that consumers are insensitive to price changes. In the telecommunications industry, demand was inelastic because there were no good substitutes. Cell phones, e-mail, and instant messaging did not exist in the 1970s. Consumers viewed telephone service as a necessity and did not respond significantly to increases in price. Without regulation, AT&T could have charged much higher prices than a competitive firm. The lack of substitutes led the government to conclude that it must take action against AT&T's monopoly. However, the presence of scale economies made breaking up the company inefficient. As a result, the government chose to regulate the telecommunications industry.

Government Regulation of Price and Output. Government regulation of the telecommunications industry focused on the prices consumers were charged. We know from our study of competitive markets that efficiency results from setting price equal to marginal cost. However, regulators could not force such a strategy on AT&T without causing it to suffer economic losses, because marginal cost is less than average cost in a natural monopoly. In such cases, economists advise setting price and output as close to the competitive level as possible without creating losses. Figure 13.3 includes the demand and cost curves from Figure 13.2. Note that the *MC* curve crosses the demand curve at a point below the *LAC* curve. If regulators had forced AT&T to set price equal to marginal cost at 6 cents per minute and output at 200 million minutes, AT&T would have experienced losses equal to the area shaded in orange. Price would have been below long-run average cost. Thus, regulators sought a solution that would allow AT&T some level of accounting profit.

We next discuss two methods of regulating price and output: the price cap and rate of return regulation. One way to set price and output as close to the competitive level as possible is to institute a **price cap**, a maximum price that firms can charge or maximum allowable rate of increase in price.[5] A price cap effectively makes the marginal revenue curve a horizontal line at the price cap up to the point where it crosses the demand curve. In Figure 13.3, the government institutes a price cap of 8 cents per minute. With the fixed maximum price, the firm expands output above the monopoly level. The decrease in price also reduces profits, and redistributes gains toward consumers as shown by the consumer surplus area shaded in light blue. With price set where *D* crosses *LAC*, economic profits (which include opportunity costs) are zero.

Price caps are effective only when the demand curve is stable for long periods. If the demand curve fluctuates—shifting rightward and leftward—over the course of the year, the price cap will sometimes be too high or too low. When demand is

Price cap
Government regulation setting a maximum price that firms can charge or maximum allowable rate of increase in price.

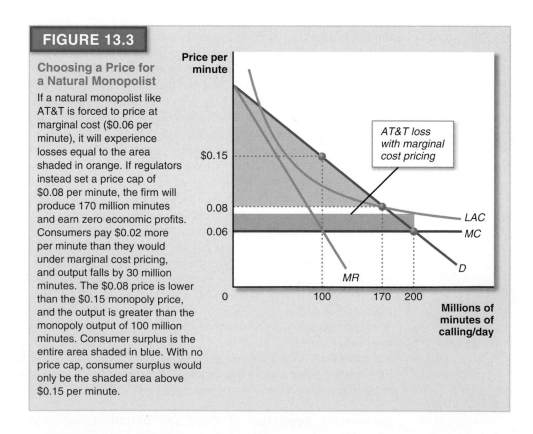

FIGURE 13.3

Choosing a Price for a Natural Monopolist

If a natural monopolist like AT&T is forced to price at marginal cost ($0.06 per minute), it will experience losses equal to the area shaded in orange. If regulators instead set a price cap of $0.08 per minute, the firm will produce 170 million minutes and earn zero economic profits. Consumers pay $0.02 more per minute than they would under marginal cost pricing, and output falls by 30 million minutes. The $0.08 price is lower than the $0.15 monopoly price, and the output is greater than the monopoly output of 100 million minutes. Consumer surplus is the entire area shaded in blue. With no price cap, consumer surplus would only be the shaded area above $0.15 per minute.

---

[5] Price caps that are defined over multiple years typically have an adjustment built in to account for changes in the overall rate of inflation. In this example, we assume that the price cap is a simple fixed price.

low, the price cap may be above the equilibrium price, and so will not affect the equilibrium. When demand is high, the price cap may be too low, resulting in a shortage.

Rate of return regulation
Government regulation setting a prespecified amount of profit that a firm may earn in a given time period.

The government could also try to increase output and decrease prices by regulating how much profit a firm of a given size can earn. **Rate of return regulation** allows the firm to earn a prespecified amount of profit in a given time period. In practice, rate of return regulation is very complex and difficult to monitor. As we will see in Chapter 14, the higher the risk, the greater return (profit) an investor expects to receive. If the allowable profit rate is set too low, AT&T will have trouble attracting investors. If the rate is set too high, it will be overcompensated for its level of risk.

▶ Deregulation

Deregulating
Removing regulations and allowing market forces to have a greater impact on prices, output, profits, and industry structure.

The current trend is for the government to favor deregulation rather than regulation, which bodes well for Ticketmaster. **Deregulating** a market means removing regulations and allowing market forces to determine prices, output, profits, and industry structure. In this section, we turn to situations in which government regulation inhibits competition rather than promoting it as intended. We discuss the conditions that should precede the deregulation of a market, and examine how some of the newly deregulated markets have fared.

Factors Favoring Deregulation

One factor encouraging deregulation is the difficulty of choosing an effective regulatory strategy. Another consideration is advances in technology that have allowed new firms to enter and compete successfully in many industries. Technological changes in the telecommunications industry have eliminated many of the scale economies that once dominated the industry. Consumers now have many options regarding equipment, long-distance calling, and even local calling. In addition, wireless networks and voice-over-Internet phone service provide close substitutes for hardwired local and long-distance carriers. These advances in technology have changed the definition of the market by increasing the number of substitutes. Instead of a single, massive firm serving everyone, we now see vigorous competition in many areas of the telecommunications market.

The airline industry was deregulated in 1978, followed by the trucking and railroad industries in 1980, and long-distance telecommunications in 1984. Recently, some states have opened electricity generation to competition. These changes are not universally accepted as beneficial. However, the Mercatus Center at George Mason University estimates that the consumer benefits resulting from deregulation exceed $50 billion annually.[6]

Reasons for Deregulation

When the government considers deregulating an industry, it must determine how the market dynamics will change. The government must be confident that the private market outcomes will be more efficient than the regulated outcomes. Thus, it must

---

[6] Jerry Ellig, "Electricity: Reliability and Competition," in "Deregulation and the Electric Industry," June 19, 1997, www.mercatus.org/article.php/171.html, accessed March 31, 2005. Jerry Ellig is a Senior Research Fellow at the Mercatus Center, George Mason University. The Mercatus Center represents a conservative point of view.

LifeLessons

Two Wrongs Don't Make a Right

Large-volume discounters such as Sam's Club and Costco are an accepted part of the American retail landscape that you might take for granted. They offer very low prices and low-frills service on everything from groceries to office equipment to personal products. Some consumers struggle with the oversized and bundled portions (three-packs of salsa, and toothbrushes by the dozen). In return, consumers pay prices that are sometimes much lower than those at smaller retail stores. For large families in particular, the savings often outweigh the inconvenience.

In the not-so-distant past, consumers did not have the discount-pricing option. In the 1930s, many states passed "fair trade" laws that allowed manufacturers to set minimum retail prices for goods. These laws were specifically aimed at the large-volume discounters that had begun to emerge as an alternative to the small retail shop. The reasoning was that allowing the discounters to set their own prices would enable them to undercut small shops and put them out of business. Surprisingly, the federal government embraced these state laws by passing a law that exempted such actions from prosecution under the Sherman Act. This exemption was very much at odds with the overall goal of U.S. antitrust policy of promoting competition. It effectively outlawed low prices. As such, it was an effort to have two wrongs make a right: Charge consumers higher prices to save retail stores from bankruptcy.

Beginning in the 1950s, minimum-price agreements began to unravel because they were so hard to enforce. Finally, in 1975, Congress passed the Consumer Goods Pricing Act, eliminating fair trade pricing policies. While competition from large-volume discounters may be a difficult challenge for small retailers, they do give consumers the opportunity to pay lower prices for many goods.

---

determine whether existing firms or potential entrants can create and maintain competition in the industry. Finally, it must ask the following questions:

- Will deregulation affect product safety or reliability?
- Will deregulation eliminate service for some consumers?
- Will the benefits of deregulation accrue for only a few consumers?

Deregulation of the Airline Industry

Get Ahead of the Curve
Compare antitrust policy in Mexico with what you have learned about U.S. antitrust policy.

The airline industry is a case in point. It was once heavily regulated but has been deregulated, resulting in substantial benefits to consumers. During the early years of civilian air travel, competition among carriers was so intense that some feared the industry would collapse. To prevent this, airlines successfully sought regulation by the Civil Aeronautics Board (CAB). In 1978, the U.S. Airline Deregulation Act removed the strict regulations that the CAB had exercised over prices, number of carriers, and route assignments for nearly 40 years. During much of that time, a few large airlines dominated the U.S. market. Prices were high. Barred from price competition, airlines engaged in intense competition over the quality of in-flight services. In effect, customers were paying for tie-in sales without even realizing it. Customers' airfares included the cost of expensive meals, drinks, movies, relatively empty flights, and other amenities they had no choice but to pay for.

Deregulation revolutionized the airline industry. Major carriers like Pan Am, Braniff, TWA, Continental, and Eastern filed for bankruptcy. Some carriers that remain from that era, such as US Airways, have struggled to be profitable. Others merged and consolidated. Immediately after deregulation, there was a flood of new entrants. Although few of them survived, the average number of carriers per route increased. Much of the new competition came from existing firms that entered each other's markets. Because they used price to compete for passengers, savings for consumers have been remarkable. Alfred Kahn, who presided over the deregulation, notes that 96 percent of passengers fly on discount tickets. Accounting for inflation, airline passengers save between $17 and $20 billion per year.[7] These benefits have not come completely without cost. Flights are booked to capacity, airports and runways are crowded, flight delays are typical, and the quality of in-flight service has decreased. Despite these inconveniences, Kahn argues that the benefits of deregulation far outweigh the costs. Concerns that deregulation would cause the airlines to skimp on safety and reliability have not materialized.

Deregulation Has Forced USAir to Cut Costs

Benefits of Deregulation

One benefit of regulation is that regulators can monitor prices in all submarkets of an industry. For example, regulators watch airline routes between cities to ensure that fares between cities are not extremely high in one market and extremely low in another. In an unregulated market, when prices are based on the forces of supply and demand, there are no such guarantees. In the airline and telecommunications industries, all consumers appear to have benefited greatly from increased competition. Airline price competition benefits all passengers. Although there are some restrictions on the cheapest tickets, discounts are available to all who meet the

---

[7] Kahn's remarks were made during a PBS special entitled "Commanding Heights: Deregulation." The text of his remarks can be found at www.pbs.org/wgbh/commandingheights/shared/minitextlo/ufd_deregulation_full.html.

restrictions. In telecommunications, virtually all consumers have benefited enormously from competition in cellular and long-distance service.

Strategy and Policy
The Department of Justice Takes on the Cingular–AT&T Wireless Merger

In early 2004, Cingular (which is itself a joint venture of BellSouth and SBC Communications) agreed to purchase AT&T Wireless. Unrestricted, the resulting company would have been a true wireless giant. According to the U.S. Department of Justice, even before the merger, the HHI in some geographic markets was as high as 5,000. This HHI was already above the 1,800 threshold for compromised competition discussed earlier. After the merger, the HHI would be as high as 8,000 in some markets, close to the maximum of 10,000 indicating complete monopoly. As a result, consumers would likely face higher prices for phones and access (especially given that phones and access to wireless networks are typically sold together). In addition, there might be insufficient competitive pressure on the new firm to maintain appropriate customer service. Imagine consumers being unwillingly transferred from one company's network to another when the new firm drops duplicated service.

The final judgment, issued in March 2005, required the newly merged firm to sell off (divest) the entire AT&T Wireless network in the 13 markets in which the combined market share of Cingular and AT&T Wireless would be highest. The goal of divesting assets is to restore a competitive atmosphere to each of the most concentrated markets. With more than 140 million wireless customers and more cell phones than landlines, the U.S. Department of Justice has a strong incentive to ensure that consumers are protected, and that competition is preserved.

Critical-Thinking Questions

1. Should the U.S. Department of Justice consider traditional wired phone lines as substitutes for wireless networks? What would be the effect on the HHI if they were to do so?
2. Under what circumstances would it have been better to allow the merger of Cingular and AT&T Wireless and regulate the newly formed company instead of forcing the divestiture?

SUMMARY

- **The government's role in promoting efficiency.** The U.S. government may intervene in the private sector to promote productive efficiency, innovation, or allocative efficiency. Problems can occur when a single firm has control over a market, or when there is an insufficient number of firms to generate the benefits of a competitive market. In some cases, the natural structure of the industry is not competitive, as in the case of natural monopoly. In other cases, there may be few enough firms in an industry that they are able to collude and set output and price similar to a monopoly.

- **The legal framework of the U.S. antitrust policy.** The framework rests primarily on three pieces of legislation: the Sherman Act, which forbids collusion aiming to control a market or monopolizing a market; the Clayton Act, which prohibits price discrimination and establishes more detailed guidelines for conduct and penalties; and the Federal Trade Commission Act, which establishes an agency to work with the Justice Department on enforcement of antitrust law.

- **Enforcement of antitrust policy.** Some actions are *per se* illegal, meaning that simply engaging in them is enough to find guilt. The rule of reason in which the courts consider the merits of each case separately applies more often today. This approach requires some judgment to determine whether antitrust action is justified.

- **Mergers.** Mergers are sometimes investigated by the government. In some circumstances, the courts disallow them. Conglomerate mergers are not usually challenged. Vertical and horizontal mergers may be challenged if they could substantially lessen competition.

- **Regulation.** Government regulation of an industry may be preferable to antitrust action aimed at creating competition. In some cases, economies of scale are so great that having more than one firm in the industry would reduce efficiency. The government can leave such monopolies intact. It can also create a monopolist and monitor its behavior by setting maximum prices or determining a maximum allowable rate of profit.

- **Deregulation.** Deregulation of an industry may be appropriate if changes in the technology of production have occurred that make it more efficient to open markets to competition. Since the 1970s, a number of industries have been deregulated, including the airlines, telecommunications, and trucking industries.

▶KEY TERMS

Capture theory *344*
Clayton Act (1914) *339*
Conglomerate merger *342*
Deregulating *347*
Federal Trade Commission (FTC) *339*
Horizontal merger *342*
Innovation *335*

Merger *341*
Natural structure *335*
Optimal structure *335*
Per se illegality *340*
Predatory pricing *338*
Price cap *346*
Product tie-in *339*
Public interest theory *343*

Public utility commissions (PUCs) *344*
Rate of return regulation *347*
Rule of reason *341*
Treble damages *339*
Vertical merger *342*

▶PROBLEMS

1. What is deadweight loss? Use a graph to show that even if marginal cost is constant (a horizontal line) monopoly pricing results in a deadweight loss. What is the source of this loss?

2. Early in the 2000s, there was substantial debate in the United States over whether the federal government should prevent the mergers that allow news media markets to become highly concentrated. The market for television news might be subject to almost unlimited scale economies, as the marginal cost (to the media outlet) of another viewer is zero. With such a clear case for natural monopoly, why would citizens want the government to intervene?

3. Could a monopolist achieve the same level of allocative efficiency that occurs naturally with competition (i.e., marginal cost pricing) if it wanted to? Or is competition required for this level to be reached?

4. The bookstore at many small schools is a monopolist in the market for sweatshirts with the college logo on them, but at large schools, there are many suppliers. Use a natural monopoly argument to show that both the small-school monopoly and large-school competitive market structures are optimal.

5. Suppose that the sole local pizza box supplier agrees to sell boxes only to the largest local pizza shop.
   a. Who would be harmed, and how?
   b. Would it be more appropriate to pursue this case under Section 1 or Section 2 of the Sherman Act? Why?

6. Suppose that Microsoft decided to give away the first 10 million copies of the next release of its Windows operating system (but not any added software that Microsoft produces).
   a. Who would benefit and who would suffer under such a strategy?
   b. Should the government intervene?
7. Maria calls the box office to inquire about purchasing season tickets for the Baltimore Ravens football games. In order to purchase eight regular season games at $20 per ticket, she must also purchase the same tickets at the same price for two preseason games, in which no star players will participate. What type of restriction is this?
8. Suppose that the long-run average costs in the baking industry are constant (that is, the *LAC* curve is a horizontal line).
   a. What is the likelihood of a single firm coming to dominate this industry?
   b. If a monopolist exists in such an industry, should the government break it into smaller firms? Why or why not?
9. Under what circumstances should the Federal Trade Commission and the Department of Justice block a vertical merger?
10. Suppose two firms that presently supply separate markets (for example, the East Coast and the West Coast) in the same industry want to merge. They each currently have a 10 percent share of their respective markets. The firms argue that the merger will increase efficiency, and so should go unchallenged. Should the government allow the merger or consider blocking it? Explain your reasoning.
11. In most communities, the market for water is not competitive. Rather, water is supplied through a local water authority, operating as a regulated monopoly. Why does such an arrangement increase overall economic efficiency?
12. As part of the push to increase domestic security that occurred in 2002, the federal government took over airport security checkpoints. Why might this approach be more efficient than allowing competition in this industry?
13. In 2003, consumers gained the right to retain their portable cell phone numbers (a specific phone number that a consumer can keep, even when changing providers). Industry insiders claimed that such a change in policy would significantly increase competition in the cell phone industry. Why might this be true?
14. If the oil cartel OPEC described in Chapter 12 were subject to U.S. law, what section of the Sherman Act could be applied to break up the cartel? What would you predict about prices and oil output if the cartel were successfully broken up?
15. Suppose that for a bottled water monopolist, the only cost of production is a $100,000 fixed cost. The marginal cost of producing additional output is $0 per unit no matter how many units are produced.
   a. Make a graph, with output measured in increments of 100-gallon units, that shows the average total cost curve.
   b. What are firm losses if a regulator forces the monopolist to price at marginal cost and sell 500 units (50,000 gallons)?
   c. What price cap will allow the firm to break even at that output level?
16. Why might a hospital regulatory board insist that a potential entrant into the hospital industry demonstrate that there is sufficient demand to support a new hospital, rather than allowing the market to make that determination? Why might a regulator want to *prevent* competition in the hospital market?

17. Are consumers better off if firms make their pricing information widely available to the public through the Internet, as airlines do? Give a reason why this could help consumers, and one reason why consumers could be harmed by such a policy.

18. Draw a graph showing a firm that is a natural monopoly in the farm tractor industry. Show on the graph the point at which the monopolist would price and earn zero economic profits. Show the point where the firm would price at efficient levels. Which output level is higher?

HERE'S HOW MyEconLab CAN HELP YOU GET A BETTER GRADE

1. Log into MyEconLab and take Practice Test chapter-A (to log in for the first time, see page 30 for instructions.)

2. Based on your test results, MyEconLab will identify the areas where you need further work and create a personal Study Plan for you.

3. Your Study Plan contains the exercises listed below and others like them that will target the specific chapter topics you need to focus on. You'll receive instant feedback and find links to tutorials, animations, and the online textbook to help you study.

4. When you're ready, go take Practice Test chapter-B and demonstrate how your results have improved.

Section 13.1, Exercise 1 What are the three factors that antitrust authorities are interested in promoting?

Section 13.1, Exercise 2 Explain the difference between allocative and productive efficiency.

Section 13.2, Exercise 1 Identify the major provisions of the Sherman Act and the Clayton Act.

Section 13.3, Exercise 1 What is the difference between *per se* illegality and the rule of reason?

Section 13.3, Exercise 2 For each of the following actions, identify whether it is *currently* likely to be considered (1) *per se* illegal, (2) rule of reason, or (3) not a violation of antitrust law.

   a. Tie-in sales
   b. Price fixing
   c. Price discrimination
   d. A firm that is a monopoly because it has a superior product
   e. A firm that is a monopoly because it has driven rivals out of business through predatory pricing

Section 13.4, Exercise 1 Why is the U.S. Department of Justice more concerned about horizontal mergers than about other types of mergers?

Section 13.4, Exercise 2 For each of the following examples, identify the type of merger involved.

   a. McDonald's buys a cattle ranch.
   b. McDonald's buys Burger King.
   c. McDonald's buys a chain of gas stations.

Section 13.5, Exercise 1 The following graph shows a monopoly firm that has economies of scale over a wide range of output. Identify:

   a. The efficient price
   b. The price that regulators (using price cap regulation) would choose
   c. The deadweight loss if the market is regulated

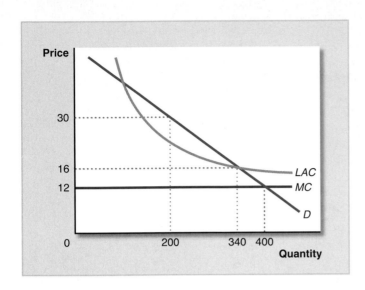

Section 13.5, Exercise 2 Suppose that demand fluctuates frequently in a regulated industry. Show the effect on firm profits if there is a price cap.

Section 13.6, Exercise 1 Under what circumstances is industry deregulation desirable?

Section 13.6, Exercise 2 Describe the effects of deregulation on the airline industry.

14

Firms and Financial Markets

Can you imagine life—especially at school and at work—without the benefits of Internet search engines? The companies that provide search engines are now giant firms, but they weren't always so large. Before Google became a household name, it was a graduate-school project. Today, Google is a major corporation and such a part of daily life that its name has become a verb. Google has developed and grown because various forms of financing were available at crucial points in its development. Most recently, on August 19, 2004, shares of Google were first made available to the general public. The sale made the firm's founders, Larry Page and Sergey Brin, instant billionaires.

As graduate students, Page and Brin, like most students, had little cash to spare and few sources of loans. They operated out of a dorm room, scrounged equipment from Stanford University's computer science department, and raised funds by borrowing against their credit cards at high interest rates. They were finally able to expand their operations when Andreas Bechtolsheim, a founder of Sun Microsystems, saw promise in their venture. He provided $100,000 for a share of ownership in Google. This funding, and the credibility it provided, enabled Page and Brin to raise the money they needed to grow Google from a class project to an ongoing enterprise and then to a corporate giant.

Google's story is not unique. Most major corporations started as small businesses. As demand for a product grows, the firm that supplies it grows in turn. Growth brings the opportunity for more revenue and profit. However, firms generally need money to fund the increases in plant, equipment, and research that allow them to expand. Even large companies can need periodic infusions of funds to maintain their competitiveness. A small, high-tech startup may want to grow. A large auto manufacturer may want to upgrade its facilities. A struggling restaurant may need funds to help it through a difficult spell. Firms of all types and sizes routinely face crucial financing decisions.

Companies can raise funds in a variety of ways. They can take out a loan, issue bonds, or sell stock. They can also accept venture capital, which is what Page and Brin did when they received financing from Bechtolsheim.

From perfect competition to monopoly, virtually all firms need physical capital. To purchase physical capital, firms need financial capital. In this chapter, we examine the various ways that firms raise financial capital. Each source has advantages and disadvantages for both the firms that seek the funds and the investors who provide them. We also consider how the choice of financing can affect the operations of a company, and the challenges when the goals of firm managers and stockholders conflict.

ALONG THE WAY, YOU WILL ALSO LEARN:

- How financial capital differs from physical capital, and how they are related.
- How firms raise financial capital by borrowing.
- How firms raise financial capital by selling bonds.
- How firms raise financial capital by selling stock.
- How firms raise financial capital through venture capital.
- How different forms of ownership affect the way a firm is run.

AT THE END OF THE CHAPTER, THE MYECONLAB LOGO WILL DIRECT YOU ONLINE

- MyEconLab is a resource-packed online homework and tutorial system that can help you perform better in your economics course. To log in for the first time, see page 30 for instructions.
- MyEconLab can help you apply important concepts from the chapter to real-world issues. Watch for the logo to indicate online features about valuing investments.
- At the end of each chapter, you'll find a special study section that will help you get the most out of your textbook and your instructor's MyEconLab course.

▶ Why Firms Seek Funds

We begin our look at firms' financial capital resources by examining firms' motivation. Whether a small project run out of a dorm room or a multinational corporation, all firms seek funds for the same basic reason: Their financial needs exceed the funds they have on hand. One of the most common reasons firms seek funds is to pay for the purchase of plant and equipment. We refer to the funding that firms obtain as *financial capital*. Recall from Chapter 2 that financial capital is the money that firms use to purchase plant and equipment (or *physical capital*). In this section, we explore the relationship between the firm's demand for physical and financial capital and the analysis that guides a firm's decision making.

The Net Benefits from an Investment

Net benefits
The difference between the revenue a project generates and the cost it imposes, including the opportunity cost.

Before Google—or any firm—makes decisions about financial capital, it must first determine what physical capital it needs. Firms invest in physical capital with the same underlying goal that drives all firm decisions: the desire to maximize profits. Recall from Chapter 8 that firms want to undertake projects that add to profits. Such projects have positive net benefits. Economists define the **net benefits** of a project as the difference between the revenue it generates and the costs it imposes, including the opportunity cost. A firm's computation of the net benefits of an investment project is complex. Physical capital by definition lasts for many periods, so firms must consider the value of such investments over time.

Time, Interest, and the Value of Investment in Physical Capital

When weighing the net benefits of an investment opportunity, firms must determine the cost of financial capital. To illustrate, suppose that Google founders Page and Brin used $50,000 of their personal savings for additional computer server memory while still working out of their dorm room. The benefits of the added memory accrued over the course of two years, totaling $28,500 per year (received at the end of each year). You might be tempted to say that the investment was worthwhile, because the sum of the benefits ($28,500 × 2 = $57,000) is greater than the $50,000 cost of the memory. However, this reasoning ignores opportunity costs. While Page and Brin paid for the servers in the current year, they had to wait for the benefits.

Interest
The payments lenders receive in addition to the repayment of their loans.

Time Value of Money. To compute net benefits correctly, we must consider the opportunity cost of using the money for the investment project. For example, Page and Brin could have left the $50,000 in the bank, where it would have earned **interest**, the payment that lenders receive in addition to the repayment of their loan. We also use the term "interest" to mean the cost of borrowing funds. When funds are deposited in the bank, the interest paid to the depositor is compensation for the right to use those funds to make loans.

Time value of money
Indicates that money paid in the present is more valuable than the same sum paid at a future date. Time value is based on the opportunity cost of use of the funds over the time period in question.

Suppose someone offered you the choice of $100 right now or $100 one year from now. The wise decision would be to accept the $100 today for one simple reason: If you had $100 today, you could always deposit that money in the bank and have more than $100 in one year. Economists use the term **time value of money** to describe the insight that money today is more valuable than the identical amount of money at a future point. Your compensation for not having the money available for your own use and instead making those funds available for lending is the interest you earn.

Lenders charge interest for a number of reasons:

1. Interest compensates lenders for not being able to use their money to buy things they want.
2. Interest compensates lenders for assuming the risk that the borrower will not repay the loan.
3. Interest protects lenders who fear that rising prices will reduce the purchasing power of the loan repayments.

Interest rate
The unit price of the loan; the cost per hundred dollars borrowed.

Principal
The dollar value of the loan from the lender to the borrower.

Lenders and borrowers both focus on the **interest rate**, the unit price of the loan determined as the cost per hundred dollars borrowed. Equation 14.1 shows the relationship between the interest rate, the interest payment, and the **principal**, or the dollar value of the loan.

$$\text{Interest rate} = 100 \times (\text{Interest payment/Principal}) \qquad (14.1)$$

For example, if the interest payment is $5 per $100 borrowed, the interest rate is:

$$\text{Interest rate} = 100(5/100)$$

$$= 5\%$$

In this case, a person will have to offer you at least $105 a year from today for you to be willing to sacrifice $100 today. Think of the interest rate as the opportunity cost of waiting a year for your money.

Present value (*PV*)
Value today of a stream of revenue or a series of payments, even if it is not received or paid today.

Future value (*FV*)
What an asset will be worth at some time in the future

Present and Future Value. The **present value (*PV*)** of future income is equal to its value today. In the case of a stream of revenue or a series of payments, it is the maximum amount that someone would pay today in order to receive that series of payments in the future. An asset's **future value (*FV*)** is what a sum of money will be worth at some time in the future, and is the opposite of the asset's present value. The formula for the future value of an asset that earns an interest rate r payable in one year is shown in Equation 14.2.

$$FV = PV\,(1 + r) \qquad (14.2)$$

If the interest rate is five percent, the future value of a current $200 payment in one year is:

$$FV = \$200(1 + 0.05) = \$210$$

We can rearrange Equation 14.2 to find the present value, shown in Equation 14.3.

$$PV = \frac{FV}{(1 + r)} \qquad (14.3)$$

We can now apply our understanding of the time value of money to determine the value of the $28,500 earned from the purchase of additional memory in the first two years. Using Equation 14.3, and assuming an interest rate of five percent, the present value of the added memory after one year is:

$$PV = \frac{\$28,500}{(1 + 0.05)} = \$27,142.86$$

Thus, the $28,500 that the memory generates at the end of the first year is worth only $27,142.86 today. The reason is that benefits received in the future are worth less than benefits received today. In general, the farther into the future the benefits are received, the less they are worth today.

Let's now determine the present value of the revenue earned from the memory after two years. If Page and Brin had to wait two years for revenue, then they must discount the benefits received in the second year twice.

$$PV_2 = \frac{B_2}{(1 + r)(1 + r)} = \frac{B_2}{(1 + r)^2}$$

Discounting
The process of determining the present value of a future stream of revenue or payments.

Discounting is the method used to determine the present value of a future stream of revenue or payments. The discounted present value of the benefits received in the second year of operation (B_2) is:

$$PV_2 = \frac{B_2}{(1 + r)^2} = \frac{\$28,500}{(1 + 0.05)^2} = \$25,850.34$$

Net Benefits Calculation. How do firms put these present value and future value equations to use? Economists are frequently interested in the net present value of an asset. The **net present value (NPV)** is the difference between the present value of an asset and the present value of expenditures on it. Proposed projects with positive net present value are profitable investments. Those with negative net present value are not profitable investments. Let's use the concept of net present value to evaluate the net benefit—the difference between the revenue the project generates and the costs it imposes—of Google investing in computer memory. Recall that Page and Brin would pay $50,000 at the start of the current year and would receive $28,500 in benefits at the end of both the current year and the next year. The net present value of their $50,000 investment is:

Net present value (NPV)
The difference between present value of an asset and present value of expenditures on it.

$$NPV = -\$50,000 + \frac{\$28,500}{(1 + 0.05)} + \frac{\$28,500}{(1 + 0.05)^2}$$

$$= -\$50,000 + \$27,142.86 + \$25,850.34 = \$2,993.20$$

The NPV of the memory is $2,993.20, so Page and Brin should make the investment. In this simple example, the asset lasts only two years. In practice, the useful life of most plant and equipment investments is much longer. Computing the net present value for such investments requires a formula that can accommodate many periods, rather than just two. The general formula for computing NPV is complex. Because we use only two-period examples in this chapter, we do not introduce the general formula here.[1] The general principle remains the same. We discount future values by a greater amount because they are not received until farther into the future.

myeconlab
Get Ahead of the Curve
Use the concept of present discounted value to assess the benefits of purchasing a monthly card for the New York subway.

Interest and the Demand for Financial Capital

NPV is a valuable tool that allows us to compare investment opportunities. The interest rate is a crucial component of NPV calculations. We noted earlier that the interest rate reflects the opportunity cost of waiting for money. It follows that a firm's demand for physical and financial capital falls as the interest rate rises. To illustrate, suppose that the interest rate has increased from 5 percent to 10 percent.

---

[1] More generally, $NPV = -C \sum_{t=0}^{T} \frac{B_t}{(1 + r_t)^t}$, where B_t is the benefit in year t.

Substituting the new interest rate into our previous calculation shows that the new net benefit of the $50,000 investment in memory is:

$$NPV = -\$50,000 + \frac{\$28,500}{(1 + 0.1)} + \frac{\$28,500}{(1 + 0.1)^2}$$

$$= -\$50,000 + \$49,462.81 = -\$537.19$$

The NPV of the memory is −$537.19 at 10 percent interest. In this case, the firm should not make the investment.

What about opportunity costs? Before purchasing the memory, Page and Brin would have considered alternative investments. The opportunity cost of capital is the best alternative use of the capital or the funds required to purchase it. Suppose that instead of buying more memory, Page and Brin could buy new servers. Let's assume that the cost of the servers is the same as that of the memory ($50,000). Servers also last for two years and generate $57,000 in revenue. Unlike memory, however, the servers take a year to install and integrate into Google's operations. Thus, the servers bring no benefits in the first year. Before discounting, the total benefit of both investment projects is $57,000. However, the NPVs differ because of the timing of the benefits. Assuming a five percent opportunity cost of capital, the NPV of benefits from the servers is:

$$NPV = -\$50,000 + \frac{\$0}{(1 + 0.05)} + \frac{\$57,000}{(1 + 0.05)^2} = \$1,700.68$$

Both investments bring in the same amount of revenue, but their $NPVs$ differ. Because the memory yields benefits in the first and second periods, its NPV is $2,993.20; the servers have an NPV of only $1,700.68. Both $NPVs$ are positive, so the investments are sound. The memory is a better investment than the server, however. Holding all else equal, the sooner benefits are received and the lower the interest rate, the higher the NPV.

Our conclusion that a firm's demand for physical and financial capital falls as the interest rate rises indicates a negative relationship. This negative relationship between the interest rate and the level of physical capital investment is consistent with the Law of Demand. The downward-sloping demand curve in Figure 14.1 shows that the quantity of physical capital demanded falls as the interest rate rises.

TEST + *E X T E N D* Your Knowledge

1. TEST Use the net present value formula to show the net present value of the memory if it earned $30,000 in the first year but only $25,000 in the second year because of frequent breakdowns. Use a five percent interest rate. Should the firm make the investment?

2. EXTEND Banks make loans to their best business customers at the lowest interest rate. This rate is known as the prime rate. Go to the U.S. Federal Reserve Board Web site at www.federalreserve.gov/releases/h15/update/ and find the current bank prime interest rate for commercial loans. Consider Google's question of whether to invest in memory that will produce earnings of $28,500 for two years. Should Google make the investment at the current value of the prime rate?

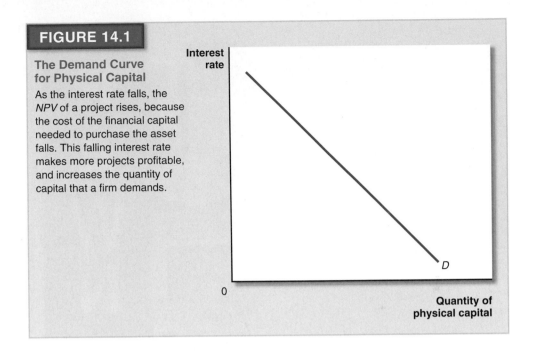

FIGURE 14.1

The Demand Curve for Physical Capital
As the interest rate falls, the *NPV* of a project rises, because the cost of the financial capital needed to purchase the asset falls. This falling interest rate makes more projects profitable, and increases the quantity of capital that a firm demands.

Using this demand relationship, we can determine the level of investment in physical capital. If the interest rate is five percent, firms will pursue all projects with an *NPV* greater than zero using five percent as the opportunity cost of capital. If rates go up or down, firms recalculate the *NPV* with the new rate to determine the level of investment.

Raising Funds with Bank Loans

We now turn to sources of funds for firms to borrow by focusing on bank loans. In our previous calculations, we assumed that Page and Brin had the $50,000 they needed to purchase the additional computer memory. In reality, when Page and Brin first formed Google, they did not have money on hand. Moreover, no bank would lend them the money. As a result, they had to borrow against their credit cards, which cost them much more in interest than a bank loan. Why was Google unable to secure a bank loan? What general lessons about bank loan terms can we learn from Google's experience?

Bank Loan Terms

Most loans are fixed obligations. With a fixed obligation, the borrower (the firm, in this case) must repay the loan plus a given amount of interest at set times. The payments made on such loans are independent of the firm's financial condition once the loan is made. Lenders do not typically have a direct say in the operation of the firm and so must make judgments about the firm's ability to repay the loan at the time it is made.

Banks typically use techniques like the *NPV* method to assess whether the project the loan will finance is worthwhile. The greatest risk a lender faces is that the borrowing firm will **default**, or fail to repay the loan. If a borrower defaults, the lender could lose both the interest payments it had expected and the principal. Banks protect themselves against default by conducting extensive credit checks to ensure that firms are

Default
Occurs when a borrower fails to repay a loan.

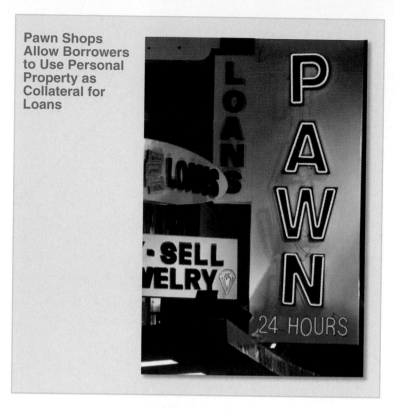

Pawn Shops Allow Borrowers to Use Personal Property as Collateral for Loans

Collateral
An asset that the borrower agrees to give the lender if he defaults on the loan.

creditworthy. Additionally, banks ask borrowers to provide collateral. **Collateral** is an asset that the borrower agrees to give the lender if he defaults on the loan. The lender can then resell the asset to recoup its losses. What if the borrower lacks sufficient assets for collateral? In Google's early days, the company did not have enough assets to satisfy potential lenders and was a poor candidate for a bank loan. Fortunately for Page and Brin, credit card companies do not ask for collateral or check a user's credit each time he uses the credit card to make a purchase. Their credit cards effectively allowed them to take out a series of short-term loans. Because credit card loans are riskier than bank loans, credit card companies charge a much higher interest rate on the loan.

Bank Loan Limitations

Today, any bank would regard Google as a good credit risk, but Google faces a different problem. Major corporations like Google often need to borrow billions of dollars, a sum that is beyond the capacity of most banks. Even if a bank could afford to make a billion-dollar loan, it would be reluctant to risk so much money on one borrower.

▶Raising Funds with Bonds

Bond
A certificate of debt that guarantees the lender a fixed payment from the borrower such that the principal plus a predetermined rate of interest is repaid by a specific date.

As an established firm, Google now has access to various forms of financing that are more attractive than a bank loan. In this section, we continue our look at the ways firms borrow money by focusing on bonds.

Bond Terms

A **bond** is a certificate of debt that guarantees the lender (the purchaser of the bond) a fixed payment from the borrower (the seller of the bond) such that the principal

Coupon payments
Interest payments made to the purchaser of a bond.

Maturity
The point at which the borrower repays the principal of the loan and interest payments cease.

plus a predetermined rate of interest is repaid by a specific date. A firm that issues bonds is a *borrower*. The interest payments it makes to the purchasers of the bond are called **coupon payments**. A bond reaches **maturity** at a set date when the firm repays the principal of the loan and interest payments cease. Maturity varies from bond to bond, lasting from a single day to decades. Bonds differ from bank loans in that a bond breaks up the loan into many relatively small IOUs. Bonds therefore reduce the burden and the risk that any one lender faces.

Why Firms Issue Bonds

A bond is a fixed obligation. A firm does not pay its lenders more if profits increase, and does not pay them less if profits decrease. A firm prefers issuing bonds if it is optimistic about its future and wants to keep the profits for itself. Bonds are less attractive to the firm that is pessimistic and expects to have trouble meeting a fixed obligation.

Bonds might also appeal to firms because they do not dilute ownership. A bondholder is a creditor with a financial claim on the company. Bondholders do not have an ownership stake in the company.

Finally, the U.S. tax structure favors bonds. Firms can list interest payments as a cost and not pay taxes on them.

Bonds and Risk

An unstable company is more likely to default on its bond payments than a stable one. Investment advisors Moody's and Standard & Poor's help investors to evaluate the likelihood that a firm will be able to meet the obligations of its bond issue. These companies assign the issuer a grade that reflects the risk involved in buying bonds from it. The two ratings systems closely resemble each other and appear in Table 14.1.

As we move down Table 14.1, the bonds become riskier. The safest investments are rated as AAA or Aaa. Bonds sold to pursue riskier investments are rated lower.

TABLE 14.1

Bond Rating Systems

Moody's Rating	Standard & Poor's Rating	Interpretation
Aaa	AAA	Best quality
Aa	AA	High quality
A	A	High to medium quality
Baa	BBB	Medium quality
Ba	BB	Uncertain quality
B	B	At risk of default
Caa	CCC	Poor quality
Ca	CC	High uncertain quality
C	C	Lowest rating
–	D	In default

Junk bonds
High-risk bonds that most analysts regard as very poor investments and that receive the lowest bond ratings.

Bonds rated as BB (or Ba) or lower are often referred to as **junk bonds**, which are high-risk bonds that most analysts regard as very poor investments and so receive the lowest ratings. If a firm's bond rating falls from high quality to low quality, its bonds must offer interest rates that are typically two to three percentage points higher in order to attract buyers.

The Bond Market

Secondary market
Provides a place (physical or electronic) where buyers and sellers can gather to exchange financial assets.

Bonds are frequently bought and sold on a **secondary market**, which allows people to buy and sell existing financial assets such as bonds and stocks. Unlike a newly issued bond, a bond sold on the secondary market does not directly benefit the firm. Google, for example, receives funds only when it sells bonds to investors. It receives no additional funds when investors sell their bonds to other investors. However, Google benefits indirectly from the secondary market because it makes the bonds that Google issues liquid. An asset is **liquid** when it is readily convertible into cash. The fact that investors can sell bonds they no longer wish to hold increases the investors' willingness to buy that bond in the first place.

Liquid assets
Assets that are readily convertible into cash.

Capital gains
Earned by an investor when selling an asset for a higher price than was paid for it.

An investor earns **capital gains** by selling an asset for a higher price than was paid for it. A bondholder who does not want to hold the bond until maturity can profit in the secondary market if the bond's price has risen.

▶ Raising Funds with Stock

Stocks are another critical form of firm fundraising. Early in the company's history, Larry Page and Sergey Brin were concerned that by selling stock they would lose control of their company. They recognized that selling stock effectively divides ownership of the company into little pieces known as **shares**—the smallest unit of ownership in a company. It entitles the stockholder to a stake in running the company and a portion of its profits.

Shares
The smallest unit of ownership in a company that entitles the bearer to a stake in running the company and a portion of its profits.

Suppose, for example, that a firm is worth $3 million. If the firm sells one million shares, each share is worth $3 and effectively entitles the bearer to one out of one million votes in the control of the firm and one-millionth of the firm's profits. This example is simplified—firms seldom pay all of their profits to stockholders. Instead, they keep some portion of profits on hand to meet everyday expenses and to use for investment projects. In Chapter 3, you saw that distributed profits are called *dividends*, which are the stockholders' share of the firm's profits. In this section, we explore the financial aspects of stock and examine the impact of selling stock on firm operations. We also examine the relationship between movements in a particular stock's price and the performance of the overall economy.

Why Firms Issue Stock

Firms often sell stock for the same reason that they sell bonds: to fund investment in physical capital. This, however, is not the only reason for selling stock. Recall that Page and Brin became billionaires when they sold stock in Google to the general public. Had they sold an equal amount of bonds, they would have had to pay all that money back to the bondholder at maturity. Stocks do not bring a fixed obligation. The owners of Google got to keep the money they raised from selling stock.

There are three reasons why investors buy stock. Large investors may hope to buy enough stock to have a say in how the company is run. Most investors, however, look instead to the financial gains of owning a piece of the company. Some investors buy stock in the hope that the firm will pay generous dividends. Others buy stock because they believe that the price of the stock will rise, and they will be able to sell the stock for a large capital gain.

The Secondary Market for Stocks

As was the case for bonds, most transactions involving stocks bring no direct benefit to the firm. Instead, investors buy and sell shares of stock from other investors. Again, firms benefit from the fact that the secondary market increases investors' willingness to purchase new issues of stock. U.S. firms have a choice of many different stock markets (also known as stock exchanges) in which to sell their stock. A **stock market** is a centralized location where buyers and sellers exchange shares. Some cities host stock exchanges that cater to local companies. Others have a national or even international profile.

The oldest and best-known U.S. stock market is the New York Stock Exchange (NYSE). Almost 2,800 companies are members of the NYSE, and about 1.5 billion shares of stock change hands every business day. The National Association of Securities Dealers Automated Quotations, better known as the NASDAQ, lists the largest number of firms of all U.S. stock exchanges. NASDAQ boasts about 3,300 member companies. Unlike the NYSE, where exchanges are typically made in person, the NASDAQ is a virtual exchange. Transactions are handled strictly by computer. Page and Brin chose to sell Google's stock on the NASDAQ exchange. Once the shares had been sold initially, investors who wished to sell or buy shares of Google could do so using NASDAQ.

Stock and Stock Market Performance

Of the thousands of companies whose stocks change hands on a typical day on the NYSE or NASDAQ, many see their stock price rise, while others see their price fall. How, then, can we say that the stock market went up or down?

Stock Indexes. When we speak about *the* stock market, we are actually talking about movements by all of the stocks that are traded on the different exchanges. To get a quick idea of how all stocks have moved, we use an **index**, a single number that summarizes the movement of many different variables.

Many different indexes sum up the movements of stock exchanges. The NASDAQ-100 summarizes movements on the NASDAQ. The *Financial Times' Footsie* index measures movements on the London Stock Exchange. The Standard & Poor's 100 captures movements on the NYSE. By far the most famous index is the Dow Jones Industrial Average (DJIA), or just the Dow. The DJIA consists of 30 stocks that repre-

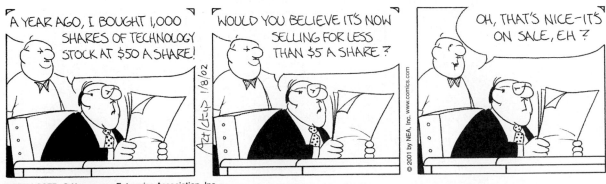

BORN LOSER: © Newspaper Enterprise Association, Inc.

sent the overall movement of stock prices. Dow Jones regularly monitors and adjusts the firms in the DJIA to reflect changes in the structure of the U.S. economy.

Stock Quotes. Investors can follow movements in companies' stock prices at various stock exchanges online at any time. The day's final position is chronicled in major newspapers. Table 14.2 shows the Google listing in the *Wall Street Journal* on February 9, 2005. For comparison, we also show the listing for Goody Family, the stock listing that immediately precedes Google in the NASDAQ listings.

A great deal of information is contained in these brief summaries of stock market activity, including:

1. The company's name and stock symbol (usually an abbreviation of the company name), appear in columns 4 and 5 of Table 14.2. The letter *n* that follows Google's stock symbol indicates that Google is new to the exchange; it first issued stock in the last 52 weeks.
2. Column 1 tells us the percentage change in the price of a share of stock to date in 2005. The price of Google stock had risen by three percent as of February 9.
3. Columns 2 and 3 show the highest and lowest closing prices that the company's stock had reached over the previous 52 weeks. The closing price is the price of the company's stock at the end of the trading day.
4. Columns 6 through 8 show the dividend that the company pays, the percentage yield that owning a share of the company's stock would bring, and the company's price-to-earnings (PE) ratio. The **yield** tells us how large the company's dividend was relative to the price of its stock. The **price-to-earnings (PE) ratio** is the value of the company's stock (the price times the number of shares) divided by the company's annual after-tax profits. Because Google, like many new companies, does not have positive profits, there is no way at this point to compute the PE ratio. The PE ratio of Goody Family tells us that the value of that company's stock outstanding is 19 times the size of its net earnings. The dividend, yield, and PE ratio columns are blank for Google. Like most start-ups, Google has focused largely on growth rather than profits. Google does

Yield
Indicates how large the company's dividend is relative to the price of its stock.

Price-to-earnings (PE) ratio
The value of the company's stock (the price times the number of shares) divided by the company's annual after-tax profits.

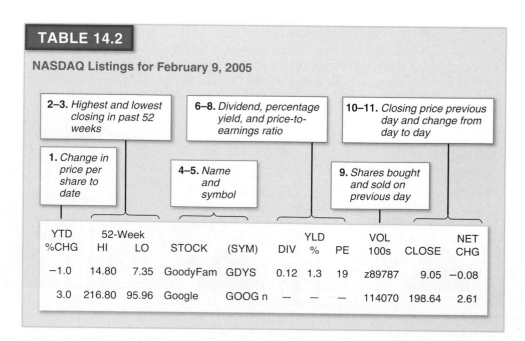

TABLE 14.2

NASDAQ Listings for February 9, 2005

2–3. Highest and lowest closing in past 52 weeks

6–8. Dividend, percentage yield, and price-to-earnings ratio

10–11. Closing price previous day and change from day to day

1. Change in price per share to date

4–5. Name and symbol

9. Shares bought and sold on previous day

YTD %CHG	52-Week HI	LO	STOCK	(SYM)	DIV	YLD %	PE	VOL 100s	CLOSE	NET CHG
−1.0	14.80	7.35	GoodyFam	GDYS	0.12	1.3	19	z89787	9.05	−0.08
3.0	216.80	95.96	Google	GOOG n	—	—	—	114070	198.64	2.61

not list a dividend, because it has retained all of its earnings and reinvested them in the company so as to maximize growth.

5. Column 9 shows how many shares of stock, in hundreds, that were bought and sold the previous day. On February 8, slightly more than 11.4 million shares of Google stock traded hands. The *z* in front of the number for Goody Family tells us that the number for that company does not have to be multiplied by 100. Only 89,787 shares of Goody Family stock were bought and sold.

6. Columns 10 and 11 show the closing price on the previous day and how much it had risen or fallen compared to the day before. Thus, the price of Google stock was $198.64 at the end of trading on February 8, 2005, which was an increase of $2.61 over the previous day's close.

Interpreting Movements in the Stock Market

The price that investors are willing to pay for a company's stock reflects their expectation of the company's future profits. However, on any given day, an investor can have other reasons for wanting to buy or sell stock. One investor may want to sell Google stock to raise enough cash to buy a house. Another may have completed a major business deal that provided enough cash to buy a stock that he's been following. As a result, on any given day, at least some of the movement in a company's stock does not reflect anything about the company. An accurate picture about people's expectations for a company therefore comes from long-term movements in its stock prices rather than its movements over a short period of time.

If a single stock's movements reveal expectations about the firm's future profits, then broad movements in a stock index reflect expectations about the overall economy. Movements in stock prices, however, do not directly cause companies to succeed or fail. Almost all stock market transactions involve shares of stock that the company has already sold. The stockholders of a company, not the company itself, become poorer when a stock price falls. The stock market crash of 1929 reflected the underlying weakness of the U.S. economy and presaged the coming Great Depression. However, it had no direct effect on the economy itself.

LifeLessons

Sometimes Good News Is Bad News

Have you ever been puzzled by the events on Wall Street? Consider, for example, what happened to the Intel Corporation in the summer of 2004. Over the months of July and August, the company's stock price steadily fell. It dropped from a high of $28 per share in late June to $20 per share in early September. This decline of close to 30 percent in stock value came despite a corporate report in early July that announced higher corporate profits. According to what we have learned, higher profits should have made Intel more attractive to investors and caused the price of its stock to rise. Instead, the price fell. How could investors react so negatively to such good news?

The answer lies in expectations. Suppose that consumers expect a firm to announce that its profits rose 10 percent over the last quarter. When consumers expect such strong performance, their demand for the stock increases before the company actually reports its profits. If the company announces that profits rose by only 6 percent, investors' expectations are not realized. People no longer think the company will be as profitable as they had expected it to be before the report was issued. As a result, the demand for the company's stock shifts to the left. The company's seemingly positive report on profits has thus become negative, because the firm did not meet expectations. When expectations are not met, even good results can be disappointing.

Stock movements can have two indirect effects on the economy. First, the stock market can create or destroy wealth. If the value of stocks (or bonds) rises, then people can use the capital gains they receive from selling their stock or bonds to make other purchases. If the value falls, the losses rule out some purchases. For example, experts believed that the rapid rise of the stock market in the late 1990s helped fuel the demand for housing, thereby stimulating the whole economy. Second, movements in the stock market do not only reflect confidence in the economy; they can *affect* confidence as well. A booming stock market gives people hope that their incomes will rise in the future. This, in turn, encourages them to make expenditures on expensive items, such as houses or cars, which they might not make otherwise. The stock market thus becomes a self-fulfilling prophecy through which the belief in good times helps produce the conditions that create good times.

Stocks and Risk

Accounting scandals of the early 2000s brought attention to the relation of firm behavior to stock prices. The crash of Enron's stock in 2001 and the sudden collapse of WorldCom in 2002 reflected an important weakness of the stock market. If investors base their decisions on incorrect or misleading information, they cannot make intelligent investment decisions. Enron and WorldCom's stock collapsed when it became evident that the management of the companies had conspired to hide massive losses from employees and investors. Such actions can undermine the ability of all firms to raise financial capital, particularly by selling stock. If investors do not believe that they are participating in a fair game, they will invest their funds elsewhere.

The U.S. government protects the interest of consumers who buy bonds and stocks. The U.S. Securities and Exchange Commission (SEC) was created in 1934 to reassure investors who had been scared away by the stock market crash of 1929. The SEC has two basic requirements of firms. First, it requires all firms that issue stocks and bonds to provide accurate and timely information about their firm's performance to the general public. As a result, corporations must submit to outside audits of their finances and make information public through, among other things, annual reports to stockholders. Second, the SEC requires that dealers who buy and sell bonds and stocks do so honestly and act in the best interest of the public. For example, the SEC does not want investment counselors to advise their clients to buy stock in a specific company that they believe is a poor risk.

The recent corporate scandals have led some to claim that the SEC's requirements are not strict enough. Outside audits and published annual reports, for example, do little good if the auditors do not tell the truth and the annual reports are misleading. The Sarbanes-Oxley Act, which was enacted in 2002, is the latest attempt to

TEST + *EXTEND* Your Knowledge

1. TEST Go to finance.Yahoo.com and use the Google stock symbol GOOG to find out how well did Google do on the stock market on the most recent trading day. What, if anything, does this tell you about the profitability of Google?

2. EXTEND Do you think that most investors regard stocks and bonds as complements or substitutes? Suppose that the overall price of stocks as measured by the major indexes rises. Use supply and demand curves to show what you would expect to happen to the overall price of bonds.

combat the danger of misinformation. Among its many provisions, the bill bans auditors from performing other work (such as consulting) for the companies they audit. The bill also imposes severe civil and criminal penalties for firm officials who knowingly publish incorrect financial statements.

Venture Capital

The final form of firm financing we discuss here is illustrated by a turning point in Google's fortune. As mentioned earlier, when the founders of Google needed additional capital but were not ready to begin selling stocks or issuing bonds, they turned to Andreas Bechtolsheim, a co-founder of Sun Microsystems. He provided Page and Brin's fledgling enterprise with $100,000 in exchange for an ownership stake in Google. The funds that Bechtolsheim provided are known as venture capital.

Venture capital
Funds and expertise that investors contribute to a firm; as compensation, venture capitalists typically receive either stock or bonds that can be converted into stock.

Venture capital refers to both funds and expertise that investors bring to a new firm. In return for their money and expertise, venture capitalists investors typically receive either stock or bonds that can be converted into stock. Venture capitalists are typically interested in rapidly increasing the value of the company and turning this increase in value into capital gains. The long-term return on either stocks or bonds is less appealing to them. In order to impose their vision of rapid growth on the company, venture capitalists often insist on a leadership role within the company.

The Asymmetric Information and Principal–Agent Problem

We close the chapter by examining the implications of information on the firm's structure and operations. As noted earlier, a major reason for Page and Brin's reluctance to sell stock was their fear that selling stock to the general public would change Google's character. As long as ownership was restricted to a small circle of people, Page and Brin could ensure that Google was run the way they wanted.

In Chapter 3, we encountered the three basic forms of ownership: *sole proprietorships, partnerships, and corporations.* For most corporations, ownership is so widely spread that no single owner can make all the day-to-day decisions. If the firm's stockholders do not decide whom to hire or what price to charge for output, then who does? The modern corporation is able to flourish because it has replaced owners with **managers**, employees who oversee the day-to-day operations of the firm.

Managers
Employees who oversee the day-to-day operations of a firm.

Asymmetric Information

Asymmetric information
Occurs when one party to a contract or transaction has more information than another.

The fundamental problem of stockholders in their efforts to control managers is that information is asymmetric. **Asymmetric information** exists when one party has more information related to a contract or transaction than another party. Asymmetric information can affect the behavior of individuals (such as employer and employee) either before the contract is made or after. A classic asymmetric information problem appears with the purchase of a used car. When an individual uses a car for many years and then decides to sell it, the seller has much more information about the quality of the car than the potential buyer. A dishonest seller may not reveal known problems with a car and instead overstate its condition and value. The buyer has no way to easily check the claims of the seller, and this lack of information may cause a buyer to pay more for the car than if its true history were known.

The Principal–Agent Problem

The information asymmetry between shareholders and managers regarding how managers allocate their time and use resources gives rise to what economists call the principal–agent problem.

The **principal–agent problem** is the conflict that can arise when one person or group relies upon another to maximize its well-being, but has no way to directly control the other's behavior. For corporations, the conflict stems from the different incentives facing the owner of the firm, also called the *principal*, and the manager, who is called the *agent*. In a corporation, the stockholders want to maximize the return on their investment in the form of profits. Managers may have different goals, such as maximizing their own income, minimizing the effort required to earn a satisfactory rating, or earning promotions instead of working as effective team members. If the stockholders do not structure the incentives facing the agents carefully, the firm's managers might work to achieve their own goals rather than those of the owners. Workers cannot readily be expected to work against their own self-interest. As a result, the challenge for the stockholders is to structure the compensation of the managers such that by working to further their own self-interest, they also work to further the goals of the firm.

Principal-agent problems can occur either at the time that the contract is formed or after, as discussed in the following sections.

Adverse Selection. **Adverse selection** occurs when one party fails to fully disclose information before the contract is agreed upon and makes choices based on its information advantage. Consider a management candidate who has a prior history of stealing from her employer. She may be especially interested in positions where large quantities of cash are typically on hand and individual accountability is difficult. That same person may also hide her past criminal record information from an employer to gain access to such a position.

Moral Hazard. **Moral hazard** results when information asymmetry leads one of the parties to act against the interests of the other party after the contract is written. Consider auto insurance. Insurance companies offer auto insurance policies to individuals based on the assumption that the individual, motivated by self-interest in his own safety, will drive carefully. But some individuals might see insurance differently. They might drive very carefully if they have no insurance, knowing that they are personally liable for the results of any accident they cause. After insured, however, they might drive more recklessly, because the insurance company now bears most of the cost of any accident they cause.

In the context of firm management, managers might not act in the best interest of the stockholders if the terms of their employment are not structured so that they are rewarded according to the profits of the firm. Consider managers who are paid a fixed wage per year with guaranteed increases in pay that are based on length of employment rather than performance goals. They might act in ways that run contrary to the interests of the stockholders. They might decide to slack off or shirk their responsibilities instead of working diligently at all times.

Board of Directors. Stockholders attempt to resolve the principal-agent problem by appointing a **board of directors**, which sets rules of behavior for managers and employees of the firm. It also decides what projects the firm should pursue, and how the firm should raise funds. If board members adopt unpopular or unprofitable policies, the stockholders can, in principle, vote them out of office. Unlike most elected officials, however, most board members do not actively seek office. Instead, they

---

Principal–agent problem
The conflict that arises when one person or group relies upon another to maximize its well-being.

Adverse selection
Results when one party does not fully disclose information before a contract is agreed upon and makes choices based on its information advantage.

Moral hazard
Results when asymmetric information after a contract is written leads one of the parties to act against the interests of the other party.

Board of directors
Sets the rules of behavior for managers and employees of the firm; decides which projects the firm should pursue; and determines how the firm should raise funds.

CONFLICT OF INTEREST

WHEN THE UNDERTAKER IS ALSO YOUR LIFE INSURANCE SALESMAN

THE BOOK OF PHRASES

THE BOOK OF PHRASES

©2005 CREATORS SYNDICATE, INC. www.creators.com

8-17

B.C.: By permission of John L. Hart, and Creators Syndicate, Inc.

come to the attention of a nominating committee through their achievements in government, academia, or the business world. As a result, board members seldom devote their whole attention to representing the interests of the people who voted them into office. Like the investors they represent, board members leave the day-to-day operations of the firm to management. Thus, the principal-agent problem also exists for boards of directors with respect to the managers of the firms as their agents.

Boards must structure the compensation of top managers such that they have the incentive to make the best decisions regarding the future of the firm. Suppose the board wants managers to concentrate on maximizing long-run profits. It might not want to give managers bonuses based on short-term performance, such as quarterly bonuses based on sales. Such a system could, for example, cause managers to rush delivery of products that are not up to the firm's quality standards.

Strategy and Policy
Colleges and Universities Need Capital, Too

The cost of a new classroom building complete with modern teaching and learning technology can easily exceed $10 million. Where does a college or university obtain the capital to build a new classroom building? Because most institutions are organized as non-profit institutions, and many are state-owned, selling stock is not an option. For some public universities, the state pays part or all of the cost. But for other public institutions, as well as private colleges and universities, donations are the primary funding source.

To raise funds for a specific project such as a dormitory, science center, or student center, institutions often organize a capital campaign. If you look around your own school, you will likely find that many of the buildings are named for an individual. In many cases, those names represent major donors who have given either all or a substantial portion of the funds for the building. In some cases, the donation is so large that the entire school is renamed. Rowan University, for example, used to be known as Glassboro State College. It changed its name in 1992, after industrialist Henry Rowan gave the New Jersey school $100 million. As alumni of your school, you will certainly hear from the fundraising office.

In addition to donations, schools can also raise funds by issuing bonds. The advantage of bonds is that a school can raise a large amount of financial capital in a very short amount of time. It can take many years to raise the funds needed for a new building using donations if no single major donor steps forward. The disadvantage of bonds is that they represent debt that the school must repay. The more debt a school has, the less flexibility it has to adopt new strategies in the future.

Critical-Thinking Questions

1. Are bonds issued by colleges and universities high-risk or low-risk? Why?
2. What is the incentive for alumni to supply the financial capital that colleges and universities demand, given that they are no longer students?

►SUMMARY

- **Why firms seek funds.** Firms use financial markets to raise funds when they do not have enough cash on hand to purchase needed physical capital. Because physical capital typically lasts for many periods, the value of the capital must be determined by calculating the present value of the intended investment and comparing it to the cost. The net present value of a stream of revenue received in the future must take into account the opportunity cost of capital. Firms should pursue only those projects with a positive net present value.

- **Raising funds using loans.** Firms can raise financial capital using loans from financial institutions such as banks. The advantage to the firm of using a loan is that it does not dilute the ownership of the company. Banks set the interest rates on the loans in part based on how risky they believe the loan to be. As the probability of default increases, the interest rate charged increases as well.

- **Raising funds using bonds.** A bond is a debt that requires the borrower to repay the lender over a set time period. In the case of a bond, the firm borrows directly from many lenders. Bonds pay a fixed coupon payment over the life of the bond, plus a fixed sum when the bond matures. As with a bank loan, the sale of bonds does not dilute the ownership of the company.

- **Raising funds through stock sales.** Firms can raise funds by selling a share of ownership in the form of shares of stock. When stocks are initially issued, the firm receives the proceeds. Stocks are also traded in secondary markets such as the NASDAQ. When stocks are bought and sold in the secondary market, the original firm is uninvolved in the transaction. Stocks do not carry with them a promise of repayment as in a bond or loan, but they do dilute the ownership of the firm, distributing it among shareholders.

- **Venture capital.** Firms can also obtain financial capital through venture capitalists, who offer expertise and financial resources in exchange for a share of ownership in the firm.

- **The asymmetric information and principal–agent problem.** When ownership and management are separated, as in the case of a public corporation in which ownership is determined by stock shares, principal–agent problems can arise due to information asymmetry. Shareholders must work to ensure that the managers of the firm are working in the best interest of the shareholders. To do so, they appoint a board of directors to oversee the management team.

PROBLEMS

1. If the current interest rate is eight percent, which of the following would make you better off: receiving $300 today or receiving $325 in one year?

2. Which is more profitable, an investment that pays $1,000 in year one and $1,500 in year two, or an investment that pays $1,300 in year one and $1,100 in year two? Assume that no initial expenditure is required and that the interest rate is six percent. Does your answer change if the firm must make an initial expenditure of $2,000 at the beginning of year one?

3. A city is thinking of building a new aquarium. The building will cost $1 million to build and will bring the city net revenues of $525,000 for each of the next two years. For simplicity, assume that the expense of building the aquarium occurs immediately and that all revenues are paid once a year starting one year from today.
   a. If interest rates are five percent, should the city build the aquarium?
   b. What happens to your answer if the interest rate is three percent?

4. Why do banks insist on collateral from their borrowers? How might the need for collateral prevent banks from some socially desirable loans, such as those made to college students for their tuition?

5. Why might a firm borrow by issuing bonds rather than going to a bank? Why might it prefer issuing bonds to selling stock?

6. Why might an investor prefer buying bonds to buying stock?

7. What benefits, if any, does a firm receive when a bondholder sells for $125 a bond that the firm had issued the previous year for $100?

8. Would a firm with a AAA bond rating pay a higher or lower interest rate than a firm with a Caa rating? Why?

9. Why would an investor choose to purchase a bond with a higher risk rating than one with a lower risk rating?

10. How did Google benefit from the venture capitalist Andreas Bechtolsheim? How did Bechtolsheim benefit from his actions?

11. How do corporations avoid some of the risks that a sole proprietorship or partnership faces?

12. Why might an investor prefer buying stock to buying bonds?

13. How does the stock market provide information about investors' expectations regarding a firm's future performance?

14. a. Which company in Table 14.2 experienced a larger increase in the price of its shares on February 8, 2005? Justify your answer.

    b. Which company in Table 14.2 had experienced a larger year-to-date increase in its share price?

15. How does the separation of ownership from management lead to the principal–agent problem? How can boards of directors help to resolve the problem?

16. What problems sometimes prevent boards of directors from resolving the principal–agent problem?

17. Why might an auto insurance company not want to insure drivers of a new car that is advertised as being almost impossible to damage in an accident?

18. Use supply and demand curves to explain what would happen to a company's stock price when it reports losing money in the previous quarter. Can you think of a reason why the company might actually see its stock price rise when it makes the announcement?

HERE'S HOW MyEconLab CAN HELP YOU GET A BETTER GRADE

1. Log into MyEconLab and take Practice Test chapter-A (to log in for the first time, see page 30 for instructions.)

2. Based on your test results, MyEconLab will identify the areas where you need further work and create a personal Study Plan for you.

3. Your Study Plan contains the exercises listed below and others like them that will target the specific chapter topics you need to focus on. You'll receive instant feedback and find links to tutorials, animations, and the online textbook to help you study.

4. When you're ready, go take Practice Test chapter-B and demonstrate how your results have improved.

Section 14.1, Exercise 1 Identify each of the following items as an example of financial capital, physical capital, or neither.

a. 100 shares of Kodak stock
b. A factory
c. A computer
d. An apple
e. A $10,000 bond issued by the State of New York

Section 14.1, Exercise 2 Congratulations! You have won the lottery. You have a choice of receiving a $1,500 payment every year for the next three years (beginning right now), or receiving instead a lump-sum payment of $4,000 now. Which would you prefer:

a. . . . if the interest rate is 10 percent?
b. . . . if the interest rate is 20 percent?

Section 14.1, Exercise 3 Find the net present value of each of the following projects. Assume that the interest rate is 10 percent.

    a. A $10,000 investment now will bring revenue of $15,000 in two years.

    b. A $10,000 investment now will bring a payment of $7,000 one year from now and a second payment of $8,000 two years from now.

Section 14.1, Exercise 4 Identify each of the following statements as true or false.

    a. As the interest rate increases, investment will rise.

    b. If you don't have to borrow money to invest in a project, the interest rate is zero.

Section 14.2, Exercise 1 Why do credit cards charge higher interest rates on loans than banks do?

Section 14.3, Exercise 1 Why would a firm sell bonds rather than issuing stock?

Section 14.3, Exercise 2 A firm issues a bond that matures in one year. The maturity value of the bond is $1,000. If your opportunity cost of funds is 10 percent, what is the most that you would be willing to pay for the bond?

Section 14.4, Exercise 1 Why would a firm issue stock rather than selling bonds?

Section 14.4, Exercise 2 What determines the price that investors are willing to pay for a stock?

Section 14.4, Exercise 3 Identify each of the following statements as true or false.

    a. A rising stock market can make consumers feel more wealthy, and therefore they will spend more.

    b. A rising stock market can be seen as a sign of optimism about the economy and future income, and thus cause consumers to spend more.

    c. The value of every stock will rise when the stock market is rising.

    d. A profitable year for a company might not cause the value of its stock to rise.

    e. A rise in the value of a stock makes company profits rise.

Section 14.5, Exercise 1 Why would a company raise money through venture capital rather than through stock or bonds?

Section 14.6, Exercise 1 In corporations, management is generally separate from ownership. How does this create a principal–agent problem?

15

Labor Markets

In preceding chapters, you saw how price and output were determined in a single output market. We examined the unique characteristics of the fish, baseball, cheesesteak, and video game console markets and showed how these characteristics are influenced by the nature of the good being bought and sold. In these examples, we focused strictly on the output. In Chapter 14, we turned our attention to decisions made inside the firm to examine capital investment choices. In this chapter, we examine labor markets and a firm's need to create the optimal mix of labor and capital to meet the larger goal of profit maximization. Whether it's Pike Place Fish Market, the Atlanta Braves, John's cheesesteaks shop, or any other business, profit-maximizing firms must decide how much capital and labor they need. To see how these decisions are made, we focus on the dilemma of Marlon, owner of Convenient Carriers, Inc. Marlon's first product is a nylon carrying case for MP3 players.

Marlon is focused on increasing his profits. The business has been earning a small profit that he'd like to increase for as long as the MP3 player boom lasts. Marlon knows he must create the largest difference possible between total revenue and total cost to maximize profits, but how? We'll assume that there is no product differentiation, creating a perfectly competitive market. Thus, raising prices is not a viable option. To increase profits, he must concentrate on keeping costs to a minimum. Marlon has already gotten the best deals he can on the materials for the player cases.

His hiring strategy—increasing production through increased spending on labor resources—is the main variable under his control. Marlon must determine if additional labor costs would result in higher profits for the company.

As we focus on the labor market in this chapter, you will see that he can use some very simple rules to ensure that he chooses the best combination of inputs. On the demand side of the labor market, we will generalize Marlon's hiring decisions to create a profit maximization rule for all firms. On the supply side, we will develop a simple model of how workers decide how much labor to supply at any given wage rate. We then briefly discuss the firm's input choices in the long run. Finally, we will apply our labor market model to determine the impact of education and training on workers' wages and discuss the influence of unions.

ALONG THE WAY, YOU WILL ALSO LEARN:

- How the marginal product of labor and marginal revenue together determine the demand for labor.
- How the value that workers place on their leisure time affects the supply of labor.
- How product price and marginal product affect equilibrium in the labor market.
- How firms decide on the optimal mix of capital, technology, and labor in the long run.
- Why some workers are paid more than others.
- The purpose of unions and their effect on labor market outcomes.

AT THE END OF THE CHAPTER, THE MYECONLAB LOGO WILL DIRECT YOU ONLINE

- MyEconLab is a resource-packed online homework and tutorial system that can help you perform better in your economics course. To log in for the first time, see page 30 for instructions.
- MyEconLab can help you apply important concepts from the chapter to real-world issues. Watch for the logo to indicate online features about the labor market.
- At the end of each chapter, you'll find a special study section that will help you get the most out of your textbook and your instructor's MyEconLab course.

▶The Demand for Labor in the Short Run

In this section, we use the supply and demand model to show how Marlon's firm chooses the optimal amount of labor in the short run when it operates with a fixed amount of capital. How many workers should Marlon hire to maximize his firm's profits? Later in the chapter, we examine the long-run demand for inputs.

Derived demand
Labor demand is derived from consumers' demand for the final product.

We analyze the demand for labor in a market first by considering the demand for labor by individual firms. Labor demand is a **derived demand**: The demand for labor is derived from consumers' demand for the final product. When consumers demand more output, the price of the output produced increases. When the price of output increases, labor services become more valuable to the firms. Firms respond by demanding more labor. Specifically, the quantity of labor that a firm demands is determined by two factors: labor productivity and output price.

Labor Productivity

A key component of a firm's demand for labor is the productivity of labor. Recall from Chapter 8 that economists measure worker productivity as the additional output produced by one more unit of labor. This additional output is called the marginal product of labor, or *MPL*. In the short run, the *MPL* may increase at first. It eventually declines due to the Law of Diminishing Marginal Returns. Recall that the Law of Diminishing Marginal Returns states that as more and more units of a variable input are combined with a fixed quantity of other inputs, the marginal product of the variable input must eventually decline. As more and more units of labor are added, capital becomes increasingly overutilized. Each added unit of labor is therefore less productive than the last.

To illustrate, let's return to Convenient Carriers, Inc. When Marlon increases the number of sewing-machine operators he employs in the short run, each additional employee increases total output by less and less. We can see the impact of additional machine operators on output in columns 1 and 2 of Table 15.1, which show the quantity of labor and marginal product of labor at Convenient Carriers, Inc.

In the short run, there is a fixed number of sewing machines, cutting machines, and packing machines. Each additional employee that Marlon adds must use the equipment more and more intensively. Initially it may be highly advantageous from an efficiency standpoint to add labor. Eventually, however, inefficiency results when some workers are idle, waiting for their turn to use the equipment and space. As a result, after diminishing returns set in, the additional labor is less and less productive. When Marlon employs one machine operator, his firm produces only two MP3 player cases per hour. The marginal product of the second worker is four cases per hour. Together, the two workers produce a total of six cases per hour. For now, though, we'll stay focused on the marginal benefit of adding another worker, not on the total benefit. The third worker causes output to increase by seven MP3 player cases per hour, and

TABLE 15.1

Profit-Maximizing Choice of Labor for Convenient Carriers, Inc.

L, Quantity of Labor (1)	MPL, Marginal Product of Labor (in MP3 cases per hour) (2)	P, Price of MP3 Cases (in dollars) (3)	VMPL = P × MPL (in dollars) (4)	W, Hourly Wage Rate (5)
0	—	8	—	24
1	2	8	16	24
2	4	8	32	24
3	7	8	56	24
4	9	8	72	24
5	10	8	80	24
6	8	8	64	24
7	5	8	40	24
8	3	8	24	24
9	2	8	16	24
10	1	8	8	24
11	0	8	0	24

so on. In this case, *MPL* is highest for the fifth worker and decreases thereafter. Diminishing marginal returns thus set in after the fifth worker. The marginal product of labor reaches zero at the eleventh worker. Thus, diminishing *total* returns set in after the eleventh worker. Hiring more than 11 workers would not make sense under any circumstances. Any additional workers would cause output to fall. There would be so many workers that they would end up interfering with one another.

Marginal Revenue Product of Labor

We now examine the influence of output price on labor demand. The marginal product of labor is only one factor in Marlon's decision of how many workers to hire. The measure of *MPL* in column 2 of Table 15.1 uses physical units—cases produced per hour. To determine the change in revenue resulting from a change in the quantity of labor employed, Marlon must translate the amount of cases an additional worker produces into the dollar value this output brings. He can then compare that value to the cost (the wages of another worker).

Marginal revenue product of labor (MRPL)
The product of the marginal revenue and marginal product (MR × MPL).

The additional revenue that results from employing an additional unit of labor is called the **marginal revenue product of labor (MRPL)**. *MRPL* is determined by multiplying the marginal revenue by the marginal product ($MR \times MPL$). We showed in Chapter 9 that $MR = P$, in perfectly competitive markets. In industries that sell their output in perfectly competitive markets, the *MRPL* is computed by multiplying the price per unit and the marginal product ($P \times MPL$). Because the output price is the market value of the output, the *MRPL* is also known as the **value of marginal product of labor (VMPL)** for a perfectly competitive market. The *MRPL* and *VMPL* tell the firm the dollar value of the additional output produced by one more worker. If MP3 player cases sell for $8 each, we multiply the marginal product figures from column 2 of Table 15.1 by the $8 price in column 3 to find the *VMPL* of Convenient Carriers, shown in column 4.

Value of marginal product of labor (VMPL)
The product of the price per unit and marginal product ($P \times MPL$), which tells a firm in a perfectly competitive market the dollar value of the additional output produced by one more worker.

The Short-Run Labor Demand Curve and Hiring Decisions

Now that we've determined the *VMPL* of Marlon's workers, we can address the issue of how many workers he should hire. We know that Marlon maximizes his profits when he produces output until the marginal revenue of the last unit produced just equals the marginal cost of producing the last unit. By this reasoning, he should hire labor up to the point where the extra revenue generated by the workers just equals the extra cost they impose. In terms of our model, *VMPL* is the marginal benefit, and the wage rate, *W*, is the marginal cost. Thus, Marlon continues to hire labor until the *VMPL* in column 4 of Table 15.1 is just equal to the cost of the labor, *W*, shown in column 5. For now, let's assume that the equilibrium wage in this market is $24 per hour. We explore how this wage rate is determined later in the chapter. At $24 per hour, Marlon will hire eight workers (the highlighted row in Table 15.1).[1] Recall that demand is the quantity that consumers (here, the firm is the consumer) purchase at various prices, all else equal. In this case, "all else equal" implies that capital is fixed. The *VMPL* curve is therefore the firm's short-run demand curve for labor. Based on the data in Table 15.1, if wages rise to $40 per hour, the firm hires seven workers. If wages fall to $16 per hour, the firm hires nine workers.

---

[1] For most workers, actual cash wages are only a portion of the total compensation that they receive. Our $24 per hour as compensation is a simplifying assumption that overlooks employee benefits.

Although the *VMPL* of the second worker is also $16, no employer will want to stop hiring workers if adding another worker *increases* marginal product. For example, the marginal product of labor rises when Marlon increases his workforce from three to four workers. As a result, the fourth worker is more valuable to Marlon than the third (as long as the wage and the price of output do not change). Thus, employers search for the point where *VMPL* = *W* on the portion of the curve where *VMPL* is decreasing.

We plot hourly wage rates and the *VMPL* information from Table 15.1 on a graph in Figure 15.1. Marlon hires labor at a wage rate of $24 until the added cost of the last worker just offsets the revenue the worker generates. This occurs at the eighth worker. Although he might be tempted to do so, Marlon should not stop hiring when he reaches the worker with the highest marginal product (the fifth worker). Hiring the sixth worker adds more to Marlon's revenue ($64) than to his cost ($24).

Short-Run Market Demand Curve for Labor

What does our information about Marlon's short-run labor demand indicate about the market for sewing-machine operators? If the demand curve for labor is downward-sloping for each firm, we know that the market demand for labor is also downward-sloping. All firms in the market demand more labor as wages fall. Figure 15.2 shows the market demand curve for sewing-machine operators in the Dallas area. This demand curve includes Marlon's employees as well as those of all the other local firms that hire sewing-machine operators. If there are 25 firms in the Dallas area with demand curves identical to that of Convenient Carriers, and all employees work 8 hours per day, the market demand for labor is 1,600 hours of labor (25 firms × 8 workers × 8 hours per day) at a wage of $24 per hour.

So far, we have assumed that the going wage for sewing-machine operators is $24 per hour. As with the prices of most goods and services, the forces of supply and demand together determine the price of labor. We must therefore turn to the supply of labor to complete our labor market model.

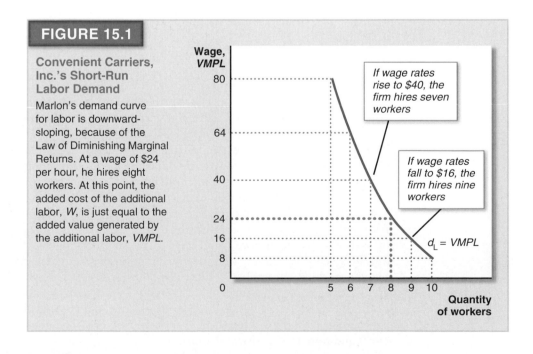

FIGURE 15.1

Convenient Carriers, Inc.'s Short-Run Labor Demand

Marlon's demand curve for labor is downward-sloping, because of the Law of Diminishing Marginal Returns. At a wage of $24 per hour, he hires eight workers. At this point, the added cost of the additional labor, *W*, is just equal to the added value generated by the additional labor, *VMPL*.

If wage rates rise to $40, the firm hires seven workers

If wage rates fall to $16, the firm hires nine workers

$d_L = VMPL$

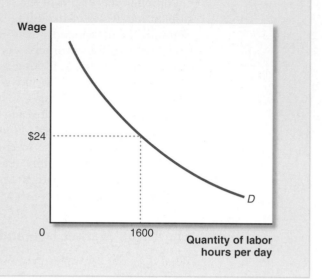

FIGURE 15.2

Market Labor Demand in the Dallas Area

The market demand curve for sewing-machine operator labor is the combined demand of all firms in the Dallas area. It is downward-sloping, because each firm's demand curve for labor is downward-sloping. If all employees work 8-hour days and there are 25 firms (including Marlon's) the total demand for labor is 8 × 8 × 25 = 1,600 hours per day when the wage is $24 per hour.

The Supply of Labor in the Short Run

We now focus on the supply side of the labor market. In product markets, profit-maximizing firms decide how much output they are willing to supply by comparing marginal revenue (which equals price in competitive markets) with marginal cost. Workers make a similar comparison based on how they value their time. We begin by illustrating the workers' decisions with the individual labor supply curve.

Individual Labor Supply

The first step in determining the individual labor supply curve is considering how individual workers allocate their time between work and leisure. We assume that individuals allocate their time to maximize their utility or happiness, rather than their profits or income. There are only 24 hours in a day, and each of us must divide those hours among competing uses. When you spend more time working for pay, you earn more money. As you increase the number of hours spent working for pay, you have less time to enjoy leisure and perform household duties.

Work Time Versus Leisure Time. To simplify the model, we assume that an individual worker can either work in the labor market for an hourly wage or consume leisure. Time spent working for pay provides income, but no utility. It may seem odd to say that someone "consumes leisure." Recall, however, that people allocate resources to activities that increase their utility. Leisure certainly provides utility. Although we do not pay for it directly, it is not free. The *opportunity cost* of an hour of leisure is the income we could have earned by working for that hour. To see the link between labor supply and the consumption of leisure, suppose that Aditya is a sewing-machine operator in Dallas. He allocates his time between working for pay and reading books (his favorite leisure activity). If Aditya had unlimited financial resources, he would always choose to read rather than work. However, he needs to earn money to support himself, and so he must work. The question is how much to work and how much leisure to consume?

Aditya can best allocate his time by comparing the marginal value of the last hour spent at each activity. The opportunity cost of an additional hour of leisure is equal to the wages he would earn if he spent the hour working. For now, we continue to assume that sewing-machine operators earn $24 per hour. Thus, the opportunity cost of each hour of leisure is constant at $24. The opportunity cost of an additional hour of work is the value of the lost leisure time, which must equal $24 in equilibrium.

In Chapter 7, we learned that the marginal utility derived from consuming an additional unit of any good eventually declines. The same principle holds for consuming leisure. The more time Aditya spends reading, the less he values yet another hour of reading. Thus, in Table 15.2, we see that as labor hours decrease (and time spent consuming leisure increases), the value Aditya places on the marginal utility of the additonal leisure falls. When Aditya supplies no labor, his leisure time is equal to 24 hours. Because he has so much leisure, the value of the first hour of leisure lost when Aditya works 1 hour is very low: only $4. Because he can earn the wage rate of $24 by sacrificing leisure worth only $4, he happily works that hour. For the first 7 hours that Aditya works, the value of his leisure lost is less than the wage. For the eighth hour of work, the value he places on the lost leisure is just equal to the wage he earns: $24. Thus, he chooses to work 8 hours and consume 16 hours of leisure. Aditya maximizes his utility by working 8 hours per day.

Individual Labor Supply Curve. We can also use the information in the second column of Table 15.2 to see how many hours Aditya would be willing and able to work at wage rates other than $24 per hour. If the wage were $11 per hour, Aditya would work only 5 hours per day. If the wage were $40 per hour, he would work 10 hours per day. We use the information in the table to plot Aditya's individual labor supply curve. Remember that a supply curve shows the quantity that a seller will offer at different prices. In this case, the individual supply curve indicates how much labor

TABLE 15.2

Marginal Utility of Leisure Versus Work

L, Quantity of Labor (in hours)	Value of Marginal Utility of Leisure Time (in dollars)	W, Wage Rate per Hour (in dollars)
0	—	24
1	4	24
2	5	24
3	6	24
4	8	24
5	11	24
6	15	24
7	19	24
8	**24**	**24**
9	32	24
10	40	24
—	—	24
24	240	24

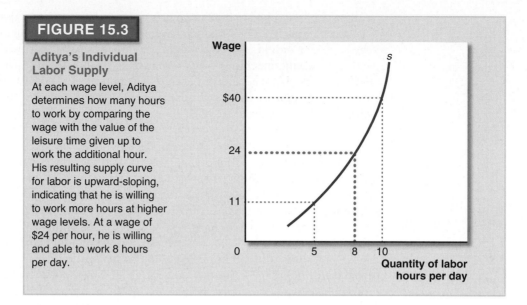

FIGURE 15.3

Aditya's Individual Labor Supply

At each wage level, Aditya determines how many hours to work by comparing the wage with the value of the leisure time given up to work the additional hour. His resulting supply curve for labor is upward-sloping, indicating that he is willing to work more hours at higher wage levels. At a wage of $24 per hour, he is willing and able to work 8 hours per day.

a worker will offer at various wages. Figure 15.3 shows Aditya's labor supply curve. Like most supply curves, it is upward-sloping. The higher the wage, the more hours Aditya is willing to work. Notice also that the curve becomes steeper at higher wages. In fact at very high wage rates, individual labor supply curves can even bend backwards as individuals decrease labor supply in order to "purchase" more leisure time.

Market Supply for the Labor Market

By adding the hours that all workers in a given market are willing to work at various wage levels, we arrive at the market labor supply. We show the market supply curve for the labor market in Figure 15.4. At a wage of $24 per hour, a total of 1,600 hours are supplied. To simplify the model, we have assumed that all workers have identical preferences. In reality, each individual has his or her own preferences for work and leisure. As a result, we cannot multiply the hours worked by one individual by the size of the labor force to obtain the total labor supply. The market supply of labor is the sum of all individual labor supply curves.

BORN LOSER: © Newspaper Enterprise Association, Inc.

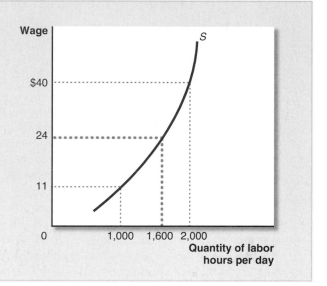

FIGURE 15.4

Market Labor Supply Curve

The market supply curve for labor is equal to the sum of all of the individual supply curves for labor. Both the individual supply curves and the market supply curve for labor are upward-sloping. When the wage is $24 per hour, the total supply is 1,600 hours per day.

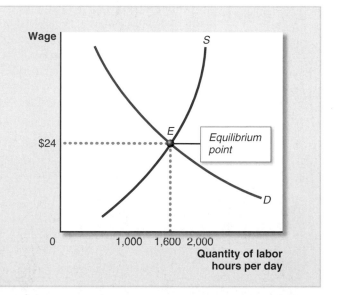

FIGURE 15.5

Equilibrium in the Labor Market

The labor market equilibrium occurs at the point of intersection of the market labor demand and supply curves. The equilibrium wage is $24 per hour, and firms utilize 1,600 worker hours per day.

▶ Equilibrium in the Labor Market

As with any market, the intersection of the supply and demand curves determines the equilibrium point in the labor market. Figure 15.5 combines the market demand curve from Figure 15.2 with the market supply curve from Figure 15.4. It shows the equilibrium wage of $24 per hour and the equilibrium quantity of labor of 1,600 hours of labor per day. Like the other market equilibria we have examined, the labor market equilibrium is stable. The wage remains at $24 per hour unless some outside force causes a change in supply or demand. And, as with a product, the equilibrium is self-correcting. If the wage were set too high, there would be a surplus of workers, and wages would fall back to $24 to restore the equilibrium. If the wage were set too low, there would be a shortage of workers and firms would bid wages back up to $24. We discuss the main factors that affect demand and supply in the following sections.

Changes in the Market Demand for Labor

We know that the competitive firm's demand for labor is determined by multiplying output price by marginal product to find *VMPL*. As a result, changes in product price and the productivity of labor at the firm level affect market demand for labor.

Product Price. If a change in the product market alters a product's price, the demand for labor also shifts. When the output price rises, labor demand rises. When the output price falls, labor demand falls. For example, in the economic slowdown from March 2001 to September 2001, many firms faced a decrease in demand for their products. The decrease in the demand for output (a leftward shift of the demand curve for the products) caused product prices to fall. The demand for the labor needed to produce and sell the products decreased as well. At the market level, the decline in demand for labor led to layoffs and unemployment. This downturn contrasted sharply with the boom of the 1990s. At that time, firms experienced increasing demand for their products. This higher demand in turn created higher demand for labor, so employment and wages both rose.

Marginal Product. The demand for labor also increases if labor becomes more productive. Suppose that a new training video demonstrates a faster way to sew an MP3 player case. All workers who see the video can now produce 30 percent more cases per hour. At the market level, suppose that all firms have access to the video and use it to improve their productivity. The market demand curve for labor will shift to the right.

During World War II, Female Labor Force Participation Increased Dramatically

(a) Rosie the Riveter.

(b) Many women worked in heavy industries such as shipbuilding.

Market Supply Changes in the Labor Market

We now turn to factors that affect the labor market supply. At the individual level, workers decide how much they want to work by evaluating the trade-off between income and time away from work. In reality, workers may not always be able to choose the amount of hours they work. They must instead choose between working full-time and working part-time. Over the length of a career, however, workers have some control over the total number of hours they work.

If workers as a group develop a greater preference for leisure, the labor market supply curve shifts to the left and wages rise. If workers develop a greater preference for income, the labor market supply curve shifts to the right and wages fall. These preferences for leisure and income affect the total labor supply. We next examine two specific trends impacting total labor supply: the participation of women and of immigrants in the U.S. workforce.

Increased Female Labor Force Participation. The single biggest change in the labor market over the last 40 years has been the dramatic increase in the female labor force participation rate, or the percentage of women who are willing and able to work. This trend is especially prevalent among married women and women with children. Few women, particularly married women with children, worked outside the home in 1960. This was not the case during the mid-1940s. The famous poster of "Rosie the Riveter" urged women to join the labor force during World War II. Many women did just that. But soon after the war ended and the men who had been fighting returned, most women returned to a more traditional role in the home. More permanent changes in the economic status of women occurred in the tumultuous 1960s. Since then, women have increasingly pursued degrees in previously male-dominated fields and applied their skills to the job market. Increases in female labor force participation over a wider variety of occupations increased the supply of labor in those fields, which helped to meet the demand for labor in the economy.

Immigration. If the demand for labor is very different in two parts of one country, or in two different countries, wages in the two areas may also vary widely. Workers then have an incentive to migrate to where the wages are highest. For example, suppose that workers in Mexico can earn much higher wages by working in the United States. Mexican workers have an incentive to cross the U.S.–Mexico border to find jobs. Ever since the industrial revolution of the 1800s, workers have immigrated in large numbers to the United States from virtually every part of the world. They have come in search of higher wages and the better living conditions made possible by those wages.

In Europe, workers often migrate from less-developed countries such as Turkey to more industrialized economies, such as Germany, Spain, and the Netherlands, in search of higher wages. These more industrialized countries experience chronic shortages of native-born workers. To meet their labor shortages, the countries have invited temporary workers to work there for long periods of time without ever becoming citizens. By the mid-1990s, temporary workers composed more than 10 percent of the total labor force in many European countries.

Our labor market model can help us understand the movement of workers across national boundaries. In Spain, for example, 25 percent of the labor force is made up of temporary immigrant workers. With no immigration and a relatively low supply of industrial labor, high wages mean high costs for firms. These high wages reduce firms' profit-maximizing output level. Immigration pushes wages down, causing the supply curve of labor to shift to the right. The new equilibrium quantity of labor is higher, causing output to increase.

Because the additional workers cause wages to fall, it is not surprising that workers in the countries that import labor oppose the free movement of labor into their countries. Over time, an influx of workers from other countries might not reduce wages if the economy is growing. Instead, it might slow the growth of wages in occupations with high concentrations of immigrants. Wages in high-immigrant occupations may fall behind other occupations, but wages may still be growing overall.

TEST + *EXTEND* Your Knowledge

1. TEST Some cities and states have reputations for granting very high jury awards in malpractice suits. These suits drive up the cost of malpractice insurance and can even make such insurance difficult to obtain. As a result, physicians are leaving those areas to pursue medical careers elsewhere. For example, between 1994 and 2001, the median award in a malpractice suit in the city of Philadelphia was $973,000, compared to a median of $410,000 for the rest of Pennsylvania. Attempts to pass legislation that would limit awards have had only limited success. What is likely to happen to the market for physicians in Philadelphia if doctors continue to leave the city? Use the supply and demand model to support your answer.

How might this change affect the price of health care?

2. EXTEND Suppose that instead of leaving the city, physicians decide to stay and pay the higher insurance costs. If the cost of the insurance is fixed (it does not change with the number of patients who are treated), what do you predict about the quantity of labor supplied to the market by physicians? Explain, using the concepts of fixed, marginal, and average total cost. To simplify the analysis, you may assume that physicians can supply more labor to the market with no decrease in the fee per visit they receive.

▶ The Demand for Labor, Technology, and Capital in the Long Run

Labor is only one of the factors of production that firms use to produce goods and services. Recall from Chapter 2 that land, physical capital, and entrepreneurship are the three other factors of production. In the short run, labor is the only input that is variable (easily changed). Therefore, in the short run, firms must produce using the physical capital and technology on hand. In the long run, all inputs are variable. In the long run, firms decide how much physical capital and labor to use in order to produce output at the lowest possible cost. In this section, we look at the demand for labor and capital. In the process, we complete our picture of the labor market with the long-run view.

Technology as an Input

Embedded technology
Technology that is part of capital rather than being a physical commodity in and of itself.

Technology is not itself a physical commodity. Economists thus usually refer to **embedded technology** in machinery to indicate that technology is part of the capital itself. When a firm purchases a new computer, its stock of capital and technology both increase. The purchase may add to the existing stock of computers, or it may replace an old machine. In both cases, the computer and the current technology (as measured by factors like processor speed, hard drive size, and monitor resolution) embedded in the machinery increase the productive capacity of the firm. For the remainder of this chapter, we will consider technology to be part of capital.

The Demand for Capital

In the long run, firms must determine the optimal combination of all inputs. The demand for capital is based on the firm's desire to minimize the cost of producing output. Thus, it employs both labor and capital up to the point where the extra output it receives in return for the expenditure on the input is the same. For example, Marlon would not want to continue to hire another operator if he could purchase a new machine that, at lower cost, would increase output by more than that extra worker. This concept is very similar to the equimarginal principal that we encountered in Chapter 7, in which consumers maximized utility by consuming each good up to the point where the marginal utilities per dollar were equal.

In the case of a firm engaged in production, the firm is attempting to minimize cost. The firm would like to employ each input up to the point where the marginal productivity per dollar is equal. Thus, the cost-minimizing rule for any given level of output is:

- If the marginal product of capital per dollar is greater than the marginal product of labor per dollar, add more capital.
- If the marginal product of labor per dollar is greater than the marginal product of capital per dollar, hire more labor.
- If the marginal product of capital per dollar is equal to the marginal product of labor per dollar, the cost of producing that output level is minimized.

We summarize the demand for inputs as follows:

- As the demand for output increases, product price increases, which increases the demand for inputs.
- As the productivity of an input increases, its value to the firm increases, which increases the demand for that input.

Firms demand more of an input when it becomes more productive. How does an increase in demand for one input affect the demand for the other inputs? The following sections discuss the two possible effects related to whether capital is a complement to or substitute for labor.

Capital as a Complement to Labor. If a firm increases its stock of capital, labor may become more productive, resulting in an increase in the demand for labor. If the new machinery is a complement to labor, it will make labor more productive. The increase in the marginal product of labor increases *VMPL*, leading to a higher demand for labor. For example, a new automobile paint sprayer that works faster and that can improve the finish on cars may increase the demand for auto painters. In the long run, when more capital is added, labor productivity increases and firms therefore have the incentive to add more labor.

Capital as a Substitute for Labor. New technologies may also result in decreased demand for certain types of labor, as firms elect to substitute capital for labor. That is, it may be cheaper for the firm to use more machines and fewer people. A good example of this type of substitution is the use of precut or prefabricated materials in the home construction industry. Around the world, the use of these materials has greatly reduced the need for onsite labor. In Sweden, the working time per cubic meter of new construction has thus fallen by more than 30 percent since 1960.

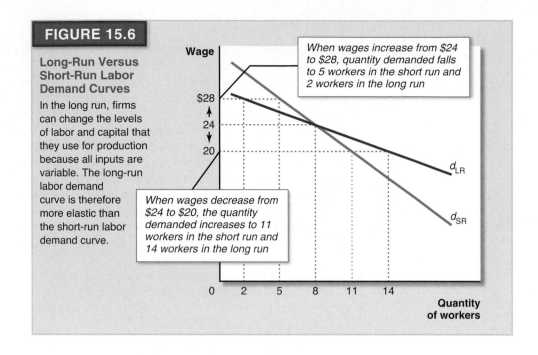

FIGURE 15.6

Long-Run Versus Short-Run Labor Demand Curves

In the long run, firms can change the levels of labor and capital that they use for production because all inputs are variable. The long-run labor demand curve is therefore more elastic than the short-run labor demand curve.

When wages increase from $24 to $28, quantity demanded falls to 5 workers in the short run and 2 workers in the long run

When wages decrease from $24 to $20, the quantity demanded increases to 11 workers in the short run and 14 workers in the long run

Short-Run Versus Long-Run Labor Demand Curve

The net effect of technology on labor demand is that the long-run demand curve for labor is more sensitive to price changes (more elastic) than the short-run demand curve. Figure 15.6 shows a long-run (d_{LR}) and a short-run demand curve (d_{SR}) for labor. In the short run, when wages fall from $24 to $20, firms demand more labor but cannot combine that labor with a different level of capital. In the long run firms can switch from capital to the now less-expensive labor and use a more labor-intensive input mix when wages fall. Thus, instead of labor demand increasing from 8 to 11, labor demand increases to 14 workers. We observe a larger change in the long run than in the short run, because firms have more freedom to choose the least costly way to produce in the long run. When wages rise from $24 to $28, the short-run labor demand curve shows that the quantity of labor demanded falls to 5 workers. In the short run, firms are unable to substitute capital for the now more-expensive labor. In the long run, firms reduce the quantity of labor demanded to 2 workers, switching to a more capital-intensive mix, because labor is now relatively more expensive.

Education and Training

Now that we've built a model to analyze the market for labor, we can put it to use. However, we cannot analyze *the* market for all labor as if labor were a single, homogeneous input. Instead, the labor market is composed of many submarkets that are divided by occupation, skill level, and geography. Here, we focus on differences in skills. Keep in mind that the skills required to perform well in a specific occupation often help to determine the geographic limits of the market as well.

The existence of many labor markets means that we must define a specific labor market before we can analyze it. We also must be aware that not all workers are substitutes for one another. In this section, we clarify the characteristics that economists use to identify specific labor markets and then focus on the implications of education and training differences from the perspective of the firm (demand) and the worker (supply).

Human Capital and the Labor Market

Recall from Chapter 2 that economists refer to the skills that workers acquire as *human capital*. Human capital results from investment in education, training, and experience, which increase worker productivity. We use the word "capital" to indicate that workers invest in their skills, just as a firm might invest in its capital stock. A firm might purchase a new computer to improve productivity. A worker might invest in computer training to be able to make use of the new computer.

There are important differences in the skills required to perform various jobs. Nevertheless, occupation, skill level, and geography are all key components in defining a specific labor market. To see why, consider that neurosurgeons do not compete with sewing-machine operators for jobs. Similarly, the market for sewing-machine operators in San Francisco operates independently from the market for sewing-machine operators in Dallas. The geographic boundaries of the market for some occupations may be national or even international. However, these occupations tend to be highly specialized, such as the market for professors of Renaissance literature. Conversely, at lower or broader skill levels, markets tend to be more localized. If Marlon needs another sewing-machine operator in Dallas, he is unlikely to advertise in the *New York Times*.

The Firm's Perspective

We know that a firm's demand for labor stems in part from the productivity of labor. Workers invest in education and training to increase their productivity. The skills they acquire enable them to organize the work of others, perform complex tasks, and work in a wide variety of environments. Thus, customer service firms in Southern California are willing to pay more for workers who are fluent in both English and Spanish than for workers who can speak only one language. An architectural firm is willing to pay more for an architect who is trained to use computer-aided design (CAD) software than for one who draws by hand only.

Suppose that Marlon's firm wants to hire a new production supervisor with a specific skill set. As for any supervisory position, communication skills are essential. At the MP3 player case company, good communication skills require fluency in both English and Spanish. Marlon's firm could also produce more cases per hour if the manager were able to install and use a computer-based electronic inventory system. Finally, a candidate with production management experience would be able to coordinate effectively the activities of other workers.

The demand for managerial candidates varies with the skills that candidates possess. Labor productivity and labor demand rise as skills increase. Demand is greatest for individuals who are bilingual, have computer training, and have management experience.

The Workers' Perspective

Firms are not the only beneficiaries of increases in human capital. When workers invest in human capital, they gain access to occupations for which demand is high. Figure 15.7 presents the demand curves based on our example of Marlon's managerial candidates and the corresponding supply curves. To keep the focus on

FIGURE 15.7

Equilibrium in the Labor Market for Manager Candidates of Varying Skill Levels

Notice that the demand curves shift rightward from panels (a) through (d) as the skill level and labor productivity of managers increases. For simplicity, we assume that the supply curve in each panel is the same. As the demand curve shifts, the equilibrium wage rises as firms' willingness to pay increases.

(a) Workers with no special skills

Wage

S_L

$20

D_L

0

Quantity of labor

(b) Bilingual workers

Wage

S_L

$25

D_L

0

Quantity of labor

(c) Bilingual and computer skills

Wage

S_L

$30

D_L

0

Quantity of labor

(d) Bilingual, computer skills, and managerial experience

Wage

S_L

$35

D_L

0

Quantity of labor

demand, we assume that the supply of workers in each panel is the same.[2] Wages increase with worker productivity. Workers in panel (a) of Figure 15.7 earn $20 per hour. Bilingual workers, shown in panel (b), earn $25 per hour. Panel (c) shows that the addition of computer skills increases wages to $30 per hour. Finally, the wages for workers with all these skills plus managerial experience in panel (d) is $35. Remember that Marlon is willing to pay these higher wages because the different skills increase the manager's productivity ($VMPL$) and therefore the revenue brought to the firm. In reality, more highly skilled workers earn higher wages because of both higher demand *and* lower supply. There are far fewer experienced bilingual managers with strong computer skills than there are managers with no significant experience who speak only one language. When the supply of workers with the needed characteristics is low, those workers can command higher wages.

---

[2] In reality, the supply of workers decreases as the skill set for that group increases.

Education and Training Levels in Practice

Wages are greater in markets for highly skilled labor. As a result, it might seem logical for all workers to acquire the maximum amount of skill. However, the data on education—the most general form of human capital training—indicate just the opposite. As of 2003, about one-third of the U.S. population over the age of 18 had no more than a high-school education. About 19 percent received some college education but did not receive a degree. Another 17 percent completed college, and 8 percent pursued education beyond college. Given the clear benefit of increases in human capital, why are these education levels so low?

Workers make human capital decisions by investing up to the point where the marginal benefit (MB) of human capital just equals the marginal cost (MC). The marginal benefit of increased education can be very large, particularly beyond the college level. The marginal cost of attaining education rises with the level of education. The cost of obtaining human capital includes the direct cost (such as tuition and books), opportunity cost (wages forgone while attending school), and stress and workload associated with coursework. Workers who must give up full-time employment to attend college or graduate school may face very high opportunity costs. They must forgo higher and higher earnings to attain more and more education. For example, in 2003 an individual who attended college full-time gave up $23,673 in salary (the median annual salary available to workers with high-school degrees). An individual who attended graduate school gave up $40,588 per year (the median earnings of a college graduate). The earnings of individuals with post-graduate educations are much higher than those with college degrees. However, those individuals also bear a higher cost to obtain their higher level of education, and thus earnings.

Some individuals are simply better-equipped to complete higher levels of education and training than others. Some face financial constraints. For others, the difficulty and stress of obtaining a college education is not worth the increased earnings that they could obtain after graduation. In fact, research indicates that many individuals who do not pursue higher education have made the right decision, because they would not earn enough to make the investment worthwhile. Economists call this process **self-selection**: People who are more able to benefit from investments in human capital are more likely to select the option of investing in it. We will return to the distribution of wages in Chapter 16 in the context of a broader discussion of income distribution, wealth, and poverty.

Get Ahead of the Curve

Use the ideas you have learned about investment in human capital to analyze the problem of average U.S. educational levels.

Self-selection

Occurs when people who are more able to benefit from obtaining human capital invest in it more than people who are less able to benefit from such investments.

▶ Unions

Up to this point, our examination of the labor market has assumed that each worker makes a one-on-one bargain with an employer. Each individual is offered a wage and decides to accept or reject that offer independently of the decisions of other workers. The assumptions of this model are correct for most of the U.S. workforce. However, worker–employer relationships determined by a union are an important exception. A **union** is a non-profit organization of workers that enables them to bargain with management collectively, rather than as individuals. There are many different types of unions that work to promote the welfare of workers, including actors (the Screen Actors Guild), baseball players (the Major League Baseball Players Association), and automobile workers (the United Auto Workers). In this section, we introduce the goals and types of unions. We also discuss trends in U.S. union membership.

Union

Non-profit organization in which workers bargain with management collectively, rather than as individuals, in order to maximize the utility of union members.

LifeLessons

Higher Wages Might Mean Higher Risk

Have you ever wondered why the cafeteria jobs on campus pay more than the library jobs? Have you ever thought about a specific job or occupation and said to yourself, "I would never do that; it's too dangerous!"? Employment such as being a police officer in a major city, washing skyscraper windows, or working with hazardous waste materials is dangerous. Other jobs are less dangerous, but are less desirable simply because of the working conditions, such as jobs where it is very hot or very cold, or that require working late at night. All else equal, everyone would like to have a job that is safe and pleasant. So how do employers get workers to take the jobs that aren't?

Employers pay higher wages that include a compensating differential to entice workers to accept less desirable jobs. A compensating differential is a wage premium that employers pay to make up for undesirable job characteristics. Suppose that a firm offers carpenters $20 per hour. They work either indoors at ground level, or outside on a tall building, where they are exposed to the risk of falling and harsh weather conditions. The firm needs 10 carpenters for each job, but with wages equal for each job, no workers apply for the high-risk job. If the firm raises wages for both jobs, the problem remains.

To solve its problem, the firm must offer the high-risk workers more money. How much more? The answer depends on how many workers are willing to trade some risk for additional earnings. Not all workers are as averse to risk as others. By adding just enough of a compensating differential to fill the high-risk positions, the firm will attract the workers who are least averse to risk (or have the highest preference for income). These workers are compensated by higher pay for the undesirable job characteristics such as the risk of injury or uncomfortable working conditions. As a result, we cannot say they are worse off than the workers earning less money under better conditions. They accept more of these negative job characteristics for more pay.

Underwater Welding Is Risky Business

(a) Welders at traditional construction sites can earn wages...

(b) But underwater welders earn much more.

"The workers won't be happy that you've
turned their website suggestions into origami."

Courtesy www.CartoonStock.com

Goals of Unions

Collective bargaining
When workers negotiate with employers as a group rather than as individuals over wages, benefits, and working conditions.

Stated most broadly, the goal of a union is to maximize the utility of its members. Unions achieve this goal in part through a process called **collective bargaining**, which means that workers negotiate as a group, rather than as individuals, with employers over wages, benefits, and working conditions. Unions pursue specific strategies, such as increasing wages and benefits, lobbying government officials for pro-labor legislation, and reducing layoffs and plant closings. This pragmatic approach to union–management relations is known as "bread-and-butter" unionism. To the extent that unions are able to increase wages, they create a wage differential between the union and the non-union compensation in a given occupation.

Types of Unions

Unions fall into two basic categories: craft unions and industrial unions. Both types of unions attempt to increase bargaining power with employers, but they employ very different strategies.

Craft unions
A union organized around a specific skill or occupation.

Craft Unions. Craft unions increase their bargaining power through exclusiveness. They formalize membership in their occupations, and restrict access to work and skill acquisition by non-members. For example, a roofers' union might fight to exclude non-union labor from the maintenance of government buildings. This strategy increases the union's power by restricting the supply of labor, which leads to an increase in wages.

Industrial unions
A union organized around the workers in a specific industry.

Industrial Unions. Industrial unions work to increase bargaining power through inclusiveness. They work to ensure that all members of a given industry, such as the garment workers industry, are covered by a collective bargaining agreement. The union increases the power it gets from monopolizing the labor force if firms can employ only union workers. With more market power, unions are better able to bargain for higher wages, better benefits, and better working conditions.

TABLE 15.3

Union Affiliation of Employed Wage and Salary Workers 16 and Over by Selected Characteristics in 2004

Characteristic	Total Employed (in thousands)	Total Unionized (in thousands)	Percent of Employed Unionized
All workers	123,554	15,472	12.5
Men	64,145	8,878	13.8
Women	59,408	6,593	11.1
White	101,340	12,381	12.2
African American	14,090	2,130	15.1
Asian	5,280	603	11.4
Hispanic	16,533	1,676	10.1
Full-Time	101,224	14,029	13.9
Part-Time	22,047	1,406	6.4

Source: Bureau of Labor Statistics, Table 1 at www.bls.gov/news.release/union2.t01.htm

Union Participation Rates

Table 15.3 shows unionization rates for various demographic groups in 2004. We see from the table that men are more prevalent in unions than women. That said, some unions, such as the American Federation of Teachers, have many women members. Also notice that African Americans are more likely to be members of a union than other racial groups, while Hispanics are the least unionized. Finally, although more than 13 percent of the full-time labor force is unionized, less than 7 percent of the part-time labor force is unionized. This statistic helps to explain the difference in unionization rates between men and women, as women are more likely to work in part-time jobs than men.

Decline in U.S. Union Membership

U.S. union membership has declined steadily over the last 50 years. We can illustrate many reasons for this overall decline with a supply and demand framework. In Figure 15.8, we show the market for membership in a union. The demand for unions by workers is based on workers' expectation that union membership brings higher wages, better working conditions, and more benefits. The price of union membership is measured in the monthly dues that each member pays. The demand curve is downward-sloping because as monthly dues rise, fewer workers are willing and able to pay the dues. The supply curve slopes upward because, as monthly dues rise, unions can cover the cost of organizing workers in industries that are difficult to unionize. As a result, more union memberships become available. As the desirability of union membership declines, the demand curve for union membership shifts leftward from D_0 to D_1 in Figure 15.8.

Some of the decline has resulted from factors beyond unions' control. Growing competition from international trade has stiffened employers' opposition to union demands. This opposition has reduced the increased pay and job security that unions offer. In addition, unions were historically slow to adopt positions that would make them attractive to women, such as advocating day care for children and maternity

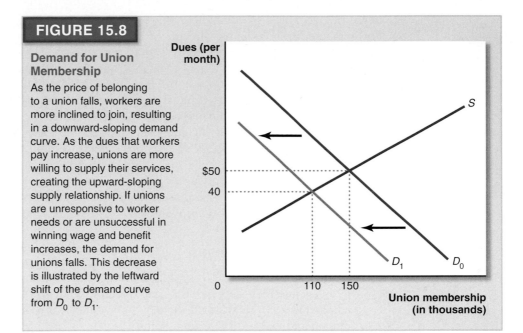

FIGURE 15.8

Demand for Union Membership

As the price of belonging to a union falls, workers are more inclined to join, resulting in a downward-sloping demand curve. As the dues that workers pay increase, unions are more willing to supply their services, creating the upward-sloping supply relationship. If unions are unresponsive to worker needs or are unsuccessful in winning wage and benefit increases, the demand for unions falls. This decrease is illustrated by the leftward shift of the demand curve from D_0 to D_1.

leave. These policies reduced the perceived value of unions to women. As the traditional base of union membership has declined, unions have begun to target women.

TEST + **E X T E N D** Your Knowledge

1. TEST Suppose that an industrial union is successful in organizing all workers in the U.S. lawnmower manufacturing industry. As a result, the union takes a very aggressive stance toward raising wages. How would this affect firms' costs and their ability to supply output?

2. E X T E N D Suppose that in response to this strategy, lawnmower manufacturers decide to move production to China, where wages are lower. Show the effect of this decision on the demand for U.S. union membership.

Strategy and Policy
Temporary Workers in the United States

As discussed earlier, many European nations have long issued temporary visas to foreign guest workers to fill the jobs that domestic employers find hard to staff. Early in 2004, President George W. Bush proposed a similar program for the United States. Under his proposal, many individuals currently working illegally in the United States would be granted temporary legal status for a period of at least three years. Some experts claim that such a policy further exploits poor workers from countries like Mexico. Others believe that the proposed law provides a steady source of workers to industries that struggle to find a willing labor force. It also offers both workers and their employers a mechanism to legitimize pre-existing relationships.

The validity of these arguments is a matter of debate. It is notable that the proposal has drawn support and opposition from both ends of the political spectrum. Some opponents of the law argue that it fails to fully legitimize foreign workers' role in the U.S. economy, granting them only temporary status fraught with uncertainty. For example, Rob Williams, director of the Migrant Farmworker Justice Project, believes that the legislation ties permission to remain in the United States too closely to proof of employment: "[When] their job runs out, they're history." Some conservative Republicans also oppose the law. They maintain that it provides added incentive for foreign workers to enter the United States illegally in an attempt to gain temporary status after having successfully entered.

Supporters of the new law include some immigrants. They view it as an opportunity to obtain legal paperwork such as driver's licenses and to educate their children in the United States. Among the strongest proponents are industry groups in the restaurant, hotel, and agricultural industries that employ millions of foreign workers. They claim that they need access to low-wage laborers because these workers fill jobs that Americans do not want.

Critical-Thinking Questions

1. Draw a graph of the U.S. unskilled labor force showing the likely effect of allowing guest workers into the United States. What will happen to wages and employment in this sector if the new policy makes it easier for noncitizens to remain and work in the United States?
2. What will happen to the market (both supply and demand) for this group of workers if the legislation is unsuccessful?

►SUMMARY

- **The demand for labor in the short run.** Labor demand is a derived demand. Firms decide how much labor to employ based on the value of the marginal product. In competitive markets, this value is determined by multiplying the marginal product by the price. When either labor productivity or output price increases, labor demand increases as well.

- **The supply of labor in the short run.** Individuals decide how much labor to supply to the market based on the opportunity cost of leisure; that is, the nonmarket work time that they forgo. Individuals who value leisure more than income will require higher wages to be induced to supply labor than individuals who value leisure less.

- **Equilibrium in the labor market.** As with product markets, the equilibrium price (wage) is determined by the intersection of the labor demand and labor supply curve. The most significant change in the U.S. labor market supply in recent times comes from the large increase in the number of women who choose to work full-time in the market.

- **The demand for labor, technology, and capital in the long run.** All inputs, including the technology that is embedded in capital, are variable in the long run. In the long run, firms have much more freedom in their choice of how to produce output than in the short run. The drastic changes in technology that have occurred over the last generation have also led to large changes in the demand for labor.

- **Education and training.** Workers demand education because it increases their productivity and therefore their wages. Not all workers receive the same level of education, in part because they have different abilities to learn and make use of education and training.

- **Unions.** Unions come in two basic forms. Craft unions are organized by skill, and get their strength by limiting access to jobs and skills. Industrial unions are organized based on the industry that employs the workers, and acquire their power by collective bargaining. Union membership and influence have declined over the last half-century.

KEY TERMS

Collective bargaining 397	Industrial unions 397	Union 395
Craft unions 397	Marginal revenue product of	Value of marginal product
Derived demand 380	labor (MRPL) 382	of labor (VMPL) 382
Embedded technology 390	Self-selection 395	

PROBLEMS

1. List two distinct labor markets that exist on your college campus. Be careful to identify groups of workers that are not good substitutes for one another. Identify the characteristic (such as a specific skill) that makes each labor market unique.

2. Complete the following table and indicate how many workers the firm would hire if the wage were $12 per hour. How would your answer change if wages increased to $21 per hour? Draw a graph of the *VMPL* curve.

L, Workers	MPL	P	VMPL
0	—	3	
1	14	3	
2	20	3	
3	13	3	
4	7	3	
5	4	3	
6	2	3	

3. How would each of the following changes affect labor demand in the cable television installation market? (*Hint:* Remember that labor demand is derived from product demand.)
   a. An increase in consumer income
   b. A decrease in the price of satellite television systems
   c. An increase in the population
   d. A new trend toward going to movie theaters rather than in-home viewing

4. Would you stop working completely if you won $10 million in the lottery? Why or why not? Explain your answer in economic terms.

5. Why are high-school teachers usually required to continue earning education credits after they have completed their undergraduate degrees?

6. Why do most organizations have fewer secretaries than in the past?

7. Use a supply-and-demand graph to show how wages and employment in the landscaping industry will change if each of the following events takes place:
   a. New, faster lawnmowers with wider cutting decks are developed.
   b. New trimmers are engineered that make a lawn look much nicer when it is finished.
   c. A drought occurs.
   d. A new grass is developed that grows twice as fast as the current popular types.
   e. A large group of unskilled workers immigrates to the area.
   f. A large group of highly skilled workers immigrates to the area.

8. At Jalpa's Manufacturing Company, the marginal product of the last worker hired is 20 units per day. Each unit sells for $3, and workers are paid $70 per day. Is the level of employment too low, too high, or just right? Justify your answer.

9. If, as discussed in the chapter, the economic returns of attending graduate school are so high, why don't more people earn graduate degrees?

10. John's parents were disappointed that he decided to attend trade school after high school rather than college. They cited statistics that average wages are higher for college grads than trade-school grads. John's reply was: "That may be so, but *I* will earn more with a trade-school degree than a college degree." Under what circumstances is this argument valid?

11. Why do economists typically assume that the level of technology is fixed in the short run?

12. Give two examples of situations in which labor might be more difficult to vary than capital.

13. Suppose the market wage for fast food workers is $6 per hour. To make the working poor better off, the government institutes a minimum wage of $8 per hour for adults working in fast food restaurants. It leaves the minimum wage at $6 for teens. Will adult fast food workers be better off? Why or why not?

14. Answer true, false, or uncertain, and explain your answer: "Minimum wages are more effective for helping the poor when capital and labor are not good substitutes for one another."

15. Why might a firm decline the opportunity to employ a college intern, even if the intern does not need to be paid?

16. Contractual agreements between major league baseball players and team owners require that team rosters be exactly 25 players. Use marginal product and value of marginal product concepts to explain why this rule might prevent teams from hiring the optimal quantity of players.

17. In Japan, some unions have historically represented workers in only a single company. How might this policy affect bargaining between labor and management?

18. Suppose that a dressmaker finds the following productivity data for her firm:

Employees	Dresses Produced per Week
0	0
1	10
2	24
3	33
4	39
5	42

   a. For each level of employment, calculate the marginal product of labor.
   b. If the dresses can be sold for $50 each, what is the value of the marginal product of labor ($VMPL$) for each level of employment? If workers earn $450 per week, how many employees should she hire?

HERE'S HOW MyEconLab CAN HELP YOU GET A BETTER GRADE

1. Log into MyEconLab and take Practice Test chapter-A (to log in for the first time, see page 30 for instructions.)

2. Based on your test results, MyEconLab will identify the areas where you need further work and create a personal Study Plan for you.

3. Your Study Plan contains the exercises listed below and others like them that will target the specific chapter topics you need to focus on. You'll receive instant feedback and find links to tutorials, animations, and the online textbook to help you study.

4. When you're ready, go take Practice Test chapter-B and demonstrate how your results have improved.

Section 15.1, Exercise 1 The following table shows the short-run hourly productivity data for production of CD players.

L (Quantity of Labor)	MPL (Marginal Product of Labor)
0	—
1	5
2	8
3	10
4	7
5	4
6	1
7	0
8	−2

a. At what point do diminishing marginal returns set in? At what point do diminishing total returns set in?
b. If the price of a CD player is $100, calculate the VMPL for each level of labor.
c. Graph the demand for labor.

Section 15.1, Exercise 2 The following table shows short-run weekly productivity data for Melissa's pie factory. Melissa's pies currently sell for $10 per pie.

L	MPL	VMPL
0	—	—
1	80	800
2	70	700
3	61	610
4	53	530
5	47	470
6	42	420
7	38	380
8	35	350
9	33	330
10	31	310

a. At a wage rate of $700 per week, how many workers will be demanded?
b. At a wage rate of $400 per week, how many workers will be demanded?
c. Suppose that the firm builds a larger plant and thus the productivity of labor doubles for each worker. What will happen to the demand for labor? At a wage of $700 per week, how many workers will be hired now?

Section 15.2, Exercise 1 Melanie has 10 hours per day in which she can choose to work or to not work (to consume leisure). The following table shows her marginal utility of leisure time.

L (Quantity of Labor, in hours)	Value of Marginal Utility of Leisure Time (in dollars)
0	0
1	1
2	3
3	6
4	10
5	15
6	21
7	28
8	36
9	43
10	51

a. How many hours will Melanie choose to work if the wage rate is $10 per hour?
b. How many hours will Melanie choose to work if the wage rate is $25 per hour?
c. Graph Melanie's supply of labor.

Section 15.2, Exercise 2 Bill works as a machine operator, and at a wage of $25 per hour, Bill supplies 40 hours of labor per week. Draw a supply curve for Bill, and show the probable effect on Bill's labor supply curve and quantity of labor supplied in each of the following situations.

a. The wage rate falls.
b. Bill buys a new boat, and thus values every hour of leisure more.

Section 15.3, Exercise 1 The following table shows market supply and demand for production workers in a small town.

Wage Rate	Quantity of Labor Demanded (in hours)	Quantity of Labor Supplied (in hours)
$22	0	2,800
20	200	2,400
18	450	2,025
16	675	1,675
14	875	1,350
12	1,050	1,050
10	1,200	725
8	1,325	475
6	1,425	250
4	1,475	100
2	1,500	0

a. Find the equilibrium wage and quantity of labor.
b. Graph the approximate shape of the supply and demand curves, and show the equilibrium point.

Section 15.3, Exercise 2 Consider the market for hospital nurses in a given geographical area. Draw representative supply and demand curves, and show the effect of each of the following changes on the equilibrium wage and quantity of labor.

a. The number of hospitals in the area decreases.
b. More nurses graduate from college.

c. Hospitals invest in new equipment that makes nurses more productive.
d. Nurses now prefer to have more leisure time at any income level.
e. The price of hospital services increases.

Section 15.4, Exercise 1 Carefully explain why the long-run demand for labor is more elastic than the short-run demand for labor.

Section 15.4, Exercise 2 Explain the effect of an increase in the firm's capital stock on its demand for labor.

Section 15.5, Exercise 1 Indicate whether each of the following pairs of examples would be considered to be part of the same labor market, and briefly explain why or why not.

a. A job at McDonald's in New York City, and a job at McDonald's in Los Angeles
b. A professor of economics at the University of California at Berkeley, and a professor of economics at Yale University in Connecticut
c. A machine operator in Boston, Massachusetts, and a nurse in Boston, Massachusetts

Section 15.5, Exercise 2 Extensive data indicate that if you choose to go to graduate school, you are likely to earn a higher annual salary than you would have if you had stopped with a bachelor's degree. Does this mean that you should go to graduate school?

Section 15.6, Exercise 1 What is the primary reason that unions may be able to achieve higher wages for workers?

Section 15.6, Exercise 2 Why has the demand for union membership declined?

16

Poverty and the Distribution of Income

Each year, *Forbes Magazine* publishes several lists of individuals who have achieved great wealth, fame, or both. The names on the list of the wealthiest Americans change very little from year to year. There is somewhat more turnover on *Forbes'* list of the top 100 celebrities. A few names, however, are fixtures on both lists. One of the most notable is Oprah Winfrey, or simply Oprah. In 2003, her annual income was $210 million, and her net worth was over $1.1 billion. Born in rural Mississippi, one of the poorest regions of the United States, Oprah had become one of the 500 richest individuals in the world by age 50.

Do you ever daydream about what it would be like to win $1 million in the lottery? Oprah earns more than that every two days. In 2004, the median U.S. household income was just under $42,000. That means that 50 percent of households lived on less than $42,000 for the year. Just 5 percent of American household incomes were over $100,000, yet the incomes of the wealthiest Americans stretch into the hundreds of millions. Clearly, income in the United States is not distributed equally.

One of the most interesting aspects of Oprah's career is her decision to share her wealth with others who are less fortunate. For many years, Oprah gave a $100,000 "Use Your Life" award every Monday on her television show to a person who was helping others lift themselves out of poverty. These people were often working to address some of the root causes of poverty, such as lack of education, discrimination, and beginning life with serious economic disadvantages. One winner was Jane Stephenson, founder of the New Opportunity School for Women in Berea, Kentucky. This school provides intensive training in job and life skills for women who live in the south-central Appalachian region whose family income is less than $10,000 a year. Oprah has also raised and distributed millions of dollars to fund other educational initiatives.

Many of us would like to have Oprah's wealth and her ability to help others, but there are very few Oprahs and an increasing number of those who have very little. You may have heard about fears that the "middle class" in the United States is dwindling, creating an increasingly polarized society. A relatively small number of individuals such as Oprah Winfrey, Bill Gates, and Warren Buffet now control a disproportionately large—and growing—share of wealth. At the same time, over the past 20 years, low-income families and individuals, such as those at the New Opportunity School for Women, have seen their incomes fall.

In this chapter, we review income distribution; that is, how the economy's total income is apportioned. We examine the role of discrimination and education in the distribution of income as well as government policies aimed at redistributing income. It is impossible to cover income, wealth, poverty, and inequality comprehensively in a single chapter, or even in an entire book. We thus offer a broad overview of this vital yet complex area of economics.

ALONG THE WAY, YOU WILL ALSO LEARN:

- How income is distributed in the United States, and which families have fared better and worse, over the last 30 years.

- What important trade-offs between equity and efficiency must be considered when fighting poverty.

- How discrimination can harm both the parties that are discriminated against and the parties that practice discrimination.

- Why and how education affects income distribution.

- What programs were created by the government in response to poverty, including minimum wages.

AT THE END OF THE CHAPTER,
THE MYECONLAB LOGO WILL DIRECT YOU ONLINE

- MyEconLab is a resource-packed online homework and tutorial system that can help you perform better in your economics course. To log in for the first time, see page 30 for instructions.

- MyEconLab can help you apply important concepts from the chapter to real-world issues. Watch for the logo to indicate online features about poverty and inequality.

- At the end of each chapter, you'll find a special study section that will help you get the most out of your textbook and your instructor's MyEconLab course.

▶ U.S. Income and Wealth Distribution

We begin our look at income distribution with trends in the U.S. economy over the last 30 years. First, we set the stage with some basic vocabulary and statistics about the U.S. economy. Then we introduce a graphical tool that economists use to summarize the distribution of income.

Income Distribution Terminology

Earned income
Income gained from work.

Unearned income
Income gained from all sources other than work, such as interest, profits on the sale of stocks, inheritance, and gifts.

Wealth
The stock of financial resources accumulated by an individual over time.

Annual income is the flow of purchasing power into a household in a given year. This income may be **earned income**, which represents income generated from work (often called *earnings*), or **unearned income**, which includes income from interest, profits on the sale of stocks, inheritance, and gifts. There is a strong relationship between earned and unearned income. With the exception of retirees, families with low earnings rarely have significant unearned income from stocks, bonds, and other financial instruments. These families are unable to save much of their income.

Wealth is the stock of financial resources accumulated by an individual over time. For example, while Oprah's income in 2003 was $210 million, her wealth was much greater: $1.1 billion. Oprah's wealth is her total accumulated savings from all lifetime income, both earned and unearned. Some people's wealth comes strictly from their own hard work or economic rent that serves as a payment for a special talent and good fortune. Oprah was born into a family with very little accumulated wealth. Thus, *Forbes* describes her fortune as "self-made." Economists would describe her earnings as economic rent that she is able to charge as a result of her unique talent as an entertainer. Others obtain wealth by inheriting it from their families, or marrying someone who is already wealthy.

U.S. Income Statistics

There is no official definition for the term "middle class." There is also considerable debate as to how the well-being of the average American has changed in the last 30 years. However, there is no doubt that the U.S. income distribution has changed. Table 16.1 breaks the U.S. income distribution into *quintiles*, or fifths. Each quintile represents 20 percent of the households in the United States, arranged from the lowest income to the highest. As shown in Table 16.1, the poorest 20 percent of U.S. households earned only 3.4 percent of U.S. total income in 2003, down from 4.1 percent in 1970. From 1970 to 2003, the income share of the highest 20 percent of households increased from 43.3 percent to 49.8 percent. The share of income earned by the top 5 percent of households also rose, increasing from 16.6 percent in 1970

TABLE 16.1

Share of Aggregate Income (Percent) of U.S. Households from 1970 to 2003

	1970	1975	1980	1985	1990	1995	2000	2003
Poorest 20 percent	4.1	4.4	4.3	4.0	3.9	3.7	3.6	3.4
Second 20 percent	10.8	10.5	10.3	9.7	9.6	9.1	8.9	8.7
Third 20 percent	17.4	17.1	16.9	16.3	15.9	15.2	14.8	14.8
Fourth 20 percent	24.5	24.8	24.9	24.6	24.0	23.3	23.0	23.4
Highest 20 percent	43.3	43.2	43.7	45.3	46.6	48.7	49.8	49.8
Top 5 percent	16.6	15.9	15.8	17.0	18.6	21.0	22.1	21.4

Source: Historical Income Tables H-2 and H-3, United States Census Bureau, at www.census.gov/hhes/income/histinc/h02.html and www.census.gov/hhes/income/histinc/h03.html

to 21.4 percent in 2003. Although it appears to have leveled off in the last 5 or 6 years, it is clear that the difference in income between the richest and poorest Americans has grown substantially over the last 30 years.

Note that Table 16.1 includes only data on the distribution of income. There are many ways to measure the well-being of groups in a society other than using their incomes. We can include the value of fringe benefits like health insurance and pensions, and government transfer programs such as Social Security payments. We can also look at accumulated wealth with savings and investments, rather than annual income. A table showing accumulated wealth would reveal an even less equal distribution than that shown in Table 16.1, which presents data on income. A table presenting income plus government transfers (such as aid to the poor) would be somewhat more equal.

While such comparisons of wealth and income over time may be very telling about the direction of change in a society, we need to be careful. Poverty has both absolute and relative components. Many people considered to be poor in the 2000s have access to goods—such as color televisions and mobile telephones—that even the well-to-do had trouble purchasing in the 1960s. People at the very bottom of the U.S. income distribution have access to health care that even the president lacked in the 1800s. We must be cautious when using emotionally charged terms like "poverty" and make our comparisons carefully. Oprah Winfrey now directs much of her charity work towards children in South Africa, where the term "poverty" takes on a stark and much more ominous meaning than in the United States.

The Lorenz Curve

Lorenz curve
A graph that shows the percentage of income that is earned by a given percent of households in a country or subgroup; it indicates how evenly income is distributed.

Economists depict information on income distribution like that shown in Table 16.1 in graph form using a tool called the Lorenz curve. The **Lorenz curve** provides a quick and easy way to understand how near or far an economy is from distributing its income absolutely equally. It effectively lines up all the households in a society from poorest to richest and asks how total income grows as we account for more and more households.

Graphing the Lorenz Curve. Panel (a) of Figure 16.1 shows a sample distribution of income. We use the data to construct the Lorenz curve. As we include more households along the horizontal axis, the percentage of total households rises from 0 to 100 percent. As we go from no households to all households, the percentage of income we account for also rises from 0 (when none of society's income is counted) to 100 percent (when all income is counted) on the vertical axis. Consider the case of exactly equal incomes. The percentage of households and the percentage of income rise at the same rate, because all households have the same income. Panel (a) of Figure 16.1 shows that adding another 20 percent of the population adds exactly 20 percent of the population's income.

Graphing the information from panel (a) of Figure 16.1, as shown in panel (b), shows that the Lorenz curve for a population with a perfectly equal income distribution is a straight line from the origin to the point (100, 100). Perfect equality never occurs in reality. However, it serves as a valuable reference point for actual distributions.

Interpreting the Lorenz Curve. We derive the U.S. Lorenz curve at various times in history by using the data in Table 16.1. Panel (a) of Figure 16.2 presents the U.S. data for 1970, 1985, and 2000 as cumulative distributions. In a cumulative distribution, we add the percentage of income for each successive fifth of the population

FIGURE 16.1

Income Distribution and the Lorenz Curve

The Lorenz curve shows the percentage of income that is earned by a given percentage of households. The 45-degree line indicates perfect equality. Income is distributed exactly evenly: 20 percent of the households earn 20 percent of total income; 40 percent of the households earn 40 percent of total income; and so on.

(a) Distribution of Income with Perfect Equality

Ranking	Percent of Households	Percent of Income
Poorest 20 percent	20	20
Second 20 percent	40	40
Third 20 percent	60	60
Fourth 20 percent	80	80
Highest 20 percent	100	100

(b) Lorenz Curve

to the lower groups. For example, in 2000, we see that a total of 12.5 (3.6 + 8.9) percent of the population was in the bottom two-fifths (the poorest 20 percent and second 20 percent in Table 16.1). Panel (b) of Figure 16.2 shows the Lorenz curves corresponding to these years. As the data show, the U.S. distribution of income is unequal, and it has become more so since 1970. The highest 20 percent of households now receive about 50 percent of the total income. The poorest 20 percent of families, like the families of the women who enter the New School for Opportunity, earn less than 4 percent of the total income.

We see from the first row of Figure 16.2(a) that the poorest households' share of total income in the U.S. economy has declined over time. In fact, only the wealthiest segment of the population, shown in the bottom two rows of the table, clearly gained between 1970 and 2000. Panel (b) of Figure 16.2 illustrates this change. Because the poorest 20 percent of households account for less than 20 percent of income, the Lorenz curves sag below the line that indicates perfectly equal incomes. All incomes are taken into account by the time all households are counted, so the Lorenz curve catches up at the end. The gap between the line of perfect equality and the actual Lorenz curve forms a "fish-eye" shape. As incomes become less equal with time, the poorest households account for less of the total income. As a result, the Lorenz curves sag farther below the straight line, making a larger fish-eye.

The changes depicted in Figure 16.2(b) may seem relatively modest, but a small movement in the Lorenz curve can mean sizable transfers of income. Moreover, changes in the distribution of income can have significant social effects. The likelihood of resentment, social unrest, or even violence or civil war grows as income

FIGURE 16.2

Lorenz Curves Sag Downward as Inequality Increases

As income is distributed more unequally, the Lorenz curves sag further downward. The lowest-income groups receive a smaller share of total income, and the highest-income groups receive a larger share. The shift of the Lorenz curves downward shows that U.S. inequality increased from 1970 to 2000.

(a) Cumulative Frequency Distributions for the United States in 1970, 1985, and 2000

Percent of Households   Cumulative Percent of Income

	1970	1985	2000
Poorest 20 percent	4.1	4.0	3.6
Second 20 percent	14.9	13.7	12.5
Third 20 percent	32.3	30.0	27.3
Fourth 20 percent	56.8	54.6	50.3
Richest 20 percent	100.0	100.0	100.0

(b) Lorenz Curves Sag Downward as Inequality Increases

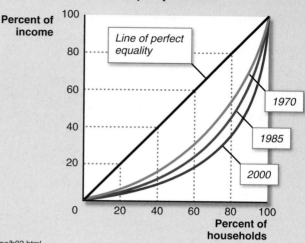

Source: Historical Income Table H-2, U. S. Census Bureau, at www.census.gov/hhes/income/histinc/h02.html

becomes less equally distributed. The people at the high end of the income distribution have a vested interest in ensuring that they do not get too far ahead of the people who earn less than they do.

TEST + **E X T E N D** Your Knowledge

1. TEST Suppose that a society consists of only 10 families. Income is distributed across the families as follows:

Family	Income
A	$ 10,000
B	50,000
C	100,000
D	100,000
E	250,000
F	300,000
G	300,000
H	490,000
I	900,000
J	1,500,000

Divide the population into five groups from the poorest to the richest, compute the percentage of income earned by each group, and show the distribution in a table. Use the data to draw the Lorenz curve for this society.

2. EXTEND Suppose that the government taxes each family's income at a rate of 20 percent. In an effort to redistribute income toward the poor, the proceeds of the tax are divided into 10 equal shares, and one share is paid to each family to create its new after-tax income. Re-create your table and show the new percentage of incomes for each group using the after-tax incomes. Does the tax have the desired effect?

▶ Income Distribution: Efficiency Versus Equity

In earlier chapters, we examined many aspects of market economies. In most cases, we emphasized efficiency. For example, when goods are exchanged in a competitive market instead of in a monopoly, we avoid the deadweight loss associated with monopoly. Output is higher and prices are lower in a competitive market. Economists are sometimes criticized for focusing too heavily on efficiency and showing too little concern for issues of equity. This disparity may stem from the nature of the two tasks: Efficiency is a relatively objective concept, while equity is much more subjective.

Nevertheless, good economic analysis takes both efficiency *and* equity into consideration. Maximizing efficiency ensures that resources are not wasted, while equity considers the potential impact of a given distribution of resources. Recall from Chapter 2 that there is no such thing as maximizing equity, because there is no single definition of "equity" or universally accepted measure of fairness. In this section, we describe the tensions and challenges policy makers face when addressing issues related to income distribution.

Measuring Poverty and Income Distribution

Policy makers must keep in mind that income distributions show *relative* well-being. Although poverty can be considered in relative terms, in real life, when establishing eligibility for social programs, governments typically measure poverty in *absolute* terms, using specific income level criteria. Consider a family that does not have enough to eat and cannot properly clothe, house, and educate their children. We may describe the family as poor, no matter what its position is on the income distribution chart. Conversely, it may be misleading to refer to families as "poor" that lie in the lower portion of the distribution yet have all basic needs met. For example, a family that is considered to be poor by American standards might be considered to be well off in some of the poorest nations of the world.

From a domestic policy perspective, the United States defines poverty in absolute terms for its own residents. For example, a family of four with an income of less than $19,484 in 2004 was considered to be below the poverty line. When a household falls below the poverty line, it becomes eligible for a variety of aid programs, which we discuss later in the chapter.

How we define "relative" poverty is meaningful from an international policy perspective. How much aid should we send to foreign countries when members of our own society cannot afford adequate food and housing? There is no objective, quantifiable answer. In the remainder of this chapter, we focus on determining who is at the low end of the U.S. income distribution and what, if anything, can be done to improve the economic well-being of these individuals. When we discuss certain absolute measures (for example, access to health care), we do so in the context of the United States.

Identifying the Poor

Poverty line
The income cutoff used to identify the poor; an individual or family of a given size below this line cannot afford the basic necessities.

Panel (a) of Table 16.2 shows the government definitions of poverty for various family sizes. As you can see, the poverty threshold rises as family size increases. The United States uses an income cutoff known as the **poverty line** to identify the poor—those with an income at or below this point. The poverty line attempts to capture poverty in an absolute sense. A family in poverty does not have enough income to meet its basic needs—food, clothing, and shelter. Panel (a) shows that in 2004, the

TABLE 16.2

Poverty in the United States

(a) Census Bureau Poverty Thresholds for 2004

Size of Family Unit	Poverty Line Threshold
One person	—
Under 65 years	9,827
65 years and over	9,060
Two people, no children present	—
Householder under 65 years	12,649
Householder 65 years and over	11,418
Three people	14,776
Four people	19,484
Five people	23,497
Six people	27,025
Seven people	31,096
Eight people	34,778
Nine people or more	41,836

Source: United States Census Bureau, Web site at www.census.gov/hhes/poverty/threshld.html

(b) Individuals and Families in Poverty in 2003

Characteristic	Number (in thousands)	Percent in Poverty
By individual		
Total	35,861	12.5
In families	25,684	10.8
White	24,272	10.5
African American	8,781	24.4
Asian and Pacific Islander	1,401	11.8
Hispanic	9,051	22.5
Under 18	12,866	17.6
18 to 64	19,443	10.8
65 and older	3,552	10.2
By family		
Total	7,607	10.0
White	5,058	8.1
African American	1,986	22.3
Asian and Pacific Islander	311	10.2
Hispanic	1,925	20.8
Married couple	3,115	5.4
Female head of household, no spouse present	3,856	28.0
Male head of household, no spouse present	636	13.5

Source: Excerpted from United States Census Bureau, Current Population Survey, 2004 Annual Demographic Supplement

myeconlab

Get Ahead of the Curve

Use your knowledge of measuring poverty in the United States to assess the United Nations' goal of halving world poverty by 2015.

poverty line was $9,827 for an individual under age 65, $12,649 for a couple under 65, and $19,484 for a family of four. Panel (b) shows a breakdown of individuals and families in poverty for the year 2003. Notice that in 2003 (the most recent year for which data are available), a total of 12.5 percent of the population (over 35 million people), or 10 percent of families, lived in poverty. In the top portion of Table 16.2(b), showing data by individual, we see that 17.6 percent of children under 18 are poor. On a percentage basis, poverty is most prevalent among African Americans (24.4 percent of whom live in poverty) and Hispanics (22.5 percent).

The lower portion of Table 16.2(b) details the status of families below the poverty line. It shows that the burden of poverty is also unequally distributed across groups. More than a quarter of female-headed households live in poverty. The likelihood of poverty rises sharply if the woman is African American or Hispanic. Indeed, a family with an African American or Hispanic female head of household is roughly eight times more likely to be poor than a white family with both spouses present.

Explaining Income Distribution Differences

Most societies regard the elimination of poverty as a central function of the government. During much of the twentieth century, centrally planned or communist governments such as the Soviet Union sought to equalize the distribution of income among its citizens. This logic led at times to a system of heavy taxes or outright confiscation of property. The stagnation and eventual collapse of most communist regimes strongly suggest that such policies are not the best long-term solutions. People living under these regimes had little reason to work diligently to improve their well-being, because they did not profit from working hard or making correct decisions. Moreover, transferring income from the wealthy to the poor treats only the symptoms of poverty. Combating hunger and inadequate housing may be necessary in the short run. To reduce poverty permanently, we must first understand its root causes and then design policies that treat those causes.

Limiting the Scope of Economic Analysis

Identifying the problem and designing the solution are beyond the scope of economics alone. Indeed, poverty also has historical, sociological, and psychological dimensions. Economists and policy makers cannot change many of the factors that lead to differences in wealth. For example, some people are wealthy because they have natural talents that set them apart as highly intelligent or physically gifted. In the United States it is unlikely that the government would want to establish new policies that discourage these individuals from making the most of their abilities. We therefore limit our discussion to policies that governments are willing and able to implement. For example, discrimination may prevent the economic advance of certain groups, such as female heads of households and minorities. Differences in access to education or technology (what some call the "digital divide") may also create a continuing cycle of poverty for families at the low end of the income distribution. Well-designed government policies might help correct these problems and create more economic prosperity for disadvantaged groups.

▶ Discrimination

Discrimination
When an individual takes actions or makes decisions based on personal prejudices.

We now turn to the effect of discrimination on the distribution of income. Debates over discrimination and the policies designed to combat it are passionately waged. Most forms of discrimination based on race, religion, ethnic background, age, and gender are illegal. In addition, discrimination is viewed by most people as morally wrong. Economists have done a great deal of work in this important area. In defining *discrimination,* economists distinguish between prejudice and discrimination. Although the two words are often used interchangeably, their meanings differ. Disliking someone because of a specific characteristic, such as race or gender, is prejudice. Treating that person differently *because* of prejudice is discrimination. Thus, **discrimination** occurs when individuals take their feelings—prejudices—and turn them into actions. In this section, we examine the economics of discrimination and government programs seeking to combat it.

Discrimination as Tastes and Preferences

While discrimination is a very serious issue, a rather mundane example may help you understand it and how governments can combat it. Imagine that you ask a friend what her favorite pizza topping is, and she says "pepperoni." If you ask her why she prefers pepperoni, she most likely will not provide a meaningful explanation beyond saying that she thinks it tastes best. If you offered her an alternative, such as mushrooms, she would be unwilling to trade a slice of pepperoni for the slice with mushrooms. Suppose that you offer to give her both $1.00 and a slice of mushroom pizza for her slice of pepperoni pizza. If she refuses, your friend is willing to sacrifice $1.00 to indulge her preference for pepperoni. If $1.00 does not change her mind, you can then offer $2.00, $3.00, and so on. Eventually, your friend will probably reach a point where she would rather have the less-preferred slice, plus the money than just the pepperoni slice. That is, your friend's desire for money will eventually overcome her preference for pepperoni pizza.

Gary Becker, a Nobel Prize–winning economist, developed a theory of discrimination that works much the same way as this example. In his path-breaking book *The Economics of Discrimination* (first published in 1957), Becker argues that when individuals discriminate, they are simply exercising their tastes and preferences through market exchanges. In other words, they express their dislikes through their willingness to pay to avoid associating with individuals they do not like. This theory is based on the concept of consumer behavior described in Chapter 7. As explained in the following discussion, researchers and policy makers can use money to measure the intensity of discrimination. We demonstrate how the model works by considering the actions of consumers, employees, and employers.

Consumer Discrimination. Consumers can be a powerful force of discrimination. If a large group of consumers decides not to shop at the businesses of a specific minority, the consequences for the minority group can be devastating. To highlight the role of consumers in the Becker model, we turn to an example of discrimination based on gender. Suppose that April owns a service garage where she repairs automobiles. She has always loved cars. Her work is as good as that of any mechanic in town. Some of her potential customers, however, are prejudiced against women working in such fields. As a result, they discriminate against her when they need car repairs. They believe she can repair their cars, but they have a distaste for interacting with a woman in the car repair business. As a result, her business is not doing as well as it could be. We can use the supply and demand model to show the effects of the discrimination by consumers.

Panel (a) of Figure 16.3 shows the market for repairs if customers do not discriminate. The supply curve, S_{all}, and demand curve, D_{all}, show the supply and demand for car repairs in the town. The equilibrium rate per hour for repairs when there is no discrimination is $60. If consumers do discriminate, there are two separate demand curves: one for service garages owned by men (D_m) and another for those owned by women (D_w), as shown in panel (b). To simplify the model, we assume that repairs are of equal quality, and that there are equal numbers of shops with identical costs owned by each gender ($S_w = S_m$). Demand for repairs is lower at shops owned by women than men. As a result, the equilibrium quantity is 10 repairs lower in the female-owned service garage market, and women must charge the lower equilibrium price of $50 per hour. In contrast, the price at male-owned service garages is $70 per hour. Thus, April and other female service garage owners are harmed by the discrimination.

Interestingly, the lower price generates a cost advantage for nondiscriminating consumers. Nondiscriminating consumers will always buy from the service garages owned by women, as long as the price is lower than at service garages owned by

FIGURE 16.3

The Car Repair Market and Discrimination

The market supply curve, S_{all}, is the sum of the supply curves of male- and female-owned service garages ($S_m + S_w$). Panel (a) presents a market in which customers do not discriminate based on gender. The demand for and supply of repairs result in an equilibrium price of $60 per hour. When consumers discriminate against service garages owned by women, the demand, D_w, is lower, as shown in panel (b). The two supply curves, S_m and S_w, are equal because we assume an equal number of each owner type. As a result, service garages owned by women can sell 10 fewer repairs than male-owned service garages, and must sell repairs at $50 per hour while male service garage owners can charge $70 per hour.

(a) No Discrimination

(b) With Discrimination

men. If the market for repairs is competitive, consumers that discriminate suffer economically for having a distaste for purchasing car repairs from women.

Overcoming this form of discrimination can be difficult. Merely educating discriminators might not be effective, as their behavior is based on tastes rather than a lack of information. In addition, it would be unrealistic to force consumers to go to specific service garages against their will.

Employer Discrimination. An employer who discriminates prefers not to hire a certain type of employee. A discriminatory employer is willing to pay higher labor costs to avoid associating with these individuals. Suppose that the producer of a local news program does not like to associate with a certain group of workers, even though he knows that they are just as productive as other workers. Thus, faced with the choice between equally talented camera operators from each group, this discriminatory executive will always choose the applicant from the group he prefers. In the context of the supply and demand model, the demand for employees in this less-preferred group of workers lies to the left of the demand curve for other workers at any given wage rate. For the remainder of this section, we refer to the group of workers who face discrimination as Type-D workers, and those who do not as Type-F workers.

A Type-D job applicant may be able to get hired by offering to work for less money than a Type-F applicant. The low wage compensates the executive for hiring a worker he does not like, just as the lower repair price at service garages compensates a non-discriminating customer for getting a car serviced by a less-preferred group. The stronger the executive's taste for discrimination, the larger the wage

A non-discriminating consumer shops only on the basis of price and quality. A consumer who discriminates also considers the personal characteristics of the individual providing the good or service.

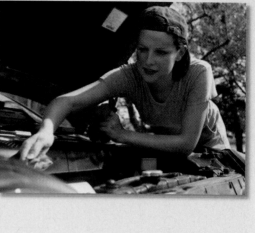

difference will have to be in order for the executive to offer the job to the Type-D applicant. Think of both situations as a side payment that the party being discriminated against must pay to attract customers or get a job.

Surprisingly, according to Becker's theory, if the market for camera operators is competitive, the government might not have to do anything to combat this form of discrimination. Market forces will cause prejudiced network executives to change their ways or risk being driven out of the market. Suppose that as a result of discrimination, the pay of Type-D camera operators falls. All stations that do not share the executive's discriminatory beliefs will hire workers from that group at a lower wage. As a result, the nondiscriminatory employer will enjoy lower costs and higher profits than discriminatory employers.

As more and more nondiscriminating employers enter the market and hire Type-D workers to take advantage of the higher profits they can earn, the wages of Type-D workers will rise. At the same time, discriminating firms with high costs will face increased competition from low-cost firms and end up going out of business.

In panel (a) of Figure 16.4, we see the market for camera operators from the perspective of an employer with no discrimination. The labor supply curve, S_{all}, and demand curve, D_{all}, show the supply and demand for all workers. The wage in the market is $30 per hour. If employers discriminate on the basis of race, ethnicity, or some other criteria, they behave as if there are two separate demand curves, one for Type-D workers (D_D) and another for Type-F workers (D_F). This scenario is shown in Figure 16.4(b). The demand curve for Type-D workers is not lower because their marginal revenue product is actually lower. Employers who discriminate merely act *as if* it were lower, because they do not want to associate with this group. We assume

FIGURE 16.4

The Labor Market and Employer Discrimination

Panel (a) shows a market where employers do not discriminate. The demand for and supply of all workers together result in a market wage of $30 per hour. When employers discriminate against Type-D workers, the demand for Type-D workers (D_D) is lower than for Type-F workers (D_F), as shown in panel (b). Type-F workers are paid the higher wage, $40 per hour, and Type-D workers receive the lower $20 per hour.

(a) No Discrimination

(b) With Discrimination

that there are equal numbers of each type of worker ($S_F = S_D$) to simplify the model. The quantity demanded is lower for Type-D workers (35) than for Type-F workers (55). Consequently, wages of workers that are discriminated against fall to $20 per hour, whereas Type-F workers now earn $40 per hour. Nondiscriminatory employers benefit from this cost advantage. Nondiscriminatory employers continue to hire Type-D workers as long as their wages are lower than the other group. Employers who discriminate pay higher wages ($40), and eventually suffer losses.

Government Action to Combat Employer Discrimination

As Table 16.2 showed, the poor are disproportionately African American and Hispanic. Consequently, discrimination is widely cited as a reason for income inequality. Discrimination against African Americans and Hispanics may explain why these minority groups are overrepresented among the poor. To combat discrimination, government laws such as the Civil Rights Act of 1964 make it illegal to hire or pay differentially based on personal characteristics such as race, religion, or gender. The goal of such legislation is to increase the cost of discrimination by imposing fines and court costs on discriminatory employers. The resulting higher cost of discriminating discourages employers from acting on their prejudices.

Employee Discrimination. Employee discrimination occurs when one worker has an aversion to working with or under another employee based on some irrelevant characteristic. Suppose Greg is a Type-F camera operator who doesn't like to work with Type-D employees. As a result, he feels as though he will earn less (because his utility is reduced) if he is forced to work with Type-D workers on the same crew. When he is forced to associate with Type-D workers, he demands higher pay to restore his utility level to what it was when he had only Type-F co-workers. One possible outcome of employee discrimination is a segregated workforce. Suppose that the network managers feel that all workers make equally good employees. They might respond to Greg's wage demand by firing him and all workers who feel as he does. Because Greg does not demand a higher wage if he works with only Type-F employees, he may find work at a company that happens to employ only those workers. What if a large number of workers share Greg's taste for discrimination? The workplace could become segregated into networks with only Type-F camera crews and networks with crews of all types.

An often-cited example of employee discrimination comes from professional baseball. For more than 50 years, African Americans were prevented from playing Major League Baseball in the United States.[1] In 1947, professional baseball was re-integrated by the inclusion of Jackie Robinson of the Brooklyn Dodgers. His first year was marred both by the rants and threats of racist fans (another example of consumer discrimination), and by poor behavior on the part of some of his own teammates (employee discrimination). Prior to the start of the season, some teammates threatened to refuse to appear in games with Robinson. He was also taunted mercilessly by some opposing players. Today, such a situation is highly unlikely in any industry in the United States. The Major League Baseball teams that were the quickest to integrate, such as the Brooklyn Dodgers, New York Giants, Cleveland Indians, and Milwaukee Braves, all improved significantly in the late 1940s and 1950s. The teams that were the slowest to integrate, particularly the Philadelphia Phillies and Boston Red Sox, experienced declines in their winning percentages.

Antidiscrimination Legislation. The Equal Pay Act of 1963 outlawed pay differences based on race, religion, sex, and national origin. A year later, the Civil Rights Act of 1964 prohibited discrimination in hiring or firing. However, the impact of past discrimination lingers. Equal opportunity is the official law of the land, but there is still no effective way to outlaw consumer discrimination. In addition, previous discrimination has limited many people's access to education and skills. Even if a particular individual is not the target of discrimination, discrimination against previous generations may limit the parents' ability to provide that individual with a high-quality education, which in turn limits what she can provide for her children. One way to combat this built-in disadvantage is **affirmative action**, which consists of policies designed to eliminate the effects of past and present discrimination. Proponents of these policies view them as an opportunity to help minority groups that suffered discrimination in the past catch up with other groups. Opponents view affirmative action as discrimination against people who are not specifically protected by the law. Whether affirmative action is a vital supplement to flawed legislation or a form of reverse discrimination remains a hotly disputed topic with no single answer.

Affirmative action
Policies designed to eliminate the effects of past and present discrimination.

---

[1] The prohibition of African Americans was accomplished through an informal agreement by team owners. Although many believe that Jackie Robinson was the first African American to play National or American League baseball, there were a few African Americans who played professional baseball in the late nineteenth century.

►Education

When Oprah gave $100,000 to Jane Stephenson and the New Opportunity School for Women, she recognized two important things. First, differences in education can lead to differences in earnings. Second, some demographic groups in this country do not receive the same quantity or quality of education as others. In this section, we trace how educational opportunities affect earning power in the job market, and hence also affect the distribution of income in society.

Quantity of Education and Income Distribution

We know from Chapter 15 that workers in competitive markets are paid a wage equal to the value of their marginal product ($W = VMPL = p \times MPL$). If increases in education result in higher marginal productivity, economic theory predicts that they will also result in higher wages. In fact, highly educated workers do earn higher salaries on average than less-educated workers. According to the U.S. Census Bureau, in 2003, a high-school dropout earned $15,610 per year on average, a high-school graduate earned $23,673, and a college graduate earned $40,588. College graduates were also more likely to have jobs than high-school graduates. Unemployment rates were lower for college grads than for high-school grads, and both groups had lower unemployment rates than high-school dropouts. These statistics suggest that if some groups receive less education, they are likely to have lower incomes and higher unemployment rates as well. The data in Figure 16.5 show the percentage of individuals 25 years old and older who had completed high school and college in 2004. According to the data, whites are more likely to complete both high school and college than African Americans or Hispanics. While these differences are large, they are much smaller than they once were. For example, in 1970, a white individual was about 1.7 times as likely to be a high-school graduate and about 3 times as likely to be a college graduate than either an African American or a Hispanic. While racial and ethnic differences remain, they have decreased substantially. In 2004, whites were only about 1.5 times as likely to graduate from high school as Hispanics and 5 percent more likely than African Americans.

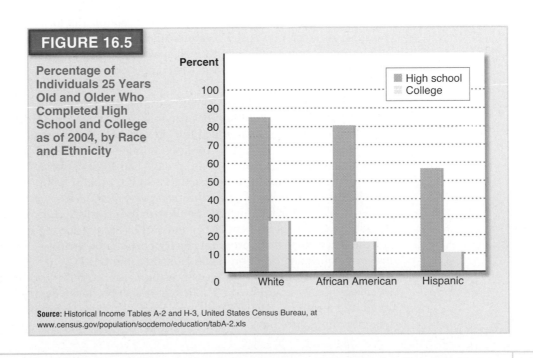

FIGURE 16.5

Percentage of Individuals 25 Years Old and Older Who Completed High School and College as of 2004, by Race and Ethnicity

Source: Historical Income Tables A-2 and H-3, United States Census Bureau, at www.census.gov/population/socdemo/education/tabA-2.xls

Quality of Education and Income Distribution

Although differences in years of schooling are important, it would be a mistake to focus only on the *quantity* of education. The *quality* of education people receive is also vital. The expenditure per student is much lower on average in high schools serving low-income areas than in high schools serving high-income suburban areas. As a result, there is less money available for equipment like computers, textbooks, and science laboratory materials in low-income areas. Qualitative differences in the education received by low-income students and wealthy students may be reflected in differences in their incomes later in life.

The superior educational experiences of children from wealthy families may help them succeed even if they do not actually learn more than low-income children. Indeed, economists have noted that the quantity and quality of a person's education demonstrates to potential employers that the individual has the intelligence and self-discipline to succeed in the workplace. Future productivity and innate ability are difficult for potential employers to observe. As a result, employers look for signals that potential employees will be highly productive. Children of wealthy families provide signals to the job market by attending prestigious private schools and by taking advantage of other costly educational activities that impress potential employers. Equally qualified individuals from poor families may be passed over simply because they never had the opportunity to demonstrate their talents or the resources to pay for schooling beyond high school. Wealthy students can thus end up with better jobs because of their wealth, and the income differences that began with their parents continue into the next generation.

Government Policy and Educational Opportunities

Differences in educational experiences at the pre-college level are important issues for government policy makers. Although a free market system cannot—and, most argue, should not—guarantee equal *outcomes* for all, an important and potentially achievable goal is equality of *opportunity*. That is, everyone should have an equal chance to succeed, even if not all actually do succeed.

One major reason why rich and poor children have such different educational experiences is that public schools generally rely on the local government for their funding. As a result, wealthy communities can afford to spend a great deal per pupil, while poor communities cannot. To make educational opportunities more equal, state and federal governments have become increasingly involved in providing funds for public schools.

At the college level, states heavily subsidize the cost of attending in-state university systems. In 2005–2006, for example, a high-school student from Hartford, Connecticut, could have attended the University of Connecticut, a public university, and paid tuition of $7,912. To attend Yale University, a private institution in Connecticut, the same student would have had to pay tuition of $31,460. One reason for the difference in tuition stems from the roughly $200 million that the state provides to the University of Connecticut every year. Higher-cost private education is easier to obtain for high-income families than for those with very limited resources. In addition, all colleges benefit from government-sponsored student loan programs. To the extent that these programs disproportionately help low-income groups, they have an equalizing effect on the income distribution.

Some non-profit groups offer educational opportunities for adults who have not been adequately served by the public school system. The federal government has also tried to improve the educational experiences of children from poor families by offering preschool programs such as Head Start. Head Start prepares children from

LifeLessons

Investing in Education—It's Not Just for Students

We have so far discussed the value of public schools for the students who are enrolled in them. But students are not the only beneficiaries. A strong public school system benefits all members of a community, regardless of whether they have school-aged children. A good school system makes a municipality more attractive than an otherwise identical town with poor schools. With more people wanting to move in, local businesses and homeowners profit. Homeowners benefit because the value of their property rises. With more and wealthier residents, local businesses are likely to see their profits rise as well. In addition, because many high-school graduates have traditionally settled in their home towns, the community gains from having an educated—and therefore employable—workforce.

Do these benefits apply to college towns? Because college graduates are more mobile than high-school graduates, they are less likely to settle locally. The benefits of providing advanced skills are thus likely to spill over into other communities. As the benefits of higher education are lost to other communities, a local government has less incentive to subsidize local postsecondary education. To keep more college graduates in the area after they complete their studies, the city of Philadelphia recently began an advertising campaign aimed at new graduates. The "Stay–Invent the Future" program is designed to showcase the benefits of making Philadelphia a permanent home after graduation.

impoverished families for grade school by providing enrichment activities. The preparation improves the educational experiences of disadvantaged children and increases their earning power. Children who take part in Head Start are more likely to graduate from high school and have high earnings. They are less likely to be charged with a crime than children from similar backgrounds who do not participate in the program.[2]

State and local governments have also turned to the private sector to improve public schools. These attempts to introduce market principles in public education have proven highly controversial. One example is a system of vouchers that families can use to help defray the cost of private or parochial schools. With this system, parents can, in effect, direct their education tax contribution to the school that their child attends, even if that school is privately run. The argument behind vouchers is that giving poor parents more options for their children forces all schools to compete for students and improve their services. Opponents of vouchers see them as a way to provide funds to parents who would send their children to private or parochial schools no matter what.

▶ Income Redistribution and the Government's Response to Poverty

Antidiscrimination legislation and public school funding are two of many ways in which the government intervenes in the private sector to alter the distribution of income. Policy makers debate the desirability and effectiveness of specific programs in decreasing poverty and reducing income inequality. Policy makers agree, however, that these programs in general are long-run solutions that do not provide immediate

---

[2] Eliana Garces, Duncan Thomas, and Janet Currie, "Longer Term Effects of Head Start," NBER Working Paper W8054, December 2000.

relief from the symptoms of poverty. Those who cannot find work, who are physically unable to work at all, or who cannot earn enough to provide themselves or their families with basic necessities need more direct assistance. In this section, we look at various forms of government assistance aimed at redistributing income.

Temporary Aid for Needy Families

Temporary Aid for Needy Families (TANF)
Provides financial assistance to families with children under the age of 18.

The government officially stopped providing welfare after reforms in the mid-1990s. However, the government still makes direct payments to individuals and families in need, although it is no longer called "welfare." **Temporary Aid for Needy Families (TANF)** provides financial assistance to needy families with children under the age of 18. This program is part of the federal Personal Responsibility and Work Opportunity Act of 1996, but is administered at the state level, so benefits and eligibility requirements vary from state to state. We will discuss the state of Georgia's administration of the program to illustrate how TANF functions. In Georgia, a family of three (for instance, a mother and two children) is eligible for TANF if their monthly income is below $784 and they have total assets worth less than $1,000. This maximum income is well below the poverty line, which is set at $1,231 per month, or $14,776 per year, for such a family. In 2004, there were on average 128,317 TANF recipients per month in Georgia, down from 377,630 welfare recipients in 1995.

Entitlements
Programs that apply, regardless of other considerations, if an individual meets certain criteria, such as having income below a threshold level.

Because TANF is not an entitlement, it can impose work requirements. **Entitlements** are programs that apply, regardless of other considerations, if an individual meets certain criteria, such as having income below a set threshold level. An individual or family that meets this condition automatically receives the benefit. The work requirement reflects the concern of policy makers that individuals who receive welfare with no work requirement have little incentive to find employment. The reduction in the number of aid recipients under TANF may result from an increase in individuals who find jobs and no longer need aid. In addition, TANF limits the amount of time families may receive assistance. Previous welfare programs had no such restrictions. Families may receive TANF funds for up to 24 months over any period of 84 consecutive months. After they reach the lifetime limit of 60 months, they may no longer receive any TANF funds, regardless of their level of need. On the positive side, work requirements should help recipients gain job experience that will reduce their need for TANF in the future.

The Income Tax System and the Earned Income Tax Credit

Progressive income tax system
Tax system in which the marginal rate at which income is taxed increases as an individual's income rises.

Marginal tax rate
The tax that an individual pays on each additional dollar of income earned.

Average tax rate
Individual's total income tax divided by the individual's total income.

Recall from Chapter 3 that income taxes are levies on personal or corporate earnings. Although not specifically designed to reduce poverty, the United States has what is known as a **progressive income tax system**, in which the marginal rate at which income is taxed increases as an individual's income increases. The **marginal tax rate** is the rate an individual pays on each additional dollar earned. An **average tax rate** is the tax paid per dollar of total income. Suppose, for example, that the marginal tax rates are as follows:

Income Level	Marginal Tax Rate
$0–$10,000	0%
$10,001–$20,000	10%
$20,001 and higher	30%

If Tamara earns $40,000 in a year, we calculate her taxes as:

Income	Tax Owed
$10,000	$0
$10,001–$20,000	$10,000 × 10% = $1,000
$20,001–$40,000	$20,000 × 30% = $6,000

Based on these calculations, her taxes are $7,000. Thus, her average tax rate is 17.5 percent ($7,000 ÷ $40,000). Any additional income she earns would be taxed at a marginal tax rate of 30 percent.

The income tax system is much less progressive than it used to be. Forty years ago, the highest marginal tax rate was 70 percent. Today's income tax system does not redistribute as large of a share of income from the wealthy to the poor as it once did. Whether this is good or bad is a normative question. With a progressive tax system, resources are redistributed from those who have more to those who have less, because wealthier individuals pay a greater share of the cost of government services. At the lowest levels of income, workers may be eligible for the **Earned Income Tax Credit (EITC)**, a major federal tax relief program, begun in 1975, that allows workers to receive tax refunds that are greater than the federal taxes they paid into the system. Eligibility is determined by income and family size. The credit is designed to reimburse workers for other types of taxes paid. In 2004, approximately 21 million families received refunds in excess of $36 billion through the EITC. The EITC effectively makes the tax system more progressive *and* makes direct payments to low-income workers. As a result, the program both redistributes income and serves as a poverty-reduction measure.

In addition to income transfers, some government programs make transfers in the form of services. For example, Medicaid is a government program designed to provide medical assistance to low-income individuals. It uses tax revenues to fund medical care. Consequently, it also serves to redistribute resources from high-income to low-income groups.

Earned Income Tax Credit (EITC)
A major federal tax relief program that allows workers to receive tax refunds that are greater than the federal taxes they paid into the system.

Unemployment Insurance

Unemployment insurance is another program administered at the state level. It aids individuals who are temporarily out of work. The benefit of such a program is that it provides some level of income for individuals while they search for a new job, rather than forcing them to take the first job available. The benefits workers receive are based in part on prior income. Those who previously had a high-paying job are eligible for greater benefits than someone who had a low-paying job. To receive unemployment benefits, individuals must be out of work for reasons other than quitting or being fired for cause. They must also be either looking for work or participating in a government-approved training program. An unemployed worker can receive benefits for up to 26 weeks, and may qualify for an extension in some circumstances. Unemployment benefits are modest—the maximum in some states is only around $300 per week. However, unemployment insurance does provide a safety net for workers and their families.

Food Stamps

TANF and unemployment benefits are direct cash transfers. In contrast, food stamp benefits are a more narrowly targeted form of government aid. They are actually no longer stamps at all, but electronic benefit transfer cards. Recipients can use these cards, which function like debit cards, to purchase food items, plants, and seeds. They cannot be used for alcohol, tobacco, medicine, nonfood items, and hot (ready-to-eat)

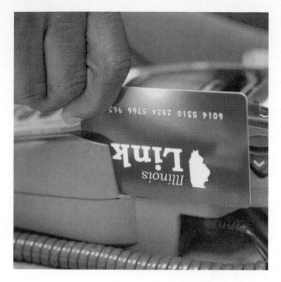

food. Eligibility for the program varies with the number of individuals in a family: In 2005, a family of five with a pretax income of less than $2,387 per month was eligible for food stamps. The narrow focus of food stamps has led some economists to oppose them as a substitute for direct monetary aid. People can use food stamps only to obtain particular kinds of food. Consequently, food stamps benefit primarily consumers who would have spent at least as much as the food stamp allotment on food. A poor family that spends a higher percentage of its income on clothing than on food would be better off receiving income or even "clothing stamps" rather than food stamps.

The Minimum Wage

The government may be able to increase the wages of the lowest-paid workers by forbidding employers from paying their employees wages below a certain level. Chapter 6 introduced the idea of a *minimum wage* as a form of a price floor. The minimum wage is a minimum hourly compensation rate for workers. The federal government sets the minimum wage, although state and local governments can impose additional provisions that further raise the minimum wage. As of January 2005, the federal minimum wage rate was $5.15 per hour.

The purpose of the minimum wage is to increase the income of the working poor. How well it achieves this goal is the subject of endless debate both in the political arena and among economists. To economists, declaring the minimum wage a good thing or a bad thing is far from simple. With our knowledge of the fundamentals of labor markets, we can see why, as the following sections examine.

Using a Graph to Analyze the Minimum Wage. Suppose a federally imposed minimum wage increased the hourly pay of all workers who had been earning less than the minimum and no workers lost their jobs. We could say that the higher minimum wage improved the well-being of low-wage workers. However, a minimum wage might not work as desired. The reason follows directly from the Law of Demand. When price increases, quantity demanded decreases. Consider the market for movie ticket–takers in Figure 16.6. As with most markets, the market demand curve for labor slopes downward, and the market supply curve for labor slopes upward. Without government intervention, the equilibrium wage is $4.65 per hour. The equilibrium quantity is 500 workers.

Recall from Chapter 6 that a *price floor* is a minimum price in a market set by the government. In any market, when the government increases the wage above the equilibrium, it creates a surplus of labor. As Figure 16.6 shows, when the price floor is set at $5.15, wages rise by $0.50 as planned. Especially in light of the policy goal of minimum wages, an unfortunate side effect of the increase in wages is that some workers lose their jobs. The demand curve for labor is downward-sloping; the new minimum wage increases the cost of production for the firm. Thus, at the new wage rate, movie theaters are willing to hire only 470 workers, and 30 workers who had been willing to work for $4.65 lose their jobs. Moreover, at the $5.15 wage rate, an additional 30 individuals are willing to work. However, no firm will hire these extra workers. In the end, the minimum wage increases the wage rate only for those who retain their jobs. However, it creates a pool of 60 workers who want to work at the

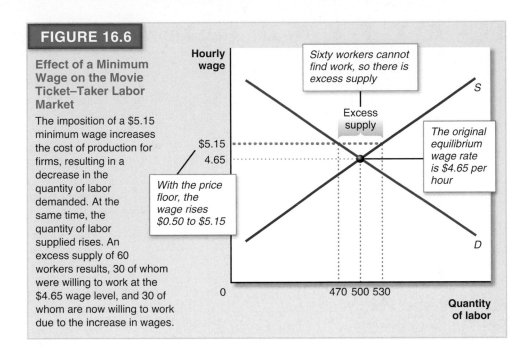

FIGURE 16.6

Effect of a Minimum Wage on the Movie Ticket–Taker Labor Market

The imposition of a $5.15 minimum wage increases the cost of production for firms, resulting in a decrease in the quantity of labor demanded. At the same time, the quantity of labor supplied rises. An excess supply of 60 workers results, 30 of whom were willing to work at the $4.65 wage level, and 30 of whom are now willing to work due to the increase in wages.

Sixty workers cannot find work, so there is excess supply

The original equilibrium wage rate is $4.65 per hour

With the price floor, the wage rises $0.50 to $5.15

going rate and cannot find work. The most frustrated of all are the workers who had been willing to work at the previous wage, but are now unemployed.

Minimum Wage Debate. The magnitude of the job loss brought about by the minimum wage is a hotly debated topic in economics literature. Some economists, such as David Card and Alan Krueger, argue that demand for unskilled labor is unresponsive to wage increases, and so does not result in lower employment.[3] Likeminded policy makers advocate large increases in the minimum wage that are designed to ensure that workers who earn the minimum wage are not below the poverty line. Advocates of a much higher minimum wage have come to refer to the higher wage as a *living wage*.

Other economists, such as David Neumark and William Wascher, claim that the findings of Card and Krueger are flawed.[4] They believe that increases in the minimum wage cause large increases in unemployment among low-wage workers. Some policy makers have used this and similar findings to advocate reductions in the minimum wage for younger and thus presumably less valuable workers.

The debate between opponents of the minimum wage and advocates of a much higher minimum wage remains unresolved. Keep in mind that the minimum wage might not ever reduce poverty rates if many minimum-wage workers are teens living in households with parents present. Constructing a policy that provides income relief for the poor without creating additional incentives that distort markets remains one of the great challenges of any government.

Get Ahead of the Curve

Apply your knowledge of labor markets and income distribution to recent U.S. trends in income growth.

---

[3] David Card and Alan Krueger, *Myth and Measurement: The New Economics of the Minimum Wage*, Princeton, NJ: Princeton University Press, 1995.

[4] David Neumark and William Wascher, "The Effect of New Jersey's Minimum Wage Increase on Fast Food Employment: A Re-Evaluation Using Payroll Records," National Bureau of Economic Research, NBER Working Paper 5224.

1. TEST Use a graph similar to Figure 16.6 to show the predicted effect of an increase in the minimum wage from $5.15 to $8.50. Label the quantity of labor supplied and demanded, and find the new employment level at the minimum wage.

2. EXTEND Log on to the Living Wage Resource Center Web site using the link at www.aw-bc.com/leeds/ch16. Read the summary statement on the main page.

Then click on the "Other Living Wage Research" link, go to the "Link to Summary of Study" page, and read through the executive summary of the results. Compare the claims made here to the statements in the article "On November 6th Vote No on Proposal C. Living Wage Harms Our Economy," using the link at www.aw-bc.com/leeds/ch16. Which claims are in line with theoretical predictions? Which claims do you think are credible?

Strategy and Policy
The "Jobless Recovery" of the Early 2000s

When the economy slows down, firms need less labor, because fewer goods and services are demanded. When the economy picks up again, an increase in employment usually follows. Unfortunately for many U.S. workers, the economic recovery that began in late 2001 was what is termed a "jobless recovery," because of the lack of job growth that accompanied the increase in GDP. Although the economy as a whole grew in 2002, employment fell by more than 350,000 jobs. The exact causes of the lack of job growth are complex and not fully understood. Widely cited reasons why firms did not add labor as demand for their goods and services increased include the (1) "offshoring" of jobs to other countries with lower wages, and (2) a switch to a more technology-intensive combination of inputs.

Offshoring occurs when firms transfer the production of goods to other countries, frequently to India or China, where workers earn much lower wages than their U.S. counterparts. Such a strategy helps firms keep costs down, which may translate into lower prices for domestic consumers. However, a subsequent economic recovery does little good to those who have lost jobs that move overseas. Consider Rockford, Illinois, where about 1,000 jobs disappeared when Motorola closed a repair plant. At the same time that it closed the repair plant, Motorola spent more than $1 billion to build a new electronics factory in China.[5] Illinois is not unique in this regard. Overall, the United States has lost over 2.8 million manufacturing jobs since 2000.[6] A Federal Reserve Bank of New York study concluded that many of these job losses are permanent.

Because many types of service jobs (such as cleaning services) cannot be performed in a remote location, offshoring hits manufacturing particularly hard. Economic recovery eventually results in higher employment nationally. However, areas that are highly dependent on manufacturing can take a long time to recover.

---

[5] "U.S. Manufacturing Heartland Struggles with Jobless Recovery," *Sydney Morning Herald*, January 13, 2004 at www.smh.com.au/articles/2004/01/12/1073877762803.html?from=storyrhs, accessed May 31, 2005.

[6] For more information on jobless recovery, please refer to Erica L. Groshen and Simon Potter, "Has Structural Change Contributed to a Jobless Recovery?" *Current Issues in Economics and Finance*, August, 2003, v9, 0.8 at www.newyorkfed.org/research/current_issues/ci9-8/ci9-8.html. Accessed August 18, 2005.

Workers who lose their jobs may face long periods of economic hardship. The challenge for U.S. policy makers is to maintain the international trade that has helped the country as a whole to prosper, while at the same time assisting workers in areas hard hit by the loss of employment.

Critical-Thinking Questions

1. Using the supply and demand model, show how employment and wages are affected in a local economy when a large employer moves its jobs elsewhere.
2. What kind of social programs might be most helpful to workers in areas like Rockford, Illinois?

►SUMMARY

- **U.S. income and wealth distribution.** Since the 1970s, some observers have noted a rising disparity between the incomes of the wealthy and the poor, with a decline in the percentage of the population defined as "middle class." As of 2003, the top 5 percent of U.S. households received 21.4 percent of all income produced, while more than 12 percent of the population fell below the poverty line. The Lorenz curve shows the extent that income in an economy deviates from a perfectly equal distribution. Minorities and immigrants are far more likely to be poor by this standard than others. Wealth is the total amount of financial resources that an individual has accumulated over a lifetime. Wealth is even more unevenly distributed than income.

- **Income distribution: efficiency versus equity.** While efficiency is measurable in an objective fashion, equity is a normative concept. As we attempt to identify and assist those at the lowest income distributions, we must first identify those we most want to help. The U.S. government uses the poverty threshold as the official definition of which families are in poverty. Qualification for most government aid is based on a family's income relative to this measure.

- **Discrimination.** Discrimination is one important cause of poverty. Discrimination denies people access to jobs and education based on their race, religion, sex, or some other characteristic that is not relevant to the performance of duties. Most economists now view discrimination as a "taste," a preference for not employing, working with, or otherwise interacting with a specific group of people for reasons unrelated to their job performance.

- **Education.** Differences in the quantity and quality of education affect a person's productivity and hence his earnings later in life. Because the children of the wealthy tend to receive superior educations, differences in income may be perpetuated.

- **Income redistribution and the government's response to poverty.** As of the mid-1990s, welfare is not an entitlement, meaning that the poor no longer automatically qualify for financial assistance. Welfare is now regarded as temporary assistance, with specific limits on how long one may receive such assistance. States may place additional work requirements on people receiving welfare. Unemployment insurance and food stamps also provide aid to people without work or adequate income. Some economists criticize food stamps as too restrictive. They would replace food stamps with cash transfers that let people purchase what they desire. Finally, a government may institute a minimum wage (a form of price floor) when it believes that the wages in a given market are too low. These price floors both increase wages and reduce the quantity of labor demanded, generating considerable debate about whether workers are truly better off with them.

Affirmative action 420
Average tax rate 424
Discrimination 415
Earned income 409
Earned Income Tax Credit
  (EITC) 425

Entitlements 424
Lorenz curve 410
Marginal tax rate 424
Poverty line 413
Progressive income tax
  system 424

Temporary Aid for Needy
  Families (TANF) 424
Unearned income 409
Wealth 409

PROBLEMS

1. Suppose that in the Kingdom of Dwark, the king owns all resources and all income earned in the economy goes directly to him. Only through charity are his subjects able to survive. Draw the Lorenz curve for the economy assuming the king decides to keep all income for himself.

2. Lotteries are often criticized as harmful to the poor. Why might a lottery reduce the well-being of poorer individuals more than the well-being of the wealthy?

3. How might family educational values, expectations for children, and the relationship between education and income combine to make incomes more unequal across time?

4. Studies have shown that discrimination tends to fall when the economy is expanding and to rise when the economy is in recession. Why do you think this is the case?

5. How would the introduction of a new, more difficult bar exam that is required to practice law affect attorneys' wages? Show your answer using a supply and demand diagram.

6. How would wages change in the nursing profession if, due to discrimination, women were forced to work only as nurses and were forbidden from becoming physicians? How would wages change in the market for physicians? Show the change in each market using a graph.

7. In the first Test and Extend problem, a tax was used to equalize income. If the tax rate were 100 percent, allowing the government to redistribute income perfectly equally, how much would each family get? How might such a tax hurt long-term growth in the economy?

8. What does the term "economic rent" mean as applied to wages earned by some individuals?

9. What was the impact on wages and living standard from the rapid expansion of most state university systems after World War II?

10. Discuss the probable effects of a new law that increases the minimum wage within the city of Chicago to $2.00 above the minimum wage in all other areas of the state. Will it help reduce poverty in Chicago?

11. Why do some economists say that we should replace $100 in food stamps with $100 in cash?

12. The *Workfirst!* program in Georgia requires TANF recipients to participate in work activities. Why might this be impractical, given the number of single-parent households? What solution to the problem can you identify?

13. Suppose that the U.S. distribution of income as shown in Table 16.1 were much more unequal, so that the rich got much richer and the poor got much poorer. How might this new distribution actually hurt the rich over time?

14. Use a supply and demand framework to show how discrimination in India against the Dalits (a group viewed as "unclean" by many in India) has led to their impoverishment.

15. Suppose the marginal tax rates are 0 percent on the first $20,000; 10 percent on the next $20,000; and 30 percent on all income above $40,000. Calculate the tax owed by an individual who earns:
    a. $10,000
    b. $30,000
    c. $100,000

16. Why do jobless recoveries hit manufacturing industries particularly hard?

HERE'S HOW MyEconLab CAN HELP YOU GET A BETTER GRADE

1. Log into MyEconLab and take Practice Test chapter-A (to log in for the first time, see page 30 for instructions.)

2. Based on your test results, MyEconLab will identify the areas where you need further work and create a personal Study Plan for you.

3. Your Study Plan contains the exercises listed below and others like them that will target the specific chapter topics you need to focus on. You'll receive instant feedback and find links to tutorials, animations, and the online textbook to help you study.

4. When you're ready, go take Practice Test chapter-B and demonstrate how your results have improved.

Section 16.1, Exercise 1 Suppose that society is divided into four income levels. Each income level represents 25 percent of the population.

Group	Income
1	$ 20,000
2	40,000
3	100,000
4	500,000

a. What percentage of total income is earned by each group?

b. Draw the Lorenz curve for this society.

Section 16.1, Exercise 2 How has U.S. income inequality changed since 1970?

Section 16.2, Exercise 1 How is poverty defined?

Section 16.2, Exercise 2 Centrally planned governments, such as the former Soviet Union, tried to reduce poverty through heavy taxation and other income redistribution programs. Why were they unsuccessful?

Section 16.3, Exercise 1 Suppose that some bakeries are run by men and some are run by women. While there is no difference in the quality of cakes from the two types of bakeries, some consumers believe that only women can bake good cakes.

a. Graph the market for cakes with consumer discrimination taken into account. What can you say about the price of cakes and the quantity sold at each type of bakery?

b. Who wins and who loses from discrimination in this market?

Section 16.3, Exercise 2 Why do economists argue that employer discrimination is not likely to be a problem if markets are competitive?

Section 16.4, Exercise 1 What is the primary reason that quality and quantity of education affect earnings later in life?

Section 16.4, Exercise 2 Why might students of wealthy families gain more from education even if they don't actually learn more?

Section 16.5, Exercise 1 Suppose that the income tax system has marginal tax rates as follows:

Income Level	Tax Rate
0–$15,000	5%
$15,001–$30,000	10%
$30,001–$45,000	15%
Over $45,000	20%

a. If a worker earns $50,000 per year, what is the marginal tax rate?
b. What is the total amount of taxes paid by this worker who earns $50,000 per year?
c. What is the average tax rate?
d. Is this a progressive tax system?

Section 16.5, Exercise 2 Assume that the labor market is currently in equilibrium.

a. Draw a graph of the current labor market, and identify the equilibrium wage and quantity of labor. In equilibrium, is there unemployment?
b. Choose an effective minimum wage, and show the effect on the market.
c. Identify workers who have been laid off due to the minimum wage, and workers who have entered the market and are now looking for a job due to the higher minimum wage.
d. Is the market with the minimum wage efficient?

17 Market Failure: Public Goods and Externalities

If you enjoy eating shellfish or boating, Chesapeake Bay is a must-see destination. At 2,500 square miles, this great natural treasure is the largest estuary in North America. Bordered by Maryland and Virginia, Chesapeake Bay offers some of the finest boating anywhere. Its shallow waters were once dotted with dozens of lighthouses that warned sailors of danger, several of which are now preserved as national landmarks. The wetlands that surround the bay form an ideal habitat for shellfish, as does the grassy bottom of the bay. In fact, the word "Chesapeake" is derived from an Algonquian word meaning "great shell-fish bay."

The very beauty and bounty that characterize Chesapeake Bay are at risk. Open access to the bay by all types of boaters means that sailors cannot insist on quiet. Noise and overcrowding by high-powered speedboats and personal watercraft spoil the serenity of sailing. Dwindling wetlands and other habitat loss, overfishing, and pollution have damaged the bay's water quality and jeopardized shellfish populations. Large-scale commercial fishing vessels challenge the remaining independent fishing vessels for shrinking fishing resources. This pressure seriously threatens the populations of the famous blue crab, along with other shellfish in the bay. So many interested groups are attempting to use the same resources in ways that often impinge on one another; it seems almost impossible to separate the "good guys" from the "bad guys."

What role does economics play in analyzing how the bay came to be at risk and in identifying a solution? How does our understanding of markets apply to the management of the bay's rich natural resources?

Throughout this book, we have discussed how markets allocate goods and services. Central to the philosophy of a market-based economy is the conclusion that competitive markets allocate resources efficiently. Chesapeake Bay, however, offers at least two examples of failures of markets to allocate resources efficiently: the protection offered by lighthouses, and the threat to the fisheries. In some cases, society devotes too few resources to the production of a good, and it is underproduced. In other cases, society devotes too many resources to the production of a good, and it is overproduced. In this chapter, we examine how such under- and overproduction occurs and how the government may intervene to improve resource allocation.

ALONG THE WAY, YOU WILL ALSO LEARN:

- The difference between private and public goods.

- The unique characteristics of pure public goods.

- The different types of externalities, and how markets fail to allocate resources optimally when externalities are present.

- How the Coase Theorem provides a mechanism through which optimal allocations can be reached.

- How the government may intervene through taxes, subsidies, or vouchers to increase the efficiency of an outcome.

AT THE END OF THE CHAPTER,
THE MYECONLAB LOGO WILL DIRECT YOU ONLINE

- MyEconLab is a resource-packed online homework and tutorial system that can help you perform better in your economics course. To log in for the first time, see page 30 for instructions.

- MyEconLab can help you apply important concepts from the chapter to real-world issues. Watch for the logo to indicate online features about externalities and public policy.

- At the end of each chapter, you'll find a special study section that will help you get the most out of your textbook and your instructor's MyEconLab course.

 ## Public and Private Goods

Market failure
Occurs when the private market allocates resources inefficiently by failing to equalize the marginal social cost of producing goods and the marginal social benefit of consuming the goods.

We begin our study of market failure by considering the idyllic lighthouses that dot Chesapeake Bay to distinguish among types of goods. **Market failure** occurs when the private market allocates resources inefficiently by failing to equalize the marginal social cost of producing goods and the marginal social value of the goods. The first lighthouse on Chesapeake Bay was built in 1792 at Cape Henry, Virginia. Many more lighthouses were built on the bay over the next 150 years to warn ship captains of treacherous rocks and shallow areas. Every ship that used the lights to pass safely through the bay benefited from these lighthouses. Without the warnings they provided, countless ships (and their cargo) would have been lost. How is the

Pure public good
A good that is non-excludable and non-rival.

Non-excludability
Exists when there is no way to prevent consumers from deriving benefits from a good.

Non-rival consumption
When one person's enjoyment or use of a good does not detract from another's.

Pure private good
A good that is excludable and rival in consumption.

owner of a lighthouse compensated for this service? The owner has no way to collect a fee from ships that use its beam. The value of the lighthouse's service does not vary based on the number of ships using it. No matter how many ships use the light at any one time, the value of the light to an additional ship does not diminish. These two characteristics set lighthouses apart from most goods.

Economists call a good such as a lighthouse a pure public good. **Pure public goods** have two primary characteristics that we've already illustrated: non-excludability and non-rival consumption. **Non-excludability** means that there is no way to prevent consumers from deriving benefits from a good, even if they do not pay any of the cost of producing the good. **Non-rival consumption** means that one person's enjoyment or use of a good does not detract from another's. In contrast, a **pure private good** is one from which producers can exclude consumers who do not pay, and for which consumers are rivals in consumption. Table 17.1 shows that in addition to pure public and private goods, some goods are excludable yet non-rival, and goods that are non-excludable but rival.

TABLE 17.1

Classification of Goods by Rivalry and Excludability

	Excludable	Non-Excludable
Rival	**Private goods** Cars, food, clothing	**Common property resources** Fisheries; public library; space on a public beach
Non-rival	**Club goods** Cable television; movie theater; rock concert	**Pure public goods** Lighthouse; national defense

Club good
A good that is excludable and non-rival in consumption.

Club goods are excludable and non-rival. These are goods such as cable television, movies shown in theaters, and concerts. With club goods, producers can prevent people who do not pay from consuming the good. In addition, they can produce the good one time for *all* consumers. They need not produce the good separately for *each* consumer. When a cable company shows a movie over its cable network, every consumer who subscribes can watch the movie without reducing the utility of others who want to watch the same film.

Common property resource
A good that is non-excludable but rival in consumption.

Goods such as the peace and quiet and the shellfish population of Chesapeake Bay are **common property resources**, and resources that are non-excludable and rival. There is no way for one consumer to prevent others' consumption. However, the consumption by one person or firm prevents others from consuming the same good. When one commercial fishing boat removes a ton of crabs from the bay, no other vessel can catch the same ton of crabs.

▶ Pure Public Goods

Now that we've classified goods by type, we turn our attention to pure public goods. In this section, we examine how to finance and determine the market demand for public goods. We then focus on the role of the government in providing them.

Free-Rider Problem

Public goods such as lighthouses can be difficult to finance. No specific party has an incentive to pay for the lighthouse. After the lighthouse is constructed, all users—even those who paid nothing—can enjoy it. Economists call this dilemma the free-rider problem. A **free rider** receives the benefits of a good without bearing a share of the cost.

Instances of the free-rider problem are all around us. Consider a group project for which everyone participating receives the same grade. Three of the four students in your group work, while the free-riding fourth student does nothing. Or suppose the residents of a development all decide to build a large swingset in a local park. Will each family pay an amount equal to the value it places on the swingset? Probably not. Free riders will let others give enough to fund the construction. The problem for society is that each consumer has an incentive to underpay in the hope that others will cover his share. As a result, relying on the private market for funding leads to underproduction. The presence of free riders means that a society will not produce as much of a public good as it actually desires. Economists say that production is below the socially efficient level.

Market Demand for Public Goods

Market demand curves show the marginal benefit for all members of society combined. In the case of private goods, market demand curves also show the combined willingness of all consumers to pay. To obtain the market demand curve for a private good, we add all individual demand curves horizontally (adding the quantity demanded at each price for all consumers). With pure public goods, the marginal benefit for each consumer is not obtained at the expense of other consumers. The consumers share one unit of the good rather than consuming separate units. As a result, we cannot determine the combined benefit to society from a public good through the horizontal summation of individual demand curves. Instead, we add the marginal benefit that each consumer receives for a given amount of the good. The combined marginal benefit to all members of society is the **marginal social benefit** (MB_s) of the good.

To illustrate, we can add the individual demand curves vertically to determine the marginal social benefit of a lighthouse. Assume that 100 ships make use of the lighthouses on the bay, and that each ship benefits equally. In panel (a) of Figure 17.1, we see that if there is only 1 ship, total demand is equal to MB_1. The marginal cost of providing lighthouses is MC, and the equilibrium quantity of lighthouses is 0. Marginal benefit is less than marginal cost (the curves do not intersect) at any positive number of lighthouses. With 3 ships, demand is equal to MB_3, and the equilibrium quantity is 1. What if we combine the benefits of all 100 ships, as shown in panel (b) of Figure 17.1? The equilibrium quantity of lighthouses is then equal to 25.

The Government Solution

The free-rider problem complicates the determination of the optimal quantity. Suppose that each consumer knows that his demand is as depicted in panel (a) of Figure 17.1. Each consumer has no incentive to tell lighthouse owners about his willingness to pay. Instead, consumers may simply hope that the efficient quantity will be built and they can free-ride on others. Thus, if society wishes to consume the socially efficient amount of pure public goods, it must find an alternative funding source. One commonly used solution is the government. Governments can impose

Free rider
An individual who receives the benefits of a good without bearing a share of the cost.

Marginal social benefit (MB_s)
The sum of the marginal private benefit and the external (social) benefit.

FIGURE 17.1

Determining the Optimal Quantity of a Public Good

With only 1 ship, total demand is equal to MB_1, and there is insufficient benefit to justify the cost of a lighthouse. With 2 or more ships, we add the marginal benefit curves vertically to determine market demand because consumption is non-rival. Panel (a) shows that with 3 ships, there is just enough demand for 1 lighthouse. We see in panel (b) that with 100 ships and non-rival consumption, summing all 100 demand curves vertically results in a total demand of MB_{100}, and the equilibrium quantity is 25 lighthouses.

taxes and license fees to force those who benefit from public goods to pay a share of the cost. National defense, national parks, air traffic control, and, more recently, airport security are publicly provided goods for which citizens contribute to the cost through taxes. In the case of national defense, part of the income tax paid by all citizens is used. The presumption is that all citizens receive the benefits of national defense, and that these benefits are non-rival. While individual taxpayers cannot choose how much national defense to purchase, they have an indirect say through the election process.

Until this point in the chapter, we have focused on how much of a good to purchase. After society decides how much to consume, it must then decide who should pay.

The Problem of the Commons

Pure public goods are non-rival. As you saw in Table 17.1, however, common property resources are non-excludable but rival in consumption. This rivalry becomes especially damaging in cases when the goods are free or sold at an artificially low price. Consumers then have an incentive to overuse the goods. In 1832, William Forster Lloyd first described the economics of this issue in the context of sheep grazing in commonly held pastures in England known as *the commons*.[1] Those who owned a flock of sheep could take it to the commons for grazing instead of grazing the sheep on their private property. The cost to residents of using the commons was

---

[1] Ronald Coase, who found that the common grounds were not freely available to all, later disputed Lloyd's conclusions. The concept of open access as set out by Lloyd, however, remains intact.

zero, while using their own property was costly. As a result, the commons were overused. In fact, they were so overused that the fields were often destroyed, and no one could further benefit from them.

The same problem occurs with local parks today. Have you ever tried to have a picnic on the weekend of July 4 at a local state park? If so, you are aware that these common resources are rival in consumption. An area that one group uses for its picnic is not available to another for a gathering at the same time. Consider the Chesapeake Bay fishing professionals who earn a living from the once-plentiful oysters and blue crabs. The problem of rival consumption puts their livelihood at risk. The same is true for firms that pump oil from underground reservoirs. In both cases, rival consumption could deplete the good they are trying to harvest. However, there are important differences. The shellfish resource is renewable, but the oil is not. We next examine this distinction in more detail.

Renewable Natural Resource. The stock of fish, such as the crabs and oysters in the bay (a public-access fishery), is a **renewable natural resource**: a resource that, if not overconsumed, has the ability to regenerate. The crab and oyster populations will continually regenerate themselves, providing a continuous stream of benefits. If overused, they cannot regenerate, and die out. A fishery population will shrink if so many fish are caught that the remaining population is unable to replace them.

This problem is so prevalent in both salt- and fresh-water fisheries that states have established strict catch limits for many species. Fishermen can fish only in certain months of the year, they can keep only a certain number of fish per day, and the fish must exceed a stated minimum length. Even with these limits, many open-access fresh-water fisheries such as trout streams must be continually restocked to ensure a supply of fish. To protect fish populations in ponds and streams, the government can also charge license fees. Anglers must gain permission to fish by purchasing licenses. However, in many cases, the fees are too low and catch limits too high to adequately protect the fish population.

Chesapeake Bay faces a greater problem than a recreational trout-fishing stream does. In the bay, commercial fishing vessels do the most intensive fishing. If the catch is too large, the population of fish will decline. The population will not be able to sustain itself. After a certain point, the more effort that is applied to fishing, the lower the fish population will be. Figure 17.2 uses a study from the National Oceanic and Atmospheric Administration to show the effects of various levels of fishing effort on the ability to harvest shellfish from the Chesapeake. Figure 17.2(a) shows that the catch rate of blue crabs appears to go up and down over time. That said, the overall quantity of crabs harvested has not changed much since the mid-1960s. Yet panel (b) shows that in order to catch the harvest shown in panel (a), fishermen have had to work increasingly hard. As a result, the catch-per-pot rate shown in panel (c) has steadily declined. The crabs cannot reproduce fast enough to allow for larger catches. Fishing professionals have to work harder and harder just to maintain their catch. Over time, if the level of effort continues to increase, the blue crab population will fall.

Nonrenewable Resources. The problem of the commons is not limited to renewable resources. The exploitation of nonrenewable resources, such as oil, is especially problematic if the oil deposits are located beneath several different plots of privately held land. Disputes over the rights to oil reserves in several nations have led to wars. In 1990, Iraq invaded Kuwait, an act that led directly to the first Gulf War and indirectly to the second. Iraq justified its invasion of Kuwait in part by claiming that

---

Renewable natural resource
If not overconsumed, these resources have the ability to regenerate.

FIGURE 17.2

The Relationship Between Effort and Catch Rates in Crab Fishing

Panel (a) shows that although there appears to be a natural cycle of increases and decreases over time, average crab harvests did not change much between 1965 and 1995. In panel (b), we see that the effort required to achieve the catch has increased steadily since the 1940s. We see in panel (c), that as a result, effort per unit of catch (pounds per crab pot, here) has steadily decreased over time. If the trend of increased effort continues, eventually the crab harvest will begin to decline as it is unable to regenerate itself at the same rate that it is harvested.

(a) Reported Baywide Blue Crab Harvest

(b) Baywide Blue Crab Nominal Fishing Effort (person-days fished)

(c) Baywide Blue Crab Catch-Per-Unit-Effort (pounds per crab pot placed)

Source: Stock Assessment of the Chesapeake Bay Blue Crab (*Callinectes sapidus*) Executive Summary Figures, noaa.chesapeakebay.net/statistics/BCfigure.html, accessed June 1, 2005

Kuwait was pumping too much oil from underground reserves that lay beneath both countries.

To remove political complexities, let's put the oil example in a narrow context. Consider an oil deposit that lies beneath a plot of land owned by one person. That individual can choose the best rate at which to remove the oil from the ground. He will take into account that after the underground reserve is empty, it will not regenerate and will produce no more revenue. Suppose that Ed, a rancher in Texas, discovers an oil reserve that lies completely under his land. The rate at which Ed pumps the oil depends on a number of factors. These include the size of the oil deposit, the future price of oil, and the rate by which he must discount future revenues. (Recall our coverage of the net present value of money in Chapter 14.) In general, the more the owner expects the price to rise in the future, the greater his incentive to pump the oil later rather than now.

What if the oil reserves lie beneath two ranches—Ed's ranch and Tanya's ranch? In this case, Ed must be concerned with both the pace at which he pumps oil and how rapidly Tanya is pumping oil. Suppose Tanya does not need the money she could earn from pumping the oil right away. She would prefer to pump a little bit of the oil each year over a long period of time. Ed, however, needs money now, so he pumps the oil as quickly as possible. At this point, Tanya has an incentive to begin pumping oil at a faster rate. If she waits, there may be nothing left to pump in future years. The result is that the oil reserve is depleted faster than either Ed or Tanya would choose if either were the sole owner.

In the case of nonrenewable resources, the rate of depletion is an important economic decision. If multiple parties have access to the same resource, that decision is greatly complicated by tension between the competition to exploit the resource and the desire to spread its use over time.

TEST + *EXTEND* Your Knowledge

1. TEST Suppose that your state seeks to discourage overfishing by charging everyone who fishes for trout a $20 fee, and by limiting their catch to eight fish per day. After implementing this fee, the state finds that the local streams are still fished out completely every year and must be restocked. Some advocate increasing the fee, while others argue that the catch limits per angler should be reduced. Could either solution work? Can you think of others?

2. EXTEND Log on to the Utah Division of Wildlife Resources site using the link at www.aw-bc.com/leeds/ch17 and find the fees for fishing licenses in Utah. You will note that there are many different prices for different groups. Can you justify these prices, in light of the problem of the commons? If not, what changes do you recommend?

▶ Externalities

Consumption externality
Arises when the consumption of a good by one individual or group affects others.

In the previous section, we discussed market failure that results from goods, being either non-excludable, non-rival, or both. We now turn our attention to a different type of market failure that we first discussed in Chapter 6: externalities. An externality occurs when the cost or benefit of the production or consumption of a good or service falls on parties that are not directly involved in (that is, are *external* to) the transaction. We focus on two types of externalities: consumption externalities and production externalities. **Consumption externalities** arise when the consumption

Production externality
When the production of a good or service that affects individuals or firms that do not directly produce or consume the good.

of a good by one individual or group affects others. **Production externalities** occur when the production of a good or service affects individuals or firms that do not directly produce or consume the good. Externalities can bring either benefits (*positive externalities*) or costs (*negative externalities*). You'll soon discover that examples of externalities are all around us. We return to the Chesapeake Bay discussion to explain several common examples of consumption and production externalities. We first describe how the presence of externalities affects the optimal level of output, and then turn to ways in which that level of output might be achieved.

Positive Externalities

Waterfront home maintenance is a private good that can illustrate a positive externality. Sun-Yee owns a home on the Chesapeake Bay shore. Her lawn runs right down to the edge of the bay. When storms hit the bay, some soil erodes from the edge of her property. This soil erosion hurts her property's value because it damages the lawn. It also damages the fishing conditions in the bay by decreasing the water quality.

Suppose that to prevent any further damage to her lawn, Sun-Yee installs a retention barrier that protects the soil from high waves. She alone pays for the renovations, and she is entitled in return to the entire increase in property value when she sells the home. Local fishermen do not help to pay for the new retention system nor receive any of the resulting profits of the home sale. They do benefit from her work, though. The decrease in soil runoff from the lawn improves the fishing in the bay. In this case, Sun-Yee's work generates a positive externality for the fishermen. A positive externality is a benefit received by individuals or groups who are not directly involved in a transaction.

Positive Consumption Externalities. When you get a flu shot, you reduce the probability that you will be stricken with the flu that season. Your increased likelihood of good health is the private benefit of consuming the shot. The benefits don't stop there, though. Because you are less likely to be sick, your roommate, family members, and others close to you are also less likely to become ill. Thus, as with the home renovations, the social benefits of flu shots exceed the private benefits, because social benefits include external benefits. The private equilibrium quantity is less than the socially optimal quantity.

Marginal external benefit
Benefit that accrues to individuals or groups not directly involved in the production or consumption of the good.

Positive Production Externalities. Producers underproduce goods that generate positive externalities, because the benefits they receive do not reflect the external benefits that accrue to bystanders. Thus, the marginal revenue they receive is less than the marginal social benefit—the benefit to society—that one more unit of their good provides. The model of supply and demand shows how this production level occurs. Figure 17.3 shows the impact of the installation of soil-retention systems by private homeowners. On the horizontal axis, we show the quantity of soil retention systems in thousands of feet. The vertical axis measures the price of the systems in dollars per foot. The demand curve ($D_p = MB_p$) shows the private demand, or marginal private benefit, for these systems by the homeowners in the neighborhood. The marginal external benefit is shown by the line labeled MB_E, which also slopes downward, reflecting declining marginal external benefit. **Marginal external benefit** is the benefit that accrues to individuals or groups not directly involved in the production or consumption of the good. The sum of the MB_p and MB_E curves represents the marginal social benefit, MB_s.

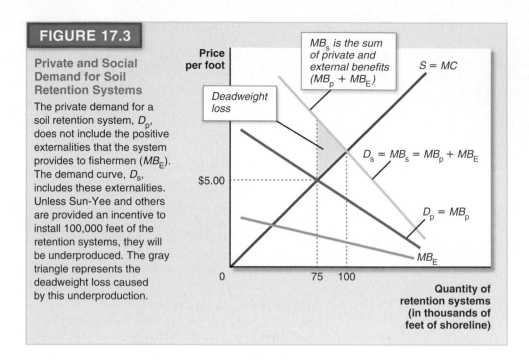

Private and Social Demand for Soil Retention Systems

The private demand for a soil retention system, D_p, does not include the positive externalities that the system provides to fishermen (MB_E). The demand curve, D_s, includes these externalities. Unless Sun-Yee and others are provided an incentive to install 100,000 feet of the retention systems, they will be underproduced. The gray triangle represents the deadweight loss caused by this underproduction.

Figure labels:
- Price per foot
- MB_s is the sum of private and external benefits ($MB_p + MB_E$)
- $S = MC$
- Deadweight loss
- $D_s = MB_s = MB_p + MB_E$
- $5.00
- $D_p = MB_p$
- MB_E
- 0   75   100
- Quantity of retention systems (in thousands of feet of shoreline)

If Sun-Yee and other local homeowners ignore positive externalities, the equilibrium quantity of waterfront renovations they produce is 75,000 feet, and a deadweight loss exists (the area shaded in gray in Figure 17.3). The deadweight loss occurs because, when Sun-Yee considers installing the retention system, she does not factor in the external benefits that flow to her neighbors. She receives only the private benefits of her repair decision. The external benefits that accrue to local fishermen increase the total social benefit of the renovations. The socially optimal demand curve, D_s, shows the marginal social benefit. The marginal social benefit curve is equal to the marginal private benefit plus the marginal external benefit. The intersection of $D_s = MB_s$ and $S = MC$ yields 100,000 feet of renovations, which is the socially optimal quantity. At the socially optimal quantity, the deadweight loss is eliminated.

Without some form of intervention that increases the equilibrium output level to 100,000 feet, the good or service—in this case, renovations—is underprovided. Overall efficiency would be improved if Sun-Yee and others had the proper incentive to produce the socially efficient quantity of soil-retention renovations. Just as we measured the deadweight loss resulting from monopoly pricing in Chapter 10, we show the deadweight loss created by ignoring the social benefits of the renovations. The area of the gray triangle, which lies above the supply curve and below D_s, between the private and socially optimal consumption levels represents the deadweight loss associated with producing 75,000 rather than 100,000 feet of soil retention systems.

Negative Externalities

In the previous section, you saw that overall social welfare is less than it could be in the presence of positive externalities because the equilibrium quantity is based solely on private benefits and costs. In contrast, transactions that generate negative externalities impose costs on people who are not directly involved in the transaction, and so lead to overprovision of a good.

Negative Consumption Externality. An example of a negative consumption externality is a boater who blasts around Chesapeake Bay in a very loud speedboat on busy weekends. The noise and traffic disturbs the peace and quiet that the people in sailboats crave. The speedboater doesn't come to the Chesapeake Bay to disturb the sailors; the negative externality is an inevitable consequence of the speed and sound produced by that boat.

Negative Production Externality. An example of a negative production externality is the runoff that flows into the bay from poultry farms. The runoff creates nutrient pollution that damages the fragile underwater environment needed to support the vast shellfish populations. As a result of this pollution, shellfish populations fall and commercial fishing suffers. Let's take a closer look at the problem caused by the poultry farmers.

In determining how much to produce, the poultry farmers set marginal private cost equal to marginal private benefit to find the profit-maximizing output level. However, the farmers do not consider the external cost that they impose on fisheries as part of their cost of production. They produce up to the point where marginal private cost (MC_p) just equals marginal private benefit (MB_p). Figure 17.4 shows how the optimal social quantity differs from the optimal private quantity in the market for poultry. The **marginal external cost (MC_E)** represents the marginal cost of production that accrues to individuals and firms not directly involved in the transaction. The upward-sloping supply curve, S_p, shows the private marginal cost of production, MC_p. The downward-sloping demand curve shows the marginal private benefit, MB_p. If they ignore the externality, the poultry farmers produce 18 million chickens per year.

The supply curve, $S_s = MC_s$, reflects the total cost to society of producing chickens. MC_s, **marginal social cost**, is equal to MC_p plus the marginal external cost of production (MC_E). It lies above the original supply curve, S_p, indicating that the full cost of production to society is greater than the private cost at every output level.

Marginal external cost (MC_E)
The marginal cost of production that accrues to individuals and firms not directly involved in the transaction.

Marginal social cost (MC_s)
Marginal private cost plus marginal external cost.

FIGURE 17.4

The Social Cost of Pollution

If poultry farmers consider only the private cost of producing chickens, MC_p, the equilibrium quantity is 18 million chickens per year. The farms also produce nutrient runoff, which runs into the Chesapeake Bay and harms the shellfish population, which is the marginal external cost, MC_E. The marginal social cost (MC_s) of production is the sum of marginal private cost, MC_p, and marginal external cost (MC_E). Because the farms produce this negative externality, the socially optimal quantity is 15 million chickens per year. The gray triangle represents the deadweight loss.

MC_s is the sum of the private marginal cost and the external marginal cost ($MC_p + MC_E$)

There are many poultry farms that border Chesapeake Bay. The farms produce nutrient runoff that can flow into the bay, damaging the environment. Because the runoff is not produced intentionally, but is a by-product of poultry production, it represents a negative externally.

Because chicken farmers do not account for the deadweight loss, the market equilibrium is 18 million chickens. The socially optimal output level, 15 million, is lower than 18 million. Notice the gray triangle that lies below S_s and above the demand curve between the private market output and the socially optimal output. It represents the social cost (deadweight loss) of the externality.

Runoff pollution is one of the most serious threats to the Chesapeake Bay ecosystem. Shellfish such as oysters cannot tolerate the changes to water and sediment quality that have accompanied the widespread development of businesses and residences along the shores of the bay. Later in the chapter, we discuss how the governments of the shoreline states have tried to tackle this issue. First, we consider whether the poultry farmers and those catching shellfish might be able to resolve the problem without outside intervention.

▶ The Coase Theorem: Private Parties Solve the Common Property Dilemma

Private ownership is one of the hallmarks of a market-based economy. Individuals have the right to own land, cars, homes, businesses, and more. In fact, the right to private ownership is an important incentive to work. For example, U.S. laws allow you to prohibit another person from growing crops on land that you own. In some cases—such as the water in Chesapeake Bay—the question of ownership is not as clear. We have no pre-established rights for using the resources of the bay. As you will learn, after these rights have been established, efficient solutions may be close at hand.

Nobel Laureate Ronald Coase developed a mechanism to analyze and resolve such problems, using a theory that now bears his name. The **Coase Theorem** states that if property rights exist and bargaining and information costs are low, the parties involved will be able to bargain among themselves to obtain an efficient outcome without governmental intervention.

Coase Theorem
When property rights exist and bargaining and information costs are low, solutions to externality problems can be resolved through bargaining to obtain an efficient outcome without governmental intervention.

Residence Hall Quiet Hours: Coase Theorem Application

An interesting (and probably familiar) application of the Coase Theorem occurs in college residence halls. Most residence halls have established quiet rules for different times of the day. Suppose that from midnight to 10:00 A.M. from Sunday through Thursday, residents have the right to a quiet environment. At all other hours, residents have the right to make noise. By establishing property rights, the college resolves the dilemma of when the residence halls will be quiet. It also creates an environment in which bargaining can occur. Students who value quiet will be willing to pay others who prefer noise either to not make noise during the day, or to go elsewhere to make it. If other students value noise, they will be willing to pay other students to put up with it at night when the residence hall is supposed to be quiet. For example, in 2003, a student with a rock band at Temple University actually paid his neighbors to tolerate his practicing.

Chesapeake Bay: Coase Theorem Application

Applying the Coase Theorem to the Chesapeake Bay runoff problem is challenging, because so many firms and individuals use it for varied purposes. We simplify matters here by assuming that chicken farmers and shellfish industry members are the only groups that use the bay's water. Suppose that those fishing in the bay have the right to a clean fishing environment. Wastewater runoff from chicken farms causes $10 million of damage per year in reduced shellfish harvest, but it costs the chicken farmers $20 million to haul the waste away from the bay for treatment. Chicken farmers are better off paying the shellfishing fleet between $10 million and $20 million to allow the runoff to go into the bay. The fishing professionals are also better off, as they receive more in payments from the chicken farmers than the value of the shellfish lost.

A fascinating twist to the Coase Theorem is that the same result occurs if the property rights are reversed. Suppose that farmers have the right to allow their runoff to enter the bay's watershed. If the value of the lost shellfish harvest exceeds the cost of paying the chicken farmers to ship the waste elsewhere, the shellfish fleet owners will be willing to pay the farmers not to allow the runoff into the bay. As long as one party has established property rights, the two parties can strike a mutually beneficial bargain.

Bargaining and information costs must be low for the Coase Theorem to work. If the resources needed to organize a bargaining solution to a problem exceed the cost of the problem itself, the economy is clearly not better off. In the case of complex environmental damage disputes such as those related to Chesapeake Bay, it is unlikely that private bargaining will work the way it would in the simple setting of the residence hall. As a result, the government might intervene in such cases.

THE BUCKETS: © United Feature Syndicate, Inc.

▶ Government Can Solve the Common Property Dilemma

Where do private parties turn when a private market fails to generate an efficient outcome because of externalities? What if the private bargaining suggested by Coase is infeasible? The government can intervene to try to improve the outcome. Governments can use legislation, taxes and subsidies, and market-based solutions such as voucher systems to resolve the inefficiency created by externalities.

In some cases, government agencies are dedicated to combating negative externalities. The U.S. agency with primary responsibility for environmental quality control at the federal level is the **Environmental Protection Agency (EPA)**. In addition, state governments have agencies or departments of environmental protection that are concerned with more localized environmental issues. In this section, we examine government tools for addressing market failure.

Environmental Protection Agency (EPA)
The U.S. agency with primary responsibility for environmental quality control at the federal level.

Get Ahead of the Curve

Apply your knowledge of externalities and public policy to evaluate recent legislation that reduces harmful emissions from New York State power plants.

Regulation

We begin with the use of legislation in the context of our Chesapeake Bay example. To solve the nutrient runoff problem in the bay through legislation, the local and state governments could force farmers to construct retention basins and treatment facilities. These actions would prevent the nutrients from reaching the bay. In fact, local governments set such requirements all the time, to force farmers to internalize the cost of the externality. That is, farmers are compelled to bear the additional cost that their actions create. Other examples of this strategy at work are mandatory technology in jet engines to reduce noise around airports and air scrubbers in smokestacks to reduce airborne pollutants from factories.

LifeLessons

Trash Travels

One of the biggest problems facing large cities today is trash disposal. Cities generate mountains of waste either buried in landfills or incinerated into ash. Cities with very limited ability to dispose of their own trash must look to other municipalities—or nations—to accept it. In March 1987, a barge named the Mobro 4000 left New York City after discovering that the landfill in Islip, New York, was full and unable to accept its load. The owners of the barge then attempted to unload the 3,200 tons of waste in Morehead City, North Carolina. But on learning that some of the refuse was hospital waste, Morehead City refused to accept the load. In all, the Mobro 4000 spent 74 days covering 6,000 miles in search of a place to dump its load. It even visited Mexico and the Bahamas. With no takers, it was forced to return to Brooklyn, New York, where the load was incinerated into 430 tons of ash that was then buried in Islip.

While this tale of trash may seem unique and sadly comical, millions of tons of waste set sail every year for other countries. A nearly identical story appeared just the year before. A ship named the *Khian Sea* set out from Philadelphia on a voyage that would take it to more than a half-dozen nations in search of a place to dump a load of already incinerated ash. After 14 months and thousands of miles, the ash was finally dumped in Haiti. After 12 years of haggling, the group who dumped the ash returned to Haiti to remove the remaining ash. The ash had been deemed hazardous waste.

When one society exports undesirable loads such as trash to another without fully compensating the other, the group on the receiving end bears the cost of the negative externality. Think twice before tossing an unwanted item in the trash!

Taxes and Subsidies

A local government can also reduce the deadweight loss associated with the chicken farm runoff with a tax or subsidy.

Pigouvian Tax. Maryland environmentalists are seeking a tax on more than 2,700 chicken farmers to help clean up Chesapeake Bay. To illustrate how such a tax may result in an efficient level of output, assume that at the socially optimal output level, the social cost of the negative externality is $1.00 per chicken produced. The tax will make chicken-farming more expensive, which will reduce the equilibrium quantity of chickens sold in the poultry market. Figure 17.5 includes the market demand for poultry and the private market supply curve from Figure 17.4. With no tax, the private market equilibrium generates a deadweight loss equal to the area shaded in gray. You know from Chapter 6 that a per-unit tax of $1.00 per chicken shifts the supply curve upward by the amount of the tax. With the tax, the new supply curve is S^t, which intersects the demand curve, D, at the optimal level of 15 million chickens. Taxes used to correct for the effects of externalities are sometimes called **Pigouvian taxes**, after the economist A. C. Pigou. The tax on chickens represents a Pigouvian tax because it shifts the supply curve to the point where the new equilibrium output is equal to the socially optimal output, eliminating the deadweight loss.

Subsidy. In the case of a positive externality, the government can bring about the efficient level of production by using a subsidy instead of a tax. Suppose that if the government rebates to residents $1.00 per foot of the cost of soil retention systems, the socially optimal quantity (100,000 feet) will be produced. If the government offers to subsidize soil retention systems, the demand for them increases. Figure 17.6 shows the soil retention systems externality of Figure 17.3. The private demand curve, D_p, now shifts rightward, so that the vertical distance between the original and the new demand curve including the subsidy, D^s, is equal to the $1.00 subsidy. The resulting equilibrium output level, where D^s crosses S_p, is at the socially optimal level of 100,000 feet.

Pigouvian taxes
Taxes used to correct for the effects of externalities; these taxes increase efficiency.

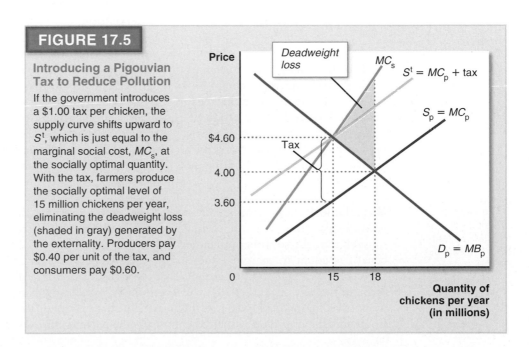

FIGURE 17.5

Introducing a Pigouvian Tax to Reduce Pollution

If the government introduces a $1.00 tax per chicken, the supply curve shifts upward to S^t, which is just equal to the marginal social cost, MC_s, at the socially optimal quantity. With the tax, farmers produce the socially optimal level of 15 million chickens per year, eliminating the deadweight loss (shaded in gray) generated by the externality. Producers pay $0.40 per unit of the tax, and consumers pay $0.60.

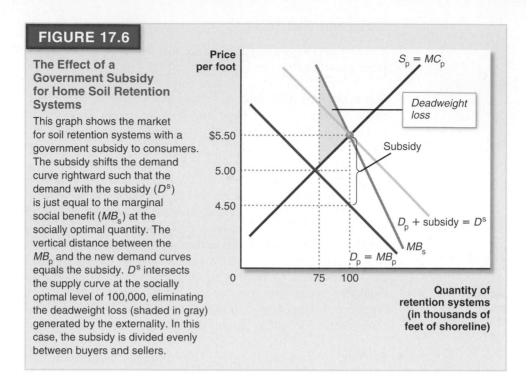

FIGURE 17.6

The Effect of a Government Subsidy for Home Soil Retention Systems

This graph shows the market for soil retention systems with a government subsidy to consumers. The subsidy shifts the demand curve rightward such that the demand with the subsidy (D^s) is just equal to the marginal social benefit (MB_s) at the socially optimal quantity. The vertical distance between the MB_p and the new demand curves equals the subsidy. D^s intersects the supply curve at the socially optimal level of 100,000, eliminating the deadweight loss (shaded in gray) generated by the externality. In this case, the subsidy is divided evenly between buyers and sellers.

Market-Based Solutions to Externalities

Legislative solutions, such as bans and quotas, as well as taxes and subsidies, represent direct government intervention in markets that produce externalities. The advantage of such methods is that they are usually straightforward. As such, they can be effective at reducing negative externalities or promoting positive ones. The downside of these methods is that they are imprecise. For example, a tax on all poultry affects the environmentally clean producer who releases no waste as well as the polluting producers that the tax aims to affect. Thus, the punishment does not always fit the crime. Governments can use the power of markets to increase efficiency as an alternative to direct market intervention.

Effluent Charges. Rather than tax the output that produces the externality, a government can charge firms per unit of effluent (emissions) produced. In the case of chicken farms, farmers would be charged per unit of nutrient runoff rather than taxed on the quantity of chickens raised. We then avoid the problem of taxing the environmentally friendly producer at the same rate as the serious polluter. With an effluent charge, the clean producer might pay no charge at all. Thus, firms have a market-based incentive to correct problems in their production. Unfortunately, programs that charge based on the quantity of emissions are cumbersome (and expensive) to administer.

Marketable permits
Allow firms that receive them to emit a certain quantity of effluents per year.

Marketable Permits. Marketable permits are tradable rights that allow firms that hold them to emit a certain quantity of effluents per year. If the level of permits is set such that the socially optimal level of output is produced (where marginal social benefit is equal to marginal social cost), deadweight loss can be eliminated. The advantage of a marketable permit is that the effluents are decreased more efficiently through the use of markets. Ideally, economists would advocate auctioning off the permits to the highest bidder at the outset. In this way, the firms that benefit most from emitting pollution will bid the most for the permits. Firms that benefit the least (because they can easily alter production methods to eliminate the pollutants) will be willing to pay the least and so will not obtain them.

Get Ahead of the Curve

Use your understanding of market-based regulation to analyze government proposals to control mercury emissions from coal-fired U.S. power plants.

Rather than auctioning permits, the government has employed other distribution means. For example, the EPA first determines how much of a particular pollutant it will allow per year. It then divides that total among producers by issuing permits. Each firm is allowed to produce a fraction of the total. When the permits are marketable, one firm can sell its permit to another, thus achieving a result similar to the auction. Marketable permits are set apart from other regulatory schemes, in that the right to emit pollution can be bought and sold. As such, they allow the firms a degree of choice regarding whether they will use an environmentally clean method and pay less, or emit more effluents and pay more. As in the case of an auction, firms with a high marginal private benefit from emitting effluents will purchase them from firms that have low marginal private benefit of effluent emission. Firms will sell their permits if they can easily reduce emissions, while they will purchase additional permits if they are less costly than emission reduction. In addition, public interest groups and individuals who wish to reduce the overall level of pollution can simply buy the permits and never use them. If it sets the quantity of permits correctly, the EPA achieves the reduction in emissions it wants at minimal cost. The result is increased overall efficiency in the economy.

Combined Strategies. The final government strategy is to combine elements of several tactics. In the case of fishing, the government combats overharvesting of renewable resources in several ways. It can require that fish caught be at least a certain size, restrict equipment by limiting net size or type, and impose an overall quota, as in the case of the Alaskan king crab. Each year, the Alaskan king crab season lasts only a few days. Over 200 commercial fishing vessels vie for the total allowable catch. One disadvantage of the overall quota is that it results in an all-out effort against rivals in a contest of manpower and equipment. The same quantity of fish could be caught with far fewer boats and less-intensive effort over more time.

The "smash-and-grab" nature of overall fishing quotas has prompted industry experts to advocate individually transferable quotas (ITQs). With ITQs, fishing professionals are assured a specific quantity per boat or per person. The transferability of the individual quotas also increases efficiency. An inefficient ITQ holder (perhaps the owner of an old, slow boat) can sell his quota to another vessel. Such a system also helps to manage the population of fish. Further, it prevents boat owners from spending too much on capital in an effort to maximize their catch in a short period of time.[2] ITQ programs in Iceland and New Zealand have successfully controlled the harvest of renewable natural resources.

Strategy and Policy
Money for Nothing—The Battle for Open Space

As the U.S. population increases, more and more land is devoted to residential and commercial space, leaving less and less land undeveloped. Land previously considered undesirable for development has come under increasing pressure, as residents push city and suburban limits outward. In some suburban and semirural areas, residents are now mounting efforts to save remaining open space through the use of

---

[2] Aaron Steelman, "Fishing for Solutions: Policymakers Struggle to Curb Overfishing in the Chesapeake Bay," www.rff.org/rff/News/Coverage/2002/August/Fishing-for-Solutions.cfm.

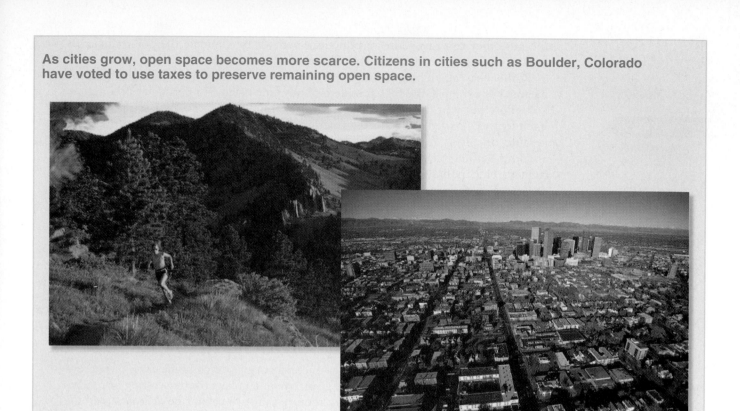

As cities grow, open space becomes more scarce. Citizens in cities such as Boulder, Colorado have voted to use taxes to preserve remaining open space.

open space initiatives. These initiatives typically use tax dollars and publicly funded bond issues to purchase open plots of land as they become available.

In Boulder, Colorado, residents have worked to preserve open space for more than 100 years. In 1898, the citizens of Boulder authorized a bond issue to preserve the land that is now Chatauqua Park. In response to population increases that threatened wilderness areas, citizens acquired additional land that now totals more than 41,000 acres. The drive to preserve open wilderness space is highly organized. Acquisitions are approved by an Open Space Board and managed by an Open Space Department. Various community groups such as the Lions Club care for the preserved lands. Residents also sought to slow development by passing a charter amendment. This amendment established a "blue line" above which water would not be supplied. Without this highly organized effort by residents and their willingness to pay to preserve open space, much of this land would certainly have been used for housing and commercial space. Because public open space is non-excludable, free riding can lead to underprovision. Attracting funding to preserve these natural resources requires residents' awareness of the potential for loss of these lands to development, and willingness to pay to preserve the lands.

Critical-Thinking Questions

1. If citizens value open space, why are land donations insufficient? Why are taxes required to preserve open space?
2. More than 3.5 million visitors come to the Boulder area Open Space and Mountain Parks land every year. If many of these visitors are from outside the area, might there be a more efficient way to fund open space in Boulder?

SUMMARY

- **Public goods and private goods.** Pure public goods are non-excludable, so there is no way of preventing consumers from deriving benefits from the good, and non-rival, meaning that one person's enjoyment or use of the good does not detract from another's. Pure private goods are both excludable and rival. Club goods are excludable and non-rival, and common property resources are non-excludable and rival.

- **Pure public goods.** To determine the market demand for a pure public good, we must add the individual demand curves vertically, because consumption is non-rival. The optimal level of the good is the point at which this market demand (marginal benefit) curve is equal to the marginal cost. The government must often step in to ensure that the optimal level of a pure public good is produced, particularly given the free-rider problem.

- **Externalities.** Externalities exist when production or consumption of a good imposes costs or confers benefits on parties not directly involved in the transaction. In the case of negative externalities, the good is overproduced in the private market outcome. With positive externalities, the good is underproduced unless the government intervenes in some way.

- **The Coase Theorem.** When property rights are not established, resources are likely to be overconsumed. Users generally consider only the private costs and benefits of their actions. The Coase Theorem provides a mechanism through which optimal solutions can be negotiated by assigning property rights to one party, and allowing bargaining.

- **Government intervention.** Government intervention in market failures may take several forms. Governments can impose Pigouvian taxes to reduce production and consumption of goods that are overproduced, and can offer subsidies for goods that are underproduced. Marketable permits and Individually transferable quotas (ITQs) are an attempt to combine market incentives and efficiency with government intervention to increase the overall efficiency of an outcome.

KEY TERMS

PROBLEMS

1. Suppose that the manufacturer of plastic toy drums has a marginal cost of $15 per drum. In addition to this private cost, the drums cause noise pollution that reduces social welfare at a rate of $5.00 per drum. Graph the marginal private cost and the marginal social cost (including the externality). Draw a market demand curve for drums on the same graph and label the socially optimal output, the private market output (ignoring the externality), and the deadweight loss that occurs from producing the private market output. How might regulators use a tax to reduce output to the socially optimal level?

2. Why do many new development communities place restrictive covenants on residences that prohibit all but a few paint-color schemes on homes?
3. Use a supply and demand graph to illustrate that in the absence of government (e.g., the local city government) intervention, a campus beautification project at your school will be underfunded. Label the social optimum.
4. Is a sidewalk a good example of a public good? Why or why not?
5. What is the economic argument for charging a toll to cross a bridge? Does the toll assign the cost appropriately? Explain.
6. Use a positive externality argument to explain why local school taxes are levied on all residents, not just on those who have children in the school system.
7. Suppose that a sawmill that creates water pollution is located upstream from a spring-water company. How can the Coase Theorem ensure that the river water is used efficiently?
8. Check your university housing rules to see what the quiet hours are for residence halls at your school. Are penalties listed? What do these penalties imply about property rights?
9. Though not actually possible, suppose that underground oil reserves regenerate themselves every year. How might this have changed the incentives of Ed and Tanya regarding the oil field that lies beneath their ranches?
10. Historically offshore fishermen have not needed to purchase a license. Offshore fishermen have staunchly fought proposals to initiate a saltwater fishing license. Why might they be unwise in their opposition?
11. Suppose that the marginal cost of steel production is $100 per ton, and that for every ton of steel a firm produces, it also produces air pollution that costs society $10. Use a graph to show the marginal private cost and the marginal social cost of steel production for 0 to 10 tons of steel.
12. Sketch a market demand curve ($MB_p = MB_s$) on your graph from problem 11 and label the socially optimal output level and deadweight loss that result if the firm produces up to the point where demand is equal to the marginal private cost of production.
13. The residents of a local community believe that too many picnics are being held in their local park. At a town meeting, the mayor considers two proposals. One limits each family in the town to one picnic per month per year. The other creates a coupon system through which each family receives 12 "picnic coupons," which they are free either to use or sell to other families. Which solution is more likely to maximize social welfare and why?
14. Why is the Coase Theorem ineffective when bargaining is expensive to carry out?

HERE'S HOW MyEconLab CAN HELP YOU GET A BETTER GRADE

1. Log into MyEconLab and take Practice Test 17-A (to log in for the first time, see page 30 for instructions).

2. Based on your test results, MyEconLab will identify the areas where you need further work and create a personal Study Plan for you.

3. Your Study Plan contains the exercises listed below and others like them that will target the specific chapter topics you need to focus on. You'll receive instant feedback and find links to tutorials, animations, and the online textbook to help you study.

4. When you're ready, go take Practice Test 17-B and demonstrate how your results have improved.

Section 17.1, Exercise 1 For the following list, identify whether each good is non-rival, non-exclusive, or both.

  a. An art museum
  b. A DVD
  c. Clean air
  d. An interstate highway
  e. A hiking trail in a public park
  f. A fireworks display

Section 17.1, Exercise 2 Identify each of the goods or services listed in Exercise 1 as a private good, a public good, a club good, or a common property resource.

Section 17.2, Exercise 1 The following graph shows the marginal benefit for a pure public good. Suppose that all citizens have exactly the same marginal benefit schedule and that the marginal cost per unit of this good is constant and equal to $50.

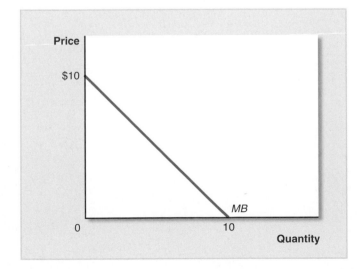

a. Suppose that there are 10 people in this community. Graph the marginal social benefit curve. How many units of this good should be provided?

b. Now suppose that there are 100 people in the community. Graph the new marginal social benefit curve.

Section 17.2, Exercise 2 Suppose that Tom, Dick, Jerry, and Sue are the only residents of Chestnut Street. Each would like to see a streetlight put on the corner, and the cost of the light would be $100. Tom values the light at $75, Dick values it at $50, Jerry values it at $30, and Sue values it at $25.

a. What is the marginal social benefit of the streetlight?
b. Would it be socially efficient to have the light?
c. Will any single resident be willing to provide the light?
d. Suppose that Tom goes to his neighbors and asks for voluntary contributions to the streetlight fund. Is he likely to collect enough money to buy the light?

Section 17.2, Exercise 3 Why are common property resources such as schools of fish likely to be overused?

Section 17.3, Exercise 1 Education is often considered to be a good with a consumption externality, because a higher number of educated people tend to have benefits for society. The following graph shows the private demand and the social marginal benefits of education.

a. Identify the equilibrium market price and quantity.
b. Identify the socially efficient price and quantity.
c. Identify the deadweight loss at the private market equilibrium.

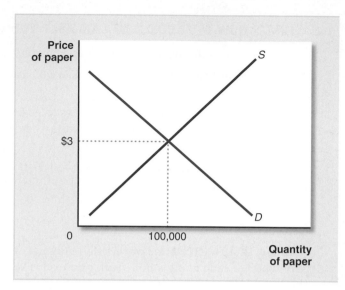

Section 17.3, Exercise 2 Paper mills are often located on rivers, so that they can easily receive logs from upstream locations and use water power to run the mill. These mills have often used the river to dispose of waste as well. The following graph shows the market supply and demand for paper.

a. Suppose that every unit of paper produced generates an additional $1.00 cost for a town downstream, which must remove waste from its water due to the pollution generated by the mills. Draw the marginal social cost curve.

b. Identify the socially efficient price and quantity on your graph.

Section 17.4, Exercise 1 Consider the situation described in the previous exercise. Describe how a bargaining solution could be achieved in each of the following cases.

a. The paper mills are given the legal right to pollute.

b. The town is given the legal right to clean water.

Section 17.4, Exercise 2 Why do bargaining solutions work only if transactions costs are low?

Section 17.5, Exercise 1 Consider again the paper mill problem described in Section 17.3, Exercise 2.

a. Show the effect on the market if the government imposes a $1.00 tax on producers.

b. Is the result socially efficient?

18

Unemployment and Employment

As he walked across the stage to receive his diploma from the University of California at Santa Cruz, in May 2001, Jason wished he could feel as excited as many of his classmates. But his future didn't seem especially bright that day. Choosing to major in computer science had seemed like a smart move back in his sophomore year. The economy had been booming, especially the tech sector, and all the seniors had landed great jobs. Two years later, however, the economy was in recession, the tech sector was in free fall, and there didn't seem to be any jobs for someone with a degree in computer science. Jason's plans to pay off his student loans quickly and to save up for a new car now seemed unrealistic.

Worried about his future, Jason turned to his advisor for help. "You have to be patient," his advisor counseled. "You've only just graduated. A good job will turn up pretty soon." Jason thought about all the time he'd spent searching for job openings and filling out applications without receiving any responses. He wondered how his advisor could believe that jobs were out there.

Jason's friend Steve had a less optimistic outlook. "Those cushy computer science jobs are gone for good," he said. "Everything has changed. You're a smart guy. There is a ton of other things you could do. Have you thought about law school?" Steve was headed for law school himself, but Jason didn't want to spend three more years in school. The thought of additional student loans made him shudder. Besides, he liked computer science and didn't want to feel that he had wasted his time studying it.

The advice from Jason's Uncle Rajan seemed to fall between the other two. "The economy is down," he told Jason, "and the tech sector is down with it. These things move in cycles. The economy will come back up eventually, and when it does, the jobs in Silicon Valley will come back, too." Jason hoped his Uncle Rajan was right, but his uncle couldn't say when the cycle would bring jobs back. Until it did, he was out of luck.

In this chapter, we explore Jason's dilemma of being ready and willing to work but unable to find employment. We will see that there may be an element of truth in the advice from each person he consulted.

ALONG THE WAY, YOU WILL ALSO LEARN:

- What it means to be employed or unemployed and how the composition of the U.S. labor force has changed in the past 30 years.

- How economists measure unemployment.

- The different kinds of unemployment.

- Why a certain amount of unemployment is inevitable and may even be desirable.

- The costs that unemployment imposes on society.

- How immigration and trade policies affect unemployment.

 AT THE END OF THE CHAPTER, THE MYECONLAB LOGO WILL DIRECT YOU ONLINE

- MyEconLab is a resource-packed online homework and tutorial system that can help you perform better in your economics course. To log in for the first time, see page 30 for instructions.

- MyEconLab can help you apply important concepts from the chapter to real-world issues. Watch for the logo to indicate online features about unemployment rates.

- At the end of each chapter, you'll find a special study section that will help you get the most out of your textbook and your instructor's MyEconLab course.

▶ Unemployment, Employment, and the Labor Force

We begin our look at unemployment with some basic vocabulary illustrated by Jason's dilemma. Jasmin, Jason's 12-year-old sister, could not understand why he was so upset. After all, she told him, she didn't work, Grandpa Vinesh didn't work, and even Mom hadn't worked for many years when they were younger. What's wrong with not working?

Jasmin had a point. As a society, we like the fact that Jason's family can support itself without sending a 12-year-old girl or an 80-year-old grandfather to work. The fact that Jason's mother did not work for 10 years is a sign of the family's prosperity, not poverty. The key difference is that Jason was desperately looking for work, but his mother and grandfather chose not to work. Jasmin would not be permitted to work even if she wished to. The U.S. economy is prosperous enough that it can afford to impose *child labor laws*. These laws sharply limit the amount and type of work that children can perform. The laws also keep children in school—gaining valuable education—until they are at least 16 years old.

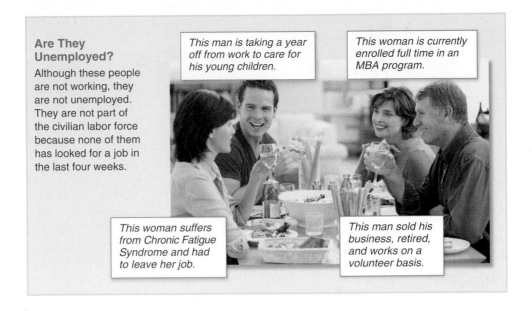

Are They Unemployed?
Although these people are not working, they are not unemployed. They are not part of the civilian labor force because none of them has looked for a job in the last four weeks.

This man is taking a year off from work to care for his young children.

This woman is currently enrolled full time in an MBA program.

This woman suffers from Chronic Fatigue Syndrome and had to leave her job.

This man sold his business, retired, and works on a volunteer basis.

Defining the Labor Force

To better understand the labor market, we must first distinguish among the characteristics of the unemployed. Because they were not working by choice or by government decree, we say that Jason's sister and grandfather are not in the **civilian labor force.** In general, the civilian labor force consists of individuals who meet all of the following criteria:

- Are at least 16 years old
- Are not in the armed services
- Are not incarcerated or otherwise institutionalized
- Have a job or have looked for work in the last four weeks

Civilian labor force
All people in an economy who are at least 16 years old; are not in the armed forces; are neither incarcerated or otherwise institutionalized; and either have a job or have looked for work in the last four weeks.

Characterizing Employment Status

Anyone who is in the labor force and working is *employed*; anyone who is in the labor force and is not working is *unemployed*. With these definitions, we can categorize each member of Jason's family. Jasmin does not have a job, but she is not unemployed, because she fails to meet the age criterion for being in the labor force. In fact, child labor laws prevent her from holding a job. Jason's grandfather is not included in the labor force because he has not looked for work recently. When Jason's mother resumed working outside the home, she went from being out of the labor force to being employed. Because Jason has no job and is actively seeking a job, he is unemployed. Figure 18.1 provides a close look at the labor force that Jason has joined.

In 2004, the U.S. population that was at least 16 years old and was neither institutionalized nor in the armed forces numbered about 223 million. Only 148 million people were in the civilian labor force. About 75 million people, one-third of the civilian, noninstitutional population was neither working nor actively seeking work. Of the 148 million people in the civilian labor force, about 140 million were employed, leaving roughly 8 million people unemployed.

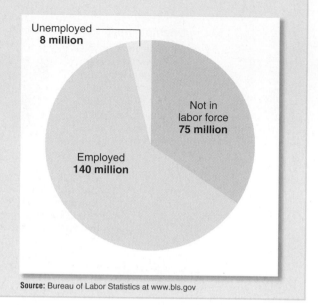

FIGURE 18.1

The U.S. Labor Force in 2004

In 2004, the U.S. civilian, noninstitutionalized population that was at least 16 years old was slightly more than 223 million. This total corresponds to the entire circle. Of these, about 75 million people (the blue wedge) were not in the civilian labor force. Of the 148 million people in the civilian labor force, about 140 million people were employed (the green wedge), and about 8 million people (the yellow wedge) were unemployed.

Unemployed
8 million

Not in labor force
75 million

Employed
140 million

Source: Bureau of Labor Statistics at www.bls.gov

The Changing Face of the U.S. Labor Force

Now that we've established the criteria for employment status, we can turn to trends in the U.S. labor force. The U.S. labor force grew substantially over the last three decades of the twentieth century. Between 1970 and 2004, the number of people holding or seeking jobs rose by over 66.5 million workers, an increase of almost 80 percent.

We can attribute some of this increase to the entry of the post–World War II baby boom generation into the labor force. In addition to growing larger, the labor force has also become far more diverse. Two major changes are the expanding representation of women and immigrants—particularly Hispanics—in the labor force.

Women in the Labor Force

Labor force participation rate
The percentage of the civilian, noninstitutionalized population that is in the civilian labor force.

In 1970, women constituted about 38 percent of the civilian labor force. Over the next three decades, however, far more women than men entered the labor force. The **labor force participation rate** is the percentage of the population (or a demographic subgroup, such as men or women) that is working or actively seeking work.

Since 1970, the labor force participation rate of women has grown steadily. In 1970, only about 43 percent of women over 16 in the civilian noninstitutional population were in the civilian labor force. By 2004, that figure had grown to over 60 percent. The number of men in the civilian labor force grew less quickly than the civilian, noninstitutional population. As a result, the labor force participation rate of men fell during this time period, from almost 80 percent to about 73 percent. Because more women than men have entered the labor force since 1970, women make up an increasing percentage of the labor force. By 2004, women constituted nearly half the labor force.

There are many reasons why women have become such a large part of the labor force. Some economists claim that women's growing labor force participation has its roots in the turn of the twentieth century. At that time, the public schooling that women received started to more closely resemble the schooling that men received. With increasingly marketable skills, women found better opportunities in the labor market and responded by working more. Other economists point to the decline of discrimination. Today's employers are more willing to hire women and pay them wages and salaries that reflect their contributions, thus providing women with a greater incentive to work. The growing U.S. divorce rate has also led women to work more. With half of all marriages ending in divorce, many women can no longer afford to perform the traditional role of homemaker. A career protects women from being "a divorce away from poverty."

Finally, marriage and children did not form as much of a barrier to work for Jason's mother as they did for his grandmother; this will probably be even less of an issue for his sister. Over the last three decades, the labor force participation rate of married women has risen much more sharply than that of single women. In 1970, only about 40 percent of married women and 40 percent of married women with children were in the labor force. By 2004, over 60 percent of married women and over 75 percent of married women with children were working or actively seeking work. The labor force participation rate of married women with children less than 18 years old has gone from less than 50 percent to more than 70 percent in the last three decades alone.

Hispanics in the Labor Force

In addition to changes in gender composition, the ethnic composition of the labor force has changed. Between 1970 and 2004, the number of whites in the labor force grew by more than 60 percent, from 74 million to over 121 million. Over this same period, the number of African Americans rose by 78 percent, from 9 million to almost 17 million. However, the fastest growth has been among Hispanics. Hispanics were such a small part of the labor force in 1970 that the government did not even collect separate data for them. By 1980, the number of Hispanics in the labor force had surpassed 6 million, more than half the number of African Americans. By 2004, the number of Hispanics in the labor force had tripled to more than 19 million.

Most of the growth of Hispanics in the labor force stems from massive immigration to the United States. According to the U.S. Census Bureau, about one-sixth of all Hispanic residents of the United States have entered the country since 1990. Hispanics now account for about half of all foreign-born U.S. residents.

▶ Changes in Jobs Held by Americans

The makeup of the U.S. labor force changed over time, so too did the nature of the jobs that workers occupy. In Chapter 3, we saw how manufacturing has played a steadily decreasing role in the U.S. economy. About 60 percent of all U.S. output is now provided by the service sector. That same shift in output is also reflected in the labor market. Fewer and fewer Americans produce tangible commodities. In the 1920s, 1 in 5 U.S. workers produced food in the agricultural sector of the economy. Figure 18.2 shows that by 1970, this number had fallen to about 1 in 25 workers. By 2000, it had dropped to 1 in 40.

Manufacturing attracted former agricultural workers earlier in the century. However, Figure 18.2 illustrates that employment in manufacturing has declined over the last three decades. Notice that the bars representing the percentage of the labor force employed in agriculture and manufacturing have grown steadily shorter, while

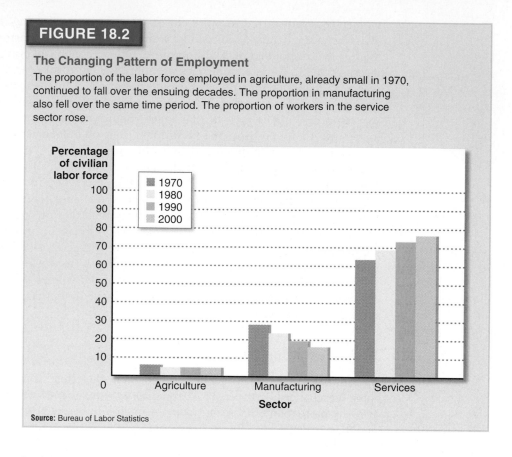

FIGURE 18.2

The Changing Pattern of Employment

The proportion of the labor force employed in agriculture, already small in 1970, continued to fall over the ensuing decades. The proportion in manufacturing also fell over the same time period. The proportion of workers in the service sector rose.

Percentage of civilian labor force

Legend:
- 1970
- 1980
- 1990
- 2000

Sector: Agriculture, Manufacturing, Services

Source: Bureau of Labor Statistics

those representing employment in services have grown steadily taller. Some of the decline in manufacturing and most of the decline in agriculture is due to technological progress. Today, it does not take as many people as it once did to produce a bushel of wheat or a fleet of automobiles. The productivity gains have been far less pronounced in the service sector than in either agriculture or manufacturing. In addition, many of the new service jobs in such areas as health care and entertainment are the result of rising standards of living. Only after people have satisfied their basic needs can they turn their attention to health care and entertainment.

Counting the Unemployed

The U.S. government sometimes provides assistance to those who, like Jason, are looking for work. However, the government must measure unemployment before it can formulate effective policies to combat it. In this section, we look at how the government measures unemployment.

Bureau of Labor Statistics

The Bureau of Labor Statistics (also known as the BLS) is a government agency devoted to collecting data regarding employment, worker compensation, and prices. It categorizes a person as unemployed if he or she meets the four criteria that we listed earlier for being in the labor force but does not have a job. However, some people who are not literally working still meet the BLS definition of having a job and some who are working are not counted. Specifically, the BLS considers people employed if they worked at least 15 hours per week without pay in a family business, or if they were temporarily absent from work due to illness, accident, or strike. However, it counts them as unemployed if they were hired and were waiting to start a new job within the month or were waiting to be recalled to a job from which they were temporarily laid off.

The Current Population Survey

Could we measure unemployment by surveying the population to find out who is employed, who is unemployed, and who is out of the labor force? The U.S. government has done this regularly since 1940 with the Current Population Survey (CPS), a joint project of the BLS and the Census Bureau. The CPS does not count all unemployed people. Instead, it formulates an estimate based on a random survey.[1]

The Unemployment Rate

Simply using the number of unemployed workers can misstate the severity of a nation's unemployment problem. For example, in 1931, about 8.0 million people were unemployed in the United States. In 1991, that figure stood at 8.6 million. While the economy was in a recession in early 1991, times were not nearly as bad as during the depths of the Great Depression in 1931. Why, then, do the unemployment numbers suggest otherwise?

While the total *number* of unemployed workers was greater in 1991 than it was in 1931, the unemployed workers themselves formed a far smaller proportion of the labor force. This was because there were so many more *employed* workers during 1991 than in 1931.

The Civilian Unemployment Rate

Civilian unemployment rate
The percentage of the civilian labor force that has unsuccessfully sought work in the previous four weeks.

Because the scale of any economy changes over time (and differs among nations), we typically measure unemployment using what economists call "the civilian unemployment rate," rather than the number of unemployed people. The **civilian unemployment rate** (u) is the percentage of the civilian labor force that has unsuccessfully sought work in the previous four weeks. We measure it as the ratio of the number of people who are unemployed to the number of people who are in the labor force:

$$u = \frac{Number\ of\ unemployed}{Civilian\ labor\ force} \times 100 =$$

$$\frac{Number\ of\ unemployed}{Number\ of\ unemployed + Number\ of\ employed} \times 100 \qquad (18.1)$$

We can use Equation 18.1 to show that the unemployment rate in 1991 was only 6.8 percent, while the unemployment rate in 1931 was 15.9 percent:

$$u_{1991} = 8.6\ million/126.5\ million = 6.8\%$$
$$u_{1931} = 8.0\ million/50.3\ million = 15.9\%$$

---

[1] For more on the Current Population Survey, go to www.bls.census.gov/cps/cpsmain.htm.

These percentages mean that fewer than seven out of every 100 people who actively sought employment were unemployed in 1991. Almost 16 out of every 100 unsuccessfully sought employment in 1931. Examining the unemployment rate rather than the absolute number of unemployed workers provides a more accurate comparison of economic conditions in 1991 and 1931.

The Unemployment Rate's Shortcomings. Although Jason had trouble finding a job, most of his classmates had no such problem, and all of his parents' friends had jobs. He was therefore surprised to learn that the unemployment rate was close to 6% in 2001. Though the unemployment rate gives economists a good overall picture of the status of the labor market, it obscures differences between subgroups of the population. Some people, such as minorities, teenagers, and high-school dropouts, have a much harder time finding employment than others do. As a result, these subgroups have much higher unemployment rates than a single measure of unemployment would imply.

Racial and Ethnic Differences in Unemployment Rates. Fortunately, we can calculate unemployment rates for narrow segments of the population to describe to the labor market conditions that they face. For example, the number of unemployed whites in the United States has always been much higher than the number of unemployed African Americans. In 2004, more than 5.8 million whites were unemployed while only 1.7 million African Americans were. Note, though, that these numbers ignore the fact that African Americans make up a much smaller portion of the overall civilian, noninstitutionalized population and hence the labor force. The Census Bureau estimates that in 2004, whites made up roughly 82 percent of the population (about 183 million people), and African Americans constituted only about 12 percent (about 26 million people). The unemployment rate for African Americans was 10.4 percent, while the unemployment rate for whites was only 4.8 percent. Thus, while fewer African Americans than whites were unemployed in 2004, unemployment was a larger problem for this subgroup of the population.

Individuals Overlooked by Unemployment Measures

Get Ahead of the Curve

Apply your knowledge of how unemployment is measured to the puzzle of recent low unemployment figures.

Sometimes people's behavior causes them to be missed by standard measures of unemployment. For example, if Jason followed his friend Steve's advice, he would give up looking for a job and enter law school. He would not be alone. Applications to M.B.A. and other graduate and professional programs rose in 2001, along with unemployment rates. Many young workers who lost their jobs decided not to bother searching for new jobs in such a bad economic climate. With the opportunity cost of forgone salaries lower due to the downturn, unemployed young executives enrolled in full-time programs that they hoped would pay off when the job market improved. While some people stopped seeking work to invest in skills, others simply gave up looking, because they could find no worthwhile employment opportunities. Either way, workers who would be counted as unemployed had they continued looking for work no longer appeared in the unemployment statistics. Individuals overlooked by unemployment measures fall into three categories, which we discuss in turn.

Discouraged workers
Workers who withdraw from the labor force rather than keep searching for jobs.

Discouraged Workers. Recall that according to the U.S. government's definition of unemployment, a person who has not sought work in the past four weeks is no longer in the labor force. Workers who withdraw from the labor force rather than continue searching for jobs are known as **discouraged workers**. Here the term *discouraged* may refer to workers who truly feel downcast about their prospects. It may also refer to workers who choose alternative activities over looking for a job. In August 2004, the government estimated that more than half a million people left the labor force because they believed there were no jobs available for them. Another million or so had stopped looking for work but did not specifically cite discouragement as the reason for leaving the labor force. Regardless of the cause, discouraged workers are no longer counted as unemployed. Because fewer people are counted as unemployed, the *discouraged worker effect* causes the unemployment rate to understate the true degree of unemployment in the economy during a downturn. By the same token, the return of formerly discouraged workers to the labor force during a recovery may cause unemployment rates to rise initially, while they search for a job.

Underemployed
Describes people who work fewer hours than they would like or at a job that requires lesser skills than they possess.

Underemployed Workers. Another source of inaccuracy in measuring unemployment stems from the BLS survey, which allows people to respond only "yes" or "no" when asked whether they are employed. This setup leaves a lot of room for ambiguity. Suppose, for example, that Jason finds part-time work at his uncle's software company. In this case, Jason would be considered underemployed. Being **underemployed** means that Jason is employed, but works fewer hours than he would like or at a job that requires lesser skills than he possesses. The decline of the steel industry has displaced large numbers of skilled steelworkers from relatively high-paying jobs. Many of these workers were forced to accept low-paying unskilled work. The unemployment statistics, however, count these workers no differently now than when they had high-paying jobs at the steel mills. Conversely, workers who hold more than one job are counted as employed only once.

Illegal Aliens. Some workers who have jobs are not counted at all. For example, many illegal aliens work long hours but go to great lengths to avoid being detected for fear of being deported. In reality, they are as much a part of the labor force as a citizen who works openly. Not counting them causes official unemployment statistics to understate the real number of employed workers.

TEST + *E X T E N D* Your Knowledge

1. TEST In 1954, there were 63,643,000 people in the labor force, of whom 3,532,000 were unemployed. In 1974, there were 91,949,000 people in the labor force, of whom 7,929,000 were unemployed. Which year experienced worse unemployment?

2. EXTEND Go to the Bureau of Labor Statistics Web site using the link at www.aw-bc.com/leeds/ch18 and look up the unemployment rate for African American and white teenagers. Compare these figures to the figures for adult African Americans and whites. Why do the unemployment rates for teenagers differ from those of adults? Why do the unemployment rates for African Americans and whites differ? Does this affect your view of the racial differences in unemployment?

▶ Types of Unemployment

Jason received a lot of advice regarding his failure to find a job. His advisor felt that his unemployment was a temporary annoyance and nothing more. His friend Steve was far more worried. He felt that Jason would never find a programming job. His Uncle Rajan was somewhere in between, feeling that jobs would eventually appear when the overall economy pulled out of its downturn. In this section, we shall follow Jason as he considers the nature of his unemployment and wonders how worried he should be. We'll examine the four main categories of unemployment along the way.

Frictional Unemployment

According to Jason's advisor, the problem is not a lack of jobs. Jobs that suit Jason's skills exist. Ideally, Jason would have found one immediately. The problem is that Jason lacks experience in looking for jobs and is unaware of all the opportunities that are available. In addition, because Jason is a new entrant to the labor force, potential employers are unaware of his talents. The system of matching employers with job seekers does not always work smoothly. It can take time for employers and employees to find one another. According to Jason's advisor, Jason is merely frictionally unemployed. **Frictional unemployment** occurs when job openings exist and people are willing to take them, but it takes some time to bring the two together.

Because frictional unemployment does not generally last for a long time, policy makers do not devote many resources to combating it. Most of the policies intended to lower frictional unemployment consist of providing information to the interested parties. With the rise of the Internet, the number and sophistication of *job banks* have grown dramatically. Job banks bring potential employers and employees together. Job banks offer a variety of services, such as resume development, which help workers prepare themselves for new careers. Many of these sites, such as America's Job Bank (www.ajb.org), have arisen from a joint effort by the public and private sectors. More recently, numerous purely private initiatives have been started, such as the widely advertised Monster.com (www.monster.com).

Frictional unemployment
When job openings exist and people are willing to take them, but it takes some time to bring the two together.

Seasonal Unemployment

In some cases, we can predict regular, brief increases and decreases in the level of unemployment. Every May and June, a large number of high school and college graduates enters the job market for the first time; Jason was a member of this group. Because they lack on-the-job experience and employment connections, first-time job-seekers like Jason are more likely to undergo temporary spells of unemployment than are more experienced workers. This recurrent rise in unemployment, however, does not imply that the economy worsens every June. Similarly, some employers regularly expand their workforces at specific times of the year. Think of the many retailers who regularly hire additional workers in November and December to handle the holiday rush. Again, a corresponding drop in unemployment in November and December does not mean that the economy has grown. These fluctuations are routine, seasonal movements that are unrelated to the true strength of the economy. **Seasonal unemployment** results from the periodic rise and fall of unemployment with the seasons of the year.

These movements are so regular and so predictable that the Bureau of Labor Statistics now automatically adjusts unemployment figures to give us seasonally

Seasonal unemployment
Results from the periodic rise and fall of unemployment with the seasons of the year.

adjusted measures of unemployment. Seasonally adjusted unemployment rates fall below the unadjusted rates in January, February, March, June, and July. Those months regularly experience higher unemployment regardless of the overall health of the economy.

Structural Unemployment

Jason's friend Steve worries that Jason's problem goes beyond temporary friction in the labor market. In particular, Steve fears that the bursting of the dot-com bubble has permanently reduced demand for people with Jason's set of skills. If the underlying structure of the economy has changed so that computer science majors can no longer find work, Jason may face an extended period of unemployment or underemployment in a job that makes lesser use of his skills.

Structural unemployment
When workers lack jobs due to a permanent mismatch of skills or deficient skills.

Such skill mismatches can have a severe effect on the economy. When workers lack jobs due to a permanent mismatch of skills or deficient skills, we categorize them as **structurally unemployed**. Structurally unemployed workers do not have a job waiting for them somewhere in the labor market. Instead, they are faced with a labor market that is unsuited to their talents. Until the structure of the labor market changes or workers like Jason develop new skills, they will remain unemployed or underemployed.

The government often attempts to retrain displaced workers. One of the main obstacles facing such retraining programs has been the government's inability to predict the future direction of the job market. Consider training programs that prepared people to work in the auto industry in the early 1970s or the information technology industry in the late 1990s. These programs suddenly found themselves teaching skills that were no longer in demand by the marketplace.

Cyclical Unemployment

Finally, as his Uncle Rajan suggests, Jason might be out of work simply because of the overall downturn in the economy. The 2001 recession caused roughly 2 million workers to be laid off. In addition, many new job-seekers such as Jason were unable to find jobs when they entered the labor force. The layoffs occurred across many industries. However, some industries are particularly sensitive to the regular ups and downs of the economy. Uncle Rajan seems to believe that the downturn in the technology sector will reverse itself when the whole economy begins to recover. If this is the case, Jason will face a longer spell of unemployment than if he were frictionally unemployed. His situation is not as hopeless, though, as it would be if he were structurally unemployed.

Cyclical unemployment
Results from a broad downturn in economic activity.

We call the unemployment that results from a broad downturn in economic activity **cyclical unemployment**, because it moves upward and downward with the overall level of economic activity. Those who are cyclically unemployed are generally the last hired when times are good and the first fired when times are bad. While temporary, these spells of unemployment can seem endless to those who are cyclically unemployed. For example, during the Great Depression of the 1930s, some began to fear that they would never find jobs.

LifeLessons

It Pays to Wear the Old School Tie

Though new entrants to the labor force frequently experience frictional unemployment, some are more likely to experience it than others. Much job searching is done through personal contacts provided by family and friends. Such informal networks serve many purposes. First, they provide access to jobs that might never be formally advertised. Second, they provide a two-way channel for information. Potential employers learn more about the applicant than they can learn from a resume or job interview, and applicants learn more about the demands of a particular job and the general state of the job market than they could otherwise. Economists attribute a portion of the higher unemployment rates among minority youths to their lack of such informal networks.

College alumni form another informal network. Colleges court their graduates as a source of both funds and jobs. Loyal alumni who attribute their success to their alma mater can smooth the path into the workforce for the graduates who will follow.

Governments combat cyclical unemployment with economic policies aimed at promoting economic growth and minimizing fluctuations in economic activity. The debate over these policies forms the core of macroeconomic theory. As a result, cyclical unemployment will be the focus of much of the remainder of this text.

TEST + *EXTEND* Your Knowledge

1. TEST If a new form of online instruction allows students to take economics courses from any Nobel Laureate they wish, what sort of unemployment will occur among economics professors?

2. EXTEND In October 2003, the unemployment rate in California was 6.6 percent, but in Nebraska, it was 3.8 percent. What form(s) of unemployment could account for this difference? Why?

▶ The Meaning of Full Employment

As long as we rely upon a market-based economy, the unemployment rate will never actually reach zero, even when it is seasonally adjusted. At any point in time, many people will be temporarily without work due to frictional unemployment. Similarly, at any given point in time, some people will lack the skills to be meaningfully employed and thus will experience structural unemployment. In this section, we explore why some unemployment is inevitable. You will also see that while Jason would clearly prefer to have a job, he might occasionally benefit from being unemployed.

Why Some Unemployment Is Inevitable

Political candidates of every persuasion promise that they will strive to provide jobs for all Americans who want to work. The government, however, has never achieved this goal, and it never will. At any point in time, there will always be workers who lack the appropriate skills for meaningful employment. Firms that hire such workers would first have to train them. Such training could prove very costly. Similarly, firms would find it prohibitively costly to eliminate frictional unemployment by immediately finding and hiring new or newly laid-off workers. Frictional and structural unemployment are difficult to eliminate, and we cannot account for them like we adjust for the regular, predictable ups and downs of seasonal unemployment. Thus we say that the economy has reached **full employment** when it has eliminated cyclical unemployment. The term "full employment" has a unique meaning to economists. It does *not* mean that everyone who wishes to work can find a job or that there is a zero unemployment rate. Instead, it means that pushing the unemployment rate lower would exceed the benefits.

Full employment
An economy reaches full employment when it has eliminated cyclical unemployment.

Most economists currently believe that, once the figures are seasonally adjusted, between 4 and 5 percent of the U.S. labor force is structurally or frictionally unemployed. Economists generally believe that we should not push the unemployment rate any lower than this. As a result, the *full employment unemployment rate* lies between four and five percent. Because structural and frictional unemployment rates have fluctuated, the full employment unemployment rate has also changed over time. In the 1970s and 1980s, for example, large numbers of women and baby boomers entered the labor force for the first time. As noted earlier in this chapter, first-time job-seekers are far more likely to be frictionally unemployed than their more experienced counterparts. In addition, periodic fluctuations in oil prices led to major restructuring of the economy as producers and consumers tried to reduce their energy costs. The decline of the U.S. auto industry in the 1970s and 1980s increased the number of structurally unemployed workers and the full employment unemployment rate.[2]

In the 1990s, new job-seekers no longer came from the baby boom generation. Instead, they came from the much smaller Generation X. At the same time, the surge of women into the labor market slowed to a more steady flow of new workers. With fewer people entering the labor force in the 1990s, the number of frictionally unemployed workers fell. With the relatively low energy prices that prevailed throughout most of the 1990s, there were few structural shocks to the economy. As a result, the full employment unemployment rate also fell.

Why Unemployment Is Not Always Bad

An increase in structural unemployment sometimes reflects broader forces that work in the economy's long-term best interest. Technological progress often puts people who were trained to use technology that has become outdated out of work. At the same time, it creates new jobs based on the new technology. The advent of the personal computer late in the twentieth century displaced some skilled typists who could not adjust to the new technology. Similarly, the invention of the typewriter destroyed the livelihood of skilled copyists at the beginning of the century. Governments have tried to minimize the pain imposed on those who are displaced from their jobs by providing training or retraining programs. Ideally, these programs help workers obtain the skills needed to master the new technology and find new jobs. Unfortunately, as we have seen, training programs often do not work out as planned.

Like structural unemployment, frictional unemployment can also serve a broader purpose. Suppose that Jason's advisor is right and Jason is frictionally unemployed. Then it is only a matter of time before he finds a programming job. The worst thing Jason can do in this situation is to panic and take a low-skill job. Because such a job would pay Jason lower wages than what he could expect from a job that uses his skills as a programmer, it would delay or prevent him from meeting his career goals. Jason will be better off if he continues searching for, and

---

[2] For all of these reasons the full employment unemployment rate rose during the 1970s and 1980s.

eventually takes, a job as a programmer. Frictional unemployment might therefore be an investment that pays off in the form of a better employment match, higher future pay for the worker, and greater output for the economy as a whole.

How Governments Increase Unemployment

The U.S. government takes an active role in reducing the pain caused by frictional unemployment. This allows workers to search for the most appropriate job. While the specific requirements vary from state to state, the general purpose of **unemployment insurance** is to provide benefits to people who are unemployed through no fault of their own; who are ready, willing, and able to work; and who are actively seeking work.

Unemployment insurance
Benefits provided to people who are unemployed through no fault of their own; who are ready, willing, and able to work; and who are actively seeking work.

Unemployment Insurance. The unemployment insurance program originated with the Social Security Act of 1935, an initiative aimed at mitigating the Great Depression. Firms fund unemployment insurance through payroll taxes. An employer's tax burden depends upon the degree of unemployment its workers experience. The U.S. Department of Labor oversees the collection of payroll taxes. The insurance benefits are administered by the individual states.

Some aspects of the individual unemployment insurance programs hold true for any state. To receive unemployment insurance benefits, an applicant must:

- Have looked for work
- Be legitimately unemployed, meaning that they cannot have quit work without just cause, been discharged for misconduct, or be involved in a labor dispute
- Be able to work and willing to accept a job that the local unemployment office finds for them, provided the job matches their skill set

The specific benefits and some eligibility provisions, however, vary from state to state. For example, if you live in Rhode Island, your unemployment insurance benefits would replace more than half your lost earnings. If you live in Alabama, your benefits would replace slightly more than 40 percent of your previous earnings. In setting the level and duration of unemployment insurance, state governments must balance the benefits of promoting the optimal search for a new job against the costs of encouraging workers to remain unemployed.

The Impact of Unemployment Insurance. Some people argue that unemployment insurance does not make the economy operate more efficiently. Instead, they argue that unemployment insurance programs reduce the opportunity cost of unemployment. The lower cost of remaining unemployed encourages more workers to stay unemployed for a longer period. As evidence, they point to the unemployment rates in Europe, where unemployment insurance is more generous and longer-lasting. Figure 18.3 shows the average unemployment rates for the United States and several other industrial economies for the years 1990 to 2004. The extremely low unemployment rates in Japan reflect in part the tradition of lifetime employment in which firms do not lay off workers in response to economic fluctuations. As a result, unlike in the United States and the European nations, there is almost no cyclical unemployment in Japan.

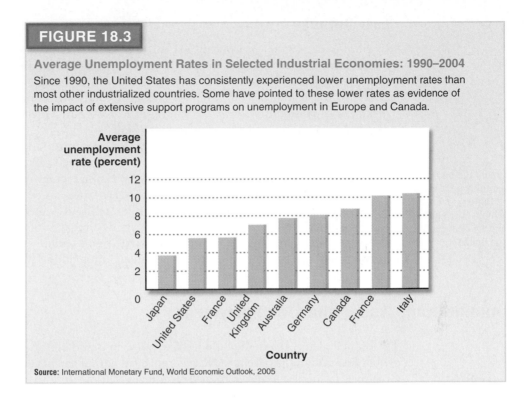

FIGURE 18.3

Average Unemployment Rates in Selected Industrial Economies: 1990–2004

Since 1990, the United States has consistently experienced lower unemployment rates than most other industrialized countries. Some have pointed to these lower rates as evidence of the impact of extensive support programs on unemployment in Europe and Canada.

Source: International Monetary Fund, World Economic Outlook, 2005

The Social Consequences of Unemployment

We've established how to categorize and quantify the various aspects of unemployment. What about the effect of unemployment on the economy as a whole?

Social Ills and Unemployment

Economists and sociologists have noted that, even in prosperous societies, a number of social ills accompany rising unemployment. Crime, domestic violence, and the incidence of mental illness all increase during periods of high unemployment.

Other indicators of societal health, like marriage and birth rates, fall as people conclude that they cannot afford to start a family without a stable job. In less fortunate nations, the consequences of widespread unemployment can be far more severe. The popular press is filled with articles linking large-scale unemployment among young workers in developing countries with radical forms of religious fundamentalism.

The worst political consequences of high unemployment in the twentieth century came in Germany during the Great Depression. As more than 3.5 million German workers lost their jobs between 1929 and 1932 and the unemployment rate rose to 26 percent, the Nazi Party steadily rose in popularity, paving the way for its ascent to power in 1933.

Some politicians blame rising unemployment rates on what they see as unfair trade practices by foreigners. Such attitudes led to the Japan-bashing of the 1980s, in which unemployed American autoworkers believed that Japan's trade policies had caused them to lose their jobs. More recently, it has led some to blame China's trade policies for the rising U.S. unemployment rate during the early 2000s.

Get Ahead of the Curve

Analyze the causes and consequences of high unemployment rates in Germany.

Lost Output

Unemployment is not a problem just for people like Jason who are without jobs. People who are unemployed do not produce anything. When an economy produces less, even people who have jobs may be worse off. In Chapter 2, we showed that failing to use resources completely or efficiently pulls a firm or economy inside its production possibilities frontier, resulting in lost output. When workers are unemployed, an economy produces less and GDP falls.

Okun's Law
A one-percentage-point rise in the unemployment rate above the full employment unemployment rate causes GDP to fall by about 2.5 percentage points.

The negative relationship between unemployment rates and GDP is known as **Okun's Law**, named for the economist who first discerned this relationship. Recent estimates of Okun's Law suggest that every percentage-point rise in the unemployment rate above the full employment unemployment rate causes GDP to fall by about 2.5 percentage points. While that may seem like a small percentage, 2.5 percent of $11.7 trillion, the U.S. GDP in 2004, amounts to almost $300 billion. That means that reducing unemployment by one percentage point could generate about $1,000 in additional production for every man, woman, and child in the United States.

Immigration, Trade, and Unemployment

Jason's challenges to finding a job strike home in a number of ways. He is proud of what his immigrant parents have accomplished and of the growing prosperity of his relatives in India. However, he also recognizes that much of the recent public debate over unemployment centers on issues related to immigration and trade. Some people have claimed that Indian immigrants like his Uncle Rajan, who now works in Silicon Valley, have taken jobs away from "native-born" Americans. Others claim that American jobs have disappeared because American firms have outsourced their programming to companies in India, such as the one that employs Jason's cousin Vijay. What is Jason to make of such accusations?

Immigrants and Unemployment

No matter how badly Jason wants a job, he has trouble blaming immigrants for his troubles. After all, his Uncle Rajan got a job with a programming company after he came from India. Did his own uncle take away a job from an American? The simplest model of immigration suggests that immigrants do have a negative impact on native-born workers. In this model, any country with high wages and open borders will attract immigrants. These immigrants then compete with native-born workers for jobs, displacing native-born workers and driving down wages. Figure 18.4 illustrates this basic model.

If U.S. workers earn $10 per hour while workers elsewhere earn only $2.50 per hour, foreign workers will migrate to the United States. When foreign workers migrate to the United States, the labor supply curve in the United States shifts to the right, and wages in the United States fall. Native-born workers who want to work at $10 per hour will find themselves priced out of a job.

In reality, the question of how immigrants affect U.S. labor markets is very hard to answer. For example, many immigrants do not compete with native workers for employment. Instead, they take jobs that native-born workers are unable or unwilling to fill. At the time Jason's Uncle Rajan accepted the job as a programmer, few native-born workers had the skills or the inclination to take such a job. Rather than displacing native-born workers, Jason's uncle filled a need in the U.S. economy and made it more productive.

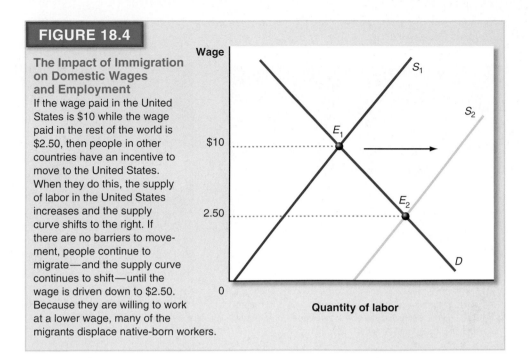

FIGURE 18.4

The Impact of Immigration on Domestic Wages and Employment
If the wage paid in the United States is $10 while the wage paid in the rest of the world is $2.50, then people in other countries have an incentive to move to the United States. When they do this, the supply of labor in the United States increases and the supply curve shifts to the right. If there are no barriers to movement, people continue to migrate—and the supply curve continues to shift—until the wage is driven down to $2.50. Because they are willing to work at a lower wage, many of the migrants displace native-born workers.

Trade and Unemployment

Suppose, for a moment, that the United States had prevented immigration in an attempt to keep wages and employment high. Closing the door to foreign workers may open the door to foreign goods and services, because high wages mean high costs of production. If workers elsewhere are able to do the same jobs at lower wages, as is Jason's cousin Vijay, then U.S. firms have an incentive to reduce their costs by importing goods and services from abroad.

The U.S. government could also restrict the amount of foreign goods and services that U.S. firms and households consume, by imposing quotas or prohibitively high tariffs. Protecting U.S. industries with high costs and preserving high prices, however, means that U.S. consumers must pay more for goods and services. Low-cost workers like Jason's Uncle Rajan and low-cost goods or services produced by Jason's cousin Vijay are no longer available. A family in the United States that has to pay more for computer software has less money to spend on movies, cell phones, and other goods and services. Such restrictions may therefore preserve jobs in the U.S. computer industry at the expense of jobs in the entertainment and telecom industries.

Finally, protection is not a one-way street. Suppose that the U.S. government bars imports of the goods and services that Vijay produces in New Delhi. The Indian government might respond by keeping out American-made goods and services. Saving American jobs in industries that compete with imports might destroy American jobs that produce exports.

Strategy and Policy
It All Depends on How You Count

In July 2004, the Bureau of Labor Statistics provided good news for the political campaigns of both President George Bush and Senator John Kerry. The BLS

Two Views of Outsourcing

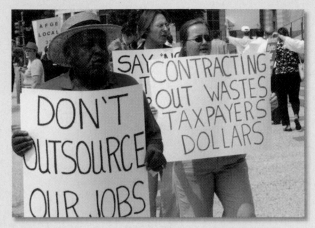

(a) Many phone centers have moved to developing countries such as India or the Philippines. These moves have reduced costs for U.S. firms. According to some estimates, they have increased U.S. employment levels.

(b) Opening phone centers abroad has displaced some U.S. workers and created anxiety among others who fear that their own jobs will be "shipped overseas."

reported that the economy had added only 32,000 new jobs in the previous month, more than 150,000 fewer than experts had predicted. The anemic job growth, the slowest reported all year, fueled Senator Kerry's claim that the economic recovery was running out of steam. At the same time, the BLS reported that the unemployment rate fell from 5.6 to 5.5 percent. The Bush campaign used this information to claim that the economy showed continued, steady improvement.

How could one government agency provide what seemed to be such inconsistent information? One explanation is that the unemployment rate and job growth data come from two different sources, each with its own advantages and disadvantages.

The BLS calculates the size of the labor force and the number of unemployed workers—and hence the unemployment rate—from the CPS. The CPS is conducted by the Bureau of the Census and is based on a sample of 60,000 households. Because this survey uses the household as its unit of observation, economists refer to it as the *household survey*. The household survey asks workers whether they have been employed and, if not, whether they have looked for work in the last four weeks. It counts an individual as employed only once, regardless of how many jobs he or she holds. In September 2004, the household survey found that about 139 million workers were employed.

The BLS also collects payroll data in a survey of 160,000 businesses and government agencies. Because of its larger sample size, the *establishment survey* is often regarded as a reliable measure of employment growth. According to the establishment survey, there were only 131 million workers employed, and the unemployment rate would have been considerably higher.

However, the establishment survey, too, has flaws. Because the establishment survey uses the workplace as its basic unit of observation, it does not capture many of the employment possibilities that the household survey captures. For example, the household survey includes agricultural workers, self-employed workers, and private household workers as employed. The establishment survey is not sent to these establishments, so it misses the workers there. Similarly,

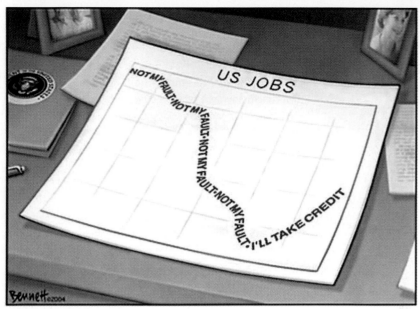

www.cartoonstock.com

because the establishment survey looks at payrolls, it misses unpaid family workers. They are counted in the household survey as long as they work at least 15 hours per week. Again, because it looks at payrolls, the establishment survey could be affected by natural disasters, such as the hurricanes that devastated Florida in the summer and early fall of 2004. As a result, the results of the establishment survey are frequently revised in light of later information. Because neither survey is perfect, the BLS continues to present results from both sets of surveys, frequently providing ammunition for both defenders and critics of current economic policy.

Critical-Thinking Questions

1. How could the household survey understate unemployment? How could the establishment survey overstate unemployment?
2. Why do the results of the establishment survey need frequent updates, while those of the household survey do not?

▶ SUMMARY

- **Unemployment, employment, and the labor force.** Not everyone who is jobless is counted as unemployed. Some people who do not work may be out of the labor force.

- **The changing face of the U.S. labor force.** The nature of the U.S. labor force has changed substantially in recent years, due to the influx of women and Hispanics into the labor market.

- **Changes in jobs held by Americans.** Jobs have also changed as U.S. workers transitioned from agricultural and manufacturing jobs to those in service industries.

- **Counting the unemployed.** The unemployment rate is a better measure of unemployment than the absolute number of unemployed workers, yet even this measure fails to capture discouraged workers or underemployed workers. The overall unemployment rate obscures substantial differences between subgroups of the population.

- **Types of unemployment.** The government pays relatively little attention to frictional unemployment, which is relatively short-term. The BLS adjusts the unemployment figures to account for seasonal unemployment, because seasonal employment does not reflect the underlying health of the economy. The government tries to reduce structural unemployment by providing skills to workers. Eliminating cyclical unemployment is a major goal of macroeconomic policy.

- **The meaning of full employment.** In a market economy, some frictional and structural unemployment will always exist. Unemployment insurance provides unemployed workers with income for support during frictional unemployment while they search for the jobs that best suit their skills. Technological progress often calls for retraining workers and for government programs designed to give workers new skills to respond to structural unemployment. Because it is impossible to eliminate all frictional and structural unemployment, we say we have achieved full employment when cyclical unemployment is zero.

- **The social consequences of unemployment.** Even moderate increases in unemployment can have negative social consequences. As unemployment rises, so does the crime rate. High levels of unemployment can destabilize democratic institutions.

- **Immigration, trade, and unemployment.** Some economists argue that the influx of workers from other countries into the United States and the outsourcing of U.S. jobs and services to workers in foreign countries have a detrimental effect on U.S. workers. Others argue that immigrants who take jobs that native-born workers are not willing or able to fill make the U.S. economy stronger. They also claim that importing goods and services from abroad helps companies produce more efficiently by reducing costs. This, in turn, lowers the prices consumers pay.

▶ KEY TERMS

Civilian labor force 461	Full employment 471	Structural unemployment 469
Civilian unemployment rate 465	Labor force participation rate 462	Underemployed 467
Cyclical unemployment 469	Okun's Law 474	Unemployment insurance 472
Discouraged workers 467	Seasonal unemployment 468	
Frictional unemployment 468		

▶ PROBLEMS

1. Why has the labor force participation rate of women risen so much in the last several decades?

2. When Jason was 5 years old, his mother didn't work and was not considered part of the labor force. When he was 20 years old, his mother didn't work and was considered part of the labor force. Why was she counted at one point and not at the other?

3. Are the following people unemployed or not? Justify each answer.
   a. An autoworker who loses his job because people stop buying cars during a recession.
   b. A lawyer who resigns from her job to tend to a sick child.
   c. The same lawyer in Problem 3b who has trouble finding a job when she returns to the labor force after her child recovers.
   d. An anthropology professor who loses his job because fewer students now major in anthropology.
   e. A pre-med student at UCLA who spends all her spare time in the lab.

4. In January 1954, the labor force had 63 million people, of whom 3 million were unemployed. In January 2004, the labor force had 147 million people, of whom 8 million were unemployed. In which year was the unemployment rate higher?

5. In a presidential debate, the challenger complains that more people are out of work now than when the incumbent took office, while the incumbent says that unemployment rate is lower than when he took office. Resolve this disagreement.

6. What might cause the official unemployment rate to understate the unemployment problem?

7. In January 2004, the unemployment rate was 8.8 percent among those who lacked a high school diploma, but only 2.9 percent for those who had at least a college degree. Explain the difference in unemployment rates.

8. Why doesn't the government have many policies in place to reduce seasonal unemployment?

9. Of the people who are unemployed in Problem 3, what type of unemployment are they experiencing? Explain each answer.

10. Statistics show that enrollments in colleges rise during a recession. Why might this be? What impact would this effect have on unemployment rates?

11. Of cyclical, frictional, seasonal, and structural unemployment, about which should the government worry most? About which should it worry least? Justify each answer.

12. What forms of unemployment would go up as a result of the massive changes in the types of jobs that exist in the U.S. economy?

13. Why doesn't "full employment" mean that everyone who wants a job has one?

14. There are 90 million people in the labor force of Florin. Of these, 1 million are structurally unemployed, 2 million are frictionally unemployed, and 1 million are cyclically unemployed.
    a. What is the unemployment rate in Florin?
    b. What is the full employment unemployment rate in Florin?

15. What impact would each of the following have on the full employment unemployment rate?
    a. The entry of a large number of young workers into the labor force due to the baby boom echo (the children of baby boomers).
    b. A decline in tourism-oriented jobs at hotels, restaurants, and theme parks due to a recession.
    c. A permanent decline in tourism-oriented jobs caused by a fear of traveling due to terrorist threats.
    d. Social Security reform provides senior citizens with an incentive to re-enter the labor force.

16. Between 2000 and 2003, the unemployment rate rose from 4.0 to 6.0 percent. Assuming that full employment corresponds to 5 percent unemployment, what does Okun's Law say would happen to real GDP?

17. The government is considering increasing unemployment insurance benefits. What positive and negative impact would this step have on the economy?

18. Why should we worry about unemployment when almost 95 percent of the labor force is employed?

19. How might trade restrictions designed to protect U.S. jobs lead to greater unemployment?

20. Use supply and demand curves to explain why some people fear the impact of immigration on native workers. Why do some people feel that this simple model overstates the impact of immigrants on native workers?

HERE'S HOW MyEconLab CAN HELP YOU GET A BETTER GRADE

1. Log into MyEconLab and take Practice Test 18-A (to log in for the first time, see page 30 for instructions).

2. Based on your test results, MyEconLab will identify the areas where you need further work and create a personal Study Plan for you.

3. Your Study Plan contains the problems listed below and others like them that will target the specific chapter topics you need to focus on. You'll receive instant feedback and find links to tutorials, animations, and the online textbook to help you study.

4. When you're ready, take Practice Test 18-B and demonstrate how your results have improved.

Section 18.1, Problem 1 Would the government count each of the following individuals in the labor force?

a. Mary, 20, a full-time college student who babysits occasionally on weekends for extra money

b. Jonathan, 40, who stays at home to take care of his two children

c. Merle, 70, a retiree who also works five hours a week at Wal-Mart to keep busy

d. Karen, 35, who quit her job two weeks ago and has been looking for a new one ever since

e. Tristan, 25, who was let go from his job six weeks ago, and hasn't started looking for a new job yet

Section 18.1, Problem 2 Which of the following individuals would the government consider to be unemployed?

a. Dorothy, who works part time at the local supermarket

b. Blanche, a full-time student who is too busy to work or look for work

c. Rose, who spends all day taking care of her two young children

d. Sophia, who is 15 but already looking for her first job for when she turns 16

Section 18.2, Problem 1 The civilian, non-institutionalized population 16 years old or older of Ecoland is 1 million. Of these, 650,000 are employed, 100,000 are unemployed, and the rest are not in the labor force. What is the labor force participation rate of Ecoland?

Section 18.2, Problem 2 Which of the following statements regarding the nature in the United States labor force is **not** true?

a. More than half of all women in the U.S. are either working or looking for work.

b. Over three-fourths of married women with children are either working or looking for work.

c. Women constitute nearly half of the U.S. labor force.

d. The labor force participation rate of males has increased over the last 30 years.

e. In terms of percentages, Hispanics have been the fastest-growing group in the labor force over the last 30 years.

Section 18.3, Problem 1 Which of the following statements regarding the types of jobs held by Americans is correct?

a. A larger proportion of Americans work in the manufacturing sector than ever before.

b. Due to technological progress, workers have moved from the services sector to the manufacturing and agricultural sectors.

c. In 2000, over 70 percent of the American labor force worked in the services sector.

d. A larger proportion of Americans work in the agricultural sector currently than the manufacturing sector.

e. Increases in the U.S. standard of living have allowed more and more workers to return to the agricultural sector.

Section 18.4, Problem 1

a. Justin works "off the books" for his family business for 20–30 hours per week, while going to college part time. Is he considered employed or unemployed?

b. Mary Alice, after spending weeks looking for work, was hired at Dell Computers and is now waiting one week before starting her new job. Is she considered employed or unemployed?

Section 18.4, Problem 2 The civilian, non-institutionalized population 16 years old or older of Ecoland is 1 million. Of these, 650,000 are employed, 100,000 are unemployed, and the rest are not in the labor force. What is the civilian unemployment rate of Ecoland?

Section 18.4, Problem 3 In the Kingdom of Far Far Away, the unemployment rate is 6 percent. If the labor force is 400,000, how many people in the Kingdom are employed and how many are unemployed?

Section 18.4, Problem 4 The civilian, non-institutionalized population 16 years old and older of Ecoland is 1 million. Of these, 650,000 are employed, 100,000 are unemployed, and the rest are not in the labor force. What is the unemployment rate of Ecoland?

a. Use the original data on Ecoland's population. What happens to Ecoland's unemployment rate if 25,000 of the unemployed become discouraged and give up looking? Calculate the new unemployment rate.
b. Use the original data on Ecoland's population. What happens to Ecoland's unemployment rate if 50,000 of those not in the labor force begin searching for employment? Calculate the new unemployment rate.

Section 18.5, Problem 1 For each of the following situations, define the type of unemployment involved.

a. Kim worked at a candied apple factory, but was recently let go because her job can now be done by a machine.
b. Kim worked at a candied apple factory, but was recently let go because a downturn in the economy resulted in reduced demand for many goods, including candied apples.
c. Kim worked at a candied apple factory, but recently quit in search of a job that better matched her skills.
d. Kim worked at a candied apple factory, but was let go in January because there is always a decline in demand for candied apples after the holidays.

Section 18.5, Problem 2 Suppose that John Doe quits his job, and takes the summer off to paint his house and read the newest John Grisham book. Is he :

a. Underemployed
b. No longer in the labor force
c. Structurally unemployed

d. Frictionally unemployed
e. Lazy

Section 18.6, Problem 1 The civilian, non-institutionalized population 16 years old and older of Ecoland is 1 million. Of these, 650,000 are employed, 100,000 are unemployed, and the rest are not in the labor force. Suppose that out of the 100,000 unemployed, 40,000 are frictionally unemployed, 10,000 are seasonally unemployed, 30,000 are structurally unemployed, and 20,000 are cyclically unemployed. What is the full employment unemployment rate of Ecoland?

Section 18.6, Problem 2 Suppose that the full employment unemployment rate is estimated to be 5.5 percent. Suppose further that the actual unemployment rate is 6.5 percent. Which of the following statements must be true?

a. Structural unemployment is greater than frictional unemployment.
b. Cyclical unemployment is one percent.
c. Structural unemployment is one percent.
d. Cyclical unemployment is greater than structural unemployment.
e. The economy is at full employment.

Section 18.6, Problem 3 Which of the following statements concerning full employment is true?

a. Full employment is reached when cyclical and frictional unemployment have been eliminated.
b. Full employment is reached when frictional unemployment has been eliminated.
c. Full employment is reached when cyclical unemployment has been eliminated.
d. Full employment is reached when the unemployment rate is zero percent.
e. Full employment is reached when frictional and structural unemployment have been eliminated.

Section 18.7, Problem 1 Suppose that in Ecoland, the current unemployment rate is 6 percent, and real GDP is $10 million. If economists estimate Ecoland's full employment unemployment rate to be 5 percent, what is the amount of lost output to Ecoland? What if they estimate full employment unemployment to be 4 percent?

Section 18.8, Problem 1 Use supply and demand analysis to depict what happens to Mexican wages and employment if there is substantial emigration of Mexican workers into the United States.

REICHSBANKNOTE 109826 *

Fünfzig Millionen Mark

zahlt die Reichsbankhauptkasse in Berlin gegen diese
Banknote dem Einlieferer. Vom 1. Januar 1924 ab
kann diese Banknote aufgerufen und unter Umtausch
gegen andere gesetzliche Zahlungsmittel eingezogen
werden

Berlin, den 1. September 1923 NF · 13

REICHSBANKDIREKTORIUM

19

Inflation and Prices

One day, Jessica came home from shopping absolutely beside herself. The new outfit she wanted for the weekend was just too expensive. "Prices just keep going up!" she exclaimed. "It seems like my paycheck can't buy anything anymore. I'm going to have to ask for a raise."

Her mother could only smile. "I wish your great-grandfather could hear you say this. You should have heard his stories about Germany in the 1920s when he was young. He used to say that his pay went up every day. At one point they gave him so much currency that he couldn't carry it—he had to take it away in a wheelbarrow. I remember his saying that prices rose so quickly that everyone insisted on being paid three times a day. Then they would run to the bakery or the grocer and spend it before it became worthless. Imagine, fifty million marks for a loaf of bread!

"Maybe they kept hoping things would improve. But money *wasn't* worth anything. One of his favorite stories was about the day he went home and left the full wheelbarrow outside. Some thieves stole the wheelbarrow—but they dumped out the money and left it. His money literally was not worth the paper it was printed on!"

Jessica's great-grandfather was not exaggerating. In the horrifying autumn of 1923, prices in Germany went totally out of control. Yet Germany's experience, while extreme, was far from unique. Runaway price increases have been recorded as far back as third-century Rome. In recent years, a wide variety of economies have all experienced unsettling price increases. Examples range from the highly developed economy of Israel to the economy of Ukraine during its transition from communism to a market economy to Angola's developing economy.

In Chapter 7, we looked at the nature and implications of unemployment. In this chapter, we will explore the causes and repercussions of another major macroeconomic dilemma that confronts policy makers: inflation. In addition to discussing how economists measure inflation, we will compare several countries' experiences with inflation and examine the impact of inflation on the economy and on society.

ALONG THE WAY, YOU WILL ALSO LEARN:

- That inflation does not necessarily make goods and services less affordable.

- The causes of inflation.

- How we measure inflation.

- What happens when inflation gets out of control.

- Why falling prices are not necessarily better than rising prices.

**AT THE END OF THE CHAPTER,
THE MYECONLAB LOGO WILL DIRECT YOU ONLINE**

- MyEconLab is a resource-packed online homework and tutorial system that can help you perform better in your economics course. To log in for the first time, see page 30 for instructions.

- MyEconLab can help you apply important concepts from the chapter to real-world issues. Watch for the logo to indicate online features about inflation in the United States and Hong Kong.

- At the end of each chapter, you'll find a special study section that will help you get the most out of your textbook and your instructor's MyEconLab course.

 ## Defining Inflation

Inflation
The general upward movement of prices in the economy.

Inflation is a general upward movement of prices. This definition is easy to memorize, but it can be hard to understand. Most people take it to mean that inflation increases the cost of living. In fact, you will see that inflation does not necessarily make goods and services less affordable. When it does, however, the impact is widespread. Because we all buy and sell goods and services, all of us are affected in some way by inflation. Thus, inflation directly affects more people than unemployment does. After all, even during the recession of 2001, almost 95 percent of the workforce was still employed. Moderate inflation hurts everyone a little, and unemployment hurts only those out of work—but hurts them a great deal. In this section, we examine the costs of inflation for consumers and firms, the causes of inflation, and the effect of inflation on incomes and interest rates.

The Relationship Between Inflation and Wages

We begin our look at inflation by considering Jessica's concerns about rising prices. Jessica is a college senior with weekly expenses of $100. She meets these expenses by working 10 hours per week at a bookstore, where she earns $10 per hour. If the overall level of prices rose by 10 percent, Jessica would need 10 percent more in income, or $110 per week, to buy the same selection of goods and services that she purchased before prices increased. Suppose that Jessica's pay does rise by 10 percent. Now the real cost of what she buys—the amount of leisure time she must sacrifice to buy a given combination of goods and services—has not changed. As long as her hourly wage rises at the same rate that prices do, Jessica is not affected by inflation.

The Costs of Inflation

Unfortunately, inflation almost never affects all goods and services equally. In Chapter 7, you saw that the unemployment rate is an overall measure that does not apply uniformly to all demographic subgroups. Just as teenagers face higher unemployment rates than older workers do, inflation reflects a variety of changes in the prices of individual goods and services.

Jessica's Costs from Inflation. Suppose that Jessica's wage instead rose by only 5 percent, to $10.50. By working 10 hours, she would now earn only $105. To earn the $110 she needs, Jessica must work an extra half-hour per week. The cost of inflation to Jessica is the extra half-hour that she must work to buy the same things she used to buy.

While she might not be happy about it, Jessica can maintain her spending by working more. Not everyone can do that. People who live on fixed incomes, such as private pensions or public assistance, have no way to increase their incomes and can be hurt badly by inflation. Workers with long-term contracts whose wages or salaries are spelled out in advance are also hurt by inflation. Households, firms, or financial institutions that receive fixed returns on savings or loans see the value of their returns decline as inflation rises.

By the same token, some people benefit from inflation. Inflation helps people who make fixed payments. Paying Jessica $10 per hour becomes less of a burden to the bookstore owner if all other prices, including the price of the books sold, also rise. Jessica also benefits if she makes a fixed-interest payment on a mortgage or a car loan. The burden of that payment falls if other prices, including Jessica's wage, rise.

Menu Costs. Another cost of inflation arises when people spend resources trying to predict exactly which prices will rise and how quickly. Producers want to produce more of the goods and services whose prices rise most quickly. Suppose that the owner of Jessica's bookstore believes that CDs will increase in price, and that book prices will not. The owner has an incentive to stock fewer books and stock more CDs. Consumers also want to predict price movements so that they can consume goods and services before the prices rise and cut back on their purchases afterwards. If Jessica knows that CDs will become more expensive in the near future, she has an incentive to buy some right now. Interestingly, the expectation of future inflation is a self-fulfilling prophecy. Recall from Chapter 4 that people demand more of a good or service if they expect its price to rise in the future. If people expect most goods and services to go up in price, the demand curve for most goods and services shifts to the right, and the price level increases. In other words, there is inflation. In addition, when consumers and producers spend resources to predict inflation, they have fewer resources with which to produce or consume goods and services. Inflation can thus lead to lower real GDP and employment.

Even if inflation is easily predicted, firms and households that continually adjust their behavior are distracted from their basic functions of production and consumption. Jessica encountered such a cost at the bookstore. Every time the price of books went up, the barcode readers at the checkout counter had to be reprogrammed. If the price of cappuccino or brownies at the bookstore's coffee bar rose, the bookstore had to print new menus. The new menus by themselves did not make the bookstore more productive or profitable. Instead, they were an expense that it incurred in order to alter prices. **Menu costs** is the name that economists give to the wide array of costs that firms encounter when they adjust to higher prices. Menu costs can be as simple as retooling a soda machine to take more coins than before. They can be as complex as intense negotiations between workers and firms over cost-of-living increases in salaries.

Causes of Inflation

Economists generally agree that inflation occurs when an economy has "too much money chasing too few goods." This simple phrase captures the idea that inflation results when either the government produces too much money, or producers cannot provide enough output. We now look at how this description applies to several historic periods of inflation.

One of the earliest examples of inflation resulted from the actions of the Roman emperors in the third century. Beset by a series of civil wars, the emperors needed funds to support their armies. However, the Roman government lacked the stability it needed to raise taxes. Instead, the emperors debased the currency. **Debasing** a currency means reducing its value. The Roman emperors debased the currency by mixing "base" elements, such as lead, with the gold used to make their coins. This process allowed the emperors to mint far more coins than before with the same amount of gold. The emperors then spent the additional coins to support the armies that kept them in power.

The extra coins in circulation meant that the people of Rome had more money to buy goods and services. Recall from Chapter 4 that as purchasing power

Inflation and Natural Disasters

Inflation results when too much money chases too few goods. Natural disasters—such as the tsunami in South Asia—can reduce an economy's ability to produce. Even if the government does not create additional money, reduction in goods and services could cause the price level to rise.

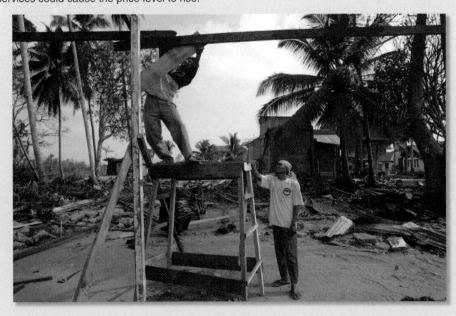

increases, the demand for a good or service typically rises. The additional demand for goods and services in turn drives up the prices charged for them. With the overall price level rising, Rome suffered from inflation.

Almost two thousand years later, in the mid-1980s, the Brazilian government faced a pressing need for funds. Rather than borrowing funds to cover its expenses, the Brazilian government printed additional currency. By the late 1980s, the Brazilian economy, like ancient Rome's, was overwhelmed by inflation. Prices in Brazil soared hundreds of percent per year for much of the next decade.

In other instances, inflation occurs because too little is produced relative to the amount of money that is available. Suppose that the general ability of society to produce goods and services falls, but the amount of money in circulation stays unchanged. There is again "too much money" for the amount of goods and services available. Households, firms, and the government bid against one another for the scarce goods and services, driving up the price level. The overall increase in prices results in inflation. One famous example of this type of inflation came in the wake of the Bubonic Plague of the fourteenth century. The plague devastated Europe, killing roughly one-third of the population. The peasants, who were responsible for most of the production in this largely agrarian society, were hit particularly hard. A food shortage resulted. The price of wheat, a basic staple and one of the few goods whose price was recorded, almost doubled within three years of the plague's peak.

In recent years, inflation has occured whenever outside events reduce the ability of an economy to provide basic goods and services. This situation occurred in late 2005 after Hurricane Katrina struck New Orleans. The disruption of the supply of basic commodities—from oil pumped in the Gulf of Mexico to coffee imported from Colombia—caused the U.S. price level to rise.

Real and Nominal Values

As you have seen, inflation can cause a good's price to increase without increasing the true cost of the item. Economists can tell whether an increase in price reflects an increase in cost by distinguishing between *real* and *nominal* values. Let's see how economists apply the difference between real and nominal values to incomes and interest rates.

Nominal income
The dollar value of a person's income.

Real and Nominal Income. Recall that Jessica's ability to buy goods and services decreased when her pay increased from $100 to $105 but what she had to spend rose from $100 to $110. Jessica's **nominal income** is the dollar value of her pay. When Jessica's pay went from $100 per week to $105 dollars per week, her nominal

DILBERT: © Scott Adams/Dist. by United Features Syndicate, Inc.

income rose by 5 percent. Jessica's **real income** is the purchasing power of her nominal income. Her real income can rise or fall depending on how much prices and her nominal income change. Consider the following possible scenarios:

1. Suppose that the prices of goods and services that Jessica buys rises by 10 percent. She must now spend $110 to get the same mix of goods and services. If Jessica's nominal income rises by only 5 percent, then she can afford to spend only $105, and her real income falls.
2. Now suppose prices rise by 5 percent; then Jessica must spend $105 to continue to consume the same mix of goods and services. If Jessica's nominal income also rises by 5 percent, then she can afford to buy exactly what she bought before prices rose, and her real income stays the same.
3. Finally, if prices rise by 5 percent, and Jessica's income rises by 10 percent, then she must spend $105 to continue to consume the same mix of goods and services. Because she can now afford to buy $110 worth of goods and services, Jessica's real income rises.

Equation 19.1 shows the relationship between nominal income, real income, and the rate of inflation.

$$\text{Percentage change in real income} = \text{Percentage change in nominal income} - \text{Percentage change in prices} \qquad (19.1)$$

Thus, a 5-percent increase in nominal income accompanied by a 2.5-percent increase in prices results in a 2.5-percent increase in real income (5 percent − 2.5 percent = 2.5 percent). A 5-percent increase in nominal income accompanied by a 10-percent increase in prices results in a 5-percent *decrease* in real income (5 percent − 10 percent = −5 percent).

LifeLessons

Sometimes It Pays to Owe Money

When buying expensive items such as a house or a car, consumers frequently go into debt. The total payments of the mortgage or the car loan are generally much higher than the purchase price. However, going into debt may be cheaper than paying the full price up front. If the loan requires fixed payments over time and prices rise quickly enough, the value of the payments may fall over time. Suppose, for example, that Jessica's car loan requires that she set aside $25 per week to pay the interest charges. When Jessica earned $100 per week, she had to devote $\frac{\$25}{\$100}$, or 25 percent of her pay, to the car loan. If inflation causes her pay to rise to $110 per week, she devotes only $\frac{\$25}{\$110}$, or 22.7 percent of her pay, to the car loan. Inflation has actually made the fixed-interest payment less burdensome.

The news for borrowers, however, is not all good. When lenders become aware of the dangers of being locked into fixed payments, they may become reluctant to lend at all. Adjustable lending rates, such as variable-rate mortgages, protect lenders from inflation. Although these innovations increase the burden on borrowers, they may help borrowers on the whole because otherwise lenders might not be willing to lend.

Nominal interest rate
The dollar amount of interest a borrower pays for every $100 borrowed.

Real interest rate
The purchasing power of the repayment the borrower makes for every $100 borrowed.

Real and Nominal Interest Rates. The Life Lesson makes clear that we must distinguish between real and nominal quantities when people borrow or lend. Interest is the extra payment a borrower makes above and beyond repaying the amount borrowed. As Equation 19.2 shows, the **nominal interest rate** is the unit price of a loan. It is the amount of interest that a borrower pays for every $100 borrowed.

$$\text{Nominal interest rate} = (\text{Interest payment/Amount borrowed}) \times 100 \quad (19.2)$$

The **real interest rate** is the purchasing power of the repayment the borrower makes for every $100 borrowed. The difference between the two is the percentage change in prices. This relationship is shown in Equation 19.3.

$$\text{Real interest rate} = \text{Nominal interest rate} - \text{Percentage change in prices} \quad (19.3)$$

Equation 19.3 shows that if nominal interest rates rise with inflation, the real interest rate does not change. If, for example the nominal interest rate is 5 percent and inflation is 2 percent, then the real interest rate is 3 percent (3 percent = 5 percent − 2 percent). If inflation rises to 12 percent and the nominal interest rate rises to 15 percent (3 percent + 12 percent = 15 percent), the real interest rate remains 3 percent. Figure 19.1 shows real and nominal interest rates from 1964 through 2004.

In the 1970s, nominal interest rates rose sharply, but real interest rates did not. In fact, real interest rates were extremely low. The difference between the two stems from the high inflation rates of the 1970s. During the late 1970s, nominal rates rose sharply from about 5 percent to over 10 percent, while real interest rates fell sharply and were even negative in 1975. A negative interest rate means that the lender is effectively paying the borrower to take out a loan. How can this be? Negative interest rates occur because borrowers and lenders typically agree on a nominal interest rate when the loan is made, before they see what actually happens to the price level. Inflation was much greater than expected in 1975. Though the nominal rate was very high, in 1975 inflation was even higher. As a result, the real interest rate was negative.

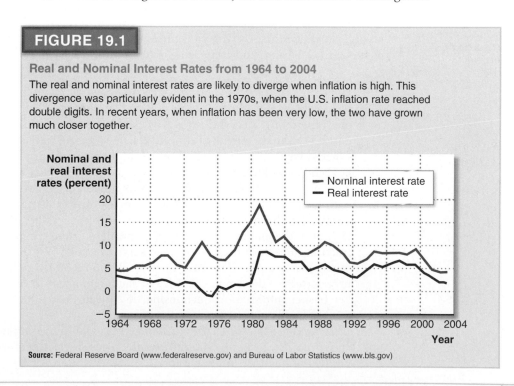

FIGURE 19.1

Real and Nominal Interest Rates from 1964 to 2004
The real and nominal interest rates are likely to diverge when inflation is high. This divergence was particularly evident in the 1970s, when the U.S. inflation rate reached double digits. In recent years, when inflation has been very low, the two have grown much closer together.

Source: Federal Reserve Board (www.federalreserve.gov) and Bureau of Labor Statistics (www.bls.gov)

TEST + *EXTEND* Your Knowledge

1. TEST What costs does inflation impose on an economy?

2. *EXTEND* Go to the Web site of the Bureau of Labor Statistics using the link at www.aw-bc.com/leeds/ch19.

Find the most recent information on prices and wages. What has happened to nominal wages over the last year? What has happened to real wages? Have nominal wages kept up?

► Measures of Inflation

Consumer Price Index
An index that summarizes movements in the prices faced by consumers.

With millions of prices changing in many different ways, how can one number tell us how the overall price level moves? Economists resolve this problem by constructing price indices to measure inflation. A price index summarizes the information provided by the prices of many different goods and services.

The **Consumer Price Index** (or **CPI**) summarizes movements in the prices faced by consumers. Economists do not rely solely on one large, nationwide measure of the CPI. Other price indices look at price movements in specific geographic regions or in other goods and services. The Producer Price Index, for example, tracks movements in the wholesale prices that firms pay to other firms. In this section, we concentrate on how economists compute the CPI. We also examine the reliability of this measure.

Calculating the CPI

Market basket
The combination of goods and services that the typical consumer purchases during a set period.

The method of calculating the CPI has undergone some important changes since the late 1990s. However, the principle behind it remains the same. We determine how much more (or less) it costs to buy a given market basket from one month, quarter, or year to the next. A **market basket** is the combination of goods and services that the typical consumer purchases during the period in question. Calculating the CPI involves four steps: surveying consumers, surveying retailers, determining the cost of the market basket, and comparing expenditures across time periods.

1. *Surveying consumers.* The BLS determines what combination of goods and services goes into the market basket by conducting extensive surveys of what consumers buy. Like any broad measure of household behavior, the market basket obscures individual differences. In fact, no individual household buys exactly what the "typical" household buys. Vegetarians don't buy meat; households in Phoenix, Arizona, buy more sun block than those in Rochester, New York; and households with infants buy diapers and formula, while those with teenagers buy designer jeans and pizza. To account for all these different purchases, the market basket consists of over 95,000 goods and services. However, the market basket of the "typical" consumer consists of only a small fraction of each of these goods and services.
2. *Surveying retailers.* The BLS surveys about 23,000 retailers in 87 different urban areas to determine the price of each item in the market basket. For market basket information on housing, it collects rent information from about 50,000 landlords or tenants.
3. *Determining the cost of the market basket.* The BLS computes the cost of the entire market basket by multiplying the price of each item in the market basket by the quantity in the basket.

4. *Comparing expenditures across time periods.* Knowing the cost of the market basket in a given year may be interesting in itself. However, it does not tell us anything meaningful unless we compare it with the cost from another time period.

Base year
The year whose price level serves as the basis for comparison with other years to form the Consumer Price Index.

Suppose that we computed the cost of a market basket in 2003, our base year, and want to compare it with the cost of a market basket in 2004. We call 2003 the **base year** because it serves as the basis for comparison with prices in another year. Suppose that the market basket cost $400 per month in 2003 and $412 in 2004.

We compute the CPI by dividing the cost of the market basket in 2004 by the cost in 2003. Equation 19.4 expresses this relationship.

$$[(Cost\ of\ market\ basket\ in\ current\ year)/ \\ (Cost\ of\ market\ basket\ in\ base\ year)] \times 100 = CPI \qquad (19.4)$$

The CPI in 2004 is:

$$(412/400) \times 100 = 103$$

Because the CPI is greater than 100 in 2004, the typical consumer spent more in 2004 than in 2003 to buy the fixed market basket of goods and services.

Equation 19.4 illustrates that the CPI is a *relative* measure of price levels. It tells us the cost of a given market basket in one year, compared to another year. Our choice of the base year is an arbitrary starting point. The CPI for our base year will always be 100, no matter what the market basket costs. In this example, the CPI for 2003 is $(400/400) \times 100 = 100$. If we had chosen 2004 as our base year, the CPI in 2004 would have been $(412/412) \times 100 = 100$. If the CPI in a given year is greater than 100, then prices are higher compared to the base year. If the CPI is less than 100, then prices are lower relative to the base year. The second column of Table 19.1 shows the CPI from 1990 through 2003, with the year 2000 as the base year. The steady rise in the CPI over this period shows that prices continually increased.

Interpreting the CPI

Inflation rate
The percentage change in the price level from one period to another.

In column 3 of Table 19.1, you can see that the difference between the CPI in 2001 and 2002 was 1.62. This is roughly the same as the change in the CPI between 1946 and 1947. Does this mean that inflation was the same between 2001 and 2002 as it was between 1946 and 1947? In fact, inflation was much worse in 1946–1947 than it was in 2001–2002. To see why, you must first understand how the yardstick with which economists measure inflation relates to the CPI. Economists define the **inflation rate** as the percentage change in the price level from one period to another. Although the price level increased by the same amount in both periods, prices—and hence the CPI—were much lower to begin with in 1946 than they were in 2001. Comparing these two periods would be like comparing Gwyneth Paltrow with a sumo wrestler. Everyone would notice if Gwyneth Paltrow gained 20 pounds. If the sumo wrestler gained 20 pounds, no one would see any difference.

To interpret Gwyneth Paltrow's and the sumo wrestler's weight gains correctly, we must use their original weights as the basis of comparison. To compute the rate of inflation between 1946 and 1947, we use the original level of the CPI as the basis for comparison. The percentage change in prices (the inflation rate) is the difference in the CPIs for the two years divided by the CPI in the comparison year:

TABLE 19.1

The Consumer Price Index: 1990–2004

Year (1)	CPI (2)	Increase in CPI (3)	Percentage Change of CPI (4)
1990	75 90	–	–
1991	79.09	3.19	4.21%
1992	81.48	2.39	3.01%
1993	83.91	2.43	2.99%
1994	86.06	2.15	2.56%
1995	88.50	2.44	2.83%
1996	91.11	2.61	2.95%
1997	93.21	2.09	2.29%
1998	94.66	1.45	1.56%
1999	96.75	2.09	2.21%
2000	100	3.25	3.36%
2001	102.85	2.85	2.84%
2002	104.47	1.62	1.58%
2003	106.85	2.38	2.28%
2004	109.69	2.84	2.66%

Source: Bureau of Labor Statistics (www.bls.gov). Base year changed to 2000

Get Ahead of the Curve

Use the Consumer Price Index to assess recent inflation in the United States.

$$Inflation\ rate = \left(\frac{CPI_{1947} - CPI_{1946}}{CPI_{1946}} \right) \times 100 = \left(\frac{1.62}{11.32} \right) \times 100 = 14.31\%$$

Inflation from 1946 to 1947 was 14.31 percent. Using the same reasoning to compute the inflation rate between 2001 and 2002 yields:

$$Inflation\ rate = \left(\frac{CPI_{2002} - CPI_{2001}}{CPI_{2001}} \right) \times 100 = \left(\frac{1.62}{102.85} \right) \times 100 = 1.58\%$$

Because prices were so much higher to begin with in 2001 than in 1946, the inflation rate in 2001, 1.58 percent, was far lower than that in 1946. When computing annual inflation rates, the base changes from year to year, so we must be careful about using the CPI to make statements about the rate of inflation.

Evaluating the CPI in Practice

As valuable a tool as the CPI is, it is not a perfect measure. We next look at three particular trouble spots that can cause the CPI to overstate inflation: it obscures individual price movements; it ignores changes in tastes and technology; and it does not allow households to adjust to price changes.

The CPI and Individual Price Movements. It is important to remember that the CPI is an index and thus does not show individual price movements. Some prices rise by more than the CPI, some rise by less, and some fall. To see why, consider a very simple world in which Jessica buys only clothing, measured in outfits, and food, measured in meals. Let us further suppose that Jessica's market basket for 2003 was

Comparing CPIs is Like Comparing Weight Gain

If Gwyneth Paltrow were to gain twenty pounds, even a casual observer would notice the difference. If a sumo wrestler were to gain twenty pounds, however, his closest friends may not notice. The reason is that twenty pounds is a much greater percentage change in Gwyneth Paltrow's weight, which is also why we convert the CPI to percentage changes when measuring inflation.

4 outfits and 10 meals. If an outfit cost $25 and a meal cost $10, then the cost of Jessica's market basket in 2003 was:

$$(4 \times \$25) + (10 \times \$10) = \$200$$

Suppose that the price of clothing rose by 20 percent to $30 in 2004, and the price of food fell by 10 percent to $9. The cost of Jessica's market basket in 2004 was:

$$(4 \times \$30) + (10 \times \$9) = \$210$$

Using 2003 as the base year and 2004 as the current year, we insert $210 in the numerator of Equation 19.4 and $200 in the denominator. The CPI for 2004 is:

$$(210/200) \times 100 = 105$$

The CPI thus rose from 100 to 105 from 2003 to 2004, which tells us that inflation in this simple example was five percent. Because it is an index, the CPI captures overall price movements. The price level rose by five percent, despite the fact that neither individual price rose by five percent. This change is summarized in the first two rows of Table 19.2.

The Impact of New and Better Goods on the CPI. Jessica's grandmother had not experienced anything like the horrible inflation that *her* father, Jessica's great-grandfather, described. However, she often complained to Jessica that prices were much higher now than when she emigrated from Germany to the United States in the 1950s. Jessica's grandfather, an avid basketball fan, often told Jessica that the

TABLE 19.2

Fixed Market Baskets and Substitution Bias

Year	Goods in Market Basket	Price per Good	Cost of Market Basket	CPI
2003	4 outfits	$25.00	$200	100
	10 meals	$10.00		
2004 (without substitution)	4 outfits	$30.00 (+ 20%)	$210	105
	10 meals	$9.00 (− 10%)		
2004 (with substitution)	2 outfits	$30.00 (+ 20%)	$204	102
	16 meals	$9.00 (− 10%)		

basketball stars of today, such as Shaquille O'Neal, were not as talented as the players he saw in the 1950s, such as the late George Mikan. A poll conducted by the Associated Press in 1950 declared Mikan as the greatest basketball player of the first half of the twentieth century, but few fans remember him today. It turns out that the comparisons made by Jessica's grandmother and grandfather have a lot in common.

We can certainly compare statistics for Shaq and Mikan. However, many changes in basketball over the years have affected player performance, yet are not found in the statistics. By the same token, the market basket from 2005 is vastly different from that of 1955. Imagine the world that your grandparents lived in when they were your age. Computers were in their infancy while PDAs, the Internet, and microwave ovens—items we now take for granted—were all the stuff of science fiction novels.

In addition to enjoying more, better, or simply different goods and services than your grandparents did, social conditions lead people to make different decisions than they would have made a generation or two ago. Relatively few married women worked outside the home in 1955. As a result, there was little reason for a family to eat out regularly at a restaurant. Today, such meals are commonplace. The fraction of the market basket devoted to eating outside the home has risen by more than a third in the last 50 years. Other changes include the growing suburbanization of the United States and the construction of the interstate highway system. These have caused the portion of the market basket spent on transportation to rise by over 50 percent and the portion spent on public transportation to fall by almost 17 percent over the same time period. Figure 19.2 summarizes some of the differences between the 1951 and 2001 market baskets.

According to Figure 19.2, food and apparel both took up a smaller fraction of the typical U.S. household's market basket in 2001 than they did a half-century earlier. U.S. households spent a smaller portion of their incomes on food and clothing and spent a greater portion on housing and transportation. The importance of recreation and, surprisingly, medical care, were relatively unchanged. With such changes in what Americans bought, it is unrealistic to calculate the CPI based on an unchanged market basket.

The market basket can change even if the goods in it are supposedly the same. Cars cost more than they did 50 years ago, but they are far safer and more comfortable today. Seatbelts, airbags, and antilock brakes are among a host of techno-

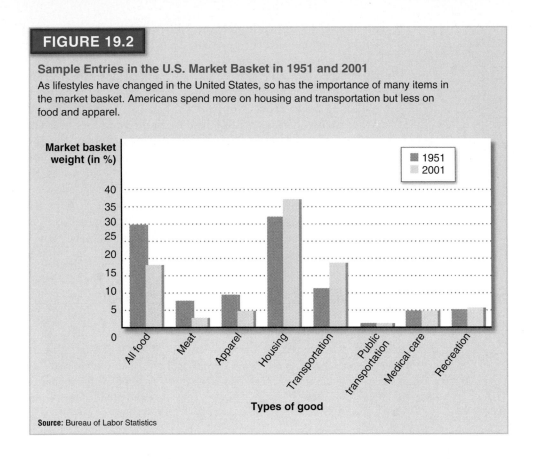

FIGURE 19.2

Sample Entries in the U.S. Market Basket in 1951 and 2001

As lifestyles have changed in the United States, so has the importance of many items in the market basket. Americans spend more on housing and transportation but less on food and apparel.

Market basket weight (in %)

Legend: 1951, 2001

Types of good

Source: Bureau of Labor Statistics

logical innovations that have made cars safer to operate. Automatic transmissions and power steering have made driving much easier. Bucket seats, individual climate controls, and CD and DVD players have made driving much more comfortable. Even today's gas "hogs" get better mileage—and pollute less—than the typical 1956 Chevy. The CPI does not account for such changes in the quality of goods and services. Although the nature and quality of goods and services purchased by the typical consumer changed greatly over 50 years, they did not change very much from one year to the next. As a result, inaccuracies are not so severe when we compare years that are close together. Such changes are cumulative, and inaccuracies based on these differences grow as the years we compare grow farther apart.

Substitution Bias and the CPI. To examine the effect of price changes, let's return to our example featuring Jessica's market basket. In the simple two-good world shown in Table 19.2, we saw that the CPI increased by 5 when the price of clothing rose from $25 to $30, the price of food fell from $10 to $9, and Jessica's market basket stayed constant. The Law of Demand tells us, however, that Jessica responds to these price changes by buying more food and less clothing. Suppose, for example, that Jessica responds by purchasing 16 meals and only 2 outfits. Jessica spends $204 on this new market basket, which is $6 less than she would have spent on a fixed market basket.

Keeping Jessica's market basket fixed has resulted in substitution bias. **Substitution bias** refers to the fact that, when consumers substitute relatively cheaper goods for relatively more expensive goods, the CPI provides an inaccurate picture of changes in the cost of living. Substitution bias and quality change led a government

Substitution bias
Causes the CPI to overstate inflation, because consumers substitute relatively cheaper goods for relatively more expensive goods.

commission to conclude that the CPI overstates increases in the cost of living by slightly over one percent per year. That is, if the CPI said prices rose by four percent, the cost of living actually rose by a bit less than three percent. Even such a small miscalculation can have serious implications for government spending. Many federal benefit programs, from food stamps to Social Security, are linked to the CPI.

In an effort to reduce substitution bias, the BLS has altered its approach to the market basket. Before, the BLS held constant purchases of each item, like frozen pizzas, ice cream, or peanut butter. The BLS now holds constant the proportion that the typical consumer spends on broad categories of goods and services. Although food and clothing are broader categories than the BLS uses, they illustrate the way the CPI now operates. In our example, the CPI now allows Jessica to respond to changes in the prices of specific foods and items of clothing. However, it still keeps the fraction that she spends on food and clothing overall constant. By allowing consumers to respond somewhat to changes in prices, the new CPI more accurately reflects changes in the cost of living.

TEST + *E X T E N D* Your Knowledge

1. TEST Compute the CPI if the price of pizza falls from $10 to $8, the price of ice cream cones rises from $2 to $4, and a typical consumer buys five pizzas per week and three ice cream cones per week.

2. EXTEND Go to the Web site of the Bureau of Labor Statistics using the link at www.aw-bc.com/leeds/ch19 and find the annual measures of the consumer and producer price indices for the last 10 years. Compare and discuss the movements in the two indices. Recall that the Producer Price Index tells us what producers charge other producers for wholesale items.

▶ The U.S. Experience with Inflation

Inflation varies from one year to the next and from one country to the next. In this section, we look at U.S. inflation rates since 1925. We then compare recent U.S. inflation rates to those of several other countries.

U.S. Inflation Rate

Deflation
The general downward movement of prices in the economy.

The inflation rate in the United States has never approached that of Germany in the 1920s, but it was much more of a problem in the United States when Jessica's parents were her age, in the 1970s. Figure 19.3 shows that inflation has fluctuated widely in the United States since 1926 and that prices have gone up every year since 1955. The only prolonged period of deflation occurred in the early 1930s during the Great Depression. Just as inflation is a general increase in prices, **deflation** is a general decrease in prices. During the depression, too little money was chasing too many goods, so prices fell. As the economy began its unsteady recovery from the depression in the mid-to-late 1930s, prices also fluctuated.

Inflation reappeared as the United States began its military build-up immediately before World War II. The production of airplanes, ships, and arms led to too much money chasing too few civilian goods. Inflation slowed but did not disappear when the government applied wartime wage and price controls in the early 1940s. These controls limited what producers could charge and what workers could demand for

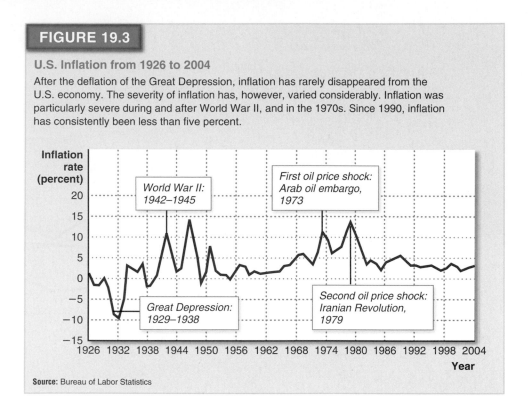

FIGURE 19.3

U.S. Inflation from 1926 to 2004

After the deflation of the Great Depression, inflation has rarely disappeared from the U.S. economy. The severity of inflation has, however, varied considerably. Inflation was particularly severe during and after World War II, and in the 1970s. Since 1990, inflation has consistently been less than five percent.

World War II: 1942–1945

First oil price shock: Arab oil embargo, 1973

Great Depression: 1929–1938

Second oil price shock: Iranian Revolution, 1979

Source: Bureau of Labor Statistics

pay for the duration of the war. When price controls were lifted after the war ended, workers and firms sought to push up wages and prices. As a result, inflation worsened in the late 1940s and early 1950s. By the mid-1950s, inflation had moderated and did not exceed three percent per year for about a decade.

Starting in the mid-1960s, inflation became an increasingly serious problem for the U.S. economy. For the next 15 years, inflation reached greater and greater highs during economic expansions. While inflation abated during downturns, it never quite returned to its previous low. In 1973, the Organization of Petroleum Exporting Countries (OPEC) first flexed its muscle by cutting off oil exports to the U.S. Inflation reached double figures for the first time since the late 1940s. U.S. inflation slowed in the wake of the economic downturn that followed the oil price shock. It quickly picked up again, reaching a peak of 13.5 percent in 1979, the year of the Iranian Revolution and the second oil price shock.

U.S. inflation fell again with the severe economic slowdown of the early 1980s. Since then, inflation has moderated, never again approaching the levels of the 1970s. Inflation did not exceed 5 percent between 1990 and 2004, averaging less than 2.5 percent.

The U.S. Inflation Rate in an International Context

With one major exception, the U.S. experience with inflation over the last decade or so closely parallels that of most industrialized countries. Figure 19.4 shows inflation in the United States and five other industrial economies from 1996 to 2004. Inflation in four countries—France, Germany, Italy, and the United Kingdom—has been very similar to that in the United States. The annual rate of inflation never exceeded four percent, and it seldom exceeded three percent. Japan is the only

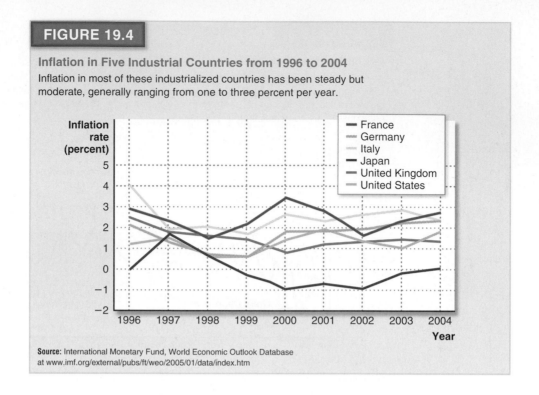

FIGURE 19.4

Inflation in Five Industrial Countries from 1996 to 2004
Inflation in most of these industrialized countries has been steady but moderate, generally ranging from one to three percent per year.

Legend:
- France
- Germany
- Italy
- Japan
- United Kingdom
- United States

Source: International Monetary Fund, World Economic Outlook Database at www.imf.org/external/pubs/ft/weo/2005/01/data/index.htm

outlier in the group. Starting in 1999, prices in Japan actually fell. We explore Japan's experience more closely later in this chapter.

Germany's Great Inflation

We conclude our examination of inflation by taking a closer look at a notable episode we've referred to several times already: Germany's inflation in the 1920s. Jessica's great-grandfather learned that inflation becomes particularly dangerous when it turns into **hyperinflation,** which occurs when inflation exceeds more than 50 percent per month. During the hyperinflation of the early 1920s, Germans lived with price increases of more than 10 percent per *hour.* In contrast, the U.S. inflation of about 10 percent a year in the 1970s seems trivial.

Hyperinflation
Exists when inflation exceeds 50 percent per month.

Origins of the German Inflation

Germany's inflation accelerated in 1914 when the government began to print more money to finance World War I. In the wake of its crushing defeat in 1918, the German government tried to finance its war debts and rebuild German society by printing even more money. With more German marks chasing fewer goods and services, the price level in 1922 escalated to 41 times its prewar level. Inflation grew completely out of control in 1923, when prices rose to several billion times their 1922 level. The writer Stefan Zweig observed that

> A pair of shoe laces cost more than a shoe had once cost, no, more than a fashionable store with two thousand pairs of shoes had cost before. . . . [1]

---

[1] Stefan Zweig, *The World of Yesterday*, New York: Viking Press, 1943, p. 313.

Inflation also affected productivity and output; workers became less productive as they had to take time out of the workday to spend their wages and salaries. Firms became as focused on coping with inflation as they were on producing goods and services. Many larger firms even devoted entire departments to tracking inflation.

Impact of the German Inflation on Society

As the economy spun out of control, so did German society. As Stephan Zweig put it:

> All values were changed, and not only material ones; the laws of the State were flouted, no tradition, no moral code was respected. Berlin was transformed into the Babylon of the world.[2]

People lived for the moment with little regard for the future. Why worry about next month or next year when "the price of soup can rise several million marks in an hour"?[3] The German people were attracted to any group that promised to restore economic and social order. It is no coincidence that Adolf Hitler first burst onto the national scene at the height of the inflation in November 1923.

The government quickly crushed Hitler's attempt to overthrow the local government in Munich. It also managed to get inflation under control by early 1924. The hyperinflation, however, crushed many people's confidence in democratic institutions. Radical parties of the right and left became increasingly popular, paving the way for Hitler's subsequent return.

Get Ahead of the Curve
Use the example of Hong Kong to contrast the effects of inflation and deflation on an economy.

Strategy and Policy
Deflation and Investment

While the United States and most other industrialized countries have experienced moderate inflation, Figure 19.4 shows that Japan has spent several years dealing with deflation. Prices in Japan began a sustained decline in 1999 after a decade of economic stagnation. In a reversal of the standard story, it resulted from too little money chasing too many goods.

At first glance, deflation may seem like a good thing. After all, as the price level falls, households' purchasing power increases. The reality is not so simple. Falling output prices increase the burden of a given wage or salary on firms. To cut their costs as revenue falls, firms reduce the wages and salaries they pay. If workers object, then the firms may have to lay off workers. After a long tradition of employment relationships that lasted a lifetime, many Japanese firms have begun to do just that. For this reason, the Japanese government has called deflation its most pressing economic problem.

Japan will have trouble breaking out of its prolonged economic slump unless its firms start spending more on new plants and equipment. Japanese firms will be reluctant to borrow the funds they need to make such investments, though, because deflation keeps raising the real burden of borrowing. When firms borrow, they typically make fixed interest payments over the lifetime of the loans. As the price level falls, the revenues of the firms fall, and the burden that these fixed payments imposes rises. Deflation thus discourages firms from borrowing. If firms borrow less than before, they cannot afford to invest as much in new plant and equipment as they once did. As a result, firms' ability to produce declines.

---

[2] Stefan Zweig, *The World of Yesterday*, New York: Viking Press, 1943, p. 313.
[3] Erich Maria Remarque, *The Black Obelisk*, New York: Harcourt, Brace, and World, 1957, p. 352.

Critical-Thinking Questions

1. How did deflation reinforce the economic downturn in Japan?
2. What barrier limited the Japanese banking authorities' ability to stimulate borrowing?

▶ **SUMMARY**

- **Defining inflation.** Inflation is an overall increase in the consumer price index. As an overall measure, it can mask widely differing movements in individual prices. Many people regard inflation as a more serious problem than unemployment, because it affects all of society and not just a small subset of the population. Inflation occurs when "too much money chases too few goods." Inflation particularly hurts those on fixed incomes, though it can benefit those who make fixed payments. Adjusting to inflation also imposes costs on firms and households. Finally, inflation creates a difference between real and nominal values of incomes and interest rates.

- **Measures of inflation.** The CPI, or consumer price index, is the most commonly used measure of inflation. It measures how the cost of a typical market basket of goods and services changes over time. To compare price levels at different times, we must keep the market basket constant. We thus cannot account for new and better products, and for the fact that consumers respond to price changes by altering what they buy. This causes the CPI to overstate inflation. The Bureau of Labor Statistics has modified the way it computes the CPI to minimize problems like substitution bias.

- **The U.S. experience with inflation.** While the price level has generally risen over the last 80 or so years, the U.S. rate of inflation has been uneven. During the 1970s, the price level rose rather quickly. Since the mid-1980s, it has risen much more gradually. During the Great Depression of the 1930s, the price level actually fell. Over the last decade, U.S. inflation has been comparable to that in other industrialized countries.

- **Germany's great inflation.** Hyperinflation occurs when the price level rises by more than 50 percent per month. Prices rose so rapidly that workers had to take time off during the day to spend their pay before it became worthless. The result was a collapse of morality and confidence in the government.

▶ **KEY TERMS**

▶ **PROBLEMS**

1. Under what conditions can we say that inflation does not increase the cost of anything?
2. How did inflation in ancient Rome differ from inflation in fourteenth-century Europe?
3. Is a retiree who relies on a pension of $500 per month helped or hurt by inflation? Explain your answer.
4. Is a young college graduate who makes car payments of $150 per month helped or hurt by inflation? Explain your answer.

5. How is it possible for a person to receive a raise but find herself worse off?

6. If the nominal interest rate is five percent and inflation is two percent, what is the real interest rate? Justify your answer.

7. Why are negative real interest rates illogical? If they are illogical, why did they occur in the 1970s?

8. Assume that we live in a world with two goods: economics textbooks and cupcakes. In 2004, textbooks cost $100 and cupcakes cost $0.50. The typical market basket consists of 2 economics textbooks and 10 cupcakes.
   a. Compute the CPI for the base year of 2004.
   b. In 2005, the price of textbooks falls to $99, and the price of cupcakes increases to $1. What is the CPI for 2005?
   c. What is the inflation rate between 2004 and 2005?

9. Assume that we live in a world with three goods: ice cream, root beer, and tunafish sandwiches.
   a. Suppose that in 2004 the typical consumer buys 4 half-gallons of ice cream, 10 large bottles of root beer, and 20 tunafish sandwiches each month. In 2004, a half-gallon of ice cream costs $2.50, a large bottle of root beer costs $2.00, and a tunafish sandwich costs $4.00. What does the typical market basket cost?
   b. Suppose that prices change in 2005 so that a half-gallon of ice cream costs $3.00, a bottle of root beer costs $1.80, and a tunafish sandwich costs $4.50. Construct a price index that shows how much prices have risen, holding the market basket constant.
   c. Why might your answer in part b overstate the increase in the cost of living?

10. In Problem 9, provide a change in the price of tunafish sandwiches that would have led to deflation rather than inflation.

11. Recalculate the values in the second column of Table 19.1 using 1990 as the base year.

12. What is substitution bias and how might it cause the values in Table 19.1 to overstate inflation?

13. Why doesn't any one consumer buy exactly what is in the market basket?

14. Why does the CPI reflect changes in the price level rather than the actual price level itself?

15. If the price of bubble gum doubles, and nothing else changes, the CPI stays almost unchanged. Why would such a large change in an item in the market basket have so little an effect?

16. If the CPI in 2002 was 175 and the CPI in 2003 was 180, what was the rate of inflation between the two years?

17. Why is the CPI comparing 2004 and 2005 more accurate than the CPI comparing 1954 and 2005?

18. How does substitution bias reflect the Law of Demand?

19. Has inflation in the United States lessened or worsened since 1970? Explain your answer.

20. Why is hyperinflation so much worse than ordinary inflation?

HERE'S HOW MyEconLab CAN HELP YOU GET A BETTER GRADE

1. Log into MyEconLab and take Practice Test 19-A (to log in for the first time, see page 30 for instructions).

2. Based on your test results, MyEconLab will identify the areas where you need further work and create a personal Study Plan for you.

3. Your Study Plan contains the problems listed below and others like them that will target the specific chapter topics you need to focus on. You'll receive instant feedback and find links to tutorials, animations, and the online textbook to help you study.

4. When you're ready, take Practice Test 19-B and demonstrate how your results have improved.

Section 19.1, Problem 1 Suppose that for the past year, inflation was four percent. For the following scenarios, specify whether each individual is worse off, better off, or the same after the price level rises.

   a. Hassan, a retired accountant who receives a fixed monthly pension
   b. Deirdre, whose boss gave her a 6-percent pay raise
   c. Clifford, who is making fixed payments on a new car
   d. Samuel, who bought a new house with a variable interest rate that is pegged to the inflation rate
   e. Carla, who just received a 2-percent pay raise
   f. Rebecca, who just signed a three-year salary contract
   g. Given your answers to parts a through e, does it make sense to say that inflation affects everyone equally?

Section 19.1, Problem 2 Suppose that you lend your friend $100 for a year. You desire a real interest rate of 4 percent.

   a. If you expect inflation to be 3 percent, how much interest should you ask for?
   b. If inflation turns out to be 5 percent instead of 3 percent, who benefits: you or your friend? Justify your answer.
   c. If inflation turns out to be 1 percent instead of 3 percent, who benefits: you or your friend? Justify your answer.

Section 19.1, Problem 3 The following table shows the inflation rate for the years 1995–1999, and the nominal wage of Sheila.

Year	Inflation Rate	Nominal Wage	Percentage Change in Real Wage
1995	—	$20.00	
1996	3%	$21.00	
1997	5%	$21.52	
1998	4%	$21.80	
1999	2%	$21.80	

Determine the percentage change in Sheila's real wage rate for 1996–1999. For each year, determine whether Sheila is actually worse off or better off. (*Hint:* you will need to calculate the percentage change in her nominal wage first.)

Section 19.2, Problem 1 Suppose that our market basket contains two goods: T-shirts and pizza. The market basket consists of 10 T-shirts and 25 pizzas. The following chart shows the prices of these goods for the years 1985–1988. Use it to answer the following questions. Let the base year be 1985.

Year	Price (T-shirts)	Price (pizza)
1985	$5.00	$15.00
1986	$4.50	$16.00
1987	$5.00	$17.00
1988	$5.25	$17.50

   a. Calculate the cost of the market basket for each year.
   b. Calculate the price index for each year.
   c. Calculate the annual inflation rate for the years 1985–1986, 1986–1987, and 1987–1988.

Section 19.2, Problem 2 Does the rate of inflation depend upon the year specified as the base year? Use the price information from Problem 1 to justify your answer. Calculate the CPI, given the base year of 1988. Calculate the annual inflation rate for the years 1985–1986, 1986–1987, and 1987–1988. Are your answers the same as in the answer to part c earlier?

Section 19.2, Problem 3 Fill in the following blanks. The two possible answers to each question are: change in quality bias or substitution bias.

    a. Ennis buys a new computer in 2000 for $1,000. Ennis's wife Barbie buys the same model computer in 2002, but with more memory and a faster central processing unit (CPU), for $1,000. This potential problem with CPI measurement is an example of _____.

    b. Lisa normally buys 5 pounds of chicken and 10 pounds of ground beef per month. However, this month the price of ground beef rose while chicken did not, and now she buys 8 pounds of chicken and 6 pounds of ground beef. This potential problem with the CPI measurement is an example of _____ .

Section 19.3, Problem 1 Which of the following statements regarding U.S. inflation is true?

    a. Since 1926, the U.S. has experienced deflation as often as inflation.

    b. Since 1926, the U.S. inflation rate has been near zero every year.

    c. Since 1926, the U.S. inflation rate has averaged around 10 percent.

    d. Since 1926, the U.S. inflation rate has been between 0 percent and 5 percent for most years.

Section 19.4, Problem 1 Which of the following is the correct definition of hyperinflation?

    a. An inflation rate of 50 percent per year

    b. An inflation rate of 50 percent per month

    c. An inflation rate of at least 10 percent per year for 5 years or more

    d. Inflation coupled with too much coffee and sugar

20 GDP and the Business Cycle

Frank and Shawna need to buy a new car for their thriving catering business. They have narrowed their choices down to a Toyota Matrix or a Ford Focus. They want a reliable car with good gas mileage, but Frank has another concern. He wants to buy American.

"I keep seeing all those stories about how Americans buy so much more from other countries than they buy from the United States," he tells Shawna. "Let's buy something that adds to the American economy."

"Okay," Shawna replies, "then we'll get the Matrix. After all, it's assembled here in the United States, while the Ford is assembled in Canada."

Frank and Shawna are facing a problem that is familiar to economists. In this era of global production and consumption, you shouldn't assume that familiar American brand names such as Ford indicate where a product is actually made. Many Ford cars are assembled in Canada, and Toyota has extensive production facilities in the United States. Buying the Toyota might or might not add more to U.S. economic activity than buying the Ford does. This complication is one of the many difficulties that economists face when they attempt to measure how much a nation produces.

In Chapter 2, you saw that economists use GDP—or, more precisely, GDP per capita—to measure a nation's economic well-being. In this chapter, we take a careful look at how economists measure a nation's output and income at the macroeconomic level. We explore what goes into such a measure, and what is left out, taking a close look at each component of GDP and the methods that economists use to measure GDP. Next, we examine the strengths and weaknesses of GDP as a measure of well-being. Finally, we look at GDP over time as an indicator of the economy's performance.

ALONG THE WAY, YOU WILL ALSO LEARN:

- Which goods and services count in GDP, and which do not.

- How to calculate GDP by measuring expenditures in the economy.

- How to calculate GDP by measuring incomes in the economy.

- How value added allows us to see what a specific product or industry contributes to GDP.

- How real GDP and real GDP per capita can help us measure social well-being, though they might not be perfect measures.

- How an economy's performance fluctuates over time.

AT THE END OF THE CHAPTER, THE MYECONLAB LOGO WILL DIRECT YOU ONLINE

- MyEconLab is a resource-packed online homework and tutorial system that can help you perform better in your economics course. To log in for the first time, see page 30 for instructions.

- MyEconLab can help you apply important concepts from the chapter to real-world issues. Watch for the logo to indicate online features about the U.S. and Brazilian economies.

- At the end of each chapter, you'll find a special study section that will help you get the most out of your textbook and your instructor's MyEconLab course.

Defining GDP

Recall that GDP measures the amount of production in an economy. More formally, we define GDP as the total market value of all new, final goods and services produced in a given country over a given period of time. We now examine each component of this definition in detail.

The Total Market Value of Goods and Services

Frank and Shawna's business purchases are a useful illustration of why GDP relies on total market value. Suppose that Frank decides to buy the Toyota Matrix for their catering business. In addition, he buys a new oven and dishwasher. Meanwhile, Shawna buys 25 tablecloths, 100 china plates, and 150 salmon fillets. Who has bought more overall output? You might be tempted to conclude that Shawna has bought more by adding the number of items that each has bought (Frank has bought 3 items; Shawna has bought 275) and then comparing the sums. Adding the items, however, raises important questions. Exactly what does one tablecloth plus one plate equal? How do you compare them to an oven plus a car? Adding and comparing such dissimilar items is a challenge. Imagine, then, how difficult it must be to determine how much an entire economy produces.

Calculating GDP. To determine how much a nation produces, we must add together many different items. Total market value provides a common yardstick with which we can measure what an economy produces. Using dollars as the common denominator allows us to compare very different output mixes. We first multiply the quantity of each good that is produced by its price to compute the overall market value of that good or service. GDP is the sum of the market values of all the goods and services that a nation has produced. It summarizes the total market value of a nation's output.

Suppose, for example, that a new Matrix costs $15,000, an oven costs $1,000, and a dishwasher costs $500. The market value of Frank's bundle of goods is:

$$(1 \times \$15,000) + (1 \times \$1,000) + (1 \times \$500) = \$16,500$$

If a tablecloth costs $100, a plate costs $50, and a salmon fillet costs $5, the market value of Shawna's bundle of goods is:

$$(25 \times \$100) + (100 \times \$50) + (150 \times \$5) = \$8,250$$

Comparing Market Values. Although Shawna bought many more items than Frank did, the market value of what she purchased ($8,250) is much less than Frank's purchases ($16,500). In dollar terms, Frank bought more than Shawna did.

New Goods and Services

Not all items are counted when calculating GDP. We include only newly produced goods and services. Before choosing between the Focus and the Matrix, Frank and Shawna thought of purchasing a vintage 1964 Ford Mustang from Frank's neighbor for $10,000. Would the Mustang count toward GDP? Unlike the Matrix, the Mustang would not count. The reason is that GDP includes the market value of only *new* goods and services.

In 1964, the neighbor's purchase of the new Mustang for $5,000 represented new production that was counted in that year's GDP. That is, a household had a $5,000 car that had not existed before. Frank and Shawna's purchase of the used car would not add to the number of cars owned by households. Instead, it would shift an existing car from one owner to another. Counting the Mustang in GDP again this year would be **double counting**, which occurs when we include the value of an item twice when calculating GDP. Economists avoid double counting because it causes them to overstate the level of production in the economy. When calculating GDP, we count the production of a good or service only once, in the year in which it was produced. Most goods and services are produced and sold in the same year. When a good is produced in one year and sold or resold in another, it is counted only in the year in which it was produced.

Double counting
Including the value of an item twice when computing GDP.

Final Goods and Services

GDP includes only *final* goods and services: counting the metal, glass, and other materials that went into the new car that Frank and Shawna bought would also result in double counting. The metal and glass that go into a car are **intermediate goods**: inputs that are used up in the creation of a final good that will be sold in the market. "Used up" means that the intermediate good becomes a part of the good it helps create. Nothing is left over. **Final goods**, by contrast, are goods (or services) that are used by the ultimate consumer and are not consumed in the production of another good.

A good can be either a final good or an intermediate good, depending on how it is used. If, for example, Frank and Shawna themselves ate the salmon that Shawna bought, it would be a final good. If they used the salmon as part of a meal they prepared for their catering business, it would be an intermediate good and would not

Intermediate goods
Inputs that are used up in the creation of a final good that will be sold in the market.

Final goods
Goods (or services) that are used by the ultimate consumer.

GDP Includes Only Final Goods and Services
If a dressmaker buys this cloth to make a dress that she sells in her shop, then the sale of the cloth does not add to GDP. If she uses it to make a dress that she wears herself, the purchase *does* count.

be counted in GDP. The Bureau of Economic Analysis (BEA), the government agency that computes GDP, must therefore first establish whether a good is final or intermediate.

Goods and Services Produced in a Given Country

As Shawna reminded Frank when they were looking for a car, the country that produces a good or service matters in our definition of GDP. Globalization complicates GDP calculations. The United States imports some cars that Ford, a U.S. car manufacturer, makes in Canada. Toyota, a Japanese company, assembles some of its cars in the United States. A Toyota Matrix that is produced in the United States constitutes part of the U.S. GDP, although it is a "Japanese" car. "American" Fords that are produced in Canada count toward Canada's GDP. More generally, a country includes an item in its GDP if the good or service is produced within its borders.

Goods and Services Produced in a Given Period of Time

Our final consideration in defining GDP concerns the period of time under examination. Because the production of goods and services occurs over time, we must specify the period over which we are measuring GDP. The time period affects our measure of GDP because the quantity produced grows as the time period lengthens.

What is the best time period over which to measure GDP? Economists typically rely on annual measures of GDP. Looking across an entire year smoothes out random fluctuations that might take place over a short period of time. It also accounts for regular, predictable swings in production over the course of the year. In order to track production more closely, many governments also provide quarterly estimates of expected yearly production.

The Expenditure Approach to GDP

We now turn to the two methods that nations generally use to calculate GDP: the expenditure approach and the income approach. In this section, we focus on the expenditure approach. We begin with the observation that output receives a market value only when it is purchased. As a result, the dollar value of the quantity of goods and services supplied by producers must equal the dollar value of the quantity demanded by different sectors of the economy. We look carefully at how expenditures demanded by households, firms, and the government relate to GDP. We examine each component separately and then show how, when taken together, they constitute a nation's GDP.

Consumption Expenditure by Households

Consumption
Household's purchases of new goods and services.

Households' purchases of new goods and services are the consumption goods we discussed in Chapter 2. We refer to these purchases as **consumption** and denote them by the symbol C. Frank and Shawna's purchases of durable goods, such as the Toyota Matrix, count as consumption. Their purchases of non-durable goods, such as the beef they buy for their own use, also count toward consumption. Consumption also includes expenditure on services, such as college tuition. Finally, consumption includes rental expenditure on housing. Even if Frank and Shawna own their own home, they are still consuming housing. To account for this consumption, the government includes an estimate of the rent that homeowners would have had to pay for their dwelling.

In 2004, U.S. households spent roughly $8.2 trillion on the consumption of new, final goods and services, making it the largest single component of GDP. Consumption spending typically accounts for more than two-thirds of all U.S. expenditures.

Investment Expenditures by Firms

Investment
The purchase of capital goods such as plant and equipment.

Although $8.2 trillion is a substantial sum, it falls far short of $11.7 trillion, U.S. GDP in 2004. From where does the remaining demand for $3.5 trillion of new, final goods and services come? One source is investment spending (denoted as I). Firms make **investment** expenditure when they buy capital goods such as plant and equipment. Recall from Chapter 2 that capital goods are used to produce other goods and services. Three categories of spending are included as investment expenditures:

- Business spending on capital goods such as machinery, equipment, and tools
- All private construction
- Changes in business inventories

In 2004, these purchases totaled roughly $1.9 trillion. Again, a purchase could be part of either household consumption or business investment, depending on how the item is used. The Toyota Matrix would be an investment expenditure if Frank and Shawna used it for their catering business. It would be part of consumption if they used it to drive to the movies.

Spending on Capital Goods. Capital goods are manmade inputs used—but not used up—in the production of final goods. Ford's purchase of a new conveyor belt or a new building, for example, constitutes investment expenditure. Unlike its purchase of intermediate goods such as tires or steel, Ford's purchases of capital goods count toward GDP.

Investment is yet another term whose economic meaning differs from its everyday meaning. When your friends or family speak of investment, they typically mean a financial transaction involving stocks or bonds. To an economist, households' and firms' purchases of stocks and bonds are a form of saving. Stocks and bonds are not newly produced goods and services. They are a way for households and firms to hold funds that they do not spend on goods and services.

Private Construction Spending. All private construction—that is, construction by firms or households—counts as investment expenditure in GDP. Some private construction, such as a new factory, is clearly business investment. Rental property, such as a new apartment complex, also is clearly a form of investment spending. Finally, we also count new construction of single-family housing as investment, even when it is owner-occupied.

Inventory Investment. So far in this discussion, the entries in GDP have resulted from a sale of some kind. Our final form of investment, additions to inventory, occurs when a firm does *not* sell what it has produced. **Inventory** is the stock of goods that a firm produces but does not sell in the same time period. Because GDP measures production and not sales, any output by a firm must be counted toward GDP. If the output is sold, it counts as consumption expenditure. If a firm produces a good that it is not sold, that unsold good counts as inventory investment.

A firm adds to its inventory for any one of three reasons:

1. *Timing.* Suppose that Toyota produced the car on December 12, 2005, but Frank and Shawna did not buy it until March 30, 2006. The car counts as an addition to inventory—and an investment—in 2005. When Frank and Shawna buy it, their purchase counts as consumption in 2006. Does this method involve double counting the value of the car? Because selling the car reduces Toyota's inventory, the sale is a negative investment for Toyota. The negative investment offsets the added consumption, so GDP does not change in 2006.

2. *Strategy.* Suppose that Ford fears that labor negotiations will break down and its workers will strike in early 2006. To protect itself against an interruption in production, Ford might increase the number of cars it has ready to ship to dealers in its warehouses. The addition to inventory increases investment and GDP. A reduction in inventory—for instance, if the dispute with its workforce is settled peacefully—lessens GDP.

   Recently, many firms have strategically reduced their inventories because improved database management, communication, and transportation have allowed them to produce goods "just-in-time." Just-in-time production methods reduce the costs of storing inputs and output by bringing the necessary inputs together just in time for immediate delivery to the consumer.

3. *Overestimated demand.* Firms add to inventory when they overestimate the demand for their products. If Toyota produces too many cars, it adds the unsold cars to inventory. This action is called *unintended* inventory

Inventory
The stock of goods that a firm produces but does not sell in the same time period.

investment, because Toyota did not expect to add the cars to inventory. Similarly, if it underestimates the demand for cars, Toyota might have to reduce its inventory below the desired level. Unplanned changes in inventory result from planning mistakes in the amount that a firm produces. Firms respond to such changes by increasing or reducing the amount they produce in the future. In a later chapter, you will see how unplanned changes in inventory affect the economy.

Government Expenditure

Like private industries, federal, state, and local governments purchase a variety of goods and services. Government expenditure (G) in 2004 totaled almost $2.2 trillion in goods and services. Government expenditure, however, does not include all spending by government. It refers strictly to state, local, and federal governments' purchases of final goods and services. In Chapter 3, you saw that such expenditure accounts for only a portion of total spending by government. Governments spend large sums on Social Security payments to retirees, unemployment benefits to workers who have been laid off, and subsidies to firms. None of these, however, counts as government expenditure. Instead, they are all government transfer payments: shifts of funds, rather than payments for goods and services. Because they involve no new production, we do not count transfer payments in GDP.

Net Exports

If we add together consumption, investment, and government expenditures in 2004, we come up with $12.3 trillion ($8.2 trillion + $1.9 trillion + $2.2 trillion = $12.3 trillion). However, we've established that GDP was only $11.7 trillion. What accounts for the $0.6 trillion disparity? The answer is that some of what households, firms, and governments buy is not produced domestically. The Ford Focus that Frank and Shawna considered buying is one example. By the same token, U.S. firms sell some of what they produce to households, firms, or governments in foreign countries. These sales do not appear in C, I, or G.

How do we focus on *domestic* production? We first add exports (X), the goods and services produced in the United States, but sold abroad, to GDP. Because U.S. GDP counts the production of U.S.-made goods and services even if they are sold elsewhere, we add exports. We then subtract imports (M), new, final goods and services bought by U.S. households, firms, or governments that are produced in another country. Expenditures on imports are included as consumption expenditure by households or investment expenditures by firms. As a result, we must subtract imports to measure U.S. production.

For example, suppose that Frank and Shawna had spent $15,000 on a new Ford Focus that was produced in Canada. Their purchase would count as U.S. consumption expenditure. Because the car was not produced in the United States, it does not belong in U.S. GDP. Subtracting the expenditure as an import negates its impact on consumption. Adding exports and subtracting imports yields a value called net exports. **Net exports** are the difference between the market value of all exports and the market value of all imports (X–M). In 2004, this figure was about −$0.6 trillion, meaning that the United States imported about $0.6 trillion more in goods and services than it exported. By including net exports, we count all items produced in the United States in GDP, and we do not count items produced elsewhere.

Net exports
The difference between the market value of all exports and the market value of all imports.

TABLE 20.1

The Components of the Expenditure and Income Approaches to GDP in 2004

Expenditure		Income	
Consumption (C)	$8.2 trillion	Labor compensation	$6.6 trillion
Investment (I)	$1.9 trillion	Rent	$0.2 trillion
Government Expenditure (G)	$2.2 trillion	Interest	$0.5 trillion
Net Exports (X–M)	− $0.6 trillion	Proprietor's income and profit	$2.1 trillion
Sum	**$11.7 trillion**	**Sum**	**$9.4 trillion**
		Plus	
		Taxes on production and imports	$0.8 trillion
		Depreciation	$1.4 trillion
		Net foreign factor income	$0.05 trillion
		Sum	**$11.65 trillion**

Source: Bureau of Economic Analysis

Get Ahead of the Curve

Use your knowledge of Gross Domestic Product to analyze recent economic growth in the United States.

The Expenditure Approach Equation

Adding together the individual GDP components gives us the total market value of purchases of new, domestically produced final goods and services by the different sectors of the economy. We can therefore express GDP as shown in Equation 20.1.

$$GDP = C + I + G + (X-M) \qquad (20.1)$$

Table 20.1 applies Equation 20.1 to the U.S. economy for 2004.

The first column of Table 20.1 applies Equation 20.1 to the U.S. economy in 2004. Net exports account for this discrepancy. Net exports have a negative impact on GDP, because the United States imported more than it exported in 2004, so (X–M) enters Table 20.1 as a negative number.

▶ The Income Approach to GDP

We can also calculate GDP by considering the incomes earned in the economy. Recall that the circular flow model of the economy in Chapter 3 shows households exchanging money for goods and services with firms in the product market. This logic was the basis for the expenditure approach. At the same time, however, firms exchange money for inputs with households in the resource market. Expenditures by consumers and producers eventually flow to households as income through the resource market. This insight forms the basis of the income approach. Because the circular flow states that expenditures on the product market must roughly equal incomes on the resource market, the two approaches to GDP should yield similar numbers.

With the income approach, we compute GDP by adding up the income received by the factors of production. Recall from Chapter 2 that the factors of production include land, labor, physical capital, and entrepreneurship.

Factor Incomes

We begin by tracing GDP—the total expenditure in the U.S. economy—in 2004 to see how GDP flows to households in the form of income. In 2004, the BEA estimated U.S. GDP to be about $11.7 trillion, meaning that roughly $11.7 trillion was spent in exchange for new, final, U.S.-made goods and services. This spending generated about $11.7 trillion of new income for all those responsible for producing that output. The second column of Table 20.1 summarizes the income that each factor of production receives. We now take a close look at each form of payment corresponding to the factors of production.

Labor Compensation. Labor compensation is by far the largest entry in the second column of Table 20.1. It includes all wages and salaries as well as fringe benefits such as pensions and health insurance that workers earn by producing output that year. In 2004, labor compensation totaled about $6.6 trillion.

Rent. Rental income includes all income earned by those who provide the property and the physical capital that produce that year's output. In 2004, this figure represented $0.2 trillion. In addition to expenditure on land and buildings, rental income includes payments for the use of intellectual property such as royalties from the rights to books or inventions. Because physical capital also includes residential housing, rental income includes an estimate of the rent homeowners would have to pay if they rented their dwellings.

Interest. Interest income consists of the net income earned by those who supply financial capital for the year's production. In 2004, this income amounted to $0.5 trillion. It is the difference between the interest households earn on their financial assets, such as checking and saving accounts, and the interest households pay on what they borrow, such as mortgages, car loans, and student loans. Because, as a whole, households earn more interest than they pay, interest income for households is positive.

Proprietor's Income and Profit. Profit earned by sole proprietors and partnerships such as Shawna and Frank's catering business is called proprietor's income. Recall from Chapter 3 that profits earned by corporations are called corporate profits. Corporations use their profits in three different ways: to pay the corporate profits tax, to pay dividends to stockholders, and to pay for new investment. The profits that firms reinvest are called retained earnings. Proprietor's income and corporate profits amounted to about $2.1 trillion in 2004.

Taxes on Production and Imports, Depreciation, and Net Foreign Factor Income

Adding together all the different forms of income in Table 20.1 yields only $9.4 trillion in U.S. income in 2004. This amount is $2.3 trillion less than the estimated GDP of $11.7 trillion. How can this be, given the basic conclusion of the circular flow that firms' revenue returns to households as income? The discrepancy results from three leakages from the circular flow: taxes on production and imports, depreciation, and net foreign factor income, as explained in the next few sections.

Taxes on Production and Imports. Taxes on production and imports are assessed on producers, but they are paid at least in part by consumers. Tariffs, property taxes, and sales and excise taxes are all examples of these taxes. Such taxes show up in the product price (which is used to calculate GDP by the expenditure approach). However, they are not captured as income for the factors of production in the income approach. For example, if there were a five-percent sales tax on catered dinners, newlyweds with a bill of $20,000 would owe an additional $1,000 tax when paying Frank and Shawna's bill ($0.05 \times \$20,000 = \$1,000$). The expenditure on the dinner thus exceeds the income that Frank, Shawna, and their employees receive from providing it. We add $1,000 in taxes to the total income generated by the dinner to match the total expenditure on it. Taxes on production and imports totaled about $0.8 trillion in 2004.

Depreciation
Occurs when capital goods wear out after extended use.

Depreciation. Depreciation is the wear, tear, and obsolescence that eventually cause some inputs to lose their value. Depreciation occurs when capital goods, such as the Toyota Matrix or the oven that Frank and Shawna purchase, begin to wear out after extended use. Firms must constantly make these purchases to continue producing the same level of output.

The replacement of capital that has depreciated is a substantial part of investment in the expenditure approach to GDP. However, because it does not add to the capital stock, replacing depreciated capital stock does not generate additional income in the resource market. In 2004, depreciation was about $1.4 trillion, accounting for much of the $2.3 trillion difference between GDP and factor income.

Net Foreign Factor Income. Because the United States is part of a global economy, some foreigners work in the United States or own U.S. factors of production. Some U.S. citizens also work overseas or own foreign factors of production that earn income overseas. GDP focuses on production within the borders of a given nation, so we must add net foreign factor income to other factor incomes. **Net foreign factor income** is the difference between the income earned by foreign-owned resources in the production of U.S. goods and services and the income earned by U.S.-owned resources used in the production of goods and services overseas. For example, the profits earned by Toyota plants operating in the United States show up on Toyota's books in Japan. Because U.S. resources generated these profits, they should be added to U.S. income. Moreover, some of the income generated by Ford's operations in other countries goes to households in the United States. We subtract this income because it does not result from U.S. production. U.S. net foreign factor income was $0.05 trillion in 2003, roughly one-half of one percent of GDP.

Net foreign factor income
The difference between the income earned by foreign-owned resources in the production of U.S. goods and services and the income earned by U.S.-owned resources used in the production of goods and services abroad.

The Income Approach Equation

Equation 20.2 summarizes the calculation of GDP as the sum of incomes in the economy.

$$\text{GDP} = \textit{Labor compensation} + \textit{Rent} + \textit{Interest} +$$
$$\textit{Proprietor's income and profit} + \textit{Taxes on production and imports} +$$
$$\textit{Depreciation} + \textit{Net foreign factor income} \qquad (20.2)$$

The second column of Table 20.1 shows that the sum of factor incomes and the three leakages between firm revenue and factor income was almost $11.7 trillion. In other words, GDP as calculated in Equation 20.2 roughly equals the calculation using the expenditure approach to GDP.

 ## The Value-Added Approach to GDP

Value added
The increase in value at each stage of a good's or service's production.

We can see how much a particular good or service adds to GDP by totaling up the value added at each stage of its production. The **value added** at a stage of production is the difference between the market value of the inputs and the market value of the output at that stage.

While it is a bit cumbersome, we can compute a nation's GDP by adding the value added for *all* goods and services. To illustrate, assume that the $15,000 price tag for Frank and Shawna's car includes a $400 high-performance tire package. That $400 of additional production counts as consumption expenditure and would generate $400 in additional income. Table 20.2 shows that the production and sale of the tires generates $400 of added value as well.

TABLE 20.2

Value Added by the Optional Tire Package

Activity	Starting Value	Final Value	Value Added
ExxonMobil pumps crude oil from the Gulf of Mexico	$0	$20	$20
INSA makes synthetic rubber from crude oil	20	100	80
Firestone makes four tires from synthetic rubber	100	320	220
Toyota sells four tires	320	400	80
Total value added			**$400**

At the first stage of production, the ExxonMobil oil company pumps crude oil from the Gulf of Mexico. It then sells the crude oil to a chemical company, INSA Rubber. Seven gallons (enough to make four tires) of crude oil sells for about $20. Thus, ExxonMobil has added $20 worth of value by extracting the crude oil. INSA uses the $20 worth of crude oil to make synthetic rubber. INSA sells this synthetic rubber to the tire manufacturer Firestone for $100. INSA has added $80 of value by transforming the oil into rubber. Firestone uses the synthetic rubber to manufacture four high-performance tires, which it sells to Toyota for $320. Transforming the rubber into tires adds $220 of value. Finally, Toyota sells the four tires to Frank and Shawna for $400. Toyota adds $80 worth of value by distributing, marketing, and mounting the tires. The total value added by all four stages of production is: $20 + $80 + $220 + $80 = $400. This amount equals Frank and Shawna's expenditure and the income earned by all the factors of production used in making the tires. Applying this approach to all the goods and services produced in the economy, we find that GDP equals the sum of the value added for all final goods and services produced in the economy in a given year.

The sum of the value added for each final good or service produced in the economy yields the market value of that good. As a result, we can total the value added for all goods to determine overall GDP.

▶ Refining GDP

Now that we've established the various methods of calculating GDP, we turn our focus to interpreting it. Because GDP is also a measure of income, it is tempting to equate GDP with the well-being of society. There are several problems with using GDP in this way. In this section, we look at the adjustments that economists make to GDP so that it accurately reflects social well-being.

Real and Nominal GDP

Nominal GDP
The market value of new output evaluated at the output's current market price.

Recall from the inflation chapter that Frank and Shawna's nominal income could rise without making them better off. Economists apply this concept to the economy as a whole by referring to **nominal GDP,** which is the market value of new output evaluated at the output's *current market price.* As was the case with nominal income, when nominal GDP goes up by 10 percent, we cannot say whether society is better off. Output could have risen by 10 percent with prices constant, prices could have risen by 10 percent with output constant, or both output and price could have risen by, say, 5 percent. How do we compare an economy's health at two different times? To do so, we need a measure that changes only when there is a change in the level of output. We must therefore negate the impact of price changes on nominal GDP.

Real GDP
The value of output in constant dollars.

Nominal GDP measures the market value of output in *current dollars*—the prices that exist at the time. For example, U.S. GDP in 2004 used the prices that prevailed in 2004. Hence, that $11.7 trillion is nominal GDP. This measure can change when either output or prices change. In contrast, real GDP changes only when output changes. **Real GDP** is the value of output in *constant dollars,* meaning that we use prices from a given base year. If 2000 is the base year, we would compute real GDP in 2005 using the prices that prevailed five years earlier. Using prices that prevailed in 2000, real GDP in 2004 was $10.8 trillion, rather than $11.7 trillion.

GDP deflator
Measures changes in the prices of all sectors of the economy.

The GDP Deflator. The difference between nominal and real GDP also provides us with a more general measure of price changes in the economy. In the inflation chapter, we used the CPI (Consumer Price Index) to measure movements in prices faced by consumers. However, consumption accounts for only a portion of GDP. To measure price movements for the overall economy, the BEA calculates the GDP deflator. The **GDP deflator** measures changes in the prices in all sectors of the economy. The BEA computes the GDP deflator by comparing nominal GDP and real GDP for a given year, as stated in Equation 20.3.

$$\text{GDP deflator} = \frac{\textit{Nominal GDP in current year}}{\textit{Real GDP in current year}} \times 100 \qquad (20.3)$$

For example, nominal GDP in 2004 was $11.7 trillion, while real GDP with 2000 as the base year was $10.8 trillion. The GDP deflator for 2004 with 2000 as the base year was:

$$\frac{\$11.7 \text{ trillion}}{\$10.8 \text{ trillion}} \times 100 \approx 108$$

A GDP deflator of 108 means that prices rose by eight percent in the U.S. economy between 2000 and 2004.

Unlike the CPI, the GDP deflator looks at all goods made in the United States, not just those bought by a typical household. Thus, the GDP deflator includes capital goods like new plant and equipment, and goods and services sold to foreign households.

The Chain-Weighted Price Index. As was the case for the CPI, it becomes increasingly difficult to compute real GDP and the GDP deflator over time. Again, the problem stems from assuming that the weights assigned to goods and services do not change over time. When computing real GDP in 2004, we assumed that the prices of goods and services had not changed since 2000. Prices *did* change, however, leading to increasingly inaccurate measures of real GDP over time. What if we changed the weights to reflect the new prices? Real GDP would change abruptly from year to year, due merely to the new weights rather than any change in production.

Chain-weighted price index

Uses the average of prices in the current year and prices in the previous year to calculate real GDP.

To avoid the problems that come with assigning fixed prices to goods and services, the BEA has developed the **chain-weighted price index.** Chain-weighting uses the average of prices in the current year and prices in the previous year to calculate real GDP. The weights used are never more than one year apart. As a result, the chain-weighted price index dramatically reduces distortions that result from keeping weights constant for many years and the abrupt changes that result from switching weights. For example, when DVD players were first sold in 1997, the average price was about $1,000. Now the average price is closer to $80. Assuming an unchanging base price for this and other goods would distort the measure of real GDP today. Chain-weighting reduces this problem by allowing the weight applied to DVDs to adjust gradually.

Real GDP per Capita

If one nation has a higher real GDP than another, we cannot be sure that its residents necessarily have higher incomes than the other nation's. The nation with higher real GDP might still be relatively poor if its real GDP is spread among many more people. In 2004, for example, Nigeria's GDP—roughly $125.7 billion—dwarfed that of Luxembourg, whose GDP was only about $27.3 billion. However, this comparison does not take into account that Nigeria's population is much larger than Luxembourg's: 140 million versus less than 500,000.

Real GDP per capita

A country's real income per person.

How can we modify real GDP to compare the production of a large nation with that of a small one? **Real GDP per capita** is a country's real income *per person*. We compute it by dividing a nation's real GDP by its population. In 2004, for example, Nigeria's real GDP per capita was only $1,000, whereas GDP per person in Luxembourg was the highest on earth—almost $59,000.

▶Real GDP and the Quality of Life

While real GDP per capita may be the best single measure of a nation's average income, many people feel it is a poor measure of a nation's standard of living. In this section, we examine the problems with using real GDP to measure welfare, and what can be done to improve upon this method.

TEST + *E X T E N D* Your Knowledge

1. TEST Use the data presented in Table 20.1 to compute the fraction of GDP from wages and salaries and the fraction from dividend income for the United States in 2004. Which is larger?

2. EXTEND Go to the International Monetary Fund's World Economic Outlook database using the link at www.aw-bc.com/leeds/ch20 to find the most recent GDP measures (in dollars) for Pakistan and Norway. Which is larger? Does the typical person have a higher income in Pakistan or Norway? How do you reconcile your answers to the two previous questions?

GDP Counts Some Production That Does Not Add to the Quality of Life

Because real GDP measures the market value only of new, domestic goods and services, it includes some transactions that society does not value greatly and, in some cases, would rather not make at all. For example, we would be much happier if we did not have to spend money on crime prevention or military weaponry. However, the locks and burglar alarms we buy for our homes, the tanks and cruise missiles our government purchases, and the police and soldiers we employ all count toward real GDP. As a result, some people question whether all expenditures make the same contribution to social well-being.

Similarly, while we count industrial output in real GDP, we do not discount it by the pollution that this production generates. A clean environment may have no place in our measure of real GDP while the goods and services we must buy to clean up oil spills, toxic waste dumps, and other ecological disasters do count. An economy that pollutes its environment and then attempts (perhaps unsuccessfully) to clean up the mess sees its GDP rise. A country that does not pollute to begin with sees no gain in GDP.

Real GDP Ignores Non-Market Productive Activities That Add to the Quality of Life

The link between real GDP and market transactions also means that it fails to account for some goods and services that we value greatly. As a result, real GDP per capita may understate social well-being. A meal that Frank prepares as a caterer counts toward GDP. Yet a meal he prepares for only himself and Shawna does not.

More generally, parents provide the services of a cook, chauffeur, babysitter, housecleaner, launderer, and tutor. Does a child pay his parents for these services? Of course not! As a result, none of these services counts toward real GDP. As women work more outside the home, married couples increasingly rely on the marketplace for the goods and services that "housewives" used to provide. Restaurants, day-care centers, and cleaning services have all prospered as a result of the shift to two-worker households. If your mother or grandmother cooked, cleaned, and stayed home to care for you, she did not charge you a fee for her services. There was no market transaction for these duties. Consequently, there was no official market value to what she provided, and her services did not count as a part of GDP.

As women work more in the marketplace and produce less in the home, the real value of market transactions gives an increasingly accurate picture of total production. Still, some economists estimate that unmeasured housework causes GDP to understate the value of production in the United States by over 20 percent.[1]

GDP Ignores the Role of Leisure in the Quality of Life

One of the great benefits of having a successful business is Frank and Shawna's ability to work less and enjoy leisure time. Leisure time, however, has no place in real GDP. Real GDP would be higher if Frank and Shawna worked more, but they would not be happier. Because leisure time implies *forgone* production, the time we spend resting at the beach or lounging around the house does not count in real GDP (although the beach towels and paperback novels we buy *do* count).

GDP Ignores Production in the Underground Economy

The fact that GDP counts only market transactions helps to explain the drastic drop in reported income in many formerly socialist countries in the early years of their transition to market economies. In Ukraine, for example, GDP fell by about 60 percent between 1990 and 2000. Official statistics suggest that Ukraine was starving. However, much of the apparent decline occurred because many transactions started taking place "under the table" so that households and firms could avoid taxes. Economists refer to the unofficial transactions that never get recorded in official statistics as the **underground economy**.

Underground economy
The unofficial transactions that are not recorded in official statistics.

Measuring activity in an underground economy is quite a challenge. After all, many people who engage in unrecorded transactions wish to hide the nature and extent of their activities. In some relatively less-developed countries like Egypt and Nigeria, the underground economy may be as large as 76 percent of the size of the official economy.

Even prosperous countries have large underground economies. The high tax rates in Scandinavian countries encourage many people to take unofficial, untaxed work. As a result, unofficial activity there is as much as one-fifth the size of the official economy. The underground economy is a much smaller percentage of overall economic activity in the United States—roughly 8 to 9 percent of official GDP. Still, over $900 billion worth of underground activity took place in the United States in 2004.[2]

Uneven Income Distribution May Affect Well-Being

Even if two nations have the same real GDP per capita, the people in those two nations are not necessarily equally well off. If one nation has a few wealthy people and many poor people, and the other has a largely middle-class population, we cannot say that the two countries are identical.

Neither real GDP nor per-capita real GDP takes the *distribution* of income into account. In 2001, Honduras and Bolivia both had real GDP per capita of $2,600. Income in Bolivia, however, was much more equally distributed than income in Honduras. Unless you were lucky enough to be rich, you would probably prefer to live in Bolivia, despite a real GDP per capita no higher than that in Honduras.

---

[1] See, for example, Robert J. Eisner, *The Misunderstood Economy: What Counts and How to Count It*, Boston: Harvard Business School Press, 1994. Moreover, this figure may be far higher in less-developed countries, where people do far more work within the home.
[2] See Friedrich Schneider and Dominik Enste, "Shadow Economies: Size, Causes, and Consequences," *Journal of Economic Literature*, vol. 38, no. 1, March 2000, pp. 77–114.

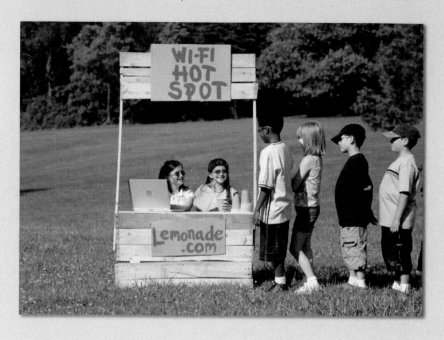

A Lemonade Stand Is an Example of an Underground Economy
The income from this stand will not be reported or taxed and so will not be counted in GDP.

TEST + *EXTEND* Your Knowledge

1. TEST Use the fact that underground economy may have been as much as 60 percent the size of Ukraine's official GDP and data from the World Bank's Web site from the link at www.aw-bc.com/leeds/ch20 to compute what Ukraine's GDP would be if we included unrecorded transactions in its calculation.

2. EXTEND During the course of a day, look for activities going on around you that contribute to people's well-being but do not count in GDP, or that count in GDP but are not desirable. Make a list of five such activities and estimate their monetary value.

▶ Growth and Fluctuations in GDP

Now that you understand what GDP is, let's look at how it has grown over time. We'll also discuss what its fluctuations indicate about the state of the economy. Figure 20.1 shows U.S. real GDP since 1929. Real GDP has grown tremendously over this period, a fact that is reflected in today's much higher standard of living. In the next chapter we take a close look at how and why economies grow. For now, we focus on the fact that the growth has been far from steady. Figure 20.1 shows that real GDP has sometimes grown much more quickly than the long-term trend. The rapid growth of real GDP in the late 1990s is the most recent example. At times, such as from 2001–2004 real GDP, it has grown much more slowly. Finally, it has sometimes declined, as in 2001. These fluctuations are not perfectly even—the expansions are generally much longer than the contractions—nor do they occur at regular intervals. Economists call the fluctuations in economic activity that causes real GDP to rise above and fall below its long-term trend the **business cycle**.

Business cycle
Reflects the ups and downs in the overall level of production.

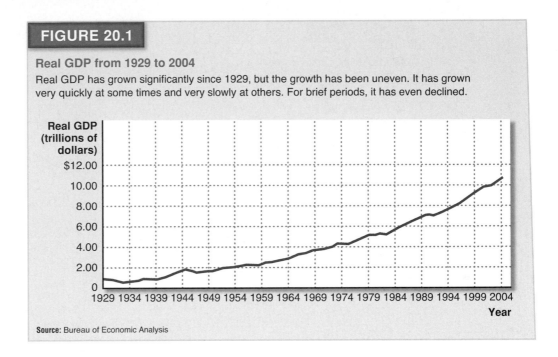

FIGURE 20.1

Real GDP from 1929 to 2004

Real GDP has grown significantly since 1929, but the growth has been uneven. It has grown very quickly at some times and very slowly at others. For brief periods, it has even declined.

Source: Bureau of Economic Analysis

LifeLessons

The Grass Isn't Always Greener, Even If the Money Is

In 2004, U.S. real GDP per capita was approximately $40,000. In France, real GDP per capita was far lower—the equivalent of less than $28,000. U.S. shores were not swamped with Frenchmen desperate to immigrate, though. In fact, many French citizens wondered why anyone would want to live in the United States.

Were the French just being obstinate? In fact, they may have had good reason to prefer life in France. While the average income is higher in the United States, it comes at a cost. The typical American has a longer work week and far fewer vacations than the typical Frenchman. Moreover, the French government provides many services—from health care to child care—for which Americans must pay individually. Although this does not mean that the services are free, the taxes that pay for them fall disproportionately on France's upper-income brackets. As a result, it is not obvious that the higher GDP per capita in the United States automatically translates to a higher quality of life.

The Business Cycle

Peak
The highest point of an economic expansion.

Trough
The lowest point of an economic contraction.

Recession
The period over which production falls.

Every business cycle consists of an expansionary phase and a contractionary phase. Figure 20.2 illustrates these phases for the United States in the mid- and late 1980s and early 1990s. Real GDP rose throughout the late-1980s. It reached its peak in the third quarter of 1990. The **peak** is the highest point of an economic expansion and the point at which the economy begins to contract. Real GDP then fell until it reached a trough in the first quarter of 1991. The **trough** is the low point of a contraction, after which the economy expands once again.

Economists call a period during which production falls a **recession**. The National Bureau of Economic Research (NBER), the body charged with determining when

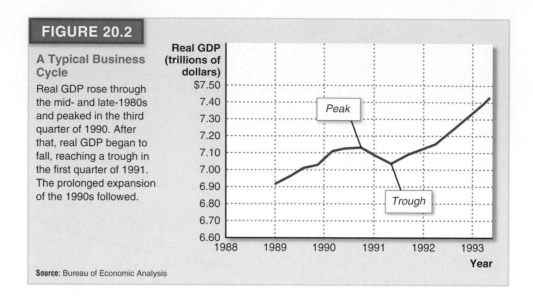

FIGURE 20.2

A Typical Business Cycle

Real GDP rose through the mid- and late-1980s and peaked in the third quarter of 1990. After that, real GDP began to fall, reaching a trough in the first quarter of 1991. The prolonged expansion of the 1990s followed.

Source: Bureau of Economic Analysis

B.C.: By permission of John Lo Hart FLP, and Creators Syndicate, Inc.

recessions begin and end, defines a recession as "a period of significant decline in total output, income, employment, and trade, usually lasting from six months to a year, and marked by widespread contractions in many sectors of the economy."[3] In practice, the NBER usually declares the economy to be in a recession when real GDP has declined for two consecutive quarters. Table 20.3 shows officially reported business cycles since 1899.

Table 20.3 shows that the U.S. economy has had many expansions and contractions. It also shows that the ups and downs do not follow a rigid pattern. Expansions have been as short as ten months and as long as ten years, while contractions have lasted from six months (as in 1980–1981) to three and a half years.

Business Cycles and the Overall Movement of the Economy

As the NBER's definition of a recession indicates, many—but not all—sectors of economic activity tend to rise and fall together during a recession. As you saw in the

---

[3] For more on how the NBER evaluates recessions, see www.nber.org/cycles.

TABLE 20.3

Business Cycles in the Twentieth-Century United States

Date of Peak	Date of Trough	Length of Contraction (months)	Length of Expansion (months)
June 1899	December 1900	18	24
September 1902	August 1904	23	21
May 1907	June 1908	13	33
January 1910	January 1912	24	19
January 1913	December 1914	23	12
August 1918	March 1919	7	44
January 1920	July 1921	18	10
May 1923	July 1924	14	22
October 1926	November 1927	13	27
August 1929	March 1933	43	21
May 1937	June 1938	13	50
February 1945	October 1945	8	80
November 1948	October 1949	11	37
July 1953	May 1954	10	45
August 1957	April 1958	8	39
April 1960	February 1961	10	24
December 1969	November 1970	11	106
November 1973	March 1975	16	36
January 1980	July 1980	6	58
July 1981	November 1982	16	12
July 1990	March 1991	8	92
March 2001	November 2001	8	120

Source: National Bureau of Economic Research

Get Ahead of the Curve

Apply your understanding of business cycles to Brazil's economic performance.

last two chapters, the unemployment rate and the inflation rate are also important measures of economic health. Together with real GDP, these measures reveal the impact of the business cycle.

Although they do not always move perfectly with GDP, unemployment and inflation tend to move in the directions indicated in Table 20.4 over the course of the business cycle. For example, in the third quarter of 1990, when the business cycle peaked, unemployment stood at 5.7 percent, and prices rose 1.7 percent over the previous quarter. At the trough in the first quarter of 1991, after a brief and relatively mild recession, unemployment had risen to more than 6.1 percent, and prices were only 0.8 percent higher than in the previous quarter. (The most recent recession, which lasted from March to September of 2001, was even shorter and more mild.)

Potential GDP. In the unemployment chapter, you learned that cyclical unemployment falls as the economy grows during an economic expansion. When cyclical unemployment falls to zero, the economy is at full employment. If unemployment fell any further, firms would have to seek out structurally or frictionally unemployed

TABLE 20.4

Outline of the Typical Business Cycle

Portion of Cycle	Unemployment Rate	Inflation Rate	Real GDP
Peak	Low	High	High
Contraction	Rising	Slowing	Falling
Trough	High	Low	Low
Expansion	Falling	Accelerating	Rising

FIGURE 20.3

Potential and Real GDP: 1980–2004

Real GDP has stayed quite close to potential GDP over the last quarter century. It has fallen below potential GDP during the recessions of the early 1980s, 1990–1991, and 2001. Real GDP has sometimes exceeded potential GDP. Most recently, this status occurred during the rapid economic expansion of the late 1990s.

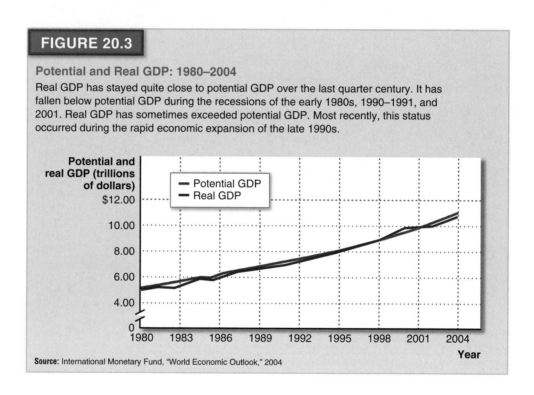

Source: International Monetary Fund, "World Economic Outlook," 2004

Potential GDP
The amount an economy produces when it is at full employment.

workers. This, in turn, would drive up the costs of production—and hence prices—at an unacceptable rate.

Because they want to avoid unemployment and inflation, policy makers try to keep real GDP at the level of potential GDP. **Potential GDP** is the level of real GDP that corresponds to the full employment of resources. As you saw in the unemployment chapter, when the unemployment rate rises above the full employment unemployment rate, GDP falls below potential GDP.

Figure 20.3 shows how potential GDP and real GDP have moved since 1980. Notice that real GDP has closely tracked potential GDP over the last few decades. It fell below potential GDP during the recessions of the early 1980s and 1990s. Because the later recession was milder, the difference between real and potential GDP was smaller in the early 1990s. Real GDP was greater than potential GDP during the boom of the late 1990s. At first, this seems impossible. How can an economy produce more than its potential? As you will see in the following section, the answer is not that everyone has a job when the economy is at full employment.

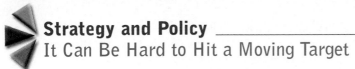

Strategy and Policy
It Can Be Hard to Hit a Moving Target

Policy makers try to keep the economy as close to potential GDP as they can. If real GDP falls below potential GDP, unemployment grows. If real GDP exceeds potential GDP, inflation increases.

Unfortunately, no one knows the precise value of potential GDP. We know that the economy is producing at its potential when cyclical unemployment is zero. However, as discussed in the unemployment chapter, it is often hard to be sure exactly whether a given worker is experiencing frictional, cyclical, or structural unemployment. This lack of clarity can lead policy makers to believe that potential GDP is higher or lower than it really is.

Recent history shows the problems that such mistakes have caused. In the 1950s, economists generally agreed that the full employment unemployment rate (when there is no cyclical unemployment) was about 5 percent. In the 1960s, many felt that this rate had fallen to 4 percent. This adjustment may seem minor. But recall that Okun's Law says that a 1-percent increase in unemployment above the full employment rate causes real GDP to fall by 2.5 percentage points below its potential. Setting a target that was 2.5 points below the true value of potential GDP in 1963 would have understated potential GDP by over $60 billion. This error would have translated to over $1,000 in income for a family of four. Recognizing this potential problem, policy makers sought to increase the level of real GDP.

At the same time that authorities were increasing their target for potential GDP, changes in the economy were pushing those targets in the other direction. As noted in the unemployment chapter, the rapid increase in the number of women and young workers in the 1970s increased unemployment rates associated with full employment. Some now attribute the inflation of the 1970s to an unrealistically high estimate of potential GDP and the slow adjustment to more pessimistic levels in that decade.

By 1980, economists had come to believe that the unemployment rate associated with full employment was higher—between 5 and 6 percent. At the same time, potential GDP was lower than previously believed. These more pessimistic estimates remained unchallenged until the mid-1990s. The strong expansion of the late 1990s, when real GDP exceeded potential GDP from 1997 through 2000, raised new concerns. Some considered the estimates of potential GDP to be too low. In particular, critics pointed to how inflation did not flare up in the late 1990s, which should happen when real GDP exceeds potential GDP. The public statements of government officials and policy makers suggest that they are now more optimistic about potential GDP and believe that the economy can tolerate lower unemployment rates without sparking inflation.

Critical-Thinking Questions

1. Why are economists concerned about understating or overstating potential GDP?
2. What factors might have led potential GDP to rise in the late 1990s?

SUMMARY

■ **Defining GDP.** GDP (gross domestic product) is the market value of all new, final goods and services produced in a given country over a given period of time. Market value gives us a common yardstick to measure combinations of different goods and services. We include only new goods because used goods were counted when they were first produced. We count only final goods because the value of intermediate goods is reflected in the price of the final good. Finally, GDP is country- and time-specific, so we look at production only within a country's borders and only over a specific time period, typically a year.

- **The expenditure approach to GDP.** We can express GDP as the sum of expenditure by all of the different sectors of the economy. Households spend money on consumption goods. We call firms' expenditure on capital goods *investment expenditure*. Government expenditure on goods and services does not include transfer payments, because no goods or services are bought or sold. Because not all domestic production is purchased domestically and because not all purchases are made from domestic producers, we must also include net exports. We can compute GDP as: $GDP = C + I + G + (X - M)$.

- **The income approach to GDP.** Each dollar of spending on this year's production generates a dollar of income for the factors used in producing that output. We can also calculate GDP by adding up all the income in the economy generated by producing this year's output. On the income side,

$$GDP = Labor\ compensation + Rent + Interest +$$
$$Proprietor's\ income\ and\ profit + Taxes\ on\ production\ and\ imports +$$
$$Depreciation + Net\ foreign\ factor\ income$$

We add the last three terms because they are leakages from the economy.

- **The value-added approach to GDP.** Value is added because the market value of output is greater than the market value of the inputs that went into production. We can calculate GDP by adding all the value added at all stages of production for all the goods and services produced in an economy.

- **Refining GDP.** GDP may rise for a number of reasons having nothing to do with production or income. Real GDP discounts increases in GDP that occur because prices rise. To compute real GDP, economists use the GDP deflator. Chain weighting allows the deflator to reflect changes in the mix of output by the economy. Per capita GDP accounts for the fact that GDP could be greater in a large country than in a small country (or in single a country whose population has grown over time) without making residents any better off. Economists frequently combine the two concepts to compute real GDP per capita. A nation's GDP may grow because prices rise rather than because it produces more. Real GDP accounts for changes in prices. GDP per capita measures how much an economy produces per person. It provides a more accurate measure of well-being than GDP does because a large but poor country may have a higher GDP than a small but rich nation.

- **Real GDP and the quality of life.** GDP may overstate well-being, because it counts goods and services that we may not value highly. GDP figures might be understated, because they do not count goods or services that do not have a market price attached to them, such as the underground economy.

- **Growth and fluctuations in GDP.** Economies do not grow at a constant rate. Instead, they fluctuate around a long-term trend. The upward and downward movements around the trend are known as the *business cycle*. The business cycle reflects overall movements in output, income, prices, and employment.

Business cycle 520
Chain-weighted price index 517
Consumption 509
Depreciation 514
Double counting 507
Final goods 507
GDP deflator 516

Intermediate goods 507
Inventory 510
Investment 509
Net exports 511
Net foreign factor income 514
Nominal GDP 516
Peak 521

Potential GDP 524
Real GDP 516
Real GDP per capita 517
Recession 521
Trough 521
Underground economy 519
Value added 515

PROBLEMS

1. Why does your purchase of the New York Philharmonic's new recording of Beethoven's Ninth Symphony count towards U.S. GDP, although Beethoven was an Austrian who has been dead for almost 200 years?

2. Why does GDP include the oven that the baker buys to bake bread in but not the flour he buys to make the bread?

3. Why shouldn't we necessarily be concerned if GDP declines between December and March?

4. Would the following be counted in GDP? If so, explain how it enters GDP (C, I, G, or (X–M)) and why. If not, explain why not.
   a. Nabisco's purchase of flour to make cookies.
   b. Your purchase of flour to make cookies for your study group.
   c. The Pentagon's purchase of flour to make cookies for soldiers.
   d. Nabisco's purchase of an oven to bake cookies.
   e. Your purchase of Hungarian hazelnuts to put in your cookies.

5. Suppose that you purchase a stereo that comes from a dealer's inventory. How does your purchase affect GDP?

6. Suppose that an economy has $100 million of physical capital and that capital depreciates at the constant rate of $10 million per year.
   a. Draw a graph with capital stock on the vertical axis and time (in years) on the horizontal axis, showing what the value of the capital stock will be if the nation does not replace its capital stock.
   b. Use your findings to explain why the economy "must run in order to keep in the same place."

7. Why does your purchase of GM stock not count as investment, whereas GM's construction of a new plant in Michigan does count?

8. Ice cream manufacturers use ice cream to make ice cream sandwiches. Why don't we count ice cream as a capital good?

9. Why does the money that the government spends on stealth bombers count toward GDP, but the money it gives to flood victims does not?

10. In the Kingdom of Florin, people live very simple lives. Each year, they buy $1,000 worth of cinnamon rolls, $2,500 worth of robes, and $3,000 worth of tapestries that are made in the neighboring state of Guilder. Guilder, in turn, buys $4,500 worth of Florin-made ox-carts. What is the GDP of Florin?

11. Suppose that the economy of Guilder consists of the following:

$$C = \$5,000 \quad I = \$1,000 \quad G = \$500$$
$$X = \$3,000 \quad M = \$4,500$$

What is the GDP of Guilder?

12. Suppose that the people in problem 12 are either laborers or landowners. If laborers receive $1,000 in income, how much rent do landowners receive? Assume that there is no depreciation, net foreign income, or taxes.

13. If we add up all the income earned by households, we get a smaller number than that nation's official measure of GDP. What can account for this shortfall?

14. To make $1,000 worth of cinnamon rolls, the bakers in Florin must first purchase $250 worth of flour, $50 worth of eggs, and $25 worth of cinnamon. What is the value added by Florin's bakers?

15. Many Europeans consider their countries to have a higher quality of life than the United States does, despite having lower real GDP per capita in Europe. Why do they feel that way?

16. If nominal GDP in Botswana was $7.4 billion in 2003 and the GDP deflator was 275 in 2003, what was real GDP in Botswana that year?

17. In 2000, the People's Republic of China, a country of about 1.2 billion people, had a GDP of about $1.1 trillion. Belgium, with population of about 10.2 million, had a GDP of about $260 billion. In which country was the average person richer? Why?

18. Victoria and Jenny are each married with two children. Victoria works outside the home and sends her children to a local day-care center, while Jenny stays home and watches her children. How do their actions affect GDP?

19. In 1995, U.S. GDP was $7.40 trillion. In 2000, it was $9.96 trillion. The GDP deflator in 1995 was 98.1, and in 2000 it was 106.9. Did real GDP rise in this time period?

20. How can an economy produce more than its potential GDP?

HERE'S HOW MyEconLab CAN HELP YOU GET A BETTER GRADE

1. Log into MyEconLab and take Practice Test 20-A (to log in for the first time, see page 30 for instructions).

2. Based on your test results, MyEconLab will identify the areas where you need further work and create a personal Study Plan for you.

3. Your Study Plan contains the problems listed below and others like them that will target the specific chapter topics you need to focus on. You'll receive instant feedback and find links to tutorials, animations, and the online textbook to help you study.

4. When you're ready, take Practice Test 20-B and demonstrate how your results have improved.

Section 20.1, Problem 1 When Yoshi buys a new car battery from Sears, is this purchase counted towards GDP? Why or why not? When General Motors buys car batteries for their new cars, is this purchase counted towards GDP? Why or why not?

Section 20.1, Problem 2 Suppose that Sally from Boston, Massachusetts, owns a car dealership company in Mexico City, Mexico. Do her sales of new cars count toward U.S. GDP or Mexican GDP?

Section 20.1, Problem 3 Which of the following transactions would count towards U.S. GDP?

a. Briana buys two tickets ($100 each) to the upcoming Jimmy Buffett concert.
b. Peter gives his neighbor $100 for his lawnmower.
c. Marsha spends $30 for dry-cleaning.
d. Kendra buys an authentic Mexican rug (for $250).
e. Greg buys chocolate chips ($3) to make cookies for her next economics club meeting.
f. Cindy buys 10 hairbrushes ($15 each) for her hair salon.
g. Kin buys a set of new Firestone tires (for $400).
h. Mike buys a "certified pre-owned" 2003 Chevrolet Corvette from the Chevy dealership.

Section 20.2, Problem 1 Determine which component the following transactions would enter into U.S. GDP (C, I, G, X, or M). If more than one component is affected, indicate all that apply. If the transaction does not affect U.S. GDP, indicate that as well.

a. Alfonzo pays $20 for a haircut.
b. The government writes Otis a $500 unemployment compensation check.

c. Floyd buys 10 new hairbrushes ($15 each) from a beauty supply store for his barber shop.
d. The government pays Private First Class Gomer Pyle $1,000 every two weeks.
e. At the end of the year, General Motors has 500 unsold cars still on its lot.
f. Aunt Bee buys a new BMW (made in Germany) for $45,000.
g. Applebee's restaurant on Main Street spends $10,000 to upgrade their computer equipment.
h. Pedro, in Mexico, buys a new Chevrolet Tahoe for $30,000.
i. Thelma buys an authentic Mexican rug for $250.
j. Manuel and Helen purchase a new $200,000 home.

Section 20.2, Problem 2

a. Ecoland is a very simple island country that produces and buys only computers. During the year, Ecoland produced a total of 500 computers valued at $2,000 each. What is the GDP of Ecoland?
b. We now have more information about Ecoland. The people of Ecoland bought 150 of the computers, businesses of Ecoland bought 200, the government bought 50, and Ecoland exported 100 to their neighboring country. Calculate each component of GDP and show that the total equals your answer from part a.

Section 20.3, Problem 1 Suppose that Ecoland experienced GDP of $1,000,000 for the year. And suppose for the year that Ecoland workers earned $600,000, property owners received rent of $15,000, those who supplied financial capital earned $40,000, business owners received income and profit of $180,000, the government collected taxes on production and imports in the amount of $70,000, and capital equipment depreciated by $120,000.

How much was net foreign factor income? Is it positive or negative? What does that mean in terms of foreign- and domestic-owned resources?

Section 20.4, Problem 1 Suppose that a wheat farmer sells $1,500 worth of wheat to a miller. The miller turns the wheat into flour and sells it to a baker for $2,750. The baker turns the flour into bread and pastries, which he sells to consumers for $3,500.

 a. How much value to GDP did the farmer, miller, and baker add?
 b. Show that the value-added approach to GDP equals the value of the final goods bought by consumers.

Section 20.5, Problem 1 Suppose that in a given country from year 1 to year 2, the general price level rises (the prices of most goods rise), and that the quantity produced (and purchased) also rises. What can we determine about the values of nominal and real GDP?

 a. Both nominal and real GDP will rise, but real GDP will increase more.
 b. Nominal GDP rises but the change on real GDP cannot be determined.
 c. Both nominal and real GDP will rise, but nominal GDP will increase more.
 d. Nominal and real GDP will increase by the same amount.
 e. Nominal GDP will rise, but real GDP will remain constant.

Section 20.5, Problem 2 The following table contains information about a small economy that produces only bikinis and Speedos. Use it to answer the next few questions. Let the base year be 1980.

Year	Price (bikinis)	Quantity (bikinis)	Price (Speedos)	Quantity (Speedos)
1980	$75	20	$50	10
1981	80	20	52	10
1982	80	25	55	12
1983	90	30	60	15

 a. What is the nominal GDP for the years 1980–1983?
 b. What is the real GDP for the years 1980–1983?
 c. What is the GDP deflator for the years 1980–1983?
 d. Is there a year when real GDP does not grow from the previous year? Did nominal GDP grow during that time? How can we explain that?
 e. How much did prices rise between 1980–1983?

Section 20.5, Problem 3 Use the following chart to answer the questions.

Year	U.S. Real GDP (in billions of dollars)	U.S. Population (in millions)
2000	9,800	282
2001	9,900	285
2002	10,100	288
2003	10,400	291

 a. Calculate U.S. real GDP per capita for each year- from 2000–2003.
 b. At any year did U.S. real GDP per capita for each year decrease? If so, how can you explain this? Did U.S. real GDP ever decrease? What about the population? (*Hint:* you should look carefully at the relationship between growth in per capita GDP against growth in real GDP and growth in population.)

21

Aggregate Demand and Aggregate Supply: The Basic Model

Is war always good news for an economy? For Joanna, this was an interesting and important question. Joanna's family has a proud tradition of military service. Her grandfather served in World War II in Europe, her father served in South Vietnam from 1967 to 1968, and her older brother Joel served with the Army during the first Gulf War in Iraq in late 1990 and early 1991. Now she was scheduled to depart for Iraq for a year with her National Guard unit, which meant leaving her new restaurant in the hands of her business partners. Worried about how her business would fare while she was gone, she held a family conference about what to expect both during her year of service and when she came back.

Joanna's father told her not to worry. "The economy did pretty well while I was in Vietnam," he said. "I didn't have any trouble getting a decent-paying job after I got back. The economy must have been growing." He hinted that inflation might have been a problem, though, when he said, "I do seem to remember that my dad and mom were complaining a bit about the high prices they were paying for basic necessities."

Joanna's older brother Joel saw things differently. He had shipped out to Kuwait in August 1990 and returned home six months after the rapid victory in Iraq in February 1991. However, he believed that the first Gulf War had not helped either him or, apparently, the U.S. economy. While he was overseas, he got a few letters from home mentioning a recession. "My experience was different from Dad's," he told his sister. "I didn't find a good job right away, probably because of the recession." One thing was much like his father's experience; as he related, "Everybody was complaining about high gas prices when I got home."

Now Joanna was puzzled. "From what both of you are telling me, the impact of war on an economy seems kind of random. Is war good for the economy or not? What will happen to my restaurant while I'm away in Iraq? If I have to find a new job, will I find a good-paying job quickly?" Joanna was naturally thinking about her own personal affairs, but she was also asking questions about important macroeconomic issues. The answers to her questions depend on the two key forces shaping the behavior of the macroeconomy: aggregate demand and aggregate supply, which represent the total spending and the total production by all the participants in the macroeconomy.

In this chapter, we explore the forces of aggregate demand and aggregate supply. We discuss the determinants of the shape and location of the aggregate demand curve and two aggregate supply curves: one representing the short run and one representing the long run. After constructing our model, we conclude our analysis by observing how aggregate demand and the two versions of aggregate supply explain macroeconomic equilibrium in both the short run and the long run.

ALONG THE WAY, YOU WILL ALSO LEARN:

- How the price level and other variables affect aggregate demand.
- How the price level and other variables affect short-run aggregate supply.
- How we determine short-run macroeconomic equilibrium.
- How long-run aggregate supply is related to full employment real GDP.
- How we determine long-run macroeconomic equilibrium.
- How short-run and long-run macroeconomic equilibriums are related.

**AT THE END OF THE CHAPTER,
THE MYECONLAB LOGO WILL DIRECT YOU ONLINE**

- MyEconLab is a resource-packed online homework and tutorial system that can help you perform better in your economics course. To log in for the first time, see page 30 for instructions.
- MyEconLab can help you apply important concepts from the chapter to real-world issues. Watch for the logo to indicate online features about economic growth in China and European oil prices.
- At the end of each chapter, you'll find a special study section that will help you get the most out of your textbook and your instructor's MyEconLab course.

 ## The Basics of Aggregate Demand

Aggregate demand
Real value of all new, final, domestically produced goods and services that households, firms, governments, and the foreign sector are willing and able to purchase at a given set of overall price levels, *ceteris paribus*.

In this chapter, we introduce the concepts of aggregate demand and aggregate supply, to see how those two economic forces bring the macroeconomy into equilibrium. The first building block of our model is aggregate demand, the focus of this section.

On a macroeconomic level, we are interested in **aggregate demand**, the real value of all new, final, domestically produced goods and services that households, firms, governments, and the foreign sector are willing and able to purchase at a given set of overall price levels, *ceteris paribus*. Aggregate demand is equal to the sum of consumption expenditure by households (*C*), investment expenditures by firms (*I*),

FIGURE 21.1

The Aggregate Demand Curve

Panel (a) shows the real GDP demanded at three price levels. By graphing the combinations, we find three specific points (A, B, and C) on a given aggregate demand curve. The resulting aggregate demand curve shown in panel (b) is downward-sloping.

(a) Relationship of the price level and real GDP demanded

Combination	Price Level	Real GDP Demanded
A	110	$4.0 trillion
B	105	$4.5 trillion
C	100	$5.0 trillion

(b) Graph of the aggregate demand curve

government expenditures (G), and net exports (X–M). These sources of aggregate demand for final goods and services should look familiar. The same list forms the expenditure approach to GDP (gross domestic product) from the prior chapter. The discussion that follows examines the relationship between aggregate demand and the price level, the slope of the aggregate demand curve, and movements in aggregate demand.

The Relationship Between the Price Level and Aggregate Demand

In the macroeconomy, the overall price level is the major determinant of spending in the economy. The aggregate demand relationship shows how total spending varies when the price level changes. Figure 21.1 shows the relationship between the price level and the amount of aggregate demand (as measured by real GDP). In panel (a), as the price level falls from 110 to 105 to 100, the total amount of goods and services demanded increases from $4.0 trillion to $4.5 trillion and finally to $5.0 trillion. This relationship is graphed in panel (b) to determine the aggregate demand curve. Note that the aggregate demand curve is a downward-sloping line, indicating an inverse relationship between the price level and the amount of goods and services demanded.

Why the Aggregate Demand Curve Slopes Downward

Why is the aggregate demand curve downward-sloping in the macroeconomy? We'll answer this question as we examine three basic reasons that, considered together, explain the downward slope: the wealth effect, the interest rate effect, and the international trade effect.

The Wealth Effect. As the price level falls, the value of the real wealth held by households in their portfolios of assets increases. If you had $1,000 in cash as a nest egg, a falling price level would increase the purchasing power of that $1,000. The increased real value of that nest egg would make you feel wealthier. When households feel wealthier, they tend to spend more on most goods and services. As a result, the quantity of aggregate output (real GDP) demanded increases as the price level falls.

The Interest Rate Effect. As the price level falls, demanders have more purchasing power for a given level of income. They do not need to spend as many dollars to purchase the same goods and services as they did before. As a result, these demanders can increase their savings, because they have income remaining after making their usual purchases. If they had been borrowing to buy some of those goods and services, they will not have to borrow as much to get the same market basket as before. The combination of more saving by some demanders and less borrowing by others puts downward pressure on interest rates. Falling interest rates encourage others to increase their borrowing to buy new goods and services. For example, lower interest rates encourage people to buy new cars and homes, and businesses to invest in new capital. Consequently, the quantity of aggregate output (real GDP) demanded increases as the falling price level causes interest rates to drop.

The International Trade Effect. As you saw in Chapter 3, trade among nations in an open economy affects the flow of imports and exports in the domestic economy. As the price level in one country falls relative to price levels elsewhere, foreign

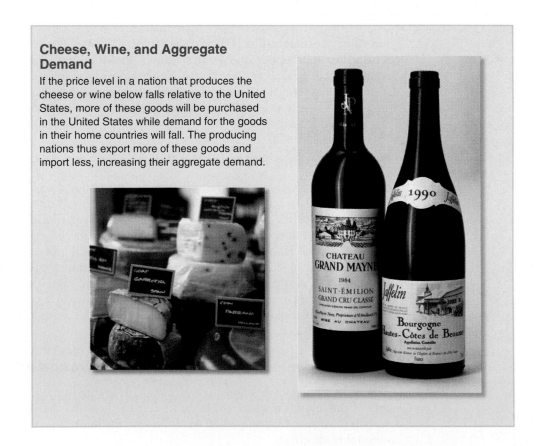

Cheese, Wine, and Aggregate Demand

If the price level in a nation that produces the cheese or wine below falls relative to the United States, more of these goods will be purchased in the United States while demand for the goods in their home countries will fall. The producing nations thus export more of these goods and import less, increasing their aggregate demand.

households, firms, and governments buy the relatively cheaper domestically produced goods and services, *ceteris paribus*. At the same time, domestic households, firms, and governments find that foreign goods have become relatively more expensive, and they buy fewer foreign goods. The combination of more exports and fewer imports means that net exports increase, and so does domestic aggregate demand. Once again, falling domestic price levels have increased the quantity of aggregate output (real GDP) demanded.

The Bottom Line. When we combine these three impacts, we see that a falling price level results in more aggregate quantity demanded in an economy. The aggregate demand curve must be downward-sloping to reflect the increase in purchases of goods and services as the price level falls.

Basic Movements in Aggregate Demand

Before using aggregate demand to analyze the overall health of a macroeconomy, we must understand two distinct reasons why more or fewer goods and services might be demanded, as described in the following sections.

Change in aggregate quantity demanded
As the price level changes along a given aggregate demand curve, there is more or less aggregate quantity demanded in the macroeconomy.

Movements Along an Aggregate Demand Curve. A **change in aggregate quantity demanded** is a situation where, as the price level changes along a given aggregate demand curve, there is more or less aggregate quantity demanded in the macroeconomy. Panel (b) of Figure 21.1 illustrates this situation. At a price level of 105, the aggregate quantity demanded in the macroeconomy is $4.5 trillion. A decrease in the price level from 105 to 100 causes movement along the given aggregate demand curve from point B to point C. That increase from $4.5 to $5.0 trillion represents an increase in the aggregate quantity demanded. If the price level rises from 105 to 110, there is movement along the aggregate demand curve from point B to point A. The decrease from $4.5 trillion to $4.0 trillion represents a decrease in the aggregate quantity demanded. *A change in aggregate quantity demanded* is always shown as movement along a single aggregate demand curve. It is caused only by a change in the price level in the macroeconomy.

Change in aggregate demand
Occurs when forces other than changes in the price level shift the entire aggregate demand curve to the left or to the right.

Shifts to a New Aggregate Demand Curve. There is a second way to examine how aggregate demand fluctuates in the macroeconomy. With a **change in aggregate demand**, forces other than changes in the price level shift the entire aggregate demand curve to the left or to the right. More or fewer goods and services are demanded at *each* price level.

In Figure 21.2, the aggregate demand curve AD_1 may shift to AD_2, indicating more is demanded at the price level of 105 ($5.0 trillion instead of $4.5 trillion) and every other price level as well. This is an increase in aggregate demand. When AD_1 shifts to AD_3, less is demanded at the price level of 105 ($4.0 trillion instead of $4.5 trillion) and every other price level. This is a decrease in aggregate demand.

What causes the aggregate demand curve to shift? Any change in the economy that encourages more or less spending by households, firms, government, or the foreign sector at a given price level can move the entire aggregate demand curve. We organize these factors into three basic categories—macroeconomic policy, expectations, and the global economy—that highlight some of the influences of these factors on aggregate demand.

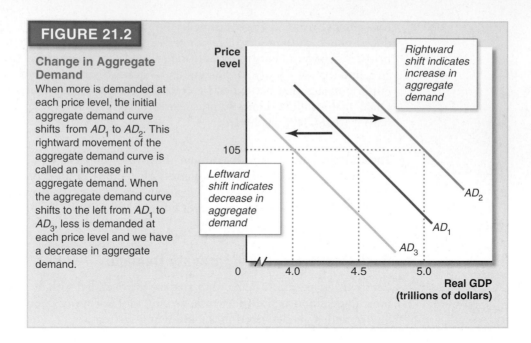

FIGURE 21.2

Change in Aggregate Demand

When more is demanded at each price level, the initial aggregate demand curve shifts from AD_1 to AD_2. This rightward movement of the aggregate demand curve is called an increase in aggregate demand. When the aggregate demand curve shifts to the left from AD_1 to AD_3, less is demanded at each price level and we have a decrease in aggregate demand.

Macroeconomic Policy Influences. We will discuss the impact of macroeconomic policy variables in much more detail in future chapters. For now, we examine the general impacts of changes in macroeconomic policy on aggregate demand. For example, at any given price level, when policy makers increase the supply of funds available to borrowers, it causes interest rates to fall. Falling interest rates encourage households to borrow and spend, especially on housing and durable goods. Businesses will invest more on new plant and equipment at lower interest rates. With more consumption and investment occurring at each price level in the economy, there will be an increase in aggregate demand, because of the increased supply of funds.

Changes in taxes can also have an impact on aggregate demand. A decrease in income tax rates, for example, gives households more disposable income. This in turn encourages them to spend more at each price level. Similarly, a decline in any kind of tax assessed on businesses will encourage firms to increase their investment spending, and overall investment will increase at every price level. The impact of lower personal and business taxes shifts the aggregate demand curve to the right, indicating an increase in aggregate demand.

Aggregate demand also increases immediately when any level of government (federal, state, or local) increases spending on goods and services. Conversely, reductions in government spending reduce aggregate demand.

Influence of Expectations. Expectations of the future are often powerful influences on present behavior. U.S. presidents go out of their way to avoid using the dreaded R-word ("recession") in public, for fear that the mere mention of that word will become a self-fulfilling prophecy.

On a household level, what would happen to Joanna's individual spending plans if she thought that she would be getting more income in the near future from an income tax cut? She probably would feel better about her own economic future and would start consuming more now in anticipation of that brighter tomorrow. This consumer optimism can increase the consumption component of aggregate

"CONSUMER CONFIDENCE CRISIS IN AISLE THREE!"

Jim Borgman, The Cincinnati Enquirer

demand. The same reasoning applies to Joanna's business. Suppose that she anticipates that business will be better in the future, with greater sales and profits down the road. Joanna and her business partners will be inclined to spend more now on their restaurant to take advantage of the improved sales and profits forecast. During periods of optimism in the business sector, the investment component of aggregate demand generally increases.

Every month, several national surveys assess consumer and business confidence about the current and future state of the economy. Wall Street investors, policy makers, and economic analysts look carefully at these surveys of optimism to gauge the mood regarding tomorrow's economy in order to predict the pattern of consumer and business spending in the near future.

Global Influences. The United States is integrated into the global economy, with the total of U.S. exports and imports exceeding $3 trillion in 2004. What happens in other nations can influence U.S. economic health by affecting the level of aggregate demand in the U.S. economy at each price level in the economy. For example, if the economies of some of the major U.S. trading partners are booming, their demand for U.S.-made goods and services will rise. Increasing incomes overseas will increase U.S. exports and overall aggregate demand. This effect occurs even if the price level in the United States does not change.

Foreign spending on U.S. goods and services can also be affected by the purchasing power of the dollar in other nations. If foreign currencies gain purchasing power in the United States, foreigners will buy more U.S. goods and services. At the same time, the dollar will lose purchasing power overseas, and U.S. households and firms will buy fewer goods and services from other nations. Increasing U.S. exports and declining U.S. imports together mean that net foreign spending ($X–M$) will increase at every price level in the United States. As a result, the aggregate demand curve shifts to the right, indicating an increase in aggregate demand. Table 21.1 summarizes the key influences on changes in aggregate demand.

Aggregate Demand in Action: Vietnam versus the First Gulf War

We now apply our knowledge of aggregate demand to Joanna's dilemma. Aggregate demand increased during both the Vietnam War from 1967 to 1969 and the first Gulf War from July 1990 through September 1991. Table 21.2 shows what was happening to the U.S. economy and the components of aggregate demand during these two wars.

Vietnam. If we look at panel (a) in Table 21.2, we can see the broad outlines of the U.S. economy from 1967 to 1969. Joanna's father's recollection about low unemployment levels in the late 1960s was essentially accurate. The unemployment rate fell, reaching a low of 3.4 percent in 1969—an unemployment rate that would not appear again for almost 30 years. Joanna's father's memory of higher prices was also correct, as the price level rose each year. The economy grew during each of those three years.

TABLE 21.1

Key Influences on Changes in Aggregate Demand

Key Influence	Specific Determinant	Direction	Impact on Aggregate Demand
Macroeconomic policy	Supply of funds available to borrowers	Increase	Increase
		Decrease	Decrease
	Taxes	Increase	Decrease
		Decrease	Increase
	Government spending	Increase	Increase
		Decrease	Decrease
Psychological	Household and business expectations	Optimistic	Increase now
		Pessimistic	Decrease now
Global	Foreign income	Increase	Increase
		Decrease	Decrease
	Purchasing power of domestic currency overseas	Increase	Decrease
		Decrease	Increase

Panel (b) demonstrates that Joanna's father was also correct in his impressions about the health of aggregate demand in the U.S. economy during and immediately after his time in Vietnam. Let's examine the period from 1967 to 1969, which covers his service in Vietnam and the year after he returned. Aggregate demand grew consistently during this time. It was fueled primarily by increases in consumption spending, investment spending by businesses, and government spending. Only net exports, a relatively small component of total aggregate demand, showed a consistent decline. Business spending reflected optimism in an economy that had not been in a recession since early 1961. Government spending increases were due to the war in Vietnam, the Apollo moon-landing program, and social programs in the War on Poverty.

First Gulf War. Joanna's brother had complained about the state of the economy during and after his service in the first Gulf War. Table 21.2(a) illustrates the problems he faced. The unemployment rate increased throughout this time. Joel's struggle to find a job was typical, as indicated by the 6.8 percent unemployment rate he found when he returned. The price level rose by more than 4 percent from July 1990 to September 1991. Finally, real GDP fell during the recession from July 1990 to March 1991.

Given the behavior of the components of aggregate demand from July 1990 to September 1991 as seen in panel (b) of Table 21.2, Joel's complaints were on target. Consumption spending was just slightly higher at the end of the period than at the

TABLE 21.2

Comparison of Key Economic Indicators and Components of Aggregate Demand

(a) Key economic indicators during 1967–1969 and from July 1990 to September 1991

Vietnam Era		First Gulf War Era	
Unemployment rate (Change from previous period)			
1967	Unchanged	Second half 1990	Higher
1968	Lower	First half 1991	Higher
1969	Lower	Second half 1991	Higher
Price level (Change from previous period)			
1967	Higher	Second half 1990	Higher
1968	Higher	First half 1991	Higher
1969	Higher	Second half 1991	Higher
Real GDP (Change from previous period)			
1967	Higher	Second half 1990	Higher
1968	Higher	First half 1991	Lower
1969	Higher	Second half 1991	Higher

(b) Components of AD during 1967–1969 and from July 1990 to September 1991 (change from previous period)

Vietnam era	Consumption	Investment	Government	Net Exports
1967	Higher	Lower	Higher	Lower
1968	Higher	Higher	Higher	Lower
1969	Higher	Higher	Lower	Lower

First Gulf War era	Consumption	Investment	Government	Net Exports
Second half 1990	Lower	Lower	Higher	Higher
First half 1991	Lower	Lower	Higher	Higher
Second half 1991	Higher	Lower	Higher	Higher

beginning. The uncertain state of the economy and anxieties about the war and its aftermath dampened consumer spending. Investment spending by businesses was lower at the end of the period than at the beginning. Government spending barely grew, even during the build-up to the invasion of Iraq and the war. Net exports grew as the trade deficit shrank. Both eras demonstrated an increase in aggregate demand. The impact on aggregate demand was greater during the Vietnam War while the impact of the first Gulf War on aggregate demand was much smaller.

The Basics of Short-Run Aggregate Supply

The behavior of aggregate demand alone is only one indication of what a war might mean for an economy. To complete the model of the macroeconomy, we must understand the behavior of aggregate supply. Producers' decisions in response to changing price levels in the economy have a significant impact on macroeconomic health.

TEST + EXTEND Your Knowledge

Aggregate supply
Real value of all new, final, domestically produced goods and services that firms are willing and able to offer for sale at various price levels, *ceteris paribus*.

Aggregate supply is the real value of all new, final, domestically produced goods and services that firms are willing and able to offer for sale at various price levels, *ceteris paribus*. There are two different aggregate supply curves: the short-run aggregate supply curve and the long-run aggregate supply curve. Each of these curves reflects a particular relationship between the price level and aggregate supply. Our focus in this section is on short-run aggregate supply. We begin by distinguishing between the short run and the long run. We then examine the relationship between the price level and short-run aggregate supply, the slope of the short-run aggregate supply curve, and movements in short-run aggregate supply.

Differences Between the Short Run and the Long Run

The short run and the long run are not measured in weeks, months, or years. The difference between the long run and the short run has to do with the ability of participants in the economy to adjust their behavior in response to changes in the overall price level.

Sticky wages
Occur when workers are unable to change their nominal wage rate easily in response to changing overall prices.

Sticky prices
Occur when firms' costs of changing the prices charged for the goods and services they produce outweigh the benefits of changing their prices.

The Short Run. The short run is any time period that is too short to permit participants in the economy to obtain and act on all the relevant information they need to adjust fully to changes in the overall price level. Workers face **sticky wages** when they are unable to change their nominal wage rate easily in response to changing overall prices. Similarly, producers face **sticky prices** when the costs of changing the prices they charge for goods and services outweigh the benefits of changing their prices. Producers also may not know how a price change in the product they produce compares to changes in the overall price level. Both workers and firms may also have a mistaken estimate of the overall behavior of nominal prices, which could lead them to make inaccurate adjustments to changing nominal prices.

We will address these concepts of wage and price stickiness more fully in the next two chapters. At this point, keep in mind that the short-run aggregate supply curve is predicated on incomplete or inaccurate responses by key participants in the economy to changes in the overall price level.

The Long Run. In the long run, participants in the economy have enough time to gain all the relevant information and enough time to act correctly on that information. There is no wage stickiness or price stickiness. Workers and producers can fully and accurately adjust their behavior in the face of changing overall price levels.

The Relationship Between the Price Level and Short-Run Aggregate Supply

We now examine the relationship between the overall price level and firms' production decisions in the short run. In the short run, a higher price level causes producers to produce more goods and services. Figure 21.3 captures the short-run aggregate supply relationship that we would expect to see in a macroeconomy when producers face a range of different price levels as they make their production decisions.

Short-run aggregate supply curve
Captures the direct relationship between the overall price level and the amount of goods and services supplied by producers, *ceteris paribus*.

The **short-run aggregate supply curve** is upward-sloping, indicating a direct relationship between the overall price level and the amount supplied by producers, *ceteris paribus*. For producers, a higher price level is an incentive to produce more. When the price level is equal to 100, the total amount of goods and services that producers are willing and able to supply in the economy will be $4.0 trillion. If the price level increases to 105, suppliers will produce more goods and services. Consequently, real GDP supplied would rise to $4.5 trillion. If the price level rises to 110, suppliers would be even more encouraged to produce goods and services. Total output supplied would rise to $5.0 trillion.

Why the Short-Run Aggregate Supply Curve Slopes Upward

Why is the short-run aggregate supply curve upward-sloping? The answer to this question is based on the process of firms' profit maximization. Producers' profit per unit is equal to the product price per unit minus the production cost per unit.

FIGURE 21.3

The Short-Run Aggregate Supply Curve

In panel (a), a higher price level provides an incentive for producers to increase production of goods and services and offer them for sale. Graphing this data in panel (b), we find three specific points (*A*, *B*, and *C*) on a short-run aggregate supply curve that is upward-sloping.

(a) Relationship of price level and short-run real GDP supplied

Combination	Price Level	Real GDP Supplied
A	100	$4.0 trillion
B	105	$4.5 trillion
C	110	$5.0 trillion

(b) Graph of the short-run aggregate supply curve

Consider the actions or any resource owner when facing incomplete information and the resulting inability to adjust the resource's price quickly or completely when the price level changes. Suppose workers did not know exactly when and how much the price level would be changing. They would find it difficult to ask for increases in nominal wages to match the increasing price level to protect their real income. Even if workers knew by how much the price level would increase, they might not be able to obtain the required increase in nominal wages because of institutional constraints such as multi-year contracts.

In short, resource prices are sticky and generally change more slowly than output prices. The price of gasoline at the pump can change almost daily, but workers in the oil industry might get a pay raise only once a year. When resource prices (like nominal wages) lag behind rising product prices, revenues rise for firms before costs do, and profits per unit increase in the short run. Producers respond to these higher price levels and increased profits by producing more goods and services.

Basic Movements in Short-Run Aggregate Supply

Change in aggregate quantity supplied
Occurs when a change in the price level causes firms to move along a single aggregate supply curve.

As with aggregate demand, there are two explanations for how more or fewer goods and services can be supplied in the macroeconomy. A change in the price level causes output to move along a single short-run aggregate supply curve. This movement is called a **change in aggregate quantity supplied**. This change in quantity supplied is portrayed in panel (b) of Figure 21.3.

At a price level of 105, the aggregate quantity supplied in the macroeconomy is $4.5 trillion. If the price level falls to 100, the aggregate quantity supplied decreases to $4.0 trillion and we move from point B to point A. This movement along the aggregate supply curve represents a decrease in the aggregate quantity supplied. If the price level increases to 110, we move from point B to point C and aggregate quantity supplied increases to $5.0 trillion. This movement along the short-run aggregate supply curve indicates an increase in the aggregate quantity supplied. *A change in the aggregate quantity supplied* is always movement along a single short-run aggregate supply curve caused by a change in the price level in the economy.

Change in aggregate supply
Occurs when forces other than changes in the price level shift the entire aggregate supply curve to the left or to the right.

The second explanation of how there can be more or less supply in the macroeconomy is called a **change in aggregate supply**, where forces other than changes in the price level shift the entire aggregate supply curve to the left or to the right. More or less goods and services are supplied at *each* price level, as illustrated in Figure 21.4.

We begin with short-run aggregate supply curve $SRAS_1$. If $SRAS_1$ shifts to $SRAS_2$, more is supplied at the price level of 105 ($5.0 trillion instead of $4.5 trillion) and every other price level as well. This is an increase in aggregate supply. If $SRAS_1$ shifts to $SRAS_3$, less is supplied at the price level of 105 ($4.0 trillion instead of $4.5 trillion) and at every other price level. This is a decrease in aggregate supply.

The short-run aggregate supply curve captures the decisions that producers make in search of profits. In general, any economic event that influences the profitability of firms can change production plans at a given price level, increasing or decreasing the short-run aggregate supply curve. Profit-altering events include:

- Changes in the nominal wage rate and other nominal resource prices that firms must pay.
- Changes in productivity.
- Changes in expectations by producers.

FIGURE 21.4

Change in Short-Run Aggregate Supply

If the short-run aggregate supply curve shifts from $SRAS_1$ to $SRAS_2$, firms are more willing to produce and sell goods and services at each price level. This represents an increase in aggregate supply. If the short-run aggregate supply curve shifts from $SRAS_1$ to $SRAS_3$, the total amount of real GDP produced falls at each price level and we have a decrease in aggregate supply.

Leftward shift indicates decrease in aggregate supply

Rightward shift indicates increase in aggregate supply

Nominal Wage Rates and Other Nominal Resource Prices. All else equal, increases in nominal wage rates mean that producers' costs of production increase relative to the income they make from sales. Wage costs are generally about two-thirds of the U.S. total costs of production. As a result, the impact of higher nominal wage rates on profits can be substantial for U.S. firms. Higher nominal wage rates will cause a decrease in aggregate supply, as less will be supplied at each price level.

Increases in other nominal resource prices can also have a negative effect on the profits of firms and their willingness to supply goods and services to the economy. The price of electricity in California soared during the summer of 2000 and into the winter of 2001. At the peak, the price per megawatt was more than 30 times as high as the price the year before. Many California businesses could not keep producing profitably in the face of such tremendous increases in energy prices, and had to shut down. Rising energy prices would have the same effect nationally as they did in California, causing a decrease in aggregate supply.

Productivity. When productivity (output per worker) increases, firms find that their costs of production are lower at a given price level. While workers are being paid the same nominal wage rate, they are producing more goods and services that add to the firm's revenue. Suppose that the average worker can produce 25 items per hour, which the firm can sell for $1 each, and that the average worker is paid $20 per hour. The firm receives $5 of profit per worker for each hour of labor. Now suppose that the average worker becomes more productive and can produce 30 items per hour that sell for $1 each. With no change in the nominal wage rate, the firm will now receive $10 profit per worker each hour. The firm will try to capitalize on this increased profit potential by producing more output. Increased productivity means higher profits and more production. This leads to an increase in short-run aggregate supply. As a result, more output will be supplied at each price level.

Supply shocks
Unforeseen events that can affect the expected profitability of firms, and thus their willingness to produce.

Changing Expectations. Changing expectations can cause **supply shocks**, which are unforeseen events that can affect the expected profitability of firms and thus their willingness to produce. Do you remember the Y2K panic? Due to problems in computer coding, there was a fear that when their internal clocks reset to 00 at the turn

LifeLessons

Is $80 for a Barrel of Oil a Supply Shock?

Typically, spikes in the price of a barrel of crude oil have adversely affected short-run aggregate supply and caused U.S. economic downturns, as in the early 1970s, the early 1980s, and the early 1990s. In each of these three cases, the nominal price of crude oil doubled in a matter of months, reaching peaks of $20 per barrel in the early 1970s, $50 per barrel in the early 1980s, and $35 per barrel in the early 1990s. Measured in nominal terms, a price of $80 per barrel for crude oil would be historically high. Could prices this high or even higher cause the U.S. to suffer another economic downturn?

Three considerations might mitigate the impact of high oil prices today and in the future. The first consideration is that the true burden of energy prices on an economy is the real price of oil, not the nominal price. A nominal price of $80 per barrel for crude oil is actually less expensive in real terms than the price per barrel during the early 1980s. The highest real price of crude oil was in 1981, when it cost nearly $90 per barrel in current dollars. Secondly, the U.S. economy is now less dependent on crude oil than before. The oil usage per dollar of GDP has fallen continuously since 1969, as American industrial production has become more energy-efficient and the production of the less oil-intensive service sector has become more important. Finally, price spikes (rapid increases over a short period) harm an economy more than gradual increases over time.

To gauge the true impact of crude oil (and gasoline prices) on the health of the macroeconomy in general and your economic health in particular, it is best to focus on the real price of crude oil, not the nominal price, and on how fast that price is increasing.

of the century, many computers would crash or turn back to 1900 instead of ahead to 2000. As a result, vast amounts of crucial software would fail. Businesses that relied extensively on computers, such as public utilities and airlines, spent huge amounts of money to correct their computers' programming to prevent any problems. This unexpected expenditure had a negative impact on the profits of those companies. In some cases, it reduced their willingness and ability to produce goods and services. Another example of a supply shock would be a wave of pessimism among producers about future earnings, which would depress profit expectations. Any perceived deterioration in the possibility of profits can cause reductions in production and thus less aggregate supply at each price level.

Table 21.3 summarizes the key influences on changes in aggregate supply discussed in this section.

TABLE 21.3

Key Influences on Changes in Short-Run Aggregate Supply

Influences	Direction	Impact on Short-Run Aggregate Supply
Nominal wage rates and resource prices	Higher	Decrease
	Lower	Increase
Productivity	Higher	Increase
	Lower	Decrease
Expectations	Positive	Increase
	Negative	Decrease

TABLE 21.4

Factors Affecting Short-Run Aggregate Supply During 1967–1969 and from July 1990 to September 1991

Nominal wage rates (Change from previous year)

Vietnam Era		First Gulf War Era	
1967	Higher	1990	Higher
1968	Higher	1991	Higher
1969	Higher		

Overall resource prices (Change from previous year)

1967	Higher	1990	Higher
1968	Higher	1991	Higher
1969	Higher		

Productivity (Change from previous year)

1967	Lower	1990	Lower
1968	Higher	1991	Lower
1969	Lower		

Short-Run Aggregate Supply in Action: Vietnam versus the First Gulf War

We now apply this knowledge of short-run aggregate supply to the experiences of Joanna's father and brother. Table 21.4 provides a snapshot of the key factors affecting short-run aggregate supply in both periods. Although her father and brother did not know it, the Vietnam period from 1967 to 1969 and the first Gulf War episode from July 1990 through September 1991 were alike in many ways, especially regarding the influences affecting the short-run aggregate supply curve. The time periods from 1967 to 1969 and from mid-1990 to mid-1991 were both characterized by higher nominal hourly wages of workers. The increase in hourly wages during the 1967–1969 period was about twice as fast as during the first Gulf War period, due to the lower unemployment rate during the Vietnam era. These nominal wage increases reinforced Joanna's father's comment that a good-paying job was relatively easy to find in 1969 when he got back from Vietnam.

The overall resource prices paid by firms for their inputs also increased during both periods. Producers faced higher costs of production. During both time periods, productivity (measured as output per unit of capital) declined. The decline in the 1967–1969 period was only about half as great as the decline during the first Gulf War period of 1990–1991.

The net effect, in terms of nominal wages, overall resource prices, and productivity, was that Joanna's father and brother each returned from overseas to face economies that had gone through similar experiences. As seen in Table 21.3, these influences would have caused a decrease in aggregate supply.

What about differences between the two periods that may have affected the short-run aggregate supply curve? Two differences stand out. First of all, Joanna's father was overseas during a time of continued economic growth, as the boom of the 1960s continued through most of 1969. The economy fell into a recession only after he returned in December 1969. However, Joanna's brother served overseas in the Gulf during a time when the economy was already in recession (which started in July 1990 and ended in March 1991). Producers during the continuing expansion of the 1960s were more optimistic and willing to increase their production plans. In contrast, the producers during the latter period were reluctant to undertake new production in the face of a sluggish economy.

The biggest difference is one that both Joanna's father and brother remembered: the behavior of energy prices. Crude oil was two and a half times as expensive in real terms for Joanna's brother as it was for her father. Producers in the period from mid-1990 to mid-1991 experienced an oil price shock as oil prices quickly and dramatically spiked after Iraq invaded Kuwait. This oil price shock, along with the more pessimistic view of the economy, means that the short-run aggregate supply curve prevailing during the first Gulf War faced more pressure to shift leftward, reflecting a decrease in aggregate supply.

▶ Short-Run Macroeconomic Equilibrium

Short-run macroeconomic equilibrium
Occurs where the forces of short-run aggregate supply and aggregate demand meet at an equilibrium price level that clears the overall market in an environment of incomplete adjustment of wages and prices.

We'll turn to the second version of aggregate supply, long-run aggregate supply, shortly. First, we combine aggregate demand and short-run aggregate supply to determine the performance of the overall macroeconomy in the short run. Households, businesses, governments, and the foreign sector desire the lowest price level for the goods and services they want to buy. Producers desire the highest price level for the goods and services they want to sell. **Short-run macroeconomic equilibrium** occurs where the forces of short-run aggregate supply and aggregate demand meet at an equilibrium price level that clears the overall market in an environment of incomplete adjustment of wages and prices. Figure 21.5 shows a market in short-run equilibrium.

Equilibrium Price and Quantity

Panel (a) in Figure 21.5 illustrates the determination of equilibrium price and quantity in the short run. At the price level of 100, aggregate quantity demanded ($5 trillion) is greater than the aggregate quantity supplied ($4 trillion). Firms' inventory of goods start to decline. Firms respond by increasing both the production of goods and services and the prices they charge. The increasing price level causes an increase in the aggregate quantity supplied and a decrease in aggregate quantity demanded until the aggregate quantity demanded equals the aggregate quantity supplied at point E with a price level of 105 and real GDP of $4.5 trillion.

At the price level of 110, aggregate quantity supplied is $5 trillion, while aggregate quantity demanded is $4 trillion. When the aggregate quantity supplied is greater than the aggregate quantity demanded, firms have unwanted increases in inventories. Firms reduce these unintended increases in inventory by decreasing production and reducing their prices. The falling price level causes a decrease in the aggregate quantity supplied and an increase in aggregate quantity demanded. The price level continues to fall until the aggregate quantity supplied equals the aggregate quantity demanded at point E. The movements along the given short-run aggregate supply and aggregate demand curves converge at the equilibrium price level of 105 with an equilibrium real GDP of $4.5 trillion.

The equilibrium price level is also known as the *market-clearing price level*. It assures that whatever quantity that suppliers desire to sell ($4.5 trillion of real GDP) at that price level is exactly equal to the quantity that households, firms, governments, and the foreign sector want to buy ($4.5 trillion of real GDP) at that price level.

Short-Run Macroeconomic Equilibrium

At any price level below the equilibrium price level, demanders want to buy more goods and services than firms are willing to supply. If the price level is greater than the equilibrium price level, the aggregate quantity supplied will be greater than the aggregate quantity demanded. Changes in aggregate quantity demanded and aggregate quantity supplied will continue until the equilibrium price and equilibrium level of real GDP are achieved.

(a) Short-run macroeconomic equilibrium

(b) Summary of the adjustment process to short-run macroeconomic equilibrium

Price level	Real GDP Demanded (*AD* curve)	Real GDP Supplied (*SRAS* curve)	Relationship Between Aggregate Quantity Demanded and Aggregate Quantity Supplied	Impact on Price Level
100	$5.0 trillion	$4.0 trillion	Aggregate quantity demanded is greater than aggregate quantity supplied	Rises to 105
105	4.5 trillion	4.5 trillion	Equilibrium (aggregate quantity demanded equals aggregate quantity supplied)	No change
110	4.0 trillion	5.0 trillion	Aggregate quantity supplied is greater than aggregate quantity demanded	Falls to 105

Characteristics of Short-Run Macroeconomic Equilibrium

Figure 21.5(b) shows that when the price level is above the short-run equilibrium price level or below the short-run equilibrium price level, changes in aggregate quantity demanded and aggregate quantity supplied move the economy toward the short-run equilibrium price level of 105 and the equilibrium level of real GDP of $4.5 trillion. The equilibrium price level is a kind of magnet for the participants in the economy, drawing both producers and all demanders to that common price level.

There are two important notions to keep in mind about the nature of short-run macroeconomic equilibrium. First, if a macroeconomy is in short-run equilibrium, that economy stays in short-run equilibrium unless the economy is disturbed by changes in the behavior of suppliers, or households, firms, governments, or the foreign sector. Second, if a macroeconomy is not in short-run equilibrium, the forces of aggregate demand and short-run aggregate supply tend to move the macroeconomy toward the short-run equilibrium point.

Any short-run equilibrium is a combination of price level and real GDP where the participants in the economy have no incentive to change their behavior. A macroeconomy in short-run equilibrium may not be generating optimal economic conditions. The short-run equilibrium level of real GDP may not be the full employment level of real GDP. Just a quick reminder: As you saw in the employment chapter, full employment in the labor force is not a zero unemployment rate. Full employment means that cyclical unemployment is absent, but other types of unemployment such as structural and frictional unemployment remain. The output produced by this situation is the full employment level of real GDP (potential GDP).

The forces of short-run aggregate supply and aggregate demand may cause the equilibrium price level to rise over time, generating unacceptably high rates of inflation. Conversely, overall prices may fall over time, generating deflation. Short-run equilibrium in the macroeconomy is where the forces of aggregate demand and short-run aggregate supply take an economy, not necessarily where policy makers want it to be. Remember too that the short-run equilibrium is predicated on the inability of all the participants in the economy to make complete and accurate adjustments to changing nominal prices.

Short-Run Equilibrium in Action: Vietnam versus the First Gulf War

We now explore the concept of short-run macroeconomic equilibrium in more detail by examining the situations faced by Joanna's father and brother. We have explored the behavior of both aggregate demand and short-run aggregate supply during the two periods. In Figure 21.6, we combine them to determine the overall health of the economy in those two eras.

Vietnam. Joanna's father came back at a time of significant increases in aggregate demand. The behavior of the short-run aggregate supply was less clear. Higher labor costs and declining productivity would have tended to decrease short-run aggregate supply, while the general optimism of business at the time would have tended to

---

FIGURE 21.6

Economic Impact of Two Wars

The dominant influence on the U.S. economy during the Vietnam War was the increase in aggregate demand, as shown in panel (a). In panel (b), the dominant influence on the U.S. economy during the first Gulf War was the decrease in short-run aggregate supply.

increase short-run aggregate supply. Thus, the major impact on short-run macroeconomic equilibrium would be the unambiguous increase in aggregate demand. This impact is shown in panel (a) in Figure 21.6.

All the economic events surrounding Joanna's father's return from service can be explained by the prominence of increasing aggregate demand in our model of the macroeconomy. As you saw in Table 21.2, from 1967 to 1969, U.S. real GDP grew, overall prices rose, and the unemployment rate fell.

First Gulf War. In the case of the 1990–1991 economy, we noted that the impact of various events on the behavior of aggregate demand was somewhat muted, indicating no significant increase in aggregate demand during this period.

When we looked at the influences on short run aggregate supply during the first Gulf War period, we found higher labor and resource prices and sluggish productivity changes. There was also a powerful oil price shock that doubled the nominal and real prices of a barrel of crude oil in a very short period of time. A lack of business optimism during the 1990–1991 recession would also have dampened short-run aggregate supply. Consequently, the major influence on the economy during and immediately after Joanna's brother's service time was a decrease in short-run aggregate supply, as shown by the shift from $SRAS_{1990}$ to $SRAS_{1991}$ in Figure 21.6(b).

Table 21.2 documented that the U.S. economy had higher prices, a higher unemployment rate, and a recession from July 1990 to March 1991. This recession with a higher price level can be explained by the dominance of decreasing aggregate supply in the macroeconomy. Again, this decrease in short-run aggregate supply was not the only influence on short-run equilibrium—just the major influence.

After listening to her father and brother, Joanna concluded that she couldn't count on the economic impact of this war to help her or her business in the short run. We have an advantage over Joanna in that we now know how the aggregate demand and the short-run aggregate supply curves affects the price level, real GDP, and employment. Knowing those influences, we can explain how real-world economies have behaved in the past and predict how they might behave in the future. The key is watching the various determinants of aggregate demand and short-run aggregate supply to see their impact on short-run macroeconomic equilibrium.

TEST + *E X T E N D* Your Knowledge

1. TEST As demonstrated earlier, the key fact in the 1967–1969 Vietnam period was an increase in aggregate demand, and the key fact in the 1990–1991 Gulf War period was a decrease in short-run aggregate supply. Demonstrate these facts by showing in a graph that even with a small decline in short-run aggregate supply, the period 1967–1969 would still have had higher overall prices and more output, and that even with a small increase in aggregate demand, the period 1990–1991 would still have had higher overall prices and less output.

2 . EXTEND Suppose, as was the case in the last half of the 1990s in the United States, that the major force in an economy happened to be an increase in the short-run aggregate supply curve because of increased technology and productivity, paired with an increase in aggregate demand. What will be the definite outcome and what will be the indeterminate outcome in terms of changing price levels and changing real GDP? Graph your answer.

FIGURE 21.7

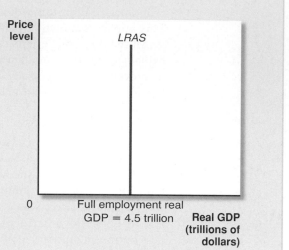

The Long-Run Aggregate Supply Curve

The long-run aggregate supply curve is vertical, because in the long run, the price level has no influence on aggregate supply. The long-run aggregate supply curve is located at the full employment level of real GDP determined by the amount of resources, the level of technology in the economy, and complete adjustments by all participants in the economy.

The Basics of Long-Run Aggregate Supply

Long-run aggregate supply curve
Level of output that occurs at full employment real GDP in the macroeconomy after adjustments to changing prices.

We now return to our discussion of aggregate supply by presenting the second version of aggregate supply. The **long-run aggregate supply curve** is the level of output that occurs at full employment real GDP in the macroeconomy after all adjustments to changing prices have occurred. In Figure 21.7, the vertical line centered over full employment real GDP ($4.5 trillion in our example) is the long-run aggregate supply curve. In this section, we examine determinants of the shape and location of the long-run aggregate supply curve.

The Shape of the Long-Run Aggregate Supply Curve

The long-run aggregate supply curve is vertical, because it reflects complete adjustment by all the participants in the economy to changing overall price levels. Earlier in this chapter you learned that when workers do not know what is happening to the price level or cannot adjust to those changing price levels, real wages lag behind. Firms then have an incentive to expand their production. In the short run, a higher price level means a greater aggregate quantity supplied. However, in the long run, workers and other resource providers have the information and time necessary to adjust their nominal wages and nominal resource prices to the changing overall price level. Firms will not have an incentive to increase real output, because in the long run, nominal wages and other resource prices move with the price level. Because everyone can adjust completely to changing overall prices, the price level has no influence over the amount of goods and services produced in the long run. Thus, the level of output that can be produced in the long run is a vertical line, independent of the overall price level.

The Location of the Long-Run Aggregate Supply Curve

Where will this vertical long-run aggregate supply curve ultimately be located? One possibility would be at some short-run equilibrium level of real GDP. However, a given short-run equilibrium level of real GDP may be below or above the optimal level of long-run real GDP for the economy. The actual unemployment rate at short-run macroeconomic equilibrium can be above or below the full employment unemployment rate in the labor market. The price level may be high or low.

What then is the optimal level of real GDP in the long run? It is the level of real GDP generated by a combination of full employment in the labor force and the use of the best available technology. Further, this level of real GDP exhibits neither underproduction nor overproduction, given the current workings of the labor market. At the full employment level of output, there is no upward or downward pressure on the price level.

In a way, we are like Goldilocks looking for the porridge that is not too hot or too cold, the rocking chair that is not too big or too small, and the bed that is not too hard or too soft. Like Goldilocks, we want everything in the macroeconomy to be just right. Economists call this "Goldilocks" point in the macroeconomy **full employment real GDP**, the level of real output generated by an economy at full employment. It is the level of real GDP that we will achieve in the presence of complete and accurate adjustments by all participants in the economy in the long run.

Full employment real GDP is sensitive to any particular estimate of what the full employment unemployment rate may be. An economist who believes that an actual unemployment rate of four percent reflects full employment will calculate a larger estimate of full employment real GDP than an economist who believes that a five percent unemployment rate represents full employment. As you will see later, disagreements over estimates of full employment real GDP can complicate the determination of the fate of the macroeconomy and the course of the business cycle.

Movement of the Long-Run Aggregate Supply Curve

The long-run aggregate supply curve is not fixed permanently at one level of real GDP. Full real GDP is a movable target that changes over time. Note that the determination of full employment real GDP parallels the determination of the maximum output generated on a production possibilities frontier. The same events that shift production possibilities also shift the long-run aggregate supply curve rightward, as shown in Figure 21.8.

Recall from Chapter 2 that the production possibilities frontier represents the amount of output that can be produced in an economy with technologically efficient full employment of all resources. Changes in technology and/or resources can shift the production possibilities frontier inward or outward (without regard to the price level in the macroeconomy). Similarly, changes in resources and/or technology can shift the entire long-run aggregate supply curve to the left or to the right. More resources and better technology would move the production possibility frontier outward. Those same changes would move the long-run aggregate supply curve to the right as well, increasing the full employment level of real GDP from $4.5 trillion to $6 trillion in our example.

Long-Run Macroeconomic Equilibrium

We've established the goal of full employment real GDP and introduced the accompanying long-run aggregate supply curve. We are now ready to determine the *long-run macroeconomic equilibrium*. The point at which the aggregate demand curve intersects both the short-run and the long-run aggregate supply curves determines the economy's position of **long-run macroeconomic equilibrium**. Figure 21.9 illustrates long-run equilibrium in the macroeconomy at point *E*. The long-run equilibrium quantity of real GDP ($4.5 trillion) is full employment real GDP—the level of

---

Full employment real GDP
Level of real output generated by an economy at full employment.

Get Ahead of the Curve
Apply the concepts of aggregate supply and aggregate demand to understanding the effects of oil price increases on the European economies.

Long-run macroeconomic equilibrium
Point at which the aggregate demand curve intersects the short-run and the long-run aggregate supply curves.

FIGURE 21.8

Production Possibilities Frontier and Long-Run Aggregate Supply

Increases in resources and/or improvements in technology are illustrated in panel (a) as a rightward shift of the production possibilities frontier from PPF_1 to PPF_2. This expansion of production possibilities means that the economy increases total output. In panel (b), when the macroeconomy has more resources and/or better technology, the amount of output that can be produced in the economy at full employment also grows. The level of output consistent with full employment will increase from $4.5 trillion to $6.0 trillion. The long-run aggregate supply curve shifts from $LRAS_1$ to $LRAS_2$.

(a) Impact on production possibilities frontier

(b) Impact on long-run aggregate supply curve

FIGURE 21.9

Long-Run Equilibrium

Long-run equilibrium in the macroeconomy occurs where the aggregate demand curve intersects the short-run and the long-run aggregate supply curves. The equilibrium level of real GDP is full employment real GDP of $4.5 trillion and the equilibrium price level is 105.

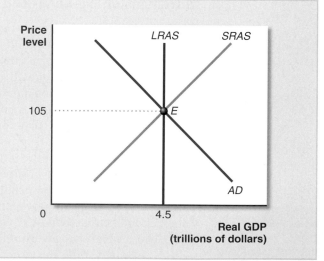

real GDP that can be produced, given current resources and technology. The equilibrium price level (105) equates aggregate quantity demanded to aggregate quantity supplied in the long run. This long-run equilibrium is the optimal resting place for the macroeconomy, because:

- The economy is now located at full employment real GDP, so no over- or underproduction is occurring.
- The economy is producing everything it is capable of producing at full employment. The actual equilibrium real GDP is equal to full employment real GDP.

- In the labor market, the actual unemployment rate is exactly equal to the full employment unemployment rate.
- The macroeconomy exhibits price stability, with no upward or downward pressure on the price level.
- All participants in the economy have obtained enough information to adjust their behavior correctly.

Short-Run Equilibrium and Long-Run Equilibrium

We have now completed our model of aggregate demand, short-run aggregate supply, and long-run aggregate supply. We conclude by reviewing the differences between long-run and short-run equilibrium in the macroeconomy.

Short-Run Equilibrium

Recall that short-run equilibrium occurs when any aggregate demand curve intersects any given short-run aggregate supply curve, as illustrated in Figure 21.5(a). At any short-run equilibrium, households, firms, governments, and the foreign sector are satisfied because the quantity demanded that they are willing and able to purchase at that equilibrium price level is being supplied. Suppliers are also satisfied, because the aggregate quantity supplied that they are willing and able to offer for sale at the equilibrium price level is equal to the aggregate quantity demanded. Both groups of participants therefore have no incentive to change their behavior by demanding or supplying more or less at the equilibrium price level.

This short-run macroeconomic equilibrium situation can still harbor economic difficulties. We might find that the economy is underperforming (with suboptimal levels of real GDP) or overheating (with above-optimal levels of real GDP). Participants in the labor market might be dissatisfied by an actual unemployment rate that is higher than the full employment unemployment rate. Not all the participants in the economy have been able to make the required adjustments to the changing level of overall prices.

Long-Run Equilibrium

Get Ahead of the Curve

Use your knowledge of long and short-run equilibrium in the macroeconomy to analyze recent economic growth in China.

Now consider an economy in long-run macroeconomic equilibrium, when the aggregate demand, short-run aggregate supply, and long-run aggregate supply curves intersect at full employment real GDP, as depicted in Figure 21.9. At the long-run equilibrium point in this economy, there is $4.5 trillion of real GDP and an overall price level of 105. Demanders and suppliers are satisfied. Neither has any incentive to change their behavior regarding consumption or production plans.

In a labor market in long-run macroeconomic equilibrium, workers find that the actual rate of unemployment is equal to the full employment unemployment rate. There is no excess labor supply to push down the nominal wage rate or excess labor demand to push it up. At the prevailing nominal wage rate, the quantity of labor supplied is equal to the quantity of labor demanded. The participants in the labor market are satisfied and have no incentive to change their behavior, and firms have no motivation to change their hiring plans. Participants in the economy have adjusted fully and accurately to the overall price level. In principle, long-run equilibrium can be quite stable. The macroeconomy is balanced on a tripod of satisfied demanders, satisfied suppliers, and satisfied workers. In reality, we find that actual macroeconomies are always moving toward long-run equilibrium, which itself presents a moving target.

Long-Run Equilibrium in Action: Vietnam versus the First Gulf War

The time periods that Joanna and her family were discussing are too short to allow us to describe in any meaningful way the impact of the long-run aggregate supply curve. However, the location of the long-run aggregate supply curve is significant in determining where an economy might be headed over time. In a sense, the short-run macroeconomic equilibrium is a snapshot of where the economy is at any particular time and how it got there. The long-run equilibrium previews how the economy will adjust over time as recessions and recoveries ebb and flow and the economy seeks out long-run macroeconomic equilibrium. For Joanna and her family, the location of the long-run equilibrium and how the economy seeks out that equilibrium will be a key determinant for their immediate economic future. In the next two chapters, we will examine how a short-run equilibrium moves toward long-run equilibrium, how the adjustment process occurs naturally, and how it occurs when aided by the intervention of the government.

Strategy and Policy
Social Security, the Long-Run Aggregate Supply Curve, and You

The location of the long-run aggregate supply curve might seem like a mere academic exercise in estimating how the macroeconomy grows over time. However, the location and movement of the long-run aggregate supply curve plays an important role in the future of the U.S. Social Security system. In reality, Social Security is essentially a pay-as-you-go system, where the Social Security taxes paid in by workers are quickly disbursed as retirement checks to current Social Security recipients. When more is paid into the fund as taxes than goes out to recipients, Social Security runs a surplus. When less is paid in than goes out, Social Security funding for future retirees is jeopardized. Currently, more funds are going into the Social Security system than are being disbursed. However, as baby boomers retire, eventually more will have to be paid out than will be coming in.

The current forecast by the Social Security Administration identifies 2017 as the year in which Social Security benefits disbursed to retirees will exceed payments into Social Security by workers. Further, by 2042 the Social Security fund surplus currently accumulating will be depleted. At that point, benefits to retirees must be cut by about 30 percent to match the inflow of Social Security taxes by workers. Alternatively, Social Security taxes could be increased now to maintain solvency.

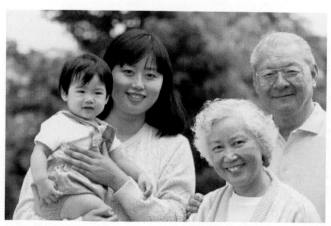

The forecast for the health of Social Security depends partly on the anticipated growth in U.S. productivity and the new inflow of immigrants. More productivity and more immigrants mean more and higher wages to tax and more funds going into the Social Security system. Productivity and immigration are also key determinants of movement in the long-run aggregate supply curve.

The estimates of the health of Social Security are based on assumptions about the average economic growth rate in the United States, which in turn are based on assumptions about productivity and annual net immigration.

Specifically, the trustees of the Social Security Administration estimate an average annual growth rate in long-run aggregate supply of 1.8 percent for the next 75 years. Their estimate of an economic growth rate of 1.8 percent is composed of predicted gains in productivity of 1.6 percent per year and a yearly net inflow of immigrants into the United States of 900,000. These predictions are pessimistic, given our past history. The U.S. economy has grown by an average of 3 percent over the last 75 years. Since 1945, U.S. productivity growth alone has averaged about 1.8 percent per year. In 2002, the United States had a net inflow of 1.4 million immigrants.

If the long-run aggregate supply curve increases faster than estimated, the solvency of Social Security can be extended much further into the future. The Social Security Administration itself estimates that with a productivity growth rate of just 1.9 percent, net immigration of 1.3 million per year, and an annual growth rate of 2.6 percent in the long-run aggregate supply curve, Social Security would be solvent for the next 75 years. The Social Security benefits that you will ultimately receive depend on what happens to the long-run aggregate supply curve between now and your retirement.

Critical-Thinking Questions

1. What economic trends might lead you to conclude that the rate of growth of long-run aggregate supply in the future might be greater than Social Security's estimate of around 1.8 percent? What economic trends might lead you to conclude that the rate of growth of long-run aggregate supply in the future might be less than the postwar average?
2. Besides the variables mentioned previously, what are some other economic or demographic factors that would affect the ability of the Social Security system to continue its solvency farther into the future?

►SUMMARY

■ **The basics of aggregate demand.** The aggregate demand relationship captures decisions made by all households, firms, governments, and foreign sector participants in the macroeconomy when confronted with a changing price level, *ceteris paribus*. The aggregate demand curve illustrating that relationship is downward-sloping, due to the wealth, interest rate, and international trade effects. An economy can experience more or less demand for goods and services when the aggregate quantity demanded increases or decreases in response to changing price levels (change in aggregate quantity demanded) or when the entire aggregate demand curve shifts so that more or less is demanded at each price level (change in aggregate demand). Macroeconomic policy changes, changes in expectations, and global effects can shift the entire aggregate demand curve.

■ **The basics of short-run aggregate supply.** The aggregate supply relationship illustrates the behavior of producers in the economy when confronted with changing prices, *ceteris paribus*. The short-run aggregate supply curve is upward-sloping as producers find increased incentives for profitable production when increases in product prices outstrip increases in resource prices. When suppliers move along a given short-run aggregate supply curve in response to a changing price level, the change in aggregate quantity supplied can result in more or less production in the macroeconomy. When changes in nominal wages and resource prices, productivity, or expectations affect producers, the entire short-run aggregate supply curve can shift, giving the economy more or less aggregate supply at each price level.

- **Short-run macroeconomic equilibrium.** When the aggregate demand curve equals the short-run aggregate supply curve at a given price level, the macroeconomy is in short-run macroeconomic equilibrium. An economy at short-run macroeconomic equilibrium tends to stay there until all market participants have correctly adjusted their wages and prices.

- **The basics of long-run aggregate supply.** The long-run aggregate supply curve represents the level of output that occurs at full employment with complete and accurate information and adjustments made by all the participants in the macroeconomy. The long-run aggregate supply curve will shift when there are changes in the amount of resources or the level of technology in the economy. Long-run equilibrium, found at the point in which the aggregate demand curve intersects the short-run and the long-run aggregate supply curves, occurs in an environment of accurate and complete adjustment to wages and prices by all the participants in the economy.

- **Short-run equilibrium and long-run equilibrium.** Short-run macroeconomic equilibrium occurs any time that the aggregate demand curve intersects the short-run aggregate supply curve. This equilibrium satisfies suppliers and demanders but might not please the participants in the labor market. Only long-run equilibrium, where the aggregate demand curve intersects both the short-run and long-run aggregate supply curves, satisfies all participants in the macroeconomy.

KEY TERMS

Aggregate demand 534	Change in aggregate supply 544	Short-run aggregate supply curve 543
Aggregate supply 542		
Change in aggregate demand 537	Full employment real GDP 553	Short-run macroeconomic equilibrium 548
Change in aggregate quantity demanded 537	Long-run aggregate supply curve 552	Sticky prices 542
Change in aggregate quantity supplied 544	Long-run macroeconomic equilibrium 553	Sticky wages 542
		Supply shocks 545

PROBLEMS

1. How will the following events affect the U.S. aggregate demand curve?
   a. The Japanese economy begins to expand rapidly.
   b. Businesses and consumers expect a slowing of economic growth.
   c. The purchasing power of the U.S. dollar increases compared to the euro.
2. How will the following actions of macroeconomic policy affect the U.S. aggregate demand curve?
   a. Social Security taxes are increased to extend the life of the Social Security system.
   b. The federal government expands its spending on prescription drug benefits under Medicare.
   c. Consumers expect more disposable income in the future as temporary tax cuts are made permanent.
3. List and briefly explain three reasons why the aggregate demand curve is downward-sloping.
4. If the total amount of savings in the U.S. economy is $50 trillion and the CPI is 100, what happens to the purchasing power of that amount of savings if the CPI rises to 110? Would households consume more or less at the new, higher price level?
5. If consumers currently spend $6 trillion on a given bundle of goods and services, would they spend more or less to purchase that bundle if the price level

falls by 10 percent? Would they tend to save more or less because of this change in the price level?

6. For a given industry, let the product price per unit = $5.00 and the production cost per unit = $3.00.
   a. Based on this information, what is the profit per unit for this producer?
   b. Now let the product price increase to $6.00 per unit, and the production cost per unit increase to $3.50 per unit. What is the profit per unit now for this producer?
   c. How should this producer change his production plans in the face of the changing profit per unit?
   d. If many producers faced the same situation, how would this affect the aggregate supply curve?

7. How will the following events affect the U.S. short-run aggregate supply curve?
   a. Increase in U.S. nominal wage rates.
   b. Decrease in the price of natural gas.
   c. Increased use of computers in the workplace improves efficiency of U.S. workers.
   d. Increase in cost of company-provided health care for workers.

8. If the macroeconomy has $10 trillion in aggregate demand and $8 trillion in short-run aggregate supply when the price level is 200, what would you expect to happen to the price level?

9. Suppose that the quantity of aggregate demand is less than the quantity of short-run aggregate supply at a given price level. What must happen to the price level to achieve equilibrium in this economy? How will this changing price level affect the quantity of aggregate demand and the quantity of short-run aggregate supply?

10. Consider the following information about aggregate demand and short-run aggregate supply in a macroeconomy:

Price Level	Aggregate Demand	Short-Run Aggregate Supply
125	$300 billion	$600 billion
120	350 billion	550 billion
115	400 billion	500 billion
110	450 billion	450 billion
105	500 billion	400 billion
100	550 billion	350 billion
95	600 billion	300 billion

   a. At which price levels are there surpluses in the macroeconomy? At which price levels are there shortages?
   b. What is the equilibrium price level? What is the short-run equilibrium level of output?
   c. Draw the aggregate demand curve and the short-run aggregate supply curve and label the equilibrium price and quantity.

11. Using the same information as in Problem 10, answer the following questions.
   a. Assume that the federal government must spend another $100 billion on national security. What will be the impact of this spending on the equilibrium price level and equilibrium level of real GDP in this economy? Graph this situation.
   b. What would happen if rising energy prices cause producers to cut back aggregate supply by $100 billion at each price level? What would be the impact on the equilibrium price level and the equilibrium level of real GDP in this economy? Graph this situation.

c.   If there is an increase in aggregate demand of $100 billion at each price level and a decrease in aggregate supply of $100 billion at each price level, what would the impact be on the equilibrium price level and the equilibrium level of real GDP in this economy? Graph this situation.

12. In the real world, economic forces move both the aggregate supply and short-run aggregate demand curve at the same time. The overall impact on the equilibrium price level and equilibrium level of real GDP depends on both the direction and relative magnitude of the changes. For each of the following cases, move both curves in the manner indicated and then determine the impact on both the equilibrium price level and the equilibrium level of output.
    a.   An increase in aggregate demand that is larger than the decrease in short-run aggregate supply.
    b.   An increase in aggregate demand that is smaller than the increase in short-run aggregate supply.
    c.   A decrease in aggregate demand that is larger than the decrease in short-run aggregate supply.
    d.   A decrease in aggregate demand that is smaller that the increase in short-run aggregate supply.

13. Some people opposed to increases in the minimum wage argue that its major impact would adversely affect short-run aggregate supply, raising the price level and reducing real GDP.
    a.   Graph the reasoning behind this argument using aggregate demand and short-run aggregate supply.
    b.   Others claim that the major impact of a higher minimum wage would be to increase overall household income and thus increase aggregate demand. Graph the reasoning behind this argument separately.
    c.   If a policy analyst asserts that the two effects happen at the same time and the increase in aggregate demand would be greater than the decrease in short-run aggregate supply, show the overall impact on the price level and real GDP in this analyst's view.

14. In the early 1990s, the Russian economy experienced a rapidly increasing price level and falling real GDP. Using the short-run macroeconomic equilibrium model, show how both the aggregate demand and the short-run aggregate supply curve could have shifted to give Russia both a higher price level and less real GDP.

15. Which of the following situations occur at short-run equilibrium?
    a.   Inventories may be increasing or decreasing.
    b.   The aggregate demand curve intersects with the short-run aggregate supply curve.
    c.   Full employment is guaranteed.
    d.   Overproduction or underproduction is possible.

16. What are the characteristics of full employment real GDP?

17. What is the economic interpretation of a vertical long-run aggregate supply curve? Why is it located at full employment real GDP?

18. How would the following activities have affected the location of the long-run aggregate supply curve in the following situations?
    a.   Increased use of computer technology in the 1990s in the United States.
    b.   Loss of population during the Potato Famine in the 1800s in Ireland.
    c.   Discovery of new oil deposits in Venezuela.

19. What are the basic characteristics of the macroeconomy at long-run equilibrium in terms of real GDP and the labor market?

20. Match each of the following descriptions to either the short-run aggregate supply curve or the long-run aggregate supply curve.
    a. Its intersection with the aggregate demand curve means the absence of overproduction or underproduction.
    b. Will occur if all wages and prices are fully flexible.
    c. Upward-sloping curve.
    d. Curve is located at the full employment level of output.
    e. Vertical curve.

myeconlab STUDY GUIDE

HERE'S HOW MyEconLab CAN HELP YOU GET A BETTER GRADE

1. Log into MyEconLab and take Practice Test 21-A (to log in for the first time, see page 30 for instructions).

2. Based on your test results, MyEconLab will identify the areas where you need further work and create a personal Study Plan for you.

3. Your Study Plan contains the problems listed below and others like them that will target the specific chapter topics you need to focus on. You'll receive instant feedback and find links to tutorials, animations, and the online textbook to help you study.

4. When you're ready, take Practice Test 21-B and demonstrate how your results have improved.

Section 21.1, Problem 1 Use the graph to fill in the blanks in the following questions.

a. A movement from point *A* to point *B* is referred to as _____ .
b. A movement from point *A* to point *C* is referred to as _____ .
c. A movement from point *A* to point *D* is referred to as _____ .
d. A movement from point *A* to point *E* is referred to as _____ .

Section 21.1, Problem 2 Refer to the graph in Problem 1 to answer the following questions. Assume that the starting point in the economy is point *A*. How will each of the following events affect U.S. aggregate demand as a move to either points *B*, *C*, *D*, or *E*?

a. The purchasing power of the dollar overseas increases.
b. The government enacts a tax increase.
c. Households and businesses have a positive future outlook.
d. There is a decrease in the price level.
e. Policy makers decrease the supply of available funds to borrowers.
f. Canada, a major trading partner with the United States, experiences a severe recession.
g. There is an increase in the price level.
h. The federal government increases spending.

Section 21.1, Problem 3 Which of the following is not a reason why the aggregate demand curve is downward-sloping?

a. As the price level rises, households feel less wealthy and therefore spend less, causing consumption (*C*) to fall.

b. As the price level rises, it puts upward pressure on interest rates, making borrowing more costly and causing investment (I) to fall.

c. As the price level rises, military equipment becomes more expensive, causing government spending (G) to fall.

d. As the price level rises, domestic goods become more expensive and foreign goods cheaper, causing exports (X) to fall and imports (M) to rise.

Section 21.2, Problem 1 Use the graph to answer the following questions.

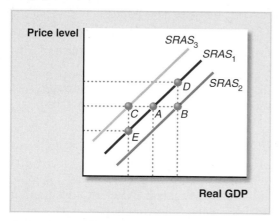

a. A movement from point A to point B is referred to as _____ .

b. A movement from point A to point C is referred to as _____ .

c. A movement from point A to point D is referred to as _____ .

d. A movement from point A to point E is referred to as _____ .

Section 21.2, Problem 2 Use the graph in Section 21.2, Problem 1 to answer the following questions. Specify whether the following events are represented by a movement along the given short-run supply curve $SRAS_1$ or a shift in the supply curve. In addition, specify whether it is an increase or decrease.

a. There is a significant rise in the cost of workers health care, paid by firms.

This is represented as a _____ (movement along/shift in) the short-run aggregate supply curve, and is a(n) _____ (increase/decrease). It is modeled as a movement from point A to point _____ (C).

b. There is a fall in the general price level.

This is represented as a _____ (movement along/shift in) the short-run aggregate supply curve, and is a(n) _____ (increase/decrease). It is modeled as a movement from point A to point _____ (E).

c. Increases in technology make workers more productive than before.

d. There is a significant increase in the nominal wages of workers.

e. There is a rise in the price level.

f. There is a wave of optimism among businesses regarding future earnings.

Section 21.3, Problem 1 For each of the following questions, explain whether the event will affect U.S. aggregate demand or short-run aggregate supply, and in which direction.

a. The U.S. government enacts a decrease in the tax rates.

b. Australia, a major U.S. trading partner, experiences significant income growth.

c. More American workers become computer-savvy, raising their level of productivity.

d. There is a decrease in the cost of fuel (an input to firms).

e. Policy makers increase the supply of available funds to borrowers.

f. All levels of government reduce their levels of spending.

Section 21.3, Problem 2 For each of the events described in Section 21.3, Problem 1, predict what will happen to the U.S. short-run equilibrium price level and equilibrium real GDP.

Section 21.3, Problem 3 Use aggregate demand and short-run aggregate supply analysis to explain each of the situations described here. That is, is the event most likely explained by a shift in aggregate demand or shift of the short-run aggregate supply curve? In which direction was the shift?

a. The country experiences an increase in output, along with an increase in the price level.

b. The country experiences a lower price level, while at the same time there is an increase in output.

c. The country experiences a higher price level of prices and a decline in output.

d. The country experiences a lower price level on prices along with a decline in output.

Section 21.4, Problem 1 Specify whether each of the following characteristics is attributed to long-run aggregate supply, short-run aggregate supply, or both.

a. Assumes full employment and equilibrium in the labor market

b. Shows production is positively related to the price level

c. Shows production is unrelated to the price level

d. Assumes market participants are unable to adjust completely to changes in the price level

e. Based on estimates of the full employment level

f. Shows production is unrelated to the price level

g. Assumes that market participants are able to adjust full to changes in the price level

h. An advance in technology shifts this curve to the right

Section 21.5, Problem 1 Which of the following is the defining characteristic of long-run equilibrium that differentiates it from short-run equilibrium?

a. In long-run equilibrium, producers are satisfied because the amount they produce is equal to the amount desired by buyers, although this may not be true in short-run equilibrium.

b. In short-run equilibrium, buyers are satisfied because the amount they desire is available, although in long-run equilibrium, there may be a shortage or excess of goods.

c. In long-run equilibrium, the amount of goods and services desired by buyers equals the amount produced, although this may or may not be true in short-run equilibrium.

d. In long-run equilibrium, the labor market is in equilibrium at the full employment level of labor, although in short-run equilibrium, the labor market may or may not be in equilibrium.

From Short-Run to Long-Run Equilibrium: The Model in Action

22

Among the world's nations, the range of economic performance from 2001 to 2004 was remarkably wide. Snapshots of the behavior of real GDP and overall price levels illustrate some stark differences among the 184 economies tracked by the International Monetary Fund (IMF). The IMF is an international agency that, among its other duties, monitors key economic indicators among its member nations. Imagine living in Equatorial Guinea in Africa and experiencing an increase in real GDP of more than 40 percent in 2001. At the other extreme, what was life like in Madagascar when its real GDP fell by 12.7 percent in 2002? What would it have been like living in Zimbabwe in 2003 when the inflation rate was 431 percent or in Libya in 2002 when overall prices declined 9.9 percent? What explains the dramatically different economic circumstances among the nations of the world?

At first, it might seem as if nothing is similar about the economic experiences of these nations. They have different endowments of land, labor, physical capital, and entrepreneurship and are located in widely different areas of the globe. Some are economically advanced, and others are not. Some are huge, technologically advanced economies, and others are small, less-developed nations dependent on a single crop or commodity. How could the economic experiences of an American, Russian, Pakistani, and Brazilian citizen ever be the same?

We will examine a number of nations around the world in this chapter. In spite of the obvious differences, there are common patterns in their economic performances. Some nations we'll examine had four years of continuous growth in real GDP combined with modestly rising prices. Others have had episodes of growing real GDP and falling prices since 2001.

Another group has exhibited periods of falling real GDP and rising price levels. A final set of nations has experienced years of both falling real GDP and a falling price level.

What is the explanation for these shared situations? Are they merely a series of coincidences, or is there some economic architecture that explains why nations with vastly different economic characteristics behave in a similar manner over time? One possible answer is that the performance of any given economy at any particular time is a truly random event. This view was captured by comedian Lewis Black in one of his signature rants: "The economy goes up, it goes down, it goes up, it goes down, it goes up, it goes down. Nobody knows why ... it happens. And I know this because I took economics. And I'd explain it to you, but I flunked that course. It's not my fault. They taught it at eight o'clock in the morning!"

It's tempting to agree with Black. It can all seem rather random. Fortunately, economists have tools to explain the behavior of real-world macroeconomies, as he would have learned it he were a morning person. In this chapter, you will see how the tools of aggregate demand and aggregate supply shape the economies of all nations to generate typical patterns of behavior. We also practice working with the concept of short-run equilibrium by exploring how economic circumstances can change equilibrium real GDP and the price level. Then we examine how an economy can transition from a given short-run macroeconomic equilibrium to the more desirable long-run equilibrium. We critically examine the workings of this long-run model of the macroeconomy and the forces that can move an economy to full employment in the long run.

ALONG THE WAY, YOU WILL ALSO LEARN:

- How changes in aggregate demand and short-run aggregate supply can explain the movements of real GDP and prices we observe in the macroeconomy.

- How the operation of the long-run model of the macroeconomy can lead to the belief that full employment is the normal state of macroeconomic health.

- How the macroeconomy can ultimately eliminate the problems of an underperforming or overheating economy.

- Issues and concerns about the workings of the long-run model.

 AT THE END OF THE CHAPTER, THE MYECONLAB LOGO WILL DIRECT YOU ONLINE

- MyEconLab is a resource-packed online homework and tutorial system that can help you perform better in your economics course. To log in for the first time, see page 30 for instructions.

- MyEconLab can help you apply important concepts from the chapter to real-world issues. Watch for the logo to indicate online features about Zimbabwe and Ireland.

- At the end of each chapter, you'll find a special study section that will help you get the most out of your textbook and your instructor's MyEconLab course.

▶ Changing Aggregate Demand and Short-Run Aggregate Supply

We begin by examining how basic changes in the position of either the aggregate demand curve or the short-run aggregate supply curve can explain four situations in the short-run macroeconomy:

- An increase in aggregate demand, which leads to a growing economy with a higher price level.
- A decrease in aggregate demand, which leads to a recession with a lower price level.
- An increase in short-run aggregate supply, which leads to a growing economy with a lower price level.
- A decrease in short-run aggregate supply, which leads to a recession with a higher price level.

Case 1: The Impact of an Increase in Aggregate Demand

myeconlab

Get Ahead of the Curve

Put your knowledge of macroeconomics to work understanding Ireland's economic boom.

What happens when there is an increase only in aggregate demand? In the real world, there are a variety of simultaneous changes in the individual components of aggregate demand as well as changes in the short-run aggregate supply decisions made by producers. To simplify this analysis, we employ the assumption of *ceteris paribus* and assume that only the aggregate demand curve increases: More realistically, we could assume a situation where the increase in aggregate demand dominates any changes in short-run aggregate supply.

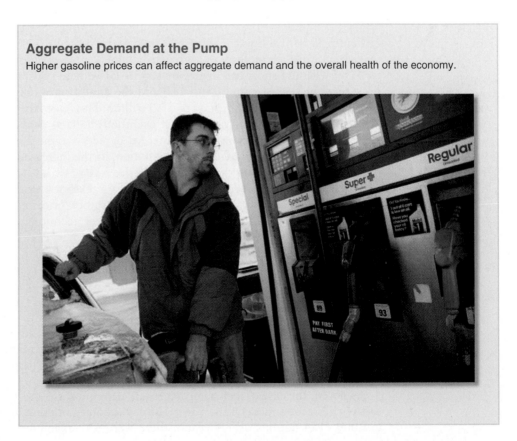

Aggregate Demand at the Pump
Higher gasoline prices can affect aggregate demand and the overall health of the economy.

FIGURE 22.1

Impact of Changing Aggregate Demand on Short-Run Equilibrium

In panel (a), the aggregate demand curve shifts rightward from AD_1 to AD_2, moving the equilibrium point in this macroeconomy from E_1 to E_2. As a result of this increase in aggregate demand, the equilibrium price level and real GDP in the economy increase. This scenario represents demand-side inflation. In panel (b), the aggregate demand curve shifts leftward from AD_1 to AD_3, causing the price level and real GDP to decrease.

Demand-side inflation

An increase in aggregate demand puts upward pressure on the equilibrium price level.

Figure 22.1(a) shows the impact of such an increase in aggregate demand on the macroeconomy. An increase in aggregate demand causes a rightward shift from AD_1 to AD_2 (with the short-run aggregate supply curve held constant). The equilibrium price level increases from 105 to 110 and the equilibrium output (as measured by real GDP) rises from $4.5 trillion to $5.0 trillion. How does the increase in real GDP affect the unemployment rate? It will eventually fall, as the increased production causes more workers to be hired. Panel (a) depicts a typical economic expansion. This situation illustrates **demand-side inflation**, as the increase in aggregate demand puts upward pressure on the equilibrium price level.

The strong U.S. recovery of the late 1990s is a textbook example of demand-side inflation. U.S. consumers were optimistic. Rising stock prices and home prices made consumers feel wealthier. Investment in computer technology increased business investment. From 1995 to 2000, the U.S. Consumer Price Index increased by approximately 10 percent, real GDP rose by about 20 percent, and the U.S. civilian unemployment rate fell from over 6 percent to around 4 percent.

Most economic expansions are the result of increasing aggregate demand. The United States, Russia, Pakistan, and Brazil all exhibited higher overall prices and rising real GDP from 2001 to 2004. The specific reasons for the increase in aggregate demand varied. In some cases, there was an increase in domestic consumer spending. In others, there was an increase in the exports of a particular raw material, agricultural good, or manufactured product. In yet other cases, new domestic investment in plant and equipment was the major force.

As noted, the case of increasing aggregate demand is the most typical case among the world's economies. Of the 736 possible outcomes in the IMF survey from 2001 to 2004 (184 nations over 4 years), there were 631 examples of this result. Thus, approximately 86 percent of observed instances in all the nations exhibited economic performance dominated by increasing aggregate demand.

Case 2: The Impact of a Decrease in Aggregate Demand

Case 2 is the polar opposite of Case 1. We show the effect of a decrease in aggregate demand, *ceteris paribus*, in Figure 22.1(b). The equilibrium price level falls from 105 to 100 and equilibrium real GDP falls from $4.5 trillion to $4.0 trillion. As a result of the reduction in real GDP, the unemployment rate eventually increases.

The most dramatic U.S. example of the impact of a major decrease in aggregate demand is the Great Depression of the 1930s. By 1929, the U.S. economy had been growing steadily for most of the decade and the unemployment rate was estimated at 3.2 percent. In 1933, the economy hit rock bottom. Consumption had collapsed, businesses had cut back on investment, governments had slashed spending and raised taxes in a futile effort to balance their budgets, and a trade war reduced U.S. net exports. All the components of aggregate demand fell simultaneously. That precipitous decline in aggregate demand caused the economy to crash. Real GDP fell by nearly 27 percent and the unemployment rate ultimately reached 24 percent of the labor force. The price level also fell by nearly 25 percent. This is the typical pattern of behavior, although to a much lesser degree, of most recessions in the United States before 1960.

This pattern of falling real GDP and falling overall prices is quite rare today. As we will see in later chapters on fiscal policy and monetary policy, governments have tools at their disposal to prevent significant and sustained declines in aggregate demand. In fact, of the 184 countries the IMF tracked over four years, only three nations exhibited this pattern: Japan, Argentina, and Singapore all had falling prices and output in 2001, and Japan repeated this pattern in 2002. In the case of Japan, uncertainty about the health of the economy in general and the banking system in particular caused both consumers and businesses to reduce spending. Similarly, Singapore is heavily dependent on the export sector for its economic growth. The slowdown in the world economy beginning in 2001—especially after September 11, 2001—reduced Singapore's net exports and overall aggregate demand. In Argentina, a lack of confidence in the government and in its monetary system led to reductions in both domestic and foreign investment in the Argentinean economy. The decline in business and consumer confidence also took its toll on aggregate demand. These four episodes in three countries represent less than 1 percent of all the examples in the IMF data during the four-year period of 2001 to 2004.

Case 3: The Impact of an Increase in Short-Run Aggregate Supply

Case 3 is characterized by the dominant influence of an increase in short-run aggregate supply on overall economic health. In Figure 22.2(a), the increase in short-run aggregate supply leads to a shift from $SRAS_1$ to $SRAS_2$. The increase in short-run aggregate supply lowers the equilibrium price level from 105 to 100 and increases equilibrium real GDP from $4.5 trillion to $5.0 trillion. Increased production generally lowers unemployment rates.

This combination of economic events has recently been relatively rare for the United States. However, we can identify such scenarios in a number of other nations. Hong Kong in Asia, Mali and Libya in Africa, and Bahrain and Oman in the Persian Gulf all exhibited both lower prices and higher real GDP for at least one year from 2001 to 2004. Indeed, this behavior occurred 48 times (of 736 possible occurrences), representing approximately 6 percent of all observations. In these

FIGURE 22.2

Impact of Changing Short-Run Aggregate Supply on Short-Run Equilibrium

In panel (a), an increase in short-run aggregate supply from $SRAS_1$ to $SRAS_2$ moves the economy from its initial equilibrium E_1 to the new equilibrium point E_2, where the economy has a lower equilibrium price level and more real GDP. In panel (b), a decrease in short-run aggregate supply causes a leftward shift from $SRAS_1$ to $SRAS_3$. The economy will move from its initial equilibrium point E_1 to a new equilibrium point E_3. This combination of a higher price level, lower real GDP, and increasing unemployment rate is called *stagflation*.

(a) Impact of an increase in short-run aggregate supply

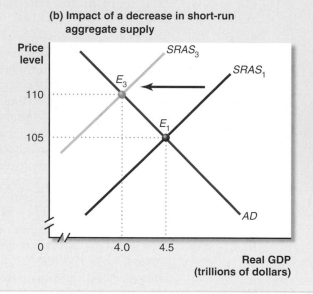

(b) Impact of a decrease in short-run aggregate supply

cases, the major positive influence on short-run aggregate supply that dominated the economy was most often the impact of new investment. This new investment increased productivity in the economy and increased business and international confidence in the economy's state of health.

Case 4: The Impact of a Decrease in Short-Run Aggregate Supply

Recent U.S. recessions have exhibited falling real GDP, rising unemployment rates, and a rising price level. What explains this triple dose of bad macroeconomic news? Consider a decrease in short-run aggregate supply that dominates the economy, as illustrated in panel (b) of Figure 22.2 by the shift from $SRAS_1$ to $SRAS_3$. In any real-world recession, aggregate demand can also decrease. However, in this case, the decrease in short-run aggregate supply is more significant than any changes in aggregate demand.

The result of a decrease in short-run aggregate supply would be less real GDP at equilibrium ($4.0 trillion instead of $4.5 trillion) and a higher equilibrium price level in the economy (110 instead of 105). Unemployment would likely increase as firms cut back production. This situation is the worst of all possible worlds for a macroeconomy. We call this painful mixture of economic misery **stagflation**, which describes a stagnant economy (reduced real GDP and increasing unemployment) with increasing price levels. It also illustrates a type of inflation called **supply-side inflation**, which occurs when the reduced production decisions by firms put upward pressure on the price level. This has been the usual pattern of U.S. recessions over the past 30 years. For example, the recent U.S. recession from March 2001 to November 2001 exhibited this pattern of falling real GDP, higher unemployment rates, and an increasing price level.

Stagflation
Stagnant economy (with reduced real GDP and increasing unemployment) with increasing inflation.

Supply-side inflation
A reduction in short-run aggregate supply by firms puts upward pressure on the price level.

Other nations also exhibit this behavior. Zimbabwe in Africa, Uruguay and Venezuela in Latin America, and the Bahamas, Grenada, and Haiti in the Caribbean all fit this pattern. Indeed, from 2001 to 2004, there are 54 examples of stagflation in the IMF data, representing a little over 7 percent of all occurrences among the nations.

What causes a decrease in short-run aggregate supply that leads to stagflation? As you recall, anything that reduces the profitability of production will decrease short-run aggregate supply. In recent U.S. recessions, economists can point to increasing business taxes, declining productivity, pessimistic business expectations, and higher energy prices as causes of reductions in short-run aggregate supply. In some of the other nations mentioned, the impact on short-run aggregate supply is more dramatic. For example, in Zimbabwe, Haiti, and Venezuela, civil unrest negatively affected the economy's productive capacity at times from 2001 to 2004. In other nations, pessimism about the future of the economy has been a dominant factor behind the decrease in short-run aggregate supply.

Table 22.1 summarizes the effects of changes in aggregate demand and short-run aggregate supply on the business cycle.

TABLE 22.1

Summary of Aggregate Demand, Short-Run Aggregate Supply, and the Business Cycle

Dominant Influence	Impact on the Price Level	Impact on Real GDP	Impact on Unemployment Rate	Real-Life Examples, 2001–2004
Case 1: Increase in *AD*	Increase = Demand-side inflation	Increase	Decrease	United States, Russia, Pakistan, Brazil
Case 2: Decrease in *AD*	Decrease = Deflation	Decrease	Increase	Japan, Singapore, Argentina
Case 3: Increase in *SRAS*	Decrease = Deflation	Increase	Decrease	Hong Kong, Mali, Libya, Bahrain, Oman
Case 4: Decrease in *SRAS*	Increase = Supply-side inflation	Decrease	Increase	Zimbabwe, Uruguay, Venezuela, the Bahamas, Grenada, Haiti

▶ The Long-Run Model of Aggregate Demand and Aggregate Supply

As established in the previous chapter, real-world economies in short-run macroeconomic equilibrium tend to gravitate toward long-run equilibrium and full employment. All the economies mentioned earlier, regardless of their short-run situation, are moving toward a long-run equilibrium. Here all the participants in the

TEST + *EXTEND* Your Knowledge

1. TEST By observing the behavior of real GDP and the price level, you can determine what has been happening to a nation's economy in the short run. Explain how economists describe each of the following situations.

  a. Real GDP and the price level have increased.
  b. Real GDP and the price level have fallen.
  c. Real GDP has increased and the price level has fallen.
  d. Real GDP has fallen and the price level has increased.

2. EXTEND Visit the Federal Reserve Bank of St. Louis's Web site for International Economic Trends using the link at www.aw-bc.com/leeds/ch22. Scroll down to the Table of Contents and click on Page 3—Economic Indicators. Check the international comparisons of the quarterly behavior of real GDP and price levels for Canada, France, Germany, Italy, Japan, the United Kingdom, and the United States over the last three years. Identify one quarterly example of each of the four cases in the TEST section using data from those countries.

Long-run model of aggregate demand and aggregate supply
Self-adjusting mechanism that illustrates how the macroeconomy moves over time to full employment real GDP.

economy have fully and accurately adjusted their behavior in response to movements in the economy's overall price level so that wage and price stickiness is removed. We now examine the **long-run model of aggregate demand and aggregate supply**, which illustrates a self-adjusting mechanism that can move the macroeconomy over time to full employment real GDP. In this section, we introduce the classical school of economic thought and examine the beliefs upon which the long-run model rests.

The Classical School of Economic Thought

Classical school of economic thought
Stresses the self-adjusting nature of the economy in the long run.

The **classical school of economic thought** explains the basic workings of the macroeconomy by stressing the self-adjusting nature of the economy in the long run. This school of thought developed in England as its economy entered the Industrial Revolution with the rise of towns and factories. The first classical economists wrote during the Age of Enlightenment from 1776 to 1850, when the world seemed a reasonable place governed by basic laws of nature. As typified by Adam Smith and his major work *The Wealth of Nations*, published in 1776, classical economists subscribe to the fundamental belief that the economy achieves full employment equilibrium in the long run. The long-run model of aggregate demand and aggregate supply thus provides the optimal level of real GDP.

The Basic Beliefs of the Long-Run Model

Three basic statements capture the essence of the long-run model of the macroeconomy:

1. Most economies at most times and in most places are at or very close to full employment real GDP. If we took a snapshot of any of the various nations mentioned earlier, the long-run model asserts that the picture would generally portray full employment.
2. If left alone, a macroeconomy tends to generate and maintain full employment without any outside help. Consequently, government intervention in the macroeconomy will do more harm than good. The government should let the

economy work out its own problems. For the economy's long-run health, the best government is the least government, limiting its impact on the economy by taxing less, spending less, and regulating less. Such *laissez faire* economics relies on the economy's natural adjustment mechanism to achieve full employment real GDP.

3. Any deviations from full employment real GDP will tend to be minor, temporary, and self-correcting. The long-run model does not promise that the macroeconomy will always generate exactly full employment real GDP. Rather, when an economy does deviate from full employment, the natural adjustment mechanisms are at work helping the economy to ultimately heal itself. Symptoms of temporary economic deviations can include overheating with inflation or underperforming with a recession and excess unemployment. The natural forces of aggregate demand and short-run aggregate supply, in particular, that are constantly at work in the economy will cure those problems over time. Although there may be short-run disruptions in the economy, full employment real GDP is the long-run norm.

The long-run model views the macroeconomy the same way that a physician views a generally healthy patient. A healthy individual will tend to stay healthy. When a healthy person does catch a cold or the flu, the physician does not need to prescribe any special surgical procedure or powerful medication. The natural recuperative powers of a normally healthy individual will usually limit the duration of the cold or flu to a few days. Medical intervention would probably do more harm than good for the patient.

Even though the classical view dates from more than two centuries ago, ideological descendents of these economists and their views exist today among politicians and policy makers. Have you ever heard a politician say that government is not the solution to our economic woes, but the problem itself? When inflation or unemployment occurs, there are economists, politicians, and policy makers who recommend a period of watchful waiting. They believe that economic problems will be temporary and that specific governmental action to cure these problems is unwise and counterproductive.

Basis for the Long-Run Model

What inner workings of the macroeconomy lead to the conclusion of the long-run model that full employment real GDP is the general rule in the long run? The long-run belief in full employment depends on three observations regarding the nature of the macroeconomy. We discuss each observation in turn.

Say's Law
Belief of classical economists that "supply creates its own demand."

Say's Law. Underpinning the conclusion that full employment is the general rule and natural state of the macroeconomy is **Say's Law**, which states that "supply creates its own demand." Popularized by Jean Baptiste Say, a French economist and influential disciple of Adam Smith, this simple five-word phrase highlights short-run aggregate supply as the main engine of change and long-run aggregate supply as the major determinant of overall economic health. The essence of Say's Law lies in the fact that the act of supplying goods to an economy generates the exact amount of income necessary to buy all those same goods and services.

To illustrate, consider a small group of people stranded on an island who form a simple economy. With the resources available on that island, all the inhabitants go to work and produce $100,000 worth of goods and services. Workers on the island who were responsible for producing those goods and services are paid in seashells for providing their resources. From our discussion in the chapter on GDP, you know that when an economy produces $100,000 worth of goods and services, it also creates exactly $100,000 of income (in the form of seashells on this island). The only place the workers can spend their seashells is on the island. Therefore, they spend their entire $100,000 of income on the island and end up buying the entire yearly output of their island.

As we saw in the previous chapter, if the aggregate quantity supplied in a macro-economy is equal to the aggregate quantity demanded in that economy, there is a short-run equilibrium. Employers on the island will not need to adjust their production plans by hiring or firing workers. The island economy begins and ends the year with the same full employment situation.

More generally, the act of supplying goods and services to the economy ultimately generates the exact amount of income that can be spent to buy those same goods and services. Say's Law leaves out the middle step in the process—the creation of income to be used for spending—for the sake of brevity.

The Loanable Funds Market. Say's Law is simplistic. One major problem is the omission of saving in the model. In our island economy, what would happen if some of the folks who earned a portion of that $100,000 in income decided to save some funds? Our little macroeconomy will still produce its $100,000 worth of yearly output and its inhabitants will still earn $100,000. However, suppose that they spend only $80,000 on the available goods and services and save the other $20,000. At the end of the year, there will be a stack of unsold goods worth $20,000. Producers will decide to cut back on their production and consequently require fewer workers. What can save our islanders from the scourge of unemployment and a departure from long-run equilibrium? How do we make up for the lost purchasing power now trapped in savings?

Loanable funds market
Market that converts saving into new spending by facilitating exchanges among suppliers and demanders of loanable funds.

The **loanable funds market** converts saving into new spending by facilitating exchanges among suppliers and demanders of loanable funds. Figure 22.3(a) illustrates how the loanable funds market works. Participants in the economy who might want to save are the suppliers of loanable funds. They have funds that they are not currently using and are seeking the highest possible interest rate for their savings. The higher the interest rate they are paid, the more they are willing to save. As a result, the supply curve for loanable funds provided by savers is upward-sloping. It indicates a direct relationship between interest rates and loanable funds supplied by savers.

Demanders for those loanable funds include individuals and firms that lack funds to spend. Perhaps the funds are needed for a business investment, for buying a new car or home, or for books and tuition. In short, these demanders for loanable funds are borrowers (in other words, investors in new plant and equipment, durable goods, or human capital). They seek the lowest possible interest rate to borrow the funds that they want to invest. Their demand curve for loanable funds is downward-sloping,

FIGURE 22.3

Operation of the Loanable Funds Market

In panel (a), the equilibrium interest rate (5 percent) is the rate that assures that what savers want to save at that rate is exactly equal to what investors want to borrow at that interest rate. The equilibrium quantity is $20,000 and the dollars of saving (S) equals the dollars of investment (I). In panel (b), the increase in saving from S_1 to S_2 moves the equilibrium from E_1 to E_2. The equilibrium interest rate falls from 5 percent to 4 percent and saving and investment both increase from $20,000 to $30,000. The decrease in the equilibrium interest rate encourages more investment, which matches the increased savings.

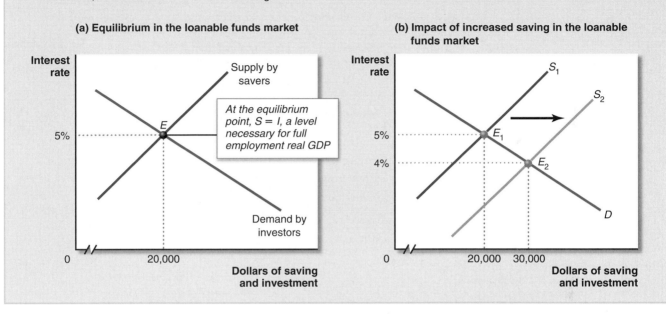

(a) Equilibrium in the loanable funds market

(b) Impact of increased saving in the loanable funds market

indicating an inverse relationship between the interest rate in the loanable funds market and the amount borrowed for investment.

The loanable funds market establishes an equilibrium interest rate, at which the quantity of funds that savers want to save at that interest rate is exactly equal to the quantity of funds that borrowers demand. In panel (a) of Figure 22.3, the 5 percent equilibrium interest rate ensures that $20,000 of saving will enter the loanable funds market, where other participants in the economy would be willing to borrow $20,000 at the equilibrium interest rate. The $20,000 of borrowed funds would then be spent. Our island economy has produced $100,000 worth of goods and services, and now total demand is again $100,000. The classical economists believed that there would always be an equilibrium interest rate in the loanable funds market to guarantee that whatever savers take out of the spending stream will exactly equal what borrowers demand at that interest rate. As a result, saving equals investment at the level necessary to assure full employment real GDP.

If more saving occurred, adjustments in the loanable funds market would permit the recycling mechanism to continue to work, as shown in panel (b) of Figure 22.3. Any increases in the supply of saving by savers automatically lowers the interest rate in the loanable funds market (from 5 percent to 4 percent, for example) and encourages an equal quantity of new borrowing by investors. At the new, lower equilibrium interest rate of 4 percent, the quantity of saving and investment increases from $20,000 to $30,000. In the view of the classical economists, an increase in the amount of saving that occurs in the economy will not ultimately jeopardize full employment.

Price and Wage Flexibility. The final reason for the long-run model's emphasis on full employment is the existence of **price and wage flexibility,** a situation in which prices and wages are equally able to go up or down. This condition is the opposite of the price and wage stickiness discussed in the previous chapter. Under what conditions would a firm accept lower prices for their products? Why would a worker accept lower wages for the same work?

Consider the degree of competition in both product and labor markets. The long-run model assumes a macroeconomy with high levels of vigorous competition in both markets. One small firm competes with many other small firms producing the same good or service in the same market. Individual workers bargain with their employers one-on-one about their wages, hours, and working conditions.

Price flexibility provides crucial support for the inevitability of full employment real GDP in the long run. Suppose that the quantity of aggregate demand becomes temporarily less than the quantity of aggregate supply. Firms quickly find that they are producing more than is being demanded. Inventories of unsold goods increase, sending a strong signal to producers to cut back on their production and to consider reducing employment levels.

However, a handful of other firms choose to cut the price of their goods in the hopes of increasing the quantity demanded for their product. After a handful of firms take this step, all other firms are forced by competition to cut their prices or risk losing market share and sales to their competitors. The result is that all firms are ultimately forced to lower prices in the face of a temporary downturn in demand. Prices are not sticky, but freely flexible. Firms do not have to cut output and employment to deal with the increasing inventory. Demand is restored as product prices fall and inventories decline, while full employment continues uninterrupted.

What is the impact on the labor market of a temporary decline in aggregate demand? Firms are producing more than is being bought at the current price level and inventories increase. Producers can cut back on production, which would reduce real GDP recession and employment.

Imagine that you are working for a firm that is facing increasing inventories. The boss regretfully informs you and all the other employees that he must let some workers go. If he picks you out as the first one to be laid off, what could you say to keep your job? You could make him an offer he couldn't refuse by offering to work at a lower wage. Your co-workers would be motivated to make the same basic offer. Workers will grudgingly accept cuts in wages and/or benefits (such as health coverage or pensions) to keep their jobs. Wage stickiness will not survive in the face of this downturn in demand. Full employment real GDP therefore continues.

The long-run model's price and wage adjustment process is sophisticated and even-handed enough that the worker is not

Courtesy www.cartoonstock.com

LifeLessons

Givebacks and Flexible Wages

Workers' nominal wages generally do not decrease. At worst, most workers find that their hourly wages or salaries remained relatively fixed during downturns in the economy. Only rarely do workers in a struggling industry (such as the airline industry) voluntarily accept cuts in their nominal wages. Still, the dynamics of the classical model play themselves out in the job market in ways that affect a worker's total compensation of wages and benefits. If workers' wages are not easily cut, companies can reduce their overall payments to workers by reducing the other part of workers' total compensation—their benefits.

Increasingly often in recent years, companies have asked workers to give up some of their benefits to maintain firms' competitiveness in the marketplace. Newer workers are finding that they are not getting the same pension plans offered to workers in the past.

Most companies that offer pensions now have defined-contribution plans, in which the size of the pension is determined by the amount the worker contributes. Workers in the past often were covered by defined-benefit plans, in which the size of the pension was determined by the years of service and the level of the workers' wages. Today's workers are also finding that their health insurance costs them more, with higher co-payments and deductibles than past health plans. Increased competition among firms in the global market is creating a U.S. job market with employee benefits reflecting the flexibility of the classical labor market.

Employer-provided health care and pensions will be more tenuous and less common in the future. Employees will find that they must take more responsibility for own economic circumstances and become more sophisticated consumers of economic information.

harmed (by accepting a lower nominal wage) and the producer is not harmed (by cutting product prices). As you saw in the chapter on inflation, what really matters to a worker's economic health is the real wage (the purchasing power of a paycheck). Suppose that there is a 10-percent reduction in nominal wages matched by a 10-percent decline in overall product prices. The workers' real wage will stay the same. If nominal wages and prices are fully and proportionately flexible in response to the same underlying decline in demand, neither workers nor business owners will lose ground economically. The adjustments in nominal wages and prices preserve real income and real profits. These adjustments that keep the economy at full employment real GDP reinforce the conclusion that the long-run aggregate supply curve is located at full employment real GDP and consistent with any price level.

▶ The Adjustment Process in the Long-Run Model

We now explore the nature of the adjustment process by observing the problems an economy might have in the short run and how the economy might transition to long-run macroeconomic equilibrium and full employment. As you have seen, the long-run model asserts that any major problems in the macroeconomy will heal themselves through price and wage flexibility without government intervention. For economic "physicians" diagnosing a macroeconomy's problems, maladies come in two versions: an underperforming economy or an overheating economy.

FIGURE 22.4

The Underperforming Economy: Identification and Elimination of the Recessionary Gap

In panel (a), actual real GDP falls short of full employment real GDP. The $0.5 trillion gap between the income we want ($4.5 trillion) and the income we have ($4.0 trillion) is called the *recessionary gap*. In panel (b), falling wages and other resource prices shift the short-run aggregate supply curve from $SRAS_1$ to $SRAS_2$. The equilibrium point ultimately moves from E_1 to E_2, achieving full employment real GDP and eliminating the recessionary gap.

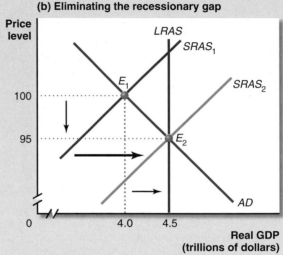

The Underperforming Economy: Eliminating Recessionary Gaps

In the underperforming economy, short-run equilibrium real GDP is less than the full employment level of real GDP. Figure 22.4(a) depicts an underperforming economy.

Symptoms of the Underperforming Economy. In panel (a) of Figure 22.4, full employment real GDP ($4.5 trillion) is greater than actual real GDP ($4.0 trillion). The intersection of the aggregate demand curve and the short-run aggregate supply curve determines short-run equilibrium real GDP. However, this output is to the left of full employment real GDP determined by the long-run aggregate supply curve. As a result, the economy is not producing at its full capability. A **recessionary gap** occurs when actual real GDP is less than full employment real GDP. It reflects a lower equilibrium price level and an unemployment rate above the full employment unemployment rate. In panel (a), this recessionary gap of $0.5 trillion is the difference between short-run equilibrium real GDP ($4.0 trillion) and full employment real GDP ($4.5 trillion).

Underproduction in the macroeconomy leads to cyclical unemployment in the labor market. The actual unemployment rate is greater than the unemployment rate consistent with full employment (which we call the full employment unemployment rate). The shortfall of income and a sluggish labor market indicate that there are no worries about excessive inflationary pressure in this underperforming economy.

Eliminating the Recessionary Gap. The long-run model demonstrates that the inner workings of the macroeconomy will end a recessionary gap. In panel (b) of Figure

Recessionary gap
Occurs when actual real GDP is less than the full employment real GDP.

22.4, at short-run equilibrium real GDP ($4.0 trillion), the sluggish labor market puts downward pressure on nominal wages. You might encounter this situation when looking for a summer job. If there are a large number of college students looking for work in your home town, nominal wages will probably be low. With many looking for a job, nominal wage rate will start to fall. These falling nominal wages put downward pressure on the overall costs of production. Other resource prices will also decrease in the face of reduced demand.

As you saw in the previous chapter, falling costs of production increase the profit potential for producers. The short-run aggregate supply curve responds to the increased profit potential by shifting. In panel (b) of Figure 22.4, the short-run aggregate supply curve continues to increase until it reaches the new equilibrium point E_2, which is long-run equilibrium. Workers and firms have made all necessary adjustments.

The Results of the Adjustment Process. In Figure 22.4(b), actual real GDP ($4.5 trillion) is now equal to full employment real GDP ($4.5 trillion). There is full employment output, so there is no over- or underproduction in the macroeconomy. The labor market is also in equilibrium, because the actual rate of unemployment is equal to the full employment unemployment rate. The new equilibrium price level is now 95 instead of 100.

The adjustment process increases real GDP, decreases the unemployment rate, causes the overall price level to fall, and causes nominal wages to fall. Wage and price flexibility is critical in making this long-run adjustment process work smoothly. Workers must ultimately accept lower nominal wages until the balance between the quantity of labor supplied and the quantity of labor demanded is reached at a lower prevailing nominal wage. Firms must ultimately be willing to lower their nominal prices in order to sell more output until the economy reaches full employment real GDP. As we showed earlier, as long as there is parity in the declines in nominal wages and the nominal price level, this adjustment process does not harm the real incomes of workers and business owners.

Notice that in our description of the entire adjustment process, you do not see the word "government." All the necessary adjustments in the labor and output market occur without any policy actions from the government. The main role of government in the long-run adjustment process is to let the natural recuperative powers of the macroeconomy eliminate the problem over time.

The Overheating Economy: Eliminating Inflationary Gaps

The overheating economy occurs when actual real GDP found in short-run equilibrium is greater than full employment real GDP due to excessive aggregate demand. In general, the overheating economy illustrated in Figure 22.5(a) is overproducing compared to its optimal productive capacity.

Inflationary gap
Gap between the higher level of real GDP at the current short-run equilibrium and the lower level of full employment real GDP.

Symptoms of the Overheating Economy   In panel (a) of Figure 22.5, full employment real GDP ($4.5 trillion) is less than actual real GDP ($5.0 trillion). Short-run equilibrium output lies to the right of full employment real GDP. Consequently, the full employment unemployment rate is greater than the actual unemployment rate. An overheating economy generates inflationary pressures as increasing incomes put upward pressure on the price level. We call this excessive production an **inflationary gap**, the gap between the higher level of real GDP at the current short-run equilibrium and the lower level of full employment real GDP.

FIGURE 22.5

The Overheating Economy: Identification and Elimination of the Inflationary Gap

In panel (a), we see a $5.0 trillion economy that has grown past full employment real GDP ($4.5 trillion) and is overheating. The excess output of $0.5 trillion represents the inflationary gap. In panel (b), at the initial short-run equilibrium of E_1, rising wages and other resource prices cause the short-run aggregate supply curve ultimately to shift from $SRAS_1$ to $SRAS_2$. The equilibrium point moves from E_1 to E_2 to eliminate the inflationary gap.

(a) The overheating economy

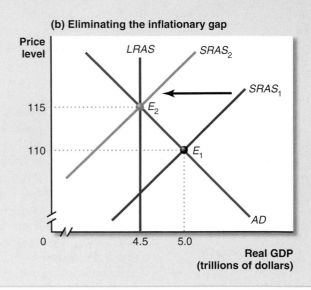

(b) Eliminating the inflationary gap

Industrial Production During World War II

The Possibility of Overproduction. Full employment real GDP represents the output generated by the full employment of all resources and the use of the most current technology. How is more output than what is achieved at the full employment level even possible? A macroeconomy can temporarily produce more than its long-run potential output if the work effort provided by the labor force increases. This increase is necessarily a temporary situation. You will soon see how natural economic forces remedy it. Further, remember that full employment real GDP is based on some small level of frictional, structural, and seasonal unemployment. A nation can exceed its full employment real GDP by having an actual unemployment rate that is less than the full employment unemployment rate.

This situation can and does occur in real-world macroeconomies. For example, actual U.S. real GDP during World War II substantially exceeded its long-run potential output because of a major increase in the labor force participation rate and an extremely low unemployment rate. The combination of these two labor market characteristics allowed the United States to produce the massive amounts of war materials needed to fight the war. In peacetime, the widespread use of mandatory overtime can also allow an economy, by overworking its labor force, to produce—temporarily—above its full employment level of production.

To fight a war, citizens may tolerate such labor market conditions. However, during peacetime, such distortions can prove problematic for the macroeconomy. In some U.S. industries, working beyond full employment has meant that employees work mandatory overtime. Workers often eventually object to mandatory overtime as too stressful, tiring, and not worth the extra income.

Eliminating the Inflationary Gap. The adjustment mechanism to eliminate an inflationary gap focuses on the impact on labor and resource markets and on the behavior of the short-run aggregate supply curve. Consider panel (b) of Figure 22.5. An overheating economy will put upward pressure on nominal wages and resource prices. If the summer job market reflects increasing labor demand in your home town, you would find that prevailing nominal wages would be higher as firms compete to hire the workers they need. Higher nominal wages and resource prices increase firms' costs of production. As costs of production start to rise, the possibility of profits declines and short-run aggregate supply decreases. This decrease is shown by the shift from $SRAS_1$ to $SRAS_2$ in panel (b) of Figure 22.5. This adjustment process will be a series of decreases in the short-run aggregate supply curve until it reaches the new equilibrium real GDP ($4.5 trillion), which is also full employment real GDP.

Results of the Adjustment Process. At the new equilibrium point E_2 in Figure 22.5(b), the intersection of the aggregate demand curve and the long-run and short-run aggregate supply curves generates full employment real GDP. At that level of output, the actual rate of unemployment equals the full employment unemployment rate. Actual real GDP ($4.5 trillion) equals full employment real GDP ($4.5 trillion). The economy has cut back on its production, incurred higher nominal wages, and increased the equilibrium price level from 110 to 115 as part of the adjustment process. The macroeconomy has again achieved full employment real GDP without any government intervention.

In the long-run model, aggregate supply is the main engine of the macroeconomy. Consequently, all the necessary adjustments required to reestablish full employment real GDP occur with changes in short-run aggregate supply over time, as workers and firms adjust their behavior. The aggregate demand curve does not have to shift to achieve full employment real GDP in long-run equilibrium.

TEST + *EXTEND* Your Knowledge

1. TEST In a recessionary gap, when the economy is underperforming, what is the relationship between actual real GDP and full employment real GDP? What is the relationship when the economy is overheating? What is the relationship when the economy is in long-run equilibrium?

2. EXTEND Go to the Web site for the Federal Reserve Bank of St.

Louis using the links at www.aw-bc.com/leeds/ch22 to see actual real GDP in quarterly data and full employment real GDP (also called real potential GDP) in quarterly data. Compare actual real GDP to full employment real GDP (real potential GDP) for each quarter in 2001 and the current year to see when the U.S. economy has been at full employment, in a recessionary gap (underperforming economy), or in an inflationary gap (overheating economy).

Real-World Difficulties of the Long-Run Model

Over time, concerns have arisen about the usefulness of the long-run model in real-world analyses. The model does not seem to work as well in practice as it does in theory. In this section, we examine some practical difficulties in relying on the long-run model.

Determining the Length of the Long-Run Period

How long does the adjustment process take in the real world? In our model and graphs, there is a presumption of rapid and seamless adjustment as the economy moves quickly and effortlessly from one equilibrium point to another. The graphs do not give us a sense of the difficult adjustments that must occur over time in the real world. Production decisions by firms cannot be—and are not—made immediately. Changes in technology, resource use, and hiring decisions take time to implement. There are usually a number of costly and time-consuming adjustments in production plans before long-run equilibrium is finally achieved. Firms and workers may initially overestimate or underestimate the necessary adjustments. If full employment real GDP is changing at the same time, the adjustment process to that new level of output could take longer still. How long will price and wage stickiness persist? Are the participants in the economy willing to wait for a number of years rather than a number of months for the economy to reestablish full employment real GDP?

Estimating the Full Employment Level of Real GDP

As you saw in the previous chapter, full employment real GDP can be a moving target, typically growing but possibly shrinking with changes in resources and technology. Increases in resources and technology can expand full employment real GDP. Therefore, while some economists may assert that a macroeconomy will ultimately achieve full employment real GDP, they can never be sure exactly what that full employment real GDP will be. In a similar fashion, full employment real GDP is very sensitive to any given estimate of the full employment unemployment rate. Suppose that Economist A thinks that full employment real GDP occurs when the unemployment rate in the macroeconomy is 4 percent. Economist A might consider the current economic situation, with a 4.5 percent actual unemployment rate, to be underperforming, and predict that the economy will adjust with lower nominal prices, more real GDP, and falling unemployment rate. Economist B might believe that full employment is consistent with an unemployment rate of 5 percent. Therefore, says Economist B, the economy is overheating when the actual unemployment rate is 4.5 percent. The long-run adjustment process to this situation would yield higher nominal prices, less real GDP, and a higher unemployment rate.

How do these different perceptions of full employment real GDP affect the predicted behavior of the macroeconomy? In Figure 22.6, suppose that $4.5 trillion is the current short-run equilibrium real GDP and $4.0 trillion is the estimate of full employment real GDP based on the belief that 5 percent is the full employment unemployment rate. This belief would yield $LRAS_1$. The economy has an inflationary gap and will adjust with a higher nominal price level, less real GDP, and a higher unemployment rate. The economy will move from its initial equilibrium of E_1 to the long-run equilibrium at E_2. Now suppose that $5.0 trillion is the estimate of full employment real GDP based on the belief that the full employment unemployment rate is only 4 percent. This belief would generate $LRAS_2$. Then the

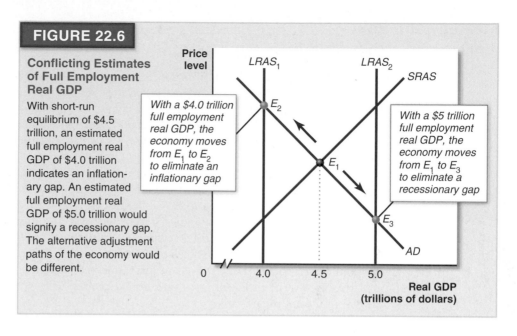

FIGURE 22.6

Conflicting Estimates of Full Employment Real GDP

With short-run equilibrium of $4.5 trillion, an estimated full employment real GDP of $4.0 trillion indicates an inflationary gap. An estimated full employment real GDP of $5.0 trillion would signify a recessionary gap. The alternative adjustment paths of the economy would be different.

With a $4.0 trillion full employment real GDP, the economy moves from E_1 to E_2 to eliminate an inflationary gap

With a $5 trillion full employment real GDP, the economy moves from E_1 to E_3 to eliminate a recessionary gap

current short-run equilibrium real GDP of $4.5 trillion represents a recessionary gap. The economy responds with a lower nominal price level, more employment, and less real GDP. The economy would now move from its initial equilibrium of E_1 to the long-run equilibrium at E_3. This path is the exact opposite of the first adjustment. The better our estimate of full employment real GDP, the more certain we would be about the future adjustment path.

Clearly, both economists and their estimates cannot be right. Their analysis and predictions are crucially linked to their estimates of full employment real GDP. Determining full employment real GDP is more of a subjective art than an objective science.

Tension Between the Long-Run Model and Government Policy

Another problem with the dependence of long-run adjustment process on changing short-run aggregate supply is that relatively few nations seem to follow its precepts by letting nature take its course. Consider the real-world cases in the IMF data where the dominant influence is either increasing or decreasing short-run aggregate supply. There are a total of 102 examples of this behavior (54 examples of decreasing short-run aggregate supply and 48 cases of increasing short-run aggregate supply). These cases represent only about 14 percent of the total cases from 2001 to 2004. In all the other cases, the behavior of aggregate demand is more influential. There must be another adjustment mechanism that accounts for the majority of the behavior of real-world economies. We examine this other mechanism, based on government policy–induced changes in aggregate demand, in an upcoming chapter on fiscal policy.

Some final related questions are the focus of the next two chapters: What happens to this model of long-run macroeconomic adjustment if we encounter a business cycle that the model cannot easily explain or quickly eliminate? What happens if the actual unemployment rate remains persistently high for a number of years if labor markets and production decisions by firms resist the required adjustments? What happens if we encounter a macroeconomic problem that is not minor, temporary, or self-correcting? The long-run model faced these questions when confronted with the U.S. Great Depression, beginning in 1929.

Zimbabwe: Lessons from a Failing Economy

In economics, we like to learn from success rather than from failure. We also tend to focus our attention on aggregate demand, because if nothing else, it is easier to measure than aggregate supply. You saw in this chapter that the typical real-world state of affairs is that macroeconomies are usually growing, generally with rising price levels due to increasing aggregate demand. We can learn important lessons about both short-run and long-run aggregate supply by looking at a failing economy.

Without a doubt, the best (or worst) example of a struggling real-world economy is Zimbabwe. Its economy shrunk by nearly 5 percent in 2004. Zimbabwe also had the world's highest rate of inflation (282 percent) in 2004. This was also more than five times as great as the next-highest rate, that of the Dominican Republic at 52 percent. At the most recent (2004) estimate, Zimbabwe's unemployment rate was 70 percent. By any reasonable measure, Zimbabwe has suffered the world's worst economic performance. And this is not just a one-year phenomenon. The nation has had this pattern of rapid inflation and falling real GDP for the last four years, as shown in the following table:

Change in	2001	2002	2003	2004
Overall price level	+76.7%	+140.0%	+431.7%	+282.4%
Real GDP	−2.7%	−6.0%	−10.0%	−4.8%

Source: International Monetary Fund *World Economic Outlook*, April 2005, Statistical Appendix, Tables 2 and 8

What is going on in Zimbabwe? In essence, Zimbabwe has felt the sting of a sharp and continuous reduction in its short-run and long-run aggregate supply curves. Some of the specific events that have led to a decrease in both aggregate supply curves are:

- A land reform program, designed to break up large commercial agricultural land holdings into smaller parcels owned by more people, has resulted in violence and chaos. Many current landowners face confiscation of their lands without compensation. As a result, they have not been planting crops. The smaller farms resulting from the government program have not been as productive as the larger farms. The cumulative result has been a major reduction in a vital sector of the economy that provides one of every four jobs in the workforce and about one-third of all Zimbabwe's export earnings. This failed land reform immediately decreased short-run aggregate supply. By reducing the full employment level of output, it decreased long-run aggregate supply as well.
- Zimbabwe has one of the highest rates of infection from HIV/AIDS in the world. The disease has reduced the size of its labor force, reducing its production possibilities and decreasing its long-run aggregate supply.
- Political problems have unnerved both local and international investors. There have been accusations of rigged elections, a four-year war with the Democratic Republic of Congo that ended in 2002, and the use of widespread labor strikes by opposition parties. These events have reduced confidence in the economy and caused reductions in short-run aggregate supply, as pessimistic businesses produce less and less.

Critical-Thinking Questions

1. Show graphically how, even if Zimbabwe could increase its aggregate demand, the persistent decline in short-run aggregate supply will still result in excessive inflation—even if real GDP manages to grow.
2. "The reliance on short-run aggregate supply as the engine for economic growth is a two-edged sword. When short-run aggregate supply grows, that growth can be great for an economy, but when it shrinks, it can really hurt." Explain this statement using aggregate demand and short-run aggregate supply to demonstrate the impact of changing short-run aggregate supply on real GDP and the overall price level.

SUMMARY

- **Changing aggregate demand and short-run aggregate supply.** Changes in aggregate demand and short-run aggregate supply explain the behavior of the different parts of the business cycle and the patterns of changing real GDP, price levels, and unemployment trends over time and among nations.

- **The long-run model of aggregate demand and aggregate supply.** The long-run model asserts that because of Say's Law, the workings of the loanable funds market, and price and wage flexibility, the economy will ultimately operate at or near full employment real GDP in the long run. Over time, participants in the economy will be able to accurately and completely adjust their decisions in the face of changing price levels to lead the economy to full employment real GDP.

- **Eliminating the recessionary or inflationary gap.** The long-run model of the macroeconomy illustrates that when an economy is either falling short of full employment real GDP (underperforming) or exceeding full employment real GDP (overheating), changes in the short-run aggregate supply curve remove these problems and restore full employment equilibrium. In the case of the underperforming economy, falling nominal wages and resource costs ultimately increase short-run aggregate supply until the economy reaches full employment. In an overheating economy, nominal wages and resource costs increase, reducing short-run aggregate supply until full employment real GDP is reached.

- **Real-world difficulties of the long-run model.** The operation of the long-run model presents some practical challenges in achieving full employment equilibrium: the length of the adjustment process based on price and wage flexibility, the difficulty of determining full employment real GDP, and the temptation for governments to manipulate aggregate demand.

KEY TERMS

Classical school of economic thought 572

Demand-side inflation 568

Inflationary gap 579

Loanable funds market 574

Long-run model of aggregate demand and aggregate supply 572

Price and wage flexibility 576

Recessionary gap 578

Say's Law 573

Stagflation 570

Supply-side inflation 570

1. From 1996 to 1997, the U.S. price level rose from 156.9 to 160.5, while real GDP rose from $7.8 trillion to $8.1 trillion. Graph this situation using a change in either the aggregate demand curve alone or the short-run aggregate supply curve alone. What economic phenomenon does this illustrate?

2. From 1948 to 1949, the U.S. price level fell from 24.1 to 23.8, while real GDP fell from $1.64 trillion to $1.63 trillion. Graph this situation using a change in either aggregate demand alone or short-run aggregate supply alone. What economic phenomenon does this illustrate?

3. From 1973 to 1974, the U.S. price level rose from 44.4 to 49.3, while real GDP fell from $4.12 trillion to $4.09 trillion. Graph this situation using a change in either aggregate demand alone or short-run aggregate supply alone. What economic phenomenon does this illustrate?

4. From 1938 to 1939, the U.S. price level fell from 14.1 to 13.9, while real GDP rose from $878 billion to $950 billion. Graph this situation using a change in either aggregate demand alone or short-run aggregate supply alone. What economic phenomenon does this illustrate?

5. What are the basic beliefs of the long-run model?

6. What are the basic characteristics of a macroeconomy in long-run equilibrium in terms of real GDP and the labor market?

7. How is long-run equilibrium determined graphically in the aggregate demand and aggregate supply model?

8. What are the three basic tenets of the long-run model of the macroeconomy?

9. Define the concepts of wage flexibility and price flexibility.

10. Under what conditions would a firm be willing to accept a lower price for its product? Under what conditions would a worker be willing to accept a lower nominal wage for the hours worked?

11. Explain how price and wage flexibility can maintain full employment real GDP even if there is a temporary downturn in demand.

12. Draw a graph of an underperforming economy and label the recessionary gap.

13. Explain graphically and in your own words how the short-run aggregate supply curve adjusts in the long-run model to eliminate a recessionary gap.

14. Draw a graph of an overheating economy and label the inflationary gap. Explain graphically and in your own words how the short-run aggregate supply curve adjusts in the long-run model to eliminate an inflationary gap.

15. In each case, identify which type of gap is being described:
    a. The full employment unemployment rate is greater than the actual unemployment rate.
    b. Full employment real GDP is greater than actual real GDP.
    c. The major economic problem is unemployment.
    d. When this gap is removed in the long run, the price level rises and real GDP falls.

16. In practice, what difficulties exist in applying policies based on the long-run model in solving the problems of the macroeconomy?

HERE'S HOW MyEconLab CAN HELP YOU GET A BETTER GRADE

1. Log into MyEconLab and take Practice Test 22-A (to log in for the first time, see page 30 for instructions).

2. Based on your test results, MyEconLab will identify the areas where you need further work and create a personal Study Plan for you.

3. Your Study Plan contains the problems listed below and others like them that will target the specific chapter topics you need to focus on. You'll receive instant feedback and find links to tutorials, animations, and the online textbook to help you study.

4. When you're ready, take Practice Test 22-B and demonstrate how your results have improved.

Section 22.1, Problem 1 Fill in each of the blanks in the following questions with one of the provided answers.

a. An increase in aggregate demand leads to a(n) _____ (*increase/decrease*) in the price level, a(n) _____ (*increase/decrease*) in real GDP, and a(n) _____ (*increase/decrease*) in the unemployment rate.

b. A decrease in aggregate demand leads to a(n) _____ (*increase/decrease*) in the price level, a(n) _____ (*increase/decrease*) in real GDP, and a(n) _____ (*increase/decrease*) in the unemployment rate.

c. An increase in short-run aggregate supply leads to a(n) _____ (*increase/decrease*) in the price level, a(n) _____ (*increase/decrease*) in real GDP, and a(n) _____ (*increase/decrease*) in the unemployment rate.

d. A decrease in short-run aggregate supply leads to a(n) _____ (*increase/decrease*) in the price level, a(n) _____ (*increase/decrease*) in real GDP, and a(n) _____ (*increase/decrease*) in the unemployment rate.

Section 22.1, Problem 2 During the years 2001–2004, what was the most common occurrence in world economies?

a. increasing aggregate demand
b. decreasing aggregate demand
c. increasing short-run aggregate supply
d. decreasing short-run aggregate supply

Section 22.2, Problem 1 Consider the following statements:

I. Most economies are at or very close to the full employment level of real GDP.

II. Governments often need to intervene in the economy in order to reach full employment real GDP.

III. Deviation from full employment real GDP can be significant and the economy can be out of long-run equilibrium for a considerable amount of time.

IV. Economies are essentially self-correcting and will always gravitate towards long-run equilibrium.

Which of these statements capture the basic beliefs of the long-run model?

a. I and II
b. II, III, and IV
c. I and IV
d. II, III, and IV
e. II and III

Section 22.2, Problem 2 In the loanable fund market, the supply curve is composed of _____ (*savers/borrowers*), and is _____ (*upward/downward*)-sloping. The demand curve is composed of _____ (*savers/borrowers*) and is _____ (*upward/downward*)-sloping.

Section 22.2, Problem 3 Suppose that the government enacts tax legislation than encourages investment. In the loanable funds market, we would predict this would lead to a(n) _____ (*increase/decrease*) in the _____ (*supply/demand*) curve. This leads to a(n) _____ (*increase/decrease*) in the interest rate, and a(n) _____ (*increase/decrease*) in the amount of savings.

Section 22.3, Problem 1 Suppose that the economy is in an inflationary gap. This state implies that in the labor market, there is a _____ (*shortage/excess*) of labor, causing wages to _____ (*rise/fall*). This in turn causes the (*AD/SRAS/LRAS*) to shift _____ (*left/right*), moving the economy back into long-run macroeconomic equilibrium.

Section 22.3, Problem 2 Suppose that the economy is in a recessionary gap. This state implies that in the labor market, there is a _____ (*shortage/excess*) of labor, causing wages to _____ (*rise/fall*). This in turn causes the _____ (*AD/SRAS/LRAS*) to shift _____ (*left/right*), moving the economy back into long-run macroeconomic equilibrium.

Section 22.3, Problem 3 Draw a graph of an economy during a recessionary gap. Be sure to include the *AD*, *SRAS*, and *LRAS* curves. Is output less than, equal to, or greater than full employment real GDP?

Section 22.4, Problem 1 What are some of the difficulties of using the long-run model in real-world situations?

23

The Role of Aggregate Demand in the Short Run

Movies can mirror reality, illustrating the resilience of the human spirit in the face of adversity. Many films have shown how ordinary people coped in extraordinary ways with the devastating impact of the Great Depression of the 1930s. Films as varied as *The Grapes of Wrath* (1940), *Bonnie and Clyde* (1967), *Paper Moon* (1973), *O Brother, Where Art Thou* (2000), and *Road to Perdition* (2002) all chronicled the battle between a sense of helplessness and the desire to persevere that is characteristically American. This same battle has also played out in two recent movies that you may have seen: *Seabiscuit* (2003) and *Cinderella Man* (2005). *Seabiscuit* is the story of how an underdog thoroughbred gave a sense of optimism to many Americans who otherwise had little reason to cheer. *Cinderella Man* is the story of James Braddock, who during the height of the Great Depression returned to boxing just to earn a living. He ultimately became the heavyweight champion of the world. Unifying all these movies is the theme that ordinary people facing very difficult times during the worst U.S. economic catastrophe found a way to survive—and sometimes even thrive.

Why were people feeling helpless? The economy no longer seemed to function properly. Previously, people who lost one job had the reasonable expectation that they could quickly find another. Hard work seemed to be rewarded. Prosperity was only temporarily interrupted by recessions. The state of the economy was generally healthy. But, starting with the stock market crash in 1929, the U.S. economy fell faster and further than it ever had before. No sector of the economy was untouched by the ongoing disaster. Jobs were lost and gone forever. Beset by circumstances beyond their control, everyone had to find his or her own way to survive. The economy worsened year after painful year from 1929 until it hit bottom in 1933. The full recovery of the U.S. economy waited until 1941.

The movies based on the Great Depression also show a desire among Americans to persevere in the absence of answers, without an understanding of what went wrong and how to fix it. What had happened to the promise of permanent prosperity that seemed tantalizingly close during the Roaring Twenties? More importantly, how could anyone fix an economy in such dire straits? This chapter tells the story of how these tragic economic events affected some economists' understanding of the macroeconomy. We examine a model that called for immediate action instead of passively waiting for the economy to heal itself. We also explore the components of aggregate demand at the core of this model.

ALONG THE WAY, YOU WILL ALSO LEARN:

- How the Great Depression shifted the focus of economists, politicians, and policy makers away from the long-run model of aggregate demand and aggregate supply.

- How the Keynesian short-run model of aggregate demand and aggregate supply provided a useful alternative diagnosis of the health of the macroeconomy.

- The characteristics of the short-run model and how it differs from the long-run model.

- The importance of aggregate demand in the short-run model of aggregate demand and aggregate supply.

AT THE END OF THE CHAPTER, THE MYECONLAB LOGO WILL DIRECT YOU ONLINE

- MyEconLab is a resource-packed online homework and tutorial system that can help you perform better in your economics course. To log in for the first time, see page 30 for instructions.

- MyEconLab can help you apply important concepts from the chapter to real-world issues. Watch for the logo to indicate online features about the effects of high gas prices and low business investment on the U.S. economy.

- At the end of each chapter, you'll find a special study section that will help you get the most out of your textbook and your instructor's MyEconLab course.

Emergence of the Keynesian Short-Run Model

In this section, we examine the economic trials of the United States during the Great Depression, which set the stage for a new, short-run economic model. These changes in macroeconomic thought fundamentally altered the view of the government's role in the macroeconomy.

The Great Depression's Challenge to the Long-Run Model

During the 1930s, the Great Depression swept over many of the world's leading economic powers, challenging the long-run view of a full employment level of output. The Great Depression was the most severe economic trauma in U.S. history. From the beginning of the U.S. Great Depression in 1929 to its depths in 1933, the unemployment rate rose from slightly over 3 percent of the labor force to almost 25 percent, while real GDP decreased by almost 27 percent. The seemingly endless economic decline began to convince many Americans that this depression would never end. People started to delay making the everyday decisions of life. Marriage rates and birth rates fell precipitously in the 1930s, and participation in radical political movements in both the left and the right rose. In his first inaugural address in 1933, President Franklin Delano Roosevelt referred to this "nameless, unreasoning, unjustified terror" when he declared, "The only thing we have to fear is fear itself." As vividly illustrated in many of the movies set during the Great Depression, the fear was fostered by not knowing what was happening or how to fix it.

Recall that the long-run model of aggregate demand and aggregate supply asserts that any excess, cyclical unemployment would generally be minor, temporary, and self-correcting. In the long-run model, the natural forces affecting short-run aggregate supply guarantee that the labor market and wages would completely adjust and full employment would ultimately result. For presidents elected before Roosevelt in 1932, the basic economic concerns of the federal government were balancing the budget every year if possible and holding government spending and taxation to a minimum. The natural workings of the macroeconomy, it was thought, would generate economic growth and full employment in the long run. Economists, politicians, policy makers, and the public generally exhibited an abiding faith that the economy would eventually heal itself.

However, economies did not behave in this fashion in much of the world during the 1930s. The U.S. unemployment rate of 25 percent in the depths of the Great Depression was not "minor." It remained over 10 percent throughout the entire decade of the 1930s. Most economists maintain that the massive wartime mobilization of the U.S. economy beginning in 1942 ultimately returned the U.S. economy to the full employment level of output. It seems clear that the U.S. economy did not heal itself given that it needed a world war to restore full economic health. President Franklin Roosevelt knew that he must react to the nation's suffering from the ravages of the depression.

Economists and national leaders faced stark choices. They could follow the dictates of the long-run model and patiently await its promise of a future full employment equilibrium. Given enough time, the macroeconomy would ultimately adjust as the model predicted. However, the nation's short-run suffering necessitated immediate action. Thus, it was necessary to find a new model that could explain the Great Depression and offer more effective and timely solutions. Economists base their evaluation of any economic model on its ability to predict and explain economic reality. The Great Depression was a new reality requiring a new model. After the problem was correctly identified and diagnosed with a new model of the macroeconomy, a more timely end to the Great Depression could occur.

The Keynesian Short-Run Model Emerges

Into this search for a new model of macroeconomic activity stepped John Maynard Keynes. He was an iconoclastic professor of economics at Cambridge University in England.

The Keynesian Challenge to the Long-Run Model. Keynes's book *The General Theory of Employment, Interest, and Money* was published in 1936. The **Keynesian model** is a short-run model of the behavior of the macroeconomy that emphasizes the role of aggregate demand and government action in the macroeconomy, while

Keynesian model
Short-run model of the behavior of the macroeconomy that emphasizes the role of aggregate demand and government action in the macroeconomy.

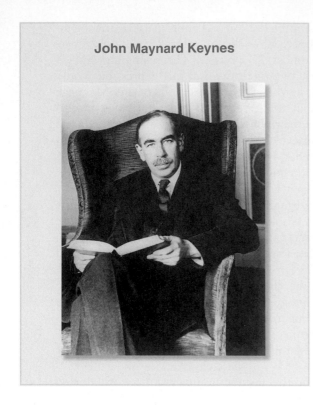

John Maynard Keynes

questioning the validity of the long-run model as an effective guide for macroeconomic policy. It challenged accepted macroeconomic thought in the following ways:

- The established classical model focuses on the long run, whereas the Keynesian model is concerned with the short run. Keynes challenged the preoccupation with the long run by proclaiming, "In the long run, we are all dead." This quotation expressed his unwillingness to wait patiently for the macroeconomy to heal itself in the long run.
- The long-run model emphasizes the aggregate supply side of the macroeconomy. The short-run Keynesian model focuses on the aggregate demand conditions that can be shaped by changes in government policy.
- Proponents of the long-run model stress that market forces will ultimately return real GDP to its full employment level. Adherents of the Keynesian short-run model believe that the economy might spend long periods below full employment when market forces cannot adjust quickly.
- Advocates of the long-run model teach that government intervention cannot improve on the natural functioning of the economy. Supporters of the Keynesian short-run model believe that government should play a prompt and important role in stabilizing the economy.

The General Theory is arguably the most important economics book of the twentieth century. It became the blueprint for macroeconomic policy in industrialized nations for the next two generations. From this point on, we refer to the Keynesian short-run model simply as the short-run model.

In 1933, during his first hundred days in office, Roosevelt proposed—and Congress passed—a wide variety of economic legislation designed to stabilize the economy and to put people back to work. Roosevelt was unwilling to wait until the natural forces of aggregate supply slowly brought the economy back to health. For the first time, a U.S. president took specific responsibility for the economic health of the nation. FDR's pragmatic approach to curing the Great Depression presaged the Keynesian theoretical emphasis in *The General Theory*.

▶ Characteristics of the Short-Run Model

The major tenet of the short-run model is that full employment is the exception, rather than the rule. Most modern economies typically fall short (and sometimes well short) of full employment real GDP. The short-run model advocates an aggressive approach to economic policy, with the intent to attack and cure short-run problems quickly and effectively. According to the short-run model, economies in the 1930s were plagued with a lengthy and lingering illness that could be cured only by the prompt use of strong economic medicine.

The short-run model is based on three pillars. Each of these pillars challenges the timeliness and efficiency of the long-run model's adjustment process used to defend its belief in the widespread achievement of full employment. In this section, we contrast the main characteristics of the short-run model with those of the long-run model.

Challenge to Say's Law

Instead of relying on Say's Law ("supply creates its own demand"), Keynes taught that demand creates its own supply. Aggregate demand is the main engine of economic performance. If something is wrong in the macroeconomy, there must be something wrong with aggregate demand. To return to full economic health, the right dose of aggregate demand is required. Aggregate demand is the major motivation for suppliers who will produce only because there is demand for that product, not just because they can produce. Indeed, during the Great Depression, U.S. manufacturers could have produced many more goods than they actually did. Movies about the Great Depression portray this fact with their depiction of empty factories, idle workers, and abandoned farms. The glaring lack of aggregate demand during the depths of the Great Depression made increased production unwise and unprofitable. Business investment fell dramatically, as firms saw no need to expand production to produce even more goods that no one would or could buy.

Challenge to the Loanable Funds Market

Recall that the loanable funds market in the long-run model takes any amount of excess saving in the economy and channels it into an equal amount of new investment spending. The common influence of the interest rate on the behavior of borrowers and savers guaranteed that saving equals investment at the level necessary to achieve full employment real GDP. In the short-run model, there is no automatic recycling mechanism for saving. Many factors influence how much savers want to save and investors want to borrow at any particular time. These factors complicate the operation of the loanable funds market.

Savers' Motivation. The level of consumers' disposable income has a major impact on the decision to save. It is much easier to save out of a large amount of disposable income than from a small amount of disposable income. Some savers are motivated by habit, perhaps putting $20 per paycheck into their savings no matter what. Other households and individuals save for a rainy day, for retirement, or for the down payment on a new car or home.

Investors' Motivation. In the short-run model, investors who want to borrow are motivated not only by interest rates, but also by the expected rate of return on the particular investment they had planned. If, for example, a business believes that the expected rate of return on building a new factory is 10 percent, would it make sense to build that factory if the business could borrow the funds it needs at 5 percent? The answer clearly is yes. If the expected rate of return on that new factory fell to 4 percent, would the business be willing to borrow funds at that same 5 percent to earn a smaller expected rate of return? The answer should be no. Any potential borrowers make the same basic comparison when they consider making an investment.

The motivations that shape the behavior of savers and borrowers can complicate and delay the adjustments in the loanable funds market necessary to achieve full employment.

Challenge to Price and Wage Flexibility

The successful operation of the long-run model assumes freely flexible prices and wages that quickly and easily adjust to re-establish full employment real GDP. The assumption is based on an economy composed of highly competitive small firms, workers individually negotiating their own wages and benefits, and limited government. In contrast, the short-run model saw a modern industrial economy populated by large firms with some control over the prices that they charge. They were price setters, and not price takers. Workers represented by strong unions had the power to strike when it came time to bargain over wages, hours, working conditions, and benefits.

These developments affected the nature of price and wage flexibility. In describing the long-run model, we stressed freely flexible prices and wages, which easily adjust up or down without any stickiness. In the short-run model, prices and nominal wages are free to rise. What firm would not accept a higher price for its product? What worker would not gladly receive a higher wage rate? In a vivid and telling phrase, Keynes believed that nominal prices and wages in modern economies are "sticky downward." Firms that dominated a particular market could and would resist cutting prices on their output if possible. Unionized workers could successfully resist wage cuts.

Price Inflexibility. We first look at how price inflexibility places a critical roadblock in the achievement of full employment real GDP in the long-run model. A temporary lack of aggregate demand has the potential to generate unemployment and recession. Firms quickly find that they are producing more than is being demanded. Inventories of unsold goods increase, signaling producers to somehow accommodate the declining demand.

In the long-run model, consider one firm in a highly competitive climate that cuts its product prices to sell more and to exhaust excess inventories. All the producers are forced by vigorous competitive pressure to do the same. Overall product prices fall. Firms need not cut back on output or employment.

Now consider the short-run model's view. If the firms have even a modest amount of control over the prices they charge, there is less competitive pressure for them to cut their prices. These firms will respond to the falling aggregate demand by cutting output and employment rather than the prices that they charge. Full employment production disappears in the face of falling aggregate demand. Until prices can adjust fully, the economy will remain at a less-than-full employment situation. There is no natural competitive pressure in the product market to restore full employment real GDP.

Wage Inflexibility. We now examine the same situation of diminished demand and observe its impact in a labor market where the workers are represented by unions. In the long-run model, when firms are producing more than is being demanded, individual workers, bargaining only for themselves, each accepted lower nominal wages to keep their jobs. Now imagine what would happen if the boss tells the employees that the firm has fallen on some tough times and asks the employees to sacrifice some wages, hours, and benefits to help the company through the crisis. Union workers typically would vigorously fight any reductions in the terms of the contract for which they had originally bargained. This wage stickiness—the reluctance to accept lower nominal wages and fewer benefits—will hinder the ability of the economy to make the adjustments that are necessary to achieve full employment. Employers will have to lay off some workers to deal with the accumulating inventory. Unemployment and recession might prove to be persistent and stubborn as wage rigidities delay the adjustments required by the long-run model.

TEST + *E X T E N D*   Your Knowledge

▶ The Importance of Aggregate Demand in the Short-Run Model

The most fundamental difference between the long-run and short-run models is the reliance on aggregate supply and aggregate demand, respectively. The long-run model stresses the role of aggregate supply as both the engine of the economy and the cure for any and all temporary problems that the economy might face. In contrast, we will see that in the short-run model, the cause and the cure of the macro-economy's problems lies in the behavior of aggregate demand.

By providing the right amount of aggregate demand at the right time, the problems of an underperforming or overheating economy can be cured without waiting for the necessary changes in nominal wages and prices to affect aggregate supply. Figure 23.1 reiterates the impacts that increases or decreases in aggregate demand can have on the performance of the economy.

Panel (a) of Figure 23.1 illustrates the impact of an increase in aggregate demand. As the result of this new aggregate demand, the level of real GDP increases, as does the equilibrium price level. Eventually, this new production level requires more workers. As a result, the unemployment rate ultimately falls. Panel (b) shows the effect of a decrease in aggregate demand. The level of real GDP and overall price level both decline. The reduction in real GDP ultimately causes the unemployment rate to increase.

These two graphs capture the cause of and a cure for the Great Depression. The lack of aggregate demand caused the U.S. economy to suffer falling output, falling prices, and increasing unemployment rate. For the economy to grow again, the short-run model recommends an infusion of aggregate demand to raise output and lower unemployment. In theory, any of the four components of aggregate demand could contribute the right amount of aggregate demand in a timely fashion:

- Consumption expenditures by households (C)
- Investment spending by business firms (I)
- Net foreign spending ($X - M$)
- Government spending on goods and services (G)

In practice, only one of these components has the necessary characteristics that make it the preferred vehicle for changing aggregate demand. To discover that preferred method, we examine each component in the following sections.

FIGURE 23.1

Impact of Changing Aggregate Demand on Short-Run Equilibrium

Increases or decreases in aggregate demand can move equilibrium real GDP higher or lower and also raise and lower the price level. In panel (a), the increase in aggregate demand from AD_1 to AD_2 increases real GDP from $4.5 trillion to $5.0 trillion and the price level to 110. In panel (b), the decrease in aggregate demand from AD_1 to AD_3 decreases real GDP from $4.5 trillion to $4.0 trillion and the price level to 100.

(a) Impact of an increase in aggregate demand

(b) Impact of a decrease in aggregate demand

Get Ahead of the Curve

Apply the model of aggregate demand to analyze the effect of high gasoline prices on the U.S. economic performance.

The Role of Consumption

Consumption is the largest single component of aggregate demand in the U.S. economy, generally representing around 70 percent of total GDP. Theoretically, changes in consumption spending could cure any problem with an overheating or underperforming economy. However, consumption spending is usually very stable and difficult to change. Figure 23.2 illustrates the pattern of U.S. consumption behavior from 1995 to 2004. As you can see, consumption expenditures grew each year within a narrow range of 2.5 percent to 5.1 percent.

Consumption and Income. There are many variables that affect how much households are willing and able to consume, including household wealth and debt, consumers' optimism or pessimism about their economic futures, the ability to borrow and the level of real interest rates, the overall price level, and households' current stock of durable goods. These determinants can have an impact at any particular time. Economists believe that the single most important variable that explains how much households spend is disposable income. Recall that disposable income is the income that remains after all taxes have been paid. In general, as disposable income increases, households typically spend more dollars. However, they spend a smaller percentage of each additional dollar of disposable income. We next quantify this important relationship between changing disposable income and consumption.

Measuring Consumption Behavior: MPC and MPS. How does consumption change as disposable income changes? Consider households that receive more take-home pay as the result of a cut in income tax rates. Economists must determine the impact of that new disposable income on overall consumption in the economy. The concept

FIGURE 23.2

Changes in Consumption and Investment, 1995–2004 (in constant 2000 dollars)

While changes in consumption spending have varied within a fairly narrow range, changes in investment spending by firms have varied more widely during this period.

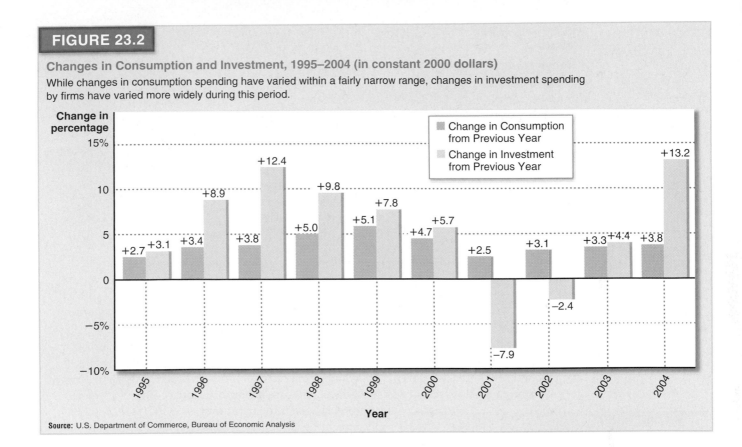

Source: U.S. Department of Commerce, Bureau of Economic Analysis

---

Marginal propensity to consume (MPC)
Fraction consumed of additional income.

that gives us that important information is the **marginal propensity to consume (MPC),** the fraction consumed of additional income. Equation 23.1 shows how economists determine MPC.

$$\text{MPC} = \textit{Change in consumption/Change in disposable income} \qquad (23.1)$$

Suppose that a family receives a tax rebate check for $600 from the federal government and spends $400 of that check as consumption expenditure. The MPC for that family is $400/$600 = 0.67 = 67 percent. This family consumes 67 percent of its new disposable income. In 2004, disposable personal income in the United States increased by $487 billion and consumption expenditures increased by $483 billion. The MPC for the U.S. economy in 2004 was $483 billion/$487 billion = 0.99 = 99 percent. U.S. households consumed 99 percent of their additional disposable income that year.

Typically, as disposable income increases, the percentage of that new income that is consumed (MPC) will fall. For example, an additional $10 in disposable income for an impoverished family will, in all likelihood, be entirely consumed. The same $10 given to a millionaire will probably not be spent. As a household's income and consumption rise, it satisfies more of its basic needs and can begin to save more. As revealed dramatically in many of the films about the Great Depression, households do not think much about saving for the future when they are worried about their next meal. Households that already enjoy a high level of income might prefer saving to buying another diamond wristwatch.

Marginal propensity to save (MPS)
Fraction saved out of additional income.

The complementary concept of the **marginal propensity to save (MPS)** measures the fraction saved out of additional income. Equation 23.2 illustrates how we calculate MPS.

TABLE 23.1

Measurement of Consumption and Saving Behavior

Measure of Consumer Behavior	Definition	Equation	Expected Relationship to Changing Income
MPC = Marginal propensity to consume	Fraction consumed of additional disposable income	Change in consumption/Change in disposable income	MPC tends to fall as disposable income increases
MPS = Marginal propensity to save	Fraction saved of additional disposable income	Change in saving/Change in disposable income	MPS tends to rise as disposable income increases

$$MPS = \textit{Change in saving/Change in disposable income} \qquad (23.2)$$

Consider again the family who receives $600 of new disposable income in the form of a tax rebate check. Because the family spends $400 of that new disposable income, it must have saved $200 of that check. (The only two activities that can occur as a result of this new disposable income are new consumption or new saving.) Therefore, the MPS for that family is $200/$600 = 0.33 = 33 percent. The family saves 33 percent of that additional income. For the United States in 2004, the change in disposable income was $487 billion and the change in saving was $4 billion. Based on this information, the U.S. MPS in 2004 was 1 percent. The value of the MPC plus the value of the MPS must equal 100 percent, because any new disposable income can be only consumed or saved. In the U.S. economy in 2004, the MPC of 99 percent and the MPS of 1 percent totaled 100 percent of disposable income. The expectation is that as disposable income increases, the MPS will increase, because the higher levels of income promote more saving among households.

Table 23.1 summarizes the information about the measurement and expected behavior of typical household consumption and saving patterns.

Households become accustomed to a certain pattern of spending and saving and are often reluctant to alter their consumption behavior. When disposable income declines, households attempt to maintain the previous level of spending. Many of the families and individuals featured in depression-era movies made a valiant attempt to live as they did before the Great Depression, to put up a brave front, and to avoid letting circumstances overwhelm them and their families. Today, in much more prosperous times, Americans tend to be the world's best spenders and worst savers among the major industrial nations, spending nearly

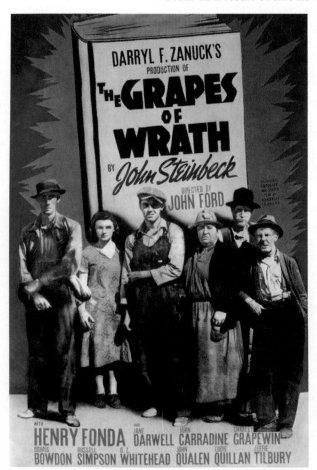

all their disposable income. As a result, there is little opportunity to substantially increase household spending, even if such spending might improve macroeconomic health.

Economists also believe that households look at their expected flow of income when they make their basic spending and saving plans. Any large, unexpected increases in disposable income will not add to a household's estimation of typical income over time and will not cause a household to change its spending pattern significantly. The lesson for policy makers is that it is difficult to change consumption patterns quickly enough to address short-run fluctuations in the economy.

myeconlab

Get Ahead of the Curve

Use your knowledge of the short-run model to analyze how the sluggish performance of business investment contributes to the poor performance of the U.S. economy.

The Role of Investment

Unlike household consumption, investment spending by businesses (gross private domestic investment) can and does easily change. Looking again at Figure 23.2, we can observe the behavior of investment in the United States from 1995 to 2004. The change in investment ranged from an increase of more than 13 percent in one year to a decline of nearly 8 percent in another.

LifeLessons

Are You Saving Early Enough?

When you think of saving, what is your objective? A down payment on a new car, or a flat-panel TV perhaps? It might come as a surprise that it's never too early to start thinking about retirement savings. Americans are notoriously poor savers. Yet savings will be needed for retirees to supplement whatever Social Security income is available. Retirement counselors typically estimate that a retiree in 2045 will need more than $1 million in total savings to fund a comfortable retirement.

Many people focus on this total savings and are very discouraged to see how much they have to save. It seems as if successful saving for retirement requires a high marginal propensity to save. The amount you save can be much less of a problem if you start saving at the right time. The earlier a household starts to save for retirement, the less it must save at any given time to achieve its goals. Consider someone who saves $1,000 a year at a 5 percent rate of return, starting at age 22. That saver would have over $124,000 in 40 years. However, a person who saved the same $1,000 a year starting at age 42 would accumulate only a little over $33,000 in 20 years. The moral of the story is that for an adequately funded retirement, save early to make sure you save enough.

DILBERT: © Scott Adams/Dist. by United Features Syndicate, Inc.

Reasons for Volatility of Investment Spending. The amount of planned investment in an economy, as you saw in the discussion of aggregate demand, depends partly on the degree of optimism in the business community. Businesses need to determine their expected rate of return on each investment project. John Maynard Keynes described the emotions that cause business expectations about the economic outlook to swing wildly from optimism to pessimism and back again as "animal spirits." Investment spending is as volatile and changeable as the moods of business executives. Investment is also sensitive to changing interest rates. Consider the typically large amount of borrowing involved in business investment and the length of the loans. Relatively small changes in interest rates can dramatically affect the expected profitability. Tax policies that reward firms' investment in new plant and equipment with tax reductions can also encourage investment by business firms.

Thus, although gross private domestic investment changes frequently, it cannot be reliably manipulated. As a result, it is not a good option for policy makers seeking to provide the right amount of aggregate demand at the right time.

The Role of Net Exports

Another contender for altering aggregate demand in the face of changing economic circumstances is net exports. Total U.S. exports and imports represent a huge amount of spending for the economy. If we add the total U.S. exports (X) to the total U.S. imports (M) in 2004, we get $3.1 trillion of total spending in nominal terms, a large amount of spending power that can affect overall aggregate demand.

Net Exports and the Purchasing Power of the Dollar. If the dollar is gaining purchasing power, as we saw in our introduction to aggregate demand, foreign goods cost less in the United States and U.S. exports cost more overseas. The combination of these two events would decrease U.S. net exports. The change in the purchasing power of the dollar internationally explains a great deal of the movement in U.S. total net exports. U.S. policy makers can do little to affect the purchasing power of the dollar. The purchasing power of the dollar is established in a market where more than $1 trillion of foreign currencies are traded every day. Given the huge size of this market, the ability of U.S. policy makers to control the purchasing power of the dollar on a timely basis is minimal. You also saw in our discussion about the determination of U.S. net exports that the economic health of other nations affects their willingness and ability to buy U.S. exports. There is also little that U.S. policy makers can do to improve the health of trading partners in order to increase U.S. net exports and thus overall aggregate demand.

The Role of Government

By process of elimination, the government remains as the last best hope for altering aggregate demand. As seen in Table 23.2, during the early days of the Great Depression in the United States, consumption, investment, and net exports all suffered major declines. Consumption, the major component of U.S. aggregate demand, fell during all four years. U.S. families and households had no ability to increase their spending and provide more aggregate demand. Investment, the other major component of aggregate demand, fell by huge percentages for three of the first four years of the Great Depression. Businesses were wracked with pessimism and had no incentive to invest in new plant and equipment to produce even more goods that they could not sell. Policy makers could see no way to encourage the aggregate demand needed for the recovery of the economy.

TABLE 23.2

Components of U.S. Aggregate Demand, 1930–1933

Year	Consumption Expenditures (C)	Investment Spending (I)	Net Exports (X – M)
1930	−5.3%	−33.3%	−2.1%
1931	−3.1%	−37.2%	0
1932	−8.9%	−69.8%	+5.2%
1933	−2.2%	+47.5%	−12.1%

Source: U.S. Department of Commerce, Bureau of Economic Analysis

Franklin Delano Roosevelt in 1933 and John Maynard Keynes in 1936 both arrived at the same conclusion: Government, through its own spending and tax cuts, could and should provide the aggregate demand needed to cure the economy's short-run problems. The federal government itself could be the spender of last resort, willing and able to spend when all other spending units will not or cannot spend more. At a minimum, the federal government could cut taxes in order to prompt new consumption or investment spending. The short-run model concludes that the government must provide the needed dose of aggregate demand. In the following chapter, we examine the tools of fiscal policy employed by economic policy makers to alter aggregate demand and therefore the performance of the macroeconomy.

TEST + E X T E N D Your Knowledge

1. TEST Following are the figures for the change in disposable income and household spending in the United States from 2001 to 2004. Based on these data, calculate the MPC in each year.

Year	Increase in Disposable Income (in billions of current dollars, from previous year)	Increase in Household Spending (in billions of current dollars, from previous year)
2001	$292.8	$328.9
2002	340.9	314.0
2003	332.2	380.8
2004	487.0	482.6

Source: U.S. Department of Commerce, Bureau of Economic Analysis

2. EXTEND In two of the years listed in the table, the actual MPC was greater than 1.0. What does that indicate about household spending patterns? Explain how MPC can be greater than 1.0 by analyzing MPS during those two years. What might explain the behavior of the MPS in those two years?

Strategy and Policy
All Demand-Fueled Growth Is Not the Same

A large economy needs a powerful engine to make it grow. But not every major economic power relies on the same fuel for its economic engine. Two of the largest economies in the world today are the U.S. economy and the Chinese economy. In 2004, the Chinese economy grew at an annual growth rate of more than 9 percent, over twice the U.S. growth rate. The components of aggregate demand that fuel these two massive economies are dramatically different. In the United States, the major source of increasing aggregate demand and economic growth is the willingness and ability of American consumers to demand goods and services. Consumption expenditures by households represent 70 percent of U.S. GDP. As consumption expenditures grow steadily over time, so does the U.S. economy. Both investment and government spending each represented a little less than 20 percent of total U.S. GDP in 2004. The U.S. trade deficit actually reduced its GDP by about 6 percent.

The Chinese economy, with its much lower per-capita income ($5,600, compared to over $40,000 in the United States), cannot rely on consumption expenditures by their citizens to fuel economic growth. Although China has a huge trade surplus with the United States, its overall trade surplus does not contribute substantially to its economic growth. Instead, the Chinese have relied on investment spending to fuel economic growth. Investment spending has increased dramatically, yielding major increases in economic activity. In 2004, investment in new plant and equipment was 46 percent of total spending in China, the greatest percentage of any major economy in the world. The Chinese government has worked hard to attract foreign investment into China while also investing heavily in their own state-owned enterprises.

The lesson is that it does not matter what component of aggregate demand is growing in a nation, as long as some component of aggregate demand is growing strongly. There is no single correct way to stimulate an economy though growing aggregate demand. The boom in the investment component of aggregate demand fuels Chinese economic growth, whereas consumption fuels the U.S. economy.

Critical-Thinking Questions

1. Using the production possibility frontier, explain the difference between the future of an economy that grows through increasing investment and an economy that grows through increasing consumption?
2. How might the future of Chinese economic growth change as China's economy matures?

► SUMMARY

■ **Emergence of the Keynesian short-run model.** The long-run model of the macroeconomy predicts that in the long run, real-world economies will heal themselves and that any short-run problems will quickly disappear. The Great Depression demonstrated limitations in the operation of this model. The Keynesian short-run model emerged as an explanation of and cure for the problems of the macroeconomy by challenging the adjustment process employed in the long-run model.

■ **Characteristics of the short-run model.** The short-run model of the economy is based on the idea that full employment is not the general rule. Problems with the loanable funds market and sticky prices and wages can postpone the adjustment process so that an economy might not quickly or easily reestablish full employment real GDP.

■ **The importance of aggregate demand in the short-run model.** According to the short-run model, aggregate demand is the main engine of the macroeconomy. The key to understanding the model is the behavior of the various components of aggregate demand. When macroeconomic problems occur, aggregate demand can be adjusted to cure the problem. Consumption spending is not easily changed by policy makers, and investment and net exports cannot be reliably changed by policy makers. Government action to change its own spending and change the spending of households and businesses by tax changes is the preferred way to change aggregate demand.

▶ **KEY TERMS**

Keynesian model 593
Marginal propensity to consume (MPC) 599

Marginal propensity to save (MPS) 599

▶ **PROBLEMS**

1. Why did the U.S. Great Depression cast doubt on the effective operation of the long-run model?
2. Compare and contrast the views of the long-run model and the short-run model about the role of aggregate demand and aggregate supply in the adjustment process.
3. Compare and contrast the behavior of the loanable funds market in the long-run and short-run models of the macroeconomy.
4. Based on the following information, calculate the MPC.

Income	Consumption
$12,000	$12,100
12,300	12,350
12,600	12,600

   a. What is the MPS for this sample household?
   b. If the income increases to $12,900 and the MPC remains the same, what will be amount of consumption at that new level of income?
5. Explain why MPC + MPS must always equal 100 percent.
6. What is the major influence on the behavior of consumption expenditures by households? Why does this influence tend to stabilize consumption expenditures?
7. What is the major drawback of relying on consumption expenditure as the source of needed aggregate demand in the short-run model?
8. What are the influences on the behavior of investment spending by businesses? Why do these influences tend to make investment spending unstable over time?
9. What are the major influences on the behavior of net exports? Why do these influences make it difficult for a nation's policy makers to control its net exports?
10. Why should we expect MPC to fall and MPS to increase as disposable personal income in the economy becomes greater?
11. In what ways did the economic policies of President Roosevelt in 1933 foreshadow the policy recommendations of the Keynesian short-run model?
12. How might one explain the dramatic increase in investment spending in the U.S. in 1933 as shown in Table 23.2?
13. How did the Keynesian short-run model challenge Say's Law?
14. How did the Keynesian short-run model challenge the concept of wage and price flexibility?
15. What does it mean that the government should be the "spender of last resort"?
16. Why can aggregate demand be described as both the cause of and the cure for the Great Depression in the U.S.?

The Keynesian Cross

Keynesian Cross
A model of the economy that focuses on the relationship of aggregate expenditures and total production to determine equilibrium real GDP.

We can gain a greater appreciation for the workings of the Keynesian model by focusing more specifically on the components of aggregate expenditures. We do so by employing the **Keynesian Cross**, a model of the economy that focuses on the relationship between aggregate expenditures and total production to determine equilibrium real GDP. In this appendix, we illustrate the components of Keynesian aggregate expenditures and then include total production to provide an alternative view of macroeconomic equilibrium.

 ## Consumption

Consumption function
The relationship between income and consumption.

We begin by modeling the behavior of consumers. As you saw in this chapter, the major influence on how much households are willing to consume is the level of income. We illustrate this relationship between consumption and income by formulating a simple relationship between income and consumption, known as the **consumption function**. It is shown in Equation A23.1.

$$C = c_0 + c'y \qquad (A23.1)$$

Autonomous consumption
The amount of consumption that is independent of income; that is, the amount a household will consume even if its income is zero.

In this equation, c_0 is the amount that households would spend on consumption even if their incomes (y) equaled zero. We call this irreducible level of consumption **autonomous consumption**, because it is independent of the household's level of income. The idea behind c_0 is that you need food, clothing, and shelter, no matter what your income is. If you find yourself in the unfortunate position of having little or no income, you spend any wealth you have accumulated, such as savings accounts, and eventually borrow, in order to support a minimum level of consumption.

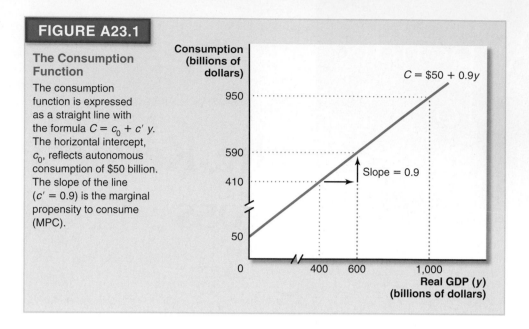

FIGURE A23.1

The Consumption Function

The consumption function is expressed as a straight line with the formula $C = c_0 + c'y$. The horizontal intercept, c_0, reflects autonomous consumption of $50 billion. The slope of the line ($c' = 0.9$) is the marginal propensity to consume (MPC).

Consumption (billions of dollars)

$C = $50 + 0.9y$

950

590

410

Slope = 0.9

50

0   400   600   1,000

Real GDP (y) (billions of dollars)

As your income rises from zero, your consumption expenditure rises beyond this minimum amount of consumption. For simplicity, we assume that it rises at the constant rate of c'. If, for example, c' equals 0.9, then every dollar of extra income leads you to spend $0.90 more than before. We called c' the marginal propensity to consume (MPC) in this chapter, because it measures how much of the marginal or extra dollar of income you spend on consumption.

Equation A23.1 assumes that the consumption function is linear. That is, it assumes that consumption rises by a fixed amount for every dollar increase in income. This is a simplifying assumption that we use to make graphing easier. In Figure A23.1, real GDP and consumption expenditure rise together in a straight line starting at $50 billion of consumption on the vertical axis. The consumption function has a slope of 9/10 = 0.9. As income increases by $200 billion (from $400 billion to $600 billion), for example, consumption spending increases by $180 billion (from $410 billion to $590 billion).

In our example, $C = $50 + 0.9y$. When real GDP is zero, consumption expenditures are $50 billion. When real GDP equals $1,000 billion, consumption expenditures equal $950 billion.

45-Degree Line

We gain greater insight into the consumption function when we compare it with a reference line that rises at a 45-degree angle—that is, with a slope equal to 1.0—from the origin. We plot this reference line in panel(a) of Figure A23.2. Because we measure both the vertical and horizontal axes in billions of dollars, in panel (a) both quantities rise by the same amount as we move along the 45-degree line. For example, as we move from the origin to point A, the level of consumption and income both rise from 0 to $1,000 billion. As we go from A to B, both rise to $2,000 billion. Everywhere and anywhere on this reference line, consumption equals income as households spend all their income and saving is zero.

The 45-degree Line and the Consumption Function

In panel (a), the 45-degree line has a slope of 1.0. That means that real GDP and consumption rise by the same amount as we move along it. At point *A*, both consumption and real GDP equal $1,000 billion, while at point *B* they both equal $2,000 billion. In panel (b), the consumption function lies above the 45-degree line for lower levels of real GDP, and lies below the 45-degree line for higher levels of real GDP. People who receive a low income thus spend more than they earn, while individuals with a high income save part of what they earn. When real GDP is equal to $500 billion, consumption also equals $500 billion and saving equals zero.

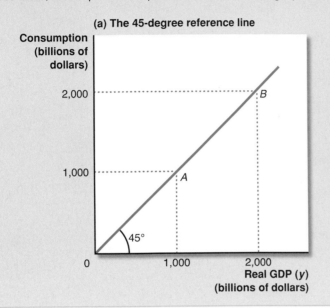

(a) The 45-degree reference line

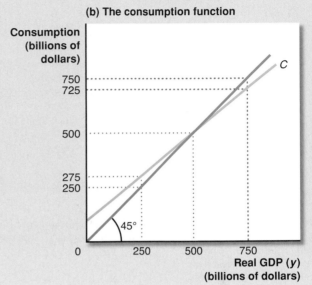

(b) The consumption function

Consumption and Income Comparisons

When we superimpose the consumption function on the 45-degree reference line, as in panel (b) of Figure A23.2, we can compare consumption to income over a wide range of incomes.

At a relatively low level of income, such as $250 billion, the consumption function lies above the 45-degree line. This is because households have income of $250 billion but use their savings or other sources of funds to spend $275 billion on goods and services. The vertical distance of $25 billion between the consumption function and the 45-degree line measures this gap between consumption and income. At a relatively high level of income, such as $750 billion, household income exceeds consumption ($725 billion) by the amount of the vertical distance between the consumption function and the 45-degree line. That same distance measures the amount of saving ($25 billion) that occurs at that level of income. When the consumption function and the 45-degree line intersect at an income level of $500 billion, households are spending all their income on consumption and they neither add to nor withdraw from their savings.

▶ Investment

Unlike consumption, investment in our simple Keynesian model is not assumed to depend on real GDP. Using this simplifying assumption, we will portray the

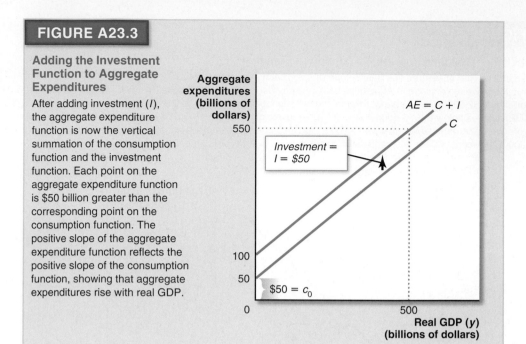

FIGURE A23.3

Adding the Investment Function to Aggregate Expenditures

After adding investment (*I*), the aggregate expenditure function is now the vertical summation of the consumption function and the investment function. Each point on the aggregate expenditure function is $50 billion greater than the corresponding point on the consumption function. The positive slope of the aggregate expenditure function reflects the positive slope of the consumption function, showing that aggregate expenditures rise with real GDP.

Investment function
The linear relationship based on the simplifying assumption that investment spending is independent of the level of income.

investment function as the amount of planned investment in the economy (i_0), which is independent of the level of income in the economy. Equation A23.2 is our investment function.

$$I = i_0 \qquad (A23.2)$$

In this example, we let *I* = $50 billion. The assumption is that although many variables can affect the level of investment, firms are planning to invest $50 billion at any and all levels of real GDP.

In the simplest Keynesian model, including only households and firms, aggregate expenditures equal consumption expenditures by household (*C*) plus investment spending by firms (*I*). Because *I* is constant, adding the two components of aggregate expenditures together consists of adding vertically the layer of investment to the consumption function, as seen in Figure A23.3. Thus, when real GDP is $500 billion, aggregate expenditures are composed of $500 billion in consumption expenditures and $50 billion in investment.

The upward-sloping line *C* + *I* shows that aggregate expenditures increase as real GDP rises. We label our aggregate expenditure function as *AE*.

Government Spending and Net Exports

Exogenous variable
An economic activity decided by outside factors.

We incorporate government expenditure to the model by adding yet another layer to the aggregate expenditure function. If government spending is an **exogenous variable**, or decided by outside factors, then adding the **government spending function** (*G*) to the model augments the aggregate expenditure function without changing its slope, as shown in Equation A23.3.

$$G = g_0 \qquad (A23.3)$$

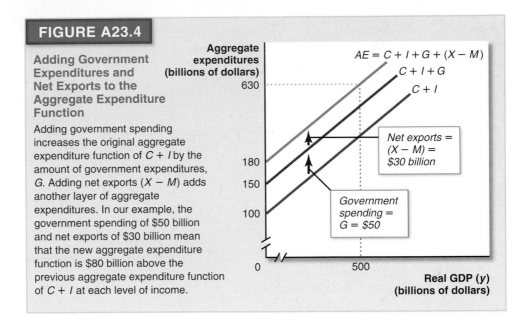

FIGURE A23.4

Adding Government Expenditures and Net Exports to the Aggregate Expenditure Function

Adding government spending increases the original aggregate expenditure function of $C + I$ by the amount of government expenditures, G. Adding net exports $(X - M)$ adds another layer of aggregate expenditures. In our example, the government spending of $50 billion and net exports of $30 billion mean that the new aggregate expenditure function is $80 billion above the previous aggregate expenditure function of $C + I$ at each level of income.

Aggregate expenditures (billions of dollars)

$AE = C + I + G + (X - M)$
$C + I + G$
$C + I$

Net exports = $(X - M)$ = $30 billion

Government spending = $G = $50

Real GDP (y) (billions of dollars)

Government spending function
The linear relationship based on the simplifying assumption that government spending is independent of the level of income.

Net export function
The linear relationship based on the simplifying assumption that net exports are independent of the level of income.

Similarly, net exports $(X - M)$ add a final layer of aggregate expenditures when exports exceed imports, and reduce the amount of aggregate expenditures when exports are less than imports. In our simple model, we will assume that the **net export function** is independent of income and is not affected by changes in a nation's income, as seen in Equation A23.4.

$$(X - M) = (x - m)_0 \qquad (A23.4)$$

This too is a simplifying assumption, because imports typically rise with income, and therefore net exports tend to fall as real GDP rises.

Figure A23.4 adds government spending as $G = $50 billion and $(X - M) = $30 billion to derive the complete aggregate expenditure function with all the major components of spending. In essence, we have added the layers of spending like layers on a cake to obtain the overall aggregate expenditure function of $C + I + G + (X - M)$. Thus, when real GDP is equal to $500, aggregate expenditures equal $630 billion ($500 billion of consumption, $50 billion of investment spending, $50 billion of government spending, and $30 billion of net exports).

Equilibrium in the Keynesian Cross Model

Even after we include all the various components of aggregate expenditures, there is no guarantee that what consumers, firms, and governments want to buy equals what firms want to sell. Recall that the value of goods and services that households and firms are willing and able to buy may not equal the value of newly produced domestic goods and services (real GDP) that firms desire to sell. Given our expanded model, the 45-degree reference line takes on a more important interpretation. Everywhere on that 45-degree line, total production is designed to satisfy total aggregate expenditures. Because the 45-degree line measures the production plans of producers, we will label it as total production (TP).

FIGURE A23.5

Equilibrium in the Keynesian Cross Model

In this figure, we assume that total production is equal to real GDP. Thus the 45-degree line represents total production for the macroeconomy. At $1,800 billion (equilibrium real GDP), aggregate expenditures equal total production at point E, so there are no changes in output or inventory that need occur. At points above and below $1,800 billion, changes in inventory move the economy back toward the equilibrium real GDP.

We can illustrate equilibrium in the macroeconomy by noting where the aggregate expenditure function and total production intersect. The diagram represents the Keynesian Cross. Figure A23.5 illustrates this approach to macroeconomic equilibrium.

At relatively low levels of real GDP, such as $1,700 billion, to the left of the intersection of the aggregate expenditure function and total production at point E, aggregate expenditures are greater than total production. Since households, firms, governments, and the foreign sector want to buy more than firms have produced, inventories unexpectedly fall, and production will rise. To the right of point E (at an income level like $1,900 billion), aggregate expenditures are less than what firms produce, so inventories unexpectedly rise, and production will fall. Only at point E with real GDP equal to $1,800 billion do the actions of buyers and sellers align. There are no unexpected changes in inventory and no required change in output. The macroeconomy is at equilibrium.

To see how changes in aggregate expenditures affect the Keynesian Cross and macroeconomic equilibrium, suppose that the U.S. economy is initially in equilibrium at the income level of $1,800 billion, as in Figure A23.6. New trade policies in Japan and China open those economies to U.S. exports so that U.S. net exports increase by $50 billion to a total of $80 billion.

The increase in net exports adds to the previous aggregate expenditure function, moving the economy from AE_1 to AE_2. Now the level of aggregate expenditures ($1,850 billion) exceeds production at $1,800 billion. Inventories unexpectedly fall, and firms increase production as a result. The higher production also increases incomes. Higher incomes, in turn, increase consumption. Because consumption does not rise as fast as income, though, real GDP eventually catches up with aggregate expenditures at $2,300 billion. A $50 billion increase in aggregate expenditures ultimately increased equilibrium real GDP by $500 billion.

The fact that all adjustments affect output and not prices underscores an important aspect of the Keynesian Cross framework. It is based on the assumption that prices are fixed. Thus, while the Keynesian Cross provides a deeper understanding

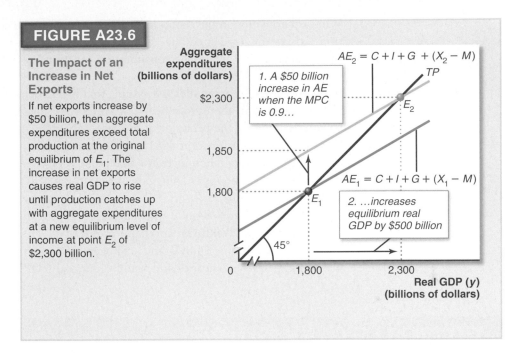

FIGURE A23.6

The Impact of an Increase in Net Exports

If net exports increase by $50 billion, then aggregate expenditures exceed total production at the original equilibrium of E_1. The increase in net exports causes real GDP to rise until production catches up with aggregate expenditures at a new equilibrium level of income at point E_2 of $2,300 billion.

Aggregate expenditures (billions of dollars)

$AE_2 = C + I + G + (X_2 - M)$

TP

1. A $50 billion increase in AE when the MPC is 0.9…

$2,300

E_2

1,850

$AE_1 = C + I + G + (X_1 - M)$

1,800

E_1

2. …increases equilibrium real GDP by $500 billion

45°

0   1,800   2,300

Real GDP (y) (billions of dollars)

of the forces of aggregate expenditures at work in the economy than the long-run model, the Keynesian Cross accurately depicts an economy only for very short periods of time or when it is mired in a deep recession.

SUMMARY

■ Consumption in the Keynesian Cross model is composed of both autonomous consumption and consumption brought about by rising incomes. Investment (I), government spending (G), and net exports ($X - M$) are all autonomous spending in the Keynesian Cross model. Aggregate expenditures are found by vertically adding all the components of total spending.

■ Equilibrium occurs in the Keynesian Cross model where the aggregate expenditure function intersects the 45-degree line, which represents total production. Any changes in any component of aggregate expenditures will change equilibrium real GDP.

KEY TERMS

Autonomous consumption 607
Consumption function 607
Exogenous variable 610

Government spending function 611
Investment function 610
Keynesian Cross 607

Net export function 611

PROBLEMS

1. In Figure A23.1, we found that if the consumption function = $50 + 0.9y$, then when income was $1,000 billion, total consumption was $950 billion.
   a. If the consumption function is now $40 + 0.9y$, what would consumption be if income were $1,000 billion?
   b. If the consumption function is now $50 + 0.8y$, what would consumption be if income were $1,000 billion?
2. Explain why autonomous consumption is a positive amount, so that even when your income is zero, you will still consume.

3. What is happening in the economy at the point where the consumption function crosses the 45-degree line? where the consumption function lies above the 45-degree line? where the consumption function lies below the 45-degree line?

4. In the Keynesian cross model, we assume that investment is unaffected by the level of income in the economy. What would be a more likely effect of the level of income on the behavior of investment?

5. If the consumption function is $100 + 0.5y$, the investment function = $80, the government spending function = $200, and the net export function = $10, what would the amount of aggregate expenditures be if income were $1,000, $2,000, and $3,000?

6. If total production = $4,000 and aggregate expenditures = $4,500, what would happen to inventories and equilibrium real GDP?

7. If total production = $4,000 and aggregate expenditures = $3,500, what would happen to inventories and equilibrium real GDP?

⟨myeconlab⟩ STUDY GUIDE

HERE'S HOW MyEconLab CAN HELP YOU GET A BETTER GRADE

1. Log into MyEconLab and take Practice Test 23-A (to log in for the first time, see page 30 for instructions).

2. Based on your test results, MyEconLab will identify the areas where you need further work and create a personal Study Plan for you.

3. Your Study Plan contains the problems listed below and others like them that will target the specific chapter topics you need to focus on. You'll receive instant feedback and find links to tutorials, animations, and the online textbook to help you study.

4. When you're ready, take Practice Test 23-B and demonstrate how your results have improved.

Section 23.1, Problem 1 In what ways did the Keynesian short-run model challenge the long-run model?

Section 23.2, Problem 1 Which of the following statements is true?

a. The long-run model holds that "supply creates its own demand," that the loanable funds market is self-correcting, and that prices and wages are "sticky downward."

b. The long-run model holds that supply creates its own demand, and the short-run model stresses that demand creates supply.

c. The short-run model maintains that wages are sticky but prices are flexible, and the long-run model holds that wages are flexible but prices are sticky.

d. The long-run model holds that prices and wages are flexible, but that the loanable funds market may be slow to adjust.

e. The short-run model holds that the loanable funds market is self-correcting, but prices and wages may be slow to adjust.

Section 23.2 Problem 2 Categorize each of the following assumptions as corresponding to either the long-run model or the short-run model.

a. The output market is highly competitive, composed of small firms with little market power.

b. The output market is composed of large firms with some market power.

c. Workers, through union representation, have some power over their wages.

d. Workers have little power over their wages.

e. Prices and wages can be slow to adjust.

f. Prices and wages adjust quickly.

Section 23.3, Problem 1 Suppose that the Burke family receives a monthly pay raise of $750. If their marginal propensity to consume is 90 percent, how much of their new income will they spend? How much will they save?

Section 23.3, Problem 2 Which of the aggregate demand components is the preferred method of changing aggregate demand in the short-run model?

a. Consumption
b. Investment
c. Government spending
d. Imports
e. Exports

Section 23.3, Problem 3 Which of the following statements is true regarding components of aggregate demand?

a. The interest rate is the single most important variable that determines consumption.
b. Investment is the largest and most stable component of aggregate demand.
c. Policy makers can easily manipulate and control net exports.
d. Investment depends on interest rates as well as business expectations, so it is an unreliable component for policy makers to manipulate.
e. American households have a relatively high savings rate and low level of consumption.

Section 23.4, Problem 1 The consumption function, investment, government spending, and net exports are as follows for the country of Ecoland:

Consumption: $C = \$150 + 0.80y$
Investment: $I = \$35$
Government spending: $G = \$40$
Exports: $X = \$15$
Imports: $M = \$10$

a. What is the level of aggregate expenditures if income were $1,000?
b. What is the level of aggregate expenditures if income were $1,200?
c. Solve for the equilibrium level of income (output). (*Hint:* Set up the equation as $Y = C + I + G + (X - M)$, and then solve for Y.)

Section 23.4, Problem 2 Use the same information as in Problem 1, but suppose that investment increases by $10 to $45.

a. Calculate the new equilibrium level of income (output).
b. Use the original values for C, I, X, and M from Section 23.4 Problem 1, but suppose that G increases by $10 to $50. Calculate the new equilibrium level of income (output).
c. Does it matter which component of aggregate expenditures changes? That is, would you get a different answer if X had increased by $10? Or if M had decreased by $10?

24

Fiscal Policy

"**A**re you better off now than you were four years ago?" Ronald Reagan first posed this question in the 1980 presidential election when he challenged Jimmy Carter. The simple question reveals a set of assumptions and beliefs held by Americans about their economy and their political leadership. The question is now a common component of U.S. presidential campaigns. Incumbents running for re-election during good economic times use the question to claim credit for any improvements in macroeconomic health during their tenure. Challengers raise the question when the past four years have been rough economic times for the average citizen.

Reagan's question addressed the impatience of many voters and politicians who are unwilling to let the economy take its natural course toward long-run equilibrium. The question also expressed the widely held beliefs that a U.S. president bears a major responsibility for the overall health of the economy and can undertake policies to cure quickly whatever ails it.

Why do voters generally believe that a president should lose his job if too many U.S. citizens lose theirs? How much control does a president actually have over the health of the economy and the business cycle? Should the president be blamed when economic times are bad or re-elected when the economy is doing well? Since 1980, two incumbent presidents (Jimmy Carter in 1980 and George H. W. Bush in 1992) have been defeated, each in part because of perceived economic ills that occurred on their watches. Two other presidents, Bill Clinton and George W. Bush, were re-elected during economic expansions. Politicians have become less concerned about the long-run stewardship of the macroeconomy and more focused on short-run economic policy.

In this chapter, we investigate the role that government can play in the performance of the macroeconomy. We focus on how changes in government taxation and spending can move an economy that is underperforming or overheating in the short run to a long-run full employment equilibrium. You will learn that some economists believe that the government has a crucial role to play in achieving and maintaining overall economic health. We also examine the difficulties that the government encounters in choosing, implementing, and timing macroeconomic policy.

ALONG THE WAY, YOU WILL ALSO LEARN:

- The goals for the government's role in macroeconomy.

- What changes should occur in government taxation and spending to implement an expansionary policy to address an underperforming economy.

- What changes should occur in government taxation and spending to implement a contractionary policy to address an overheating economy.

- The difference between discretionary and automatic changes in government taxation and spending.

- Difficulties that occur in the use of government taxation and spending to cure the economy.

AT THE END OF THE CHAPTER,
THE MYECONLAB LOGO WILL DIRECT YOU ONLINE

- MyEconLab is a resource-packed online homework and tutorial system that can help you perform better in your economics course. To log in for the first time, see page 30 for instructions.

- MyEconLab can help you apply important concepts from the chapter to real-world issues. Watch for the logo to indicate online features about the U.S. and German economies.

- At the end of each chapter, you'll find a special study section that will help you get the most out of your textbook and your instructor's MyEconLab course.

▶ The Goals of Fiscal Policy

The question "Are you better off now than you were four years ago?" implies a short-term time horizon and voices the voters' belief that economic problems should be addressed immediately and answers provided quickly. The Keynesian focus on the short-run behavior of the macroeconomy has therefore colored and shaped the public's perception of the responsibility of a president. Very few presidents will now wait for an overheating or underperforming economy to cure itself. Whether the economy improves immediately or not, voters want to see expressions of concern and an activist approach to the problems of inflation, recession, and unemployment. Since Franklin Delano Roosevelt's first term, the public has believed that presidents have control over the economic machinery of government.

Fiscal policy
Intentional use of governmental powers to tax and spend in order to alter aggregate demand to quickly achieve full employment real GDP.

Fiscal policy is the intentional use of governmental powers to tax and spend in order to alter aggregate demand to quickly achieve full employment. The government uses its powers to tax and spend to provide the amount of aggregate demand necessary to correct two basic economic problems: an underperforming economy and an overheating economy. Government taxing and spending plans can be more quickly and reliably adjusted than the spending plans of households, businesses, and the foreign sector. We discuss the implications of government taxation and spending for the federal government's budget position and the impact of government taxation and spending on interest rates in the following chapter.

The short-run model's goal is the same as the long-run model's: achieve full employment real GDP. The short-run model's approach to achieving that goal, though, is dramatically different in terms of both the medicine prescribed and the recuperation time required.

To address the problems of the underperforming or the overheating economy, we must determine the right fiscal medicine to use and the correct dosage. If we prescribe the right medicine but an excessive dosage, we could move from an economy with one problem to an economy with the other problem without ever achieving the full employment level of real GDP. If we prescribe too weak a dosage, we might not cure the original problem.

▶ Expansionary Fiscal Policy

Expansionary fiscal policy
Use of increased government spending and decreased taxes to increase aggregate demand and real GDP.

Recall from the previous chapter that the underperforming economy's short-run equilibrium real GDP is less than full employment real GDP. This economy needs to be prodded to grow. The solution suggested when utilizing the short-run model is **expansionary fiscal policy**, the use of increased government spending and decreased taxes to increase aggregate demand and thus real GDP.

In Figure 24.1, the economy is initially in short-run equilibrium at point E_1 where aggregate demand curve AD_1 intersects the short-run aggregate supply curve. The short-run equilibrium level of real GDP is $4.0 trillion while the full employment real GDP indicated by the long-run aggregate supply curve is $4.5 trillion. As a result, the economy is underperforming. There is a $0.5 trillion recessionary gap—the income gap between where the economy currently is ($4.0 trillion) and the $4.5 trillion full

FIGURE 24.1

Curing the Underperforming Economy with Expansionary Fiscal Policy

The initial short-run equilibrium is $4.0 trillion, while full employment real GDP is $4.5 trillion. The resulting $0.5 trillion recessionary gap is labeled as *RG*. The government can increase aggregate demand by either increasing its own spending or decreasing taxes to shift the aggregate demand curve from AD_1 to AD_2. With the new equilibrium at E_2, we reach full employment real GDP ($4.5 trillion) at a price level of 105.

employment real GDP. The short-run model calls for expansionary fiscal policy to increase aggregate demand from AD_1 to AD_2. The resulting new long-run equilibrium is at E_2 where $AD_2 = SRAS = LRAS$. Actual real GDP is now $4.5 trillion, the full employment real GDP.

How can the government provide the needed aggregate demand to cure the recessionary gap? It can increase its own spending on goods and services, which will directly and immediately increase aggregate demand. Alternatively, or additionally, it can cut taxes on either households or businesses—or both—to eventually increase aggregate demand. If any of these fiscal policy initiatives is undertaken, aggregate demand will increase. If the proper amount of aggregate demand results, the economy will achieve full employment real GDP. The economy will grow, the price level will be higher, and the unemployment rate will fall to the full employment unemployment rate.

The Multiplier Principle

How do policy makers determine the precise amount of aggregate demand to provide? If the government adds too much to aggregate demand, the new short-run equilibrium real GDP could occur beyond full employment real GDP and yield an inflationary gap. We would then have an overheating economy. However, if the government provides an insufficient amount of aggregate demand, the new short-run equilibrium of real GDP will still be short of the full employment real GDP and the recessionary gap (though smaller) would still exist.

Multiplier principle
Concept that changes in one component of aggregate demand will lead to a magnified change in real GDP.

The concept of the multiplier gives fiscal policy makers the tool they need to provide the right amount of aggregate demand. The **multiplier principle** reflects the fact that changes in one component of aggregate demand will lead to a magnified change in level real GDP. The multiplier principle is based on the interaction of two very basic economic ideas: (1) each $1.00 of new spending generates $1.00 of new income, and (2) each $1.00 of new income generates some new consumption spending (as measured by the MPC).

The Multiplier Effect. Consider what happens when someone in the economy spends just $1.00 more. That $1.00 of new spending means $1.00 of new income for someone else (round 1). That individual with $1.00 of new income will now spend some of that new income. Assume that the marginal propensity to consume is 0.90; households spend 90 percent of any new income. The $1.00 of new income

will generate $0.90 of new spending (round 2). This $0.90 of new spending by one person will generate a ripple of $0.90 of new income for someone else. The $0.90 in new income will generate $0.81 of new spending as the recipient of the income spends 90 percent of that new income (round 3). That $0.81 of new spending generates another ripple of new income for someone else (round 4). This multiplier process will continue as long as someone in the macroeconomy gets new income to spend. The overall result of this multiplier process is shown in Table 24.1. The total amount of new GDP generated will be $10.00 (measured as either new expenditures or new income).

TABLE 24.1

The Multiplier Process

	New Spending =	New Income =	New Consumption +	New Saving
Round 1	$1.00	$1.00	$0.90	$0.10
Round 2	$0.90	$0.90	$0.81	$0.09
Round 3	$0.81	$0.81	$0.73	$0.08
Round 4	$0.73	$0.73	$0.66	$0.07
All remaining rounds	$6.56	$6.65	$5.90	$0.66
Total	$10.00	$10.00	$9.00	$1.00

The Multiplier Formula. A simple formula for the multiplier process allows us to determine the total impact of new spending on income without individually measuring and adding each new ripple of income and spending. The formula for the multiplier is based on the fact that as more of each dollar of new income is saved, the multiplier process weakens. In our example, if each individual spent only 80 percent of any new income (MPC = 0.80), the multiplier process would not have gone on so long and been nearly so strong. We capture the inverse impact that the MPS has on the ripple effect in the Equation 24.1: The basic spending multiplier (m) = 1/MPS, or, because MPC + MPS = 1, as 1/1 – MPC.

$$Basic\ spending\ multiplier\ (m) = 1/MPS = 1/(1 - MPC) \qquad (24.1)$$

To find the overall impact on real GDP of any given change in aggregate demand, we use the simple spending multiplier formula in Equation 24.2.

$$Change\ in\ real\ GDP = Change\ in\ any\ component\ of\ aggregate\ demand \times m \quad (24.2)$$

In our example in Table 24.1, the initial change in aggregate demand was $1.00, and with an MPC = 0.90, the basic spending multiplier is $1/0.10 = 10$. Therefore, our total change in real GDP (measured as either new income or new spending) was $10.00.

The Government Spending Multiplier Process

The solution for the underperforming economy in Figure 24.1 required that the government increase aggregate demand to restore the missing amount of income—the recessionary gap. In Figure 24.1, fiscal policy has to close a recessionary gap of $0.5 trillion. Assume that the marginal propensity to consume for this economy is 0.90. By how much must government increase its spending to close this recessionary gap of $0.5 trillion of missing real GDP? The government spending multiplier process (shown in Equation 24.3) needed to cure a recessionary gap is a specific application of Equation 24.2 where the government spending multiplier = *m*.

$$Increase\ in\ government\ spending = Size\ of\ the\ recessionary\ gap/$$
$$Government\ spending\ multiplier \qquad (24.3)$$

In our example, the size of the recessionary gap is $0.5 trillion and the multiplier is 10. Using Equation 24.3, we find that the increase in government spending must equal the size of the recessionary gap ($0.5 trillion) divided by the government spending multiplier of 10. Therefore, the government must increase its spending by $0.05 trillion ($50 billion). The multiplier process ensures that the total addition to real GDP will be $0.5 trillion, which will exactly close the recessionary gap. The multiplier process allows the government to increase its spending by less than the size of the recessionary gap and rely on the multiplier effect to achieve the desired new real GDP.

The Tax Multiplier Process

The government can also lower taxes to increase aggregate demand. Recall that decreases in personal taxes for individuals will cause more consumption spending and that decreases in business taxes will cause more investment spending. If the government wants to close the same $0.5 trillion recessionary gap in Figure 24.1, by how much should it lower total taxes?

Effect of Taxes on Household Consumption. The impact of tax cuts on households is diluted, because some of the new disposable income will be saved. Therefore, the amount saved will not be available for new consumption and aggregate demand. Suppose that you receive a tax cut that increases your disposable income by $100 per month and that your marginal propensity to consume is 0.90. You will add only $90 dollars of new spending each month to aggregate demand. The other $10 is saved. The effect of a tax cut depends on whose taxes are cut. High-income households have a lower MPC than households with less income. To get the largest impact on aggregate demand of a given tax cut, the tax cut should be focused on lower-income households.

With any tax cuts for households, the decrease in taxes will be partly spent (which affects aggregate demand) and partly saved (which doesn't). Therefore, the multiplier for a change in taxes is inherently smaller in absolute value than the corresponding change required for government spending. In our simple model of the macroeconomy, the size of the tax multiplier will be the basic spending multiplier (m) minus 1. Also, the tax multiplier must be negative to reflect the inverse relationship between taxes and real GDP, because increasing taxes ultimately reduces real GDP and decreasing taxes ultimately increases real GDP. Thus, the tax multiplier = $-(m - 1)$.

Tax Multiplier Equation. The tax multiplier formula allows us to calculate how much taxes must decrease in order to eliminate a given recessionary gap, as shown in Equation 24.4.

"I know we said we'd get you a laptop...
But this will have to do until business is better."

$$\text{Decrease in taxes} = \frac{\text{Size of the recessionary gap}}{\text{Tax multiplier}} \qquad (24.4)$$

Using Equation 24.4, the required decrease in taxes will equal the size of the recessionary gap ($0.5 trillion) divided by the size of the tax multiplier (which is equal to the basic spending multiplier of 10 − 1 = 9). Therefore, to cure a recessionary gap of $0.5 trillion, taxes must be cut by $0.055 trillion ($55 billion). Notice the $0.005 trillion ($5 billion) difference compared to an increase in government spending of $0.05 trillion ($50 billion) to cure the same-size recessionary gap. It takes more in tax cuts than government spending increase to generate a given amount of new real GDP.

Tax cuts also take longer to affect aggregate demand than government spending. Any new government spending is directly and immediately injected into the economy as new aggregate demand. Tax cuts, though, must first increase the amount of disposable income available to consumers and/or the profit outlook for businesses. After households are convinced that the new disposable income is permanent, they will increase their consumption. After business firms decide to undertake new investment in the improved (lower-tax) business environment, it will take some time for the actual new investment to take place.

Table 24.2 summarizes our cure for the recessionary gap using expansionary fiscal policy.

TABLE 24.2

Expansionary Fiscal Policy

Basic problem:	Not enough aggregate demand to achieve full employment real GDP
Cure using government spending:	Increase government spending to directly and immediately increase aggregate demand Correct dose: Increase in government spending = Size of the recessionary gap/Government spending multiplier
Cure using taxation:	Decrease taxes to eventually increase consumption and investment and therefore aggregate demand Correct dose: Decrease in taxes = Size of the recessionary gap/Tax multiplier

▶ Contractionary Fiscal Policy

Contractionary fiscal policy
Use of reductions in government spending and increases in taxes to reduce aggregate demand and real GDP.

The other short-run problem that can plague an economy in our short-run model is the inflationary gap that is characteristic of an overheating economy. The cure for this problem is **contractionary fiscal policy**, which is the use of reductions in government spending and increases in taxes to reduce aggregate demand and real GDP.

In Figure 24.2, the economy is overheating. The actual level of real GDP ($5.0 trillion) at E_1 is greater than the desired level of full employment real GDP ($4.5 trillion) indicated by the long-run aggregate supply curve. The long-run model calls for waiting for the short-run aggregate supply curve to ultimately adjust in the long run to restore full employment real GDP. In contrast, the short-run model calls for

1. TEST During most of the 1990s, the federal budget process employed a PAYGO system. Any new spending in one area of the federal budget had to be matched by an equal decrease in spending in another area of the budget or by an equal increase in taxes. The basic rule was that the government would pay as it goes for new programs by cuts in other programs or by increasing taxes. Suppose that the government wanted to spend $100 billion more on the military under a PAYGO system. What changes would the government have to make in either federal expenditures or in taxes to fund this increased military spending? Which change would you prefer?

2. EXTEND

a. In one scenario, the $100-billion increase in national defense is paid for by a $100-billion reduction in government spending on education. Using a government spending multiplier of 3, what would be the effect on real GDP of this PAYGO process?

b. In a second scenario, the $100-billion increase in defense spending is paid for by a $100 billion increase in taxes. Using the same government spending multiplier and calculating the corresponding tax multiplier, what would be the short-run impact on real GDP of this PAYGO process?

c. If you were interested in increasing real GDP in the short run, which PAYGO process would you prefer and why?

FIGURE 24.2

Curing the Overheating Economy with Contractionary Fiscal Policy

The initial short-run equilibrium real GDP is $5.0 trillion and $4.5 trillion is full employment real GDP. The resulting $0.5 trillion inflationary gap is labeled as *IG*. The government can reduce aggregate demand by either decreasing its own spending or increasing taxes until AD_1 shifts to AD_2. At the new equilibrium E_2, we reach full employment real GDP ($4.5 trillion) with a price level of 105.

the government to intervene in the economy to reduce aggregate demand by the correct amount to restore full employment real GDP.

Government Spending and Taxes

To reduce aggregate demand, the government should either cut its own spending or raise taxes. If done in the correct amount, the aggregate demand curve will decrease, shifting from AD_1 to AD_2, and full employment will be restored, where $AD_2 = SRAS = LRAS$.

Based on our discussion of the multiplier process, we know that the government does not have to decrease its spending or raise taxes by the full size of the inflationary gap. Using Equation 24.5, we can calculate the required reduction in amount of aggregate demand that government spending must provide.

$$\textit{Decrease in government spending = Size of the} \\ \textit{inflationary gap/Government spending multiplier} \quad (24.5)$$

Assuming again an MPC of 0.9 and the size of the inflationary gap of $0.5 trillion, as in Figure 24.2, we know that the amount of the reduction in government spending must equal $0.5 trillion (the size of the inflationary gap) divided by 10, the size of the multiplier. Thus government spending must be reduced by $0.05 trillion or $50 billion to remove the inflationary gap.

We can also find the size of the tax increase necessary to remove the inflationary gap by using Equation 24.6.

$$\textit{Increase in taxes =} \\ \textit{Size of the inflationary gap/Tax multiplier} \quad (24.6)$$

Using this equation, the required decrease in taxes must equal the size of the inflationary gap ($0.5 trillion in Figure 24.2) divided by the size of the tax multiplier (which is equal to the basic spending multiplier of 10 – 1 = 9). In this example, to cure an inflationary gap of $0.5 trillion, taxes must be raised by $0.055 trillion ($55 billion).

The multiplier process assures that small reductions in aggregate demand are multiplied into greater reductions in real GDP. In our simple model of the macroeconomy, we can determine the precise size of the decrease in government spending or increase in taxes necessary to eliminate the inflationary gap.

Table 24.3 summarizes the fiscal policy cure for an inflationary gap.

TABLE 24.3

Contractionary Fiscal Policy

Basic problem:	Too much aggregate demand to achieve full employment real GDP
Cure using government spending:	Decrease government spending to directly and immediately decrease aggregate demand
	Correct dose: Decrease in government spending = Size of the inflationary gap/Government spending multiplier
Cure using taxation:	Increase taxes to eventually decrease consumption and investment and therefore aggregate demand
	Correct dose: Increase in taxes = Size of the recessionary gap/Tax multiplier

LifeLessons

▶ Discretionary Fiscal Policy versus Automatic Stabilizers

Discretionary fiscal policy
Congress and the president take explicit legislative actions to change government spending or taxes.

Table 24.4 summarizes our discussion of fiscal policy thus far. Notice that this table charts only **discretionary fiscal policy**, where Congress and the president take explicit legislative action to change government spending or taxes. In this section, we preview the effect of discretionary fiscal policy on the federal government's budget position and look at a second version of fiscal policy called automatic stabilizers.

Budget Deficits and Surpluses

The federal government is the largest spending and taxing component of any U.S. governmental unit. We examine the impact of discretionary fiscal policy on the federal budget position in detail in the following chapter. For now, note that with expansionary fiscal policy, as the government spends more and/or taxes less, a federal budget deficit will grow or any federal budget surplus will shrink. Contractionary fiscal policy, which decreases aggregate demand in the economy, has the opposite effect. To decrease aggregate demand, the federal government could decrease its own spending and/or increase taxes. A combination of less spending and increased taxes will reduce any existing federal budget deficit or increase any existing budget surplus. There are many issues concerning other economic impacts of the federal budget that we discuss in detail in the following chapter.

Automatic Stabilizers

Automatic stabilizers
Government taxation and spending programs that trigger appropriate increases or decreases in the amount of aggregate demand based on the state of health of the economy—without new legislative action.

Another fiscal policy is the use of **automatic stabilizers**, government taxation and spending programs that trigger automatic increases or decreases in the amount of aggregate demand based on the state of health of the economy—without new legislative action.

Unemployment Benefits. Unemployment benefits are one such automatic stabilizer. When an economy is in a recessionary gap, the short-run model calls for increased government spending to stimulate aggregate demand. With rising unemployment in

TABLE 24.4

Summary of Discretionary Fiscal Policy

Type of Fiscal Policy	Desired Impact on Aggregate Demand	Government Spending	Taxes	Impact on Federal Budget Position	Goal
Expansionary	Increase	Increase	Decrease	Increasing deficit or decreasing surplus	1. Full employment real GDP 2. Eliminate recessionary gap 3. Reduce high unemployment rate
Contractionary	Decrease	Decrease	Increase	Decreasing deficit or increasing surplus	1. Full employment real GDP 2. Eliminate inflationary gap 3. Reduce high inflation rate

a recession, the government pays out more unemployment benefits. This increase in government spending cushions the decrease in aggregate demand that occurs in a recession.

Tax Systems. Tax systems can be another automatic stabilizer. Under a progressive tax system, the tax rate varies directly with the level of income. Those with higher levels of income pay higher tax rates, and those with low income pay a lower tax rate. The U.S. income tax system is a progressive tax system. An underperforming economy reduces taxable income of households, moving individuals into brackets with lower tax rates, and thus preserving some of their disposable income. Consumption spending based on disposable income tends to remain more stable, cushioning some of the pain of an economic downturn. Conversely, during an overheating economy, individuals moving into higher income tax brackets help to cool off the economy without any need for new legislation.

Effectiveness of Automatic Stabilizers. Automatic stabilizers by themselves do not completely cure the problems of recessionary or inflationary gaps. Unemployment insurance payments, for example, do not completely replace the income lost by unemployed workers in an underperforming economy. Higher tax rates in an overheating economy do not reduce aggregate demand enough to eliminate the inflationary gap. Yet automatic stabilizers do keep the economy from moving too far too fast in any one direction. These adjustments limit upward and downward movements of the economy and occur without any specific action by policy makers.

In recent years, several policies have lessened the cushioning effect of automatic stabilizers on the economy. Federal legislation has reduced both the number of tax brackets and the tax rates charged in each bracket. Currently there are six federal income tax brackets, ranging from 10 percent for the lowest-income individuals to 35 percent for those with the highest incomes. Yet because the tax brackets are so wide and the number of tax rates relatively few, large changes in individual incomes due to changing economic conditions generally do not move many individuals from one tax bracket to another. For example, an individual with $70,000 in taxable income would have to lose more than $40,000 in taxable income in order to move to a tax bracket with a lower tax rate. Consequently, the impact of changes in tax rates on disposable income has weakened the role of taxes as an automatic stabilizer. In addition, many public assistance programs have been eliminated, reduced, or made more restrictive. These changes have reduced the impact that changes in the economy have on outlays by the government for transfer payments.

Real-World Difficulties with Fiscal Policy

Get Ahead of the Curve

Evaluate the intended and unintended economic consequences of President Bush's economic policy.

Our discussion of fiscal policy may give the impression that fiscal policy is an effective and precise macroeconomic tool: It seems that all a policy maker must do is calculate the size of the inflationary or recessionary gap, find the relevant government spending or tax multiplier, and implement the correct change in government spending and taxes to restore full employment real GDP. The public perception is that a president, with control over government spending and taxes, should be able to provide the proper policy at the right time. Any lingering problem is the fault of a president who must not be interested in curing that particular problem. Fiscal policy is not that simple for policy makers in the real world. In this section, we examine several practical complications.

Stagflation

President Carter in the late 1970s faced the problem of stagflation, which combined generally rising rates of inflation with higher rates of unemployment. Recall that stagflation is caused by a decrease in short-run aggregate supply. Presidents have very little control over the behavior of the short-run aggregate supply curve. President Carter was the unlucky victim of a supply-side shock from relentlessly increasing oil prices. There was little, if anything, that he could have done to stop the rising energy prices that were causing the stagflation. The use of expansionary fiscal policy to reduce the unemployment rate and stimulate economic growth would have exacerbated the increasing rate of inflation. Using contractionary fiscal policy to fight inflation would have made unemployment worse.

Political Considerations

Government taxation and spending is part of the political process. Getting members of Congress and the president to limit the amount of new spending or tax cuts to the economically appropriate level is easier said than done. Increasing spending or reducing taxes as part of expansionary fiscal policy is politically popular. Given this political bias toward expansionary fiscal policy, we should not be surprised that fiscal policy generally does a good job in fighting unemployment and recessions. Over the years, the United States has had less frequent, milder, and shorter recessions, partly because the correct fiscal policy to fight recessions is also the politically attractive policy. Presidential candidates often find themselves taking pledges to not raise taxes if they are elected and promising new spending programs for important voting blocs. As a result, their options in fighting an overheating economy with contractionary fiscal policy are limited.

Over the last 20 years, U.S. presidents have found it difficult to implement the fiscal policy that they wish. All presidents must rely on Congress for the approval of any discretionary fiscal policy. They can only submit a budget or a tax bill to Congress. During the legislative process, government spending bills tend to increase, due to "pork barrel" spending added by the legislators to benefit their constituents. Tax legislation often ends up with more tax cuts than proposed by a president, as legislators seek to please their constituents. The president's only recourse on spending bills or tax bills that exceed his preferences is the use of the presidential veto of unwanted spending or tax legislation. However, the veto is a very blunt instrument, because the president must veto the entire spending or tax bill, even if the legislation has other spending or tax changes that the president desires. Also, Congress can, by a two-thirds majority vote, override any presidential veto.

Multiplier Problems

Suppose that policy makers could exactly determine the size of the inflationary or recessionary gap and politicians could discipline themselves to vote for only the economically appropriate level of taxes and government spending. The use of fiscal policy would still be muddled by the real-world behavior of the multiplier. Recall that in our examples, we could exactly determine the size of the multiplier. With that multiplier, we then exactly determined the right dose of fiscal policy. The real-world multiplier process is not nearly so precise and predictable. Several limitations of the multiplier process in the execution of fiscal policy compromise its effectiveness and the success of fiscal policy in general.

Size of the Multiplier. The exact size of the multiplier is unknown. Other leakages from the spending stream that occur in the real world are ignored in our model. The real multiplier will be less than the size implied by the value of MPS or MPC. In 2004, the MPS for the U.S. economy was 1 percent. This MPS suggests a government spending multiplier of 100 and a tax multiplier of 99. Many economists estimate the real-world basic spending multiplier to be between 2 and 3. The range of this estimate means that the range of the potential impact of spending on real GDP will be quite large in real economies. For example, a $100-billion increase in some component of government spending would mean that the U.S. economy would have between $200 billion and $300 billion more new real GDP. That is a wide range of error, even in a $12-trillion economy.

Length of the Multiplier Process. The exact length of the multiplier process required to obtain the complete impact of the multiplier in the real world is unknown. The short-run model asserts that the time from the start of new government spending to its complete effect on real GDP is fairly brief and definitely shorter than the time required for the supply-side adjustment required in the long-run model. But is the length of time one month, six months, one year, two years, or longer? Not knowing the timing of fiscal policy in practice makes it difficult to have the right fiscal policy working at the right time. An expansionary fiscal policy designed to increase aggregate demand and jump-start an underperforming economy might end up having its major impact in a subsequent expansion. The increased aggregate demand would then feed inflation.

Overlapping Multiplier Effects. Multiplier effects can and do overlap in the real world. In our model of the macroeconomy, we observe only one change in one component of aggregate demand setting off one multiplier effect. In the real world, there are many multipliers in motion at the same time. At any given time, changes in the direction and amount of consumption, investment, net exports, government spending, and taxes may all create separate multiplier effects of differing strengths. There are major differences, in terms of clarity and control, between the ripples caused by dropping one rock in a pond and by throwing a handful of different-sized rocks in the same pond at the same time. In the latter case, it would be difficult to observe the impact of any specific rock, given the overall turbulence in the pond. In the same way, simultaneous increases and decreases in different components of aggregate demand by varying amounts make it difficult for policy makers to predict the precise impact of any given fiscal policy. At any one time, a president and his economic advisors may be facing a number of competing or complementary trends in aggregate demand, which complicates policy making.

Fiscal Policy Lags

Lags
Time gaps between the origination of a problem in the macroeconomy and the ultimate solution of the problem.

Another complication to using fiscal policy is that the U.S. legislative mechanism is ill-suited to devising and implementing policy that affects the economy in a timely manner. In general, the process of discretionary fiscal policy is subject to **lags**, or time gaps, between the origination of a problem in the macroeconomy and the ultimate solution of the problem. The existence of these lags makes it even more difficult to have the right policy take effect at the right time.

When conducting discretionary fiscal policy, a number of time lags naturally occur. It takes time for policy makers to identify a problem. For example, U.S. GDP statistics are issued every three months by the Department of Commerce. An economic problem could be undetected for three months before appearing in the GDP statistics. After the problem is identified, policy makers must agree on a policy to solve the problem. Then legislation has to be introduced in Congress, fully debated, and finally, signed by the president. Only then will the impact of the fiscal policy begin to be felt in the actual performance of the economy.

For example, the 2001 recession started in March. President Bush called for tax cuts to cure the recession at the end of October, about the time that the recession ended. Congress finally passed the tax cuts in March of 2002, well after the recovery had begun. Any impact of the tax cuts on the economy started to occur exactly one year after the recession began and about four months after the recession ended. The inability of the government's executive and legislative branches to act quickly led some to question the value of discretionary fiscal policy as a useful tool in managing the health of the economy.

Is it fair to ask, "Are you better off now than you were four years ago?" as a political tactic? The short-run model and its emphasis on the effectiveness of fiscal policy seem to suggest that a president can, by altering taxation and spending, control the performance of the macroeconomy. The short-run model also implies that four years should be enough time to cure the economy's problems. However, there are sufficient complications in the conduct of modern fiscal policy to suggest that presidents are not in full control of the U.S. macroeconomy. Presidents are more captives than controllers of the behavior of the macroeconomy. Fiscal policy works well in principle, but not nearly so well in practice.

TEST + *EXTEND* Your Knowledge

1. TEST As you have seen, the goal of tax cuts is ultimately to increase aggregate demand. Using the formula for the simple tax multiplier, calculate the impact of a $500-billion tax cut when the MPC is (a) 0.80, (b) 0.85, (c) 0.90, and (d) 0.95.

2. EXTEND If you were an economic advisor to the president, what would you hope for in terms of the public's use of the additional income provided by a tax cut to maximize the increase in aggregate demand? Check out President Bush's published statement about the possible uses of the tax cut that was eventually passed in 2001 in the section "Real Tax Relief for Real Families," using the links at www.aw-bc.com/leeds/ch24. How do the expectations in President Bush's statement compare to yours?

Strategy and Policy
Is There a Political Business Cycle?

Political business cycle
Theory that politicians will try to manipulate fiscal policy for maximum political and electoral advantage.

In the opinion of many political scientists, voters in U.S. presidential elections focus on the short-run performance of the economy when voting for a candidate. A politician might be tempted to adopt a fiscal policy to accommodate this focus by voters. The **political business cycle** is the theory that politicians will try to manipulate fiscal policy for maximum political and electoral advantage. This temptation is especially great for an incumbent president who can exert some influence over fiscal policy. The politically desirable pattern for a sitting president would be to get all the economic bad news out of the way early in the first presidential term and then engage in aggressively expansionary fiscal policy in the latter half of first term. Only after re-election would it be politically prudent to slow down the economy to control the inflation and to reduce the budget deficits associated with expansionary fiscal policy.

There is only mixed evidence of this pattern of policy in the United States. However, that does not mean that there is no manipulation of fiscal policy. Instead, it might be that manipulation was not completely successful. Certainly, there is temptation to use fiscal policy for political purposes. There is much evidence that presidents and Congress increase government spending in specific states and for certain constituencies in hope of winning their votes.

Presidents ignore this politically sensible pattern of policy at their peril. Presidents Jimmy Carter and George H. W. Bush both adopted a deliberately contractionary fiscal policy in the second half of their term to restrain inflation and reduce the federal budget deficit. In both cases, they were defeated for re-election. President Clinton raised taxes to cut the deficit early in his first term and set the stage for vigorous growth in his re-election year of 1996. President George W. Bush was able to pass tax cuts and government spending increases during his first term. The growth rate of real GDP rose during his first term from 0.8 percent in 2001 to 1.9 percent in 2002 to 3.0 percent in 2003 and 4.4 percent in the election year of 2004.

The impact of fiscal policy can be weak or at least delayed. That possibility has not stopped recent presidents who know that voters hold them accountable for their economic fortunes from trying to schedule tax cuts and spending increases to maximize the political advantages of incumbency.

Critical-Thinking Questions

1. Members of the U.S. House of Representatives are elected every two years, not every four years. Like presidents, incumbents in Congress also like to run on a strong economy. What differences would you expect in the attitude of U.S. representatives in terms of their general willingness to cut taxes and increase government spending compared to that of a president in his first term?

2. In the United States, presidential elections are held at regularly scheduled four-year intervals. In a parliamentary system of government, which is common in many other nations, prime ministers have the discretion to call for new parliamentary elections at any time of their choosing. Would you expect a political business cycle under this electoral system? If so, how might it differ from that in the United States?

►SUMMARY

- **The goals of fiscal policy.** The government, through its taxation and spending, can provide the right amount of aggregate demand in the short run to cure the economy's problems.

- **Expansionary fiscal policy.** When an underperforming economy is suffering from a recessionary gap, government spending should be increased and/or taxes should be cut. The use of the multiplier process illustrates the right amount of aggregate demand that should be added to the economy.

- **Contractionary fiscal policy.** When an economy is overheating and has an inflationary gap, the correct fiscal policy is to decrease the amount of government spending and/or increase taxes. The government spending and tax multipliers reveal the correct dosage of contractionary fiscal policy.

- **Discretionary fiscal policy versus automatic stabilizers.** Discretionary fiscal policy is the deliberate use of legislated changes in government taxation and spending to manipulate aggregate demand. Discretionary fiscal policy takes time to implement. Some changes in government spending and tax rates, called automatic stabilizers, are built into the structure of government spending and taxes and respond immediately and automatically to changing economic circumstances. Automatic stabilizers are not strong enough to prevent inflationary or recessionary gaps, but automatic stabilizers do moderate the severity of those problems.

- **Real-world difficulties with fiscal policy.** In the real world, there may be complications when using fiscal policy. These complications include the existence of problems with aggregate supply not susceptible to government policies, political considerations that affect the ability to cut government spending or raise taxes, uncertainties surrounding the operation of the multiplier, and the existence of fiscal policy lags.

►KEY TERMS

Automatic stabilizers 626

Contractionary fiscal
  policy 623

Discretionary fiscal
  policy 626

Expansionary fiscal
  policy 619

Fiscal policy 618

Lags 630

Multiplier principle 620

Political business cycle 631

1. Complete each of the following statements using the formula given in this chapter for the government spending multiplier.
   a. If the increase in government spending is $100 billion and the MPC is 0.75, the increase in real GDP will be $___ billion.
   b. If the increase in government spending is $50 billion and the resulting increase in real GDP is $400 billion, the MPC must be ___.
   c. If the MPC is 0.9 and the increase in real GDP is $400 billion, government spending must have increased by $___ billion.

2. Explain why the tax multiplier is inherently weaker than the government spending multiplier.

3. Draw a graph of a recessionary gap and show how the use of expansionary fiscal policy can help this economy attain full employment real GDP.

4. Draw a graph of an inflationary gap and show how the use of contractionary fiscal policy can help this economy attain full employment real GDP.

5. Assuming an economy with a full employment real GDP of $600 billion, an actual real GDP of $500 billion, and an MPC = 0.9, answer the following questions.
   a. What type of gap exists in this economy?
   b. What is the size of that gap?
   c. To cure this gap using only changes in government spending means that government spending must (increase, decrease) by $___ billion.
   d. To eliminate this gap using only changes in taxes means that taxes must (increase, decrease) by $___ billion.

6. Assuming an economy with a full employment real GDP of $400 billion, an actual real GDP of $500 billion, and an MPC = 0.75, answer the following questions.
   a. What type of gap exists in this economy?
   b. What is the size of that gap?
   c. To eliminate this gap using only changes in government spending means that government spending must (increase, decrease) by $_____ billion.
   d. To cure this gap using only changes in taxes means that taxes must (increase, decrease) by $_____ billion.

7. What is the difference between discretionary fiscal policy and automatic stabilizers?

8. Why is it more difficult to use the government spending or tax multipliers in the real world than in the short-run model?

9. Complete each of the following statements using the formula given in this chapter for the tax multiplier.
   a. If the increase in taxes is $100 billion and the MPC is 0.75, the decrease in real GDP will be $_____ billion.
   b. If the increase in taxes is $50 billion and the resulting decrease in real GDP is $200, the MPC must be _____.
   c. If the MPC is 0.9 and the increase in real GDP is $450 billion, taxes must have have decreased by $_____ billion.

10. What are the two basic economic ideas that lie behind the operation of the multiplier principle?

11. If there was an increase in spending of $2.00 and the MPC was 0.75, illustrate the first three rounds of new spending and income with a table such as Table 24.1.

12. What is the impact of an expansionary fiscal policy on the federal budget position, of a contractionary fiscal policy on the federal budget position?

13. Historically speaking, has the United States done a better job fighting recessions with fiscal policy it has fighting inflation?

14. What problems does the existence of fiscal policy lags present for policy makers?

myeconlab STUDY GUIDE

HERE'S HOW MyEconLab CAN HELP YOU GET A BETTER GRADE

1. Log into MyEconLab and take Practice Test 24-A (to log in for the first time, see page 30 for instructions).

2. Based on your test results, MyEconLab will identify the areas where you need further work and create a personal Study Plan for you.

3. Your Study Plan contains the problems listed below and others like them that will target the specific chapter topics you need to focus on. You'll receive instant feedback and find links to tutorials, animations, and the online textbook to help you study.

4. When you're ready, take Practice Test 24-B and demonstrate how your results have improved.

Section 24.1, Problem 1 How is the ultimate goal of the short-run model different from that of the long-run model?

a. The long-run model is concerned with unemployment, and the short-run model is more concerned with the re-election of policy makers.

b. The long-run model is more concerned with controlling rising prices than the short-run model is.

c. The short-run model is more focused on problems with inflation, and the long-run model is mainly focused on the problems of unemployment.

d. Both models have the same goal—achieving the full employment level of real GDP.

e. The short-run model is more focused on maintaining a high level of output, and the long-run model is concerned with keeping employment high.

Section 24.2, Problem 1 Expansionary fiscal policy is needed for an _____ (*underperforming/overheating*) economy. It consists of either _____ (*increasing/decreasing*) government spending or _____ (*increasing/decreasing*) taxes.

Section 24.2, Problem 2 Suppose that the level of real GDP is currently $150 billion in Ecoland. Economists estimate full employment real GDP to be $175 billion, and the marginal propensity to consume (*MPC*) to be 0.80. As the leader of Ecoland, should you increase or

decrease government spending in order to push the economy back to the full employment level of output? By how much?

Section 24.2, Problem 3 Use the same scenario as in Section 24.2, Problem 2. However, instead of changing the level of government spending, this time use tax cuts. Should you increase or decrease taxes in order to reach the full employment level of output? By how much?

Section 24.3, Problem 1 Contractionary fiscal policy is needed for an _____ (*underperforming/overheating*) economy. It consists of either _____ (*increasing/decreasing*) government spending or _____ (*increasing/decreasing*) taxes.

Section 24.3, Problem 2 Suppose that the level of real GDP is currently $216 billion in Ecoland. Economists estimate full employment real GDP to be $200 billion, and the marginal propensity to consume (*MPC*) to be 0.75. As the leader of Ecoland, should you increase or decrease government spending in order to push the economy back to the full employment level of output? By how much?

Section 24.3, Problem 3 Use the same scenario as in Section 24.3, Problem 2. However, instead of changing the level of government spending, this time use tax cuts. Should you increase or decrease taxes in order to reach the full employment level of output? By how much?

Section 24.4, Problem 1 Suppose that the economy is in long-run macroeconomic equilibrium. Diminished future expectations then reduce consumption and investment, causing aggregate demand to fall from AD_1 to AD_2, as shown in the following graph.

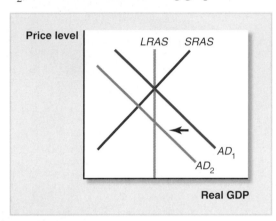

Automatic stabilizers would:

a. Make the situation worse by decreasing aggregate demand (shifting AD_1 left).
b. Move the economy back to long-run equilibrium by increasing aggregate demand back to AD_1.
c. Move the economy back to long-run equilibrium by increasing $SRAS$.
d. Move the economy towards long-run equilibrium by increasing aggregate demand to somewhere between AD_2 and AD_1.
e. Shift aggregate demand to the right of AD_1.

Section 24.5, Problem 1 Which of these graphs shows the stagflation?

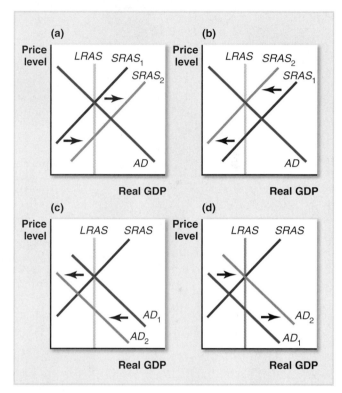

Section 24.5, Problem 2 Which of the following are reasons that fiscal policy is difficult to implement in the real world?

a. The true size of the government spending and tax multipliers is unknown, making precise manipulation difficult.
b. It is politically unpopular to combat an overheating economy with contractionary policies.
c. During times of stagflation, the correct fiscal policy to fight inflation makes unemployment worse, and the correct policy to fight unemployment makes inflation worse.
d. There are significant time lags between the time that a macroeconomic problem occurs and when the policies enacted actually take effect.
e. All of the above are difficulties in using fiscal policy.

25 The Federal Budget and the National Debt

The Smiths and the Joneses are neighbors with annual incomes of $100,000 each. The Smiths have annual expenses of $90,000, while the Joneses have annual expenses of $110,000. It's clear that the Smiths have a prosperous future ahead of them and that the Joneses will soon be in deep trouble. A household cannot live beyond its means for very long. However, that is precisely what the United States government seems to be doing. With the exception of the period from 1998 to 2001, the U.S. federal government has spent more than it has taken in for most of the last half century. In 2004 alone, the federal government had to borrow $412 billion in order to cover its expenses. This amounts to every man, woman, and child in the United States taking out a $1,400 loan (on top of a loan of more than $1,000 the year before that). Critics say such borrowing cannot go on forever. Eventually, these loans would have to be repaid with interest. Repaying these loans, in turn, would bring an abrupt halt to economic growth and would be a crushing burden on future generations. When the U.S. government runs such large deficits, it is as if the Joneses are having a party and sticking their children with the bill.

Many see the Joneses' party as equivalent to the tax cuts enacted by the Bush administration in 2001. In the words of Senator John Kerry, "the president's fiscal policies ... have driven up the biggest deficits in American history."[1]

Others claim that such thinking misrepresents the policies of the Bush administration. Going into debt is not always bad, and in some cases, can

---

[1] Quotes from the presidential debate come from: "The Presidential Candidates' Second Debate: 'These Are the Differences,'" The *New York Times*, nytimes.com. October 8, 2004.

actually be desirable. While being chronically in debt may be a problem, the Joneses might have good reason to be in debt for a short period. Taking out loans in bad times—say, when Mr. Jones has been laid off—and paying off the loan in good times might allow the Joneses to keep their standard of living relatively steady. Temporarily going into debt could also be necessary when there is a family emergency, such as an unexpected illness, or a short-term financial pressure, such as sending a child to college. Without a loan, the family would not be able to afford these important expenses.

President Bush made precisely these claims when he asserted that the $412-billion deficit was due to the economic downturn of 2001 and the national emergency posed by the "war on terror" following the terrorist attacks of 2001. He commented, "We have a deficit because this country went into a recession. . . . The stock market started to decline dramatically six months before I came to office and then the bubble of the 1990s popped. And that cost us revenue. . . . Secondly, we're at war and I'm going to spend what it takes to win the war." According to President Bush, continued economic prosperity and success in the war on terror would quickly eliminate the deficit.

In this chapter, we examine the causes and consequences of the federal budget deficit. To analyze the impact of the deficit, we must build a theoretical framework that allows us to analyze the impact of government budget deficits on the other sectors of the economy. We will show that sometimes economists believe that deficits are justifiable—even necessary. We also demonstrate why most economists believe that large, prolonged budget deficits endanger the well-being of an economy. Finally, you will see when the behavior of households like the Smiths and the Joneses serves as a useful analogy of government behavior and when it does not.

ALONG THE WAY, YOU WILL ALSO LEARN:

- The relationship between the federal budget deficit and the national debt.
- How federal budget deficits can affect interest rates.
- About the debates over the effect of U.S. budget deficits and the national debt.

AT THE END OF THE CHAPTER, THE MYECONLAB LOGO WILL DIRECT YOU ONLINE

- MyEconLab is a resource-packed online homework and tutorial system that can help you perform better in your economics course. To log in for the first time, see page 30 for instructions.
- MyEconLab can help you apply important concepts from the chapter to real-world issues. Watch for the logo to indicate online features about the U.S. federal budget deficit.
- At the end of each chapter, you'll find a special study section that will help you get the most out of your textbook and your instructor's MyEconLab course.

▶ The Federal Budget Deficit and the National Debt

We begin this section by contrasting budget deficits at the state, local, and federal levels. The Jones family's borrowing is an illustrative starting point. When Mr. and Mrs. Jones borrow money, the debt could be as large as a second mortgage on the house. Generally, Erin Jones, a college freshman, has far less access to credit than her parents. After all, Erin has only a part-time job, has no home or car against which she can borrow, and has only recently obtained a credit card. Like the Jones family, governments at the local, state, and federal levels all face the problem of budget deficits. As is the case with Erin, state and local governments face far greater restrictions on how much and how often they can borrow.

U.S. State and Local Government Deficits

Some states have strict rules against borrowing any funds. Such states must cut spending or raise taxes in order to meet any budget shortfalls. Most states have more flexibility, but they still operate within very tight limits. Some states cannot draw up a budget that anticipates a deficit. They are permitted to have a deficit, however, if the shortfall results from an unanticipated economic downturn that has caused expenditures to rise and revenues to fall. Other states allow a budget deficit, but do not permit it to be larger than surpluses that the state has accumulated in previous years. Such restrictions significantly limit the size of deficits at the state level. The projected total deficit for all 50 states in 2005 was roughly $40 billion, about one-ninth the size of the projected federal budget deficit. Because the federal deficit dwarfs the deficits at other levels of government, we restrict our attention in the remainder of this chapter to the federal budget deficit.

The U.S. Federal Budget Deficit

Figure 25.1 shows that over the last 75 years, the United States has run deficits far more often than surpluses. The figure also shows that federal budget deficits are frequently associated with war. When at war, a government needs immediate access to massive amounts of funds to equip and pay armies. While such expenditures are often desirable, and sometimes necessary, governments are generally reluctant to fund them by raising taxes. The areas shaded in red in Figure 25.1 show large increases in the U.S. federal budget deficit during its involvement in conflicts, particularly World War II (1941–1945). Lesser spikes occurred during the Korean War (1950–1953), the Vietnam War (1965–1975), and the first Gulf War (1991). Some of the current deficit is due to government spending on the conflict in Iraq and the war on terrorism.

Though war explains many of the federal budget deficits, deficits have also occurred during peacetime. Many of the peacetime deficits result from the business cycle. Recessions that lasted more than 12 months are shaded in blue in Figure 25.1. The link between deficits and the ups and downs of the economy is less obvious, but no less important, than the link between deficits and war. The first major peacetime deficit in Figure 25.1 occurred during the Great Depression of the 1930s. More recently, deficits have coincided with the recessions of 1981–1982, 1990–1991, and 2001.

Notice also in Figure 25.1 that the deficits of the 1980s and the 2000s are much larger than previous deficits. In 2004, the U.S. federal government spent roughly $412 billion more than it raised in taxes. This figure is more than eight times greater than the deficit of $47.6 billion that the U.S. government ran in 1944 at the height of World War II. Further, it is more than 100 times greater than the $3.6 billion deficit of 1934, when the U.S. economy was begginning to recover from the Great Depression.

While frightening at first glance, these figures are in some ways misleading. For example, although the deficit of 2004 was much larger than the deficit of 1934 or 1944, the price level was also much higher. A $50-billion deficit today is a much smaller claim on resources than it was 60 or 70 years ago and is therefore much less

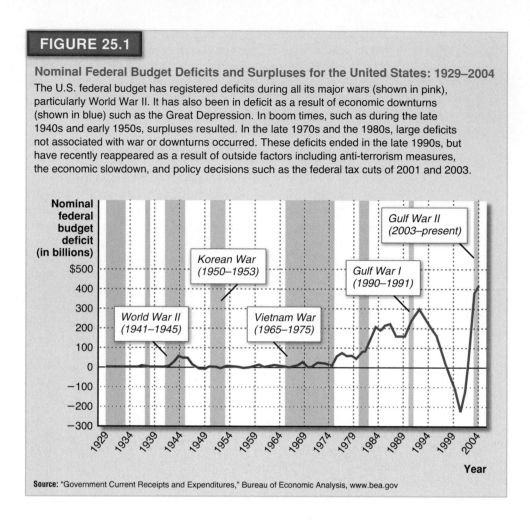

Nominal Federal Budget Deficits and Surpluses for the United States: 1929–2004

The U.S. federal budget has registered deficits during all its major wars (shown in pink), particularly World War II. It has also been in deficit as a result of economic downturns (shown in blue) such as the Great Depression. In boom times, such as during the late 1940s and early 1950s, surpluses resulted. In the late 1970s and the 1980s, large deficits not associated with war or downturns occurred. These deficits ended in the late 1990s, but have recently reappeared as a result of outside factors including anti-terrorism measures, the economic slowdown, and policy decisions such as the federal tax cuts of 2001 and 2003.

Source: "Government Current Receipts and Expenditures," Bureau of Economic Analysis, www.bea.gov

burdensome today than it once was. Because it does not account for inflation, Figure 25.1 shows the **nominal deficit**, the dollar value of the federal budget deficit. To compare such widely separated years, we use the real deficit, a measure of the deficit that accounts for inflation. The **real deficit** represents the purchasing power of the federal budget deficit. Figure 25.2 shows that accounting for inflation moderates the extreme rise of the deficit in recent years. Still, the deficits since 1980 rival those of World War II, and they dwarf those of any other year, including years during the Great Depression.

The National Debt

The federal budget deficit shows how much the federal government borrows in any one year. The federal government's total obligations are given by the **national debt**, the sum of all prior federal deficits and surpluses. The U.S. national debt reflects all the accumulated federal budget deficits and surpluses from George Washington to George W. Bush. As Figures 25.1 and 25.2 show, the U.S. government has run many more deficits than surpluses in the last 75 years. As a result, its national debt is much larger than the federal budget deficit in any one year, surpassing $8 trillion in 2005. Over $1 trillion of debt was added by the deficits that occurred between 2002 and 2005. What is the impact of such large budget deficits and the national debt on the economy? To answer this critical question, we must first establish a framework in which to evaluate that impact.

Nominal deficit
The dollar value of the federal budget deficit.

Real deficit
The purchasing power of the federal budget deficit.

National debt
The sum of all prior federal deficits and surpluses.

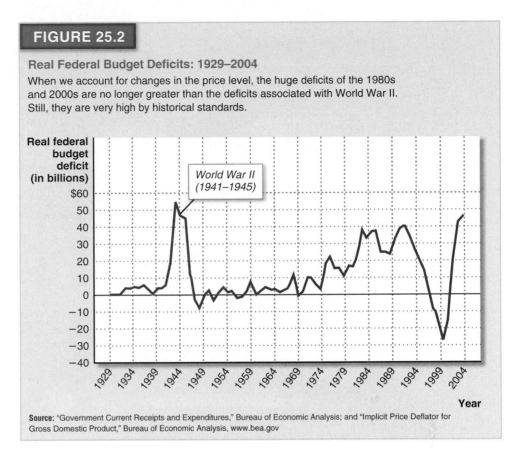

FIGURE 25.2

Real Federal Budget Deficits: 1929–2004

When we account for changes in the price level, the huge deficits of the 1980s and 2000s are no longer greater than the deficits associated with World War II. Still, they are very high by historical standards.

Source: "Government Current Receipts and Expenditures," Bureau of Economic Analysis; and "Implicit Price Deflator for Gross Domestic Product," Bureau of Economic Analysis, www.bea.gov

►The Impact of Budget Deficits on Interest Rates

One reason that economists worry about the deficit is their concern about its effect on interest rates. Unlike the Joneses, the U.S. government is such a large borrower that its behavior affects the terms at which firms and households are able to borrow. In this section, we review how interest rates are set in the loanable funds market and use that framework to see how the federal budget deficit can affect interest rates.

The Federal Government and the Loanable Funds Market

When the federal government (or any state or local government) spends more money than it receives in tax revenue, it must somehow acquire additional funds. In the United States, the government does not directly control either the quantity of money in circulation or the quantity of loanable funds. As a result, it can make up the shortfall only by borrowing on the loanable funds market.

Unlike the Joneses, the U.S. government has no discretion regarding the amount it borrows. Much of its spending is set ahead of time; if tax revenues do not cover its obligations, the government has no choice but to borrow. It *must* borrow the full amount of the deficit, regardless of the interest rate. Consequently, the government seldom considers the costs and benefits of borrowing. Households (such as the Joneses) and firms are much more sensitive to interest rates when deciding how much to borrow. If interest rates are high, the Joneses might decide to borrow less and buy a used car rather than a new one. When interest rates are low, they might borrow more and buy a new car.

The National Debt Clock

Growing concern over the national debt has led concerned groups to remind us of how much the federal government owes. This publicity has taken the form of Web sites and this sign, which shows the debt in mid-2003. By mid-2005, the debt had surpassed $8 trillion.

FIGURE 25.3

A Higher Federal Budget Deficit Leads to Higher Interest Rates

If the government runs a budget deficit, then it must borrow, and the supply curve for private loanable funds shifts to the left by $400 billion. ($0.4 trillion), from S_1 to S_2, the amount of the deficit. Because the supply curve has shifted to the left, the equilibrium real interest rate rises from three percent to five percent. Firms and consumers borrow less and spend less on investment and consumption, which in turn results in crowding out.

When the government runs a budget deficit of $400 billion, it reduces the supply of loanable funds available for private borrowers in the loanable funds market by $400 billion. In Figure 25.3, the supply of loanable funds available for the private sector shifts to the left from S_1 to S_2 by $400 billion ($0.4 trillion), the amount of the government borrowing. The leftward shift of the supply curve creates excess demand at the original equilibrium interest rate of three percent. Private borrowers are willing and able to borrow $1.0 trillion, but private lenders are willing and able to make only $0.6 trillion available. The excess demand causes the equilibrium interest rate to rise from three percent to five percent. At this higher interest rate, borrowing by the private sector falls from $1.0 trillion to $0.8 trillion.

Crowding Out

Crowding out
Occurs when deficit spending by the government displaces private spending.

Decreased private borrowing means that investment by firms in new plant and equipment and the consumption of items like cars and houses by households both fall. **Crowding out** occurs when deficit spending by the government displaces spending by firms and households.

Short-Run Crowding-Out Effects. In the short run, crowding out makes expansionary fiscal policy less effective. Consider federal government tax cuts intended to stimulate the economy. As you saw in the prior chapter, the tax cut stimulates aggregate demand. Because lower taxes add to GDP, the tax multiplier is negative. Suppose, for example, that it equals –4. A tax cut of $100 billion would cause real GDP to increase by $400 billion: –4 × (–$100 billion) = $400 billion.

Figure 25.4 illustrates the effect of the tax cut as a rightward shift of the aggregate demand curve from AD_1 to AD_2. In this case, the equilibrium level of GDP rises from $11.4 trillion to $11.8 trillion. The story, however, does not end with the increase in real GDP. The tax cut also increases the federal budget deficit. As in Figure 25.3, the greater deficit causes the supply of loanable funds to fall and the interest rate to rise. Because the interest rate is the price of borrowing, higher interest rates also cause the amount of borrowing by households and firms to fall. This decline, in turn, causes consumption by households and investment by firms to fall. Because consumption and investment are components of aggregate demand, aggregate demand falls as well. The expansionary impact of the tax cut is therefore partly offset by the decline in private spending that results from higher interest

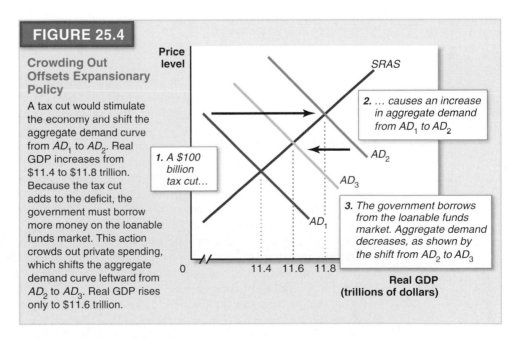

FIGURE 25.4

Crowding Out Offsets Expansionary Policy

A tax cut would stimulate the economy and shift the aggregate demand curve from AD_1 to AD_2. Real GDP increases from $11.4 to $11.8 trillion. Because the tax cut adds to the deficit, the government must borrow more money on the loanable funds market. This action crowds out private spending, which shifts the aggregate demand curve leftward from AD_2 to AD_3. Real GDP rises only to $11.6 trillion.

Price level

SRAS

2. ... causes an increase in aggregate demand from AD_1 to AD_2

1. A $100 billion tax cut...

AD_2

AD_3

AD_1

3. The government borrows from the loanable funds market. Aggregate demand decreases, as shown by the shift from AD_2 to AD_3

0   11.4 11.6 11.8

Real GDP (trillions of dollars)

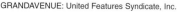
GRANDAVENUE: United Features Syndicate, Inc.

FIGURE 25.5

The Long-Run Impact of a Federal Budget Deficit

When the federal government cuts taxes, it increases the deficit in order to expand income and consumption. In effect, it moves the economy from point A_1 inside PPF_1 to point B_1 on the boundary. Point B_1, however, shows that expanding current consumption comes at the expense of capital goods. As a result, the economy may not be able to produce as much in the future. PPF_1 (in dark green) expands only to PPF_2 (in green) due to the shift from capital goods to consumption goods, and output grows only to point B_2 rather than to point A_2 on PPF_3 (in light green).

(Graph: Consumption goods on vertical axis, Capital goods on horizontal axis. Curves PPF_1, PPF_2, PPF_3 shown. Points: A_1 below B_1; B_1 on PPF_1; B_2 on PPF_2; A_2 on PPF_3.)

---

rates. In Figure 25.4, crowding out reduces the rightward shift of the aggregate demand curve to AD_3. In this example, real GDP rises to only $11.6 trillion as opposed to $11.8 trillion.

Long-Run Crowding-Out Effects. Crowding out may also have longer-term effects. Suppose, for example, that a tax cut succeeds in restoring the economy to full employment. We illustrate the increase in production by moving the amount of capital goods and consumption goods produced from point A_1 inside the economy's initial production possibilities frontier (PPF_1, shown in dark green) to point B_1 on the frontier of PPF_1, as shown in Figure 25.5.

When tax cuts crowd out private investment, they increase the overall level of production and alter the mix of goods produced. Suppose that the expansionary fiscal policy crowds out only private investment. The economy then produces fewer capital goods and more consumption goods, so point B_1 lies above and to the left of point A_1. As you saw in Chapter 2, an economy that produces fewer capital goods reduces its future capacity to produce. In terms of Figure 25.5, it might grow only to point B_2 on PPF_2 (in green) rather than to point A_2 on PPF_3 (in light green). Increasing consumption at the expense of investment today could mean that the economy will be on a lower PPF in the future. That is, it will be able to produce fewer capital goods *and* fewer consumption goods.

TEST + *E X T E N D* Your Knowledge

1. TEST Suppose that the federal government wishes to expand real GDP by increasing spending. If the government spending multiplier is 3, how much must it spend to increase real GDP by $642 billion? If the government does not change any other policy, what happens to the federal budget deficit as a result of the additional spending? What does the change in the federal budget deficit do to the market for the loanable funds market? How would the changes in the loanable market funds affect the impact of the increased government spending on real GDP?

2 . E X T E N D Suppose that the government is trying to cool off an overheated economy. It does so by reducing government spending by the same amount as in the left column's TEST question. How would a tax *increase* affect the federal budget? How would the change in the federal budget affect the loanable funds market? How would the change in the market for the loanable funds market affect the ability of the government to reduce economic activity?

▶ Debate Over the Federal Budget Deficit and the National Debt

Get Ahead of the Curve

Evaluate former Federal Reserve Chairman Alan Greenspan's argument that federal budget deficits are "unsustainable."

Democrats and Republicans have feuded for generations over the dangers posed by the federal budget deficit. Ironically, the parties have switched sides in recent decades. For many years, Republicans fiercely opposed federal budget deficits. They had even proposed amending the Constitution to outlaw them. Democrats had fought such attempts to balance the budget. They felt that the restrictions on spending that would result from imposing a balanced budget on the federal government would do more harm to the economy than the deficits themselves. With the election of Ronald Reagan in 1980, those positions began to change. Today, Democrats bemoan the deficit, while Republicans claim that raising taxes would cause greater harm than the deficit does. Is the deficit a clear and present danger to your future, or is it just a passing annoyance? In this section, we present two opposing views of the deficit. One argument downplays the significance of deficits in general. The other notes that, while deficits may be undesirable, the deficits of the 2000s are not particularly dangerous.

Why We Should Not Worry About the Federal Budget Deficit and the National Debt

Some economists believe that the reappearance of deficits in 2001 does not endanger the economy. While these economists generally do not favor deficits, they feel that the deficits were unavoidable, given the state of the economy and the military actions taken in the wake of September 11. Moreover, they believe that the dollar amount of the deficit overstates the burden it imposes, even when one accounts for inflation.

Cyclical Deficits and Automatic Stabilizers. As you saw earlier, the Joneses might want to borrow money from time to time if they know that cash-strapped times will be followed by prosperous times. Farmers frequently face this situation. The bulk of their expenses—planting, tending, and harvesting their crops or raising their livestock—comes long before they can sell their produce and generate any revenue. They often bridge the gap between sowing and reaping by taking out loans. The same can be said of the U.S. economy. A downturn, such as the 2001 recession, naturally causes the federal budget deficit to rise. The recovery that follows reduces the deficit, and might even result in a budget surplus. According to this reasoning, federal budget deficits are countercyclical—rising in bad times and falling in good times. The budget might not be in balance at any one moment. However, periodic deficits and surpluses offset each other over time.

The regular movement of the deficit occurs because government receipts are procyclical: Tax revenues rise in good times as the incomes of firms and households increase, and they fall in bad times. In contrast, many government transfer payments are countercyclical. They rise as the incomes of firms and households decline. As the economy contracts, cyclical unemployment rises, and an increasing number of workers become eligible for unemployment insurance. At the same time, more families sink into poverty. As a result, they become eligible for Temporary Assistance for Needy Families (TANF), a federal program designed to provide short-term aid to families in economic distress. With tax revenues falling and transfer payments rising, deficits naturally arise. We call such deficits **cyclical deficits** because they rise and fall over the business cycle. Because they will disappear as the economy recovers, cyclical deficits should not add significantly to the national debt. During economic expansions, revenue rises and transfer payments fall, resulting in a surplus. The surpluses in good times offset the deficits in bad times, leaving the overall debt unchanged.

According to this point of view, trying to balance the budget during an economic downturn would be irresponsible and self-defeating. Cutting spending or raising taxes during a recession would put contractionary pressure on the economy at a time when the government wants the economy to expand. In addition, reinforcing the downturn causes transfer payments to rise and tax receipts to fall. As a result, pursuing a balanced budget by trying to eliminate a cyclical deficit could cause the deficit to increase. Advocates of this point of view say that the government should take a broader view of the federal budget deficit. Rather than balancing the budget every year, it should seek a balance over the course of the business cycle, allowing for periodic surpluses and deficits.

In addition, as you saw in an earlier chapter, the cyclical deficit provides the economy with automatic stabilizers. The decline in tax revenues and increase in government outlays during a recession increase aggregate demand. This process stimulates economic activity even if the government undertakes no new discretionary policy. During an expansion, higher taxes and lower outlays help to cool off the economy without any need for further legislation. Trying to balance the budget when deficits or surpluses arise naturally would reduce the ability of the economy to right itself automatically.

The recession of 2001 lasted only from March to October, so the cyclical deficits should not have lasted long. It certainly does not explain a turnaround of more

Cyclical deficits
Deficits that result from the movement of the business cycle.

than $650 billion between 2001 and 2004. The end of the recession, however, roughly coincided with the terrorist attacks of September 11, 2001. Since then, the United States has had to finance wars in both Afghanistan and Iraq and vastly increase domestic antiterrorist spending. Military expenditures in Iraq have averaged about $64 billion per year, while expenditures in Afghanistan have averaged about $14 billion. In addition, spending by the U.S. Department of Homeland Security in 2004 was just over $36 billion. If we assume that none of this spending would have taken place in the absence of the "war on terror," then these costs have added about $100 billion per year to federal government expenditure. In the absence of additional revenue, they have added $100 billion to the deficit. Although $100 billion is a substantial sum, it accounts for less than one-fourth of the total deficit in 2004 and less than one-sixth of the about-face from the surplus between 2000 and 2004.

The Current Debt and Deficit Figures are Deceiving. While the theory illustrated in Figure 25.3 looks logical enough, economists have failed to establish a clear link between the size of government deficits or the national debt and interest rates in reality. For example, the federal budget went from a surplus of almost $130 billion in 2001 to a deficit of over $400 billion in 2004, a net decline of over a half-trillion dollars. However, the real interest rate fell from over six percent to about three percent. The seeming conflict between theory and reality has been the subject of heated debate in macroeconomics.

Some argue that the deficit has not caused interest rates to rise, because the deficit is not as large as the dollar figure suggests. They claim that the effects shown in Figure 25.1 and even Figure 25.2 give a misleading impression of the burden of the deficit, because neither of them shows the ability of the government to pay its debts. While the nominal and real deficits may have increased, so have nominal and real GDP. As the U.S. economy has grown, its ability to repay its debt has also grown.

To see the relationship between the deficit and GDP, let's consider two mortgages taken out by the Joneses. When they bought their first home, the Joneses took out a $50,000 mortgage and made monthly payments of $350. When they bought a new home ten years later, they took out a $125,000 mortgage and made monthly payments of $875. At first glance, it seems obvious that the debt burden of the second mortgage is the heavier of the two. Yet this assessment ignores the fact that the Joneses' combined income was only $30,000 per year when they took out their first mortgage. The annual burden imposed by the mortgage payments, 12 × $350 = $4,200, was 14 percent of their annual income ($4,200/$30,000 = 0.14). With a current income of $100,000, the Joneses find the annual mortgage payments, 12 × $875 = $10,500, more affordable even though they are more than twice as high. The reason is that the current payments are only 10.5 percent of their current annual income ($10,500/$100,000 = 0.105).

We apply the same reasoning to the U.S. economy in Figure 25.6, which shows the ratio of the federal budget deficit to GDP from 1929 through 2004.[2] Notice that the ratio of the deficit to GDP since 2001 is not very large by historical standards. Recall that Figure 25.1 showed that the federal budget deficit in 1944 was about $48 billion, less than one-eighth the size of the deficit in 2004. Figure 25.6 shows

---

[2] Because we discount both nominal GDP and the nominal deficit by the same factor when we compute real GDP and the real deficit, it does not matter whether we use the ratio of the nominal deficit to nominal GDP or the real deficit to real GDP. The answer in both cases is the same.

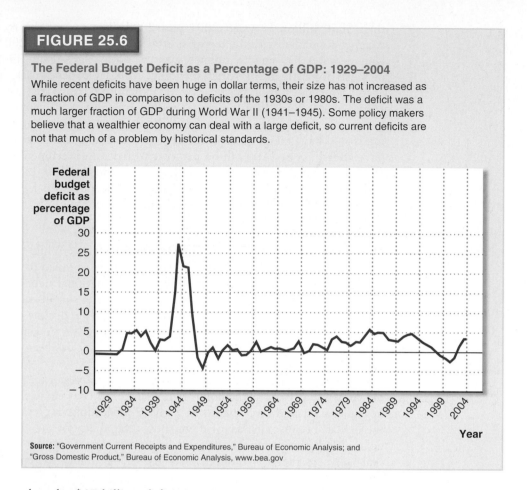

FIGURE 25.6

The Federal Budget Deficit as a Percentage of GDP: 1929–2004

While recent deficits have been huge in dollar terms, their size has not increased as a fraction of GDP in comparison to deficits of the 1930s or 1980s. The deficit was a much larger fraction of GDP during World War II (1941–1945). Some policy makers believe that a wealthier economy can deal with a large deficit, so current deficits are not that much of a problem by historical standards.

Federal budget deficit as percentage of GDP

Year

Source: "Government Current Receipts and Expenditures," Bureau of Economic Analysis; and "Gross Domestic Product," Bureau of Economic Analysis, www.bea.gov

that the $47 billion deficit in 1944 was over 20 percent of GDP, while the much larger deficit of 2004 was much more affordable, about 3.5 percent of GDP.

Household Debt versus National Debt. Defenders of the deficit also point out that the national debt differs from household debt in two important ways. First, while the Joneses must eventually repay their loans, the government does not ever have to repay its debt. The federal government can raise funds much more readily than any household (or firm or state or local government). If it has to do so, the federal government can repay its debts by raising taxes and reducing its spending. As long as lenders believe that the government *can* raise taxes or cut spending to repay its debts, they are unlikely to insist that it do so. As a result, the government can effectively pay off its old loans by taking out new loans. This process allows the government to be in debt forever if it so chooses.

The federal government can go on borrowing indefinitely because repaying much of the debt is only a transfer, not a net burden on the economy. The government owes about one-third of its debt to private U.S. lenders, such as banks, insurance companies, and pension funds. The effect is roughly like Erin Jones's borrowing money from her parents to buy a car. She is in debt to her parents and might be poorer in the future because of it, but the Joneses as a whole are no worse off. Whatever Erin pays, her parents receive, so there is no change in the well-being of the family as a whole.

At the federal level, some of the higher taxes you must pay as a result of the federal debt go toward paying off that savings bond you got for your birthday. As long as repaying the debt does not impose a huge burden on the economy, lenders will be

LifeLessons

Life Is Short, Unless You're the Government

As noted earlier, the government never has to get out of debt. Corporations can also owe money indefinitely. Why, then, can't the Joneses? One important reason lies in a key difference between governments and corporations on the one hand, and households on the other.

At least in theory, governments and corporations can live forever. When the Bush administration leaves Washington, another administration will take its place. When Bill Gates steps down at Microsoft, another CEO will step up to replace him. The U.S. government and most corporations are not tied to one individual. Lenders are willing to extend credit even in the waning days of a corporate or presidential administration, because they know that the next administration will assume the debts of the previous one. When the Joneses take out a car loan or a mortgage, lenders know that they will have relatively few ways to collect their funds if that person dies before the loan is repaid. Lenders recognize that life is short, and they structure their loans accordingly.

willing to extend new loans. The new loans allow the government to continue borrowing indefinitely.

In addition, the federal government effectively owes about half of its debt to itself, which reinforces the internal nature of the debt. Although the government might have to cut spending to pay its debts, some of its creditors are federal agencies and state and local governments. Thus governmental bodies supply and demand loanable funds. Borrowing from government agencies or other levels of government reduces the federal government's need to borrow on the loanable funds market and reduces the crowding out of private borrowing. Consequently, defenders of the Bush administration say that the debt has little effect on the economy. The facts seem to bear them out. Interest rates actually declined when budget surpluses turned into deficits during the first four years of George W. Bush's presidency.

Why We Should Worry About the Federal Budget Deficit and the National Debt

Despite the arguments in the previous section, many people remain concerned about the federal budget deficit. While they concede that interest rates did not rise in response to the reappearance of budget deficits, they claim that crowding out still exists. It just has been obscured by outside forces. Some of these forces pose additional dangers for the economy. In this section, we examine additional sources of crowding out and the impact of borrowing from foreign lenders.

Crowding Out Revisited. Figure 25.3 showed that an increase in the federal budget deficit causes interest rates to rise, if all else in the economy remains equal. Some economists claim that other events in the early 2000s prevented interest rates from rising as much as our theory would predict. One such event was the decline in investment by firms in the early 2000s. According to this view, the long expansion of the 1990s led business to build too much capacity in the form of plant and equipment. The sudden decline of high-tech firms and the recession of 2001 caused firms to cut back their investment spending, and therefore their borrowing. Private investment spending declined from $1.74 trillion in 2000 to $1.57 trillion in 2002 and did not surpass its 2000 level until 2004. Although government borrowing was

The Changing Politics of the Deficit

Members of both political parties have expressed outrage over the federal budget deficit and the national debt, though seldom at the same times.

FIGURE 25.7

Government Deficits and Declining Investment in the Loanable Funds Market

A $400-billion federal budget deficit causes the supply curve for loanable funds to shift to the left from S_1 to S_2. If, however, a recession causes private spending to fall, the demand curve would also shift to the left (from D_1 to D_2). The declining demand for loanable funds could offset the impact of the declining supply of loanable funds, leaving interest rates unchanged at three percent.

increasing due to the federal budget deficits, borrowing by private firms was decreasing, dampening the impact of the deficit on interest rates.

Figure 25.7 shows the impact of the decline in private sector investment on the loanable funds market. The declining supply of loanable funds would ordinarily cause interest rates to rise from three percent to five percent. The recession, however, causes investment and consumption by firms to decline. Because firms and households spend less, they demand fewer funds to undertake investment. The demand curve for loanable funds shifts to the left, reducing the total amount of funds borrowed and lent from $1 trillion to $0.6 trillion but keeping interest rates stable at three percent.

Critics also point out that large budget deficits crowd out public as well as private spending. In 2004, the federal government paid about $160 billion in interest on the debt, roughly seven percent of all federal expenditure, about six times what it spent on international affairs, and almost twice what it spent on education, training, employment, and social services combined. Given current deficits, the government estimates that interest payments will rise to over $300 billion, more than 10 percent of total expenditure, by 2010. As the federal government spends more on interest payments, it has less money to spend on current programs. Some, for example, point to the U.S. Education Department's reduction of the number of Pell Grants to college students as one effect of the deficit on government spending. On the whole, however, federal spending grew quite rapidly, despite the deficit. Between 2001 and 2004, federal spending rose an average of 8.8 percent per year, about eight times the average annual growth in expenditure during the Clinton administration.

Any crowding out of government spending would not affect everyone equally. Diverting spending to interest payments transfers funds from people who used to benefit from government programs to people or institutions that hold government debt. Because wealthier households have the funds to buy government securities (recall from Chapter 3 that a security is a certificate that promises to pay the bearer a specific sum of money on a particular date), interest payments often redistribute income from poorer households to wealthier households.

The Globalization of the National Debt. A major concern for those who worry about the debt is the growing importance of **external debt**, the amount of money that the federal government owes to residents and institutions of foreign countries. In 2004, the U.S. government owed about 20 percent of its total debt to foreigners, almost double the percentage held by foreigners in 1994. The increasing reliance on external debt helps explain why interest rates have not risen with large deficits since the 1980s. However, critics believe that the United States does itself greater harm by borrowing from abroad.

Figure 25.8 shows that externalizing the debt has increased the supply of loanable funds available to the U.S. economy. Government deficits shift the supply curve for loanable funds to the left from S_1 to S_2. As a result, interest rates rise from three percent to five percent. When the U.S. government sells securities to foreign investors, it enlarges the supply of loanable funds. The supply curve of loanable funds shifts rightward from S_2 to S_3. The increase in supply due to the reliance on foreign creditors offsets the reduction in supply due to the deficit, so the interest rate rises only to 3.5 percent.

While external debt helps keep interest rates low, repaying the interest on external debt imposes a new burden on the economy. When the United States pays interest to foreigners who are holding U.S. government securities, funds leave the country. That leaves less money in the hands of domestic households and reduces the standard of living.

In addition, when a country borrows heavily from abroad, it becomes reliant on the actions of foreign investors. Today, the United States is a very attractive investment opportunity for foreigners. What happens if opportunities elsewhere become more attractive? Or if foreign investors begin to doubt the ability of the U.S. government to

External debt
The amount of money that the federal government owes to residents of foreign countries.

Get Ahead of the Curve

Apply your understanding of macroeconomics to analyze how China and other Asian countries may play a role in the growing U.S. budget deficit.

FIGURE 25.8

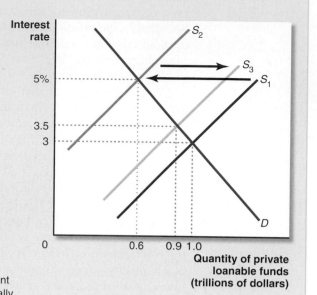

The Impact of Externalizing the Debt on Interest Rates

If the government must borrow $400 billion ($0.4 trillion) to cover its deficit, the supply curve for loanable funds shifts left from S_1 to S_2, and the interest rate rises from three percent to five percent. If the government is able to borrow $300 billion ($0.3 trillion) from foreign lenders, then the supply curve for loanable funds also shifts to the right from S_2 to S_3, which limits the increase in interest rates to 3.5 percent. The quantity of loanable funds that are available to the private sector falls to only $0.9 trillion. It would have fallen to $0.6 trillion if the government had borrowed the entire sum internally.

repay its debts? Foreign funds could rapidly disappear, forcing the government to raise taxes and cut spending drastically to pay interest on its debt. The sudden disappearance of foreign lenders caused the Mexican government to default on its loans in 1982. Similar crises caused Russia to default in 1998 and Argentina to do the same in 2001. Some fear that the United States could face a similar fate if its external debt continues to rise.

Structural Deficits. While opponents of deficits do not deny that the latest recession adversely affected the federal budget, they point out that the recession ended in 2001. Meanwhile, the deficit has continued to grow. They believe that the tax cuts of 2001 and 2003 have fundamentally changed the nature of the deficit, making it independent of the state of the economy. Prior to the 1980s, deficits could be attributed to temporary traumas such as war or recession. However, the recent deficits have become part of the structure of the economy. Economists call deficits that are independent of the state of the economy structural deficits. More formally, a **structural deficit** is the deficit that would occur even if the economy were at peace and full employment. The total federal budget deficit thus consists of the cyclical deficit and the structural deficit. Analyses of the $650-billion turnaround from surplus to deficit have concluded that as much as $250 billion of the change is due to the tax cuts of 2001 and 2003 and not to outside economic or political conditions. As additional features of the tax cut legislation are phased in, this cost could rise to as much as $400 billion per year.[3]

Structural deficits and their impact on the economy do not disappear when the economy recovers. As a result, economists and policy makers worry more about

Structural deficits
Deficits that are independent of the state of the economy.

---

[3] See William Gale and Peter Orszag, "The Cost of Tax Cuts," Brookings Institution, www.brookings.edu/views/articles/20040919galeorszag.htm and Joel Friedman, Ruth Carlitz, and David Kamin, "Extending the Tax Cuts Would Cost $2.1 Trillion," Center for Budget and Policy Priorities, www.cbpp.org/2-2-05tax.htm.

structural deficits than cyclical deficits. Opponents of the tax cuts fear that we have entered an era of large structural deficits that will increase interest rates, which will crowd out both private and government spending.

TEST + *E X T E N D* Your Knowledge

1. TEST In 2002, the U.S. federal budget went from a surplus to a deficit. State two factors that could have contributed to this turnaround and explain why each affected the budget the way it did.

2 . EXTEND Find the data on government expenditure and revenue for 2005 at the Bureau of Economic Analysis Web site using the link at www.aw-bc.com/leeds/ch25. How has the deficit changed? What economic forces have caused it to change in this way?

Strategy and Policy
What to Cut?

Entitlements
Government programs that automatically provide benefits if the individual meets the eligibility requirements.

Suppose that you, the president of the United States, wish to reduce the deficit. That means you will have to raise taxes or cut spending. Raising taxes seems too controversial, so you decide that cutting government spending is the way to go. Unfortunately for you, your options here are limited. An increasing proportion of the federal budget consists of **entitlements**, meaning that a person who meets the eligibility requirements for a benefit program has the right—is *entitled*—to receive the benefits of the program. The government has no discretion as to whether it will spend the money.

Consider the growing importance of the two largest entitlement programs, Social Security and Medicare, in the federal budget of the United States. In 1954, federal spending on Social Security amounted to only $4.4 billion, about eight percent of the total spent on defense. Medicare did not even exist. By 2004, spending on Social Security and Medicare had risen to $764 billion, more than the federal government spent on defense, education, foreign aid, transportation, and the environment combined.

The growth of Social Security and Medicare helped make transfer payments an increasingly important part of the federal budget. Figure 25.9 shows the steadily growing importance of transfer payments. In 1954, transfer payments accounted for less than 20 percent of total government outlays. Since that time, transfer payments have steadily grown in importance until, in 2004, they accounted for almost 40 percent of the federal budget. If current trends continue, transfer payments will soon be greater than government expenditure on all other goods and services combined.

Because many transfer payments are entitlements, increasing pressure is placed on the government to reduce spending in other areas of the budget, such as education and the environment. The growth of spending on Social Security and Medicare is one reason why the government is so concerned with how these programs will be financed as the baby boom generation now begins to retire. Unless the government changes the basic structure of entitlement programs—such as by altering the eligibility requirements or the level of benefits—they will continue to take up an ever-increasing share of the federal budget.

FIGURE 25.9

The Growing Importance of Transfer Payments in the Federal Budget

Over the last half-century, transfer payments have grown much more quickly than government expenditure on goods and services. In 1954, transfer payments took up less than 20 percent of the federal budget. In 2004, they took up almost 40 percent.

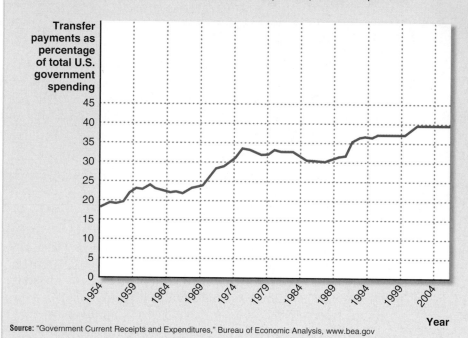

Source: "Government Current Receipts and Expenditures," Bureau of Economic Analysis, www.bea.gov

Critical-Thinking Questions

1. Why is it so much harder to balance the budget than it was 50 years ago?
2. Go to the summary of the U.S. budget for 2004 at www.aw-bc.com/leeds/ch25. What programs would you have cut to eliminate the $412-billion federal budget deficit?

![triangle]

▶SUMMARY

■ **The federal budget deficit and the national debt.** Federal budget deficits have become a major political controversy. Deficits tend to rise with wars and economic downturns. The sum of all budget deficits and surpluses is the national debt. Except for a brief decline in the late 1990s, the national debt deficit has grown significantly since the 1980s.

■ **The impact of budget deficits on interest rates.** Economic theory predicts that government budget deficits reduce the supply of loanable funds that are available to the private sector. This reduction causes interest rates to rise and crowds out private borrowing. Crowding out can reduce the effectiveness of expansionary fiscal policy. It can also reduce long-run growth by reducing the amount of capital stock that is available to the economy.

■ **Debate over federal budget deficit and the national debt.** The impact of the federal budget deficit is the subject of debate among economists and policy makers. Some believe that the deficits will disappear as the economy grows and military conflicts decline. They claim that cyclical deficits are not a long-term problem, as they are offset by cyclical surpluses. They also note that the ratio of the deficit to GDP is not high by historical standards and that the national debt is not so important as long as it is internal. Others claim that the deficits are now structural in nature and will not disappear with peace and economic recovery. They also note that a growing portion of the debt is now owed to foreigners. This could keep interest rates from rising on the loanable funds markets. Payments to foreigners leave the U.S. economy, however, making people worse off.

▶ KEY TERMS

Crowding out 643	External debt 651	Real deficit 640
Cyclical deficits 646	National debt 640	Structural deficit 652
Entitlements 653	Nominal deficit 640	

▶ PROBLEMS

1. What is the difference between a federal budget deficit and the national debt?
2. In 2000, the federal budget had a $240 billion surplus. In 2003, it had a $375 billion deficit. What happened to the national debt in each year? Why?
3. Why does the federal budget deficit in the United States dwarf the deficits run by state governments?
4. If the U.S. military presence in Iraq were to end, what would be the likely impact on the federal budget deficit?
5. If the economy were to slide into a recession, what would be the likely impact on the federal budget deficit?
6. The federal budget deficit in 1985 was $212 billion. The federal budget deficit in 1986 was $221 billion. If prices rose by 1.9 percent, did the real budget deficit rise or fall?
7. Show what happens in the loanable funds market if the government runs a $100-billion budget deficit.
8. Show what happens in the loanable funds market if the government runs a $100-billion budget surplus.
9. How would a budget deficit crowd out private sector spending? How would this effect change the impact of expansionary fiscal policy on the economy?
10. How would crowding out affect the economy in the long run?
11. Why do some people believe that efforts to balance the budget during a recession reduce real GDP still further?
12. Why do some people regard efforts to balance the budget during a recession as self-defeating in that it worsens the deficit?
13. Why do some people say that we shouldn't we worry about cyclical deficits?
14. The federal budget deficit in 1943 was about $54.5 billion. In 2003, it was $375 billion. GDP in 1943 was about $1.6 trillion, and GDP in 2003 was about $11.0 trillion. In which year was the deficit more of a burden on the economy?
15. Why do some say that the ratio of the deficit to GDP is a better measure of the deficit than the dollar amount of the deficit?
16. Why is crowding out less of a problem during a recession than during an economic expansion?

17. What distinguishes a structural deficit from a cyclical deficit? Why is a structural deficit more of a danger than a cyclical deficit?
18. Under what circumstances would repaying the federal budget deficit be a transfer rather than a net burden on society?
19. How does the government's borrowing from foreign lenders affect the loanable funds market?
20. In what sense does borrowing from foreigners help the U.S. economy? In what sense does borrowing from foreigners harm the U.S. economy?

⟨X myeconlab⟩ STUDY GUIDE

HERE'S HOW MyEconLab CAN HELP YOU GET A BETTER GRADE

1. Log into MyEconLab and take Practice Test 25-A (to log in for the first time, see page 30 for instructions).

2. Based on your test results, MyEconLab will identify the areas where you need further work and create a personal Study Plan for you.

3. Your Study Plan contains the problems listed below and others like them that will target the specific chapter topics you need to focus on. You'll receive instant feedback and find links to tutorials, animations, and the online textbook to help you study.

4. When you're ready, take Practice Test 25-B and demonstrate how your results have improved.

Section 25.1, Problem 1 The table shows economic data for the Kingdom of Ecoland.

Year	Nominal Deficit	National Debt	Price Level	Real Deficit
1999	——	$20 billion	——	——
2000	$5 billion (deficit)		100	
2001	1 billion (surplus)		101	
2002	4 billion (deficit)		105	
2003	8 billion (deficit)		107	
2004	6 billion (deficit)		110	

a. Fill in the rest of the table. That is, calculate the national debt each year, and also calculate the real deficit (or surplus) for each year (round to two decimal places).
b. In real terms, is the $5 billion deficit in 2000 larger or smaller than the $6 billion deficit in 2004?

Section 25.1, Problem 2 Which one of the following is true regarding historical U.S. budget deficits and surpluses?

a. The U.S. has run a budget deficit every year since 1929.

b. In nominal amounts, the U.S. deficit for 2004 was lower than the annual deficits during World War II.
c. In real amounts, the U.S. deficit in 2004 was close to the deficits during World War II.
d. In real dollars, the U.S. 2005 budget deficit is twice as large as the deficits run during World War II.
e. The U.S. ran the greatest budget deficits during the Great Depression.

Section 25.2, Problem 1 Which of the following statements regarding budget deficits and the interest rate is true?

a. The government carefully considers the costs of borrowing before running a budget deficit.
b. When the government runs a budget deficit, it causes the private supply of loanable funds to decrease (shift left), raising the interest rate.
c. Crowding out occurs when the government runs a budget surplus.
d. When the government runs a budget deficit, it causes an increase in the private demand for loanable funds, causing the interest rate to rise.

e. When the government runs a budget deficit, it causes a decrease in demand for loanable funds, causing interest rates to fall.

Section 25.3, Problem 1

Year	Nominal Deficit	Nominal GDP	Deficit as a Percentage of GDP
2000	$5 billion (deficit)	$75 billion	
2001	1 billion (surplus)	80 billion	
2002	4 billion (deficit)	82 billion	
2003	8 billion (deficit)	90 billion	
2004	6 billion (deficit)	93 billion	

a. Fill in the last column of the table.
b. In terms of percentage of GDP, was the $5 billion deficit in 2000 larger than the $6 billion deficit in 2004?

Section 25.3, Problem 2
Which of the following are reasons why we should not be concerned about federal budget deficits and the national debt?

a. Cyclical deficits are a normal byproduct of the business cycle, creating budget deficits during recessions and surpluses during expansions.
b. Recently, there has been little evidence linking budget deficits to rising interest rates and crowding out.
c. Although nominal deficits have grown, so has U.S. national income, or our ability to pay them.
d. Much of the government's debt is actually to itself, meaning that there is not much crowding out of private borrowing.
e. All of the above are reasons why we should not be concerned.

Section 25.3, Problem 3
Which of the following are reasons why we should be concerned about federal budget deficits and the national debt?

a. The government will eventually have to pay back all loans, which would bankrupt the nation.
b. Interest paid by the government on debt is money that could have been spent on other programs and seems to be rising.
c. The amount of the external debt has risen to over 50 percent of the total national debt.
d. The structural deficit, the part of the deficit not caused by business cycles, is currently almost 90 percent of the total deficit.
e. None of the above is correct.

26 Basics of Money and Banking

Believe it or not, it's perfectly **legal to print your own money. As long as you don't copy an existing currency, printing money is not considered counterfeiting. But who would accept your** money? Then again, what makes that one-dollar bill in your pocket more acceptable than what you can print on your color inkjet?

A group of people in Ithaca, New York, has been successfully printing and circulating their own currency since 1991. Their privately issued paper money is called Ithaca Hours. It was created when a community activist decided that if the town had its own currency, it would keep local spending at home, stimulating the town's economy. Going from door to door, he signed up local merchants who agreed to accept Ithaca Hours in payment for their goods and services. Some individuals also agreed to be paid in Ithaca Hours.

As townspeople and local businesses began to trust the value and usefulness of Ithaca Hours, their acceptability began to spread. Currently, more than $100,000 worth of Ithaca Hours is circulating in the Ithaca area. A local governing board issues the private money to local groups and civic projects as loans and grants. Businesses and individuals that agree to accept Ithaca Hours also receive additional Ithaca Hours for their participation.

Ithaca did not invent the idea of a local currency. During the Great Depression in the United States, cities, school districts, businesses, and even individuals issued their own paper money, which was called scrip. There are dozens of other examples of local, privately issued currency in the United States today. If it is perfectly legal to print your own private currency, why doesn't everyone do it? As we examine the definition of money, you will see that it takes much more than some paper and a printing press (or personal printer) to issue private money. Private money such as Ithaca Hours must meet a stringent set of legal and practical requirements to function as money.

In this chapter, we explore the principles and functions that describe money. Using those principles and functions, we determine the assets that constitute the U.S. money supply. Then we look at the role of depository institutions and the principles that have evolved to govern their behavior. We observe the requirements of a safe banking system. Finally, we investigate the role of a central bank in regulating and maintaining the safety of the banking system.

ALONG THE WAY, YOU WILL ALSO LEARN:

- The basic principles, functions, and desirable characteristics that define money.
- How the United States measures its money supply.
- How the process of financial intermediation facilitates borrowing and lending, and how simple deposits and receipts evolved into modern fractional reserve banking.
- That the safety and stability of modern banking depend on the public's attitude toward banks and the cautious behavior of banks when making loans.
- The reason why a banking system needs a central bank and how the United States established its central bank.

AT THE END OF THE CHAPTER, THE MYECONLAB LOGO WILL DIRECT YOU ONLINE

- MyEconLab is a resource-packed online homework and tutorial system that can help you perform better in your economics course. To log in for the first time, see page 30 for instructions.
- MyEconLab can help you apply important concepts from the chapter to real-world issues. Watch for the logo to indicate online features about Cuba's use of the U.S. dollar and the influence of short-term interest rates.
- At the end of each chapter, you'll find a special study section that will help you get the most out of your textbook and your instructor's MyEconLab course.

The Principles, Functions, and Desirable Characteristics of Money

Money
Any item that is generally acceptable for use in exchange by both buyers and sellers of goods and services.

What is money? On a daily basis, we use certain pieces of paper and metal as money. What makes dollar bills and quarters money while paper napkins and nails are not money? The standard definition of **money** is that it is generally acceptable for use in exchange by both buyers and sellers of goods and services. That same definition also illustrates the difficulty of defining money. Over time and across cultures, a bewildering array of items has been successfully used as money. In this section, we discuss the principles, functions, and characteristics that allow specific items in specific economies to function as money.

Principles that Define Money

Principle #1: All money is an asset but not all assets are money. What do we mean when we say that all money is an asset to the person who holds it, but not all that person's assets are money? Imagine conducting an inventory of everything you own. By putting a price tag on all those items, you have constructed your portfolio of assets, representing your wealth. Your portfolio of assets contains a wide variety of items that have value to you, such as a baseball card collection, clothes, a car, books, a TV, bank accounts, and dollar bills. We can divide the portfolio into two basic components: assets that behave as money (the bank accounts and dollar bills) and assets that do not behave as money (the baseball cards, car, books, and television). The goal in defining money is to determine the dividing line that separates money from nonmoney assets.

Money is an *asset*; that is, it has value to its holder. Things other than money have value to us as well. Are your most prized possessions your money assets? Probably not. When individuals have only a few minutes to enter their homes to save their most cherished possessions in the face of an approaching flood or forest fire, they rarely (if ever) leave carrying their money. In almost every case, people grab their family photographs since money assets are far easier to replace than treasured photographs.

The portfolio of assets also illustrates that individuals need more than just money assets to survive. Remember the fable of King Midas. Everything he touched turned to gold. This power quickly became a curse. King Midas found he needed nonmoney assets such as food and drink to survive. We, too, need to balance our holdings of money and nonmoney assets in our portfolio to be content.

Principle #2: Money is socially defined. Individual societies at particular times and places determine their definitions of money. In North America since the 1600s, dried fish functioned as money in the Massachusetts Bay Colony, tobacco leaves were money in the Virginia Colony, wampum (beaded Native American jewelry made from polished shells) served as money on the frontier, and gunpowder and bullets were money assets in the American West. Any asset that a society chooses to use as money is money. **Currency** is the coin and paper money component of money. A government cannot dictate which assets its people will actually use as the money assets. For example, Russian citizens in the early 1990s rarely used the ruble, although it was their official currency. Rapid inflation quickly eroded the purchasing power of the ruble. Russians preferred to use a variety of currencies from other nations and even traded one good for another to make their exchanges. When there is a conflict between what a society wants to use as money and what government wants that society to use as money, society always wins.

Because money is a social convention, it is possible for any society to issue its own money, as long as members of that society are willing to use that asset in exchanges. In Ithaca, the "society" that accepts this local currency in payment for goods and services is composed of approximately 1,600 individuals and businesses located, for the most part, within 20 miles of Ithaca. However, these same Ithaca Hours are not generally acceptable in other towns and regions.

In general, we define money by observing it in action. Whatever assets perform the functions of money and have the desirable characteristics of money are money.

Currency
The coin and paper money component of money.

Money Is a Social Convention

A wide range of assets has functioned as money in North America, including dried fish, tobacco leaves, wampum, and bullets.

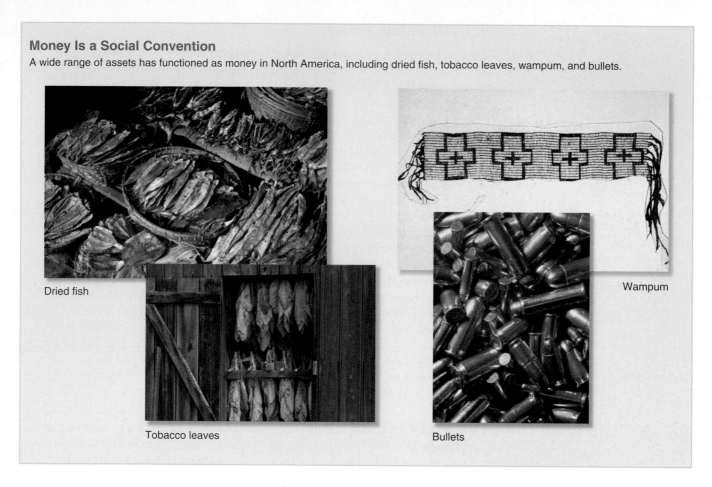

Dried fish

Wampum

Tobacco leaves

Bullets

BIG NATE: Newspaper Enterprise Association, Inc.

The Functions of Money

We now return to the example of the portfolio of assets to discover how the functions of money distinguish money assets from nonmoney assets. To be generally acceptable in exchange for goods and services, money must perform certain functions in the economy. Those roles are generally performed more successfully by money assets than by other assets such as cars, baseball cards, and real estate. To examine the roles that money plays in an economy, we first look at an economy that does not use specific money assets—a barter economy—and then compare it to an economy that uses money.

FIGURE 26.1

Typical Transactions in a Barter Economy and in a Money Economy

In the barter economy in panel (a), the basic transaction appears simple. An individual trades a good that he has (bushels of wheat) for another good provided by someone else (winter coat). In the money economy transaction shown in panel (b), an individual exchanges the goods she possesses (wheat) or the services she can provide (labor) for money assets of $150. With those money assets, an individual can buy the winter coat that she wants.

(a) Barter economy

Individual who has wheat and wants a winter coat — Wheat → Individual who has a winter coat and wants wheat — Coat ←

(b) Money economy

Individual who wants a winter coat — Labor or wheat → Money assets received = $150 — Money → Store selling winter coats — Winter coat ←

Barter economy
An economy where goods and services are directly exchanged for other goods and services without the use of a specific money asset.

Double coincidence of wants
Requirement that each participant in the trade has a good or service that the other person wants and desires a good or service that the other person has; and that the participants are willing to give up their goods or services.

Barter Economy. In a **barter economy**, goods and services are directly exchanged for other goods and services without the use of a specific money asset. In principle, every good or service can be accepted in exchange for any other good or service. Thus for each good or service, multiple prices are quoted in terms of all other goods and services.

Panel (a) of Figure 26.1 depicts such an exchange in a barter economy. Suppose that you have 50 bushels of wheat that you grew, and that you want to trade that wheat for a winter coat. This transaction seems simple and straightforward. In practice, there are significant obstacles. A barter economy requires a double coincidence of wants for a trade to occur. A **double coincidence of wants** means that each participant in the trade has a good or service that the other person wants and desires a good or service that the other person has. The participants must also be willing to give up their good or service. Imagine the difficulty of finding someone who had a coat you desired and who was willing to exchange it for the wheat you have. Carrying bushels of wheat from store to store in town would prove quite time-consuming and awkward. A barter economy has many such costs of time and resources that must be incurred in exchanging goods and services.

To overcome the difficulty of trading goods and services for all items an individual wants, a barter economy encourages individuals to be more self-sufficient. Given the difficulty of trading wheat for a coat, you might be tempted to try to sew your own winter coat. However, if you have greater skill and are more productive at producing wheat, you—and the economy—suffer when you take the time and effort to sew your coat instead.

Money Economy. A typical transaction in a money economy appears more complicated than a transaction in a barter economy. In a money economy, people still offer to exchange the goods and services they possess, but they receive money for them. In turn, they use their money assets to purchase the goods and services they want.

Figure 26.1(b) illustrates a typical transaction in a money economy. If you want that winter coat, you must first obtain money assets. There are several ways to do this. You could work for pay to obtain the $150 needed to buy the coat. You could also sell some of the wheat that you grew on your farm to the local grain elevator. In either case, you can take the $150 in money assets that you obtain from selling your goods or services to any store that sells winter coats and pay for the coat of your choice.

A money economy has a significant advantage over a barter economy—there is no need for a double coincidence of wants. Money assets are widely acceptable in payment for goods and services. You would not have to look far to find a store that would willingly accept your money in exchange for a new winter coat. This typical money transaction also has significantly lower costs of time and transportation. Finally and most importantly, a money economy encourages specialization. Individuals will specialize in the activity at which they are the most productive in order to secure the highest income possible, and then exchange money assets for the goods and services they desire. Recall from Chapter 2 that individuals and the economy both benefit from specialization through increased productivity and expanding production possibilities.

We now examine the three specific functions that money assets perform in a modern money economy: a medium of exchange, a unit of account, and a store of value.

Medium of exchange
Money is useful and acceptable in transactions for both the buyer and the seller.

A Medium of Exchange. Money is a **medium of exchange** because it is useful and acceptable in transactions for both the buyer and the seller. The buyer must be willing to part with money assets in exchange for the goods and service desired. Equally important, the seller must be willing to accept the money assets in exchange for the goods provided. As you saw in panel (b) of Figure 26.1, money assets are in the middle of the ultimate exchange of some goods and services for other goods and services.

Ithaca Hours are a medium of exchange in the Ithaca community. A local newsletter lists 300 businesses that accept Ithaca Hours along with any limitations on that acceptance. (For example, some merchants may accept a maximum of $50 of Ithaca Hours per transaction or perhaps limit payment in Ithaca Hours to half of the bill.) Individuals in Ithaca also acquire Ithaca Hours by providing goods and services. Some workers receive part of their pay in Ithaca Hours and others accept the currency in exchange for goods sold at garage sales or flea markets. Ithaca Hours holders know that this privately printed currency is useful and acceptable in many transactions in and around town.

Unit of account
The value of all other assets is measured in terms of the money asset.

A Unit of Account. Money also functions as a **unit of account**, meaning the value of all other assets is measured in terms of the money asset. This function is sometimes called the *price tag function*, because the price tag on an item portrays the item's value in terms of the money assets of the economy. This function of money allows us to compare the value of different goods and services. A brand new economics text costs about $100. However, a first edition of John Maynard Keynes's historic economics book *The General Theory of Employment, Interest, and Money* in good condition sells for about $10,000. Although you cannot judge a book by its cover, you can judge it by its price tag.

The basic unit of account for Ithaca Hours sets one Hour equal to $10 of U.S. currency; this is the average hourly wage in the Ithaca area. Therefore, a $100 economics textbook would have a price tag of 10 Ithaca Hours.

Store of value
Money assets can retain
purchasing power for
future use.

A Store of Value. Money functions as a **store of value** meaning that money assets retain purchasing power for future use. If you do not spend the money you have in your wallet right now, it will not immediately lose its purchasing power. That dollar in your wallet represents a link between you as the current holder and some unknown person who will accept that dollar in a future exchange. Money assets retain some purchasing power for years into the future. However, money is an imperfect store of value, because inflation eats into the real value of the dollar and can significantly reduce its purchasing power over time. Other nonmoney assets might better hold their real value over time. Another disadvantage that limits money's ability to serve as a store of value is that it does not earn interest.

A second feature of money as a store of value is that money assets are useful and acceptable in paying off debt. Thus money also functions as a medium of exchange into the future. If you have not already bought a home, you will probably work with a mortgage lender sometime in the future to do so. The standard length of a home mortgage is 30 years. In theory, you and the lender must agree on some asset that you will be willing to pay and the lender will be willing to accept over the next 30 years to discharge that debt. The fact that dollars are such an acceptable asset makes obtaining your mortgage less complicated.

The Desirable Characteristics of Money Assets

The two principles of money and the three functions of money are helpful in distinguishing money assets from nonmoney assets. No matter how much you treasure a family photograph, it will never have the general acceptability required to function as a medium of exchange, a unit of account, or a store of value. On the other hand, a dollar bill fits all the criteria of money assets. What about other assets that generally meet these criteria only in a broad sense, falling in the gray area between the assets that are definitely money and assets that are definitely not money, such as an ounce of gold? Gold is clearly a standard of value. We say something is "as good as gold" or "worth its weight in gold." If we put a gold bar into a safety deposit box, it would hold some of its value for years. To distinguish clearly between money and nonmoney assets, we now examine desirable characteristics of money assets. These desirable characteristics help make money generally acceptable in exchange for goods and services:

- Divisibility
- Durability
- Portability
- Relative scarcity
- Uniformity
- Liquidity

Divisibility

Divisibility means that the money assets can be denominated into large and small units. These large and small denominations make a money asset acceptable in a wide variety of circumstances and in transactions of many different magnitudes. U.S. coins and currency in circulation meet this characteristic by ranging from the penny to the one-dollar coin and from the $1 bill to the $100 bill.

Gold lacks this divisibility. At a market price of $400 per ounce, a $10 gold piece would weigh only 0.025 of an ounce—it is literally gold dust. It would be very difficult for both buyers and sellers to use gold dust in transactions.

Ithaca Hours embody the desirable characteristic of divisibility. As mentioned earlier, each Ithaca Hour is worth $10.00. Ithaca Hours come in five different denominations: Two Hours (worth $20.00), One Hour (worth $10.00), One-Half Hour (worth $5.00), One-Quarter Hour (worth $2.50), and One-Eighth Hour (worth $1.25). Ithaca Hours must also follow the federal regulations for issuance of private money, which specify that any privately issued money must be issued in denominations worth $1.00 or more.

Durability

Money assets should also be durable. To function as a store of value, they must be able to hold some value over a considerable period of time. Dried fish in the Massachusetts Bay Colony worked well as a money asset, but fresh fish did not. A money asset with better durability is more widely accepted in transactions than a fragile asset. Merchants prefer to accept long-lasting assets that retain their value and usefulness over time.

Portability

Money assets ought to be portable. To be useful and acceptable as a medium of exchange, money should be easily carried from one place to another for use in transactions. Portability also reduces the costs of an exchange by making it easy and convenient to carry around the purchasing power necessary to engage in a variety of purchases of goods and services.

Relative Scarcity

Relative scarcity means that money assets should not be easily reproduced or counterfeited. As previously noted, in the Virginia Colony, tobacco leaves were used as money. Colonists literally grew their own money. Eventually, almost every farmable acre in the colony was devoted to tobacco cultivation. The Virginia colony was nearly destroyed by rampant inflation, as there was too much tobacco money chasing too few goods. Money that can be counterfeited or created with little effort or expense loses its usefulness. U.S. currency was, for a long time, one of the easiest currencies to counterfeit. Anyone with a color copier, a computer, and some bond paper could do a passable job of counterfeiting. In recent years, the U.S. Bureau of Engraving and Printing, under the direction of the U.S. Secret Service and the U.S. Treasury, has been redesigning the paper currency. Without such anti-counterfeiting measures, U.S. currency would be in danger of losing its usefulness as a medium of exchange.

The Ithaca Hours also have built-in protections against counterfeiting. They are made of a special paper produced from local reeds. Each Ithaca Hour bears a unique serial number. Special inks give each note a distinctive color. Some believe that Ithaca Hours are actually harder to counterfeit than U.S. dollars. A local council carefully controls the amount of Ithaca Hours issued. Issuing too many Ithaca Hours would adversely affect the value and ultimate acceptability of the currency in the local economy.

Uniformity

Money assets are uniform, so they are readily recognized as money assets. The lack of a uniform national currency significantly hampers to the effective operation of an economy. Uniformity increases the general acceptability of money assets in exchange for goods and services. Ithaca Hours are easily recognized as a distinctive currency in their area of circulation. This privately printed paper money is designed to increase its use and acceptability in and around town. Standard Ithaca Hours depict local scenes and there are commemorative Ithaca Hours that honor local citizens. This local flavor improves Ithaca Hours acceptability in transactions in its trading area.

Liquidity

Liquidity
The ease of converting a given asset into a medium of exchange.

The last important desirable characteristic of money assets is **liquidity**, which reflects the ease of converting a given asset into a medium of exchange. Some assets already are a medium of exchange and therefore are perfectly liquid. You can spend the dollar bill in your pocket at a moment's notice. All assets you hold in your portfolio of assets possess some degree of liquidity. For example, you can convert your car into cash by selling it. You must first advertise your car in the local paper or on a Web site, meet with any prospective buyers, haggle over the price, and transfer the title to the buyer in exchange for cash or a check. All these steps take some time, which means that your car does not have as much liquidity as that dollar bill.

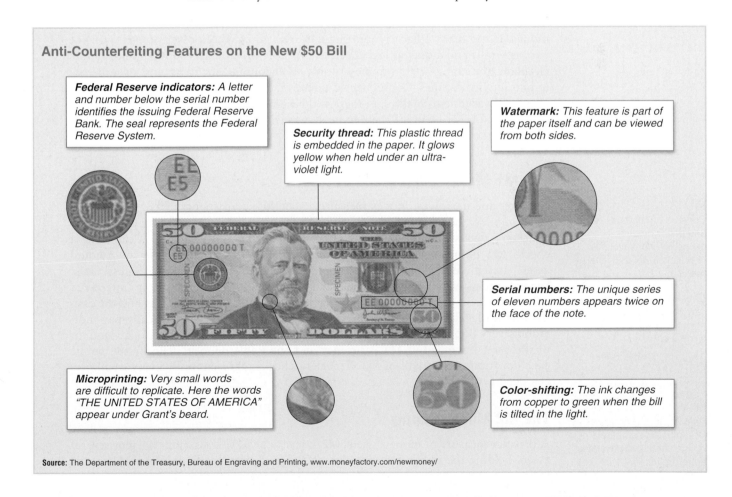

Anti-Counterfeiting Features on the New $50 Bill

Federal Reserve indicators: A letter and number below the serial number identifies the issuing Federal Reserve Bank. The seal represents the Federal Reserve System.

Security thread: This plastic thread is embedded in the paper. It glows yellow when held under an ultra-violet light.

Watermark: This feature is part of the paper itself and can be viewed from both sides.

Serial numbers: The unique series of eleven numbers appears twice on the face of the note.

Microprinting: Very small words are difficult to replicate. Here the words "THE UNITED STATES OF AMERICA" appear under Grant's beard.

Color-shifting: The ink changes from copper to green when the bill is tilted in the light.

Source: The Department of the Treasury, Bureau of Engraving and Printing, www.moneyfactory.com/newmoney/

Ithaca Hours have liquidity. At many local merchants, they are an accepted means of payment and do not have to be converted into U.S. national currency to be spent. However, this liquidity is confined to the local economy.

TEST + *EXTEND* Your Knowledge

1. TEST In what societies could the following privately issued currencies function as money: (a) A $100 bill of Monopoly money, or (b) Your own handwritten $5 promise to pay (an IOU)? Why would these pieces of paper not be considered money by society at large?

2. EXTEND In prisoner-of-war camps during World War II, cigarettes often circulated as money among the prisoners and guards. What characteristics of cigarettes made them an effective money asset in these camps holding prisoners from many nations? What problems might occur when using cigarettes as money?

▶ The Current Measures of Money

Money supply
The amount of money assets circulating in an economy.

Measuring the size of the **money supply**, the amount of money assets circulating in an economy, is important. As you learned in the chapter on inflation, too much money chasing too few goods causes inflation and reduces the purchasing power of money. If too many Ithaca Hours circulate, the purchasing power of each piece of currency falls and money is less effective as a store of value. If too few Ithaca Hours circulate, the ability of the money supply to encourage spending and overall economic activity declines. Consequently, policy makers need to monitor this important economic variable to make sure there is the right amount of money in an economy. In this section, we examine the two most frequently charted measures of the money supply in the United States.

The M1 Money Supply

M1
Consists of currency (coins and paper money), checkable deposits, and traveler's checks held by the general public.

Checkable deposits
Any deposits in any bank account on which you can write a check.

The first and narrowest money measure, called **M1**, consists of currency (coins and paper money), *checkable deposits*, and traveler's checks held by the general public. **Checkable deposits** are any deposits in any bank account on which you can write a check. M1 money assets share two key features. First, they are the most liquid assets, a medium of exchange that people can spend directly for goods and services. Second, the assets in M1 earn little or no interest. Cash balances pay no interest at all. The coins in your piggy bank did not multiply when you were little, and the cash in your wallet does not earn interest today. Checkable deposits typically pay individuals very little, if any, interest. Panel (a) of Figure 26.2 shows the dollar amount of the assets included in M1. Currency and checkable deposits held by the public each constitute about half of M1. Traveler's checks represent only a very small percentage of total M1.

The M2 Money Supply

M2
Consists of all the assets in M1, plus several assets held by the public that are also quite liquid.

A broader measure of money assets, **M2**, consists of all the assets in M1 plus several assets held by the public that are also quite liquid, but less liquid than M1 assets.

FIGURE 26.2

Components of the M1 and the M2 Money Supplies

In panel (a), we see that the U.S. M1 money supply is composed primarily of currency and checkable deposits held by the public. In panel (b), the M2 money supply is a broader measure of the money supply and includes M1 supply along with some other highly liquid assets.

(a) The M1 money supply
(seasonally adjusted, as of August, 2005)

Currency	$ 711.6 billion
Checkable Deposits	$ 628.5 billion
Travelers' Checks	$ 7.2 billion
Total	$1,347.3 billion

(b) The M2 money supply
(seasonally adjusted, as of August, 2005)

M1 Money Supply	$ 1,347.3 billion
Savings Deposits	$ 3,565.7 billion
Money Market Mutual Funds	$ 700.5 billion
Small-Denomination Time Deposits	$ 920.3 billion
Total	$6.533.8 billion

Source: www.FederalReserve.gov/Releases/H6/

Certificate of deposit
A commitment by a depositor to keep the funds on deposit for a specific period of time at a financial institution.

Money market mutual funds
Deposits by individuals into a financial firm that pools those individual deposits to buy short-term financial assets such as U.S. government securities.

These other assets include savings accounts, small-denomination time deposits (also known as certificates of deposit or CDs), and money market mutual funds. A **certificate of deposit** is a commitment by a depositor to keep the funds on deposit for a specific period of time at a financial institution. **Money market mutual funds** represent deposits from individuals into a financial firm, which then pools those individual deposits to buy short-term financial assets such as U.S. government securities.

In general, these money assets are less useful and acceptable as a medium of exchange and bear some costs when converted into currency and checkable deposits to be used in exchange. Withdrawing your funds from a CD before it matures results in a penalty paid for that early withdrawal. Withdrawing funds from a savings account or a money market account incurs no such penalty, but it can be inconvenient. You typically cannot write a check on a savings account. Instead, you must go to the trouble of withdrawing the cash personally. While you can generally write checks on money market mutual funds, the checks often carry limitations (such as a minimum withdrawal of $500 per check or the ability to write only two checks per month).

Figure 26.2(b) illustrates the dollar amounts of the assets that constitute M2. M1 assets represents about 21 percent of the total of M2. Savings deposits are the largest component of the M2 (approximately 55 percent), and money market mutual funds and small-denomination time deposits represent approximately 11 percent and 14 percent, respectively, of M2.

A key requirement of our measures of money is that the monetary asset must be held in the hands of the general public to be counted in the money supply. The dollar bill in your pocket is counted as part of both M1 and M2. However, a dollar bill in the vault of your credit union would not be counted as part of M1 and M2 until it ended up in the public's hand. This distinction becomes important in the next chapter when we explore the process of money creation.

Role of Credit Cards, Debit Cards, and Electronic Money in the Money Supply

Why aren't credit cards and debit cards listed as money assets? Some means of payment that we use to make purchases, such as credit cards and debit cards, are not money. When we use credit cards, we are—in effect—taking out a loan. All money is an asset to its holder and a loan is a liability to the borrower. As a result, credit cards are not a money asset for the user. The company that issued the credit card, often a bank or financial institution, pays for our purchases, and we, in turn, pay the company. Many credit cards charge substantial interest rates to users who do not pay the balance of their loans on time. A debit card is neither money nor a loan. It is simply a way to transfer funds from the buyer's bank account to the seller's bank account—the electronic equivalent of a check. The funds in the buyer's checking or savings account are part of the money supply, but the means of accessing those funds, the debit card, is not.

In one sense, money is a way of transferring ownership of a good or service from one individual to another. In many cases, people transfer ownership by a tangible means of payment such as coins or paper money or a check. In our increasingly technologically sophisticated economy, people are more frequently using **electronic money (or e-money)**, which pays for goods and services in electronic, not physical, form. E-money, despite its name, is not a new money asset. Instead, it is a more convenient way to make payments.

You probably use one or more versions of e-money already—such as the debit card mentioned earlier or a stored value card. With the stored value card (such as prepaid phone cards), individuals load the card with purchasing power using either cash or funds from bank accounts. The card itself can then be used as a means of payment, transferring ownership of those funds from the card user to the seller. Instead of dollar bills and checks exchanging hands, e-money such as debit cards and stored value cards transfers payments electronically.

Electronic money (e-money)
The means of payment for goods and services in electronic, not physical, form.

▶ The Role of Financial Intermediaries and the Rise of Modern Depository Institutions

Financial intermediaries
Institutions which facilitate the transfer of money from savers to investors in an economy.

Depository institution
A financial intermediary that accepts deposits from savers, lends money for a variety of loans, and offers checkable deposits to depositors.

We now examine institutions called **financial intermediaries**, which facilitate the transfer of money from savers to investors in an economy. The financial intermediary brings together the ultimate source of funds, the savers, and the ultimate users of funds, the investors. Financial intermediaries include a large group of institutions that do everything from selling insurance to managing mutual funds. Our focus is on one specific type of financial intermediary: the **depository institution**, which accepts deposits from savers, lends money for a variety of loans, and offers checkable deposits to depositors. Depository institutions include the institutions where you do your banking: banks, thrift institutions (both savings and loan associations and mutual savings banks), and credit unions. We begin this section by establishing the role of depository institutions. To illustrate the rise of the modern depository institution, we follow the evolution of a goldsmith into a bank. We trace the major

LifeLessons

activities of modern banks—accepting deposits and making loans—to the practices of goldsmith banks. The history of banking also uncovers the evolution of many of our modern money assets. We also show the rationale for the amount of funds depository institutions maintain to meet customers' demand for funds.

The Role of Depository Institutions

Individuals who have funds but are not using them are the savers in the economy. These savers, as the ultimate lenders of funds, deposit their excess funds in banks (or other depository institutions) to earn interest on their savings. Individuals and firms who need funds but do not have them are the borrowers or investors in the macroeconomy, borrowing from banks at a given interest rate to invest in a wide range of projects. The bank profits from its role of financial intermediation by charging the borrower a higher interest rate than it pays to depositors.

The bank matches savers with surplus funds to investors who want to put those funds to work. Without depository institutions, if you have $1,000 in savings and wish to put it to profitable use by lending it out and charging interest, you would have to find someone to borrow those funds from you. It would be inconvenient and time-consuming for you to go door-to-door in your neighborhood to find potential borrowers. Putting an ad in the newspaper would be costly and bothersome as well. There would also be a risk that your borrowers might not pay you back. Instead, you can earn interest by depositing your funds in your local bank. The depository institution also makes borrowing large sums more efficient. Imagine the complications of borrowing small amounts from a large number of savers at different terms and interest rates. A borrower can go to the bank to borrow needed funds with only one loan, a single interest rate, and a set time frame for repayment.

---

[1] *Undergraduate Students and Credit Cards in 2004: An Analysis of Usage Rates and Trends*, Nellie Mae, New England Educational Loan Management Association www.nelliemae.com/library/research_12.html.

FIGURE 26.3

Simplified Balance Sheet for the Deposit Function

When a depositor brings in $1,000 of gold to the goldsmith for safekeeping, the goldsmith has a new asset (the gold in the vault) and issues a receipt to the depositor for the gold. This deposit receipt is an asset to the depositor but a liability to the goldsmith, who owes the gold to the owner of the deposit receipt on demand.

Goldsmith Bank
(Deposit Function)

Assets	Liabilities
Gold on deposit + $1,000	Receipts in circulation + $1,000 (to depositor)

The Deposit Function

Our story of goldsmith banking begins in London around 1650, as wealthy individuals began to deposit their gold and silver with goldsmiths for safekeeping. For a fee, this goldsmith held the precious metals and issued a receipt to the depositor. This receipt in the depositor's name allowed the depositor to reclaim the gold and silver on deposit at any time.

Goldsmith Balance Sheet. A simplified balance sheet for the goldsmith bank and the deposit function is shown in Figure 26.3. The left side contains the goldsmith bank's assets, which are items in the bank's possession or owed to the bank. The assets represent the goldsmith bank's use of funds. The righthand side contains the goldsmith bank's liabilities—what the bank owes to others. The liabilities represent the bank's sources of funds. On the simplified balance sheet, assets must equal liabilities at all times. Because the bank now has gold in its possession, its assets have increased by $1,000. The $1,000 in deposit receipts (claims on the gold that the bank owes to the depositor) are the bank's liabilities.

Changes in Goldsmith Receipts. As noted previously, the deposit receipts were originally issued in the depositor's name so only the depositor could collect the gold. This requirement made deposit receipts inconvenient to the depositor. Suppose that the depositor found a good or service in one part of town and the merchant demanded gold or silver as payment. The depositor would have to take the deposit receipt to the bank, withdraw some gold or silver, travel back across town, and complete the purchase.

To increase the usefulness of the depositor's receipts in transactions, the banks allowed depositors to endorse the deposit receipt to a third party. Now if the depositor were shopping in one part of town and wanted to pay for an item, the depositor could write on the deposit receipt, "Pay to the order of _____" and sign that endorsement. The merchant then would have access to the gold or silver by presenting the signed deposit receipt to the issuing bank. This financial instrument is equivalent to the modern check. When you write out a check to a local merchant, you are effectively transferring the ownership of funds you have on deposit to the merchant by filling in the merchant's name on the line "Pay to the order of" and signing your name.

As helpful as this change was to depositors, the deposit receipts introduced complications for the merchants. In the course of a week, merchants might accumulate many deposit receipts from different banks. To retrieve the gold or silver, the merchant would have to travel to each bank and present deposit receipts. To better serve the merchants, the banks made the deposit receipts "Payable to the bearer." A deposit of $1,000 in gold would generate $1,000 of deposit receipts that could ultimately be used by anyone holding those receipts. This use of deposit receipts made payable to bearer became the basis of paper money issued under the gold standard. Until 1933 domestically in the United States and 1971 internationally, anyone with U.S. paper money had the right to exchange that paper money for a certain amount of gold. In essence, the bearer of U.S. paper money had a receipt payable to the bearer for the face value in gold.

Fractional Reserve Banking

Fractional reserve banking
A system in which the amount of a depository institution's circulating liabilities can be safely backed by only a fraction of its value with readily available funds as reserves.

With the deposit receipts increasingly useful and popular in circulation, the goldsmith banks noticed that the gold generally stayed in the bank vault, and the deposit receipts remained in circulation. The deposit receipts were generally acceptable in exchange for goods and services. As a result, people preferred to use the deposit receipts in transactions. Rarely did anyone bring in a deposit receipt and actually claim the gold.

This important observation became the basis of all modern banking—known as the principle of **fractional reserve banking**, a system in which the amount of a depository institution's circulating liabilities can be safely backed by only a fraction of its value with readily available funds as reserves. Suppose that the goldsmith bankers noticed that due to the popularity and usefulness of the deposit receipts, at most only 10 percent of the receipts were ever presented for gold. The banks could actually issue more deposit receipts than there was gold on deposit and still be confident that it could honor those receipts.

The Loan Function

How did the banks make use of the ability to issue additional deposit receipts? If borrowers came in seeking money for a loan, a bank could issue receipts to those borrowers for the amount of that loan. The borrowers were happy to get the new receipts that were readily accepted for goods and services in the economy. Because of fractional reserve banking and the loan, the simplified balance sheet of the original banker now appeared as in Figure 26.4. On the asset side, there are now two categories of assets: the gold on deposit as reserves held by the bank ($1,000) and the loans owed by the borrowers to the bank ($9,000). On the liability side, there are now two sources of receipts in circulation: the receipts issued to the original depositor ($1,000) and the receipts issued to the borrowers ($9,000). Each dollar of receipts in circulation is now backed by only 10 percent of its value with gold on deposit as reserves. We calculate this percentage by taking the dollar amount of gold on deposit and dividing by the total receipts in circulation. With $1,000 of gold as reserves and $10,000 of total receipts in circulation, we obtain $1,000/$10,000 = 10 percent backing with gold reserves.

Banks soon realized that the more deposits they received, the more reserves they obtained. The more reserves they had, the more loans and profits they could make. To attract more deposits, banks began to pay interest to their depositors, instead of charging them a fee to safeguard their gold.

FIGURE 26.4

Simplified Balance Sheet for the Loan Function (Fractional Reserve Banking)
Here the goldsmith bank has made loans by issuing an additional $9,000 of receipts to borrowers. This is fractional reserve banking because the receipts in circulation ($10,000) are greater than the gold on deposit as reserves ($1,000). Each $1 of receipts in circulation is backed by only a fraction of its value with gold on deposit as reserves.

Goldsmith Bank
(Loan Function)

Assets		Liabilities	
Gold on deposit as reserves	+ $1,000	Receipts in circulation	+ $1,000 (to depositor)
Loans	+ $9,000		+ $9,000 (to borrowers)
	+ $10,000		+ $10,000

Commodity money
A money asset that also has value as a commodity.

Convertible paper money
A money asset that can be used to claim the valuable commodity that backs its value.

Fiat money
A money asset because of its usefulness and acceptability in exchange and not because of any asset that is used to back its value.

Modern Money Assets

The story of goldsmith banking covers much of the evolution of modern money assets. The gold itself is an example of a **commodity money**, a money asset that also has value as a commodity. The deposit receipts issued by goldsmiths are an example of a **convertible paper money**, a money asset that can be used to claim the valuable commodity that backs its value. When the United States was on the gold standard, the holder of U.S. paper money could exchange it for a specified amount of gold.

Later, other money assets developed that were not backed by the value of any commodity or precious metal. **Fiat money** is a money asset because of its usefulness and acceptability in exchange, and not because of any asset that is used to back its value. Some fiat moneys are decreed to be so by a nation's government. Mexican pesos, Japanese yen, British pounds, and U.S. dollars are all fiat moneys.

TEST + *E X T E N D* Your Knowledge

1. TEST Which of the following simplified balance sheets does *not* illustrate the concept of fractional reserve banking?

2 . E X T E N D Of the two examples of fractional reserve banking portrayed among Banks A, B, and C, which one would a goldsmith bank most likely use, and why?

	Bank A				Bank B				Bank C		
	Assets		Liabilities		Assets		Liabilities		Assets		Liabilities
Gold	$100	Receipts	$5100	Gold	$300	Receipts	$900	Gold	$200	Receipts	$200
Loans	$5000			Loans	$600						
	$5100		$5100		$900		$900		$200		$200

Safety of Fractional Reserve Banking

How can a bank issue more claims than it has funds readily available to honor those claims? If any bank cannot honor all its promises to depositors at a given time, the bank will fail. There are two prerequisites that keep fractional reserve banking safe: public faith and trust in the banks, and cautious lending.

Public Faith and Trust

Bank run
A large number of depositors withdrawing their funds from a depository institution at one time.

The first requirement for successful fractional reserve banking is that the public must have faith and trust in their banks (and other depository institutions). When depositors believe that their deposit claims will be honored, they have no incentive to withdraw their funds. What if that confidence in the ability of the bank to honor its deposit claims is lost? The survival of that bank (and many other depository institutions) is at risk. Hearing of a problem elsewhere in the banking system, people might hasten to withdraw their deposits before their own bank fails. A **bank run** occurs when a large number of depositors withdraw their funds from a bank at one time. In a fractional reserve system, that bank might lose most or all of its reserves, putting its very existence in jeopardy. A bank run can happen even when the bank's loans are sound and they have enough cash on hand to meet normal day-to-day transactions.

In the early 1930s, people in the United States lost trust in the safety of their deposits. Because no depository institution then (or now) has enough funds available to satisfy all its depositors at once, depository institutions started to collapse. From 1929 to 1933, thousands failed; thus causing a worsening wave of bank panics. Even healthy depository institutions were forced to close.

Federal Deposit Insurance Corporation (FDIC)
A federal agency that insures bank deposits.

One of Franklin Roosevelt's first actions as U.S. president in 1933 was to declare a "bank holiday," temporarily closing all banks to save the remaining healthy banks from further failures. Later that year, his administration proposed legislation that created the **Federal Deposit Insurance Corporation (FDIC)**, a federal agency that insures bank deposits. If an insured bank fails, depositors currently get some or all of their funds back. Deposits are currently guaranteed up to $100,000 per depositor per insured bank. Today, the FDIC insures deposits at most banks. Other federal deposit insurance funds insure deposits at savings and loan associations and credit unions. Since 1933, there have been no widespread bank runs, even though individual depository institutions still can and do fail.

FRANK & ERNEST: Thaves/Dist. by Newspaper Enterprise Association, Inc.

Cautious Lending

Default
When borrower fails to repay a loan.

The second requirement is that depository institutions be cautious and conservative in their lending. Conservative lending helps them to maintain public confidence in their safety and stability, and to keep an adequate amount of funds available as reserves. Suppose that a bank does a poor job of evaluating its borrowers. Some of its borrowers may **default**, or fail to repay their loans. If defaults happen, the bank might not have enough cash on hand to pay depositors who wish to withdraw their funds, and a bank failure can occur. Depository institutions can increase their risk of failure if they make too many loans, even if they are good loans to creditworthy borrowers. If a bank lends too much, it might not have enough cash on hand as reserves. In addition, it may not be able to turn its loans into cash quickly enough to meet the demands of its depositors. The problem is the liquidity of the bank's assets, rather than the size of those assets. Still, a bank that cannot meet the withdrawal demands of its depositors is in danger.

The U.S. savings and loan crisis of the 1980s was caused, in part, by ill-advised loans made by many savings and loan associations. Before 1980, savings and loan associations specialized in mortgage loans to home buyers. Because the savings and loans knew this market well, they were able to make safe and conservative loans. Beginning with a new law in 1980, savings and loans were permitted to make many more types of loans to many more borrowers. Lacking experience in these loans, the savings and loan associations often made poor loan decisions. Many loans soon went bad, falling into foreclosure and default. A large number of the savings and loans became insolvent and had to be merged into healthy depository institutions or closed. Although the FDIC's deposit insurance fund for banks remained sound, a similar federal deposit insurance fund for savings and loans was nearly depleted. The ultimate cost to U.S. taxpayers to close down failed savings and loans and to pay deposit insurance compensation claims to their depositors was hundreds of billions of dollars.

▶ The Need for a Central Bank

As we observe the workings of the fractional banking system, notice the temptation for a bank to keep too little cash in reserves. This lack of reserves jeopardizes the safety of the individual bank and, if the lack of trust spreads, the entire banking system. Struggling depository institutions need an emergency source of liquidity so that they can obtain the funds they need to honor their depositors' claims and retain the public's trust in their depository institution individually and the banking system in general. If the entire banking system is under stress, how do depository institutions obtain that needed liquidity? The problem of insufficient reserves and the need for emergency liquidity can be addressed by a single institution: a central bank. A **central bank** is a financial institution whose major responsibilities include regulating depository institutions to assure that they do not abuse the fractional reserve system and providing emergency liquidity as a lender of last resort to depository institutions needing reserves. In this section, we introduce the U.S. central bank and provide an overview of the U.S. banking system.

Central bank
A financial institution whose major responsibilities include regulating depository institutions and providing emergency liquidity to depository institutions needing reserves.

The Federal Reserve System and Fractional Reserve Banking

Federal Reserve System
The central bank of the United States.

The U.S. central bank is the **Federal Reserve System**, usually called the Fed. The Fed provides a number of safeguards for the fractional reserve banking system. The Fed sets a reserve requirement to specify how many dollars of reserves each individual

Reserve requirement
A percentage of deposits that must be held by a depository institution in a form readily available to depositors.

depository institution should hold to honor its depositors' claims. This **reserve requirement** is a percentage of deposits that must be held by a depository institution in a form readily available to its depositors.

The Fed is also the lender of last resort for depository institutions. A depository institution facing unexpected depositor withdrawals needs a dependable source of emergency reserves to satisfy its depositors and to restore public trust in its ability to meet depositors' demands. The Fed is the ultimate provider of emergency liquidity for the U.S. banking system.

A Short History of American Central Banking

The history of U.S. central banking goes back to the very beginning of the nation. In 1791, Congress established the First Bank of the United States to perform the duties of a central bank. It was given a 20-year charter that Congress refused to renew in 1811. Just five years later, Congress changed its mind and chartered the Second Bank of the United States. Congress refused to renew its 20-year charter in 1836. By that time, many policy makers believed that the nation did not need a central bank to control the behavior of other U.S. banks or provide emergency liquidity. Many Americans feared the concentration of banking power evident in these first two attempts at central banking. Both the First and Second Banks of the United States were the largest corporations in the nation at the time. Both had numerous branches throughout the nation as well, extending their influence and power throughout the economy.

The United States did not have a central bank from 1836 to 1913. This period exposed the economy to the dangers inherent in fractional reserve banking. With no effective national regulator of the banking system, widespread abuse, fraud, and mismanagement by the nation's banks was common. With no institution controlling the behavior of banks and size of the money supply, there were a series of highly inflationary episodes. At other times, recessions and banking panics were the order of the day. After an especially damaging bank panic in 1907, policy makers determined that the United States needed central bank to ensure the safety of the banking system and to control the money supply. Legislation passed in 1913 authorized the U.S. Federal Reserve System.

The Structure of the U.S. Banking System

Get Ahead of the Curve

Use your knowledge of money and the structure of the U.S. financial system to examine some consequences of the rise in short-term interest rates.

We now discuss briefly the current structure of American banking system that the Fed regulates and controls. As we saw earlier, the major categories of U.S. depository institutions are commercial banks, thrift institutions (savings and loan associations and mutual savings banks), and credit unions. Since a major change in federal legislation in 1980, these depository institutions have become increasingly alike, conducting the same basic activities, accepting the same types of deposits, and making the same types of loans.

Figure 26.5 illustrates several key elements of the current structure of the U.S. banking system. Of the nearly 18,000 depository institutions with federal deposit insurance (which includes almost every depository institution), slightly more than half are credit unions. Commercial banks represent about 40 percent of the total number of depository institutions, and thrift institutions are less than 10 percent of the total. Notice that a depository institution may choose to be chartered either by the federal government or by its home state government. No matter which government charters the depository institution, the Federal Reserve System is ultimately the major regulator and lender of last resort for that institution.

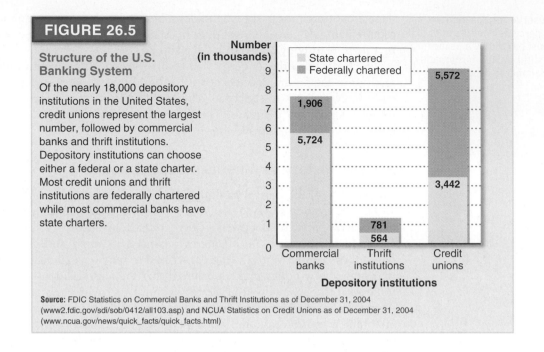

FIGURE 26.5

Structure of the U.S. Banking System

Of the nearly 18,000 depository institutions in the United States, credit unions represent the largest number, followed by commercial banks and thrift institutions. Depository institutions can choose either a federal or a state charter. Most credit unions and thrift institutions are federally chartered while most commercial banks have state charters.

Number (in thousands)

■ State chartered
■ Federally chartered

Commercial banks: 1,906 / 5,724
Thrift institutions: 781 / 564
Credit unions: 5,572 / 3,442

Depository institutions

Source: FDIC Statistics on Commercial Banks and Thrift Institutions as of December 31, 2004 (www2.fdic.gov/sdi/sob/0412/all103.asp) and NCUA Statistics on Credit Unions as of December 31, 2004 (www.ncua.gov/news/quick_facts/quick_facts.html)

The structure of the U.S. banking system is unusual in several respects. Most nations have a banking system dominated by a small number of huge banks with nationwide branches that provide most of the banking services for the nation. In the United States, a large number of small depository institutions compete with a small number of huge banks. American banking legislation in the past was designed to protect small, local depository institutions from competition and domination by larger depository institutions from other regions.

The historical pattern of American banking is changing. In recent years, the U.S. banking system has been consolidating into a system of fewer and larger depository institutions with more branches, resembling more closely the pattern found in other nations. The United States now has fewer banks than at any time in the last hundred years. Currently, of the nearly 9,000 FDIC-insured depository institutions (banks and thrift institutions), about 72 percent have multiple branches. The total number of branches for banks and thrifts is over 82,000.

In the next chapter, you will see how the Federal Reserve System is structured to provide the necessary liquidity for the banking system and how the Fed acts as the chief regulator of the U.S. banking system. You will also see how the Fed controls the money supply in the public interest.

Strategy and Policy

The One-Dollar Coin One More Time?

In spite of the less-than-spectacular success of the Susan B. Anthony dollar coin and the "gold" Sacagawea dollar coin, the U.S. Congress has again contemplated issuing a new one-dollar coin. A bill called the Presidential $1 Coin Act of 2005 passed the U.S. House of Representatives in April 2005 with a vote of 422–6 in favor of minting a new one-dollar coin. As of August 2005, the bill was awaiting action in the Senate. Past efforts to circulate a one-dollar coin in the United States have not been successful. The Susan B. Anthony dollar was minted primarily from 1979 to 1981 when the U.S. Mint produced nearly one billion of them. The public indifference to that first dollar coin led the mint to end its production. Three years after first issuing the new Sacagawea dollar coin in 1999, a federal government survey found that 97 percent of Americans had not used the new dollar coin in the last 30 days and 74 percent could not remember ever using one. In many other nations, a coin of fairly large value circulates widely, such as the $1.00 and $2.00 coins in Canada and Australia, a one-pound (value, not weight!) coin in the United Kingdom, and one-euro and two-euro coins in the European Union.

There are benefits of a circulating one-dollar coin for the United States. By using $1 coins instead of $1 bills, consumers would not face the same wear and tear on a frequently used monetary denomination. There would be less danger of counterfeiting. A $1 coin lasts for decades while a $1 bill typically lasts 18 months. Consequently, the U.S. Mint estimates that it could save more than half a billion dollars each year in printing costs.

The new dollar coin being considered by Congress would have images of former U.S. presidents on its face. Four new presidential dollar coins would be issued per year, starting in 2007, with the first four U.S. presidents: George Washington, John Adams, Thomas Jefferson, and James Madison. The presidential dollars would be issued in the order in which the presidents served. Public acceptance of any new money asset is critical to its use and success. Congressional supporters anticipate that these presidential dollars would be as popular and accepted by the public as the continuing issue of the new state quarters.

Critical-Thinking Questions

1. What are some disadvantages that banks, individuals, and businesses might experience with the widespread use of any one-dollar coin? Which desirable characteristics of money assets might be compromised with a one-dollar presidential coin?
2. Because money is socially defined, if the new one-dollar coin is considered to be collector's item and is used rarely in transactions, would you count it as part of the money supply? Why or why not?

SUMMARY

- **The principles, functions, and desirable characteristics of money.** Two basic principles help determine the money assets in an economy:

  Principle #1: All money is an asset, but not all assets are money.

  Principle #2: Money is socially defined.

  Money assets perform certain activities better than nonmoney assets do. The three primary functions of money are: a medium of exchange, a unit of account, and a store of value. To perform well as a money asset, an asset should possess certain desirable characteristics: divisibility, durability, portability, relative scarcity, uniformity, and liquidity.

- **The current measures of money.** In the United States, there are two frequently charted measures of the money supply: M1 and M2. Each measure contains assets that meet the basic principles, perform the functions, and possess the desirable characteristics of money assets. M1 consists of currency, checkable deposits, and traveler's checks held by the general public. M2 comprises M1 plus savings deposits, small-denomination time deposits, and money market mutual funds.

- **The role of financial intermediaries and the rise of modern depository institutions.** A financial intermediary is an institution that accepts deposits and makes loans. Depository institutions such as banks, thrifts, and credit unions are examples of one group of financial intermediaries. By examining goldsmith banks, we observe how the two basic activities of modern depository institutions (accepting deposits and making loans) developed. These two activities gave rise to the principle of fractional reserve banking, which is still at the heart of modern banking. Many modern money assets (such as commodity money, checkable deposits, and convertible paper currency) evolved from the activities of early banking as well.

- **Safety of fractional reserve banking.** The safe operation of a fractional reserve banking system requires public trust and confidence in ability of depository institutions to honor their deposit claims and conservative lending by those institutions. If either criterion is unmet, there is a danger of a bank run or banking panic.

- **The need for a central bank.** Given the dangers inherent in fractional reserve banking, a central bank is an important financial institution. The U.S. central bank, the Federal Reserve System, plays an important role as a regulator of depository institutions and the ultimate source of liquidity in the banking system. The U.S. banking system is characterized by its large number of depository institutions.

►KEY TERMS

Bank run 675

Barter economy 663

Central bank 676

Certificate of deposit 669

Checkable deposits 668

Commodity money 674

Convertible paper money 674

Currency 661

Default 676

Depository institution 670

Double coincidence of wants 663

Electronic money (e-money) 670

Federal Deposit Insurance Corporation (FDIC) 675

Federal Reserve System 676

Fiat money 674

Financial intermediaries 670

Fractional reserve banking 673

Liquidity 667

M1 668

M2 668

Medium of exchange 664

Money 660

Money market mutual funds 669

Money supply 668

Reserve requirement 677

Store of value 665

Unit of account 664

►PROBLEMS

1. Consider five pieces of paper that are commonly held in a portfolio of assets: a $20 bill, a U.S. Savings Bond, a stock certificate, a high school diploma, and the title to a car. Which, if any, of these pieces of paper are money assets?
2. The $2 bill does not circulate widely in the United States. Using the principle that money is socially defined, explain why this is so.
3. The following is a quotation from Aristotle about money: "Everything, then, must be assessed in money; for this enables men always to exchange their services, and so make society possible." What functions of money are found in this statement from more than 2,500 years ago?
4. The People's Republic of Dyspepsia has outlawed money, so barter is their only form of exchange. Ann grows apples and wants candy. Bob makes bicycles and wants golf balls. Carl makes candy and wants a bicycle. Danielle makes golf balls and wants apples. What trades could these people make to get the goods they want with the goods that they make?

5. What are three disadvantages of a barter economy?

6. What are three advantages of a money economy?

7. In each of the following cases, decide whether the statement refers to a situation that would occur under a barter or money economy.
   a. Requires a double coincidence of wants
   b. Encourages specialization
   c. High costs of making exchanges
   d. Promotes self-sufficiency
   e. Leads to a multiplicity of prices for each good

8. Economists talk about "hedges against inflation." These assets hold their real value in the face of rising prices. What are some nonmoney assets that can serve well as stores of value when prices are rising?

9. Match the historical examples of American monetary assets listed below to a desirable characteristic of money assets.
   a. The Susan B. Anthony dollar coin was an attempt by the U.S. government to improve this characteristic of U.S. monetary assets.
   b. Gold coins when gold is $400 per ounce would have trouble satisfying this characteristic.
   c. The bulk and weight of a dollar coin defeats this characteristic.
   d. Tobacco money in the Virginia colony lacked this important characteristic.
   e. Bank notes issued by thousands of individual U.S. banks prior to 1860 had problems with this characteristic.
   f. U.S. paper currency is being redesigned to prevent this problem.

10. Explain why credit cards, ATM cards, and debit cards are not counted as part of either M1 or M2.

11. Explain the evolution of the deposit receipts issued by goldsmith bankers and how this evolution improved the general acceptability and usefulness of these deposit receipts in transactions.

12. Your hometown asks you whether it should create its own currency. Make a case for and against this idea.

13. In the process of financial intermediation, who are the ultimate suppliers of funds and who are the ultimate demanders of funds?

14. What are the two prerequisites for safe fractional reserve banking?

15. What are two lessons about modern banks that can be learned from the story of goldsmith banks?

16. What is the role of a central bank in the safeguarding of fractional reserve banking?

17. Looking at the balance sheet of the goldsmith bank in Figure 26.4, show how it would change if the banker wanted to have each $1.00 of deposit receipts backed by 25 percent of its value with gold on deposit as reserves.

18. Looking again at the balance sheet of the goldsmith bank in Figure 26.4, show what would happen to the bank's gold reserves if individuals presented $1,500 of the $10,000 of deposit receipts for gold on a particular day. For simplicity, assume that $500 of deposit receipts came from depositors and $1,000 from deposit receipts originally given to the borrowers.

HERE'S HOW MyEconLab CAN HELP YOU GET A BETTER GRADE

1. Log into MyEconLab and take Practice Test 26-A (to log in for the first time, see page 30 for instructions).

2. Based on your test results, MyEconLab will identify the areas where you need further work and create a personal Study Plan for you.

3. Your Study Plan contains the problems listed below and others like them that will target the specific chapter topics you need to focus on. You'll receive instant feedback and find links to tutorials, animations, and the online textbook to help you study.

4. When you're ready, take Practice Test 26-B and demonstrate how your results have improved.

Section 26.1, Problem 1 When money is accepted as payment for goods and services, it is being used as a _____; if money is used to express the value of goods and services, it is being used as a _____; and when it is used to hold purchasing power for future use, it is being used as a _____.

Section 26.1, Problem 2 Which one of the following assets is the most liquid?

   a. A savings account
   b. An ounce of gold
   c. Real estate
   d. Stock of IBM
   e. U.S. government bond

Section 26.2, Problem 1 Which one of the following is *not* included in M2?

   a. Cash held by the general public
   b. Savings accounts
   c. Time deposits (certificate of deposits)
   d. Money market mutual funds
   e. All of the above are included in M2.

Section 26.2, Problem 2 Classify each of the following as part of M1, M2, both, or neither:

   a. Money market mutual funds
   b. Small-denomination time deposits
   c. Cash held inside bank vaults
   d. Checking accounts (checkable deposits)
   e. Credit cards
   f. Cash held by the general public
   g. One ounce of gold
   h. Traveler's checks

Section 26.2, Problem 3 Ecoland has the same measures of the money supply as the United States. The following table shows a breakdown of monetary assets as of last month in Ecoland.

Currency held by the public:	$1,500,000
Currency held as reserves in bank vaults:	$750,000
Savings deposits:	$1,200,000
Money market mutual funds:	$800,000
Checking deposits:	$600,000
Government bonds held by public:	$250,000
Gold held by public:	$400,000

   a. What is the size of M1?
   b. What is the size of M2?

Section 26.3, Problem 1 The primary role of financial intermediaries is to:

   a. Equilibrate future consumption with current consumption
   b. Facilitate the transfer of money from savers to borrowers
   c. Ensure that everyone who wants a loan gets one
   d. Sell shares of corporations to the general public
   e. Represent the interests of insurance companies

Section 26.3, Problem 2 For each of the following, specify whether it would appear on the left or the right of a typical bank's balance sheet, and whether they would be an asset or liability to a bank.

   a. Cash held in vaults
   b. Checking deposits
   c. Saving deposits
   d. Loans

Section 26.3, Problem 3 Which of the following could *not* be commodity money?

    a. Gold
    b. Salt
    c. Cigarettes
    d. Paper money
    e. Rum

Section 26.4, Problem 1 One of the main reasons why there have been few bank runs since the early 1930s is that:

    a. There have been no bank failures since the Great Depression.
    b. Bank presidents are more cautious about lending.
    c. The creation of the Federal Deposit Insurance Corporation protects the public's deposits.
    d. U.S. presidents closely monitor banking practices.
    e. Banks are no longer allowed to lend money, and must hold all deposits on reserve.

Section 26.5, Problem 1 Which of the following statements regarding the Federal Reserve and the U.S. banking system is true?

    a. The Federal Reserve was established to monitor and regulate the U.S. banking system, and to serve as a lender of the last resort to depository institutions.
    b. The Federal Reserve is responsible only for regulating depository institutions that are federally chartered. State-chartered institutions are the sole responsibility of the individual states.
    c. Seventy-five percent of the U.S. banking system is composed of commercial banks, with credit unions and thrift institutions making up the rest.
    d. The U.S. has had a central bank continually since the beginning of the nation in 1791.
    e. All of the above statements are true.

27

Money Creation and Monetary Policy

In the days following the terrorist attacks of September 11, 2001, the United States narrowly avoided a second disaster related to the economy. The tragic attacks killed thousands of innocent people and caused billions of dollars of property damage. In addition, they came perilously close to bringing the U.S. and global financial systems to ruin. As in any time of uncertainty, people hurried to their banks and ATMs to withdraw cash, severely draining cash reserves in some areas. A failure by the banking system to meet individual depositors' demands at such a time could easily have set off a major bank panic.

Communication, the lifeblood of the U.S. financial system, and travel were severely disrupted, especially by the grounding of flights over the continental United States. Firms were also threatened by a possible lack of liquidity, the ability to turn their assets into cash. They needed their clients' deposits processed quickly so they could pay their own bills. The disruptions in communication and air travel slowed banking operations. On the international front, the interruption of communication and transportation networks delayed the movement of U.S. dollars into foreign banks, jeopardizing international trade in goods and services.

Adding to the danger of a crisis of confidence, Alan Greenspan, the renowned chairman of the Federal Reserve Board, was at a banking conference in Switzerland, on September 11. Roger Ferguson, the vice chairman of the Federal Reserve Board and a man few people would recognize, announced to the world: "The Federal Reserve System is open and operating ... [and] available to meet liquidity needs." These few, well-chosen words reassured the financial system and prevented a liquidity crisis.

Vice chairman Ferguson made his announcement the very morning of the attacks. However, it takes more than words to ensure that the world's largest economy continues to function. The Federal Reserve System's role in stabilizing the U.S. economy and, by extension, economies worldwide, is unfamiliar to many people. The Fed has many important daily responsibilities designed to preserve the ongoing health of the banking system and the overall economy. The tools the Fed used immediately after the terrorist attacks are the same ones it uses every day. One of the Fed's key tasks is to intervene in the operation of the financial system in order to maintain the liquidity necessary to preserve faith and trust in the banking system.

In this chapter, we explore the structure of the Fed and its key relationships with the federal government, the banking system, and the public. You will see how the everyday actions of individual banks affect the supply of money in the national economy. We explain the cumulative impact on the money supply of the actions of individual banks. You will also see how the Fed provides the liquidity required for the safe operation of our fractional reserve banking system and uses its monetary tools to help the economy move toward its goals of full employment, price stability, and economic growth.

ALONG THE WAY, YOU WILL ALSO LEARN:

- How the Federal Reserve System is structured.

- About the Fed's interactions with the federal government, the banking system, and the public.

- How individual banks create money by accepting deposits and making loans.

- How the banking system expands the money supply through the multiplier process.

- How the Federal Reserve System can provide the right amount of money at the right time using its three major monetary tools.

- How the federal funds market captures the Fed's intentions for monetary policy and influences the behavior of the money supply.

AT THE END OF THE CHAPTER, THE MYECONLAB LOGO WILL DIRECT YOU ONLINE

- MyEconLab is a resource-packed online homework and tutorial system that can help you perform better in your economics course. To log in for the first time, see page 30 for instructions.

- MyEconLab can help you apply important concepts from the chapter to real-world issues. Watch for the logo to indicate online features about the U.S. and Chinese central banks.

- At the end of each chapter, you'll find a special study section that will help you get the most out of your textbook and your instructor's MyEconLab course.

▶ The Structure of the Fed and Its Defining Relationships

The focus of this chapter is **monetary policy,** which consists of actions by the Fed to change the size of the money supply in order to achieve macroeconomic goals.

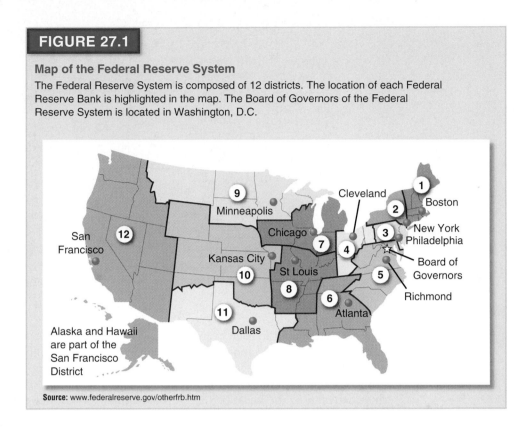

FIGURE 27.1

Map of the Federal Reserve System

The Federal Reserve System is composed of 12 districts. The location of each Federal Reserve Bank is highlighted in the map. The Board of Governors of the Federal Reserve System is located in Washington, D.C.

Source: www.federalreserve.gov/otherfrb.htm

Monetary policy
Actions by the Fed to change the size of the money supply in order to achieve macroeconomic goals.

Before examining the tools the Fed used to stabilize the economy in the midst of the crisis after September 11, we must explain its decision-making structure and key relationships.

The Fed's Structure

In creating the U.S. Federal Reserve system, Congress sought to balance competing regional interests within the United States and to address the general suspicion of a centralized monetary authority. As you saw in the previous chapter, many Americans were wary of concentrating economic power in a central bank. No one wanted that bank to ignore the special needs and interests of their particular region of the nation. Consequently, Congress created the Federal Reserve *System* rather than a single central bank. This system consists of a central body and 12 Reserve Banks that are distributed throughout the nation. Figure 27.1 shows a map of the Federal Reserve districts and the cities in which the Reserve Banks are located.

Board of Governors
The central authority that runs the Fed.

Board of Governors. The seven-member **Board of Governors** is the central authority that runs the Fed. Although the President of the United States appoints members of the Board of Governors (subject to confirmation by the Senate), his power to staff the Board is constrained. By law, a presidential appointment to the Board of Governors must balance "the financial, agricultural, industrial, and commercial interests and geographic divisions of the country." To ensure geographic balance, no more than one member of the Board may come from a given Federal Reserve district.

To further limit presidential influence, each member's term lasts for 14 years. Board members cannot be removed because of disagreements over policy. One

Courtesy www.CartoonStock.com

member's term ends in each even-numbered year. If each member serves a complete term, no president can appoint more than two members in each presidential term.

The president then appoints—and the Senate must confirm—one of the members to be chairman of the Board and another to be vice chairman. The chairman and vice chairman of the Federal Reserve Board each serve four-year renewable terms. Alan Greenspan has served as chairman of the Board of Governors since his appointment to the Board in 1987. His last term as a Board member and chairman ends on January 31, 2006. At that point, Alan Greenspan will have served nearly 19 years completing the final five years of another member's term and one 14-year term of his own on the Board of Governors.

Federal Open Market Committee. The members of the Board of Governors fill 7 of the 12 positions on the **Federal Open Market Committee (FOMC),** which sets the overall direction of U.S. monetary policy.

As you learned earlier, the Federal Reserve Act established a Reserve Bank in each of the 12 Federal Reserve districts to diffuse the power of the central bank and accommodate regional economic needs. The Reserve Banks provide their local perspectives to the Federal Reserve Board and represent the policy interests of their districts in Board decisions. One important way in which the Reserve Banks provide this local perspective is through their representation on the FOMC. Five of the 12 FOMC members are Reserve Bank presidents. Four of them serve rotating one-year appointments as voting members of the FOMC. Because the Fed's major monetary policy takes place at the New York Fed, the president of the New York Reserve Bank is a permanent voting member. The remaining Reserve Bank presidents attend FOMC meetings as nonvoting members. The Reserve Banks also supervise local banks and respond to localized banking concerns.

The Fed's Defining Relationships

The U.S. central bank, the Fed, is distinguished from any other U.S. financial institution by a series of special relationships. We complete our introduction to the Fed by examining its relationships with the federal government, depository institutions, and the public.

Federal Open Market Committee (FOMC)
The group within the Federal Reserve System that sets U.S. monetary policy.

The Fed and the Federal Government. The Fed is the federal government's bank. The U.S. Treasury has its checking account at the Fed, into which the Treasury deposits tax revenues and from which it disburses the funds that it spends. Given the massive flows of government tax revenue and spending, this checking account is a crucial mechanism in fiscal policy. When the federal government borrows funds to finance a budget deficit, the Fed aids the Treasury in its borrowing process by issuing and redeeming U.S. government securities as well as performing many of the routine bookkeeping functions required in the sale and redemption of those securities.

The Fed and Depository Institutions. The Fed is a banker's bank. As an individual, you deposit funds and borrow funds from your bank. In the same way, your bank can deposit reserves and borrow reserves from the Fed. The Fed is the lender of last resort for the banking system. As we discussed in the previous chapter, all depository institutions are fractional reserve institutions. As such, none of them has enough reserves readily available to satisfy all its depositors at once. Rapid and massive deposit outflows jeopardize depository institutions' safety and survival. The Fed stands ready to provide emergency reserves for an individual bank or the entire banking system. This responsibility became especially important in the immediate aftermath of 9/11. Because of the disruptions to the financial infrastructure, there was a critical need for sufficient liquidity to preserve the safety of the U.S. banking system.

The Fed and the Public. The Fed has a series of special relationships with the public, including the following:

1. The Fed provides all the paper money currently in circulation in the U.S. economy. The U.S. Bureau of Engraving and Printing prints these Federal Reserve Notes for the Fed. The Fed is responsible for making sure that this currency is put into circulation. It also removes and destroys tattered and dirty currency from circulation.

2. The Fed is responsible for **check clearing**, which involves deducting deposits and reserves from the bank on which the check was written and crediting both deposits and reserves to the bank where the check was deposited. In 2004, the Fed processed slightly more than 14 billion checks—about half of all checks cleared within the U.S. banking system. Suppose that you write a check and send it to someone in another part of the country. In the past, this activity involved physically moving the check from where it ended up to where it started, usually by flying it overnight in one of the Fed's jets. It was several days before the issuing bank received the check and could debit the depositor's account. The grounding of all air transportation after the 9/11 attacks compromised the Fed's ability to clear checks. Since October 2004, under a system called Check 21 (after the Check Clearing for the 21st Century Act), banks have been able to send electronic copies of checks to the issuing bank. Under this arrangement, checks will be cleared in one day or less.

3. The Fed is the major regulator of depository institutions. It administers a series of laws designed to make sure that bank customers are treated fairly. The Truth in Lending Act requires each lender to tell potential borrowers the **annual percentage rate (APR)** on any loan they are offered. The APR is the actual annual interest rate that the borrower must pay under the terms of the loan. A potential borrower can then compare the costs of loans from different lenders to obtain the best terms. The Truth in Savings Act mandates that

Check clearing
The process which involves deducting deposits and reserves from the bank on which the check was written and crediting both deposits and reserves to the bank where the check was deposited.

Annual percentage rate (APR)
The actual interest rate that the borrower must pay under the terms of the loan.

Annual percentage yield (APY)
The actual rate of return on a deposit based on how often the bank pays interest to the depositor.

depository institutions disclose the **annual percentage yield (APY)** on any deposit they offer. The APY is the actual rate of return on a deposit based on how often the bank pays interest to the depositor. In general, the more frequently the bank pays interest, the greater the APY. Each depositor knows the exact annual rate of return on any kind of deposit. This information makes it easier for a depositor to obtain the highest possible interest rate on a deposit.

4. Most importantly, the Fed controls the money supply with the public interest in mind. The Fed is responsible for supplying the economy with the right amount of money at the right time. Too much money can lead to rapid inflation. Economic growth can stagnate if there is too little money.

The Creation of Money by Individual Depository Institutions

Now that we've established the Fed's basic structure and responsibilities, we turn our focus to the day-to-day workings of banks and other depository institutions to see how those activities affect the size of the money supply. By accepting deposits and making loans, a bank, thrift institution, or credit union can literally create money, as explained in this section. The Fed uses the money creation process to provide the economy with the appropriate money supply. In this section, we illustrate the money creation process in an example featuring three banks. By exploring the money creation process through the activities of individual depository institutions, we will also uncover the means by which the Fed can harness this money-creating potential in the best interests of the economy. Our example is based on three assumptions:

1. The public does not wish to hold currency.
2. Banks hold only required reserves.
3. Banks are always willing and able to make loans.

Although we focus the discussion on banks, the principles apply to any depository institution.

Accepting a Deposit

We begin with a very simple situation. Suppose that you have $1,000 in currency and deposit it at a local depository institution, Academia National Bank. In Figure 27.2(a), we see that Academia National Bank now has an additional $1,000 in currency, which it holds as reserves. Academia National Bank also now has an additional $1,000 liability in the form of the new checkable deposit. Recall that M1 consists of currency, checkable deposits, and traveler's checks that are in the *hands of the public*. As a result of this transaction, the amount of currency in the hands of the public has decreased by $1,000, while the amount of checkable deposits in the hands of the public increased by $1,000. Money was not created. Only the composition of the money supply changed.

Calculating the Reserve Position

In the previous chapter, you learned that the Fed sets reserve requirements for all depository institutions. Banks must hold a percentage of deposits to meet the needs

FIGURE 27.2

Impact of Initial Deposit on the Balance Sheet

Panel (a) shows that when an individual deposits $1,000 in currency into a checking account at Academia National Bank, the currency becomes an asset to the bank while checkable deposits are a liability. Each $1 of new deposits initially generates $1 of new total reserves for the bank. In Panel (b), Academia National Bank calculates its reserve position to determine how many dollars of excess reserves resulted from the $1,000 deposit.

(a) Academia National Bank accepts a deposit

Assets	Liabilities
Total reserves + $1,000	Checkable deposits + $1,000 (to depositor)

(b) Academia National Bank calculates its reserve position

Assets	Liabilities
Total reserves Required reserves + $100 Excess reserves + $900	Checkable deposits + $1,000 (to depositor)

Total reserves
Those funds held by a bank in readily available form to meet depositors' withdrawal demands.

Required reserves
The dollar amount of reserves that a bank must hold in readily available form.

of their depositors. A bank's **total reserves** are those funds held by a bank in readily available form to meet depositors' withdrawal demands. Reserves may be held as vault cash in the bank itself or as deposits at the Federal Reserve System. **Required reserves** are the dollar amount of reserves that a bank must hold in readily available form. The reserve requirement is the percentage of deposits that must be held by the bank as either vault cash or deposits at the Fed. The amount of required reserves is determined at each bank by multiplying its deposits by the reserve requirement. When Academia National Bank receives your $1,000 deposit, it calculates its reserve position using Equation 27.1.

$$\text{Total reserves} = \text{Required reserves} (\text{Deposits} \times \text{Reserve requirement}) + \text{Excess reserves} \qquad (27.1)$$

For simplicity, suppose that the reserve requirement is 10 percent. Academia National Bank must hold 10 percent of the new $1,000—or $100—as additional required reserves. The remainder of the new total reserves, $900, counts as **excess reserves,** or reserves held by a bank beyond the amount required by the Fed.

Excess reserves
Reserves held by a bank beyond the amount required by the Fed.

Figure 27.2(b) shows the results of Academia National Bank's calculation of its reserve position on the asset side of its simplified balance sheet. The total reserves it received from the initial $1,000 deposit are composed of an additional $100 of required reserves and the remaining $900 of additional excess reserves.

Making a Loan and Creating Money

How does a bank decide how much to lend? Loans are the major source of bank profits. However, as you saw in the previous chapter, conservative lending ensures the safety of fractional reserve banking. Issuing too many loans sacrifices safety. Making too few loans sacrifices profits. We show you how banks resolve this dilemma by examining the lending decisions of Academia National Bank and two other banks: Bookville National Bank and Collegetown National Bank.

Academia National Bank. How much should Academia National Bank lend? A single bank can safely lend an amount equal to its excess reserves. This guideline stresses safety rather than profit maximization for the bank. Based on this lending guideline, Academia National Bank could safely lend $900—the amount of its new excess reserves. A current customer of Academia National Bank, who has a checking account with the bank, wants to borrow $900 for a camping vacation to Yellowstone National Park. After checking the applicant's credit history, the loan officer decides to make the loan.

Panel (a) of Figure 27.3 illustrates that because of this loan, Academia National Bank now has $900 more in loans on the asset side of its balance sheet. Notice that Academia National Bank does not lend its excess reserves. The excess reserves merely provide guidance to the bank about how much it can lend. On the liability side, Academia National Bank now has an additional $900 of checkable deposits that it owes to the borrower. Academia National Bank credits $900 into the borrower's checking account. The significant item on this balance sheet is the $900 in new deposits. That is literally newly created money that did not exist anywhere in the economy until Academia National Bank credited those funds to the depositor's account. When a bank makes a loan, it creates an equal amount of new money.

Bookville National Bank. If a bank has the power to create money, why would it limit its loan and money creation to $900? After all, more loans would mean more profits. The answer is that each bank must assume that the funds it lends will ultimately be deposited in another bank. When the $900 check clears, Academia National Bank loses an equal amount of deposits and reserves due to the check collection process. In a fractional reserve system, where the Fed insists on a certain level of required reserves, losing reserves can be uncomfortable for a depository institution. To protect against any negative impact from the loss of reserves, Academia

---

FIGURE 27.3

Academia National Bank Makes a Loan and Clears a Check

In Panel (a), by lending an amount equal to its excess reserves, Academia National Bank creates $900 of new money. In Panel (b), the check written on Academia National Bank is deposited in Bookville National Bank. Academia National Bank loses $900 of deposits and reserves to Bookville National Bank. By following the lending guideline, Academia National Bank still meets the reserve requirement while maximizing its profits.

(a) Academia National Bank makes a loan

Assets		Liabilities	
Total reserves		Checkable deposits	
Required reserves		+ $1,000 (to depositor)	
	+ $100	+ $900 (to borrower)	
Excess reserves		*Newly created money*	
	+ $900		
Loans	+ $900		
	+ $1,900		+ $1,900

(b) Academia National Bank loses deposits and reserves to Bookville National Bank

Academia National Bank

Assets		Liabilities	
Total reserves		Checkable deposits	
Required reserves		+ $1,000 (to depositor)	
	+ $100		
Excess reserves			
	+ $0		
Loans	+ $900		
	+ $1,000		+ $1,000

Bookville National Bank

Assets		Liabilities	
Total reserves		Checkable deposits	
	+ $900		+ $900

National Bank will lend only what it can ultimately afford to lose through the check clearing process that is, its excess reserves.

To illustrate, suppose that the borrower uses the $900 loan money to buy camping supplies from a sporting goods store. The merchant takes the check written by the borrower and deposits it into his or her depository institution, Bookville National Bank. The simplified balance sheet for Bookville National Bank is shown in Figure 27.3(b). Bookville National Bank now has $900 in new deposits and $900 in new total reserves. Academia National Bank has to be careful about the impact of this $900 check being cleared against it. The total number of deposits at Academia National Bank falls back to the original $1,000 owed to the original depositor. Academia National Bank also loses its $900 of excess reserves to Bookville National Bank. Academia National Bank's reserve position falls back to $100: It now has the required reserves of $100 and no excess reserves. The borrower must still repay the $900 loan. Academia National Bank is maximizing its profits while maintaining its safety. As a result of this new $900 deposit, Bookville National Bank has received an injection of a new deposit and new reserves. It begins to think about making new loans. Bookville National Bank calculates its reserve position. Bookville National Bank's balance sheet, shown in panel (a) of Figure 27.4, reveals that it has $810 of new excess reserves. Following the same lending guideline as Academia National Bank, Bookville National Bank is now able to lend $810 safely.

Bookville National Bank takes on this new liability by crediting a borrower with an additional $810 of checkable deposits, as shown in Figure 27.4(b). At the same time, Bookville National Bank has acquired a new asset: the $810 loan. Notice that Bookville National Bank has also created money by putting $810 more checkable deposits into the hands of the public.

Collegetown National Bank. Bookville National Bank will lose deposits and reserves when the borrower spends the funds. The merchant who receives the $810 check deposits the check into its account at Collegetown National Bank. When the

---

FIGURE 27.4

Bookville National Bank Calculates Its Reserve Position and Makes a Loan

In Panel (a), with a reserve requirement of 10 percent, Bookville National Bank must keep $90 of new required reserves to back up its new $900 deposit. The rest of the new total reserves, $810, are excess reserves. Panel (b) shows that Bookville National Bank can safely lend an amount equal to its excess reserves. With this $810 loan, Bookville National Bank has also created money.

(a) Bookville National Bank calculates its reserve position

Assets	Liabilities
Total reserves	Checkable deposits
Required reserves	+ $900 (to depositor)
+ $90	
Excess reserves	
+ $810	

(b) Bookville National Bank makes a loan and creates money

Assets	Liabilities
Total reserves	Checkable deposits
Required reserves	+ $900 (to depositor)
+ $90	+ $810 (to borrower)
Excess reserves	*Newly created money*
+ $810	
Loans + $810	
+ $1,710	+ $1,710

check clears and Collegetown National Bank collects the $810 from Bookville National Bank, Collegetown National Bank will gain that amount of deposits and reserves at the expense of Bookville National Bank. As long as Bookville National Bank follows the lending guideline, it will avoid any problems on its balance sheet when the check is cleared against it. Collegetown National Bank will now calculate its reserve position, lend out an amount equal to its excess reserves and thereby create more money.

TEST + *EXTEND* Your Knowledge

1. TEST As you just learned Collegetown National Bank gains $810 of new deposits and new reserves. Show the impact of this transaction on the balance sheet of Collegetown National Bank. Calculate the reserve position for Collegetown National Bank.

2. EXTEND How much money is Collegetown National Bank now safely able to lend? Show the balance sheet for Collegetown National Bank after it makes a loan for this amount. Why is this new loan also newly created money? Show what happens to Collegetown National Bank's balance sheet if a check for the amount of the new loan is cleared against it.

► Money Creation by the Banking System

We have illustrated the money creation process at the individual bank level. What is the total impact of this money creation by the banking system? In this section, we answer this question by constructing equations that capture the total impact of the money creation process. Our goal is to highlight the role that excess reserves play in the money creation process, as these excess reserves are crucial to the Fed's ability to control the money supply in the public interest. We begin by analyzing the impact of our money creation example at the individual bank level. We then generalize these lessons to the banking system and calculate the overall effect of the money creation process.

Insights from the Bank-Level Money Creation Process

Table 27.1 illustrates the total impact on the banking system of our initial deposit of $1,000 in currency. Let's recap the key details from our example involving the Academia, Bookville, and Collegetown National Banks based on the initial deposit of $1,000 at Academia National Bank:

1. Academia National Bank had to maintain $100 of new required reserves for the initial deposit of $1,000. Academia National Bank was able to create new money by lending $900.
2. The $900 loan was ultimately deposited in Bookville National Bank. Bookville National Bank had to maintain $90 of new required reserves on the new $900 deposit. It could then lend $810.
3. Collegetown National Bank received a new $810 deposit. It lent $729 while holding $81 of new required reserves.

This example process illustrates two important facts. First, the process is powerful. That initial deposit of $1,000 in one bank has already increased the money

TABLE 27.1

Impact on the Banking System of $1,000 Initial Deposit of Currency

Bank	Change in Deposits	New Loans = Newly Created Money	New Required Reserves
Academia National Bank	+ $1,000	+ $900	+ $100
Bookville National Bank	+ $900	+ $810	+ $90
Collegetown National Bank	+ $810	+ $729	+ $81
All other banks combined	+ $7,290	+ $6,561	+ $729
Total	+ $10,000	+ $9,000	+ $1,000

supply by $2,439, composed of the $900 created by Academia National Bank, the $810 by Bookville National Bank, and the $729 by Collegetown National Bank. Many banks will participate in the process down the line. Second, this process creates less new money with each step. Each subsequent bank gets a smaller deposit, yielding fewer excess reserves, and creating less money. If we were to continue for all the rest of the banks, we see in the fourth row of Table 27.1 that the cumulative new deposits at these remaining banks would equal $7,290. Thus the remaining banks increase the money supply by an additional $6,561, the amount of the new loans. All these remaining banks must hold a combined total of $729 of new required reserves against their cumulative new deposits of $7,290 to meet the reserve requirement. The total for the banking system at the end of the entire process of money creation is impressive: $10,000 of total new deposits, $9,000 of new loans (newly created money), and $1,000 of new required reserves.

How does the lending rule employed by the banking system compare to the lending guideline employed by each individual bank? Each individual bank in this process can safely lend an amount equal to its excess reserves. The banking system itself, however, can safely lend a multiple of its excess reserves. In our example, the banking system received an initial deposit of $1,000 in the form of the initial deposit into Academia National Bank. Given the 10-percent reserve requirement, that initial deposit meant an initial amount of excess reserves of $900 for the banking system. When all was said and done, the banking system was able to lend $9,000 based on $900 of initial excess reserves. Why is the lending guideline so much more generous for the banking system? The answer is that, while an individual bank has to fear a check being collected against it, the banking system as a whole does not. Any check that you write on a U.S. bank will, in all probability, end up deposited somewhere else in the U.S. banking system.

The Simple Money Creation Process

We next focus on summarizing the money creation process without laboriously calculating what each of many banks will do in terms of new deposits and new loans. The flow of new deposits from bank to bank is very similar to the flow of new spending from person to person illustrated by the spending multiplier in our fiscal policy chapter. A few simple formulas, described in the following sections, allow us to quickly determine the impact of money multiplier process.

Simple Money Multiplier. The **simple money multiplier** calculates the strength of the money creation process in the banking system. Note that each bank in Table 27.1 held some required reserves. The greater the amount of required reserves, the weaker the money multiplier process will be. We capture this influence with Equation 27.2.

$$\text{Simple money multiplier} = 1/rr \qquad (27.2)$$

where rr = reserve requirement imposed by the Fed. In our example, the reserve requirement = 10 percent, so the simple money multiplier = $1/0.10 = 10$.

After determining the strength of the simple money multiplier, we can focus on the impact on new checkable deposits and new loans (newly created money) in Equations 27.3 and 27.4.

$$\text{Change in initial deposit} \times \text{Simple money multiplier} =$$
$$\text{Maximum change in new checkable deposits} \qquad (27.3)$$

$$\text{Change in initial excess reserves} \times \text{Simple money multiplier} =$$
$$\text{Maximum new loans} = \text{Maximum newly created money} \qquad (27.4)$$

In the beginning of this process, the banking system received $1,000 of new deposits, so $1,000 \times 10$ (the simple money multiplier) = $10,000 of new checkable deposits, as shown in Table 27.1. When the banking system received that initial $1,000 of new deposits, it also initially obtained $900 in new excess reserves. Equation 27.4 tells us that $900 \times 10 = 9,000 of new loans = $9,000 of newly created money.

Reverse Multiplier Effect. When loans are repaid, the multiplier effect works in reverse. If the loan is repaid with a check from another bank, this repayment triggers a multiple contraction in the money supply. Suppose our vacationer pays off the $900 loan at Academia National Bank with a check written on an account at Bookville National Bank. Bookville National Bank now has $900 less in checkable deposits and $900 less in reserves. With this loss of reserves and a 10-percent reserve requirement, Bookville National Bank has a reserve deficiency of $810 and must accumulate new reserves to meet the reserve requirement. One way to accomplish this is to use the funds coming in from loan repayments to eliminate the reserve deficiency. What if the loan repayment of $810 comes from another bank? That bank then has a reserve deficiency that causes the money supply to fall by $729; this series of events is our money creation process in reverse. Funds are progressively contracted as banks accept loan repayments to rebuild their reserve positions. Funds are drawn from deeper and deeper in the banking system to repay loans and rebuild reserve positions. Ultimately, the money supply increases only when the amount of new loans made by the banking system is greater than the amount of existing loans being repaid in the banking system.

The Realistic Money Creation Process

Notice that we are using the *simple* money multiplier to find the *maximum* in new deposits, new loans, and newly created money. The three simplifying assumptions that we made at the beginning of our example yielded the maximum anticipated impact. Relaxing those earlier assumptions, as shown in the following sections, provides a more realistic look at the money creation process.

Public Holds Currency. We assumed that the public held no currency. Other than the initial deposit, all participants in the money creation process used checkable deposits in all their transactions. If the public does hold currency, the flow of deposits from one bank to another is reduced. For example, if the Bookville National Bank customer received that $900 check and decided to keep $50 in currency when he deposited the check, Bookville National Bank would have only $850 of new deposits to work with, instead of $900. As a result, the actual change in the money supply would be less than the maximum change. The actual money multiplier will be less than the simple money multiplier.

Banks Hold Excess Reserves. We also assume that the banks held no excess reserves. In our example, each bank lends an amount equal to its excess reserves. After the check cleared, each bank desired zero excess reserves. Banks can and do hold excess reserves for enhanced safety. Doing so reduces the flow of deposits from one bank to another, which reduces money creation. For example, suppose that Academia National Bank wants to hold $100 of new excess reserves along with the $100 of new required reserves. It is now willing to lend only $800 instead of $900. As a result, the actual change in the money supply would be less than we find in our equations shown earlier. Such excess reserves weaken the money creation process.

Banks' Reluctance to Make New Loans. We assumed that banks are always willing and able to lend. In our example, when Academia National Bank wanted to lend $900, a customer immediately appeared who wanted to borrow $900. All the banks in our example always made their loans for exactly the amount they were willing and able to lend. In reality, if bad times are expected, banks are often reluctant to make loans. At other times, loan customers are lacking. In the early 1980s, the interest rate on a 30-year fixed-term mortgage was 15 percent. Most borrowers were not willing to pay that historically high nominal interest rate. The money creation process is weakened when banks are unwilling or unable to lend.

The bottom line is that the actual money multiplier is always less than the simple money multiplier. Because there are leakages and slippages in the money creation process, the actual impact of a given amount of new excess reserves or new deposits on money creation is much less than our simple money multiplier formulas suggest. Currently, the actual average reserve requirement is approximately six percent. This implies a simple money multiplier of 16.7. In reality, the actual size of the M1 money multiplier is less than 2.0.

The Fed's Control of the Money Supply

Through its monetary policy, the Fed aims to provide the correct amount of money for the economy to function successfully. We have established that excess reserves fuel money creation. If the Fed wishes to increase the money supply, it must increase the amount of excess reserves in the banking system. If the Fed wants to decrease the money supply, it must remove excess reserves from the banking system. In this section, we examine the Fed's three major tools for adding or subtracting excess reserves on bank balance sheets. We discuss the limitations of these monetary policy tools in practice. Finally, we also show how the Fed applied these specific tools in response to the 9/11 attacks.

Open Market Operations

Open market operations
The Fed's buying or selling of U.S. government securities.

The first of these three tools of monetary policy is called **open market operations,** which involve the Fed's buying or selling of U.S. government securities. This tool is the most frequently used Fed monetary tool conducted every business day.

Effect on the Balance Sheet of Banking System. To see how the buying and selling of government securities by the Fed changes the reserve position of banks and their ability to create money, consider the following simplified example. Suppose that the reserve requirement is 10 percent and that the Fed buys $1,000 of U.S. government securities from banks. The impact on the banking system's balance sheet is shown in panel (a) of Figure 27.5.

The banks sell $1,000 in U.S. government securities from their assets to the Fed. How does the Fed pay the banks for these securities? Banks want reserves from the Fed. In a fractional reserve banking system, reserves are important both for bank safety and as a basis for new loans. The banks want to be credited with $1,000 of new reserves. On the asset side of the banks' balance sheets, they receive $1,000 in new total reserves from the Fed.

In examining the banks' balance sheets, we can see that the banks have received $1,000 in new total reserves. Excess reserves fuel money creation, so the banks want to know how much of that $1,000 of new total reserves is excess reserves. The banks have no new deposits as a result of this open market operation. As a result, they do not need to hold any new excess reserves. *All* the new total reserves they received from the Fed are excess reserves. With this open market operation, the banking system has traded securities to the Fed to obtain an equal amount of new excess reserves. When the Fed buys U.S. government securities in the open market, it engages in **expansionary monetary policy,** which involves providing the banking system with more excess reserves to expand the money supply. However, if the Fed sold U.S. government securities, the banks would end up with more government securities and less reserves on their balance sheets. This situation would limit their ability to make loans and thus restrict monetary growth. When the Fed sells U.S. government securities, it engages in **contractionary monetary policy,** which reduces

Expansionary monetary policy
Fed actions that provide the banking system with more excess reserves to expand the money supply.

Contractionary monetary policy
Fed actions that reduce the amount of excess reserves in the banking system and curtail the ability of banks to create money.

FIGURE 27.5

Impact of Open Market Operations and the Discount Rate on the Banking System

In panel (a), when the Fed buys $1,000 worth of U.S. government securities from the banking system, it receives $1,000 in new total reserves from the Fed. Because the banking system has no new deposits against which reserves must be held, all those new total reserves are excess reserves. In panel (b), banks borrow $1,000 in new reserves from the Fed. These new total reserves may be all required reserves, all excess reserves, or some combination of the two.

(a) Open market operation

Assets	Liabilities
U.S. government securities − $1,000	
Total reserves + $1,000	

(b) Discount rate

Assets	Liabilities
Total reserves + $1,000	Discount loans + $1,000

the amount of excess reserves in the banking system and curtails the ability of banks to create money.

Effectiveness of Open Market Operations. Open market operations are an efficient and effective way of conducting monetary policy. They are flexible, responsive, and immediate. Each morning, officials at the New York Federal Reserve Bank consult with officials at the Federal Reserve System in Washington. The officials at the New York Reserve Bank then contact about 30 securities dealers and tell them how many U.S. government securities the Federal Reserve system wishes to buy or sell that day. The dealers have about 15 minutes to respond to the Fed with their offers of how much they would charge for U.S. government securities (if the Fed is buying) or pay for securities (if the Fed is selling). Approximately five minutes after they receive the responses, the Fed officials in New York decide which transactions they are willing to make, the dealers are notified, and the open market operations for that day conclude.

Open Market Operations After 9/11. The New York Federal Reserve Bank is located only blocks from the site of the World Trade Center. On September 11, 2001, Reserve Bank employees observed firsthand the devastation and disruption in lower Manhattan, the center of the American banking system. They knew that the banking system would need a huge injection of new reserves to accommodate the extraordinary financial pressures resulting from the attacks. On the day after the terrorist attacks, expansionary open market operations pumped $38 billion of new reserves into the banking system. On a typical day, the New York Federal Reserve Bank generally conducts open market operations worth about $3.5 billion. The Fed dramatically increased its open market purchases to infuse the banking system with emergency liquidity.

Changing the Discount Rate

Discount rate
The interest rate that the Fed charges depository institutions that borrow reserves from the Fed.

The second of the Fed's major monetary tools is its ability to change the **discount rate,** or the interest rate that the Fed charges depository institutions that borrow reserves from the Fed. For example, assume that the Fed lowers the discount rate and banks then borrow $1,000 more from the Fed. Panel (b) of Figure 27.5 shows the impact on the balance sheet of the banking system as a result of this discount loan.

Effect on the Balance Sheet of Banking System. On the balance sheet of the banking system, we see $1,000 more reserves on the asset side and $1,000 of new liabilities, representing the loan from the Fed. How much of the new $1,000 of reserves on the banking system's balance sheet are required reserves that must be held? How much are excess reserves that can fuel money creation? Depository institutions have the right to borrow from the Fed. They may borrow reserves that are all required reserves, reserves that are all excess reserves, or any combination of the two. Lowering the discount rate is expansionary monetary policy because banks can acquire more excess reserves and in turn create more money. Raising the discount rate is contractionary monetary policy that discourages banks from acquiring more excess reserves.

Each time the FOMC meets to discuss monetary policy, the Fed can change the discount rate. The Fed can also change the discount rate between scheduled FOMC meetings, if conditions warrant. The Fed has averaged three to four changes per year recently, with a high of eleven changes in 2001 and a low of zero changes in 2003.

Effectiveness of Discount Rate Changes. Changing the discount rate is the Fed's weakest major monetary tool. One problem with this tool is that it is a passive policy: The Fed must wait for banks to act. The Fed lowers the discount rate and hopes that the banking system will decide to borrow more excess reserves to make more loans and create more money. Raising the discount rate is a weak contractionary tool. The Fed cannot prohibit depository institutions from borrowing from the Fed. Even if the Fed raises the discount rate to higher levels, banks can always borrow reserves from other sources, such as their fellow depository institutions.

Banks typically borrow very small amounts of reserves from the Fed. The Fed and the banking community often view borrowing from the Fed as a sign of poor performance and management at the borrowing bank.

Discount Policy After 9/11. Even though banks generally do little borrowing from the Fed, the availability of such loans proved vital in the wake of the September 11 attacks. On a normal day, Federal Reserve Banks lend about $100 million to the U.S. banking system. On September 12, 2001, Federal Reserve Banks made $45 *billion* worth of loans to ensure that banks had all the reserves and liquidity they needed to operate. The Fed effectively told the banking system that it could borrow whatever reserves it needed for as long as it needed. The FOMC also met in an emergency meeting on September 17, 2001, to lower the discount rate by an additional one half of one percent.

Changing Reserve Requirements

The final major monetary tool at the Fed's disposal is the ability to change reserve requirements. Currently, there are reserve requirements only on checkable deposits.

Effect on Money Creation. As the Fed raises reserve requirements (with a given amount of deposits and total reserves in the banking system), the banking system has more dollars of required reserves and fewer dollars of excess reserves. That reduction in excess reserves reduces the ability of banks to create money. However, raising the reserve requirements also reduces the size of the simple money multiplier. Each dollar of excess reserves is less powerful in expanding the money supply. Recall the formula shown in Equation 27.4.

$$\textit{Change in initial excess reserves} \times \textit{Simple money multiplier} =$$
$$\textit{Maximum new loans} = \textit{Maximum newly created money} \qquad (27.4)$$

With fewer excess reserves in the banking system and a small simple money multiplier, the contractionary impact on the money supply from raising the reserve requirement is magnified. Lowering the reserve requirement has a magnified impact on expanding the money supply.

Effectiveness of Reserve Requirement Changes. Changing the reserve requirement is the only Fed tool that simultaneously alters both the level of excess reserves and the size of the simple money multiplier. As a result, it is the Fed's most powerful monetary tool. The Fed rarely resorts to this tool. The Fed last changed reserve requirements when it lowered them in February 1992. The Fed views changes in reserve requirements as a disruptive force on the balance sheets and behavior of banks.

Reserve Requirements After 9/11. The Fed did not change reserve requirements after September 11, 2001. The banks did not need more *excess* reserves after the terrorist attacks they needed more *total* reserves. Lowering reserve requirements would have rearranged the composition of total reserves and not created any additional reserves in the banking system.

Get Ahead of the Curve

Use your knowledge of the Federal Reserve to assess former Chairman Alan Greenspan's performance.

Summary of Monetary Policy Tools

We summarize the impact of these three major tools in expansionary and contractionary monetary policy in Table 27.2. The table shows the relative strength of each tool and the frequency of use. Note that the use of open market operations is labeled the most effective monetary tool. Even though it does not have the most powerful

TABLE 27.2

Fed's Major Monetary Tools

(a) Expansionary Monetary Policy

Monetary Tool	Strength	Frequency of Use
Open market operations (Fed buys U.S. government securities)	Most effective	Every business day
Lowering the discount rate	Weakest	Generally 3–4 times a year
Lowering reserve requirements	Strongest	Very infrequently; last changed in 1992

(b) Contractionary Monetary Policy

Monetary Tool	Strength	Frequency of Use
Open market operations (Fed sells U.S. government securities)	Most effective	Every business day
Raising the discount rate	Weakest	Generally 3–4 times a year
Raising reserve requirements	Strongest	Very infrequently; last changed in 1992

impact on the banks' reserve position, its ease and efficiency make it the Fed's preferred tool of monetary policy.

The use of these tools of monetary policy has several significant advantages for policy makers. As you have seen, the Fed was able to respond to the 9/11 crisis within minutes of the attacks on the World Trade Center and the Pentagon. In the normal course of business, the Fed is able to respond quickly to changing economic circumstances. Unexpected changes in employment, real GDP, or inflation can be addressed very quickly. The intended direction of monetary policy can switch from expansionary to contractionary in very short order. These monetary tools allow the Fed to conduct policies of both large and small scale with relative ease.

Limitations of Monetary Policy

Monetary policy can be nimble and responsive in the hands of policy makers. However, monetary policy might not work effectively in some circumstances. Although the Fed's goal is to manipulate the money supply in the public interest, it does not directly control the money supply. The Fed depends on the behavior of the banking system and the public to transmit the impact of monetary policy to the economy.

To illustrate, imagine that the Fed sees signs of weakness in the economy and implement an expansionary monetary policy to overcome this weakness. The Fed supplies more excess reserves to the banking system in the hope of reducing interest rates and stimulating aggregate demand. For this policy to succeed, the banking system must use these new excess reserves as the basis of additional lending. What if the banks, seeing the weakness in the economy, became reluctant to make new loans? The public, wary of the economic future, might decide to hold on to more currency. The amount of new money created would be curtailed as banks held more excess reserves and the public more currency. Both of these actions would weaken the money creation process. Even though the Fed might undertake the correct monetary policy, the transmission of that expansionary policy to the economy through the public and banking system might be disrupted.

One example of such a disruption was the recession of 1990–1991. The Fed lowered the discount rate 10 times in 1991. Yet borrowers found it difficult to obtain loans from banks, and loans that were made had high nominal interest rates. Many banks held any new reserves provided by the Fed's expansionary monetary policy to gain more safety in difficult economic times. The problems of the savings and loan associations in the 1980s had made many other depository institutions very cautious about granting loans. The stock market crash of 1987, coupled with declining real estate prices, had further reduced the banks' willingness to lend. In spite of the significant reduction in the discount rate and the increase in bank reserves, the money supply in 1990 and 1991 grew very slowly. The banks received the fuel for money creation but did not use that fuel to facilitate money creation. As a result, the Fed's correct monetary policy was unable to prevent the economy from sliding into a recession.

▶The Federal Funds Market

Federal funds market
The market in which banks can lend reserves to other banks.

To illustrate the impact of the Fed's monetary policy more concretely, we must explore an important financial market. The **federal funds market** is the market in which banks lend reserves to other banks. This market captures the influence of the Fed's monetary policy on the availability and cost of reserves. In our simple money creation example, we assumed that the banks that possessed excess reserves could earn no interest on them. In reality, if a bank has excess reserves, it can lend them for very short periods (usually overnight) to other banks. In this section, we examine this market for reserves and the Fed's procedure for announcing its monetary policy through the behavior of this market. Although monetary policy is usually described as changing the money supply, the most immediate impact of monetary policy is usually transmitted through changing interest rates. The Fed uses the interest rate in the federal funds market to signal and transmit its monetary policy decisions.

The Federal Funds Rate

Federal funds rate
The interest rate charged on reserves borrowed in the federal funds market.

The demand for excess reserves is inversely related to the interest rate charged on reserves borrowed in the federal funds market, which is the **federal funds rate.** The supply of reserves by other banks is directly related to the federal funds rate.

Operation of the Federal Funds Market. Each business day, borrowing and lending banks notify a brokerage house in New York of their willingness to supply or demand reserves. The brokerage house matches those offers, announces the equilibrium federal funds rate, and notifies successful borrowers and lenders of these federal funds.

Figure 27.6 illustrates the operation of the federal funds market. The banks that want excess reserves are the demanders in this market. As the federal funds rate falls, they increase the quantity of federal funds demanded. The suppliers of federal

FIGURE 27.6

The Federal Funds Market

In panel (a), demanders for federal funds want to borrow more reserves as the federal funds rate falls. Lenders will supply more reserves as federal funds rate rises. The equilibrium federal funds rate is 3 percent and the equilibrium quantity of federal funds borrowed and lent is $50 billion. In panel (b), the federal funds market is initially in equilibrium at E_1 with a federal funds rate of 3 percent and an equilibrium quantity of federal funds of $50 billion. If the Fed conducts an expansionary monetary policy, the demand for federal funds decreases from D_1 to D_2. The new equilibrium federal funds rate is 2.5 percent and fewer federal funds are borrowed ($45 billion).

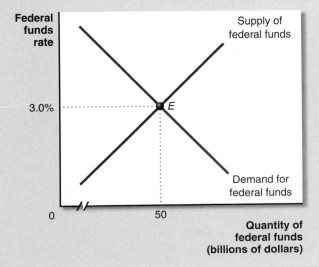

(a) Equilibrium in the federal funds market

(b) Impact of expansionary monetary policy in the federal funds market

TABLE 27.3

The Fed's Monetary Policy

Type of Monetary Policy	Intended Impact on Money Supply	Intended Impact on the Federal Funds Rate	Open Market Operations	Change in the Discount Rate	Change in the Reserve Requirement
Expansionary	Increased growth rate	Lower	Fed buys U.S. government securities	Fed lowers	Fed lowers
Contractionary	Decreased growth rate	Raise	Fed sells U.S. government securities	Fed raises	Fed raises

funds are banks that have reserves to lend. As the federal fund rate increases, they increase the quantity of federal funds supplied. The equilibrium federal funds rate equates the quantity demanded of reserves to the quantity supplied. In Figure 27.6(a), the equilibrium federal funds rate is three percent and the quantity of federal funds borrowed and lent equals $50 billion.

The Fed's Role in the Federal Funds Market. The Fed plays the determining role in the federal funds market. With the three tools of monetary policy, the Fed can exert significant control over the total amount of reserves in the banking system. When the FOMC meets, it sets a target for the federal funds rate. The Fed then uses its tools of monetary policy to add or subtract excess reserves to meet that target. Figure 27.6(b) shows the impact of an expansionary monetary policy by the Fed. Typically, an expansionary monetary policy means that the Fed buys U.S. government securities. These Fed purchases increase the amount of excess reserves in the banking system. As a result, banks have more reserves and will want to borrow fewer reserves at every federal funds rate. The demand for federal funds will decrease. As a result, the amount of federal funds borrowed falls from $50 billion to $45 billion and the equilibrium federal funds rate decreases from 3.0 percent to 2.5 percent.

What if the Fed conducts a contractionary monetary policy? There is more demand for reserves and upward pressure on the federal funds rate. As a result, the federal funds rate increases and the quantity of federal funds borrowed is greater.

The Fed's 9/11 Response. On September 17, 2001, the Fed held an emergency meeting to lower the targeted federal funds rate from 3.5 percent to 3.0 percent. However, the Fed also announced that it would push the actual federal funds rate below this target rate if circumstances warranted. By September 19, the federal funds rate had fallen to 1.9 percent. For the next six days, the actual federal funds rate was well below its target rate, as the Fed flooded the banking system with excess reserves.

We summarize the impact of the Fed's monetary policy on the economy in Table 27.3. The Fed's monetary policy comes in two basic versions: expansionary and contractionary. Expansionary monetary policy happens when the Fed steps on the monetary gas pedal, increasing the growth rate of the money supply and lowering the federal funds rate. The Fed accomplishes this acceleration in monetary growth and reduction in the federal funds rate by providing more reserves to the banking system and the federal funds market. To do so, it buys U.S. government securities, lowers the discount rate so that banks are encouraged to borrow more reserves, and/or reduces the reserve requirement to create more excess reserves.

A contractionary monetary policy is designed to reduce the amount of reserves in the banking system. The Fed accomplishes this goal by selling U.S. government securities, raising the discount rate, and/or raising the reserve requirement. This contractionary impact involves the Fed stepping on the monetary brakes, slowing the growth of the money supply and raising the federal funds rate.

The FOMC Directive and the Conduct of Monetary Policy

FOMC Directive
Document that gives the New York Fed officials directions about how to conduct monetary policy and provides the public with insight into the Fed's view of future monetary policy.

Every six to eight weeks, business reporters breathlessly report that the FOMC is meeting to decide upon the future of interest rates. Unexpected changes announced by the FOMC in the direction or magnitude of change in interest rates can be disconcerting to the financial community and cause brief but powerful changes in financial markets.

Why do reporters focus their attention on these periodic meetings of FOMC, when open market operations take place every business day? The answer is that the FOMC meets eight times a year to decide whether to change its intentions for the magnitude of its open market operations and the direction of interest rates. After each meeting, the FOMC issues a press release summarizing the Fed's monetary policy decisions made that day and why the decisions were made. This announcement is called the **FOMC Directive,** a document that gives the New York Fed officials directions about how to conduct monetary policy while providing the public with insight into the Fed's view of future monetary policy. After the Directive is issued, the Federal Reserve Bank of New York engages in open market operations every business day to execute the FOMC's interest rate decision.

In this chapter, we have explored the role the Fed plays in monetary policy. We have seen how individual depository institutions actually create money by accepting deposits and making loans. Through the money multiplier process in the banking system, potentially large and disruptive changes in the money supply can occur. Using expansionary or contractionary monetary policy, the Fed seeks to provide the right amount of money and the right level of interest rates to achieve its goals of full employment, price stability, and sustainable economic growth. In the next chapter, we examine the role that the money supply and interest rates play in achieving overall macroeconomic health.

TEST + *EXTEND* Your Knowledge

1. TEST Banks obtain additional reserves to make new loans in the federal funds market. Would you expect the federal funds rate to be higher or lower than other interest rates? Would you expect the federal funds rate to move in the same direction as other interest rates? Why or why not?

2. EXTEND The Board of Governors of the Federal Reserve System's Web site lists a number of interest rates in the U.S. economy (www.aw-bc/leeds/ch27). Check this Web site to see whether your predictions were accurate by comparing the federal funds rate to the bank prime rate (the lowest loan rate on commercial loans) and the interest rate on mortgage loans.

At various points in his tenure as chairman of the Federal Reserve Board, Alan Greenspan has been called "the most powerful man in Washington." In part, his power reflects the traditional independence of the Federal Reserve System from the oversight of the legislative and executive branches of government. As you have learned, the members of the Board of Governors serve terms of office that insulate them from the political considerations of Congress or the president. The Fed is also financially independent, as it does not rely on federal appropriations to support its activities. Instead, it supports itself primarily with earnings from its holdings of U.S. government securities and from fees received from the banking system for the services the Fed provides.

The chairman of the Federal Reserve Board has more impact on monetary policy than any other individual. The chairman benefits from substantial independence from short-term political pressures. Alan Greenspan began his term under Ronald Reagan, a conservative Republican, yet Bill Clinton, a Democrat, felt compelled to reappoint him.

From time to time, the Fed conducts monetary policy that slows monetary growth, raises interest rates, reduces economic growth, and raises the unemployment rate. At such times, politicians become critical of the Fed and may seek to impose more political accountability on the Fed. Periodically, Congress has tried to impose its will on the Fed, threatening to set targets for monetary growth, interest rates, or the growth rate of real GDP and to control more of the Fed's finances through audits and oversight.

The Fed enjoys considerably greater independence than many other central banks. The Bank of England, for example, can set interest rates, but the British government can overrule those interest rate changes. The Bank of Japan is also subject to the authority of its Ministry of Finance. However, the Ministry's role has been in flux with the recent banking crisis. An earlier study by Alberto Alesina and Lawrence Summers found the Federal Reserve System to be more independent than the central banks of 12 of 14 other industrialized nations.[1]

Inflation targeting
The Fed solely commits its monetary policy to achieve a certain rate of inflation for a given time period.

Some critics of the Fed's independence believe that the Fed should adopt **inflation targeting** where the Fed solely commits its monetary policy to achieve a certain rate of inflation for a given time period. For example, the Fed might set a target rate of inflation of 2 percent for the next two years. For critics of Fed independence, inflation targeting has two major benefits: (1) increased transparency as the Fed must publicly divulge its precise target for monetary policy and (2) increased accountability as the Fed's successes and failures would be readily apparent to all. To date, the Fed has resisted inflation targeting in favor of a more eclectic set of macroeconomic targets that includes controlling inflation as a primary but not sole target of monetary policy.

Because the Fed does not have to worry about who wins the next election, it can take a longer perspective on policy issues. In the late 1970s and early 1980s, then-chairman Paul Volcker tightened the screws on the growth of the money supply. As

---

[1]Alberto Alesina and Lawrence Summers, "Central Bank Independence and Macroeconomic Performance: Some Comparative Evidence," *Journal of Money Credit, and Banking*, vol. 25 (May 1993) pp. 151–162. Alesina and Summers found the Fed was less independent than the central banks in Switzerland and Germany and more independent than the banks in Spain, New Zealand, Italy, the United Kingdom, Australia, France, Norway, Sweden, Denmark, Japan, Canada, Belgium, and the Netherlands. This study pre-dated the European Monetary Union.

the theory would predict, the Fed's policy induced high interest rates and a severe recession that had many members of Congress calling in vain for Volcker's dismissal. The Fed stuck to its guns, however, and the policy is now credited with ending the severe inflation of the 1970s. The ability of the Fed to withstand political pressure and combat inflation reflects its independence. Alesina and Summers found that inflation rates were substantially lower in nations with more independent central banks.

Independence, however, comes at a potential cost to the American people. The U.S. government is built on a system of checks and balances that makes its policy makers answerable to the voters. The Fed's policy makers have no such obligation or accountability. Ideally, insulation from the political process allows the Fed to pursue necessary but unpopular policies. At worst, a lack of oversight and transparency allows the Fed to pursue wrongheaded policies with no pressure to reverse course. As a result, the Fed can implement policies that create widespread unemployment without any fear of retribution, even if such a policy is contrary to the wishes of the American people.

Critical-Thinking Questions

1. Fed's monetary powers are ultimately subject to the discretion of Congress, which created the Fed in 1913. Under what conditions might Congress be more likely to consider reducing the Fed's current monetary independence? What specific legislative steps might Congress consider to limit the Fed's independence and increase the Fed's accountability in monetary policy?
2. Why might Congress be reluctant to tamper with the Fed's independence even when the Fed is pursuing policies with which Congress disagrees?

SUMMARY

- **The structure of the Fed and its defining relationships.** The central bank of the United States, the Federal Reserve System, is designed to provide the economy with the right amount of money at the right time. The Board of Governors is the Fed's central authority while the FOMC sets the overall direction of monetary policy. The Fed is characterized by a series of special relationships with the federal government, the banking system, and the public. These special relationships give the Fed a unique place in the U.S. economy.

- **The creation of money by individual depository institutions.** Individual depository institutions can create money. Depository institutions receive new deposits, calculate reserve positions, and then lend amounts equal to their excess reserves. When a depository institution makes a loan, it creates an equal amount of money.

- **Money creation by the banking system.** As each depository institution accepts new deposits and makes new loans, the cumulative effect on new checkable deposits and loans in the banking system grows. The simple money multiplier process captures the impact of the injection of new reserves into the banking system. The formula used to determine the size and strength of the process is: *Simple money multiplier* $= 1/rr$ where rr = the reserve requirement imposed by the Fed.

- **The Fed's control of the money supply.** The Fed has three major tools for controlling the money supply: open market operations, changing the discount rate, and changing reserve requirements. Each of these tools has the ability to alter the amount of excess reserves in the banking system and the ability of banks to create money.

- **The federal funds market.** The impact of the Fed's monetary tools and intentions is captured in the behavior of the federal funds market, where banks borrow and lend reserves. Through expansionary monetary policy, the Fed can provide more reserves and thus lower the federal funds rate. Contractionary monetary policy ultimately increases the federal funds rate. The FOMC Directive announces the Fed's current and future monetary policy intentions.

KEY TERMS

Annual percentage rate (APR) 689
Annual percentage yield (APY) 690
Board of Governors 687
Check clearing 689
Contractionary monetary policy 698
Discount rate 699

Excess reserves 691
Expansionary monetary policy 698
Federal funds market 702
Federal funds rate 703
Federal Open Market Committee (FOMC) 688
FOMC Directive 705
Inflation targeting 706

Monetary policy 686
Open market operations 698
Required reserves 691
Simple money multiplier 696
Total reserves 691

PROBLEMS

1. With a simplified bank balance sheet, illustrate the impact on an individual bank when it receives a deposit of currency into a checkable deposit.
2. Why is there no change in M1 when an individual deposits currency into a checkable deposit?
3. A single bank receives $1,000 in currency deposited by an individual into her checking account. The required reserve ratio is 5 percent.
   a. Initial change in the bank's total deposits = $_____
   b. Initial change in the bank's total reserves = $_____
   c. Change in the bank's required reserves = $_____
   d. Change in the bank's excess reserves = $_____
4. Why will an individual bank lend only an amount equal to its excess reserves?
5. What happens on the balance sheet of an individual bank when the bank has a check cleared against it?
6. Why does the strength of money creation for each bank decrease as the money creation process continues?
7. Following are simplified balance sheets for two individual banks. Consider each bank and each case independently from the other. Use the situation described to show the numerical changes that would result from the specified activity in each case. Show decreases with "−," increases with "+," and no change with "0."
   a. A small business writes a check drawn on its bank to pay back a $2,000 loan from that same bank.

Academia National Bank		
Total reserves $ _____	Checkable deposits $ _____	
Loans $ _____		
Impact of this activity on M1 = $ _____		

b. You cash a $25 check drawn on this bank:

Bookville National Bank Balance Sheet

Total reserves	$ _____	Checkable deposits	$ _____
Loans	$ _____		

Impact of this activity on M1 = $ _____

8. Answer the following questions based on the money creation process.
   a. If an individual bank receives an initial deposit of currency of $15,000 into a checkable deposit when the reserve requirement is 10 percent, how much can this individual bank safely lend?
   b. If the banking system receives the same deposit with the same reserve ratio, by how much can the banking system potentially expand its deposits?
   c. A bank has total checkable deposits of $100,000 and total reserves of $37,000. The reserve requirement is 25 percent. The maximum amount by which the bank can safely increase its loans = $_____. The maximum amount by which the banking system can safely increase its loans = $_____.
   d. A bank initially has no excess reserves. A customer deposits $900 of currency into a checking account in the bank. The bank then lends $500 to a borrower. As a result of these two transactions, M1 has (increased, decreased) by $_____ .

9. You are given the following simplified balance sheet for a local commercial bank. Assume that the reserve requirement is 10 percent.

Assets		Liabilities	
Total reserves	$ 100,000	Checkable deposits	$ 700,000
Loans	$ 600,000		

   a. Required reserves = $_____ and excess reserves = $_____.
   b. This single bank can safely lend an additional $_____.
   c. If the bank is willing and able to make the loan for the full amount in the previous question, show how its balance sheet will look immediately after the loan is made:

Assets		Liabilities	
Total reserves	$ _____	Checkable deposits	$ _____
Loans	$ _____		

d. If this bank then has the check cleared against it for the full amount of that loan, show the bank's balance sheet after the check is cleared:

Assets		Liabilities	
Total reserves	$ _____	Checkable deposits	$ _____
Loans	$ _____		

10. Why is the size of the actual money multiplier less than the simple money multiplier?

11. What are some of the checks and balances in the structure of the Federal Reserve System?

12. Why is the Fed the government's bank?

13. What do the Truth in Lending Act and the Truth in Savings Act mean for consumers of banking services?

14. Describe the impact of open market operations on the balance sheets of both the Fed and the banking system.

15. Why is changing the discount rate generally considered the Fed's weakest monetary tool?

16. Why is changing the reserve requirement generally considered the Fed's strongest monetary tool?

17. The Fed has three major monetary tools. In the first column below, list these three tools in order of their frequency of use (from the most frequently used to the least frequently used). In the second column, list the three tools in order of their strength (from the strongest to the weakest).

Frequency	Strength
1. _____	1. _____
2. _____	2. _____
3. _____	3. _____

18. Who are the demanders and the suppliers in the federal funds market?

19. How would a contractionary monetary policy of the Fed selling U.S. government securities to the banking system affect the demand for federal funds, the equilibrium federal fund rate, and the amount of federal funds borrowed and lent?

20. Would you support legislation to increase the Fed's accountability and reduce some of its independence? Why or why not?

HERE'S HOW **MyEconLab** CAN HELP YOU GET A BETTER GRADE

1. Log into MyEconLab and take Practice Test 27-A (to log in for the first time, see page 30 for instructions).

2. Based on your test results, MyEconLab will identify the areas where you need further work and create a personal Study Plan for you.

3. Your Study Plan contains the problems listed below and others like them that will target the specific chapter topics you need to focus on. You'll receive instant feedback and find links to tutorials, animations, and the online textbook to help you study.

4. When you're ready, take Practice Test 27-B and demonstrate how your results have improved.

Section 27.1, Problem 1 Which of the following statements is correct?

a. The Federal Reserve System is divided into 7 regional banks. The Board of Governors has 12 members who serve 14-year terms.

b. The Federal Reserve System is divided into 12 regional banks. The Board of Governors has 14 members who serve 7-year terms.

c. The Federal Reserve System is divided into 7 regional banks. The Board of Governors has 14 members who serve 12-year terms.

d. The Federal Reserve System is divided into 14 regional banks. The Board of Governors has 7 members who serve 12-year terms.

e. The Federal Reserve System is divided into 12 regional banks. The Board of Governors has 7 members who serve 14-year terms.

Section 27.2, Problem 1 Are required reserves, excess reserves, deposits, and loans shown on a bank's balance sheet as assets or liabilities?

Section 27.2, Problem 2 Following is the balance sheet for The First National Bank.

The First National Bank

Assets	Liabilities
Total reserves:	Deposits: $500,000
Required reserves: $20,000	
Excess reserves: $80,000	
Loans: $400,000	
Total Assets: $500,000	Total Liabilities: $500,000

a. What is the reserve requirement?

b. How much can the The First National Bank safely lend?

Section 27.2, Problem 3 Suppose that Althea deposits $500 of loose change into her bank, Bank A. Suppose that the reserve requirement is 5 percent.

a. Fill in the values for Bank A's balance sheet:

Bank A

Assets	Liabilities
Total reserves:	Deposits:
Required reserves:	
Excess reserves:	
Total Assets:	Total Liabilities:

b. How much can Bank A safely lend?

c. Suppose that Bank A loans the amount from the previous question to Jonathan, one of its customers. Jonathan then spends all of that money on sweets at Barry's Bakery. Barry, the owner, deposits this money into his account at Bank B. Fill in the missing values in the following balance sheets for Bank A and Bank B.

Bank A

Assets	Liabilities
Total reserves:	Deposits:
Required reserves:	
Excess reserves:	
Loans:	
Total Assets:	Total Liabilities:

Bank B

Assets	Liabilities
Total reserves:	Deposits:
Required reserves:	
Excess reserves:	
Total Assets:	Total Liabilities:

d. How much can Bank B safely lend?

Section 27.3, Problem 1 Suppose that Sally deposits $1,000 into her checking account at Bank A. Also suppose that the reserve requirement is 10 percent and that banks hold no excess reserves and the public holds no currency.

  a. What is the value of the simple money multiplier?
  b. What is the maximum change in new checkable deposits?
  c. Now suppose that the reserve requirement is lowered to 5 percent. What is the value of the simple money multiplier? What is the maximum change in new checkable deposits?
  d. What is the relationship between the reserve requirement and the simple money multiplier?

Section 27.3, Problem 2 Suppose that Albert finds $2,000 in change in his couch that he deposits into his checking account at Bank A. Also suppose that the reserve requirement is 5 percent and that banks hold no excess reserves and the public holds no currency.

  a. What is the value of the simple money multiplier?
  b. Immediately after Albert makes the deposit, how has the money supply changed?
  c. What is the maximum change in new checkable deposits?
  d. What is the maximum amount of newly created money?

Section 27.4, Problem 1

  a. If the Fed wishes to pursue expansionary monetary policy, then it could (*buy/sell*) U.S. government securities, or (*raise/lower*) the discount rate, or (*raise/lower*) the reserve requirement.
  b. If the Fed wishes to pursue contractionary monetary policy, then it could (*buy/sell*) U.S. government securities, or (*raise/lower*) the discount rate, or (*raise/lower*) the reserve requirement.

Section 27.4, Problem 2 Suppose that the reserve requirement is five percent, banks hold no excess reserves, and the public holds no currency.

  a. If John deposits $10,000 into his checking account, what is the maximum change in new checkable deposits? What is the maximum newly created money?

  b. If the Federal Reserve buys $10,000 worth of U.S. securities from banks, what is the maximum change in new checkable deposits? What is the maximum newly created money?
  c. What is the difference between those two scenarios?

Section 27.5, Problem 1 If the Federal Reserve wanted to pursue expansionary policy, it would buy U.S. securities. In the federal funds market, this would cause the:

  a. Supply of federal funds to increase, causing the federal funds rate to fall.
  b. Supply of federal funds to decrease, causing the federal funds rate to rise.
  c. Demand for federal funds to increase, causing the federal funds rate to rise.
  d. Demand for federal funds to decrease, causing the federal funds rate to fall.
  e. Demand for federal funds to increase, causing the federal funds rate to fall.

Section 27.5, Problem 2

Which of the following graphs shows the effects of contractionary monetary policy on the federal funds market? Which shows expansionary monetary policy?

28

Money in the Macroeconomy

Have you ever daydreamed about money falling from the sky or about finding money growing on a tree in the woods? You might think that this shower of dollars or new pile of cash would make you rich. Yet if everyone had the same experience, you wouldn't be richer after all. Why is that?

Suppose that the Federal Reserve decided to double the size of the U.S. M1 money supply. Suppose, too, that the serious, responsible members of the Fed decided that they were tired of being serious and responsible. Rather than wait for expansionary monetary policy to work its way through the banking system, they take a shortcut and order the U.S. Bureau of Engraving and Printing to deliver enough crisp, new $100 bills to double the size of the current money supply. This would be about $1.5 trillion in brand-new $100 bills, or approximately 400 stacks of $100 bills that are ten feet tall, ten feet long, and ten feet wide. The Fed then hires a fleet of C-140 transport planes to fly across the country one night, dropping all those bills over cities and towns. The next morning, you wake up to see $100 bills all over the landscape. Everyone is out grabbing as many as they can, and you naturally join right in. Would your financial worries be over? How would all this new money affect the U.S. economy? What would happen to prices, interest rates, employment, and real GDP?

Although this is a fanciful situation, the answers to these questions reveal the role of money. There have been times when a nation—and indeed the world—experienced a huge increase in the money supply over a relatively short period of time. Around the turn of the twentieth century, the United States and most other industrial nations were still using a gold standard. Beginning in 1896, substantial new gold discoveries in the

Klondike region of Alaska and in South Africa created a major, sustained increase in the amount of gold available for the money supply. More gold meant more money in the United States and the world. The U.S. stock of monetary gold more than tripled from 1897 to 1914, and the overall world gold stock more than doubled. This increase was not exactly money falling from the sky, but these gold discoveries ultimately pumped vast amounts of new money into world economies. In this chapter, we examine the effects of such increases in the money supply.

Our focus in this chapter is on the role of money in the macroeconomy. We begin by examining the concept of money demand to determine why individuals hold money. We combine this understanding of money demand with a discussion of money supply to determine equilibrium conditions in the money market. Next, we explore the long-run impact of money on the macroeconomy. We proceed to a discussion of the short-run impact of money on such key economic variables as the price level, interest rates, employment, and real GDP. Finally, we compare the differences that changes in the money supply have in the long run and the short run.

ALONG THE WAY, YOU WILL ALSO LEARN:

- The reasons why individuals demand money assets.

- About the money market, where money demand and money supply determine the level of interest rates in the economy.

- How changes in the money supply affect the macroeconomy in the long run.

- How changes in the money supply affect the macroeconomy in the short run through various channels of monetary influence.

- The key differences in the long-run and short-run impacts of money in the macroeconomy.

AT THE END OF THE CHAPTER, THE MYECONLAB LOGO WILL DIRECT YOU ONLINE

- MyEconLab is a resource-packed online homework and tutorial system that can help you perform better in your economics course. To log in for the first time, see page 30 for instructions.

- MyEconLab can help you apply important concepts from the chapter to real-world issues. Watch for the logo to indicate online features about inflation fighting and the impact of high interest rates.

- At the end of each chapter, you'll find a special study section that will help you get the most out of your textbook and your instructor's MyEconLab course.

▶ The Money Market

Money market
Where money demand and money supply determine the equilibrium rate of interest.

All those $100 bills on the ground that one magical morning would not stay there very long. There would be a mad scramble as all of us tried to gather as many of them as we could. To see how the money supply affects the economy, we must examine the **money market**, where money demand and money supply determine the equilibrium rate of interest. We begin this section by explaining what money does for individuals and why individuals hold money. We then look at money demand and money supply in the economy as a whole. After establishing equilibrium in the money market, we examine the real-world challenges that changing money demand and money supply generate for monetary policy.

Holding Money

Holding money imposes costs and provides benefits to the holder. The first cost is the opportunity cost of forgone interest earnings. In M1, coins, currency, and traveler's checks all earn no interest. Though checkable deposits can earn interest, that interest rate is typically very low. Money assets converted to stocks, bonds, or even other bank deposits could earn a higher rate of return than M1 assets.

Money assets also bear the cost of declining purchasing power over time. As the price level rises, the purchasing power of the money we hold decreases. Even at a modest rate of inflation, the purchasing power of a dollar can decline substantially over time. At an inflation rate of just 3 percent, the purchasing power of money will be cut in half in 24 years.

Money also provides benefits to the holder. By holding money, individuals can prepare for everyday events, be protected when things go wrong, and have the ability to pursue investment opportunities.

Individuals compare the costs and benefits of holding money when deciding how much money to hold. They hold money only if the benefits are greater than the costs. If the benefits of holding money increase or the costs of holding money decline, individuals will hold more money assets.

Money Demand

Now that we've introduced the costs and benefits of holding money at the individual level, we can examine the overall demand for money in the macroeconomy. **Money demand** is the desire to hold money to obtain the benefits of preparedness, safety, and increased opportunities. There are three distinct types of money demand, each reflecting a specific motivation for holding money assets: transactions demand, precautionary demand, and speculative demand.

Transactions Demand. Transactions demand is the demand for money assets for use in everyday, expected transactions. Transactions demand reflects the benefit of preparedness. When you go out the door each morning with money in your wallet, you are prepared for the expected transactions that you regularly face. You might buy your lunch at school every day, put gas in your car once a week, and pay for textbooks every term. The money you hold for such purchases is transactions demand. How much money do you typically hold for transaction purposes? The amount varies for each individual. Determining factors include the following:

1. *Frequency of payment of income:* The lower the time period between paychecks the more money you need to set aside to meet everyday, expected transactions.
2. *Economy's payment mechanism:* The increasing popularity of electronic money has caused transactions demand to decline. Credit cards and stored value cards are popular alternatives to holding money.
3. *Individual income:* As an individual's income increases, transactions demand also increases. Individuals with high incomes tend to do more spending and to spend more on each given transaction than lower-income individuals.

Money demand
The desire to hold money to obtain the benefits of preparedness, safety, and liquidity.

Transactions demand
The demand for money assets for use in everyday, expected transactions.

Income Level and Transactions Demand

A family eating at a fast food restaurant will not need as much money for transactions demand as a family dining at a more upscale restaurant.

Precautionary demand
The demand for money assets as an insurance policy against unexpected transactions.

Precautionary Demand. Precautionary demand is the demand for money assets as an insurance policy against unexpected transactions. Money held as precautionary demand enables the holder to deal with emergency situations without much difficulty. Suppose that your car were towed after being illegally parked and that the towing company accepts only cash. You will have a minor inconvenience if you are carrying sufficient cash but a major problem if you are not carrying cash. Precautionary demand is higher for risk-sensitive individuals than for those comfortable with risk. Further, the greater an individual's income, the greater is his precautionary demand.

Holding money for precautionary purposes is inversely related to the interest rate. A higher interest rate means a higher cost of obtaining the insurance provided by precautionary demand. As a result, individuals hold low amounts of precautionary demand at high interest rates.

Speculative demand
The demand for money as a type of investment asset in an individual's portfolio.

Speculative Demand. Speculative demand is the demand for money as an investment asset in an individual's portfolio. In this type of money demand, individuals desire to hold money because it is a store of value. In any portfolio of financial assets, money has a low risk of a loss of value, yet it also has a very low—perhaps even zero—nominal rate of return. The major determinant of the amount of money that an individual holds as speculative demand is the level of interest rates in the economy. The speculative demand for money is inversely related to interest rates. When interest rates are high, the speculative demand for money in a portfolio of investment assets is low, because the rate of return on other, nonmoney assets is greater than for holding money. When interest rates are low, the speculative demand for money is high.

FIGURE 28.1

Money Demand and Money Supply

In panel (a), the money demand curve shows the total amount of transactions, precautionary, and speculative demand for money at each interest rate in the money market. At an interest rate of 5 percent, the quantity of money demanded is $1.5 trillion. If the interest rate increases to 7 percent, the quantity of money demanded will fall to $2.0 trillion. If the interest rate falls to 3 percent, the quantity of money demand increases to $1.8 trillion. In panel (b), because the supply of money provided by the Fed's monetary policy is constant at any given time, the interest rate has no effect on money supply. As a result, the money supply curve is a vertical at $1.5 trillion.

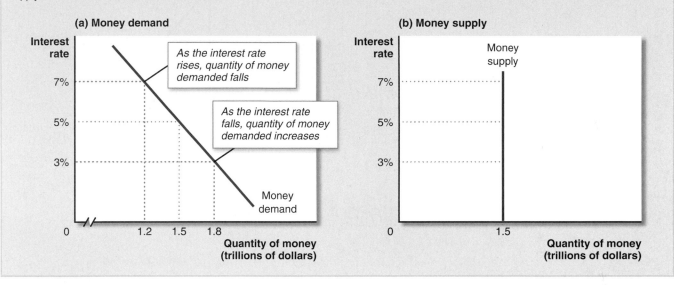

Overall Money Demand. Individuals will use some of the $100 bills from the Fed's imaginary money drop for transactions, precautionary, and speculative purposes. All we know for sure is that the new quantity demanded will exactly equal the quantity supplied of new money, because no $100 bills will be left on the ground. A common denominator in all three types of money demand is that interest rates affect money demand. Figure 28.1(a) shows the impact of the interest rate on money demand. An increasing interest rate means less transactions, less precautionary, and less speculative demand for money. At a higher interest rate, individuals reduce their quantity of money demanded. At a lower interest rate, individuals can obtain the benefits of holding money at a lower opportunity cost and respond by increasing their quantity of money demanded.

Money Supply

To complete our picture of the money market, we must incorporate money supply. The money supply is determined by the Fed's monetary policy, along with the decisions made by banks and borrowers. Recall that the Fed undertakes a given monetary policy to provide a certain amount of money to the economy. At any one time, there is some constant amount of M1 in the economy. In Figure 28.1(b), the money supply is represented as a vertical line centered at the given size of M1, $1.5 trillion. The interest rate has no effect on the size of the money supply. The money supply would be $1.5 trillion at a 3-percent, 5-percent, or 7-percent interest rate.

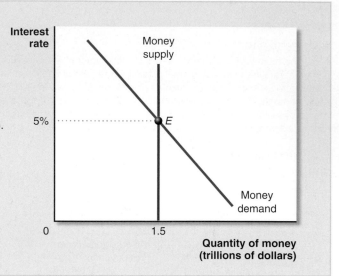

FIGURE 28.2

Equilibrium in the Money Market

The point where the quantity of money supplied equals the quantity of money demanded is the money market equilibrium (labeled *E*). The equilibrium interest rate is 5 percent, and the equilibrium quantity of money is $1.5 trillion.

LifeLessons

How Do You Feel About Charging Interest?

Would you—and should you—charge interest to a friend who borrows money from you? Such diverse thinkers as Aristotle, Thomas Aquinas, and Karl Marx shared an intense dislike of charging interest on loans. In fact, all the major Western religions and many social movements have condemned lending at interest at one time or another. Today, Christianity and Judaism have accommodated themselves to the notion of charging interest, and Marxist economies have largely disappeared. Islam, however, still objects to charging interest because lending at interest allows the individual with funds to lend to take advantage of the individual forced to borrow out of necessity or unfortunate circumstances. Lenders should not gain from the misfortune of others. But what incentive do lenders have to lend if they can't charge interest? Islamic banks have addressed this situation in recent years through an innovation known as Profit-and-Loss Sharing, in which borrowers pay a share of the earnings on their investment back to the lenders. Borrowers thus resemble a corporation paying stock dividends rather than fixed interest payments. Ultimately, you can lend to a friend without charging interest and still be fair to yourself if you employ the principles of Islamic banking.

Money Market Equilibrium

By graphing money supply and money demand in Figure 28.2, we find the equilibrium interest rate and the equilibrium money supply in the money market. The intersection of the money demand curve and the money supply curve occurs at point *E*, the equilibrium point in the money market. The equilibrium interest rate is 5 percent and the equilibrium quantity of money in the economy is $1.5 trillion.

In any market, if the quantity supplied is greater than the quantity demanded, there is downward pressure on the price. In the money market, if the quantity of money supplied by the Fed is greater than the quantity of money demanded by the public, the interest rate falls until it reaches the equilibrium interest rate. If the quantity of money demanded is greater than the quantity of money supplied by the Fed, the interest rate in the money market increases until the equilibrium interest rate is achieved.

FIGURE 28.3

Impact of Changing Money Demand

In panel (a), an increase in money demand from MD_1 to MD_2 changes the equilibrium point in the money market from E_1 to E_2. The increase in money demand causes the equilibrium interest rate to rise from 5 percent to 7 percent. In panel (b), a decrease in money demand from MD_1 to MD_3 moves the equilibrium point from the original E_1 to the new money market equilibrium of E_3. The result is a reduction in the equilibrium interest rate from 5 percent to 3 percent.

The Impact of Changing Money Demand. What happens in the money market if there is an increase in the demand for money? Panel (a) of Figure 28.3 contains the answer. An increase in money demand shifts money demand from MD_1 to MD_2 and causes the equilibrium interest rate in the money market to rise to 7 percent. The equilibrium quantity of money remains at $1.5 trillion. Figure 28.3(b) illustrates that a decrease in money demand causes the equilibrium interest rate to fall from 5 percent to 3 percent. Notice that changes in money demand do not change the given size of the money supply. The money supply is determined by the monetary policy actions of the Fed and the behavior of the banks and borrowers.

The Impact of Changing Money Supply. If the Fed conducts an expansionary or contractionary monetary policy, what is the effect on the interest rate and on the equilibrium quantity of money in the money market? Figure 28.4 illustrates the impact of expansionary and contractionary monetary policies in the money market. The Fed can conduct an expansionary monetary policy by buying U.S. government securities, lowering the discount rate, or lowering the reserve requirement. In panel (a), the money supply increases from MS_1 to MS_2 as a result of expansionary monetary policy. There is a greater equilibrium quantity of money ($1.8 trillion instead of $1.5 trillion) and a lower interest rate (3 percent instead of 5 percent). The new equilibrium established at the lower interest rate encourages an increase in the quantity of money demanded. In the money market, individuals move down the given money demand curve to the intersection of the original money demand curve and the new money supply curve. Note that this result occurs if there is a one-time increase in the money supply. If the money supply increases consistently, nominal

FIGURE 28.4

Impact of Changing Money Supply

In panel (a), an increase in the money supply by the Fed moves the money market equilibrium from E_1 to E_2 where the new equilibrium interest rate (3 percent) is lower and the new equilibrium quantity of money ($1.8 trillion) is now greater. In panel (b), when the Fed decreases the money supply from MS_1 to MS_3, the new equilibrium is E_3 with a higher interest rate (7 percent) and a lower equilibrium quantity of money ($1.2 trillion).

(a) Increasing money supply

(b) Decreasing money supply

interest rates will eventually rise as lenders factor in the impact of increasing price levels in the nominal interest rates they charge.

In panel (b) of Figure 28.4, the Fed's contractionary monetary policy decreases the money supply to $1.2 trillion. As a result, the equilibrium interest rate increases from 5 percent to 7 percent.

In our example, the one-time doubling of the money supply by the Fed during its flyover of the U.S. countryside would, other things equal, significantly decrease the equilibrium interest rate in the money market.

Real-World Complications

It is important to remember that the Fed does not directly set interest rates. Rather, the Fed affects the level of interest rates in the economy through its use of the tools of monetary policy and their impact on the size of the money supply. The Fed directly sets only one interest rate (the discount rate) and controls only one other rate (the federal funds rate). The rest of the interest rates are influenced by the actions of the Fed but are not determined by Fed mandate. The Fed does not directly set or control such key interest rates as the prime rate (the rate banks charge their best commercial customers), mortgage interest rates, the rates charged on credit cards, the rates paid by depository institutions to their depositors, or the rates charged to their borrowers.

Fed actions do place upward or downward pressure on interest rates. However, the behavior of money demand, which is determined by individuals, could interfere with the movement in interest rates intended by the Fed. Figure 28.5 illustrates this situation. The Fed will undertake monetary actions to increase the money supply

FIGURE 28.5

Money Demand and Money Supply Changes

The Fed wants to lower the equilibrium interest rate to stimulate the economy and so increases the money supply from MS_1 to MS_2. If the public increases its demand for money from MD_1 to MD_2 at the same time, money market equilibrium moves from E_1 to E_2. Although there is more money supply ($1.8 trillion instead of $1.5 trillion), the equilibrium interest rate will stay at 5 percent despite the Fed's monetary policy initiative.

and lower interest rates in the money market during a sluggish time in the economy. The money supply then increases from MS_1 to MS_2. The Fed's expectation would be that a general reduction of interest rates would stimulate economic activity. Money demanders could take steps to weaken or offset the desired impact of this policy. If, for example, there were an increase in precautionary demand due to uncertainty in the economy, money demand would increase from MD_1 to MD_2, just enough so that the increase in the money supply would not lower interest rates. The Fed's intended effect on the behavior of interest rates could be completely thwarted by the actions of money demand as the interest rate remains at 5 percent.

In our money supply example at the start of the chapter, it is possible that the new money that fell from the Fed's plancs would not result in lower interest rates. This major infusion of money into the economy could increase transactions demand, precautionary, and speculative demands. It is possible, although not very likely, that such a massive increase in the money supply would not lower the level of interest rates much, or even at all.

The Long-Run Effects of Money on the Economy

The remaining question in our discussion of money and monetary policy is this: What is the influence of money on key economic variables in the macroeconomy, such as the price level, interest rates, employment, and real GDP? Although the situation of the Fed dropping $100 bills from airplanes is invented, there have been examples when new money entered the economy in massive amounts. Earlier, we referred to major gold discoveries in the Klondike and in South Africa over 100 years ago that caused the money supply to grow rapidly. How did the U.S. economy respond to this new money flowing so abundantly into the economy? We now address this question in terms of the long run and short run. In this section, we examine how increases in the money supply affect the basic measures of economic health—prices, real GDP, and employment—in the long run.

The Quantity Theory of Money

We illustrate the long-run influence of money in the macroeconomy by exploring the **quantity theory of money**. The quantity theory of money is the view that, in the long run, changes in the money supply lead to proportional changes in the price level. A large increase in the money supply, according the quantity theory of money, will eventually lead to a large increase in the price level.

The Equation of Exchange and Velocity. The quantity theory of money is based on the observation that, in every market transaction, money must change hands. Consider, for example, a very simple economy consisting of two people, Stan and Dan. They each run a store in which everything costs $1.00. Each makes all his transactions by going to the other's store during his lunch hour (Dan closes from noon to 1:00 P.M. and Stan closes from 1:00 P.M. to 2:00 P.M.). Suppose further that there is exactly one $1.00 bill in circulation. That means, in effect, that Dan buys one item from Stan at noon, and, an hour later, Stan buys one item from Dan. On Monday, Dan buys a one-dollar carton of chocolate milk from Stan, and then Stan buys a one-dollar bag of potato chips from Dan. In one day, the dollar bill changes hands twice and $2.00 worth of transactions takes place. Over the course of a five-day workweek, the two engage in $10 (5 days × $2.00) worth of transactions, and in a year they undertake $520 ($10 per week × 52 weeks) worth of transactions. We capture all this activity with the **equation of exchange**, an identity that states the relationship between the money supply (M), velocity (V), the price level (P), and the number of transactions (T) in a given time period, as given in Equation 28.1.

$$MV = PT \qquad (28.1)$$

On the lefthand side, M is the nominal amount of money in circulation; in this case, $1.00. V, the **velocity of money**, is the number of times a dollar changes hands in a given period. It measures the turnover rate of money—how fast money moves from one person to another in the economy over time. In our example, we measure velocity by taking the dollar amount of transactions that have occurred during the week and dividing by the size of the money supply. Thus, V = $10/$1 = 10, so we now know that the dollar bill changes hands 10 times over the course of the week.

Velocity is the opposite of money demand. Money demand measures how long the average person holds onto the average dollar. Velocity measures how quickly the average person gets rid of the average dollar. Based on this relationship, if the velocity of money is high, the demand for money must by definition be low.

On the righthand side of Equation 28.1, P is the price level (in this case, $1.00), and T is the number of transactions that take place over a given time period. In this example, 10 transactions took place each week, so PT—the dollar value of transactions—is $1 × 10 = $10.

If the Fed doubled the money supply to two one-dollar bills in our example, what would happen in the long run? Following are just a few of the possible long-run outcomes consistent with the equation of exchange:

- The price level could double, and the velocity and the number of transactions could stay the same.
- The price level and velocity could stay the same and the number of transactions could double.
- The velocity of money could fall by 50 percent, while the price level and the number of transactions stay the same.

There are many other combinations of changes in velocity, price levels, and number of transactions that can occur in the long run while still maintaining the validity of the equation of exchange. The equation of exchange has no unique ability to predict or explain what will happen in the long run if the money supply is changed.

Quantity Theory of Money Equation

To predict the long-run role of money in the macroeconomy, we need to make two alterations in the operation of the equation of exchange:

1. We must generalize and apply the example to the overall economy by replacing the single price we have been using with a price index such as the Consumer Price Index (CPI). In addition, we must replace the number of transactions with real GDP (Q), the actual physical amount of goods and services produced in the macroeconomy.
2. We will assume that the velocity of money is constant and that the level of real GDP is fixed at or near the full employment level of real GDP. This assumption of full employment is consistent with the long-run model's outcome, which predicts that full employment is the general rule after all adjustments have been made.

After incorporating these two alterations, the equation of exchange becomes the quantity theory of money, an explanation of the role of money in the macroeconomy as stated in Equation 28.2.

$$MV = PQ \qquad (28.2)$$

where M = the nominal money supply, V = the *constant* velocity of money, P = the overall price level, and Q = *fixed* level of real GDP in the economy.[1]

What happens if the Fed's monetary policy causes the money supply to increase by 5 percent? Given our assumptions of constant velocity and the full employment level of real GDP, the only possible long-run result is that the price level also increases by 5 percent. If the money supply shrinks by 2 percent, the quantity theory of money predicts that the price level in the long run will also decrease by 2 percent. A strict application of the quantity theory of money is unambiguous: The percentage change in the money supply results in an equal percentage change in the price level in the long run.

If velocity and real GDP are not constant, the strict proportionality of the quantity theory of money is lost, but its implication remains: In the long run, changes in the money supply result mostly in price changes with minimal impacts on real GDP and employment.

The Quantity Theory in the Long-Run Model of Aggregate Demand and Aggregate Supply

We can incorporate the quantity theory of money into the long-run model of aggregate demand and aggregate supply. The quantity theory of money assumes a

---

[1] The bold type used for velocity and the level of real GDP is to remind you that those two variables are considered constant in the quantity theory of money.

FIGURE 28.6

The Impact of Increasing Money Supply in the Long-Run Model

If the Fed increases the money supply, aggregate demand will increase from AD_1 to AD_2 and macroeconomic equilibrium will shift from E_1 to E_2. In the long run, the level of output will stay the same at $4.5 trillion while the overall price level will increase from 105 to 110.

constant real GDP at the full employment level in the long run. The long-run aggregate supply curve is the reference line for that level of real GDP. Recall that the initial aggregate demand curve is based on a given size of the money supply. If there is an increase the size of the money supply, the amount of spending in the economy increases as well. The aggregate demand curve increases, as shown in Figure 28.6. The initial long-run equilibrium point economy in the economy is at point E_1, where the equilibrium price level is 105 and the equilibrium real GDP is $4.5 trillion. When more money is introduced into the economy, there is an increase in aggregate demand from AD_1 to AD_2 and the new equilibrium is established at E_2.

The result is that the economy in the long run still has the full employment level of real GDP of $4.5 trillion, but the price level is higher at 110. The ultimate result of an injection of new money into the economy is a higher price level with no change in either real GDP or employment. There is no need to worry about inflationary or recessionary gaps, because in the long run, the economy is functioning at or near the full employment level of real GDP.

The Quantity Theory and the Role of Money in the Long Run

Money neutrality
Changes in the nominal money supply affect only nominal prices, not real GDP or employment.

The major conclusion of the quantity theory of money is that in the long run, money is neutral. **Money neutrality** means that changes in the nominal money supply affect only the nominal price level and not real GDP or employment. On a more practical level, the quantity theory of money states that much of the impact of new money ultimately shows up as price changes, rather than as improvements in either economic growth or employment. Any existing problems with low real GDP and high unemployment rates would remain. The lesson of the quantity theory of money is that a nation cannot simply print money to achieve prosperity in the long run. Although some nations have tried that approach, more money merely leads to a higher price level in the long run.

In our hypothetical example of the Fed injecting money into the economy, the prediction made by the quantity theory of money is unambiguous. An overnight doubling of the U.S. money supply would, in the long run, also double the price level in the U.S. economy. There would be no long-run impact on employment or the amount of real GDP produced by the economy. An introduction of a massive amount of new money in an economy would not cure an underperforming economy.

The gold discoveries in the last few years of the nineteenth century and the resulting increase in the money supply led to a steady increase in the U.S. price level from 1897 to 1914. This sustained increase in the price level due to the flood of new gold became a global economic phenomenon.

TEST + *E X T E N D* Your Knowledge

1. TEST As you might expect, different denominations of currency have different velocities. Indicate which of the following denominations of U.S. currency should have the fastest velocity and which should have the slowest velocity: the $1 bill, the $100 bill, and the $2 bill. Why?

2 . E X T E N D To see if your intuition is correct, go to the "Where's George?" Web site using the link at www.aw-bc.com/leeds/ch28. Look at the travels of the $1, $2, and $100 bills with the greatest velocity to see whether the number of times each bill has changed hands in the last three years is consistent with your answer.

▶ The Short-Run Influence of Money in the Macroeconomy

Given the predictions of the quantity theory of money, why do governments or central banks try to improve an economy's performance by increasing the money supply? In the short run, money can affect real GDP and employment as well as the price level. Money influences the economy in the short run through three mechanisms: the interest rate channel, the net export channel, and the portfolio channel, as discussed in the following sections.

The Interest Rate Channel

Interest rate channel
The primary influence of the money supply on the economy flows through its impact on interest rates and interest-sensitive investors.

The first view of the short-run impact of money is the **interest rate channel**, where the primary influence of the money supply on the economy flows through its impact on interest rates and interest-sensitive investors, and ultimately on aggregate demand. As you saw in our discussion of the money market in Figure 28.4, increasing the nominal money supply through expansionary monetary policy can lower the interest rate. A falling interest rate encourages more investment spending by businesses and consumption expenditures by households. After new aggregate demand appears, the basic spending multiplier activates. More real GDP and employment result in the short run because of expansionary monetary policy.

Money Is Not Neutral. In the view of the interest rate channel, money is not neutral. The increase in the money supply means that, in the short run, the level of real GDP and the price level will grow. More workers will be hired and employment will grow.

Money Has a Narrow Impact. An implication of the interest rate channel is that money has a narrow impact on the macroeconomy. Only interest-sensitive borrowers are initially affected by changes in the interest rate. A decrease in the interest rate of 1 percent can change an investment project from unprofitable to profitable for some businesses. Other possible investors might not be affected at all. For example, many businesses are not interested in investing in a particular economic climate even if interest rates are falling.

Money Has a Delayed Effect. The interest rate channel also suggests that money has a delayed effect in the macroeconomy. For example, if the Fed increases the money supply this week, the interest rate can fall almost immediately in the money market. However, the impact on the interest rates paid by borrowers in other financial markets might take some time to appear. Financial intermediaries might not immediately lower the interest rates they charge on business, personal, and mortgage loans. Interest rates on credit cards are notoriously sticky, even in the face of generally falling interest rates elsewhere. It might be some time before borrowers experience lower interest rates. Even after the additional expenditures on new investment or consumer durables are made, it takes additional time for the full multiplier effect to be felt on real GDP.

Liquidity Trap. Another possible hindrance to the influence of interest rates on economic activity is the **liquidity trap**, which occurs when even large increases in the money supply do not lower interest rates, stimulate business spending, or increase real GDP and employment. Under certain circumstances, all this new money supply might be simply hoarded as new money demand. If interest rates are already extremely low, the opportunity cost of holding additional money is minimal. In a very weak economy where participants fear the worst, the most rational thing to do with any new money is often simply to hold it. If the entire amount of new money supply were held as increased money demand, interest rates would not fall. Without declining interest rates, the impact of an increased money supply would be lost on the economy.

In our "money-from-heaven" example of expansionary monetary policy, what does the interest rate channel tell us about the impact of doubling the money supply? The first lesson is that if there were a liquidity trap present, all that new money would not lower already minimal nominal interest rates. The impact of new money on interest rates would be zero. There would be a break in the chain of influence from the Fed's monetary policy to interest rates and the entire economy. Another possible break in the chain could occur if investment spending were interest-insensitive. Then even a large decline in interest rates brought about by a doubling of the money supply might not induce much additional new spending. However, the most likely scenario is that the doubling of the money supply in our extreme example would cause the level of interest rates to fall and spending to increase, generating more real GDP, employment, and a higher price level.

The Net Export Channel

The second short-run channel of monetary influence is the **net export channel**, the path through which changes in the domestic money supply affect the exports and imports of a given nation, and thus aggregate demand. For example, if the United States increased its money supply, U.S. interest rates would decline. These falling interest rates would make investing in U.S. financial assets less desirable for foreign investors. As a result, foreign investors would not need as many dollars to invest and the demand for U.S. dollars will fall in international currency markets. The purchasing power of the dollar would fall internationally. Foreigners would then find that their currencies have greater purchasing power when buying U.S. goods, so they would buy more U.S. exports. However, Americans in this case see that their dollars

Liquidity trap
Occurs when even large increases in the money supply do not lower interest rates, stimulate business spending, or increase real GDP and employment.

Net export channel
The path through which changes in the domestic money supply affect the exports and imports of a given nation.

have less purchasing power overseas and will buy fewer imports. The U.S. net exports (U.S. exports minus U.S. imports) would then increase, increasing U.S. aggregate demand. Through the multiplier effect, the level of real GDP in the United States would grow as would U.S. employment and the price level.

The Portfolio Channel

Portfolio channel
The path through which changes in the money supply affect individual portfolios of assets in the economy.

The third short-run channel of monetary influence is the **portfolio channel**, the path through which changes in the money supply affect individual portfolios of assets in the economy and thus aggregate demand. As you saw in our first chapter on money, each of us has a portfolio of assets. Each portfolio has a preferred ratio of money and nonmoney assets. Our portfolio must contain some money assets that serve as a medium of exchange. We also need a certain amount of nonmoney assets, because we cannot wear or eat money. Suppose that the Federal Reserve undertakes an expansionary monetary policy and increases the money supply. Everyone's portfolio of assets (wealth) is now a little larger because of the influx of new money into the economy. That's the good news. However, everyone's preferred portfolio is also a little unbalanced as well, with too many money assets compared to nonmoney assets. The typical portfolio has too much liquidity. To deal with this excess liquidity, we must take some money assets and convert them into nonmoney assets. In other words, everyone can spend a little of the new money to buy some new goods and services. The increase in the money supply therefore affects the typical portfolio by encouraging more spending in the economy. This new spending generates new aggregate demand, leading to more real GDP, employment, and a higher price level.

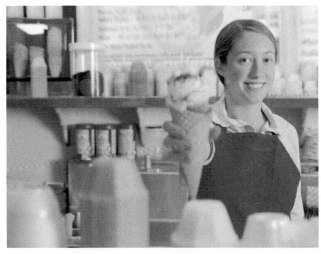

Although we may not always be aware of this portfolio effect, we all use it when making key economic decisions. Consider your situation at college. At the beginning of the fall term, suppose that your portfolio has the preferred ratio between money and nonmoney assets. As the term goes on, your money assets dwindle as you buy nonmoney assets such as textbooks, clothes, DVDs, and CDs. By the end of the fall term, your portfolio no longer has the preferred ratio, with too many nonmoney assets and too few money assets. You feel quite uncomfortable being so cash-poor. To restore your desired ratio of money and nonmoney assets, you find a job during the holidays. The money that you earn at that job will replenish your money assets and help you restore the preferred ratio in your portfolio for the start of the next term.

In the short run, an influx of money increases the amount of real GDP and the level of employment. Money has a broad impact on the macroeconomy in the portfolio channel. Because everyone has a portfolio of assets, changes in the money supply cause a change in the ratio of money and nonmoney assets in all portfolios.

Impact of the Short-Run Channels

Figure 28.7 shows how the interaction of these three channels affects the behavior of the macroeconomy. Panel (a) summarizes the impacts of the various short-run channels of monetary influence. For all three short-run channels, the initial event is a change in the money supply brought about by the Fed's monetary policy actions. This change in the money supply will cause changes in the level of interest

myeconlab

Get Ahead of the Curve

Put your knowledge of money and monetary policy to work analyzing the efforts of European and U.S. central banks to fight inflation.

FIGURE 28.7

The Short-Run Impact of Money

In panel (a), changes in the money supply affect aggregate demand through each of the channels and ultimately the level of real GDP. In panel (b), the Fed conducts an expansionary monetary policy to lower interest rates and increase aggregate demand, which causes aggregate demand to shift from AD_1 to AD_2. The new short-run equilibrium level of real GDP is $5.0 trillion and the new equilibrium price level is 110.

(a) Channels of monetary influence

(b) Impact of an increase in the money supply

rates, the amount of net exports for a nation, and the portfolio of assets of individuals and firms. These changes will alter the amount of aggregate demand in the economy. Finally, through the multiplier effect, a change in aggregate demand will have a magnified impact on real GDP. In the case of an expansionary monetary policy, the increase in the money supply will lower interest rates, reduce the purchasing power of a nation's currency, and unbalance portfolios. There will be more consumption expenditures, more investment spending, and more net exports.

Panel (b) of Figure 28.7 illustrates the result of new money supply in the context of the short-run model of aggregate demand and aggregate supply. The initial equilibrium point is E_1, with $4.5 trillion in real GDP and a price level of 105. The expansionary monetary policy increases aggregate demand from AD_1 to AD_2 as consumption, investment, and net exports all increase. The new equilibrium is at E_2, with more real GDP ($5.0 trillion) and a higher price level (110), because of the new money injected into the economy. The impact of money in the macroeconomy is not neutral: The increased money supply has increased the price level, the amount of real GDP, and employment in the short run.

Comparing Long-Run and Short-Run Influences

We have investigated different impacts of money on the macroeconomy in this chapter: the quantity theory, the interest rate channel, the net exports channel, and the portfolio channel. The quantity theory of money states that money is neutral in the long run. Changes in the money supply ultimately affect only the price level, not real GDP and employment. However, the other three channels emphasize that money is not neutral in the short run. At least temporarily, changes in the money

TEST + *EXTEND* Your Knowledge

1. TEST In many states, individuals can participate in a state-sponsored lottery such as Powerball™. Imagine that someone has just won a Powerball jackpot of $50 million. In terms of our discussion of the portfolio effect, what has happened to the size of that individual's portfolio and the ratio in that portfolio between money and nonmoney assets?

2. *EXTEND* Based on our discussion of the portfolio effect, what do you predict the winner of $50 million will do with many of those new funds? Go to the Powerball Web site using the link at www. aw-bc.com/leeds/ch28. Read the stories of the last five winners of major Powerball jackpots to see if they behaved in a way that you predicted.

supply can cause changes not only in the price level, but also real GDP and employment. It appears that the ability of money to affect the level of real GDP and employment erodes over time.

How can changes in the money supply affect real GDP, employment, and the price level in the short run, but only the price level in the long run? Figure 28.8 provides the answer to this question. We start at long-run equilibrium (where AD_1 equals $SRAS_1$ equals LRAS), at point E_1. The full employment level of real GDP is $4.5 trillion and the equilibrium price level is 105. If there is an increase in the money supply, you now know that through the interest rate, net export, and portfolio channels, aggregate demand will increase. As a result, the aggregate demand curve will increase from AD_1 to AD_2, and the economy is now in an inflationary gap at point E_2. Recall that the inflationary gap represents the difference between the full employment level of real GDP ($4.5 trillion) and the higher short-run equilibrium level of real GDP associated with equilibrium point E_2 ($5.0 trillion). Because of the injection of new money into the economy, real GDP is higher and the price level has increased from 105 to 110. The short-run influence of more money is more real GDP, a higher price level, and more employment. Money is not neutral.

FIGURE 28.8

Relationship of the Short-Run and Long-Run Influences of Money

In the short run, an increase in the money supply causes the aggregate demand curve to shift from AD_1 to AD_2 and equilibrium moves from E_1 to E_2. At E_2, the overall price level is now higher (110) and there is more real GDP ($5.0 trillion). There is now an inflationary gap so wages and resource prices increase. In response, short-run aggregate supply will decrease. After all adjustments have occurred in the economy in the long run, the new equilibrium will be at E_3. The new equilibrium real GDP is back at the original level, $4.5 trillion. Only the overall price level is greater now at 115.

With an overheating economy generating an inflationary gap, there is upward pressure on nominal wage rates. These rising wages increase the costs for producers and decrease short-run aggregate supply. This decrease in the short-run aggregate supply continues until the short-run aggregate supply curve reaches $SRAS_2$ where the economy establishes a new long-run equilibrium at point E_3. The equilibrium level of real GDP is once again the full employment level of $4.5 trillion and the new equilibrium price level is 115. Because the ultimate effect of more money supply is only a higher price level, money is neutral in the long run.

The result of the injection of new money supply into the economy is a temporary stimulus to real GDP and employment. In the short run (at E_2), there is an increase in real GDP, employment, and the price level. After the economy fully adjusts to the increase in the money supply, the new long-run equilibrium has the same real GDP and employment as before the injection of new money. The only difference is that the overall price level in the economy is now higher at 115 instead of 105.

It is not a contradiction to say that money is not neutral in the short run but is neutral in the long run. Figure 28.8 indicates that the impact of expansionary monetary policy on the real economic variables of real GDP and employment erodes over time, as participants in the macroeconomy adjust to the impacts of the increased money supply. Any gains in real GDP and employment are only temporary. In our fictional example, the Fed's massive increase in the money supply would lead to short-term gains as the new money leads to more real GDP and employment. And all that new money would also lead to long-term pain, as the price level would increase more and more as time went on, while the gains in real GDP and employment retreat. Ultimately, only the price level would be higher.

How long is the long run and how short is the short run? There is no definite answer. Most economists believe that the transition from short-run impacts to long-run impacts takes about two years after the start of an expansionary monetary policy. The key practical point of this discussion is that no monetary policy can have a permanent effect on either real GDP or employment, once all economic adjustments are made. Ultimately, as the quantity theory of money predicts, changes in the money supply are ultimately translated into price level changes.

Strategy and Policy
Japan and the Liquidity Trap

For many years, the liquidity trap was thought to be an interesting theoretical possibility, but not a practical concern for the conduct of monetary policy. However, in recent years, the liquidity trap has emerged as a valid concern for policy makers. During the 1990s, interest rates in Japan fell to an extremely low level. In 1990, Japanese banks were paying their customers an average of 7.7 percent on three-month certificates of deposit. By 1995, the rate on three-month CDs had fallen to 0.6 percent. By the middle of 1999, Japanese banks were paying 0.1 percent on three-month CDs. The Japanese economy also suffered through a persistent and painful recession during the second half of the 1990s. The Bank of Japan, the nation's central bank, undertook expansionary monetary policy in the hope of stimulating economic growth. But in the face of interest rates that were already extremely low, any new money provided by the Bank of Japan did not lower interest rates or increase spending. Nominal interest rates could not be pushed below zero. Any new money furnished to the economy ended up as new savings rather than new spending.

There were several reasons for this dramatic increase in the demand for money. Increasing pessimism about the future of the economy led both business and consumers to save for the expected emergency, instead of spending. Japan also had entered a period of deflation, where the price level was actually falling. As a result, it made sense to save now rather than spend, because prices would likely be lower in the future. Any new money provided by the actions of the Bank of Japan went into cash hoards by businesses and households. In the minimal interest rate environment of the liquidity trap, monetary policy in Japan could not rely on the interest rate channel to influence the Japanese economy in the short run.

Critical-Thinking Questions

1. The Japanese central bank was hoping that increases in the money supply would cause inflation. If Japanese citizens expected more inflation, what would this expectation do to their desire to hoard money?
2. Changes in the money supply can work through channels other than the interest rate channel. Explain how increases in the money supply in Japan might work through the portfolio effect and the net export effect to stimulate the Japanese economy.

SUMMARY

- **The money market.** The money market is composed of money supply and money demand. Money held by individuals imposes the opportunity cost of forgone interest earnings and cost of declining purchasing power on the holder. The benefits of holding money are preparedness, safety, and increased opportunities. Individuals demand money for the benefits it provides them. There are three types of money demand: transactions, precautionary, and speculative. Transactions demand is based on the use of money in everyday, expected activities. Precautionary demand focuses on the use of money for unexpected expenditures, and speculative demand relates to the role of money as an investment asset. The money supply is determined by monetary policy and is unaffected by the level of interest rates. Changes in money supply and money demand affect the equilibrium level of interest rates and the equilibrium quantity of money in the money market.

- **The long-run effects of money on the economy.** The equation of exchange spells out the relationship of money supply, velocity, the price level, and the number of transactions. The quantity theory of money illustrates the long-run impact of money on the macroeconomy, assuming a constant velocity and full employment of real GDP. An increase in the money supply will, in the long run, cause the economy to maintain the full employment level of real GDP, but the price level will be higher. Money is neutral in the long run.

- **The short-run influence of money in the macroeconomy.** The short-run influence of money is captured in the interest rate, the net export, and the portfolio channels of monetary influence. These three channels demonstrate that money is not neutral in the short run, instead affecting real GDP and employment as well as the price level. Expansionary monetary policy can increase real GDP and employment as well as the price level. Contractionary monetary policy can have the opposite effect.

- **Comparing long-run and short-run influences.** When the money supply changes, the initial impacts are felt in employment and real GDP as well as in the price level. As time goes on, the economy adjusts to the changing money supply, so that in the long run, the impact of a changing money supply is confined to changing the price level.

Equation of exchange 724   Money neutrality 726   Quantity theory of money
Interest rate channel 727   Net export channel 728   724
Liquidity trap 728   Portfolio channel 729   Speculative demand 718
Money demand 717   Precautionary demand 718 Transactions demand 717
Money market 716   Velocity of money 724

PROBLEMS

1. What are two costs individuals incur by holding money assets?
2. What are major benefits do individuals obtain by holding money assets?
3. What is transactions demand for money? What three determinants affect the amount of transactions demand by individuals?
4. What is precautionary demand for money? What three determinants affect the amount of precautionary demand by individuals?
5. What is speculative demand for money? What is the major determinant of the amount of speculative demand by individuals?
6. Why is the money supply curve drawn as a vertical line in the money market?
7. Show in a graph of the money market why a decrease in the quantity of money supplied by the Federal Reserve System might not raise interest rates.
8. In your own words, describe the equation of exchange.
9. Find the value for the missing part of the following examples using equation of exchange.
   a. If, in time period 1, $M = \$100$, $V = 6$, and $P = \$2$, what is the amount of real GDP?
   b. If, in time period 2, $M = \$150$, $P = \$3$, and real GDP $= \$300$, what is the velocity of money?
   c. If, in time period 3, $V = 5$, $P = \$3$, and real GDP $= \$150$, what is the size of the money supply?
   d. If, in time period 4, $M = \$100$, $V = 5$ and real GDP $= \$100$, what is the price level?
10. What are the assumptions that lie behind the quantity theory of money?
11. In Problem 9, is money neutral when the economy moves from period 1 to 2, from period 2 to 3, from period 3 to 4? Explain your answer.
12. What are three short-run channels by which money can affect the macro-economy?
13. What is the liquidity trap and what is its significance for the interest rate channel?
14. Supposes that you find a $5.00 bill on the sidewalk. Using the portfolio of assets approach, explain the results of this bit of good luck by determining what happens to the size of your portfolio of assets, the ratio of money to nonmoney assets, and your willingness to spend.
15. Using the short-run model of aggregate demand and aggregate supply of Figure 28.7(b), show what happens in the short run if the Fed decreases the money supply.
16. What is money neutrality? How does the long-run impact of money differ from the short-run impact of money in terms of money neutrality?

17. What does the following quotation from Henry Ward Beecher, famous U.S. clergyman and editor, tell us about the role of money in the macroeconomy: "Money is like snow. If it is blown up into drifts, it blocks up the highway and nobody can travel; but if it is diffused over all the ground, it facilitates every man's travel."

18. Using the graph in Figure 28.8, explain why a decrease in the money supply by the Fed lowers real GDP temporarily, but lowers the price level permanently.

(myeconlab) STUDY GUIDE

HERE'S HOW MyEconLab CAN HELP YOU GET A BETTER GRADE

1. Log into MyEconLab and take Practice Test 28-A (to log in for the first time, see page 30 for instructions).

2. Based on your test results, MyEconLab will identify the areas where you need further work and create a personal Study Plan for you.

3. Your Study Plan contains the problems listed below and others like them that will target the specific chapter topics you need to focus on. You'll receive instant feedback and find links to tutorials, animations, and the online textbook to help you study.

4. When you're ready, take Practice Test 28-B and demonstrate how your results have improved.

Section 28.1, Problem 1 Answer the following questions based on money market as shown in Figure 28.2.

   a. How will a decrease in money demand by the public affect the equilibrium interest rate and the quantity of money in the money market?

   b. How will a decrease in the money supply by the Federal Reserve affect the equilibrium interest rate and the quantity of money in the money market?

Section 28.1, Problem 2 In the money market, what factors affect the money supply?

Section 28.1, Problem 3 Suppose that the money market, as shown in the figure, is at equilibrium with an interest rate of five percent. If the Federal Reserve wished to increase the interest rate to seven percent, then it could:

   a. Sell U.S. securities, lower the reserve requirement, or lower the discount rate.

   b. Buy U.S. securities, lower the reserve requirement, or raise the discount rate.

   c. Sell U.S. securities, raise the reserve requirement, or raise the discount rate.

   d. Buy U.S. securities, lower the required reserve, or lower the discount rate.

   e. The Federal Reserve exerts no control in the money market.

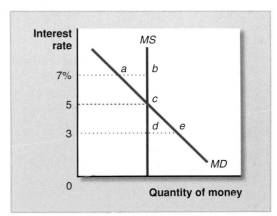

Section 28.1, Problem 4 In the money market, what would happen to the quantity of money and the equilibrium interest rate if the Federal Reserve decreased the money supply, while at the same time there was an increase in money demand by the public?

Section 28.2, Problem 1 According to the quantity theory of money, if real output is 1,000 units, the price level is $6.00, and the supply of money is $1,500, what is the velocity of money?

Section 28.2, Problem 2 Money neutrality implies that changes in the money supply have no effect on:

   a. Real GDP
   b. Employment
   c. Prices
   d. Only options a and b are correct.
   e. Options a, b, and c are all correct.

Section 28.3, Problem 2

   a. Fill in the blanks in the following sentences concerning the short-run effect between the money supply and the net export channel.

      A decrease in the U.S. money supply leads to a(n) *(increase/decrease)* in the purchasing power of the U.S. dollar and a(n) *(increase/decrease)* in the purchasing power of foreign currency. This in turn, leads to a(n) *(increase/decrease)* in net exports and aggregate demand.

   b. Fill in the blanks in the following sentences concerning the short-run effect between the money supply and the interest rate channel.

      A decrease in the money supply leads to a(n) *(increase/decrease)* in interest rates. This, in turn, leads to a(n) *(increase/decrease)* in investment spending by firms and consumption spending by households and thus aggregate demand.

Section 28.3, Problem 3 The liquidity trap is a special case in which increases in the money supply by the Federal Reserve no longer decrease the interest rate. Which of the following graphs shows the most likely explanation for this phenomenon?

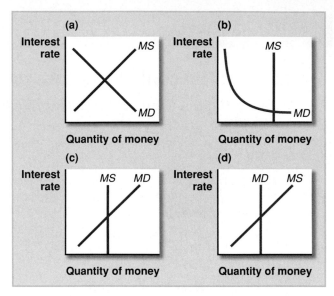

Section 28.4, Problem 1

   a. Suppose that the economy is in long-run macroeconomic equilibrium. What would be the short-run effect on the economy (prices, real GDP, and employment) if the Federal Reserve were to decrease the money supply?

   b. Suppose that the economy is in long-run macroeconomic equilibrium. What would be the long-run effect on the economy (prices, real GDP, and employment) if the Federal Reserve were to decrease the money supply?

29 Long-Run Implications of Macroeconomic Policy

During August 2001, those who watched the U.S. economy were worried. After 10 years of uninterrupted growth, real GDP had begun to fall. The unemployment rate, which during the last quarter of 2000 had dipped below 4 percent, was at 4.5 percent and rising. By September 2001, the major stock exchanges had fallen thousands of points below the previous year's high. Policy makers and the business community began to ask how long it would take for the economy to turn around. How many companies would fail and households suffer before the turnaround came?

These concerns quickly led politicians to call for a variety of monetary and fiscal policies intended to stabilize the economy. The approaches differed, but the basic point of each policy was the same: to stimulate aggregate demand and increase real GDP. No one seemed inclined to wait for the economy to right itself. According to long-run economic models, however, waiting is the one policy that is guaranteed to work. Economists have learned that after households and firms have time to adjust, real GDP and employment both return to their long-run levels for all but the most severe recessions. Moreover, the delays in formulating and implementing policy can result in bad timing that leads the policy to backfire.

Those who believe in immediate action to combat a recession maintain that waiting for the economy to right itself imposes economic hardships that can be eliminated by the appropriate policies. The key question is how long we must wait for economic forces to return the economy to its long-run position. If the long-run equilibrium is far off, then waiting might not be such a good idea. If the long run comes fairly soon, then acting in the short run may produce undesired outcomes.

In this chapter, we look at several different arguments that economists presented regarding the appropriate response to the recession of 2001. We find that there is no consensus among economists over what the government and the Fed should do to stabilize the economy.

ALONG THE WAY, YOU WILL ALSO LEARN:

- That economists remain divided on the effectiveness of stabilization policy.

- What the Phillips curve reveals about the relationship between the inflation and unemployment rates.

- How economists use rational expectations to explain the declining impact of stabilization policy.

- How the real business cycle model explains fluctuations in real GDP.

- How the supply-side model justifies tax cuts.

- How fixed-wage contracts and skill acquisition might cause short-run policy to have a lasting impact on the economy.

AT THE END OF THE CHAPTER, THE MYECONLAB LOGO WILL DIRECT YOU ONLINE

- MyEconLab is a resource-packed online homework and tutorial system that can help you perform better in your economics course. To log in for the first time, see page 30 for instructions.

- MyEconLab can help you apply important concepts from the chapter to real-world issues. Watch for the logo to indicate online features about the 2004 Nobel Prize in Economics and the prospect of stagflation.

- At the end of each chapter, you'll find a special study section that will help you get the most out of your textbook and your instructor's MyEconLab course.

Stabilization Policy

In the preceding chapters, you have seen that an economy's GDP follows a long-run growth path, yet it can temporarily deviate from that path. These deviations can take the form of a recession that pulls the economy below its long-run path or robust growth that pushes it above its long-run path. Neither deviation is desirable. A recession causes the unemployment rate to rise and results in lower real GDP. If the economy grows too fast, inflation could result. If the deviations from the trend last for several years, they could impose considerable pain on households and firms and endanger the political futures of elected officials. As a result, since the Great Depression of the 1930s, the federal government and the Federal Reserve have implemented **stabilization policies**, which are designed to limit both the size and the duration of deviations from the U.S. economy's long-run trend.

In the preceding chapters, we have discussed a number of fiscal and monetary stabilization policies. We have also shown, however, that economists often disagree on the effectiveness of stabilization policies. In previous chapters, we have also encountered a number of practical objections to stabilization policies. For example, fiscal policy is subject to long and variable lags that may cause the policy to take effect after the need for it has already passed.

Stabilization policies
Actions taken by policy makers to limit the size and duration of the economy's deviation from its long-term trend.

GRAND AVENUE: United Features Syndicate

In this chapter, we discuss the debate over stabilization policy: some economists believe that stabilization policies would not work even if they were perfectly implemented. The opponents of stabilization policies have constructed theoretical models that show that any active attempt to stabilize the economy is doomed to fail. They conclude that policy makers should focus on ensuring long-run growth and not respond to short-run deviations from the long-run path. Other economists believe in the power of stabilization policies. They, too, have constructed theoretical models, which they use to justify an active role for policy makers.

The disagreement between those who believe in active short-run intervention or restrict attention to long-run goals is one of the most vigorous debates over economic policy. In this chapter, we look at the nature of this disagreement and examine some of the theories the opposing sides have developed in the context of the 2001 recession in the United States.

The Trade-Off Between Inflation and Unemployment

We begin by looking at an active stabilization policy based on the belief that the U.S. government could prevent recessions like the one that struck in 2001. We focus on the tradeoff faced policy makers between two key macroeconomic variables: inflation and unemployment.

The Phillips Curve

Phillips curve
A graph showing a negative relationship between the rate of inflation and the unemployment rate.

In 1958, the economist A. W. Phillips plotted data for the unemployment rate and the rate of increase in wages in the United Kingdom for the period 1861–1957. The **Phillips curve** showed an inverse relationship between wage movements and unemployment. Other economists soon found a similar negative relationship between U.S. inflation and unemployment rates. The U.S. Phillips curve for the years 1950 through 1969 is shown in Figure 29.1. If the government had been willing to accept an annual inflation rate of 5.5 percent, it could have driven unemployment down to about 3.5 percent. If it had been willing to tolerate an inflation rate of only 1.6 percent, then there would have been unemployment of about 4.5 percent. The opportunity cost of a lower unemployment rate was higher inflation, and vice versa.

The Phillips curve appeared to provide policy makers with a menu of inflation and unemployment from which they could choose. By implying that policy makers

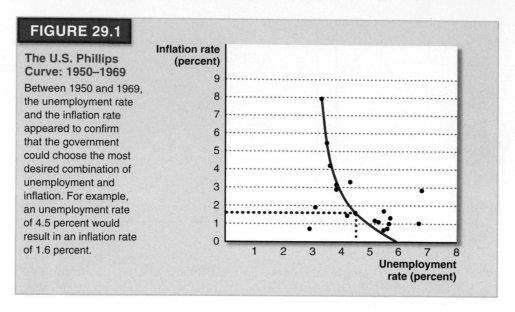

FIGURE 29.1

The U.S. Phillips Curve: 1950–1969

Between 1950 and 1969, the unemployment rate and the inflation rate appeared to confirm that the government could choose the most desired combination of unemployment and inflation. For example, an unemployment rate of 4.5 percent would result in an inflation rate of 1.6 percent.

could maintain their ideal unemployment-inflation combination indefinitely, the Phillips curve indicated that policy makers could choose from a variety of long-run equilibria. Moreover, by keeping real GDP and the unemployment rate steady, the government could avoid recessions such as the one in 2001. Further, the Phillips curve led policy makers to believe they could maintain these trade-offs forever.

The Phillips Curve and Unemployment

The point where the Phillips curve crosses the horizontal axis shows the unemployment rate at which there is no inflation. In Figure 29.1, zero inflation occurs when the unemployment rate equals about 6 percent. This point corresponds to the notion of full employment. The zero-inflation (seasonally adjusted) unemployment rate includes only frictionally unemployed and structurally unemployed workers. Frictional unemployment has no impact on inflation, because it consists of workers who simply have trouble locating existing job openings. Workers seeking jobs put downward pressure on wages. Employers seeking workers put upward pressure on wages. The net impact is that wages, production costs, and the price level stay about the same.

Structural unemployment also places no downward pressure on wages because the structurally unemployed lack the skills to bid for jobs that others hold. Unemployed workers with inappropriate skills or who lack even the most basic skills are not competing for jobs. Cyclical unemployment *does* affect wages and the price level. Cyclically unemployed workers create increased competition for the remaining jobs, causing costs and the price level to rise more slowly or even fall.

When cyclical unemployment disappears, firms can hire more workers only by tapping into the pool of frictionally or structurally unemployed workers. Seeking out frictionally unemployed workers and training or retraining structurally unemployed workers adds to firms' costs of production. As a result, the price level increases. The price increase pushes the economy back along the Phillips curve and causes inflation. The more the government reduces the unemployment rate, the higher the inflation rate.

The End of the Phillips Curve Relationship

In the early 1970s, U.S. policy makers almost universally agreed that the government could successfully fine-tune the economy. Ironically, by the 1970s, the U.S.

FIGURE 29.2

The U.S. Phillips Curve: 1970–1989

In the 1970s and 1980s, the negative relationship between the inflation rate and the unemployment rate seemed to disappear. Instead, unemployment averaged 7 percent at various rates of inflation.

government's efforts to increase real GDP seemed to do nothing but feed inflation. In particular, as Figure 29.2 illustrates, the Phillips curve relationship between inflation and unemployment seemed to vanish. Rather than tracing out a downward-sloping curve, the Phillips curve was a vertical line at about 7 percent unemployment. There was no longer a trade-off between inflation and unemployment. Instead, only inflation fluctuated.

A downward sloping Phillips curve meant that policy makers could choose the combination of inflation and unemployment rated that society most preferred. By the 1970s, they seemed to have no choice at all. Instead, there was a **natural rate of unemployment**, the full employment unemployment rate, toward which the economy gravitated regardless of governmental policy. With the economy stuck at the natural rate of unemployment, a tax cut, such as the one implemented in 2001, would not reduce the unemployment rate. Instead, it would only feed inflation.

Natural rate of unemployment
The unemployment rate to which the economy moves regardless of the initiatives of policy makers.

Rational Expectations

The inability of the government or the Fed to stabilize the economy in the 1970s led economist and Nobel laureate Robert Lucas to formulate a critique of stabilization policy that denied any role for active stabilization policy. The *Lucas critique* stemmed from the observation that many policies fail because they do not account for people's reaction to a new situation. Existing models of the economy had assumed that people respond to macroeconomic policy in precise, mechanical ways. According to these models, expansionary policy causes firms and consumers to spend more, leading to an increase in real GDP. The opposite occurs for contractionary policy. Lucas noted that workers might adapt to a new policy in ways that negated its intent.

Rational Expectations on a Microeconomic Level

Long-run and short-run macroeconomic models are based on strong assumptions about how workers perceive and respond to government policy. The long-run model assumes that workers recognize changes to their real wages and behave accordingly.

When workers see their real wages fall, it is assumed that they work less or insist on higher pay. Their behavior drives the real wage and the unemployment rate back to their original levels.

The short-run model assumes that workers either do not recognize or do not respond to changes in their real wages. The rational expectations model takes a middle ground. **Rational expectations** theory maintains that people are uncertain about the conditions under which they operate, and that as a result, they formulate expectations about government policy and its impact on them. They then respond to these expectations in an economically rational manner. We next illustrate rational expectations at the microeconomic level in the context of a single person's decision. We then consider how rational expectations apply to a single market.

Rational expectations
A theory that states that households and firms make rational economic decisions using whatever information they have about the state of the economy.

Rational Expectations: A Single Person's Decision. In Frank R. Stockton's classic short story, "The Lady or the Tiger," a young courtier stands in a packed arena, facing a difficult choice. He has been (correctly) accused of having an affair with the king's daughter. According to the custom of the land, he must decide his own fate by choosing one of two doors. Behind one stands a ravenous tiger that would instantly kill and eat him. Behind the other stands a beautiful maiden who would instantly become his bride. Seeking guidance, the young man looks up to the royal box where the princess sits. Subtly but clearly, she points to the door on the right. The young man now must decide. Would the princess prefer seeing him killed or in the arms of another woman? The young man must make his decision based on all the information he has regarding the princess and then take the rational action based on his expectation.

Rational Expectations in a Single Market. The companies that hold the concession rights at Soldier Field in Chicago face a less serious decision on eight Sundays each fall. They must decide how many hot dogs, how many cold drinks, and how much hot cocoa to stock for each Chicago Bears football game. The firms must order all the items several weeks in advance. As a result, they do not know with certainty what the weather or the records of the two teams will be on the day of the game. However, they have already faced many situations like this, so their expectations are based on solid information. The firms use their years of experience to form expectations regarding weather patterns and the Bears' performance. They have also formulated expectations regarding how each of these factors affects the demand for food and drink. Consequently, a dull game on a cold and dreary day might depress sales of everything but hot cocoa. However, a game with playoff implications on warm fall afternoon will probably bring high sales of food and cold drinks.

Though the firms have more information than the young courtier did, they can still make serious errors. Suppose that in mid-November, the firms must place their orders for a mid-December game against the Minnesota Vikings. At the time, the two teams might appear playoff-bound, and the weather outlook might be favorable. After the orders are placed, however, both the Vikings and Bears could go on losing streaks, while an arctic front suddenly moves down from Canada. Having more information does not always mean that the firms' expectations are exactly on target. It does mean they are usually close.

Rational Expectations on a Macroeconomic Level

The key contribution of rational expectations to macroeconomics is that while households make the best possible use of whatever information they have, their information might be limited or incorrect. Especially over short periods of time, households might not perceive the true state of the economy. They can therefore be "fooled" into behaving the way that policy makers want them to.

Money Illusion. Consider employees who believe that higher nominal wages also mean higher real wages. In fact, their real wages could be falling. Rational expectations theory explains why stabilization policies can be effective in the short run. Suppose that workers do not realize that tax cuts actually cause prices to rise along with wages. They will therefore not insist on pushing wages still higher. Economists call workers' misperception of their well-being **money illusion**, which means that workers focus on their nominal wages rather than their real wages. Workers who are subject to money illusion are less likely to insist on higher wages to protect their purchasing power. As a result, workers' actions will not offset expansionary polices that cause employment and real GDP to rise and real wages to fall.

Expectations Become Rational. After discerning the goals of policy makers, people act in ways that offset the expansionary effect of the policy. Figure 29.3 shows how a tax cut increases aggregate demand, as shown by the rightward shift from AD_1 to AD_2. Workers respond to higher prices by demanding higher nominal wages to restore their standards of living. The higher wages bring higher nominal production costs, which cause aggregate supply to decrease. The aggregate supply curve shifts to the left from $SRAS_1$ to $SRAS_2$, where equilibrium reaches the original level of real GDP at $11 trillion. In the long run, the tax cut has no impact on employment or output. Real GDP and employment both return to their original levels. Meanwhile,

Money illusion

Occurs when workers worry about their nominal wages rather than their real wages.

FIGURE 29.3

Rational Expectations and the Long-Run Aggregate Supply Curve
The rational expectations model says that workers may at first be fooled by a tax cut that increases aggregate demand, as shown by the rightward shift from AD_1 to AD_2. As a result, real GDP may rise at first from $11 trillion to $12 trillion. Eventually, however, workers catch on that higher prices have eroded the purchasing power of their wages and insist on higher wages. The higher cost of production reduces short-run aggregate supply, as shown by the leftward shift from $SRAS_1$ to $SRAS_2$. The vertical long-run aggregate supply curve (*LRAS*) at the original $11 trillion level of real GDP appears sooner and sooner.

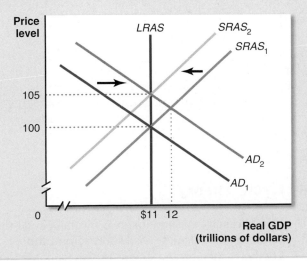

the price level rises in this example from of 100 to 105, which means inflation of 5 percent has occurred.

The Effect of Rational Expectations on Policy

The difference between the rational expectations model and the long-run model lies in the ability of households to learn about the economy, and their corresponding ability to respond to policy changes more quickly. According to this view, government policy became predictable in the second half of the twentieth century. Economic downturns brought expansionary fiscal or monetary policy, and periods of inflation brought contractionary policies. Households and firms were able to anticipate the stabilization policies, and the slow process of learning about the state of the economy accelerated. Workers therefore came to base their wage demands on what the economy was going to be like and not merely on its current state.

Eventually, households and firms became so good at anticipating stabilization policy that their reactions practically coincided with the policy itself. When this happened, even the short-run impact of economic policy disappeared. Instead of the slow move back to the full employment level of GDP, workers short-circuited the process. The short run aggregate supply curve in Figure 29.3 shifted to the left almost immediately. According to this viewpoint, workers and firms would have fully anticipated the 2001 tax cut, most of whose provisions did not even come into effect until well after the recession ended. Workers' actions would offset any expansionary impact of the tax cut. Aggregate demand would increase and short run aggregate supply would decrease simultaneously. Employment would not expand, and real GDP would not rise. Only the price level would rise.

According to the rational expectations model, for stabilization policy to consistently have its intended effect, it must be completely unpredictable. To accomplish this objective, policy makers would have to implement policies in secret and pursue inappropriate policies as often as they pursued appropriate ones. That is a very steep price to pay to ensure that a policy succeeds. Rational expectations thus provides a strong theoretical argument for opponents of stabilization policy.

TEST + *EXTEND* Your Knowledge

1. TEST Suppose that the Federal Open Market Committee tries to stimulate the economy by increasing the money supply. Use aggregate demand and the appropriate aggregate supply curves to show the impact that increasing the money supply would have on the economy according to someone who believes in rational expectations. Then show what would happen according to someone who does not believe in rational expectations.

2 . EXTEND Some proponents of the rational expectations model claim that workers' ability to anticipate changes in policy allows the government or the Fed to cool off an overheated economy at no cost of greater unemployment. Show how the policy would affect aggregate demand and aggregate supply in the rational expectations model.

► Real Business Cycle Theory

Real business cycle theory
A model of the economy that attributes economic expansions and contractions to technological innovations and slowdowns.

Like rational expectations, real business cycle theory takes a long-run view of the economy and denies a role for stabilization policies. **Real business cycle theory** attributes the ups and downs of the economy to changes in productivity—the ability of the economy to produce goods and services. In particular, the theory asserts

LifeLessons

Good Intentions Sometimes Lead to Bad Results

The graduate programs at many universities have special requirements for their graduate students. Because they expect graduate students to be experts in their fields of study, the universities hold them to a higher grading standard than undergraduates. In particular, many universities require that graduate students maintain at least a C average. Most professors agree with the policy's goal. However, a policy's goal is no guarantee of its success. In particular, the policy fails to take into account that the people subject to the policy may respond in ways that subvert it. Rather than holding graduate students to a higher standard, professors and graduate students at many schools now regard Cs as Fs. As a result of this grade inflation, all grades have risen in graduate classes, even though the students' performance has not improved. Because the policy failed to take into account how the professors adapted their grading standards in light of the new requirements, the policy did not cause the students to work harder. Instead, the policy produced inflated grades.

that good and bad times are sparked by technological innovation and not by monetary or fiscal policy. Innovation causes the productivity of inputs to rise and increases long-run aggregate supply. The increase in long-run aggregate supply causes employment and real GDP to rise.

Figure 29.4 shows how technology affects the economy. When labor becomes more productive, the economy can produce more at any given price level, and long-run aggregate supply increases. In Figure 29.4, the long-run aggregate supply curve shifts to the right from $LRAS_1$ to $LRAS_2$. and real GDP rises from $10 trillion to $12 trillion.

Real Business Cycles and the 2001 Recession

A period of rapid technological advance, such as the mid- to late-1990s, brings about higher wages and lower unemployment and inflation. When the rate of technological advance slows, precisely the opposite happens. Slowing technological

myeconlab

Get Ahead of the Curve

Apply your understanding of the debates over stabilization policy to assessing the work of the 2004 recipients of the Nobel Memorial Prize in Economics.

FIGURE 29.4

Technology Spurs an Economic Expansion

Technological change increases productivity. As a result, the long-run aggregate supply curve shifts to the right from $LRAS_1$ to $LRAS_2$. Assuming no change in aggregate demand, the price level falls from 105 to 100. The equilibrium level of GDP rises from $10 trillion to $12 trillion.

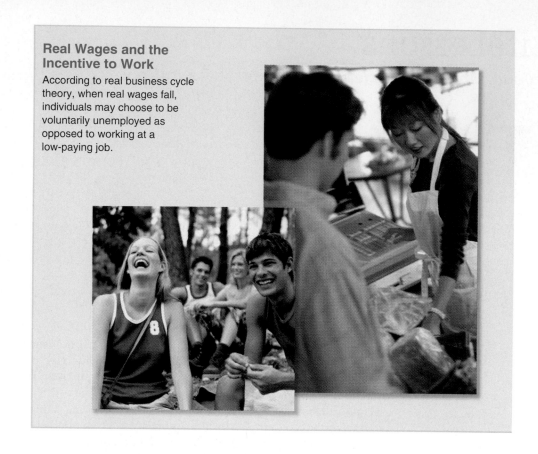

Real Wages and the Incentive to Work
According to real business cycle theory, when real wages fall, individuals may choose to be voluntarily unemployed as opposed to working at a low-paying job.

advances cause the productivity of labor to stagnate. According to this point of view, the 2001 recession reflected a slowdown in technological innovation. No tax cut or other expansionary policy would reverse the decline in productivity.

Economists who believe in real business cycles also believe that the unemployment that accompanies recessions is not a serious problem. They base this conclusion on the commonly held assumption that workers decide how much labor to supply by weighing the benefits of working (the wages they receive) against the value of forgone activities such as schooling or leisure.

Real Business Cycles and the Unemployment Rate

When real wages fall due to a technological slowdown, people's incentive to work falls as well. Households, in turn, work less because the benefit of working falls. Some people leave the labor force, and others choose to be unemployed. People who cannot find jobs because they will not accept the prevailing wage are *voluntarily* unemployed. When high-paying jobs become more plentiful, people leave school, the home, or their leisure activities to accept job offers, and the unemployment rate thus falls. Proponents of real business cycles regard the higher unemployment rate in 2001 as a decision by households to take time off rather than work for low wages.

▶ Supply-Side Economics

Supply-side economics
Policies designed to increase aggregate supply.

Unlike either rational expectations or real business cycle theory, **supply-side economics**—the use of policies designed to increase aggregate supply—prescribes an active role for government. Supply-side economics emerged in the 1980s and fell out of favor rather quickly, but it has resurfaced in recent U.S. policy. Although President George W. Bush never openly embraced supply-side theory, many of the basic principles of supply-side economics became cornerstones of his administration's economic agenda. In particular, they appear to be the basis for the 2001 tax cuts.

Supply-Side Theory

As its name suggests, supply-side economics focuses on the long-run aggregate supply curve rather than the aggregate demand curve. It starts from the widely accepted notion that the economy improves when long-run aggregate supply increases. As Figure 29.4 showed, a rightward shift of the long-run aggregate supply curve increases real GDP and puts downward pressure on the price level. All economists would endorse a policy that shifts the long-run aggregate supply curve to the right. What sets supply-side economics apart is its claim that the best policy to increase long-run aggregate supply is to reduce taxes.

Supply-Side Tax Policy

When you received your first paycheck, were you taken aback by the amount withheld for taxes? To illustrate the tax burden U.S. citizens face, the Tax Foundation determines how long it would take Americans to meet their tax obligations each year if they sent every paycheck to the federal, state, or local government until all taxes were paid. Taxpayers would not be free to keep their paychecks for their own uses until after their taxes were paid. In 2005, the typical worker would not have been able to keep his or her earnings until April 17.

Supply-side economists believe that high tax rates and the resulting tax burden reduce the incentive to work and encourage unproductive activity aimed at reducing taxes. They believe that cutting tax rates would unleash a wave of productive activity that would boost real GDP. The increase in productive activity would be so great that tax revenues—the amount of money collected in taxes—would actually rise, as a result of the lower tax rates.

Even critics of supply-side economics believe that it accurately depicts behavior at extremely low or extremely high tax rates. Both very low tax rates and prohibitively high tax rates result in little tax revenue. The critics are much more dubious about what goes on between the extremes. Studies of the U.S. economy and comparisons with other nations have found little evidence to support the claim that lowering tax rates increases tax revenues.[1]

The experience of the 1980s seemed to bear out the critics of supply-side economics. Under President Ronald Reagan, the government cut income tax rates in accordance with supply-side beliefs. The Economic Recovery Tax Act of 1981 reduced all **marginal tax rates**—the amount of tax paid on an extra dollar of taxable income—by 25 percent. However, the expected surge in tax revenues never occurred. Instead, deficits rose to levels never before seen in our nation's history.

Marginal tax rates
The tax paid on an additional dollar of earned income.

The 2001 Tax Cuts

Many of the descriptions of the 2001 tax cuts made it sound as if they were designed to increase aggregate demand. Even President George W. Bush claimed that the tax

---

[1] See, for example, N. Bruce and S. J. Turovsky, "Budget Balance, Welfare, and the Growth Rate: Dynamic Scoring of the Long-run Government Budget," *Journal of Money Credit and Banking*, vol. 31. pages 162–186.

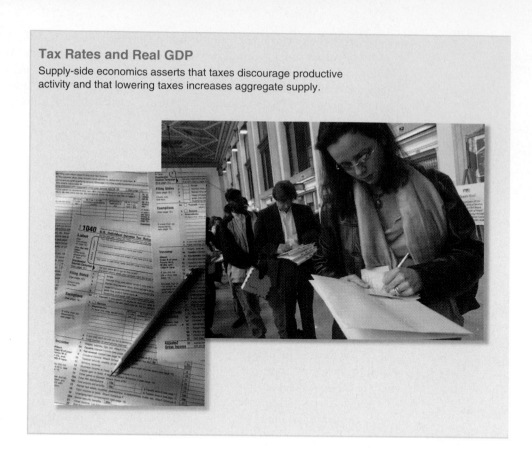

Tax Rates and Real GDP
Supply-side economics asserts that taxes discourage productive activity and that lowering taxes increases aggregate supply.

cuts would put more money into the hands of consumers and stimulate spending. However, the details of the policy suggest that it has more in common with supply-side theory than with any of the aggregate demand-based policies we encountered in earlier chapters. A tax cut designed to stimulate aggregate demand would be most effective if it were directed at those with low incomes. Low-income households spend more (and save less) of each dollar of income than high-income households. As a result, the ripple effects of the multiplier are greatest if the tax cut is aimed at the households with the lowest income. By contrast, supply-side theory says that a tax cut should provide incentives to those people most capable of increasing output and employment in the economy. These people are at the upper end of the income distribution. The 2001 tax cut targeted such high-income households.

▶ "New Keynesian" Models

From the early 1970s into the 1990s, rational expectations and real business cycle theories dominated the debate over macroeconomic policy. Slowly, however, those who favored stabilization policy began to find additional theoretical tools and observations to justify their stand. Our focus in this section is on the "New Keynesian" models that provide fuel for proponents of active stabilization policies.

FIGURE 29.5

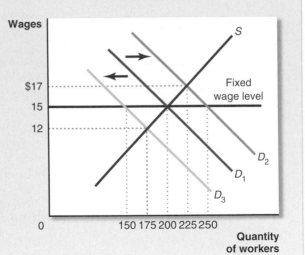

Labor Market with Fixed-Wage Contracts

If a contract fixes the wage at $15 per hour, the supply of labor becomes a horizontal line at $15. If the demand for labor shifts from D_1 to D_2, the company will increase its workforce from 200 to 250 rather than to 225. Similarly, when the demand for labor shifts from D_1 to D_3, the quantity of workers declines from 200 to 150 rather than to 175. Fixed-wage contracts increase the volatility of employment and outputs.

Money Illusion Revisited

Economists generally agreed that the impact of the 2001 tax cut or any expansionary policy would disappear after workers recognized the actual impact of the tax cut on their real wages. Rational expectations led many economists to believe that workers would catch on very quickly, causing the tax cut to have only a very brief effect on the economy. Most economists now believe that workers eventually catch on to the impact of stabilization policy, returning the economy to its natural level. However, some believe that workers and firms have developed agreements that keep real wages from adjusting for long periods of time, as discussed in the following sections.

Fixed-Wage Contracts. One economic argument is that wages adjust slowly to changes in economic policy because of fixed-wage contracts between workers and employers, rather than because workers do not know what is happening. Suppose that a company has a long-term contract with its employees. It can keep wages fixed or rising at a predetermined rate for extended periods, as in Figure 29.5.

For simplicity, suppose that a firm agrees to set a fixed wage of $15 per hour. This turns the supply of labor into a horizontal line at $15 per hour. The firm and its workforce can change the wage only when the contract comes up for renewal. An expansionary policy increases the demand for labor. As a result, the demand curve shifts rightward from D_1 to D_2. If wages could rise to $17, the firm would hire only 25 more workers, increasing employment from 200 workers to 225 workers. If, due to the contract, wages do not rise, employment expands all the way to 250 workers. In bad times, labor demand falls, as shown by the leftward shift from D_1 to D_3. If wages fall to $12 per hour, fewer workers are displaced and employment falls to only 175 workers. With a fixed-wage contract, employment falls to 150 workers, because wages do not fall in response to the lower demand for labor. As long as the contract is in effect, the wage stays fixed while employment and output change. In such a situation, a tax cut can therefore have a prolonged effect.

Such contracts typically occur when labor and management conduct formal negotiations over wages, salaries, and working conditions. As a result, they are usually associated with a unionized labor force. This may have been a reasonable picture of the labor market in the late 1940s and early 1950s when more than one-third of the civilian, nonfarm labor force was unionized. However, it is not a realistic picture of the labor market today, when about 12.5 percent of the civilian labor force is unionized.

Implicit Contracts. Because formal, explicit contracts have become less common, workers and firms are more likely to engage in **implicit contracts**, informal understandings that do not require formal negotiation. One theory of implicit contracts suggests that workers and firms agree to keep wages relatively fixed because workers do not like to see their wages or salaries rise and fall. They prefer a stable wage, even if it is lower than the average wage that would prevail if their pay fluctuated. By accepting a lower average wage, workers effectively purchase an insurance policy that protects them from fluctuating wages.

Implicit contracts
A set of informal understandings between labor and management that do not require formal negotiations.

Hysteresis and Crowding In

Even if the tax cuts of 2001 had no lasting impact and the short-run aggregate supply curve quickly shifts to the left, some economists claim that expansionary policy could have had a lasting effect. Economists call the lasting effect of a short-run policy **hysteresis**.

Hysteresis
The lasting impact of short-run policy.

To see the lingering effect of a temporary expansion, consider how an individual firm might respond to the tax cut. If the tax cut succeeds in stimulating demand for its output, the firm hires additional workers. The on-the-job training that the new workers receive might take the form of highly specialized training, such as learning computer software that was designed specifically for the firm. Alternatively, it might be basic training, such as learning the importance of reporting to work on time. Either set of skills makes the new workers more productive than they had been before they were hired.

As workers become more productive, long-run aggregate supply increases. This rightward shift of the long-run aggregate supply curve causes the long-run equilibrium to shift to the right, increasing full employment real GDP and reducing the full employment unemployment rate.

Economic downturns can also have lingering effects. When a firm lays off workers, the workers' skills begin to erode. Lower productivity causes long-run aggregate supply to decrease, reducing real GDP and employment even when the initial downward pressure on the economy has ended.

Hysteresis thus represents something of a middle ground between those who believe that active stabilization can have only a passing effect on the economy and those who believe that the government has a role to play in the economy. It also combines elements of all the models we have encountered in this chapter. This theory concedes that a policy like the tax cut of 2001 might not have a lasting effect on the economy. Firms and households will adjust to the increase in aggregate demand by reducing short-run aggregate supply. However, it asserts that even if the impact of the tax cut itself passes quickly, it can have a lasting impact on the employability of workers. As a result, short-run aggregate supply decreases, but it will not fall back to its original level, and real GDP will be higher as a result of the tax cut.

▶ Evaluating Policy Options

What policy should the U.S. government and the Fed follow when the macroeconomy is facing a recession as the United States did in 2001? The answer depends on

1. TEST If workers understand that their real wage differs from their nominal wage, why are wages slow to fall during economic expansions and slow to rise during downturns?

2. EXTEND Go to the Bureau of Labor Statistics Web site using the links at www.aw-bc.com/leeds/ch29 to see how wages have changed since the recession of 2001. How responsive were nominal wages to the downturn? What theory do the wage movements support?

your view of the economy. Table 29.1 spells out the choices that policy makers face. Unfortunately, neither economists nor politicians can hold outside factors constant and isolate the impact of a specific policy. As a result, it is difficult to determine conclusively whether a policy really works.

Perhaps as a result, policy choices often reflect the philosophical views of the policy makers as much as the implications of economic models. Individuals who believe that government should be committed to social programs to help struggling households might advocate active stabilization policy even if the economic evidence suggests that such policy is ineffective. Individuals who believe that "big government" is bad might oppose stabilization policy even if economic models favor active policy.

Finally, there are no guarantees that the policy will work as advertised. Stabilization policy is more art than science. The tools of macroeconomic theory provide the basic list of ingredients for a successful policy. But how each of these ingredients is to be used involves more than following a recipe from a cookbook. Each policy maker must try to find the right recipe for the particular economic situation. Unfortunately, though the same combination typically yields the same result each time in the kitchen, there are many factors beyond the control of policy makers that could lead the same elements of economic policy to succeed or fail at different times. The economic policies of foreign governments, technological

TABLE 29.1

Economic Models and Policy Prescriptions

Economic Model	View of Economy	Policy Prescription
Phillips curve	Inflation and unemployment rates are inversely related	Choose optimal mix of inflation and unemployment
Rational expectations	Workers catch on to systematic stabilization policy	Stabilization policy doesn't work; focus on long run
Real business cycles	Increases in real per-capita GDP stem from increases in technology	Stabilization policy doesn't work; focus on technological progress
Supply-side economics	Productive activity is discouraged by high taxes	Cut taxes to encourage productive activity
Optimal contracts	Long-term contracts prevent quick adjustments to policy	Stabilization policy can work for substantial periods
Hysteresis	Workers become more productive when employed	Stabilization policy can promote long-term growth

innovation, and even the weather can alter the effectiveness of economic policy. All of these influences create a challenge for the economist trying to cook up a cure for whatever ails the economy.

Strategy and Policy
Adjusting to Inflation

Advocates of rational expectations face a major institutional obstacle to their claim that stabilization policy is ineffective because the short-run aggregate supply curve shifts instantly to the left. In order for this to happen so quickly, workers must immediately recognize the policy and force employers to raise their wages. Suppose that workers were so observant that they could recognize the policy being implemented right away. They still would have to convince employers to raise their wages. Given the time it takes to renegotiate contracts, it seems unlikely that employees could arrange for their pay to rise on a moment's notice.

In response, supporters of rational expectations point to a contractual innovation that dates back to the 1970s: the cost of living adjustment, or COLA. The high inflation of the 1970s badly eroded the real incomes of people who received government transfer payments as well as workers with fixed nominal wages. In order to protect the purchasing power of recipients of entitlements such as Social Security or food stamps, Congress mandated that payments rise as a cost of living index, such as the CPI, rose. Automatic cost of living adjustments have also been applied to salaries, particularly in the public sector. COLAs protect federal and some state employees' real wages. Wages and salaries are adjusted for these employees with no need for an explicit renegotiation of the employment contract. Firms in the private sector have been more reluctant to implement COLAs for their employees. Most workers and firms still negotiate wage rates that are fixed or that rise at predetermined increments for the length of the contract. As a result, at least a short run trade-off between inflation and unemployment remains possible.

Critical-Thinking Questions

1. What is the advantage of a COLA over renegotiating a contract?
2. Use aggregate supply and aggregate demand to show the impact of an expansionary policy if workers are covered by COLAs that cause wages to rise at the same rate as prices.

SUMMARY

- **Stabilization policy.** Large deviations from the long-run trend of GDP growth can result in high unemployment rates or severe inflation. Governments have tried to stabilize the economy by minimizing the deviation from the long-run trend. Economists are divided as to whether such active attempts to stabilize the economy can really affect the economy as intended.

- **The trade-off between inflation and unemployment.** For much of the second half of the twentieth century, most economists and policy makers felt that the government could affect the level of economic activity for long periods of time. The Phillips curve showed a continual trade-off between inflation and unemployment rates. In the 1970s, the trade-off between inflation and unemployment rates seemed to disappear.

- **Rational expectations.** According to rational expectations, government policies become less effective as households and firms adjust to the impact of the policies. If the government's policies become predictable, these adjustments might completely offset the government policies in the short run.

- **The real business cycle model.** According to the theory of real business cycles, people work when wages are high and spend a longer time looking for work or engage in nonlabor activities when wages are low. Much of the decline in employment during recessions comes from people choosing not to work.

- **Supply-side economics.** Some economists believe that the government can increase real GDP by increasing aggregate supply rather than aggregate demand. Cutting taxes would increase the reward for working hard and engaging in productive activity rather than trying to avoid taxes. Because they believe that the most productive people earn the most, supporters of supply-side economics generally advocate cutting the taxes of households with high incomes.

- **"New Keynesian" models.** Some economists believe that short-term gains have long-term effects, because they provide workers with skills that make the workers more productive in the long run. These economists also claim that explicit and implicit contracts prevent workers from adjusting wages in the short term, even if the workers correctly anticipate the government's policy.

- **Evaluating policy options.** It is difficult to say what the correct policy should have been in 2001. Macroeconomic policy does not operate under strict laboratory conditions. As a result, policy sometimes reflects the beliefs of policy makers as much as the evidence that they face.

►KEY TERMS

Hysteresis 752	Natural rate of	Real business cycle theory
Implicit contracts 752	unemployment 743	746
Marginal tax rates 749	Phillips curve 741	Stabilization policies 740
Money illusion 745	Rational expectations 744	Supply-side economics 748

►PROBLEMS

1. Using the Phillips curve pictured below, what inflation rate must policy makers be willing to tolerate if they want to reduce the unemployment rate from 6 percent to 2 percent? Suppose that society is willing to tolerate inflation of only 4 percent per year. How far can it reduce unemployment?

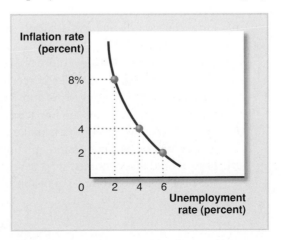

2. Which form of unemployment—cyclical, structural, or frictional—lies behind the inflation-unemployment trade-off of the Phillips curve? Why is it this one and not the others?

3. In the 1970s, many women and baby boomers entered the labor force for the first time. What is the likely impact of such a change on the Phillips curve?

4. Studies have shown that antilock braking systems (ABS) help cars stop more quickly and safely than regular brakes. Other studies have shown, however, that cars with ABS are no less likely to get into accidents than cars with regular brakes. What light does the Lucas critique shed on this paradox?

5. "The rational expectations model assumes that people can predict the future. Because we never know exactly what the future will bring, the rational expectations model makes no sense." Do you agree or disagree with this statement? Explain your reasoning.

6. According to the theory of rational expectations, the government or the Fed can cool off an overheated economy without creating unemployment if households and firms correctly anticipate the policy. Show how this can occur when the Fed engages in a policy designed to reduce aggregate demand.

7. Suppose that more students start to take macroeconomics courses, where they learn how monetary and fiscal policy operate and how these policies affect output, employment, and prices. How would this change in course choices affect the applicability of rational expectations?

8. How would an economist who believes in rational expectations explain the fact that the short-run aggregate supply curve immediately shifts to the left?

9. How would the real business cycle model explain the fact that enrollment in M.B.A. programs rose during the 2001 recession?

10. Do economists who believe in real business cycles believe that official unemployment rates overstate or understate the problems faced by the economy? Why?

11. According to the theory of real business cycles, how did the "Internet revolution" affect the overall economy? Use aggregate demand and aggregate supply curves to explain your answer.

12. What would an economist who believes in real business cycles say about the impact of the technology bust that occurred in the early 2000s on the economy?

13. Why do advocates of supply-side economics believe that whose taxes the government cuts is so important?

14. How can you distinguish a supply-side tax cut from one designed to stimulate aggregate demand?

15. Why was money illusion a more reasonable assumption in 1935 than in 1975?

16. Union membership has fallen in recent decades, reducing the number of long-term contracts between firms and workers. How could this trend change in the labor market affect the impact of a tax cut?

17. How do fixed wage contracts make unemployment more sensitive to the ups and downs of the economy than contracts that allow wages to fluctuate?

18. How would an economist who believes in hysteresis analyze the aftermath of the prolonged economic expansion of the late 1990s?

HERE'S HOW MyEconLab CAN HELP YOU GET A BETTER GRADE

1. Log into MyEconLab and take Practice Test 29-A (to log in for the first time, see page 30 for instructions).

2. Based on your test results, MyEconLab will identify the areas where you need further work and create a personal Study Plan for you.

3. Your Study Plan contains the problems listed below and others like them that will target the specific chapter topics you need to focus on. You'll receive instant feedback and find links to tutorials, animations, and the online textbook to help you study.

4. When you're ready, take Practice Test 29-B and demonstrate how your results have improved.

Section 29.1, Problem 1 Which of the following sttements are true? Stabilization policies attempt to:

a. Keep inflation under rigid control.
b. Ensure that fiscal policy and monetary policy closely follow one another.
c. Make sure that everyone has a job.
d. Diminish the size and the duration of deviations from the economy's long-run trend.
e. Increase the rate of the long-term growth trend of real GDP.

Section 29.2, Problem 1 The Phillips curve initially showed evidence _____ (*for/against*) active stabilization policies, and showed a _____ (*positive/negative*) relationship between inflation and employment.

Section 29.2, Problem 2 The presence of which types of unemployment affect wages and ultimately the price level:

a. Frictional unemployment only
b. Frictional and structural unemployment
c. Frictional and cyclical unemployment
d. Frictional, structural, and cyclical unemployment
e. Cyclical unemployment only

Section 29.3, Problem 1 Which one of the following statements is true?

a. Both the Phillips curve and the rational expectations model provide strong evidence in favor of active stabilization policies.
b. The Phillips curve provides support for active stabilization, while rational expectations argues against it.
c. The Phillips curve argues against active stabilization, and rational expectations supports it.

d. Both models provide theoretical arguments against active stabilization policies.
e. Both models provide support for active fiscal stabilization policies, but against active monetary policy.

Section 29.3, Problem 2 Which one of the following explains the rational expectations model of workers' reactions to repeated expansionary policies?

a. Workers will begin to recognize the change in their real wages sooner and sooner, rendering the policy nearly ineffective over time.
b. Workers will always take the same amount of time to recognize the change in their real wage, rendering the policy temporarily effective.
c. Workers will immediately recognize the change in their real wage the first time, rendering the policy completely ineffective.
d. Workers will never recognize the change in their real wage, rendering the policy completely effective.
e. Workers are unpredictable, and sometimes will recognize the change in their real wage, and sometimes not, rendering the effectiveness completely random.

Section 29.3, Problem 3 Which one of the following statements is true regarding the effectiveness of stabilization policies of the short-run model, the long-run model, and the rational expectations model?

a. All three models show support for active stabilization policies.
b. The long-run and rational expectations models provide theoretical arguments against active stabilization, and the short-run model supports it.

c. Only the rational expectations model promotes active stabilization.
d. All three models show theoretical support for opponents of active stabilization.
e. The long-run and short-run models provide theoretical arguments against active stabilization, and the rational expectations model supports it.

Section 29.3, Problem 4 The graph shows an increase in *AD* caused by expansionary policy in aggregate demand. Which one of the following statements about the reaction of workers is true of the rational expectations model?

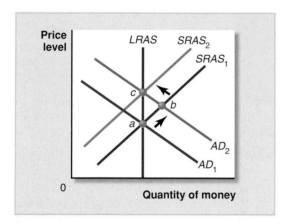

a. At first, workers may not realize that the increase in the price level has lowered their real wages. The economy moves from point a to point b.
b. Eventually, workers will realize the change in their real wages, and make adjustments such that the economy moves from point b to point c.
c. If policy makers try expansionary policy again, workers will make the adjustments sooner than before, and the economy will move from point a to point b to point c.
d. If policy makers continue with expansionary policy, workers will automatically understand the implications, make the necessary adjustments immediately, and the economy will move straight from point a to point c.
e. All of the above statements are true.

Section 29.4, Problem 1 Which one of the following statements regarding the real business cycle theory is true?

I. The theory predicts regular cycles of economic activity around the long-run trend, due to natural fluctuations of aggregate demand.
II. The theory provides theoretical support against active stabilization policies.
III. The theory provides theoretical support for active stabilization policies.
IV. The theory explains cycles of economic activity due to changes in productivity and shifts in aggregate supply.

a. I and II are correct
b. I and III are correct
c. II and IV are correct
d. III and IV are correct
e. None of the statements is correct.

Section 29.4, Problem 2 The real business cycle theory states that:

a. Workers might be more concerned with their nominal wages than with their real wages.
b. Workers make the best decisions possible based on available information.
c. Economic expansions and contractions are due to technological innovations and slowdowns.
d. Economic expansions and contractions are due to changes in worker incentives, such as tax cuts.
e. There is a short-run trade-off between inflation and unemployment.

Section 29.5, Problem 1 Supply-side economics favors _____ (*increasing/decreasing*) tax rates as a means of expanding the economy. This implies an _____ (*active/passive*) role of the government in the economic arena.

Section 29.5, Problem 2 How are supply-side economics and real business cycle theory similar?

a. Both models emphasize the effects of changes in aggregate demand in the economy.
b. Both models show strong theoretical support for active stabilization policies.
c. Both models offer theoretical evidence against active stabilization policies.
d. Both models emphasize the effects of changes on aggregate supply in the economy.

e. There is nothing similar between the two models.

Section 29.6, Problem 1 Which of the following statements regarding optimal contracts theory is correct?

Optimal contract theory predicts that active stabilization policies will be:

a. Effective, because workers are unable to change their real wages due to long-term or fixed-wage contracts.
b. Effective, because workers are quick to adjust their real wages in response to price changes.
c. Effective, because workers are uninformed about market conditions and changes to their real wages.
d. Ineffective, because workers care more about their nominal wages than about their real wages.
e. Ineffective, because workers immediately react to price changes by renegotiating their contracts to adjust their real wages.

Section 29.6, Problem 2 Hysteresis, in economics, refers to:

a. The theory that workers might react to stabilization policies in unpredictable ways, resulting in unpredictable effects on the economy.
b. Informal understandings between labor and management that do not require formal negotiations.
c. The theory that workers might be more concerned about their nominal wages than about their real wages.
d. The prolonged after-effects on the economy after stabilization policies, such as a permanent increase in productivity after expansionary policy.
e. Short-term policies designed to minimize economic deviations from the long-run trend.

Section 29.7, Problem 1 Classify each of the following models as either advocates or opponents of active fiscal and monetary stabilization policy:

Short-run model
Long-run model
Phillips curve
Rational expectations model
Real business cycle model
Supply-side model
Optimal contracts model
Hysteresis model

30

Economic Growth

The United States and Mexico are economic and political partners as well as neighbors. The two nations are bound together economically by the North American Free Trade Agreement (NAFTA) and share democratic ideals. Even so, the border between the United States and Mexico sometimes seems as though it separates enemies rather than friends. Guard towers and high-tech surveillance mechanisms loom at regular intervals. Armed guards patrol the border. The goal, however, is not to keep out Mexican soldiers. It is to prevent poor Mexicans from entering the United States illegally to seek work and a better life for themselves and their children.

Hispanics now form the largest U.S. minority population, and close to 60 percent of U.S. Hispanics are of Mexican heritage. It may not surprise you that over 30 percent of Los Angelenos are Mexican-American, as are more than 40 percent of New Mexicans. But did you know that over 20 percent of the people in Chicago are Mexican-American? Or that cities such as Omaha, Nebraska, and Portland, Oregon, have large Mexican-American populations? This large-scale immigration is driven by the markedly different standards of living in Mexico and the United States. Real GDP per capita in the United States is more than three times that of Mexico. At first glance, there seems to be little reason for such differences. The climate, terrain, and cultural history of Mexico and the southwest United States are so similar that you could easily be confused as to which side of the border you were on. One of the great economic puzzles of the last half-century is why real GDP has grown so much more rapidly in some nations than in others.

In this chapter, we see that economic theory offers several explanations for why some economies grow faster than others. We find, however, that standard economic models do not explain the difference in growth very well. Only when we include broader economic forces and institutions, such as market economies and private property, can we fully grasp why some economies have prospered and others have not.

ALONG THE WAY, YOU WILL ALSO LEARN:

- Why countries are so concerned about economic growth.

- How population, capital, and technology affect a nation's economic growth.

- What role markets and incentives play in determining how quickly an economy grows.

**AT THE END OF THE CHAPTER,
THE MYECONLAB LOGO WILL DIRECT YOU ONLINE**

- MyEconLab is a resource-packed online homework and tutorial system that can help you perform better in your economics course. To log in for the first time, see page 30 for instructions.

- MyEconLab can help you apply important concepts from the chapter to real-world issues. Watch for the logo to indicate online features about World Bank programs and Latin America.

- At the end of each chapter, you'll find a special study section that will help you get the most out of your textbook and your instructor's MyEconLab course.

The Elements of Economic Growth

Until now, our study of macroeconomics has focused on stabilization, or keeping real GDP from rising above or falling below full employment real GDP. In this chapter, we consider how and why full employment real GDP grows over time. We begin by looking at why economic growth is so important and how it differs from economic development.

Defining and Measuring Economic Growth

Economic growth
A sustained increase in output and income by an economy.

Most people agree that economic growth is a good thing, but what is it that is growing? **Economic growth** refers to a sustained increase in output and income by an economy. In terms of the model presented in Chapter 2, growth causes a country's production possibilities frontier (PPF) to shift outward. Panels (a) and (b) of Table 30.1 show the combinations of coffee and computers that a hypothetical economy is capable of producing before and after it grows. As we move down panel (a) of Table 30.1, the economy produces more coffee. However, this comes at the expense of producing fewer computers. Points G_1 and H_1 on PPF_1 in Figure 30.1 correspond to combinations G_1 and H_1 in panel (a) of Table 30.1. These points illustrate that the economy can produce more coffee only by moving down and to the right along PPF_1, which means giving up some computers. When the economy grows, it can produce more coffee *and* more computers. Moving down panel (b) of Table 30.1 again shows a trade-off between computers and coffee, but the economy is now able to produce more of both goods. We see this in Figure 30.1, as PPF_1 shifts out to

TABLE 30.1

Production Possibilities for Coffee and Computers Before and After Growth

(a) Before growth

	Coffee (tons)	Computers (thousands)
A_1	0	100
B_1	10	99
C_1	20	97
D_1	30	93
E_1	40	87
F_1	50	79
G_1	60	69
H_1	70	57
I_1	80	43
J_1	90	27
K_1	100	0

(b) After growth

	Coffee (tons)	Computers (thousands)
A_2	0	110
B_2	11	109
C_2	22	105
D_2	33	99
E_2	44	91
F_2	55	81
G_2	66	69
H_2	77	55
I_2	88	39
J_2	99	21
K_2	110	0

FIGURE 30.1

Economic Growth and the Production Possibilities Frontier

Economic growth increases the ability of an economy to produce. Moving along PPF$_1$ from point G_1 (60 tons of coffee and 69,000 computers) to point H_1 (70 tons of coffee and 57,000 computers) means that the economy produces more coffee. But the economy then produces fewer computers. Growth allows the economy to operate at G_2 on PPF$_2$. It can now produce 66 tons of coffee and 69,000 computers, a combination that is not possible with the original trade-off.

PPF$_2$. Growth allows the economy to move from point G_1 to point G_2, increasing the amount of coffee from 60 tons to 66 tons without reducing the amount of computers produced.

Real GDP per Capita. Although a PPF provides useful insights, we cannot apply such a simple model to an economy with thousands of goods. Instead, we use real

GDP to measure the economic growth of an entire economy. Specifically, economists measure economic growth by the percentage change in a nation's real GDP per capita. Recall that real GDP per capita is the standard measure of a nation's production and income. It is often used (despite the numerous flaws that we have discussed earlier) to measure a nation's well-being.

According to statistics from the International Monetary Fund (IMF), an international lending agency discussed earlier, U.S. real GDP per capita grew at an annual rate of about 2.1 percent between 1981 and 2004. In Mexico, the average growth rate during this same period was about 0.5 percent per year. A difference of about 1.6 percent per year may seem small. However, a small annual difference can have a big impact over time, as shown by Figure 30.2.

Figure 30.2 assumes that two individuals, one in Mexico and one in the United States, start with the same annual income of $20,000 in 1980. Suppose that the Mexican's income grew at the average growth rate of the Mexican economy. He would earn slightly more than $22,500 in 2004. Now suppose that the American's income grew at the rate of the U.S. economy. Her income would surpass $22,500 in 1985. By 2004, her income would be almost $33,000, more than 45 percent higher than her Mexican counterpart's.

In addition to growing more slowly on average, the Mexican economy was subject to much wider swings than the U.S. economy. GDP per capita in Mexico grew by more than 5 percent in 1981, 1997, and 2000. It fell by more than 5 percent in 1982, 1985, and 1994. By contrast, the U.S. economy grew by more than 5 percent only once, in 1984, and its sharpest decline was less than 3 percent, in 1981. The recession of 2001 caused U.S. real GDP per capita to fall by less than three-tenths of a percent, but a simultaneous recession in Mexico caused its real GDP per capita to fall by more than twice as much.

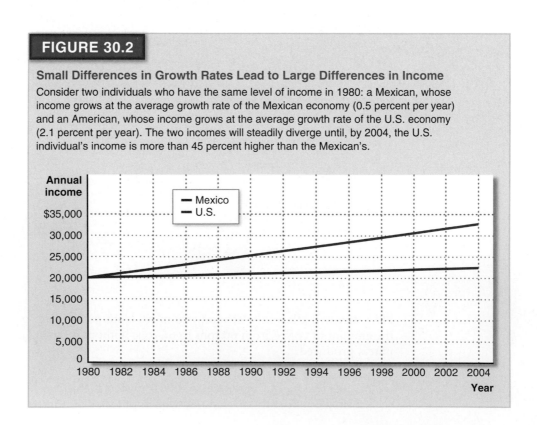

FIGURE 30.2

Small Differences in Growth Rates Lead to Large Differences in Income

Consider two individuals who have the same level of income in 1980: a Mexican, whose income grows at the average growth rate of the Mexican economy (0.5 percent per year) and an American, whose income grows at the average growth rate of the U.S. economy (2.1 percent per year). The two incomes will steadily diverge until, by 2004, the U.S. individual's income is more than 45 percent higher than the Mexican's.

Rule of 72
Mathematical relationship that states that the rate at which a country's income grows times the number of years it takes that income to double equals 72.

The Rule of 72. Another way to illustrate the impact of different growth rates is with a concept known as the rule of 72. The **rule of 72** states that the rate at which a country (or a person's or a firm's) income grows multiplied by the number of years it takes that income to double equals the number 72. Using this rule, we see that it would take 144 years for real GDP per capita in Mexico to double if the economy grows at the rate of 0.5 percent per year ($0.5 \times 144 = 72$). By contrast, U.S. real GDP per capita would double in only 34 years if its economy grows by 2.1 percent per year ($2.1 \times 34 = 72$). In 144 years, U.S. real GDP per capita would be almost 20 times its original level, about 10 times the increase of the Mexican economy.

The Importance of Economic Growth

Slow growth in Mexico has had a large human cost. Roughly 40 percent of all Mexicans live below its official poverty line. That is more than three times the percentage of people living in poverty in the United States. Poverty itself has had dire consequences. According to estimates by the United Nations, Mexico recorded 23 infant deaths for every 1,000 live births in 2003, while the United States had about 7 per 1,000.[1] In general, developing nations have higher infant mortality rates than advanced nations, and the poorest developing nations have far higher rates.

Poor countries also suffer greater political unrest. In 1994, Mexico experienced an open revolt by indigenous peoples in the Mexican state of Chiapas. The uprising was fueled by anger over land privatization that had displaced thousands of people and by fear that the recently negotiated NAFTA would result in widespread unemployment. The rebellion has continued in one form or another since then, leaving hundreds dead and tens of thousands without homes.

More generally, slow growth, poverty, and violence seem to reinforce one another. In the 1990s, 30 countries experienced civil wars or insurgencies. Of these, 28 had real GDP per capita below $3,000 per year and 22 had real GDP per capita below $1,000 per year.

Economic Growth and Economic Development

Using real GDP per capita as a yardstick, it is relatively easy to define and measure growth. Defining growth in terms of GDP, though, means that the definition of growth shares many of GDP's weaknesses. In particular, because GDP is an imperfect measure of a nation's well-being, the growth rate of real GDP per capita may not fully capture changes in a nation's welfare.

Development
The creation of an environment in which people can develop their full potential and lead productive, creative lives in accord with their needs and interests.

Economists broaden the measure of a nation's well-being by referring to its state of development. The United Nations defines **development** as the creation of "an environment in which people can develop their full potential and lead productive, creative lives in accord with their needs and interests."[2] This broad definition can mean different things to different people. Almost everyone agrees that development involves increases in real GDP per capita. Beyond that, however, many people disagree over exactly what constitutes development. Some believe that people cannot

---

[1] This is the most recent year for which U.S. data are available. See "Survival: Progress and Setbacks," *U.N. Human Development Reports*, hdr.undp.org/statistics/data/indicators.cfm?x=93&y=1&z=1.
[2] United Nations, "What Is HD?," *Human Development Reports*, hdr.undp.org/hd/.

develop their full potential unless they are free from government interference in their personal and business decisions. Others view development as the elimination of poverty, provision of primary education, reduction of child mortality, and improvement of maternal health and the environment. All these initiatives generally imply a large role for government. As these examples indicate, measuring development involves both positive factors (movements of real GDP per capita provide an objective measure) and normative factors (does economic freedom matter more than maternal health?). The values a person brings to the process thus affect how he or she views a nation's level of development.

One of the mandates of the United Nations (UN), likely the best known international organization, is to promote the economic progress of its member states. To measure progress towards this goal, it has created one of the more popular measures of development: the United Nations' Human Development Index (UNHDI). This index combines a nation's real GDP per capita with measures of its population's education and life expectancy to formulate a single number that summarizes a country's developmental level. Panels (a) and (b) of Figure 30.3 show the 10 least developed and 10 most developed economies according to the UNHDI. It also compares each nation's UNHDI with its GDP per capita. According to the UNHDI, the United States is the eighth most advanced nation. Mexico ranks at 53, well below the United States but far more advanced than the bottom 10.

The UNHDI index is highly correlated with, but not identical to, real GDP per capita. The countries with the highest UNHDI all have high real GDP per capita. Though the least developed country (Sierra Leone) has a higher real GDP per capita than Ethiopia, all the least developed countries have among the world's lowest measures of real GDP per capita. No matter what measure of development you choose, it is closely linked to our measure of economic growth. Because there is greater agreement on what economic growth means than on what development means and because it is so closely linked to most measures of development, we focus on economic growth for the remainder of this chapter.

TEST + *E X T E N D* Your Knowledge

1. TEST Between 2003 and 2004, real GDP per capita in Ireland grew by 2.8 percent while in Pakistan it grew by 5.0 percent. Assuming that these growth rates remain unchanged, how long would it take each country's real GDP per capita to double?

2 . E X T E N D Go to the World Bank's *Data Profile* tables and the *Country at a Glance* tables using the links at www.aw-bc.com/leeds/ch30. Examine the most recent data on the quality of life (life expectancy), the status of women (female illiteracy), and the state of technology (education) for Ireland and Pakistan. How do the three sets of variables differ for the two countries? What do they say about each country's level of development?

▶ Economic Models of Growth

In order to analyze how an economy's real GDP grows, we must first determine how much it produces. In this section, we focus on the tools that economists use to model economic growth. We outline the key elements of economic models of growth and explore each in turn.

FIGURE 30.3

GDP Per Capita for the Ten Least Developed and Ten Most Developed Nations

Because the UN Human Development index consists of many factors, this measure is not perfectly correlated with GDP per capita. Still, we see that the GDP per capita of the most developed countries is far higher than for the least developed countries.

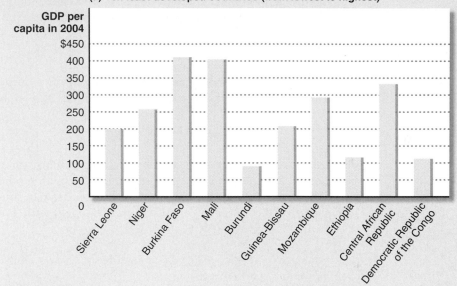

(a) Ten least developed countries (from lowest to highest)

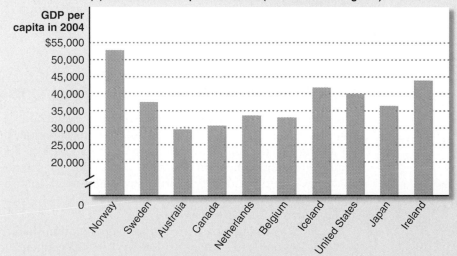

(b) Ten most developed countries (from lowest to highest)

Source: Human development ranking from United Nations, Human Development Report, www.hdr.undp.org. GDP per capita from International Monetary Fund, World Economic Outlook, www.imf.org/external/pubs/ft/weo/2004/02/data/dbhnim.cfm

Aggregate Production Function

Aggregate production function
Relates real GDP to the inputs that households provide on the resource market.

Economists typically use an aggregate production function to model how a nation produces real GDP (y).[3] On a microeconomic level, a production function relates the output of a firm to the inputs it uses. On a macroeconomic level, the **aggregate production function** relates real GDP to the inputs that households provide on the resource market. For simplicity, we consider only three of the many inputs used in the economy: the size of its stock of physical capital (K), the size of its labor force (L), and the state of its technology. For now, we assume that the level of technology is constant. We write the aggregate production function as shown in Equation 30.1.

$$y = f(K, L) \qquad (30.1)$$

where $f(K, L)$ is the function that transforms inputs into output. Dividing real GDP by the population (N) yields real GDP per capita, as shown in Equation 30.2.

$$real\ GDP\ per\ capita = \frac{y}{N} = \frac{f(K,L)}{N} \qquad (30.2)$$

Because we define growth as the percentage change in real GDP per capita, Equation 30.2 forms the basis of most economic growth models. The dependence of real GDP per capita on physical capital, labor, technology, and population allow us to summarize the findings of most growth models with four simple but crucial observations:

- All else equal, increasing the labor force (L grows while N does not) promotes economic growth.
- All else equal, an increase in the population (N grows while L does not) hinders growth.
- All else equal, increasing the stock of physical capital (K) promotes growth.
- All else equal, technological improvements promote growth.

We next explore each of these observations in detail.

The Role of Population and the Labor Force in Economic Growth

It is a matter of arithmetic that real GDP per capita falls if population (N) rises faster than real GDP (y) in Equation 30.2. In this equation, the number of workers (L) appears in the numerator, but population (N) appears in the denominator. A steadily growing population eventually contributes to growth—today's children are tomorrow's workers. Yet high birth rates might mean that the nonproductive population—effectively, the number of mouths to feed—is growing more rapidly than the labor force that feeds them.

Mexico, for example, has a far younger population than the United States does. In 2004, Mexico had 21.5 births for every 1,000 people, and almost one-third of the population was under the age of 15. The United States had 14 births per 1,000 people, and barely over one-fifth of the population was younger than 15. The large number of children hinders economic growth in Mexico because young children are not as productive as adults.

---

[3] Economists use the lower case y to refer to *real* GDP. An upper case Y would denote nominal GDP.

Slow economic growth and poverty can be a cause as well as a result of rapid population growth. In a poor country with few government transfer payments, children can provide an extra source of income. When the children grow up, they can support their elderly parents. This logic can be an important consideration in an economy whose households are too poor to save and whose government does not have the resources to aid the elderly. As incomes rise, the need for children to work falls. Parents can save for their own old age and do not need to rely heavily on their children. A self-reinforcing cycle thus occurs, as growth moderates population growth, which in turn spurs further growth. In addition, the provision and use of birth control can be difficult in a poor country with low levels of education.

Limits to the Impact of Labor Force Growth

Equation 30.2 suggests that an economy grows as its labor force grows. Experience and economic theory show, though, that an economy cannot continue to grow at a given rate merely by adding workers. For one thing, additional workers contribute to real GDP only if there is work for them to perform. In fact, developing nations supply "guest workers," temporary workers who receive long-term temporary visas to fill jobs that domestic employers find hard to staff. They supply these workers to advanced countries, such as Germany, or to oil-rich countries, such as Kuwait. The large number of legal and illegal immigrants from Mexico to the United States and recent negotiations between the two countries over creating their own guest worker program suggests that Mexico probably cannot depend on using additional workers to fuel economic growth. In fact, it suggests that the workers are more valuable in the United States, where there there are better job opportunities than in Mexico.

Additional workers add relatively little to real GDP in Mexico because of diminishing marginal returns to labor. To illustrate this concept, imagine the impact of studying economics this evening. The first hour you spend studying economics will probably have a large impact on your grade. The fifth hour you spend studying will have a much smaller impact. On the macroeconomic level, adding labor to the existing fixed capital and technology in the economy brings large returns at low levels of employment, but the returns decline as employment rises. Figure 30.4 shows the impact of diminishing marginal returns on an aggregate production function.

At first, adding workers to a fixed amount of capital and fixed technology causes real GDP to rise very quickly, so the curve in Figure 30.4 has a steep slope. In this example, going from 100 million workers to 150 million workers causes real GDP to rise by $2 trillion. As diminishing marginal returns set in, real GDP rises more slowly, and the curve flattens out. Thus, adding another 50 million workers to go from 150 million workers to 200 million workers causes real GDP to rise by only $0.5 trillion. Eventually, additional workers might have nothing to do, and they would add nothing to real GDP. At this point, the aggregate production function becomes a horizontal line. Adding workers without adding capital or advancing technology can therefore increase real GDP, but only to a certain point. After that, additional growth must come from another source.

The Role of Physical Capital in Economic Growth

An alternative to adding workers is to make existing workers more productive. If each worker can produce more goods and services, then there is more for each person to consume. One way to increase productivity is to increase the stock of physical capital, K. When labor has more physical capital at its disposal, productivity

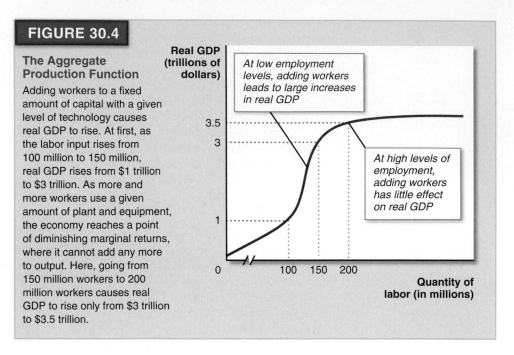

FIGURE 30.4

The Aggregate Production Function

Adding workers to a fixed amount of capital with a given level of technology causes real GDP to rise. At first, as the labor input rises from 100 million to 150 million, real GDP rises from $1 trillion to $3 trillion. As more and more workers use a given amount of plant and equipment, the economy reaches a point of diminishing marginal returns, where it cannot add any more to output. Here, going from 150 million workers to 200 million workers causes real GDP to rise only from $3 trillion to $3.5 trillion.

At low employment levels, adding workers leads to large increases in real GDP

At high levels of employment, adding workers has little effect on real GDP

grows, and real GDP per capita grows. Studies of the U.S. economy have shown that, all else equal, a 1 percent increase in the amount of physical capital available per hour of labor causes output per worker to rise by one-third of a percent, a relationship known as the **one-third rule**.

Physical Capital and the Loanable Funds Market. Though simple in principle, investing in physical capital may be difficult in practice. In particular, how do producers obtain physical capital? In earlier chapters, we have seen that firms get the funds they need for investment on the loanable funds market. The demand and supply of loanable funds determine the quantity of funds available for private investment. As an economy saves more, the supply of loanable funds increases. This, in turn, encourages borrowing and investment by firms. In addition, we have seen that government budget deficits decrease the supply of loanable funds available for private borrowing, reducing the level of borrowing by firms. The low saving and high government budget deficits in Mexico and the United States reduce the funds available in Mexico and the United States, as shown in panels (a) and (b) of Figure 30.5.

Because of their relatively low incomes, saving is beyond the means of most Mexican households, so the supply curve S_{Mexico} in panel (a) of Figure 30.5 is to the left of the supply curve for a country with higher income, such as the United States, S_{US}. This difference causes the quantity of funds borrowed and invested by firms in a poor country such as Mexico to be lower than for a richer country such as the United States. The equilibrium quantities shown in Figure 30.5 show the total amount saved by each country in 2003 (the most recent year for which data are available). Mexico saved about $114 billion, and the United States saved $1,890 billion. Even accounting for the larger U.S. population, the United States was able to generate about 5.5 times as much saving per person as Mexico.

Although U.S. incomes are very high, the U.S. supply of funds is still relatively low. U.S. households currently save only about one percent of their disposable income, and the federal government has a large budget deficit. Panel (b) of Figure 30.5 shows that the deficit shifts the supply of funds available to private borrowers leftward from S_1 to S_2. As a result, private firms have fewer funds available for investment.

FIGURE 30.5

Loanable Funds for Private Investment

Firms in Mexico and the United States have trouble raising the funds for investment for very different reasons. Panel (a) shows that Mexico is a poor country with little ability to save. Mexico's inability to generate savings limits its supply of loanable funds, S_{Mexico}, and the equilibrium quantity of loanable funds, which is $114 billion. Panel (b) shows the consequences of a large federal budget deficit. Federal budget deficits reduce the supply of loanable funds in the United States, shifting the supply of loanable funds leftward from S_1 to S_2. The total amount available for private borrowing falls from $1.5 trillion to $1.2 trillion. Low savings due to poverty or large federal budget deficits cause interest rates to rise and private borrowing to fall.

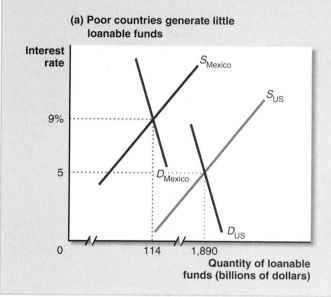

(a) Poor countries generate little loanable funds

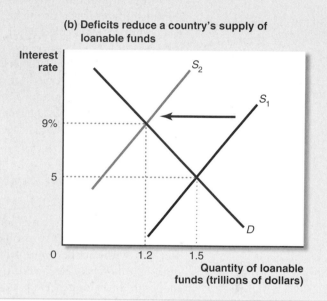

(b) Deficits reduce a country's supply of loanable funds

The Financing Gap. Neither Mexico nor the United States generates enough funds internally for firms to borrow and invest, so both countries rely on foreign sources. As of 2003, the World Bank, a prominent international lending agency whose role we shall examine shortly, reported that Mexico experienced a shortfall of roughly $10 billion in domestic savings. The United States had a shortfall of almost $500 billion. Despite great need for funds in the United States, foreign investors see it as a relatively safe investment. Consequently, U.S. firms and the U.S. government have had little trouble raising the funds they seek. Like many poor countries, Mexico is regarded as a less safe investment and has had difficulty in raising funds. Mexico faces a chronic **financing gap**, a shortage of funds that it needs to make investments so it can grow and develop. The governments of wealthy countries sometimes provide poor ones with loans or outright aid. According to World Bank figures for 2003, Mexico received about $100 million in aid.[4]

The ongoing financing gap is a major reason for the existence of the **World Bank**, an international agency whose mission is "to fight poverty and improve the living standards of people in the developing world."[5] It does so by providing impoverished countries with loans and other forms of assistance. According to a World Bank

Financing gap
A shortage of funds that a country needs to make the investments it needs to grow and develop.

World Bank
An international agency that provides loans and grants to developing nations to improve the well being of people in the developing world.

---

[4] The World Bank Group, *Mexico Data Profile*, devdata.worldbank.org/external/CPProfile.asp?SelectedCountry=MEX&CCODE=MEX&CNAME=Mexico&PTYPE=CP.
[5] Quoted from the World Bank Web site, www.worldbank.org

annual report, it approved more than $18.5 billion in loans and grants for projects around the world in the fiscal year that ended June 30, 2003. Although few criticize the World Bank's goals, its policies have had mixed results. Today, roughly three-fourths of its loans to African nations are in default. The World Bank thus finds itself in a difficult position. Refusing to make further loans to countries that have not made good use of their borrowed funds generates resentment among developing countries and stirs protests worldwide. Yet continuing to lend money to countries that run a high risk of default could damage the World Bank's ability to make future loans.

As is the case with labor, capital is subject to diminishing marginal returns. Given the small amount of physical capital in many less-developed countries, why are diminishing returns a problem? Diminishing marginal returns can rapidly take hold if a country lacks skilled labor and other inputs that it must combine with the capital stock.

In addition, the lock-step relationship between investment and economic growth in the one-third rule does not necessarily apply in all cases. For example, between 1960 and 1985, the amount of capital per worker more than doubled in Nigeria. The one-third rule predicts that output per worker would have then increased by over 33 percent. In fact, it rose by only 12 percent. Clearly, other forces must also be at work.

The Role of Human Capital and Technology in Economic Growth

Having more machines will accomplish little if a nation does not have a workforce that is capable of operating them. An educated worker might be able to repair damaged equipment or solve problems that arise in the production process. However, workers without the appropriate training or skills are able to cope with only the most routine tasks. As a result, physical capital is much more likely to sit idle or be inoperable for long periods in countries with unskilled labor. More machines will also fail to promote economic growth if they are obsolete or incapable of producing output that meets today's standards. The technological level of a nation's physical capital and the ability of workers to use it limit the impact of increases in labor or capital alone on economic growth. We now take a close look at the role of human capital and technology in economic growth models.

The Role of Human Capital. In addition to having less physical capital at their disposal than U.S. workers have, Mexican workers also have less human capital. Recall

DILBERT: © Scott Adams/Dist. by United Features Syndicate, Inc.

that human capital refers to the skills or knowledge acquired through education and training that increases individuals' output. Workers acquire human capital through formal training programs and informal on-the-job training. The most important source of human capital is schooling. Education levels in Mexico have improved significantly over the last decade. However, half the labor force still has no more than a primary school education, and less than one-third have a high school diploma. In contrast, over three-fourths of the U.S. labor force have a high school diploma.

The gap in schooling would cause Mexico to lag behind the United States even if the two countries had the same amount of physical capital, because human capital and physical capital are often complementary. In other words, skilled workers and physical capital make each other more productive. In contrast, many machines are used to perform the tasks once performed by unskilled workers. Thus, physical capital is often viewed as a substitute for unskilled labor. For example, robots replace assembly-line workers but require computer programmers and engineers to operate them and technicians to maintain them.

The Role of Technology. An economy's technology refers to the quality of its inputs and its ability to combine those inputs to form output. A number of economists, most notably Nobel laureate Robert Solow, have traced economic growth to advances in technology. This research focuses on improvements in technology, such as more highly skilled workers, more effective machines, or better managerial techniques. These advances allow a country to produce more with a fixed amount of labor and capital.

Remarkably, large differences between advanced and developing countries have arisen only in the last 200 years. For the United States and much of Europe, the last two centuries have been marked by unprecedented growth. High school history classes teach that the key to Western prosperity was the Industrial Revolution of the early nineteenth century. Technological advances, though, occurred at many different times and in many different places without spurring economic growth. China developed paper, the printing press, the spinning wheel, and gunpowder long before Europe did. Only now, though, is China approaching Western standards of living. A working steam engine existed in ancient Rome, yet Rome remained an agrarian society with no industry. Clearly, some other factors allowed England and the United States to turn a technological revolution into an economic revolution.

As we have seen, countries can increase the quality of their workforces by investing in the skills of their workers. They can also add to the quality of their physical capital and to the way in which they combine labor and capital by engaging in research and development (R&D), the discovery and implementation of new products and ways to produce them. Some economists point to the greater expenditure on R&D by firms in the United States and other advanced nations as a reason for why their real GDP per capita has grown more rapidly than that of developing countries such as Mexico.

Limits to the Impact of Human Capital and Technology. Although increases in human capital can increase productivity and promote economic growth, a poor nation's investment in education can backfire if workers leave the country after receiving it. As workers acquire additional skills, they may become more valuable to advanced countries than to their home country.

The "brain drain" has resulted in a migration of talent from developing countries to industrialized countries. Some of these take the form of the guest workers discussed earlier, such as skilled blue-collar workers from Pakistan who work in the oil fields of Kuwait. Other migration is more permanent. Many graduates of the India Institute of

The Brain Drain and Investment in Education
The India Institute of Technology is one of the world's finest technical universities, but many of its graduates have taken jobs in California's Silicon Valley.

Technology, one of the premiere engineering universities in the world, now hold prominent positions in U.S.-based Fortune 500 firms. Mexico will not benefit from promoting education if the beneficiaries of the education end up working in Los Angeles.

Although differences in R&D used to explain why some countries grew faster than others, they do not explain as much as they once did. From the dawn of the Industrial Revolution until well into the twentieth century, countries treated human capital and technology as a treasure that they should conceal from others. Nations and individual firms went to great lengths to establish and maintain their technological advantages. Today, that is no longer the case. While a handful of countries engage in most of the world's research and development, others are able to keep up, due to the rapid diffusion of technology. The time span between the introduction of a new product and the appearance of competing products has fallen from more than thirty years to about three years.[6]

Get Ahead of the Curve
Apply the model of economic growth to assess proposed changes in World Bank programs.

▶ The Role of Markets and Incentives in Economic Growth

Limiting population growth, investing in capital stock, and promoting access to technology and education all play important roles in promoting economic growth. As you have seen in this chapter, though, Mexico and other struggling countries

---

[6] William J. Baumol, *The Free-Market Innovation Machine*, Princeton University Press (Princeton), 2002, page 74.

TEST + *EXTEND* Your Knowledge

1. TEST The population of Guatemala grows at an annual rate of about 2.6 percent. Go to the World Bank Web site using the links at www.aw-bc.com/leeds/ch30 to find the real GDP of Guatemala. If the population of Guatemala continues to grow at its current rate, what real GDP must it achieve next year if it is to maintain living standards? What will it have to be in five years?

2. EXTEND The United Nations Human Development Index is closely related to real GDP per capita, but it is not the same. Why do the two measures differ?

have had trouble meeting the conditions for growth. If anything, Mexico is losing workers—particularly highly skilled workers—rather than increasing its labor force. It also faces great difficulty in raising the funds needed to invest in physical capital or in human capital. Finally, even if Mexico were able to increase all of these factors, there is no guarantee that its economy would grow as a result. As we have shown, many economies have failed to grow despite meeting the necessary conditions. In this section, we explore what many economists now recognize as the missing link in economic growth: incentives provided by the market mechanism.

Economies Respond to Incentives

As emphasized in Chapter 1, one of the primary lessons of economics is that consumers and producers respond to incentives to make themselves as well off as possible. Incentives, though, apply to more than individual markets. Evidence suggests that a nation's well-being may result from a system that encourages people to save, consume, produce, and invest wisely.

Earlier in this chapter, you learned that ancient Rome and China made startling technological breakthroughs but failed to capitalize on them. The prevailing ethic in these countries discouraged productive commercial activity. As a result, neither economy translated inventions and skills into economic growth.

More recently, Mexico's experiences in the twentieth century show how a government can provide the wrong incentives as well as the consequences of those incentives. For much of the twentieth century, the Mexican economy was highly regulated. The lack of economic freedom coincided with a lack of political freedom, as one political party, the Institutional Revolutionary Party (PRI) ruled Mexico from 1929 to 2000. Initially devoted to socioeconomic reform, the PRI eventually became identified with entrenched economic interests. The Mexican government kept out foreign-made goods, thereby protecting Mexican firms from international competition. The government also discouraged domestic competition by creating many large, state-run or state-affiliated firms. As a result, Mexican firms had little incentive to innovate until the reforms of the 1980s and 1990s. These reforms opened the economy to trade by limiting the ability of the government to keep out foreign-made goods and services. Reforms also curtailed the government's role in key sectors of the economy and liberalized the financial sector, so that the market, rather than the government, directed funds to their most efficient use.

A number of people have tried to quantify the degree to which governments interfere with the free operation of markets. Although these measures differ in their specifics, they all share some basic features. Among the most important features of a free economy are:

- Prices fluctuate freely.
- The government does not restrict imports.
- Inefficient producers are allowed to go out of business.
- Banks are privately owned.

As a result, while the indices occasionally disagree on a specific country's ranking, they are very similar. Despite efforts to lessen government intrusion in the Mexican economy over the last 10 to 15 years, an index compiled by James Gwartney and Robert Lawson for the Fraser Institute still ranks Mexico 59th out of 127 countries in the freedom of its markets. By contrast, the United States ranks third in economic freedom. These data suggest that Mexican firms still feel far less pressure to use resources productively than do their American counterparts. The economic freedom rankings correspond very closely to the UNHDI rankings of 53 for Mexico and 8 for the United States. Table 30.2 compares the economic freedom rankings for the five countries with the highest and the lowest GDP per capita. Except for Norway, which ranked 24th in economic freedom, each of the five richest economies in Table 30.2 had economies that were among the thirteen freest in the world. All of the poorest economies had economies whose economic freedom was ranked lower than 100.

LifeLesson

Maximizing Profit Can Serve the Public Well Being

We often think of profit maximizers as greedy individuals who will happily shortchange the public. According to this view, only vigilant government oversight protects households from greedy, unscrupulous producers. In fact, although government measures do serve an important role in protecting consumers, the presence of a free market is also important. History has shown that profit-maximizing producers generally provide better, safer products than producers in centrally planned economies. The lack of an incentive to please consumers led firms in communist countries to produce shoddy, unsafe output. One classic example came from the auto industries of the two Germanys. While West Germany produced a wide range of desirable cars, including models from the Volkswagen to the Mercedes, East Germany produced the Trabant.

The Trabant, a subcompact car that was sold throughout the Eastern bloc, was both unsafe and unreliable. Drivers were not the only victims of the Trabant. Its two-stroke engine was *100 times* more polluting than an equivalent American car. No wonder economists believe that the lack of a profit motive leads producers to provide goods that consumers do not want and to produce them inefficiently. Some economists have gone so far as to say that firms in such an environment created "negative value added," in which firms' final output is worth less than the inputs they use to make it. Profit maximizers may be greedy, but in the right setting, one can serve the public interest by pursuing profit.

TABLE 30.2

The Economic Freedom and GDP per Capita

(a) Nominal GDP per capita and economic freedom for the five richest countries in 2004

Country	GDP per Capita	Economic Freedom Rank
1. Luxembourg	$69,929	9
2. Norway	54,521	24
3. Switzerland	49,305	3
4. Denmark	44,929	13
5. Ireland	44,888	8

(b) Nominal GDP per capita and economic freedom for the five poorest countries in 2004

Country	GDP per Capita	Economic Freedom Rank
1. Burundi	$91	122
2. Democratic Republic of Congo	112	124
3. Ethiopia	116	Unranked
4. Eritrea	138	Unranked
5. Malawi	151	103

Source: World Economic Outlook Database, International Monetary Fund, www.imf.org/external/pubs/ft/weo/2005/01/data/index.htm; and James Gwartney and Robert Lawson, Economic Freedom of the World: 2005 Annual Report; The Fraser Institute (Vancouver), www.freetheworld.com

Property Rights and Security

Economic freedom is a precondition for economic growth, yet a government cannot simply declare an economy to be free. Specific social conditions must already exist to make free markets possible.

Property rights
The rights of people to ownership and control over what they produce and purchase.

Two conditions in particular are necessary for markets to function properly. First, individuals must have **property rights**, which give people ownership and control over what they produce and purchase. If people do not gain from developing a better product or a better way to produce a given product, then they have little reason to innovate. Second, households must be assured of personal and political security. Even if people have property rights, they have little incentive to be productive if these rights are not adequately protected. Accumulating wealth can make an individual a target for violence if the government is unable or unwilling to provide the safety and stability needed to secure property rights. Lawlessness discourages productive activity and economic growth.

Strategy and Policy
China's Population Experiment

China has sought to promote both development and economic growth by adopting a rigid one-child policy in which parents who have more than one child face stiff penalties. The program has succeeded in sharply curtailing population growth. As of 2003 (the most recent year for which data are available), birth rates were less

控制人口数量　提高人口素质

Control the growth of the Population　Improve the qualities of the Population

than 1.8 per mother, well below the 2.1 births needed to maintain zero population growth. Estimates suggest that China would have about 300 million more people if it had not implemented this policy.

The policy, however, has had unexpected side effects. The cultural preference for sons has led families to take actions, ranging from selective abortion to abandonment to infanticide, to ensure that their one child is a boy. These actions have distorted the ratio of boys to girls in China. Because boys are less likely to survive to adulthood, most societies need about 104 boys for every 100 girls to ensure a rough equality at adulthood. Thanks to the one-child policy, the ratio in China is 118 boys per 100 girls. The lack of marriageable women will place great strains on a society still struggling with the transition from a centrally planned economy to a market economy.

In addition, the one-child policy may have succeeded too well. China is now the most rapidly aging nation in the world. Thirty-five years ago, there were eight times as many people in China between the ages of 15 and 59 as there were over 60. Today, there are only six times as many. Estimates predict that, in another 35 years, there will be *half* as many people between 15 and 59 as over 60.[7] The problems of a decline in the working age population are already beginning to show. China is beginning to experience labor shortages in key areas—a potentially serious problem for a nation that has based much of its recent economic growth on the availability of cheap labor. More serious problems will arise when the older workers begin to retire and to rely on the taxes paid by younger workers for support. Observers refer to China's dilemma as the "4-2-1" problem, in which one child must support two parents and four grandparents. The United States faces a similar problem over how to finance Social Security when the baby boom generation retires. However, China faces a much larger demographic challenge with far fewer resources. Its fiscal difficulties will dwarf those of the United States in the years ahead.

---

[7] Richard Jackson and Neil Howe, "The Graying of the Middle Kingdom: The Demographics Economics of Retirement Policy in China," Center for Strategic International Studies, April 2004.

Critical-Thinking Questions

1. Use Equation 30.2 to show why Chinese authorities instituted the one-child policy.
2. What was the unintended, undesirable consequence of the policy for the Chinese economy.

 SUMMARY

- **The elements of economic growth.** Economic growth increases the economic well being of a nation. We measure it by percentage changes in real GDP per capita. Per capita GDP accounts for the fact that more populous countries can have higher GDP without being better off. This measure of growth shares the advantages and disadvantages of our GDP measure. Development is a complex term that refers to a variety of economic, social, and legal factors.

- **Economic models of growth.** Some economists believe that increasing the workforce and controlling population growth are essential for promoting economic growth. Others believe that countries grow when they invest in their capital stock. Poor countries have difficulty generating enough savings to fuel the necessary investment in capital, leading to a financing gap. Industrialized countries and international organizations such as the World Bank provide loans and aid to promote investment. Economic growth may also result from technological advances and education.

- **The role of markets and incentives in economic growth.** While other factors play an important role, sustained economic growth on a level equal to that of the last few centuries requires a functioning market mechanism.

KEY TERMS

Aggregate production function 768	Economic growth 762	Property rights 777
	Financing gap 771	Rule of 72 765
Development 765	One-third rule 770	World Bank 771

PROBLEMS

1. The following table shows estimated real GDP and population for three countries in 2002. Rank the countries from richest to poorest. Justify your answer.

Country	Real GDP	Population
Brazil	$1,340,000,000,000	176,029,560
Estonia	14,300,000,000	1,415,681
Nigeria	105,900,000,000	129,934,911

2. Suppose that a nation's economy grows by 100 percent over the course of a decade. Illustrate this growth using PPFs.
3. Why is economic growth more important to a poor country like Bangladesh than it is to a rich one like Switzerland?
4. Why do we use the growth rate of real GDP per capita to measure the growth of an economy?
5. Why is economic development harder to define than economic growth?
6. Some economists claim that reducing birth rates in developing countries will raise their standard of living. Use Equation 30.2 to justify this reasoning.
7. A United Nations study of development in the Arab world claimed that allowing women to work would spur economic growth. Use Equation 30.2 to explain the study's reasoning.

8. An ecological organization warns that if current trends continue, the earth will soon run out of petroleum, resulting in worldwide chaos. Evaluate the organization's claim.

9. Why do poor countries have such trouble generating enough savings to increase their stock of physical capital?

10. How do government budget deficits affect the amount of funds available for firms to invest?

11. The United States saves far less than many other industrial nations. Why doesn't it face the same financing gap problem as Mexico?

12. Why do people from developing countries protest World Bank policies? Why doesn't the World Bank give in to the protestors' demands?

13. What limits the impact of increasing a nation's stock of physical capital on its growth rate?

14. If output is determined by the equation $y = f(K, L)$, how can education lead to greater output?

15. What problems could arise if Mexico tries to spur development by founding a world-class engineering school?

16. Canada, Hong Kong, and Norway all spend far less on research and development than the United States does, so why do they have comparable standards of living?

17. Why won't additional labor, capital, or technology lead to strong economic growth in the Democratic Republic of the Congo?

18. Suppose an idealistic sociologist suggests that society would be better off if all workers, from the janitor to the CEO, were paid the same salary. What would the implications of such a policy be for economic growth?

19. Why are property rights a precondition for economic freedom?

20. What unintended consequences can result from reducing birth rates?

myeconlab STUDY GUIDE

HERE'S HOW MyEconLab CAN HELP YOU GET A BETTER GRADE

1. Log into MyEconLab and take Practice Test 30-A (to log in for the first time, see page 30 for instructions).

2. Based on your test results, MyEconLab will identify the areas where you need further work and create a personal Study Plan for you.

3. Your Study Plan contains the problems listed below and others like them that will target the specific chapter topics you need to focus on. You'll receive instant feedback and find links to tutorials, animations, and the online textbook to help you study.

4. When you're ready, take Practice Test 30-B and demonstrate how your results have improved.

Section 30.1, Problem 1 Use the rule of 72 to answer the following questions.

a. If a county's real GDP per capita doubles in 18 years, what was its annual growth rate?

b. If a country achieves a sustained annual growth rate of 3 percent in real GDP per capita, how long will it take for real GDP per capita to double?

c. If a country achieves a sustained annual growth rate of 3.6 percent in real GDP per capita, how many times will it double in 100 years?

Section 30.1, Problem 2 Why do policy makers use real GDP per capita as a means of calculating a nation's development and welfare, despite the numerous drawbacks of this approach? Is it because

a. Explicitly defining economic development and welfare is difficult.
b. Real GDP and real GDP per capita are relatively easy to measure.
c. Real GDP and real GDP per capita are closely linked to measures of welfare, such as life expectancy.
d. All of the above are reasons why we use real GDP to approximate development and welfare.

Section 30.1. Problem 3 The population and real GDP for the Kingdom of Ecoland is shown in the following table. Use this information to answer the following questions.

Year	Population	Real GDP
1985	750,000	$4,500,000,000
1986	765,000	4,635,000,000
1987	780,300	4,820,400,000
1988	811,500	4,916,800,000
1989	827,700	5,064,300,000

a. Calculate real GDP per capita for each year.
b. Calculate the growth rate for each year of real GDP per capita.
c. Was there ever a year when Ecoland did not experience economic growth?

Section 30.2, Problem 1

a. In general, an increase in the stock of capital, all else equal, leads to a(n) _____ (*increase/decrease*) in real GDP per capita.
b. In general, an increase in the size of the labor force, all else equal, leads to a(n) _____ (*increase/decrease*) in real GDP per capita.
c. In general, an increase in population, all else equal, leads to a(n) _____ (*increase/decrease*) in real GDP per capita.
d. In general, a technological advance, all else equal, leads to a(n) _____ (*increase/decrease*) in real GDP per capita.

Section 30.2, Problem 2 Which one of the following statements is false?

a. Increases in the size of the labor force cause real GDP to rise, but eventually diminishing marginal returns set in.
b. Increases in the size of the capital stock cause real GDP to rise, but eventually diminishing marginal returns set in.
c. Studies of the U.S. economy have shown that, all else equal, a one-percent increase in the amount of physical capital available per hour of labor causes output per worker to rise by three percent.
d. Historically, advances in technology have not always led to significant economic growth.
e. Government budget deficits (or borrowing) discourages a country's level of investment and its growth of capital, and therefore hinders economic growth.

Section 30.3, Problem 1 Which one of the following is *not* a feature of a free economy?

a. Limits to population growth
b. Privatization of banks
c. Free fluctuation of prices
d. Free trade
e. Natural elimination of inefficient producers

Section 30.3, Problem 2 Property rights refer to which one of the following:

a. The ownership of land
b. The people's ownership and control over what they choose to produce and consume
c. The government's ownership and control over what people choose to produce and consume
d. The government's right to seize property when necessary
e. Public ownership of goods, where the good is owned by everyone and by no single person

31

International Trade

In November 1999, a group of antiglobalization activists gathered in Seattle with the aim of disrupting a meeting of the *World Trade Organization* (WTO). As its name indicates, the WTO is an international organization that promotes trade among member countries. It has become a lightning rod for groups that oppose the effects of globalization on trade, labor, immigration, the environment, and other issues. The participants in these spirited and sometimes violent protests wanted to spark a revolution against entrenched global economic interests. In the words of one activist, "Trade unionists, environmentalists, human rights activists, church groups, AIDS activists, family farmers, and grassroots organizers from around the world are all united against the WTO, because it supports the interests of large corporations over the interests of people and nature."[1] Protests against the WTO and world trade in general have continued. A protest in Miami in 2003 involved about 10,000 demonstrators opposed to the WTO and a proposed Free Trade Area of the Americas (FTAA) that would promote trade among nations in North America and South America. The FTAA, which is still being negotiated, would eliminate government policies designed to limit trade between nations in North America and South America.

Many of the groups protesting the WTO have little else in common. For example, the Amalgamated Clothing and Textile Workers Union (ACTWU) maintains that free trade sends U.S. jobs to developing nations. Marching alongside it might be members of the Mexico Solidarity

---

[1] Kevin Danaher and Roger Burbach, eds., *Globalize This: The Battle Against the World Trade Organization and Corporate Rule*, Monroe, ME, Common Courage Press, 2000.

Network, who claim that free trade exploits workers in developing nations. Yet another group, the Rainforest Action Network, believes that free trade degrades the environment, in part through its effects on the production of textiles.

Economists also have strong opinions about international trade. Most of them agree with Adam Smith's words from more than 200 years ago: "All commerce that is carried on betwixt any two countries must necessarily be advantageous to both … and free commerce and liberty of exchange should be allowed with all nations."[2] The protesters generally maintain that current rules promoting global trade benefit special interests. Economists, however, usually regard efforts to restrict trade as favoring special interests at the expense of the economy as a whole. Clearly, both sides cannot be right. In this chapter, we develop models of trade to explain why economists advocate free trade and why many non-economists object to it.

ALONG THE WAY, YOU WILL ALSO LEARN:

- The size of the U.S. trade deficit.
- Two ways that economists model the impact of free trade.
- The implications of protecting domestic industries with tariffs and quotas.
- The arguments that domestic producers use when they call for government protection.
- The claims that free trade harms developing countries and the environment.
- The role of international organizations in promoting free trade.

AT THE END OF THE CHAPTER, THE MYECONLAB LOGO WILL DIRECT YOU ONLINE

- MyEconLab is a resource-packed online homework and tutorial system that can help you perform better in your economics course. To log in for the first time, see page 30 for instructions.
- MyEconLab can help you apply important concepts from the chapter to real-world issues. Watch for the logo to indicate online features about trade in the United States, Canada, and South America.
- At the end of each chapter, you'll find a special study section that will help you get the most out of your textbook and your instructor's MyEconLab course.

The U.S. Trade Deficit

As you learned in Chapter 3, the United States has a large trade deficit, meaning that it imports far more than it exports. In this section, we explore the history of the U.S. trade deficit and several explanations for it. We then take a close look at the current U.S. trade deficit and some of the commonly cited reasons for its recent growth. (We discuss additional reasons for the trade deficit in the following chapter, where you will learn about exchange rates and currency markets.)

---

[2] Adam Smith, *An Inquiry into the Nature and Causes of the Wealth of Nations*, Oxford, Clarendon Press (1976 printing), pages 511 and 514.

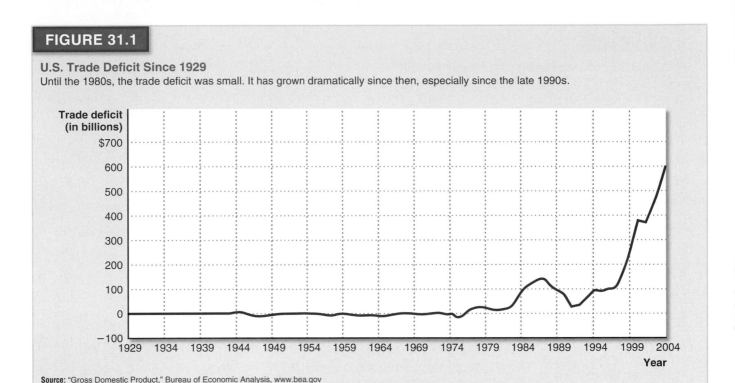

FIGURE 31.1

U.S. Trade Deficit Since 1929
Until the 1980s, the trade deficit was small. It has grown dramatically since then, especially since the late 1990s.

Source: "Gross Domestic Product," Bureau of Economic Analysis, www.bea.gov

A Historical Perspective on the Trade Deficit

In 2004, the U.S. economy imported over $600 billion more in goods and services than it exported. Figure 31.1 shows that, except for the years 1946 to 1950, when much of the industrialized world was recovering from World War II, the United States has consistently imported more than it has exported. However, until the 1980s, the trade deficit was small. The size of the deficit has grown tremendously since the late 1990s.

Trade has also become much more important to the U.S. economy in recent years. The market value of trade (imports plus exports) in the United States was 26 percent of GDP in 2004—about twice what it was in 1984. Trade has become such a prominent part of the U.S. economy that we cannot afford to ignore its impact.

The U.S. Trading Partners

The United States has a trade deficit with the rest of the world as a whole, but this does not mean that it has a deficit with every nation. The United States exports more than it imports for several nations. Panel (a) of Figure 31.2 shows the 10 countries with which the United States had the largest trade surplus; panel (b) shows the 10 countries with which it had the largest trade deficit in 2004. As the large overall deficit suggests, the surpluses in panel (a) are smaller than the deficits in panel (b).

Figure 31.2 also shows that there are no easy explanations for the U.S. trade deficit. Some analysts speculate that it is solely the result of low-wage labor in poor countries. Yet the U.S. trade deficit with Germany, a country with highly paid workers, was almost identical to its deficit with Mexico, a country with much lower-paid workers. Low-cost labor might help explain the huge trade deficit with China. However, it does not explain why the next three highest deficits are with Japan,

FIGURE 31.2

U.S. Trade Surplus and Deficit with Selected Countries

The United States has trade surpluses and deficits with many different countries. The pattern of the deficits and surpluses yields no easy explanation for the large overall trade deficit. The United States has surpluses and deficits alike with poor countries (Egypt and China), rich countries (the Netherlands and Japan), and even with oil-exporting countries (United Arab Emirates and Venezuela).

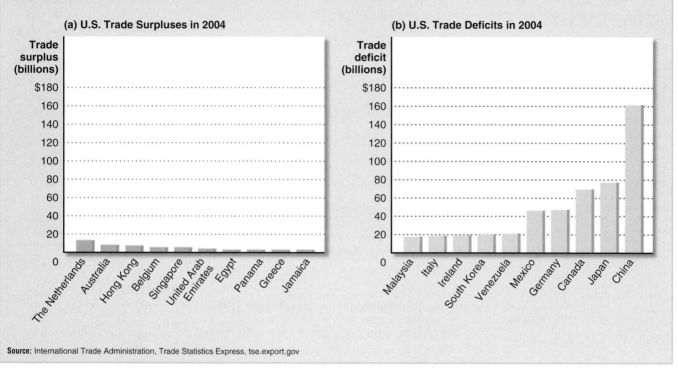

Source: International Trade Administration, Trade Statistics Express, tse.export.gov

Canada, and Germany. Panel (a) of Figure 31.2 shows that the United States had a trade surplus with several low-wage countries, such as Egypt, Panama, and Jamaica.

Oil imports are another commonly cited cause of the U.S. trade deficit. However, of the countries with which the United States has the largest deficits, only Venezuela is a major oil exporter. The United States even has one of its largest surpluses with the United Arab Emirates, another major oil exporter. In fact, more than one-third of the overall U.S. trade deficit results from our deficits with China and Japan. These deficits are not related to oil, because China and Japan are major oil *importers*.

Figure 31.1 indicates that part of the U.S. trade deficit may stem from its own prosperity. The last three declines in the trade deficit (early 1980s, early 1990s, and early 2000s) roughly coincide with economic downturns. During a downturn, incomes decline. Households and firms cut back on their purchases of all items, including imported goods and services. A decline in imports naturally reduces the trade deficit. Over the last decade, the U.S. economy has generally grown more quickly than the economies of most of its major trading partners. This, in turn, contributes to the trade deficit. In sum, the U.S. trade deficit has many possible sources.

TEST + *E X T E N D* Your Knowledge

▶ Economic Models of Free Trade

Free trade
The sale of goods made in one country to consumers in another country without any artificial barriers imposed by governments.

We begin our examination of the debate over free trade by looking at the models economists use to analyze international trade. In this section, we present two common economic justifications for **free trade**, which is the exchange of goods and services between nations with no artificial barriers, such as numerical limits or taxes on imports. The first model builds on the model of comparative advantage that we presented in Chapter 2. The second uses consumer and producer surplus from Chapter 6 to illustrate the impact of trade on society.

Comparative Advantage and the Benefits of Trade

To illustrate the benefits of free trade, consider the production of laptop computers and textiles in the United States and China. Columns 2 and 3 in panels (a) and (b) of Table 31.1 show hypothetical production possibilities for China and the United States if the two nations do not trade.

Notice that China cannot produce as many laptops (250 million laptops) as the United States (500 million laptops) in this example if both countries specialize in laptops and do not produce any textiles. Similarly, when specializing in textiles, the United States can produce only 250 million yards of textiles, far less than China's potential output of 500 million yards of textiles. To see the opportunity cost of a laptop in China, consider columns 2 and 3 of panel (a), which show that the quantity of laptops increases by 50 million when the quantity of textiles falls by 100 million yards. As a result, the opportunity cost of a laptop is 2 yards of textiles (100 million/50 million = 2/1). For now, we asume that this trade-off is constant—it holds when China produces 200 million laptops and when it produces none at all.

In the United States, the opportunity cost of one more laptop is one-half yard of textiles. Moving down columns 2 and 3 of panel (b), we see that the quantity of laptops in the third column increases by 100 million, and the quantity of textiles in the second column falls by 50 million yards (50 million/100 million = $^1/_2$). Again, this trade-off is constant over the entire range of production possibilities.

The Production Possibilities Frontier. Figure 31.3 shows the information from columns 2 and 3 in Table 31.1 for both countries in graph form.

As in Chapter 2, constant opportunity costs mean that the production possibilities frontiers (PPFs)—the blue lines in Figure 31.3—are straight lines. Giving up two yards of textiles for one laptop means that the PPF for China goes down twice as fast as it goes to the right. The United States gives up one-half yard of textiles for each laptop, so its PPF goes down one-half as fast as it goes to the right. The PPF

TABLE 31.1

Production and Consumption Possibilities in China and the United States

(a) China

Combination (1)	Textiles (millions of yards; with and without trade) (2)	Laptops (millions; without trade) (3)	Laptops (millions; with 1-for-1 trade) (4)
A	500	0	0
B	400	50	100
C	300	100	200
D	200	150	300
E	100	200	400
F	0	250	500

(b) United States

Combination (1)	Textiles (millions of yards; without trade) (2)	Laptops (millions; with and without trade) (3)	Textiles (millions of yards; with 1-for-1 trade) (4)
A	250	0	500
B	200	100	400
C	150	200	300
D	100	300	200
E	50	400	100
F	0	500	0

for China is thus much steeper than the U.S. PPF. This steepness reflects the fact that laptops are much cheaper in the United States because they "cost" fewer textiles.

The simple model of comparative advantage in Chapter 2 tells us that the United States and China can both be better off if they both specialize and trade. If the United States produces only laptops, it can export some of them to China in exchange for more textiles than it would have been able to produce at home. Because a laptop costs one-half yard of textiles in the United States, Americans would be better off if China paid more than one-half yard of textiles in exchange for each laptop. The Chinese are happy to pay up to two yards of textiles for a laptop, because that is what they would have to give up without trade. If, for example, the United States and China agree to exchange one laptop for one yard of textiles, they are both better off.

The Consumption Possibilities Frontier. In effect, trade lifts each country off its *production* possibilities frontier and allows it to choose a point on a *consumption* possibilities frontier that is farther out than its PPF. The **consumption possibilities frontier (CPF)** shows what a nation is able to consume when it specializes and trades with another nation.

The fourth column in Table 31.1 shows the consumption possibilities in China and the United States when the countries exchange one laptop for one yard of textiles. Trade allows China to consume more laptops and the United States to consume more textiles than either could without trade. The red lines in Figure 31.3 show the

Consumption possibilities frontier (CPF)
Shows what a nation can consume when it specializes and trades with another nation.

FIGURE 31.3

Trade, Production Possibilities, and Consumption Possibilities

Without trade, China and the United States are restricted to their respective PPFs (the blue lines). The opportunity cost of producing additional laptops—the amount of textiles forgone—is relatively high in China, so the PPF in panel (a) is relatively steep. The opportunity cost in the United States is relatively low, so the PPF in panel (b) is relatively flat. If the two countries trade, they can consume more than they are capable of producing in isolation, so the CPF (the red lines) for each nation lie to the right of the PPFs.

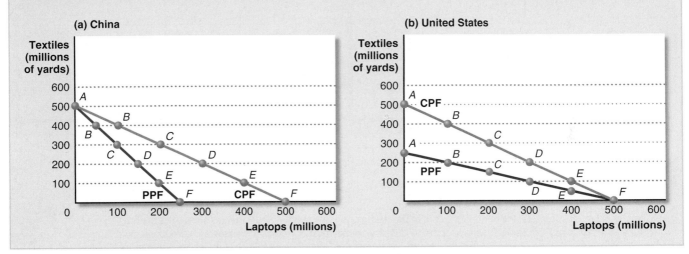

CPF for each country. Because trade allows each country to consume more than it can produce by itself, the CPF swivels out to the right of the PPF.

From what you learned about comparative advantage in Chapter 2, you know that that if laptops cost relatively less in the United States than in China, then the United States has a comparative advantage in producing laptops. It also means that textiles cost relatively more in the United States than in China. That, in turn, means that China has a comparative advantage in producing textiles. The two nations make themselves better off by producing the good at which they have a comparative advantage and importing the good at which they have a comparative disadvantage.

Comparative Advantage and Increasing Opportunity Costs. When we illustrate the impact of trade with straight-line PPFs, we are saying laptops are always relatively cheaper in the United States than in China. It also means that the United States has a comparative advantage in laptops and China has a comparative advantage in textiles, no matter how much each produces. As a result, the United States would specialize completely in producing laptops and import all of its textiles from China. China would specialize completely in textiles and import all of its laptops from the United States. You also learned in Chapter 2, however, that PPFs are not usually straight lines. Opportunity costs generally rise as a firm or country produces more of a good, which means that PPFs are typically concave, or bowed out.

Table 31.2 shows what happens if opportunity costs increase as China or the United States produces more of a good. Looking at combinations A and B of panel (a), we see that sacrificing the first 100 million yards of textiles allows China to produce 120 million laptops. Moving down successive combinations, we see that as China produces more and more laptops, the opportunity cost of producing an additional laptop rises. In combination F of panel (a), sacrificing the final 100 million yards of textiles brings China only 10 million more laptops than in combination E.

TABLE 31.2

Production and Possibilities with Increasing Opportunity Costs

(a) China

Combination (1)	Textiles (millions of yards) (2)	Laptops (millions) (3)
A	500	0
B	400	120
C	300	180
D	200	220
E	100	240
F	0	250

(b) United States

Combination (1)	Textiles (millions of yards) (2)	Laptops (millions) (3)
A	250	0
B	240	100
C	220	200
D	180	300
E	120	400
F	0	500

FIGURE 31.4

Incomplete Specialization with Concave PPFs

As China specializes in textiles, the opportunity cost of producing one more laptop falls. Panel (a) shows the decreasing cost of laptops as a concave PPF. Panel (b) shows that the U.S. opportunity cost of laptops increases as it produces more laptops. When China reaches point B on its PPF and the United States reaches point E on its PPF, it is no longer cheaper for China to produce textiles and the United States to produce additional laptops.

(a) China

(b) United States

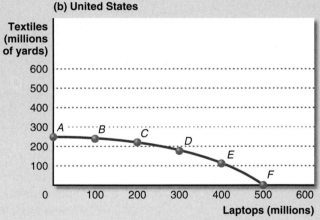

Similarly, moving down panel (b), you can see that the United States has to give up more and more textiles to get an additional 100 million laptops.

Figure 31.4 graphs the information in Table 31.2. The PPFs for both countries start out relatively flat at the upper left and become steeper as we look down and to the right. This reflects the fact that each nation can produce the first laptops relatively cheaply, but laptops become increasingly expensive as they produce more of them.

The PPF in Figure 31.4(a) is generally steeper than the PPF in Figure 31.4(b), because the opportunity cost of laptops is usually higher in China than in the United States. However, it is not always higher. Moving upward in panel (a) from point F to point E, the figure shows China beginning to produce textiles. At first, the curve is very steep, showing the very low opportunity cost of textiles in China. As China shifts to producing textiles, it moves up the PPF. As it moves from point E to point D, the curve becomes flatter, showing that the opportunity cost of textiles is rising. Similarly, as the United States shifts to producing laptops, it moves down the PPF. As it moves from point A to point B to point C of panel (b), the PPF steepens, and the opportunity cost of textiles falls. Finally, at point B in panel (a) and point E of panel (b), the slope of China's PPF becomes flatter than the United States' PPF. At this point, the opportunity cost of textiles is greater in China than in the United States and neither country wants to specialize any further. While both countries are better off importing most of one good, China finds it cheaper to produce the last 120 million laptops than to trade. Likewise, the United States finds it cheaper to produce the last 120 million yards of textiles than to trade. Increasing opportunity costs thus explain why countries do not completely specialize.

Consumer Surplus, Producer Surplus, and the Impact of Trade

We begin the second model of trade with the insight that most opponents of free trade rightly point to the costs it imposes. Even the advocates of free trade concede that free trade hurts some segments of the economy while benefiting the overall economy. The benefits from trade in our prior example are not compelling if you are a U.S. textile producer or a Chinese laptop manufacturer—one reason why U.S. textile workers protest free trade, but employees of Intel, a major exporter of semiconductors, do not.

Trade causes countries to reduce activities at which they are less efficient and expand activities at which they are more efficient. When firms in declining industries downsize or disappear, workers must find new jobs. Points on a PPF fail to show the microeconomic costs of such moves to individual firms and households. How do we measure the impact of trade on consumers and producers? In this section, we use the consumer and producer surplus tools from Chapter 6 to show who gains and who loses from trade.

U.S. Textile Market Without Trade. We begin our analysis by examining the U.S. market for textiles in a world without trade. Domestic producers must satisfy the entire U.S. demand for textiles.

Figure 31.5 shows that if there were no trade, U.S. producers would sell 5 million yards of textiles to domestic consumers at an equilibrium price of $6.00 per yard. We show the gains from exchange—the consumer and producer surplus—to the buyers and sellers of textiles with the blue and red triangles. Recall from Chapter 6 that the area of a triangle is given by the following equation:

$$\text{Area} = \frac{1}{2}\,\text{Base} \times \text{Height}$$

Using this formula, the areas of the blue triangle and the red triangle are each $12.5 million.[3] Adding the two yields total surplus of $25 million.

U.S. Textile Market with Trade. If the United States produces textiles less efficiently than other nations, then other countries would be able to sell textiles at a lower price in U.S. markets. When we open the U.S. economy to trade, the price that U.S. producers charge cannot be higher than the price charged in the rest of the world, which is known as the **world price**. In our example, as shown in Figure 31.6, the world price for textiles is $3.00. In effect, U.S. consumers can buy all the textiles

World price
The price charged for a good in the rest of the world. If a country engages in free trade, this price will prevail in that country as well.

---

[3] The consumer and producer surplus need not be equal. In fact, they rarely are! We choose this example solely for its simplicity.

FIGURE 31.5

The U.S. Textile Market Without Trade

In the absence of trade, U.S. textile makers produce 5 million yards of textiles, which they sell for $6.00 per yard. This level results in consumer surplus given by the blue triangle and producer surplus given by the red triangle. Using the equation for the area of a triangle, we find that consumer surplus and producer surplus are both $12.5 million. Total surplus is therefore $25 million without trade.

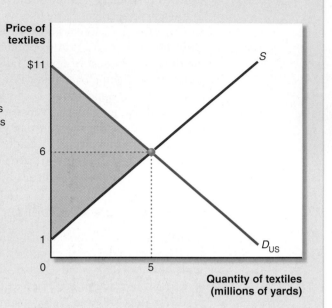

FIGURE 31.6

Consumption and Production with Free Trade

The $3.00 world price of textiles is below the U.S. price of $6.00. As a result, U.S. textile makers cut back production from 5 million to 2 million yards. The lower world price induces consumers to buy 8 million yards of textiles instead of 5 million. The 6-million-yard gap between domestic consumption and domestic production is filled by imports. The rise in consumer surplus is greater than the fall in producer surplus, so overall social well-being rises. Producer surplus (red triangle) falls from $12.5 million to $2 million, while consumer surplus (blue triangle) rises from $12.5 million to $32 million. Total surplus rises from $25 million without trade to $34 million with trade, so trade makes the economy better off.

Get Ahead of the Curve

Use the concepts of comparative advantage and trade liberalization to analyze the recent boom in South American agricultural exports.

they want at the world price of $3.00 per yard. The supply curve remains upward-sloping at prices below $3.00. This part of the supply curve reflects some very efficient U.S. producers who are willing and able to produce textiles at a price at or below the world price. These producers remain in business and enjoy the producer surplus given by the red triangle.

Figure 31.6 shows that with free trade, the supply curve is horizontal once the world price reaches $3.00. Many U.S. textile producers cut back or stop producing

LifeLessons

Comparative Advantage in the Household

One of the first questions that young couples starting a family ask themselves is, "who will take care of the children?" A few decades ago, even asking this question would have seemed absurd. Husbands went to work and wives gave up whatever jobs they had to stay home with the children. Today, an increasing number of families are sharing parental duties more equally or even reversing the traditional family roles. More men than ever are opting to stay home with children. Some see this change in roles as a blow against sexist oppression. Others see it as one more sign of the decay of Western civilization. Many economists see it as nothing more than changes in the pattern of comparative advantage within the family.

For centuries, most households lived at the subsistence level—the slightest drop in their level of consumption could prove fatal. They did whatever they could to maximize their ability to produce and consume. Moreover, most men had a comparative advantage in working outside the home, so they specialized in those activities, while women generally worked in the home. These traditional roles could have resulted from a variety of factors, from innate differences between the sexes to policies and attitudes that limited women's opportunities to acquire skills.

Today, two factors have reduced the impact of comparative advantage on traditional household roles in industrialized societies. First, because most households are much wealthier, they do not need to be so efficient in their production and consumption of goods and services. The added consumption that results from specialization may take a back seat to other considerations, such as personal fulfillment. Second, the direction of comparative advantage may have changed for many couples. As women's and men's educations became more and more alike, so did their earning potential outside the home. The comparative advantage of men working outside the home has narrowed, and, as the growing number of stay-at-home dads indicates, it has disappeared for some.

when the price falls to $3.00. Foreign firms that can produce textiles more cheaply displace these U.S. producers. As a result, the equilibrium quantity of textiles bought and sold rises from 5 million yards to 8 million yards. However, the amount of U.S.-made textiles falls to 2 million yards, and the United States imports 6 million yards. Because U.S. producers now sell less at a lower price, the producer surplus for U.S. textile makers (the red triangle) falls from $12.5 million to $2 million.

Trade harms U.S. textile producers. However, it helps U.S. consumers who want to buy textiles. When the price of textiles falls to the $3.00 world price and the quantity of textiles bought by U.S. consumers rises to 8 million yards, consumer surplus (the blue triangle in Figure 31.6) grows from $12.5 million to $32 million. Total surplus therefore rises from $25 million (as in Figure 31.5) to $34 million. Table 31.3 summarizes consumer, producer, and total surplus with and without free trade.

TABLE 31.3

Summary of the Impact of Trade

Setting	Producer Surplus	Consumer Surplus	Total Surplus
No trade	$12.5 million	$12.5 million	$25 million
Free trade	$2 million	$32 million	$34 million

TEST + *EXTEND* Your Knowledge

1. TEST Explain why the United States imports textiles, despite the fact that importing them costs Americans jobs.

2. EXTEND Use supply and demand curves to show what happens to trade and the gains from trade if the U.S. textile market is as shown in Figure 31.5, but the world price is $8.00 per yard.

▶ Protectionist Trade Policies

Opponents of free trade often turn to the government to help them protect domestic producers from imports. In this section, we examine the two most popular protective measures: tariffs and quotas. We then analyze the effect of each policy on the well-being of the economy using the models of trade that we have developed.

Tariffs

Tariff
A tax on imported goods.

One way to block imports is to raise their price by imposing a **tariff**, or a tax on imported goods. A tariff makes the price of imported goods less attractive to consumers, and thus encourages consumers to buy domestically produced goods instead. Tariffs also raise tax revenue. If the tax revenue is redistributed to consumers, it can, in part, compensate them for the higher prices they pay. Yet the effect of tariffs on the economy is not clear-cut. If foreign producers reduce the prices they charge, they may be able to compete with domestic producers despite the tax. Moreover, a U.S. tariff on textiles can raise a great deal of revenue only if it fails to discourage textile imports. If, however, the tariff succeeds in discouraging textile imports, then it cannot raise much tax revenue. As we focus on tariffs' impact on trade, we shall see that their impact on the federal budget plays an important role in our evaluation of them.

To illustrate, suppose that claims by the ACTWU and the textile industry that imports are harming U.S. firms and costing U.S. workers their jobs lead Congress to place a tariff of $1.00 per yard on foreign-made textiles. Using the numbers from our earlier example, the tariff would cause the U.S. price of textiles to rise to $4.00 per yard. At the higher price of $4.00, U.S. producers are willing and able to sell more textiles. Figure 31.7 shows that the tariff causes U.S. production to increase from 2 million to 3 million yards.

As Figure 31.7 shows, when the price of textiles rises from $3.00 to $4.00, the quantity of textiles demanded by U.S. consumers falls from 8 million yards to 7 million yards. Greater domestic production and lower consumption cause imports to fall from 6 million to 4 million yards.

U.S. textile producers and their employees clearly benefit from this policy, as they are selling more textiles at a higher price. The red producer surplus triangle in Figure 31.7 is larger than it was in Figure 31.6. The area of the triangle representing producer surplus rises from $2 million to $4.5 million. Because consumers buy less and pay more, their consumer surplus falls. The blue triangle is smaller than in Figure 31.6, shrinking from $32 million to $24.5 million. The sum of consumer surplus and producer surplus falls from $34 million to $29 million.

The decline in the sum of consumer surplus and producer surplus from $34 million to $29 million after the tariff understates the impact. Recall that the tariff adds $1.00 in tax payments to the price of textiles and that the extra $1.00 goes to the

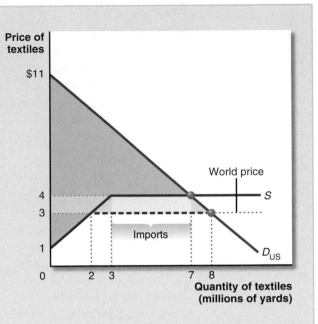

FIGURE 31.7

The Impact of a Tariff on the Market for Textiles

A tariff increases the U.S. textile price from $3.00 to $4.00. Domestic textile producers increase production from 2 million to 3 million yards, domestic consumers buy 7 million rather than 8 million yards, and imports fall from 6 million to 4 million yards. Producer surplus, the red triangle, gets larger, growing from $2 million to $4.5 million. Consumer surplus, the blue triangle, falls from $32 million to $24.5 million. The sum of consumer and producer surplus is now $29 million, but we must also account for the revenue generated by the tariff. The yellow rectangle represents the $4 million U.S. tax revenue.

U.S. government. The yellow rectangle has a width of $1.00 and a length of 4 million, the amount of imported textiles. The area of the yellow rectangle—$1 × 4 million yards = $4 million—is the total tax revenue received by the U.S. government. We assume that the government uses this revenue to benefit U.S. citizens in some way. As a result, the area of the rectangle may be a loss in one sense to U.S. consumers, but it is not a loss to U.S. citizens as a whole. The total surplus is thus the sum of consumer surplus ($24.5 million), producer surplus ($4.5 million), and tax revenue ($4 million). This sum, $33 million, is greater than the total surplus without trade, but less than the total surplus with free trade ($34 million). We can conclude that imposing a tariff harms the economy, but that some trade is better than no trade.

The deadweight loss caused by the tariff is given by the two gray triangles on either side of the yellow rectangle. The triangle on the right exists because U.S. consumers are buying fewer textiles. It is the deadweight loss from inadequate consumption. The triangle on the left exists because U.S. consumers are buying some textiles from U.S. producers, who have displaced foreign producers who would have been able to sell textiles at a lower price. The area of each triangle is $0.5 million, so the total loss is $1 million. Table 31.4 summarizes the gains and losses from the tariff.

Voluntary restraint agreement (VRA)
A negotiated arrangement that a country makes with foreign producers or foreign governments over restrictions on the quantity of goods that those countries will export.

Quotas

Recall from Chapter 6 that a quota is a maximum quantity of a good or service that can be bought and sold over a specific period of time. Countries can set these numerical limits on imports unilaterally. At other times, they negotiate with foreign producers or governments to restrict the quantity of goods that those countries export. We call negotiated restrictions **voluntary restraint agreements (VRAs)**. U.S. VRAs restrict U.S. imports of foreign products ranging from Japanese autos to Chinese textiles.

TABLE 31.4

Summary of the Impact of Tariffs and Quotas

Setting	Consumer Surplus	Producer Surplus	Tax Revenue	Total Surplus	Deadweight loss
No trade	$12.5 million	$12.5 million	$0	$25 million	$0
Free trade	$32 million	$2 million	$0	$34 million	$0
$1-per-yard tariff	$24.5 million	$4.5 million	$4 million	$33 million	$1 million
4-million-yard quota	$24.5 million	$4.5 million	$0	$29 million	$5 million

Like tariffs, quotas limit imports in order to protect domestic production and employment. The protection they provide, however, comes at a cost. Domestic consumers fund the added jobs by paying higher prices for the product. The increases in price can be substantial. One study of legislation that had been proposed to protect the steel industry found that higher prices would have cost the U.S. economy as much as $732,000 over a five-year period for every job saved.[4]

To illustrate the impact of a quota on society, suppose that the U.S. government imposes a quota of 4 million yards of textiles. If the United States allows foreign countries to sell only 4 million yards of textiles, then the difference between what U.S. producers sell and what U.S. consumers buy must be only 4 million yards. In essence, the new supply is shifted to the right by 4 million yards (at the new U.S. price of $4.00), as shown by the red supply curve in Figure 31.8. It shows that such a restriction looks almost exactly like the $1.00 tariff in Figure 31.7.

Producer surplus again rises to $4.5 million, while consumer surplus falls to $24.5 million. Unlike the tariff, however, the quota does not generate $4 million in tax revenue for the U.S. economy. Like the tariff, the quota in Figure 31.8 causes prices to rise by $1.00, from $3.00 to $4.00. However, this revenue goes to foreign producers (and becomes part of their producer surplus, which we do not capture here) rather than to the U.S. government. What had been a transfer (the yellow rectangle in Figure 31.7) is part of deadweight loss in Figure 31.8, so the deadweight loss increases by $4 million. The size of the gray area is now $5 million ($0.5 million + $0.5 million + $4 million = $5 million). Total surplus falls to $29 million. Table 31.4 shows that a quota harms the economy more than a tariff does, but it, too, is a better solution than a world with no trade. To summarize the impact of tariffs and quotas:

- Both tariffs and quotas help domestic producers.
- Both tariffs and quotas harm domestic consumers.

---

[4] Joseph Francois and Laura Baughman, "Cost to American Consuming Industries of Steel Quotas and Taxes," Washington, D.C., The Trade Partnership, 2001.

FIGURE 31.8

The Impact of a Quota on the Market for Textiles

A 4-million-yard textile quota directly limits the quantity of imported textiles to 4 million yards. As with the $1.00 tariff, the price of textiles on U.S. markets rises from $3.00 to $4.00; domestic production rises from 2 million to 3 million yards; domestic consumption falls from 8 million to 7 million yards; and imports fall from 6 million to 4 million yards. Producer surplus, the red triangle, again increases to $4.5 million, and consumer surplus, the blue triangle, again decreases to $24.5 million. The main difference from the tariff is that quotas generate no government revenue. The yellow rectangle in Figure 31.7 disappears, and the entire gray area is now a loss to the U.S. economy. Total surplus is $29 million. This approach leaves the economy worse off than with free trade or with a tariff. Some trade, however, is still better than none.

- The harm done to consumers exceeds the benefits to producers.
- Tariffs result in tax revenue that can help the economy. Quotas do not.

Arguments for Government Protection from Trade

Domestic producers who call for government protection justify their request in a variety of ways. In this section, we examine industries that demand special treatment to combat unfair trade practices, to support national interests, or to provide temporary assistance while the firms start producing or get their house in order.

Dumping

Dumping
Occurs when a firm sells a product in a foreign market at a lower price than in its domestic market.

The World Trade Organization (WTO) says that **dumping** occurs when producers in one country sell a good in another country at a lower price than it charges at home. This seems to provide an easy test for dumping—just compare the prices the firm charges in the two countries. However, the WTO acknowledges that it is rarely, if ever, easy to determine the appropriate price in the firm's home market (the "normal value") and the appropriate price in the foreign country's market (the "export price").

To see the complications that can arise in determining dumping, suppose that domestic shoemakers claim that the Italian shoemaker, Salvatore Ferragamo, is dumping its products on U.S. markets. As evidence, they show that the prices of Ferragamo shoes are lower in the United States than they are in Italy. While this may reflect dumping, it could also reflect differing market conditions in the two countries. Suppose, for example, that a recession in the United States has decreased the demand for luxury footwear. Domestic producers respond to the lower demand by reducing their prices. If Ferragamo also lowers its prices in the U.S. markets, its shoes' export prices might well be below their normal value, leaving it open to accusations of dumping. Adding to the complication is the fact that Salvatore Ferragamo shoes may sell for a variety of prices in Italy. If the shoes are cheaper in Chicago than in Milan but more expensive in New York than in Rome, is Ferragamo guilty of dumping?

Alternatively, some U.S. producers claim that dumping can often go undetected. They assert that the market price of a foreign-made good in the foreign country could understate its normal value if foreign profit margins are much lower than in the United States. The foreign producer may be able to charge a higher price in the United States than in its home country but still undercut domestic producers. In sum, while it seems easy to determine whether a country is dumping, it can often be extremely difficult to prove or disprove in practice.

Trade Restrictions in the National Interest

Some industries ask for protection from free trade because they claim that they produce products that are vital to the national interest. The steel, aircraft, and energy industries have all called for protection on these grounds in recent years.

Such arguments tend to overstate the level of protection that the industry needs. For example, government statistics show that sales to the United States armed forces accounted for only a fraction of one percent of the domestic steel industry's sales. The U.S. steel industry could dramatically reduce its production level without jeopardizing the nation's military preparedness.

Some producers make the related claim that they are a vital part of a nation's identity. Canada's magazine industry fears domination by U.S. periodicals and tries to keep them out of Canadian markets. U.S. agricultural interests promote the historical domestic role of the "family farmer" and try to keep out imported agricultural products, including those from Canada. Both groups have appealed to national identity. Their arguments may have merit, but the benefits are largely non-economic. Such policies have both positive and normative aspects. Economists focus on the positive problem of identifying the costs of the protection. Society decides whether protection is worthwhile by the policies it creates.

Infant Industries

Infant industry
A justification for protective policies based on the assumption that some industries need time to reorganize, grow, or establish themselves.

Infant industries claim that they need governmental protection to provide time to reorganize, grow, or establish themselves. At that point, they will be able to compete with foreign producers without governmental protection. The notion of temporary protection has been a part of U.S. policy since the nation's inception.

Policies based on the infant-industry argument can produce short-term benefits by protecting domestic jobs. However, they can also bring long-term costs. Industries that are sheltered from international competition may never grow up and become efficient. Temporary protection has been granted to the U.S. steel industry in the 1970s, 1980s, and, most recently, in 2002. The temporary protection effectively became permanent, because it masked deeper underlying problems related to changes in the industry.

▶ The Impact of Free Trade on Developing Countries and the Environment

Opponents of free trade in industrialized countries frequently claim that free trade sends domestic jobs to poor countries. Opponents of free trade in poor countries point to the negative aspects of these jobs. Many environmentalists claim that free trade causes countries to ignore environmental damage. In this section, we examine the impact of trade on developing countries and the environment.

Trade and Developing Countries

Multinational corporation
A company whose operations span several countries.

The Mexico Solidarity Network is a militant group in Mexico and the United States dedicated to forcing social change. It maintains that U.S. firms and households have exploited low-cost Mexican workers. It also claims that free trade allows the wealthy industrialized countries to become still richer by taking advantage of poor, developing nations. Further, large **multinational corporations**—companies that operate in several countries—force impoverished nations to compete with one another, resulting in substandard pay and working conditions.

Abuses of workers in developing (or advanced) countries may occur. Even so, such analyses make two inappropriate comparisons. Critics maintain that, on average, workers in, say, Mexico and the Philippines are paid less than one-tenth what American workers are paid. Yet, on average, these workers are roughly one-tenth as productive as U.S. workers. The difference is due to factors ranging from the lack of appropriate plant and equipment in developing countries to differences in education. In addition, the wages that multinational firms pay in developing nations are often far higher than the average wage in those nations. Statistics compiled by the World Bank show that firms in developing countries that are affiliated with American multinationals pay roughly double the average local income. Nike, in particular, has drawn considerable fire for its treatment of workers in its plants in Vietnam. Nike paid its Vietnamese workers an average annual wage of $670 in 2000, extremely low pay by U.S. standards. However, the average Vietnamese who worked for Nike earned an income that was almost twice the national average in 2000.

Lower trade barriers generally increase the opportunities available to workers in developing countries. Buyers and sellers from industrial nations challenge the authority of the local elites that had previously dominated the workforce. Developing countries that have opened themselves to trade have generally grown more rapidly than countries that have used tariffs and quotas to limit trade. According to one study, developing countries that lowered trade barriers saw the average level of income per person rise by 67 percent ($1,488 to $2,485) from 1980 to 1997. In contrast, developing countries that retained high barriers to trade grew by less than 10 percent ($1,947 to $2,133) over the same period.[5]

---

[5] Figures from D. Dollar, "Globalization, Inequality, and Poverty Since 1980," Washington, D.C., World Bank, 2001.

Trade and the Environment

The Rainforest Action Network group is dedicated to the protection of rainforests and the rights of the indigenous people who live there. It is one of many environmentalist organizations that have protested free trade. They argue that multinational corporations put pressure on poor countries and rich countries alike to relax their environmental standards and that such companies reduce their production costs by operating in countries with lax environmental laws. As a result, they further degrade the environments of the nations with which they do business.

There is, however, little empirical evidence that free trade harms the environment in this way. The costs imposed by environmental protection are generally small compared to other production costs and do not have much impact on the location decisions of multinational corporations.[6] In fact, precisely the opposite may be true. Countries that try to protect their domestic producers may actually do greater harm to the environment than countries that are more open to trade. Protecting inefficient domestic producers encourages the protected industries to make wasteful use of resources that in turn damage the environment. One example of the damage done by protectionist policies is the overuse of fertilizers that inflict environmental damage. Studies have shown that nations that provide little protection to their agricultural sector, such as Australia, use less artificial fertilizer. Countries that provide greater tariff protection to their relatively inefficient farmers, such as South Korea, tend to rely more heavily on fertilizers. The reason for the difference is that only efficient producers survive in countries that do not protect their farmers.[7] Trade barriers encourage inefficient producers to use artificial means to boost production.

▶ International Trade Organizations

Despite the efforts of protestors, nations have come to recognize the gains from free trade. Accordingly, nations have generally tried to lower the barriers to trade with one another. International organizations such as the WTO, bilateral agreements between individual nations, and multinational agreements are examples of such initiatives.

The World Trade Organization

Much of the antitrade protestors' animosity is directed at the WTO. At the same time, many policy makers regard it as vital for ensuring global prosperity. Given the controversy surrounding it, the WTO is worth examining. How did the WTO come to be, and what has it done to stimulate such disagreement?

The U.S. Constitution gives Congress the power "to regulate Commerce with foreign Nations." For about 150 years, Congress guarded this power and frequently

---

[6] See Adam Jaffe, Steven Peterson, Paul Portney, and Robert Stavins, "Environmental Regulation and the Competitiveness of U.S. Manufacturing: What Does the Evidence Tell Us?" *Journal of Economic Literature*, vol. 33, no. 1, March 1995, pages 132–163.

[7] See Kym Anderson, "Agricultural Trade Reforms, Research Initiatives, and the Environment," in E. Lutz, ed., *Agriculture and the Environment: Perspectives on Sustainable Rural Development*, Washington, D.C., The World Bank, 1998; and Gary Sampson, *Trade, Environment, and the WTO: The Post-Seattle Agenda*, Washington, D.C., Overseas Development Council, 2000.

erected trade barriers. During the Great Depression, the United States and many other industrial nations raised tariffs to try to aid domestic producers. These tariffs succeeded in discouraging imports. As a result, the volume of world trade fell dramatically in the 1930s.

The Great Depression led many U.S. policy makers to question the wisdom of past policies. One result was the Reciprocal Trade Agreements Act (RTAA) of 1934. The RTAA gives the president authority to negotiate joint tariff reductions with foreign nations, which are then renewed every three years. The desire to extend bilateral reductions in tariffs and other trade restrictions to a broad group of nations led 23 nations to meet in 1947 and produce the first General Agreement on Tariffs and Trade (GATT). The GATT reduced tariffs and other restrictions on trade. However, it failed to create an oversight body to rule on claims that nations had violated the terms of the treaty.

The WTO was formed after GATT negotiations in 1995. Its goals are to provide a forum for trade negotiations, enforce WTO-sponsored trade agreements, and monitor the trade policies of the 144 member nations.

Many of the WTO's opponents believe that it is a powerful international organization that can force nations to import goods, agree to exploitative labor contracts, and gut environmental protections. In fact, the WTO has far less power than its critics or defenders attribute to it. Its small staff and budget reflect its limited mandate. It neither makes policy nor writes rules of behavior, and its director-general cannot even comment on the policies of member nations. It also has little authority to deal with the needs and difficulties of developing countries and of formerly communist countries making the transition to market-based economies. Thus, it cannot deal with the contentious issue of trade barriers that industrialized nations have erected to protect their farmers from competition with developing countries.

myeconlab

Get Ahead of the Curve

Use evidence from the North American Free Trade Agreement to evaluate the case for free trade.

Free trade area
A group of nations that have agreed to eliminate all barriers to trade between them but retain barriers for nonmembers.

Regional Trade Agreements

Recently, the global economy has been moving toward a middle ground between those who favor and those who oppose free trade. Nations have been forming regional trade agreements in which several countries agree to trade freely but retain barriers against nonmembers. The best-known agreements are the North American Free Trade Agreement (NAFTA) and the European Union (the EU).

"It stands for 'North American Free Lunch Agreement'"

Courtesy www.CartoonStock.com

The North American Free Trade Agreement. The North American Free Trade Agreement (NAFTA) created a free trade area. A **free trade area** is a group of nations that have agreed to eliminate all trade barriers among them. Each nation, however, is free to pursue whatever trade policies it wishes regarding other countries. The three nations in NAFTA—Canada, Mexico, and the United States—each had distinct motives for entering into the agreement. NAFTA enabled Mexico to secure access to two prosperous economies for its exports. Because the United States and Canada already had a bilateral free trade agreement, NAFTA did not affect trade between them. Mexico had far higher trade barriers than either the United States or Canada. As a result, the prices of exports to Mexico fell dramatically. U.S. and Canadian trade with Mexico expanded, and Mexico became less likely to pursue trade with other partners. The shift of trade

TABLE 31.5

Former Currencies of Countries that Have Adopted the Euro

Country	Former Currency
Austria	schilling
Belgium	franc
Finland	markkaa
France	franc
Germany	mark
Greece	drachma
Ireland	pound
Italy	lira
Luxembourg	franc
The Netherlands	guilder
Portugal	escudo
Spain	peseta

Trade diversion
The shift of trade from a country outside a free trade area to a country inside the area.

Economic union
Consists of countries in a free trade area that also coordinate both external and internal economic policies.

from a country outside the free trade area to a country inside the area is known as **trade diversion.**

The European Union. Like NAFTA, the European Union (EU) is a free trade area. Unlike NAFTA, it is also an **economic union.** Members of an economic union coordinate external and internal economic policies. Examples of such policies include trade agreements with nations outside the union and tax levels and limits on the federal budget deficits of member nations. Members even reduce the barriers to international migration, so that a citizen of one nation in the EU is free to work or live in any other member nation. In 1993, the EU solidified this fusion of economies by agreeing to adopt a common currency—the *euro*—to replace the individual currencies. The countries that have adopted a common currency and their old currencies appear in Table 31.5.

The close coordination of the economies in the EU has created what some people have called "the United States of Europe." This fusion of economies has had three main goals. First, the elimination of trade barriers and the free movement of workers and other productive resources within Europe would make production more efficient and make the continent more prosperous. Second, the creators of the EU hoped that economic unity would bring political unity to a continent that experienced two major wars in the first half of the twentieth century and the Cold War for most of the second half. Third, some of the creators of the EU believed that coordinating their economic and political strategies would enable the European nations to exercise more economic and political power on the world stage.

Recent events have cast the future of the EU into question. In 2005, voters in France and the Netherlands resoundingly rejected a proposed European Constitution that would have clarified and extended political and economic unification. There were many reasons for the "no" votes, some of them dealing with domestic political

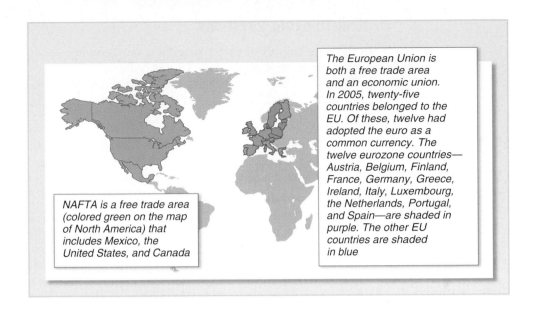

The European Union is both a free trade area and an economic union. In 2005, twenty-five countries belonged to the EU. Of these, twelve had adopted the euro as a common currency. The twelve eurozone countries—Austria, Belgium, Finland, France, Germany, Greece, Ireland, Italy, Luxembourg, the Netherlands, Portugal, and Spain—are shaded in purple. The other EU countries are shaded in blue

NAFTA is a free trade area (colored green on the map of North America) that includes Mexico, the United States, and Canada

unrest rather than dissatisfaction with the European Union. The impact, however, has been to slow the move toward greater economic and political unity.

Strategy and Policy
Why Sugar Isn't Sweet in Holland, Michigan

In January 2002, Lifesavers Candy, a division of Kraft Foods Global, Inc., announced that it would close its 600-person plant in Holland, Michigan, and move its operations to Quebec, Canada. Kraft explained that it was closing the plant because it could no longer afford the high price of sugar in the United States. Quotas imposed on imported sugar caused U.S. sugar prices to be two to three times as high as the price charged in other countries. An artificial increase in the price of sugar increases the cost of producing the candy. Lifesavers would reduce its costs of production by about $13 million per year if it could buy sugar at the world price.

Trade restrictions have two basic impacts on the market for Lifesavers candies. First, part of the higher cost is passed along to consumers, in the form of higher prices. Second, the higher cost of producing Lifesavers reduces Kraft's incentive to produce them. As a result, the price of Lifesavers rises, and the amount of Lifesavers produced and consumed falls. The lost jobs in the U.S. candy industry might prove worthwhile if there were comparable gains in the U.S. sugar industry. There is little evidence, however, that the protection offered by sugar quotas has widespread benefits. The domestic sugar industry has enjoyed about $1 billion in benefits. However, the U.S. Government Accountability Office estimates that almost half of these benefits accrue to one percent of all U.S. sugar growers and that one sugar grower alone received over $30 million in benefits annually. Because consumers (both individuals and other industries that use sugar) spend so much more on sugar and so few jobs are at stake, the cost to consumers per job saved is staggering. One estimate is $600,000 per job. Worst of all, the policy denies impoverished nations in South and Central America access to the world's largest sugar consumer (the United States).

Critical-Thinking Questions

1. Show the impact of the sugar quotas on consumer surplus, producer surplus, and overall well-being in the United States.
2. What other U.S. industries would be affected by higher domestic sugar prices?

► SUMMARY

- **The U.S. trade deficit.** The United States imports far more than it exports. This pattern does not hold, however, for all countries and all goods. The United States has a trade deficit with both high-wage and low-wage nations.

- **Economic models of free trade.** According to the theory of comparative advantage, countries are able to consume more than they can produce by specializing in producing what they are relatively best at. This approach allows them to move off their production possibilities frontiers and onto their consumption possibilities frontiers. Because of increasing opportunity costs, they might not specialize completely. Instead, they might continue to produce some goods that they import. Imports cause domestic producer surplus to fall, but they cause consumer surplus to rise by an even larger amount. As a result, trade increases overall economic well-being.

- **Protectionist trade policies.** Governments use tariffs and quotas to protect domestic industries. Each results in gains for domestic producers. The costs they impose on consumers and taxpayers more than offset the gains, leaving society worse off than before the restrictions were imposed.

- **Arguments for government protection from trade.** Domestic industries present a number of arguments for protection. They claim that domestic producers need protection from dumping by foreign competitors. The standard for determining whether dumping has occurred, however, might sometimes classify reasonable business practices as dumping. Other industries claim that the goods they produce are vital for the nation's security or identity, so the government cannot allow them to be displaced by imports. This claim, however, is frequently overstated. Finally, some industries claim that they need temporary protection. After they stabilize, they will be able to compete. In reality, most of these "infant industries" fail to develop.

- **The impact of trade on developing countries and the environment.** Many opponents of free trade maintain that trade allows large multinational corporations to exploit poor workers. These firms, however, generally offer higher pay than local employers. Studies show that countries that have opened themselves to trade have generally prospered more than countries that have not. Some environmental groups claim that trade causes companies to seek nations with lax environmental laws. In fact, protectionist policies seem more likely to lead to environmental degradation.

- **International trade organizations.** The World Trade Organization (WTO) was created in 1995. Since the end of World War II, governments have sought to create an organization that would adjudicate international disputes over trade and generally promote free trade. The WTO has become the focal point of much of the opposition to international trade. This opposition, however, overstates the importance and power of the WTO. Agreements like NAFTA and the EU lower trade barriers for nations covered by the agreement, but leave them intact for other nations. While lower tariffs and relaxed quotas bring gains, they can also distort trade by causing countries to buy from higher-cost nations that are members of the agreement rather than from lower-cost nations that are not.

Consumption possibilities
 frontier (CPF) 788
Dumping 797
Economic union 802
Free trade 787
Free trade area 801

Infant industry 798
Multinational corporation
 799
Tariff 794
Trade diversion 802

Voluntary restraint
 agreement (VRA) 795
World price 791
World Trade Organization
 (WTO) 783

PROBLEMS

1. The Bureau of Economic Analysis reported that during the first six months of 2002, the United States exported $10 billion of goods and services to Australia and imported $6 billion of goods and services from Australia. Is there a trade surplus or deficit for the United States?

2. Why is low-cost foreign labor an incomplete explanation for the U.S. trade deficit?

3. Consider a simple world that consists of only two countries: Latvia and Cameroon. These two countries can produce either coffee or fur coats. Cameroon can produce 600,000 pounds of coffee beans in a given year or 10,000 fur coats. Latvia can produce 10,000 pounds of coffee beans or 200,000 fur coats.
   a. Draw linear PPFs to show what each country can produce if it does not trade. Which country has a comparative advantage in coffee? In fur coats? Justify each answer.
   b. How can specialization and trade make Latvia and Cameroon better off?

4. If the United States has a comparative advantage in laptops and China has a comparative advantage in textiles, then why does each country still produce some of both products?

5. "Because Bangladesh is so far behind the United States technologically, it does not have a comparative advantage at anything, so the U.S. has no reason to trade with it." Do you agree or disagree with this statement? Justify your answer.

6. Use Table 31.1 to explain which Chinese workers and firms lose out with free trade? What can you propose to help them?

7. If U.S. textile producers lose out because of imports, and U.S. textile consumers gain, how can we say that the economy as a whole is better off?

8. In the 1980s and 1990s, many poor, developing countries abandoned protectionist policies in favor of free trade. What was their motivation?

9. Why is a quota more harmful to society than a tariff, even if both restrictions cause imports to fall by the same amount?

10. Assume that the United States wants its citizens to eat more domestically produced oranges and fewer of the less expensive imported oranges.
    a. Use consumer and producer surplus to show the impact that a quota on imported oranges would have on the well-being of U.S. producers and consumers.
    b. Show the impact that a tariff on imported oranges would have on the well-being of U.S. producers and consumers.
    c. Use consumer and producer surplus to explain why economists prefer a tariff to an equally restrictive quota.

11. Suppose that the United States lowers tariffs on imported sugar. Who is likely to benefit from such a policy? Who is likely to be hurt? Why?

12. Use consumer surplus and producer surplus to illustrate the impact of increasing the textile tariff cited in this chapter from $1.00 to $1.50 per yard.

13. If a quota on foreign-made textiles saves American jobs, how can it be harmful to Americans?

14. Use consumer surplus and producer surplus to show the impact of increasing the textile quota cited in this chapter from 4 million to 5 million yards.

15. The U.S. shoe industry requests protection from imports based on the U.S. military's need for footwear.
    a. Would you favor such a request? Why or why not?
    b. If a U.S. shoe manufacturer claimed that Japanese shoemakers were guilty of dumping because they were selling identical footwear at a lower price, would you agree, disagree, or request more information? Justify your response.

16. What is wrong with the infant industry argument if a country is asking for only temporary help?

17. Multinational firms pay workers in developing nations a small fraction of what they would have to pay workers in the United States. What would you say to someone who cites this as evidence that multinationals exploit their workers?

18. Why do some environmentalists object to free trade? How might one respond?

19. In what ways might an organization like the WTO help economies? In what ways might an organization like the WTO harm economies?

20. How might economic unions be beneficial for the world economy? How might they be harmful?

myeconlab STUDY GUIDE

HERE'S HOW MyEconLab CAN HELP YOU GET A BETTER GRADE

1. Log into MyEconLab and take Practice Test 31-A (to log in for the first time, see page 30 for instructions).

2. Based on your test results, MyEconLab will identify the areas where you need further work and create a personal Study Plan for you.

3. Your Study Plan contains the exercises listed below and others like them that will target the specific chapter topics you need to focus on. You'll receive instant feedback and find links to tutorials, animations, and the online textbook to help you study.

4. When you're ready, go take Practice Test 31-B and demonstrate how your results have improved.

Section 31.1, Exercise 1 Explain how the United States trade deficit has changed:

a. In absolute size.
b. As a percentage of GDP.

Section 31.1, Exercise 2 Cheap foreign labor is often blamed for the loss of U.S. jobs in industries such as steel. Why might this hypothesis be incorrect?

Section 31.2, Exercise 1 Suppose that China and the United States can each produce either computers or clothing, or some combination of these goods. China can produce 10,000 units of clothing or 1,000 computers or any intermediate combination. The United States can produce 4,000 units of clothing or 8,000 computers or any intermediate combination.

a. Graph linear production possibilities frontiers for each country. Put computers on the horizontal axis.

b. What is the comparative advantage of each country?

c. Suppose that one computer can be traded for one unit of clothing. Draw the consumption possibilities frontier for each country.

Section 31.2, Exercise 2 The following graph shows a country's domestic market for shoes, without trade.

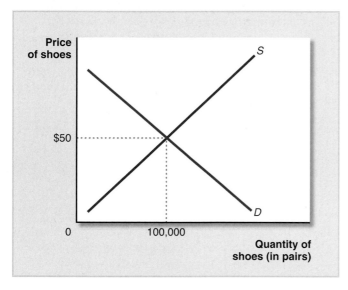

a. Identify consumer and producer surplus without trade.

b. Suppose that this country now begins to trade at a world price per pair of $18. Show the new price on the graph, and identify the quantity supplied and demanded.

c. Identify consumer and producer surplus with trade.

d. Show the net gain from trade.

Section 31.2, Exercise 3 We can demonstrate that exporting countries gain from trade. The following graph shows the domestic market of the exporting country, without trade.

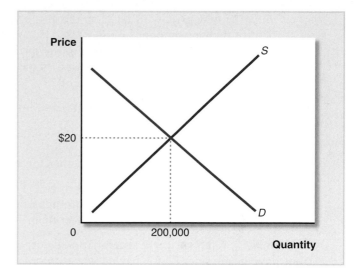

a. Identify consumer and producer surplus without trade.

b. Suppose that this country now begins to trade at a world price per pair of $25. Show the new price on the graph, and identify the quantity supplied and demanded.

c. Identify consumer and producer surplus with trade.

d. Show the net gain from trade.

Section 31.3, Exercise 1 Suppose that the shoe market is in equilibrium at a world price per pair of $18, as shown on the following graph. The government imposes a $10-per-pair tariff on shoes.

a. Show the new price with tariff on the graph, and identify the new amount of imports.
b. Identify the deadweight losses due to the tariff.
c. Who gains from the tariff? Who loses? Is the country as a whole better or worse off?

Section 31.3, Exercise 2 What is a quota, and how is it different from a tariff?

Section 31.4, Exercise 1 How does the U.S. Department of Commerce determine whether foreign firms are dumping?

Section 31.4, Exercise 2 What are infant industries, and why do governments choose to protect them?

Section 31.5, Exercise 1 U.S. multinational corporations have been criticized for paying wages in other countries that are less than the wages that they pay in the United States. What are two reasons that this criticism may be unfair?

Section 31.5, Exercise 2 Does evidence support the claim that multinational countries produce in less-developed countries to avoid environmental laws in developed countries?

Section 31.6, Exercise 1 Suppose that the United States has two trading partners that produce tomatoes: Mexico and Canada. The price of tomatoes in Canada is $2.00 per pound, and the price of tomatoes in Mexico is $1.00 per pound. Both prices are below the U.S. domestic price of $6.00 per pound.

a. If there is free trade, which country will the United States buy tomatoes from?
b. Now suppose that there is a $3.00-per-pound tariff on tomatoes. What is the new price of tomatoes, and which country will the United States buy tomatoes from?
c. The United States creates a free trade area with Canada, which means that there is now no tariff on Canadian tomatoes. Who will the United States trade with now, and what will the price of tomatoes be?
d. Is the free trade area a good idea?

32

International Finance

Imagine waking up one morning to find that you have suddenly become poor. Your job? Gone. Your bank account? Worthless. Even the cup of coffee that you used to purchase every morning now seems like the height of opulence. It might sound like a nightmarish movie plot, but it really happened in Argentina.

Throughout 2001, Argentineans were following the financial news with increasing anxiety. The government had long been supporting a policy that fixed the value of the peso at one-to-one with the U.S. dollar. It was widely recognized in international financial circles that this policy had become more than just unwise; it was unsustainable. The economy was stalling, joblessness and prices were rising, and the government was on the verge of bankruptcy. Ordinary people could only watch and worry.

Over the course of a few months in late 2001 and early 2002, joblessness and prices both skyrocketed, while real per-capita income fell by 12 percent. Households, firms, and the Argentinean government all found themselves unable to pay their bills. The government took the unusual step of declaring bankruptcy. An entire country effectively went broke.

It is hard to believe that Argentina had entered the 1990s as the leading economic power of South America. After decades of mismanagement, its economy had finally stabilized. It had become the darling of international investors. The **International Monetary Fund (IMF)**, an international organization that provides loans to promote development and ease financial crises, held Argentina up as an example to other emerging economies. What went so very wrong?

International Monetary Fund (IMF)
An international organization that provides loans to promote development and ease financial crises in emerging economies.

In this chapter, we explore the financial side of the international sector. International financial markets make possible the trade we discussed in the prior chapter. However, when a country's international finances are severely mismanaged, these markets can break down and cause economic crises like the one that beset Argentina. It is important for us to understand how international financial markets help economies and occasionally harm them.

ALONG THE WAY, YOU WILL ALSO LEARN:

- How exchange rates are determined on currency markets and how they can affect a nation's economic well-being.

- How economists measure international monetary flows and how these flows affect currency markets.

- Alternative approaches that nations take to setting exchange rates.

- How the IMF manages financial crises.

AT THE END OF THE CHAPTER, THE MYECONLAB LOGO WILL DIRECT YOU ONLINE

- MyEconLab is a resource-packed online homework and tutorial system that can help you perform better in your economics course. To log in for the first time, see page 30 for instructions.

- MyEconLab can help you apply important concepts from the chapter to real-world issues. Watch for the logo to indicate online features about Brazil and China.

- At the end of each chapter, you'll find a special study section that will help you get the most out of your textbook and your instructor's MyEconLab course.

Exchange Rates and Currency Markets

In the previous chapter, we treated international trade as the exchange of goods and services without using money. However, such exchanges of goods between individuals are usually impractical, if not impossible. The difficulty becomes still greater when the exchange crosses international boundaries. Consider Brad, a college student with a new DVD, who wants Argentinean beef for dinner. Trading as an individual, he would have to locate an Argentinean farmer who is willing to trade some beef for a DVD, agree on a trade, and complete the exchange—all by dinnertime.

The existence of money eliminates the need for such trades. However, a new question arises when consumers buy foreign-made products: Which country's money should they use? Brad has dollars, but Marta, the Argentinean farmer, wants to be paid in pesos, which she can spend in the stores in Buenos Aires. To buy that beef, Brad (or, more realistically, an importer or distributor) must first obtain Argentinean pesos.

Currency Markets

Currency market
The market in which people buy and sell a nation's money.

The easiest way to understand how Brad obtains Argentinean pesos is to think of a nation's currency as a commodity, just like socks or orange juice. The market in which people buy and sell currencies is known as a **currency market**. It functions

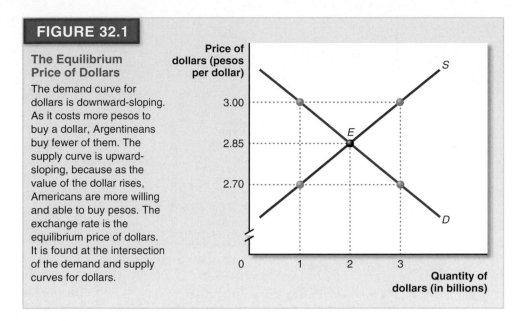

FIGURE 32.1

The Equilibrium Price of Dollars

The demand curve for dollars is downward-sloping. As it costs more pesos to buy a dollar, Argentineans buy fewer of them. The supply curve is upward-sloping, because as the value of the dollar rises, Americans are more willing and able to buy pesos. The exchange rate is the equilibrium price of dollars. It is found at the intersection of the demand and supply curves for dollars.

similarly to the market for any other good or service. Brad obtains pesos by supplying dollars on the currency market. Thus, the supply side of this currency market consists largely of people like Brad who want to buy items made in another country. The demand side in this case consists of people like Marta who want dollars, which they can spend on U.S.-made goods and services. Figure 32.1 shows the market for U.S. dollars.

The supply curve for dollars is upward-sloping, like any other supply curve. As the price of dollars rises—say, from 2.70 pesos per dollar to 3.00 pesos per dollar—Americans receive more pesos for every dollar they provide. This means that Brad has to spend fewer dollars to buy the beef he desires. Argentinean goods and services in general become cheaper to Americans. According to the Law of Demand, Americans respond by buying more Argentinean products. To buy more Argentinean goods, however, Americans need more Argentinean currency. They get that by supplying more dollars on currency markets. As a result, the quantity of dollars supplied in Figure 32.1 rises from $1 billion to $3 billion.

The demand curve for dollars is downward-sloping, because it reflects the desire and ability of Argentineans to buy U.S.-made goods and services. Argentineans demand dollars so that they can buy U.S.-made items. As the dollar becomes more expensive, rising from 2.70 to 3.00 pesos per dollar, it takes more pesos to buy dollars. Marta must spend more pesos to buy a U.S.-made DVD, and U.S.-made goods and services in general become more expensive to Argentineans. As a result, Argentineans can afford fewer U.S.-made goods and services, and the quantity of dollars they demand declines from $3 billion to $1 billion.

The equilibrium price in this market occurs where the demand and supply curves for dollars intersect. In this case, the equilibrium quantity is $2 billion, and the equilibrium price is 2.85 pesos per dollar. We call the equilibrium price the **exchange rate**, because that is the rate at which people give up one currency to get another.

Exchange rate
The equilibrium price on a currency market.

Courtesy www.CartoonStock.com

Appreciation and Depreciation

If Americans' demand for Argentinean goods and services rises, then they will need more pesos to buy those goods and services. This shifts the supply curve for dollars to the right, as shown in Figure 32.2.

When the supply curve shifts to the right from S_0 to S_1, an excess supply of dollars arises. At the original exchange rate of 2.85 pesos per dollar, Americans supply \$4 billion, but Argentineans continue to demand \$2 billion. The excess supply causes the exchange rate to fall from 2.85 to 2.70 pesos per dollar. If the demand for Argentinean goods and services falls, the supply curve shifts left from S_0 to S_2. At 2.85 pesos per dollar, Americans supply no dollars at all while Argentineans demand \$2 billion. The excess demand causes the exchange rate to rise from 2.85 to 3.00 pesos per dollar.

When the equilibrium price of the dollar rises, we say the dollar appreciates. A currency **appreciates**, or becomes stronger, when it becomes more valuable relative to another currency. When the equilibrium price of the dollar falls, it **depreciates**, or becomes weaker, meaning that it has become less valuable compared to another currency. Note that appreciation and depreciation are relative terms. If it takes more pesos to buy one dollar (the dollar appreciates) then it takes fewer dollars to buy one peso (the peso depreciates).

Appreciate
When the price of a currency rises.

Depreciate
When the price of a currency falls.

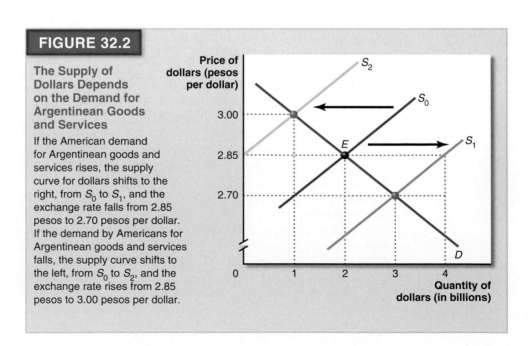

FIGURE 32.2

The Supply of Dollars Depends on the Demand for Argentinean Goods and Services

If the American demand for Argentinean goods and services rises, the supply curve for dollars shifts to the right, from S_0 to S_1, and the exchange rate falls from 2.85 pesos to 2.70 pesos per dollar. If the demand by Americans for Argentinean goods and services falls, the supply curve shifts to the left, from S_0 to S_2, and the exchange rate rises from 2.85 pesos to 3.00 pesos per dollar.

Many people equate a strong currency with a strong economy. In fact, a strong currency helps some households and firms in the country and hurts others. A strong dollar means that Americans can buy a lot of foreign currency, and a lot of foreign-made goods and services, with relatively few dollars. That is great news if, like Brad, you want to buy Argentinean beef. It is bad news if you want to sell U.S.-made DVDs in Argentina. A strong dollar means that it takes more foreign currency to buy U.S.-made goods, thereby discouraging exports. Thus, some Americans want a strong dollar, while others prefer a weak one.

▶The Balance of Payments

The discussion of appreciation and depreciation shows that, holding all else equal, any event that causes Americans to spend more money on Argentinean-made goods and services causes the dollar to become weaker relative to the peso. Any event that causes Argentineans to spend more money on U.S.-made goods and services causes the dollar to become stronger relative to the peso. The United States and Argentina thus have a clear interest in knowing how much money is flowing between them. In this section, we show how nations track international monetary flows and how these flows affect exchange rates.

Measuring the Flows of Funds Between Nations

Measuring monetary flows between nations allows us to compare the many disparate goods and services that cross international boundaries. How can we say whether a college education that an Italian student receives at the University of Arizona offsets an imported Ferrari that an executive buys in Phoenix? The market value of these goods and services provides a common yardstick that allows us to compare the value of a nation's imports with the value of its exports. In the previous chapter, we saw that the value of U.S. imports far exceeds the value of its exports, resulting in a trade deficit. However, exports and imports constitute only a portion of the payments that flow between nations.

Think of the flow of money in international transactions in the same way you think of individual purchases. You cannot buy a car, a home, or even an ice cream cone unless you first have funds in hand from some other source. On the international level, the total payments that one nation makes to other nations must be balanced by the payments it receives from abroad. We shall see that the flow of funds out of the United States to pay for its trade deficit is offset by other flows of payments into the United States. The equality between the inflow of funds and the outflow of funds is called the **balance of payments**. We express the balance of payments as the rule shown in Equation 32.1.

Balance of payments
Equality between a country's inflow of funds and outflow of funds.

Total payments to other countries = Total receipts from other countries   (32.1)

The following sections examine both sides of the equation in detail.

Total Payments to Other Countries. Payments to other countries take one of four forms:

1. *Purchases of imports by households, firms, or the government.*
2. *The return on assets owned by foreign investors.* Examples include rent paid

by American tenants to landlords in Argentina and stock dividends paid by Ford Motor Company to Argentinean investors.

3. *Transfers by households, firms, or the government of a country to other countries.* This type of payment includes the money an Argentinean immigrant sends to his parents so they can afford to visit him, and the military aid the U.S. government provides to the Argentinean government.

4. *Purchases of physical or financial capital in other countries by households, firms, or the government.* This payment type occurs when Ford builds a plant in Buenos Aires, or when American investors buy bonds issued by an Argentinean firm.

A country's total payments abroad is the sum of these four factors, as shown in Equation 32.2.

$$\text{Total payments to other countries} = \text{Purchases of imports}$$
$$+ \text{ Returns on assets owned by foreigners} + \text{Transfers abroad}$$
$$+ \text{ Purchases of foreign capital} \qquad (32.2)$$

Total Receipts from Other Countries. A country's receipts are the opposite of these payments. The United States receives payments for:

1. *The export of goods and services to other countries.*
2. *The return on foreign assets owned by domestic households or firms.*
3. *Transfers received from foreign households, firms, or governments.*
4. *The purchase of domestic physical or financial capital by foreigners.*

The sum of these receipts yields a country's total receipts, as shown in Equation 32.3.

$$\text{Total receipts from other countries} = \text{Sale of exports}$$
$$+ \text{ Returns on domestically owned foreign assets} + \text{Transfers received}$$
$$\text{from foreigners} + \text{Purchases of domestic capital by foreigners} \qquad (32.3)$$

The balance of payments (Equation 32.1) indicates that the sum of payments, (Equation 32.2) equals the sum of receipts (Equation 32.3):

$$\text{Purchases of imports} + \text{Returns on assets owned by foreigners}$$
$$+ \text{ Transfers abroad} + \text{Purchases of foreign capital} = \text{Sale of exports}$$
$$+ \text{ Return on domestically owned foreign assets} + \text{Transfers received}$$
$$\text{from foreigners} + \text{Purchases of domestic capital by foreigners} \qquad (32.4)$$

Equation 32.4 combines Equations 32.1, 32.2, and 32.3 to show the individual components of the balance of payments.

Current account
Shows current payments for goods and services and transfers.

Capital account
Shows the net sale of physical and financial assets.

The Current Account and the Capital Account

The current and capital accounts allow us to study the nature of the payments a country makes and receives. The **current account** reflects payments for goods and services as well as transfers made between nations. As its name suggests, the **capital account** includes a country's net sale of physical and financial assets to other nations.

To gain a clearer understanding of the current account, we first compute the net flow of payments into and out of the economy by subtracting the first three terms of Equation 32.4 from the last three terms. Equation 32.5 shows that the net flow of payments must be zero.

$$\text{Net exports} + \text{Net return on assets} + \text{Net transfers}$$
$$+ \text{Net purchase of capital} = 0 \qquad (32.5)$$

where

Net exports = Sale of exports − Purchases of imports

Net return on assets = Returns on domestically owned foreign assets − Returns on assets owned by foreigners

Net transfers = Transfers received from foreigners − Transfers abroad

Net purchases of capital = Purchases of domestic capital by foreigners − Purchases of foreign capital

The sum of the first three terms in Equation 32.5 (net exports, net return on assets, and net transfers) is the *current* account. Because the three terms can be either positive or negative, the current account can be either positive or negative. Recently, the sum of the first three terms in Equation 32.5 has been negative for the United States; that is, more funds are flowing out of the U.S. economy in these categories than is flowing in. However, a nation, like a household, cannot spend more money than it has. If funds are flowing *out* on the current account, they must be flowing *in*, often as a loan, from somewhere else.

Over the last several years, funds have flowed into the United States from the last term in Equation 32.5—net purchases of capital. This last term constitutes the *capital* account. Suppose that a country runs a current account deficit, spending or transferring more funds out than it takes in; it must then run a surplus on the capital account that is equal to the current account deficit. That is, the country must sell more financial or physical assets to other countries than it buys from them. Table 32.1 shows the balance of payments for the United States in 2004.

TABLE 32.1

The U.S. Balance of Payments, 2004

Category	Surplus or Deficit
Net exports	− $624 billion
Net return on assets	+ $36 billion
Net transfers	− $80 billion
Current account balance	− $668 billion
Net purchases of capital (capital account balance)	+ $584 billion
Statistical discrepancy	+ $84 billion
Net balance	$0

Source: Bureau of Economic Analysis, U.S. International Transactions Accounts Data, at www.bea.doc.gov

The table shows a current account deficit of $668 billion. (Note that the trade deficit is higher than in the prior chapter on international trade. This difference occurs in part because transfers are listed separately in the balance of payments.) This deficit is largely offset by the capital account surplus of $584 billion. The Bureau of Economic Analysis, which collects these data, attributes the remaining $84 billion to statistical error.

The Balance of Payments and Economic Behavior

The idea that the United States must accumulate in its capital account surplus the funds it spends on the current account deficit is easy to envision in theory. It is harder to see exactly how the United States coordinates such decisions in practice. After all, unlike a household, a market economy does not plan all its purchases from abroad based on a budget. When Japanese investors decide to buy more U.S. Treasury securities, they do not explicitly insist that American consumers buy more Toyotas. The two decisions are made by different groups of people with different goals and different constraints. How can we be sure that American consumers and Japanese investors will behave in a coordinated fashion?

In fact, the two sets of decisions are connected through currency markets, like the one illustrated earlier in Figure 32.2. In recent decades, the United States has had a large trade deficit with Japan. This has caused a large current account deficit and has caused the dollar to depreciate against the Japanese yen.

A weaker dollar, in turn, makes debt issued by U.S. firms or the U.S. government cheaper and thus more attractive to Japanese investors. The purchase of U.S. securities results in a capital account surplus, which offsets the current account deficit.

TEST + *E X T E N D* Your Knowledge

1. TEST Suppose that Japan has a capital account surplus of 250 billion yen and is experiencing no net currency inflow or outflow. What must be true of its current account?

2. EXTEND Go to the Bureau of Economic Analysis Web site at www.aw-bc.com/leeds/ch32 to find the latest figures on the U.S. balance of payments. What is the status of the current and capital accounts?

► Exchange Rate Systems

Today, the exchange rates of most currencies are determined in markets similar to those we've described. Sometimes, however, countries follow different policies. We now consider two recent crises: the implosion of the Argentinean economy in 2001, mentioned earlier, and the confrontation between the United States and China in 2005. Both resulted from government attempts to set a constant value for its currency in terms of the dollar. In this section, we look more closely at two different ways of how exchange rates can be determined: floating and fixed exchange rates. We also examine the current state of the dollar on currency markets and the consequences of the policies followed by Argentina and China.

Floating Exchange Rates

Up to this point in the chapter, we have assumed that the equilibrium price of a nation's currency moves up or down with free market forces. An increase in the demand for a country's products increases the demand for its currency, which makes the currency stronger or more valuable. If the government does not intervene to block or change the outcome of this process, we say that it has a **floating exchange rate**, or one that moves freely to determine the equilibrium exchange rate. With the dollar rising and falling against so many different currencies, is it possible to find any general patterns?

Factors Affecting the Demand and Supply of Currencies. Recall from Chapter 4 that relative prices, incomes, and expectations can shift the demand curve. These factors also play a key role in determining the demand and supply for a currency. We now consider how each of the above forces affects the demand for pesos as shown in Figure 32.3.

1. *Prices.* Suppose Argentinean goods rise in price but U.S.-made goods do not (or at least rise more slowly in price). If U.S. and Argentinean goods are substitutes for one another, American consumers will find Argentinean goods less attractive. The demand for Argentinean goods will fall, the supply of dollars shifts left from S_0 to S_1. Moreover, the demand by Argentineans for U.S.-made goods rises, so the demand for dollars shifts right from D_0 to D_1. As a result, the equilibrium price of dollars rises from 2.85 to 4.00 pesos per dollar. Figure 32.3 shows the equilibrium quantity of dollars rising slightly, from $2 billion to $2.5 billion. The precise quantity depends on how much the supply and demand curves shift. It could be more or less than $2.5 billion.

2. *Incomes.* When household income and firm revenue fall in the United States, so do purchases by both sectors. U.S. demand for all goods and services (including those made in Argentina) falls. Once again, the supply of dollars

FIGURE 32.3

The Impact of Price and Income Changes on the Demand for Pesos

If prices rise in Argentina but remain stable in the United States, Argentinean goods become less attractive and U.S. consumers buy fewer of them. The supply curve for dollars shifts to the left. At the same time, U.S.-made goods become more attractive to Argentineans, who demand more dollars to buy goods from the United States. This drives the price of dollars up from 2.85 pesos to 4.00 pesos. The same would happen if incomes in the United States fell while incomes in Argentina rose.

Floating exchange rate A system that allows the equilibrium price on a currency market to move up or down freely due to market forces.

shifts left. The opposite happens when incomes rise, so if incomes in Argentina rise, the demand for dollars shifts right.

3. *Expectations.* Finally, just as the price of ice cream today depends in part on what we expect the price of ice cream to be in the future, the price of a currency also depends on what we expect to happen in the future. The supply of dollars will fall today if Americans expect the dollar to appreciate in the future. If people think they will soon be able to sell dollars at a higher price, those who can put off selling dollars will do so. The demand for dollars rises today because people who buy dollars want to do so before the price rises. Such *speculation* causes the current demand for dollars to rise, the current supply to fall, and the current price to rise.

The Law of One Price. Because the currency markets operate like any other market, one of the most basic market principles—the law of one price—applies to them. The **Law of One Price** states that if markets are allowed to operate freely, identical goods and services will sell for identical prices. For example, two identical gas stations located across the street from one another cannot sell identical gas at different prices.[1] If one station charges $2.75 per gallon and another charges only $2.25, no one would buy the more expensive gas. To stay in business, the station charging $2.75 must lower its price. At the same time, the station charging $2.25 would see a surge in demand, giving it an incentive to increase its price. The two stores would adjust their prices until both charged the same price.

On an international level, suppose that Argentina and the United States make identical leather wallets (we will ignore complicating factors like transportation costs). Consumers should not spend more to buy Argentinean wallets than to buy U.S.-made wallets. For example, suppose that Brad faces the choice of purchasing Argentinean wallets that cost 28.50 pesos each or identical U.S. wallets at $10 each. For wallets to cost the same in the two countries, the exchange rate between the peso and the dollar must be 2.85 pesos per dollar. At this exchange rate, buying a wallet

that costs 28.5 pesos requires $\dfrac{28.5 \text{ pesos}}{2.85 \text{ pesos per dollar}} = \$10$, which is what Brad

would have to pay in the United States. The cost of the two items is thus identical, no matter where Brad buys them.

What would happen if the price of a U.S.-made wallet rose to $12? At the exchange rate of 2.85 pesos per dollar, a 28.5-peso Argentinean wallet would still cost only $10. Because Argentinean wallets are now cheaper than U.S.-made wallets, people like Brad would buy them instead. As Americans buy more Argentinean goods, the supply of dollars shifts right and the price of dollars falls. The price of the dollar stops falling when the exchange rate is 2.38 pesos per dollar. At this price,

a 28.5-peso wallet costs $\dfrac{28.5 \text{ pesos}}{2.38 \text{ pesos per dollar}} = \$12$, the same as it costs in the

United States.

Purchasing Power Parity. The previous example highlights two important features of floating exchange rates. First, a country's currency depreciates when the prices of

Law of One Price
If markets are allowed to operate freely, identical goods and services tend to sell for identical prices.

---

[1] Sometimes we do see differences, but that is typically because one station offers services—such as doing repair work—or additional goods that the other does not, which means the stations are not identical.

goods and services rise faster there than in other countries. Its currency appreciates when its prices rise more slowly than in other countries. Second, exchange rates rise or fall to restore equality—or parity—of consumers' purchasing power. After exchange rates have adjusted, U.S. consumers cannot buy wallets more cheaply in Argentina (and vice versa).

Purchasing power parity (PPP)
The principle that exchange rates rise and fall to equate purchasing power across countries.

The principle that exchange rates rise and fall to equate purchasing power across countries is known as **purchasing power parity (PPP)**. While economists commonly assume PPP to hold, two warnings are in order. First, PPP is a *long-run* concept. Transportation costs and a variety of domestic policies, such as taxes or tariffs, cause prices to vary across countries for extended periods. As a result, exchange rates seldom move immediately to the new equilibrium level. Second, changes in exchange rates reflect differences in overall prices. As a result, exchange rates generally do not change in response to the rise or fall in the price of a single product. Wallets are only one of countless products that countries export and import, so their impact on exchange rates is limited. As a result, even in the long run, PPP is unlikely to make the prices of wallets precisely equal in the United States and Argentina. Still, the general principle remains: As prices in one country rise relative to another, that country's currency depreciates to offset the movement in prices.

Since 1986, *The Economist* magazine has maintained a Big Mac Index, a lighthearted way to verify the predictions of PPP. If PPP holds, a Big Mac sandwich should cost roughly the same anywhere. Figure 32.4 shows the prices of Big Macs for several countries in U.S. dollars.

As the figure shows, with the exception of China and Switzerland, the price of a Big Mac generally fluctuates within relatively narrow bounds. We shall explore the reason for low prices in China later in this chapter.

The Weakening U.S. Dollar. In 2004 and 2005, many American households and firms had reason to dislike floating exchange rates. As the dollar steadily weakened, European vacations, Japanese cars, and Ugandan coffee all became increasingly

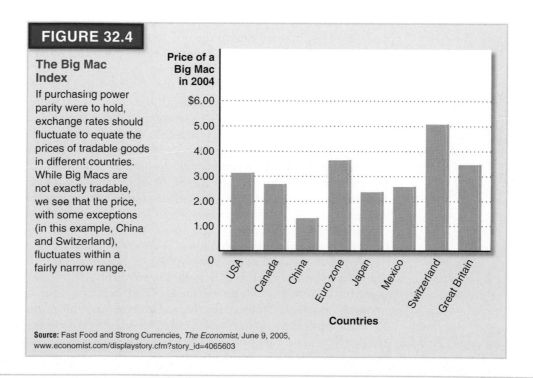

FIGURE 32.4

The Big Mac Index

If purchasing power parity were to hold, exchange rates should fluctuate to equate the prices of tradable goods in different countries. While Big Macs are not exactly tradable, we see that the price, with some exceptions (in this example, China and Switzerland), fluctuates within a fairly narrow range.

Source: Fast Food and Strong Currencies, *The Economist*, June 9, 2005, www.economist.com/displaystory.cfm?story_id=4065603

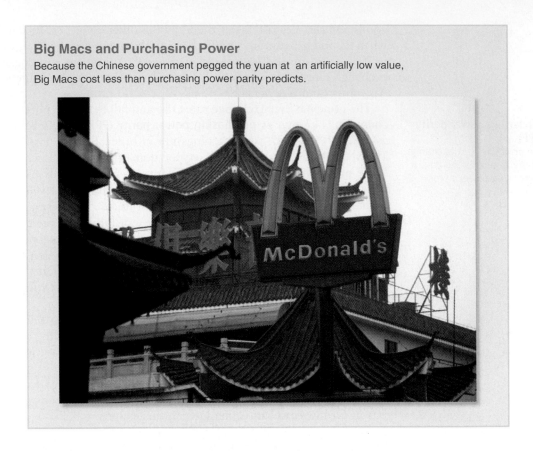

Big Macs and Purchasing Power
Because the Chinese government pegged the yuan at an artificially low value, Big Macs cost less than purchasing power parity predicts.

expensive. Other Americans, however, welcomed a weaker dollar. In this section, we explore some reasons for and consequences of the weakening dollar.

In early 2005, the dollar stood near record lows against the euro, the yen, and most other foreign currencies. The cause is not hard to find: The record current account deficits seen in Table 32.1 created an excess supply of dollars on currency markets. This, in turn, caused the dollar to weaken.

The declining value of the dollar also had political fallout. It led to resentment among Europeans, who were irate at the fact that their products were now more expensive, and thus harder to sell, on the U.S. market. They blamed the U.S. government for tolerating the declining value of the dollar. Some more extreme parties even went so far as to say that the U.S. government had engineered the decline of the dollar by buying euros on currency markets, thereby artificially pushing the supply of dollars to the right. In essence, they accused the United States of following a **beggar-thy-neighbor policy**, which seeks to boost a nation's economy at the expense of its trading partners. One way to do this is by systematically undervaluing its currency. Foreign countries are unlikely to be understanding when faced with such a policy. Sure enough, some EU countries threatened to retaliate with tariffs, quotas, or other policies designed to protect their own industries. The declining value of the dollar may have damaged political and economic relations with several European countries.

A weak dollar could also damage the U.S. economy, even if the European Union did not respond in kind. U.S. households and firms are hurt, because they must pay more for imported goods as well as for domestically manufactured goods that use imported inputs. Unfortunately, there is no easy way out of this dilemma. Any policy to strengthen the dollar would only worsen the trade deficit that caused the initial problem. The continued deficit would cause the dollar to weaken again.

Beggar-thy-neighbor policy
When a nation seeks to boost the domestic economy at the expense of a country's trading partners.

LifeLessons

Profiting from Price Differences

While the law of one price and purchasing power parity hold in the long run, short-term differences frequently appear. These can be due to institutional factors, such as taxes or governmental regulations, or due to market imperfections, such as the lack of complete information. Suppose that some individuals or firms have better information than is generally available on the market or are better positioned to act on the available information. They can exploit differences in price and make significant profits. The simple rule is to "buy low and sell high"—buy the good where it is selling at a low price and then sell it in places where it is selling at a high price. In terms of the Big Mac Index in Figure 32.4, suppose you could buy 10,000 Big Macs in Beijing for $1.20 each and quickly transport them to Zurich, Switzerland. If you then sell them in Zurich for $5.02 each, you could make a quick profit of over $38,000. The purchase and sale of goods—ranging from oil to currencies—to exploit differences in prices on markets is known as **arbitrage**. Arbitrage shifts goods and resources from places where they have less value (as reflected by the low price) to places where they have greater value (the high price). Arbitragers are thus in the enviable position of making a profit and helping society as a whole by following the simple maxim "buy low and sell high."

Fixed Exchange Rates

Arbitrage
Buying a good where its value is low, and selling where its value is high.

Fixed exchange rate
A system that sets the price of currencies at a predetermined level.

In a **fixed exchange rate** system, each nation's currency trades at a predetermined price. Early in the twentieth century, most nations rigidly fixed their exchange rates. Today, only a few countries do so. Moreover, these countries typically fix their exchange rates against a single currency, such as the U.S. dollar. In this section, we review past and contemporary examples of fixed exchange rate systems, including the gold standard and recent events in China and Argentina.

The Gold Standard. At the dawn of the twentieth century, most industrial nations had set their exchange rates according to the *gold standard*. The gold standard set the value of a country's currency in terms of gold. With an ounce of gold worth a fixed amount of each country's currency, the countries effectively fixed the value of their currencies against each other as well. Suppose that the United States set the price of gold at $400 per ounce while Argentina set the value of gold at 1,140 pesos per ounce. You could effectively exchange dollars for pesos by buying and selling gold. In this case, one dollar would buy $\frac{1}{400}$ ounce of gold, which one could sell in Argentina for $\frac{1}{400} \times 1,140$ pesos, or 2.85 pesos.

Devalue
Reduce the value of a nation's currency.

During the Great Depression of the 1930s, many countries tried to stimulate their economies by devaluing their currencies. A country **devalues** its currency when it reduces the value of its currency. The United States might, for example, have devalued the dollar to 2.50 pesos per dollar. This step would make Argentinean imports more expensive and U.S. exports to Argentina cheaper, presumably stimulating U.S. production and employment. Unfortunately, in the 1930s, as soon as one country devalued its currency, other countries did the same to protect their own industries.

So many countries devalued their currencies that fixed exchange rates effectively disappeared.

The Bretton Woods Agreement. In July 1944, as World War II was drawing to a close, representatives of the Western industrial nations assembled at the New Hampshire resort town of Bretton Woods and attempted to replace the gold standard. Because the United States held three-fourths of the world's gold reserves after World War II, it was no longer possible to return to the gold standard. Instead, the international community effectively replaced gold with the U.S. dollar as the international yardstick for fixed exchange rates. While all currencies were defined in terms of gold, only the U.S. dollar was convertible into gold (at the price of $35 per ounce).

The new fixed exchange rates system eventually broke down, due to persistent U.S. trade deficits. Because of these deficits, the United States was continually sending dollars or gold abroad. In 1971, U.S. gold holdings became so low that it feared it would not be able to pay for its imports. To prevent a crisis, the United States declared that it would no longer exchange dollars for gold. In addition, it would no longer fix the exchange rate at $35 per ounce.

Get Ahead of the Curve

Assess China's July 2005 decision to revalue its currency after many years of fixing its exchange rate.

Pegged exchange rate
Fixes the value of one currency against one or several other currencies.

China's Pegged Exchange Rate. In the first half of 2005, U.S. concern over China's attempt to fix its exchange rate came to a head. Ironically, the United States' complaints about China sounded almost exactly like Europe's complaints about the United States. Much of Europe complained that the U.S. dollar was declining against the euro, making their goods and services more expensive than Europeans felt they should be. The United States complained that the dollar did *not* decline against China's yuan despite the record trade deficits (noted in the previous chapter), making U.S.-made goods and services more expensive than Americans felt they should be. The dollar failed to decline because the Chinese government followed a policy of *pegging* the yuan to the dollar. A **pegged exchange rate** fixes the value of one currency against one or several other currencies. Since the mid-1990s, the yuan had been pegged at 8.28 yuan per dollar. The Chinese government had managed the peg by buying U.S. dollars on currency markets, as illustrated in Figure 32.5.

The U.S. trade deficit with China would ordinarily cause the price of dollars to fall. The demand for Chinese goods would shift the supply of dollars right from S_0 to S_1 and cause the price of dollars in Figure 32.5 to fall from 8.28 to 8.00 yuan per dollar and the quantity of dollars exchanged to rise from $3 billion to $4 billion. When the Chinese government buys dollars, it offsets this supply shift by shifting the demand for dollars rightward from D_0 to D_1. As a result, the exchange rate remains 8.28 yuan per dollar, while the equilibrium quantity of dollars exchanged rises to $5 billion.

With China pegging its currency at 8.28 yuan per dollar, the dollar did not weaken against the yuan, and the United States continued to import far more from China than it exported. This led to economic and diplomatic tensions with China, as U.S. industries called for protection against what they regarded as unfair trade practices. Facing threats of retaliation by the United States, China slightly relaxed its peg in July of 2005, allowing the yuan to rise to about 8.11 yuan per dollar.

Argentina's Pegged Exchange Rate

Like China, Argentina tried to peg its currency to the dollar. Unfortunately, its attempt led to more than strained diplomatic relations. The collapse of Argentina's economy in the early 2000s stemmed in part from its attempt to keep the peso unrealistically strong.

FIGURE 32.5

The Pegged Exchange Rate Requires Intervention

If exchange rates were free to float, the U.S. trade deficit with China would shift the supply of dollars to the right from S_0 to S_1. The resulting equilibrium price of dollars drops from 8.28 yuan per dollar to 8.00 yuan dollar. The Chinese government did not allowed this to happen. It pegged the yuan to the dollar by buying dollars on currency markets. The policy shifted the demand for dollars to the right, from D_0 to D_1, pushing its price back up to 8.28 yuan/per dollar and the quantity up to $5 billion.

As part of its effort to stabilize prices in the 1990s, the Argentinean government pegged the peso to the U.S. dollar at a level of one peso per dollar. The peg did not automatically stabilize prices in Argentina. Instead, it provided a public commitment by the Argentinean government to keep prices stable and a readily observable signal as to whether the government was living up to its commitment. Recall that if prices rose faster in Argentina than in the United States, the peso would depreciate if exchange rates float. By pegging the peso to the dollar, the Argentinean government was effectively promising to adopt policies that would keep prices stable.

Initially, the policy seemed a remarkable success, and Argentinean prices stayed in check from 1994 through 2000. Unfortunately, trouble loomed. The precise origins of the disaster that followed remain subject to debate. Most economists, however, agree that by the late 1990s the peso had become severely **overvalued**, meaning the official value of the peso was higher than its equilibrium price would have been on currency markets. Had floating exchange rates been in effect, the peso would have been worth only about 28 cents.

Setting the price of the peso artificially high made Argentinean exports to the United States artificially expensive and made imports from the United States artificially inexpensive. To make matters worse, the U.S. dollar itself had appreciated relative to many of the world's currencies in the late 1990s. Pegging to a strong dollar made the peso strong against other nation's currencies as well. Pegging the peso at one peso per dollar encouraged Argentineans to buy imported goods and discouraged foreigners from buying Argentinean goods. The result was a steadily worsening trade imbalance, as imports far outpaced exports. Lower international demand for Argentinean goods contributed to a severe economic downturn in Argentina in the late 1990s.

To maintain the overvalued exchange rate when the equilibrium price was much lower, the Argentinean government had to continually buy pesos on currency markets. As a result, Argentina began to deplete its holdings of foreign currency. In effect, it maintained the artificially high price of the peso relative to the dollar (and

Overvalued
Describes a currency whose official value is greater than its equilibrium price on currency markets.

other currencies) by doing the opposite of the Chinese government in Figure 32.5. China bought dollars to keep the yuan weak. Argentina supplied dollars (and other currencies) to international currency markets to keep the peso strong. The key difference was that the Chinese could print increasing amounts of yuan to buy dollars. The Argentineans, on the other hand, had only a limited amount of foreign currency with which to buy pesos.

The Argentinean government's policy of buying pesos could not have gone on forever. The government was deeply in debt to foreign lenders. Eventually, its lenders demanded repayment *in their own currencies*. Because Argentina had already depleted its supply of foreign currencies, it needed to buy foreign currencies with pesos. Doing so, however, would undermine the pegged rate of the peso. Buying foreign currencies, rather than selling them, would drive the value of the peso below the pegged level. Argentina was unwilling to abandon the policy of pegging its currency to the dollar in order to repay its loans. Instead, it took out additional loans in order to repay the ones that were currently due, and the debt grew larger and larger. Finally, in 2001, Argentina's debt was so great that it could no longer pay even the interest on its loans, so it defaulted on them. When it finally reached an agreement on repaying its loans in early 2002, Argentina had to abandon the pegged rate of one peso per dollar. The value of the peso fell sharply, which caused the prices of Argentina's imports to rise steeply. Because the Argentinean economy depended so heavily on imports, many Argentinean firms and households were suddenly unable to afford basic goods and services, and an entire country was impoverished overnight.

TEST + *EXTEND* Your Knowledge

1. TEST Go to the Yahoo! Currency Converter at finance.yahoo.com/currency to find the current exchange rate between the currencies of the nations listed in Figure 32.4 and the U.S. dollar. Do the values in the Big Mac Index still reflect PPP?

2. EXTEND Use what you have learned about PPP and China's pegging of the yuan to the dollar to explain why the price of Big Macs in Beijing was so much lower than prices elsewhere.

▶ Financial Crises and the International Monetary Fund

One of the most disturbing aspects of the Argentinean disaster was the inability of the international community to prevent it. In this section, we look at the international institution charged with preventing such financial crises, the International Monetary Fund (IMF).

The International Monetary Fund

From its founding in 1944 until the world adopted floating exchange rates in 1971, the IMF's mission was to support the system of fixed exchange rates. In particular, it provided assistance to nations that were having difficulty maintaining their exchange rates. It supplied loans to help countries through temporary trade imbalances and aid to countries that had to devalue their currencies.

The Changing Role of the International Monetary Fund. With most of the world using floating exchange rates, there has been less need for exchange rate stabilization over the last 35 years. The IMF now sees itself as "a manager of financial crises in emerging markets, a long-term lender to many developing countries and former Communist countries, an advisor and counsel to many nations, and a collector and disseminator of economic data on its 184 member countries."[2] The IMF thus plays an increasingly large role in the economic affairs of countries that face financial difficulties. The shifting mission of the IMF and the controversy over how it has performed its new tasks have put it at the center of the debate over globalization.

Debates Over the International Monetary Fund. Critics of the IMF claim that it has overstepped its authority and dictated policy to democratically elected governments. Further, they maintain that the IMF's policies have often done more harm than good. Supporters of the IMF respond that such criticism is unjust. They point out that the IMF does not push aside national governments. Instead, it intervenes only when invited to assist a nation in crisis. Frequently, these crises result from unwise or corrupt economic practices by the member nation itself. Cutting back on bloated government bureaucracies or eliminating subsidies to inefficient industries that a nation can no longer afford may create considerable short-term hardship. However, according to IMF supporters, such measures are necessary to stimulate long-term growth.

Both sides in the debate over IMF policies have found plenty of evidence for their positions in the IMF's handling of the Argentinean crisis. After supplying a steady stream of loans to Argentina's government, the IMF refused to supply any more without major economic reforms. Rather than submit to the IMF's demands, the government defaulted on its loans. Critics say the IMF bullied successive governments and undermined the democratic process in Argentina. Defenders point out that the Argentinean government's failure to manage its budget contributed greatly to the crisis and led directly to the IMF's intervention.

Strategy and Policy
The Asian Meltdown

International financial crises need not be restricted to a single nation. In some cases, sudden international monetary flows can cause an economic crisis to spread like an epidemic that knows no international boundaries. In 1997 and 1998, just such a contagion struck several East Asian economies.

In the summer of 1997, the citizens of South Korea had great reason to be proud. In about two generations, their country had gone from being one of the poorest countries in the world to being a major economic power. That July, the price of Thailand's currency, the baht, suddenly collapsed in international currency markets. Initially, observers thought this was a relatively minor, local financial hiccup that would have little lasting impact. Within a year, however, real GDP per capita in Thailand and four other East Asian countries (South Korea, Malaysia, Indonesia, and the Philippines) had fallen and unemployment had risen sharply. The sudden decline was even more remarkable because there was no obvious weakness in the East Asian economies.

Some of the blame for the sudden financial collapse must be laid at the countries' own doorsteps. A lack of openness in business dealings (what analysts call

---

[2] The Meltzer Commission Final Report: "The Future of the IMF and the World Bank," www.house.gov/jec/imf/meltzer.htm.

transparency) had allowed many banks and related financial institutions to engage in unwise investment strategies and outright corruption.

The crisis began when a major real estate developer in Thailand declared bankruptcy and was unable to pay back its loans to several local banks. While unwise, these loans were not large enough that defaulting on them would necessarily touch off a financial disaster. The problem was that the banks, and other Asian businesses, had taken out large short-term loans from foreign lenders. With no income coming in from their bad loans, the banks had trouble paying back their own debts. Fearing that other banks would also have trouble repaying their loans, foreign lenders cut back sharply on the loans they made to Thai banks and to other banks in the region. The lenders' insistence on being repaid in their own currencies further compounded the problem. Many banks did not have sufficient foreign currencies on hand.

Another possible cause of the crisis was the deregulation of the countries' financial markets. The deregulation allowed lenders and investors to deposit and withdraw funds quickly and easily. Unfortunately, these countries had yet to develop safeguards to cope with the instability that such flows introduced. Thailand's crisis spread to other countries when lenders began to fear that Thailand would not be able to repay its loans and that nearby countries, which had also borrowed heavily, would soon be in similar danger. In an attempt to protect themselves, lenders tried to pull their money out of Thailand and other East Asian nations. However, this behavior increased the likelihood that the countries would default on their loans, despite being financially healthy. The behavior resembled a bank run, when depositors try to withdraw all of their money at once.

The IMF responded to the East Asian nations' pleas for help in repaying their creditors by setting several conditions for aid. It insisted on much-needed structural reforms that would increase the transparency or openness of financial transactions. In addition, the IMF demanded that the countries cut government spending to balance their budgets. A balanced budget would assure investors that the country was solvent and improve the investment climate. Unfortunately, balancing the budget often means that governments must cut back on expenditures. The cuts frequently come from programs that help the nation's poorest citizens.

Critical-Thinking Questions

1. In what way was the Asian crisis like a typical run on a bank? In what way did it differ?
2. What policies would you recommend to prevent a future sudden collapse in exchange rates?

▶ SUMMARY

- **Exchange rates and currency markets.** Currency markets allow people in one country to buy goods and services produced in another country. Currency markets determine the exchange rate based on the forces of supply and demand.

- **The balance of payments.** The balance of payments measures flows of money across a nation's borders. Economists divide the balance of payments into the current account and the capital account. A surplus or a deficit on one of these accounts must be balanced by a deficit or a surplus on the other account, so the balance of payments is always zero. Currency markets ensure that a balance occurs.

- **Exchange rate systems.** A country whose exchange rates are set on currency markets follows a floating exchange rate system. Purchasing power parity (PPP) holds that in the long run, identical goods cost the same in countries with flexible exchange rates. In the past, countries relied on the gold standard and a system of fixed exchange rates. In recent years, China and Argentina pegged their currencies, keeping a fixed exchange rate with the U.S. dollar.

- **Financial crises and the International Monetary Fund.** The IMF was founded to help countries deal with fixed exchange rates. Today, it helps nations deal with financial crises. Its critics say that its policies have made problems worse, while others believe that the IMF is unduly blamed for the bad policies of the countries it tries to help.

►KEY TERMS

Appreciate 814
Arbitrage 823
Balance of payments 815
Beggar-thy-neighbor policy 822
Capital account 816
Current account 816

Currency market 812
Depreciate 814
Devalue 823
Exchange rate 813
Fixed exchange rate 823
Floating exchange rate 819

International Monetary Fund (IMF) 811
Law of One Price 820
Overvalued 825
Pegged exchange rate 824
Purchasing power parity (PPP) 821

►PROBLEMS

1. How do currency markets make it easier to buy goods and services produced in a foreign country?
2. Suppose that the price of a dollar on Japanese currency markets was 150 yen per dollar in 2005.
   a. Use supply and demand curves to show how this exchange rate might arise.
   b. Show what happens to the price of a dollar if the demand for dollars falls.
   c. Why is the demand curve for dollars by Japanese downward-sloping? Why is the supply curve of dollars to the Japanese upward-sloping?
3. Suppose that a new Japanese videogame craze strikes the United States and that millions of U.S. consumers buy this Japanese-made item. Use supply and demand curves in the market for U.S. dollars to show the impact of the game on the price of the dollar in terms of yen.
4. Consider what happens in Figure 32.2 from Marta's point of view. That is, look at the market for pesos rather than the market for dollars.
   a. Who is demanding pesos? Who is demanding dollars?
   b. What happens on this market when Americans decide to buy more Argentinean goods and services?
5. Which of the following people is helped by a weaker dollar and which is hurt? Justify your answer.
   a. An American tourist in Singapore
   b. An American farmer who wants to sell wheat to Danish bakers
   c. A Volvo dealer in Wisconsin
6. Suppose that people expect the dollar to depreciate against the euro. How will this expectation affect currency markets?
7. If the dollar depreciates relative to the euro, what is happening at the same time to the euro relative to the dollar? Justify your answer.
8. Assume that Canadian hockey teams receive their revenue in Canadian dollars and pay their salaries in U.S. dollars. What happens to the profits of Canadian hockey teams when the Canadian dollar depreciates relative to the dollar?

9. The kingdom of Florin spends $100 billion on imports and receives $85 billion for its exports. It pays $5 billion more to other countries than it receives in interest. It receives $10 billion more than it makes in transfer payments. What is the status of its current account? of its capital account? of its balance of payments?

10. Using the data from Table 32.1, suppose that the weakening dollar caused net exports to go from –$624 billion to –$450 billion, and that aid to Iraq and poor countries in Asia caused net transfers to go from –$80 billion to –$150 billion. Assuming that the net return on assets and the statistical error were unchanged, what would happen to the capital account?

11. How would an increase in the capital account surplus affect a household in Idaho that is trying to decide whether to buy an imported or domestically produced car?

12. How does the fact that the U.S. government borrows so much from other countries affect its capital account? How would this borrowing translate through currency markets to affect the U.S. current account?

13. Suppose the 2006 World Cup soccer tournament attracts large numbers of American tourists to Germany to watch the tournament.
    a. What would be the impact on Germany's current account for the balance of payments? On its capital account?
    b. Show the impact on the exchange rate between the dollar and the euro.

14. Why does the law of one price hold for a single product in a local market? Why does it hold across national boundaries?

15. How does the Big Mac Index reflect purchasing power parity? Why doesn't it reflect PPP perfectly?

16. How did beggar-thy-neighbor policies acquire their name? What dangers are there in following such a policy?

17. How did the gold standard encourage international trade in the nineteenth and early twentieth centuries?

18. Both depreciation and devaluation of the dollar result in a lower value of the dollar versus other currencies. What is the difference between these two terms?

19. Pegging the yuan to the dollar seemed to work for China, but pegging the peso to the dollar was disastrous for Argentina. Why did these policies have such different outcomes?

20. Why do critics of the IMF say that it worsened Argentina's economic crisis? How would defenders of the IMF respond?

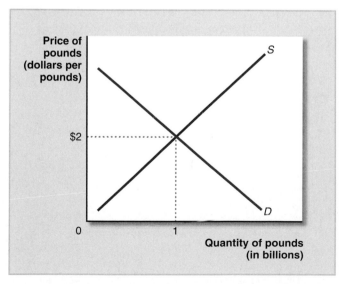

STUDY GUIDE

myeconlab

HERE'S HOW MyEconLab CAN HELP YOU GET A BETTER GRADE

1. Log into MyEconLab and take Practice Test 32-A (to log in for the first time, see page 30 for instructions).

2. Based on your test results, MyEconLab will identify the areas where you need further work and create a personal Study Plan for you.

3. Your Study Plan contains the exercises listed below and others like them that will target the specific chapter topics you need to focus on. You'll receive instant feedback and find links to tutorials, animations, and the online textbook to help you study.

4. When you're ready, go take Practice Test 32-B and demonstrate how your results have improved.

Section 32.1, Exercise 1 Consider the market for British pounds (£) as shown in the following graph. Draw a new graph showing the effect of each of the following changes, and state what happens to the value of the dollar and the value of the pound in each case.

a. More U.S. tourists wish to visit London.
b. British citizens wish to buy fewer U.S. computers due to improved products at home.
c. U.S. movies become more popular overseas.
d. U.S. consumers discover that British jam tastes better than U.S. jam.

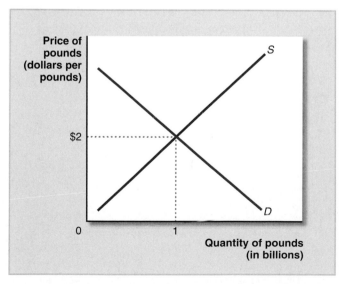

Section 32.1, Exercise 2 A high price of the dollar in terms of other currencies is known as a strong dollar. Is a strong dollar a desirable thing for everyone in the U.S.?

Section 32.2, Exercise 1 Indicate whether each of the following transactions is part of the U.S. current account or the U.S. capital account, and whether each is a receipt from the rest of the world or a payment to the rest of the world.

a. Your grandmother in Paris, France, sends you some money for your birthday.
b. A U.S. citizen buys a Ferrari automobile from Italy.
c. You buy stock in Sony, a Japanese corporation.
d. A citizen of the United Kingdom buys U.S. treasury bills.

Section 32.2, Exercise 2 Suppose that the U.S. balance of payments is zero at the current exchange rate. If U.S. consumers increase their demand for foreign goods, what will happen to:

a. The balance of payments if the exchange rate is constant?
b. The value of the dollar, once exchange rates have time to adjust?
c. The balance of payments, once exchange rates have time to adjust?

Section 32.3, Exercise 1 Suppose that £1 trades for $2. If the price of gold is $400 per ounce in New York, and there are no transportation costs, what must the price of gold in London be?

Section 32.3, Exercise 2 Now suppose that £1 trades for $1.82. The price of a Big Mac in New York City is $3.99.

a. According to purchasing power parity, what should the price of a Big Mac be in London, England?

b. The actual price of a Big Mac in London is £1.99. Would it be better (in terms of being able to buy relatively more things) to be a London tourist coming to New York or a New Yorker going to London?

Section 32.3, Exercise 3 Refer to the currency market presented in Section 32.1, Exercise 1. Draw a new graph showing the effect of each of the following changes, and state what happens to the value of the dollar and the value of the pound in each case.

a. U.S. citizens expect the value of the pound to be lower in the future.
b. The British central bank buys dollars and sells pounds in exchange.
c. Higher U.S. interest rates make U.S. stocks and bonds more attractive to overseas investors.

Section 32.4, Exercise 1 Why do countries want to borrow funds from the IMF?

Credits

Page 2–3, David Young-Wolff/Photo Edit; Page 6, Getty Images; Page 9 (left), Rebecca Ferris-Caruso; Page 9 (top center), PhotoDisc; Page 9 (bottom center), Brand X Pictures; Page 9 (far right), PhotoDisc Red; Page 15, Reuters NewMedia Inc./Corbis/Bettmann; Page 32–33, Getty Images; Page 36 (left), PhotoDisc Blue; Page 36 (right), PhotoDisc Red; Page 40, K. J. Historical/Corbis; Page 59, Getty Images; Page 69 (top left), Corbis RF; Page 69 (bottom left), Photo courtesy of Peter von Allmen and Jacob Schneck (Keith Brown pictured); Page 69 (right), PhotoDisc Blue; Page 71, AP/WideWorld Photos; Page 78–79, © Ariel Skelley/Corbis; Page 87 (left), Coca-Cola C2, the Contour Bottle design and the Dynamic Ribbon are trademarks of The Coca-Cola Company and used with its express permission; Page 87 (right), Pepsi-Cola North America; Page 102 (right), Barnes & Noble.com; Page 112–113, Getty Images; Page 127 (left), Dennis MacDonald/Photo Edit; Page 127 (right), © David H. Wells/Corbis; Page 136, AP/WideWorld Photos; Page 142–143, © G. Schuster/zefa/Corbis; Page 154, © Will & Deni McIntyre/Corbis; Page 158, AP/WideWorld Photos; Page 166–167, HIRB/IndexStock; Page 173, Ingolf Pompe/Aurora; Page 180, © NBAE/Getty Images; Page 198–199, Photo courtesy of C. F. Martin & Co., Inc.; Page 204, Photo courtesy of C. F. Martin & Co., Inc.; Page 226–227, © Dave Bartruff, Inc./Corbis; Page 242 (left and right), AP/WideWorld Photos; Page 244, AP/WideWorld Photos; Page 252–253, © Reuters/Corbis; Page 264 (left), © Terry Auspitz; Page 264 (right), Sumeet Garg, M.D.; Page 280–281, © Bob Krist/Corbis; Page 284 (left), © Royalty-Free/Corbis; Page 284 (top right), Getty Images; Page 284 (bottom right), Richard Embery/Pearson Education/PH College; Page 295 (left), Marjorie Farrell/The Image Works; Page 295 (right), Laimute Druskis/Pearson Education/PH College; Page 304–305, © JLP/Sylvia Torres/zefa/Corbis; Page 312, David Parket/Omni-Photo Communications, Inc.; Page 313, (left) © L. Nelson/Stock Photos/zefa/Corbis; Page 313 (right), Rob Melnychuk/Getty Images Inc.; Page 332–333, Getty Images; Page 349, Getty Images; Page 356–357, © Kim Kulish/Corbis; Page 364, © Randy Faris/Corbis; Page 378–379, © Jon Feingersh/Corbis; Page 388, © Corbis; Page 388, © Bettmann/Corbis; Page 396 (left), © Natalie Fobes/Corbis; Page 396 (right), Alexis Rosenfeld/Photo Researchers, Inc.; Page 406–407, AP/WideWorld Photos; Page 418 (left), © Helen King/Corbis; Page 418 (center), © Royalty-Free/Corbis; Page 418 (right), LWA-Dann Tardif/Corbis; Page 420, © Bettmann/Corbis; Page 426, Tim Boyle/Getty Images; Page 434–435, © Lowell Georgia/Corbis; Page 446 (right), © George D. Lepp/Corbis; Page 452 (left), Phil Mislinski/SuperStock; Page 452 (right), James Havey/IndexStock; Page 458–459, photo courtesy of University of Houston Cullen College of Engineering; Page 461, Flying Colours Ltd/Getty Images; Page 469, AP photo/Stuart Ramson; Page 476 (left), © Corbis; Page 476 (right), Getty Images; Page 482–483, Marketing Communications Pearson Addison-Wesley; Page 486, Getty Images; Page 493 (left), Getty Images; Page 493 (right), © Corbis; Page 504–505, © Corbis; Page 508, AP/WideWorld Photos; Page 520, © Corbis; Page 532–533, Anderson Ross/Getty Images; Page 536 (left), Lisa Romerein/Getty Images; Page 536 (right), Dorling Kindersley Media Library; Page 556, Ken Huang/Getty Images; Page 567, The Image Works; Page 574, Richard I'Anson/Getty Images; Page 580, Hulton Archive/Getty Images; Page 590–591, Universal/The Kobal Collection; Page 594, © Bettman/Corbis; Page 600, The Advertising Archives; Page 616–617, Marketing Communications Pearson Addison-Wesley;

Answers to Odd-Numbered Problems

Chapter 1

1. The economic factors include the tuition, room, board, and transportation costs; the amount of financial aid that you are offered; and the salary you might expect to earn from employment based on attending that school. Non-economic factors are things such as whether you have friends that attend the school, how much you like the campus atmosphere, the available social activities, and the quality of the sports teams.

3. Positive decisions include comparing the cost of this form of disposal (including the cost of the drums and the cost of transporting them to the area of the ocean where they will be dumped) to other available disposal methods, such as a land-fill. Normative issues include whether citizens of a particular country should have the right to use the open ocean for dumping and the value of the aquatic environment that would be spoiled if a container leaked.

5. Central planning does not work well as an economic system because it does not allocate resources based on market forces. Thus it ignores the opportunity cost of resources used to produce goods and services. As a result, materials that might have been put to a highly valued use (due to high consumer demand) might instead be used to produce goods that consumers do not value as highly. In a market economy, producers have an incentive (profits) to use resources in such a way as to maximize their value.

7. The number of classes you would take would depend on the opportunity cost of your time and the cost of necessary textbooks and supplies. All else equal, the more valuable your time is, the fewer classes you would choose to take.

9. To maximize your level of satisfaction, you will continue to consume slices of pizza until the marginal benefit declines to the point where it is below the marginal cost.

Chapter 1 Appendix

1A. The slope of the line is 2. For every one-unit increase in X, there is a two-unit increase in Y.

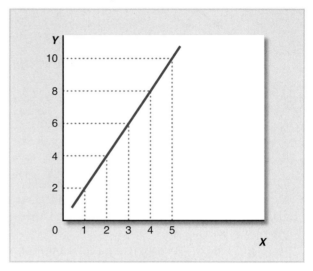

3A. The Y-intercept of the original line is 20. It reaches the X-axis where X = 10. When the intercept increases to 30, the line shifts to the right, remaining parallel to the original line, with no change in slope.

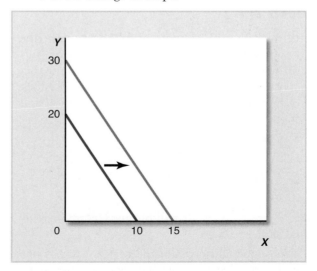

5A. When the slope of the line doubles, the line becomes steeper at every point. The Y-intercept does not change. When X increases from 4 to 5, Y increases by 2, from 18 to 20.

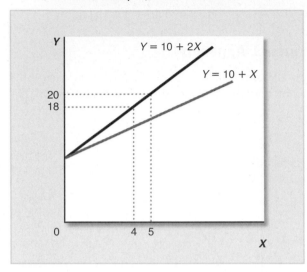

7A. To calculate the percentage change in income, we subtract the original value from the new value, divide by the original value, and then multiply the result by 100:

Percentage change = [($800 − $400)/$400]100 = 100%

9A. False. We cannot determine the number of individuals employed using only the percentage of workers who are unemployed.

Chapter 2

1. People typically acquire human capital (the knowledge that allows them to produce output) through education and training. A nation with a constant population can thus increase its stock of human capital by fostering the education and training of its population.

3. a. Coal: land.

   b. Reading ability: labor (human capital)

   c. A cement mixer: capital

   d. An auto mechanic: labor

   e. A president of a small business: entrepreneurial skill

5. The opportunity cost of the first hot dog is one hamburger, because hamburger production must fall from 10 to 9 in order to produce the first hot dog. The opportunity cost of increasing hot dog production from 2 to 3 is 2 hamburgers, because hamburger production must fall from 8 to 6 to achieve the increase in hot dog production.

7. An allocation demonstrates productive efficiency when all the resources in the economy are fully employed in the most efficient manner: that is, when no resources go unused, and we cannot increase the production of any good without sacrificing production of another good.

   A productively efficient solution, however, is not necessarily equitable. Indeed, consider a shared pizza. Giving the whole pizza to one person is productively efficient (as long as the person eats it all), as none of the pizza is wasted. Few people would agree that such a solution is equitable or fair, particularly if everyone else is hungry.

9. The benefit of specializing in consumption goods in the near term is that consumers will have more goods and services such as appliances, clothing, automobiles, and furniture. The cost of this decision is that the nation's productive capacity will not increase as much as that of a nation that specializes in capital goods.

11. The greater wealth of some members of society does not necessarily mean that economic activity was either allocatively or productively inefficient. Allocative efficiency, or when an economy produces the combination of goods and services that it values most highly, and productive efficiency, or when all of the economy's resources are fully employed, may still hold. Their increase could result from making use of special talents or from good luck. Further, the greater wealth of some members of society does not necessarily either mean that the economic activity was inequitable. The differences in wealth might be an indication of inequity or unfair allocations, but might also reflect that society's particular concept of fairness.

13. a. With no trade, the marginal cost of producing an additional shirt for Rodney is the number of hats he does not produce when he makes the shirt; that is, three hats. Conversely, the marginal cost to Rodney of producing an additional hat is $1/_3$ shirt. The marginal cost of producing an additional shirt for Laura is the number of hats she does not produce when she makes the shirt, or one hat. The marginal cost for Laura to produce an additional hat is one shirt.

    b. Rodney has a comparative advantage in producing hats, as his marginal cost is lower in terms of shirts forgone. Laura has a comparative advantage in producing shirts, as her marginal cost is lower in terms of hats forgone.

Chapter 3

1. a. Wages and salaries are a payment from firms to labor in the resource market of the circular flow.

   b. Medicare payment is a transfer payment to households.

3. The circular flow model shows that if businesses are taxed, households will be affected also. The taxes that the firm pays leak out of the circular flow. It has less to spend on the resource market, so less money flows to households.

5. When Becky purchases the doll, she sends funds from the household sector to the firms in the product market. The firm in turn pays some of those funds to Becky's neighbor (back into the household sector) through the resource market in the form of wages. Other households receive funds from the interest, rent, or profits that the firm pays on the resource market.

7. Net exports are the difference between the market value of exports minus the market value of imports. They are negative when a nation has a trade deficit.

9. The remaining goods and services are purchased by firms as investment, purchased by the government, or sold as exports to other countries.

11. When the government runs a deficit, it must borrow. It borrows the funds it needs by selling securities.

13. They are not included as expenditures because no goods or services are exchanged in return. Instead, they are counted as transfer payments.

15. When you deposit savings in a bank, most of those funds become available for the bank to make loans to borrowers. These loans help people to make expenditures that they wouldn't otherwise be able to afford. The leakage from the circular flow that your savings causes is replaced by the expenditures of the borrowers who receive the funds.

17. a. During that period, the United States would have a $4 billion trade surplus ($10 billion − $6 billion = $4 billion) with Australia.

    b. The net surplus increases the level of economic activity in the United States by adding to the payments to firms. These funds in turn also flow to households as wages.

Chapter 4

1. a. Cream is a complement of coffee. A decrease in the price of cream for use with coffee thus causes an increase in demand for coffee at each price. The demand curve shifts to the right.

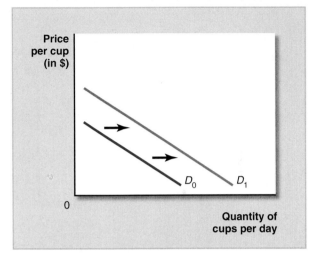

   b. Assuming that coffee is a normal good, a decrease in income causes a decrease in demand for coffee at each price. The demand curve shifts to the left.

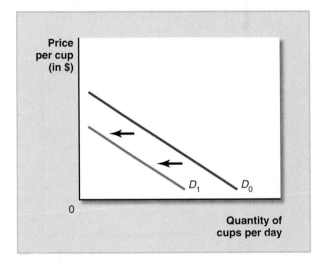

c. The development of a new drink that is caffeinated and tastes similar to coffee causes a decrease in demand for coffee at each price, because some people who initially drank coffee have now switched to the new drink, a coffee substitute. The demand curve shifts to the left.

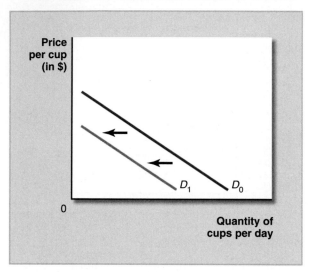

d. An expectation on the part of coffee buyers of future higher prices causes an increase in demand for coffee at each price, as people stock up on coffee in the present to avoid future higher prices. The demand curve shifts to the right.

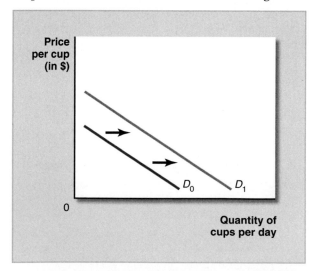

3. A change in the quantity demanded of running shoes results from a change in price. It is illustrated by a movement along the demand curve. A change in the demand for running shoes results from a change in consumers' incomes, in

prices of complements or substitutes, in tastes and preferences, in expectations about future prices, or in the number of consumers in the market. It is illustrated by a shift in the entire demand curve.

5. When the number of consumers in the market increases, demand increases. We show this as a rightward shift of the demand curve. The equilibrium price and quantity both increase. Here, we show the price increasing to $\$P_1$ per cup, and the equilibrium quantity increasing to Q_1 cups per day.

7. a. At $30 per pair of shorts, quantity demanded falls to zero.

b. If shorts are free, consumers would take 600 pairs of shorts.

c. When the price increases from $20 to $25 per pair of shorts, quantity demanded falls from 200 to 100.

d. Assuming that shorts are a normal good, the entire demand curve will shift to the right if consumer income increases: Consumers will buy more pairs of shorts at every price.

9. a. The equilibrium price is $2,000. The equilibrium quantity is 2,000 tractors.

b.

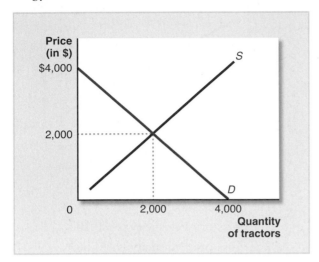

11. If a hurricane destroys much of the crop, the supply of coffee in the United States will fall, which we show as a shift of the supply curve leftward from S_0 to S_1. Producers from other countries are actually made better off, because the decrease in supply causes prices to rise. Consumers are worse off, because prices increase from P_0 to P_1.

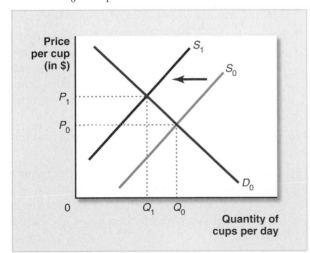

13. The original equilibrium is labeled E_0. The destruction of the coffee crop decreases supply, shifting the supply curve leftward to S_1. The introduction of the new importing country increases supply, shifting the supply curve rightward to S_2. The introduction of the new caffeinated drink that many consumers prefer to coffee causes a decrease in demand, shifting the demand curve

leftward to D_1. We cannot say with certainty where quantity and price will end up, because the final directions of change depend on the relative size of the shifts in demand and supply. In the following graph, the new equilibrium is E_1, at which price is lower than the initial equilibrium, but quantity is unchanged.

15. If the price were set above the equilibrium price, the quantity demanded would be less than the quantity supplied, resulting in a surplus. In order to restore the market to equilibrium, price would have to fall.

17. If supply were fixed at 300 pairs, the supply curve would be a vertical line at that quantity. The equilibrium price would be $15 per pair.

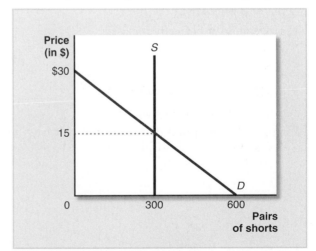

19. Without the Internet, the market for the book *Murder at Ebbets Field* is a thin market: There are so few buyers and sellers that demand and

supply are sporadic, and the buyers and sellers are not always in close contact with each other. The lack of known, well-defined supply and demand makes determining a fair price for the book difficult. The Internet now helps solve this problem by providing more information about demand and supply for different out-of-print books, and by bringing buyers and sellers into closer contact.

Thirty-three copies of *Murder at Ebbets Field* are available through the Barnes & Noble "Out of Print" book section of www.bn.com, starting at a price of $15.62 at the time of the writing of this text.

Chapter 5

1. a. Location and availability of other stations. Price differences are usually not large enough to justify driving significant distances to save merely a few cents per gallon.

   b. The product is highly perishable. As a result, the market is local.

   c. The cost of the product relative to the transportation cost of moving it makes its market worldwide.

   d. Live music must be consumed as it is produced. Because of this, the market is completely local.

   e. Books are relatively inexpensive to ship, making it easy for consumers to search nationally for the best prices over the Internet.

3. a. Demand is perfectly inelastic.

   b. The elasticity of demand is 0.6.

   c. The elasticity of demand is 0.5.

   d. Demand is perfectly elastic.

   e. The elasticity of demand is 1.0.

5. Using the midpoint formula, the elasticity of demand is $[(8 - 12)/10]/[(6 - 4)/5] = 1$.

7. a. The price elasticity is 1.5

   b. The cross-price elasticity is +0.10.

   c. The cross-price elasticity is +0.60.

   d. The cross-price elasticity is –0.60.

   e. The cross-price elasticity is –0.40.

   f. The cross-price elasticity is 0.

   Based on the cross-price elasticities, we can say that salads are weak substitutes for chicken sandwiches. Many consumers consider burgers to be substitutes for chicken sandwiches. Drinks and fries are complements to chicken sandwiches, and baked potatoes are independent.

9. For economists, the terms "luxury" and "necessity" are simply designations of elasticity values, rather than normative statements about goods. The concern is that what one consumer might believe is a necessity would be considered a luxury by another.

11. The cross elasticity is +0.80, indicating that butter and margarine are substitutes.

13. Although we expect to be positive, facial tissue is likely to have a very small income elasticity, as it is not the type of product that a consumer would seek to purchase more of when his or her income increases.

15. a. The cross-price elasticity is +2.0, indicating that the goods are substitutes.

    b. The cross-price elasticity is +1.0, indicating that the goods are substitutes.

    c. The cross-price elasticity is –2.0, indicating that the goods are complements.

    d. The income elasticity is +1.25, indicating that iPods are a normal good.

e. The price elasticity is 2.5, indicating that demand for iPods is elastic.

17. The elasticity of supply is 1.75, which is in the elastic range.

19. The supply elasticity is $[(37 - 30)/30]/[(\$6 - \$5)/\$5] = 1.167$.

Chapter 6

1. In panel (a) of the following figure, consumer surplus is shaded blue and producer surplus is shaded red. In panel (b), the $10 tax reduces both consumer and producer surplus. Most of the lost surplus becomes tax revenue for the government (shaded yellow). The area shaded in gray is deadweight loss. Although this is not always the case, we show the incidence of the tax split evenly between consumers and producers.

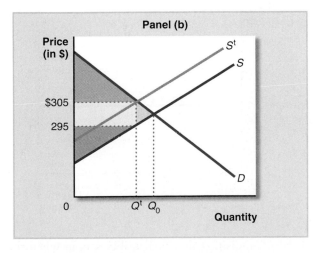

3. The following table shows the surplus for each consumer. The total surplus is $65.

Consumer	Marginal Benefit	Price	Consumer Surplus
Juanita	$50	$20	$30
James	45	20	25
Sunni	30	20	10
Marco	20	20	0

5. A marginal consumer is one for whom the price is just equal to the marginal benefit received by that consumer.

7. Some governments do not tax food and clothing because these are viewed as goods and services that consumers need for survival. Thus, a tax on food or clothing would have a disproportionately negative impact on consumers with low incomes, who must devote a very large share of their annual incomes to such goods.

9. The size of the deadweight loss triangle (shaded gray in the figure) is $\frac{1}{2}$ ($1.00 × 100), or $50 per day.

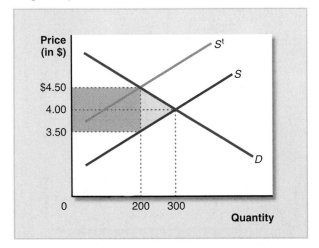

11. The short side of the market is the lesser of the quantity supplied or the quantity demanded. In the case of a market intervention, such as a price floor or ceiling, the new equilibrium quantity is determined by the short side of the market.

13. At an equilibrium price of $7.50, a price ceiling set at $8.00 would have no effect on the market.

15. In each panel in the following figure, the initial equilibrium price is P and the equilibrium quantity is Q. In panel (a), a price floor of P_f is set below P. Because the existing equilibrium is above the set floor, the price remains at P, and the equilibrium is unaffected. In panel (b), the price ceiling P_c is set above the equilibrium price, and so does not alter the equilibrium. In panel (c), the quota (Q_{max}) is greater than the equilibrium quantity, and so does not affect the equilibrium.

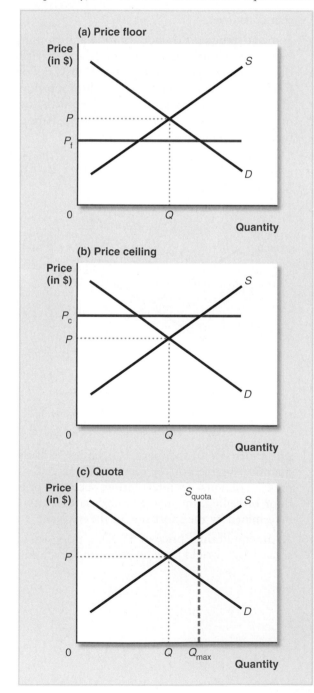

(a) Price floor

(b) Price ceiling

(c) Quota

Chapter 7

1. a.

b.

Pieces of Gum	Marginal Utility
0	–
1	20
2	25
3	15
4	10
5	5
6	0
7	−15

c.

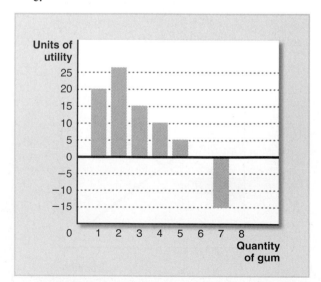

d. Diminishing marginal utility sets in when the marginal utility from the last unit consumed is less than the marginal utility of the previous unit. Diminishing marginal utility thus sets in after the second piece of gum: The marginal utility at three pieces of gum, 15, is smaller than the marginal utility at two pieces of gum, 25.

e. The marginal utility reaches 0 at the sixth piece of gum.

f. Gum costs $0.05 per piece. We divide the marginal utility by 0.05 to get the marginal utility per dollar spent.

Pieces of Gum	Marginal Utility	Marginal Utility Per Dollar Spent
0	–	–
1	20	400
2	25	500
3	15	300
4	10	200
5	5	100
6	0	0
7	–15	–300

3. a. Ignacio has $500 to allocate toward consumption of skateboards and books. Skateboards cost $100 each, so the maximum number of skateboards Ignacio can buy is $500/$100 = 5.

b. Books cost $50 each, so the maximum number of books Ignacio can buy is $500/$50 = 10.

c.

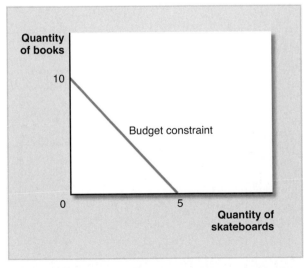

d. The slope of the budget constraint is $-P_S/P_B = -10/5 = -2$. The slope describes the trade-off Ignacio faces between skateboards and books: For every two books he gives up, he can get one skateboard.

5. The initial budget constraint intersects both the horizontal and the vertical axes at 10, as Jacob can buy a maximum of $5.00/$0.50 = 10 baseball card packs or candy bars. The slope is –1.

After the price change, the budget constraint still intersects the horizontal axis at 10, because the price of candy bars has not changed, but the budget constraint now intersects the vertical axis at 5, as Jacob can buy a maximum of $5.00/$1.00 = 5 baseball card packs. The new slope is $-^1/_2$.

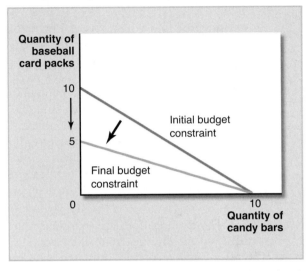

7. Ice-cream cones cost $2.00 each. We thus divide the marginal utility by 2 in order to get the marginal utility per dollar spent.

Ice-Cream Cones	Total Utility	Marginal Utility	Marginal Utility Per Dollar Spent
0	0	–	–
1	25	25	12.5
2	55	30	15
3	70	15	7.5
4	77	7	3.5
5	77	0	0
6	70	–7	–3.5

9. Diminishing marginal utility implies that the added utility received per drink decreases with each additional drink until it becomes zero or even negative. Even at a price of $0, consumers will come to a point when they do not want more to drink, and stop asking for free refills because the marginal utility has reached zero; thus marginal utility per dollar reaches zero also. The same logic applies to all-you-can-eat buffets.

11. Someone buying a newspaper from a newspaper vending machine only takes one newspaper, because he normally has no use for more, assuming that he does not take more than one newspaper and then sells the extras to others. Someone who purchases candy from a candy vending machine, however, might want more than the quantity of candy usually dispensed by the machine, and thus has an incentive to take more than the set quantity if the candy vending machine allows it. Newspaper and candy vending machines are therefore designed differently.

13. a. In spending the first dollar, you can buy a hot dog and receive 30 units of utility, or buy two sodas and receive 29 units of utility, so he should buy the hot dog. He can then purchase a second hot dog and get 18 units of utility, or purchase two sodas, and get 29 units of utility, so he purchases the two sodas. With the final dollar, he can buy a hot dog and receive 18 units of utility, or buy two sodas and receive 11 units of utility, so he should buy the hot dog. To maximize utility, Darius spends his $3 on two hot dogs and two sodas.

b. At his chosen allocation, the marginal utility per dollar spent on the final soda is (29 – 20)/$0.50 = 9/$0.50 = 18, and the marginal utility per dollar spent on the final hot dog is (48 – 30)/$1 = 18/$1 = 18. The marginal utilities per dollar spent on each good are thus equal, satisfying the first requirement for consumer equilibrium.

15. The equimarginal principle states that the marginal utilities per dollar spent on each good are equal. The consumer equilibrium condition for four commodities can thus be written as:

$$MU_X/P_X = MU_Y/P_Y = MU_Z/P_Z = MU_M/P_M$$

17. If store-brand sneakers are less durable or comfortable than name-brand sneakers, the marginal utility of store-brand sneakers is smaller than that of name-brand sneakers. Store-brand sneakers cost less, however, so their marginal utility per dollar spent might be greater. Shoe stores can therefore sell store-brand sneakers even if they are not as durable or comfortable as name-brand sneakers.

19. It does not mean that you should buy only the third good. You should follow the rule of choosing the good with the highest marginal utility per dollar, as always. Thus, at first you might purchase only the first two goods. Eventually, once the third good had the highest marginal utility

per dollar, you would purchase that good with all remaining income.

Chapter 7 Appendix

1A. a. Indifference curves are typically negatively sloped, because for any two goods that provide utility, the consumer must trade one for another if utility is to remain constant. They are typically convex, because marginal utility of any good declines as more and more units of the good are consumed. Thus, the trade-off is non-linear.

3A. a.

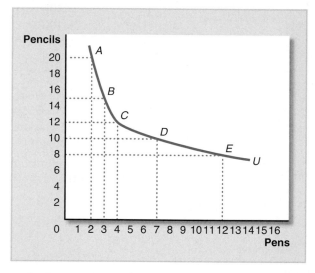

b. Between *A* and *B*, *MRS* = –5. Between *B* and *C*, *MRS* = –3. Between *C* and *D*, *MRS* = –$^2/_3$. Between *D* and *E*, *MRS* = –$^2/_5$.

5.

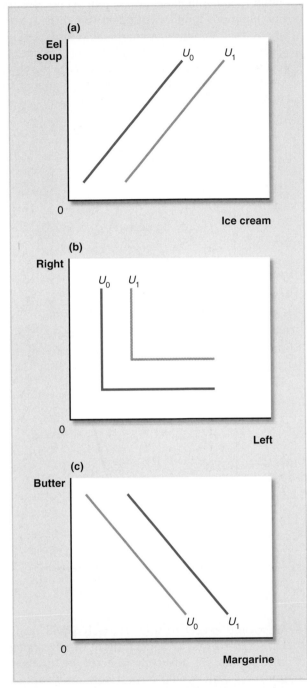

(a)

Eel soup

U_0 U_1

0

Ice cream

(b)

Right

U_0 U_1

0

Left

(c)

Butter

U_0 U_1

0

Margarine

In each case, $U_0 < U_1$. In panel (a), the indifference curves are positively sloped, because eel soup decreases your utility. Thus, in order for utility to remain constant if you have more eel soup, you must also have more ice cream. In panel (b), the indifference curves are right angles, because the goods are useful only in pairs. One right shoe and one left shoe provide utility level

U_0. Having an additional left shoe with no right shoe to accompany it does not increase utility. In panel (c), the indifference curves are straight lines, because consumers are always willing to trade butter for an equal amount of margarine, because they cannot taste the difference.

Chapter 8

1. The short run is that period of time in which at least one input is fixed. In the long run, all inputs are variable.

3. Specialization of labor means that workers specialize in one area of production rather than performing many different tasks in the production process. The practice increases productivity, because workers spend less time switching tasks and often increase the speed at which they can perform their tasks with experience.

5. In the short run, we typically assume that capital is fixed and labor is variable. Changes in capital are usually assumed to be more difficult, because they often involve the purchase and installation of new equipment and the construction of new facilities, both of which are difficult to do on short notice. In some cases, when labor inputs are characterized by very high skill and training levels, such as for brain or heart surgeons, it can be more difficult to change labor quickly than to increase capital, such as the number of operating rooms.

7. Economists do not specify a set time limit for the short run, because the length of time required to change capital depends greatly on the nature of the production process.

9. a.

Output	Fixed Cost (TFC)	Variable Costs (TVC)	Total Cost (TC)
0	$2,000	$0	$2,000
1	2,000	200	2,200
2	2,000	400	2,400
3	2,000	600	2,600
4	2,000	800	2,800
5	2,000	1,000	3,000
6	2,000	1,200	3,200
7	2,000	1,400	3,400
8	2,000	1,600	3,600
9	2,000	1,800	3,800
10	2,000	2,000	4,000

b.

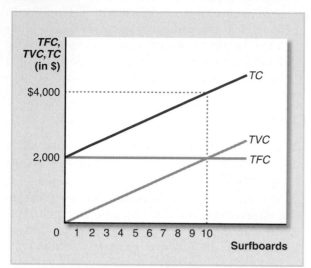

11. This statement is true. Each additional unit of output adds $10 to total cost. Thus the marginal cost is always $10. For every added unit of output, if we calculate the average variable or average total cost, they will be the same, as there are no fixed costs. AVC and ATC will also increase by $10 for each unit.

13. b.

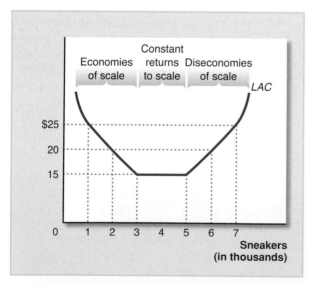

Economies of scale are present for the first 3,000 units of output. Between the 3,000 and 5,000 units of output, returns to scale are constant. Beyond the 5,000th unit of output, there are diseconomies of scale.

15. When output increases from zero, the marginal productivity of labor typically increases, as workers make better and better use of the capital on

hand. When marginal product reaches its maximum (point A in panel (a)), marginal cost reaches its minimum (point A in panel (b)). It is at this point that diminishing marginal returns set in. After point A, the marginal product begins to decrease, which causes marginal cost to increase, as greater and greater labor effort is required to achieve additional increases in output.

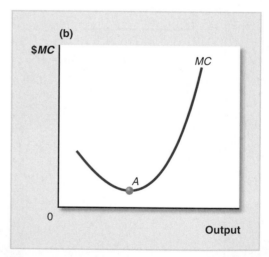

17. We would expect to find relatively small firms. Larger firms that are operating in the size range where they are adversely affected by diseconomies of scale would have a cost disadvantage relative to smaller firms.

19. Because cost is increasing more than proportionally relative to output, Pat's is experiencing diseconomies of scale.

21.

Q	TFC	TVC	TC	AFC	AVC	ATC	MC
0	$50	$0	$50	—	—	—	—
1	50	20	70	50	20	70	20
2	50	30	80	25	15	40	10
3	50	37	87	16.67	12.33	29	7
4	50	47	97	12.50	11.75	24.25	10
5	50	60	110	10	12	22	13
6	50	76	126	8.33	12.67	21	16
7	50	96	146	7.14	13.71	20.86	20
8	50	122	172	6.25	15.25	21.50	26
9	50	158	208	5.55	17.55	23.11	36
10	50	208	258	5	20.80	25.80	50

Chapter 9

1. a. and b. The initial equilibrium price is $20. When the new section of homes opens, it represents an increase in the number of consumers in the market, which shifts the demand curve to the right. As a result, price increases to P_1 and quantity increases to Q_1.

c. If the boys adopt a new technology, they will have a productivity advantage over other teams of shovelers. As a result, they will be able to earn positive profits at lower prices than other teams. Unless the other teams adopt the same technology, they may be driven out of business in the long run.

3. a.–f. See table on page 14.

5. If perfect information does not hold, buyers and sellers are not familiar with all market conditions; in particular, prices. A seller can thus charge a higher price for a good than the other sellers in the market charge, without buyers knowing that they are paying more than they need to. As a result, there is no single market equilibrium price, creating market power for sellers.

7. a. See table on page 14.

The best level of output occurs when economic profit is maximized. When the market price is $4, the best level of output for the firm is 6. When the market price is $6, the best level of output for the firm is 7. When the market price is $2, the best level of output for the firm is either 4 or 5. At this level of output, the firm incurs losses. In the short run, it should continue operations, because losses are less than fixed costs.

3. a. Table

	Running Shoes	Laptop Computers	Shoeshine Stands	Ground Beef	No. 2 Pencils	Gold
Homogenous commodity	No; varying levels of quality are associated with different running shoe brands.	No; laptop computers have varying levels of quality, of technical support availability, and different warrantees.	Yes.	No; ground beef may have varying levels of quality.	Yes.	Yes.
Many buyers and sellers	No; a small number of manufacturers dominate the running shoe market.	Many buyers, but not many sellers.	Yes, although in some markets, there may be few suppliers.	Yes.	Yes.	Yes.
Perfect information	No; consumers are not always well informed about product differences	No; consumers must search to find price information, and qualitative differences in machines make comparisons difficult.	No; consumers usually have little ability to compare prices from one stand to another.	Yes; consumers typically have good access to price information from sale circulars, and prices are easy to compare.	Yes.	Yes.
Free entry and exit	No; considerable investments, particularly in plants and R&D, must be made in order to enter the market. These initial investments are very large, and some costs are sunk, precluding free exit.	No; considerable investments, particularly in plants, must be made in order to enter the market.	Yes; unless one must purchase a permit in order to use a shoeshine stand, precluding free entry.	No; although there are few restrictions to entering the livestock industry, meat packing requires large plants and equipment.	No; considerable investments, particularly in plants and equipment, must be made in order to enter the market. These initial investments generate sunk costs that preclude free exit.	Yes; gold is a freely traded commodity, allowing any investor to buy and sell.

7. a. Table

Q	TR for P=$4 (in dollars)	TR for P=$6 (in dollars)	TR for P=$2 (in dollars)	TFC (in dollars)	TVC (in dollars)	TC (in dollars)	Profit for P=$4 (in dollars)	Profit for P=$6 (in dollars)	Profit for P=$2 (in dollars)
0	0	0	0	10	0	10	−10	−10	−10
1	4	6	2	10	2	12	−8	−6	−10
2	8	12	4	10	4	14	−6	−2	−10
3	12	18	6	10	5	15	−3	3	−9
4	16	24	8	10	6	16	0	8	−8
5	20	30	10	10	8	18	2	12	−8
6	24	36	12	10	11	21	3	15	−9
7	28	42	14	10	16	26	2	16	−12
8	32	48	16	10	23	33	−1	15	−17

b.

c.

Firm Output = q	MR	MC	Profit
0	–	–	–
1	$4.00	2	–8
2	4.00	2	–6
3	4.00	1	–3
4	4.00	1	0
5	4.00	2	2
6	**4.00**	3	3
7	4.00	5	2
8	4.00	7	–1

Because the marginal cost of the seventh unit is greater than the marginal revenue it produces, the firm should stop selling at the sixth unit.

9. At the market equilibrium, the quantity demanded and quantity supplied of bottled water are equal. If we set demand as $Q = 1,000 - 100p$, equal to supply as $Q = 100p$, we find the equilibrium price of $5.00 per hundred gallons. Plugging $5.00 back into the demand or supply equation gives us the equilibrium output level of 50,000 gallons. To maximize profits, the firm sets its marginal cost, $MC = q$, equal to the market equilibrium price, $5.00. It thus supplies 500 gallons of water.

11. To maximize profits, the firm sets its marginal cost as $MC = 10 + q$, equal to the market equilibrium price, $40. The firm should produce $q = 30$. If total cost of this output level is $1,500, it earns an economic profit of $(30 \times \$40) - \$1,500 = -\$300$. At this level of output, the firm incurs losses even though it is making the best output

choice. If fixed costs are $450, the firm's best strategy is to stay in the market in the short run, because it will then incur a loss of $300 rather than $450 if it shuts down.

13. The long-run supply curve of an industry may be upward-sloping if production costs increase as the industry expands; that is, for an increasing-cost industry. If input prices rise as firms demand more of them, then average production costs increase as the industry expands, resulting in an upward-sloping long-run supply curve for the industry.

15. If consumers do not have good information about prices, then they may not know if they are being charged a price that is higher than the price charged by another seller. As a result, if information is difficult to obtain, firms have some degree of market power.

17. The wedding gown industry is not perfectly competitive. Although entry and exit may not be difficult, the product is highly differentiated and consumers cannot easily obtain information about prices.

19. The benefits of perfect competition for consumers are that sellers are forced to compete for buyers by offering a price equal to the marginal cost of production. Thus no lower price is possible. The drawback of this market structure is that there is no differentiation in the product.

Chapter 10

1. Your answer depends on the type of school you attend, but consider which types of schools are the best substitutes for your school type, and which are the least similar. For example, if you attend a four-year public university, possible substitutes include other nearby public universities, private universities, private colleges, community colleges, and professional training schools.

3. In addition to musical talent, barriers to entry include the funds required to pay for the studio time needed to produce a CD. In order to have access to consumers through large retail outlets, a performer would also likely need to be associated with a major record label that has the ability to distribute the music widely.

5. Consumers might prefer that Microsoft monopolize the operating system market for compatibility reasons. If there were a large number of

popular operating systems, it would be more difficult for individuals and firms to share files such as documents, spreadsheets, and photos. As the number of operating systems increased, the sophistication of translation software would have to increase as well in order to maintain transferability. The cost of such capability might not be worth the benefits of having competing operating system(s).

7. If a new team entered the market, it would create a viable substitute for the monopoly team. This substitute would diminish the team's monopoly power, shifting the demand curve down and making it more elastic (flatter). In the graph, the new demand curve and marginal revenue curve are shown as the dashed lines.

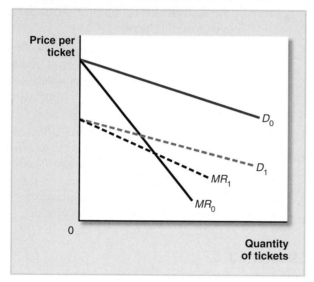

9. A monopolist that is losing money in the long run will exit the industry. Once demand falls (or costs rise) to the point that at the optimal output level, total revenue is less than total cost based on the LAC curve, the firm will exit the industry. In the following, the firm's best output level is Q^* if they produce. But producing that output level leads to a loss (the area shaded orange). In this case, the firm should exit the industry.

11. The distance between price and marginal cost is greater when demand is more inelastic. In the figure, the demand curve D_1 is more inelastic at any given price than D_0. At any output level, such as Q, the distance between price and marginal cost is lower when demand is more elastic.

13. False. When ATC is flat, $MC = ATC$, but the monopolist does not set $P = MC$. (Note that in a competitive industry, the answer to this question is true. The monopolist sets $MR = MC$ as shown in the graph.)

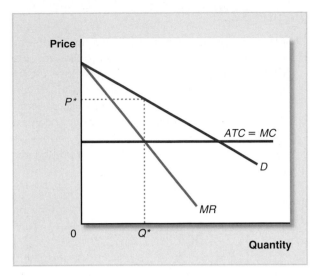

Price

P^*

ATC = MC

D

MR

0   Q^*

Quantity

15. In order for a firm to practice third-degree price discrimination, it must have market power in both markets and different demand in the two markets, and it must be able to prevent reselling of its products.

17. a. The monopoly price and quantity are labeled P^* and Q^* in the graph.

b. If the firm sets prices as a competitive firm would (where $P = MC$), it would sell Q_C units for $40 each.

c. The deadweight loss is shaded in gray.

d. If the firm were able to practice first-degree price discrimination, it would sell Q_C units of output.

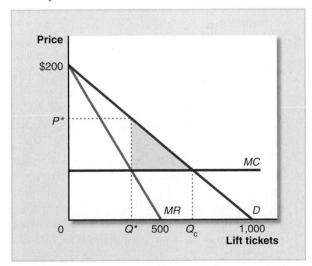

Price

$200

P^*

MC

MR   D

0   Q^* 500 Q_c 1,000

Lift tickets

Chapter 11

1. a. In the model of monopolistic competition, the product is differentiated. In the model of perfect competition, the product is identical across sellers.

b. The addition of new firms decreases the market power of the existing firms. Demand for their products typically will decrease and become more elastic.

c. Economic profits are driven to zero in the long run, because new firms are free to enter. New firms will enter as long as economic profits are greater than zero.

d. A manufacturer may choose to produce goods that are of lower quality as a form of product differentiation. This practice allows the firm to attract customers with lower prices.

3. The waterfront houses, although located very near much cheaper ones that are inland, are different in that they border the lake. As a result, they offer opportunities for boating, fishing, and better scenery than inland homes.

5. The market for college education is characterized by a wide variety of schools. Schools vary by size, location, degree programs offered, and state or religious affiliation. If the market were perfectly competitive, all colleges would be identical. Although this type of market would standardize quality, the loss of variety would be a problem.

7. In order to attract fans, new bands want to appeal to a certain market. Doing so helps them to get radio playtime and successful appearances in local clubs. However, in order to distinguish themselves from existing bands, they want to offer music that is different. The constant drive to be different leads to the evolution of musical styles over time.

9. The patent does, in and of itself, create a barrier to entry to the industry. The firm could become a monopolist in the product market if the product were not highly differentiated and the new technology created enough scale economies. If not, the firm would still increase its market share and profits if the new technology decreased production costs.

11. New products that do not create genuine differences in quality or characteristics but increase market power reduce allocative efficiency. Because they create market power through perceived differences, they create deadweight loss.

13. The new product characteristic would increase demand for the firm, and also likely make demand more inelastic at every price (assuming that consumers view the new yarn to be superior to the existing product). On the graph, demand shifts from D_0 to D_1. Price will increase. Here, price increases from P_0 to P_1. In the graph shown below, output does not change, although that is not necessarily true in all such situations.

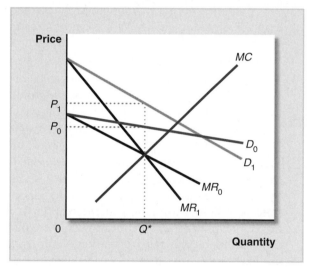

15. Ice cream is usually advertised using persuasive techniques. Informational advertising would not be effective for this product, because consumers must actually taste ice cream to determine its most meaningful characteristics (the flavor quality and the texture).

17. As long as consumers are able to discern low quality from high quality, consumers are worse off if the government prohibits the sale of low-quality goods. Consumers might prefer to spend less and buy lower-quality goods. In some cases, however, where consumers must experience a product to know its characteristics and safety is an important characteristic, such as with medical care and pharmaceutical products, the government may make consumers better off by restricting sales.

Chapter 12

1. Once the price is set at $100 per hour, if Jones increases her price and Smith does not also increase his price, quantity changes along D_{NR} to Q_1. Jones will lose market share, and revenue and profits will likely fall. If Jones decreases her price and Smith matches the price decrease, quantity will increase along D_R to Q_2. Jones will not gain market share. The lower price will generate lower profits.

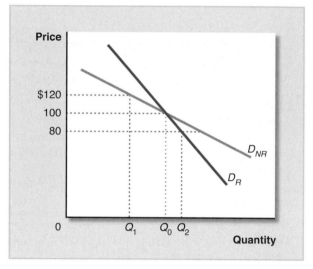

3. This statement is true. Informational advertising increases efficiency, because it increases competitiveness. Persuasive advertising decreases efficiency, because it expends resources without changing product characteristics or consumer information.

5. The advantage of the new disk is that it holds more data. The disadvantage is that it is incompatible with existing products. If your competitors have a large market share, your new product will not work with many of the drives on the market, which will reduce demand for the new disk.

7. The competitive price is set where the supply and demand curves cross. The cartel price treats the sum of the marginal costs curves as the monopoly marginal cost curve rather than the supply curve and sets output and price based on where this marginal cost curve is equal to marginal revenue.

9. Centralized cartels are unstable because firms are asked to produce at a point where marginal revenue (the cartel price) is much greater than MC, violating the profit-maximizing condition of $MR = MC$. Thus firms have an incentive to increase output. In the following, firm 1 is asked to produce Q_1. At that output level, $MR > MC$.

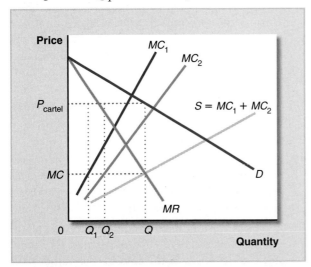

11. This is an example of the prisoners' dilemma. For each store, having a sale is the dominant strategy, yet both players would be better off by not having a sale. Thus collusion could alter the outcome because both stores could agree on not having a sale.

13. a. Initially, the CR4 is 90 and the HHI is 2,600. After the change in market shares, the new CR4 is still 90, but the new HHI is 2,125.

b. Based on the CR4, the market concentration has not changed. Based on the HHI, the market concentration has decreased. Thus, it is very unlikely that the government will take action based on the protest.

15. The maximum possible value for the HHI is $10,000 = 100^2$, which is consistent with a monopoly.

17. If surfboard buyers use the site as a way to compare prices, and manufacturers are unable to collude, each will have a strong incentive to offer the lowest price. If manufacturers are able to collude, each will have an easy way to determine whether the price agreement is being followed, which will lead to higher prices.

Chapter 13

1. Deadweight loss represents a loss of value from a market exchange as a result of deviation from the competitive outcome. A deadweight loss would exist even if marginal cost is constant, because monopolists set $MR = MC$. The source of the loss is entirely from consumer surplus. In the graph, the deadweight loss is shaded gray.

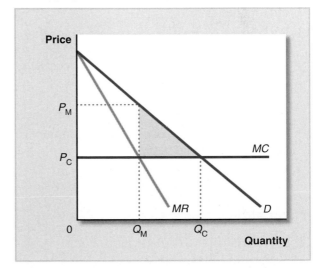

3. A monopolist could achieve the same level of efficiency as if the industry were competitive by setting price equal to marginal cost instead, of setting $MR = MC$ to set output, and then choosing price based on that output as they normally do.

5. a. If the pizza box seller supplies only one shop with boxes, all other shops will be hurt, as they either will have no supply of boxes, or will have to have boxes shipped from farther away. To the extent that the additional shipping increases costs, these firms will be at a cost disadvantage relative to the shop that can buy boxes locally. Their consumers will also be worse off, because some of those added costs will be passed on to them in the form of higher prices.

b. Section 1 would be most appropriate here, as this represents a restraint of trade.

7. The requirement to purchase tickets to more games than she wants represents a product tie-in.

9. A vertical merger might be challenged if a firm gains control over a resource needed to manufacture its final product. Such control could prohibit other firms from producing the same final product.

11. Such an arrangement increases overall efficiency, because of the high cost of setting up a water delivery network. The fixed costs of installing a set of underground pipes is so high relative to the marginal cost of delivering water through the pipes that water authorities are likely natural monopolies.

13. Portability of numbers increases competition, because it reduces a barrier to exit. When consumers must pay a cost (even just the cost of the inconvenience of having to tell friends of a new number), it creates a switching cost that is a barrier to exit.

15. The average total cost curve is continuously downward-sloping.

a.

b. Pricing at marginal cost implies a price set at $0. At 500 units of 100 gallons, the losses would equal 500×200, or $100,000.

c. Price would have to be set at $200 in order for the firm to break even.

17. Consumers may be better off if information is widely available through the Internet, because they can shop for the best price very easily. Consumers may also be made worse off if Internet pricing makes it easier for firms to monitor each other if they collude to set higher prices.

Chapter 14

1. At eight percent, in one year the $300 will be worth $324. You are better off with the $325.

3. a. The *NPV* at five percent is –$1,000,000 + $976,190.48 = –$23,809.52. Because the *NPV* is negative, the city should not make the investment.

b. If the interest rate is three percent, the *NPV* is –$1,000,000 + 1,004,571.59 = $4,571.59. In this case, the city should make the investment.

5. A firm can use bonds to raise a large quantity of financial capital. A bank (or any single lender) might be unable or unwilling to make such a large loan. Unlike stock, bonds do not dilute ownership.

7. The firm does not receive any benefits from the increased value of the bond. Those benefits go to the seller of the bond.

9. Investors might choose a bond with a higher risk rating because it pays a higher interest rate. They are compensated for the higher risk with the potential for greater return.

11. In a corporation, stockholders are not liable for the debts of the firm. The maximum risk that a stockholder faces is the loss of the value of the stock.

13. The stock market is a measure of expected future performance, because the prices of stocks incorporate investors' expectations about the future prospects of firms.

15. Separation of ownership from management can lead to the principal-agent problem, because the managers of the firm might not pursue the goals of the owners, and the owners (shareholders) cannot effectively supervise the managers to know when this occurs. A board of directors can provide oversight of the management team to

monitor management practices and activities. They have the power to remove managers that are not acting in accordance with firm goals.

17. Such a car creates an adverse selection problem, in that poor drivers who are prone to accidents might be more likely to purchase it. It also creates a potential moral hazard problem in that drivers, once they own the car, might be tempted to drive recklessly, injuring others.

Chapter 15

1. There are many different labor markets on campus. Distinct labor markets include the market for economics professors, the market for biology professors, the market for research librarians, and the market for RAs (Residence Hall Advisors).

3. a. An increase in consumer income will increase demand for cable television, and so also increase demand for installers.

   b. A decrease in the price of satellite television systems will decrease demand for cable installers.

   c. An increase in the population will increase demand for installers.

   d. A new trend toward going to movie theaters rather than in-home viewing will decrease demand for installers.

5. Human capital, like any other form of capital, can depreciate over time if it is not maintained. In order to remain current in their field and aware of new teaching techniques, teachers pursue continuing education.

7. a. When new, faster lawnmowers with wider cutting decks are developed, demand for labor falls, and the demand curve shifts leftward to D_1 as firms substitute capital for labor. The new equilibrium wage and employment are W_1, L_1.

   b. The new trimmers that are engineered to make a lawn look much nicer when it is finished increase demand for lawn services and so also labor, and the labor demand curve shifts rightward to D_2. The new equilibrium wage and employment are W_3, L_2.

   c. The drought decreases demand, and the demand curve shifts leftward to D_1. The new equilibrium wage and employment are W_1, L_1.

d. The new grass increases demand. The labor demand curve shifts rightward to D_2. The new equilibrium wage and employment are W_3, L_2.

e. When the large group of unskilled workers immigrates to the area, the supply of workers increases, and the labor supply curve shifts rightward to S_1. The new equilibrium wage and employment are W_2, L_2.

f. An increase in the supply of highly skilled workers will not affect the labor market for lawn services.

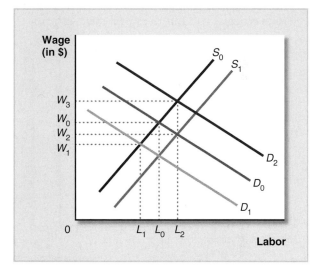

9. Individuals should pursue education up to the point where the marginal benefit is equal to the marginal cost. For some individuals, the cost of pursuing a graduate education is greater than the benefit that they would receive.

11. Technology is usually assumed to be fixed in the short run, because technology is usually embedded in the firm's physical capital, which is also typically assumed to be fixed in the short run.

13. If employers perceive teens and adult workers to be good substitutes for one another, adult workers as a group will likely be worse off, as employers switch from adult workers to lower-priced teen labor. Those adults who keep their jobs will be better off, but those who lose their jobs will be much worse off.

15. If the marginal product of the additional unit of labor is zero or negative, the firm would not want to hire the intern, even at a wage of $0 per hour. If the MPL is negative, the additional worker would reduce overall labor productivity.

17. When the workers are unionized by company rather than by industry across many companies, workers are more likely to want to work closely with management to improve the firm's fortunes, because increases in demand for the firm's products will increase demand for labor at that firm.

Chapter 16

1. In this case, income is distributed as unequally as possible. The Lorenz curve follows the horizontal axis across to a point where it nearly touches the vertical axis, and then becomes vertical.

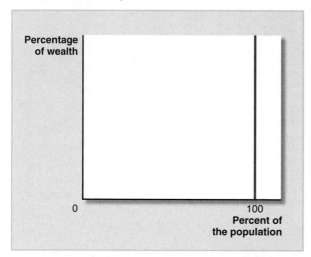

3. Incomes, wealth, and poverty can be reinforced across generations if children of the wealthy are expected to succeed in attaining high levels of education, and if children of the poor do not have high expectations and so do not pursue higher education. Because income increases with education, the differences in the quantity and quality of education obtained can perpetuate income differences.

5. If the new bar exam makes it more difficult to gain access to the field of law, the supply of lawyers will decrease, which we show as a leftward shift of the supply curve in the following graph. The equilibrium quantity decreases and wages rise.

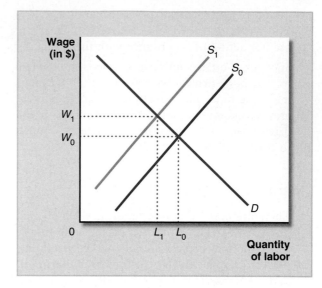

7. Each family would receive $400,000. A tax that redistributes income perfectly equally could be bad for the economy in the long run if some individuals decide not to put as much effort into work, knowing that they will receive income from others.

9. Although higher taxes required to finance the universities may have initially lowered incomes, wages and the standard of living increased once those attending the universities entered the labor force. The increased education that they received increased their productivity, and so also their wages.

11. If we give an individual $100 in food stamps that include many restrictions on the goods that they can purchase, the individual might not be able to purchase what she or he most wants. If individuals are given $100 in cash, they are free to make their own decisions regarding what they should purchase.

13. If income distributions become too unequal, it can be destabilizing for an economy. Individuals with little or no income have little incentive to follow laws of society if they cannot earn even a subsistence income.

15. The taxes owed are:
    a. $0
    b. $1,000
    c. $20,000

Chapter 17

1. The marginal social cost of the drums is greater than the private cost, because the sound creates a negative externality. A tax of $5.00 per drum would result in the socially optimal quantity Q_S.

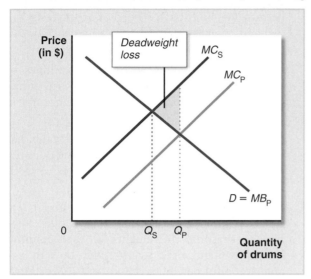

3. In this case, the marginal social benefit exceeds the marginal private benefit, as other members of the community also enjoy the improved campus, and it increases the value of their homes. The socially optimal quantity is Q_S.

5. The argument for a bridge toll is that individuals who cross the bridge receive private benefits. If the price is set such that the marginal private benefit is exactly offset by the marginal private cost of crossing, externalities are ignored. There are positive externalities associated with public roads

and bridges. Individuals who never cross the bridge still benefit from the economic activity that occurs, because others can cross the bridge.

7. The Coase Theorem can help to ensure efficient use of the water if property rights are established for either the sawmill or the spring water company. If the sawmill has the right to use the river, but the value of the river is greater to the water company, the water company will be willing to pay the sawmill enough that the sawmill is willing to avoid polluting it. If the water company has the property rights, and the value of the resource is greater for the sawmill, the sawmill will be willing to pay the water company enough that the water company will allow them to pollute it.

9. If oil were a renewable resource, the two ranchers, Ed and Tanya, would not be in competition with each other for the oil that lies beneath their properties. Instead, each could decide independently how much oil to remove from the ground in any given period.

11. The marginal cost of the pollution is $10 per ton. To obtain the marginal social cost MC_S, we add the $10 per ton to each quantity. Thus, the MC_S curve is above the MC_P curve at every point.

13. The coupon system is more likely to maximize social welfare, because coupons can be bought and sold. Those who value picnics the most will be willing to buy coupons from those who value them the least. If each family is given coupons independent of demand, it is very unlikely that they will end up distributed optimally.

Chapter 18

1. The labor force participation rate of women has risen for a number of reasons. First, the skills that women bring to the labor market more closely resemble those of men than they once did. Second, because discrimination against women in the labor market has fallen, women have more of an incentive to enter and stay in the labor market. The rise of institutions providing services such as child care has meant that family formation is not the barrier to work that it once was. Finally, the rising divorce rate has given women an added incentive to establish independent careers.

3. Not all people without jobs are unemployed.

   a. An autoworker who loses his job due to a recession is unemployed as long as he actively seeks work.

   b. The lawyer who resigns her job to take care of a sick child is not looking for work and therefore is not in the labor force. She is not unemployed.

   c. The lawyer is now looking for work, so she is unemployed.

   d. The anthropology professor is unemployed as long as he continues to look for work.

   e. A full-time college student might not be looking for a job, in which case she is not in the labor force. Alternatively, she might be looking for her first job and would therefore be unemployed.

5. Both may be right. The unemployment rate is the ratio of the number of unemployed people divided by the number of people in the labor force. The number of people unemployed could grow while the unemployment rate falls, if the labor force grows more quickly than does the number of people who are unemployed.

7. College graduates generally have more skills than high school graduates, so the demand for their services is higher. At the same time, fewer people have college degrees than high school degrees, so the supply of college graduates is lower. Both factors mean that a college graduate who seeks work is more likely than a high school graduate to find work.

9. The types of unemployment are as follows:

   a. The autoworker experiences cyclical unemployment. He was harmed by the movement of the economy into recession and will regain his job when the economy recovers.

   b. The lawyer has left the labor force, so she is not unemployed.

   c. As long as the lawyer is unemployed just because she is having temporary trouble locating an opening, she is experiencing frictional unemployment. If she cannot find employment because her skills have eroded or are no longer in demand, then she could be structurally unemployed.

   d. If the anthropology professor continues to look for work, he is likely to be structurally unemployed, because anthropologists are not in demand.

   e. If the student is looking for her first job, she is likely to be unemployed, because she does not know exactly where to look. In that case, she is frictionally unemployed.

11. The government should worry least about seasonal unemployment because that is due to the regular, seasonal movements of the economy. Unemployment rises every June due to the appearance of new high school and college graduates in the labor market. Frictional unemployment is also a low priority. It causes many people to be unemployed for a short period of time. Eventually, they will all find jobs. Structural unemployment is probably the biggest concern. The lack of (appropriate) skills could lead to long-term unemployment. Unfortunately, the government has had a difficult time eliminating structural unemployment. Providing the right skills can be tricky because no one can predict exactly what skills will be desired in the future.

13. Full employment corresponds to the unemployment rate that exists when there is no cyclical unemployment. Because seasonal, frictional, and structural unemployment are so difficult and so costly to eliminate, we allow them to exist when the workforce is "fully employed."

15. The full employment unemployment rate would:

    a. Rise. New workers typically have less information about the labor market and are likely to experience frictional unemployment. Frictional unemployment still exists when the economy is at full employment.

    b. Stay unchanged. Cyclical unemployment is affected by the rise and fall of unemployment due to overall movements in the economy. Cyclical unemployment causes the unemployment rate to rise above the full employment level.

c. Rise. If tourism declines permanently, then structural unemployment rises because people with skills specific to the tourist industry will be unable to find jobs. Higher structural unemployment causes the full employment unemployment rate to rise.

d. A policy that encourages seniors to re-enter the labor force will bring a rise in frictional unemployment. The seniors have been out of the labor market for a while and will have trouble locating jobs. Some structural unemployment may also occur if the seniors possess skills that are no longer in demand.

17. Increasing unemployment benefits will obviously make the people who are unemployed better off. It might also help the overall economy by reducing the pressure on unemployed workers to take any job that becomes available. A better match means that workers will be more productive, increasing the goods and services available to the economy. On the other hand, the higher benefits could induce workers to take their time while looking for a job, imposing greater costs on the economy.

19. Keeping out foreign-made goods would increase the price of domestically produced goods. Moreover, if people have to spend more money to buy cars then they have less money left over to buy computers. Trade restrictions designed to protect jobs in the auto industry could therefore reduce employment in the computer industry. In addition, if other nations respond to our trade restrictions by imposing their own, then firms that sell goods and services to other nations could be harmed.

Chapter 19

1. If all prices rise by exactly the same percentage, then wages, salaries, and interest income all rise along with the prices of goods and services. Real wages and real interest rates stay the same. People's purchasing power stays the same. People do not have to work more in order to afford the same combination of goods and services they bought before prices rose. (*Note*: This answer assumes that there are no "menu" costs or other costs associated with inflation.)

3. A retiree who receives a pension of $500 is on a fixed income that does not automatically rise if prices rise. The purchasing power of this income will decline as prices rise, leaving the retiree

worse off. To see why, consider the following equation relating real income to nominal income:

% change in real income = % change in nominal income − % change in prices

In this case, the percentage change in nominal income is 0. If prices rise by 10 percent, then real income declines by 10 percent. For someone on a fixed income, this relationship is true for any increase in prices.

5. A raise may not be enough to offset the rise in prices. Again using the equation

% change in real income = % change in nominal income − % change in prices,

suppose a person receives a 5-percent raise, but prices rise by 10 percent. The change in real income is 5% − 10% = -5%. The 5-percent increase in nominal income leaves the person able to afford 5-percent less than before.

7. If real interest rates are negative, then lenders are effectively paying borrowers to take their money. The purchasing power of the money that borrowers pay back is less than the purchasing power of the money that they borrowed. Negative real interest rates arose because nominal interest rates were set based on the expected rate of inflation. Recall that lenders charge a higher nominal rate when they expect higher inflation, in order to preserve the purchasing power of the money that borrowers repay. The relationship between the real and nominal rates of interest is thus:

Real interest rate = Nominal interest rate − % change in prices

Because no one knows what the true rate of inflation will be, lenders actually add the *expected* rate of inflation to the real interest rate. In the mid-1970s, inflation was much greater than expected. To see what resulted, we rearrange the equation slightly, yielding:

Real interest rate = Nominal interest rate − % change in prices

The premium that lenders added to the desired real rate was too small, the nominal interest rate was too low, and the real interest rate that actually existed was negative.

9. All of these questions involve the computation of a price index:

a. To compute the cost of the market basket in 2004, we multiply the price of each item in the basket by its price. This yields: $2.50 × 4 +

$2.00 × 10 + $4 × 20. In this case, the cost equals $10 + $20 + $80 = $110.

b. Holding the market basket constant in 2005, the new prices mean that the market basket will cost: $3.00 × 4 + $1.80 × 10 + $4.50 × 20, or $12 + $18 + $90 = $120. Recall that the price index is given by: *[(Cost of market basket in current year)/(Cost of market basket in base year)] × 100*. Using the numbers from this problem yields a price index of ($120/$110) × 100 = 109. If 2004 is the base year then the inflation rate is (109–100)/100 × 100 = 9% between 2004 and 2005.

c. Part (b) could overstate inflation if the price of ice cream and tuna fish rose because of improvements in the quality of the products. Perhaps the ice cream is now tastier and the tuna fish now has no mercury, making it less of a health risk. Inflation could also be overstated because keeping the market basket constant introduces the possibility of *substitution bias*. Consumers will respond to changes in prices by switching away from items that become relatively more expensive to items that become relatively less expensive. In this example, households might respond to the changes in prices by buying more root beer (which has become cheaper) and buying less ice cream (which has become more expensive).

11. To compute the CPI with 1990 as the base year, we divide all the values by the CPI in 1990 (75.90) and then multiply 100, which yields:

Year 1	CPI 2	CPI with New Base 3
1990	75.90	100.00
1991	79.09	104.20
1992	81.48	107.35
1993	83.91	110.55
1994	86.06	113.39
1995	88.50	116.60
1996	91.11	120.04
1997	93.21	122.81
1998	94.66	124.72
1999	96.75	127.47
2000	100.00	131.75
2001	102.85	135.51
2002	104.47	137.64
2003	106.85	140.78
2004	109.69	144.52

13. No one consumer buys what the "typical consumer" buys, because the "typical consumer" reflects the purchases of many different people who are different ages, live in different areas, have different incomes, and live very different lives from each other. As a result, the market basket has many items that no one consumer would buy. The weights reflect that fact, as many weights are small fractions. People do not actually buy a small part of a car or a laptop, but that is what appears in the market basket.

15. Most people buy little, if any, bubble gum. As a result, it receives a very small weight in the market basket. In addition, because bubble gum costs so little, even a large percentage change in its price (unlike, say, a doubling of the price of housing) results in a very small change in the overall cost of the market basket. For both these reasons, the CPI would barely change if the price of bubble gum doubled and nothing else changed.

17. It is much more realistic to hold the market basket constant for short periods of time rather than long periods of time. As time goes on, however, new goods are introduced, existing goods change, and consumers' tastes change. Thus, people in the United States bought a very different array of goods and services in 2005 than they did in 1954. By contrast, much less changed between 2004 and 2005, so the market baskets were very similar in those years.

19. In the early 1970s, inflation moved above 5 percent per year and stayed above that level for most of the next decade. On occasion, it topped 10 percent. Starting in the early 1990s, inflation fell below 5 percent and stayed below that level through mid-2005. Inflation was much lower from 2000–2005 than it was from 1970–1975. See Figure 19.3.

Chapter 20

1. Although the symphony was written in nineteenth-century Austria, the CD of the performance is a new product, produced in the United States and belonging in GDP for the United States.

3. The decline in GDP could be due to seasonal factors. For example, construction work in much of the country declines during the winter months, and there is a natural lull in retail sales after the

rush of holiday shopping in November and December. Data gathered over a longer period, such as a year, smoothes out such predictable, seasonal swings in GDP.

5. Overall, your purchase does not affect GDP. More specifically, your purchase represents added consumption. The added consumption, however, is offset by negative investment that occurs when the dealer reduces his inventory.

7. To an economist, investment is an addition to a firm's physical assets. Your purchase of GM stock does not add to GM's physical assets. It is income that you do not spend on consumption. Moreover, the stock is not a new product or service.

9. Government expenditure on goods and services counts toward GDP; transfer spending does not. The aid to flood victims is not a market transaction; it is a transfer. The aid affects the income and consumption of the flood victims. The added consumption will count in GDP.

11. Recall that GDP = $C + I + G + (X-M)$. Using the numbers given:

$$GDP = \$5,000 + \$1,000 + \$500 + (\$3,000 - \$4,500) = \$5,000$$

13. Three factors make up the difference between the market value of transactions and the sum of all incomes in an economy. These are:

a. Depreciation: the wear, tear, and obsolescence that eventually cause some inputs to lose their value.

b. Taxes on production and imports: these taxes show up in the prices paid by households and firms, but they are not received by the firms and hence leave the circular flow.

c. Net foreign factor income: some income that is generated in the United States accrues to foreigners and leaves the country. Similarly, some income in foreign countries is earned by U.S. citizens and comes here. This could add to or subtract from the sum of incomes in the United States.

15. GDP is an imperfect measure of well-being. Many items, such as leisure time or a clean environment, do not show up in GDP. To the extent that a person values such things more than the market value of goods and services, he or she might prefer to live in a country with lower real GDP per capita.

17. The key is that China has a larger GDP but many more people. China has a GDP per capita of $\frac{\$1,100,000,000,000}{1,200,000,000} \approx \$917$. Belgium has a GDP per capita of $\frac{\$260,000,000,000}{10,200,000} \approx \$25,490$. The average Belgian is much better off.

19. U.S. GDP was much higher in 2000 than it was in 1995, but prices were also higher. We can account for the price increase by computing real GDP for both years. Using the GDP deflator, we find that real GDP in 1995 was $\frac{\$7.4}{98.1} \times 100 \approx$ $7.54 trillion. Real GDP in 2000 was $\frac{9.96}{106.9} \times 100 \approx$ $9.32 trillion. Thus, real GDP rose between 1995 and 2000, but it rose by less than nominal GDP.

Chapter 21

1. a. There will be an increase in U.S. aggregate demand as U.S. net exports increase at each price level.

b. There will be a decrease in U.S. aggregate demand as pessimistic expectations reduce consumption and investment spending at each price level.

c. There will be a decrease in U.S. aggregate demand as U.S. net exports decrease at each price level.

3. a. The wealth effect: as the price level falls, the purchasing power of household wealth increases. As households feel wealthier, they demand more and aggregate demand increases.

b. The interest rate effect: as the price level falls, demanders save more, lowering interest rates. As interest rates fall, other firms and households demand more and aggregate demand increases.

c. The international trade effect: as the price level in one country falls relative to prices in other countries, demanders buy more goods and services domestically and fewer goods in other countries, so net exports increase and aggregate demand increases domestically.

5. Other things being equal, consumers would need to spend fewer dollars to buy the same bundle of goods and services at the lower price level. As a result, they would tend to save more dollars at each price level.

7. a. There will be a decrease in short-run aggregate supply as the higher nominal wages increase the costs of production and reduce the amount of aggregate supply at each price level.

b. There will be an increase in short-run aggregate supply as the lower nominal resource prices decrease the costs of production and increase the amount of aggregate supply at each price level.

c. There will be an increase in short-run aggregate supply as the increased productivity decreases the costs of production and increases the amount of aggregate supply at each price level.

d. There will be a decrease in short-run aggregate supply as the increased health care costs increase the costs of production and decrease the amount of aggregate supply at each price level.

9. If the quantity of aggregate demand is less than the quantity of short-run aggregate supply at a given price level, downward pressure is placed on the price level. The falling price level encourages an increase in the aggregate quantity demanded and a decrease in the aggregate quantity supplied.

11 a. As a result of this increase in aggregate demand of $100 billion, the new equilibrium price level will be 115 and the new equilibrium level of real GDP will be $500 billion.

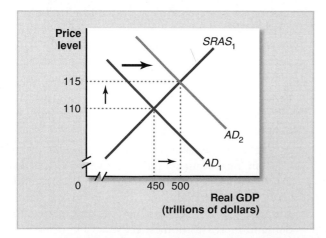

b. As a result of the higher energy prices, short-run aggregate supply would decrease by $100 billion at each price level. The new equilibrium price level will be 115 and the new equilibrium level of real GDP will be $400 billion.

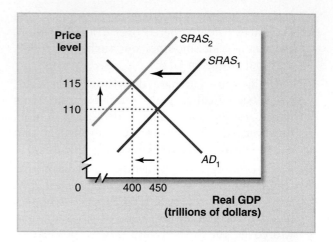

c. As a result of an increase in aggregate demand of $100 billion and a decrease in short-run aggregate supply of $100 billion, the new equilibrium price will be 120 and the new equilibrium level of real GDP will be $450 billion.

13. a.

b.

15. a, b, and d occur at short-run equilibrium.

17. The long-run aggregate supply curve is the level of real GDP that occurs at full employment output. It is located at full employment real GDP because this is the maximum amount that can be produced with full employment in the labor force and the use of the best available technology. It results after all adjustments to changing prices have occurred in the macroeconomy. Because of this complete adjustment, the price level has no impact upon the amount of goods and services produced in the long run. Thus, the long-run aggregate supply curve is vertical, indicating that real GDP is independent of the price level.

19. In long-run equilibrium, the macroeconomy is at full employment real GDP, so demanders and suppliers are satisfied. In the labor market, because all of the adjustments have been made to the changing price level, the actual unemployment rate is equal to the full employment unemployment rate.

Chapter 22

1.

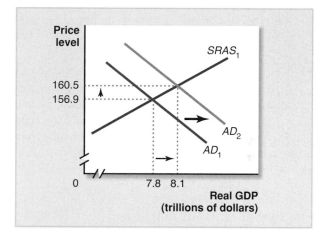

This is an example of a typical business expansion with demand-side inflation.

3.

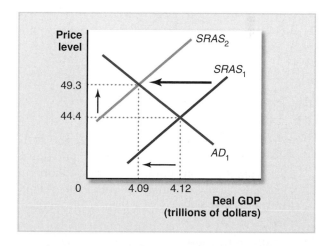

This is an example of stagflation, which generates supply-side inflation.

5. The long-run model asserts that most economies are at or near full employment real GDP; that, if left alone, economies tend to maintain full employment; and that any deviations from full employment real GDP will be minor, temporary, and self-correcting.

7. Long-run equilibrium is the intersection of a given aggregate demand curve, a given short-run

aggregate supply curve, and the long-run aggregate supply curve.

9. Wage flexibility is a situation in which nominal wages are freely flexible, so increases and decreases in nominal wages are equally likely to occur. Price flexibility is a situation in which product prices are freely flexible, so they will be equally likely to decrease when aggregate demand declines as they are to increase when aggregate demand grows.

11. When there is a temporary downturn in demand, firms will respond by reducing their prices and maintaining output and employment. In the same situation, workers will respond by accepting lower nominal wages to keep their jobs. As a result, full employment continues.

13.

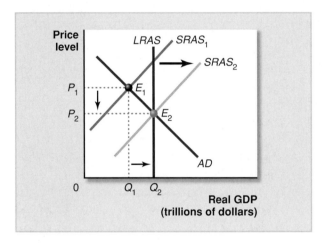

When the economy is in a recessionary gap at E_1, the conditions in the labor market put downward pressure on nominal wages. Short-run aggregate supply will increase until the new equilibrium is reached at Q_2, which is full employment real GDP.

15. a. Inflationary gap
    b. Recessionary gap
    c. Recessionary gap
    d. Inflationary gap

Chapter 23

1. The long-run model states that an economy's normal condition is full employment and any recessions would be minor, temporary, and self-correcting. The Great Depression did not involve a minor, temporary, or self-correcting economic downturn.

3. In the long-run model, both borrowers and lenders in the loanable funds market respond to the interest rate. The equilibrium interest rate works automatically to channel any amount of new saving into the new investment necessary to maintain full employment. In the short-run model, saving and investing is done by two different groups for different reasons, which makes it more difficult to achieve the amount of saving and investing necessary for full employment.

5. Because saving and spending are the only two uses of disposable income, the percentage of any new disposable income that is saved (MPS) and the percentage of any new disposable income that is consumed (MPC) must equal 100 percent of any new disposable income.

7. Although consumption spending is the largest component of aggregate demand in the United States, it is difficult to change. Consumers spend nearly all their income, so increasing consumption would be difficult. Consumers also resist reducing their current consumption, even if their income falls.

9. The amount of U.S. net exports depends on the purchasing power of the dollar established in foreign currency markets and on the economic health of U.S. trading partners. There is little that U.S. policy makers can do to manipulate the foreign currency market or improve the macroeconomies of our trading partners.

11. In 1933, President Roosevelt used increases in government spending in a variety of new programs to provide jobs for the unemployed. By doing so, these new spending programs increased aggregate demand in the U.S. economy. The federal government provided more aggregate demand when the other components of aggregate demand were falling.

13. The Keynesian model challenges Say's Law by focusing on the role of aggregate demand in the macroeconomy. In contrast to Say's Law, which identifies aggregate supply as the main engine of the economy, the Keynesian model argues that aggregate demand is the major reason for the performance of the macroeconomy.

15. In a typical recessionary gap, consumption expenditures cannot be easily changed, investment spending by businesses is lacking due to pessimistic expectations, and net exports are beyond the control of domestic policy makers. In

that situation, the government, by spending more when others are unwilling or unable, can provide the needed aggregate demand to cure an underperforming economy.

Chapter 23 Appendix

1. a. $940
   b. $850

3. When the consumption function crosses the 45-degree line, all income is consumed and saving in the economy is zero. When the consumption function lies above the 45-degree line, households consume more than their income and must withdraw funds from savings or other sources. When the consumption function lies below the 45-degree line, households consume less than their income and are able to add to their savings.

5. Aggregate expenditures are $890 when income is $1,000, $1,390 when income is $2,000, and $1,890 when income is $3,000.

7. Since total production is greater than aggregate expenditures, inventories of unsold goods will be increasing. Producers respond to this situation by producing less and equilibrium real GDP will decrease.

Chapter 24

1. a. $400 billion
   b. 0.875
   c. $40 billion

3.

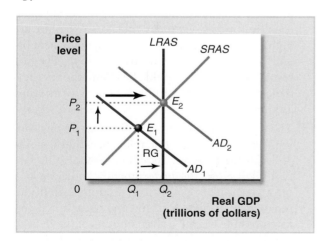

An expansionary fiscal policy of increasing government spending and/or cutting taxes will increase aggregate demand from AD_1 to AD_2, so the economy now achieves full employment real GDP at Q_2.

5. a. Recessionary
   b. $100 billion
   c. Increase, $10 billion
   d. Decrease, $11.1 billion

7. Discretionary fiscal policy requires specific legislative action to change the amount of government spending or taxes. Automatic stabilizers are changes in the amount of government spending and taxes that occur when there are changes in the underlying health of the economy without the necessity of specific new legislation.

9. a. $300
   b. 0.80
   c. $50

11.

Round	New Spending =	New Income =	New Consumption +	New Saving
1	$2.00	$2.00	$1.50	$0.50
2	1.50	1.50	1.13	0.37
3	1.13	1.13	0.85	0.28

13. Expansionary fiscal policy requires increased government spending and/or decreased taxes, both of which are politically popular. Therefore, presidents and Congress are more willing to propose and pass these measures than the spending cuts or tax increases required to fight inflation.

Chapter 25

1. The federal budget deficit is the difference between the amount of money spent by the federal government—both on goods and services as well as on transfers—and the tax revenue that the federal government collects in a given year. If this number is positive, the federal government has run a deficit. If the number is negative, the federal government has run a surplus. The national debt is the sum of all accumulated deficits and surpluses.

3. The federal government has much larger deficits than state and local governments do, because it is able to borrow much more. Most state governments, for example, face strict limits on whether or how much they can borrow.

5. If we were to enter a recession, tax revenues would fall as incomes fall and transfers would rise as unemployment and poverty rise. The result would be an increase in the federal budget deficit.

7. If the federal government runs a $100-billion deficit, the supply of loanable funds would shift to the left by $100 billion. This shift would cause the equilibrium interest rate to rise (for example, from three percent to five percent) and the equilibrium quantity of private borrowing on the loanable funds market to fall (in this example, from $500 billion to $425 billion).

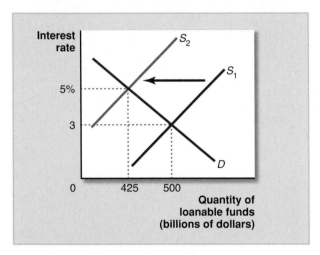

9. A federal budget deficit reduces the supply of loanable funds as seen in the answer to Problem 7. This reduction causes the equilibrium interest rate to rise and the equilibrium quantity of funds loaned to private borrowers to fall. With firms and consumers able to borrow less, investment and consumption fall. The declines in investment and consumption partly offset the expansionary impact of an increase in government spending or a tax cut. The aggregate demand curve thus shifts out only to AD_3 rather than to AD_2.

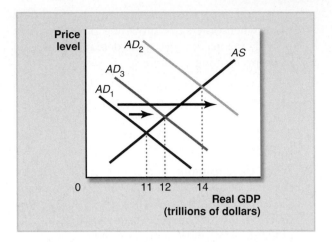

In this example, the expansionary fiscal policy would cause real GDP to rise to $14 trillion without crowding out. Because consumption and investment have fallen, tough, real GDP rises to only $12 trillion.

11. Because revenues fall and spending rises during a recession, the federal budget naturally goes into deficit. If the government sought to balance the budget, it would have to raise taxes or cut spending. Both policies reduce aggregate demand. The policies would therefore worsen the recession rather than end it.

13. Cyclical deficits arise because government revenues fall and government spending rises during a recession. Revenues fall because people's incomes fall during recession, reducing the taxes they pay. Spending rises because more people become eligible for unemployment benefits and for temporary assistance to the needy. Cyclical deficits should disappear and be replaced by surpluses when the economy recovers. During good economic times, incomes and tax revenues are high, while spending on unemployment benefits and assistance to the needy are low. The net result over time should be that the cyclical deficits and cyclical surpluses offset one another. Taking a broad view, there is no need to worry.

15. The dollar amount of the deficit can be misleading, because it does not take the ability of the government to repay its debts into account. As real GDP rises, the government's ability to pay off a given debt rises, just as a family's ability to repay its debt rises as its income rises. It is therefore possible for the dollar amount of the debt to rise but for the burden it imposes to fall. The

ratio of the deficit to GDP accounts for the ability of the government to cope with the addition to its debt.

17. A structural deficit does not disappear in good times. As its name implies, it is the result of the structure of the government budget. Because the structural deficit does not disappear during economic expansions, the national debt continues to grow. This debt imposes a growing burden on the government.

19. Borrowing from foreign lenders increases the supply of loanable funds to the economy. If the government borrowed strictly from domestic lenders, the supply of loanable funds would be S_1. If it borrowed from domestic and foreign lenders, the supply would be S_2. The impact of the deficit would therefore be smaller. In this example, interest rates would be three percent rather than five percent, and the quantity of loanable funds available for use by the private sector would be $12 billion rather than $10 trillion.

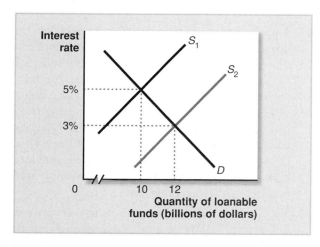

Chapter 26

1. Only the $20 bill performs all the functions of money.

3. "Everything, then, must be assessed in money" = the unit of account function

   "Enables men always to exchange their services" = medium of exchange function

5. A barter economy needs a double coincidence of wants; has high costs of time and transportation, and promotes self-sufficiency, which harms productivity.

7. a. Barter economy
   b. Money economy
   c. Barter economy
   d. Barter economy
   e. Barter economy

9. a. Durability
   b. Divisibility
   c. Portability
   d. Relative scarcity
   e. Uniformity
   f. Relative scarcity

11. Deposit receipts were first issued only in the depositor's name, while later the depositor was permitted to sign the deposit receipt over to a third party. Finally, the deposit receipt was made payable to the bearer. This evolution improved the acceptability and usefulness of deposit receipts by allowing them to circulate more widely without the necessity of redeeming the deposit receipt for the gold when making a purchase.

13. The ultimate suppliers of funds are the savers, and the ultimate demanders for funds are the investors (borrowers).

15. All modern depository institutions are fractional reserve institutions. Safe and successful fractional reserve banking requires public faith and trust in the banks and cautious lending by banks.

17.

	Assets		Liabilities	
Gold on deposit as reserves	+ $1,000		Receipts in circulation	+ $1,000 (to depositor)
Loans	+ $3,000			+ $3,000 (to borrowers)
	+ $4,000			+ $4,000

Chapter 27

1. A deposit of currency into an individual bank adds an equal amount of new reserves as an asset and new checkable deposits as a liability. For example, a $20 deposit of currency would affect the simplified balance sheet as follows:

Assets	Liabilities
Total reserves + $20	Checkable deposits + $20

3. a. +$1,000

   b. +$1,000

   c. +$50

   d. +$950

5. The bank against which the check is cleared loses both deposits and reserves equal to the amount of the check. For example, if a bank has a $20 check cleared against it, the balance sheet has the following changes:

Assets	Liabilities
Total reserves − $20	Checkable deposits − $20

7. a.

Academia National Bank

Assets	Liabilities
Total reserves no change	Checkable deposits − $2,000
Loans − $2,000	

M1 falls by $2,000, due to the reduction in checkable deposits in the hands of the public.

   b.

Bookville National Bank

Assets	Liabilities
Total reserves − $25	Checkable deposits − $25
Loans no change	

M1 does not change, because the reduction in checkable deposits in the hands of the public is offset by the increase in currency in the hands of the public.

9. a. Required reserves = $70,000 and excess reserves = $30,000.

   b. This single bank can safely lend an additional $30,000.

   c.

Assets	Liabilities
Total reserves $100,000	Checkable deposits $730,000
Loans $630,000	

   d.

Assets	Liabilities
Total reserves $70,000	Checkable deposits $700,000
Loans $630,000	

11. The President appoints the members of the Board of Governors but the Senate confirms those appointments. The members of the Board of Governors must reflect a certain geographical balance. The terms of the members of the Board of Governors are 14 years to insulate the members from political pressure. The twelve Reserve Banks are located in different regions of the country. Voting members of the FOMC include both members of the Board of Governors and presidents of Reserve Banks.

13. The Truth in Lending Act means that consumers will always know the annual percentage interest rate that they are paying on any given loan. The Truth in Savings Act means that consumers will always know the annual interest rate they are earning on their deposits. Such information enables them to find the best possible rates on both loans and deposits.

15. The Fed cannot force banks to borrow when the Fed wants the money supply to grow. The Fed cannot prohibit banks from borrowing reserves when the Fed wants to conduct a contractionary policy. Banks typically do not borrow much from the Fed.

17. Frequency

    1. Open market operations

    2. Changing the discount rate

    3. Changing reserve requirements

    Strength

    1. Changing reserve requirements

    2. Open market operations

    3. Changing the discount rate

19. A contractionary monetary policy will increase the demand for federal funds, increase the federal funds rate, and increase the amount of federal funds borrowed and lent.

Chapter 28

1. The opportunity cost of lost interest earnings and the cost of lost purchasing power over time.

3. Transactions demand is the use of money in everyday, expected transactions. The amount of money demanded for transactions purposes depends on the frequency of payment of income, the payments mechanism employed in the economy, and the level of income of the individual.

5. Speculative demand is the use of money as an investment asset in the portfolio of assets held by individuals. The major determinant is the level of interest rates in the economy. As interest rates rise, speculative demand falls.

7.

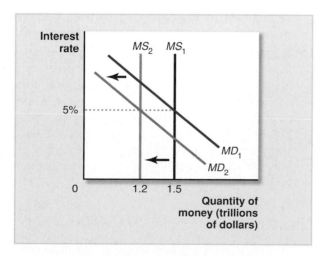

If the decrease in the money supply is matched by a decrease in money demand, the equilibrium interest rate will not change.

9. a. Real GDP = $300

    b. Velocity = 6

    c. Money supply = $90

    d. Price level = 5

11. As the economy moves from period 1 to period 2, money is neutral, because the increase in the money supply does not affect real GDP—only the price level increases. As the economy moves from period 2 to period 3, money is not neutral, because the decrease in the money supply reduces real GDP. As the economy moves from period 3 to period 4, money is not neutral, because it does affect real GDP.

13. The liquidity trap is a situation that typically occurs at very low levels of interest rates. In a liquidity trap, any new money supplied to the economy is held as new money demand. No new spending or investment will occur as the result of the newly supplied money. When the liquidity trap occurs, interest rates do not fall in response to an expansionary monetary policy, so the interest rate channel is not effective.

15.

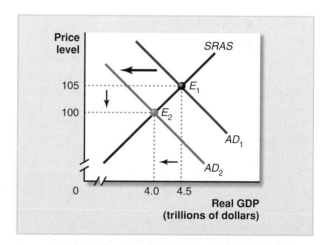

17. Like the money dropped from the planes, if the new money ends up being held by a few individuals who do not spend it, the economy will not benefit from the new money. On the other hand, if the new money supply is widely disbursed, spent, and invested, its impact on economic activity will be beneficial and will allow the economy to prosper.

Chapter 29

1. The Phillips curve goes through the point (6,2), which corresponds to six percent unemployment and zero percent inflation and through the point (2,8), which corresponds to two percent unemployment and eight percent inflation. If the government reduces unemployment to two percent, it will have to live with eight percent inflation. Because the Phillips curve goes through the point (4,4), it can reduce inflation to four percent by allowing the unemployment rate to rise to four percent.

3. The large-scale entry of women to the labor force in the 1970s increased frictional unemployment, because first-time entrants to the labor force typically have a hard time finding employment. This trend increased the full-employment unemployment rate, which shifted the Phillips curve to the right.

5. The rational expectations model does not say that everyone always knows what the future will bring. Instead, it says that most households and firms eventually come to anticipate what the government or the Fed will do if the government follows predictable policies. The statement mischaracterizes rational expectations.

7. The greater understanding of governmental policy should allow households and firms to catch on to government policy more quickly. It would cause the aggregate supply curve to shift and offset the fiscal or monetary policy more quickly than before.

9. Believers in real business cycles would say that people are allocating their time according to the incentives provided by the labor market. With fewer opportunities available on the labor market during a recession, the opportunity cost of going back to school falls. As a result, many workers withdraw voluntarily from the labor force and become full-time students.

11. The "Internet economy" made the labor force more productive. This development shifted out the long-run aggregate supply curve, keeping inflation low and increasing real GDP in the 1990s. Assuming for simplicity that the aggregate demand curve stays put, we see that the shift of the long-run aggregate supply curve causes real GDP to rise and the price level to fall.

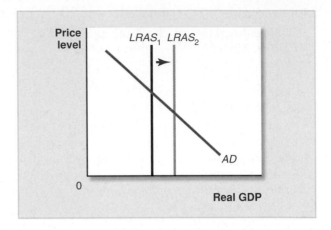

13. Advocates of supply-side economics believe that the biggest tax cut should be given to the people who will respond most strongly to a tax cut. This is likely to be the people who face the highest tax rates and the people who are most productive. Both factors point to cutting the taxes of the people with the highest income.

15. The money illusion concept is that people pay attention to nominal wages rather than real wages. In 1935, there had not been systematic inflation for many years. In fact, prices had been falling during the early 1930s. Workers were not likely to anticipate that increasing nominal wages might not translate into increased purchasing power. In 1975, inflation had been a part of the economy for decades. Workers were much more likely to understand that rising nominal wages did not necessarily make them better off.

17. A fixed wage contract prevents the cost of labor from falling during a recession and prevents it from rising during an economic expansion. If the cost of labor does not fall, employers will have even more reason to lay off workers, as seen in Figure 29.5. Similarly, in good times, the fixed wage contract keeps the cost of labor relatively low, which gives employers even more reason to hire workers.

Chapter 30

1. To determine the richest economy, we must compute real GDP per capita. We do so by dividing real GDP by population. Doing the division, we find GDP per capita to be $7,612 in Brazil, $10,101 in Estonia, and $815 in Nigeria. Thus, Estonia is the richest country and Nigeria is the poorest.

3. Economic growth can make a much bigger difference to the lives of the citizens of a poor nation such as Bangladesh. Economic growth can have a major impact on infant mortality and life expectancy in Bangladesh. In Switzerland, it leads to slight improvements to an already high standard of living.

5. Development means different things to different people. For example, some people regard individual freedom as an important feature of development, while others regard education and other services typically provided by government as more important. Depending upon how important one considers different features of development, different people can regard the same country as being at different stages of development. Economic growth is a much more clear-cut measure. The rate of growth of real GDP per capita is a number one can compute and compare with numbers for other nations.

7. Equation 30.2 tells us that, all else equal, increasing the labor force for a given population increases GDP per capita. Higher GDP per capita means higher incomes and higher standards of living.

9. In poor countries, households have low incomes and must spend most of their incomes merely to survive. Governments in these countries cannot generate significant budget surpluses, because they cannot generate large tax revenues. Both of these factors mean that the pool of savings available for the loanable funds market is very low.

11. Lenders regard a rich country like the United States as a good credit risk. They are far more willing to lend money to the United States than they are to poor countries like Mexico.

13. Just adding physical capital will do little good if the capital is not put to proper use, or if the country lacks a functioning market mechanism to allocate physical capital. Lenders have little incentive to provide capital to the most productive borrowers, and borrowers have little incentive to put the capital to the best use. Moreover, like labor, capital is subject to diminishing returns, so additions to the capital stock have less and less of an impact on output.

15. If Mexico builds a world-class engineering school without ensuring that the graduates will have jobs that pay a high enough salary, then the graduates might seek employment in other countries. The result would be a waste of resources.

17. The government of the Democratic Republic of Congo is unable to protect the property rights of its citizens. Property rights are a prerequisite for a functioning market mechanism. Without a functioning market mechanism, neither firms nor households have an incentive to make the most productive use of the resources at their disposal. If resources are not used productively, growth will stall.

19. Without property rights, neither firms nor households have any guarantee that they will see the reward for making productive use of the resources at their disposal. If there is no reward for making good decisions and working hard, then people have no incentive to do so.

Chapter 31

1. There will be a trade surplus for the United States. The United States exports more good and services to Australia than it imports from Australia.

3. a. The country that has a lower opportunity cost of producing fur coats will have a comparative advantage in the production of fur coats. The country that has a lower opportunity cost of producing coffee has a comparative advantage in the production of coffee.

   Cameroon must give up 10,000 fur coats in order to produce 600,000 pounds of coffee beans. That means that Cameroon has to give up $1/60$ fur coats in order to produce one pound of coffee. Latvia must give up 200,000 fur coats in order to produce 10,000 pounds of coffee. That means that Latvia has to give up 20 fur coats in order to produce one pound of coffee. The opportunity cost of producing coffee is greater in Latvia than it is in Cameroon. Therefore, Cameroon has a comparative advantage in the production of coffee.

   Similarly, it costs Latvia $1/20$ pounds of coffee to produce one fur coat, and it costs Cameroon 60 pounds of coffee to produce one fur coat. Therefore, Latvia has a comparative advantage in the production of fur coats.

Latvia

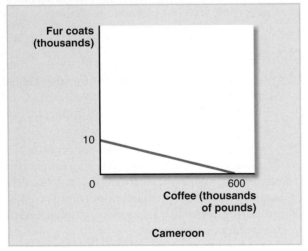

Cameroon

b. Trade allows both Cameroon and Latvia to consume more of each good, which makes them both better off than they were before trade. If each country specializes in the production of the good in which it has a comparative advantage, Latvia produces 200,000 fur coats and no coffee, and Cameroon produces 600,000 pounds of coffee and no fur coats. The total amount available for consumption in both countries is now bigger than it was before, so if the two countries trade, they will each be able to consume more, which makes them both better off. If, for example, they trade three pounds of coffee for one fur coat, then the cost of a fur coat in Cameroon is three pounds of coffee and not 60 pounds of coffee, as it was before trade. Similarly, the cost of one pound of coffee in Latvia is $1/3$ of a fur coat and not 20 fur coats.

5. Disagree. The United States may have an absolute advantage at all activities, but its absolute advantage is typically greater at some goods than at others. Bangladesh's *comparative* advantage will be in producing the good at which its absolute disadvantage is smallest. The opportunity cost of producing that good is lower than in the United States. Therefore, the United States will be able to get the good more cheaply by trading with Bangladesh, even though it is more efficient at producing everything.

7. We can say that the society as a whole is better off if the increase in consumer surplus exceeds the loss in producer surplus.

9. The quota is more harmful because the deadweight loss is greater in the case where quotas are used as trade barriers than it is if tariffs are imposed. This happens because a country receives tax revenue when it imposes a tariff but receives no tax revenue from a quota.

11. Reducing the tariff will cause the price of imported sugar to be more attractive to consumers. Consumers are thus more likely to buy foreign sugar. Therefore, foreign producers and domestic consumers will gain, while domestic producers will be hurt.

13. Domestic consumers pay for the added jobs by paying higher prices for the product. This leaves them with less money to spend on other goods. The revenue from this higher price is redistributed to the foreign producers rather than to the U.S. government. This creates a deadweight loss to the society.

15. a. They are asking for protection from free trade based on the claim that they produce products that are vital to the national interest. The U.S. footwear industry could dramatically reduce its production level without jeopardizing the nation's military preparedness. I would respond negatively to their request.

b. Lower prices are not in themselves proof of dumping. Japan might be able to produce DVD players more efficiently. It is possible that the Japanese manufacturer is charging low prices in order to drive domestic producers of DVD players out of business. However, there is not yet enough evidence to justify the claim. Further study is required.

17. The wages that multinational firms pay in developing nations are often far higher than the average wage in those nations. Also, the workers in developing nations may not be as well trained or educated, and could lack appropriate plants and equipment, so they may not be worth as much as workers in the United States.

19. One of the roles of the WTO that would help economies is adjudication of international disputes over trade and general promotion of free trade. Free trade helps the economies overall by increasing the total amount of surplus. However, it is not without cost. Individual sectors will contract out, and the firms and employees in these sectors will become worse off.

Chapter 32

1. International financial markets provide us with currency markets that make the trade possible. Currency markets allow people in one country to buy goods and services produced in another country by giving them access to the money that the producers want.

3. Americans supply dollars in order to buy yen. This transaction shifts the supply curve of dollars to the right and drives down the price of dollars. Dollars depreciate in value. In the example shown, the value of the dollar falls from 120 yen to 110 yen.

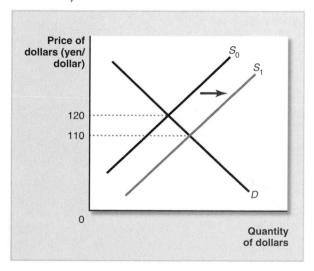

5. a. An American tourist in Singapore is hurt by a weaker dollar. The tourist needs more dollars now to purchase the same amount of goods and services in Singapore.

b. An American farmer is helped by a weaker dollar, because it takes less foreign currency to get the same amount of his baked goods.

c. If the Volvos are imported from Sweden, the Volvo dealer in Wisconsin is hurt by a weaker dollar, because its cars are now more expensive relative to comparable American-made cars.

7. If the dollar depreciates relative to the euro, the euro appreciates relative to the dollar. When the dollar depreciates, it costs more dollars to buy one euro. If that is the case, it must take fewer euros to buy one dollar.

9. The current account relates payments for goods and services as well as transfers, which amounts to –$10 billion: Net exports are –$15 billion; net interest payments are –$5 billion; and net transfers are +$10 billion. These add up to –$10 billion. Because the balance of payments must total $0, the capital account must offset the current account deficit. Therefore Florin's net sale of physical and financial assets must total +$10 billion.

11. If the United States is running a capital budget surplus, that means that foreigners owe the United States money. To buy this debt, they need U.S. dollars. That need shifts the demand for dollars on the currency market to the right. The higher demand for dollars causes the price of dollars in the currency markets to rise. A household in Idaho might decide to buy an imported car due to appreciation of the dollar and depreciation of the foreign currency. It becomes cheaper for a household in Idaho to purchase a foreign-made car.

13. a. If this is the only change in the economy, the large number of tourists would cause a current account surplus. A capital account deficit would have to result to restore the balance of payments.

b. The increased demand for German goods and services increases the supply of dollars. This increase causes the dollar to depreciate and the euro to appreciate.

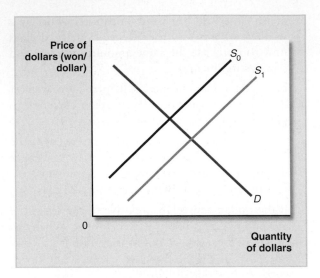

Price of dollars (won/dollar)

S_0
S_1

D

0

Quantity of dollars

15. If PPP holds, a Big Mac should cost roughly the same anywhere, so exchange rates rise and fall to equate purchasing power across countries. There are two reasons why it does not reflect PPP perfectly. First, prices vary across countries for extended periods due to transportation costs and a variety of domestic policies, such as taxes or tariffs. Second, changes in exchange rates reflect differences in overall prices. As a result, they generally do not change in response to the rise or fall in the price of a single product.

17. The gold standard set the value of a country's currency in terms of gold. With an ounce of gold worth a fixed amount of each country's currency, the countries effectively fixed the value of their currencies against each other as well. This allowed people in one country to know how much a good in another country cost. It also gave them a way to obtain the foreign currency.

19. The peso had become severely overvalued, meaning that the official value of the peso was higher than its equilibrium price on currency markets. Had floating exchange rates been in effect, the peso would have been worth only about 28 cents. China pegged the yuan to the dollar when the dollar was depreciating, so the yuan also became cheaper. This step kept the price of Chinese-made goods cheap and allowed China to continue to export goods to the United States.

Glossary

A

Absolute advantage When an individual or group is able to produce more of a good than another individual or group.

Accounting profits A measure of profit that takes into account explicit costs and the cost of interest payments on loans and depreciation.

Adverse selection Results when one party does not fully disclose information before a contract is agreed upon and makes choices based on its information advantage.

Affirmative action Policies designed to eliminate the effects of past and present discrimination.

Aggregate demand Real value of all new, final, domestically produced goods and services that households, firms, governments, and the foreign sector are willing and able to purchase at a given set of overall price levels, *ceteris paribus*.

Aggregate production function Relates real GDP to the inputs that households provide on the resource market.

Aggregate supply Real value of all new, final, domestically produced goods and services that firms are willing and able to offer for sale at various price levels, *ceteris paribus*.

Allocative efficiency When an economy produces the combination of goods and services that it values most highly.

Annual percentage rate (APR) The actual interest rate that the borrower must pay under the terms of the loan.

Annual percentage yield (APY) The actual rate of return on a deposit based on how often the bank pays interest to the depositor.

Appreciate When the price of a currency rises.

Arbitrage Buying a good where its value is low, and selling where its value is high.

Arc elasticity See *Midpoint elasticity*.

Assumptions Simplifications used to construct an economic model.

Asymmetric information Occurs when one party to a contract or transaction has more information than another.

Automatic stabilizers Government taxation and spending programs that trigger appropriate increases or decreases in the amount of aggregate demand based on the state of health of the economy—without new legislative action.

Autonomous consumption The amount of consumption that is independent of income; that is, the amount a household will consume even if its income is zero.

Average fixed cost (*AFC*) The total fixed cost divided by output.

Average product of labor (*AP*) The total product divided by the number of workers who produced it.

Average revenue Total revenue divided by output. For perfectly competitive firms, average revenue equals marginal revenue.

Average tax rate Individual's total income tax divided by the individual's total income.

Average total cost (*ATC*) The firm's total cost divided by the quantity of output it produces.

Average variable cost (*AVC*) The total variable cost divided by output.

B

Balance of payments Equality between a country's inflow of funds and outflow of funds.

Balanced budget When a government's expenditures equal its revenues.

Bank run A large number of depositors withdrawing their funds from a depository institution at one time.

Barter economy An economy where goods and services are directly exchanged for other goods and services without the use of a specific money asset.

Base year The year whose price level serves as the basis for comparison with other years to form the Consumer Price Index.

Beggar-thy-neighbor policy When a nation seeks to boost the domestic economy at the expense of a country's trading partners.

Board of directors Sets the rules of behavior for managers and employees of the firm; decides which projects the firm should pursue; and determines how the firm should raise funds.

Board of Governors The central authority that runs the Fed.

Bond A certificate of debt that guarantees the lender a fixed payment from the borrower such that the principal plus a predetermined rate of interest is repaid by a specific date.

Brand identity A consumer's ability to recognize a product and associate it with a specific name.

Brand loyalty A consumer's willingness to remain with a specific product despite the existence and advertisements of competitors.

Budget deficit The excess of spending by the government over tax revenue.

Budget line Shows all the consumption opportunities available to a consumer, given income and fixed prices. Its slope represents the trade-offs that the consumer faces when deciding how much to spend on each good or service.

Budget surplus The excess of tax revenue over government spending.

Business cycle Reflects the ups and downs in the overall level of production.

C

Capital account Shows the net sale of physical and financial assets.

Capital gains Earned by an investor when selling an asset for a higher price than was paid for it.

Capital goods The buildings and equipment used to produce other goods and services.

Capital stock The set of usable productive capital.

Capture theory Regulation theory based on the idea that firms benefit from regulation because they eventually capture the regulators, so that consumers are made worse off by regulation.

Cartel A group of firms that agree to work together to increase their profits.

Central bank A financial institution whose major responsibilities include regulating depository institutions and providing emergency liquidity to depository institutions needing reserves.

Centralized cartel A group of firms that collude in order to charge the monopoly price by agreeing to individual production quotas.

Centrally planned economy An economy in which the government, rather than the market, allocates resources.

Certificate of deposit A commitment by a depositor to keep the funds on deposit for a specific period of time at a financial institution.

Ceteris paribus A Latin phrase that means "all else equal."

Chain-weighted price index Uses the average of prices in the current year and prices in the previous year to calculate real GDP.

Change in aggregate demand Occurs when forces other than changes in the price level shift the entire aggregate demand curve to the left or to the right.

Change in aggregate quantity demanded As the price level changes along a given aggregate demand curve, there is more or less aggregate quantity demanded in the macroeconomy.

Change in aggregate quantity supplied Occurs when a change in the price level causes firms to move along a single aggregate supply curve.

Change in aggregate supply Occurs when forces other than changes in the price level shift the entire aggregate supply curve to the left or to the right.

Change in demand A change in the quantity that consumers will purchase at each price. A change in demand shifts the entire demand curve.

Change in quantity demanded A change in the amount of a good or service that consumers are willing and able to buy as a result of a price change.

Change in quantity supplied A change in the amount that producers are willing and able to sell when price changes.

Check clearing The process which involves deducting deposits and reserves from the bank on which the check was written and crediting both deposits and reserves to the bank where the check was deposited.

Checkable deposits Any deposits in any bank account on which you can write a check.

Circular flow model Represents goods, services, and incomes in the economy as flowing in a circle, from households to firms and back again.

Civilian labor force All people in an economy who are at least 16 years old; are not in the armed forces; are neither incarcerated or otherwise institutionalized; and either have a job or have looked for work in the last four weeks.

Civilian unemployment rate The percentage of the civilian labor force that has unsuccessfully sought work in the previous four weeks.

Classical school of economic thought Stresses the self-adjusting nature of the economy in the long run.

Clayton Act (1914) Legislation prohibiting price discrimination and establishing more detailed guidelines for monopoly and collusion-related conduct and penalties.

Closed economy An economy in which households and firms do not engage in international trade.

Club good A good that is excludable and non-rival in consumption.

Coase Theorem When property rights exist and bargaining and information costs are low, solutions to externality problems can be resolved through bargaining to obtain an efficient outcome without governmental intervention.

Collateral An asset that the borrower agrees to give the lender if he defaults on the loan.

Collective bargaining When workers negotiate with employers as a group rather than as individuals over wages, benefits, and working conditions.

Collusion Occurs when supposedly competing firms form joint strategies to maximize profits.

Commodity money A money asset that also has value as a commodity.

Common property resource A good that is non-excludable but rival in consumption.

Comparative advantage When one individual or group has a lower opportunity cost of pursuing an activity than does another individual or group.

Complements Goods or services that consumers use together in some way.

Conglomerate merger Occurs when firms in unrelated industries merge; rarely challenged by government.

Constant-cost industry Industry in which costs do not change as it expands. The long-run supply curve is horizontal.

Constant returns to scale Occur when the average cost of output remains the same as output increases.

Constrained maximization The process of maximizing utility subject to the constraint of the consumer's budget.

Consumer behavior The decision-making process that consumers use to allocate their scarce resources.

Consumer equilibrium The point where the marginal utility per dollar spent is equal across all goods or services consumed.

Consumer Price Index An index that summarizes movements in the prices faced by consumers.

Consumer surplus The combined difference for all units purchased between the marginal benefit for consumers and the price.

Consumption Household's purchases of new goods and services.

Consumption basket The combination of goods or services a consumer can choose, given prices and income.

Consumption externality Arises when the consumption of a good by one individual or group affects others.

Consumption function The relationship between income and consumption.

Consumption goods Goods that can only be consumed and cannot be used to produce other goods.

Consumption possibilities frontier (CPF) Shows what a nation can consume when it specializes and trades with another nation.

Contestable Describes a market in which entry barriers are low enough that firms can gain entry to the industry.

Contractionary fiscal policy Use of reductions in government spending and increases in taxes to reduce aggregate demand and real GDP.

Contractionary monetary policy Fed actions that reduce the amount of excess reserves in the banking system and curtail the ability of banks to create money.

Convertible paper money A money asset that can be used to claim the valuable commodity that backs its value.

Copyright Protects authors and publishers of literary, musical, dramatic, and artistic work against others copying their work.

Corporate profits The net income of corporations.

Corporations Firms that have a large number of owners, each of whom has only a small share of the overall responsibility for the firm.

Cost-benefit analysis Systematically compares costs to benefits to determine whether an activity should be pursued and, if so, the extent to which it should be pursued.

Coupon payments Interest payments made to the purchaser of a bond.

Craft unions A union organized around a specific skill or occupation.

Cross-price elasticities Show the percentage change in quantity demanded of one good given a percentage change in the price of a different good.

Crowding out Occurs when deficit spending by the government displaces private spending.

Currency The coin and paper money component of money.

Currency market The market in which people buy and sell a nation's money.

Current account Shows current payments for goods and services and transfers.

Cyclical deficits Deficits that result from the movement of the business cycle.

Cyclical unemployment Results from a broad downturn in economic activity.

D

Data Facts or information organized in a manner suitable for display, processing, or analysis.

Deadweight loss A loss in consumer and/or producer surplus that results when the price and quantity are not set at the competitive equilibrium.

Debasing Reducing a currency's value.

Decreasing-cost industry Industry in which production costs fall as it expands. The long-run supply curve is downward-sloping.

Decreasing returns to scale Occur when long-run average costs rise as output increases, or when the average cost of output increases as the size of the firm increases.

Default Occurs when a borrower fails to repay a loan.

Deflation The general downward movement of prices in the economy.

Demand The willingness and ability to pay for a certain quantity of a good or service at a given set of prices over a given period of time.

Demand-driven economy An economy in which producers are forced to respond to the desires of consumers, rather than one in which consumers are forced to mold their choices to what producers want to produce. Market-based economies are demand-driven.

Demand-side inflation An increase in aggregate demand puts upward pressure on the equilibrium price level.

Dependent variable A variable that is influenced by external forces (independent variables).

Depository institution A financial intermediary that accepts deposits from savers, lends money for a variety of loans, and offers checkable deposits to depositors.

Depreciate When the price of a currency falls.

Depreciation The allowance that a firm makes for the decrease in the value of its capital stock over the course of a year.

Deregulating Removing regulations and allowing market forces to have a greater impact on prices, output, profits, and industry structure.

Derived demand Labor demand is derived from consumers' demand for the final product.

Devalue Reduce the value of a nation's currency.

Development The creation of an environment in which people can develop their full potential and lead productive, creative lives in accord with their needs and interests.

Diminishing marginal utility The decrease in marginal utility associated with consuming successive units of a good. As consumers consume more of a good or service, holding consumption of all other goods and services constant, the marginal utility they derive from each additional unit must eventually decline.

Discount rate   The interest rate that the Fed charges depository institutions that borrow reserves from the Fed.

Discounting   The process of determining the present value of a future stream of revenue or payments.

Discouraged workers   Workers who withdraw from the labor force rather than keep searching for jobs.

Discretionary fiscal policy   Congress and the president take explicit legislative actions to change government spending or taxes.

Discrimination   When an individual takes actions or makes decisions based on personal prejudices.

Diseconomies of scale   Occur when long-run average costs rise as output increases.

Dividends   Periodic payments to shareholders that are determined by the number of shares of stock one holds.

Dominant strategy   A strategy that is best for a player regardless of his rival's actions.

Dominant strategy equilibrium   Each player has a single strategy that is optimal under all circumstances; a form of Nash equilibrium.

Double coincidence of wants   Requirement that each participant in the trade has a good or service that the other person wants and desires a good or service that the other person has; and that the participants are willing to give up their goods or services.

Double counting   Including the value of an item twice when computing GDP.

Dumping   Occurs when a firm sells a product in a foreign market at a lower price than in its domestic market.

Duopoly   An industry comprising two firms that supply an entire market.

Durable goods   Goods that typically last for a long time. Short-run demand for durable goods is usually more elastic than long-run demand.

Dynamic model   Looks at changes that occur in markets over time.

E

Earned income   Income gained from work.

Earned Income Tax Credit (EITC)   A major federal tax relief program that allows workers to receive tax refunds that are greater than the federal taxes they paid into the system.

Economic forecasting   The science of making predictions about future conditions based on past and present information.

Economic growth   A sustained increase in output and income by an economy.

Economic model   A tool that economists use to understand and explain economic events, and to predict the outcome of economic actions.

Economic profits   Are calculated as revenue minus explicit costs, depreciation, and opportunity costs.

Economic system   Set by national governments to establish the basic ground rules according to which consumers and producers interact to allocate goods and services among competing uses.

Economic union   Consists of countries in a free trade area that also coordinate both external and internal economic policies.

Economics   The study of how scarce resources are allocated among competing uses.

Economies of scale   Exist when the average cost of output falls as the size of the firm expands.

Elastic   When demand is elastic, consumers are relatively sensitive to price changes. Elasticities greater than 1 fall in the elastic range.

Elasticity   A measure of consumer sensitivity to changes in prices and income. Elasticities are calculated as the percentage change in quantity that results from a percentage change in another variable, such as price or income.

Elasticity of supply   Shows the percentage change in quantity supplied that results from a percentage change in price.

Electronic money (e-money)   The means of payment for goods and services in electronic, not physical, form.

Embedded technology   Technology that is part of capital rather than being a physical commodity in and of itself.

Entitlements   Programs that apply, regardless of other considerations, if an individual meets certain criteria, such as having income below a threshold level.

Entrepreneurs   Individuals who apply their creative talent and resources to start and operate businesses.

Entry barrier   Obstacles that firms must overcome to compete in a market. Entry barriers can be exogenous, meaning that they are not created by incumbent firms, or strategic.

Environmental Protection Agency (EPA) The U.S. agency with primary responsibility for environmental quality control at the federal level.

Equation of exchange The relationship between the money supply (M), velocity (V), the price level (P), and the number of transactions (T), in a given time period is such that $MV = PT$.

Equilibrium price The price at which the quantity demanded is equal to the quantity supplied.

Equimarginal principle Consumers maximize their utility when purchasing goods or services such that the marginal utility per dollar of the last unit of all goods or services are equal and all income is spent.

Equity When an allocation is fair or just. Different people may have very different conceptions of what truly is fair or just.

Excess capacity An output level in an industry wherein the firm could increase output without making losses.

Excess demand See *Shortage*.

Excess reserves Reserves held by a bank beyond the amount required by the Fed.

Excess supply See *Surplus*.

Exchange rate The equilibrium price on a currency market.

Exogenous variable An economic activity decided by outside factors.

Expansionary fiscal policy Use of increased government spending and decreased taxes to increase aggregate demand and real GDP.

Expansionary monetary policy Fed actions that provide the banking system with more excess reserves to expand the money supply.

Experience goods Must be consumed in order for the consumer to determine their quality.

Explicit costs The costs of inputs that are incurred through payment to the owner of the resource.

Exports Goods that domestic producers sell to foreign households, firms, and governments.

External debt The amount of money that the federal government owes to residents of foreign countries.

Externalities Events that occur when the production or consumption of a good or service generates unintended and uncompensated costs or benefits.

F

Factor endowment The amount of the factors of production a nation possesses.

Factors of production (inputs) Resources used to produce goods and services that fall into one of four categories: land, labor, physical capital, and entrepreneurship.

Federal Deposit Insurance Corporation (FDIC) A federal agency that insures bank deposits.

Federal funds market The market in which banks can lend reserves to other banks.

Federal funds rate The interest rate charged on reserves borrowed in the federal funds market.

Federal Open Market Committee (FOMC) The group within the Federal Reserve System that sets U.S. monetary policy.

Federal Reserve System The central bank of the United States.

Federal Trade Commission (FTC) Agency created in 1914 by the Federal Trade Commission Act; works with the Department of Justice to enforce antitrust law.

Fiat money A money asset because of its usefulness and acceptability in exchange and not because of any asset that is used to back its value.

Final goods Goods (or services) that are used by the ultimate consumer.

Financial capital The money that a firm raises.

Financial intermediaries Institutions which facilitate the transfer of money from savers to investors in an economy.

Financing gap A shortage of funds that a country needs to make the investments, it needs to grow and develop.

Firm An organization that employs resources (capital, labor, and materials) to produce goods and services.

First-degree price discrimination Also known as personalized pricing, occurs when firms take advantage of differences in consumers' willingness to pay for the same item, and each consumer is charged the maximum that they are willing and able to pay.

Fiscal policy Intentional use of governmental powers to tax and spend in order to alter aggregate demand to quickly achieve full employment real GDP.

Fixed costs (*FC*) Costs that cannot be changed in the short run and that do not change as the quantity of output produced rises or falls.

Fixed exchange rate A system that sets the price of currencies at a predetermined level.

Fixed input An input that a firm is incapable of increasing or decreasing in the time period under consideration (usually capital).

Floating exchange rate A system that allows the equilibrium price on a currency market to move up or down freely due to market forces.

FOMC Directive Document that gives the New York Fed officials directions about how to conduct monetary policy and provides the public with insight into the Fed's view of future monetary policy.

Four-firm concentration ratio (CR4) Measures market concentration by adding the market shares of the four largest firms in an industry.

Fractional reserve banking A system in which the amount of a depository institution's circulating liabilities can be safely backed by only a fraction of its value with readily available funds as reserves.

Free entry and exit Ensures that firms can easily enter or leave an industry if they wish. This assumption is sometimes referred to as perfectly mobile resources, meaning that firms can easily add and remove labor and capital.

Free rider An individual who receives the benefits of a good without bearing a share of the cost.

Free trade The sale of goods made in one country to consumers in another country without any artificial barriers imposed by governments.

Free trade area A group of nations that have agreed to eliminate all barriers to trade between them but retain barriers for nonmembers.

Frictional unemployment When job openings exist and people are willing to take them, but it takes some time to bring the two together.

Full employment An economy reaches full employment when it has eliminated cyclical unemployment.

Full employment real GDP Level of real output generated by an economy at full employment.

Future value (*FV*) What an asset will be worth at some time in the future

G

Game theory Analyzes firms' strategies by recognizing the interdependence of their actions; used to show the outcomes of various strategies chosen by the firms.

GDP deflator Measures changes in the prices of all sectors of the economy.

GDP per capita GDP divided by the number of people in the population; in other words, output per person.

Goods and services Resources and activities that consumers, firms, and the government consider to have value.

Government expenditure A market transaction in which the government spends money to acquire goods and services on the product or reserve market.

Government spending function The linear relationship based on the simplifying assumption that government spending is independent of the level of income.

Gross Domestic Product (GDP) The value of all the new final goods and services produced annually in an economy.

H

Herfindahl-Hirschman Index (HHI) Measures market concentration as the sum of squared market shares.

Horizontal merger When firms that are in the same industry or market merge.

Human capital Skills or knowledge acquired through education and training that increases individuals' output.

Hyperinflation Exists when inflation exceeds 50 percent per month.

Hysteresis The lasting impact of short-run policy.

I

Implicit contracts   A set of informal understandings between labor and management that do not require formal negotiations.

Implicit cost   A cost of production that requires no direct money payment by the firm.

Imports   Goods and services that domestic households, firms, and governments buy from foreign producers.

Incidence of a tax on consumers   The increase in the price that consumers pay due to a tax.

Incidence of a tax on producers   The decrease in the price received by producers as a result of a tax.

Income effect   The increase in a consumer's purchasing power that results from a decrease in the price of a good or service that the consumer purchases.

Income elasticity of demand   Shows the percentage change in quantity demanded that results from a percentage change in income.

Income tax   A tax levied on personal income or corporate earnings.

Increasing-cost industry   Industry characterized by increasing production costs as it expands. The long-run supply curve is upward-sloping.

Increasing returns to scale   See *economies of scale*.

Independent goods   Two goods between which the cross-price elasticity is equal to zero, indicating that there is no relationship between them.

Independent variable   A variable thought to influence the value of another variable (the dependent variable).

Index   Provides a single number that summarizes the movement of many different variables.

Indifference curve   Compares consumption alternatives for two goods or services, showing combination baskets that each give the consumer the same level of total utility.

Indifference map   The set of all a consumer's indifference curves, which covers all possible consumption combinations.

Individual demand   The willingness and ability of a specific person to pay for a particular good or service at various prices over a given period of time.

Individual demand curve   A graph that shows the quantity of a good or service that an individual will demand at various prices.

Individual demand schedule   Tells what quantity of a good or service a consumer would purchase at each price.

Individual firm supply curve   A graph that shows the quantity that a given firm is willing and able to supply at each price over a specific time period.

Individual firm supply schedule   A table shows the quantity that a firm is willing and able to supply at various prices over a specific period of time.

Industrial unions   A union organized around the workers in a specific industry.

Industry standard   An agreement on a common size, shape, or configuration across all manufacturers.

Inelastic   When demand is inelastic, consumers are relatively insensitive to price changes. Elasticities between 0 and 1 are considered inelastic.

Infant industry   A justification for protective policies based on the assumption that some industries need time to reorganize, grow, or establish themselves.

Inferior good   A good for which increases in income result in lower demand.

Inflation   The general upward movement of prices in the economy.

Inflation rate   The percentage change in the price level from one period to another.

Inflation targeting   The Fed solely commits its monetary policy to achieve a certain rate of inflation for a given time period.

Inflationary gap   Gap between the higher level of real GDP at the current short-run equilibrium and the lower level of full employment real GDP.

Informational advertising   Contains objective information about the characteristics of a good or service that is useful to the consumer making product choices.

Initial public offering (IPO)   The first sale of stock by a firm to the general public.

Innovation   The creation of new technology and the application of that technology to the production process.

Interest   The payments lenders receive in addition to the repayment of their loans.

Interest rate The unit price of the loan; the cost per hundred dollars borrowed.

Interest rate channel The primary influence of the money supply on the economy flows through its impact on interest rates and interest-sensitive investors.

Intermediate goods Inputs that are used up in the creation of a final good that will be sold in the market.

International Monetary Fund (IMF) An international organization that provides loans to promote development and ease financial crises in emerging economies.

Inventory The stock of goods that a firm produces but does not sell in the same time period.

Investment The purchase of capital goods such as plant and equipment.

Investment function The linear relationship based on the simplifying assumption that investment spending is independent of the level of income.

J

Junk bonds High-risk bonds that most analysts regard as very poor investments and that receive the lowest bond ratings.

K

Keynesian Cross A model of the economy that focuses on the relationship of aggregate expenditures and total production to determine equilibrium real GDP.

Keynesian model Short-run model of the behavior of the macroeconomy that emphasizes the role of aggregate demand and government action in the macroeconomy.

Kinked demand curve Combines two demand curves: one in which the rival firm responds to price changes, and one in which it does not.

L

Labor and labor force The number of people willing and able to work. Labor is also the entire pool of physical and mental talents available for the production of goods and services.

Labor force participation rate The percentage of the civilian, noninstitutionalized population that is in the civilian labor force.

Lags Time gaps between the origination of a problem in the macroeconomy and the ultimate solution of the problem.

Land A natural resource that can be used for agriculture, mining, housing, industrial production, and recreation. Economists also include in this definition other natural resources, such as water, gas and oil deposits, minerals, and forests.

Law of Demand The negative or inverse relationship between price and quantity demanded. When the price increases, quantity demanded decreases; when the price decreases, quantity demanded increases, *ceteris paribus*.

Law of Diminishing Marginal Returns As more and more units of the variable input (labor) are combined with the fixed input (capital), the marginal product of the variable input must eventually decline.

Law of Increasing Opportunity Cost States that as we devote more and more resources to the production of one good at the expense of another, the opportunity cost of producing more of that good increases.

Law of One Price If markets are allowed to operate freely, identical goods and services tend to sell for identical prices.

Law of Supply States that, all else equal, an increase in price will result in an increase in the quantity supplied.

Line graph An algebraic representation of the relationship between two variables using a single line.

Liquid assets Assets that are readily convertible into cash.

Liquidity The ease of converting a given asset into a medium of exchange.

Liquidity trap Occurs when even large increases in the money supply do not lower interest rates, stimulate business spending, or increase real GDP and employment.

Loanable funds market Market that converts saving into new spending by facilitating exchanges among suppliers and demanders of loanable funds.

Long run The time period in which a firm can change all inputs.

Long-run aggregate supply curve Level of output that occurs at full employment real GDP in the macroeconomy after adjustments to changing prices.

Long-run average cost (*LAC*) Long-run total cost divided by output.

Long-run equilibrium Describes a firm and industry when quantity supplied is equal to quantity demanded at the market level, and firms are earning zero economic profits.

Long-run macroeconomic equilibrium Point at which the aggregate demand curve intersects the short-run and the long-run aggregate supply curves.

Long-run model of aggregate demand and aggregate supply Self-adjusting mechanism that illustrates how the macroeconomy moves over time to full employment real GDP.

Long-run supply curve Shows the quantity that sellers will offer to the market at various prices over time, such that each firm earns zero economic profit.

Lorenz curve A graph that shows the percentage of income that is earned by a given percent of households in a country or subgroup; it indicates how evenly income is distributed.

Luxury A commodity with an income elasticity that is greater than one.

M

M1 Consists of currency (coins and paper money), checkable deposits, and traveler's checks held by the general public.

M2 Consists of all the assets in M1, plus several assets held by the public that are also quite liquid.

Macroeconomics The study of the major spending and producing units in the economy.

Management A form of labor and a science where certain highly trained workers organize, supervise, and lead others.

Managers Employees who oversee the day-to-day operations of a firm.

Marginal analysis Compares the costs and benefits of the last unit of an activity, rather than of all units combined.

Marginal benefit The benefit of consuming or producing an additional unit.

Marginal consumer A consumer who is indifferent between buying and not buying, and who receives no consumer surplus from purchasing the good or service.

Marginal cost The cost of consuming or producing an additional unit.

Marginal external benefit Benefit that accrues to individuals or groups not directly involved in the production or consumption of the good.

Marginal external cost (*MC_E*) The marginal cost of production that accrues to individuals and firms not directly involved in the transaction.

Marginal product of labor (*MP*) The change in output that results from a one-unit increase in the quantity of labor. Because it measures changes in actual output (as opposed to changes in sales revenue from output), it is also sometimes called the marginal physical product of labor.

Marginal propensity to consume (MPC) Fraction consumed of additional income.

Marginal propensity to save (MPS) Fraction saved out of additional income.

Marginal rate of substitution (*MRS*) The rate at which an individual will exchange the good or service on the vertical axis for the good or service on the horizontal axis, holding utility constant. This exchange rate also describes the slope of the indifference curve.

Marginal revenue (*MR*) The additional revenue that a firm gains from selling one more unit of output. For perfectly competitive firms, marginal revenue equals price and thus also equals average revenue.

Marginal revenue product of labor (*MRPL*) The product of the marginal revenue and marginal product ($MR \times MPL$).

Marginal social benefit (*MB_s*) The sum of the marginal private benefit and the external (social) benefit.

Marginal social cost Marginal private cost plus marginal external cost.

Marginal tax rate The tax that an individual pays on each additional dollar of income earned.

Marginal utility The change in total utility associated with a one-unit change in consumption.

Marginal utility per dollar The marginal utility of a given unit of consumption of a good or service divided by the price of the good or service.

Market basket The combination of goods and services that the typical consumer purchases during a set period.

Market concentration Refers to size and distribution of firm market shares and the number of firms relative to the market.

Market definition The process of identifying a product and the buyers and sellers of that product.

Market demand The quantity that all consumers are willing and able to buy of a particular good or service at various prices over a given period of time.

Market demand curve A graph that shows the quantity demanded at each price for all consumers in the market combined.

Market demand schedule A table that tells the quantity of a good or a service that all consumers purchase at each price.

Market edges Identify the firms and the commodities that form the supply side of the market.

Market failure Occurs when the private market allocates resources inefficiently by failing to equalize the marginal social cost of producing goods and the marginal social benefit of consuming the goods.

Market power The ability of a firm to set price.

Market structure The number and size of buyers and sellers in the market.

Market supply curve A graph that shows the quantities that sellers are willing and able to sell at various prices over a specific time period.

Market supply schedule A table that shows the quantity of a good or service that all firms in a market are willing and able to produce and sell at various prices over a given period of time.

Marketable permits Allow firms that receive them to emit a certain quantity of effluents per year.

Market-based system Allocates resources based on prices determined by the forces of supply and demand.

Market-sharing cartel Formed from agreements to split markets along a definable boundary.

Maturity The point at which the borrower repays the principal of the loan and interest payments cease.

Medium of exchange Money is useful and acceptable in transactions for both the buyer and the seller.

Menu costs The wide array of costs that firms encounter when they adjust to changing prices.

Merger When two companies formally combine into a single firm. There are three basic types of mergers: conglomerate, vertical, and horizontal.

Microeconomics The study of how individual consumers or households interact with firms in markets.

Midpoint elasticity The change in quantity divided by the average of the old and new quantities, divided by the change in price divided by the average of the old and new prices.

Minimum efficient scale The smallest output at which the firm can achieve the lowest possible average cost.

Mixed economy Allocates most goods and services using markets, but some goods and services are allocated by the government.

Monetary policy Actions by the Fed to change the size of the money supply in order to achieve macroeconomic goals.

Money demand The desire to hold money to obtain the benefits of preparedness, safety, and liquidity.

Money illusion Occurs when workers worry about their nominal wages rather than their real wages.

Money Any item that is generally acceptable for use in exchange by both buyers and sellers of goods and services.

Money market Where money demand and money supply determine the equilibrium rate of interest.

Money market mutual funds Deposits by individuals into a financial firm that pools those individual deposits to buy short-term financial assets such as U.S. government securities.

Money neutrality Changes in the nominal money supply affect only nominal prices, not real GDP or employment.

Money supply The amount of money assets circulating in an economy.

Monopolistic competition A market structure in which there are many sellers of products that are similar, but not identical.

Monopoly When a single firm is the sole supplier of a good or service to a market. A monopolist typically restricts the quantity of output and charges a price that is greater than marginal cost, generating deadweight loss.

Moral hazard Results when asymmetric information after a contract is written leads one of the parties to act against the interests of the other party.

Multinational corporation A company whose operations span several countries.

Multiplier principle Concept that changes in one component of aggregate demand will lead to a magnified change in real GDP.

N

Nash equilibrium Exists when the optimal strategy of a firm is to keep its strategy constant, given the strategy of the other firms.

National debt The sum of all prior federal deficits and surpluses.

Natural monopoly Exists if, due to scale economies, a monopoly will emerge if the market is left undisturbed.

Natural rate of unemployment The unemployment rate to which the economy moves regardless of the initiatives of policy makers.

Natural structure The degree of competition in a market that would occur if the market operated on its own, with no intervention.

Necessity A commodity with an income elasticity that is between 0 and +1.0.

Negative externality When the production or consumption of a good or service generates unintended costs.

Net benefit The difference between the cost and the benefit of a proposed action.

Net export channel The path through which changes in the domestic money supply affect the exports and imports of a given nation.

Net export function The linear relationship based on the simplifying assumption that net exports are independent of the level of income.

Net exports The difference between the injection of exports and the leakage of imports.

Net foreign factor income The difference between the income earned by foreign-owned resources in the production of U.S. goods and services and the income earned by U.S.-owned resources used in the production of goods and services abroad.

Net present value (NPV) The difference between present value of an asset and present value of expenditures on it.

Network externality Exists when consumers' utility from consuming a good increases with the number of other individuals consuming the same good.

Nominal deficit The dollar value of the federal budget deficit.

Nominal GDP The market value of new output evaluated at the output's current market price.

Nominal income The dollar value of a person's income.

Nominal interest rate The dollar amount of interest a borrower pays for every $100 borrowed.

Non-excludability Exists when there is no way to prevent consumers from deriving benefits from a good.

Non-rival consumption When one person's enjoyment or use of a good does not detract from another's.

Normal good A good for which increases in income result in increased demand.

Normal profit When a firm's earnings just cover all of its costs, including opportunity cost (also called zero economic profit).

Normative Type of economic analysis, often can be described as "what ought to be." Normative economic analysis is subjective.

O

Okun's Law A one-percentage-point rise in the unemployment rate above the full employment unemployment rate causes GDP to fall by about 2.5 percentage points.

Oligopoly A market structure in which there are relatively few sellers, each with a large share of the total market.

One-third rule A 1 percent increase in the amount of physical capital available per hour of labor causes output per worker to rise by one-third of a percent, all else held equal.

Open economy   An economy in which households and firms engage in international trade.

Open market operations   The Fed's buying or selling of U.S. government securities.

Opportunity cost   The most desired alternative you have forgone to obtain or do something else.

Optimal structure   The degree of competition in a market that maximizes allocative efficiency.

Overvalued   Describes a currency whose official value is greater than its equilibrium price on currency markets.

P

Parameters   Numerical constants that have a set value not determined by the researcher.

Partnerships   Firms led by a small number of people who share the firm's profits and responsibility for its failures.

Patent   Gives inventors exclusive rights to produce and sell a new product for 20 years.

Payoff matrix   Shows the outcomes for each strategy that a player might follow.

Peak   The highest point of an economic expansion.

Pegged exchange rate   Fixes the value of one currency against one or several other currencies.

Perfect competition   A market structure in which there are many sellers and buyers of an identical product.

Perfect information   All the buyers and sellers are aware of market conditions; namely, the prices charged by other sellers and the quality of the various goods for sale.

Perfectly elastic   Demand is perfectly elastic (or infinitely elastic) when its elasticity approaches infinity.

Perfectly inelastic   Describes demand that occurs when the elasticity is zero, so consumers are completely insensitive to price changes.

Per se **illegality**   Legal standard establishing some actions as illegal in and of themselves. Actions that always reduce competition are generally illegal *per se*.

Persuasive advertising   Focuses on affecting consumer tastes through the use of subjective information.

Per-unit tax   Adds a fixed dollar amount to the price of each unit of a good sold.

Phillips curve   A graph showing a negative relationship between the rate of inflation and the unemployment rate.

Physical capital   See capital goods.

Pigouvian taxes   Taxes used to correct for the effects of externalities; these taxes increase efficiency.

Political business cycle   Theory that politicians will try to manipulate fiscal policy for maximum political and electoral advantage.

Portfolio channel   The path through which changes in the money supply affect individual portfolios of assets in the economy.

Positive   Type of economic analysis that involves "what is," or purely objective relationships that can be tested with data.

Positive externality   When the production or consumption of a good or service generates unintended benefits.

Potential GDP   The amount an economy produces when it is at full employment.

Poverty line   The income cutoff used to identify the poor; an individual or family of a given size below this line cannot afford the basic necessities.

Precautionary demand   The demand for money assets as an insurance policy against unexpected transactions.

Predatory pricing   Occurs when a firm sets the price of its product below its own costs to drive a rival out of the industry.

Present value (*PV*)   Value today of a stream of revenue or a series of payments, even if it is not received or paid today.

Price and wage flexibility   Prices and wages are equally likely to go up or down.

Price cap   Government regulation setting a maximum price that firms can charge or maximum allowable rate of increase in price.

Price ceiling A maximum price that a producer may charge for a good or service, imposed by the government.

Price discrimination Separating customers into groups based on their willingness to pay, and then charging them different prices.

Price elasticity of demand Expresses the sensitivity of the quantity demanded for a good or service to changes in its price.

Price floor A minimum price imposed by the government to redistribute income from buyers to sellers.

Price taker A firm that accepts the price as set by the market.

Price-to-earnings (PE) ratio The value of the company's stock (the price times the number of shares) divided by the company's annual after-tax profits.

Principal The dollar value of the loan from the lender to the borrower.

Principal-agent problem The conflict that arises when one person or group relies upon another to maximize its well-being.

Prisoners' dilemma A payoff matrix in which the dominant strategy leads all players to an outcome in which all players could be made better off through collusion.

Producer surplus The combined difference for all units sold between the market price and the marginal cost of production.

Product differentiation Variation in the characteristics of products that are substitutes.

Product market The system of markets in which households purchase goods and services from firms.

Product proliferation Occurs when a firm introduces many related products so that it has a variant for every consumer, regardless of his or her tastes.

Product tie-ins Require a customer purchasing one product to also buy another product.

Production The transformation of inputs-capital, labor, and materials-into output.

Production externality When the production of good or service that affects individuals or firms that do not directly produce or consume the good.

Production function A description of the relationship between the quantity of inputs used and the output produced, using either a table or a graph.

Production possibilities frontier (PPF) The curve that shows the combinations of goods and services that an economy can produce in a given time period.

Productive efficiency When all of the economy's resources are fully employed, no resources go unused, and the production of any good cannot be increased without sacrificing production of another good.

Profits The difference between the total revenue that a firm receives from selling its output and the total cost it incurs to produce that output.

Progressive income tax system Tax system in which the marginal rate at which income is taxed increases as an individual's income rises.

Property rights The rights to gains from firms' and individuals' inventions and innovations.

Property tax A tax on land and structures.

Proprietor's income The profit earned by a sole proprietorship or partnership.

Public goods Can be freely consumed by anyone whether they pay for it or not and one person's consumption of the good does not detract from another's doing so.

Public interest theory Regulation theory based on the idea that governments must address the interests, needs, or demands of the public; maintains that government should regulate firm behavior to increase overall welfare and make consumers better off.

Public utility commissions (PUCs) Set the guidelines for firm behavior through public hearings at which they consider the opinions of both consumers and the firm on appropriate action.

Purchasing power parity (PPP) The principle that exchange rates rise and fall to equate purchasing power across countries.

Pure private good A good that is excludable and rival in consumption.

Pure public good A good that is non-excludable and non-rival.

Q

Quantity demanded   The quantity that consumers are willing and able to purchase at a given price.

Quantity theory of money   The view that, in the long run, changes in the money supply lead to proportional changes in the price level.

Quota   A maximum quantity of a good or service that can be bought and sold over a specific period of time.

R

Rate of return regulation   Government regulation setting a prespecified amount of profit that a firm may earn in a given time period.

Rational expectations   A theory that states that households and firms make rational economic decisions using whatever information they have about the state of the economy.

Rational self-interest   Quality that causes consumers to endeavor to make choices that give them the greatest satisfaction.

Real business cycle theory   A model of the economy that attributes economic expansions and contractions to technological innovations and slowdowns.

Real deficit   The purchasing power of the federal budget deficit.

Real GDP   The value of output in constant dollars.

Real GDP per capita   A country's real income per person.

Real income   The purchasing power of a person's income.

Real interest rate   The purchasing power of the repayment the borrower makes for every $100 borrowed.

Recession   The period over which production falls.

Recessionary gap   Occurs when actual real GDP is less than the full employment real GDP.

Regulated industry   An industry in which the government oversees a specific aspect of the firms' behavior, such as occupational safety, product safety, entry conditions, or pricing.

Renewable natural resource   If not overconsumed, these resources have the ability to regenerate.

Rent   Payment to owners of land.

Rent seeking   The expenditure of resources to transfer wealth or income from one group to another that does not result in increased production.

Required reserves   The dollar amount of reserves that a bank must hold in readily available form.

Reserve requirement   A percentage of deposits that must be held by a depository institution in a form readily available to depositors.

Resource market   The system of markets for factors of production.

Rivals   Firms in the same industry that do not cooperate with one another.

Rule of reason   Legal standard advocating that each case be judged on its own merits. Rival firms or consumers who claim to be damaged by a firm's anti-competitive practices must demonstrate both that such actions were taken and that they caused economic damages.

Rule of 72   Mathematical relationship that states that the rate at which a country's income grows times the number of years it takes that income to double equals 72.

S

Sales tax   A tax on transactions between merchants and customers.

Say's Law   Belief of classical economists that "supply creates its own demand."

Scarcity   There are not enough resources available to produce and consume all the goods and services we desire. We therefore must make choices about *what* to produce, *how* we produce it, and *for whom* we produce.

Search goods   Goods that have characteristics that can easily be described to and verified by consumers.

Seasonal unemployment   Results from the periodic rise and fall of unemployment with the seasons of the year.

Secondary market   Provides a place (physical or electronic) where buyers and sellers can gather to exchange financial assets.

Second-degree price discrimination   Also known as quantity discounting, when firms sell output at more than one price by taking advantage of each consumer's different willingness to pay for different quantities.

Security A certificate that promises to pay the bearer a specific sum of money on a particular date.

Self-selection Occurs when people who are more able to benefit from obtaining human capital invest in it more than people who are less able to benefit from such investments.

Shares The smallest unit of ownership in a company that entitles the bearer to a stake in running the company and a portion of its profits.

Sherman Anti-Trust Act Outlaws monopolizing an industry and firms' working together to restrain trade in an effort to control an industry.

Shortage Exists if the quantity demanded is greater than the quantity supplied at the current price.

Short run A span of time so brief that there is at least one fixed input.

Short-run aggregate supply curve Captures the direct relationship between the overall price level and the amount of goods and services supplied by producers, *ceteris paribus*.

Short-run macroeconomic equilibrium Occurs where the forces of short-run aggregate supply and aggregate demand meet at an equilibrium price level that clears the overall market in an environment of incomplete adjustment of wages and prices.

Shutdown point The point at which total revenue is just equal to total variable costs.

Simple money multiplier The measure of the strength of the money creation process in the banking system; equal to $1/rr$ where rr = the reserve requirement imposed by the Fed.

Slope A measurement of the rate of change along a line. The slope of a line is equal to the change in Y divided by the change in X.

Sole proprietorships Firms with only one owner, who bears full responsibility for the firm's success or failure.

Specialization of labor Instead of each worker performing multiple tasks, each worker devotes his time to a single task or a few related tasks.

Speculative demand The demand for money as a type of investment asset in an individual's portfolio.

Spurious product differences Perceived and often intentionally created product differences that have no impact on the quality of the good or service.

Stabilization policies Actions taken by policy makers to limit the size and duration of the economy's deviation from its long-term trend.

Stagflation Stagnant economy (with reduced real GDP and increasing unemployment) with increasing inflation.

Static model Designed to look at a market at a given moment in time.

Sticky prices Occur when firms' costs of changing the prices charged for the goods and services they produce outweigh the benefits of changing their prices.

Sticky wages Occur when workers are unable to change their nominal wage rate easily in response to changing overall prices.

Stock A certificate representing partial ownership of a firm.

Stock market A centralized location where buyers and sellers exchange shares.

Store of value Money assets can retain purchasing power for future use.

Structural deficits Deficits that are independent of the state of the economy.

Structural unemployment When workers lack jobs due to a permanent mismatch of skills or deficient skills.

Substitutes Goods or services that are similar to one another from the consumer's perspective.

Substitution bias Causes the CPI to overstate inflation, because consumers substitute relatively cheaper goods for relatively more expensive goods.

Substitution effect Indicates that consumers almost always substitute away from the good or service that has become relatively more expensive and toward the good or service that has become relatively cheaper.

Sunk cost A special kind of fixed cost that is not recoverable.

Supply The quantity of a good or service that producers are willing and able to produce or offer at a given set of prices over a given period of time.

Supply shocks Unforeseen events that can affect the expected profitability of firms, and thus their willingness to produce.

Supply-side economics Policies designed to increase aggregate supply.

Supply-side inflation A reduction in short-run aggregate supply by firms puts upward pressure on the price level.

Surplus Exists if the quantity demanded is less than the quantity supplied at the current price.

T

Tangent Describes a curved line that just touches a straight line at one single point. The slopes of tangent lines are equal at the point of tangency.

Tariff A tax on imported goods.

Temporary Aid for Needy Families (TANF) Provides financial assistance to families with children under the age of 18.

Third-degree price discrimination When a firm charges different prices in different markets for the same product or service. To put this strategy into practice, a firm needs three things: market power in both markets, different demand in the two markets, and the ability to prevent reselling.

Time value of money Indicates that money paid in the present is more valuable than the same sum paid at a future date. Time value is based on the opportunity cost of use of the funds over the time period in question.

Total cost (*TC*) The sum of all fixed costs plus the sum of all variable costs.

Total product (*TP*) A synonym for the quantity of output, Q, in discussions of production and cost.

Total product curve Shows the relationship between the quantity of labor used (on the horizontal axis) and the quantity of output produced (on the vertical axis) for a fixed amount of capital.

Total reserves Those funds held by a bank in readily available form to meet depositors' withdrawal demands.

Total revenue Price times the quantity sold; it represents the total amount of money that sellers receive for their output.

Total utility The total satisfaction that a consumer derives from the consumption of goods or services.

Trade deficit The excess of imports over exports.

Trade diversion The shift of trade from a country outside a free trade area to a country inside the area.

Trade surplus The excess of exports over imports.

Transactions costs The costs of making all the exchanges necessary to produce an item.

Transactions demand The demand for money assets for use in everyday, expected transactions.

Transfer payments Funds shifted from one group or sector to another without involving an exchange or transaction.

Transition economies Economies in the process of switching from an allocation scheme that relies on central planning to one that uses markets.

Transitivity A logical property requiring that if a consumer prefers A to B, and B to C, he or she must also prefer A to C.

Treble damages Damages equal to three times the actual damage inflicted. Plaintiffs have a right to recover treble damages in antitrust cases under the Clayton Act.

Trough The lowest point of an economic contraction.

U

Underemployed Describes people who work fewer hours than they would like or at a job that requires lesser skills than they possess.

Underground economy The unofficial transactions that are not recorded in official statistics.

Unearned income Income gained from all sources other than work, such as interest, profits on the sale of stocks, inheritance, and gifts.

Unemployment insurance Benefits provided to people who are unemployed through no fault of their own; who are ready, willing, and able to work; and who are actively seeking work.

Union Non-profit organization in which workers bargain with management collectively, rather than as individuals, in order to maximize the utility of union members.

Unit-elastic Describes demand when the percentage change in price and quantity demanded are the same, so that elasticity equals 1.

Unit of account The value of all other assets is measured in terms of the money asset.

Utility Well-being, including the benefits that consumers derive from consuming goods and services.

V

Value added The increase in value at each stage of a good's or service's production.

Value of marginal product of labor (VMPL) The product of the price per unit and marginal product ($P \times MPL$), which tells a firm in a perfectly competitive market the dollar value of the additional output produced by one more worker.

Variable A letter, symbol, or name that represents a value or an economic concept.

Variable costs (VC) Costs that vary with output-if output increases, variable costs rise, and if output decreases, variable costs fall.

Variable input An input that can be changed in the short run (usually labor).

Velocity of money The number of times a dollar changes hands in a given period.

Venture capital Funds and expertise that investors contribute to a firm; as compensation, venture capitalists typically receive either stock or bonds that can be converted into stock.

Vertical merger When one firm purchases another firm that lies either above or below it in the production stream.

Voluntary restraint agreement (VRA) A negotiated arrangement that a country makes with foreign producers or foreign governments over restrictions on the quantity of goods that those countries will export.

W

Wealth The stock of financial resources accumulated by an individual over time.

World Bank An international agency that provides loans and grants to developing nations to improve the well being of people in the developing world.

World price The price charged for a good in the rest of the world. If a country engages in free trade, this price will prevail in that country as well.

World Trade Organization (WTO) An international organization that promotes free trade among member countries.

Y

Yield Indicates how large the company's dividend is relative to the price of its stock.

Index

demand-side, 568
in Germany, 483, 498–499
measurement of, 490–497
and real and nominal values, 487–489
supply-side, 570–571
and unemployment, 741–743
and wages, 484–485
Inflationary gap, 579, 731, 732
Inflation rate
defined, 491–492
in international context, 497–498
in United States, 496–497
Inflation targeting, 706
Information, asymmetric, 371–372
Informational advertising, 294–295, 296
Initial public offering (IPO), 63
Innovation, 335
Inputs. *See* Factors of production
Intel Corporation, 369
Intercept, 23–25
Interdependent firms, 307
Interest, 359
Interest rate
and aggregate demand, 536, 538
and budget deficit, 641–645
defined, 360
equilibrium, 575, 720–721
and Federal Reserve System, 722–723
fixed, 485, 488, 499
as income in GDP, 513
in net present value, 361–362
in present value, 360
real and nominal, 489
Interest rate channel, 727–728
Intermediate goods, 507–508
Internalized transactions, 202
International inflation rate, 497–498
International Monetary Fund (IMF)
debates over, 827
and East Asian crisis, 828
role of, 565, 811, 826–827
statistics on Mexican economy of, 764
survey on aggregate demand by, 568–569
International sector, 71
International trade. *See also* Free trade
and aggregate demand, 536–537
based on specialization, 49, 50
in circular flow model, 71–73
and comparative advantage, 50–51

government regulation of, 797–799, 803
organizations for, 800–803
and quotas, 158, 803
and unemployment, 475
and union membership, 398
Internet addresses, tracking, 273–274
Inventory
defined, 510
investment in, 510–511
unintended, 510–511
Investment
defined, 509
expectations-based, 104–105
by firms, in GDP, 509–511
in Keynesian Cross, 609–610
in short-run economic model, 595, 601–602
IPO (initial public offering), 63
Iraq War, 647
Ithaca Hours, 659–660, 661, 664, 666, 668
ITQ (individually transferable quota), 451

J

Japan
aggregate demand in, 569
deflation in, 499
economic choices by, 43
inflation rate in, 497–498
and liquidity trap, 732–733
trade deficit with, 785–786
trade quotas for, 158
unemployment rates in, 472–473
Job banks, 468
"Jobless recovery," 428
Jobs, nature of, 463–464
Jobs, Steve, 37
Junk bonds, 366

K

Kahn, Alfred, 349
Keynes, John Maynard, 593–594, 603, 664
Keynesian Cross, 607–613
Keynesian short-run economic model, 592–594, 603. *See also* Short-run economic model
Kinked demand curve, 308–309
Korean War, 639
Krueger, Alan, 427

L

Labor. *See also* Labor demand; Labor market; Labor supply
defined, 203
as factor of production, 35
payments to, 65
in resource market, 65
as variable input, 203
Labor compensation, 513
Labor demand. *See also* Labor market
effect of output price on, 382–383
and labor productivity, 381–382, 393
in long run, 390–392
overview of, 380
and product price, 388
in short run, 382–383, 392
Labor force
African Americans in, 463
BLS calculation of, 476
and changes in jobs held, 463–464
defined, 35, 461
and economic growth, 768–769
Hispanics in, 463
men in, 462
women in, 462–463, 471
Labor force participation rate, 462
Labor market. *See also* Labor demand
and education/training, 392–394
equilibrium in, 387–390
female participation in, 389
and human capital, 393
and immigration, 389–390
market supply changes in, 389–390
market supply for, 386–390
Labor supply
and immigration, 474–475
individual, 384–386
market, 386–390
LAC. See Long-run average cost
Lag, fiscal policy, 630
Land, as factor of production, 35
Land development, 451–452
Landowners, payments to, 65
Law of Demand
defined, 84, 115
for interest rate/physical capital relationship, 362, 363
in monopolies, 259

The Addison-Wesley Series in Economics